GROLIER
ENCYCLOPEDIA
OF KNOWLEDGE

Grolier Incorporated
Danbury, Connecticut

1993 Printing

ISBN 0-7172-5300-7 (complete set)
ISBN 0-7172-5312-0 (volume 12)

Printed and manufactured in the United States of America.

This publication is an abridged version of the *Academic American Encyclopedia*.

3 4 5 6 7 8 9 10

Mm

M *M/m* is the 13th letter of the English alphabet. Both the letter and its position in the alphabet are derived from the Latin forms, which in turn were derived from the Greek by way of the Etruscan. The Greeks call the letter *mu,* and the name, form, and position of the letter were taken by them, along with the rest of the alphabet, from a Semitic writing system, where the name of the sign was *mem. M/m* is a voiced labial nasal continuant and is made by closing the lips and allowing the breath to go through the nasal passage while vibrating the vocal chords, as in *me, smile,* and *hammer.*

Ma Yuan (Ma Yüan) [mah yoo-ahn] The Chinese painter Ma Yuan (fl. 1190–1225), together with Xia Gui, is credited with bringing the lyrical mode of Song landscape art to its culmination during the Southern Song period (1127–1279). Working in the tradition of Li Tang, Ma evolved a new painting style distinguished by assymmetrical compositions, simplification of forms, and the use of delicate gradations of color. His distinctive painting style was much imitated in later periods. (See CHINESE ART AND ARCHITECTURE.)

Maastricht [mahs'-trikt] Maastricht, the capital city of Limburg province, is located on the Meuse River in the southeastern corner of the Netherlands, just north of the border with Belgium. The city has a population of 115,782 (1987). Glass, crystal, ceramics, chemicals, and beer are manufactured in Maastricht. Architectural landmarks include the Church of St. Servatius, the oldest church in the Netherlands, begun in the 6th century; a 13th-century bridge; a 15th-century town hall (now a museum); and a 17th-century town hall.

The Romans first built a settlement there to guard the river crossing. In 1204, Maastricht fell to the dukes of Brabant and was subsequently held by the bishops of Liège. In 1579, during the Dutch Revolt against Spanish rule, the Spanish massacred 8,000 of the residents.

Maazel, Lorin [mah-zel'] A child prodigy, the noted conductor and violinist Lorin Maazel, b. France, Mar. 6, 1930, led the New York Philharmonic at the age of 9 and made his violin recital debut in 1945, at 15. In 1949 he became apprentice conductor to the Pittsburgh Sympho-

ny, the orchestra to which he returned as music director in 1986. Maazel has headed other such major orchestras and opera companies as the Deutsche Oper (1965–71), the Berlin Radio Symphony Orchestra (1965–75), the Cleveland Orchestra (1972–82), and the Vienna State Opera (1982–84)—the first American ever invited to conduct there.

Mabuse, Jan   see GOSSAERT, JAN

macadamia nut [mak-uh-daym'-ee-uh] The commercial macadamia nut comes from two species of large, evergreen, subtropical Australian trees: *Macadamia tetraphylla* and *M. integrifolia.* The first commercial orchards were planted in Hawaii in 1921–22, which today is the principal producer of macadamia nuts. Up to 40 fruits develop from pendant clusters of 300 to 500 flowers, which are cream-colored or pink in *M. tetraphylla,* white in *M. integrifolia.* The squarish white nuts—usually sold without their round, brown shells—have a uniquely crisp texture and a pleasant, mild flavor.

McAdoo, William G. [mak'-uh-doo] William Gibbs McAdoo, b. near Marietta, Ga., Oct. 31, 1863, d. Feb. 1, 1941, a prominent American public official and Democratic politician, served President Woodrow WILSON as secretary of the treasury from 1913 to 1918. A New York City lawyer and businessperson, he had managed Wilson's 1912 presidential campaign. McAdoo helped write the Federal Reserve Act (1913), which placed the nation's banking system under public control. During World War I he headed the Federal Reserve Board, the Federal Farm Loan Board, and the War Finance Corporation; he was director general of the nation's railroads while they were under government operation (1917–19). McAdoo resigned from government in 1919 and a few years later moved to California. In 1924 he sought the Democratic presidential nomination, advocating conservation, lower tariffs, and public regulation of business, but did not win. He served as U.S. senator from California (1933–38).

Macao [muh-kow'] Macao, or Macau (Chinese: Aomen), is a special territory of Portugal covering only 15.5 km² (6 mi²) at the tip of the Macao Peninsula on the Chinese mainland, about 115 km (70 mi) east of Guangzhou (Canton). Macao's short land border (approximately 200 m/660 ft) is thus with China. Macao is located to the west of the Pearl River estuary (which flows past Guangzhou to the South China Sea), and the British crown colony of Hong Kong lies to the east of the estuary. Macao's territory includes the two small islands of Taipa and Coloane, which are situated offshore in the South China Sea.

Land, People, and Economy

Macao is an almost totally urban area. Only 10% of the land is devoted to agriculture, and Macao possesses no sources of fresh water. The climate is tropical, with an average annual temperature of 22° C (72° F); annual precipitation averages about 1,800 mm (71 in).

The population of 441,691 (1990 est.) is about 95% Chinese and 3% Portuguese. Although Portuguese is the official language, Cantonese Chinese is most widely spoken. The great majority of the inhabitants are Buddhist, with a Roman Catholic minority.

Literacy among the Portuguese and Macanese is virtually 100%. Life expectancy is high (79 years for females and 75 years for males in 1990) and the infant mortality rate is low (7 per 1,000 live births in 1990).

Manufacturing is the most profitable sector of the economy, employing more than 40% of the labor force. Textiles are by far the leading product, although the percentage of nontextile exports (chiefly toys, electronics equipment, and artificial flowers) increased from 13% to nearly 27% in 1987. Tourism and gambling (illegal in nearby Hong Kong) are major contributors to the economy. More than 5 million tourists visited Macao in 1987. Macao is heavily dependent on China and Hong Kong for food imports, but because it exports so much of its industrial output, it maintains a favorable foreign-trade balance. In 1989 exports totaled $1.7 billion; imports totaled $1.6 billion. In that year Macao had a gross national product of $2.7 billion and a per capita income of $6,300.

History and Government

The Portuguese settled Macao in 1557 as a base for commercial and missionary activities in China. Portuguese sovereignty was acknowledged by the Chinese in 1887 and reaffirmed in 1979, although the land border has never been precisely delineated. In 1987, Portugal and China agreed that Macao would be returned to China in 1999.

Macao's government, which was granted internal autonomy in 1976, is headed by a governor appointed by the Portuguese government. Although the 1987 agreement did not spell out Macao's future political system, the Chinese agreed not to interfere in the enclave's capitalist economic system for 50 years.

macaque [muh-kahk'] The 12 species of large, strong monkeys called macaques are members of the genus *Macaca* in the primate family Cercopithecidae. The Barbary ape, *M. sylvanus,* and the rhesus monkey, *M. mulatta,* are macaques. Male macaques are larger than females and grow to about 40 to 70 cm (16 to 28 in) in head and body length and weigh from 3.5 to 18 kg (8 to 40 lb), depending on the species. The tail may be longer than the head and body length, as in the bonnet macaque, *M. radiata,* or absent, as in the Barbary ape.

Macaques have brown or black fur, doglike muzzles, and pink skin on faces or rumps. They are native to southern Asia from eastern Afghanistan, Tibet, and southern China through Southeast Asia to the Philippines and the East Indies, with one species each in North Africa (Barbary ape) and northern Japan (Japanese macaque). Macaques typically live in large troops. They live partly on the ground, partly in trees; all are excellent swimmers. They are omnivorous, eating fruits, grains, insects, and vegetable matter. Extra food is carried in cheek pouches. The crab-eating macaque, *M. fascicularis,* eats clams and crabs.

Mating appears to be seasonal. The female bears one, rarely two, young after 5½ to 6 or possibly 7 months' gestation. Sexual maturity is reached at 3 to 4 years of age.

The Japanese macaque has a thick fur appropriate to its northern habitat. Like other macaques, the Japanese macaque travels in troops, with the older males as leaders and guardians. Each troop has a territory of 2 to 15 km² (0.75 to 5.75 mi²).

Macarius the Egyptian, Saint [muh-kair'-ee-uhs] Called both Macarius the Great and Macarius the Elder, Saint Macarius the Egyptian, c.300–c.390, was an Egyptian ascetic and solitary, preeminent among the early desert fathers. At about age 30 he joined a colony of monks in the desert of Scété and became widely known for his holiness and miracles. He was ordained a priest about 340.

MacArthur, Douglas A brilliant and controversial figure, Douglas MacArthur, b. Little Rock, Ark., Jan. 26, 1880, d. Apr. 5, 1964, was one of America's greatest military leaders. He graduated (1903) from West Point with the highest honors in his class. A series of engineering assignments—including service in the Philippines and a stint as aide to President Theodore Roosevelt—culminated (1914) in his participation in the occupation of Veracruz, Mexico.

World War I. During World War I, MacArthur was chief of staff, brigade leader, and then commander of the 42d (Rainbow) Division of the Allied Expeditionary Force in France. He served as superintendent (1919–22) at West Point and subsequently held two Philippine commands and two corps area commands. In 1928 he headed the U.S. Olympic Committee.

MacArthur was advanced to full general on becoming army chief of staff in 1930. During this appointment he was criticized for harshly carrying out President Hoover's orders to expel the BONUS ARMY from Washington, D.C., in 1932. He was appointed (1935) military advisor to the Philippines, and a year later Philippine President Manuel QUEZON named him field marshal of the Philippine Army. MacArthur retired from the U.S. Army in 1937, and until 1941 he struggled to build up Philippine Army strength.

World War II. With war threatening, MacArthur was recalled to active duty in 1941 by President Franklin D. ROOSEVELT. When the Japanese invaded the Philippines in December of that year, the general conducted a skillful and valiant defense on Bataan Peninsula and Corregidor Island until he was ordered (March 1942) to Australia to become supreme Allied commander in the Southwest Pacific theater. For his actions in the Philippines, MacArthur was awarded (March 1942) the Medal of Honor. Five months later MacArthur launched a daring major counteroffensive against the enemy in Papua New Guinea. Operations along the northeast coast of that huge island culminated triumphantly in 1944. Other Japanese forces and bases were bypassed in a simultaneous campaign through the Solomon, Bismarck, and Admiralty islands.

In a significant meeting at Pearl Harbor with President Roosevelt, MacArthur—who questioned his superior's strategy of emphasizing the war in Europe so heavily—won approval to reconquer the Philippines instead of continuing to Formosa. His troops invaded (October 1944) Leyte and then other islands of the archipelago, decisively defeating the Japanese forces on Luzon in August 1945. In April of that year, MacArthur had been made commander of all U.S. Army forces in the Pacific; he had been promoted to five-star rank four months earlier. He accepted the surrender of Japan aboard the U.S.S. *Missouri* in Tokyo Bay on Sept. 2, 1945.

As director of the Allied occupation of Japan, MacArthur governed (1945–51) autocratically but progressively. He introduced such far-reaching reforms as land redistribution, disarmament, and inauguration of a liberal constitution.

Korean War. When North Korean troops invaded South

General Douglas MacArthur launched the decisive amphibious assault on Leyte Island, the Philippines, on Oct. 20, 1944, more than two years after he had been ordered to leave the Philippines in March 1942.

Korea in June 1950, MacArthur was named supreme United Nations commander. In September he conducted a masterful amphibious landing at Inchon and rolled the shattered foe back toward the Manchurian border. The massive Chinese Army invaded South Korea in November; MacArthur managed to halt it by the spring of 1951. Disagreeing with his superiors, he called for aggressive action—including bombardment of Chinese bases in Manchuria—to eliminate Communism from the Far East. When MacArthur communicated his sentiments to public officials in the United States, President Harry S. TRUMAN charged the general with insubordination and on Apr. 11, 1951, relieved him of his command.

Postwar Career. Returning to the United States, MacArthur resolutely defended his actions and views in a dramatic speech to Congress (Apr. 19, 1951). Some conservative Republicans tried unsuccessfully to nominate him for the presidency in 1952. For the last 12 years of his life MacArthur resided in New York City.

MacArthur Foundation The John D. and Catherine T. MacArthur Foundation of Chicago was established after the death of John D. MacArthur (1897–1978). He had developed and owned an array of businesses, principally Bankers Life and Casualty Co., and his wife, Catherine, worked with him. The foundation has supported programs concerned with mental health, international affairs, the environment, and public policy. Since 1981 its unique MacArthur Fellows Program has granted generous awards to exceptionally creative individuals in any field of endeavor.

Macaulay, Thomas Babington Thomas Babington Macaulay, b. Oct. 25, 1800, d. Dec. 28, 1859, English historian, essayist, and politician, was a founder of the

Thomas Babington Macaulay, English writer and statesman, appears in this 1856 photographic portrait. His greatest work, the History of England from the Accession of James the Second *(1849–61), became a best-seller in Britain and the United States because of its evocative dramatization of historical events.*

length and are brightly colored, with large, hooked bills and long tails. Some species have bare skin areas on the sides of the head. Macaws are found in Central and South America. Several species are familiar as pets and zoo animals. Probably the best known is the scarlet macaw, *Ara macao*, which is bright red with yellow and blue wing areas. The hyacinthine macaw, *Anodorhynchus hyacinthinus*, is cobalt blue with bright yellow skin around the eye and base of the lower mandible.

The blue-and-yellow macaw, a brightly plumaged bird of Central and South American rain forests, is a favorite pet and zoo bird. It has a powerful bill and feeds on fruit and nuts.

Whig school of history. His parents were active in the fight to abolish slavery; when Macaulay entered Parliament in 1830 he argued vigorously for ending restrictions on Jews, and during the debates on the Reform Bill of 1832 he made eloquent and forceful speeches in favor of extending the franchise. From 1834 to 1838 he served in British India, where he helped establish a British-style educational system and drafted a penal code that became the basis of India's criminal law.

Macaulay again won a seat in Parliament on his return to England, but he devoted most of his energies to writing. His collection, *Critical and Historical Essays* (1843), gained him celebrity. He intended, in his *History of England from the Accession of James the Second,* to write the history of his country from 1685 to his own era, but he had not yet completed the reign of William III (d. 1702) when he died. Five volumes were published between 1849 and 1861. One of the great works of English literature, Macaulay's *History* exalts the Glorious Revolution of 1688 as a cornerstone of English liberty.

McAuliffe, Christa   Christa McAuliffe, b. Sharon Christa Corrigan in Boston, Sept. 2, 1948, d. Jan. 28, 1986, was a high school teacher in Concord, N.H., when selected in July 1985 to ride the SPACE SHUTTLE as a private citizen. A graduate of Framingham State College in 1970, the year of her marriage, McAuliffe also obtained an M.A. in 1978 while raising a family and pursuing her career. Following her astronaut training, she was one of the seven crew members aboard the Shuttle *Challenger* when it was destroyed during launch from Cape Canaveral in January 1986.

macaw [muh-kaw']   Macaws are among the largest PARROTS, family Psittacidae, order Psittaciformes; they belong to either the genus *Anodorhynchus* (3 species) or *Ara* (14 species). They average 76–102 cm (30–40 in) in

Macbeth   William SHAKESPEARE's *Tragedy of Macbeth*, probably written in 1605 or 1606 and first published in 1623 in what may be a shortened version, is based on historical material in Raphael Holinshed's *Chronicles of England, Scotland, and Ireland* (1587). The play may have been intended to gratify James I, King of England, who claimed descent from Banquo, Macbeth's friend, who is hailed by the three witches as the ancestor of kings. Macbeth is a brilliant psychological portrait of a villain-hero who feels his own guilt acutely but eventually loses all moral sensitivity. Lady Macbeth, who goads her husband into murdering King Duncan, commits suicide under the guilty stress depicted in her sleepwalking scene.

Macbeth, King of Scotland The life of Macbeth, king of Scots, b. *c.*1005, d. Aug. 15, 1057, formed the legendary basis of Shakespeare's tragedy *Macbeth*. He succeeded (*c.*1031) his father, Finlay, as *moarmaer* (provincial governor) of Moray. Macbeth probably had a personal claim to the crown of Scotland, but he acquired a more direct claim by his marriage to Gruoch, granddaughter of King Kenneth III (r. 997–1005). Macbeth killed King Duncan I in battle near Elgin in 1040 and took the crown. An attempt to dethrone Macbeth in favor of Malcolm Canmore, the son of Duncan, was defeated in 1046, but in 1057, Malcolm killed Macbeth at the Battle of Lumphanan. The following year he became king as MALCOLM III. Macbeth was buried at Iona as a legitimate monarch.

Maccabees (family) [mak'-uh-beez] The Maccabees were a family of village priests from Modein near Jerusalem who, in 168 BC, instigated an uprising to defend Judaism against both the SELEUCIDS, the Hellenistic rulers of Syria-Palestine, and Jews who had become Greek assimilationists or Hellenists. The name is derived from the epithet Maccabeus ("hammerer" or "extinguisher") bestowed on the most famous member of the family, **Judas** (d. 161 BC). The uprising began when the aged **Mattathias**—father of Judas and great-great-grandson of Hasmon (hence the name Hasmoneans also applied to the family)—killed an apostate Jew who was about to offer sacrifice to Zeus on an altar set up by the Seleucid King ANTIOCHUS IV EPIPHANES in the Temple precincts at Jerusalem. Mattathias's five sons carried on the uprising.

Assisted by the HASIDEANS and an army of 6,000, Judas won several victories over Syrian armies and, in 164 BC, occupied the Temple in Jerusalem, building a new altar and fortifying the area. This remarkable event continues to be celebrated as the Feast of CHANUKAH or Rededication (sometimes also called the Feast of Lights).

The struggle nevertheless continued as Judas and his brothers sought political as well as religious liberty. Judas fell in battle in 161 BC, but his brother **Jonathan** (d. 143) became (151) high priest and captured Ashkelon and Gaza. **Simon** (d. 135), the last of the brothers, subdued Acre and was appointed (140) hereditary high priest. Finally, in 139 BC, Judean ambassadors to Rome brought back a senatorial decree recognizing the independence of the Jewish state. Simon was murdered in 135, but his son **John Hyrcanus** (d. *c.*105) consolidated the gains of his father and uncles. The family ruled until 63 BC when Jerusalem was taken by the Roman general Pompey.

Maccabees, books of The books of Maccabees consist of four Jewish books named after Judas Maccabeus, the hero of the first two. The books do not appear in the Hebrew Bible, but 1 and 2 Maccabees are included in the Greek and Latin canon and in the Protestant Apocrypha. Books 1 and 2 provide a vivid account of Jewish resistance to the religious suppression and Hellenistic cultural penetration of the Seleucid period (175–135 BC). They also contain partial records of the Hasmonean (or Maccabean) dynasty, which achieved Jewish political independence during the resistance to the Seleucids and maintained it until 63 BC. The third book is an account of the persecution of Egyptian Jews by Ptolemy IV (r. 221–204 BC). The last book, 4 Maccabees, originally written in Greek probably about AD 25, is primarily a philosophical discussion of the primacy of reason, governed by religious laws, over passion.

McCardell, Claire see FASHION DESIGN

McCarran Act The Internal Security Act of 1950, sponsored by Senator Patrick A. McCarran (1876–1954) of Nevada, was a product of the era of Alger Hiss, Klaus Fuchs, Julius and Ethel Rosenberg, and McCarthyism and represented a congressional effort to eliminate suspected Communist subversion within the United States. The act provided that Communist-front and Communist-action organizations must register with the U.S. attorney general. It denied their members employment within the federal government or its defense industries and the right to use U.S. passports. It also created a Subversive Activities Control Board to determine whether organizations and individuals were Communist. Passed over President Harry S. Truman's veto, the act's provisions were later dismantled piecemeal.

McCarthy, Eugene Eugene Joseph McCarthy, b. Watkins, Minn., Mar. 29, 1916, became a national figure in 1968, when, as a U.S. senator from Minnesota, he ran for the Democratic presidential nomination in opposition to U.S. policy in Vietnam. His strong showing in the New Hampshire primary was a factor in President Lyndon Johnson's decision not to seek reelection. McCarthy's candidacy ended, however, with the Democratic nomination of Hubert H. Humphrey. McCarthy had served five terms in the U.S. House of Representatives (1949–59) before becoming a senator in 1959. He retired from the Senate in 1971. In 1976 he made another bid for the presidency as an independent.

McCarthy, Joe Hall of Fame member Joseph Vincent "Marse Joe" McCarthy, b. Philadelphia, Apr. 21, 1887, d. Jan. 13, 1978, never played a major league baseball game but managed the New York Yankees to eight pennants and seven World Series titles. He first managed (1926–30) the Chicago Cubs, winning the 1929 pennant. In 1932, his second season as Yankee manager, New York won the World Series in four straight games over the Cubs. McCarthy had his tense moments with Babe Ruth, but his authority was never challenged. He managed the Yankees through 1946 and the Boston Red Sox in 1948–50.

McCarthy, Joseph R.   The U.S. senator Joseph Raymond McCarthy, b. Grand Chute, Wis., Nov. 14, 1908, d. May 2, 1957, attacked alleged Communist subversion within the administrations of Presidents Harry S. Truman and Dwight D. Eisenhower. His activities gave rise to the term *McCarthyism*—using sensational and highly publicized personal attacks, usually based on unsubstantiated charges, to discredit people thought to be subversive.

McCarthy received (1935) a law degree from Marquette University. In 1939, running as a Republican, he won election as a state circuit judge. McCarthy joined the Marine Corps in 1942 and served in the South Pacific. In 1946 he was elected to the Senate.

At first an undistinguished legislator, McCarthy captured national attention in February 1950 by arguing that the State Department was riddled with card-carrying members of the Communist party. Moving from one charge to another and shrewdly manipulating the media, McCarthy cowed his opponents and evaded demands for tangible proof as he developed a large and loyal following. Encouraged by many Republicans, he accused the Franklin D. Roosevelt and Truman administrations of "twenty years of treason." His most prominent individual target was Gen. George C. Marshall.

Reelected in 1952, McCarthy leveled similar charges at members of the Eisenhower administration from his new post as head of the Senate's Government Operations Committee and its permanent investigations subcommittee. His failure to substantiate claims of Communist penetration of the army in the nationally televised Army-McCarthy hearings in 1954 discredited him; that December the Senate voted to censure him, 67-22. Thereafter, McCarthy's influence declined sharply.

U.S. senator Joseph McCarthy launched (1950) a campaign to expose alleged Communists in the State Department. McCarthy contributed to the anti-Communist hysteria of the early 1950s with wide-ranging accusations and sensational tactics.

McCarthy, Mary   The novelist, critic, and short-story writer Mary Theresa McCarthy, b. Seattle, Wash., June 21, 1912, d. Oct. 25, 1989, was in the forefront of American intellectual life for more than 40 years. As a book reviewer for *The Nation* and *The New Republic* following her graduation (1933) from Vassar and as theater

Mary McCarthy's acid wit won her accolades as both critic and author. Her loosely autobiographical novel The Group *(1963) became a best-seller and was filmed in 1966.*

Photo Jill Krementz © 1974

critic (1937–48) for the *Partisan Review* she demonstrated wit and fine powers of analysis. When she turned to fiction these traits were devastatingly applied to the pretensions of American college communities in *The Groves of Academe* (1952) and to the fads that influenced women's lives in the 1930s and '40s in her best-selling *The Group* (1963; film, 1966). These works, together with another novel, *A Charmed Life* (1955), and two books of short stories, *The Company She Keeps* (1942) and *Cast a Cold Eye* (1950), drew on her personal experience, and *Memories of a Catholic Girlhood* (1957) bitterly describes her orphaned life with two sets of elderly relatives. In a different vein are her two book-length essays on Italian art and history: *Venice Observed* (1956) and *The Stones of Florence* (1959). McCarthy turned her attention to national politics in the essay collections *Vietnam* (1967) and *Hanoi* (1968), followed by *Mask of State: Watergate Portraits* (1974). Another novel, *Cannibals and Missionaries* (1979), deals with terrorism, while *Ideas and the Novel* (1980) surveys the novel form and attacks postmodern developments.

McCartney, Paul   see BEATLES, THE

McCarty, Maclyn   Maclyn McCarty, b. South Bend, Ind., June 9, 1911, an American bacteriologist, collaborated with Oswald T. Avery and Colin MacLeod in 1944 to show that genetic information in cells is carried in deoxyribonucleic acid (DNA). Working with pneumococcus bacteria, they removed the DNA from a smooth (encapsulated) strain and added it to a strain of rough (nonencapsulated) cells. The offspring of the rough cells were smooth, demonstrating a process known as transformation.

McClellan, George B.   George Brinton McClellan, b. Philadelphia, Dec. 3, 1826, d. Oct. 29, 1885, was a

George B. McClellan, a U.S. general and presidential candidate, here affects a Napoleonic pose, perhaps to live up to his sobriquet, "Little Mac, the Young Napoleon."

Union general and a presidential candidate during the U.S. Civil War. He graduated second in his class at West Point in 1846, won two brevets in the Mexican War, and designed a new saddle for the army.

At the start of the Civil War, McClellan secured western Virginia for the Union. Given command of the troops around Washington later in 1861, he molded the Army of the Potomac into an effective force. He served briefly as general in chief of all the Union armies in 1861–62. His PENINSULAR CAMPAIGN of 1862 just failed to capture Richmond. McClellan adeptly reorganized the Army of the Potomac after the disastrous Second Battle of Bull Run and scored a qualified success at ANTIETAM. President Abraham Lincoln, however, relieved him of his command in November 1862. McClellan ran unsuccessfully as the Democratic presidential candidate in 1864 and served (1878–81) as governor of New Jersey.

McClintock, Barbara Geneticist Barbara McClintock, b. Hartford, Conn., June 16, 1902, d. Sept. 2, 1992, won the 1983 Nobel Prize for physiology or medicine for discovering that genes can transfer their positions on chromosomes. McClintock earned (1927) a Ph.D. in botany from Cornell University and taught and did research at several institutions before joining (1941) the Carnegie Institution of Washington. Her discovery of mobile genetic elements, published in 1953, proved significant in the understanding of several human diseases and of hereditary processes in general.

McCloskey, John John McCloskey, b. Brooklyn, N.Y., Mar. 10, 1810, d. Oct. 10, 1885, was the first native New Yorker to serve as priest in his diocese and the first American Roman Catholic to be elevated to the rank of cardinal. In 1847, McCloskey became the first bishop of Albany, N.Y., a position he held for 17 years. In 1864 he succeeded John Hughes as archbishop of New York. Pius IX named him a cardinal in 1875. Saint Patrick's Cathedral in New York City was completed while he was archbishop.

McCormack, John The celebrated Irish tenor John McCormack, b. June 14, 1884, d. Sept. 16, 1945, attained enormous popularity first in opera and later in his solo recitals of classical songs and popular ballads. At age 18, with no formal training, he won first prize at the Irish National Festival in 1902. In 1907 he made his formal concert debut in London and began his operatic career at Covent Garden in Mascagni's *Cavalleria Rusticana*. He sang with the Metropolitan Opera and the Boston Opera during the 1910–11 season and with the Chicago Opera in 1912–13. Thereafter he made few operatic appearances and concentrated on solo recitals. McCormack became a U.S. citizen in 1917.

McCormack, John W. John William McCormack, b. Boston, Dec. 21, 1891, d. Nov. 22, 1980, represented the 12th and 9th districts of Massachusetts in the U.S. House of Representatives from 1928 to 1971. He was Democratic majority leader (1940–47, 1949–53, and 1955–61) and Speaker of the House (1962–71). McCormack earlier served in the Massachusetts legislature (1920–26).

McCormick, Cyrus Hall Cyrus Hall McCormick, b. Rockbridge County, Va., Feb. 15, 1809, d. May 13, 1884, developed a mechanical reaper in 1831. In 1834, learning that Obed Hussey had patented a reaper the previous year, McCormick hastened to obtain his own patent. McCormick and Hussey machines met in hundreds of competitions over the years. The results in the fields were inconclusive, but in the marketplace McCormick was the victor. He moved (1849) his operation to Chicago, where he built an automated steam-powered plant and inaugurated modern sales methods, installment buying, and a repair and spare-parts department. After his death, his firm merged with others to form the International Harvester Company.

McCormick, Patricia Patricia Keller McCormick, b. Seal Beach, Calif., May 12, 1930, is considered the greatest woman diver to participate in the Olympics. She was the first person to win gold medals in both the platform and springboard events in two Olympics (Helsinki, 1952, and Melbourne, 1956). She also won 25 national Amateur Athletic Union (AAU) diving titles and gold medals in the 1951 and 1955 Pan American Games. She retired after 1956 and is a charter honoree (first year) in the International Swimming Hall of Fame.

McCosh, James James McCosh, b. Ayeshire, Scotland, Apr. 1, 1811, d. Nov. 16, 1894, was an American educator and philosopher. An ordained minister, he taught (1852–68) logic and metaphysics at Queen's College, Belfast, before becoming president of the College of

New Jersey, now Princeton University. During his tenure (1868–88), Princeton rose to national academic prominence: a graduate department was established (1877); the number of students and faculty increased; the endowment grew tremendously; and 14 new buildings were constructed.

McCoy, Joseph   The American pioneer cattleman Joseph Geating McCoy, b. Sangamon County, Ill., Dec. 21, 1837, d. Oct. 19, 1915, opened northeastern beef markets to Texas ranchers. He selected Abilene, Kans., on the Kansas Pacific Railway, as his headquarters and purchased the town in 1867. With the help of surveyors, he laid out a trail to Corpus Christi, Tex., and convinced ranchers to drive their cattle to railroad shipping points in Abilene. McCoy also helped open the CHISHOLM TRAIL. When the cattle trade moved west in the early 1870s, he established drives to Cottonwood Falls and Wichita, Kans.

McCullers, Carson   The novelist, playwright, and short-story writer Carson Smith McCullers, b. Columbus, Ga., Feb. 19, 1917, d. Sept. 29, 1967, established her reputation for insight and sensitivity with her first published novel, *The Heart Is a Lonely Hunter* (1940; film, 1968), a study of the psychological isolation of a deaf-mute. *Reflections in a Golden Eye* (1941; film, 1967), deals with a latent homosexual army officer baffled and made savage by his faithless wife. In *The Member of the Wedding* (1946; film, 1952), McCullers drew her most memorable portrait in the figure of 12-year-old Frankie Addams, a lonely tomboy on the brink of adolescence. With the modern Gothic tale *The Ballad of the Sad Cafe* (1951), a story of the frustrated love of a middle-aged café owner for her cousin, a pathetic dwarf, McCullers both extended her gallery of grotesques and underscored her basic pessimism.

McCulloch, Hugh   Hugh McCulloch, b. Kennebunk, Maine, Dec. 7, 1808, d. May 24, 1895, was a financier who, as U.S. secretary of the treasury (1865–69), helped restore fiscal stability during the critical RECONSTRUCTION period. An Indiana banker, he was appointed (1865) Abraham Lincoln's secretary of the treasury, retaining that office through Andrew Johnson's term (until 1869). Within six months of his appointment he had begun to reduce the national debt and reestablish federal taxation in the South; he also advocated a speedy return to the gold standard to prevent overspeculation. McCulloch served again (1884–85) as treasury secretary under Chester A. Arthur.

McCulloch v. Maryland   The case of *McCulloch* v. *Maryland* (1819) was one of several major decisions in which Chief Justice John MARSHALL defined the extent and relationship of federal and state powers. In 1816, Congress authorized the creation of a national bank, one branch of which was subsequently located in Baltimore. The Maryland legislature, in an attempt to protect its own banks from competition, levied a tax of 2 percent on all notes issued by any bank operating in Maryland not chartered by the state. McCulloch, the cashier of the Baltimore branch of the Bank of the United States, was convicted under the statute for refusing to pay the tax.

The Supreme Court reversed his conviction. Marshall maintained that the specific authority to charter a bank could be reasonably implied from the specifically enumerated powers of Article I, Section 8, in conjunction with the power of Congress to make all laws that are necessary and proper to execute the enumerated powers. He went on to hold that Maryland could not tax the bank because in the event of conflict between normally valid federal and state laws, the federal law must take precedence under the supremacy clause of Article VI. Marshall thus promulgated two major rules: the doctrine of implied powers and the concept of national supremacy.

Macdonald, Dwight   Dwight Macdonald, b. New York City, Mar. 24, 1906, d. Dec. 19, 1982, was an American political and cultural writer. He worked as editor and writer for *Fortune* (1929–36), *Partisan Review* (1937–43), his own journal, *Politics* (1944–49), *Esquire* (1960–66), and *The New Yorker* (1951–71). *Memoirs of a Revolutionist* (1957) is about the radical politics of the 1930s and '40s. Many of his writings on popular culture were collected in *Against the American Grain* (1962; repr. 1983) and in *Dwight Macdonald on Movies* (1969).

MacDonald, J. E. H.   The English-born painter James Edward Hervey MacDonald, b. May 12, 1873, d. Nov. 26, 1932, who immigrated to Canada in 1887, was the chief spokesman for the GROUP OF SEVEN, an association of landscape painters who brought the influence of modern European art to their depictions of northern Canada. Using the dramatic colors and simplified forms of the symbolists, MacDonald captured the splendors of Algonquin Park as well as the Georgian Bay and Algoma regions. In 1924 he made his first sketching trip to the Rockies, still seeking the true spirit of the North American landscape.

MacDonald, Jeanette   see EDDY, NELSON, AND MAC-DONALD, JEANETTE

Macdonald, Sir John A.   John Alexander Macdonald, b. Jan. 11, 1815, d. June 6, 1891, one of the principal founders of the Dominion of Canada, was its first prime minister (1867–73, 1878–91) and its leading political figure from 1867 until his death. Born in Glasgow, Scotland, Macdonald immigrated to Upper Canada (now Ontario) with his parents in 1820. He was elected to the Legislative Assembly of the Province of Canada (present Ontario and Quebec) in 1844. Macdonald played a major role in transforming the old Tory party into a broader Conservative grouping that was willing to cooperate with French

Sir John A. Macdonald, the first prime minister of the Dominion of Canada, was the leading proponent of the Canadian Confederation achieved in 1867. Despite accusations of bribery that interrupted his ministry in 1873, he was returned to office in 1878.

Canadians to achieve a union of all British North America. In 1857 he became prime minister of the Province of Canada. As the leader of the English-speaking Conservatives, Macdonald, with his Quebec colleague Sir George Etienne CARTIER and the Liberal George BROWN, formed the coalition administration (1864–67) that achieved Confederation. Macdonald's vital role in this process earned him the post of first prime minister of the Dominion of Canada in 1867. During Macdonald's tenure, Manitoba, British Columbia, and Price Edward Island became provinces of the Dominion. Macdonald's first efforts to organize a transcontinental railway company led to his political defeat in 1873, but he returned to office five years later. The Canadian Pacific Railway was completed in 1885. Meanwhile, Macdonald launched his National Policy for strengthening Canada through protective tariffs and encouragement of western settlement. He was last elected in 1891 but died the same year.

MacDonald, John D. John Dann MacDonald, b. Sharon, Pa., July 24, 1916, d. Dec. 28, 1986, was the author of almost 70 books and recipient of the Mystery Writers of America Edgar Grand Master Award (1972). Several of his works, including *The Executioners* (1958), were made into movies. Although MacDonald's popularity rested largely on his detective novels featuring the character Travis McGee, other works such as *A Flash of Green* (1962) and *Condominium* (1977) also won acclaim.

Macdonald, John Sandfield John Sandfield Macdonald, b. Saint Raphael, Upper Canada (now Ontario), Dec. 12, 1812, d. June 1, 1872, was a Canadian political leader. An Ontario lawyer, he sat (1841–67) in the legislature of United Canada (composed of Ontario and Quebec), leaning first toward the Conservatives and later toward the Reformers. He was copremier with Louis Victor Sicotte (1862–63) and Sir Antoine Aimé Dorion (1863–64). Although Macdonald opposed Confederation

of the Canadian provinces at first, he soon realized its inevitability. After Confederation, he served as Ontario's first premier from 1867 until 1871.

MacDonald, Ramsay James Ramsay MacDonald, b. Scotland, Oct. 12, 1866, d. Nov. 9, 1937, was a founder of the British LABOUR PARTY, from which he was eventually expelled for collaborating with the Conservatives in the coalition National government. He was also Great Britain's first Labour prime minister. MacDonald converted to socialism and in 1894 joined the Independent Labour party. A party secretary since 1900, MacDonald won a seat in Parliament in 1906 and was the Labour leader in the House of Commons from 1911 to 1914. Opposed to Britain's participation in World War I, he lost his parliamentary seat in the 1918 election. In 1922, MacDonald returned to Parliament as Labour party leader. He became prime minister and foreign secretary of Britain's first Labour government in 1924, but the minority ministry held office only nine months. Its accomplishments included an important housing act, improved unemployment benefits, and increased British participation in the LEAGUE OF NATIONS. With his enthusiasm for the labor movement fading, MacDonald took little part in the abortive 1926 general strike.

MacDonald's second term as Labour prime minister (1929–31) was dominated by the unemployment issue as his government proved incapable of dealing with the worsening depression. Confronted with a financial crisis in August 1931, MacDonald and a few senior colleagues formed a National government in coalition with the Conservatives and Liberals. This action cost MacDonald the support of the Labour party, however. He remained prime minister until 1935, but his prestige and influence diminished steadily, while the Conservative lord president of the council, Stanley BALDWIN, assumed effective leadership. MacDonald served as lord president of the council from 1935 to 1937, but after a humiliating personal defeat at the polls in 1935, he retired from public life.

Ramsay MacDonald was one of the earliest leaders of Britain's Labour movement and, in 1924, formed Britain's first Labour government. MacDonald served as prime minister in 1924 and from 1929 to 1935, demonstrating considerable ability in foreign affairs.

Macdonald, Ross   Ross Macdonald, the pseudonym of Kenneth Millar, b. Los Cralos, Calif., Dec. 13, 1915, d. July 11, 1983, was a detective writer known for his series of novels featuring private eye Lew Archer. In *The Chill* (1964), *Black Money* (1966), *The Goodbye Look* (1969), and *The Underground Man* (1971) he explored today's affluent but discontented society by having Lew Archer search for clues to present mysteries among the ghosts of his clients' pasts. Macdonald's last novels were *Sleeping Beauty* (1973) and *The Blue Hammer* (1976).

Macdonough, Thomas   Thomas Macdonough, b. New Castle County, Del., Dec. 31, 1783, d. Nov. 10, 1825, U.S. naval commander in the WAR OF 1812, scored a crucial victory over the British in the Battle of Lake Champlain. He entered the navy in 1800 and served in the TRIPOLITAN WAR against the Barbary pirates (1801–05). Later, during the war with Britain, Macdonough defeated (Sept. 11, 1814) a British squadron under Capt. George Downie on Lake Champlain, thus forestalling an invasion of New York.

McDougall, William   William McDougall, b. near York, Upper Canada (now Ontario), Jan. 25, 1822, d. May 29, 1905, was a Canadian Liberal politician of long service. Elected to the Canadian assembly in 1858, he was commissioner of crown lands in the Liberal administration of 1862–64, then provincial secretary in the Confederation coalition of 1864–67. A father of Confederation, McDougall was minister of public works (1867–69) in the first Dominion cabinet until appointed lieutenant governor of Rupert's Land in 1869. Unable to assume office because of the rebellion there of Louis RIEL, he gradually lost political influence, although he continued to sit in the House of Commons almost without interruption until 1882.

MacDowell, Edward   The American composer Edward Alexander MacDowell, b. New York City, Dec. 18,

Edward MacDowell, America's foremost composer of the 19th century, gained international recognition with his piano compositions and orchestral works. MacDowell's European musical education infused his music with a romantic lyricism.

1860, d. Jan. 23, 1908, helped raise American musical standards higher than they had ever been before. At the age of 15 he went to Paris in search of advanced musical training, and three years later he entered the Frankfurt Conservatory, where he studied composition with Joachim Raff.

MacDowell settled in Boston in 1888. In 1896 he became the first professor of music at Columbia University. He resigned in 1904, and the following year he suffered a complete mental breakdown. After his death his summer residence in Peterborough, N.H., became the site of the annual summer Peterborough Festival of the arts and the MacDowell Colony for musicians, artists, and writers.

MacDowell is best known for his descriptive piano pieces, such as "To a Wild Rose" and the collections *Forest Idyls* (1884) and *Woodland Sketches* (1896), and his two piano concertos. His other works include piano sonatas, symphonic poems, songs, and choral works.

McDowell, Irvin   Irvin McDowell, b. Columbus, Ohio, Oct. 15, 1818, d. May 4, 1885, was a Union general in the U.S. CIVIL WAR. In May 1861, McDowell, an 1838 graduate of West Point, became commander of the Union army south of Washington, D.C. In July he attacked and was defeated by the Confederates in the First Battle of BULL RUN. Relieved of command, he was later a corps commander in the Union defeat at the Second Battle of Bull Run (August 1862). McDowell saw no further combat, but he headed (1864–82) various U.S. military departments. He was later parks commissioner in San Francisco.

Mace   A form of TEAR GAS that is sprayed from a hand-held can, Mace is used by the police and military to subdue individuals during close encounters. It causes temporary blindness and, if sprayed in the face at distances of less than 1.8 m (6 ft), it can cause permanent injury. Adopted by U.S. police forces in the late 1960s as an effective substitute for billy clubs, the spray gas has been used primarily in riot control. In many states Mace is categorized as a nonlethal weapon, and its use is subject to stringent controls.

mace   Mace is the fleshy red, netlike skin that covers the NUTMEG, *Myristica fragrans,* and that is used as a spice. Its flavor is reminiscent of both nutmeg and cinnamon. Ground mace is used to flavor cakes, fish dishes, meat stuffings, and pies. The alcohol extract of mace is used in pickles and sauces and as a perfume fragrance.

Macedonia [mas-uh-dohn'-ee-uh]   Macedonia is a region on the south central Balkan Peninsula, bordering the Aegean Sea. Two mountain systems cross the area: the Pindus Mountains, a continuation of the Alps, in the west, and the Rhodope Mountains in the center and in the east.

Greeks predominate in the south, and Slavs in the north. The population is largely Eastern Orthodox, but it also includes many Muslims. The overall population den-

The approximate boundaries of Macedonia, a historical region on the Balkan Peninsula, are indicated on the map. During the 4th century BC, Macedonia became the center of the Hellenic empire. It remained so until conquered (168–146 BC) by Rome.

sity is low. The chief cities are SKOPJE in former Yugoslavia and SALONIKA in Greece.

Macedonia is an agricultural region. Rye, barley, corn, wheat, fruits, vegetables, and cotton grow in the extensive river valley lowlands. In the south tobacco growing is important. Goats and sheep are grazed in mountainous areas. Some copper, iron, and lead are mined.

Macedonia was the heart of the ancient Macedonian kingdom. During the 6th century it was overrun by Slavs, and in the 14th century it was conquered by the Turks. It remained part of the Ottoman Empire until 1912, at which time it was divided among Bulgaria, Greece, and Serbia.

The Republic of Macedonia, until 1992 part of Yugoslavia, is a newly independent nation, with an area of 25,720 km² (9,930 mi²) and a population of 1,950,000 (1991). It has been recognized by only a few countries, however, largely because of the opposition of Greece, which claims that the name *Macedonia* is part of the Greek heritage.

Macedonia, Kingdom of   The ancient Kingdom of Macedonia, situated in the north of modern Greece, was established by Perdiccas I about 640 BC. Originally a semibarbarous and fragmented power, Macedon became tributary to Persia under the Persian kings DARIUS I and XERXES I and thereafter struggled to maintain itself against Thracians and other barbarians as well as against Sparta, Athens, and the Greek cities southeast of modern Salonika.

Archelaus (d. 399 BC) centralized the kingdom by a system of roads and forts and fostered the Hellenization of his people by inviting famous Greek artists, Euripides among them, to his court. PHILIP II (r. 359–336) made Macedon the greatest power in the Greek world. Becoming the champion of Delphi in the "Sacred War" of 355–346, he extended his power into Greece itself. In 338 he decisively ended Greek liberty by defeating Thebes and Athens at Chaeronea.

Philip's son, ALEXANDER THE GREAT, won a vast empire; on Alexander's death (323), however, this empire was divided into four separate kingdoms of which Macedon was

one. Contending with the rival kingdoms and with newly formed Greek federal leagues, Macedonia remained the dominant power in Greece until conquered by Rome in a series of wars waged by PHILIP V and his son PERSEUS. The kingdom was abolished in 168 BC and, after a revolt, became a Roman province in 146 BC.

Macedonian language   see SLAVIC LANGUAGES

McEnroe, John   John Patrick McEnroe, Jr., b. Wiesbaden, West Germany, Feb. 16, 1959, established himself in the late 1970s and early 1980s as one of the world's leading tennis players. McEnroe grew up in Douglaston, N.Y. As an amateur he reached the semifinals in his first Wimbledon tournament (1977). He turned professional in 1978, winning the Masters tournament. In 1979–81 he won three consecutive U.S. Open singles championships—the first man to do so since Bill Tilden—then a fourth in 1984. By winning the 1981 Wimbledon title as well as the 1981 U.S. Open, beating Björn Borg in both finals, McEnroe gained the world's number-one ranking for 1981. He also won at Wimbledon in 1983–84, ranking first in the world twice more. During the period 1978–84 he and Peter Fleming were the top-ranked doubles team in the world. McEnroe began a comeback in the late 1980s, and he and Mark Woodforde of Australia won the U.S. Open doubles championship in 1989.

The career of U.S. tennis star John McEnroe was characterized both by remarkable accomplishments and by irascible behavior on the court. McEnroe won the NCAA singles title (1978) as a college freshman, led the U.S. team to 4 Davis Cups (1978–79, 1981–82), and won 4 U.S. Open championships (1979–81, 1984) and 3 Wimbledon titles (1981, 1983–84).

McEwen, Sir John   Sir John McEwen, b. Mar. 29, 1900, d. Nov. 20, 1980, was prime minister of Australia (Dec. 19, 1967–Jan. 10, 1968) during the brief interregnum after the drowning of Prime Minister Harold Holt. A farmer in Victoria, McEwen entered Parliament in 1934. He became leader of the Australian Country party (1958–71) and also served as deputy prime minister (1958–71) and minister for trade and industry (1963–71).

As deputy prime minister, McEwen played a major role in building up the power of the Country party—to such an extent, in fact, that the Liberal governments of the 1950s and '60s could not govern without its support. The price that the Country party exacted for its help was considerable. Under McEwen's leadership, the value of the Australian dollar was kept low to encourage exports of wool and wheat until the development of mining and manufacturing reduced Australia's dependence on primary industries. McEwen retired from politics in 1971.

McGee, Thomas D'Arcy The Canadian politician and writer Thomas D'Arcy McGee, b. Ireland, Apr. 13, 1825, d. Apr. 7, 1868, argued eloquently for a Canadian nationhood based on a federal union. In 1857, McGee, who had immigrated to the United States, moved to Montreal and was elected to the Canadian legislature as an independent. He joined the Conservatives in 1864 and later sat in the first Dominion Parliament. A supporter of continued ties with Britain, he was assassinated by a Fenian extremist.

McGill University Established in 1821 by the will of James McGill (1744–1813), McGill University is a coeducational institution in Montreal, Quebec. It has faculties of arts, music, religious studies, agriculture, medicine, dentistry, sciences, engineering, and education, all with undergraduate and graduate programs. Macdonald College (1907) teaches agricultural sciences, and the Labour College of Canada, sponsored in part by the university, trains trade unionists. McGill has three affiliated theological colleges: Montreal Diocesan (1873, Anglican), United (1926, United Church of Canada), and Presbyterian (1865).

McGillivray, Alexander Alexander McGillivray, b. 1759, d. Feb. 17, 1793, was head chief and diplomat of the CREEK. Of mixed descent (his mother was French-Creek, his father Scottish), McGillivray was well educated and polished and moved with authority among the English, Spaniards, and Americans. During the Revolutionary War he supported England. In 1784 he made a profitable trade agreement with Spain, acquiring Spanish weapons to resist U.S. territorial expansion. Later he met with President George Washington and signed a peace treaty with the United States, although he was still on the Spanish payroll.

McGinley, Phyllis The writer Phyllis McGinley, b. Ontario, Oreg., Mar. 21, 1905, d. Feb. 22, 1978, moved to New York in 1928 and was soon turning out such books of light verse as *One More Manhattan* (1937) and *A Pocketful of Wry* (1940; rev. ed., 1960). The poems of these and five other volumes were collected as *Times Three: Selected Verse from Three Decades* (1960) and won the 1961 Pulitzer Prize—the first time a writer of light verse

had been so honored. *The Horse Who Lived Upstairs* (1944) was the first of McGinley's many children's books.

McGovern, George S. George Stanley McGovern, b. Avon, S.Dak., July 19, 1922, was the Democratic nominee for president of the United States in 1972. He served (1957–61) in the U.S. House of Representatives, was Director of the Food for Peace program in 1961–62, and was elected to the U.S. Senate in 1962. McGovern won the 1972 Democratic presidential nomination with the support of younger delegates and opponents of the Vietnam War but lost the election to the incumbent, Richard M. Nixon, receiving only 38% of the popular vote. He was defeated (1980) in his bid for a fourth Senate term, and ended his bid for the 1984 Democratic nomination after trailing in early primary elections.

McGraw, John As a third baseman primarily with the professional baseball team the Baltimore Orioles, Hall of Fame member John Joseph McGraw, b. Truxton, N.Y., Apr. 7, 1873, d. Feb. 25, 1934, had a .334 career batting average (1891–1906) but is most noted as manager of the New York Giants. Beginning in 1903, his first full season, he guided the Giants for three decades, winning 10 pennants and 3 World Series. McGraw frequently feuded with players and umpires. Bill Terry, a player who had not talked to him for years, replaced McGraw as manager when the latter became ill in 1932.

McGuffey, William Holmes William Holmes McGuffey, b. Washington County, Pa., Sept. 23, 1800, d. May 4, 1873, was an American educator who edited a widely used series of reading textbooks, the Eclectic Readers. He was professor of languages (1826–36) at Miami University, Oxford, Ohio, president (1836–39) of Cincinnati College, president (1839–43) of Ohio University at Athens, and professor of moral philosophy (1845–73) at the University of Virginia.

Between 1836 and 1857, McGuffey compiled six readers for Truman and Smith, publishers in Cincinnati; more than 120 million copies were sold. Containing maxims and stories about industry, honesty, and truthfulness and illustrated with engravings, McGuffey's readers promoted a moral education in much of the United States. McGuffey was also a founder of the common-school system in Ohio.

Mach, Ernst [mahk, airnst] The Austrian philosopher and scientist Ernst Mach, b. Feb. 18, 1838, d. Feb. 19, 1916, one of the most profound thinkers in 19th-century physics, was largely responsible for providing the impetus to Albert Einstein's formulation of relativistic physics. A professor of physics at Graz (1864–67) and professor of inductive philosophy at Vienna (1895–1901), Mach asserted a realistic positivistic philosophy based upon the actual physiology of sensations. His many published works range from classical treatments of heat and mechanics to comparisons of physics with metaphysics. He is popularly known for the Mach number, relating speed to the velocity of sound, which emerged from his experiment on airflow published in 1887.

Mach did not accept any statement without empirical verification; he paved the way for Einstein by challenging Newton's model of absolute space and time, and by agreeing to the abandonment of an undetectable "ether."

Mach number   The Mach number is the dimensionless ratio of the speed of an object to the speed of sound in an undisturbed medium through which the object is traveling. An airplane flying at 0.9 times the speed of sound is moving through the air at Mach 0.9. If it flies at twice the speed of sound its speed is Mach 2. The former flight is subsonic; the latter, supersonic.

The air flowing around an object has a local Mach number that depends on the local flow speed and that varies inversely with the local speed of sound; hence it changes from point to point.

Machado de Assis, Joaquim Maria [mah-chah'-doh day ah-sees', hoh-ah-keem' mah-ree'-ah]   Joaquim Maria Machado de Assis, b. June 21, 1839, d. Sept. 29, 1908, Brazil's most revered writer, was the son of a black father and a Portuguese mother. He received scant education before entering the printer's trade and then becoming a journalist. Although Machado wrote poetry, drama, chronicles, criticism, and political works, he was known above all for his novels and short stories depicting life in Rio de Janeiro during the Second Empire (1822–89). Because for Machado life was a tragic dream, his writings are underlined by bitter pessimism, as in *Epitaph of a Small Winner* (1881; Eng. trans., 1952) and his greatest work, *Dom Casmurro* (1900; Eng. trans., 1953).

Machado y Morales, Gerardo [mah-chah'-doh ee moh-rah'-lays]   Gerardo Machado y Morales, b. Sept. 29, 1871, d. Mar. 29, 1939, was the Cuban head of state from 1924 to 1933. He gained national recognition in the Cuban War of Independence (1895–98). Popular with all classes, he came to be regarded as the leader most capable of uniting the island politically, broadening its economic base, and checking corruption.

Elected president as the Liberal party candidate in 1924, in 1927, Machado assumed personal control of all political parties. He won reelection in 1928 despite strong opposition from students, professionals, and workers and afterward resorted to brutal repression. In 1933 open rebellion, a general strike, and U.S. pressure forced him into exile.

Machaut, Guillaume de [mah-shoh', gee-yohm' duh]   Guillaume de Machaut, b. Machault, Champagne, *c.*1300, d. 1377, was a French poet and the most ac-

complished and versatile composer of the 14th century. A member of the household of King John of Bohemia from 1323, Machaut later became a canon of Reims, where he resided from 1340 until his death. As a young man he accompanied the king on military expeditions and developed a distinct fondness for noble pursuits. His later patrons, to whom he presented richly illustrated manuscripts of his poetry and music, included the king's daughter, Bonne of Luxembourg, Charles of Navarre, and King Charles V of France.

Machel, Samora Moises [mah-shel']   Samora Moises Machel, b. Sept. 29, 1933, d. Oct. 19, 1986, was president of Mozambique from 1975, when it gained independence from Portugal, until his death in a plane crash in South Africa. He joined the Mozambique Liberation Front (Frelimo) in 1963, becoming the group's military commander in chief in 1968 and its sole president in 1970. Although a Marxist, Machel set aside ideology in an attempt to solve his country's desperate economic problems.

McHenry, Fort   see FORT MCHENRY

McHenry, James   James McHenry, b. Ireland, Nov. 16, 1753, d. May 3, 1816, was U.S. secretary of war (1796–1800) under Presidents George Washington and John Adams. After serving in the American Revolution, he became a prominent political figure in Maryland, representing the state in the Continental Congress (1783–86) and at the Constitutional Convention (1787). As war secretary McHenry was a supporter of Alexander Hamilton. This led to his resignation at the demand of President Adams. Baltimore's FORT MCHENRY was named in his honor.

Machiavelli, Nicolò [mahk-ee-uh-vel'-lee, nik-koh-loh']   Nicolò Machiavelli, b. Florence, May 3, 1469, d.

Nicolò Machiavelli, Italian Renaissance author and statesman, is famed for his portrait of the ruthless and opportunistic ruler in The Prince *(1513). Machiavelli's political writings depict the maintenance of power as the sole consideration governing political behavior.*

June 22, 1527, was a celebrated political and military theorist, historian, playwright, diplomat, and military planner whose most famous works are The PRINCE (1513; Eng. trans., 1602) and *Discourses on the First Ten Books of Titus Livius* (1513–21; Eng. trans., 1636).

Machiavelli's active political career began in 1498, when he became secretary and second chancellor to the Florentine Republic. After the republic was overthrown (1512) by the Medici, Machiavelli was imprisoned and tortured. On his release in 1513 he began work on his major writings.

The tumultuous events of the Renaissance were the experiences on which Machiavelli's political thought was based. The Italian peninsula was a scene of intense political conflict involving four dominant city-states—Florence, Milan, Venice, and Naples—the Papacy, France, Spain, and the Holy Roman Empire. Each city attempted to protect itself by playing the larger powers off against each other and by hiring armies of foreign mercenaries. The result was massive political intrigue, blackmail, and violence.

In Florence a reform movement inspired by Girolamo SAVONAROLA resulted in the ouster of the ruling MEDICI family and the establishment (1494) of a republic that lasted until the citizen militia, which Machiavelli had organized (1506), was defeated by Spanish troops in 1512. The rule of the Medici was restored until 1527, when a second republic was established. That republic survived until 1530, when the Medici, aided this time by German troops, returned and overthrew it. These events are clearly reflected in Machiavelli's preoccupation with military affairs.

The Prince and the *Discourses* differ significantly in emphasis because they discuss two different types of political systems. In *The Prince,* Machiavelli was concerned with a principality, a state in which one ruler or a small elite governs a mass of subjects who have no active political life. Machiavelli addressed a monarchical ruler and offered advice designed to keep that ruler in power. He recommended policies that would discourage mass political activism and channel the subjects' energies into private pursuits. Machiavelli's aim was to persuade the monarch that he could best preserve his power by using violence carefully and economically, by respecting the persons, property, and traditions of his subjects, and by promoting material prosperity.

In the *Discourses,* Machiavelli was mainly concerned with a republic, a state collectively controlled by a politically active citizenry. His concern was to preserve the liberty and independence of a self-governing citizenry. He emphasized the idea that a republic needed to foster a spirit of patriotism and civic virtue among its citizens if it were to survive.

One of the most distinctive and controversial characteristics of Machiavelli's thought is that he did not devote much attention to the values that define the ends of political action. In his view, political life cannot be governed by a single set of moral (or religious) absolutes, and the political agent may sometimes be excused for performing acts of violence and deception that would be ethically indefensible in private life. Other works by Machiavelli include *The Art of War* (1521; Eng. trans., 1560–62) and *History of Florence* (1532; Eng. trans., 1595).

machine   The term *machine* can be defined in a number of ways. This article will consider a rather narrow definition for a machine: a device that replaces human or animal effort for the accomplishment of a specific physical task. Most machines are combinations of the SIMPLE MACHINES—the LEVER, wedge (inclined plane), WHEEL and axle, PULLEY, and SCREW. Simple machines are discussed in separate entries, as are MACHINE TOOLS. This article describes the general components by which all machines function.

The cam and the crank were two important developments of the Middle Ages. One use of cams involved the operation of a bellows (A). A rotating octagonal shaft (1) alternately raised and lowered a pivoted lever (2) and cam (3). As the cam forced a slat (4) downward, a connecting strip (5) compressed the bellows (6). During the cam's upward cycle, a weighted plank (7) opened the bellows. Cranks were initially used for turning grindstones (B), windlasses (C), and a carpenter's brace (D). In the 15th century, metal connecting rods were used with single (E) or double (F) metal cranks to convert the rotary motion of the crank into a straight-line motion, or vice versa.

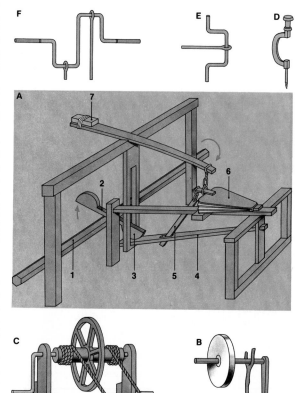

The source of power that all machines require was first provided by humans, then by animals, and later by such devices as the waterwheel, steam engine, electric motor, and internal-combustion engine. Along with the power source, the machine must have means for transmitting and modifying forces and motions in order to carry out its task.

The manner in which a machine transmits and modifies motion is known as the mechanism of the machine. Although the variety of forms of mechanisms is unlimited, motion can be mechanically transmitted from one member of a mechanism to another in only three basic ways: by a linkage such as a crank and a connecting rod; by direct contact between gear teeth or a cam and follower; or by a wrapping connector such as a belt, rope, or chain. Some machines use more than one method.

Crank. Next to the wheel, the crank is the most important motion-transmitting device, because with the connecting rod it provides means for converting linear to rotary motion and vice versa. The first crank appeared in China in the 1st century AD. The first complete crank was the carpenter's brace, invented about 1400 by a Flemish carpenter; it had four right-angle bends, with the arm and wrist of the operator forming the connecting rod. Later, when the first mechanical connecting rods were introduced, a heavy wheel known as the FLYWHEEL was needed to carry the members over the "dead" positions when the rod and crank arm were in line.

Gears. GEARS are direct-contact bodies; operating in pairs they may be used to transmit force and motion from one rotating shaft to another by means of successively engaging profiles on teeth. A gear can also be mated with a straight row of teeth on a slide called a rack. The earliest known gears were those in the Chinese South-Pointing Chariot, invented about 2600 BC. The teeth in this mechanism were wooden pins, and it contained a statuette geared always to point south regardless of the direction in which the chariot was moving. If N_2 and N_3 are the numbers of teeth on a gear pair and n_1 and n_2 are the revolutions per minute of the gears, the product $N_2 n_2$ must equal the product $N_3 n_3$, so that the speed ratio is given by $n_3/n_2 = N_2/N_3$.

Gears are used to transmit power from one shaft to another, to increase or decrease rotational speeds of machine components, to change the direction of rotation, and to produce a mechanical advantage. Spur gears (A) are the most common and are designed to transfer power between parallel shafts. Bevel gears (B) are made for transferring motion between two shafts whose axes intersect, usually at right angles. A worm gear (C) connects shafts that are at right angles but that do not intersect, and consists of a helically threaded worm (1) and spiral gear (2).

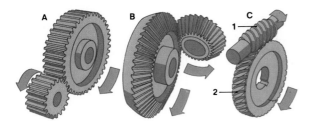

When two rotating shafts are parallel they can be connected by a spur-gear pair, which have straight teeth parallel to their axes, or by a helical-gear pair, which are basically twisted spur gears.

In many cases a gear box, or transmission, is used with a machine to change (usually, to reduce) the speed of rotation. Because the speeds of alternating-current electric motors are limited by line frequency and by the number of poles, gear reducers are commonly used between the driving motor and a machine. On geared-turbine ships the turbine may rotate at 1,500 revolutions per minute (rpm), even though the propeller shaft should rotate at only 180 rpm. Double-helical gear reducers are usually employed between turbine and shaft.

Cams. A cam and its follower are a direct-contact pair in which the cam is so shaped that it imparts a specified motion to the follower. The follower may be flat-faced or it may have a roller in contact with the cam, and the follower may move back and forth (reciprocate) or oscillate about a fixed axis. Among the diverse types are cams in the form of drums or cylinders with an endless groove cut in their peripheries, in which a roller-tipped follower may reciprocate or oscillate. Cams are widely used in textile machines, sewing machines, printing machines, and automatic machine tools.

Brakes and Clutches. These machine components usually have metallic and friction surfaces, and they control motion in machines by the direct application of forces usually created by mechanical friction; BRAKES arrest or stop the flow of motion, whereas clutches either start or stop the flow. Before a brake or a clutch is engaged, one of the two elements in the device is moving while the other is stationary; after the application of a brake the moving element is either stationary or slowed down, while after the application of a clutch both elements move at the same speed.

Springs. A spring is an energy-storing device that can tolerate large deflections under load and recover its initial size and shape when the load is removed. Most springs are metallic, but hydraulic and air springs are also available. Springs are used for a wide variety of purposes, such as cushioning transport vehicles, making resilient connections, supplying power in clocks and watches, launching and retarding missiles and vehicles, and measuring weights.

The most common type of spring is the helical spring, which is coiled in the shape of a spiral staircase and is designed to resist pushes, pulls, or twists. In most modern automobile SUSPENSION SYSTEMS, helical springs are used on the front wheels, while the rear axles are carried on semielliptic leaf springs.

Bearings. All BEARINGS have two surfaces that move relative to one another. To reduce FRICTION the surfaces may be separated by a film of a lubricant or by an assemblage of balls or rollers. The former are known as sliding-contact bearings; the latter are known as rolling-contact or antifriction bearings.

Ropes, Belts, and Chains. Wrapping connectors in the form of ropes, belts, or chains are used when a force must be transmitted over larger distances than can be accom-

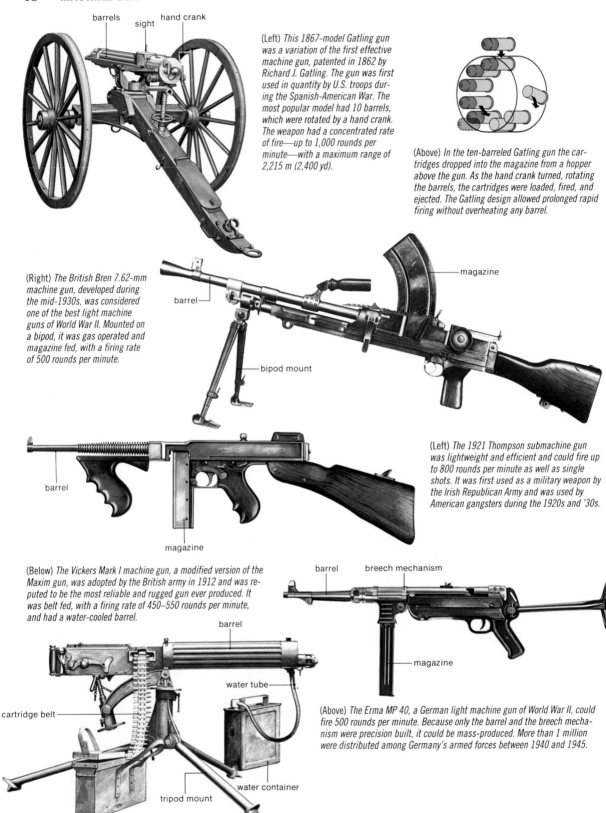

barrels   sight   hand crank

(Left) *This 1867-model Gatling gun was a variation of the first effective machine gun, patented in 1862 by Richard J. Gatling. The gun was first used in quantity by U.S. troops during the Spanish-American War. The most popular model had 10 barrels, which were rotated by a hand crank. The weapon had a concentrated rate of fire—up to 1,000 rounds per minute—with a maximum range of 2,215 m (2,400 yd).*

(Above) *In the ten-barreled Gatling gun the cartridges dropped into the magazine from a hopper above the gun. As the hand crank turned, rotating the barrels, the cartridges were loaded, fired, and ejected. The Gatling design allowed prolonged rapid firing without overheating any barrel.*

(Right) *The British Bren 7.62-mm machine gun, developed during the mid-1930s, was considered one of the best light machine guns of World War II. Mounted on a bipod, it was gas operated and magazine fed, with a firing rate of 500 rounds per minute.*

magazine

barrel

bipod mount

(Left) *The 1921 Thompson submachine gun was lightweight and efficient and could fire up to 800 rounds per minute as well as single shots. It was first used as a military weapon by the Irish Republican Army and was used by American gangsters during the 1920s and '30s.*

barrel

magazine

(Below) *The Vickers Mark I machine gun, a modified version of the Maxim gun, was adopted by the British army in 1912 and was reputed to be the most reliable and rugged gun ever produced. It was belt fed, with a firing rate of 450–550 rounds per minute, and had a water-cooled barrel.*

barrel   breech mechanism

barrel

water tube

cartridge belt

magazine

water container

tripod mount

(Above) *The Erma MP 40, a German light machine gun of World War II, could fire 500 rounds per minute. Because only the barrel and the breech mechanism were precision built, it could be mass-produced. More than 1 million were distributed among Germany's armed forces between 1940 and 1945.*

plished by other mechanisms. Ropes were probably the first elements used in this way, and they are still in use today. Belts are used in conjunction with pulleys; a common example is the fan belt in an automobile. Chain drives are most familiar in their use on bicycles, where they transmit the force from the pedal to the wheels.

See also: INVENTION; TECHNOLOGY, HISTORY OF.

machine gun The machine gun fires small-arms ammunition in a rapid, continuous stream as long as its trigger is held back. This mechanical weapon revolutionized infantry tactics by making frontal or head-on assaults by massed infantry virtually suicidal.

First Models. Early inventions, dating as far back as an English model of 1718, included multiple-barrel guns, usually with hand-cranked mechanisms for loading and firing. In 1862, Richard J. GATLING introduced his gun, which used a hand-cranked ring of gun barrels. With brass cartridges, Gatling's model became the most successful mechanically operated gun. The U.S. Army used it in the battle of Santiago, Cuba, in 1898. Other nations used it in colonial wars in Africa and Asia until the beginning decades of the 20th century.

Fully Automatic Guns. A fully automatic machine gun can use the explosive energy that propels the lead slug to feed, load, fire, extract, and eject the shell. Harnessing the recoil's impact on the barrel or the gas pressure inside the barrel provides the energy to operate the weapon.

The first practical automatic weapon was the recoil-operated machine gun patented by Hiram Maxim (see MAXIM family) in 1884. Belt-fed and water-cooled, this heavy gun, or similar models, including the Maxim-Vickers and Vickers Mark I, was used by every major country.

John M. BROWNING demonstrated a gas-operated machine gun in 1890, and in 1901 he patented a gun that operated on a short-recoil principle. Browning's inventions were used in the U.S. M1917 water-cooled and the M1919 air-cooled weapons as well as in World War II aircraft machine guns.

Aircraft Machine Guns. Although most early models used rifle ammunition (.30 caliber in most American arms), heavier weapons soon were needed for aircraft, especially for use against ground targets such as trucks and locomotives. The Germans found the 20-mm Becker effective, and the British adopted the 20-mm Oerlikon gun for their aircraft and ships. U.S. planes used .50 caliber Browning-like guns; some carried a 37-mm cannon.

In the Korean War, rockets and guided missiles replaced the machine gun as a heavy-attack aircraft weapon. Machine guns, however, are still widely used. For example, helicopters flown in the Vietnam war and Gulf War were armed with machine guns used as defensive weapons.

See also: FIREARMS.

machine tools Powered machines that shape metals and other materials through a variety of cutting or grinding processes, machine tools operate on unfinished metal parts, such as rough metal castings or forgings, and

Although modern lathes incorporate refinements such as electric motor drives and special attachments, the basic operating principles have not changed in nearly 3,000 years. The metal or wood workpiece (1) is rotated (red arrows) and unwanted material is removed by means of a cutting tool (2) that is slowly moved (blue arrows) against the work. Levers were once used to move the tools; today, a hand operated or automatic screw feed is employed. The invention of the turret lathe in 1850 made possible the mass production of duplicate parts by unskilled labor. As many as eight cutting tools can be arranged in the turret (3) and rapidly rotated into position.

perform shaping and finishing operations that produce precisely dimensioned parts. The most sophisticated machine tools are capable of exactly replicating their work on a very large number of parts and can do so automatically.

Development of Machine Tools. James Watt's STEAM ENGINE—the invention that triggered the Industrial Revolution—required large cylinders that had to be precise in interior size so that steam could not leak between cylinder and piston. In 1769, when Watt took out his first patent, cylinders of the size he required could not be accurately bored. It was only with the invention (1775) by John Wilkinson of a precision metal-boring machine that efficient steam engines could be produced. What was

A shaper (A) is a machine tool used for the planing of flat surfaces. It comprises a reciprocating ram (1), which carries a toolhead (2) that holds a cutting tool. The toolhead can be swiveled and the tool adjusted to cut horizontally, vertically, or at any angle. The work is usually held in a vise (3) that is fastened to an adjustable table (4). In making a straight cut (B), the tool is lowered to the proper level (5) and moved forward (6) to peel off a chip. After the return stroke (7), the work is moved into position (8) for the next cutting stroke.

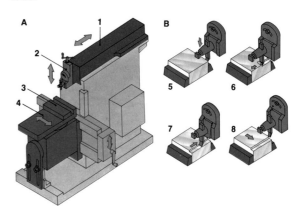

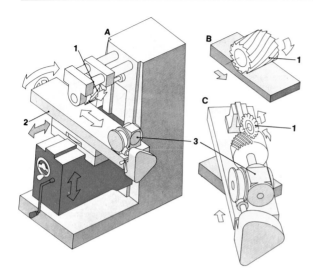

Milling machines produce a variety of shapes in metal workpieces by means of a multitoothed rotary cutting tool (1). In a universal milling machine (A), the cutter rotates in a fixed position above the workpiece, which is clamped onto a table (2) that may be moved in three dimensions or swiveled horizontally. The work may be fixed to an index, or dividing, head (3), which rotates the piece as the table moves horizontally. In addition to cutting rounded edges and grooves, the machine can mill flat surfces (B). Helical threads on a cylindrical workpiece (C) are cut by using an index head to rotate the work as it moves against an angled cutting tool.

true of the steam-engine cylinder was equally true of all the basic inventions of the Industrial Revolution: they could not be manufactured until machine tools had been devised that were capable of producing accurate parts in quantity.

The early machine tools were largely invented in England. Henry MAUDSLAY's invention (1797) of a constant-speed screw cutting machine permitted identical standard gauge screws to be mass produced. Improvements to the lathe were made by a number of machinists, including Joseph Whitworth, who became a leading manufacturer of machine tools. Planing, milling, and shaping machines—many similar to some in use today—were invented in England during the first half of the 19th century by a group of extraordinarily talented men, many of whom had worked with Maudslay.

In the United States the turret lathe and various types of gear-cutting and grinding machines were all introduced before 1850. A copying machine for turning the stocks of rifles, using a model to key the machine, was invented in 1818 by Thomas Blanchard of Worcester, Mass. Although small gear-cutting machines had long been used to make clockwork gears, improved machines began to appear during the 1830s and 1840s both in England and in America. By 1850 the basic types of grinding machines were all in use, and grinding technology was limited only by the lack of suitable ABRASIVES, many of which were invented during the latter part of the 19th century. The first milling machine was the invention (1818) of Eli

WHITNEY, and milling machines for industrial use were being produced by the 1850s. In fact, by mid-century, machines had been devised that could carry out all the basic machine-tool operations. Later developments were largely confined to refining these operations, such as increasing machine speed and inventing cutting materials that would keep their edge at higher temperatures.

During the 20th century, machine-tool advances have occurred primarily in two large areas: first, machine-tool control has been gradually automated, and today machines exist that can perform every operation automatically; second, new "chipless" techniques have been developed that use ultrasonics, lasers, high-voltage sparks, chemicals, plasma gases, and high-speed electrochemical processes to machine metals.

Fundamentals of Conventional Machine Tools. All machine tools that use metal to shape metal or other materials have similar parts to carry out the shaping process: a tool holder, to keep the shaping tool in place; and a work holder, called a table or slide, to hold the part that is to be shaped and to move or feed it at a fixed speed against the tool. In some machines the table is stationary, and the tool moves. In addition, a means of controlling the depth and angle at which the tool cuts the workpiece

A drilling machine produces holes in a securely held workpiece by means of a rotating cutting tool, usually a helically grooved twist drill (A). The standard, or knee and column, drill press (B) is found in most machine shops; a hand-feed lever is generally used to advance the drill into the work. The arrows indicate the directions in which the various components can be moved. For mass-production work a multiple-spindle drilling machine (C) can drill many holes simultaneously. A foot pedal is used to move the worktable. A radial-arm drilling machine (D) is capable of handling larger and heavier workpieces and is more versatile than the standard drill press.

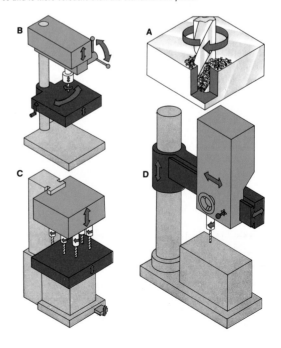

must be provided. Both the rate of feed and the position of the workpiece and the tool in relation to one another can be varied. Cutting tools must be made of materials that are harder than the metals to be cut and are capable of maintaining their cutting edge at the friction temperatures that result from the cutting operation. The most common materials used are high-speed steel, a steel-tungsten-chromium-vanadium-molybdenum alloy; nonferrous alloys containing tungsten, chromium, and cobalt; tungsten carbide in a cobalt binder; ceramicized aluminum oxide; and diamonds. Water and various types of oil are used to reduce friction temperatures and to provide LUBRICATION of the cutting area.

Most machine tools function in one or more of several basic categories: DRILLING, turning (see LATHE), shaping, planing, boring, milling, and grinding.

Automatic Control. Completely automatic machine-tool control uses code-punched or magnetic tapes to activate a particular sequence of machine operations and to instruct the machine as to the types of tools to be used, the rate of feed, cutting speed, size of cut, and finished dimensions of the workpiece. Called Numerical Control Systems, they often require computers to develop the programs for complex machining operations.

New Machining Technologies. Unlike conventional machining techniques, the new, "chipless" technologies do not use metal to cut metal. Electrical-discharge machining, for example, uses negatively charged electric sparks to remove particles of metal from the workpiece. In the ultrasonic method the disintegrating effect of high-speed vibrations is used to remove material. Laser-beam machining drills extremely small holes in super-hard materials. Plasma-arc torches, which use ultra-high-temperature ionized gas (up to 28,000° C/50,000° F), melt metal to produce a cut. Electrochemical and chemical techniques that were originally developed for printing, plate-making, and plating metals are now also used to shape metal parts.

machines, simple   see SIMPLE MACHINES

Machu Picchu [mah'-choo peek'-choo]   Machu Picchu, situated about 80 km (50 mi) northwest of Cuzco, Peru, is an ancient INCA town, one of the most famous archaeological monuments in the world. The ruins are located about 2,400 m (7,875 ft) above sea level on the eastern slopes of the Andes, near the edge of the warm humid Montaña region. The abandoned site was covered with dense vegetation and remained essentially unknown until its discovery by the American archaeologist Hiram Bingham in 1911.

Machu Picchu is best known for its architecture, which combines fine stone buildings with extensive agricultural terraces, creating the appearance of a settlement literally carved into the mountainsides. The style of its buildings and pottery as well as its careful planning suggest that the town was built under the supervision of the Inca state, which was centered at Cuzco. Perhaps the most famous feature of the site is a carved natural stone, known as *Intihuatana*, enclosed by curved walls of

The city of Machu Picchu, built atop a mountain in the Peruvian Andes, had been forgotten for more than three centuries when it was discovered by Hiram Bingham in 1911. Its actual function is not fully understood. Since it was unknown to the early Spanish invaders of the region, their documents do not identify it. Its location may mean that it served as a frontier outpost.

dressed stone with trapezoidal windows. The stone and its complex of surrounding walls are probably related to the sun religion of the Inca as well as to their veneration of certain natural stones.

Macintosh, Charles   The Scottish chemist Charles Macintosh, b. Dec. 29, 1766, d. July 25, 1843, devised a method of waterproofing (patented 1823) by sandwiching RUBBER between two layers of wool cloth. He discovered (1819) that coal-tar NAPHTHA was an effective solvent for rubber, and he then began manufacture of the raincoat that bears his name. The mackintosh became successful after the vulcanization of rubber was discovered (patented 1839) by Charles Goodyear.

Mack, Connie   The professional baseball manager Cornelius Alexander McGillicuddy, b. East Brookfield, Mass., Dec. 22, 1862, d. Feb. 8, 1956, was better known as Connie Mack. A Hall of Fame member, Mack was a manager for 53 years, a major-league record—3 (1894–96) as a playing manager for the Pittsburgh Pirates and an unequaled 50 (1901–50) as the first manager (and later owner) of the Philadelphia Athletics. Mack's teams won 9 pennants (1902, 1905, 1910–11, 1913–14, and 1929–31) and 5 World Series (1910–11, 1913, 1929–30). He twice sold off many of his best players—in 1914, after the Athletics lost four straight Series games to the Boston "Miracle" Braves, and in 1931, for financial reasons, although the Athletics had just won 3 straight pennants.

MacKay (family) The American financier and mine developer **John William MacKay**, b. Dublin, Nov. 28, 1831, d. July 20, 1902, was a pioneer in telecommunications. After immigrating to the United States with his parents in 1840, he worked as a miner in California and Nevada from 1851 to the early 1860s. In 1872, MacKay and three partners acquired the Consolidated Virginia Mine, from which they eventually mined gold and silver worth $150 million. Having become one of the richest men in the world, MacKay cofounded the Commercial Cable Company in 1883 and the Postal Telegraph Cable Company in 1886.

MacKay's son, **Clarence Hungerford MacKay**, b. Apr. 17, 1874, d. Nov. 12, 1938, inherited his father's wealth and continued his cable-laying ventures. In 1904 he completed the trans-Pacific cable begun by his father and later laid a cable between New York and Cuba (1907).

McKay, Claude Claude McKay, b. Jamaica, Sept. 15, 1890, d. May 22, 1948, was educated in the United States and became one of the most eloquent poets of the HARLEM RENAISSANCE. His collected poems, *Harlem Shadows* (1922) voiced anguish over injustice to blacks and painted skillful character sketches. McKay lived abroad from 1921 to 1944, creating controversy over his interest in Communism and his writing of such novels as *Home to Harlem* (1928) and *Banana Bottom* (1933). He also wrote two autobiographical works, *A Long Way from Home* (1937) and *My Green Hills of Jamaica* (1977).

McKay, Donald An American naval architect, Donald McKay, b. Sept. 4, 1810, d. Sept. 20, 1880, is most noted for building CLIPPER SHIPS of great beauty that set records never surpassed by sailing craft. Born in Nova Scotia, McKay established his own shipyard in east Boston in 1845. The first of his clippers, the *Stag Hound*, was launched in 1850, followed by the *Lightning*, which established a world record by traveling 807 km (501 mi) in a single day. His *Great Republic*, launched in 1853, was the largest clipper ship ever built (4,500 tons). McKay's last clipper, the *Glory of the Seas*, launched in 1869, remained under sail until 1923.

Macke, August [mah'-ke, ow'-gust] August Macke, b. Jan. 3, 1887, d. Sept. 26, 1914, was a leading German expressionist painter whose career was cut short by World War I. In 1911, Macke became a founding member of Der BLAUE REITER group. Although he was influenced by his colleagues' intensity, Macke's temperament was more restrained; he was particularly responsive to the color harmonies of Robert Delaunay's orphic cubism. Macke's views of parks and city streets sparkle with high-toned reds, yellows, and greens within a space defined by firm linear patterns.

McKean, Thomas Thomas McKean, b. New London, Pa., Mar. 30, 1734, d. June 24, 1817, was an American political figure and a Delaware signer of the Declaration of Independence. A member of the CONTINENTAL CONGRESS (1774–76, 1778–83), McKean broke the deadlock over independence in the Second Continental Congress in July 1776 by sending for Caesar Rodney, who rode in from Delaware to break that state delegation's tie vote. McKean was president of Congress in 1781 and served as chief justice of Pennsylvania's Supreme Court from 1777 to 1799. In 1787 he influenced Pennsylvania's decision to ratify the Constitution. A Jeffersonian Republican, he served three terms (1799–1808) as governor of Pennsylvania.

Mackenzie, Sir Alexander (1764–1820) Sir Alexander Mackenzie, b. Scotland, c.1764, d. Mar. 12, 1820, was a Canadian fur trader and explorer. His family brought him to New York in 1774, and he was sent to Canada after the outbreak of the American Revolution. In 1779, Mackenzie entered a Montreal fur trading firm which was subsequently absorbed (1787) by the North West Company. Mackenzie was sent to what is now the province of Alberta, where he established Fort Chipewyan on Lake Athabaska.

Interested in exploration, Mackenzie headed north from Chipewyan in June 1789. He traveled by way of the Slave River and Slave Lake, entering the river that bears his name and following it to the Arctic Ocean. By September he was back at Chipewyan, having traveled about 4,800 km (nearly 3,000 mi) by canoe in 102 days. Mackenzie undertook a second journey in 1793, this time following the Peace, Parsnip, Fraser, Blackwater, and Bella Coola rivers. He reached the Pacific Ocean at Dean Channel in July 1793, thus becoming the first European to cross the continent north of Mexico. In 1799, Mackenzie left the North West Company; he joined the XY Company, a rival organization, as a leading partner in 1802. He was knighted the same year. In 1808, Mackenzie returned to Scotland and spent the remainder of his life there.

Mackenzie,   Alexander (1822–92) Alexander Mackenzie, b. Scotland, Jan. 28, 1822, d. Apr. 17, 1892, Liberal party leader, was prime minister of Canada from 1873 to 1878. He immigrated to Upper Canada (now Ontario) in 1842. From 1852 to 1854, Mackenzie was editor of the *Lambton Shield*, a Liberal newspaper. An adherent of George BROWN's Reform party, he was elected to the Legislative Assembly of Canada in 1861. In 1867 he won a seat in the first Dominion House of Commons. Soon after, he became leader of the opposition Liberal party.

When the Conservative government of Sir John A. Macdonald fell in 1873, Mackenzie became prime minister. His government's popularity was eroded, however, by the depression of 1874–78, delays in construction of

Alexander Mackenzie, a member of Canada's first federal Parliament from 1867, assumed leadership of the Liberal party and became the nation's first Liberal prime minister in 1873. Although Mackenzie enacted significant legislation, the Liberals were voted out of power in 1878.

the Pacific railway, and Mackenzie's inability to negotiate trade reciprocity with the United States. In 1878 the Conservatives returned to power. Mackenzie remained his party's leader until 1880 and retained his seat in Parliament until his death.

Mackenzie, William Lyon William Lyon Mackenzie, b. Scotland Mar. 12, 1795, d. Aug. 28, 1861, was a Canadian journalist, politician, and rebel. He immigrated to Upper Canada (now Ontario) in 1820, where he founded a newspaper, the *Colonial Advocate*, in 1824. He became a leader in the Reform party and was elected to Upper Canada's legislature in 1828, but his harsh rhetoric led to his repeated expulsion and reelection.

In 1835, Mackenzie became Toronto's first mayor. The same year he was once again in the legislature, and his Committee of Grievances issued its *Seventh Report*, a major indictment of Family Compact government. British opposition to further home rule; political interference by the new governor, Sir Francis Bond Head; and his own defeat in 1836 made Mackenzie despair of peaceful reform, however. He founded the *Constitution*, an extreme organ of the Reform party, in 1836.

In December 1837, Mackenzie led a badly organized, easily suppressed uprising aimed at capturing Toronto and overthrowing the government (see REBELLIONS OF 1837). He fled to the United States, where he was briefly imprisoned for violating U.S. neutrality laws (see CAROLINE AFFAIR). He returned to Canada in 1849 under an amnesty, and in 1851 he was once again reelected to the legislature, where he resumed his role as government critic until his resignation in 1858.

Mackenzie River The Mackenzie River flows through the northwestern part of Canada. Rising in GREAT SLAVE LAKE (Northwest Territories), the Mackenzie flows north-northwest for about 1,700 km (1,060 mi) to the north coast of Canada and into Mackenzie Bay off the Beaufort Sea of the Arctic Ocean; its delta is more than

160 km (100 mi) long and 72 km (45 mi) wide. The entire Mackenzie River system, the second longest in North America (after the Mississippi-Missouri system), is 4,240 km (2,635 mi) long, includes the SLAVE, PEACE, and Finlay rivers, and drains an area of about 1,840,000 km² (711,000 mi²). The Mackenzie also receives the ATHABASCA and Liard rivers and drainage from the Great Bear and Athabasca lakes. Settlements along its course include Fort Good Hope, Fort Norman, Fort Simpson, Fort Providence, Norman Wells, and Oklavik.

The river is frozen from November to June, but during the ice-free season it is used for shipping petroleum and uranium. The Mackenzie was explored by Sir Alexander Mackenzie in 1789; the delta and coastal area were charted by Sir John Franklin in 1825–26.

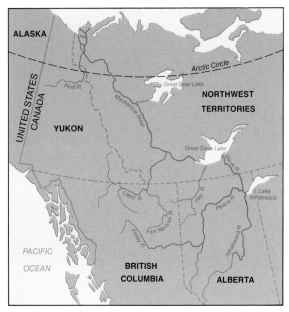

mackerel The name mackerel is commonly applied to a number of species in the mackerel and tuna family, Scombridae, and to at least two species in the jack family, Carangidae. The family Scombridae includes the true mackerels, genus *Scomber*; the Spanish mackerels, *Scomberomorus*; the frigate mackerels, *Auxis*; and the pygmy mackerels, *Rastrelliger*.

The Atlantic mackerel, *Scomber scombrus*, is found on both sides of the North Atlantic. It averages between 35 and 45 cm (14 and 18 in) long and about 500 g (1 lb) or less in weight. It has unspotted, silvery blue sides, a greenish blue back marked with wavy black lines, and white undersides. Its scales are tiny. There are two widely separated dorsal fins and four to six finlets running from both the second dorsal fin and the anal fin to the tail. The teeth are small and there is no air bladder. In the warmer months Atlantic mackerels travel in large schools off-

The Atlantic mackerel is an important commerical fish. Although the female lays about 500,000 eggs, only about three mackerel larvae in 1 million survive to the age of 3 months.

shore, feeding on shrimplike crustaceans, fish, and squid. During the winter mackerels are inactive, spending much time in trenches or gullies on the sea bottom.

The chub mackerel, *Scomber japonicus*, also known as Pacific mackerel, Japanese mackerel, and sometimes Spanish mackerel, is found worldwide. It is similar to the Atlantic mackerel but has black spots on its sides and an air bladder.

Spanish mackerels include the king mackerel, *Scomberomorus cavalla*; the Spanish mackerel, *S. maculatus*; and the cero, *S. regalis*. These are fairly large fishes with bladelike teeth and a sharp downslope of the lateral line.

Frigate mackerels, *Auxis*, are thick-bodied, tunalike fishes averaging about 30 cm (1 ft) long and 1 kg (2 lb) in weight, with distinct scales on the forepart of the body. Pygmy mackerels, *Rastrelliger*, are deep-bodied, small fishes usually less than 38 cm (15 in) long.

The jack-family mackerels, *Trachurus*, are called horse mackerels or jack mackerels. They include a Pacific species, *T. symmetricus*, which grows to about 60 cm (2 ft) long and 1.8 kg (4 lb) in weight, and a somewhat smaller Atlantic species, *T. trachurus*.

McKim, Mead, and White   The firm of McKim, Mead, and White was one of the largest and most influential American architectural firms practicing around the turn of the 20th century. Charles Follen McKim, b. Aug. 24, 1847, d. June 14, 1909; William Rutherford Mead, b. 1846, d. June 20, 1928; and Stanford WHITE, b. Nov. 9, 1853, d. June 25, 1906, went into partnership in New York City in 1879. The firm developed an elegant and historically precise classical style, which they complemented with sumptuous interior decoration. The Boston Public Library (1887–92), followed by the University Club (1899–1900) and The Pierpont Morgan Library (1906) in New York City, were all variations on Renaissance themes. They also evolved a simple, columnar monumental style appropriate to such vast public ensembles as their design for Columbia University (1893) in New York City and New York's Pennsylvania Station (1906–10; demolished).

Mackinac, Straits of [mak'-in-aw]   The Straits of Mackinac connect Lake Huron and Lake Michigan. The channel, 6 km (4 mi) wide and 48 km (30 mi) long, separates the Upper and Lower peninsulas of Michigan. The two large islands in the strait are Bois Blanc and Mackinac. The straits were discovered by Jean Nicolet in 1634. The Mackinac Bridge, one of the longest suspension bridges in the world, crosses the straits.

Mackinder, Sir Halford John   Sir Halford John Mackinder, b. Feb. 15, 1861, d. Mar. 6, 1947, is perhaps the best-known British geographer. The first reader in geography appointed (1887) to the University of Oxford since Elizabethan times, he did much to build the Oxford School of Geography and was its first director (1899). Mackinder's most influential work was *Democratic Ideals and Reality* (1919), which stressed the inherent power of the Eurasian heartland. In German translation, it may have shaped German and ultimately Nazi geopolitical views (see GEOPOLITICS).

McKinley, Mount   Mount McKinley (or Denali), in south central Alaska, is the highest mountain in North America. Located in the Alaska Range about 240 km (150 mi) south of Fairbanks, Mount McKinley is a twin-peaked mountain; the higher South Peak (6,190 m/ 20,320 ft) was first climbed by the Hudson Stuck expedition in 1913, and the North Peak (5,934 m/19,470 ft) was first climbed by the Sourdough party in 1909. The mountain was named for future President William McKinley in 1896 by W. A. Dickey, a prospector; the peak was previously called Densmore's Peak. Earthquakes sheared off much of the south face in 1912. McKinley National Park, established in 1917, was renamed Denali National Park in 1980.

McKinley, William   William McKinley, the 25th president of the United States (1897–1901), elected when the prestige and influence of the presidency was low, restored and expanded the power and authority of his office. In the aftermath of the Spanish-American War he was the first chief executive to confront the responsibilities of world power in Latin America and Asia.

Early Life. William McKinley was born on Jan. 29, 1843, in Niles, Ohio, the seventh child of William and Nancy McKinley. He spent his early years in Poland, Ohio, and briefly attended Allegheny College. In the Civil War he served at Antietam and in the Shenandoah Valley, leaving the army with the brevet rank of major. After his admission to the bar he opened (1867) a law office in Canton, Ohio, and became prosecuting attorney of Stark County two years later. McKinley married Ida Saxton on Jan. 25, 1871.

Congressman and Governor. McKinley ran for Congress as a Republican in 1876 and for the next 14 years, with one short interruption, sat in the House of Representatives. Identified with protective tariffs, McKinley believed that high tariffs, by protecting U.S. industry from foreign competition, benefited all segments of society. In 1889

AT A GLANCE

WILLIAM McKINLEY
25th President of the United States (1897–1901)

Nickname: "Idol of Ohio"

Born: Jan. 29, 1843, Niles, Ohio

Education: Allegheny College

Profession: Lawyer

Religious Affiliation: Methodist

Marriage: Jan. 25, 1871, to Ida Saxton (1847–1907)

Children: Katherine McKinley (1871–75); Ida McKinley (1873)

Political Affiliation: Republican

Writings: *The Tariff in the Days of Henry Clay and Since* (1896)

Died: Sept. 14, 1901, Buffalo, N.Y.

Buried: Canton, Ohio (adjacent to Westlawn Cemetery)

Vice-Presidents: Garret A. Hobart (1897–99); Theodore Roosevelt (1901)

he became chair of the Ways and Means Committee and architect of the McKinley Tariff (see TARIFF ACTS) of 1890.

McKinley lost his House seat in the Democratic sweep of 1890. He was subsequently elected (1891) governor of Ohio and served two terms. An effective state executive, he campaigned widely for national party candidates in 1894, and he left office a front-runner for the 1896 Republican presidential nomination. With the help of Mark HANNA, a Cleveland businessperson and close friend who mobilized support on his behalf, McKinley achieved an easy first-ballot victory. When the Democrats nominated William Jennings BRYAN on a platform of FREE SILVER, the McKinley forces pressed for maintenance of the less inflationary GOLD STANDARD, endorsed high protective tariffs, and stressed social harmony amid the economic unrest of the 1890s. Campaigning from his front porch in Canton, McKinley addressed 750,000 visitors, while the well-financed Republican organization, under Hanna's expert direction, distributed millions of pieces of campaign literature. McKinley won with 271 electoral votes to Bryan's 176.

Presidency. Although schooled in domestic issues, McKinley dealt primarily with foreign policy during his four and one-half years in office. By March 1897, Spain had been trying for two years to suppress a revolt by the Cubans in a manner that Americans regarded as brutal and economically destructive. McKinley pressed the Spaniards to withdraw from the island, but Spain would not yield to U.S. insistence on an independent Cuba. The resulting war between the United States and Spain, which Congress declared on Apr. 25, 1898, was ignited by popular pressure and by the destruction of the U.S. battleship MAINE on Feb. 15, 1898, in Havana harbor.

The SPANISH-AMERICAN WAR was brief, and when the fighting ended (August 1898) the United States was a world power. The president had played a large role in coordinating the nation's military effort, functioning directly as commander in chief. After the armistice McKinley faced decisions regarding Cuba, Puerto Rico, and the Philippines—Spanish possessions that the United States occupied or dominated when the conflict stopped. Peace negotiations with Spain resulted in U.S. occupation of Cuba until it became independent (1902) and U.S. acquisition of Puerto Rico. Unwilling to let the strategically located Philippines fall into enemy hands, McKinley directed his emissaries to acquire the islands. After receiving news of Adm. George DEWEY's victory over the Spanish fleet at Manila Bay on May 1, 1898, McKinley deftly managed a campaign to convince the American people that the islands must become the possession of the United States. Despite the opposition of antiimperialists, McKinley engineered Senate ratification (February 1899) of the Treaty of Paris (see PARIS, TREATIES OF), a milestone in the broadening of presidential influence. Earlier he had signed (1898) a bill to annex Hawaii.

The consequences of the Spanish-American War shaped the rest of McKinley's presidency. In the Philippines the army dealt with a native revolt in a prolonged and nasty guerrilla war while William Howard TAFT was setting up a civil government for the new U.S. dependency. Cuba and Puerto Rico also received governmental guidance from American administrators. To further protect U.S. interests in the Caribbean, Secretary of State John M. HAY negotiated with Great Britain to clear the way for the eventual construction of the PANAMA CANAL. In China, Hay championed the OPEN DOOR POLICY in 1899 to maintain access to that country's trade. During the BOXER UPRISING (1900), the administration sent 2,500 American soldiers with the international relief expedition that rescued Westerners caught in the surge of Chinese nationalism.

Renominated for the presidency in 1900, with Theodore ROOSEVELT as his running mate, McKinley could point to the Dingley Tariff (1897) and the Gold Standard Act (1900) as his domestic achievements. In keeping with tradition, the incumbent president did not campaign. A prosperous, assertive, self-confident nation gave McKinley 292 electoral votes to Bryan's 155. In his second term McKinley intended to push for reciprocal trade treaties, a departure from Republican adherence to the protective tariff. Speaking at the Pan-American Exposition in Buffalo, N.Y., McKinley said, "Isolation is no longer possible or desirable. The period of exclusiveness is past." The next day, Sept. 6, 1901, an anarchist, Leon Czolgosz, shot the president; McKinley died on Sept. 14, 1901.

Mackintosh, Charles Rennie In rejecting the then-current "period" styles and creating functional styles, the Scottish architect and designer Charles Rennie Mackintosh, b. June 7, 1868, d. Dec. 10, 1928, became a pioneer of modern design. He was also among the first British designers to adapt ART NOUVEAU to his own work. Both innovations are seen in his best-known work, the Glasgow School of Art (1898–99), with its Art Nouveau metalwork on the facade. Mackintosh's gifts as a furniture designer, interior decorator, and muralist were displayed in the tearooms he built (1896–1912) for Catherine Cranston in Glasgow.

Mackintosh's designs were exhibited throughout Europe and were so greatly admired that he was invited to take part in the 1900 exhibition of the Vienna Secession. He is said to have influenced the architecture of Adolf Loos as well as Russian constructivism and the Dutch de Stijl. Less appreciated in Scotland, Mackintosh confined himself after 1914 mainly to the design of textiles and furniture and to painting watercolors.

MacLaine, Shirley The actress Shirley MacLaine, b. Shirley MacLean Beatty in Richmond, Va., on Apr. 24, 1934, is respected for her facility in musical, dramatic, and comedic roles. Nominated for Academy Awards for her parts in *Some Came Running* (1958), *The Apartment* (1960), *Irma La Douce* (1963), and *The Turning Point* (1977), MacLaine finally won for *Terms of Endearment* (1983). Other notable roles were in *Can-Can* (1960), *Sweet Charity* (1969), *Being There* (1979), and *Post-*

cards from the Edge (1990). She also has written several books, including *Out on a Limb* (1983) and *Going Within* (1989).

McLaren, Norman The Canadian film director Norman McLaren, b. Stirling, Scotland, Apr. 11, 1914, d. Jan. 26, 1987, greatly advanced the art of animated films during the 1940s and '50s with such innovative one- and two-reelers as *Dots* and *Loops* (both 1940), *Hoppity Pop* (1946), *Fiddle-de-Dee* (1947), and, in 3-D, *Around Is Around* (1950). In 1941 he became director of experimental films for the National Film Board of Canada, with which he remained until 1984. His later work includes the shorts *Parallels* (1960), *Mosaic* (1965), and *Pas de Deux* (1967). McLaren's innovations and new uses of old techniques exercised considerable influence over television advertising during the formative years of the medium.

MacLeish, Archibald The works of the poet Archibald MacLeish, b. Glencoe, Ill., May 7, 1892, d. Apr. 20, 1982, reflect both the dominant concerns of American thinkers and the development of poetic form during a major part of the 20th century. *The Pot of Earth* (1925) shows the influence of Sir James Frazer's *The Golden Bough; The Happy Marriage* (1924) and *The Hamlet of A. MacLeish* (1928), the influence of T. S. Eliot and Ezra Pound. MacLeish centered on vital American social issues in the satiric *Frescoes for Mr. Rockefeller's City* (1933), *Public Speech* (1936), and anti-Fascist radio plays such as *Air Raid* (1938). Sometimes called "the poet laureate of the New Deal," MacLeish was appointed librarian of Congress by President Franklin Roosevelt in 1939. He served in this capacity until 1944 and in various government positions until 1949. In 1953 he received a second Pulitzer Prize for poetry for *Collected Poems 1917–52* (1952). In the 1950s, MacLeish again raised a universal voice in *Songs for Eve* (1954) and *J. B.: A Play in Verse* (1958), based on the book of Job. *J. B.* won the 1959 Pulitzer Prize for drama.

MacLennan, Hugh Hugh MacLennan, b. Glace Bay, Nova Scotia, Mar. 20, 1907, d. Nov. 7, 1990, one of Canada's most honored writers, analyzed such "essential Canadian clashes and values" as English-Canadian colonialism, English-French relations in Canada, and Scottish-Canadian Calvinism. His best novel, *The Watch That Ends the Night* (1959), dealt movingly with events from his own life and what he called the "conflict... between the spirit and the human condition." Other novels include *Barometer Rising* (1941), *Two Solitudes* (1945), *The Precipice* (1948), *Return of the Sphinx* (1967), and *Voices in Time* (1980).

MacLeod, Colin M. [mik-lowd'] Colin Monroe MacLeod, b. Jan. 28, 1909, a Canadian-born American medical biochemist, is best known for his work with Oswald T. Avery and Maclyn McCarty. In 1944 these three scientists demonstrated in experiments using pneumococcus bacteria that genetic information in cells is carried in the molecule deoxyribonucleic acid (DNA). Later, MacLeod studied drug resistance using the same type of bacteria.

McLoughlin, John [mik-lahk'-lin]   A Canadian fur trader, John McLoughlin, b. Rivière du Loup, Quebec, Oct. 19, 1784, d. Sept. 3, 1857, became known as the father of Oregon. He joined the Hudson's Bay Company, which sent (1824) him to the Pacific Northwest. He built Fort Vancouver (now Vancouver, Wash.) and competed successfully with U.S. traders. McLoughlin's cooperative policies toward American settlers in the Columbia River country angered his superiors, and he retired (1846) to Oregon City. Settlement of the Oregon Question (1846) gave most of the area to the United States, and McLoughlin became (1849) a U.S. citizen.

McLuhan, Marshall [muh-kloo'-uhn]   The Canadian writer and teacher Herbert Marshall McLuhan, b. Edmonton, Alberta, July 21, 1911, d. Dec. 31, 1980, generated widespread controversy during the 1960s with his theories of the effects of the media on society. In *The Mechanical Bride: Folklore of Industrial Man* (1952), he proposed that the "grammar" of electronic technology corresponds to the human central nervous system and that the characteristics of a medium such as television, much more than its content, determine what a viewer will experience. His subsequent books, notably *Understanding Media* (1964) and *The Medium Is the Message* (1967), develop and refine these theories. From 1946 to 1966, McLuhan taught at the University of Toronto.

MacMahon, Marie Edme Patrice Maurice de [mahk-mah-oh']   Patrice MacMahon, b. July 13, 1808, d. Oct. 17, 1893, was a marshal of France and the second president of the Third Republic. Beginning his army career in 1827 in Algeria, he won a victory at Magenta in the Italian war of 1859, for which he was created duc de Magenta. After defeat at Sedan in the FRANCO-PRUSSIAN WAR (1870–71), MacMahon crushed the COMMUNE OF PARIS in 1871.

In 1873, when Adolphe THIERS resigned as president of the newly created Third Republic, right-wing monarchists persuaded MacMahon to accept the presidency. Hoping to recapture France for the monarchy, they passed a law giving him a seven-year term. This action marked the beginning of a struggle between republicans and rightists that lasted for a quarter century. After MacMahon forced Premier Jules SIMON, a moderate republican, out of the cabinet on May 16, 1877, many of the previously indifferent French converted to republicanism. MacMahon resigned in 1879 after the republicans gained a Senate majority.

McMahon, William [mik-man']   William McMahon, b. Sydney, New South Wales, Feb. 23, 1908, d. Mar. 31, 1988, was prime minister of Australia in 1971–72. He replaced John GORTON as leader of the Liberal party and prime minister after the party rejected Gorton's leadership. Previously McMahon had been treasurer (1966–69) and minister for foreign affairs (1969–71) in the Gorton government, where he won much praise for skillfully adapting Australia's economic policies to new international requirements. A member of the House of Representatives from 1949 to 1982, McMahon held numerous government posts and was deputy leader of the Liberal party from 1966 to 1971. In his brief tenure as prime minister, McMahon was beset with crises. With the loss of the elections of December 1972 to the labor party, 23 years of Liberal party rule came to an end.

McMaster, John Bach   John Bach McMaster, b. Brooklyn, N.Y., June 29, 1852, d. May 24, 1932, was a pioneering American social historian. The first volume of his *History of the People of the United States* (8 vols., 1883–1913) led to his appointment (1883) as professor of history at the University of Pennsylvania, where he remained until his retirement in 1920. His emphasis on social conditions and economic developments marked an important new approach in the writing of American history.

Macmillan, Harold   Maurice Harold Macmillan, b. Feb. 10, 1894, d. Dec. 29, 1986, was prime minister of Britain from 1957 to 1963. He was educated at Eton and Balliol College, Oxford. Macmillan became a Conservative member of Parliament in 1924, lost his seat in 1929, regained it in 1931, and kept it until the Labour party sweep in 1945. During World War II, Macmillan was sent (December 1942) to North Africa as resident minister at Allied headquarters.

The British statesman Harold Macmillan became one of the Conservative party's most important figures during the postwar era. On Sir Anthony Eden's resignation in 1957, Macmillan became prime minister. He led his party to victory in the general election of 1959 but resigned in 1963 because of failing health.

Early in 1945 Macmillan became secretary of state for air. His term in government ended abruptly in July 1945 when Labour won the general election and he lost his parliamentary seat. He returned in November, however, after winning a different seat in a by-election, and he held that seat until his retirement from politics in 1964. When the Conservatives regained power, Macmillan became minister of housing and local government (October 1951), minister of defense (October 1954), foreign secretary (April 1955), and chancellor of the exchequer (December 1955).

When Sir Anthony EDEN resigned as prime minister following the SUEZ CRISIS of 1956, Macmillan succeeded him as prime minister. His first objective was to mend relations with the United States, which had been strained by the crisis. His second was to strengthen Britain's ties with Europe by joining the European Economic Community. In this he suffered a sharp rebuff from France's President DE GAULLE, who vetoed British entry in January 1963.

In 1959, Macmillan and the Conservatives won a landslide victory because of the healthy state of the British economy. Great Britain began to experience balance-of-payments problems, and in 1961 an austerity program was established. After undergoing surgery in October 1963, Macmillan resigned as prime minister. He retired from Parliament in 1964. In 1984 he took the hereditary title earl of Stockton.

MacMillan, Kenneth   The career of the choreographer, company director, and dancer Kenneth MacMillan, b. Dunfermline, Scotland, Dec. 11, 1929, d. Oct. 29, 1992, was closely linked with Britain's Royal Ballet. A charter member (1946) of the Sadler's Wells Theatre Ballet (SWTB), he joined the senior company, the Sadler's Wells Ballet (now Royal Ballet), in 1948. He choreographed for both companies; early works include *Danses Concertantes* (1955), *Le Baiser de la Fée* (1960), *The Invitation* (1960), and *Le Sacre du Printemps (The Rite of Spring,* 1962). From 1966 to 1969 he directed the Deutsche Oper Ballet in Berlin, where he introduced productions of the Maryinsky (now Kirov) classics, *The Sleeping Beauty* (1967) and *Swan Lake* (1969). In 1970 he succeeded Frederick Ashton as director of the Royal Ballet. In 1977 he relinquished the directorship to devote himself to the post of principal choreographer.

MacMillan created both compact dramatic ballets and pure dance works that display his musical intelligence and his skill in deploying an ensemble. His evening-length narrative works, the mainstay of a large opera-house company, include *Romeo and Juliet* (1967), *Manon* (1974), *Mayerling* (1978), and *Anastasia* (1971).

McMurtry, Larry   Larry McMurtry, b. Wichita Falls, Tex., June 3, 1936, raised in a family of ranchers and cowboys, has specialized in novels that explore the fading of the American frontier spirit as it clashes with a more complex modern reality. His 1961 novel, *Horseman, Pass By* (filmed as *Hud* in 1963), pits a successful and callous modern Westerner against the more humane values

represented by his father, his housekeeper, and his young nephew. *The Last Picture Show* (1966; film, 1971) evokes growing up in a drab Texas town among the survivors of a past glory, a site revisited in *Texasville* (1987; film, 1990). *Terms of Endearment* (1975; film, 1983) depicts a 30-year mother-daughter relationship with humor and tragedy. The Pulitzer Prize–winning *Lonesome Dove* (1985; TV miniseries, 1989) is an epic account of an 1870s cattle drive. Other novels include *Cadillac Jack* (1982), *Anything for Billy* (1988), *Some Can Whistle* (1989), and *Buffalo Girls* (1990).

MacNab, Sir Allan Napier   Sir Allan MacNab, b. Newark, Upper Canada (now Niagara-on-the-Lake, Ontario), Feb. 19, 1798, d. Aug. 8, 1862, was copremier of Canada (1854–56). He sat (1830–57) in the Upper Canada legislature and later the United Canada legislature, where he led the Conservatives and served as speaker (1837–41, 1844–48). MacNab became (1854) copremier, first with Augustin Morin and then with Étienne Paschal Taché. His involvement with railroad interests (he was director of the Great Western Railway) led to questions about his objectivity, however, and he resigned (1856). He was again elected (1860) to the legislature, becoming speaker for the third time in 1862.

McNamara, Robert S.   Robert Strange McNamara, b. San Francisco, June 9, 1916, served as U.S. secretary of defense (1961–68) and president of the World Bank (1968–81). He taught business administration at Harvard (1940–43) and became an air-force systems expert during World War II. In 1946, McNamara joined the Ford Motor Company and instigated important model and marketing changes. In 1960 he became Ford's first nonfamily president. As secretary of defense during the escalation of the Vietnam War, he was responsible for strengthening U.S. military capacity in both conventional and nuclear weapons. As president of the World Bank, McNamara redirected its programs to give more emphasis to the problems of world poverty.

MacNeice, Louis   [mik-nees']   The Irish poet Louis MacNeice, b. Belfast, Ireland, Sept. 12, 1907, d. Sept. 3, 1963, studied classics and philosophy at Oxford. Throughout the 1930s he taught at the Universities of Birmingham and London but devoted most of his career to writing and producing radio programs for the BBC. Although linked early with such left-wing poets as W. H. Auden, Stephen Spender, and C. Day Lewis, MacNeice always remained a fundamentally private and often ironic poet. In his work, gathered in *Collected Poems* (1967), he depicts the multiplicity of the world. An autobiography, *The Strings Are False,* was published posthumously in 1965.

McNickle, D'Arcy   The author of several important works about the struggles of American Indians to survive,

William D'Arcy McNickle, b. Saint Ignatius, Mont., Jan. 18, 1904, d. October 1977, was himself a member of the Flathead tribe. His works include the novels *The Surrounded* (1936), *Runner in the Sun* (1954), and *Wind from an Enemy Sky* (1977), plus such nonfiction as *They Came Here First* (1949; rev. ed., 1975), *Indians and Other Americans* (1959; rev. ed., 1970), and *Native American Tribalism* (1973).

Macon [may'-kuhn]   Located in central Georgia at the head of navigation on the Ocmulgee River, Macon is the seat of Bibb County and one of Georgia's largest cities. Its population is 106,612 (1990), and that of the metropolitan area is 281,103. First laid out in 1823, the city is a manufacturing, processing, and shipping center for an extensive farming region.

Macon, Nathaniel   Nathaniel Macon, b. Edgecombe (now Warren) County, N.C., Dec. 17, 1758, d. June 29, 1837, was an American congressional leader during the administrations of Thomas Jefferson and James Madison. He began his political career in the North Carolina Senate (1781–85) and later served as U.S. representative (1791–1815) and U.S. senator (1815–28). A staunch Jeffersonian and leader of forces opposing the Federalist party, he was Speaker of the House from 1801 to 1807. As head of the House Foreign Relations Committee in 1810, he gave his name to "Macon's Bill No. 2" (although he was neither its author nor its supporter). This measure aimed at protecting U.S. commerce during the quarrels with Britain that preceded the War of 1812.

MacPhail, Agnes Campbell   Agnes Campbell MacPhail, b. Proton Township, Ontario, Mar. 24, 1890, d. Feb. 13, 1954, was the first woman to be elected to the Canadian House of Commons. A member of the United Farmers of Ontario party, she served in the House from 1921 to 1940 and took a great interest in social legislation. She was a member of the Canadian delegation to the League of Nations (1929) and sat in the Ontario legislature (1943–45, 1948–51).

McPhee, John   A nonfiction writer, John McPhee, b. Princeton, N.J., Mar. 8, 1931, wrote television plays and worked as an editor for *Time* before becoming a staff writer for the *New Yorker* in 1964. McPhee's first book, *A Sense of Where You Are* (1965), was about basketball star Bill Bradley. His later works include *The Pine Barrens* (1968), about a unique area of New Jersey; *The Deltoid Pumpkin Seed* (1973), about experimental aircraft; *Coming into the Country* (1977), about Alaska; *Basin and Range* (1981), *In Suspect Terrain* (1983), and *Rising from the Plains* (1987), about geology; *Table of Contents* (1985), a group of essays; and *The Control of Nature* (1989), about humanity's wars with nature.

McPherson, Aimee Semple   Evangelist Aimee Semple McPherson, b. near Ingersoll, Ontario, Oct. 9, 1890, d. Sept. 27, 1944, founded the International Church of the Foursquare Gospel. Converted by her first husband, Robert Semple, a Pentecostal evangelist, she joined him in revival campaigns and then in the mission field in Asia. When he died in 1910, she returned to the United States with her infant daughter, married Harold McPherson, a Rhode Island grocery salesman, and began to hold revivals. In 1923 she opened Angelus Temple, a 5,300-seat auditorium. She subsequently founded a radio station, a Bible college, an evangelistic association, and the International Church of the Foursquare Gospel (1927).

Scandal repeatedly touched her personal life—most notably in 1926 when she disappeared for a month, reappeared with the story that she had been kidnapped, and was tried (case dismissed) for perjury. She died in 1944 from an accidental overdose of barbiturates.

Aimee Semple McPherson, an American evangelist, founded the International Church of the Foursquare Gospel shortly after settling in Los Angeles in 1918. The highly theatrical sermons of "Sister" Aimee attracted thousands of followers and considerable financial support.

Macpherson, James   James Macpherson, b. Oct. 27, 1736, d. Feb. 17, 1796, was a controversial poet of what is often called the preromantic period. He was born in the Highlands of Scotland, became a schoolmaster, and after making his fortune through his poetry, became active in politics. In 1760, Macpherson published his translations of Gaelic poetry, *Fragments of Ancient Poetry Collected in the Highlands of Scotland*; this immensely popular volume was followed by *Fingal* (1762) and *Temora* (1763), which purported to be translations of the epic poems of the 3d-century Gaelic bard OSSIAN. The question of their authenticity raised a furious controversy. The poems were, in fact, a blend of fragments from old Scottish and Irish poetry, tinged with 18th-century sentimentality and diction.

macrame [mak'-ruh-may]   Macrame, which takes its name from the Arabic, is a form of decorative knotting, in which basic knots, such as the square knot and hitch, are tied in horizontal and perpendicular lines to create intricate geometrical patterns. The craft is thought to have been developed by Middle Eastern weavers as a decorative means for binding off the warp threads of completed carpets. Some contemporary artisans have created wall macrame hangings of massive proportions.

Macready, William Charles [mik-ree'-dee]   One of the finest English tragic actors, William Charles Macready, b. Mar. 3, 1793, d. Apr. 27, 1873, first appeared on the London stage in 1816 at Covent Garden. Within four years he was the principal rival of Edmund Kean—the foremost Shakespearean actor of the time—appearing in such roles as Lear, Hamlet, and Macbeth and countering Kean's demonstrative manner with a more intellectual and restrained acting style. He managed both Covent Garden (1837–39) and the Drury Lane theater (1841–43), where he sought to improve production methods.

macroeconomics   see ECONOMY, NATIONAL

macromolecule [mak'-roh-mahl'-uh-kuel]   A macromolecule is any very large molecule but is usually defined as having a molecular weight of over 10,000. Macromolecules exist in various forms. Organic polymers consist of large numbers of repeating units and are classified as macromolecules. PROTEINS and nucleic acids occur naturally; PLASTICS are synthetic in origin. Inorganic MINERAL crystals are also considered to be macromolecules. Scientists measure the viscosity of macromolecules to determine their general shape.

Madagascar [mad-uh-gas'-kur]   Madagascar, formerly called the Malagasy Republic, is an island nation in the Indian Ocean, located about 400 km (250 mi) across the Mozambique Channel from the southeastern coast of Africa. Approximately the same size as Texas, Madagascar is the fourth largest island in the world, including its five small offshore island dependencies. Because of its location and unique settlement history, Madagascar has remained fairly isolated from nearby East Africa.

Land and Resources

Madagascar's dominant topographic feature is a high upland region in the center of the island called the central plateau. Its average elevation is about 1,400 m (4,500 ft), but it is characterized by hills, deep gorges, and volcanic outcroppings that hinder transportation. ANTANANARIVO, the capital and principal city, is on the plateau. During recent centuries the plateau was deforested for its timber and by slash-and-burn agricultural practices. The highest point in the country is Mount Maromokotro (2,876 m/9,436 ft).

Between the plateau and the Indian Ocean, to the east, a plain about 50 km (30 mi) wide occurs. This is

DEMOCRATIC REPUBLIC OF MADAGASCAR

Land: Area: 587,041 km² (226,658 mi²). Capital and largest city: Antananarivo (1990 est. pop., 802,400).

People: Population (1990 est.): 11,800,524. Density: 20.1 persons per km² (52.1 per mi²). Distribution (1989): 22% urban, 78% rural. Official languages: Malagasy, French. Major religions: traditional religions, Christianity, Islam.

Government: Type: republic. Legislature: Popular National Assembly. Political subdivisions: 6 provinces.

Economy: GNP (1988): $1.7 billion; $155 per capita. Labor distribution (1985): agriculture—26%; domestic service—17%; commerce—14%; construction—11%; services—9%; transportation—6%; other—2%. Foreign trade (1988): imports—$319 million; exports—$284 million. Currency: 1 Malagasy franc = 100 centimes.

Education and Health: Literacy (1985): 67.5% of adult population. Universities (1990): 6. Hospital beds (1982): 20,800. Physicians (1982): 940. Life expectancy (1990): women—53; men—50. Infant mortality (1990): 97 per 1,000 live births.

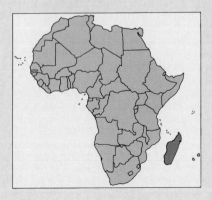

the most densely populated part of the country; Toamasina, the leading port, is there. In the sparsely populated west, hills descend from the plateau to the Mozambique Channel. Madagascar's major rivers, the Betsiboka, Tsiribihina, and Mangoky, descend from the plateau to the west coast, creating fertile, intensively cultivated valleys.

The east and southeast experience the greatest rainfall, about 3,710 mm (146 in) annually. The central plateau is the coolest part of the country, and the average annual temperature is 18° C (65° F) at Antananarivo. The plateau receives about 1,360 mm (53 in) of rain annually. The west and southwestern areas are the driest regions. Rainfall is irregular and unpredictable throughout Madagascar.

Madagascar's dwindling forests are home to an enormous variety of unique plant and animal life, including more than 6,000 species of flowering plants, half the world's chameleon varieties, and most surviving LEMURS (monkeylike primates). An international effort to preserve the island's unique ecosystem has been launched. Chromium, salt, graphite, mica, beryl, zircon, gold, and garnets are mined.

People

The basic racial stock of the people is Malayo-Polynesian, although there has been a great deal of mixture with black Africans and Arabic peoples. The Malagasy are divided into 18 ethnic groups, and conflict among them constitutes a major problem today. The largest group, the Merina, live primarily on the plateau. The other major tribes include the Betsileo, the Betsimisaraka, the Antandroy, and the Tsimihety. About 98% of the population are Malagasy, but there are small minorities from the nearby Comoros, as well as some French, Indians, and Chinese.

Like the people, the Malagasy language is of Malayo-Polynesian origin, although it has borrowed from the Bantu languages of southern Africa and from Arabic and French. About 40% of the population are Christian; a Muslim minority also exists. The rest of the population practice the traditional religion, in which ancestor worship plays a central role.

Primary education is free and compulsory between the ages of 6 and 14, but many children do not attend school. The University of Madagascar (1961) is at Antananarivo.

Economic Activity

Madagascar's economy is almost entirely agricultural. The country relies heavily on foreign aid, supplied primarily by France and other western European nations.

Rice and cassava are the leading subsistence crops. Coffee is the principal export crop, and Madagascar is the world's leading producer of cloves and vanilla. Food processing and textile manufacture are the chief industries. After 1972 the government nationalized many key industries, although restrictions imposed on foreign investment and private enterprise have been eased in recent years.

History and Government

Most scholars believe that Madagascar was inhabited about the 1st century AD, when Indonesian seafarers arrived. Arab traders later established coastal trading posts.

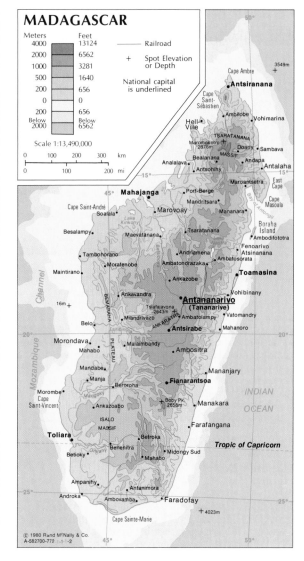

In 1500, Diogo Dias, a Portuguese navigator, was the first European to visit the island. In 1643 the French established a trading post at Fort-Dauphin.

The Merina kingdom, founded in the late 16th century, controlled the island, with fluctuating degrees of European influence, until the end of the 19th century. In 1890 the British relinquished their interests in Madagascar to France, and in 1895, Madagascar became a French protectorate. During World War II, Madagascar was occupied by British and South African forces; in 1943 it was turned over to the Free French. In 1947 a revolt against the French was harshly suppressed; estimates of those killed range from 11,000 to 80,000. A 1958 referendum on the question of independence was overwhelmingly supported.

Antananarivo is Madagascar's capital and largest city. Located on the central plateau, Antananarivo is also the center of Madagascar's commerce and industry.

In 1960 the Malagasy Republic became an independent nation. Didier Ratsiraka, who became president in 1975 after years of turmoil, was reelected in 1982 and 1989. The 1975 constitution changed the name of the country from Malagasy Republic to Democratic Republic of Madagascar. It provides for an elected president, who appoints members of the Supreme Revolutionary Council (the principal policy-making body) and a prime minister. Members of the legislature are elected by universal suffrage. The requirement that all political parties belong to the umbrella group known as the National Front for the Defense of the Malagasy Socialist Revolution was lifted in March 1990.

Madama Butterfly   see PUCCINI, GIACOMO

Madame Bovary   see FLAUBERT, GUSTAVE

▬

Maddox, Lester G.   Lester Garfield Maddox, b. Atlanta, Ga., Sept. 30, 1915, was Democratic governor of Georgia (1967–71) and then lieutenant governor (1971–75). He became nationally known as an avowed segregationist during the early 1960s, when he refused to serve black patrons in his fried-chicken restaurant near Atlanta. He closed his business rather than desegregate it in accordance with civil rights legislation. Maddox's political career followed this action.

▬

Madeira Islands   [muh-dir'-uh]   The Madeira Islands, a volcanic archipelago in the Atlantic Ocean 645 km (400 mi) west of Morocco, constitute the Portuguese autonomous region of Madeira. They comprise the inhabited islands of Madeira and Porto Santo and the uninhabited Desertas and Selvagens, having a total land area of 798 km² (308 mi²) and a population of 271,400 (1988 est.). FUNCHAL, the capital and largest town, is on Madeira.

Madeira, the largest island, is mountainous with a subtropical climate. The island is famous for its wine and for the embroidery and wickerwork produced; it is also a popular resort. On Porto Santo Island, northeast of Madeira, wheat, barley, and grapes are cultivated.

Explored by Phoenicians and Genoese, the islands were colonized in 1420 by Portuguese sponsored by Prince Henry the Navigator.

The map indicates the location of the Madeira Islands, a Portuguese-governed archipelago off the northwest coast of Africa. Only two islands of the group, Madeira and Porto Santo, are inhabited.

▬

Madeira River   The Madeira River, chief tributary of the AMAZON, is formed on the border between Brazil and Bolivia by the confluence of the Mamoré and Beni rivers. With the Mamoré, it is 3,380 km (2,100 mi) long; the Madeira proper is 1,883 km (1,170 mi). The river flows primarily northeast. About 145 km (90 mi) east of MANAUS, it joins the Amazon. Navigable for 1,288 km (800 mi), the Madeira carries rain-forest products. It was first explored by Europeans in the 16th century.

▬

Maderna, Bruno   Bruno Maderna, b. Apr. 21, 1920, d. Nov. 13, 1973, was an eminent Italian composer and conductor. In 1955, Maderna founded, with Luciano Berio, the Studio di Fonologia Musicale of the Italian Radio in Milan, an important electronic music center. In 1961 he founded and conducted the International Chamber Ensemble in Darmstadt. Maderna's earliest serial works were written in 1951; most of his electronic works also include parts for live performance.

Maderno, Carlo The work of Carlo Maderno, b. 1556, d. Jan. 30, 1629, one of the great architects of 17th-century Rome, foreshadowed the baroque style in architecture. His first independent design, for the facade of Santa Susanna (1596–1603) in Rome, is marked by a clear progression of elements—pilaster, column, and double columns—the whole being enlivened by rich yet tightly controlled sculptural details.

In 1603, Maderno was appointed architect of SAINT PETER'S BASILICA. In 1607 he won the competition to enlarge the basilica by transforming Michelangelo's Greek-cross plan into a Latin cross; he did this by adding a three-bay nave and fronting it with a vast nine-bay facade. There was much criticism of this scheme, most obviously because it obscured the original plan and the dome. So far as the commission allowed, however, Maderno tried to be true to Michelangelo's conception. The facade was completed and consecrated in 1626.

Madero, Francisco I. The Mexican political leader Francisco Indalecio Madero, b. Oct. 30, 1873, d. Feb. 22, 1913, led his country in the revolution of 1910 and became its president (1911–13). The son of wealthy landowners, Madero was educated in California and Paris. He became a champion of Mexican liberalism, and, as a political writer he criticized the regime of Mexican dictator Porfirio DÍAZ. In 1910 he ran for the presidency against Díaz but lost the election through electoral fraud. He was arrested but escaped across the border into Texas. From San Antonio he declared himself provisional president on Oct. 7, 1910, and in his Plan of San Luis Potosí he called for a revolution to overthrow Díaz. With the help

Francisco Madero, a Mexican revolutionary, organized the political uprisings that led to the collapse of Porfirio Díaz's autocratic regime. Madero won election to the nation's presidency in 1911 but was deposed within 15 months.

of Pancho VILLA, Emiliano ZAPATA, and Pascual Orozco, the revolution triumphed in May 1911, and a few months later Madero, hailed as the "apostle of democracy," was elected president.

Beset by plots and outbreaks of disorder during his tenure, Madero was overthrown and killed in a military coup led by Victoriano HUERTA. He was subsequently revered as a martyr and a symbol of Mexican democratic opposition to dictatorship.

Madhya Pradesh [mahd'-yuh prah'-dish] Madhya Pradesh is a state in central India, lying between the Ganges River valley to the north and the Deccan Plateau to the south. It covers 443,460 km^2 (171,220 mi^2) and has a population of 52,178,844 (1981). The capital is BHOPAL. The main crops are wheat, rice, legumes, peanuts, and cotton. Coal, iron ore, manganese, and bauxite are mined. Iron and steel, heavy electrical equipment, textiles, and food products are manufactured.

The region was ruled by Hindu dynasties until 712, when it was invaded by Muslims. Muslim control was solidified during the 12th century, and in the 17th century the Moguls assumed power; the British ruled from 1820 until 1947. The state received its present boundaries in 1956.

Madison Madison, in south central Wisconsin, is the state capital and the seat of Dane County. Wisconsin's second largest city, Madison has a population of 191,262 (1990); that of the metropolitan area is 367,085. Madison has a diversified economy; it is a commercial and manufacturing center in a rich agricultural region. Manufactures include food products, machinery, and medical equipment. Its skyline is dominated by the classic white granite dome of the state capitol. Many recreational parks along the lakefronts are within the city limits. The First Unitarian Church was designed by Frank Lloyd Wright. The University of Wisconsin (1849) has long been an important factor in the community. The site was acquired and named by James Duane Doty and Stevens T. Mason in 1836. In the same year the Territory of Wisconsin was established with Madison, although unsettled, as the capital. The town was laid out in 1837.

Madison, Dolley Dolley Payne Madison, b. May 20, 1768, d. July 12, 1849, the wife of President James Madison, was one of the most famous first ladies in U.S. history. She acted as White House hostess while her husband was secretary of state under Thomas Jefferson, a widower, and later during Madison's own two terms in the presidency (1809–17). She was noted for her graciousness and charm and for her ability to entertain guests and preside at dinners. During the British invasion of Washington in 1814, she escaped to Virginia carrying important state papers, a Gilbert Stuart portrait of George Washington, and other personal valuables.

AT A GLANCE

JAMES MADISON
4th President of the United States (1809–17)

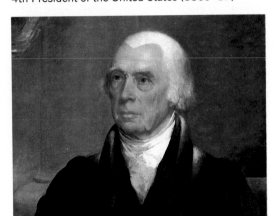

Nickname: "Father of the Constitution"

Born: Mar. 16, 1751, Port Conway, Va.

Education: College of New Jersey (now Princeton University; graduated 1771)

Profession: Lawyer

Religious Affiliation: Episcopalian

Marriage: Sept. 15, 1794, to Dolley Dandridge Payne Todd (1768–1849)

Children: None

Political Affiliation: Democratic-Republican

Writings: *Writings* (9 vols., 1900–10), ed. by Gaillard Hunt; *The Papers of James Madison* (1962–), ed. by W. T. Hutchinson, R. A. Rutland, et al.

Died: June 28, 1836, Montpelier, Va.

Buried: Montpelier, Va. (family plot)

Vice-Presidents: George Clinton (1809–12); Elbridge Gerry (1813–14)

James Madison

Madison, James   James Madison was the foremost architect of the U.S. Constitution, a leading theorist of republican government, and the fourth president of the United States (1809–17).

Early Life. Madison was born at Port Conway, Va., on Mar. 16, 1751, into a family that had been in Virginia since the mid-17th century. At preparatory school and the College of New Jersey at Princeton, from which he graduated in 1771, Madison was greatly influenced by the works of such thinkers as Joseph Addison, David Hume, John Locke, Isaac Newton, and Voltaire.

As the American Revolution approached, Madison served (from 1774) on the Orange County Committee of Safety. Two years later he was elected to the Virginia convention that voted for independence and that drafted a constitution for the new state. During 1778 and 1779 he served on the council of state under governors Patrick HENRY and Thomas JEFFERSON.

Nationalist-Federalist. Elected to the CONTINENTAL CONGRESS in December 1779, Madison became a leader of the so-called nationalist group, which advocated a strong central government. By the time he retired from Congress in 1783 he was regarded as its best-informed and most effective legislator and debater. Three years (1784–86) in the Virginia legislature convinced him that the ARTICLES OF CONFEDERATION were too weak to bind the states together in the face of domestic and foreign threats to the unity

of the new nation. At the ANNAPOLIS CONVENTION in 1786 he took a lead in the call for the CONSTITUTIONAL CONVENTION that met the following year in Philadelphia. There Madison was a persuasive proponent of an independent federal court system, a strong executive, and a bicameral legislature with terms of differing length and representation according to population.

Madison worked with Alexander HAMILTON and other supporters of the Constitution to win its ratification. He contributed several papers in the FEDERALIST series. Serving in the new House of Representatives from 1789, Madison sponsored the BILL OF RIGHTS and was one of President George WASHINGTON's chief advisors.

Democratic-Republican. In January 1790, Madison broke with the administration to oppose the financial program of Hamilton, now secretary of the treasury. Madison felt that Hamilton's policies favored commerce and wealth and allowed the executive department to dominate the other branches of government. He now began to work closely with Jefferson and his supporters. The opposition of the Jeffersonians deepened, and America's first political-party system began to emerge as the FEDERALIST PARTY sought stronger commercial bonds with Great Britain and withdrew support from revolutionary France. The Jeffersonians, known later as Democratic-Republicans, feared that a commercial faction, caring little for the nation's republican ideals, had temporarily gained control. During this period of political discouragement, however, Madison found private happiness by his marriage in 1794 to a lively widow, Dolley Dandridge Payne Todd.

Madison left Congress in disgust in 1797. As a private citizen he drafted the Virginia Resolutions (1798; see KENTUCKY AND VIRGINIA RESOLUTIONS) in protest against the ALIEN AND SEDITION ACTS, sponsored by John ADAMS's administration. In 1799–1800, he served in the Virginia legislature. In 1801, Madison was appointed secretary of state by the new president, Jefferson. These two men and the new secretary of the treasury, Albert GALLATIN, formed a Republican triumvirate that led the nation for the next eight years. Madison adroitly guided the negotiations that resulted in the LOUISIANA PURCHASE (1803) and supported American suppression of the Barbary pirates in the TRIPOLITAN WAR (1803–05). In the war between France and Britain, however, both were inflicting heavy damage on American shipping; Britain, moreover, was stopping American ships and impressing sailors on the high seas. Confronted by overwhelming British naval power, Madison supported the EMBARGO ACT (1807), which forbade American ships to trade abroad.

Presidency. Madison was easily elected president in 1808, although the Embargo Act cost him the electoral votes of commercial New England. Furthermore, the unity of the Democratic-Republican party under Jefferson was diminished under Madison and in the face of the continuing dilemmas posed by the Napoleonic Wars.

Since neither France nor Britain saw any need to respect a distant and disunited republic, Madison's diplomacy and efforts at commercial retaliation floundered ineffectively for three years. Finally, under pressure from the newly elected "war hawks" in Congress, a group led by Henry CLAY, John C. CALHOUN, and Richard M. JOHNSON, Madison asked for and received a declaration of war on Britain in June 1812. Although he was reelected president that year, factious strife within his own party and a determined (some thought treasonous) opposition from the Federalists in New England plagued Madison throughout the WAR OF 1812.

By 1814 greatly improved American armies successfully defended the Niagara frontier against the enemy, but Washington itself was captured by the British and burned. Madison watched the flames from the other side of the Potomac. Soon afterward, however, the British were defeated in Baltimore harbor and repulsed in their invasion of New York State via Lake Champlain.

These setbacks persuaded the British government to seek peace, but Madison did not know this fact in the fall and winter of 1814. In this gloomy period he faced the prospect of national bankruptcy; the apparent threat of secession in New England, where the HARTFORD CONVENTION met in December 1814; and the menace of a powerful British force approaching New Orleans. Then, in February 1815, news of both Andrew JACKSON's victory at New Orleans and the peace treaty signed at Ghent on Dec. 24, 1814, reached Washington. Joy replaced gloom, and the threat of disunion was ended. The Treaty of Ghent ensured the United States an equal and respected place in the post-Napoleonic world. At last free of foreign worries, Madison proposed wide-ranging domestic pro-

grams in December 1815: recharter of the Bank of the United States, a moderate tariff, creation of a national university, and federal support for roads and canals. Although Congress accepted only part of this program, the public acclaimed Madison on his retirement.

Later Life. Handing over the presidency to yet another member of the so-called Virginia dynasty, James MONROE, Madison retired (1817) to his Virginia estate, Montpelier. He subsequently helped Jefferson found the University of Virginia and served Monroe as a foreign-policy advisor.

Madonna   A dominant force in pop music of the 1980s and '90s, Madonna Louise Ciccone, b. Bay City, Mich., Aug. 16, 1958, achieved stardom primarily through her music videos. Not an outstanding singer or dancer, she has used music videos from her hit records *Madonna* (1983), *Like a Virgin* (1985), *Like a Prayer* (1989), and *I'm Breathless* (1990) to reinvent her image from street waif to sex symbol to glamorous star. She has acted in movies and on stage with limited success, doing best in roles close to her image at that time. Films include *Desperately Seeking Susan* (1985), *Dick Tracy* (1990), the documentary *Madonna, Truth or Dare* (1991), and *A League of Their Own* (1992).

Madras (city) [mah-drahs']   Madras is the capital of the state of Tamil Nadu in southern India. It lies on the Bay of Bengal, about 650 km (400 mi) northeast from the tip of the subcontinent. Its population is 5,361,468 (1991). Industries include filmmaking and the manufacture of cotton textiles, aluminum utensils, matches, hand-woven cloth, and cigarettes. The main exports are leather, iron ore, textiles, and coffee.

Madras University (1857) is one of the finest in India. Other cultural institutions include the Madras Music Academy, the Fort Saint George Museum, and the National Art Gallery. Southwest of the city stands Saint Thomas Mount, where the apostle Saint Thomas is said to have been martyred. Modern Madras was founded in 1639 when Francis Day of the British East India Company built Fort Saint George in the village of Madras Patnam.

madras [mad'-ruhs]   India madras is a coarse-spun, hand-loomed cotton fabric that originated in India's Madras state (now Tamil Nadu). The yarn is often dyed with vegetable dyes that "bleed" when washed; after several washings, true India madras cottons will exhibit a softness and subtlety of color that result from such bleeding.

Madrid   The capital and largest city in Spain, Madrid (1990 est. pop., 3,120,732) is in the geographical heart of the country on the Manzanares River, a tributary of the Tagus. During the 16th century the former Moorish fortress was made the capital because of its location. Today Madrid is the commercial, cultural, and transportation center of Spain, as well as the capital of Madrid province.

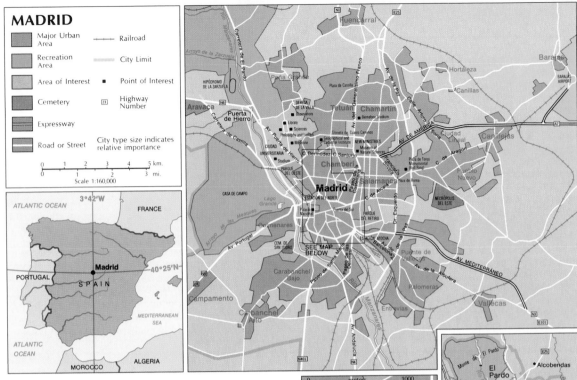

MADRID

Legend:
- Major Urban Area
- Recreation Area
- Area of Interest
- Cemetery
- Expressway
- Road or Street
- Railroad
- City Limit
- Point of Interest
- Highway Number
- City type size indicates relative importance

Scale 1:160,000

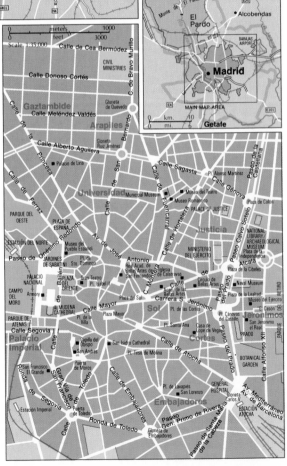

Scale 1:35,000

Contemporary City

The center of Madrid, the old city, built around the original fortress, has narrow, twisting streets. Until 1868 this portion of the city was enclosed by walls. Madrid's main thoroughfares radiate from the Plaza del Sol in the old city. The modern city center, to the east, is distinguished by wide, straight avenues and large plazas, the finest of which is the Plaza Mayor, built in the early 17th century. Ciudad Universitaria (University City) is in the northwest, and Madrid's famous bull ring lies to the east.

Madrid developed as an administrative city, but today it is Spain's leading manufacturing center. Industries include transportation equipment; textile, leather goods, chemicals, and plastics manufacturing; food processing; and mechanical and electrical engineering. Printing, publishing, and filmmaking are also important, and Madrid is the banking and financial center of Spain.

The University of Madrid was established in 1836. The most famous of the many important museums located in Madrid is the PRADO, one of the world's outstanding art museums. Other sites of interest include the former National Palace (built 1737–64); the Biblioteca Nacional; the Archaeological Museum; and the 17th-century San Isidro Cathedral. Madrid also has splendid parks.

History

Although prehistoric and Roman remains have been found, Madrid was first mentioned in written sources during the 10th century. At that time it was called Majrit and was a Moorish fortress. In 1083, Majrit fell to Castile and became a Spanish fortress maintaining the frontier against the Moors. Occasionally it served as a meeting place for the Castilian court. In 1561, Philip II made Madrid his capital, and in 1607 it became Spain's permanent capital. It then began to grow rapidly. The court attracted many of Spain's leading artists and writers to Madrid, including Cervantes, Lope de Vega, and Velázquez. During the reign (1759–88) of Charles III, many of Madrid's finest buildings, including the Prado, were constructed. In 1808, during the Peninsular War, the French took Madrid. The French were driven out briefly by a popular uprising during the same year, but they returned and ruled the city until 1813. The major republican stronghold during the SPANISH CIVIL WAR (1936–39), Madrid was beseiged by Francisco Franco's Nationalist forces for two and a half years. When the city finally fell the civil war ended.

madrigal   Madrigal is the name given to two important types of secular vocal music: one cultivated in 14th-century Italy, the other in 16th-century Italy and early-17th-century England. The former consists of two or three tercets of verse, each followed by a couplet called ritornello, with music mirroring the verse form. The main melodic interest is in the top voice, which is usually more florid than the lower parts. Chief composers were Giovanni da Cascia and Jacopo da Bologna (fl. 1350) and Francesco LANDINI.

Poetically, the 16th-century madrigal is much freer in form than its earlier counterpart. The musical setting emphasizes the mood and meaning of individual words and phrases of the text rather than formal structure. The first collection of madrigals was printed in 1530. More than 3,000 others followed within the next century.

The earliest composers included the Italian Costanzo Festa (c.1490–1545) and the Franco-Netherlanders Philippe Verdelot (d.1567), Adrian Willaert, Jacob Arcadelt (c.1514–68), and Cipriano de Rore (1516–65).

Madrigals were written for as few as three and as many as eight parts. They were often sung by solo voices, one to a part, sometimes reinforced by instruments. By the late 16th century the madrigal had become the dominant form of secular music in Europe; progressive composers such as Carlo GESUALDO, Claudio MONTEVERDI, Luca Marenzio, and Giaches de Wert used it to make their boldest harmonic and motivic experiments. In England, about 1590, native musicians created an English madrigal form that enhanced Elizabethan and Jacobean music.

maenads   [mee'-nadz]   In Greek mythology maenads were women votaries of DIONYSUS, the god of wine. Waving the thyrsus—an ivy-entwined staff—as they sang while draped in the skins of animals, the maenads abandoned themselves to orgiastic dancing and festivals.

Maes, Nicolaes   [mahs]   Nicolaes Maes, 1634–93, a Flemish painter of genre scenes and portraits, was a follower of Rembrandt, in whose studio he worked during the late 1640s. Maes's early work, much indebted to his master's treatment of light and shade, depicts women

engaged in domestic tasks, but he later became more anecdotal, producing popular renderings of amorous incidents. Finally, he took to the lucrative practice of portraiture and evolved a proficient style of characterization.

Maeterlinck, Maurice   [mah'-tur-lahnk, moh-rees']   Maurice Maeterlinck, b. Aug. 29, 1862, d. May 6, 1949, was a Belgian poet, dramatist, and essayist whose major works anticipate the contemporary theater of the absurd. His plays—The Intruder (1891; Eng. trans., 1896), The Blind (1891; Eng. trans., 1896), Pelléas and Mélisande (1892; Eng. trans., 1864)—give primacy to ritual, myth, gesture, and the world of the occult. Three dramas for marionettes—Alladine and Palomides, Interior, and The Death of Tintagiles (all 1894; Eng. trans., 1895, 1894, 1898)—are groundbreaking in their symbolist techniques. His realistic and philosophical plays, such as the feminist Ariane et Barbe-Bleue (Ariadne and Bluebeard, 1901), lack the intensity, poetry, and authenticity of his early works. Only The Blue Bird (1909; Eng. trans., 1909), reverting to fairy-tale dimensions, is of the same superior quality. Entomology, philosophy, war, religion, mathematics, physics, psychometrics, and the occult were the subjects of Maeterlinck's essays. In 1911, Maeterlinck won the Nobel Prize for literature.

Mafeking   [maf'-uh-king]   Mafeking (Mafiking; 1980 pop., 6,775) is a town in South Africa, in northern Cape Province, near the border with Botswana. The town is an important rail junction, with railroad repair shops, a creamery, and markets for cattle, sheep, and corn. Founded in 1885, Mafeking was for 80 years the administrative headquarters of the British Protectorate of Bechuanaland (now Botswana). It was the starting point of the Jameson Raid (1895; see JAMESON, SIR LEANDER STARR), and under Col. Robert BADEN-POWELL's command it withstood a siege during the SOUTH AFRICAN WAR (1899).

Mafia   The Mafia is a secret criminal organization that wields great economic and political power over large segments of Sicilian society and operates both criminal and legitimate U.S. enterprises. It is believed to have originated during the late Middle Ages; separate bands of strong-arm enforcers hired by local landowners eventually evolved into a network of autonomous groups ruling over a peasantry that was largely neglected by foreign royal rulers.

The Mafia is now a loose alliance of many small local groups, each bound by kinship and the Mafia code of omertà, which requires absolute silence about Mafia activities and absolute obedience to the hierarchical Mafia authority. Until recent years—and despite the efforts of the Italian Fascists to destroy it in the 1920s and '30s—the Mafia flourished in the Sicilian countryside. When the Fascists fled Sicily during the Allied invasion of World War II, the Mafia worked closely with U.S. forces. Today it dominates much of the business and industry in Sicily's cities.

With the Sicilian immigrations of the late 19th century, the Mafia began to operate in several large U.S. cities. During Prohibition (1920–33) it monopolized the trade in bootleg liquor and controlled loan-sharking, gambling, and prostitution. Competing Mafia "families" established mutually recognized territories, reaching agreement by negotiation or by intimidation. By the mid-1930s the Mafia had taken on the institutionalized structure that is now typical of ORGANIZED CRIME in the United States.

Magdalen Islands [mag'-duh-luhn] The Magdalen Islands, in eastern Quebec, Canada, are a group of islands and islets in the Gulf of St. Lawrence about 288 km (179 mi) southeast of the Gaspé Peninsula. Their total area is 202 km^2 (79 mi^2), and the population is 14,532 (1986). Fishing and sealing are important. The islands were reached in 1534 by the French explorer Jacques Cartier.

Magdeburg [mahg'-de-boork] Magdeburg, the capital of the German state of Saxony-Anhalt, lies about 130 km (80 mi) southwest of Berlin. Its population is 289,778 (1988 est.). It is a major inland port along the Elbe River and two canals. Magdeburg's industries produce steel, textiles, chemicals, fertilizer, and light and heavy machinery. The city's Gothic cathedral (begun 1209) and the Church of Our Lady (1070) are landmarks.

A trading village, possibly founded by Charlemagne, existed on the site in 805. It grew in prominence after becoming (962) the seat of a powerful archbishopric. In the 13th century Magdeburg obtained a charter from the ruling archbishops that allowed it essential self-govern-

ment. It became a leading member of the Hanseatic League and asserted increasing independence. In 1524, Magdeburg adopted Protestantism, and during the THIRTY YEARS' WAR it was sacked and burned (1631) by imperial forces under Johann von TILLY. The Treaty of Westphalia (1648) made Magdeburg a secular duchy, which passed to the electorate of Brandenburg in 1680. Magdeburg surrendered to the French in 1806 and became part of the Kingdom of Westphalia. Restored to Prussia, it was capital of the Prussian province of Saxony from 1816.

Magellan, Ferdinand [muh-jel'-uhn] Ferdinand Magellan was the leader of the first expedition to circumnavigate the world. In Portuguese, his native tongue, his name was Fernão de Magalhães, but the Spanish rendered this as Fernando de Magallanes.

Magellan was born c.1480 in northern Portugal. Of noble parentage, he became a page at the Portuguese court. In 1505 he sailed for India under Francisco de ALMEIDA. He apparently took part in fighting on the East African coast and in the great Portuguese naval victory over the Arabs off Diu (1509) in the Indian Ocean. He is also believed to have served in the fleet commanded by Afonso de ALBUQUERQUE that captured Malacca and gained control of the Strait of Malacca in 1511.

In 1517, Magellan went to Spain to offer his services to King Charles I. By the Treaty of Tordesillas (1494), Spain and Portugal had agreed to divide the non-Christian world between them; all territories to the west of the demarcation line in the Atlantic Ocean were to be Spanish; all those to the east, Portuguese. In 1513, Vasco Núñez de Balboa had found an ocean on the far side of the New World discovered

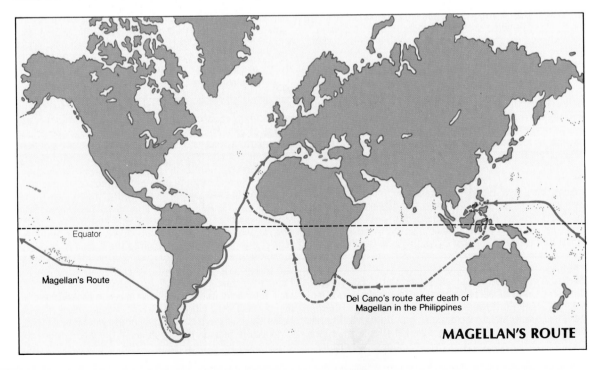

Magellan's Route

Del Cano's route after death of Magellan in the Philippines

MAGELLAN'S ROUTE

by Christopher Columbus. Magellan now proposed to the Spanish an expedition to find a passage through to this ocean and to sail west to the Moluccas, thus proving that the Spice Islands lay on the Spanish side of the line of demarcation. King Charles approved the plan, and the expedition left Seville on Sept. 20, 1519.

The five ships, carrying about 270 men, reached the Bay of Rio de Janeiro on December 13. They then sailed south, probing the estuary of the Río de la Plata for the passage. One ship, the *Santiago*, was wrecked, and its crew was taken aboard the other vessels. On Oct. 21, 1520, the ships entered the passage later to be called the Strait of Magellan. The captain of the *San Antonio* deserted and returned to Spain with the ship. On November 28, however, the three remaining vessels emerged into what Magellan named the Pacific Ocean.

They sailed north along the South American coast and then, on December 18, headed west into the unknown ocean, reaching Guam, in the Marianas, on Mar. 6, 1521. After reprovisioning, Magellan then sailed to the islands later named the Philippines. He persuaded the ruler of the island of Cebú to accept Christianity, but he became involved in a local war, and on Apr. 27, 1521, Magellan was killed in a fight with natives on Mactan Island.

Juan Sebastián del Cano assumed command. Abandoning his now unseaworthy ship, the *Concepción*, he took over the *Victoria* and sailed to the Moluccas with the *Trinidad*. Spices were purchased, and the ships were refitted. Leaving the leaky *Trinidad* behind to follow later, del Cano departed for Spain with 47 Europeans and 13 natives of the islands aboard the *Victoria*. After a voyage across the Indian Ocean, around the Cape of Good Hope, and north through the Atlantic Ocean, the *Victoria* reached Seville on Sept. 8, 1522. Only 17 Europeans and 4 East Indians were still alive.

Although Magellan did not actually complete the first circumnavigation, his skill and determination made that achievement possible. He had crossed the Pacific from east to west and discovered the vast size of that ocean.

Magellan, Strait of   The Strait of Magellan (Spanish: Estrecho de Magallanes), a 564-km-long (350-mi) passage between the Atlantic and Pacific oceans, separates the southern tip of South America and TIERRA DEL FUEGO. The Portuguese explorer Ferdinand Magellan sailed through the 3- to 32-km-wide (2- to 20-mi) strait and entered the Pacific in 1520, the first European to do so. The strait, surrounded by snow-covered mountains, is often difficult to navigate because of wind, fog, tidal rips, and a tidal range of 18 m (60 ft). The only large settlement on the strait is PUNTA ARENAS, Chile.

Magellanic Clouds [maj-uh-lan'-ik]   The Magellanic Clouds are the galaxies nearest to our own galaxy (see GALAXY, THE). Named in honor of the Portuguese navigator Ferdinand Magellan, they are visible to Southern Hemisphere observers even with the unaided eye. Until the early 1980s two galaxies were recognized: the Large Mag-

The Large Magellanic Cloud (top) *and the Small Magellanic Cloud are small satellite galaxies of our own Milky Way, visible in the Southern Hemisphere.*

ellanic Cloud (LMC), at a distance of 150,000 light-years; and the Small Magellanic Cloud (SMC), at a distance of 173,000 light-years. Recent studies, however, indicate that a third galaxy, the Mini Magellanic Cloud (MMC), lies behind the SMC and was torn from it about 200 million years ago by a near collision between the LMC and the SMC. Although superimposed in the Earth's sky, the SMC and the MMC are actually separated by a distance of some 20,000 light-years and are continuing to separate.

The Large Magellanic Cloud (LMC) is in the constellation Doradus and has a diameter of 31,000 light-years. The Small Magellanic Cloud (SMC) is in Tucana and has a diameter of 24,000 light-years.

In 1987 astronomers were able to observe closely a rare SUPERNOVA occurring in the LMC. The brightest known supergiants that have been spectroscopically studied in great detail are in the Magellanic Clouds. The brightest stars in these galaxies can be sorted out from foreground stars in our own galaxy by their large radial velocities.

Because the objects in the Magellanic Clouds are all at essentially the same distance from the Sun, relative sizes and luminosities reflect true differences in sizes and absolute magnitudes. Thus the Magellanic Clouds are ideal regions for studying sizes, absolute magnitudes, and the genetic relationships existing among various types of objects. The period-luminosity relation, the most accurate method for determining large distances in the universe, was discovered in the SMC by Henrietta Leavitt in 1912 from plates taken at the Harvard southern observing station in Peru.

See also: EXTRAGALACTIC SYSTEMS; LOCAL GROUP OF GALAXIES.

Maggiore, Lake [mah-joh'-ray]   Lake Maggiore separates the regions of Lombardy and Piedmont in northern Italy and extends into Ticino canton, Switzerland. About 54 km (34 mi) long, it has a maximum width of 12 km (7 mi) and a maximum depth of 372 m (1,220 ft). It is fed and drained by the Ticino River. Although located among Alpine foothills, it has a mild climate and many resorts, including LOCARNO, Stresa, Verbania, Arona, and Cannobio.

maggot   see FLY

Maghrib [mah'-grib]   The Maghrib (also Maghreb) is a region in North Africa between the Mediterranean Sea and the Sahara. It comprises the ATLAS MOUNTAINS and the coastal plain of northwest Africa. The name—Arabic for "west"—generally refers to Morocco, Algeria, Tunisia, and sometimes Libya and Egypt. Spain was included at the time of Moorish domination (8th–15th centuries).

magi   The magi (singular: magus) were the priestly hierarchy of ancient ZOROASTRIANISM. The name was originally that of the tribe to which they belonged. Like the Brahmans of India, the magi were keepers of the cult and of sacrificial power and exercised considerable political power while Zoroastrianism was the state religion of Persia.

In the Hellenistic world the name *magi* was applied to Eastern astrologers and interpreters of dreams, men considered "wise in the things of God." (Hence the derivation of the word *magic*.) It is in this sense that the name came to be applied to the "wise men from the East" who followed the star to Bethlehem to worship the infant Jesus, presenting him with gifts of gold, frankincense, and myrrh (Matt. 2). Later tradition called them kings and named them Gaspar, Melchior, and Balthazar. The Christian church honors them as the first Gentiles to believe in Christ and celebrates their visit by the feast of EPIPHANY.

magic   The use of a certain ritual action to bring about the intervention of a supernatural force for a specific purpose is called magic. The term has a wide range of reference, from major ritual performances to conjuring tricks (see MAGIC ACTS), and the relationship between magic and religion is particularly complex. Nineteenth-century anthropologists sought to assign magic to an earlier stage of cultural development. It has been suggested that religious acts generally involve a personal approach to spiritual powers, whereas magical activity is largely impersonal, a ritual technology that constrains and controls rather than supplicates the powers it wields.

The role of magic varies from culture to culture, from a central position in primary rituals involving the well-being of an entire community—as with some major hunting or agricultural rituals (see FERTILITY RITES)—to minor, peripheral, private acts of magic. Both public and private magic can and do exist within single societies. Black magic or sorcery (see VOODOO) may be used destructively to bring misfortune or death, and it is often distinguished from WITCHCRAFT by its use of magical techniques, such as spells or charms. Witchcraft relies on an internal quality or disposition of the witch. Beneficial, or white, magic is used to ward off such attacks as well as to prevent natural calamities; magical healing is among its aspects (see SHAMAN). Love charms are also considered white magic.

In casting spells, the appropriate use of words is sufficient to release or activate a power. The importance of the words is variable. Some Melanesian and Polynesian societies consider the precise wording of a spell crucial. In other cultures, such as that of the Azande of the Sudan,

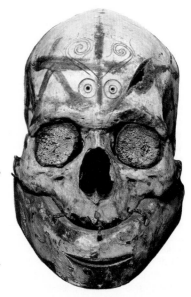

In societies that practice magic, special objects called fetishes or talismans are often thought to possess magical powers. This skull fetish belonged to a head-hunting tribe in Borneo. Among some headhunters, the head is thought to contain soul matter or spiritual force, and acquiring a head may add to an individual's or group's power. (Museum für Volkskunde, Berlin.)

conveying the spell's general meaning is adequate; magical objects such as special woods and roots are of greater significance. The objects used in magic are regarded as repositories for or symbols of the powers engaged, or, as with the destruction of wax figures of victims in sorcery, symbolically connected to the aims of the magic.

Sir Edward TYLOR and Sir James FRAZER, who advanced influential anthropological theories of magic in the late 19th and early 20th centuries, saw it as pseudoscientific. Tylor proposed that magic was based in the erroneous equation of physical causality with the association of ideas. This notion was elaborated by Frazer, who saw two basic principles in magical thought: that like produces like and that an effect resembles its cause, and that things formerly in contact continue to act on each other. The magic based on similarity he termed *homeopathic*, that based on contact *contagious*. The destruction of a victim's likeness is homeopathic magic, the burning of a lock of his hair for the same destructive purpose is contagious magic. These are the two forms of sympathetic magic. Frazer fitted magic into an evolutionary scheme in which, as its techniques were found unproductive, magic would be succeeded by religion, which in turn would be followed by scientific enlightenment. The influential sociologist Émile DURKHEIM, however, stressed the dependence of magic on collective religious belief and ritual. After working (1914–18) among the Trobriand Islanders, the anthropologist Bronislaw MALINOWSKI developed a pragmatic theory of magic that stressed its psychological value: it reduces anxieties. An account of magic functioning in a full social context as part of a logically coherent belief system was provided by Sir Edward EVANS-PRITCHARD's work in the 1920s and '30s with the Azande.

magic acts   Magic acts originated with jugglers who baffled people with deft trickery and with sorcerers who claimed that their secret spells controlled the wonders of nature and the laws of science. Today such tricks are presented only as entertainment by performers who—with few exceptions—deny any occult or supernatural power.

Modern magic dates from 1784, when the Chevalier Joseph Pinetti, self-styled "Professor of Natural Magic," exhibited in Paris such marvels as an orange tree that blossomed and bore fruit at his command. His wife, when blindfolded, described objects that spectators showed him. During the 19th century other magicians developed marvels involving optical devices, electromagnets, and forms of stage lighting that baffled audiences.

Stage magic reached a peak by 1876 when a German, Alexander Herrmann, known as Herrmann the Great, began regularly to tour the United States with a full evening show using all types of magic, from manipulative skill such as card tricks to huge contrivances like his Noah's Ark, from which all sorts of animals miraculously appeared. Herrmann not only produced and made disappear his numerous assistants, he also floated them in midair. After his death in 1896, his place was taken by Harry Kellar, who continued as America's most prominent magician for the next 12 years.

Meanwhile, vaudeville achieved great popularity, and specialty acts—T. Nelson Downs, "King of Koins"; Howard Thurston, master card manipulator; Harry HOUDINI, "Handcuff King and Escape Artist"—had become box-office attractions. Thurston invested his profits in a big show that merged with, and succeeded, Kellar's (1908) and dominated the American magic scene for 25 years. Houdini was equally famous with his spectacular escape act, but in 1926 he suffered a serious injury and died. Thurston closed his large show as theatrical business slumped during the Great Depression.

Following World War II, magic revived rapidly because of new enthusiasts and amateur performers whose work was sponsored by magical societies throughout the United States. Magicians were featured at nightclubs, on cruise ships, and at all types of conventions, including their own. In 1974, Doug Henning appeared on Broadway in *The Magic Show*. David Copperfield and others have adapted magic to the medium of television, where spectaculars now surpass the great shows of the past.

Magic Flute, The   see MOZART, WOLFGANG AMADEUS

Magic Mountain, The   see MANN, THOMAS

magic square   A magic square is a square array of integers with the property that the sum of each row, each column, and each diagonal is the same. Magic squares have been found in ancient writings from many parts of the world; in some cultures they were thought to possess magical or supernatural powers.

In the 19th century, Leonhard Euler and others developed a related square, the Latin square. This square is an array of *n* distinct elements in which each element occurs exactly once in each row and each column (*n* is the order of the square).

$$\begin{array}{cccc} 1 & 2 & 3 & 4 \\ 2 & 1 & 4 & 3 \\ 3 & 4 & 1 & 2 \\ 4 & 3 & 2 & 1 \end{array}$$

Latin squares are used to design statistical experiments so that three different sources of variability can be controlled.

Maginot Line   [mah-zhee-noh']   The Maginot Line was a system of fortifications built by France along its eastern border during the 1930s and extending more than 300 km (200 mi) from the Swiss border to a point near the Belgian frontier. Named for André Maginot, the French minister of war (1922–24, 1926–29, 1929–31), it was the most elaborate fortification in history. Its purpose was to prevent a German invasion, and the French regarded it as impregnable. The system included a network of gun emplacements and antitank obstacles, all connected by underground railroads, barracks, command posts, hospitals, and supply depots. Despite these obstacles the Germans invaded France with little difficulty in

magma Magma is a complex, mobile mixture of crystals, rock fragments, liquid, and gases deep within the Earth. The source of IGNEOUS ROCKS, it can intrude into adjacent rocks or extrude at the surface. Never directly observed, magmas are inferred from volcanic material, such as LAVA and natural volcanic glass, and from solid rocks that presumably crystallized from a melt at depth. Through experimental studies with artificial melts geologists seek to determine how magmas form and evolve.

Formation. The ultimate cause of magma formation is the internal heat of the Earth, originating either from decay of radioactive material or from residual heat remaining from the initial formation of the planet (see EARTH, HEAT FLOW IN). Magmas originate at many levels within the Earth (see EARTH, STRUCTURE AND COMPOSITION OF). Melting begins wherever temperature and pressure reach the melting point of any components. If these conditions are maintained, the body of melt grows. When a melt migrates to cooler areas or zones of different pressure, the melt can begin to crystallize.

The order in which various minerals melt and crystallize in a magma of given composition depends on the local temperature and pressure. A single magma type can thus produce different kinds of rocks at different levels in the Earth. As crystals form in a melt they may sink or float, depending on relative densities. The removal of some crystals produces physical and chemical changes within the remaining melt.

Basaltic magmas (see BASALT) probably form mainly in the lower part of the crust and the upper mantle. Because granitic magmas (see GRANITE) can form by chemical differentiation of a basaltic melt, basaltic magma was formerly thought to be the parent magma of other rock types. Geologists now believe that most granitic magma forms by melting of sedimentary rocks in lower parts of the Earth's crust.

Composition. Studies of large igneous complexes suggest that magma is neither uniform nor homogenous.

Parts may be largely crystalline and others largely liquid. The chemical composition in different parts of a melt may also vary, but most magmas are rich in silica and ALUMINA and contain variable amounts of water.

Glassy volcanic rocks originate from magma that was probably a mixture of liquid and gas alone (see VOLCANO). Volcanic rocks with various proportions of crystals and glass suggest magmas containing many solids. The various lava types indicate a range of fluid to viscous magmas. In the latter, liquid and gas may make up as little as 5 percent of the total volume.

Magna Carta Magna Carta, the great charter of liberties exacted from the English King JOHN by his rebellious barons and sealed at Runnymede on June 15, 1215, is famous as an embodiment of resistance to monarchy unregulated by law.

The rebellion of the barons stemmed from John's demand for overseas service that they felt was not owed, from John's policies of ensuring their personal loyalties by intimidation, and from increased financial exactions not only of John himself but also of his predecessors HENRY II and RICHARD I. The baronial opposition initially intended to restore what it regarded as the good old days of the Norman kings (William I, William II, and Henry I); however, realistic considerations led to an insistence on pragmatic reforms. The charter, some of it framed by Stephen LANGTON, archbishop of Canterbury, set forth the law on points raised by the rebels and attempted to reform specified abuses.

The church, stated the charter, was to be free. Magna Carta then specified liberties for all freemen so that all might be defended from royal whim. Certain taxes were not to be levied without the common consent of the kingdom, whose representatives' decisions were binding on all (a forerunner of "no taxation without representation"). The evolution of DUE PROCESS was reflected in the requirements that proper trial be held before execution of sentence and lawful judgment in royal courts.

Many of Magna Carta's 63 clauses dealt with feudal privileges of benefit only to the barons. The charter was soon violated by King John, bringing a resumption of civil

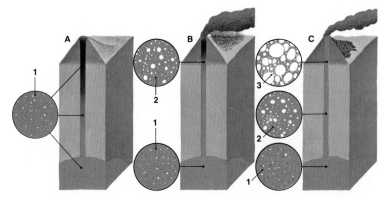

Volcanic eruptions involve ejection of magma at the Earth's surface. Magma is found under pressure in pockets deep within the Earth (A) as a hot semiplastic mixture of minerals and dissolved gases (1). If the pressure is decreased in any way, the magma will liquefy and the dissolved gases will escape to form small bubbles within the melt (2), which will rise and push out any obstructing rocks (B). As the mass rises and the overhead pressure decreases further, the bubbles will expand and coalesce to form larger bubbles (3). With increasing bubble size, the magma decreases in density and rises faster. When the surface is reached, lava and gases pour out (C).

war; nonetheless, John's successor, HENRY III, reissued it, and by 1225, when it received its final form, Magna Carta was accepted by all the parties. It remains a major symbol of the supremacy of law.

magnesite see MAGNESIUM

magnesium

Magnesium is a silvery white metallic element of the ALKALINE EARTH METAL group, which lies in Group IIA of the periodic table. Its chemical symbol is Mg, its atomic number is 12, and its atomic weight is 24.312. In 1808, Sir Humphrey Davy announced that he had isolated a new element, magnesium, from the hitherto unknown magnesium oxide, which he discovered. Antoine Bussy, who is credited with discovery of the metal, isolated larger and purer amounts in 1828.

Occurrence. Magnesium is the eighth most abundant element on Earth, constituting about 2.5% of the Earth's crust. Because of its high reactivity, magnesium is found naturally only in the combined state. The most important magnesium minerals are brucite, $Mg(OH)_2$; dolomite, $CaMg(CO_3)_2$; magnesite, $MgCO_3$; and olivine, $(Mg,Fe)_2SiO_4$. Seawater is about 0.13% magnesium. In fresh water, dissolved magnesium and calcium salts are responsible for the hardness of water.

Production. Approximately 20% of the magnesium produced in the world is extracted from roasted dolomite, $MgO \cdot CaO$, by thermal reduction. About 80% of the magnesium produced in the world is extracted from seawater. The seawater flows through tanks to which calcium hydroxide, $Ca(OH)_2$, has been added. The magnesium is precipitated as magnesium hydroxide, $Mg(OH)_2$, and is converted to magnesium chloride with hydrochloric acid, HCl. The $MgCl_2$ is dried and electrolyzed to yield magnesium metal and chlorine gas.

Properties. Pure magnesium is a soft, ductile, malleable metal that oxidizes in air, producing a grayish oxide layer that protects the rest of the metal from corrosion. Magnesium is highly reactive; in compounds it is nearly always in the +2 oxidation state. Magnesium dissolves in acids and slowly decomposes boiling water.

Uses. Magnesium is used as a galvanic anode to prevent CORROSION in pipelines, storage tanks, the hulls of ships, home water heaters, and oil tanks. Finely divided magnesium burns in air with an intense white light, so the metal is used as the source of light in some flashbulbs and pyrotechnics. Magnesium is also used in incendiary bombs, in the production of titanium and zirconium, and in the manufacture of copper and nickel alloys.

Magnesium has little structural strength and must be alloyed with other metals such as aluminum, zinc, or manganese when it is to be subjected to stress. Because of its light weight, magnesium ALLOYS are used widely as structural materials.

Biological Significance. The body of an average adult contains about 25 g (0.9 oz) of magnesium. It is known to be an activator of many enzyme systems and acts as a depressant of the central nervous system when it is injected intravenously. For this reason, magnesium and some of its compounds are used to control convulsions resulting from tetanus and childbirth. Magnesium is found in many foods, and the average adult ingests about 300 mg (0.01 oz) of magnesium per day. Magnesium deficiency results in weakness, dizziness, and convulsions. Abnormal levels of magnesium in the body have been linked to hypertension and hypotension. The kidneys regulate the amount of magnesium, and overdose may result from kidney failure, hormonal disruption, or use of too much magnesium as a drug. Magnesium is found in the chlorophyll molecules of plants, where it plays an important structural and electrochemical role in photosynthesis.

Magnesium Compounds. Magnesium carbonate, $MgCO_3$, is a white powder that is used as a filler for paper, in cosmetics and fire-resistant and insulating materials, for clarifying drinking water, and as an antacid. Magnesium sulfate, $MgSO_4$, is used for tanning leather, dyeing textiles, and in ceramics, explosives, and matches. The heptahydrate $MgSO_4 \cdot 7H_2O$, known as epsom salts, is used in treating arthritis and burns and as a local analgesic and a laxative. Milk of magnesia, $Mg(OH)_2$, is used as an antacid and a laxative.

magnet

A magnet is a body composed of ferromagnetic or ferrimagnetic material (see MAGNETISM). If suspended in a magnetic field, a magnet will align itself along the field like a magnetic compass in the Earth's field. A magnet has two poles, called north and south, with the

A magnetizable substance can be made into a magnet by repeatedly stroking it in one direction with a magnet (A) or in opposite directions with two magnets (B). The material can also be magnetized by hammering it in the direction of the Earth's magnetic field (C) or by placing it within a current-carrying wire coil (D). Magnetic field lines run radially from the north pole to the south pole (E). Unlike magnetic poles attract each other, but like poles repel (F).

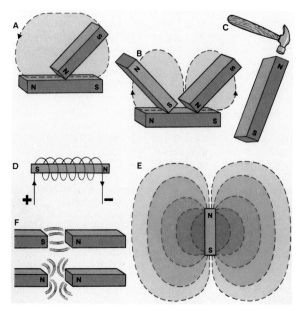

property that unlike poles attract and like poles repel one another. The principal physical characteristic of a magnet is that a high concentration of lines of magnetic force pass through its body, due to the alignment of its constituent atomic magnetic dipoles. This leads to a relatively strong field in the external space, or gap, between poles. The physical properties of a magnet can be explained in terms of the fundamental principles of magnetism.

A permanent magnet is prepared by initially being magnetized in an external magnetic field. When the field is removed or turned off, the magnet retains its magnetization for a long time. Permanent magnets are made from alloys and compounds of ferromagnetic metals, mainly iron, nickel, and cobalt. Alnico, Alcomax, and Ticonal are commonly used permanent-magnet materials. Extremely strong magnets are now being made from compounds of ferromagnetic metals with rare-earth metals.

An ELECTROMAGNET must be excited continuously by an external magnetic field in order to maintain its magnetism. If the external field is turned off, the magnetism collapses almost completely. Since the 1960s much higher magnetic fields than are obtainable with ordinary electromagnets have been made possible through the development of superconducting solenoids, which do not require iron cores (see SUPERCONDUCTIVITY).

___

magnetic moment   A magnetic dipole moment is created whenever an electric current flows around a closed loop. The strength of the moment equals the product of the number of turns by the current by the area of the loop. At the atomic level, it arises from the orbital motions of the electrons around atomic nuclei and from the intrinsic spin of the electron itself. The term *dipole* is used because the magnetic field has the same appearance as the electric field of an electric DIPOLE (see MAGNETISM). The physical units of the magnetic moment in the Gaussian system are esu-cm or ergs/gauss (see ELECTROMAGNETIC UNITS). The magnetic moments of atoms are normally expressed as multiples of the BOHR MAGNETON, which has a value of 9.27×10^{-24} joules/tesla. The spin moment of the electron is almost exactly one Bohr magneton.

___

magnetic resonance imaging   Magnetic resonance imaging (MRI) is a sophisticated medical diagnostic technique based on the principles of NUCLEAR MAGNETIC RESONANCE imaging. A patient is placed inside a cylinder that contains a strong magnet. Radio waves are then introduced into the cylinder, which cause the atoms of the body to resonate. Each type of body tissue emits characteristic signals from the nuclei of its atoms, and a computer translates these signals into a two-dimensional picture.

Unlike traditional X rays or CAT scans used in RADIOLOGY, MRI does not use ionizing radiation. It also does not require the use of radioactively labeled dyes. In addition, MRI can see through bone and produce images of blood vessels, cerebrospinal fluid, cartilage, bone marrow, muscles, and ligaments. MRI is particularly useful for detecting tumors in the posterior fossa (the region at the back of

the brain between the ears), lesions associated with multiple sclerosis, joint injuries, and herniated disks. MRI is a harmless procedure except for persons with metal objects implanted in their bodies, such as pacemakers, joint pins, or artificial heart valves. These objects may be dislodged by the powerful magnetic field.

___

magnetic storm   The transient variations of the magnetic field of the Earth, which may last from a few hours to ten days, are called geomagnetic disturbances or, when severe, magnetic storms. These variations occur because a part of the magnetic field of the Earth originates from complicated electric current systems set up by the interaction between the SOLAR WIND and the Earth's magnetic field. These systems are located on the surface and inside the MAGNETOSPHERE, which surrounds the Earth (see VAN ALLEN RADIATION BELTS). A gusty solar wind disturbs such electric current systems and also generates new ones. Any such changes give rise to magnetic disturbance fields separate from those produced by the quiet solar wind (see EARTH, GEOMAGNETIC FIELD OF).

When a typical magnetic storm occurs in middle and low latitudes, it begins with a sharp increase of the field lasting only several minutes. This is followed by a new steady condition, called the initial phase, which lasts for a few hours. This in turn is followed by the main phase, during which a large decrease in field intensity develops over a period of 6 to 12 hours. The entire storm lasts for up to 10 days.

The initial increase is caused when a shock wave generated by the gusty solar wind compresses the magnetosphere. The main phase begins when the gusty wind itself engulfs the magnetosphere, causing great instability. Charged particles (protons and ionized oxygen atoms) then become energized inside the magnetosphere and generate a westward electric ring current as they drift around the Earth at distances of 4 to 6 Earth radii (see PLASMA PHYSICS).

In high latitudes much more intense magnetic disturbances, called polar magnetic substorms, occur intermittently, particularly during the period when the main phase is developing. These substorms, which last from 1 to 2 hours, can decrease the primary geomagnetic field by as much as 5 percent. They occur concurrently with auroral activity, called the auroral substorm (see AURORAS). As the ring current increases the auroral oval expands equatorward so that auroral displays may be seen even in middle latitudes. The ionosphere is greatly disturbed by the aurora, resulting in radio-communication and navigation difficulties. Radar facilities and satellite performance are also affected. The transient magnetic disturbances induce electric currents in electric power-distribution systems and in oil and gas pipelines, particularly in the higher latitudes.

Intense magnetic storms tend to occur during the rising, peak, and early declining epochs of the SUNSPOT cycle. They have also been associated with solar flares, but a recent theory links them to "holes" in the solar corona.

magnetic tape   see INFORMATION STORAGE AND RETRIEVAL; TAPE RECORDING; VIDEO RECORDING

magnetism   Magnetism, in physics, is a general term that refers to the effects originating from the electromagnetic interactions of particles. Magnetic phenomena have been recognized since ancient times, but understanding of magnetism began only with developments in physics in the 19th century.

Basic Concepts. The magnetic field is the central concept used in describing magnetic phenomena. If a moving, charged particle experiences a force always at right angles to its direction of motion (with the exception that the force is zero when moving along one particular line), then it is moving in a magnetic field. The field lies along the particular line. This force is called the Lorentz force, named for the Dutch physicist Hendrik LORENTZ. A magnetic field originates from moving charges or electric currents, according to the law discovered by André AMPÈRE (see ELECTRICITY). The Biot-Savart law, named for French physicists J. B. Biot and Félix Savart, permits the calculation of the magnetic field from any arbitrarily shaped current paths. The laws of electricity and magnetism are summarized in elegant but simple fashion by Maxwell's equations, named for the 19th-century physicist James Clerk MAXWELL.

Many important magnetic effects originate from the flow of charge in a circular loop. This flow gives rise to a characteristic distribution of magnetic lines of force, called a dipole. A dipole can be thought of as looking and behaving like a small bar MAGNET. One end, or pole, is called north, the other end south. Lines of magnetic force flow around the dipole from north to south, just as in a bar magnet. The so-called magnetic moment is the measure of the strength of the dipole. Thus far all experimental evidence indicates that magnetic poles come in pairs that can never be separated, even though quantum theory predicts the existence of a unit magnetic charge called a MONOPOLE. At the atomic level a magnetic dipole moment arises from the orbital motions of the electrons around the nucleus and from the intrinsic spin of the electron. The magnetic moments of atoms are expressed as multiples of BOHR MAGNETONS. A Bohr magneton has a value of 9.27×10^{-24} joules/tesla.

The effects that are more specifically associated with the terms *magnetism* and *magnets* and that will be treated in the following sections are those displayed by material objects when subjected to magnetic fields. The attraction between the unlike poles of two iron bar magnets is a consequence of the interaction of the magnetic moments of the atoms in each magnet with the field produced by atoms in the other magnet. The bar magnet, or horseshoe magnet, has the property of permanent magnetism and is an example of ferromagnetism. Other types of magnetism exist, called ferrimagnetism, antiferromagnetism, paramagnetism, and diamagnetism.

For ferromagnetism and ferrimagnetism, three important physical quantities can be defined: the magnetic induction, or B-field, which is the magnetic flux density within the magnetized material; the magnetization, which is the sum of moments over all the atoms in a unit volume; and the permeability, which is the ratio of the B-field to the applied field. For paramagnetism, antiferromagnetism, and diamagnetism, the important quantities are the magnetization and the magnetic susceptibility; the susceptibility is the ratio of magnetization to applied field.

History. The lodestone was the first permanent magnetic material to be identified and studied. The Greeks were aware of the power of this mineral, now called MAGNETITE (Fe_3O_4), to attract pieces of iron. The name *magnet* is thought to be derived from Magnesia, a district in Thessaly where the lodestone was mined in ancient times.

Credit for inventing the magnetic compass is variously given to the Chinese, the Arabs, and the Italians during the first ten centuries AD (see COMPASS, NAVIGATIONAL). By the 12th century, mariners were using the instrument for navigation. In the 13th century Peter Peregrinus of France determined that the two poles of a spherical lodestone were the regions of strongest force, and he found that like poles repel whereas unlike poles attract. In 1600 the English scientist William GILBERT confirmed these discoveries and concluded, correctly, that the Earth itself is a magnet (see EARTH, GEOMAGNETIC FIELD OF). Another English scientist, John Michell (1724–93), discovered in 1750 that the attractive and repulsive forces between the poles of a magnet vary inversely as the square of the distance of separation. Charles COULOMB of France verified Michell's experiments in 1785 and also showed that the same law is applicable to the forces between electrical charges. Coulomb concluded that regardless of how small the pieces into which a magnet might be subdivided, each piece would always retain a north and a south pole.

In 1820, Hans Christian Oersted of Denmark discovered a direct relationship between electricity and magnetism by showing that an electric current flowing in a wire causes a nearby compass needle to be deflected. Ampère and François Arago demonstrated later that same year that an electric current flowing in a solenoid (a coil of wire carrying direct current) increases the permanent magnetism of an iron needle within the solenoid. In 1825, Ampère generalized that a current-carrying loop is equivalent to a magnet, and he proposed that the origin of permanent magnetism resides in the many molecular-sized current whorls within the magnet.

During the 1830s the English scientist Michael FARADAY introduced the idea of representing the magnetic field by lines of flux that extend through the space surrounding a magnet, running from the north pole to the south. This pictorial model was to prove extremely useful in understanding ELECTROMAGNETIC INDUCTION—the generation of an ELECTROMOTIVE FORCE in a closed circuit when the lines of flux pass through the circuit change. In the 1870s, James Clerk Maxwell of Scotland unified all electromagnetic phenomena under a single theory.

In addition to the ferromagnetism of permanent magnets, other types of magnetism became known after the middle of the 19th century. In 1845, Faraday found that bismuth and glass are repelled from magnetic fields. He classified this behavior as diamagnetism. Faraday also discovered that some substances clearly not permanent magnets are nevertheless attracted by magnetic fields, a behavior he called paramagnetism. These opposite characteristics stem from fundamental differences at the atomic level and require separate theoretical explanations. In the 1930s two other forms of magnetism were recognized and described: ferrimagnetism and antiferromagnetism. Theoretical explanations of the behavior of magnetic materials began with the formulation of the quantitative theories of paramagnetism and diamagnetism by Paul Langevin (1872–1946) in 1905, and of ferromagnetism by another French scientist, Pierre Ernest Weiss (1865–1940), in 1907. The subsequent application of quantum theory after 1925 has provided a more exact understanding of these phenomena of magnetic behavior.

Diamagnetism. A substance is diamagnetic if its magnetic susceptibility is negative. This property is displayed by a repulsion of the sample from a magnetic field. The magnetization persists only as long as the external field is present. Diamagnetism is very weak, compared to ferromagnetism, and it is virtually independent of temperature. Some metals are diamagnetic, such as bismuth, copper, gold, silver, and lead, with bismuth being the strongest. Water and most organic compounds are also diamagnetic, as are many nonmetals.

Paramagnetism. A paramagnetic substance is characterized by a positive susceptibility. Like a diamagnet, it can acquire a magnetization only from induction by an external magnetic field. The magnetization, however, is in the same direction as the inducing field, and a sample will be attracted toward the strongest part of a field. In 1895, Pierre CURIE first determined experimentally that the paramagnetic susceptibility is directly proportional to the strength of the field, and inversely proportional to the temperature.

Paramagnetism is found in the iron group (the so-called transition metals) and in the rare earth, palladium, platinum, and actinide groups in the periodic table. Almost all compounds and alloys containing elements from the above groups exhibit paramagnetic behavior at high temperatures but undergo phase transitions to the magnetically ordered states of ferromagnetism and antiferromagnetism at sufficiently low temperatures.

Ferromagnetism. Ferromagnetism is characterized by a spontaneous magnetism that exists in the absence of a magnetic field. This retention of magnetism distinguishes ferromagnetism from the induced magnetisms of diamagnetism and paramagnetism. When ferromagnets are heated above a critical temperature, the ability to possess permanent magnetism disappears. Pierre Curie first identified this effect in iron as occurring at 770° C, and his name is now attached to this characteristic temperature. Other ferromagnetic elements and their Curie temperatures include nickel (358° C), cobalt (1,130° C), gadolinium (16° C), and dysprosium (−188° C).

A distinctive characteristic of a ferromagnet is its HYSTERESIS curve, an indication of how difficult it is to magnetize and demagnetize a given material.

Ferromagnetism has been found in many compounds. These materials are generally put in two categories: hard and soft. Hard magnets are used in those devices where a strong magnetic field is required for an indefinite period of time. This is what is popularly called a permanent magnet. Many commercial permanent magnets are of the Alnico group (composed of iron, nickel, cobalt, and aluminum). In recent years, cobalt-samarium and neodymium-iron-boron magnets have also proved successful in permanent-magnet applications. Magnetically soft materials find application in such devices as lifting electromagnets and the power transformers that convert standard 60-cycle commercial electric power from one voltage

Seated within a chamber that is shielded against external magnetic influences, this man is having the magnetic fields in his brain mapped by a detector seen in part behind and above him. The detector is called the SQUID (for superconducting quantum interference device). The electric currents that occur in the tissues of all living organisms produce magnetic fields that are called biomagnetic fields. Until devices such as the SQUID were developed in the 1970s, however, such fields were very hard to observe because they are extremely weak. Research into biomagnetism is now rapidly expanding, and its techniques are proving useful in medical diagnosis.

to another. The cores of such transformers are usually made of iron-silicon alloys. An extensive technology has evolved to synthesize ferromagnetic and ferrimagnetic materials with specific properties to meet a wide variety of needs.

Ferrimagnetism. Ferrites are similar to ferromagnets in that they undergo transitions to ordered arrangements of magnetic moments below Curie temperatures. They form magnetic domains, have hysteresis curves, and possess sizable permanent magnetism. Above their Curie temperatures they behave as paramagnets. The important difference from ferromagnetism is that not all the moments are aligned in the same direction in the ordered state.

The excellent electrical insulating properties of ferrites have led to their use in components that operate in high-frequency devices with low electrical losses, such as transformers and phase shifters.

Antiferromagnetism. Antiferromagnetism is characterized by an antiparallel pattern of magnetic moments below a critical temperature called the Néel temperature, named for French physicist Louis Néel. A large number of compounds—many of the insulators—containing iron-group, rare earth, and actinide metals are antiferromagnets.

Ferromagnetism, ferrimagnetism, and antiferromagnetism are all representative of more general phenomena in solids, called phase transitions. A phase transition occurs when cooling through a critical temperature is accompanied by a significant change in a physical property. Other examples of phase transitions are ferroelectricity, in which a spontaneous electrical polarization develops, and SUPERCONDUCTIVITY.

magnetite Magnetite is one of the most widespread and abundant minerals and an important ore of iron. An OXIDE MINERAL (Fe_3O_4), it crystallizes in the isometric system as do the four other members of the spinel group. The naturally magnetic variety, lodestone, was well known to the ancient Greeks. Magnetite forms iron-black octahedral and dodecahedral crystals, as well as granular or laminated masses. Hardness is 5½–6½, streak is black, and specific gravity is about 5.2. Often formed at high temperature, magnetite is a common constituent of crystalline rocks, forming abundant grains in ferromagnesian igneous rocks and disseminated crystals in metamorphic rocks. It also occurs in beach sand, in meteorites, and in EMERY. The world's largest deposits are in Sweden.

magnetohydrodynamics [mag-neet'-oh-hy'-droh-dy-nam'-iks] Magnetohydrodynamics (MHD) is the study of the motion of electrically conducting fluids (liquids and gases) in the presence of a magnetic field. The subject is also called hydromagnetics or magnetodynamics. When the conducting fluid is compressible it is referred to as magneto-gas dynamics. Magnetohydrodynamics is the result of the fusing of two branches of physics—electromagnetic theory and hydrodynamics (see FLUID MECHANICS). Electromagnetic theory is governed by Maxwell's equa-

tions, and hydrodynamics is governed by Navier-Stokes fluid dynamic equations. Their combination constitutes the subject of magnetohydrodynamics.

One of the most interesting aspects of MHD is the interaction between the field and the motion of the fluid. Electric currents induced in the field as a result of its motion modify the field, and at the same time their flow in the magnetic field produces mechanical forces that modify the motion.

Alfvén Waves. In 1942 the Swedish physicist Hannes ALFVÉN reported a new type of wave motion, which now bears his name. By combining Maxwell's equations with the fundamental equation of hydrodynamics, Alfvén was able to predict the existence of a new type of wave, dubbed the magnetohydrodynamic wave. The work of S. O. Lundquist in 1951 and later experiments demonstrated the existence of MHD waves. When a perfectly conducting fluid moves transverse to the magnetic lines of force, it carries them with it. Therefore, the tube of magnetic lines of force behaves like an elastic string. This situation is analogous to the propagation of waves along a stretched elastic string.

Alfvén waves are unimportant in liquids, where the relatively high inertia damps them strongly, but are common in plasmas. They occur in the Earth's Van Allen belts and in the solar wind. They are believed to be responsible for transporting energy from the Sun's interior to sunspots and to be a principal mechanism for heating the solar corona. On Earth they have been used experimentally to heat plasmas.

The situation for compressible fluids is much more complicated. More general types of MHD waves exist when the magnetized medium can propagate both the transverse Alfvén waves and the longitudinal magneto-acoustic waves. When an MHD wave is propagating at an arbitrary angle with respect to the magnetic field, the complexity increases. In contrast to ordinary fluid dynamics, three "sound" velocities exist, classified according to their propagation velocities as fast, slow, and intermediate waves.

MHD Power Generators. In ordinary conventional electric generators, electric power is generated through the motion of metal conductors in a magnetic field. Similarly, in MHD generators electric power is generated as a result of the passing of a gaseous conductor (plasma) through a magnetic field. The motion of the ionized gas produces an electric field between the two electrodes. An electric current will flow from one electrode through an external load to the other electrode, and the system will operate as a generator. In the MHD generator the potential working temperature is much higher (about 2500 K) than the conventional generator, and by a suitable arrangement the heat energy of the ionized gas can be directly converted into flow energy. The intermediate step of going through the prime mover (steam turbines) is therefore avoided, resulting in higher efficiency. MHD generators are divided into generators with open and closed cycles. In the former case the products of combustion are supplied directly to the generator; in the latter case the same working gas is constantly recirculated.

Plasma Propulsion. The basic principle of electromagnetic pumps and electromagnetic plasma accelerators is the same. A conducting fluid in a pipe is forced to move by the Lorentz force created when mutually perpendicular magnetic fields and electric currents are applied perpendicular to the pipe. MHD plasma accelerators are used to simulate and study reentry conditions for hypersonic vehicles into the atmosphere, as well as to study more basic aerodynamic problems. Accelerators are also undergoing research and development as propulsion devices in which plasmas are accelerated and then expelled to produce a thrust. In the 1980s the United States, the Soviet Union, and Japan all had such MHD projects under way, with Japan planning to launch a small prototype MHD-powered ship in the early 1990s. The basic principle of such a ship is to pass seawater, which conducts electricity well, through a pair of large electrodes. At right angles to the current, a large magnetic field generated by a superconducting magnet produces the thrust.

magnetosphere   The magnetosphere, a gigantic natural generator of about 100 billion watts of power, results from the SOLAR WIND, a conductor, moving through the magnetic field of the Earth (see EARTH, GEOMAGNETIC FIELD OF). This power produces major geophysical phenomena such as AURORAS, MAGNETIC STORMS and the VAN ALLEN RADIATION BELTS.

The magnetosphere is an invisible comet-shaped cavity surrounding the Earth. The Earth is located at about 10

In astronomy, the magnetosphere refers to the magnetic-field region above a planet in which electrically charged particles are trapped. The Earth's magnetosphere is compressed by the solar wind on the day side and stretched into a long, cometlike tail on the night side.

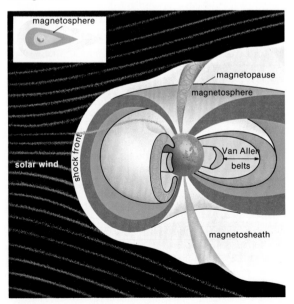

Earth radii from the blunt-nosed front, which faces the oncoming solar wind. The magnetosphere has an extensive tail extending a few thousand Earth radii along the downstream direction of the solar wind. It also has a bowshock, or shockwave, extending a few Earth radii upstream from the blunt-nosed front.

The theory that the magnetosphere is formed by the interaction of the solar wind with the Earth's magnetic field was first formulated by British geophysicists Sydney Chapman and V. C. A. Ferraro in 1931. Their idea was proved by the discovery of the Van Allen belts by the *Explorer 12* satellite in 1961. Space-probe observations indicate that other planets with magnetic fields, such as Mercury, Jupiter, and Saturn, also have a magnetosphere.

magnetron   The magnetron is an OSCILLATOR that operates in the lower portion of the MICROWAVE frequency range—up to about 30 GHz. It finds application in a number of devices, including radar transmitters and MICROWAVE OVENS. Magnetrons can be constructed in a variety of configurations, but the fundamental geometry is a hollow cylindrical plate with a coaxial, cylindrically shaped hollow cathode inside.

Magnificat   [mag-nif'-i-kat]   The Magnificat is the canticle of the Virgin (Luke 1:46–55), to which is added the Lesser Doxology, "Glory be to the Father. . . ." Its name comes from the opening words, *Magnificat anima mea Dominum* ("My soul doth magnify the Lord"). In the Catholic church it forms a part of vespers, one of the most important canonical hours, and was therefore traditionally said daily. It was recited in alternating verses; when sung, the alternation could be between plainsong and polyphony.

Chanting was done to musical formulas (Magnificat Tones) that were the same for all verses, the Tones serving as cantus firmi for the polyphonic settings. In the 17th century and later, elaborate motet settings were composed for soloists, chorus, and orchestra; for example, by Monteverdi and Bach. The Anglican church adopted the Magnificat as part of the Evening Service; Lutherans used it regularly at Advent.

Magnitogorsk   [muhg-neet'-uh-gohrsk]   Magnitogorsk is a city in Chelyabinsk oblast of Russia, a republic of the USSR. Its population is 422,000 (1985 est.). Located in the upper reaches of the Ural River, on the east slopes of the Ural Mountains, Magnitogorsk is the USSR's largest iron and steel center. It also manufactures coke-based chemicals and mining machinery.

The city was founded in 1929 in conjunction with the construction of the iron and steel plant at the foot of an iron-bearing mountain known as Magnitnaya Gora, or "magnetic mountain," for which the city was named.

Magnitogorsk grew at first around the plant, on the east bank of the Ural River; the west bank was developed later. Because of the depletion of iron ore in the local deposit, the city's steel plant has become dependent on ore shipped from the Rudny mines in northwest Kazakhstan and from the Kursk district, more than 1,500 km (900 mi) to the west.

magnitude In astronomy, magnitude is a measure of the brightness of a celestial body. The modern system of magnitudes is an extension of the system developed in ancient Greece and Rome, when STARS were grouped in five classes of brightness. The star catalog of the Greek astronomer Ptolemy, which was a recompilation of an earlier catalog by Hipparchus, used these classes. The brightest stars were assigned magnitude 1; those slightly fainter, 2; down to magnitude 5. The faintest star that can be seen without a telescope is about magnitude 6.

The English astronomer Norman Robert Pogson established (1850) that each magnitude step corresponds to a ratio of 2.5 in brightness. Thus a star of magnitude 1 is 2.5 times brighter than a star of magnitude 2, 2.5^2 times brighter than a star of magnitude 3, and 2.5^5, or 100, times brighter than a star of magnitude 6.

According to the system described above, the fainter a star is, the greater its magnitude. A star of the 21st magnitude is $21 - 6 = 15$ magnitudes fainter than the faintest star seen with the unaided eye. Stars, galaxies, and quasars of such faintness have been observed with large telescopes, but a limit exists on what can be seen. With good visibility, a stellar image is spread over a circle of about one second in diameter, so that extremely faint stars cannot be distinguished when viewed against the sky background.

The brightness of a celestial object as seen in the sky is expressed as its apparent magnitude. The brightest star, Sirius, has an apparent magnitude of −1.6, the full moon is −12.7, and the Sun's brightness, expressed on a magnitude scale, is −26.78. The zero point of the apparent magnitude scale is arbitrary; it depends ultimately on the magnitudes given in Ptolemy's catalog.

The term *absolute magnitude* is used to define the intrinsic brightness of a star. This is the magnitude a star would have if it were placed at a distance of 10 parsecs, or 32.6 light-years. The Sun has an absolute magnitude of +4.79; at a distance of 10 parsecs it would just be visible on Earth on a clear moonless night away from surface light. A star of absolute magnitude zero is 82.4 times as bright as the Sun. The brightest stars have absolute magnitudes around −7 or −8; the faintest have absolute magnitudes greater than +15, which means that they are more than 10,000 times fainter than the Sun.

magnolia [mag-nohl'-yuh] Magnolias include about 80 species of trees and shrubs in the genus *Magnolia*, in the magnolia family, Magnoliaceae. They are native to the Americas from the eastern United States to the West Indies and Venezuela, and to Asia from the Himalayas to Japan, Indonesia, and the Philippines. Magnolias have the largest leaves and flowers of any trees in the temperate region. The leaves are undivided and usually smooth-edged and leathery, and the flowers are solitary and bisexual. Each flower has numerous male stamens and female pistils spaced spirally along its raised central portion (receptacle), an outer whorl of three petallike sepals, and two or more inner whorls of usually three petals each. After the petals fall, many small, dry, podlike fruits, called follicles, develop, each containing one to two seeds. The outer coat of each seed becomes fleshy and red as the fruit ripens, and when the follicle splits open the seed dangles from it by a slender thread formed from the seed stalk (funiculus).

The southern magnolia tree is a temperate-climate plant with large leaves and flowers. A beautiful ornamental tree, it bears lotuslike blossoms throughout the spring and summer.

Magnus VI, King of Norway (Magnus the Law-Mender) [mag'-nuhs] Magnus VI, also called Magnus Lagabøter (Law-Mender), b. 1238, d. May 9, 1280, revised the legal system of Norway. Succeeding his father, HAAKON IV, as king in 1263, Magnus ended a lingering war with Scotland in 1266. His general code of laws, introduced in 1274, replaced local systems with a unified code for the entire kingdom. It strengthened the position of the monarch by treating crime not as a private matter but as an offense against king and country. Magnus also promulgated municipal laws and accepted an independent status for the church. He was succeeded by his son Eric II (r. 1280–99).

Magnus VII, King of Norway (Magnus Eriksson) Magnus VII of Norway (Magnus Eriksson), b. April 1316, d. Dec. 1, 1374, was the first king to unite the crowns of Sweden and Norway. His paternal uncle was King Birger of Sweden, and his maternal grandfather was King Haakon V of Norway. Both kingdoms fell to Magnus in 1319. Magnus modernized administration and justice. In 1355 he left Norway to his son and successor, Haakon VI. In Sweden, Magnus then fought with the mighty aristocracy, which eventually deposed him in 1363. Imprisoned until 1371, he spent his last years in Norway as coregent with Haakon.

magpie   Magpie is the common name for 11 species of long-tailed, black-and-white birds of the family Corvidae, related to the JAYS and CROWS. The black-billed magpie, *Pica pica*, is abundant throughout western North America, Europe, Asia, and North Africa. It averages 50 cm (20 in), with its wedge-shaped tail accounting for more than half its length. The yellow-billed magpie, *P. nuttalli*, similar in appearance to the black-billed magpie except for bill color and smaller size, inhabits a small region of the California coast.

The black-billed magpie is found in open, brushy regions, frequently near sheep and cattle. Its large, often domed nest is usually built on the ground.

In René Magritte's painting The Red Model (1935), the strangely frightening yet humorous world of the imagination is rendered in dreamlike images. (Claude Spaak collection, Paris.)

Magritte, René [muh-greet', ruh-nay']   René Magritte, b. François Ghislain Magritte, in Lessines, Belgium, Nov. 21, 1898, d. Aug. 15, 1967, was a leading painter and theorist of SURREALISM. Almost all of Magritte's paintings feature some sort of visual paradox: a restless blue sky with a hole in it, a human body with a fish's head, a hat suspended in midair. His seas and skies seem bright and sunny, but there is a disturbing artificiality about the too-regular clouds and the too-glassy water. The point of this interplay between precisely drawn objects and abnormal settings and features is that the common-sense perception of reality is only one way of looking at the world. In *The Human Condition I* (1934; Claude Spaak Collection, Choisel, France), Magritte forcefully demonstrates the paradoxes of perception by placing a painting showing a landscape view within the window overlooking an identical view.

Magritte's matter-of-fact way of depicting anomalies and incongruities in the fabric of reality often seems as humorous as it is disturbing. Many of his paintings are laden with visual jokes—such as the woman with a fish's head in *Le Chant d'Amour* (1948; private collection, Chicago), who is simply a mermaid with the piscine half above instead of below. Underlying the humor, however, is a serious attempt to demonstrate the multifaceted character of perceived reality.

Magsaysay, Ramón [mahg-sy'-sy, rah-mohn']   Ramón Magsaysay, b. Aug. 31, 1907, d. Mar. 17, 1957, was the third president (1953–57) of the independent Philippine Republic. A guerrilla leader during the World War II Japanese occupation and then a congressman (1946–50), he became secretary of defense under President Elpidio QUIRINO in 1950. In this post, Magsaysay broke the back of the major uprising (1950–53) of the Communist Hukbalahap (Huk) movement by encouraging insurgents to surrender and promising to resettle them on government-provided land.

In 1953, Magsaysay quit Quirino's Liberal party, charging his administration with corruption; he joined the opposition Nationalist party and won the 1953 presidential election by a landslide. An advocate of land reform and peasant welfare, Magsaysay died in a plane crash before he could carry out many of his policies.

Magyars [mag'-yahrz]   The Magyars, known also in the English-speaking world as Hungarians, are descended from the people who conquered the Carpathian Basin in the late 9th century and founded the kingdom of Hungary. Along

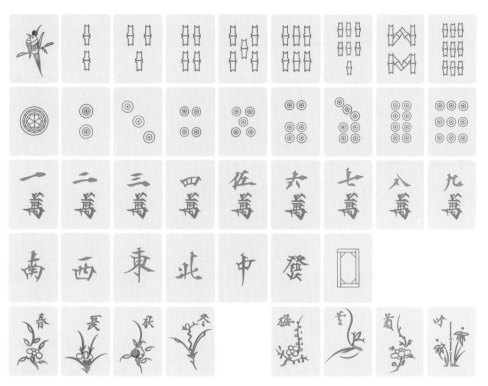

A Mah-Jongg set comprises 144 dominolike tiles divided into suit tiles, honor tiles, and bonus tiles. The 3 suits each contain 36 tiles and are called bamboo, circles, and characters. The 28 honor tiles comprise 16 wind tiles (4 for each of the 4 winds) and 12 tiles of colored dragons: 4 red, 4 green, and 4 white. The 8 bonus tiles comprise flower tiles (4) and season tiles (4, one for each season). The players try to form sets of tiles in a manner similar to the card game rummy.

with the Finns and Estonians, they speak a Finno-Ugric tongue, a subdivision of the URAL-ALTAIC LANGUAGES.

The original homeland (3000 BC–AD 500) of the Magyars was in northeastern Europe at the confluence of the Volga and Kama rivers. In the early centuries of the Christian era they mixed with various Turkish tribes, and, beginning in the 7th century, moved southwest to the Azov Sea area. Under the leadership of Árpád and Kukszán, they occupied the Carpathian Basin in 895–96. For the next 60 years they made devastating raids farther west until they were finally halted by the German king OTTO I in the Battle of Lechfeld (955).

Under STEPHEN I (r. 997–1038), the Magyars were Christianized and established a strong national state. In the course of the 12th–15th centuries they extended their control into the northern Balkans, while at home they developed a constitutional, elective monarchy. Turkish inroads, beginning in the 14th century, culminated in the trisection (1526–1699) of Hungary among the Turks, the Austrian HABSBURGS, and the Magyar rulers of TRANSYLVANIA. Subsequently all of Hungary became part of the Habsburg Empire, which in 1867 was transformed into AUSTRIA-HUNGARY.

The rise of national consciousness among the minorities in Hungary resulted after World War I in the loss of two-thirds of the former Hungarian territory. Today there are more than 15 million Magyars, of whom about 10.5 million live in Hungary, 3.5–4 million in the neighboring states of Romania, Czechoslovakia, Yugoslavia, the USSR, and Austria, and 1 million in the United States.

Mah-Jongg [mah-jawng']   Mah-Jongg is the U.S. adaptation of the 19th-century Chinese game Ma Jiang and is similar to rummy. It is best played by four people. Each player begins with 13 tiles except the player designated "East," who has 14. The players draw from a square with walls that are 18 tiles long and 2 tiles high. Play opens with East discarding a tile and proceeds as each player, in turn, either takes a discarded tile or draws one from the wall. A player wins with a complete hand (woo) of four sets plus a pair.

A set of three tiles in one suit is a chow; three tiles of one suit and rank, or dragons, or winds make a pung. And a pung plus a fourth like tile makes a kong.

Mah-Jongg was invented by an American, Joseph P. Babcock. He used the rules of Western card games and features of the Chinese tile game of the same name and patented (1920) his game, which enjoyed great popularity in the 1920s.

Mahabalipuram [muh-hah'-buh-li-pur-uhm]   An ancient seaport situated on the eastern coast of India, about 55 km (35 mi) south of Madras, Mahabalipuram was developed as the principal harbortown of the Tondai-mandalam by the Pallava kings who ruled the region from their princely capital of Kanchipuram a few miles inland. The period of its greatest magnificence spans the 7th and 8th centuries; it was the conduit for the eastward extension of Pallava power and civilization as well as a principal place of disembarkation for travelers from East and Southeast Asia. Among the archaeological remains are a series of rock-cut caves and freestanding shrines hewn from rock outcroppings during the 7th century, and the 8th-century Shore Temple.

Mahabharata, The see HINDUISM

Mahan, Alfred Thayer [muh-han'] The writings of Alfred Thayer Mahan, b. West Point, N.Y., Sept. 27, 1840, d. Dec. 1, 1914, a naval officer and naval historian, profoundly influenced U.S. naval strategy. A graduate of the U.S. Naval Academy class of 1859, Mahan had an unremarkable career until 1885, when the president of the newly established Naval War College, Stephen B. Luce, invited him to join the faculty. Mahan later served (1886–89, 1892–93) as president himself. In lectures at the War College, Mahan developed his thesis of the importance of sea power, which he published in his book *The Influence of Sea Power upon History, 1660–1783* (1890). Impressed by the British example, Mahan argued that a nation could be great only if it maintained a navy powerful enough to control the seas in the face of any adversary. This thesis received further expression in *The Influence of Sea Power upon the French Revolution and Empire, 1793–1812* (2 vols., 1892). These two works soon became standard reading for officers in all navies.

Maharashtra [muh-hah-ruhsh'-truh] Maharashtra is a state on the west central coast of India along the Arabian Sea. Comprising an area of 307,477 km^2 (118,717 mi^2), Maharashtra has a population of 62,784,171 (1981). BOMBAY is the capital and principal port; other important cities are NAGPUR, POONA, and Sholapur. The Western GHATS mountain range runs in a north-south direction, and the DECCAN PLATEAU is located in the east. Agriculture is the mainstay of the economy, and lumbering and fishing are also important. Manufactured goods include cotton textiles, petrochemicals, tools, machinery, and electrical appliances.

Part of the Gupta kingdom from the 5th to 7th century, the region was ruled by Muslim dynasties from the 14th to the 17th century, when the MARATHA leader Sivaji (1627–80) established an independent kingdom that existed until 1749. The British assumed control in 1808. Bombay state was formed in 1947 and after extensive land acquisitions was split in 1960; the southern portion became Maharashtra state.

Mahavira see JAINISM

Mahayana Buddhism see BUDDHISM

mahdi [mah'-dee] Mahdi is an Arabic word meaning literally "the [divinely] guided one." It refers to the popular Muslim concept that a messianic deliverer, the mahdi, will arise to restore security and justice to the Islamic

community when it is threatened with destruction either through conquest by unbelievers or from neglect or misrule by Muslims. The concept is a Muslim folk belief that has endured since early Islam.

The title has most often been claimed by would-be reformers seeking to restore Islam's political power or religious purity, including the Sudanese Muhammad Ahmad (1844–85), whose followers killed (1885) Gen. Charles George GORDON at Khartoum but were finally defeated by British forces under Herbert KITCHENER at Omdurman in 1898.

Mahfouz, Naguib [mah-foos', nah-geeb'] Winner of the 1988 Nobel Prize for literature, the Egyptian Naguib Mahfouz is the most famous writer of fiction in the Arab world. Mahfouz produced most of his 40 novels and short-story collections while an employee of the Egyptian civil service (1934–71), winning broad fame with his *Cairo Trilogy* (1956–57). A supporter of Anwar al-Sadat's 1979 peace treaty with Israel, Mahfouz has seen his novels banned several times in Arabic-speaking countries, but many have been translated into Hebrew, as well as into French and English.

Mahican [muh-hee'-kuhn] The Mahican (or Mohican) are an Algonquian-speaking North American Indian tribe who traditionally inhabited the Upper Hudson River valley north to Lake Champlain and east to the Housatonic River valley in New York and Connecticut. When first contacted (1609) by Dutch traders they were at war with the MOHAWK, who defeated them in the late 17th century, forcing them to abandon their eastern lands. By the 1730s most surviving Mahican had migrated to western Pennsylvania and the Kankakee River valley in Indiana. Eventually, part of this society was assimilated into the DELAWARE confederation; another group settled near a mission at Stockbridge, Mass. Additional Mahican and other eastern Algonquian speakers, under the auspices of the ONEIDA, later joined the Stockbridge colony and moved west to a reservation in north central Wisconsin. There, next to the Menominee reservation, the descendants of the Mahican live today in the Stockbridge-Munsee Indian community, whose population was about 850 in 1989.

Mahler, Gustav [mah'-lur, gus'-tahf] Gustav Mahler, b. Kališt, Bohemia, July 7, 1860, d. May 18, 1911, was an Austrian composer and conductor. His compositions are few in number—they consist chiefly of nine completed symphonies and seven song cycles—but vast in scale, often taking an hour or more to perform and calling for a very large orchestra, sometimes with a chorus and vocal soloists. Little appreciated in his own time, Mahler's music is now seen as an important link between the lyrical impulse of the romantic era and the more ironic attitudes of the arts in the 20th century.

Mahler studied in Vienna, taking courses at both the conservatory and the university and attending the lectures

The Austrian composer and conductor Gustav Mahler is shown here in his youth as conductor of the Prague opera. Mahler gained international recognition as a conductor and a composer whose emotional expression was typical of late romantic music.

of composer Anton Bruckner. In 1880, shortly before making his conducting debut at a summer theater in the Austrian spa of Hall, Mahler completed his first mature composition, the cantata *Das Klagende Lied*. For the next decade or so, Mahler accepted conducting posts at one opera house after another, wearing out his welcome in each new place with his authoritarian discipline and his devotion to serious opera. His first masterpieces, the song cycle *Lieder eines Fahrenden Gesellen* (1883–85) and the First Symphony (1884–88; revised 1893–96), slowly took shape during this period.

Mahler read *Des Knaben Wunderhorn*, a collection of German verse modeled on folk poetry, in 1887, and in the years following, he set the poems as songs, incorporating some of the songs into his Second, Third, and Fourth symphonies; these are sometimes called his "Wunderhorn" symphonies. From 1891 to 1897 he was conductor of the opera in Hamburg and—after the death in 1894 of conductor Hans von Bülow—of the symphony as well. It was while attending von Bülow's funeral (1894) that Mahler conceived the spectacular choral finale of his Second Symphony ("Resurrection"), his best-loved work during his lifetime and long afterward.

His ten years at the Court Opera, 1897–1907, and particularly his collaborations with the stage designer Alfred Roller, are considered a high-water mark in opera history and the culmination of an exceptionally fertile period in Vienna's cultural life. In 1901, Mahler married Alma Schindler. His Fifth through Eighth Symphonies were written with unaccustomed speed over the next five years. The huge Eighth Symphony (1906), and *Das Lied von der Erde* (1908–09), the "symphonic" song cycle that followed, are considered his ultimate achievements, summing up a lifetime of musical concerns and preoccupations.

Anti-Semitism and charges of absenteeism combined to drive Mahler from Vienna in 1907. The death of his eldest daughter and the diagnosis of his own life-threatening heart condition produced an attitude of resignation and a turning inward. His Ninth Symphony (1908–09) and the incomplete Tenth (1910) are heartrending documents from this period. (He was treated briefly by Sig-mund Freud in 1910.) During the last four years of his life, Mahler maintained a strenuous schedule of conducting on tour and at the Metropolitan Opera and the Philharmonic in New York City.

By infusing the symphony with the poetic, psychological, and religious content of vocal music, especially the German Lied, Mahler took up the challenge to expand the symphonic form that Beethoven had laid down in his Ninth Symphony. Unsurpassed as an orchestrator, he was also, in his later works, a prefigurer of atonality.

—

Mahmud II, Sultan of the Ottoman Empire

[mah'-mood] Mahmud II, b. July 20, 1785, d. July 1, 1839, ruled the OTTOMAN EMPIRE from 1808 until his death and began the modern reforms that transformed the empire during the 19th century. He used defeats at the hands of the Serbian and Greek national revolutions to discredit the JANISSARIES, and in 1826 he ordered the massacre of that elite corps, thus removing the military arm of the reactionaries. Intensive reforms followed in the tax system, the army, and the bureaucracy.

Mahmud recognized the virtual autonomy of Serbia in 1815, and after defeats by the European allies of Greece in the Battle of Navarino (1827) and by Russia in the RUSSO-TURKISH WAR of 1828–29 he accepted Greek autonomy as well. He had been aided against the Greeks by the modern Egyptian army of MUHAMMAD ALI PASHA. When he refused to reward the latter with Syria, the Egyptian army was turned against Mahmud in 1831–33, and Constantinople was saved only by Russian intervention. Another war (1839) with Egypt ended in Turkish defeat days before Mahmud's death.

—

Mahmud of Ghazni

[guhz'-nee] Mahmud, 971–1030, the most renowned ruler of the Ghaznavid Muslim dynasty of Afghanistan, was a great conqueror. Coming to power in 998, he widened his realm to include not only the area of modern Afghanistan but also most of present-day Iran and Pakistan. Between 1001 and 1026 he fought 17 campaigns in a holy war to conquer India for Islam; his mounted armies would sweep across the northern Indian plains, demolishing Hindu temples, defacing idols, and carrying treasures back to his ancient capital, Ghazni. Although Mahmud is best known as a warrior, he was also a lover of literature who brought intellectuals to the city.

—

mahogany

[muh-hahg'-uh-nee] The name *mahogany* is applied to a number of timber trees in the mahogany family, Meliaceae, and to their wood. True mahogany wood is the product of the approximately six species of trees in the genus *Swietenia* of the mahogany family. The original mahogany of commerce is the West Indies mahogany, *S. mahogoni*, native to the West Indies and southern Florida. Its compact, hard, handsomely grained heartwood is generally a deep reddish brown and has been used for fine furniture since about 1500. Because of overcutting, it has been replaced by the Honduras ma-

The West Indies mahogany tree bears opposite leaves, small flowers in clusters, and fruit that splits open from the base.

hogany, *S. macrophylla,* as the primary source of true mahogany. African mahogany is obtained from two genera of trees also in the mahogany family: *Khaya* and *Entandrophragma.*

The generally soft, stringy wood of at least half a dozen species of Asiatic trees is marketed as Philippine mahogany. These include the Philippine cedar, *Cedrela;* the lauans, *Shora* and *Parashorea;* and the lumbayao, *Heritiera.* Two Australian eucalyptus trees used for timber are also known as mahoganies: *Eucalyptus acmenioides,* the white mahogany, and *E. resinifera,* the red mahogany.

Mahre (brothers) [mair] The fraternal twins Phillip and Steven Mahre, b. Yakima, Wash., May 10, 1957, are two of the best U.S. ski racers ever. Phil won (1981–83) three consecutive overall World Cup championships, a feat equaled by only two other men in ski-racing history. When Phil won his first title, Steve was fourth. Phil captured a silver medal in the slalom at the 1980 Winter Olympics, and he and Steve won gold and silver medals, respectively, at the 1984 Olympics in the same event.

Maiden Castle Maiden Castle, located 3 km (2 mi) southwest of Dorchester, Dorset, is the largest and most spectacular of the prehistoric hill forts of southern England. The Iron Age defensive structure developed from a single-rampart, or univallate, enclosure of about 6 ha (15 acres) in the 4th century BC to a massive fortress with four concentric ramparts enclosing three times that area by the 1st century BC. The stronghold is believed to have succumbed to the Second Roman Legion under Vespasian shortly after AD 43; a military engagement at this time is substantiated by a war cemetery and by caches of slingstones, one of which contained over 22,000 stones.

Prior to the Iron Age occupation, Neolithic constructions at the site included a causewayed camp and an enormous earthen mound some 550 m (1,805 ft) in length, probably related in function to the long BARROWS of the same period.

Maidstone Maidstone (1987 est. pop., 134,500) is a city in Kent in southeastern England, situated on the River Medway about 48 km (30 mi) southeast of London. The city is the market center for the surrounding agricultural region, and its industries include brewing and the manufacture of paper and agricultural machinery. Historical landmarks include the Church of All Saints (begun 1395) and a grammar school founded in 1549. A Roman post, Maidstone became a thriving market town.

mail-order business Mail-order companies are retail distributors that solicit orders primarily through the mails. The mail-order business in the United States began in the late 19th century and became one of the chief sources of supply to rural areas. The early catalogs usually advertised only a few items. The mail-order giants that emerged from that era (Montgomery Ward, founded 1872; Sears, Roebuck and Co., founded 1886) came to feature almost every type of consumer item in their catalogs. Smaller mail-order firms usually concentrate on a single product or a group of closely related items.

In recent years the mail-order business has assumed a new name, DIRECT MARKETING, which today encompasses sales made via the telephone and through videotex systems, as well as sales engendered by direct mail, by newspaper and magazine coupons, and by radio and television ads.

Mailer, Norman Norman Mailer, b. Long Branch, N.J., Jan. 31, 1923, one of the best postwar American writers, has enjoyed an erratic reputation. His popular first novel, *The Naked and the Dead* (1948), based on of his combat experience in the Pacific, is considered among the finest modern war novels. *Barbary Shore* (1951) and *The Deer Park* (1955), his Hollywood novel, are less important, but many regard his fourth novel, *An American Dream* (1965), as a black-comic masterpiece.

Equally brilliant as an essayist and journalist, Mailer has published several collections of miscellaneous writings, among them *Advertisements for Myself* (1959), *The Presidential Papers* (1963), and *Pieces and Pontifications* (1982), which deal with issues from boxing to politics and race relations. *The Armies of the Night* (1968), a personal narrative of the 1967 peace march on the Pentagon, won Mailer the Pulitzer Prize and the National Book Award. It was followed by *Miami and the Siege of Chicago* (1969), Mailer's account of the traumatic Republican and Democratic conventions of 1968. His other longer journalistic writings include *Of a Fire on the Moon* (1970), an account of the *Apollo II* moon landing, and

The American writer Norman Mailer has earned critical and popular acclaim for his singular, sometimes apocalyptic vision of Americans and their world.

The Prisoner of Sex (1971), his highly personal and idiosyncratic response to the women's liberation movement. *The Executioner's Song* (1979) is Mailer's ambitious novelistic treatment of the 1977 execution of murderer Gary Gilmore in Utah.

Mailer's fictional style has progressed from the naturalistic to the surreal, whereas his journalism has usually taken an experimental and autobiographical direction. *Ancient Evenings* (1983), a novel set in ancient Egypt, was not a critical success. Neither was the murder mystery *Tough Guys Don't Dance* (1984), of which Mailer directed a film version (1987).

Maillol, Aristide [my-ohl', ahr-ees-teed']   The French sculptor and graphic artist Aristide Maillol, b. Dec. 8, 1861, d. Sept. 27, 1944, is chiefly known for his female nudes, which exude a languorous feeling of repose. Maillol did not begin to sculpt until he was almost 40 years old. He produced small wooden or ceramic figures initially but soon turned to large sculptures such as *The Mediterranean* (c.1901; Museum of Modern Art, New York City) and *Action Enchained* (c.1905; Musée National d'Art Moderne, Paris). Maillol's carefully balanced, serene female figures, characterized by massiveness and smoothly carved contours, provide a transitional link to such younger sculptors as Constantin Brancusi and Raymond Duchamp-Villon, who worked to abstract the human form even further. Maillol created woodcut illustrations for Vergil's *Eclogues* (1926–27), Ovid's *Art of Love* (1935), and Verlaine's *Chansons pour elle* (1939).

Maiman, Theodore Harold [my'-muhn]   Theodore Harold Maiman, b. Los Angeles, July 11, 1927, an American physicist, was the first to demonstrate successful operation of a LASER. The first pulse of coherent optical radiation from Maiman's ruby laser was generated in May 1960 at Hughes Research Laboratories. Ruby had been considered previously for use as a laser medium but had been rejected for various reasons. Maiman, who had worked with ruby in other applications, reexamined these reasons, decided that laser action in ruby was not precluded, and went on to construct a working laser using this material.

Maimonides [my-mahn'-i-deez]   The outstanding medieval Jewish philosopher Maimonides (Moses ben Maimon; or Rambam, from the initials of Rabbi Moses ben Maimon), 1135–1204, was physician to the Sultan Saladin and communal leader of Egyptian Jewry, as well as an important figure in the codification of Jewish law. His formulation of the basic principles of Judaism in a series of 13 creedal affirmations, in the hope of clarifying the differences between Judaism and both Islam and Christianity, occasioned great controversy when it was first composed; it has since been accepted widely and incorporated into most Jewish prayer books. His *Mishneh Torah* (Second Law; often known in English as the *Strong Hand*), an organization of Jewish oral law, also became enmeshed in controversy, partly because of its rigorously systematic rearrangements of traditional rabbinic law, and partly because Maimonides did not indicate the sources on which he based his interpretations.

The greatest controversy, however, developed over Maimonides' major philosophic work, *Moreh Nebukhim* (*Guide for the Perplexed*), in which he attempted to interpret many biblical and rabbinic themes in the light of the philosophy of Aristotle as known to him through the Arabic philosophers al-FARABI and AVICENNA. An important purpose behind his undertaking was to supply allegorically philosophic translations of the anthropomorphic expressions used with reference to God in many biblical passages. This departure from literal reading of the sacred text was deeply resented by many of the religious leaders of the age. In some contexts Maimonides was ready to abandon his Aristotelian commitment—for example, with regard to the eternity of the world, because this doctrine in his view restricted God's absolute freedom of will to create or not to create the world.

Main River   The Main River, an important tributary of the RHINE RIVER in Germany, is 525 km (326 mi) long. It begins in northeastern Bavaria near Bayreuth and then zigzags west past WÜRZBERG, Aschaffenburg, and FRANKFURT AM MAIN to join the Rhine River at MAINZ. Grapes for wine are grown along the Main, and it is an important source of hydroelectric power. It is navigable by barge for about 385 km (240 mi) to Bamberg, where the Ludwig Canal connecting the Main to the Danube begins.

main sequence   see STELLAR EVOLUTION

Main Street   *Main Street* (1920), the novel that established Sinclair LEWIS as a major writer, presents a satiric portrait of Gopher Prairie, Minn., a typically dull and conservative midwestern town modeled on Lewis's native Sauk Centre. Carol Kennicott, a physician's wife, finds life in Gopher Prairie intellectually deadening and her relationship with her husband emotionally unfulfilling. When her attempts to kindle the town's interest in music and drama fail, she leaves in hopes of realizing a more independent life in a large city. Although the novel is generally read as an attack on middle-class life, Carol's dilemma can also be seen as feminist: an intelligent woman with nothing at home to challenge her and no skills with which to earn a living in the larger world.

Maine (ship) [mayn]   The explosion and sinking of the U.S. battleship *Maine* in the harbor of Havana, Cuba, on Feb. 15, 1898, with the loss of 260 lives, helped precipitate the outbreak of the SPANISH-AMERICAN WAR. The U.S. press, particularly the newspapers of William Randolph HEARST and Joseph PULITZER, accused Spain of responsibility and rallied prowar sentiment in the United States with the slogan "Remember the *Maine,* to hell with Spain." At the time, official U.S. investigators concluded that the explosions were probably triggered by a floating mine. A modern reinvestigation attributes the explosions to a spontaneous fire in the *Maine*'s coal bunkers that spread to the ammunition stores; this finding confirms the results of Spain's 1898 investigation.

Maine (state)   Located in the extreme northeastern section of the United States, Maine is bordered by the Canadian provinces of Quebec on the northwest and New Brunswick on the north and east, by New Hampshire on the west, and by the Atlantic Ocean on the southeast and south. Although Maine is a relatively small state, it constitutes almost half of New England.

The state's name is believed to be a contraction of the word *mainland*. Early explorers of the region described it as "The Main" to distinguish it from the offshore islands. Maine became the official name of the state when it joined the union in 1820. Residents of New England sometimes call Maine "Down East" because ships sailing north from Boston to Maine were sailing downwind.

About 90% of the state is covered with forests, and trees are a major resource for Maine's paper, pulp, and wood industries. Farming—including the cultivation of the famous Maine potatoes—is also important to the economy, as are fishing and tourism. The state's natural beauty, especially its rugged coast, attracts many tourists.

Land and Resources

Maine can be divided into four physiographic regions that run from southwest to northeast: the coastal lowland, the interior hilly belt, the mountains, and the dissected upland.

The coastal lowland, a narrow belt of low rolling land

AT A GLANCE

MAINE

Land: Area: 91,653 km² (35,387 mi²); rank: 39th. Capital: Augusta (1990 pop., 21,819). Largest city: Portland (1990 pop., 61,800). Counties: 16. Elevations: highest—1,605 m (5,267 ft), at Mount Katahdin; lowest—sea level, at the Atlantic coast.

People: Population (1990): 1,233,223; rank: 38th; density: 15.4 persons per km² (39.8 per mi²). Distribution (1990): 44.6% urban, 55.4% rural. Average annual change (1980–90): +0.9%.

Government (1993): Governor: John R. McKernan, Jr., Republican. U.S. Congress: Senate—1 Democrat, 1 Republican; House—1 Democrat, 1 Republican. Electoral college votes: 4. State legislature: 35 senators, 151 representatives.

Economy: State personal income (1989): $19.9 billion; rank: 41st. Median family income (1989): $32,422; rank: 27th. Agriculture: income (1989)—$447 million. Fishing: value (1989)—$133 million. Lumber production (1991): 847 million board feet. Mining (nonfuel): value (1988)—$68 million. Manufacturing: value added (1987)—$5.3 billion. Services: value (1987)—$4 billion.

Miscellany: Statehood: Mar. 15, 1820; the 23d state. Nickname: Pine Tree State; tree: eastern white pine; motto: *Dirigo* ("I direct"); song: "State of Maine Song."

Eastern White Pine Cone and Tassel

Chickadee

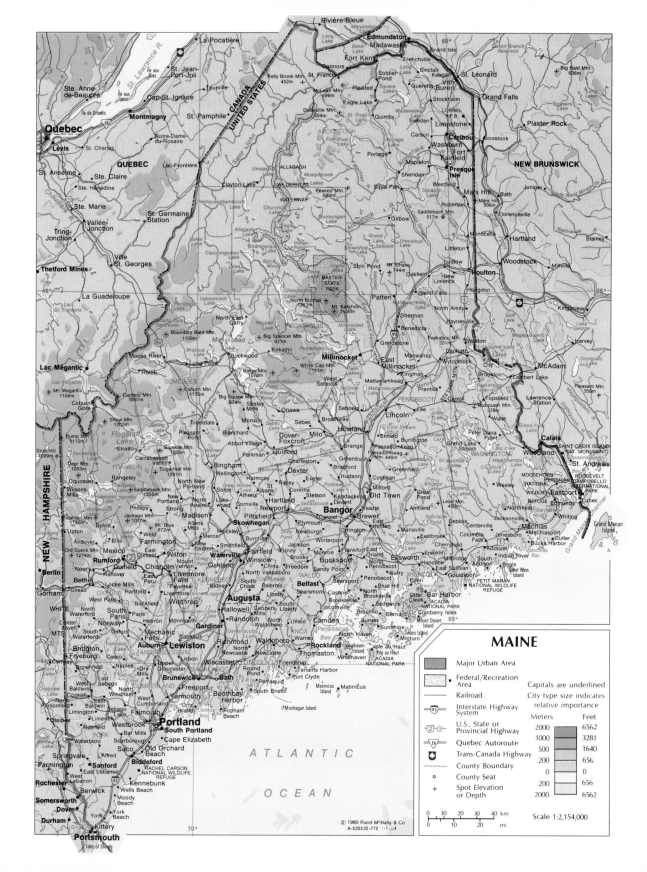

MAINE

- Major Urban Area
- Federal/Recreation Area
- Railroad
- Interstate Highway System
- U.S., State or Provincial Highway
- Quebec Autoroute
- Trans-Canada Highway
- County Boundary
- County Seat
- Spot Elevation or Depth

Capitals are underlined
City type size indicates relative importance

Meters	Feet
2000	6562
1000	3281
500	1640
200	656
0	0
200	656
2000	6562

Scale 1:2,154,000

0 10 20 30 40 km
0 10 20 mi

© 1980 Rand McNally & Co.
A-520520-772 -1-.|-1

ATLANTIC OCEAN

Acadia National Park, a diverse combination of mountains, fresh-water lakes, and rocky seashore, covers half of Mount Desert Island. Offering numerous recreational facilities and stunning views, Acadia is New England's only national park.

best-known lakes are Sebago, the Belgrades, Grands, Rangeleys, and the largest, Moosehead (303 km²/117 mi²).

Climate. Maine's climate is characterized by rapid weather changes, large ranges of annual and diurnal temperatures, and great differences in the same season in different years. The average annual temperature ranges from 4° C (40° F) in the north to 7° C (44 ° F) along the coast. The most marked differences are in the winter when northern Maine has January averages of –12° C (10° F) and the coast averages –7° C (20° F). Summer temperatures are more uniform over the state with July averages of about 20° C (68° F). Precipitation decreases from 1,170 mm (46 in) along the coast to 1,020 mm (40 in) in the north.

Vegetation and Animal Life. About 7.2 million ha (17.7 million acres), or 90% of Maine's land area, are forested. The major forest type in the state is spruce-fir, followed by mixed hardwoods and white pine.

Maine's abundant forests and rivers have made it a haven for many kinds of wildlife. Among the fur-bearing animals are black bears, beavers, foxes, lynx, and marten. Game animals such as deer attract hunters. More than 300 varieties of birds are found in the state.

Resources. Granite mined in the state has been used to decorate buildings all over the United States. In addition, sand and gravel, stone, and zinc are mined. Maine ranks as an important producer of beryllium concentrate. The state has abundant hydroelectric power for industry. Only in a few areas in the state (such as Aroostook County in the north) are the physical conditions conducive to large-scale farming.

People

Maine has a population of 1,233,223 (1990). The number of inhabitants grew slowly between 1860 and 1970, the growth rate averaging only 4.3% per decade in comparison to 12.9% for New England as a whole and 18.7% for the United States. This slow growth was the result of heavy emigration for better economic opportunities in other parts of the nation. During the 1970s and '80s, however, this trend was reversed, and Maine has had unprecedented population growth due to both significant in-migration and a decrease in out-migration.

Maine's population is not evenly distributed. About two-thirds of the population live in a six-county area, particularly in a 48-km-wide (30-mi) corridor along the principal interstate highway stretching from Kittery to Bangor. Despite the concentration of a large portion of the population in a small part of the state, Maine is not highly urbanized. The largest cities, according to the 1990 census, are Portland (64,358, 1990), Lewiston (39,757), Bangor (33,181), Auburn (24,309), and Augusta (21,325), the state capital.

Maine's population is made up of people from a variety of ethnic backgrounds, chiefly English, French Canadian, Irish, Scottish, Italian, and German. Only a small number of nonwhites live in Maine. To a large degree the blending of these many groups into the "Yankee culture" has hidden their ethnic origins. The exception is Americans of French-Canadian descent, who live mostly in the

about 30 to 50 km (20 to 30 mi) wide, runs along the coast from Kittery to Eastport. This region is penetrated extensively by ocean inlets. In the Bar Harbor and Camden areas, where the interior hills reach the coast, no lowlands are found. Cadillac Mountain (466 m/1,530 ft) on Mount Desert Island is the highest point on the Atlantic coast of the United States.

The interior hilly belt, which runs parallel to the coastal lowland, is a region of low hills averaging about 500 m (1,600 ft) in elevation. The region is narrow in the west but widens as it extends toward the New Brunswick border.

The mountain region of Maine is a portion of the Appalachian Mountains known as the Longfellow Mountains. This range runs from western Maine, north of Fryeburg, to just east of Mount Katahdin in the central part of the state. Fourteen peaks exceed 1,200 m (3,936 ft), including Maine's highest point, Mount Katahdin, which rises to 1,606 m (5,268 ft). The dissected upland, which has an average elevation of about 350 m (1,140 ft), is located in most of Aroostook and northern Somerset, Piscataquis, and Penobscot counties.

Rivers and Lakes. In addition to approximately 5,000 rivers and streams, Maine has more than 2,500 lakes and ponds. Most of the state is drained by south-flowing rivers, the larger ones from west to east being the Androscoggin, Kennebec, Penobscot, and Saint Croix. In the mountainous area the Saint John River and its major tributaries, the Allagash and Aroostook, drain northward. The upper Saint John Valley of northern Maine.

Roman Catholics constitute the largest single religious group in Maine. More Protestants than Catholics live in the state, however. The largest Protestant groups are Baptists, Episcopalians, Methodists, and members of the United Church of Christ.

Education. Public elementary and secondary education in Maine has shifted from small schools located in each community to consolidated school districts made up of two or more towns. Institutions of higher education include several private colleges, seminaries, and junior colleges. The oldest private colleges are Bowdoin (1794), Colby (1813), and BATES (1855). Public higher education is offered at the University of Maine (1865) with its main campus at Orono; the University of Southern Maine (1878) at Portland; and the Maine Maritime Academy (1941) at Castine.

Cultural Institutions. Maine's largest public libraries are in Bangor and Portland. The State Library in Augusta and the Maine Historical Library in Portland are known for their collections about Maine history. Among the state's best-known museums are the Maine State Museum in Augusta and the Portland Museum of Art. Bangor and Portland are known for their symphony orchestras. Summer-stock theaters are at Boothbay Harbor, Ogunquit, Kennebunkport, Camden, and Skowhegan.

Historical Sites. The oldest of Maine's rich array of historic sites and landmarks is the Old Gaol (a jail until 1860 but now a museum) in York, which dates to 1653. Revolutionary War sites include Fort Western (1754), where Benedict Arnold and his troops began their march on Quebec in 1775; and Burnham Tavern in Machias, where colonists met in 1775 to plot the capture of the British ship *Margaretta*. Other unique landmarks include Portland Head Light (1791), one of the oldest lighthouses in the United States, and the Wadsworth-Longfellow House in Portland, the boyhood home of Henry Wadsworth Longfellow.

Communications. Maine has about 100 radio stations, most of which serve primarily the communities in which they are located. Seven commercial television stations and a five-station public educational system provide programming for most of the state. Of the state's nine newspapers, the *Bangor News* has the largest circulation. The *Maine Sunday Telegram* is a statewide weekly newspaper.

Economy

Among Maine's leading sources of personal income are manufacturing, tourism, and trade. Manufacturing takes place primarily in the southwestern part of the state. The major tourist attractions are Maine's coastal regions and the lakes, rivers, and mountains of the interior. Maine also has an agricultural sector of some importance.

Agriculture. Although farming has declined in importance, agriculture still accounts for many of the export goods from the state. The greatest portion of the farm income in Maine comes from livestock and livestock products. Eggs are the leader in this category. The state also is a major producer of broilers—chickens from 9 to 12 weeks old. Dairy products and cattle raising are also important.

Maine ranks as the nation's third most productive potato-growing state (after Idaho and Washington). Other important crops are oats, hay, cattle corn, dry beans, peas, sugar beets, and fruits, mostly apples and blueberries.

Forestry and Fishing. Trees are the chief resource for Maine's industrial sector, but its lakes, rivers, and coastal

The picturesque village of Boothbay Harbor is situated on a peninsula in southern Maine between the Sheepscott and Damariscotta rivers. Originally developed as a center of trade and shipbuilding, Boothbay Harbor is more important today as a summer resort.

waters contribute a fish catch worth about $100 million per year. The annual lobster catch is the largest of any state.

Mining. Mining in Maine is relatively insignificant to the state's economy. Among the minerals found in the state are sand and gravel, stone, clays, copper, and zinc. The state is the leading garnet producer in the nation.

Manufacturing. Paper, including newsprint, is the state's major product, and Maine's paper-production capacity is greater than that of any other U.S. state. Other major manufactures are food products, leather goods, lumber and wood products, ships, and textiles. In recent years the electrical-machinery, rubber-and-plastic-goods, nonelectrical-machinery, apparel, and electrical-components-and-accessories industries have grown in importance.

A sector of the economy that continues to grow is food processing. Leading frozen products are blueberries, chicken, and french-fried potatoes. Sardines are an important canned product.

Tourism. One of the most significant components of the state's economy is tourism. In addition to its coastal and inland resorts, Maine has an abundance of wildlife that attracts hunters and anglers. State parks, as well as memorials, historical sites, and New England's only national park—Acadia National Park at Bar Harbor—also attract visitors.

Transportation. The state's transportation facilities include two major highways—the Maine Turnpike and I-95; the Boston and Maine railroad, a freight-carrier line; Portland International Jetport, the largest airport in Maine; and several deepwater harbors.

Energy. Most of Maine's electricity is generated by nuclear power. The remainder comes from hydroelectric and steam plants, and considerable potential for expansion exists.

Government

The constitution of Maine was adopted in 1819, and since that time about 150 amendments have been added. The chief executive is a governor elected every 4 years. The bicameral legislature is composed of a 35-member Senate and a 151-member House of Representatives. The judiciary is made up of a three-level court system: the district court, superior court, and state supreme court. Maine is represented in the U.S. Congress by two senators and two representatives. City and town governments have considerably more authority than the 16 county governments. Most decisions affecting local taxes, school budget appropriations, and many other local issues are made directly by citizens attending annual and special town meetings.

Until the rise of the Republican party just before the Civil War, politics in Maine was dominated by the Democrats. Republicans then controlled Maine politics until 1954; between 1860 and 1954 few Democratic senators and representatives represented the state in Augusta or in the Congress in Washington. In 1958, Edmund Muskie became the first Democrat popularly elected to the U.S. Senate from Maine.

History

Shell heaps left by early inhabitants may date from the 4th millennium BC. By the time European explorers reached Maine, the land was occupied by ABNAKI Indians.

Exploration and Settlement. Norse explorers may have reached Maine about AD 1000, but the first European settlement was a short-lived one, established by the sieur de MONTS and Samuel de CHAMPLAIN in 1604. The French established a settlement on Mount Desert Island in 1613 but were soon expelled by the English. Permanent English settlement began after 1622, when the Council for New England granted the territory between the Kennebec and Merrimack rivers to Sir Ferdinando GORGES and John MASON. In 1652 the Massachusetts Bay Colony assumed jurisdiction over Maine, but settlement was hindered by repeated conflicts with the Indians and the French (see KING PHILIP'S WAR; FRENCH AND INDIAN WARS). The granting of a new charter to Massachusetts in 1691 reaffirmed its control of Maine. In the 18th century the foundations for Maine's prosperous fishing, lumbering, and shipbuilding industries were laid.

The Revolution. Maine men were among the first to fight in the Revolutionary War; many coastal communities were attacked by the British, and the coastal town of Falmouth was destroyed. Although all areas east of the Penobscot River were occupied by the British, strong resistance was made by the colonists near Machiasport, where the first naval battle of the Revolution took place on June 12, 1775, resulting in the capture of the British ship *Margaretta*. In 1775, Benedict ARNOLD led his unsuccessful expedition against Quebec through Maine. Britain retained control of the area throughout the war.

Statehood. Maine did not win statehood until 1820, after eastern Maine had once again been occupied by the British during the WAR OF 1812. According to the MISSOURI COMPROMISE of 1820, Maine was admitted to the union as a free state balanced by Missouri as a slave state. Maine's capital was at Portland but was moved (1832) to Augusta.

The new state grew rapidly in population and prosperity, largely through timber trade with Asia, Europe, and the West Indies, and as a center of shipbuilding, notably at BATH. Maine made important contributions of men and supplies to the Union during the Civil War.

Following the Civil War, Maine's population growth slowed significantly despite considerable immigration of English-speaking Canadians, French Canadians, Irish, and other Canadians. The economy of Maine gradually shifted from agriculture, fishing, and lumbering, which peaked between 1865 and 1880, to manufacturing, which became the leading sector by 1900.

The developments in Maine in the 20th century mirrored those of the nation as a whole, although at a slower rate. There has been a continued shift from primary economic activities to manufacturing, with the most significant growth in trade, service, and government employment. Tourism grew tremendously after the 1930s, and several defense facilities were constructed during World War II, many of which were later phased out.

During the later 20th century Maine's population

growth, jobs, income, and other elements of development lagged behind those in most of the rest of the nation. The recent growth of the state's population, however, as well as increasing emphasis on industry and tourism, suggest that Maine's economic growth will continue at a faster rate.

Maine coon cat   The Maine coon cat is one of the oldest American breeds and is probably descended from long-haired Angora cats brought to New England by seamen. These Angoras randomly interbred with local short-haired cats and established the breed type. Some early settlers thought that the cat was part raccoon. The Maine coon cat is large, sometimes weighing more than 13.5 kg (30 lb). Its coat, which may be any color, is long and lies close to the body instead of away from it, as in Persian cats.

The Maine coon cat appears in many colors, often displaying a raccoonlike striped tail. One of the largest of American cats, it may carry a weight of 13.5 kg (30 lb) on its broad paws.

Maintenon, Françoise d'Aubigné, Marquise de [man-tuh-nohn', frahn-swahz' doh-been-yay', markeez' duh]   Françoise d'Aubigné, marquise de Maintenon, called Madame de Maintenon, b. Nov. 27, 1635, d. Apr. 15, 1719, was the second wife of King LOUIS XIV of France. She was born into an impoverished noble family, married the poet Paul Scarron in 1652, and was widowed in 1660. Later she became (1669) the trusted governess of Louis XIV's children by Madame de MONTESPAN.

After Queen Marie Thérèse's death in 1683, the king married Madame de Maintenon secretly and morganatically—that is, her rank remained unchanged. Following Louis's death in 1715, she devoted herself to the school for poor noble girls at Saint Cyr.

Mainz [mynts]   Mainz, the capital of the German state of Rhineland-Palatinate, is situated on the left bank of the Rhine opposite its junction with the Main River, 32 km (20 mi) southwest of FRANKFURT AM MAIN. The population is 189,000 (1987 est.).

Mainz is the center of the Rhine wine trade. Industrial production includes machinery, chemicals, shipbuilding, leather and plastic goods, paper, glassware, and processed foods. Although 80% of the city was destroyed during World War II, several historical landmarks remain, including the Cathedral of Saint Martin and the church of Saint Stephan (begun 975), and the grand-ducal palace (built 1627–78). Johannes Gutenberg University is there.

Mainz was settled by Celts before a Roman military camp (Mogontiacum) was built there late in the 1st century BC. In the 8th century the first German archbishopric was established at Mainz under Saint BONIFACE. Made a free city in 1244, Mainz was soon the center of a powerful league of Rhenish towns. The upheavals of the French Revolutionary period brought secularization, the loss of some lands, reduction to the rank of bishopric, and passage (1816) to Hesse-Darmstadt.

Maisonneuve, Paul de Chomedey, Sieur de [may-zawn-urv', pohl duh shohm-day', sur duh]   The French nobleman Paul de Chomedey, sieur de Maisonneuve, b. February 1612, d. Sept. 9, 1676, founded Montreal and was its first governor (1642–63). Originally a small missionary settlement called Ville-Marie, Montreal was plagued by wars with the Iroquois Indians. Maisonneuve sailed to France in 1651 to secure aid. He returned with troops in 1653 and remained governor until 1663, retiring to France in 1665.

maize   see CORN

majolica [muh-jahl'-ik-uh]   Majolica, spelled *maiolica* in Italian, the tin-oxide-glazed, painted earthenware pottery of Italy, reached a summit of artistic quality during the late 15th and early 16th centuries. Majolica resulted from the grafting of the Islamic ceramic tradition of tin-glazing onto the ancient traditions of native Italian pottery. This occurred early in the 15th century, when sophisticated Hispano-Moresque wares from Valencia were imitated by Italian potters. The name *majolica* is derived from the island of Majorca, the headquarters of trading vessels sailing between Spanish and Italian ports. One of the principal Italian centers of majolica production, the town of Faenza, later gave its name to the French term for the ware, FAÏENCE.

Majolica is first "thrown" or molded and then baked to a "biscuit" or terra-cotta condition. The porous ware is lead- and tin-oxide glazed. Decoration is applied to the dry glaze; its absorbent qualities require great skill and confidence of the painter because alterations are impossible. A second baking fuses the glaze and decoration to an even, glossy surface.

The most common surviving pieces from the earliest period of majolica are storage vessels made for monastic pharmacies, usually labeled to indicate their contents and decorated with contemporary Hispano-Moresque motifs or the symbols of saints credited with healing powers. In the late 15th century majolica became more decora-

A 16th-century majolica dish from Urbino, Italy, portraying a scene from Homer's Iliad, exemplifies the pictorial narrative common to the majolica of Urbino during the late 15th and early 16th centuries. (Metropolitan Museum of Art, New York City.)

tive and less functional. Dishes and vases were designed primarily for display, especially the pictorial narrative styles associated with Urbino. Sixteenth-century majolica decoration evolved away from pictorialism; from the East, by way of Venice and Islamic metalworkers there, came the arabesque style, a continuous interlacing of formalized leaves and branches. In the early 17th century, the tin-glaze technique was used to imitate Chinese porcelain.

Major, Clarence   The American writer and editor Clarence Major, b. Atlanta, Ga., Dec. 31, 1936, is known for his powerful poetry of black consciousness and for the complexity and vitality of his fiction. In such volumes of poetry as *Swallow the Lake* (1970) and *Inside Diameter* (1984) he mixes dialect, rhythms, and moods. His novels include *All-Night Visitors* (1969), *No* (1973), *Reflex and Bone Structure* (1975), *Emergency Exit* (1979), and *My Amputations* (1986). *Surfaces and Masks* (1988) is a book-length poem inspired by a visit to Venice.

Major, John   John Major, b. Mar. 29, 1943, succeeded Margaret Thatcher as prime minister of the United Kingdom on Nov. 28, 1990. From a lower-middle-class family, Major pursued a career in banking and was elected to Parliament as a Conservative in 1979. He became a protégé of Thatcher, who appointed him chief treasury secretary (1987–89), foreign secretary (1989), and chancellor of the exchequer (1989–90). As chancellor, Major proposed the "hard Ecu" plan for the European Community, which provided for a single European currency to exist side by side with the monetary systems of the member countries.

Majorca   [muh-johr'-kuh]   Majorca (Spanish: Mallorca), one of Spain's BALEARIC ISLANDS, is located in the western Mediterranean Sea about 225 km (140 mi) from the Spanish mainland. Covering 3,639 km² (1,405 mi²), Majorca is the largest island of the group. The population is 561,215 (1981). PALMA, located on the east coast, is the leading city and port of Majorca and the capital of the Balearics' autonomous community.

Limestone, marble, coal, iron, and lead are mined in the mountains along the east and west coast. At lower elevations and in the fertile central lowland, farming and livestock raising are leading activities. Tourism and fishing are important along the coast.

Many stone monuments date from the 2d millennium BC. The island was subsequently held by Phoenicians, Carthaginians, Romans, Byzantines, and, starting in 797, by the Moors. In 1229, James I of Aragon took Majorca from the Moors. From 1276 to 1343, Majorca was an independent kingdom, after which it became part of Aragon.

Makarios III   [mah-kah'-ree-ohs]   Makarios III (Michael Christodoulos Mouskos), b. Aug. 13, 1913, d. Aug. 3, 1977, was archbishop of the Greek Orthodox church of Cyprus and president of the Republic of Cyprus from 1960 until his death. He organized a movement for the union (*enosis*) of Cyprus, then under British rule, and Greece. The British deported him in 1956. With the creation of the independent Republic of Cyprus, Makarios became (1960) president, being reelected in 1968 and 1973. In July 1974, Makarios was deposed by Greek Cypriots who still favored union with Greece; this provoked a Turkish invasion of the island in support of the Turkish Cypriot minority, who opposed *enosis*. Makarios returned to power in December 1974 and sought to ease the conflict between the two communities, but he was unable to prevent the partition of Cyprus.

Makarova, Natalia   Natalia Makarova, b. Leningrad, Nov. 21, 1940, is considered one of the most dramatically enthralling and technically perfect ballerinas of her generation. She joined the Kirov Ballet company in 1959 dancing mostly in the full-length classical ballets such as *Swan Lake*, *Sleeping Beauty*, and *Raymonda*. On Sept. 4, 1970, during a Kirov European tour, Makarova chose to remain in London, giving as her reason a search for artistic freedom. She joined American Ballet Theatre (ABT) in November of that year and had great success in contemporary works—such as Anthony Tudor's *Lilac Gar-*

Natalia Makarova is seen performing in American Ballet Theatre's production of Jerome Robbins's Other Dances. Makarova was acclaimed for her lyrical interpretations in both contemporary and classical ballet.

den, *Dark Elegies*, and *Pillar of Fire*—as well as in the classics. From 1972 she also danced with Britain's ROYAL BALLET, with particular success in Kenneth MacMillan's *Manon* and Sir Frederick Ashton's *Cinderella*. Her staging of act 4 of *La Bayadère* for ABT in 1974 was widely admired. In 1983, Makarova danced in the Broadway musical *On Your Toes*. She retired in 1986.

Makemie, Francis [muh-kem'-ee] Francis Makemie, b. Ireland, 1658, d. 1708, was the founder of American Presbyterianism. He established (1684) the first Presbyterian congregation in America at Snow Hill, Md. In 1706, Makemie brought together Presbyterians of different backgrounds—Scotch-Irish, Scottish, and New England—to form the presbytery of Philadelphia. Lord Cornbury, New York's governor, arrested Makemie in 1707 for preaching without a license in a private home on Long Island. The event gained new followers for the Presbyterians and new support for the idea of religious freedom.

Malabar Christians [mal'-uh-bahr] The Malabar Christians are an ancient and numerous Christian community in southwestern India. They take their name from the Malabar Coast where, according to tradition, Christianity was first brought to India by Saint THOMAS the Apostle. Verifiable records, however, connect early Indian Christianity with the 5th-century missionary activity of the church in Persia, which embraced NESTORIANISM. For almost a millennium the Malabars survived, with a liturgy in the Syriac language, as an intermittently persecuted minority in India.

Great confusion resulted from the arrival of the Portuguese at the end of the 15th century. Some of the Malabar Christians were converted outright to Western Christianity; others, although preserving parts of their liturgy and some of their customs, recognized the supremacy of the pope. Force and coercion were widely used to achieve these results. When Portuguese rule ended in the 17th century, a majority of Malabar Christians affiliated themselves with the JACOBITE CHURCH. In the years following World War I, although remaining independent, they joined in communion with the other Monophysite churches (see MONOPHYSITISM).

Malabo [mah-lah'-boh] Malabo (1983 pop., 37,500), formerly called Santa Isabel, is the capital of Equatorial Guinea. It is located along the northern coast of Macías Nguema Biyogo island, in the Gulf of Guinea. Malabo is the nation's principal commercial center; its port exports cacao, coffee, and timber. The city was founded in 1827 by the British, who named it Port Clarence.

Malacca see MELAKA

Malacca, Strait of [muh-lak'-uh] The Strait of Malacca is located between the Malay Peninsula and Sumatra, connecting the South China Sea to the Indian Ocean. It is 800 km (500 mi) long and ranges from 50 to 320 km (30 to 200 mi) in width. The strait is one of the world's busiest shipping channels; its principal ports are Penang, Malaysia, Belawan, Indonesia, and Singapore.

Malachi, Book of [mal'-uh-ky] Malachi is the last of the 12 books of the Minor Prophets in the Old Testament of the BIBLE. Malachi means "my messenger" in Hebrew, and few scholars believe that it is the actual name of the prophet. The prophet's themes include the ritual purity of sacrifices, the evils of mixed marriages and divorce, and the coming day of judgment. The book, consisting of six oracles, is believed to have been written after the reconstruction of the Temple (516 BC) and before the reforms of EZRA AND NEHEMIAH (*c.*450 BC).

malachite [mal'-uh-kyt] The common hydrous copper CARBONATE MINERAL malachite, $Cu_2CO_3(OH)_2$, is a minor ore of copper; it has been used as a decorative stone, a semiprecious gem, and a green pigment. It forms tufts of needlelike prismatic crystals (monoclinic system) as well as granular, earthy, or fibrous masses intergrown with AZURITE and rounded, banded crusts. All have a distinctive bright green color and an adamantine to silky luster. Hardness is 3½–4, streak is pale green, and specific gravity is 3.9–4.1.

Malachite, a common copper carbonate nearly always combined with azurite, is mined as a minor ore of copper. It is usually found in botryoidal form (spherical masses) and may reveal bands of color when fractured.

Malachy, Saint [mal'-uh-kee] Saint Malachy, or Máelmáedoc úa Morgair, *c.*1094–1148, was an Irish abbot and bishop who reformed the church in Ireland. He disciplined the clergy and established the Roman liturgy in Ireland. Aided by Saint Bernard of Clairvaux he introduced the Cistercian order into the country with the founding of the abbey of Mellifont. He was the first Irishman formally canonized, in 1190. Feast day: Nov. 3.

Málaga [mah'-lah-gah]   Málaga is the capital of Málaga province in southern Spain. Located at the mouth of the Guadalmedina River on the Mediterranean Sea, the city is an important port and agricultural center. The population is 566,330 (1987 est.). Industries include the manufacture of textiles, food products, building materials, and fertilizer. Because of Málaga's location along the Costa del Sol, tourism is of major economic importance.

Málaga was settled by Phoenicians during the 12th century BC and then held in succession by the Carthaginians, Romans, Visigoths, and, after 711, the Moors. It subsequently served as the capital of the Moorish kingdom of Granada until 1487, when Spanish Christians captured the city. In 1937, during the Spanish Civil War, a decisive loyalist defeat took place at Málaga. The artist Pablo Picasso was born there.

Malagasy language   see MALAYO-POLYNESIAN LANGUAGES

Malagasy Republic   see MADAGASCAR

Malamud, Bernard [mal'-uh-muhd]   The novelist and short-story writer Bernard Malamud, b. Brooklyn, N.Y., Apr. 26, 1914, d. Mar. 18, 1986, created fiction that focused on Jews living in New York City, transforming ordinary people into symbols of the victory of the human spirit. Malamud's first novel, *The Natural* (1952), the story of a baseball player, is his least typical. In *The Assistant* (1957), the author's most highly praised novel, the young Italian assistant of an aged and suffering Jewish grocer moves from scorn to sympathy and eventual mythic identification with the old man and his religious values.

After graduating (1936) from the City College of New York (CCNY) and earning an M.A. (1942) from Columbia University, Malamud taught evening high school in New

The 20th-century American author Bernard Malamud received the 1967 Pulitzer Prize for his novel The Fixer *(1966). Malamud's works focus on the Jewish tradition and its influence on contemporary culture.*

Photo Jill Krementz © 1974

York until 1949, when he accepted a position in the English department at Oregon State College in Corvallis. From 1961 he taught literature at Bennington College in Vermont. A fictionalized account of his years in the northwest is presented in his third novel, *A New Life* (1961). A novel set in Russia during 1913, *The Fixer* (1966), which earned Malamud the Pulitzer Prize and his second National Book Award, is his only extended treatment of Jews outside America or of noncontemporary events. In *The Tenants* (1971), set in an abandoned tenement in New York, a Jewish-American writer and an African-American revolutionary debate each other's values. The autobiographical *Dubin's Lives* (1979) and the allegorical, neo-biblical fable of fallen humanity, *God's Grace* (1982), were his last novels. His first collection of short fiction, *The Magic Barrel* (1958), won the National Book Award; subsequent collections include *Idiots First* (1963), *Pictures of Fidelman* (1969), and *Rembrandt's Hat* (1973).

malamute   see ALASKAN MALAMUTE

Malan, Daniel F. [muh-lahn']   Daniel François Malan, b. May 22, 1874, d. Feb. 7, 1959, was a principal architect of the policy of APARTHEID in South Africa. A Dutch Reformed clergyman and later editor of a nationalist Afrikaner newspaper, he was elected to Parliament as a member of the NATIONAL PARTY in 1918. He served in Gen. James HERTZOG's government from 1924 to 1934 but broke with Hertzog when the latter fused the Nationalists with Jan SMUTS's South African party. Malan led a splinter Nationalist group until the party reunited in 1939. In 1948, after a National party victory, Malan became prime minister. He worked for racial segregation and the development of separate black "homelands"; he also outlawed the Communist party. Malan served as prime minister until 1954, when he retired from politics.

---

malaria   A PROTOZOAL DISEASE, malaria is a widespread and often fatal infection in humans; it also infects primates, rodents, reptiles, and birds. It occurs mostly in tropical regions of the world, with an estimated annual rate of incidence at more than 50 million cases, about 1 million of which are fatal.

Malaria means "bad air" in Italian, reflecting the pre-1880 view that the disease is caused by gases from the swampy regions where many cases occur. In 1880, Charles LAVERAN observed a protozoal parasite in the blood of an afflicted patient. In 1898, Ronald Ross found that the bite of the female MOSQUITO of the genus *Anopheles* transmits the parasites into the bloodstream.

Symptoms. The main symptoms of malaria are intermittent fever and chills, which occur at intervals of 24 to 72 hours, depending on the type of Plasmodium parasite (subphylum SPOROZOA) responsible. Other symptoms are headache, weakness, and an enlarged spleen.

Various human RACES have developed genetic defenses against malaria. African and Mediterranean peoples, for instance, have genes for altered hemoglobin, on which the parasite cannot thrive as easily as it does on normal hemoglobin. People having one normal hemoglobin gene and one altered gene lessen their chances of acquiring malaria. Unfortunately, people who inherit two altered genes are subject to either SICKLE-CELL DISEASE or thalassemia—particularly COOLEY'S ANEMIA—depending on the type of gene inherited.

Cure and Prevention. Until the first half of the 20th century, an extract from the bark of the South American cinchona tree, QUININE, and a related drug, quinidine, were the only antimalarial drugs. Current treatment includes the drug chloroquine as the first choice, as well as pyrimethamine and chloroguanide. Parasites have developed resistance to chloroquine, however, although combined use with the drug desipramine is helping to overcome this resistance. Similar development of resistance is feared with two newer drugs, halofantrine and mefloquine.

Genetic engineering techniques have led to the development of a method for diagnosing malaria. It is hoped that such techniques will also lead to a practical malarial vaccine.

People who have had malaria often suffer relapses, which may occur years after the initial infection. The cause of such relapses is not yet understood.

Malawi [muh-lah'-wee]   Malawi is a landlocked nation in southeastern Africa. It is bordered by Mozambique on the east and south, Zambia on the west, and Tanzania on the north. Formerly the British protectorate of Nyasaland, Malawi became independent in 1964.

Land

Malawi covers a long, narrow area; it extends about 840 km (520 mi) from north to south and has a maximum width of 160 km (100 mi). Nearly 20% of its area is covered by Lake NYASA (also called Lake Malawi), the third largest lake in Africa. Rich soils deposited by the lake around its shores are some of the most fertile in Africa. The country lies within the East African Rift System, part of the enormous GREAT RIFT VALLEY, which extends from Syria to Mozambique. Malawi's average elevation is 1,200 m (3,900 ft); Mount Mulanje (Mlanje; also Sapitwa), the highest point in the country, rises to 3,000 m (9,843 ft) in the south. The major river is the Shire.

Malawi has a subtropical climate. The dry, cool season lasts from May to October, and the warm, humid season lasts from December to March. At Mzuzu, in the northern highlands, the average annual temperature is 19° C (66° F) and annual rainfall averages 1,500 mm (59 in). At Chikwawa in the Shire River valley in the south, the average annual temperature is 26° C (79° F) and rainfall averages 840 mm (33 in). The tropical savanna vegetation in the north gives way to bushveld along Lake Nyasa and thornbush in the Shire valley.

People

The Chewa, the largest ethnic group, are descended from

AT A GLANCE

REPUBLIC OF MALAWI

Land: Area: 118,484 km^2 (45,747 mi^2). Capital: Lilongwe (1987 pop., 220,300). Largest city: Blantyre (1987 pop., 402,500).

People: Population (1990 est.): 9,157,528. Density: 77 persons per km^2 (200 per mi^2). Distribution (1988): 13% urban, 87% rural. Official language: English. Major religions: traditional religions, Roman Catholicism, Presbyterianism, Islam.

Government: Type: one-party state. Legislature: National Assembly. Political subdivisions: 3 regions.

Economy: GNP (1989): $1.475 billion; $180 per capita. Labor distribution (1985): agriculture and fishing—81%; mining, manufacturing, construction, utilities, transportation, and communications—7%; trade, services, and government—12%. Foreign trade (1988): imports—$402 million; exports—$292 million. Currency: 1 Malawi kwacha = 100 tambala.

Education and Health: Literacy (1985): 41.2% of adult population. Universities (1989): 1. Hospital beds (1986): 12,119. Physicians (1984): 262. Life expectancy (1990): women—50; men—48. Infant mortality (1990): 130 per 1,000 live births.

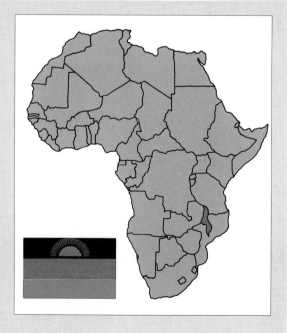

the Maravi—a Bantu tribe that first entered the region about 600 years ago and for which the country is named. The other major ethnic groups are the YAO, Nyanja, Tumbuka, Lomwe, and Sena. Small minorities of British and Indians also live in Malawi. Chichewa, the Chewa language, and English are the principal languages. About 75% of the population is nominally Christian, and 20% is Muslim; the majority practices traditional animistic religions along with other religions.

More than half of the population are concentrated in the south, and most of the urban population lives in BLANTYRE, the largest city and leading industrial and commercial center. LILONGWE has been the official capital since 1975.

Education is not required; 42% of all children attend primary school. Malnutrition is widespread.

Economic Activity

Malawi is one of the world's poorest countries. The government promotes agriculture, which provides more than 90% of all exports, but its policies favor large holdings where cash crops are grown. Because most farms are small, rural poverty is widespread. Recently, the economy has been adversely affected by drought, floods, insect

pests, overpopulation, and the civil war in Mozambique. By 1990 the war had driven nearly 800,000 Mozambicans into Malawi, giving it one of the world's highest ratios of refugees to indigenous people. From 1984 to 1989 the railway linking Malawi to Nacala, Mozambique, was closed by rebel activity, forcing landlocked Malawi to transport goods along the more costly route to and from South African ports. In 1987, Malawi was forced to import food for the first time in 20 years.

History and Government

The Maravi kingdom, centered in the Shire River valley, arose during the 15th century. At the peak of its power it reached as far south as present-day Zimbabwe. During the late 18th century the kingdom declined as a result of warfare and internal conflicts. In 1859, David LIVINGSTONE, the British explorer, visited the area, and this paved the way for the arrival of British and Scottish settlers. In 1891 the British protectorate of Nyasaland was created. In 1953, Nyasaland became part of the Federation of Rhodesia and Nyasaland. Internal opposition to the federation led to the birth of a nationalist movement. In 1963 the federation was dissolved, and in 1964 the independent nation of Malawi was declared.

According to the constitution of 1966, Malawi is a republic. The Malawi Congress party (MCP) is the sole legal political party. Dr. H. Kamuzu BANDA, who has served as leader of the MCP since 1958 and as president since 1966, was declared president-for-life in 1971. Because there is no prime minister he also serves as head of the cabinet and holds several cabinet posts. The unicameral National Assembly is composed of members of the MCP elected to serve 5-year terms. Malawi, the only black African nation with formal diplomatic relations with South Africa, moved to improve relations with neighboring black-ruled states in the late 1980s.

Malay Archipelago [may'-lay ahr-chuh-pel'-uh-goh]

The Malay Archipelago, the world's largest island group, considered a bridge between Asia and Australia, extends 6,100 km (3,800 mi) from the Indian Ocean off the coast of southeast Asia in the west to the southwestern Pacific in the east. The archipelago consists of the Philippines, Indonesia, Brunei, parts of Malaysia, and Papua New Guinea.

Malay language   see MALAYO-POLYNESIAN LANGUAGES

Malay Peninsula   The Malay Peninsula is the southernmost portion of the mainland of Southeast Asia. It covers about 181,300 km^2 (70,000 mi^2) and is bounded by the South China Sea on the east and the Indian Ocean and the Strait of Malacca on the west. Parts of Burma and Thailand and much of Malaysia are located on the narrow peninsula, and Singapore lies at its southern tip.

Malaya   see MALAYSIA

MALAWI

— Railroad
+ Spot Elevation or Depth

National capitals are underlined

City type size indicates relative importance

Meters	Feet
4000	13124
2000	6562
1000	3281
500	1640
200	656
0	0
200	656
2000	6562

Scale 1:7,440,000

© 1980 Rand McNally & Co.
A-586000-772

Malayo–Polynesian languages

The Malayo-Polynesian language family, also commonly called the Austronesian family (from the Latin root *austro*, "southern," and the Greek word *nesis*, "island"), includes between 600 and 1,000 languages, probably more than any other language family in the world. It encompasses most languages of Malaysia, Indonesia, the Philippines, and Madagascar; a fifth of the approximately 1,000 languages spoken in New Guinea and neighboring islands; and most languages spoken in the islands of the Pacific, which are traditionally grouped into three regions: Melanesia (Solomon Islands, New Caledonia, Vanuatu, and Fiji), Micronesia (Mariana Islands, Caroline Islands, Marshall Islands, and Kiribati), and Polynesia (Tonga, Niue, Samoa, Wallis and Futuna, Tuvalu, Tokelau, Cook Islands, Hawaii, French Polynesia, Easter Island, and New Zealand). The Austronesian family also includes the Aboriginal languages of Taiwan and a few isolated languages of Vietnam and Cambodia; the Aboriginal languages of Australia, however, and the Papuan languages of New Guinea, are not related to the Austronesian family.

Two of the world's major languages belong to the Austronesian family: Indonesian-Malay, spoken as a lingua franca by 150 million people in Indonesia and Malaysia; and Javanese, spoken natively by 60 million in Java. Other Austronesian languages with large numbers of speakers include Tagalog (also called Pilipino), the official language of the Philippines (10 million native and second-language speakers); Cebuano, also spoken in the Philippines (10 million speakers); Sundanese, spoken in West Java (15 million speakers); Madurese, spoken in East Java (7.5 million speakers); and Malagasy, a chain of dialects spoken in Madagascar (10 million speakers).

Historical Development and Genetic Subgrouping. All Austronesian languages derive from a single language or group of dialects called Proto-Austronesian, spoken about 5,000 years ago somewhere in the islands of Southeast Asia by a seafaring people.

The most ancient division in the Austronesian family separated 3 groups of about 20 Formosan languages from all other languages of the family. Most of the remaining Austronesian languages fall into a Western and an Eastern, or Oceanic, group. Members of the Western group include all the Austronesian languages spoken in Southeast Asia, Indonesia, Madagascar, the Philippines, Guam, and Palau. The Oceanic group extends over the coastal areas of Papua New Guinea into the islands of the Pacific.

While many attempts have been made to link Austronesian languages to other language families, there is no solid evidence that the family has any external relatives. An ancient genetic link may have existed with the Papuan languages of New Guinea or possibly even with Tai languages, but such relationships are so remote that natural language change has obliterated any evidence of them. Other theories linking Austronesian languages to the Semitic languages, the Indo-European family, the languages of South America, or to Japanese have been dismissed as fanciful.

Structural Characteristics. For the most part, Austronesian inflectional morphology is simple: verb and noun inflections are rare. Verbal categories such as voice, tense, and agreement are usually marked with affixes or with independent function words, particularly in the Oceanic languages. Typically verbs can be used as nouns or adjectives without any change in form; to a lesser extent the reverse is also true. Reduplication is commonly used to mark categories like plurality, repetition, and moderation; for example, the Fijian word *levu*, "big", reduplicates as *lelevu* to refer to several objects and as *levulevu* to mean "biggish." Many Austronesian languages have two forms of the first-person plural pronouns: an exclusive form ("we excluding you") and an inclusive form ("we including you"). Some languages like Fijian have complex pronoun systems in which the exclusive-inclusive contrast and several number categories are marked: singular, dual (for two people), paucal (for a few people), and plural (for many people).

The constituent order of basic transitive clauses in Austronesian languages is typically subject-verb-object or verb-subject-object, but the family also includes an unusual number of languages (for example, Fijian, Malagasy, Batak, Palauan, and Kiribati) in which the basic order is verb-object-subject. Austronesian languages typically place adjectives and relative clauses after their head nouns, but articles before nouns. Formosan languages, Philippine languages, and Malagasy have developed a "focus" system, in which the verb changes its form to encode the grammatical function (subject or direct object, for example) of the noun phrase with the greatest importance in the clause.

Patterns of Language Use. Important written traditions are associated with some Western Austronesian languages, including Indonesian-Malay, Tagalog, and Javanese. A sizable body of ancient religious texts exists in Javanese, for which a now-obsolete syllabic writing system was devised in the 9th century. In contrast to Western Austronesian languages, most Oceanic languages are handicapped by the small size of their speech communities from gaining wider acceptance as literary languages or languages of the media. In Fiji, Samoa, and Kiribati the indigenous languages serve as one of the working languages of government, education, and the press alongside English, though in many respects English holds a privileged position. With the exception of Javanese, Austronesian languages lacked writing systems before contact with Europeans, and today most of them are written in the Roman alphabet.

Some Austronesian languages have different "speech levels," wherein certain words can be used only in addressing persons of particular social rank. Complex speech-level systems are found in Balinese and Javanese, and, to a lesser extent, in certain Polynesian languages like Tongan and Samoan. The imprint of Sanskrit and Arabic on the languages of Indonesia bears witness to the different waves of religious influence. European languages (principally English, French, and—in the Philippines and Micronesia—Spanish) have also left their mark on many Austronesian lexicons.

MALAYSIA

Land: Area: 329,749 km² (127,317 mi²). Capital and largest city: Kuala Lumpur (1985 est. pop., 1,103,200).

People: Population (1990 est.): 17,510,546. Density: 53.1 persons per km² (137.5 per mi²). Distribution (1990): 35% urban, 65% rural. Official language: Bahasa Malaysia. Major religions: Islam, Buddhism, Daoism, Hinduism, Christianity.

Government: Type: constitutional monarchy. Legislature: Parliament. Political subdivisions: 13 states, 2 federal territories.

Economy: GDP (1989): $37.9 billion; $2,270 per capita. Labor distribution (1990): agriculture and fishing—30.8%; manufacturing—17.3%; commerce and services—27.6%; government and public authorities—13.5%; construction—6%. Foreign trade (1989): imports—$20.2 billion; exports—$24.4 billion. Currency: 1 ringgit = 100 sen.

Education and Health: Literacy (1988): 76% of adult population. Universities (1989): 7. Hospital beds (1986): 32,960. Physicians (1987): 5,794. Life expectancy (1990): 68. Infant mortality (1990): 30 per 1,000 live births.

Malays   see MALAYSIA

Malaysia [may-lay'-zhuh]   Malaysia is the southernmost nation of mainland Southeast Asia. It is composed of two parts that are separated by more than 650 km (400 mi) of the South China Sea. Most of Malaysia occupies the southern tip of the Malay Peninsula, south of Thailand. It is sometimes called Malaya, or Peninsular or West Malaysia. East Malaysia, composed of the two states of SABAH and SARAWAK, occupies the northern portion of the island of BORNEO, the rest of which is part of Indonesia. Malaysia was a British colony until 1957, when it became independent. As a nation it has faced the problem of unifying its diverse population, composed of Malays, Indians, and Chinese.

Land and Resources

Peninsular Malaysia is dominated by a mountainous core consisting of several parallel north-south ranges. The highest, the Main Range, has peaks over 2,100 m (7,000 ft). Coastal plains are found between the mountains and the sea in the west and east. Sarawak consists largely of coastal plain. In Sabah the narrow coastal plain gradually gives way to a mountainous region that divides Malaysia from Indonesia. Mount Kinabalu, at 4,101 m (13,455 ft) the highest point in Malaysia, is in Sabah. Malaysia is drained by an abundance of short rivers and streams, many of which flood seasonally.

Malaysia has a tropical climate. Temperatures through-out the year average 21° to 32° C (70° to 90° F), although they are lower in mountainous zones. Rainfall averages from 2,030 mm (80 in) to 2,540 mm (100 in) annually and occurs mosly during two monsoon seasons.

The major resources exploited in Malaysia are tin, timber, petroleum, bauxite, copper, iron ore, and gold.

People

The indigenous population are the Malays, who compose more than 50% of the population. They are predominantly rural and traditionally have held the greatest political power. Another 32% of the population are Chinese, the descendants of late-19th- and early-20th-century immigrants. Primarily urban dwellers, the Chinese have traditionally dominated the economy. About 8% of the population are composed of Malaysians of Indian descent who came to the area during the colonial period to work on the rubber plantations. Non-Malay indigenous tribal peoples, who represent 8% of the population, are heavily concentrated in East Malaysia.

The official language, Bahasa Malaysia, is written in both a Roman alphabet and an Arabic script. English is also widely spoken. Various Chinese and Indian languages are common. The state religion is Islam. Malays are Sunnite Muslims of the Shafi'ite school of Islam who maintain some of their pre-Islamic beliefs in ghosts and spirits. Buddhism and Hinduism are the predominant religions among the Chinese and Indians, respectively.

The bulk of Malaysia's population lives in West Malaysia, particularly in the western coastal plain. Most of Malaysia's largest cities are there, including KUALA LUMPUR (the capital), George Town, Ipoh, and Johor Baharu. About 40% of Malaysia's people are under 15 years of age.

The state provides 13 years of free education. The largest of the country's universities is the University of Malaya (1962) at Kuala Lumpur.

Economic Activity

Malaysia has one of the soundest economies of the developing nations of Asia, although its rate of economic growth slowed in the 1980s due to decreasing prices and demand for its chief export commodities. Until the 1960s about two-thirds of Malaysia's export earnings came from rubber and tin. In recent years, however, petroleum from offshore reserves and palm oil have become more important.

Agriculture is the largest sector of the economy, and Malaysia is the world's leading producer of natural rubber and palm oil; rice is the major subsistence crop. The country supplies about one-fourth of the world's tin. The industrial sector has expanded rapidly since the 1960s. Electronic components (particularly semiconductor chips), electrical machinery, and textiles and clothing are the leading manufactures. Also important to the economy are forestry and tourism.

Government

Malaysia's government is modeled on the British system, somewhat modified because Malaysia's federal structure incorporates 13 states and the federal capital territory. A monarch, the supreme ruler, is elected every 5 years by the 9 traditional rulers of Malaya, the sultans. Real power, however, is in the hands of the prime minister and the cabinet. The bicameral parliament is composed of a partially appointed senate and a house of representatives elected by universal adult suffrage. The leading party, the National Front, is a coalition of primarily ethnic political parties.

History

The Buddhist Srivijaya Empire, centered in Sumatra, ruled most of the Malay Peninsula from the 9th to the 13th century. During the 14th century most of the population was converted to Islam under a Muslim Malay state centered at Malacca, on the west coast of the peninsula. In 1511, Malacca was taken by the Portuguese, and in 1641 it passed to the Dutch. By 1786 the British had acquired Penang Island, and gradually their influence spread. In 1895 they created the colony of the Federated Malay States. Under British governance, the rubber plantations were established and tin mining began.

During World War II the Japanese held the peninsula, but in 1946 the British resumed control. In 1948 the Malayan Communist party began a guerrilla insurrection called the Emergency, which was not suppressed until 1960. In 1957 the Federation of Malaya attained independence, and Tunku ABDUL RAHMAN became the first prime minister. The Federation of Malaysia, consisting of Malaya, Singapore, Sarawak, and Sabah, was created in 1963. As a result of conflicts, Singapore seceded in 1965 and became an independent state.

In 1969, rioting between Malays and Chinese precipitated Abdul Rahman's resignation. A Communist insurgency in 1975 threatened political stability, as did sporadic Chinese-Malay tensions, which in 1987 led the government, headed since 1981 by Dr. Mahathir Mohammed, to imprison alleged proponents of unrest; all were released by 1989. Mahathir, who headed the dominant party in the ruling National Front coalition, retained the prime ministership following elections in 1982, 1986, and 1989. In 1989, although facing for the first time an opposition coalition that included Malays and losing control of two state governments, his National Front retained its two-thirds majority in parliament.

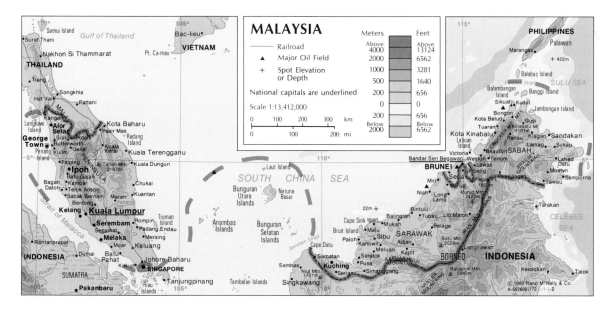

Malcolm X, an American black nationalist, became a disciple of Elijah Muhammad, the spiritual leader of the Nation of Islam, or Black Muslims, and rose to prominence as minister of the group's Harlem mosque. In 1963, Malcolm X left the Nation of Islam to found a rival organization. He was assassinated in 1965.

Malcolm X

Malcolm X, b. Malcolm Little in Omaha, Nebr., on May 19, 1925, d. Feb. 21, 1965, was an influential American advocate of BLACK NATIONALISM, and—as a pioneer in articulating a vigorous self-defense against white violence—a precursor of the black-power movement of the late 1960s. He became a rebellious youth and at age 16 drifted to New York City, where he got involved in the Harlem underworld. In prison for burglary from 1946 to 1952, he read widely and was converted to the teachings of Elijah MUHAMMAD. On his release, he embraced the BLACK MUSLIM movement and changed his name to Malcolm X.

Diverging ideologically from the more conservative Elijah Muhammad, Malcolm was suspended (1963) as a minister of the Black Muslims. After a pilgrimage to Mecca, he announced (1964) that he had become an orthodox Muslim and founded the rival Organization for Afro-American Unity. His travels in the Middle East and Africa gave him a more optimistic view regarding potential brotherhood between black and white Americans; Malcolm no longer preached separation between the races. His career ended abruptly when he was shot and killed in New York City in 1965 by assassins thought to be connected with the Black Muslims.

Malcolm III, King of Scotland

(Malcolm Canmore) Malcolm III, b. *c.*1031, d. Nov. 13, 1093, founded the house of Canmore, which ruled Scotland for more than 200 years. The son of Duncan I, who was killed (1040) by MACBETH, Malcolm lived in exile until he defeated and killed (1057) Macbeth near Lumphanan in Aberdeenshire. He succeeded to the throne in 1058 after the death of Lulach, Macbeth's stepson. Malcolm's second wife was Margaret (later canonized as MARGARET OF SCOTLAND) of the English royal house of Wessex, who fled to Scotland after the Norman conquest (1066).

Malcolm invaded England many times, after 1068 supporting the claim of his brother-in-law Edgar Atheling to the English throne. In 1072, however, he was forced to pay homage to William I, and he was finally defeated and killed by Norman forces at Alnwick in 1093. Four of his sons succeeded to the throne—Duncan II (r. 1093–94), Edgar (r. 1097–1107), Alexander I (r. 1107–24), and DAVID I (r. 1124–53).

Maldives, Republic of

[mal'-dyvz] The Republic of Maldives (formerly Maldive Islands) is located in the northern Indian Ocean about 500 km (300 mi) southwest of the tip of India. It consists of more than 1,000 small, low-lying coral islands (only about 200 are inhabited), forming a chain of atolls about 800 km (500 mi) long.

The climate is hot and humid, with an average temperature of about 27° C (80° F). Annual rainfall ranges from 2,540 mm (100 in) in the north to 3,800 mm (150 in) in the south. Monsoon rains occur twice a year. Because of climatic conditions, malaria is widespread.

The people are of mixed Singhalese (from Sri Lanka), Indian, and Arab stock, and they speak Divehi (Maldivian), which is related to Singhalese. Almost the entire population adheres to Islam, which is the official religion. About 25% of the population live in Male, the capital. The remainder live mostly on scattered coral islands, where they fish and collect coconuts. Because resources are limited, the Maldives rely heavily on imports for most necessities, including rice, the staple food. Fishing for tuna and bonito is the primary industry. Since 1985, foreign fleets have been able to fish Maldivian waters, paying a royalty on their catch. Tourism (now the leading earner of foreign exchange) and shipping also provide income.

The Maldives were thought to have been settled during the 5th century AD by people from Sri Lanka, but in 1982 archaeologist Thor HEYERDAHL claimed to have discovered

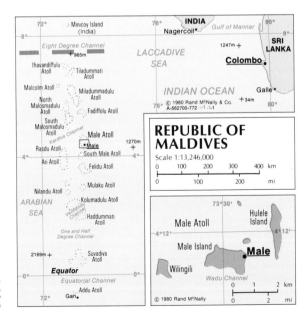

REPUBLIC OF MALDIVES

Scale 1:13,246,000

AT A GLANCE

REPUBLIC OF MALDIVES

Land: Area: 298 km^2 (115 mi^2). Capital and largest city: Male (1985 est. pop., 46,334).

People: Population (1990 est.): 217,945. Density: 731 persons per km^2 (1,895 per mi^2). Distribution (1990): 26% urban, 74% rural. Official language: Divehi. Major religion: Islam.

Government: Type: republic. Legislature: Majilis (Citizen's Council). Political subdivisions: 19 atolls.

Economy: GNP (1989): $87 million; $420 per capita. Labor distribution (1990): agriculture and fishing—17%; manufacturing—13%; construction—3%. Foreign trade (1988): imports—$95.4 million; exports—$44.6 million. Currency: 1 rufiyaa (Maldivian rupee) = 100 laaris.

Education and Health: Literacy (1990): 95% of adult population. Universities (1987): none. Hospital beds (1985): 121. Physicians (1985): 23. Life expectancy (1990): women—65; men—60. Infant mortality (1990): 76 per 1,000 live births.

evidence of a nearly 3,500-year-old settlement established by sailors from the prehistoric INDUS CIVILIZATION. Arab traders first arrived in the 12th century and introduced Islam. Beginning in the 12th century the islands were ruled by a sultan. From 1887 to 1965 the Maldives were a British protectorate. In 1965 the islands became independent, and in 1968 the sultanate was abolished.

The Maldive government is headed by a president, who is elected every 5 years and appoints and heads the cabinet. There is no prime minister. Ibraham Nasir, president from 1968 to 1978, was succeeded by Maumoon Abdul Gayoom. In November 1988, Gayoom survived a coup attempt—his third—with the aid of Indian troops. The troops were withdrawn within a year.

Malebranche, Nicholas [mahl-brahnsh', nee-koh-lah'] Nicholas Malebranche, b. Aug. 6, 1638, d. Oct. 13, 1715, a French Christian philosopher, was intent upon understanding his religion in the light of both Saint Augustine and René Descartes.

According to Malebranche, ideas cannot come from the senses, nor from the soul itself; rather, "we see all things in God." Malebranche's theory of occasionalism holds that God is the sole true cause of phenomena. Natural causes are merely apparent or occasional reflections of a constant conjunction of events in accordance with universal laws. Only through the activity of God can an event follow from the perceived cause.

In his discussions of the problem of CAUSALITY Malebranche anticipated some of the arguments later set forth by David HUME.

Malenkov, Georgy M. [muhl-ying-kawf, gay-ohr'-gee] The Soviet politician Georgy Maksimilianovich Malenkov, b. Jan. 8, 1902, d. Jan. 14, 1988, succeeded Joseph STALIN as premier of the USSR in March 1953. Malenkov joined the Soviet Communist party in 1920 and was one of the young bureaucrats picked by Stalin to replace the men he had eliminated in the GREAT PURGE from 1936 to 1938. As director of personnel administration of the central committee, Malenkov collected the evidence used to justify the executions of many of his party colleagues.

During World War II, Malenkov played a leading role in carrying out Stalin's directives. Considered Stalin's heir apparent in 1952, Malenkov assumed the dual role of leader of the party and the government after Stalin's death. He was forced to yield the former position after a few days, however (Nikita KHRUSHCHEV assumed the post six months later), and he was ousted as premier in February 1955. In 1957 he was banished to Siberia as head of a power station.

Malevich, Kasimir [mahl-yay'-vich, kah'-sim-eer] Russian painter Kasimir Malevich, b. Feb. 11 (N.S.), 1878, d. May 15, 1935, was a key figure in the development of abstract art. By 1915 he had carried cubism to its logical limits by eliminating all references to pictorial representation and by reducing forms to basic geometric shapes painted in flat, pure colors against plain backgrounds. He called (1913) this style SUPREMATISM, positing that pure feeling without any reference to the visual

The rectilinear structure of Kasimir Malevich's suprematist composition Eight Red Rectangles (c.1915) reveals how early abstract painting developed from cubism. (Stedelijk Museum, Amsterdam.)

world was the supreme concern of art. Pursuing this theory, he embarked (1917–18) on a series of paintings in which white geometric shapes were set against white backgrounds, as in his *Suprematist Composition: White on White* (1918; Museum of Modern Art, New York City).

For a few years after the Bolshevik Revolution of 1917, Malevich and his followers dominated Soviet art, and Malevich set himself up as director of the art school in Vitebsk. After 1921, however, abstract art fell out of favor in the USSR, and Malevich's suprematist paintings were stigmatized as decadent by the government. Only in

1989, with the mounting of a major retrospective exhibition in Moscow, was the artist rehabilitated and accorded full recognition in his homeland.

Mali [mah'-lee]   The Republic of Mali is a landlocked state located on the edge of the Sahara in West Africa. Bordering on Senegal and Mauritania in the west, Algeria in the north, Niger and Burkina Faso in the east, and Ivory Coast and Guinea in the south, Mali was a French colony until 1960, when it achieved independence. The nation is located in the SAHEL, the transitional zone between the Sahara (to the north) and tropical Africa (to the south); the dry environment is a major influence on Mali's economy.

Land and Resources

The topography of Mali consists of plateaus and plains. The plateaus, found in the southwest, south, and southeast, are extensions of the Fouta Djallon and Guinea highlands. In the south alluvial lowlands with some marshy areas are located along the Niger River. In the north the wastes of the SAHARA are interrupted only by the Adrar des Iforas, an extension of the Ahaggar (Hoggar) Plateau in Algeria, with an elevation of about 885 m (2,900 ft). The NIGER RIVER and its tributaries comprise the principal drainage system.

The climate is tropical, and the year is divided into a wet season (July to October) and a dry period (November to June). The south receives the most rain (890 mm/35 in annually); temperatures there average 27° C (81° F). In

AT A GLANCE

REPUBLIC OF MALI

Land: Area: 1,240,192 km^2 (478,841 mi^2). Capital and largest city: Bamako (1987 pop., 646,163).

People: Population (1990 est.): 8,142,373. Density: 6.6 persons per km^2 (17.0 per mi^2). Distribution (1989): 18% urban, 82% rural. Official language: French. Major religions: Islam, traditional religions.

Government: Type: under military rule. Legislature: National Council (suspended). Political subdivisions: 7 regions, capital district.

Economy: GNP (1989): $2.11 billion; $260 per capita. Labor distribution (1985): services—19%; agriculture—80%; industry and commerce—1%. Foreign trade (1987): imports—$493 million; exports—$260 million. Currency: 1 C.F.A. franc = 100 centimes.

Education and Health: Literacy (1991): 20% of adult population. Universities (1990): none. Hospital beds (1983): 4,215. Physicians (1983): 283. Life expectancy (1990): women—47; men—45. Infant mortality (1990): 116 per 1,000 live births.

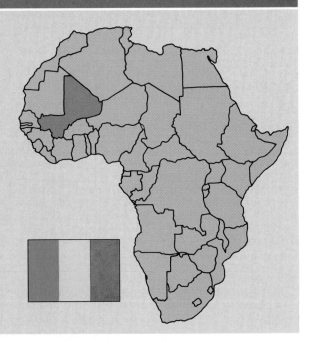

the Sahel region of central Mali it rains less (350 mm/14 in), and the average temperature is higher (29° C/84° F). In the northern desert, which receives almost no rain, temperatures exceed 47° C (117° F) during the day. The rainy season has been shorter than its historic average since the late 1960s, and the country experienced severe droughts in the early 1970s and again in the mid-1980s, aggravating already serious problems of soil erosion and desertification.

Mineral wealth includes enormous, but undeveloped, reserves of iron ore, bauxite, gold, and manganese. Marble, limestone, and phosphates are exploited, and camel caravans still transport salt across the desert from northern mines.

People

Mali's inhabitants may be divided into Berber-speaking pastoralists in the Sahara and the Sahel (including TUAREG and BERBERS); FULANI cattle herders in the Sahel; agriculturalists speaking Mande and Voltaic languages in the Sahel and the south; and Songhai fishermen living along the Niger.

Although 90% of the people are Muslims, nearly 10% still adhere to traditional African religions. Bambara serves as an important lingua franca.

Mali is one of the most sparsely settled nations in Africa. Most of the people live in the south near the Niger and Senegal rivers, and years of drought have increased migration to urban areas, particularly BAMAKO, the capital.

Education is free and compulsory for all children between the ages of 6 and 15, but only a small percentage of school-age children attend because of a shortage of facilities. Malnutrition is a problem, and health care is limited.

Economic Activity

The economy rests primarily on subsistence agriculture and livestock raising, although only about 2% of the land is suitable for cultivation and less than 25% is pasturage. Cotton, groundnuts, sorghum, and rice are important crops. Drought has decimated Mali's large herds of cattle,

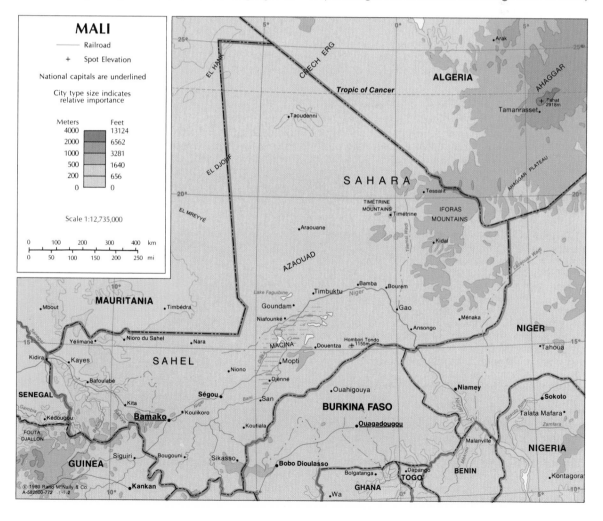

sheep, and goats, driving many nomads into refugee camps on the outskirts of towns where they can receive food aid. The drought that began in 1983 affected almost all of the country, drastically reducing crop yields and the fish catch.

Industry is small scale and limited generally to food processing and the production of light consumer goods and some building materials (primarily cement). Mali has a chronic trade deficit and depends heavily on foreign aid.

History and Government

Beginning in the 5th century the region now comprising Mali was part of several empires whose great cities near the Niger River, including TIMBUKTU, prospered because of their location on the trans-Saharan trade routes. Under the first of these states, the Ghana empire, Islam was introduced; after an Almoravid invasion during the 10th century, Ghana declined.

The Mali empire (for which the modern nation is named) soon arose, reaching its peak during the 14th century under MANSA MUSA, who became famous after making a lavish pilgrimage to Mecca (1324–25). By the 16th century the Mali empire had disintegrated but was followed by the SONGHAI empire. The non-Muslim Bambara kingdoms arose during the late 17th century. During the 19th century the region was swept by Islamic holy wars and the Bambara rulers were deposed by Muslim Fulani of Maçina. These rulers were, in turn, defeated by the army of the Islamic reformer al-Hajj UMAR during the 1850s.

The modern era began with the arrival of the French at Ségou in 1866. By 1898 the French had conquered all of Mali despite opposition by the inhabitants. Initially part of Senegal, the area finally became a separate colony called the French Soudan, a part of the Federation of French West Africa (established 1904). In 1959 the colonies of Soudan and Senegal joined to form the Mali Federation, which became independent in 1960. The federation collapsed shortly thereafter, and Soudan became the Republic of Mali.

In 1960, Mali took its present name and became an independent state led by President Modibo Keita. Discontent with Keita's socialist policies led to his overthrow in a 1968 coup led by Col. Moussa Traoré. A military council then ruled the country until 1979, when Mali became a one-party state with an elected president and legislature. Traoré was elected president in 1979 and reelected in 1985. After years of economic decline and demands for political reform sparked widespread unrest, Traoré was overthrown in March 1991. The new ruling military council named a civilian prime minister to oversee a transitional government and pledged to hold Mali's first multiparty elections since independence by year's end.

malice   Malice, in law, is the state of mind of a person who intentionally does a wrongful act (either civil or criminal) with evil intent. *Malice aforethought* is the common law term that establishes premeditation in murder cases. The term is sometimes used to mean ill will toward a particular person, as in the TORTS of malicious libel or malicious prosecution.

Malinowski, Bronislaw [mal-in-ahf'-skee, brahn'-ee-slahf]   Polish-born Bronislaw Malinowski, b. Apr. 7, 1884, d. May 16, 1942, was an influential British anthropologist and early proponent of the "functionalist" approach in the study of culture (see SOCIAL ANTHROPOLOGY). His first anthropological fieldwork (1915–18), in the southwest Pacific among the TROBRIAND ISLANDERS, was marked by rigorous empirical methods and a holistic approach to the study of social institutions and their interaction. *Argonauts of the Western Pacific* (1922), Malinowski's analysis of Trobriand trade, is an ethnographic landmark. He later conducted fieldwork in many parts of the world, including Africa (1934) and the Oaxaca Valley, Mexico (1941–42). He was a professor at the University of London from 1927 and a visiting professor at Yale from 1939. His works include *The Dynamics of Culture Change* (1945) and *Magic, Science and Religion* (1948).

mallard   The mallard, *Anas platyrhynchos*, is a widespread species of wild DUCK (order Anseriformes, family Anatidae), inhabiting lakes and marshes of Europe, Asia, and North America. It is up to 71 cm (28 in) in length. The male has an iridescent green head, white neck band, and rust-colored breast. The female is mottled brown. Both have wings with a metallic blue band. Mallards eat invertebrates, including numerous mosquito larvae, and plants. A shallow nest is built at the edge of ponds or in the open grassland and contains from eight to ten eggs. The female alone cares for the eggs and young. Several varieties of domestic duck were developed by selective breeding of the mallard.

The mallard is the ancestor of the domestic duck. The female (front) has a brown body and white tail; the male has a white band between its green head and rust breast.

Mallarmé, Stéphane [mahl-ahr-may', stay-fahn']   Stéphane Mallarmé, b. Paris, Mar. 18, 1842, d. Sept. 9, 1898, was the exquisite poet and master of French SYMBOLISM. His Tuesday evening receptions were attended by many famous artists and literary figures. He began as one of the Parnassians but after a spiritual crisis in 1866 developed into a hermetic poet preoccupied with eternity and nothingness. Some of Mallarmé's finest poetry is written in the compressed form of the sonnet. Of his longer poems, *Herodias* (1869; Eng. trans., 1940), *L'Après-midi d'un faune* (The AFTERNOON OF A FAUN, 1876), and *Un Coup de dés jamais n'abolira le hasard* (A Throw of the Dice Will Never Eliminate Chance, 1897) demand ever-increasing efforts of comprehension. The last of these is considered one of the most obscure poems in the French language. Mallarmé also translated the poetry of Edgar Allan Poe into French and produced a series of remarkable prose poems and essays in *Divagations* (1897) and a considerable amount of vivid personal correspondence.

Malle, Louis [mahl] Louis Malle, b. Oct. 30, 1932, is a French film director known for his eclecticism, unconventional themes, and willingness to experiment. In 1957, Malle directed his first film, *Frantic* (French title: *L'Ascenseur pour l'échafaud*), which introduced actress Jeanne Moreau and photographer Henri Decäe to the cinema-going public. Later films noted for characterization include *The Lovers* (1958); *Zazie in the Métro* (1960); *The Fire Within* (1963), a penetrating study of an alcoholic; and *Viva Maria* (1965), a musical-comedy romp set in revolutionary Mexico. Malle's fascination with human behavior has prompted him to tackle the subjects of incest (*Murmur of the Heart*, 1971), collaboration with the enemy (*Lacombe, Lucien*, 1974), and child prostitution (*Pretty Baby*, 1978). The not-quite-sentimental *Atlantic City* (1980) was a popular success, as was *Au Revoir les Enfants* (1988), a portrayal of life in German-occupied France.

Mallet-Joris, Françoise [mahl-ay'-zhor-ee', frahn-swahz'] Françoise Mallet-Joris, b. July 6, 1930, is a Belgian novelist writing in French who first achieved literary recognition at the age of 17 with a book of poems. Her first novel, *The Illusionist* (1951; Eng. trans., 1952), which dealt frankly with lesbianism, became a controversial success. In 1958 she received the Prix Fémina for the novel *Café Céleste* (1958; Eng. trans., 1959). Other novels include *The Underground Game* (1973; Eng. trans. 1975) and *Un Chagrin d'amour et d'ailleurs* (An Affliction of Love and More, 1981).

Mallorca see MAJORCA

Mallory, Stephen Russell Stephen Russell Mallory, b. Trinidad, *c.*1812, d. Nov. 9, 1873, was Confederate secretary of the navy throughout the U.S. Civil War. As a U.S. senator from Florida (1851–61) he had served on the Naval Affairs Committee. Appointed to Jefferson Davis's cabinet in 1861, Mallory developed the effective program of commerce raiding by Confederate cruisers. He believed strongly in ironclad warships, which he first sought to buy in Europe and then had built at home. He later resumed the practice of law.

mallow Mallows are plants of several genera in the mallow family, Malvaceae. The genus *Malva* comprises about 30 species of annual, biennial, and perennial herbs native to Europe, North Africa, and temperate Asia. These plants are characterized by flowers with five typically heart-shaped petals, five sepals, and three small bracts below the sepals. The stamens of the flower are united into a tube around the elongated pistil.

Musk mallow, *M. moschata*, is a perennial herb with showy, usually pink (sometimes white or bluish) flowers and mostly deeply cut leaves of five main segments. It grows to more than 60 cm (2 ft) high and is found from southeastern Canada to Nebraska and North Carolina.

The marsh mallow, *Althaea officinalis*, is similar to *Malva* species but has six to nine bracts below the sepals. It is an erect perennial, growing to 1.2 m (4 ft) high, with gray green velvety leaves and pale pink flowers. It is native to Europe but is now also found on the borders of marshes along the eastern coast of the United States. The roots of this plant were the source of the original marshmallow candy, which was made by boiling pieces of the soft inner root pulp with sugar until very thick, straining, and then cooling.

Malmö [mal'-mur] Malmö, one of Sweden's largest cities, is located near the southern end of the Swedish peninsula, 26 km (16 mi) across the Öresund (Sound) from Copenhagen. The population is 231,575 (1989 est.). Malmö is the transportation and commercial center for the surrounding agricultural region; industries produce ships, foodstuffs, textiles, chemicals, paper, leather, tobacco, and dairy products. Landmarks include Saint Peter's Church (1319), the town hall (1546), and Malmöhus Castle (first built 1434, rebuilt 1537–42).

Malmö was chartered as a city during the 13th century, at which time the region belonged to Denmark. In 1658 it passed to Sweden. Port facilities were improved in 1775; after 1800, Malmö began to develop as an industrial city.

malnutrition see NUTRITIONAL-DEFICIENCY DISEASES; STARVATION

Malory, Sir Thomas Sir Thomas Malory, d. 1471, the author of the *Morte Darthur*, made available in English a major portion of the traditional romances of ARTHUR AND ARTHURIAN LEGEND. In his manuscript the author says that he finished his work in the ninth year of the reign of Edward IV (1469 or 1470) and prays for "good delyueraunce" from prison. On this basis scholars have identified two possible Thomas Malorys, the most widely accepted candidate being a knight of Newbold Revell, Warwickshire, who was committed to prison for attempted murder and who died there Mar. 14, 1471.

malpractice   Malpractice is misconduct by any professional. Although the term is usually applied to physicians and surgeons, it is also used in connection with lawyers, public officials, architects, engineers, pharmacists, or any other persons (even clergy) who practice a profession and furnish skilled services.

Although professionals are not held liable under the law for NEGLIGENCE, they are held responsible for acts of malpractice. Negligence is an act or omission in which a reasonably prudent person would not have engaged, whereas malpractice is the failure to live up to the minimum standard of practice of which similar professionals would be capable. A professional may be found legally guilty of malpractice for any injury caused to a client from a lack of the requisite knowledge and skill, the failure to use reasonable care and diligence, or the failure to exercise good judgment. The standards of practice that apply are generally those followed by other professionals in the same locality. Legal action for malpractice can arise only if there is an agreement between the professional and the person claiming the malpractice. The agreement may be expressed, written, or implied from words or conduct.

In the late 1960s the number of malpractice suits against U.S. doctors, and the size of awards in successful cases, began to increase greatly. This resulted in higher medical costs as doctors increased their fees to cover larger premiums for malpractice insurance.

Malraux, André [mal-roh', ahn-dray']   The French novelist, art philosopher, and political activist André Malraux, b. Nov. 3, 1901, d. Nov. 23, 1976, first achieved fame as the recipient (1933) of the Goncourt Prize for *Man's Fate* (1933; Eng. trans., 1934), a novel fusing reportage of the Chinese revolution of 1927 with philosophical reflections on revolutionary action and the meaning of life. These preoccupations were already present in *The Conquerors* (1928; Eng. trans., 1929) and *The Royal Way* (1930; Eng. trans., 1935), which recounts a dramatic search for Khmer temples in the jungles of Cambodia.

From Malraux's fight against fascism came *Days of Wrath* (1935; Eng. trans., 1936), denouncing the debasement of human dignity in Nazi jails, and *Man's Hope* (1937; Eng. trans., 1938), celebrating the democratic hopes born of the Spanish Civil War. Taken prisoner during World War II, Malraux escaped to southern France and became commander of a Free French unit. Whereas in the 1930s Malraux had shown Communist sympathies, in 1945 he joined the government of General Charles de Gaulle as minister of information and between 1958 and 1968 served as minister of cultural affairs in de Gaulle's second government.

Malraux's philosophy of art, already present in his final novel, *The Walnut Trees of Altenburg* (1948; Eng. trans., 1952), now infused a series of critical works—*The Voices of Silence* (1951; Eng. trans., 1953), *Le Musée imagi-*

André Malraux, a French novelist and humanist, expressed in an active political life the heroic ideals of his novels. A participant in the Spanish Civil War and the French resistance during World War II, he believed in the power of art and heroism to transcend human isolation.

naire de la sculpture mondiale (The Imaginary Museum of World Sculpture, 1953–54), *The Metamorphosis of the Gods* (1957; Eng. trans., 1960)—expounding the thesis that in the artistic achievements of successive civilizations can be seen the universality of humankind. Malraux also wrote a revealing autobiography, *Anti-Memoirs* (1967; Eng. trans., 1968).

malt   see BEER

Malta [mawl'-tuh]   Malta is a country composed of a group of islands lying 93 km (58 mi) south of Sicily in the Mediterranean Sea between Italy and North Africa. The islands are Malta (the largest), Gozo, Comino, and the uninhabited rocks of Comminotto and Filfla. Valletta, the chief city and capital located on the island of Malta, possesses one of the finest harbors in southern Europe. Because of its strategic importance, Malta has been subject to numerous invasions. It was a British colony until 1964, when it became independent.

Land and People

The islands are mostly composed of low-lying limestone hills. Dingli Cliffs, the highest point, rises to 253 m (829 ft). Because there are no rivers, the vegetation, which includes species indigenous to both Italy and North Africa, is sparse in some areas. Malta has a Mediterranean climate. Summers are warm, with an average temperature of 25° C (77° F) in July; winters are mild, with an average temperature of 13° C (56° F) in January. Rainfall averages about 510 mm (20 in) annually, with about three-quarters falling during the winter. The islands are often exposed to violent winds.

Malta's ethnically mixed population has been increasing rapidly, giving it one of the highest population densities in the world. The chief spoken language, Maltese, is

AT A GLANCE

REPUBLIC OF MALTA

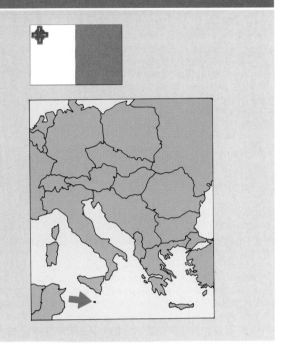

Land: Area: 316 km² (122 mi²). Capital: Valletta (1990 est. pop., 9,196). Largest city: Birkirkara (1990 est. pop., 20,963).

People: Population (1990 est.): 352,430. Density: 1,115 persons per km² (2,889 per mi²). Distribution (1985): 85% urban, 15% rural. Official languages: Maltese, English. Major religion: Roman Catholicism.

Government: Type: republic. Legislature: House of Representatives. Political subdivisions: none.

Economy: GDP (1989): $2.04 billion; $5,280 per capita. Labor distribution (1987): services and public administration—38.5%; manufacturing—28.1%; construction—4.6%; utilities, transportation, and communication—8.5%; agriculture—2.5%; other—17.8%. Foreign trade (1988): imports—$1,360 million; exports—$710 million. Currency: 1 Maltese lira = 100 cents.

Education and Health: Literacy (1985): 96% of adult population. Universities (1990): 1. Hospital beds (1988): 3,217. Physicians (1988): 710. Life expectancy (1990): women—78; men—74. Infant mortality (1990): 8 per 1,000 live births.

the only Semitic language in the world normally using the Latin alphabet. Almost the entire population is Roman Catholic, the official religion. Education is compulsory between the ages of 6 and 16.

Economic Activity

Malta's economy was long dependent on income from British military installations. By 1979, however, all British forces had withdrawn and Malta faced the need to diversify its economic base. Light manufacturing, including traditional craft industries, is now the largest source of income. Tourism has become a major industry. Shipping and shipbuilding are expanding, and a new harbor is being constructed at Marsaxlokk Bay. About half of Malta's land is devoted to agriculture, but because farms are small and the soil is poor, output is low, and 70% of Malta's food must be imported. Because of the overpopulation and unemployment problems, Malta has instituted a program of sponsored emigration. Malta is an associate member of the EUROPEAN COMMUNITY.

History and Government

Malta is notable for its prehistoric monuments, including the temple complex of tarxien, which show that a high level of civilization had been reached there by the Copper Age. The islands were subsequently occupied by the Phoenicians and Carthaginians. With the defeat of Carthage in 218 BC they became part of the Roman Empire. According to Acts 28, Saint Paul was shipwrecked

on Malta and planted the Christian faith there. In 870 the Arabs took the islands and introduced Arabic. In 1090, Malta was conquered by the Normans, and in 1530 it was acquired by the Knights of St. John (see HOSPITALERS). The knights transformed the islands by building extensively and in 1565 successfully resisted an Ottoman attack. In 1798, Malta was taken by Napoléon Bonaparte. Captured by the British in 1800, it later became the headquarters

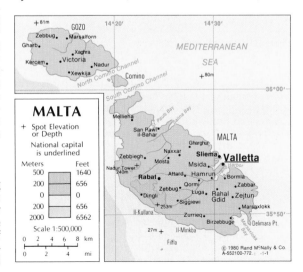

Valletta, the capital of Malta since 1571, is situated on a promontory between two deep-water harbors, Grand Harbor, shown here, and Marsamxett Harbor. This strategic position made Valletta an important naval base for Britain until 1979, when the base was closed.

of Britain's Mediterranean fleet. During World War II, Malta was subjected to heavy bombing by German and Italian forces, and in 1942 King George VI awarded it the George Cross for valor. Malta became self-governing in 1947. Full independence was achieved in 1964, and Malta became a member of the Commonwealth of Nations.

According to the most recent constitution, instituted in 1974, Malta is a republic headed by a president. The 65-member unicameral House of Representatives elects the president every five years. The president appoints the prime minister, who is the head of the majority party of the house. Dominic Mintoff, a Labourite, was prime minister from 1971 to 1984. His successor, Labourite Carmelo Misfud Bonnici, continued Mintoff's neutralist foreign policy and settled a dispute with the church over education. In 1987 the opposition Nationalists came to power under Eddie Fenech Adami.

Malta, Knights of   see HOSPITALERS

Maltese [mawl-teez'] The Maltese is a tiny dog, with a coat of long, silky, white hair that hangs straight almost to the ground. The hair on its head is usually tied with ribbons into two topknots. The Maltese stands about 13 cm (5 in) high at the shoulder and should weigh less than 3 kg (7 lb), with 1.8 to 2.7 kg (4 to 6 lb) being the preferred size. The small size, glamorous appearance, and lively temperament of the Maltese have made it an extremely popular breed, particularly in Japan.

The breed is so ancient that its precise origins have been obscured. Whether the breed is named for the island of Malta, as would appear likely, or for the Sicilian town of Melita is uncertain. During World War I and shortly afterward, the Maltese faded nearly to the point of extinction; however, the breed recovered well, particularly in the United States.

Maltese Falcon, The *The Maltese Falcon* (1930), a novel by Dashiell HAMMETT, is considered the first of the "hard-boiled" school of detective fiction. An adept portrayal of the seediness of the private detective's work and milieu, it introduced Hammett's best-known character, Sam Spade. Spade is hired by a seemingly vulnerable young woman to find an ancient, priceless jeweled falcon. As the mystery unravels the circumstances become more and more sordid, and Spade, for all his cynicism, is revealed as the last incorruptible force. Much admired for its prose style, the novel was made into a memorable film (1940) starring Humphrey Bogart and Mary Astor.

Malthus, Thomas Robert [mal'-thuhs] The English economist Thomas Robert Malthus, b. Feb. 14, 1766, d. Dec. 29, 1834, was one of the earliest thinkers to study population growth as it relates to general human welfare. Educated in philosophy, mathematics, and theology at Cambridge (1784–88), Malthus took holy orders (1790) and became (1805) professor of history and political economy at East India College near London. In 1798 he anonymously published *An Essay on the Principle of Population, As It Affects the Future Improvement of Society*. It was an attack on William Godwin's and the marquis de Condorcet's theories of eternal human progress. Malthus argued that the standard of living of the masses cannot be improved because "The power of population is indefinitely greater than the power of the earth to produce subsistence for man." Population, he asserted, when unchecked by war, famine, or disease, would increase by a geometric ratio but subsistence only by an arithmetic one. Malthus's identification of population growth as an obstacle to human progress was bitterly resisted in the Enlightenment climate of the day. In 1803, Malthus published a revised edition of his work, in which he added "moral restraint"—late marriage and abstinence—as a factor that might limit population growth, and he provided empirical evidence to back up his theories.

In the middle of the 19th century neo-Malthusianism emerged, a movement that, partly influenced by Robert Owen, advocated BIRTH CONTROL for the poor.

Malvern, Godfrey Huggins, 1st Viscount [mawl'-vurn] The white Rhodesian statesman Godfrey Martin Huggins, b. England, July 6, 1883, d. May 8, 1971, served as prime minister (1933–53) of Southern Rhodesia and as the first prime minister (1953–56) of the short-lived Federation of Rhodesia and Nyasaland. Trained as a physician, he emigrated to Southern Rhodesia (now Zimbabwe) in 1911. In 1923, when Southern Rhodesia became a self-governing colony, he was elected to the Legislative Assembly, and in 1933 he became prime minister.

An advocate of social segregation, Huggins was more pragmatic in his acceptance of the idea of shared political power for blacks and whites. During World War II he supplied troops and minerals to aid the British war effort. He subsequently helped create the Federation of Rhodesia and Nyasaland (1953–63), serving as its prime minister until 1956, when he retired. In 1955 he was made 1st Viscount Malvern of Rhodesia.

mamba Mambas, genus *Dendroaspis,* are venomous African snakes in the same family, Elapidae, as the cobras. They are quick-moving, slender snakes with narrow heads and very large eyes. The four or five species are typically arboreal and large in size, averaging between 1.5 and 2.2 m (5 and 7.25 ft) in length; the black mamba, *D. polylepis,* is the largest poisonous snake in Africa, reaching a length of 4.27 m (14 ft). Because they may be found on low-lying branches, can move vigorously and rapidly, and possess an extremely potent venom, mambas are the most feared snakes in Africa.

The black mamba, found in Africa, does not have the hood that characterizes its Indian relatives. It strikes its enemy with a poisonous bite that is almost always fatal.

Mamelukes [mam'-uh-looks] The Mamelukes, a military, landholding aristocracy, long figured prominently in

Middle Eastern history. They were originally recruited from non-Arab slaves imported to serve various traditional Muslim rulers as soldiers and officials. Until 1382 the dominant Mamelukes were mostly of Turkish ethnic origin; after that date, the majority was generally of Circassian origin.

The Egyptian Mamelukes overthrew the Ayyubid dynasty in 1250 and inaugurated a line of more than 50 independent sultans, who presided over an unruly but culturally brilliant era until the Ottoman conquest of 1517. From their capital in Cairo they ruled parts of Syria, Arabia, Libya, and Sudan. An awesome cavalry force, the Mamelukes checked the MONGOL invasions of Syria, defeated the Crusaders, and suppressed the ASSASSINS. When no outside threats loomed, however, they divided into quarreling factions.

Ottoman rule did not hurt the Mamelukes as a class. They continued to share effectively in the rule and wealth of Egypt. On the eve of the French invasion in 1798, Egypt's 20,000 Mamelukes enjoyed virtual independence. MUHAMMAD ALI, who consolidated his own control over Egypt following the French occupation, destroyed the Mamelukes in 1811.

Mamet, David [ma'-mit] A noted American playwright, David Alan Mamet, b. Chicago, Nov. 30, 1947, began his career as an actor and director before achieving acclaim in 1976 for two Off-Off Broadway plays, *Duck Variations* and *Sexual Perversity in Chicago* (Obie award, 1976). *American Buffalo* (1976; Obie, 1976; New York Drama Critics Circle Award, 1977), a satire on business executives, was highly praised and subsequently revived on Broadway. *The Woods* (1977) and *Edmond* (1982) were followed by two enormously successful plays, the Pulitzer Prize–winning *Glengarry Glen Ross* (1984), a scathing representation of American business practices, and *Speed-the-Plow* (1988), which as savagely reveals the amoral underside of the film industry. Mamet's interest in films has produced screenplays for *The Postman Always Rings Twice* (1981), *The Verdict* (1982), and *Tin Men* (1987). He directed as well as wrote the screenplays for *House of Games* (1987) and *Things Change* (1988).

mammal [mam'-ul] Mammals are the dominant lifeforms on Earth today and have been for many millions of years, even though the number of living species (somewhat more than 4,000) is small when compared to the 750,000 species of insects. Over much of the world, the character of the landscape has been transformed by the activities of humans and the other mammals that they have introduced into new environments.

The class Mammalia includes about 19 living orders of mammals and an equivalent number of extinct ones. The individual species are widely distributed, from the edges of the Arctic ice cap in the north, down through temperate, desert, and tropical areas, to the edge of the Antarctic continent in the south; they also occupy the oceans and major river systems of the world. Mammals span an incredible range of sizes, from shrews and bats

Despite differences in size and form, all mammals share a number of internal features. A muscular diaphragm, unique to mammals, aids breathing. A four-chambered heart pumps blood separately to the lungs and to the rest of the body. Most mammals have a large brain with a well-developed cerebral cortex. This diagram shows major internal organs of a male lion.

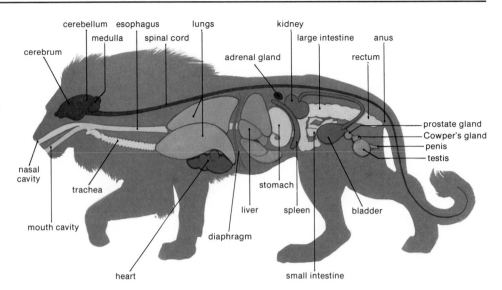

Labels: cerebellum, esophagus, medulla, spinal cord, lungs, kidney, large intestine, anus, cerebrum, adrenal gland, rectum, prostate gland, Cowper's gland, penis, testis, nasal cavity, trachea, stomach, bladder, mouth cavity, liver, spleen, diaphragm, heart, small intestine

that weigh but a few grams (a fraction of an ounce) to the blue whale, weighing more than 100 tons, the largest mammal that has ever lived.

Characteristics

Mammals as a group can be defined by certain diagnostic features, even though some of these features are shared by other groups, and not every feature is found in all mammals. Viewed broadly, mammals are vertebrate animals that (1) are endothermic (warm-blooded), able to maintain a constant body temperature by internal regulation of either heat production or heat loss, or both; (2) bear living young that are nourished by milk; (3) have large brains, allowing for quick learning and comparatively flexible behavior; (4) produce at least a partial covering of hair; (5) contain sweat glands in the skin; (6) develop external ears (pinnae), which increase hearing acuity; (7) have a single bone making up each side of the lower jaw; (8) possess a four-chambered heart; and (9) have three middle-ear bones (auditory ossicles).

Mammals alone possess mammary glands, from which the term *mammal* is derived. Mammary glands produce nutritious milk that allows the young to develop rapidly. The social bond between the mother and her young during and often after the suckling period facilitates training of the young. During this time the rudiments of social behavior are learned, and the young's ability to survive is enhanced by indoctrination into foraging techniques and choice of food.

Sweat glands wet the surface of the skin and allow for evaporative cooling, especially under conditions of high temperatures or exertion. Hair in most mammals forms an insulating coat (the pelage) that entraps air and reduces both heat loss from the body and heat gain from the environment.

Compared to living reptiles and to amphibians, mammals are unusually active, and the cost in energy of maintaining an even body temperature is high. This cost is partly met by several features that increase efficiency of circulation and respiration. Unlike the arrangement in fishes, amphibians, and most reptiles, in mammals oxygenated and deoxygenated blood does not mix in the heart: oxygen-depleted blood from the body enters the right atrium and is pumped to the lungs by the right ventricle; oxygen-rich blood from the lungs enters the left atrium and is pumped by the left ventricle to the body. The thoracic cavity (the chamber that holds the lungs and heart) is separated from the abdominal cavity by a muscular sheet, the diaphragm. When relaxed, the diaphragm bows into the thoracic cavity, decreases the volume of the cavity, and with contraction of abdominal muscles forces air out of the lungs; when the muscles of the diaphragm contract, it becomes taut and flat, increasing the volume and lowering the pressure of this cavity, drawing air into the lungs. To support their high energy demands for oxygen, mammals must be able to breathe while they suckle, chew food, or clutch prey in their jaws. This capacity is provided by the secondary palate, a shelf of bone forming the roof of the mouth, which separates the mouth from the nasal passages.

The skeleton of mammals differs most markedly from the skeletons of other vertebrates in being highly simplified. The mammalian skull lacks bones present in the reptilian skull. The lower jaw, which in other vertebrates consists of a mosaic of several bones on each side, is formed by one bone, the dentary, on each side in mammals. The jaw–skull joint in mammals is between the dentary and the squamosal, the skull bone immediately in front of the ear opening. The two bones that form the jaw–skull joint in reptiles became modified during evolution into part of the mammalian hearing apparatus. These bones, teamed with the stapes, a bone used for sound transmission in reptiles, form a short chain of bony ossicles across the mammalian middle-ear chamber. This

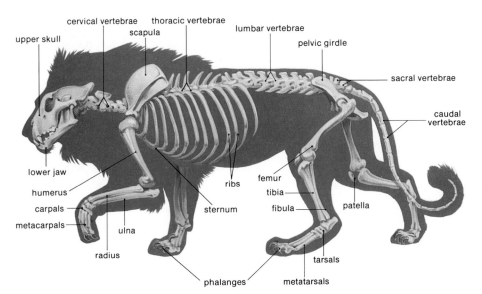

upper skull · cervical vertebrae · scapula · thoracic vertebrae · lumbar vertebrae · pelvic girdle · sacral vertebrae · caudal vertebrae · lower jaw · humerus · carpals · metacarpals · ulna · radius · phalanges · ribs · sternum · metatarsals · tarsals · femur · tibia · fibula · patella

The mammalian skeleton, which contains more than 200 bones, consists of a skull, or cranium; an axial skeleton, which includes the vertebral column, ribs, and sternum (breastbone); and an appendicular skeleton, comprising bones of the limbs and the shoulder and pelvic girdles. Compared with other vertebrate skeletons, the simplified skeleton of a mammal permits greater speed and range of movement.

chain—consisting of the malleus, incus, and stapes—occurs only in mammals. The bony protective casing enclosing the chain is itself derived in part from another reptilian jawbone.

Ecological Adaptation. A primary key to the success of mammals is their ability to adapt to and occupy a spectrum of environments. Some mammals that occupy Arctic areas or frigid seas have thick insulating coats of fur or envelopes of blubber (fat) to reduce heat dissipation. The oryx, an antelope that inhabits almost waterless deserts of Africa, has a system whereby the blood flowing to the brain on a hot day is cooled by inhaled air, thereby maintaining the brain at a temperature lower than that of the overheated body, avoiding brain damage. Kangaroo rats of the deserts of the U.S. Southwest can live on a diet of dry seeds and no drinking water. This ability depends in part on three adaptations: (1) kidneys that produce highly concentrated urine containing low amounts of water, (2) a lack of sweat glands, and (3) the ability of the nasal passages to withdraw some moisture from air exhaled from the lungs before this moisture is lost from the body. Deep-diving whales conserve energy, and thus oxygen, during prolonged dives by slowing down their heart and metabolic rate, by reducing blood flow to certain parts of the body, and by allowing the muscles to store oxygen.

Some small mammals can avoid the intense cold and food shortages of winter by hibernating. Some species of ground squirrel store much of the energy derived from feeding in the summer as fat, which provides the energy that sustains the squirrels during six months of winter dormancy. Conversely, a similar adaptation to the harshness of some summer habitats is estivation, or summer dormancy.

Social Behavior. A remarkably interesting aspect of the biology of mammals is their complex social behavior. For example, in some species the social order is controlled by a dominance hierarchy. One individual, usually a male, is the dominant animal; remaining members are arranged in a hierarchy according to their ability to dominate others, and each animal recognizes its place in the system.

The establishment and maintenance of the hierarchy is often by means of ritualized combat and threat displays. Such threats include the threat yawn of the baboon, which displays the hugh canine teeth, and the high-head posture of the Grant's gazelle, which displays the animal's powerful neck and horns. Facial markings in some antelopes serve to increase the conspicuousness of such displays. Communication between individuals or groups takes place by means of such visual displays, by scents, or by vocalizations.

Displays have seemingly evolved for a purpose. By means of threats, an animal can assert or demonstrate its dominance without risking the serious injury that often accompanies fighting. An injured animal under natural conditions is generally doomed to a short life, with little chance to reproduce.

A variety of types of social groups occur among social mammals. In some mammals the male and female and their young are the social unit. In lions the pride, an expanded kinship group, is the unit. The pride is usually controlled by two or three adult males that are brothers, and includes a number of adult females, most of which are closely related, and their offspring. In the hyena "clan," by contrast, the adult females are the dominant animals; the units include up to 30 or more assorted adult females, adult males, and young.

As a rule, male mammals compete strongly among themselves for access to females, and the largest and strongest individuals are usually the most successful breeders. The reproductive life of the male may be short, however, relative to that of the female. Dominant male lions, for example, generally maintain their position in a pride for no more than 2 to 3 years, after which they are deposed by younger and more vigorous males. The effective reproductive life of the male does not begin until he becomes a dominant member of the pride, and it ends when he is deposed. Thus, the reproductive life of the male may be as short as 2 years, whereas that of the female is usually more than 10 years.

Fossil History

The FOSSIL RECORD shows that mammals appeared more than 190 million years ago in the Triassic Period, and their ancestry goes even further back. Mammallike reptiles, from which the mammals evolved, dominated the terrestrial scene about 280 million years ago during the Permian Period, long before the first dinosaurs arose. These reptiles were members of the subclass Synapsida, characterized by the presence of a single opening on each side of the skull behind the eye to allow more room for the jaw muscles. Synapsids showed indications of development of a mammallike ability to maintain a constant body temperature. Their limbs developed a mammallike posture, and their dentition showed the mammalian trend toward the division of labor between front teeth adapted

to grasping and killing prey and back teeth adapted to crushing or chopping food. Synapsid reptiles gradually became extinct as dinosaurs gained dominance over the Earth. Their unspectacular descendants, the mammals, survived.

The earliest mammals were no larger than mice and probably ate insects. As do all mammals to this day, these primitive mammals had lower jaws made of a single bone on each side and used the three bony ossicles as transmitters of sound in the middle ear.

For more than 100 million years—the vast sweep of time when dinosaurs dominated the Earth—mammals persisted, perhaps by being inconspicuous and nocturnal. But mammalian evolution continued, and refinements in reproduction and tooth, skull, and brain design were incorporated into the mammalian structural plan. When the dinosaurs became extinct approximately 65 million years ago, at the end of the Cretaceous Period, mammals inherited the Earth.

Before long, different groups of mammals had become adapted to a great variety of ecological niches, many pre-

Various mammals show adaptation to their environment. The killer whale has a streamlined form and paddlelike limbs for aquatic life. A layer of fat insulates the walrus against arctic conditions. Desert inhabitants, such as camels, are resistant to dehydration. Kangaroos have long, powerful legs adapted for jumping. Large front claws and touch-sensitive rays on its nose equip the star-nosed mole for underground living. Bats have front limbs modified for flight. The gerenuk, a long-necked antelope, stands on its hind legs to reach foliage.

killer whale
Orcinus orca

long-eared bat
Plecotus

camel
Camelus

gerenuk
Litocranius walleri

walrus
Odobenus rosmarus

kangaroo
Macropus

star-nosed mole
Condylura cristata

mammoth
Mammuthus

woolly rhinoceros
Coelodonta antiquitatus

Brontotherium

eohippus
Hyracotherium

Tritemnodon

saber-toothed cat
Smilodon

Triconodon

Triconodon, *one of the most primitive mammals, lived during the Upper Jurassic Period, which ended about 135 million years ago. Mammals of the Eocene Epoch (54–38 million years ago) include the eohippus, a fox-sized browsing horse, and* Tritemnodon, *a slender, carnivorous animal with a small brain.* Brontotherium, *a horned titanothere that stood 2.4 m (8 ft) tall, lived during the Early Oligocene, which began about 38 million years ago. Pleistocene (2.5 million-10,000 years ago) mammals include the mammoths; the woolly rhinoceros; and the saber-toothed cats, such as* Smilodon, *which had daggerlike upper canine teeth.*

viously occupied by dinosaurs. The key to mammalian success in their wide variety of life-styles was an amazing structural and functional plasticity. Limbs were variously modified into flippers, shovels, wings, and pillars; teeth became adapted to dealing efficiently with diets ranging from a myriad of plant matter through a variety of animal material; and sensory systems were modified so that even dwellers of murky waters or those active at night could perceive their environment.

The Cenozoic Era, the period from about 65 million years ago to the present, has been termed the Age of Mammals. During this time the Earth has been populated by a succession of assemblages of mammals: as environments have changed, species unable to adapt have been replaced by species able to exploit the new conditions.

During the early parts of the Cenozoic, climates over broad regions of the world were warm and rainfall was high. The widespread forests in North America supported many subtropical species of plants. Under these conditions all of the orders of mammals that survive today underwent their early evolution; however, many of the early representatives would seem unusual and unfamiliar. Small primates called lemurs, early ancestors of man, inhabited the forests. Horses were the size of small dogs;

they were forest dwellers and had four toes on each front foot and three toes on each hind foot. Also in the forests were huge rhinoceroslike beasts called titanotheres. Not all of the early Cenozoic mammals, however, would be unfamiliar today. Bats, identical in general appearance to the bats of the present, flew erratically across the twilight sky, and rodents looking essentially like present-day mice and rats occupied a broad array of habitats.

The mild conditions of the early Cenozoic were gradually replaced by more temperate conditions. Grasslands expanded, bringing possibilities for new ways of life and new food sources. To horses, the ability to move fast and far to avoid predators and to seek widely separated water holes or concentrations of food became important. Correspondingly, the side toes of the three-toed feet of the plains-dwelling *Merychippus* were reduced, and when moving on firm ground this animal was functionally one-toed. Appearing at this time in Europe, and later spreading to the New World, were the first representatives of the family Bovidae, which today includes antelope, bison, and sheep. The long, slender limbs and cloven-hoofed feet of these animals were well adapted to moving rapidly and efficiently over open grassland, and these animals prospered and diversified. In Africa some primates occu-

The 19 Orders of Living Mammals

Monotremata · platypus · opossum · **Marsupiala** · koala · kangaroo · Australian native cat · solenodon · **Insectivora** · hedgehog · **Dermoptera** · flying lemur · shrew · leaf-nosed bat · patas monkey · **Chiroptera** · fruit bat · chimpanzee · marmoset · **Edentata** · lemur · **Primates** · anteater · **Lagomorpha** · **Pholidota** · aardvark · **Tubulidentata** · pangolin · arctic hare

Rodentia

porcupine

capybara

naked mole-rat

pygmy mouse

Mysticeti

blue whale

Odontoceti

dolphin

manatee

Sirenia

Proboscidea

polar bear

fur seal

Carnivora

maned wolf

margay

elephant

Hyracoidea

hyrax

mountain goat

rhinoceros

Artiodactyla

camel

hippopotamus

moose

Perissodactyla

zebra

pied grasslands or savannas, assumed a ground-dwelling style of life, and founded the evolutionary line that eventually led to humans.

By 7 million years ago, in the middle Pliocene Epoch, mammals had become "modernized." Roughly 80 percent of the families of mammals of that time still have living representatives.

A spectacular segment of mammalian history occurred during the Pleistocene Ice Age. This epoch, from about 2.5 million years ago to about 10,000 years ago, was characterized by mammalian faunas that were not only more diverse than those today but also contained many large and spectacular species. Four glacial advances occurred, separated by relatively warm periods when the glaciers receded. With each advance, mammals were pushed southward before the front of ice, and with each retreat they moved northward again. The musk ox, for example, an animal that now occupies arctic parts of Canada and Alaska, occurred as far south as Colorado and Arkansas in the United States during one glacial advance. Many of the species alive today had closely related Pleistocene counterparts, but in addition to these somewhat familiar types there were a number of spectacular giants. Elephants were widely distributed in Europe and North America, some larger than living elephants and bearing enormous tusks with tips that crossed in some old males. Huge bison, with horns spanning more than 1.8 m (6 ft), and beavers the size of bears inhabited North America.

With the end of the Pleistocene, the huge mammals became extinct over most of the world. Only in Africa does a mammalian fauna resembling that of the Pleistocene remain.

Classification

The class Mammalia is often divided into two subclasses, the Prototheria and the Theria. The subclass Prototheria, in turn, is divided into three infraclasses, the extinct Eotheria and Allotheria and the living Ornithodelphia, (monotremes).

The subclass Theria is also divided into three infraclasses, the extinct Pantotheria and the living Metatheria (marsupials) and Eutheria (placental mammals). The marsupials and placental mammals are separated, as the name implies, on the general basis of the presence or absence of a placenta, a special organ that develops between the mother and the fetus during pregnancy. All living mammals, except the marsupials and egg-laying monotremes, are placental mammals. About 19 orders of living mammals are commonly recognized.

Subclass Prototheria. This subclass is represented by only one living order, containing the most primitive mammals.

Infraclass Ornithodelphia. The order **Monotretata** (2 families and 3 to possibly 6 species) includes the duck-billed platypus and the spiny anteaters, or echidnas. Monotremes are the only mammals that lay eggs, but they nourish the young with milk. They are largely insectivorous. They live in Australia, Tasmania, and New Guinea.

Subclass Theria. This subclass comprises all living mammals that bear their young alive.

Infraclass Meratherie. The **Marsupialia** (12 families and 242 species) contains the opossums, kangaroos, koalas, wombats, and bandicoots. Baby marsupials are rudimentary when born, and each newborn grasps a nipple with its mouth and remains attached during the early part of its life. Many marsupials have pouches that retain the young. Marsupials utilize many types of food. They occupy Australia and some nearby islands, South America, and much of North America.

Infraclass Eutheria. The **Insectivora**, the third largest mammalian order (8 families and 406 species), comprises shrews, moles, and hedgehogs. These are generally small mammals with sharp-cusped teeth adapted to an insect diet. Insectivores prefer moist habitats and occur in Europe, Asia, Africa, North America, and parts of South America.

The **Dermoptera** (2 families and 2 species) contains the colugos, or flying lemurs. These are restricted to tropical forests in Southeast Asia and the Philippine Islands. A membrane between the forelimbs and hind limbs enables them to glide.

The **Chiroptera** (18 families and about 850 species), or bats, have wings formed by membranes stretched between the four fingers of the hand and between the last finger and the body. Most bats use echolocation in addition to vision for perceiving their environment. Bats occur almost everywhere except in polar regions and exploit a great array of foods.

The **Primates** (11 families and about 166 species) include the lemurs, lorises, tarsiers, monkeys, apes, and humans. Primates usually have dextrous hands with nails instead of claws, large eyes that face forward, and large brains. Most are arboreal and occupy forests, but some live in grasslands or deserts. Primates are mostly herbivorous, and their range (exclusive of that of humans) includes tropical parts of both the Eastern and Western hemispheres.

The **Edentata** (3 families and 31 species) includes the sloths, anteaters, and armadillos. All members lack front teeth; some have no teeth; and when teeth are present they lack enamel. Armadillos have a jointed, bony shell. Edentates occur from the central United States southward through most of South America; most species occupy tropical areas. Sloths eat leaves; armadillos and anteaters eat mostly insects.

The **Pholidota** (1 family and 8 species) comprises the pangolins. Found in Africa and Southeast Asia, pangolins are covered with scales, lack teeth, and feed on termites.

The **Tubulidentata** (1 family and 1 species) comprises the aardvarks. These burrowing African mammals have a compact piglike body, a long snout, and reduced teeth. The aardvark uses its stout claws to dig for termites, which it gathers up, anteaterlike, with its long tongue.

The **Lagomorpha** (2 families and 63 species) contains the hares, rabbits, and pikas. Lagomorph dentition is similar to that of a rodent, but in back of each of the two prominent upper front teeth (incisors) is a second, peglike tooth. The rabbits typically have long ears, and many have long, slim limbs adapted for running. Pikas have small ears and short legs. These mammals occupy environments ranging from Arctic to desert and are nearly worldwide in distribution.

The **Rodentia** is the largest mammalian order (34 families and more than 1,700 species). Due to introductions by human beings, rodents are nearly worldwide in distribution. They have four prominent front teeth that are used for gnawing, a broad space with no teeth (canines are lacking), and a series of back teeth used for grinding food; they utilize a tremendous variety of foods.

The **Mysticeti** (3 families and 10 species), or baleen whales, lack teeth, having instead fringed plates of horny material (baleen) growing downward from the upper jaw. Water rich with small marine organisms is brought into the mouth and forced out through the baleen by the tongue; organisms are strained out and swallowed. Hind limbs are absent; the front limbs are modified into flippers. Propulsion is accomplished by the horizontally oriented tail (fluke).

The **Odontoceti** (7 families and 74 species) are the toothed whales, which include porpoises and dolphins. Odontocete jaws typically bear large numbers of simple, conical teeth. These social animals have a highly developed ability to echolocate. The limbs and tail are like those of baleen whales. Odontocetes occupy all oceans and many large rivers and lakes; they feed on many kinds of prey.

The **Carnivora** (10 families and 284 species) comprises dogs, cats, civets, seals, walruses, and others. Terrestrial carnivores (fissipeds) have large canine teeth, and most have one upper and one lower "carnassial" tooth on each side of the jaw. The carnassial teeth function to shear, or slice, meat in most carnivores but are flattened in omnivores, such as bears and raccoons. Terrestrial carnivores have clawed feet and are often swift runners or adroit climbers. Seals, sea lions, and walruses (often considered a separate order, Pinnipedia) usually have simple conical teeth, and the limbs are flipperlike. The upper canines of walruses are enlarged into huge tusks. Carnivores eat a wide assortment of animals and some plant material and are found nearly worldwide.

The **Proboscidea** (1 family and 2 species) contains the elephants, the largest living terrestrial mammals. The animal's snout is extended into a trunk, and one upper incisor on each side develops into a huge tusk. The rear grinding teeth emerge in sequence; only one on each side of each jaw is functional at a time. The limbs, which must bear great weight, are built like pillars. Elephants eat vegetation and live in forested or partly forested parts of Africa and Southeast Asia.

The **Hyracoidea** (1 family and 11 species) comprises the hyraxes. These rabbit-sized animals of Africa and the Middle East resemble rodents but are more closely related to elephants. Hyraxes have an incisor tooth on each side of the upper jaw that forms a short tusk, and feet with nails instead of claws. These almost tailless herbivores are nimble climbers.

The **Sirenia** (2 families and 5 species) includes the dugongs and manatees. Like those of whales and porpoises, the forelimbs of these fully aquatic creatures are flippers and the tail is a horizonal fluke. Dugongs and manatees graze on aquatic plants in coastal waters, lakes,

or rivers, along many tropical coastlines.

The **Perissodactyla** (3 families and 16 species) encompasses horses, rhinoceroses, and tapirs. These animals all have hooves or broad nails. The skull is long, and the back teeth are adapted to grinding vegetation. Perissodactyls are native to parts of Africa, Asia, and Central and South America.

The order **Artiodactyla** (8 families and 171 species) contains the cloven-hoofed mammals, such as camels, giraffes, sheep, and cattle. There is a good deal of variation in foot structure and in the head. Many species, such as deer and antelopes, have antlers or horns. Hippopotamuses, pigs, and peccaries lack these weapons but have tusklike canine teeth. Artiodactyls are nearly worldwide in distribution but are absent from Antarctica, the Australian region, and remote islands.

Exploitation. Human beings have a long history of exploiting their fellow mammals, and their impact has been devastating. Today more than 100 species of mammals are threatened with extinction, and within the last 400 years some 36 species have become extinct, mostly because of the destructive acts of human beings (see ENDANGERED SPECIES).

mammary glands see BREAST; MAMMAL

---

mammography Mammography is an X-ray technique used to aid in the diagnosis of breast CANCER in women. Tactile examinations of a BREAST may be able to distinguish between well-defined and freely mobile tumors, which are generally benign, and fixed, firm lumps that blend with surrounding tissue, which may be malignant. When any suspicious lump is detected, however, a mammogram should be taken. If doubt remains, a biopsy, or surgical removal of a sample of suspected tissue for examination, can determine its nature with certainty. If cancer is confirmed, a MASTECTOMY (removal of part or all of the breast) may be performed to prevent the spread of cancer to other parts of the body; various other modes of treatment are also available.

Medical organizations are in agreement that women of age 50 or older should all have yearly mammograms. They also agree that in women younger than the age of 35, obtaining a so-called baseline mammogram—one to which later mammograms can be compared—has not proved of statistical significance in aiding the later diagnosis and treatment of patients. For the age period of 35 to 50, however, varying opinions exist as to the need for yearly mammograms. Some organizations, such as the U.S. National Cancer Institute, recommend mammographic screening for women under 50 only if they are in high-risk groups (those who have already had breast cancer, who exhibit what may be precancerous conditions, or who have relatives with the cancer).

---

mammoth [mam'-uhth] Mammoths are a group of extinct elephants that were common in northern Eurasia and North America during the Pleistocene Epoch (2.5

The mammoth of the Pleistocene Epoch was a contemporary of early humans. Several specimens, found preserved in ice, are displayed in museums.

million to 10,000 years ago). During the Pleistocene Epoch (see ICE AGES), the woolly mammoth was widely distributed over the Earth and was well adapted to glacial climates. The imperial mammoth, *Mammuthus imperator,* measured as much as 4.6 m (15 ft) high at the shoulder and was probably the largest elephant of all time.

Specimens well preserved by natural refrigeration have been found in the Arctic permafrost of Alaska and Siberia; some flesh is so well preserved that it has been eaten by animals. Since the first frozen mammoth was reported in 1400, about 40 have been found, 5 of them almost complete. The Berezovka mammoth, excavated in 1901 and now at the Zoological Institute in Leningrad, is more than 39,000 years old.

The discovery of frozen body tissue has provided much information about the woolly mammoth and the evolution of the elephants, and DNA fragments that have been extracted from the remains may provide further data.

Mammoth Cave   Mammoth Cave is a system of underground caves in Mammoth Cave National Park, located in west central Kentucky, about 140 km (85 mi) west of Louisville. The park covers 208 km² (80 mi²). Passages through the caves extend for more than 245 km (150 mi) and occur at five different levels. Created by dissolution of limestone, the caves are noted for their stalagmites and stalactites and gypsum and onyx formations. Many underground rivers and streams flow through the caves. The national park was established in 1941.

man, early   see PREHISTORIC HUMANS

Man, Isle of   see ISLE OF MAN

mana [mah'-nah]   *Mana* is a Melanesian term for a diffuse supernatural power or influence that is believed to be embodied in certain objects or persons and to account for their extraordinary qualities or effectiveness. The arbitrary, uncontrollable force may also be attached to songs, dreams, or ideas. Mana was first described by English anthropologist R. H. Codrington in 1891.

Management and Budget, U.S. Office of   The U.S. Office of Management and Budget (OMB) is the president's administrative arm for supervising the performance of the federal agencies and controlling their budget requests. It was established in 1970, replacing the Bureau of the Budget, which was created in 1921. The new agency has management duties as well as budgetary ones. As part of the executive office of the president, it oversees and coordinates the work programs of federal agencies and tries to improve their statistical services and information systems. It also prepares the annual budget recommendations for the president.

Managua [mah-nah'-gwah]   Managua is the capital and largest city of Nicaragua, located in the west central part of the country along the south shore of Lake Managua. Its population is 682,111 (1985 est.). Managua serves as the commercial and transportation center of the nation. The National Palace, the modern cathedral, and Darío Park are well-known landmarks.

Managua was a large Indian town by the 16th century when it was taken by the Spanish. In 1857 it was chosen as the capital of Nicaragua. Managua was destroyed by a severe earthquake and fire in 1931, and subsequently rebuilt. In 1972 another earthquake resulting in more than 10,000 casualties occurred. A new commercial center is being built 10 km (6 mi) away from the former city center.

Manama [ma-nam'-uh]   Manama (1987 est. pop., 146,994), the capital, chief city, and port of Bahrain, is located at the northeast tip of Bahrain Island in the Persian Gulf. Petroleum refining is the principal industry. Manama's free port, with a deepwater harbor, exports petroleum and serves as transshipment point for cargo bound for Saudi Arabia. Manama was first mentioned in 14th-century written texts.

Manasseh ben Israel [muh-nas'-uh]   Although baptized in infancy by his Marrano parents, Manasseh ben Israel, b. Portugal, 1604, d. Nov. 20, 1657, was at the age of 18 appointed rabbi in Amsterdam, where he started the first Hebrew press. The crowning achievement of his varied career was in securing Oliver Cromwell's tacit permission for Jews to settle in England (for the first time since 1290). Manasseh was a prolific author. His portrait was etched by his friend Rembrandt.

manatee see SIRENIA

Manaus [mah-nows'] Manaus (also Manáos) is a city in Brazil, situated on the Rio Negro 11 km (7 mi) from its junction with the Amazon River. It is the capital of Amazonas, Brazil's largest state. Manaus has a population of 809,914 (1987 est.). A major transportation hub, it has long been an important river port and is linked by road with the Trans-Amazonian Highway and Venezuela. Rainforest products are exported. Oil refining and diversified manufacturing of light consumer goods takes place. The University of Amazonas (1965) and the city's famous opera house, the Teatro Amazonas, are there.

In 1669 the Portuguese established a fortress in Manaus. About 1890, Manaus became the wealthy center of a rubber boom that lasted three decades.

Manchester (England) Manchester is a large industrial city in northwestern England that was the center of Great Britain's Industrial Revolution. Formerly a part of Lancashire, it was incorporated into the metropolitan county of Greater Manchester in 1974. Manchester lies along the River Irwell and is linked to the port city of LIVERPOOL, 35 km (20 mi) to the west, by the Manchester Ship Canal. The population of the city is 445,900, and of the metropolitan county, 2,577,000 (1988 ests.).

Cotton textile manufacturing, which originally dominated the economy, has declined, but Manchester remains the focus of the Lancashire synthetic textile industry. Docks on the canal handle imported raw materials used in Manchester's diverse industries. Steel, machine tools, electrical equipment, and chemicals are manufactured, and petroleum is refined. The well-known Victoria University of Manchester developed from a college founded there in 1851. The city is also the home of the Hallé Orchestra.

The earliest settlement there was the Roman town of Mamucium, from which the city derives its name. In 1359, Manchester was declared a market town. A locally important textile industry specializing in woolens developed in the 16th century. Manchester's first steam-powered textile mill opened in the 1760s. Because of the proximity to coal, used to power the mills, and to the port of Liverpool, Manchester soon became the largest producer of textiles in the world. During the 19th century, Manchester was a center of liberal economic and political thought; the free-trade economists of the period were called the Manchester school. The influential liberal newspaper the *Guardian* (originally the *Manchester Guardian*) was founded in 1821.

Manchester (New Hampshire) Manchester, the largest city in New Hampshire, is located in the southern part of the state on the Merrimack River. Its population is 99,567 (1990). The Amoskeag Manufacturing Company, one of the largest textile firms in New England, was the economic mainstay of Manchester for more than a century until 1935, when it went bankrupt. Today Manchester's diversified industries produce electronic and electrical equipment, shoes, automobile parts, paper, tires, and textiles; several printing companies are also there. Saint Anselm's College was founded in 1889. Currier Gallery of Art is well known.

A settlement was established in 1722 on the site of an Indian fishing village, and it was incorporated as Derryfield in 1751. In 1805 a textile mill was established, and in 1807 a canal was opened that permitted barge traffic to Boston. In 1810, after the city's industrial growth had begun, it was named Manchester, for the city in England.

Manchester terrier The Manchester terrier was developed in the 19th century in Manchester, England, apparently by crossing English terriers with whippets. The breeding intention was to develop an accomplished rat killer, principally for sporting use in pits. The Manchester terrier was also used to course rabbits, again for sport. The dog has a smooth, glossy, short coat, jet black with rich mahogany tan markings, which accounts for the original name of *black-and-tan-terrier*. It stands about 40 cm (16 in) high at the shoulder and comes in two varieties for show purposes: standard and toy. The standard weighs at least 5.4 kg (12 lb) but not more than 9.9 kg (22 lb) and may have cropped ears. The toy variety must be less than 5.4 kg (12 lb) and cannot have cropped ears.

Manchu see QING (DYNASTY)

Manchu-Tungus language see URAL-ALTAIC LANGUAGES

Manchuria [man-chur'-ee-uh] Manchuria, a region in northeastern China, is one of the most important economic areas of the country. In Chinese it is called Tung Pei, which means "north east." Manchuria borders the USSR in the north and west, Mongolia in the west, North Korea in the southeast, and the Yellow Sea in the south.

Manchuria, the most intensively developed industrial region of China, is situated in the extreme northeastern portion of the nation.

Central Manchuria consists of a fertile plain hemmed in by forested mountains. The Lesser and Greater Khingan Mountains are in the north and west. In the east the Changpai Mountains reach 2,744 m (9,003 ft) at Paitou, on the Korean border. In the southeast the Liaotung Peninsula juts into the Yellow Sea. Drainage is provided by the AMUR, Sungari, Liao, and YALU rivers.

The population of Manchuria is mostly Chinese. The Manchu, from whom the English name for the region is derived, constitute a small minority, as do Koreans and Mongols. Manchuria's largest cities, among the most important in China, are CHANGCHUN, Haerbin, Lüda (comprising LÜSHUN and DALIAN), and SHENYANG.

Manchuria's heavy industries include agricultural machinery, chemicals, locomotives, machine tools, and steel manufacturing. Agriculture takes place in the central plain and river valleys, and coal and iron mining are important.

The Manchus, a people of the Tungu group, were originally known as the Jurzhen. A nomadic people in Manchuria, they conquered northern China in the 12th century but were forced to withdraw in 1234. In 1606 the chieftain NURHACHI united the Jurzhen tribes into one powerful khanate. His successor undertook the conquest of China, and in 1644 a Manchu was proclaimed Chinese emperor, inaugurating the QING dynasty.

While the Manchu ruled China, the Russians began to encroach upon Manchuria because of its rich resources. In the late 19th century they met with Japanese competition. This led to the RUSSO-JAPANESE WAR (1904–05), fought in Manchuria and ending in Japanese victory. In 1931, Japan occupied all of Manchuria and made it the puppet state of Manchukuo. During this period much of Manchuria's economic development took place.

Following World War II and the defeat of Japan, Manchuria was occupied by the USSR. The Soviets soon withdrew, however, and Manchuria became a battleground between China's Communist and Nationalist forces. By 1948 the Communists were in control. Today Manchuria is divided into the provinces of Jilin, Liaoning, and Heilongjiang.

Manco Capac [mahnk'-oh kah-pahk']

Manco Capac was the legendary founder of the royal dynasty that ultimately ruled the INCA empire. According to tradition, he originally came from south of CUZCO, eventually establishing there the settlement that was to become the imperial capital. Manco Capac supposedly turned to stone, and that stone became one of the Inca's most revered objects.

Whether or not Manco Capac actually existed has never been confirmed. The Inca left no written records, and the precise dates of his life or possible reign cannot be determined. If Manco Capac were a real person, however, he would have lived in the 14th century.

Mandaeans [man-dee'-uhnz]

The Mandaeans, also known as Nazoreans, are a gnostic (see GNOSTICISM) sect that originated in Mesopotamia or Palestine in the 1st or 2d century AD, or possibly in pre-Christian times. Today they number no more than a few thousand, living in southwest Iran and southern Iraq. They are sometimes called the Christians of Saint John because of their claim that John the Baptist was a member of the sect and because ritual cleanliness is their principal concern.

Mandaean religion draws from Christianity, Judaism, and Islam, but rejects all three. Their sacramental meal resembles that of the PARSIS, whereas their astrological system has much in common with that of the Babylonians. They differ from other gnostics in their emphasis on fertility.

The Mandaeans believe in a world of light and splendor beyond the visible heavens where the king of light is enthroned. This earthly abode is one of darkness and pollution but is connected to the world of light by the living waters that descend to earth through mountains in the north that reach to the heavens. The planets and the signs of the zodiac stand between humankind and the world of light and are therefore regarded as evil.

mandala [muhn'-duh-luh]

A mandala (Sanskrit for "circle") is a symbolic diagram of the universe used for ritual purposes in tantric Buddhism (see TANTRA). Frequently represented in Chinese, Japanese, and Tibetan Buddhist art, the mandala generally consists of a group of cosmic deities (or their symbols or associated magic syllables) that are arranged in one or more circles surrounded by a square and oriented toward the points of the compass. Some of the earliest mandalas were laid out architecturally, as at the Samye monastery (c.780) in Tibet. They were also frequently drawn in powder on the ground for use in initiation rites. From the 9th century mandalas were painted on walls or on cloth or paper.

Mandalay [man'-duh-lay]

Mandalay, the second largest city in Burma, is situated in the central part of the country. Its population is 532,895 (1983). Located along the Irrawaddy River and on major railroad lines, it is an important transportation and commercial center. Mandalay's principal industries are silk weaving, food processing, and traditional crafts.

Mandalay is a major center of Burmese Buddhism. Its religious buildings include numerous monasteries, the complex called the 730 Pagodas, and the Arakan Pagoda. The University of Mandalay was founded in 1958.

Mandalay, established in 1857 as the capital of the Burmese kingdom, was taken by the British in 1885. Occupied by Japan during World War II, it suffered extensive damage in fighting between Japanese and Allied forces in 1945.

mandamus [man-day'-mus]

Mandamus (Latin, "we command") is a WRIT issued by a court of superior jurisdiction commanding a lower court, a public official, a corporation, or a private person to perform a certain act. The writ of mandamus can be either peremptory or alternative. If it is peremptory, the defendant is compelled to perform the specific act; if it is alternative, the defendant can choose either to appear in court to contest the issuance of the writ or to comply with it immediately. Usually a court will issue an alternative writ first.

Mandan [man'-dan]   The Mandan are a Siouan-speaking North American Indian people of the Upper Missouri River valley. A village-dwelling people, they cultivated maize, squash, and beans and hunted wild game. Villages ranged from 10 to 100 earth lodges. Mandan economics and politics were organized through clans by descent through the mother's line. The major Mandan ceremony, the *Okipa*, celebrated the Lord of Life who lived in the Sun; to induce a holy vision, the Mandan practiced such sacrifices as fasting and self-torture.

In 1738 white traders contacted the Mandan. Bison and other furs were exchanged for guns and steel tools. Epidemic disease followed, and the Mandan suffered several epidemics before the LEWIS AND CLARK EXPEDITION arrived (1804). In 1837 smallpox reduced nearly 2,000 Mandan to less than 200. They joined the ARIKARA and HIDATSA for protection from the SIOUX. After 1866 the merged tribes lost most of their land; the remaining land became the Fort Berthold Reservation in North Dakota. The merged tribes on or near the reservation numbered about 2,660 in 1989.

Mandela, Nelson [mahn-del'-ah]   Nelson Rohihlahla Mandela, b. July 18, 1918, is South Africa's most prominent black nationalist leader. Trained as an attorney, he helped form the Youth League of the AFRICAN NATIONAL CONGRESS (ANC) in 1944. In 1961 he abandoned peaceful protest and became commander of the ANC's newly formed political wing. After being sentenced to life imprisonment for conspiracy to overthrow the government in 1964, Mandela came to symbolize black political aspirations. He was named head of the ANC after his release on Feb. 11, 1990, and began negotiations with President F. W. DE KLERK to end APARTHEID and reshape the political system.

Mandelstam, Osip Emilievich [mahn'-dul-shtahm', aw'-sip em-yeel'-yuh-vich]   The Russian poet Osip Emilievich Mandelstam, b. Jan. 15 (N.S.), 1891, d. Dec. 27, 1938, who "brought to the Revolution gifts it did not need," is today recognized as a major 20th-century writer whose poetry—about 400 lyrics—is regarded as an immense contribution to Russian literature. In his lyrics Mandelstam's reactions to his time, history, and art are synthesized with earlier perspectives drawn from the entire range of Western culture. His books of verse are *Stone* (1913), *Tristia* (1922), and *Poems* (1928). His prose writing includes *The Noise of Time* (1925) and such es-

says on poetry as *Conversations about Dante* (c.1933). He was arrested in 1934 and 1938, and his works were unpublished during the Stalin era.

mandolin   The most prominent type of the musical instrument known as the mandolin is the Neapolitan, a small lute about 60 cm (2 ft) long with deeply vaulted ribs and a table slanted downward at the lower end. It has four double rib-fastened metal strings suspended across a low bridge and a fretted neck to pegs inserted into a rectangular peg-box. A small flexible plectrum is used to vibrate the strings. A feature of mandolin playing is the constant reiteration of all long pitches, which counteracts its weak sustaining power.

The mandolin emerged from the medieval-Renaissance mandola possibly as early as the 15th century and enjoyed a vogue in concert music furing the 18th century; Handel, Mozart, Vivaldi, and Auber all composed for it. By 1900 it had become a popular folk instrument in Germany and America.

The mandolin has been used for vocal accompaniment as well as for classical composition since the 18th century. Development in Italy from the mandola, the modern mandolin has four pairs of strings tuned to violin pitch and produces a clear, bright tone.

mandrake   Mandrake, *Mandragora officinarum,* is an old European medicinal plant of the nightshade family, Solanaceae. Because its thick root is often forked, suggesting human legs, with side roots appearing to be arms, many superstitions have been associated with the mandrake. The roots contain the alkaloid hyoscyamine, which can interfere with the transmission of nerve impulses.

Mandrake is a perennial herb with long, wavy-margined leaves arising from the rootstock and large, bell-shaped, greenish yellow or purplish flowers borne in the center of the leaves. The flowers mature into fleshy berries.

In North America the perennial herb *Podophyllum peltatum,* of the barberry family, Berberidaceae, commonly called the mayapple, sometimes has a divided rootstock and has also been known as a mandrake.

mandrill   The mandrill, *Mandrillus sphinx*, is a terrestrial Old World MONKEY in the family Cercopithecidae, order Primates. It lives in the jungle of equatorial West Africa. The adult male has a long, narrow muzzle with cheeks of bright blue and purple to violet, centered by a scarlet nose. The buttock pads are lilac to pink, with reddish purple and blue at the sides. When a male is frightened, angry, or excited, the colors become brighter. Females are more sedately colored. The brow ridges of both sexes are prominent and are topped in the male by a crest and a mane. Males are about 90 cm (36 in) long and weigh up to 54 kg (120 lb); females are smaller. Mandrills eat mainly vegetation and insects.

The strikingly colored mandrill travels in groups of from 3 to 50 or more. It can climb and may sleep in trees.

Manet, Édouard   [mah-nay', ay-dwahr']   Édouard Manet, b. Paris, Jan. 23, 1832, d. Apr. 30, 1883, has often been called the first modern artist to conceive of a painting as a flat surface covered with pigment, and purposely to draw attention to the process of painting. Although he was not completely unconcerned with subject matter, Manet used the traditional concept of content only as a point of departure—one that led him in many different directions.

His early works, such as *The Spanish Guitarist* (1860; Metropolitan Museum of Art, New York City), reveal a debt to Diego Velázquez and Francisco de Goya, but they also display the two-dimensional directness that would mark Manet's more controversial paintings. Once he moved away from the general influence of baroque art he embarked on a series of provocative challenges to the official Salon art of the day. The first of these unconventional works was the *Déjeuner sur l'Herbe* (1862; Musée d'Orsay, Paris), refused by the Salon of 1863 but shown that year at the famous Salon des Refusés. Although Ma-

net manifested his admiration for past art by basing the *Déjeuner* poses on Marcantonio Raimondi's print (*c.*1525–30) after Raphael's lost cartoon for the *Judgment of Paris*, the general public was shocked both by the bohemian candor of the subject matter and by the very summary way in which the brushwork suggested lighting and textures. The painting looks unfinished and gives the impression of an informal moment captured as if by a camera.

Manet again caused public scandal with his *Olympia* (1863; Musée d'Orsay), a candid presentation of a courtesan posing naked on her bed. The homage paid here to Titian's famous *Venus of Urbino* (*c.*1538; Uffizi Gallery, Florence) only aggravated the outcry created by the suggestive props accompanying the nudity and by the use of bright color-patches juxtaposed without transitions of modeling.

Manet's thoroughly unconventional treatment of traditional subjects represents a turning point in modern painting. Even more than the proponents of realism, led by Gustave Courbet, Manet devalued the importance of what was painted in favor of stressing the process by which a painting was created. His later works ranged in subject matter from beach and outdoor subjects to city scenes, all of which he rendered with increasingly free brushstrokes and bolder use of color and light. Although he maintained close contacts with the emerging impressionists, his predilection for strong black-and-white contrasts and his feeling for clear outlines kept him outside the mainstream of IMPRESSIONISM. The crowning masterpiece of his last years, *A Bar at the Folies-Bergère* (1881–82; Courtauld Institute Galleries, London), acknowledges the triumph of impressionism in its use of quick, vibrant strokes to enhance the fall of light onto textures and sur-

In The Fifer *(1866), Édouard Manet used broad, flat areas of undifferentiated color to make the figure appear on the same surface plane as its environment. This redefinition of the canvas as a 2-dimensional painted surface, earned Manet his important position in modernist art. (Musée d' Orsay, Paris.)*

faces, but it also testifies to Manet's personal, inventive brilliance in the way in which different aspects of visual experience are combined in startling and illogical ways. By the time of his death, Manet was recognized as a pioneer of the modern movement in painting.

manganese

manganese [mang'-guh-neez] The chemical element manganese is a silver gray metal of the TRANSITION ELEMENTS and a member of Group VIIB in the periodic table. Its chemical symbol is Mn, its atomic number is 25, and its atomic weight is 54.938. Manganese was first recognized as an element in 1774 by the Swedish chemist Carl Scheele and isolated in the same year by his coworker, Johan Gahn. It is essential for plant growth and is found in trace elements in higher animals, where it activates many of the enzymes involved in metabolic processes.

Occurrence. The Earth's crust contains 850 ppm manganese in chemically bonded form. By far the most important manganese mineral is pyrolusite, which consists largely of manganese dioxide, MnO_2. Pyrolusite is brown black in color and often somewhat magnetic; the name "manganese" is a corrupted form of the Latin word for a form of magnetic stone, *magnesia*. Although manganese ores are not scarce, extraction is economically feasible only with open-cast mining. In addition, extensive deposits of manganese nodules are found at many sites on the ocean floor.

Uses. Pure manganese is rarely used, as it is a moderately reactive and brittle metal. About 95% of the world's annual production of manganese is used by the iron and steel industry. Manganese reduces iron oxide to form manganese oxide, which dissolves well in molten slag and is easily separated from the iron. In alloys, manganese increases the durability and corrosion resistance of iron and steel and makes steel more malleable when forged.

Important manganese alloys that do not contain iron include the Heusler alloys (18–25% manganese, plus copper and aluminum or zinc), which are the strongest nonferrous metals; manganese copper (approximately 75% copper and 25% manganese), which has great electrical resistance; and manganin (about 83% copper, 14% manganese, and 3% nickel), which has a very slight heat-expansion coefficient and an electrical resistance nearly independent of temperature.

Manganese Compounds. The most frequently occurring valence of manganese is +2, but +4, +6, and +7 are also common, and +1, +3, and +5 are known.

The Mn^{2+} ion has a light pink color in water because it forms $Mn(H_2O)_6^{2+}$. Manganese chloride ($MnCl_2$) and manganese sulfate ($MnSO_4$), are added to commercial fertilizers. Manganese carbonate, $Mn(CO_3)_2$, yields the pigment manganese white. Manganese salts are used in the paint industry to accelerate the hardening of drying oils.

Adding sulfuric acid to the intensely green potassium manganate (K_2MnO_4) produces the intensely purple potassium permanganate ($KMnO_4$), used for bleaching and removing color from fabrics that are able to tolerate strong oxidation, and to clear clogged drains.

The most important manganese compound, pyrolusite, or manganese dioxide (MnO_2), is also an oxidizing agent. Pyrolusite is used extensively in the electrodes of dry batteries. It is also used as an oxygen source in fireworks and as a chemical catalyst. All other manganese compounds are made from pyrolusite.

manganese nodule

manganese nodule   see OCEANIC MINERAL RESOURCES

Mangas Coloradas

Mangas Coloradas   Mangas Coloradas (Spanish for "Red Sleeves"), b. *c.*1791, d. Jan. 18, 1863, emerged as a prime leader of the Mimbres APACHE in southwestern New Mexico after the Mexican-instigated massacre of many Mimbres Indians in 1837. He sought friendly relations with Americans but unrelentingly raided Mexicans. In 1861, when he tried peaceably to persuade American gold miners to leave Santa Rita, he was lashed nearly to death. Upon recovery, Mangas gathered his forces and drove the miners out. With his son-in-law, COCHISE, he defended Apache Pass against Gen. James H. Carleton's California Column in 1862. In 1863 goldseekers tricked him into captivity. At Fort McLane he was killed; his head was cut off, boiled, and exhibited as a curio at public lectures.

mange

mange   Mange is the common term for several mite infestations of mammals in which the mites burrow beneath the skin and lay eggs, causing irritation and often loss of hair. Some mite forms are species specific; others can be exchanged among several mammal species, including humans. The latter forms include species of the mite genus *Sarcoptes*. In humans, sarcoptic mange is known as scabies (see SKIN DISEASES). It is characterized by intense itching, as are chorioptic mange (caused by *Chorioptes* species that typically infest the lower legs and feet of animals) and ear mange (caused by *Otodectes* and *Psoroptes* species). These infestations can spread rapidly in herd animals, but they are readily treated.

Demodectic mange, or red mange, caused by *Demodex* mites, is not serious in humans but can be fatal to dogs. Although a normal inhabitant of hair follicles in many healthy dogs, *D. canis* causes severe problems in animals that apparently have some form of immunodeficiency.

mango

mango   A tree of East Asian origin that is widely cultivated in tropical areas for its fruit, the mango, *Mangifera indica*, belongs to the cashew family, Anacardiaceae. The genus *Mangifera* contains about 60 species of jungle trees whose fruits are fibrous, acrid, and sometimes toxic, with a flavor that has been likened to turpentine. Centuries of selection have produced varieties that are free of both fibers and offensive flavor.

In the regions where they are grown, mangoes are an important food crop. Their principal growing area is still tropical Asia, although they were introduced into the Western Hemisphere in the early 1700s and are now successfully cultivated in the Caribbean countries as well as

The mango tree bears a sweet fruit that is an important food source for the inhabitants of tropical countries. The tree is an evergreen that grows up to 27 m (90 ft) tall.

in Florida and California. The tree is tolerant of a wide range of rainfall but needs a period of dry weather at the time the fruits are formed.

mangrove Mangroves are trees or shrubs typically forming dense thickets along warm, muddy, brackish or saltwater shorelines. The mangrove family, Rhizophoraceae, contains about 15 genera and 120 species distributed throughout the tropics. The genus *Rhizophora,* the mangroves proper, contains 3 to possibly 7 species, including the red or American mangrove, *R. mangle,* found

The American mangrove tree, found along tropical coasts, is distinguished by its abovewater roots. Seeds develop roots (top) *while still attached to the parent tree. When a seed drops to the mud, its root grows to the ground below and takes hold.*

from southern Florida and the West Indies into South America and, according to some authorities, along the Atlantic coast of Africa. Rarely exceeding 6 m (20 ft) high in Florida, the red mangrove in the tropics may reach approximately 30 m (100 ft) tall, with trunks up to 1 m (3 ft) in diameter. Its hard, dense, red-colored wood is used in wharf pilings and for fuel; the thick bark is an important source of tannin. The red mangrove sends out stilt-like prop roots from its trunk to the ground for additional support. These aerial roots form tangled thickets that catch and hold sediment; extensive growths of mangroves along coasts are thus valuable for stabilizing and slowly extending the shoreline. Red mangrove has thick, leathery, elongated oval leaves and pale yellow flowers. The flowers mature into brownish berries that begin to germinate while still on the tree. When the fruit drops from the tree it floats until it contacts mud, where it immediately begins growth.

The combretum family, Combretaceae, often called the white mangrove family, contains about 15 genera and 600 species of trees and shrubs. The genus *Avicennia,* family Avicenniaceae, contains about 14 species also collectively known as white mangroves. The genus *Sonneratia,* family Sonneratiaceae, contains 5 species similar to *Rhizophora* that are commonly also called mangroves.

Manhattan Most of Manhattan, one of the five boroughs of NEW YORK CITY, is a long narrow island bounded by the Hudson, Harlem, and East rivers and Upper New York Bay. A small portion of the borough, which is coextensive with New York County, is on the mainland to the north. Manhattan covers 57 km² (22 mi²) and has a population of 1,487,536 (1990). It is the commercial and cultural heart of New York City.

In 1524, Giovanni da Verrazano was the first European explorer to visit Manhattan. In 1626, Peter MINUIT, a Dutchman, is said to have purchased the island for the equivalent of $24 in trade goods from the Manhattan Indians. A Dutch settlement, New Amsterdam, was soon established. In 1664 it was taken by the British and renamed New York. Manhattan comprised the entire city until 1898 when the other four boroughs (Brooklyn, the Bronx, Queens, and Staten Island) became part of New York.

Manhattan Project The Manhattan Project was the code name for the U.S. effort during World War II to produce the ATOMIC BOMB. It was named for the Manhattan Engineer District of the U.S. Army Corps of Engineers, because much of the early research was done in New York City. Sparked by refugee physicists in the United States, the program was slowly organized after nuclear fission was discovered by German scientists in 1938, and many U.S. scientists expressed the fear that Hitler would attempt to build a fission bomb.

The program was first under the leadership of Vannevar BUSH, head of the National Defense Research Committee and the Office of Scientific Research and Development, and then under Gen. Leslie Groves of the Army

Corps of Engineers. Groves immediately purchased a site at Oak Ridge, Tenn., for facilities to separate the necessary uranium-235 from the much more common uranium-238, and he consolidated the research done in many East Coast universities under the direction of Arthur COMPTON at the University of Chicago. He also appointed theoretical physicist J. Robert OPPENHEIMER as director of the weapons laboratory, built on an isolated mesa at Los Alamos, N.Mex. After much difficulty a porous barrier suitable for separating isotopes of uranium was developed and installed in the Oak Ridge gaseous diffusion plant. Finally, in 1945, uranium-235 of bomb purity was shipped to Los Alamos, where it was fashioned into a gun-type weapon. In a barrel, one piece of uranium was fired at another, together forming a supercritical, explosive mass.

Another type of atomic bomb was also constructed using the synthetic element plutonium. Enrico Fermi built a reactor at Chicago in late 1942, the prototype of five production reactors erected at Hanford, Wash. These reactors manufactured plutonium by bombarding uranium-238 with neutrons. At Los Alamos the plutonium was surrounded with high explosives to compress it into a superdense, supercritical mass far faster than could be done in a gun barrel. The result was tested at Alamogordo, N.Mex., on July 16, 1945—the first explosion of an atomic bomb.

----

manic-depressive psychosis Manic-depressive psychosis, now more accurately called bipolar disorder, is a psychological disorder characterized by episodes of euphoria or depression, or alternating episodes of each. In the positive-affect phase the person is elated and inappropriately optimistic; grossly overestimates his or her own abilities and other positive attributes; shows speeded movement, thought, and speech; undergoes intellectual disorganization; and has pathologically bad judgment. In the negative-affect phase the individual experiences sadness, slowed speech and movements, and self castigation. Some individuals alternate between the two states, usually with healthy periods between the two; others, however, have only one or the other. In either phase it is not unusual for hallucinations, delusions, or both to occur.

The causes of bipolar disorder are unknown. Researchers have sought to demonstrate that genetic defects might be the root cause. Significant progress was made in this area in the late 1980s. Stressful life experiences, however, may also be contributing factors, although episodes of the disorder seldom appear to be triggered by life events.

Lithium salts (see LITHIUM, drug) are a common medical treatment, but side effects can be severe. New drugs such as Prozac (approved by the Food and Drug Administration in 1987) and Anaframil (approved in 1990) have shown great promise in treating the disorder. Even without treatment, more than 90 percent of patients with bipolar disorder recover, but the majority have recurrences.

Manichaeism [man'-ik-ee-izm] Manichaeism was a gnostic (see GNOSTICISM) religion that originated in Baby-

lonia in the 3d century AD. Its founder was a Persian of noble descent called Mani (or Manes), c.216–c.276.

At about the age of 24, Mani received a special revelation from God, according to which he was called to perfect the incomplete religions founded by earlier prophets—Zoroaster, Buddha, and Christ. About the year 242, he undertook an extensive journey as an itinerant preacher, proclaiming himself the "Messenger of Truth," the Paraclete promised by Christ. Traveling throughout the Persian Empire and as far as India, he gathered a considerable following. He met with increasing hostility from the Zoroastrian priests and was finally executed for heresy.

The essence of Manichaeism was the principle of absolute DUALISM: the primal conflict between God, represented by light and spirit, and Satan, represented by darkness and the material world. Human beings, created by God, were divine in spirit, but they carried within them seeds of darkness, sown by Satan, because of their material bodies.

Salvation, as taught by Mani, requires liberating the seed of light, the soul, from the material darkness in which it is trapped. This is achieved by strict celibacy and ascetic practices. Those who would become perfect are to set three "seals" on their lives: on the mouth, to speak only truth and to abstain from meat or impure food of any kind; on the hands, to refrain from war, killing, or injuring life; and on the breast, to render impossible the works of the flesh. This triple seal applies only to the elect or pure; hearers follow a less demanding code. The imperfect are destined to continual rebirth in a world of material bodies.

Manichaeism disappeared in the West in about the 6th century, although its doctrines reappeared in the teachings of the BOGOMILS, ALBIGENSES, and other sects during the Middle Ages. In the East, Manichaeism survived until the 13th century.

Manifest Destiny The term *Manifest Destiny* came into use among Americans in the 1840s as a defense for U.S. territorial expansion. Ever since the 17th century Americans had been pushing westward, and many Americans believed that a celestial design lay behind the extension of American institutions. A new optimistic spirit of confidence in the rightness of the expansion of the United States developed in the 19th century, however, and in 1845 a New York editor, John L. O'Sullivan, coined a phrase that captured this mood when he wrote that it was "the fulfillment of our manifest destiny to overspread the continent allotted by Providence for the free development of our yearly expanding millions." His immediate concern was the annexation of Texas, but soon the term *Manifest Destiny* was used in the dispute with Great Britain over Oregon (see OREGON QUESTION).

O'Sullivan believed that the United States should not confine its territorial ambitions to the continent of North America, and historians have debated since then whether Manifest Destiny was a screen for imperialism. The term was used to justify the Mexican War (1846–48), the Alaska Purchase (1867), and the Spanish-American War (1898)—all of which resulted in U.S. territorial gains.

Manila is located on Manila Bay, on the western coast of Luzon, the largest of the Philippine Islands. The city's land-locked harbor is the main port of the country.

Manila   Manila is the capital and largest city of the Philippines and the second largest metropolitan area in Southeast Asia (after Jakarta, Indonesia). It is situated in southwestern Luzon, on Manila Bay. The Pasig River flows through the city.

In 1975 the city of Manila merged with 16 surrounding communities to form one governmental unit. The National Capital Region, with an area of 636 km² (246 mi²), has a population of 7,766,000 (1989 est.).

Manila's diverse industries include chemical, textile, shoe, rope, and coconut oil manufacturing, as well as shipbuilding and food and tobacco processing. Because of its fine, protected harbor, Manila serves as the principal port of the Philippines. It is also the financial and publishing center of the nation. Universities in Manila's metropolitan area include the University of the Philippines (1908) and the University of Santo Thomas (1611). The National Museum, Rizal Park, the presidential palace, San Agustin Church (16th century), and the walled old city are landmarks.

By the early 16th century a walled Muslim city called Maynilad was there. In 1571 the Spanish destroyed the Muslim settlement and built a walled city and churches. Manila soon became the center of Roman Catholicism in Asia. The Spanish held Manila (except for a British occupation, 1762–63) until 1898. In that year, during the Spanish-American War, the United States defeated the Spanish fleet in Manila Bay and took the Philippines. In 1942, during World War II, the Japanese took Manila. When it was recaptured by U.S. forces in 1945 it suffered heavy damage. In 1948 the capital was moved to Quezon City, but in 1976 it was returned to Manila.

Manila Bay   Manila Bay, an inlet of the South China Sea, extends into southwestern Luzon Island in the Philippines. Covering about 2,000 km² (775 mi²), it is considered one of the finest harbors in the world. The city of Manila is on its eastern shore. In 1898, during the SPANISH-AMERICAN WAR, the Spanish fleet was decisively defeated there by U.S. forces.

manioc [ma'-nee-ahk]   Manioc, or cassava, is a tropical plant widely cultivated as an important source of starch and staple food among many tropical peoples. Manioc, *Manihot esculenta*, also sometimes known as the tapioca plant, is a member of the spurge family, Euphorbiaceae, and native to South America. It was one of the first plants domesticated in the Western Hemisphere and was later introduced into Europe and Africa. Its large, tuberous roots are processed into cassava flour, or tapioca, or they may be fermented into an alcoholic beverage. Cassava products are also used as laundry starches and fabric sizings and in the manufacture of explosives and glues.

Manioc is grown principally in Africa, Latin America, Indonesia, Malaysia, and the Philippines. Many varieties and closely related species contain the poison hydrocyanic acid, which can be removed only by cooking the root.

Manitoba [man-i-toh'-buh]   Manitoba, the easternmost of Canada's prairie provinces, stretches north from its southern border with Minnesota and North Dakota to the Northwest Territories. The province has a 644-km (400-mi) coastline along Hudson Bay in the northeast; Ontario lies to the east. On the west Manitoba adjoins Saskatchewan. The name *Manitoba* is thought to have come from the Ojibwa Indian word *manitou*, meaning "Great Spirit."

Land and Resources

Manitoba contains four physiographic regions. The flat tundra plain along the shores of Hudson Bay—the Hudson Bay Lowland—is the lowest in elevation. The land rises toward the CANADIAN SHIELD region to the west, which covers 60% of the province. The shield is drained by the CHURCHILL RIVER and the NELSON RIVER, both of which flow into Hudson Bay.

The Manitoba Lowland, located in the south central area, contains the province's largest lakes—Lake WINNIPEG (24,389 km²/9,417 mi²), Lake Winnipegosis (5,374 km²/2,075 mi²) and Lake Manitoba (4,646 km²/ 1,794 mi²). It is drained by the ASSINIBOINE RIVER and the

AT A GLANCE

MANITOBA

Land: Area: 649,950 km² (250,947 mi²); rank: 6th. Capital and largest city: Winnipeg (1991 pop., 616,790). Municipalities: 201. Elevations: highest—832 m (2,730 ft), at Baldy Mountain; lowest—sea level, along the coast of Hudson Bay.

People: Population (1991): 1,091,942; rank: 5th; density: 2 persons per km² (5.2 per mi²). Distribution (1991): 72.1% urban, 27.9% rural. Average annual change (1986–91): +0.54%.

Government (1992): Lieutenant Governor: George Johnson. Premier: Gary Filmon, Progressive Conservative party. Parliament: Senate—6 members; House of Commons—7 Progressive Conservatives, 5 Liberals, 2 New Democrats. Provincial legislature: 57 members. Admitted to Confederation: July 15, 1870, the 5th province.

Economy (monetary figures in Canadian dollars): Total personal income (1990): $21 billion; rank 5th. Median family income (1990): $42,880. Agriculture: farm cash receipts (1987)—$2.1 billion. Fishing: value (1987)—$28.3 million. Forestry: lumber production (1988)—105 million board feet. Mining: value (1988)—$1.7 billion. Manufacturing: value added (1988)—$2.9 billion.

Red River of the North. Along Manitoba's western border, the land rises to form the province's only upland region of three small mountain ranges. The smallest and most fertile region in Manitoba is the treeless prairie of the Saskatchewan Plain in the southwest.

Soils. Soils in the south vary from prairie soils in the southeast to chernozems in the Red River valley. Dark-brown soils are dominant in the southwest, while the northern parts of the province contain mostly gray brown podzols and peat.

Lakes and Rivers. Downstream from its junction with the Assiniboine, the Red River of the North flows into Lake Winnipeg. The lake empties into the Nelson River, which flows into Hudson Bay. The Churchill River crosses northern Manitoba from the Saskatchewan border to Hudson Bay. Lakes and rivers cover more than 15% of Manitoba's area.

Climate. Because of its continental climate and its soils, Manitoba can support agriculture only in the area south of 53° north latitude. Winnipeg has an average January temperature of –19° C (–3° F) and an average July temperature of 19° C (67° F), while at Churchill the average January temperature is –28° C (–19° F), and the average July temperature is 12° C (54° F).

Vegetation and Animal Life. Forests dominate the landscape north of the agricultural areas in Manitoba. Spruce, jack pine, balsam poplar, aspen, and white-birch trees predominate. Caribou, moose, elk, deer, beaver, and fox

inhabit the northerly zone, and deer, coyote, and rabbits are found close to urban areas.

Resources. Manitoba's forests and deposits of nickel, copper, gold, silver, lead, and zinc are among its major resources. Petroleum reserves underlie the southwestern region. An abundant water supply has made inexpensive electricity possible. Lakes support a thriving fishing industry.

People

More than half of Manitoba's people live in the WINNIPEG metropolitan area. Other major cities are Brandon, Portage la Prairie, and Thompson. By ancestry, about 43% of the residents are from the British Isles. Other ethnic groups include Germans, Ukrainians, Dutch, Scandinavians and Finns, French Canadians, and Indians.

Education and Cultural Activities. The University of Manitoba (1877), the University of Winnipeg (1871), and Brandon University (1899) are the major universities. The province has eight newspapers. Radio and television stations broadcast in both English and French. Cultural activities, centered in Winnipeg, include the Royal Winnipeg Ballet, the Winnipeg Symphony Orchestra, the Manitoba Theatre Centre, and the Winnipeg Art Gallery.

Economic Activity

Two patterns of activity have dominated Manitoba's economy since the end of World War II: the rapid growth

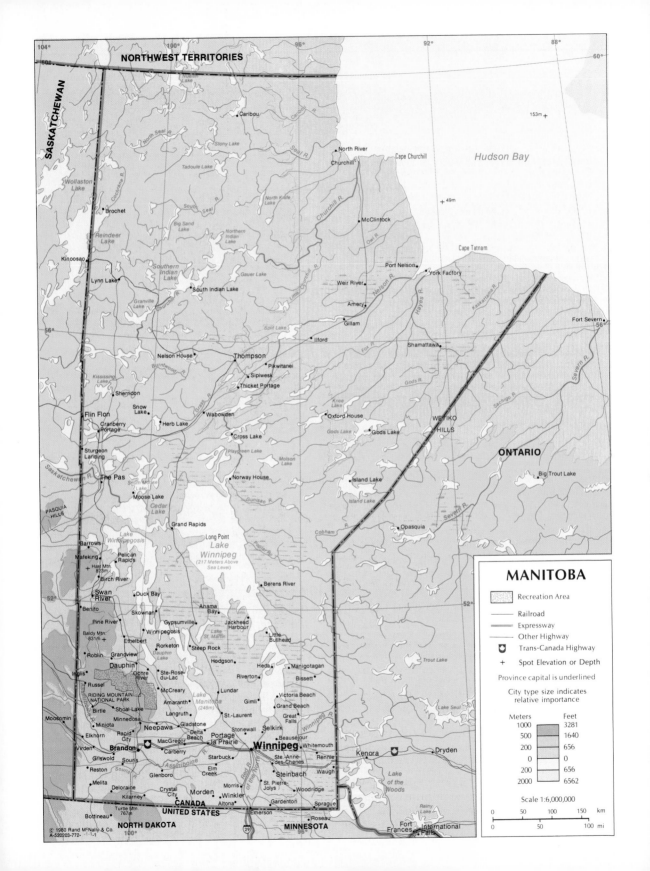

Churchill, at the Churchill River's mouth on Hudson Bay, is an important railroad terminus and a major grain shipping port even though its harbor is ice-free only 14 weeks a year. The site was originally settled as a trading post of the Hudson's Bay Company.

of manufacturing and the provincial government's increasing participation in the economy.

Manufacturing and Mining. Nickel, gold, zinc, and copper are Manitoba's most important minerals. With the exception of pulp and paper manufacturing, centered at The Pas, and the mining-smelting-refining complexes at Flin Flon and Thompson, Manitoba's industries are concentrated in the Winnipeg area. Meat packing, flour milling, petroleum refining, and the manufacture of transportation equipment, clothing, chemicals, iron and steel products, and electrical goods are of significance.

Agriculture and Forestry. Wheat, oats, barley, vegetables, sugar beets, and sunflowers are Manitoba's most important crops. Cattle raising and dairying, concentrated around Winnipeg, are of great importance. Lumbering is concentrated in the north, and about half of the timber is processed into paper and paperboard.

Fishing. Freshwater fishing is a major industry. Much of the total catch comes from Lakes Winnipeg, Manitoba, and Winnipegosis. Major types of fish caught are pickerel, whitefish, and pike.

Tourism. Manitoba's lakes are its biggest tourist lure. Visitors are attracted by the canoeing and sport-fishing opportunities. Riding Mountain National Park receives many summer visitors.

Energy. Manitoba is self-sufficient in energy, produced chiefly at government-owned hydroelectric plants. Natural gas from Alberta is used for commercial and industrial heating.

Transportation. All of Canada's rail lines and the TRANS-CANADA HIGHWAY converge at Winnipeg. Railway links to the United States and water routes to the port of Churchill make Winnipeg an international city.

Government

Manitoba has a parliamentary form of government in which the leader of the majority party in the legislature serves as premier. The province has a unicameral Legislative Assembly of 57 members. The formal head of the provincial government is the lieutenant governor. The two major political parties are the New Democratic party (NDP) and the Progressive Conservative party (PCP).

History

Eskimo near Hudson Bay and the Blackfoot, Ojibwa, and Assiniboin Indians in the south were the first inhabitants of Manitoba. In 1612, Sir Thomas Button explored the territory. In the 1670s the HUDSON'S BAY COMPANY began to establish fur-trading settlements on the shore of Hudson Bay. French traders were also active until the Treaty of Paris (1763) ending the French and Indian War left Britain in control of Canada. The first agricultural settlement was begun in the Red River Valley in 1812 by the earl of SELKIRK. This RED RIVER SETTLEMENT was opposed by the NORTH WEST COMPANY, and violent hostilities occurred until the merger (1821) of the North West Company with the Hudson's Bay Company. By 1836 the Manitoba area came firmly under the control of the Hudson's Bay Company.

After the creation (1867) of the Dominion of Canada, the confederation government bought the lands of the Hudson's Bay Company. Fearing loss of their lands, the métis and Indians of the Red River area rebelled in 1869 under the leadership of Louis RIEL. The Red River Rebellion soon collapsed, however, and in 1870, Manitoba became the first province created from the former domains of the Hudson's Bay Company. Settlement accelerated in the 1880s after the coming of the railroads. The province's economic growth after World War II resulted from increased urbanization and industrialization.

Manitoulin Islands [man-uh-too'-lin]   The Manitoulin Islands are a group of islands in northern Lake Huron. The largest of the group, Manitoulin, covering 2,766 km^2 (1,068 mi^2), is the largest island located in a freshwater lake in the world. Drummond Island is part of Michigan; the other islands are part of Ontario. Tourism, fishing, and lumbering are the economic mainstays.

Manley (family)   Two generations of the Manley family have provided political leadership in Jamaica. Of black and Irish descent, **Norman Washington Manley**, b. July 4, 1893, d. Sept. 2, 1969, founded (1938) the People's National party, based on principles of moderate socialism. He served as chief minister of Jamaica (1955–59) and prime minister (1959–62), but when the country became independent in 1962 the premier was Sir Alexander BUSTAMANTE of the Labor party.

In 1972 the People's National party returned to power under the leadership of **Michael Norman Manley**, b. Dec. 10, 1924. He adhered to his father's socialist principles. Economic problems and political unrest and violence contributed to his 1980 election defeat, but he won reelection in 1989.

Mann, Heinrich   The German novelist, dramatist, and political essayist Heinrich Mann, b. Mar. 27, 1871, d. Mar. 12, 1950, was the elder brother of Thomas Mann. His animus against German society first appeared in *Im Schlaraffenland* (1900; trans. as *In the Land of Cockaigne*, 1925). *Professor Unrat* (1905; trans. as *The Blue Angel*, 1932), a satire on education and bourgeois society, reached a wide audience through a film version (1930). Mann's finest novel is perhaps *Der Untertan* (1918; trans. as *The Patrioteer*, 1921), in which King William II (1888–1918) is parodied and satirized in the decadent, amoral Diederich Hässling. Most of Mann's dramas and essays, including his study (1915) of the French novelist Émile Zola, were completed between 1911 and 1932. Deprived of his German citizenship by the Nazis in 1933, Mann took refuge in France, but in 1940 he settled in the United States. In his later writing, which includes the novels of French history *Young Henry of Navarre* (1935; Eng. trans., 1937) and *Henry, King of France* (1938; Eng. trans., 1938), his acerbic political views became more skeptical.

Mann, Horace   Horace Mann, b. Franklin, Mass., May 4, 1796, d. Aug. 2, 1859, was an influential American educator and public official. A graduate (1819) of Brown University, he was admitted to the bar in 1823 and served in the Massachusetts House of Representatives (1827–33) and the State Senate (1834–37). He was active in codifying the state laws, in establishing the first public hospital for the insane, and in forming the first state board of education in the country. As the first secretary of this board (from 1837), he fought for free public schools against those who opposed tax-supported education. He protected schools from sectarianism, sponsored a compulsory education bill, thus striking a blow at child labor, and established public high schools over the opposition of private schools. He fought for the establishment of a state normal school (1839) to train teachers and for the acceptance of women teachers and advocated the abolition of corporal punishment in the schools.

Mann played a major role in informing citizens about education. He established the *Common-School Journal*, and his 12 annual reports (1837–48) were milestones in American education. He argued that an educated citizenry was essential for a democracy.

Mann was elected to the first of two terms in the U.S. House of Representatives in 1848 as an antislavery Whig. In 1852, he became the first president of Antioch College in Yellow Springs, Ohio.

Mann, Thomas   Thomas Mann, the foremost German novelist of the 20th century, was born of a patrician family in the north German city of Lübeck on June 6, 1875. The setting of his youth was one of gradual decline, especially after the death of his father in 1891. His mother, who was of Brazilian origin, then moved to Munich, where Mann worked briefly in an insurance agency, attended lectures at the University of Munich, and became a contributor to *Simplicissimus,* a satirical literary journal, which he subsequently edited.

Mann's first collection of short stories, *Little Herr Friedemann* (1898; Eng. trans., 1972), won acclaim; his autobiographical first novel about the decline of a patrician family, *Buddenbrooks* (1901; Eng. trans., 1924), established his European reputation. *Tristan* (1903), a collection of novellas that includes "Tonio Kröger" (1903; Eng. trans. in *Stories of Three Decades*, 1936), portrays the artist as an exile from society. Mann's marriage (1905) to Katja Pringsheim, daughter of a wealthy Jewish family, fulfilled his ambition to become a father (he and Katja had six children) and also secured his financial independence. Mann satirized his engagement in *The Blood of the Walsungs* (1906; Eng. trans., 1921) and celebrated his marriage, with gentle irony, as the union of a German prince and an American heiress in *Royal Highness* (1909; Eng. trans., 1916).

Mann lived in or near Munich until 1933, taking up his country's cause during World War I and arguing against his own doubts and the beliefs of his pacifist, democratic brother, Heinrich, in *Betrachtungen eines Unpolitischen* (Reflections of a Non-Political Man, 1918). During the Weimar Republic, however, Mann became a spokesperson for liberal democracy and an antagonist of fascism—a role he continued to play during the early years of Nazi government.

In 1933 he emigrated to Switzerland, where he edited a periodical, *Mass und Wert* (Measure and Values, 1937–39), and then to the United States, where he lived first in Princeton, N.J. (1938–40), and subsequently at Pacific Palisades, Calif. (1941–52), acquiring U.S. citizenship in 1944. The tetralogy *Joseph and his Brothers* (1933–42; Eng. trans., 1934–44) and *Lotte in Weimar* (1939; trans. as *The Beloved Returns,* 1940) reflect Mann's attempt to rid himself of cultural pessimism. *Doktor Faustus* (1947; Eng. trans., 1948), a symbolic novel concerning the German catastrophe and defeat, reverts to a pessimistic view of Western civilization, as does the serenely cynical *Confessions of Felix Krull, Confidence Man* (1954; Eng. trans., 1955), a picaresque account of a crook. After the

Thomas Mann, a leading German writer of the early 20th century, was awarded the Nobel Prize for literature in 1929 for such works as the novella Death in Venice *(1912) and his masterpiece,* The Magic Mountain *(1924).*

war and during the McCarthy era Mann became increasingly dissatisfied with the United States and frequently returned to Europe. In 1952 he settled in Switzerland and died near Zurich on Aug. 12, 1955. He received many honors, including the Nobel Prize for literature in 1929.

Mann was deeply aware of the Western cultural tradition, whose values he both shared and questioned. Like Tonio Kröger, the artist-hero of the novella of that title, Mann believed that spiritual gifts make the artist an exile from life while longing to share its passions. The spirit thrives as the artist's vitality declines. In *Death in Venice* the artist's longing for life is depicted as a diseased and fatal passion, but Tonio Kröger is saved from sterile isolation by his love for the "blond and blue-eyed," the normal, healthy, average humans who, in all their banality, relish the passions of life. The artist's intermediary position between animal nature and spiritual aspiration make the artist the true representative of a universal human dilemma.

In *The Magic Mountain* (1924; Eng. trans., 1927) Mann alludes to the decline of a diseased Western civilization through an account of the inmates of a Swiss sanatorium. Hans Castorp, the protagonist, dreams of a synthesis between the forces of darkness and light. It is typical of Mann's ironic detachment, however, that at the conclusion of the novel he carries his vision into the trench warfare of 1914.

A more positive notion of a humanist synthesis inspired *Joseph and His Brothers* and *The Beloved Returns,* which deal with men blessed by both spirituality and physical vitality. In *Doktor Faustus,* however, Mann brought his exploration of the artist's relation to society to a tragic conclusion. The composer Adrian Leverkühn makes a pact with the devil to achieve an artistic breakthrough. His nihilistic bargain and its consequences are a symbolic parallel to Germany's pact with a political devil, Hitler, who gave the nation vitality but led it to destruction. Mann's life-long theme, as he observed in the essay "On Myself" (1940), is the breakdown of civilization—the invasion of the carefully cultivated and disciplined defenses of Western culture by the elemental power of Dionysian urges.

Mann Act   The Mann Act (the White Slave Traffic Act), authored by Illinois Republican Representative James Mann and passed by the U.S. Congress in 1910, prohibits the transportation, coercion, or enticement of females across state lines for the purpose of prostitution or other immoral activities. Those convicted may be fined $5,000 or imprisoned for up to 5 years, or both; the punishment may be doubled if the victim is a minor.

manna   In the Bible manna, described as "a thing white, powdery, as fine as hoarfrost," was the natural food provided by God to the Israelites as they fled Egypt for the Promised Land (Exod. 16). Manna fell from the sky every day except the Sabbath, for which an extra portion was gathered the previous day. The biblical accounts portray this as a miraculous deliverance from hunger, but this desert phenomenon can still be observed on a small scale in the Near East, where certain insects secrete a sticky honeydew. In Christian symbolism, manna is held to prefigure the Eucharist, on the basis of John 6:31–40.

Mannerheim, Carl Gustaf Emil [mahn'-ur-hym, kahrl gus'-tahv ay'-mil]   One of the great soldiers of the 20th century, the Finnish baron Carl Gustaf Emil von Mannerheim, b. June 4, 1867, d. Jan. 27, 1951, defended his country against the Soviet Union in World War II and then served as Finland's president. A wealthy member of the Swedish ethnic minority in the Russian province of Finland, he entered the Russian army in 1889 and was commander of the tsar's personal army when World War I began. When Finland declared its independence in 1917, Mannerheim returned home, organized the White (anti-Bolshevik) army, and with German help won the short, bloody civil war of 1918. Regent of Finland for six months, he lost the election for president in 1919 and retired from politics. In 1931 he was put in charge of Finnish defense. He built the famous Mannerheim Line, an unsuccessful attempt to block a Soviet invasion of Finland through the Karelian Isthmus. He led Finnish forces, which were greatly outnumbered, in a brilliant battle against the USSR in the RUSSO-FINNISH WAR of 1939–40. During World War II he also led Finland (in alliance with Germany) in a second war (1941–44) against the Soviets but was again defeated. Appointed marshal of Finland in 1942, he served as president from 1944 to 1946.

Mannerism   The art of the High Renaissance in Rome and Florence tended to idealize nature, especially the human figure. Michelangelo and Raphael were regarded by their contemporaries as exponents of the perfect *maniera,* or "style." Later artists, emulating their achievements, were inclined to pursue virtuosity not as means of representing nature but as an end in itself. Mannerism, the deliberate cultivation of *maniera,* loosely defines a period (c.1520–c.1570) between the Renais-

(Right) *The Ma-donna with the Long Neck (1534) by Parmigianino reflects the re-markable elonga-tion, arbitrary scale, and fluid movement charac-teristic of Manner-ism. (Uffizi, Florence.)*

(Below) *Bronzino's Allegory, or Venus, Cupid, Folly, and Time (c.1546), is representative of Mannerism. (National Gallery, London.)*

VASARI named *maniera* as the distinguishing mark of the arts of his own time. By the 17th century the word had become pejorative and, until quite recently, Mannerism was regarded as a style that, while overvaluing technical skill and bizarre effects, had departed from the standards of classical art. The grace of this style and its tendency to abstract from nature, however, frequently produced works of extraordinary beauty. PARMIGIANINO's *Madonna with the Long Neck* (1534; Uffizi, Florence) and ROSSO FIORENTI-NO's *Dead Christ with Angels* (c.1535; Museum of Fine Arts, Boston) are paintings in which mastery of style over-comes objections to distortion of anatomy and color.

Mannerism originated in Rome but quickly spread, in the work of GIULIO ROMANO and Perino de Vaga, through-out Italy. Rosso Fiorentino, who left Rome in 1530 to work at the Château de Fontainebleau (see FONTAINE-BLEAU, SCHOOL OF), carried the style to France, and because works by all these artists were disseminated through en-gravings, Mannerism had become a European phenome-non by 1540. It remained a predominantly Italian style, but Jean GOUJON evolved a peculiarly French Mannerism, and in northern Europe Mannerism was reconciled to late Gothic art by Albrecht ALTDORFER. The strengths, and the weaknesses, of Mannerism as a painting style are perhaps most thoroughly exemplified by the portraits of BRONZINO or by his brilliantly erotic *Allegory* (c.1546; National Gal-lery, London)—works in which technique has overcome subject. It matters not so much what is painted, but how well it is done.

Mannerist sculpture reached a peak of virtuosity in the bronze figures of Giovanni da BOLOGNA, who resolved hu-man movement into graceful, three-dimensional patterns. In the decorative arts, Benvenuto CELLINI and the mem-bers of the Jamnitzer family created household articles encrusted with fantastic forms that verge on the grotesque.

A similar love of decoration divorced from function, of sheer delight in fertility of invention, characterizes the Italian architecture of the mid-16th century. Giorgio Vasari and Bartolommeo AMMANATI, working in Florence in the 1550s and '60s on the Uffizi and Pitti palaces, ex-tended a development that can be discerned in Michel-angelo's Laurentian Library (1524; Florence), where elements of classical architecture are used for ornamen-tation, without regard to their original purpose.

Mannheim [mahn'-hym] Mannheim is an industrial city and port in the German state of Baden-Württemberg, on the Rhine River at its confluence with the Neckar Riv-er. Mannheim's population is 294,600 (1987 est.). Its principal products are iron and steel, chemicals, automo-biles, electrical equipment, and tobacco products. The University of Mannheim (1907) is there, as are many 18th-century baroque buildings.

By the 8th century a village existed there. In 1606, Mannheim was established as a market center and forti-fied site by Elector Palatine Frederick IV. The city was destroyed in 1622, during the Thirty Years' War, and again in 1689, when the French devastated the Palati-nate. In 1720, Mannheim became the residence of the

sance and the baroque. It was not, however, an artistic movement with definable principles.

In 14th-century Italy *maniera*—implying sophistica-tion, grace, and self-assurance—was a desirable attribute of the cultivated person. By the mid-15th century the term was used in the visual arts, and in 1550, Giorgio electors Palatine, who made the city a leading 18th-century center, notable especially for the Mannheim school of music. Mannheim became part of Baden in 1802. During World War II it suffered heavy damage.

Manning, Henry Edward   The English cardinal Henry Edward Manning, b. July 15, 1808, d. Jan. 14, 1892, greatly strengthened the Roman Catholic church in Britain. He was ordained (1833) in the Anglican ministry but moved from a Low Church position to become prominent in the OXFORD MOVEMENT. Convinced that royalty should not head the Church of England, he converted (1851) to Roman Catholicism and was ordained a priest.

Manning was named a cardinal in 1875. He devoted himself to Catholic education, prison reform, and improving the conditions of the poor through the society of Oblates of St. Charles, which he had established in 1857. Manning is remembered for his support of the strikers in the London dock strike of 1889, which he settled.

Manolete   [mah-noh-lay'-tay]   Manolete (Manuel Laureano Rodriguez Sánchez), b. July 5, 1917, d. Aug. 28, 1947, was a Spanish bullfighter who was considered one of the greatest classicists to fight in the ring. His style was marked by extreme economy of movement and complete composure. In his brief but much-publicized career, Manolete killed more than 1,000 bulls. At the age of 30 he was fatally gored. After his death, which had the impact of a national tragedy, he was awarded La Cruz de la Beneficencia, Spain's highest civilian decoration.

manorialism   [muh-nohr'-ee-ul-izm]   Manorialism, also known as seignorialism, was the economic, social, and administrative system that prevailed in Europe in the MIDDLE AGES. Manorialism had its origins in the 4th century, reached its zenith in the 11th and 12th centuries, and then began a long decline that ended only in modern times. Manorialism was essentially a system whereby the land, or manor, was owned by the lord and was parceled out to individual peasants who farmed it. In return, payments in the form of money, crops, and services were made to the lord.

Manorialism often existed alongside FEUDALISM but should not be confused with it. Feudalism was a political and legal structure regulating the relations among the various levels of the nobility.

This fortified manor house from the reign (1154–89) of Henry II of England retains some features of a castle, including a moat and enclosing wall. The lord of the manor lived in the central two-story house; the ground-floor storage room was called the undercroft. Dairy cattle and beehives were kept in the courtyard, or bailey. The kitchen and blacksmith's forge are shown along the near wall.

Development. The origins of manorialism can be traced to the period of economic decline that characterized the late Roman Empire. Imperial laws had bound some farmers to the soil. By about the 4th century, however, the centralized authority of Rome and its great commercial empire had become largely extinct. All over Europe the economy had reverted primarily to subsistence farming. The chaotic political and economic conditions of this period (sometimes called the Dark Ages) led to the subjection of the weak by the strong. Small farmers found themselves increasingly forced to seek the protection of more powerful neighbors. In return for this protection, they gave up certain rights and a portion of their income. As a result, the farmers became more firmly tied to the land with the evolution of a formalized manorial system of landlord and tenant, of lord and peasant.

The Structure of Manorialism. In the classic manor, the usable land was divided into the demesne, which was the land retained by the lord for his own use; the arable, which was land parceled out to the peasants, or tenants, whose right to the land was known as tenure; and the meadow lands, which were used for grazing livestock and were available to all the tenants.

Tenants' rights to the arable land were generally heritable as were the complicated systems of payments to the lord. In addition to rent in crops and money, each tenant was required to donate a specific number of days of labor each year to the lord for such public-service tasks as building roads, bridges, and dams. The tenants were also required to give military service in times of need. In addition to providing the land, the lord was expected to provide military protection and economic security in the form of credit and foodstuffs during years of crop failure. The lord was the dispenser of justice in the form of a local, or manorial, court.

The legal position of the peasants differed in time and place. Some were free; others were serfs, or villeins, who were actually bound to the land. The status of the peasant, whether free or serf, was bleak. Ideally, the manor was a complete and closed economic system with benefits accruing to both landlord and tenant. In practice, however, most of the wealth flowed in the direction of the landlord.

Decline of the Manor. Various factors led to the eventual decline of manorialism. One was the severe problem of overpopulation that gradually worsened the condition of the peasantry and created an atmosphere of social unrest. At the same time, more and more economic and political power was being concentrated in the crown instead of in the hands of local lords. The rise of commerce and industry brought new power and prosperity to the cities, and peasants increasingly left the land for these new urban areas. At the same time, personal obligations were more and more frequently converted into financial ones. Many peasants were freed from their bondage to the lord; others purchased their freedom; some simply escaped.

By the 14th and 15th centuries the great wars of the Middle Ages, such as the Hundred Years' War, and plagues such as the Black Death (see BUBONIC PLAGUE)

had depleted the population of the countryside, resulting in a rural labor shortage and thereby strengthening the peasants' position once more. In addition, ENCLOSURES—whereby former meadowlands and arable lands farmed by tenants were fenced, in particular for sheep raising—greatly accelerated the breakdown of the manors, especially in Britain.

By the end of the 16th century the effective end of the manorial system in Western Europe had been reached. Vestiges lingered into the modern era, however. In the Austrian Empire, the serfs were not freed until 1781, and in France the remaining pockets of manorialism were swept away by the French Revolution. Serfs were not emancipated until 1861 in Russia, where the last elements of the manorial system remained until the Revolutions of 1917.

___

Mansa Musa, Emperor of Mali [mahn'-sah moo'-sah]   Mansa Musa, d. 1337, ruled the ancient West African empire of Mali from 1312 to 1337 and won fame in North Africa and Europe as the monarch who controlled the world's richest gold mines. This reputation was enhanced when, around 1324–25, he undertook the pilgrimage to Mecca and spent gold lavishly during a sojourn in Cairo. He also established cordial relations with Muslim rulers in North Africa and became noted for his efforts to spread Islam among his subjects. Mansa Musa made TIMBUKTU a great center of commerce and learning.

___

Mansart, François [mahn-sahr', frahn-swah']   One of the most brilliant architects of his generation, François Mansart, b. Jan. 23, 1598, d. Sept. 23, 1666, played a leading role in shaping the French baroque style. Although he probably never visited Italy, he understood the Italian models instinctively and adapted them freely in his designs.

About 1623, Mansart built the Château de Berny. In Paris he built the Church of Sainte Marie de la Visitation (1632–33), combining elements of Renaissance and Mannerist detail in its ornamentation. Mansart's Hôtel de la Vrillière (1635), with its three wings enclosing a walled courtyard, became the prototype of the Parisian townhouse. Mansart also gave his name to the "mansard roof," a familiar feature of 19th-century French and American urban architecture.

___

Mansfeld, Ernst, Graf von   Ernst, graf von Mansfeld, b. 1580, d. Nov. 29, 1626, was a Roman Catholic general of mercenary troops fighting for the Protestants in the THIRTY YEARS' WAR (1618–48). From 1618 he served the rebellious Bohemians and Frederick V, elector Palatine, but his chief aim was to win a principality for himself. Mansfeld carried the war into the Palatinate, Alsace, and the Netherlands, receiving Dutch money and living on plunder. In 1626 he was defeated by the imperial general Albrecht von WALLENSTEIN and was chased to Hungary, where his army disintegrated.

Mansfield, Katherine Katherine Mansfield, the pen name of Kathleen Mansfield Beauchamp, b. Wellington, New Zealand, Oct. 14, 1888, d. Jan. 9, 1923, best known for stories in which character is revealed through a decisive moment. Educated in New Zealand and London, she left New Zealand in 1907 to establish herself in London as a writer. Her unhappy marriage in 1909 was followed by an equally unsuccessful affair and a miscarriage. Her wealthy parents then sent her to Bavaria to convalesce. These experiences produced materials for her first collection of short stories, *In a German Pension* (1911).

After writing stories and reviews under the initials KM for a number of journals, Mansfield published the collections *Prelude* (1918), *Je ne parle pas français* (1918), and *Bliss and Other Stories* (1920). Her fame was enhanced by such later volumes as *The Garden Party* (1922) and *The Dove's Nest* (1923). Following her death from consumption at age 34, her husband, John Middleton Murry, published posthumous editions of her journal (1927) and her letters (1928).

The New Zealand-born author Katherine Mansfield greatly influenced the 20th-century short story. She is shown here in a portrait by Anne Estelle Rice. (National Art Gallery, Wellington, New Zealand.)

Mansfield, Mike Michael Joseph Mansfield, b. New York City, Mar. 16, 1903, was a U.S. senator from Montana (1953–77) and majority (Democratic) leader of the Senate (1961–77). He then was the longest-serving (1977–88), and highly popular, ambassador to Japan. Before entering the Senate he worked (1922–31) as a copper miner, taught (1933–42) history at the University of Montana, and served (1943–53) in the U.S. House of Representatives.

Manship, Paul Distinctive style and superb technique made the classically inspired sculpture of Paul Manship, b. Saint Paul, Minn., Dec. 24, 1885, d. Jan. 31, 1966, a dominant influence on American sculptors during the first three decades of the 20th century. Drawing from various elements of tradition—including Greek, Roman, and Renaissance sculpture—Manship developed his own style, which combined a naturalness in the sub-

Paul Manship's Actaeon *(1924) reflects the sculptor's frequent choice of mythological subjects. (Brookgreen Gardens, Georgetown, S.C.)*

ject's pose with stylized drapery and anatomical detail. As his many casts of birds and animals attest, Manship was a close observer of nature, yet he was always guided by the classic ideal of formalized perfection. Generally working in either bronze or marble, Manship produced an enormous range of works, including public monuments, medals, and interpretations of mythological themes.

manslaughter Manslaughter, in criminal law, is the unlawful killing of a human being, either intentionally or unintentionally but without MALICE. Although U.S. state laws differ in their classification of types and degrees of manslaughter, they generally distinguish between voluntary and involuntary manslaughter. Voluntary manslaughter is an intentional homicide stemming from a provocation that would tend to arouse a spontaneous intensity of feelings in a reasonable person and cause the person to act quickly—in the heat of passion—without thinking of the consequences. Involuntary manslaughter is an unintentional homicide occurring during unlawful activity—such as reckless driving—that does not constitute a felony, or a death caused by gross NEGLIGENCE.

Manson, Charles The notorious mass killer Charles Manson, b. Cincinnati, Ohio, Nov. 12, 1934, was convicted of the murders of actress Sharon Tate and six of her friends near Bel Air, Calif. The bloody rampage on the night of Aug. 9, 1969, was the culmination of Manson's cult philosophy based on the worship of both God and the devil. He exerted total control over the so-called Manson family, mostly women, through repetitious preaching, drugs, and fear. His control was such that the Tate murders were committed at his direction but without his presence. After a widely publicized trial in Los Angeles, Manson was sentenced (Apr. 9, 1971) to death, but the sentence was later reduced to life imprisonment in keeping with the change in California law eliminating the death penalty.

The Italian early Renaissance painter Andrea Mantegna's mastery of the new science of perspective is evident in The Agony in the Garden *(c.1460–70), a complex composition incorporating figural groupings and elaborate architecture in a detailed landscape setting. (National Gallery, London.)*

Mantegna, Andrea [mahn-ten'-yah, ahn-dray'-ah]

Andrea Mantegna, 1431–1506, was one of the greatest artists of the early Renaissance period in northern Italy. His tempera paintings, frescoes, and engravings, which often depict scenes of the ancient world elaborately reconstructed from classical ruins, employed ingenious settings seen from daring points of view. These experiments in perspective influenced almost every contemporary artist in northern Italy.

In the young artist's first major project, the decoration (1449–55) of parts of the Ovetari Chapel in Padua's Eremitani Church, he made use of the new science of linear perspective. On the lower register of one wall, Mantegna illustrated the *Martyrdom of St. James* (destroyed 1944) in a perspective calculated on the basis of the spectator's eye level, which would be slightly below the bottom of the frame. Accordingly, figures and buildings loom above the ground line and seem to recede up and away from the observer. Throughout his artistic career, Mantegna displayed great interest in unorthodox or innovative forms of pictorial organization. His altarpiece (1456–59) for the church of San Zeno in Verona contains one of the first Italian versions of the enthroned Madonna format, in which patron saints flank the enthroned Madonna and child.

From 1459 until the end of his life, Mantegna worked for the ruling Gonzaga family in Mantua. At the Gonzaga's ducal palace, he decorated the *Camera degli Sposi* (completed 1474) with frescoes that display another bold experiment in perspective illusion. The Gonzaga family and their court are shown sitting or standing about the walls of the room as though they occupy a high loggia that logically extends the space of the chamber. On the ceiling Mantegna painted a circular "opening" to a "sky" surrounded by a balustrade, over which laughing women peer down and along which nude boys play. This type of ceiling illusion anticipated the fashion for such decorations in Italy. His nine large canvases, entitled the *Triumph of Caesar* (1485–92; Hampton Court Palace, London), are an impressive if pedantic series that once formed a frieze.

mantis   see PRAYING MANTIS

mantisfly   Mantisflies (family Mantispidae, order Neuroptera) resemble the praying mantis in having a lengthened prothorax and the front legs fitted for grasping prey. They are generally less than 25 mm (1 in) long, with four membranous wings. The adults eat other insects; the larvae are parasites of spiders.

mantle   see EARTH, STRUCTURE AND COMPOSITION OF

Mantle, Mickey

Mickey Charles Mantle, b. Spavinaw, Okla., Oct. 20, 1931, started his professional baseball career in the minor leagues in 1949 as a shortstop but became an outfielder on joining the New York Yan-

Mickey Mantle, a switch-hitting outfielder who played for the New York Yankees, won the American League's Most Valuable Player award 3 times (1956, 1957, 1962) and hit 536 home runs during his career. Mantle played for 18 seasons in the major leagues and was inducted into baseball's Hall of Fame in 1974.

kees in 1951. When Joe DiMaggio retired, Mantle replaced him in center field. Although frequently sidelined by injuries, the fleet, switch-hitting slugger amassed a total of 536 home runs. In 1956, Mantle won baseball's Triple Crown (with a .353 batting average, 52 home runs, and 130 runs batted in). That year, as well as in 1957 and 1962, he was the American League's Most Valuable Player. His 18 home runs in World Series play remains a record.

Mantle retired on Mar. 1, 1969, just as spring training was beginning. His uniform number, 7, was retired, as had been those of Babe Ruth, Lou Gehrig, and Joe DiMaggio. In 1974, Mantle was inducted into the Baseball Hall of Fame.

mantra   In Hinduism and Buddhism a mantra is a mystical syllable or phrase used in ritual and meditation. Mantras are believed to have a deep affinity with particular deities or spiritual forces that they represent; by chanting them, a devotee is believed able to establish a link with such forces.

Mantua   Mantua (Italian: Mantova) is the capital of Mantua province in the Lombardy region of northern Italy. Its population is 60,932 (1981). Of Etruscan origin, Mantua was an independent city from the 12th to the 18th century. It became a duchy in 1530 and was ruled by the GONZAGA family from 1328 to 1707. Its rich architectural heritage includes the basilica of Sant'Andrea, originally designed by Leon Battista Alberti (1470), the cathedral, and the ducal palace of the Gonzagas. Mantua is a center for processing farm products.

Manu [muh'-noo]   In Hindu mythology Manu is the progenitor of the human race. He is thus the lord and guardian

of the living, and his name is attached to the most important codification of Hindu law, the *Manava-dharma-sastra* (Laws of Manu). Compiled by Brahmanic legalists sometime between 200 BC and AD 200, this code is the earliest of the Vedic texts (see VEDAS) called the dharma-sutras, manuals on DHARMA, or duty. It defines the specific duties and responsibilities of the individual in terms of varna, or class—Brahman, Kshatriya, Vaisya, or Sudra (see CASTE)—and asrama, or state of life, classifications that remain fundamental to HINDUISM to the present day.

Manuel I Comnenus, Byzantine Emperor

Manuel I, b. *c.*1120, d. Sept. 24, 1180, succeeded his father, JOHN II COMNENUS, as ruler of the BYZANTINE EMPIRE in 1143. Throughout his reign Manuel sought to revive the Roman Empire. He led armies against the Turks, Serbs, Hungarians, and Armenians and against the principality of Antioch, and he sent expeditions to combat the Normans of Italy and the Egyptians. Hoping to receive the crown of the Holy Roman Empire, Manuel negotiated unsuccessfully with Pope ALEXANDER III for reunification of the Orthodox and Catholic churches. His forces were crushed by the Turks in 1176.

Manuel II Palaeologus, Byzantine Emperor

[pay-lee-oh-loh'-guhs]   Manuel II Palaeologus, b. June 27, 1350, d. June 21, 1425, succeeded his father John V Palaeologus on the throne of a diminished, impoverished BYZANTINE EMPIRE, which Manuel ruled from 1391. With the empire threatened by Ottoman Turks, Manuel visited (1399–1403) Western Europe—including Paris and London—in a largely futile appeal for military and financial aid. The defeat (1402) of the Turks at Ankara by TIMUR relieved the pressure, but the Turks besieged Constantinople again in 1422.

Manuel I, King of Portugal   (Manuel the Fortunate)

Manuel I, the Fortunate, b. May 31, 1469, d. Dec. 13, 1521, ruled Portugal during the period of its greatest glory and prosperity. He succeeded his cousin and brother-in-law, JOHN II, in 1495. Like John, Manuel encouraged overseas explorations; during Manuel's reign, Vasco da GAMA reached (1498) India, opening the East to Portuguese commerce, and Pedro CABRAL discovered (1500) Brazil.

Manuel, who restored to the BRAGANÇA family the estates that John had confiscated, attracted numerous aristocrats to his brilliant court; he subsidized the arts and embellished Lisbon with many buildings in the Manueline style. He also strengthened crown control over local administration.

Manuel's ambition to unite the thrones of Portugal and Spain led him to marry, in succession, three Spanish princesses. At the urging of his Spanish allies, Manuel expelled (1496) all unconverted Jews and Muslims from Portugal. Those who stayed became nominal Christians with the understanding that their faith would not be questioned. Many Jews were massacred in Lisbon in 1506, but the king punished those responsible. Manuel was succeeded by his son, JOHN III.

Manuelito Manuelito, c.1818–1893, a famous NA-VAJO Indian war leader, gained fame as a young warrior in the 1820s, when the Navajo were raiding white and Pueblo Indian towns in New Mexico. The raids continued after the United States took possession (1848) of New Mexico. In 1860, Manuelito joined forces with other Navajo leaders for an attack on the white Americans, but the Indians were routed by heavy losses at Fort Defiance. In 1868, Manuelito and other Navajo leaders signed a treaty with the United States that guaranteed the Navajo reservation in their homeland. Manuelito headed a native police force in 1872.

manufacturing, history of Manufacturing is the process by which raw materials or components are fabricated and assembled into finished products. Manufacturing has evolved from a relatively simple system of hand-tool production carried on within a household or workshop by individual workers into the modern FACTORY SYSTEM with its large, highly mechanized labor force. This article deals primarily with manufacturing in the United States, which in its early years in many respects recapitulates the longer span of development in Europe and then parallels Europe throughout the 19th and 20th centuries.

Colonial Manufacturing

Throughout the colonial period goods produced for local consumption were largely of household or workshop manufacture. Particularly in rural areas, the spinning and weaving of woolens were common in most households, as was the making of homespun garments and even shoes. Consumer demands in the colonial towns were usually supplied by imports or by skilled craftsmen working in small shops, who produced a variety of items, such as cloth, tailored suits, soap, candles, paper, and wine. The only power available to colonial manufacturers, aside from that exerted by men or animals, came from WATER-WHEELS, which were used principally in the production of flour and lumber.

From the Revolution to the Civil War

In 1790, Samuel SLATER, a one-time employee of Richard ARKWRIGHT who had learned the latter's methods for mechanized spinning of cotton in England, successfully built the equipment for a spinning factory in Pawtucket, R.I. Slater's success not only launched the domestic cotton textile industry but also established a pattern for the future growth of manufacturing in the United States. Initial progress was slow, however, because it was difficult to acquire patterns for the first machines for factory production, and labor and capital were scarce.

By the middle of the 19th century most of these problems had been overcome. Faced with a scarcity of accumulated funds, entrepreneurs adopted the CORPORATION as a device for assembling capital. An expanding group of skilled mechanics increased the availability of machinery, and higher wages attracted the workers to operate them. By this period the factory system had been extended to the production of woolens, lumber, flour, shoes, paper, and iron, but was still primarily dependent on water power for energy.

The pressure to economize on the use of labor prompted two technical innovations—continuous-process manufacture and interchangeable-parts production.

Continuous-Process Production. Continuous-process manufacture, in which production is so arranged that materials move smoothly through successive processing stages, was originated by Oliver EVANS, who in 1784 introduced the system in a flour mill he had built in Delaware. In order to reduce to a minimum the amount of labor involved in the milling process, Evans designed a power-driven CONVEYOR system that moved grain from one machine to another and from one floor to another. This process subsequently became a characteristic feature of factory operations.

Interchangeable Parts. At the turn of the 19th century Connecticut arms makers Eli WHITNEY and Simeon North began the experiments that led to interchangeable-parts manufacture, in an attempt to improve the long-established methods of producing firearms. Arms had previously been made with hand tools by individual craftsmen; component parts were not interchangeable, and each weapon had to be individually fitted.

Whitney and North trained employees to specialize in separate weapon parts, and developed tools and power-driven equipment capable of turning out standard, interchangeable components.

By the 1850s improvements had been made in the speed and accuracy of the machines utilized. Many of these improvements came from the expanding machine-tool industry, which by mid-century was prepared to supply standardized machines or to build special equipment for customers.

Although still subordinate to agriculture, manufacturing by 1860 had clearly earned a secure place in the U.S. economy, employing 1.3 million workers, 20 percent of the nation's entire labor force.

1860–1920

During the period between the Civil War and the end of World War I the U.S. economy took on most of its modern characteristics. The change that stands out above all others was the shift from an agricultural economy to an industrial economy, a change that by the 1890s made the United States the world's leading industrial nation.

In large part the change reflected the influence on manufacturing of several improvements in technology. One improvement was the introduction of more efficient and flexible methods of using energy, notably the widespread adoption of the high-pressure STEAM ENGINE and the utilization of electricity (see POWER, GENERATION AND TRANSMISSION OF). These developments not only relieved manufacturers of the necessity of locating at waterpower sites but also made coal the chief FUEL for industrial production. A second factor was an improved process of producing metals, particularly iron and steel (see IRON AND STEEL INDUSTRY), which increased the quality of materials used. A third development was the further growth of the MACHINE TOOL industry that supplied the necessary machines. The final improvement was the large-scale mass-production technology of Henry Ford (see FORD family), who by 1914 had combined interchangeable-parts and continuous-flow manufacture to establish what is popularly known as the ASSEMBLY LINE.

These advances were manifested by the proliferation of mechanized industries, which by World War I were turning out huge quantities of standardized products including hardware, ready-made clothing, clocks, typewriters, and farm machinery.

Between 1860 and 1920 factory employment rose from 1.3 million to just under 10 million, while output, measured in terms of value added to the gross national product, grew from $854 million to $24 billion. By the 1890s the manufacturing sector had already surpassed agriculture as a generator of national income. Basic to this expansion was a huge increase in population and per capita income. No less important in fostering a large common domestic market was the expansion of the railway network that linked consumers and producers. Widespread abuse of the labor force, such as 12- to 14-hour workdays and the exploitation of CHILD LABOR, also marked this phase of industrial development. The result was the rise and proliferation of strong LABOR UNIONS.

1920–1980

Despite fluctuations in employment and production, manufacturing grew impressively following World War I. By 1977 the manufacturing labor force of close to 20 million was more than double that for 1920, and output (measured in constant 1920 dollars) had expanded nearly sixfold.

Both the growth rate and structure of manufacturing were modified and strengthened by the introduction of a number of important innovations, which in some instances led to the creation of new industries and in others to improvements in the productive efficiency of old ones. A growing electric-power industry spawned an impressive array of electrically operated consumer products, including radios, television sets, blankets, dehumidifiers, and home freezers. The INTERNAL-COMBUSTION ENGINE in its various forms—gasoline, gas, and diesel—found increasing application in industry and in land and air transportation. Of prime importance in their industrial impact were developments in the fields of chemistry and chemical engineering. Methods were introduced by which such familiar products as fertilizer and rubber could be produced artificially. Even more innovative was the introduction of technology for the synthetic manufacture of a great variety of entirely new materials (see CHEMICAL INDUSTRY).

Increasing mechanization of labor remained the essential feature of the evolution of manufacturing methods during these years. Beginning in the 1950s the increased use of AUTOMATION—automatic controls over manufacturing processes—had great implications for large-scale

manufacturing. It involved the movement of materials through an entire production sequence under the guidance and control of a computer (see PROCESS CONTROL). An important development in the area of automation in the 1970s and 1980s was the industrial ROBOT, a computer-controlled machine capable of performing repetitive tasks.

By the 1970s, U.S. manufacturing had begun to suffer from one of the factors that had ended British industrial domination nearly a century earlier: a "maturing," or aging, physical plant. The relatively slow pace of modernization in the United States left the nation with outdated plants and machinery compared to, for example, the Japanese and West Germans, who had been forced to rebuild almost completely after World War II. The Japanese, in particular, were quick to seize upon new manufacturing technology; by 1981, for example, they employed fully half of the world's industrial robots and were rapidly overtaking the United States in the new field of microelectronics, a U.S. invention.

Another trend in U.S. manufacturing after World War II was a dramatic shift of resources to the service sectors of the economy, such as trade, transportation, and communications. This had the effect of draining employees and funds away from manufacturing and increased the difficulties of modernizing.

The Late 1980s and Beyond

Beginning in the 1980s, forward-looking U.S. manufacturers began assessing the potential of COMPUTER-AIDED DESIGN AND COMPUTER-AIDED MANUFACTURING (CAD-CAM) to create new factory systems. Originally, computers had been used in factories almost entirely to control the flow of materials. Other automated manufacturing devices, such as robots, were confined to performing repetitive and relatively simple actions such as spot welding.

Today, using advanced technologies that begin with the computer design of product parts, entire assemblies can be computer controlled, a development known as Computer Integrated Manufacturing (CIM). On its simplest level computer design produces parts that are cheaper and easier to assemble. Connected with automated machine tools, however, computers can aid in the manufacture of higher-quality, longer-lived parts that often can be robotically assembled. As machinery is automated, flexibility in manufacturing increases, allowing for a wide variety of products to be made and changeovers to take place within a short time, without the retooling that was once necessary. Smaller manufacturing units prove more efficient than the cavernous factory spaces of the past. The installation of CIM systems is costly, but manufacturers find that they pay for themselves quickly, while labor costs plummet. Although the implications of CIM for the future of the U.S. labor force are unclear, the technique's value as a manufacturing tool is already being proven.

See also: GOVERNMENT REGULATION; INDUSTRIAL REVOLUTION; POLLUTION, ENVIRONMENTAL; TECHNOLOGY, HISTORY OF.

manure   Manure is any bulky organic material, derived from animals or plants, that supplies cropland or garden soil with plant nutrients and that decomposes to form HUMUS. It is often used in combination with FERTILIZER, which contains more highly concentrated plant foods. The most common form of manure, barnyard manure—animal excreta mixed with plant refuse (bedding materials, straw, spoiled feed, and the like)—is a valuable source of nitrogen, phosphorus, and potassium, although the amounts of these components vary according to the type and feed of the animals, the plant materials added, and the method of storage. When mixed with earth, the humus-forming action of manure binds soil particles into small groups with room between them for air and water to circulate, and soil bacteria slowly convert the manure into chemical salts, which are dissolved by water and taken up as food by plant roots. The addition of humus improves the soil's tilth and water-holding capacity.

Other organic wastes that are used as manures include fish scrap, GUANO (seabird droppings), peat, cottonseed meal, seaweed, and COMPOST. Soil can also be conditioned by planting a "green manure" or cover crop—a quick-growing crop such as ryegrass or often leguminous plants, which are plowed under before maturity and which then decay rapidly in the soil. Green manures are used primarily to increase the soil's nitrogen content.

Manutius, Aldus [muh-nue'-shuhs]   An Italian printer, editor, and scholar, Aldus Manutius, b. 1449, d. Feb. 6, 1515 (family name Mannucci or Manuzio), founded the Aldine Press, a pioneering family printing firm (see BOOK). It was the first press to produce printed editions of many of the Greek and Latin classics and the first to use italic type—created for pocket-size books, another significant innovation of the Aldine Press. Aldine works became noted for their anchor and dolphin signature, or colophon, which first appeared in 1502, and their use of original woodcuts.

Manx cat   The Manx cat, from the Isle of Man—which is situated between England and Northern Ireland—is a

The Manx cat has an arched back, double coat, and long, muscular rear legs. Although some have short tails, only the rumpy, or tailless, variety (below) is recognized as a show animal.

tailless, usually double-coated breed of any color. Because its hind legs are longer than its forelegs, the Manx has a sort of hopping, rabbitlike movement and appears to have an arched back. Taillessness does not breed true, and "stumpies," with very short tails, may appear in the same litter with tailless "rumpies." There also is a lethal factor associated with taillessness, and repeated breeding of tailless to tailless results in stillborn kittens.

Manzoni, Alessandro   Alessandro Manzoni, b. Mar. 7, 1785, d. May 22, 1873, is regarded as the father of the modern Italian novel. By 1827 he had completed five *Inni sacri* (Sacred Hymns, 1812–22); two historical plays in verse (1820 and 1822); several poems, including his celebrated ode to Napoleon, *Cinque Maggio* (The Fifth of May, 1821); and his masterpiece, the novel *I promessi sposi* (1827; trans. as *The Betrothed*, 1828). Dissatisfied with its language, however, he spent the next dozen years rewriting it in the Tuscan dialect and overseeing the publication of the definitive edition (1840–42). The book is at once a charming love story of two young silk weavers, Renzo Tramaglino and Lucia Mondella, a brilliantly incisive portrait of life in Spanish-dominated Lombardy in the 17th century and a persuasive dramatization of Catholic dogma.

Mao Zedong (Mao Tse-tung) [mow' zay-dong']   Mao Zedong founded the People's Republic of China in 1949. Along with the founders of the Han and Ming dynasties, he was one of only three peasants who rose to rule all of China in a single lifetime, and he led perhaps the greatest social revolution in human history. He gave theoretical legitimacy to the continuation of class struggle in the socialist and communist stages of development and is regarded, along with Karl MARX and V. I. LENIN, as one of the three great theorists of Marxian communism.

Early Life. Mao was born on Dec. 26, 1893, into a well-to-do peasant family in Hunan province. From 1911, the year that the republican forces of SUN YAT-SEN launched the overthrow of the Qing (or Manchu) dynasty, Mao spent most of 10 years in the provincial capital, where he was exposed to the rapid political changes sweeping the country and served briefly in the republican army. By 1918 he had gone to Beijing, where he worked briefly as a library assistant at Beijing University. It may be partly due to his relative poverty during his student years that he never identified completely with cosmopolitan bourgeois intellectuals. He did establish contact with intellectual radicals who later figured prominently in the Chinese Communist party. In 1919, Mao returned to Hunan, where he engaged in radical political activity while supporting himself as a primary-school principal.

In 1920, Mao married Yang Kaihui, the daughter of one of his teachers. Yang Kaihui was executed by the Chinese nationalists in 1930. In that year Mao married He Zizhen, who accompanied him on the Long March. Mao divorced her (1937), and in 1939 he married JIANG QING.

When the Chinese Communist party (CCP) was organized in Shanghai in 1921, Mao was a founding member and leader of the Hunan branch. At this stage the new party formed a united front with Sun Yat-sen's KUOMINTANG (Guomindang). Mao worked in Shanghai, Hunan, and Guangzhou, concentrating variously on labor organization, party organization, propaganda, and the Peasant Movement Training Institute.

Conflict with the Nationalists. In 1927, CHIANG KAI-SHEK reversed the Kuomintang's policy of cooperation with the Communists. Mao was forced to flee to the mountains of south China, where he established with ZHU DE a rural base defended by a guerrilla army. It was this almost accidental fusion of Communist leadership with a guerrilla force operating in rural areas with peasant support that was to make Mao the leader of the CCP. In 1931 a Chinese soviet was founded in Jiangsu province, with Mao as chairman. A series of extermination campaigns by Chiang Kai-shek's Nationalist government forced the CCP to commence the LONG MARCH in October 1934. At Zunyi in Guizhou, Mao gained effective control over the CCP, ending the era of Russian direction of party leadership. Remnants of the Communist forces reached Shaanxi in October 1935 and established a new headquarters at Yenan.

When the Japanese invasion of 1937 forced the CCP and the Kuomintang once again to form a united front, the Communists gained legitimacy as defenders of the Chinese homeland. Mao rose in stature as a national leader and established himself as a military theorist and important Marxist thinker.

China's Leader. The soundness of Mao's self-reliance and rural guerrilla strategies was proved by the CCP's rapid growth during the Yenan period. The shaky truce between the Communists and the Nationalists broke down at the end of the war, and civil war erupted. By 1949, Chiang's government fled to Taiwan, leaving the People's Republic of China, formed by the Communists in 1949, in control of the Chinese mainland.

When Mao's efforts to open relations with the United States in the late 1940s were rebuffed, he allied himself with the USSR. The Korean War deepened hostility to the United States. During the early 1950s, Mao served as chairman of the CCP, chief of state, and chairman of the military commission. His uniqueness as a leader is evident from his commitment to continued class struggle under socialism, which led him to take a number of unusual initiatives in the late 1950s. In the Hundred Flowers movement of 1956–57 he encouraged intellectuals to make constructive criticism of the party, which revealed deep hostility to CCP leadership. At about the same time, Mao called for the elimination of the last vestiges of rural private property and the formation of people's communes, and for rapid industrial growth through a program known as the GREAT LEAP FORWARD. The suddenness of these moves led to administrative confusion and popular resistance, while adverse weather resulted in severe food shortages. As a consequence, Mao lost his position as chief of state and found his influence over the party severely curtailed.

During the 1960s Mao made a comeback, attacking the party leadership and the new chief of state, LIU SHAOQI, through a Great Proletarian CULTURAL REVOLUTION,

Mao Zedong, one of the original members of the Chinese Communist party, founded the People's Republic of China in 1949. Mao was an influential theorist whose intense nationalism and teachings on revolutionary struggle had a tremendous impact on the communist world.

which peaked from 1966 to 1969 and was largely orchestrated by Mao's wife, Jiang Qing. As events threatened to get out of hand, Mao was obliged to rely increasingly on the military, led by LIN BIAO, who was named as Mao's successor in 1969. By 1971, however, Lin was reported to have died in a plane crash after having plotted to assassinate Mao, who was once more firmly in control. During the Cultural Revolution, Mao's sayings (printed in a little red book) and buttons bearing his image were widely distributed, his word was considered ultimate authority, and his person was the subject of ecstatic adulation, although Mao continued to state his belief in the Leninist notion of collective party leadership.

Toward the end of his life, Mao stated that the world's states were divided into three groups: the underdeveloped nations, the developed nations, and the two superpowers (the United States and the USSR). This analysis underscored China's position as a leader of the Third World and helped to rationalize a rapprochement with the United States. In 1972, Mao lent his prestige to this policy change by receiving U.S. president Richard M. Nixon in Beijing.

Mao died in Beijing on Sept. 9, 1976. Although he was criticized after his death for the failure of his economic policies and the revolutionary excesses of his later years, his basic foreign policy was continued and his theories remained influential in the Third World.

Maori [mow'-ree]   The Maori, a people of New Zealand, speak a language related to Tahitian and Hawaiian. Anthropologists claim that they are descended from Polynesian canoe travelers who arrived on the island by the middle of the 12th century. At the time of Capt. James COOK's visit in 1769, the Maori population was an estimated 100,000 to 250,000, divided into about 50 tribes, each occupying separate territories. Three social classes existed: aristocrats, commoners, and slaves captured in war. Differences in rank were associated with supernatural power, or MANA. Religious knowledge and activities were also graded, with priests (*tohunga*) functioning as key figures. Traditional art forms included wood carvings—such as those decorating meeting houses and great canoes—poetry and story telling, chants, dances, and songs.

In 1840 the Treaty of Waitangi guaranteed the Maoris ownership of their land in exchange for recognition of British sovereignty. The New Zealand government subsequently bought large tracts of Maori property. In the late 1850s settlers encroached illegally on the last Maori stronghold on North Island, setting off the Maori Wars (1860–72). The defeated Maori lost much of their remaining land. They now number 300,000 (1986 est.), about 10 percent of New Zealand's population; they have many, but not all, of the same rights as other New Zealanders.

Maori language   see MALAYO-POLYNESIAN LANGUAGES

map turtle   Six or seven species of North American turtles of the genus *Graptemys*, family Emydidae, are commonly called map turtles, presumably in reference to the intricate pattern of lines or spots on their shells and heads. Map turtles are highly aquatic, ordinarily leaving the water only to bask or to lay eggs. They range from 12 to 27 cm (4.7 to 10.6 in) in shell length, and females are sometimes twice as large as males. Map turtles show a distinctive courtship behavior, the male vibrating his long claws against the head of the female. Map turtles feed primarily on mollusks, insects, and other small animals, but they also eat plant material.

The common map turtle has jaws that are adapted for breaking the shells of mollusks, its principal food.

maple   Maple is the common name for a family, Aceraceae, of trees and shrubs in the soapberry order, Sapindales. The Aceraceae contains two genera: *Acer*, the maples proper and the box elder, and *Dipteronia*, two small trees from China. Almost all maples are deciduous, dropping their leaves at the end of the growing season; a few have persistent leaves and are regarded as evergreen or semievergreen. Maples have opposite leaves, two leaves

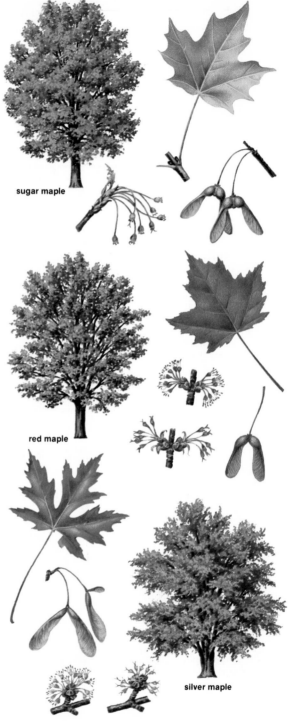

sugar maple

red maple

silver maple

The maple tree bears minute flowers that develop into winged seeds. Common to temperate zones of the world, it is a shade tree popular for its autumn foliage. The wood of the sugar maple, the most important North American maple, is used to make fine furniture and sap is used for maple syrup. Its leaf is the national emblem of Canada. The red maple is used for landscaping and lumber. The silver maple is named for the light gray underside of its leaves.

arising from the same level but on opposite sides of the stem. The leaves are either simple or divided into leaflets. The simple leaves are usually long-stemmed and palmately lobed, somewhat like an outstretched hand, and have toothed margins. The flowers are either unisexual (either male or female) or bisexual, and both kinds may occur within a species. The flowers are generally small and inconspicuous and are borne in clusters; they may appear before or with the leaves. The fruit, called a samara, commonly consists of paired, winged nutlets.

The genus *Acer* is widespread throughout the northern temperate region and also grows on mountains in the tropics. Authorities differ on the number of species, which is variously given as 115 to 200. Most species are found in China and Japan. Thirteen species are native to the United States, and 5 of these are important for timber products. A number of maples, including the Norway maple, *A. platanoides*, have been introduced into the United States.

Maples are generally divided into two groups: the hard maples, such as sugar maple and black maple, and the soft maples, such as the silver maple, red maple, and box elder. Soft maples grow more rapidly than hard maples but are brittle and often break in high winds and in ice storms. For this reason the stronger and longer-lived hard maples are preferable as shade trees. Maple wood is used principally for lumber, distilled products, veneer, crossties, and pulpwood. Most of the lumber is used for flooring, furniture, crates, and interior finishing. A certain amount of maple wood is crushed or chipped and distilled to produce acetic acid and alcohol.

Sugar maple, *A. saccharum*, also called rock maple, is widely distributed in the northeastern United States and southeastern Canada. The leaf, which appears on Canada's national flag, usually has five lobes separated by rounded, shallow indentations. The margins of the leaves have sparse, pointed teeth. The sap taken from the trunk in late winter or early spring is used to make maple syrup and maple sugar.

Red maple, *A. rubrum*, is distributed throughout eastern North America from southeastern Canada to Texas and Florida. Its leaves commonly have three lobes, occasionally five; the lobes are coarsely toothed.

Silver maple, *A. saccharinum*, has a distribution similar to that of the sugar maple, but its range extends farther south. The silver maple's leaves are deeply separated into five large-toothed lobes. The leaves are bright green on the upper surface and silvery white below.

Japanese maple, *A. palmatum*, has about 80 varieties ranging from shrubs to trees. Popular as ornamentals, they are small and have leaves that are deeply divided into five to nine narrow, toothed lobes. Summer foliage colors vary from green through yellow to pink and red.

maple syrup and sugar Maple syrup is made from the "sweetwater" sap of North American maple trees, primarily the sugar maple (*Acer saccharum*) but also the black and the red maple (*A. nigrum* and *A. rubrum*), all of which are native to the eastern half of the continent. Because of a physiological process that is not yet clearly un-

derstood, these maples will bleed quantities of sap through wounds in the trunk under conditions of alternate freeze and thaw in late winter and early spring. The sap may contain up to 10 percent sugar. It is reduced by boiling to a sweet syrup, or, with further boiling, to a solid sugar. Both the syrup and the sugar have a distinctive flavor and color not present in the sap but developed through boiling.

The syrup has been made in Canada and the United States since the first colonial settlers learned the art from the Indians. Both syrup and sugar were important items of trade until the late 1800s, when white cane sugar became less expensive to use as a sweetener. Nowadays the Canadian province of Quebec produces by far the largest amount of syrup.

Maple sap is harvested during a 4- to 6-week period between January and April, although in some years warm nighttime temperatures may cut short the harvest. Mature trees are tapped by drilling two or three 7.6-cm (3-in) holes around the trunk, into which are inserted metal or plastic spouts. The sap drips from the spouts into buckets, or into plastic tubing that connects a stand of trees with a storage tank in the sugarhouse. The sap is then boiled in an evaporator to reduce its water content. Depending on the amount of sugar in the sap, between 115 and 190 l (30 and 50 gal) of sap are required to make 3.8 l (1 gal) of syrup.

maps and mapmaking Because its surface is nearly spherical, the Earth is most accurately represented by a GLOBE. However, a map, a flat image of the Earth, is more practical to use, more portable, and less costly to produce. Mapmaking, or cartography, attempts to reproduce the Earth, or a portion of it, with a minimum of distortion so that the information contained in the map will be as accurate as possible.

This 15th-century map of the world was based on the theories of the 1st-century Greek astronomer Ptolemy, whose Geographia *was a major source of information for medieval scholars.*

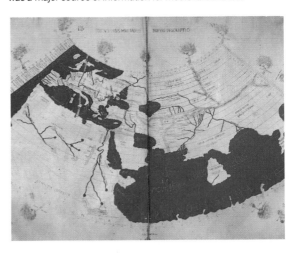

Gerardus Mercator (left) and Jadocus Hondius, Dutch cartographers of the 16th century, produced well-plotted maps that contributed to increased sea trade and exploration.

History of Mapmaking

The first known map, a small clay tablet portraying an estate, was made late in the 3d millennium BC by the Sumerians. About the 14th century BC, Egyptians made maps showing boundaries of property for use in taxation. The earliest important phase in the development of cartography can be traced to the ancient Greeks, who in turn are believed to have borrowed from the earlier cultures of the Middle East.

The Greek and Roman Period. As early as the 8th century BC, the Greeks had already established a reputation as accomplished sailors and colonizers. By the early 6th century BC, Greece had become the leading center of geographical knowledge. The first book on geography, describing a circular, flat Earth surrounded by ocean waters, appeared at the end of the 6th century BC. In the 3d century BC the famous scholar and mathematician ERATOSTHENES OF CYRENE calculated the Earth's circumference with remarkable accuracy. He and his contemporary HIPPARCHUS laid the foundations for scientific cartography, developing a system of LATITUDE and LONGITUDE.

Much of what is known about ancient Greek cartography comes from the writings of STRABO and PTOLEMY. The latter's *Geographia* included map projections and coordinates for places in the known world. The Romans, inheritors of the Greek knowledge of geography, surveyed their empire.

The Middle Ages. During the Middle Ages cartographers relied heavily on classical references and religious scripture for information and showed the Earth as a flat disk. The *mappae mundi*, derived from a 1st-century BC map, was a commonly used style, depicting a flat Earth with Jerusalem at the center, Asia at the top, Europe to the lower left, and Africa in the lower right corner. An ocean surrounded the clustered landmasses. Portolanos (manuals comprising sea charts), introduced in the 13th century, showed detailed shorelines and were used for navigation into the 17th century.

The Renaissance. Between the 15th and the 17th centuries, great advances in cartography were related to discoveries by explorers such as John CABOT, Christopher COLUMBUS, and Ferdinand MAGELLAN. The invention of the printing press and the perfection of copper-plate engraving allowed distribution of less expensive maps rendered in fine detail. The earliest map showing the New World was drawn in 1500 by the Spanish explorer Juan de la COSA. In 1507, Martin Waldseemüller prepared the first map on which the name *America* appeared, referring to the South American continent.

By the middle of the 16th century, Europe had several major centers of cartographic activity. Italy was the principal mapmaking center. The Netherlands achieved superiority about 1570 and retained it through most of the 17th century. Gerardus MERCATOR founded a mapmaking house, and Abraham Ortelius published the first modern atlas in 1570.

The Modern Period. The first national survey was begun in France by the Cassini family in 1733, establishing mapping as a government-sponsored pursuit. Such surveys included both topographic maps and marine charts.

When lands in the United States west of Pennsylvania were opened for settlement, surveyors were faced with the problem of delimiting land parcels on a terrain with no features such as hills and trees. A system of townships and ranges was established, and some evidence of this system remains in the rectangular road pattern common in areas west of the Appalachians. In 1879 the U.S. Geological Survey began a national mapping program that continues today.

International cooperation in mapping resulted in the International Map of the World (formulated 1891, still incomplete) and the World Aeronautical Chart, begun for strategic purposes during World War II and later completed. Both have been rendered at a standard scale and show the entire world with standard symbolization.

In recent years technology has revolutionized mapmaking, enabling cartographers to merge photo imagery from satellites and aircraft with almost any kind of data. The new computerized map technology is known as GIS (geographic information systems).

Map Scale

The scale of a map is the relationship between distance on the map and the corresponding distance on the Earth's surface. Large-scale maps show a small area and can contain much detail, whereas small-scale maps cover a large area.

Scale can be expressed in one of three ways: fractionally, verbally, or graphically. A fractional scale gives the equivalence of one unit on the map to the number of units on the ground shown within that one map unit. The fractional scale "1:24,000" indicates that one unit on the map represents 24,000 comparable units on the ground. A verbal scale states the same relationship in words: "One inch on the map is equivalent to 0.61 kilometers on the ground." A graphic or bar scale is a line located in the legend that has been marked at intervals, much like a ruler. The ground distance between two points can be determined by measuring the distance between them on the map and then comparing that distance to the distance marked along the line or bar.

Types of Maps

Theoretically, an infinite variety of map types exists. Most of the commonly used map types are either cultural or physical in nature, but some are both physical and cultural.

Distributional Maps. Distributional, thematic, or statistical maps depict the spatial variation of any phenomenon on the Earth's surface. With symbolization a map can show, for example, the occurrence of mineral deposits, animal species, or public libraries.

Some maps are drawn with isolines connecting points of equal value. In maps showing elevations, the isolines are called contour lines. If a map contains isolines, the legend gives the interval at which the isolines are drawn, such as every 10 meters of altitude. Statistical data are often mapped using choropleths, which do not attempt to relate values in adjoining areas. The information to be shown is grouped by value, and each group is assigned a color or pattern. Those areas on the map with a given value are then overlain with the corresponding color or pattern.

Geologic Maps. The areal distribution of any of several geologic subjects is the concern of geologic maps. Bedrock maps, showing the geologic formation that is either exposed at the surface or overlain by surface deposits, are essential for construction projects and mineral explora-

Distribution maps convey a wide variety of information through the use of contrasting symbols. These five maps show different kinds of data for the same section of the eastern United States. The maps fall into two main categories, qualitative and quantitative. Qualitative maps delineate the relative locations of related entities, such as political units, rock formations, or areas of colonial exploration. Quantitative maps illustrate numerical measurements of specific phenomena according to their geographical distribution. Density of population and frequency of tornadoes are two examples.

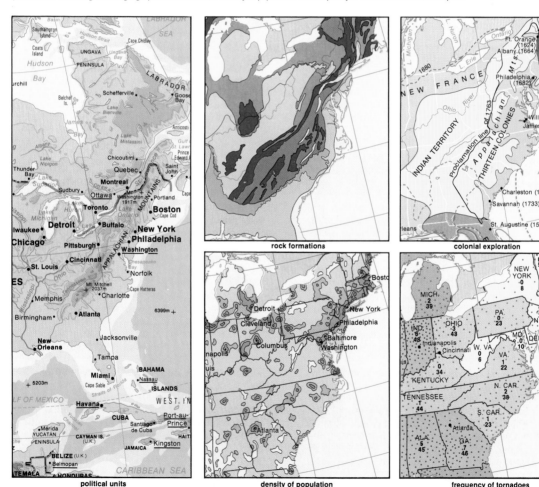

rock formations

colonial exploration

political units

density of population

frequency of tornadoes

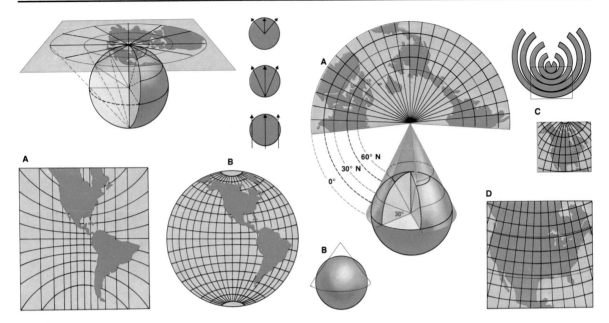

In an azimuthal, or zenithal, projection the parallels and meridians are transferred to a plane that touches the sphere at a single point. The object is to retain azimuth, or true compass bearing, along great circles. (A great circle is the shortest distance between two points on the surface of a sphere.) Azimuthal projections may be drawn from gnomonic, stereographic, or orthographic perspectives (right). In a gnomonic projection (A), all arcs of great circles appear as straight lines, enabling pilots to plot the shortest possible courses. In Lambert's equal-area projection (B), the line coordinates are adjusted to preserve equality of area (equivalence) in all sections of the map.

In a conical projection the parallels and meridians are projected from the sphere onto a cone. When the cone is opened and laid flat (A), the parallels form concentric arcs, with the meridians radiating out from the center. The cone and sphere intersect at a standard parallel (shown here at 30° N), from which all other parallels are measured. In a secant conic projection (B), the use of two standard parallels allows a greater distribution of scale error. A polyconic projection (C) renders all parallels standard; it is accurate only near the central meridian. Alber's equal-area projection (D) adjusts the standard parallels mathematically to preserve area equivalence.

tion. Surficial geology maps contain data on sediment distribution; they often include information on the geologic time interval during which sediments were deposited. Tectonic maps display the actual or projected surface resulting from such structural elements as fault planes and fold axes and the degree to which initially horizontal rock layers have been deformed. Paleogeologic maps, including paleolithic and paleotectonic maps, show the areal geology present at some previous time and may show how the shape and size of continents and oceans have changed over time. Structure contour maps indicate the elevations or depths of formations relative to a continuous surface, such as the contact between two sedimentary rock formations. Isopach maps record the thickness of a specific stratigraphic interval (such as a layer of oil shale) by using isopachs—thickness contours. Lithofacies maps show rock types in a stratigraphic unit.

Soil Maps. Soil types present within a map area can be shown using one of several classification systems. Such maps are useful in making land-use decisions.

Land-Use Maps. The variation in activities within a given area is shown on land-use maps. Residential, industrial, and agricultural areas can be differentiated to provide information useful to city planners and road builders. Local governments use such maps in establishing zoning regulations.

Economic Maps. The geographic distribution of specific economic activities such as mining, manufacturing, and agriculture is found on economic maps. Rational location decisions for economic pursuits can be made by using such maps.

Zoological and Botanical Maps. The area distributions of animals and plants are shown on zoological maps and botanical maps. Animal migration routes can also be illustrated, as well as the ecological status of an area. Such maps are useful to lumber companies and wildlife management personnel.

Statistical Maps. Quantitative information—that which may be measured—can be found on statistical maps. Patterns in the spatial variation of any given subject become evident when mapped, using symbols, bar or pie graphs, or isolines.

Political Maps. The boundaries of governmental units are found on political maps. Frequently political entities within boundaries are located and named.

Topographic Maps. The visible shape of such landforms as mountains and valleys is shown on topographic maps. These can be used by engineers during the planning stages of construction projects. Components of these maps include bench marks—points of known elevation relative to mean sea level, and contour lines connecting points of equal elevation. Orthophotoquads, another type of topographic map, are derived from aerial photographs or other remote sensors. They show a high degree of detail unobtainable by ground surveys. Bathymetric maps show marine topography by using contour lines drawn along intervals below sea level.

Cadastral Maps. Cadastral maps identify parcels of land for purposes of ownership and taxation. Since a high degree of accuracy is important, most cadastral maps can be legally produced only by a duly authorized surveyor.

Meteorological Maps. The relationship between the atmosphere and weather conditions is shown on meteorological maps. Principal components include isobars, or lines of equal barometric pressure, and isotherms, lines of equal temperature. Wind speeds and directions are symbolized by a wind rose diagram. Satellite imagery has enabled meteorologists to improve the accuracy of such maps. Photographs taken from high-altitude satellites and transmitted to Earth show frontal activity and impending storms, thus enabling forecasters to predict weather further into the future than was previously possible.

Transportation Maps. One of the most frequently used map types is the transportation map. Highways, railroads, and airports are shown along with cities and points of interest.

Historical Maps. Exploration or trade routes, military movements, and former political units can be found on historical maps. Early maps can be carefully interpreted by historians and used as a basis for drafting precise historical maps.

Map Projections

The Earth's shape is best represented by a sphere slightly flattened at top and bottom. Mapmakers, however, assume the Earth to be a perfect sphere. When transferring points from the curved Earth to the flat map surface, both equality in size and true directional relationship are impossible: the curved Earth's image suffers distortion. A cartographer must therefore select the map projection best suited to the eventual use of the map. Projections can be placed in one of three general groups, based on the method in which the information on the round Earth is transferred to the flat map—azimuthal, conic, or cylindrical—as illustrated in the accompanying diagrams. Various recent projections, such as the Robinson projection adopted by the National Geographic Society in 1988, try to reduce distortions of shape and size.

See also: SURVEYING.

Maputo [mah-poo'-toh] Maputo (formerly Lourenço Marques) is the capital of Mozambique. The country's largest and most important city, it has a population of 1,069,727 (1989 est.). Situated in the extreme southeastern part of Mozambique, Maputo has a large natural harbor on Delagoa Bay, on the Indian Ocean. It was one of the major ports in southern Africa before Mozambique gained independence in 1975, but a subsequent long civil war at times virtually halted freight transport in and out of the city. The University of Mozambique (1962) is in Maputo.

The city was founded in 1544 by a Portuguese trader, Lourenço Marques, but it remained a small settlement until railroad construction stimulated population growth after 1895. In 1907 the city replaced Mozambique City as the capital of Portuguese East Africa.

Maracaibo [mah-rah-ky'-boh] Maracaibo, the capital of Zulia state, is the second largest city and second most important port of Venezuela. Its population is 1,179,384 (1989 est.). The city lies in the northwestern part of the country on a channel linking the Gulf of Venezuela with Lake Maracaibo. The major export is petroleum, but the port also handles coffee, cacao, sugar, and lumber. Manufactures include foodstuffs, beverages, soap, clothing, and rope. The State University of Zulia (founded 1891) is located there.

Maracaibo was permanently settled in 1571. The settlement grew very slowly until the discovery of oil at Lake Maracaibo in 1917. Thereafter the population increased rapidly.

Maracaibo, Lake Lake Maracaibo, connected by narrows to the Gulf of Venezuela, lies in the Maracaibo Basin in northwestern Venezuela, one of the world's richest petroleum-producing regions. The largest lake in South America, it has an area of 12,800 km^2 (4,941 mi^2), with a maximum length of about 155 km (96 mi) and a maximum width of 121 km (75 mi). Channels 11 m (35 ft) deep have been dredged in the naturally shallow lake to permit the movement of transport ships carrying the petroleum extracted from the lake bed and shore.

Marat, Jean Paul [mah-rah'] One of the most notorious figures of the FRENCH REVOLUTION, Jean Paul Marat, b. Switzerland, May 24, 1743, d. July 13, 1793, later became a symbol of the radical aspirations of his era. After studying medicine in France, Holland, and Britain, he settled in Paris. The Revolution enabled him to emerge as a master of vituperative journalism, and from September 1789 his newspaper, *L'Ami du Peuple* ("The Friend of the People"), denounced deputies, ministers, and finally the king himself. It called for innumerable executions and the prompt appointment of a temporary dictator. Marat became immensely popular in Paris for his compassion for the poor and his concern for social justice; he also remained independent and incorruptible.

Marat was partly responsible for the beginning of the prison massacres of September 1792. He was elected a deputy for Paris to the National Convention, where his cadaverous appearance and theatrical conduct excited both horror and derision. His sympathies lay with the radical JACOBINS, and the more moderate GIRONDISTS tried to discredit Maximilien ROBESPIERRE and Paris by associating them with Marat. In the spring of 1793 the deputies dispatched Marat to the Revolutionary Tribunal for inciting "patriots." His acquittal and reinstatement (April 24) preceded his greatest personal triumph—the purging of

Jean Paul Marat rose to political power during the French Revolution as a newspaper editor and member of the National Convention. In 1793 he was murdered in his bath; his corpse is depicted here in a famous painting by Jacques Louis David. (Musées Royaux des Beaux-Arts, Brussels.)

the convention by insurrection on June 2—but the next month he was stabbed to death in his bath by Charlotte CORDAY, a young supporter of the Girondists. Marat's assassination was exploited by the Jacobins, thereby helping to lay the groundwork for the Reign of Terror.

Maratha [muh-rah'-tah]   The term *Maratha* (or Mahratta) refers generally to the Marathi-speaking peoples of Maharashtra state in India who number about 35 million. In a narrower sense the name denotes members of the dominant caste in Maharashtra, today numbering nearly 10 million people. Most Maratha are occupied as cultivators or landowners. They claim Kshatriya, or warrior, status and see themselves as equivalent to the RAJPUTS of the Punjab. The caste itself is divided into a series of regional groupings between which marriage is relatively rare. Maratha are further subdivided into a series of gotras, groups in which descent is traced through the male line.

The Maratha were the dominant class in a powerful Hindu state centered in Maharashtra in the 17th, 18th, and early 19th centuries. The Maratha fought three wars (1775–82, 1803–05, 1817–18) against the British, who finally annexed all their territory.

marathon   A marathon is a foot race that is 26 mi 385 yd (42.19 km) long. It has been a men's Olympic event since the first modern Olympic Games were held in Athens in 1896. The first women's Olympic marathon was run in 1984. A world-class male runner can complete a marathon in slightly more than 2 hours, but because of the vast differences in the courses, the International Amateur Athletic Federation does not recognize a world record.

According to legend, in 490 BC a Greek soldier named Pheidippides ran the 36.2 km (22.5 mi) from the site of the battle of Marathon to Athens, where he died after announcing the Greek victory over the Persians. The modern marathon commemorates this feat.

The length for the Olympic marathon was not standardized until 1924, when the distance used in the 1908 Olympics was adopted. That distance resulted from the British Olympic Committee's desire to have the race begin at Windsor and end at the royal box in London's White City Stadium. (For information on current marathons, see RUNNING AND JOGGING.)

Maravich, Pete   Peter Press Maravich, b. Aliquippa, Pa., June 22, 1948, d. Jan. 5, 1988, was one of the most prolific scorers in basketball history. Maravich attended Louisiana State University, where his father, "Press" Maravich, was basketball coach. In 3 seasons of eligibility (1967–68 through 1969–70) he averaged 43.8, 44.2, and 44.5 points per game—the 3 highest season averages in major college basketball. His career average was 44.2 points per game. He also set an all-time college basketball career scoring record, which still stands, accumulating 3,667 points. Nicknamed "Pistol Pete" for his shooting skills, the 6-ft 5-in (1-m 96-cm) Maravich also became a flamboyant ball-handler and dribbler. In his 10-season professional career with the Atlanta Hawks, New Orleans Jazz, and Boston Celtics of the National Basketball Association (NBA), he scored 15,948 points for a 24.2 per game average. In 1977, Maravich led the NBA in scoring (31.1 points per game). He was inducted into the Basketball Hall of Fame in 1987.

marble   Marble, a rock resulting from the metamorphism of limestone or dolostone, is commonly composed predominantly of calcite or dolomite. Marble tends to be coarser grained than the rock from which it was derived. Calcite marbles have a mosaic texture, whereas dolomite marbles are granular. Impurities such as clays and quartz in the original rock react with the calcite and dolomite to form other minerals—for example, garnet, talc, olivine, diopside, and mica. A marble's color, which may be uniform or which may appear in streaks and swirls, also comes from the presence of impurities—iron oxide produces a red color; chlorite and epidote, green.

Marble is found in the metamorphic core zones of younger mountain chains, as well as in the eroded roots of ancient mountain chains in the continental shields. In North America commercial marble comes from the Appalachians and the Rocky Mountains as well as from sites in New York and Quebec and especially at Proctor, Vt., and Sylacauga, Ala. A pure white marble is found at the Alabama site.

Because of its decorative appearance and strength, marble has long been prized for use in architecture and statuary. Michelangelo chose Carrara marble from the Italian Apennines for his *Pietà* (Saint Peter's Basilica, Rome).

marbles   Marbles are small, hard, spherical objects with which children play games. They may be made of stone, glass, steel, clay, or plastic, and they require precise handling in order to aim them accurately and attain distance in shooting. A shooter "knuckles down"—that is, places the knuckle of the forefinger on the ground—then balances the marble in the crook of the forefinger and presses the thumb behind the forefinger before snapping it in such a way as to shoot the marble at other target marbles in a ring drawn on the ground. Some variations require the shooter to hit a single, large, target marble, whereas others use the golf principle, whereby players try to shoot their marbles into a hole in the ground. In the first game, players keep the marbles they knock out of the ring; in the second game, marbles that do not hit the target marble are lost; in the last game, players lose marbles that miss the hole. These games can also be played for points.

Marbury v. Madison Chief Justice John Marshall's opinion in *Marbury* v. *Madison* (1803) is generally regarded as the single most important opinion in the history of the U.S. Supreme Court. The decision set out the arguments on the basis of which the Court exercises its power of JUDICIAL REVIEW, which means that the Court can judge whether or not statutes passed by Congress or state legislatures meet the requirements set out by the U.S. Constitution.

Marbury v. *Madison* grew out of the conflict between the Federalist presidency of John Adams and the Republican presidency of his successor, Thomas Jefferson. Just before Jefferson's inauguration (Mar. 4, 1801), President Adams named a number of Federalist politicians to newly created positions. One of them, William Marbury, was appointed a justice of the peace for the District of Columbia. Marbury had not been delivered his formal papers of appointment, however, and President Jefferson instructed his secretary of state, James Madison, not to do so. Marbury sued for an order (writ of mandamus) forcing Madison to deliver the papers.

Although Marshall found that Marbury was wrongfully deprived of his commission, he went on to declare that Section 13 of the Judiciary Act of 1789 under which Marbury had filed his suit was unconstitutional because it added to the Supreme Court's "original jurisdiction." Marshall held that Article III of the Constitution limited this original jurisdiction to the specific cases mentioned there. For this reason, Marbury's suit was thrown out and a political crisis averted. At the same time, Marshall established the right of the Supreme Court to set aside statutes of Congress when they were thought to violate the overriding commands of the Constitution.

Marc, Franz One of Germany's leading expressionist painters, Franz Marc, b. Feb. 8, 1880, died during World War I before his art could reach its full development. Marc found his direction in his early twenties, during a visit to Paris, where he saw paintings by Vincent van Gogh, Paul Gauguin, and the Fauves. By 1908, Marc had

From 1908, the German expressionist painter Franz Marc limited his subject matter to animals. Yellow Horses *(1912) typifies his use of distortion and vibrant color to symbolize the energizing life forces of his subjects. (Staatsgalerie, Stuttgart, Germany.)*

made animals his exclusive subject matter, rendering them in a sinuous, organic style related to Jugendstil, a style closely allied to Art Nouveau. In 1911, Marc became a founding member, with Wassily KANDINSKY, of Der BLAUE REITER, an association of expressionist painters that established contact with similar movements in France and Italy. Thereafter, Marc began to depict his subjects—horses, deer, tigers—in a more intellectualized, geometric manner. His series *Deer in the Forest* (1913–14; Staatliche Kunsthalle, Karlsruhe) shows recognizable images becoming progressively more enmeshed in surging diagonal lines and patterns of vivid, often clashing color. By 1914, when he enlisted in the German Army, Marc's work had become almost wholly abstract. He was killed on Mar. 4, 1916, at Verdun, France.

Marcantonio, Vito Vito Anthony Marcantonio, b. New York City, Dec. 10, 1902, d. Aug. 9, 1954, a left-wing U.S. representative from New York (1935–37, 1939–51), was at the center of controversy during the cold-war period. A member of the American Labor party, he was first elected as a Republican and subsequently ran on other tickets as well. After World War II his critics claimed that his voting record followed the Communist line, but Marcantonio always denied that he was a Communist. In 1950, running on only the American Labor ticket, he was defeated by a joint Republican-Democratic candidate.

Marceau, Marcel [mahr-soh'] Marcel Marceau, b. Strasbourg, France, Mar. 22, 1923, is the world's most popular pantomime performer. After studying with Charles Dullin and Étienne Decroux, he joined Jean Louis Barrault's company in 1946. The next year he created "Bip," the well-known stage personage he has since taken around the globe. Performing up to 300 times

Marcel Marceau, a French pantomime artist, appears as Bip, the Chaplinesque character he introduced in 1947. Marceau is internationally acclaimed for his humorous sketches and dramatic productions, called mimo-dramas, expressed without words.

a year, Marceau was largely responsible for the recent worldwide resurgence of interest in mime and pantomime.

Marcel, Gabriel   Gabriel Marcel, b. Dec. 7, 1889, d. Oct. 8, 1973, was a French dramatist and philosopher in the existential tradition, although he preferred the name *neo-Socratic* to the label *existentialist,* in order to distinguish his theistic approach from the atheistic EXISTENTIALISM of Jean Paul SARTRE. Many of the important themes in Marcel's work are directly religious, such as his concepts of man as a pilgrim (*homo viator*) and of the absolute as a personal, loving being.

Marcel distinguished between a problem and a mystery. A problem, he believed, is a difficulty that is resolved through "primary reflection," which is abstract, analytical, and objective. Once a problem is solved, there is no more interest in it, whereas a mystery, which is never completely solved, remains alive and interesting no matter how successfully one may have dealt with it in previous attempts.

Marcellus, Marcus Claudius [mahr-sel'-uhs]   The Roman general Marcus Claudius Marcellus, c.268–208 BC, won distinction in the PUNIC WARS and was elected consul five times. He waged war against the Insubres in Gaul, defeating their chief in single combat (222), and held off HANNIBAL three times at Nola (216, 214). Marcellus conquered Syracuse in 211, outwitting Archimedes' brilliantly engineered defenses. After defeating a Carthaginian force near Himera, he returned to Rome before entering the field against Hannibal once again near Venosa, where he died in battle.

march   March music probably originated as a stimulant for battle, and military marches appeared in print by the late 16th century. The martial function of marches has remained dominant, but during the 19th and early 20th centuries the march was used also as dance music, being adapted first to the quickstep, then to the two-step—which John Philip SOUSA's "Washington Post March" popularized—and, in syncopated styles, to the cakewalk and ragtime dances.

In contrast to lively military marches, slower marches are used for a variety of ceremonial purposes. Academic, inaugural, and other processional rituals often used such pieces as Elgar's stately "Pomp and Circumstance" marches. Funerals are often accompanied by the well-known march from Chopin's "Sonata in B-flat minor" or the one from Handel's oratorio *Saul.* Weddings almost invariably include the "Wedding March" from Mendelssohn's music for *A Midsummer Night's Dream,* or Wagner's march from his opera *Lohengrin.* Perhaps the most familiar American march is Sousa's "Stars and Stripes Forever."

Marche (Italy) [mahr'-kay]   Marche, a region in east central Italy, extends along the shore of the Adriatic Sea for about 160 km (100 mi). The region encompasses an area of 9,693 km^2 (3,743 mi^2) and has a population of 1,428,557 (1988 est.). The APENNINES rise to heights of more than 2,440 m (8,000 ft) on the western side of the region. ANCONA is the capital and leading port.

The chief economic activity is farming. Livestock is raised, and fishing is important to the economy. In addition to petroleum refining, chemical production, and shipbuilding, small industries manufacture textiles, musical instruments, and pottery.

Colonized by the Romans in the 3d century BC, Marche was ruled by the Byzantines and Lombards in the 6th century, by feudal families from the 12th century, by the Papal States from 1631, and by the French from 1797 until 1815. It was incorporated into the unified kingdom of Italy in 1860.

Marciano, Rocky [mahr-see-ah'-noh]   Rocco Francis Marchegiano, b. Brockton, Mass., Sept. 1, 1923, d. Aug. 31, 1969, was the only world heavyweight champion in the history of boxing who never lost a professional fight.

Rocky Marciano, the only professional world heavyweight champion in boxing history to retire undefeated, won the heavyweight crown in 1952, when he knocked out Jersey Joe Walcott.

Weighing about 84 kg (185 lb) and standing only 1 m 80 cm (5 ft 11 in) tall, he was comparatively small by modern standards, but he was a devastating puncher, winning 43 of his 49 professional bouts by knockouts. Marciano started boxing while serving in the Army Engineers and continued afterward as an amateur. In 1947 he came under the guidance of boxing manager Charley Goldman. After winning 42 professional bouts, Marciano defeated Jersey Joe Walcott for the championship in 1952. He defended his title six times, scoring five knockouts and one decision (over Ezzard Charles) before announcing his retirement in 1956. Marciano was killed in the crash of a small airplane near Newton, Iowa.

Marcion [mahr'-shuhn]   Marcion, d. AD c.160, a native of Sinope in Pontus, was the founder of a Christian sect that survived until the 4th century and beyond. A devoted Christian, Marcion made his way to Rome (c.140) and attached himself to the church there. He associated with the Syrian gnostic Cerdo and developed unorthodox views that brought him into conflict with the Roman church. Marcion was excommunicated (c.144), but his following grew rapidly into a sect that rivaled the Catholic church.

The main thesis of Marcion's system was that the gospel of Jesus Christ is entirely a gospel of love to the exclusion of the Mosaic Law. He believed that the original gospel of Jesus had been corrupted by Judaizing tendencies among the earliest disciples and that the Old Testament had no validity for Christians. According to Marcion, only Saint Paul had correctly understood the original teaching of Jesus. About 140, Marcion collected ten of Paul's letters and an edited Gospel According to Saint Luke, which he purged of all legalistic and Old Testament references. He claimed that these constituted the rule or canon of the church's teaching. Marcion's rejection of the other three Gospels compelled the Christian church to define what it accepted as the true New Testament canon (see BIBLE).

Marconi, Guglielmo [mahr-koh'-nee, gool-yel'-moh]   Guglielmo Marconi, b. Bologna, Italy, Apr. 25, 1874, d. July 20, 1937, is known as the father of wireless. The young Marconi developed a deep interest in electrical phenomena. When he read of the experiments of Heinrich HERTZ on electromagnetic waves, he became obsessed with the idea that such waves could be used for transmitting information without the need for the wire connection of the electric TELEGRAPH. In 1894, Marconi began his wireless telegraphy project by repeating some of Hertz's experiments with a number of improvements. Marconi offered his wireless communication system to the Italian government, but it was refused. He patented his system in London in 1896. In 1897, Marconi formed his wireless telegraph company. His four-circuit tuning, patented in 1900, led to widespread use of his system. In a famous experiment he received (1901) a radio-wave signal in St. John's, Newfoundland, that had been sent out from Cornwall, England.

The Italian inventor Guglielmo Marconi, photographed at 22 years of age, looks out from behind his first patented wireless receiver (1896). He detected radio waves beamed across the Atlantic in 1901, thus giving his telegraphy system credibility. In 1909, Marconi shared the Nobel Prize for physics.

As an Italian national, Marconi played an active role in World War I and represented Italy at the Paris Peace Conference in 1919. He continued to perform experiments in the new field of RADIO, which evolved from wireless telegraphy. He received many honors, including sharing the Nobel Prize for physics in 1909.

Marcos, Ferdinand E.   Ferdinand Edralin Marcos, b. Sept. 11, 1917, d. Sept. 28, 1989, was president of the Philippines from 1965 to 1986. Elected to Congress in 1949, he served as minority leader until 1959, when he was elected to the Senate. After defeating Diosdado Macapagal for the presidency in 1965, he became (1969) the first Philippine president to win a second term. Citing the need to combat student unrest, Communist terrorism, and a Muslim separatist movement, Marcos imposed martial law in 1972. He served as both prime minister and president until 1981, when he lifted martial law and won direct presidential elections under an amended constitution giving him the right to rule by decree. His party won legislative elections in 1978, 1981, and 1984.

Mounting opposition, fueled by a deteriorating economy, corruption, and outrage over the 1983 assassination of opposition leader Benigno S. Aquino, Jr., led Marcos to call early presidential elections, held on Feb. 7, 1986. When the legislature declared Marcos the victor despite widespread charges of election fraud, his opponent, Corazon AQUINO, began a campaign of nonviolent resistance to bring down the Marcos regime. Marcos and Aquino held rival inauguration ceremonies on February 25. Later that day, Marcos left the presidential palace for U.S. exile. Subsequently, several civil suits were filed against Marcos and his wife, Imelda, and in 1988 they were indicted on U.S. racketeering charges. He had died before the trial began, but she was acquitted in 1990.

Marcus Aurelius, Roman Emperor   Marcus Aurelius, b. Apr. 26, 121, d. Mar. 17, 180, ruled Rome from 161 until his death. Born Marcus Annius Verus, he

The reign (AD 161–80) of Marcus Aurelius was known as the Golden Age of the Roman Empire. A confirmed Stoic and a humanitarian ruler, Marcus Aurelius lowered the taxes of the poor and showed leniency toward political criminals. His *Meditations* provide a rare glimpse into the mind of a Stoic philosopher and king.

was adopted by the emperor ANTONINUS PIUS in 138 and married his daughter a few years later. On his succession to the throne Marcus insisted on sharing power with his brother Lucius Verus, who died in 169.

Educated by the best tutors in Rome and Athens, Marcus was a devotee of Greek learning and of the philosophy of STOICISM. Even during his campaigns (167–175, 178–180) against the Marcomanni and other Danubian tribes he kept a "spiritual diary." This document, the *Meditations,* reflects Marcus's attempt to reconcile his Stoic philosophy of virtue and self-sacrifice with his role as a warrior-sovereign.

Marcus's wars and benevolences—he lowered taxes and was charitable toward the less fortunate—were expensive and often ineffective. His son COMMODUS, who succeeded him, inherited the Danubian war, which Rome could not win, and a treasury that had been seriously depleted.

Marcuse, Herbert [mar-koo'-ze, hair'-bairt]   Herbert Marcuse, b. Berlin, Germany, July 19, 1898, d. July 30, 1979, became a U.S. social philosopher who acquired a large following among young radicals in the United States and Europe in the 1960s. Drawing on Hegel, Marx, and Freud, Marcuse put forward a theory of "the great refusal," meaning that individuals should reject the existing social order as repressive and conformist without waiting for a revolution. He came to the United States in 1934 and taught philosophy at various universities until his death. Among his books are *Eros and Civilization* (1955), *One-Dimensional Man* (1964), and *The Aesthetic Dimension* (1979), a revised translation of an earlier critique of Marxist aesthetics.

Marcy, William L.   The American political leader William Learned Marcy, b. Sturbridge (now Southbridge), Mass., Dec. 12, 1786, d. July 4, 1857, served in the cabinets of U.S. presidents James K. Polk and Franklin Pierce. He graduated from Brown University in 1808 and soon began practicing law in Troy, N.Y. Marcy moved to

Albany in 1823. As a member of Martin Van Buren's political machine, the Albany Regency, he served as New York comptroller (1823–1829), state supreme court justice (1829–1831), U.S. senator (1831–1832), and governor (1833–1839). In the 1840s, however, he sided with the conservative Hunker Democratic faction, and Polk's appointment of Marcy as secretary of war in 1845 displeased Van Buren and the antislavery Barnburners (see HUNKERS AND BARNBURNERS). His most conspicuous service was as Pierce's secretary of state (1853–1857), making the GADSDEN PURCHASE from Mexico. He is best remembered, however, for his assertion in 1832 that "to the victor belong the spoils of the enemy"—which gave rise to the term *spoils system* (see PATRONAGE).

Mardi Gras [mahr'-dee grah]   Mardi Gras (French for Fat Tuesday), or Shrove Tuesday, is the last day of the period of carnival (see CARNIVALS AND FAIRS) before Ash Wednesday, which marks the arrival of the fasting days of Lent. The name has come to represent the entire carnival period. Notable Mardi Gras celebrations take place in New Orleans, La., Rio de Janeiro, and Nice, France.

Marduk [mahr'-duk]   In Mesopotamian mythology Marduk was the chief god of Babylon. His cult became important in the reign (18th century BC) of Hammurabi. The ENUMA ELISH recounts Marduk's rise to the top of the Babylonian pantheon. He was the son of EA and Damkina. Of immense stature, with two heads and fiery breath, he was sent by the other gods to do battle with Tiamat, the primordial dragon. After killing her, he created earth, sea, and the heavens from her body. From Tiamat's consort, Kingu, he fashioned humankind. Marduk then became the king of the gods.

mare's tail (plant)   Mare's tail is an aquatic herb, *Hippurus vulgaris,* of wide distribution. It is often considered the only species in the family Hippuridaceae. Mare's tails are perennials that rise up to 60 cm (2 ft) above the water, where they bear whorls of tiny leaves at intervals along the stem.

Marey, Étienne Jules [muh-ray', ay-tee-en' zhuel]   Étienne Jules Marey, b. Mar. 5, 1830, d. May 15, 1904, a French physiologist, laid the foundations of modern CINEMATOGRAPHY in the 1880s with his photographic studies of motion. His nonphotographic studies of the movement of the horse inspired the work of Eadweard MUYBRIDGE, whose serial photographs of the 1870s in turn inspired Marey's invention (1887) of the chronophotograph. Marey's pictures superimposed the stages of action in a single picture, giving form to motion. His work appealed to Marcel Duchamp, who based some paintings on Marey's pictures. By 1892, Marey had achieved primitive motion pictures, but these were soon eclipsed by the work of Louis and Auguste Lumière.

Marfan syndrome   Marfan syndrome is a connective tissue disorder observed to some degree in one out of about every 10,000 persons. It is caused by a gene abnormality; an affected parent has about a 50 percent chance of passing it on to offspring. Symptoms include abnormal tallness compared to unaffected family members. The limbs, fingers, and head are disproportionately long, and sometimes the spine and breastbone are excessively curved. Loose joints and small muscles are other symptoms. More seriously, such persons are likely to have a weakened aorta and heart valves and to be prone to cardiac infections. Hormones may aid in reducing growth if the symptoms appear before puberty. Drugs can help to relieve stress on the aorta, but surgery is sometimes required. No diagnostic test exists for the condition prior to the appearance of symptoms.

Margaret of Anjou   Margaret of Anjou, b. Mar. 23, 1429, d. Apr. 25, 1482, was queen consort of HENRY VI of England (1445–61) and Lancastrian leader in the Wars of the Roses (see ROSES, WARS OF THE). The daughter of René of Anjou, later king of Naples, she married Henry as part of the Anglo-French peace settlement in 1445. Strong-willed in contrast to her feeble husband, she established an ascendancy at the court together with the BEAUFORT family. Her position was reinforced by the birth of a son, Edward, in 1453. She led the Lancastrian resistance to the claims to power of Richard, duke of York. After the victory of Richard's son EDWARD IV in 1461, Margaret fled with Henry to Scotland. In 1471 her son and husband died, and she was captured following another Yorkist victory. She was freed, however, and allowed to retire to France in 1476.

Margaret of Austria   Margaret of Austria, b. Jan. 10, 1480, d. Dec. 1, 1530, daughter of the Austrian archduke MAXIMILIAN, later Holy Roman Emperor MAXIMILIAN I, was regent of the Netherlands (1507–15, 1519–30) for her nephew Charles, later Holy Roman Emperor CHARLES V. She extended Habsburg control in the Netherlands and levied harsh taxes there to finance wars with France. In 1529 she negotiated the Treaty of Cambrai, or "Ladies' Peace," with Louise of Savoy, who represented her son Francis I of France.

Margaret of Navarre   Margaret of Navarre, also known as Margaret of Angoulême, b. Apr. 11, 1492, d. Dec. 21, 1549, was a sister of the French king Francis I. An important protector of John CALVIN, the poet Clément Marot, and other early reformers of the church, she expressed her intensely felt religious views in poetry and plays. Her best-known work is the incomplete *Heptaméron,* published in 1558 (Eng. trans., 1924). Modeled on Boccaccio's DECAMERON, it contains short stories told by fictional characters who probably represent Margaret and her relatives and friends.

Margaret of Scotland, Saint   Saint Margaret, b. *c.*1045, d. Nov. 16, 1093, the queen consort of MALCOLM III of Scotland, is credited with the introduction of English (Roman) usages into the Scottish church. The daughter of Edward the Exile, an English prince, she fled to Scotland after the Norman Conquest and married (*c.*1070) Malcolm. Noted for her piety and charity, she was canonized in 1250. Feast day: Nov. 16 (formerly June 10).

Margaret of Valois   [vahl-wah']   Margaret of Valois, b. May 14, 1553, d. Mar. 27, 1615, was the youngest daughter of HENRY II of France and CATHERINE DE MÉDICIS. On Aug. 18, 1572, six days before the SAINT BARTHOLOMEW'S DAY MASSACRE, she was forced to marry the Protestant Henry of Navarre (later HENRY IV) to seal a Catholic-Protestant reconciliation. Margaret was involved in a number of extramarital affairs at the courts of both her brother HENRY III at Paris and her husband at Nérac. Expelled from the royal court for her political intrigues, she returned to the unwilling Navarre in 1584. In 1599, ten years after Henry of Navarre's accession to the throne, she consented to the annulment of her marriage. In 1605, Henry IV allowed her to return to Paris. Margaret's charm and literary talent were admired by the leading writers of the age.

Margaret I, Queen of Denmark, Norway, and Sweden   One of the most powerful women of the Middle Ages, Margaret I, b. 1353, d. Oct. 28, 1412, united Denmark, Norway, and Sweden under one crown. The younger daughter of Waldemar IV of Denmark, she was married at age 10 to Haakon VI of Norway, a son of Magnus VII. In 1376 her 6-year-old son, Olaf, was elected king of Denmark; he inherited Norway on Haakon's death in 1380. Margaret, however, held the real power in both realms even after Olaf's death in 1387. In 1388 she was elected queen of Sweden.

For the rest of her life, Margaret dominated Scandinavian affairs, quelling internal violence, expanding the royal domain, patronizing religious institutions, and fostering Danish influence. Her grandnephew, Eric of Pomerania, was crowned king of all three kingdoms at Kalmar in 1397, although he remained merely a figurehead as long as she lived.

Margaret II, Queen of Denmark   Margaret II, b. Apr. 16, 1940, became Queen of Denmark in 1972. Denmark's constitution was changed in 1953 to permit female succession because her father, Frederick IX, had no sons. Margaret and her husband, Prince Henrik, have two sons.

margarine   Margarine, or oleomargarine, is a butterlike product made primarily from vegetable oils, fats, and milk. (The name *oleomargarine* was once used for margarines that contained animal fats, principally lard and oleostearin from beef.) The original margarine, developed in the late 1860s in France, used beef fat as the principal ingredient. Later margarines used animal fats and vegetable oils. Most of the margarines available today contain only vegetable oils, usually derived from SAFFLOWER, SOYBEANS, corn, and cottonseed.

In producing margarine, refined fluid oils are modified by HYDROGENATION into solids, which are then churned with skimmed milk until a substance with the consistency of butter is achieved. Carotene (provitamin A) is added both for its color and to increase the food's nutritive value. Preservatives may be used to extend shelf life. Salt and other flavoring agents are added, and the product is chilled and pressed to remove excess water.

Mari [mah'-ree]

Mari (present-day Tell Hariri), situated close to the Euphrates 11 km (7 mi) northwest of Abu Kemal, Syria, is celebrated for its splendid 2d-millennium BC palace and cuneiform archive. The city, occupied before 3000 BC, had become an important independent state by the early 2d millennium BC. Controlled by Shamshi-Adad I of Assyria between 1796 and 1780, it was finally overthrown (c.1760) by Hammurabi of Babylon. Holding a key position on the trade route between Mesopotamia and Syria, Mari depended for prosperity upon firm political control and declined after the death of Hammurabi (1750).

The city's ruins cover more than 245 ha (600 acres). A series of temples dedicated to the goddess Ishtar date from 2500 to 1800 BC; votive statues from the mid-3d-millennium BC shrines show stylistic links with the southern Mesopotamian art of Sumer. In the northeast part of the city lies the 18th-century BC palace of Zimri-lim (1779–1761 BC); measuring approximately 24,000 m^2 (260,000 ft^2), it contained nearly 300 rooms and courtyards, some of which were decorated with wall paintings including the famous *Investiture of Zimri-lim* (Louvre, Paris). The vast palace contained thousands of cuneiform tablets, which form a key Near Eastern archive.

Maria Theresa, Austrian Archduchess, Queen of Hungary and Bohemia

Maria Theresa, b. May 13, 1717, d. Nov. 29, 1780, ruled the Austrian Habsburg domains from 1740 to 1780. Archduchess of Austria, queen of Bohemia and Hungary, and consort of Holy Roman Emperor FRANCIS I, she was one of the most effective rulers of the HABSBURG dynasty.

The eldest daughter of Holy Roman Emperor CHARLES VI, Maria Theresa married Francis in 1736. In 1713 her father had promulgated the PRAGMATIC SANCTION that declared the Habsburg territories indivisible and inheritable by his female issue. When Charles died in 1740, however, his daughter's succession was challenged by several European princes, and FREDERICK II of Prussia quickly annexed the province of SILESIA.

Maria Theresa, daughter of Emperor Charles VI, ruled the Austrian Habsburg empire from 1740 to 1780. During her reign Maria Theresa centralized the administration of government, established a strong standing army, and initiated reforms in agriculture and education.

In the War of the AUSTRIAN SUCCESSION, Maria Theresa received aid only from the British and the Dutch. Meanwhile, Charles Albert of Bavaria was elected (1742) emperor as CHARLES VII. After his death in 1745, Maria Theresa secured the imperial crown for her husband, but she was not able to recover Silesia.

Determined to regain Silesia, Maria Theresa abandoned Britain in favor of an alliance with France—a traditional enemy—and Russia. As a result, Britain allied with Prussia. This "reversal of alliances"—known also as the "diplomatic revolution"—did not help Austria, and in the ensuing SEVEN YEARS' WAR (1756–63) the Austrian treasury was drained.

Maria Theresa's internal reforms were supported by able ministers such as Wenzel Anton von Kaunitz (1711–94), by her husband, and by her eldest son, Joseph. She centralized the administration, reduced the powers and privileges of the nobility, subordinated the church to the state, abolished the tax exemptions of both the nobility and the church, and established a strong standing army. She also initiated agrarian and educational reforms and a system of relief for the poor.

An intolerant woman (she was both anti-Semitic and anti-Calvinist), Maria Theresa abhorred the·ideas of the Enlightenment. After the death of her beloved husband in 1765, she came into increasing conflict with Joseph, who became emperor as JOSEPH II. She deplored the immorality of the first Partition of Poland (1772), which Joseph insisted that Austria share in. In addition to Joseph, nine of her children survived to adulthood; they included the future emperor LEOPOLD II and MARIE ANTOINETTE, the ill-fated queen of Louis XVI of France.

Maria II, Queen of Portugal (Maria da Glória)

Maria II, b. Brazil, Apr. 4, 1819, d. Nov. 15, 1853, queen of Portugal (1826–28, 1834–53), reigned in an age of great political turmoil. She was the granddaughter of King JOHN VI. After John died in 1826 his son Peter IV became king, but he wanted to remain in Brazil, where he held the title Emperor PEDRO I. Peter abdicated (1826) the crown of Portugal in favor of Maria, on condition that she become engaged to her uncle, Dom Miguel. In 1828, however, Dom Miguel usurped the crown. British and French intervention against him in 1832–33 finally brought Maria to the throne. In an atmosphere of intense rivalry between liberals and conservatives, Maria played the part of a constitutional monarch. Married (1836) to Duke Ferdinand of Saxe-Coburg, she bore 11 children and died in childbirth. She was succeeded by her sons Peter V (r. 1853–61) and Louis I (r. 1861–89).

Mariana Islands [mah-ree-ahn'-uh]   The Mariana Islands (also known as the Northern Mariana Islands) are a group of 16 islands located in the western Pacific Ocean, about 2,250 km (1,400 mi) south of Japan. Although the U.S. Territory of GUAM is geographically part of the island chain, it is not usually considered part of the Mariana group because it has long been governed as a separate entity. Only six of the Mariana Islands are inhabited, including the largest, SAIPAN (the administrative center), Tinian, and Rota. The islands have a total land area of 1,240 km^2 (479 mi^2), and the population is 22,719 (1990 est.). Tourism and the service industry provided by U.S. government and military installations are the economic mainstays.

The first European to discover the Marianas was Ferdinand Magellan in 1521, who claimed them for Spain. In 1899, Spain sold them to Germany, and in 1914, Japan assumed control. In 1944 the Marianas fell to U.S. forces. After World War II they became part of the Trust Territory of the Pacific Islands, under U.S. administration (see PACIFIC ISLANDS, TRUST TERRITORY OF THE). In 1975, Mariana residents voted for separate status in political union with the United States. They became internally self-governing in 1978. On Nov. 3, 1986, the United States proclaimed the Marianas a U.S. commonwealth.

Marianas Trench   The Marianas Trench, also called the Marianas Trough, the deepest known point on the Earth's surface, is an arc-shaped valley on the floor of the north Pacific Ocean located about 320 km (200 mi) east of the Mariana Islands. The trench, about 2,550 km (1,580 mi) long, contains a narrow, steep-sided gorge called Challenger Deep. The French oceanographer Jacques Piccard and U.S. Navy Lt. Don Walsh descended into the gorge to a depth of 10,912 m (35,800 ft) on Jan. 23, 1960. They traveled within the BATHYSCAPHE *Trieste,* designed by Piccard's father (see PICCARD, AUGUSTE) to withstand the enormous pressures while measuring the currents, salinity, and temperature of the water. The record depth of 11,034 m (36,201 ft) was sounded by Soviet scientists in 1959.

Marichal,   Juan [mah-ree-shahl']   Hall of Fame member Juan Antonio Sanchez Marichal, b. Dominican

Republic, Oct. 20, 1938, was one of baseball's dominant pitchers in the 1960s, when he won more games (191) than anyone else. The right-handed Marichal played for the San Francisco Giants (1960–73), Boston Red Sox (1974), and Los Angeles Dodgers (1975) and was known for his great control. He pitched in a record eight All-Star games and in his career had a won-lost record of 243-142 (.631 winning percentage), an earned-run average of 2.89, and 2,303 strikeouts.

Marie Antoinette   As the queen consort of King LOUIS XVI of France, Marie Antoinette, b. Nov. 2, 1755, d. Oct. 16, 1793, aroused hostile passions that helped lead to the FRENCH REVOLUTION. The daughter of Maria Theresa of Austria and Holy Roman Emperor Francis I, she married Louis in 1770. By 1774, when her husband became king, however, the beautiful, spirited Marie Antoinette had withdrawn from the restraints of French court etiquette and from her timid, aloof husband to a life of innocent but frivolous pleasure. She enchanted her small circle of friends but created the image of an untrustworthy foreigner and prodigal spendthrift opposed to the reforms proposed by the king's ministers.

Popular hatred of her obscured the fact that she advocated royal compromise with the revolutionary STATES-GENERAL. Bravely suffering her family's virtual imprisonment in the Tuileries from October 1789, she initiated their abortive attempt to flee the country in 1791 (the Flight to Varennes). Having secretly aided Austria's counterrevolutionary invasion of France, Marie Antoinette was executed by guillotine for treason.

Marie Antoinette, daughter of Maria Theresa of Austria, was the queen consort of Louis XVI of France. She was unpopular among the French, who suspected her of spying for Austria. During the French Revolution she was found guilty of treason and counterrevolutionary activity and guillotined.

Marie de France   Despite her name, the Anglo-Norman poet Marie de France lived and wrote at the court of Henry II of England sometime between 1175 and 1190. Her lais, dedicated to the king, defined the genre of the lai as a romantic story in verse, of variable length, that is related to several traditions including Ovid and Celtic folklore. The most famous of her lais are *Guigemar*, *Bisclavret* (The Werewolf), and *Le Chevrefoil* (The Honeysuckle). Her beast fables make up the *Ysopet*; the title is derived from the name of Aesop.

Marie de l'Incarnation

Marie de l'Incarnation, b. Marie Guyard at Tours, France, Oct. 28, 1599, d. Apr. 30, 1672, was the first woman to go to Canada as a Roman Catholic missionary. Married in 1617, she was widowed two years later and in 1632 entered the Ursuline convent at Tours. Marie volunteered for missionary service and in 1639 sailed for Quebec, where she taught school and compiled Indian dictionaries and catechisms. Her letters to her son, first published in 1681, have remained a valuable source of early Canadian history.

Marie de Médicis

[may-dee-sees'] Marie de Médicis, b. Apr. 26, 1573, d. July 3, 1642, was the second wife of HENRY IV of France and regent after his death. She was the daughter of Grand Duke Francesco I of Tuscany and a member of the MEDICI family. On her marriage in 1600 she came to France with a large Italian retinue. She has been accused of knowing of the plot behind her husband's assassination (1610), but her complicity remains uncertain.

As regent during the minority of her son, LOUIS XIII, she reversed Henry's anti-Habsburg policy. She came to rely on the Italian statesman Concino Concini, marquis d'Ancre, whom she made (1613) a marshal of France. Although Louis came of age in 1614, Marie's regency remained in effect until 1617, when Concini was murdered at the king's direction. She first regarded Cardinal RICHELIEU as her protégé, but he proved to be her implacable foe. Soon after her unsuccessful effort in November 1630 to secure Richelieu's dismissal, Louis banished her to Compiègne, but she fled to Brussels in the Spanish Netherlands.

Marietta

Marietta is a city in southeastern Ohio at the confluence of the Muskingum and Ohio rivers. It is the seat of Washington County and has a population of 15,026 (1990). Light manufacturing and truck, dairy, and cattle farming sustain the economy. Of interest are the Campus Martius Museum and Mound Cemetery, which contains an Indian mound. Marietta is the site of the first permanent settlement in Ohio (April 1788). A few months after its founding it was made the first capital of the Northwest Territory. The city was named for Marie Antoinette, queen of France.

marigold

Marigolds are annual or perennial herbs of the genus *Tagetes* in the sunflower family, Compositae. Although some marigolds may be called "African" or "French," these are merely popular names and do not indicate the plants' origin. Marigolds are native to the Americas from the southwestern United States to Argen-

The African marigold, an annual herb, is actually native to Mexico. If planted in a vegetable garden, marigolds ward off such pests as parasitic worms and rabbits.

tina. The flower heads, which may be a brassy yellow or orange or a reddish brown, are produced from July until frost and are borne either solitary or in flat-topped clusters.

marijuana

[mar-i-wahn'-uh] Marijuana (also spelled marihuana) is the common name given to any DRUG preparation from the hemp plant, *Cannabis sativa*. Various forms of this drug are known by different names throughout the world, such as kif in Morocco, dagga in South Africa, and ganja in India. Hashish refers to a dried, resinous substance that exudes from the flowering tops of the plant. In Western culture, cannabis preparations have acquired a variety of slang names, including grass, pot, tea, reefer, weed, and Mary Jane. Cannabis has been smoked, eaten in cakes, and drunk in beverages. In Western cultures marijuana is prepared most often as a tobaccolike mixture that is smoked in a pipe or rolled into a cigarette.

The major psychoactive component of marijuana is tetrahydrocannabinol (THC). Other cannabinoids have also been isolated, and their biochemistry is being studied. Psychoactive compounds are found in all parts of the plant, with the greatest concentration in the flowering tops. The content of these compounds varies greatly from plant to plant, depending on genetic and environmental factors.

Marijuana has its major physiological effects on the cardiovascular and central nervous systems; these effects are primarily sedative and hallucinogenic. Low doses psychologically produce a sense of well-being, relaxation, and sleepiness. Higher doses cause mild sensory distortions, altered time sense, loss of short-term memory, loss of balance, and difficulty in completing thought processes. Even higher doses can result in feelings of depersonalization, severe anxiety and panic, and a toxic psychosis, along with hallucinations, loss of insight, delusions, and paranoia. Physiologically, the heart rate increases and blood vessels of the eye dilate, causing reddening. A feeling of tightness in the chest and a lack of muscular coordination may also occur. Research suggests that marijuana smoke may have a long-term harmful effect on the lungs. Users may develop tolerance for the drug, but studies have not determined whether physical dependence results.

In 1937 possession and sale of marijuana became a criminal offense in the United States. In 1968 the possession and sale of THC was restricted to research. Despite such measures, marijuana continued to be widely used, at least until the 1980s, when surveys showed a decline in use. Cultivation of marijuana in the United States increased, however, accounting for 25 percent of the U.S. domestic market by 1990.

Medically, marijuana and THC preparations are sometimes used to treat GLAUCOMA, because they help to reduce pressure within the eye. The U.S. Food and Drug Administration has also approved the use of synthetic THC for treating the nausea and vomiting that can accompany cancer chemotherapy.

John Marin's works range from rugged seascapes to lively montages of city streets, as in Variations on Brooklyn (1932). (Whitney Museum of American Art, New York City.)

The marijuana, or Indian hemp, plant, Cannabis sativa, is native to central Asia but has been naturalized in many parts of the world. The dried flowering tops, stems, and leaves of the plants yield a mildly hallucinogenic drug that has been used since ancient times.

dium, he achieved in his early landscapes and cityscapes an individualistic, expressive style characterized by loose, spontaneous composition and transparency of color.

From 1912 to 1914 the New York City skyline was Marin's dominant theme, its buildings and bridges fused into a personal idiom of futurist energy, cubist structure, and Orphist synthesis of color and form. Spending summers in Maine beginning in 1914, he then also turned to seascapes, in which the brushwork appeared increasingly lyrical and calligraphic. From 1920 on his forms became simpler and his colors brighter; often large, abstract planes enframe these compositions, as in the celebrated *Maine Islands* (1922; Phillips Collection, Washington, D.C.).

marimba The marimba is a XYLOPHONE with a resonator under each of its wooden bars. In African music the resonators may be tin cans or gourds; in Central America, wood. The marimba in the modern orchestra (made in the United States since about 1910) has two rows of bars arranged similarly to the piano keyboard; beneath each bar is a tubular metal resonator tuned to the bar's pitch. The bars are struck with soft or padded mallets, and the sound is more mellow and resonant than that of the xylophone. Marimbas are common in percussion sections for the performance of 20th-century compositions; concerti for the instrument have been written by Paul Creston and Darius Milhaud.

Marin, John [mair'-in] John Marin, b. Rutherford, N.J., Dec. 23, 1870, d. Oct. 1, 1953, was an important member of the first generation of American modernist painters. Alfred Stieglitz first exhibited Marin's paintings in 1909. Working primarily in watercolor, his favorite me-

marine biology Marine biology is the study of ocean plants and animals, particularly of their adaptations to each other (see CORAL REEF) and to such factors as currents, waves, temperature, pressure, water chemistry, and light intensity. The field dates back to the early 19th century and is one of the main branches of OCEANOGRAPHY, the study of physical and chemical phenomena occurring in the oceans. Because marine biology provides practical benefits for the fishing industry, many maritime nations have established marine biology laboratories.

Marine Corps, U.S. The U.S. Marine Corps, within the Department of the Navy, consists of air and ground forces specially trained in AMPHIBIOUS WARFARE. The marines have been used in wartime for the seizure or defense of advanced naval bases and for the conduct of land operations involved in the prosecution of naval campaigns. The marines also provide detachments and organizations for service on naval vessels and security de-

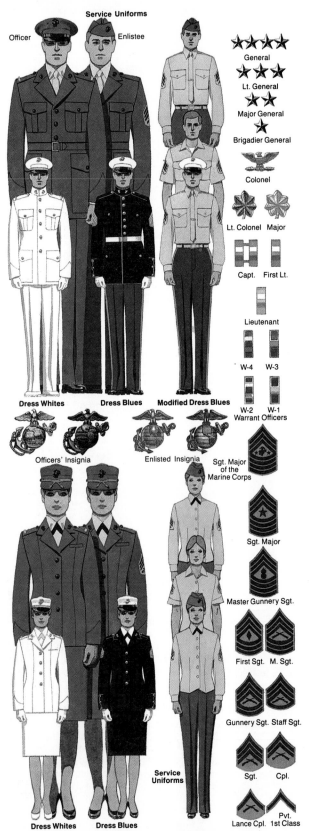

Service Uniforms

Officer — Enlistee

Dress Whites — Dress Blues — Modified Dress Blues

Officers' Insignia — Enlisted Insignia

Service Uniforms

Dress Whites — Dress Blues

★★★★ General
★★★ Lt. General
★★ Major General
★ Brigadier General
Colonel
Lt. Colonel — Major
Capt. — First Lt.
Lieutenant
W-4 — W-3
W-2 — W-1
Warrant Officers

Sgt. Major of the Marine Corps
Sgt. Major
Master Gunnery Sgt.
First Sgt. — M. Sgt.
Gunnery Sgt. — Staff Sgt.
Sgt. — Cpl.
Pvt.
Lance Cpl. — 1st Class

In the United States Marine Corps, officers and enlisted personnel wear uniforms of similar design. Formal summer uniforms known as "dress whites" are reserved for officers of either sex; "dress blues" may be worn by both officers and enlisted personnel. Rank is indicated in cap emblems and through rank insignia on the uniform. The garrison cap is standard wear for both officers and enlisted men. The service hat is worn by ceremonial units.

tachments for the protection of naval property and U.S. embassies and consulates. The commandant of the Marine Corps is a four-star general and a member of the Joint Chiefs of Staff. For more information on rank in the marines, see RANK, MILITARY.

History. "Sea soldiers" or marines have had an important role in naval warfare since the beginning of recorded history. Imperial Rome made use of marines as the fighting element of its navy. One of the oldest of modern marine corps is Britain's Royal Marines, which dates from 1664. On Nov. 10, 1775, the Second Continental Congress authorized the raising of two battalions of American marines. These Continental Marines served at sea with the Continental Navy (under John Paul JONES, in particular) and on occasion ashore with the Continental Army, as at the Battle of Princeton (1777). After the war they were disbanded, as was the Continental Navy.

The U.S. Marines came back into being in 1794, when the United States began to rebuild its navy, and they were established as a distinct and separate corps in 1798. Marines served in the Quasi-War with France (1798–1801), in actions against the Barbary pirates (see TRIPOLITAN WAR) in the Mediterranean, and in the WAR OF 1812. The Marine Corps provided a regiment in the SEMINOLE WARS, and in the MEXICAN WAR a marine battalion joined Gen. Winfield Scott's army at Veracruz and fought its way to Mexico City. During the CIVIL WAR the U.S. Marine Corps made numerous landings to enforce the blockade of the Confederacy. The Confederacy had its own small Confederate States Marine Corps.

During the SPANISH-AMERICAN WAR (1898), a U.S. Marine battalion landed at Guantánamo to seize and defend an advance base in support of naval operations against Santiago de Cuba. Interventions in Latin America and the Orient led to long-term garrisoning of marines in China (1905–41), Panama (1903–14), Nicaragua (1910–13, 1926–33), Haiti (1915–34), and the Dominican Republic (1916–24). During WORLD WAR I the Marine Corps sent (1917–18) two brigades to the American Expeditionary Force in France.

During the course of WORLD WAR II the U.S. Marines grew to six divisions and five aircraft wings, with a peak strength of about 485,000. In the KOREAN WAR the marines had one division and an aircraft wing in active combat operations. Marine Corps unit involvement in the VIETNAM WAR lasted from 1962 until 1975. In 1983, Marines served as part of a multinational peacekeeping force in Lebanon and constituted most of the U.S. force that invaded Grenada in October of that year. Half the combat strength of the Marine Corps was employed in the GULF WAR (1991).

Present Organization. The post-Vietnam Marine Corps was stabilized at a strength of 197,000 officers and enlisted personnel. Marine Corps aviation had an inventory

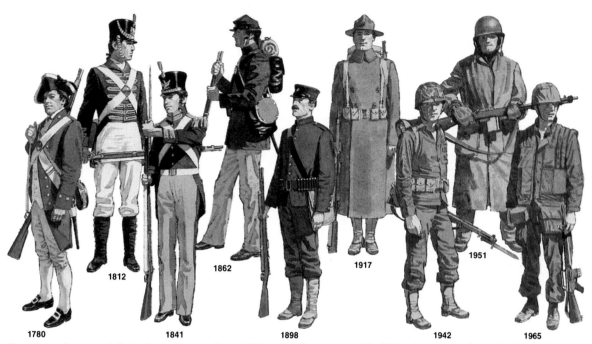

1780   1812   1841   1862   1898   1917   1942   1951   1965

The various uniforms worn by Marine Corps soldiers over the past 200 years are illustrated above. The 1780 marine wears a uniform with white coat facings and white breeches. With the exception of the change from breeches to long pants, the 1812 marine is almost identical to his Mexican War counterpart. By 1862, however, the marines had discarded these decorated uniforms in favor of simpler garb, whereas the 1898 marine wears a visored cap, a carry-over from the Civil War kepi. The 1917 marine is shown in a khaki uniform. The combat marines of 1942, 1951, and 1965 wear uniforms almost identical to their army counterparts except for minor color variations and the marine emblem.

of about 1,300 aircraft, half of them fixed-wing, the other half helicopters. The Fleet Marine Force (Pacific) has its headquarters in Oahu, Hawaii, where a Marine Corps air-ground brigade is also based. The 1st Marine Division's home base is Camp Pendleton, Calif. Most of the 3d Marine Aircraft Wing is nearby at El Toro, Calif. When not at sea or elsewhere on exercises, two-thirds of the 3d Marine Division is stationed in Okinawa. Its supporting 1st Marine Aircraft Wing is divided between the Japanese home islands and Okinawa. On the U.S. East Coast, the Fleet Marine Force (Atlantic) is headquartered at Norfolk, Va. The 2d Marine Division is at Camp Lejeune, N.C., with the 2d Marine Aircraft Wing nearby at Cherry Point, N.C. Air-ground task forces from these two units are routinely maintained afloat in the Mediterranean.

Marine Corps educational and developmental activities are centered on Quantico, Va. The corps' major logistical support bases are at Albany, Ga., and Barstow, Calif. A huge air-ground combined arms training area is maintained at Twenty-Nine Palms, Calif.

The Marine Corps Reserve consists mainly of the 4th Marine Division and the 4th Marine Aircraft Wing, with headquarters at New Orleans, La.

The Marine Corps' familiar "globe and anchor" emblem was adopted in 1868. The corps' motto since 1883 has been *Semper Fidelis* ("always faithful"). The term *Leatherneck* referring to a marine comes from the leather stocks or collars worn by marines from 1775 until 1875.

The more recent term *Devil Dogs* is a translation of the epithet *Teufelhunden* reportedly applied to the U.S. Marines by the Germans in World War I.

Mariner Mariner is a series of U.S. space probes that have provided information on the inner planets MERCURY, VENUS, and MARS. The first successful probe, *Mariner 2* (1962), was the first spacecraft to visit a planet. The last, *Mariner 10,* launched in late 1973, survived a seemingly endless series of malfunctions to accomplish the first two-planet, four-encounter space mission ever flown. The smallest Mariners weighed upward of 200 kg (440 lb), and the largest, *Mariners 8* and *9,* each weighed about 1,000 kg (2,200 lb).

The initial Mariner, because of a malfunction, veered off course shortly after liftoff on July 22, 1962. *Mariner 2,* launched on Aug. 27, 1962, passed within 34,758 km (21,598 mi) of Venus on December 14 of that year, proving that the surface temperature of Venus is about 400° C (800° F) and indicating that the planet's magnetic field is either nonexistent or extremely weak. *Mariner 5,* which flew by Venus at a distance of 3,991 km (2,479 mi) on Oct. 19, 1967, confirmed a low upper limit to the magnetic-field strength, provided some data on atmospheric composition, and detected a glowing hydrogen corona about 2,900 km (1,800 mi) above the planet. The final Mariner encounter with Venus, *Mariner 10,* passed about 5,770 km (3,585 mi) from Venus on Feb. 5, 1974. Images made through ultraviolet filters revealed a wealth of detail in the clouds, including several distinct layers. *Mariner 10* then went on to Mercury, where it had three encounters, found a weak magnetic field, and photomapped the surface.

The first successful Mars probe, *Mariner 4*, passed 9,844 km (6,118 mi) from Mars on July 14, 1965. Low-resolution photos showed few surface features, but other instruments revealed the planet's thin atmosphere and low temperatures. *Mariners 6* and *7* added better photos and more data in July 1969. In 1971, *Mariner 9* went into martian orbit and revealed huge volcanoes, canyons, rills, and many features suggestive of formation by flowing water. Photometry and spectroscopy yielded data on surface types and atmospheric structure and content and laid the groundwork for the VIKING spacecraft that encountered Mars in 1976.

A project to send two Mariner spacecraft to JUPITER and SATURN was renamed VOYAGER.

See also: SPACE EXPLORATION.

Marinetti, Filippo Tommaso The Italian playwright and poet Filippo Tommaso Marinetti, b. Alexandria, Egypt, Dec. 22, 1876, d. Dec. 2, 1944, began the aesthetic movement FUTURISM in 1909, when his "Futurist Manifesto" appeared in the Parisian daily *Le Figaro*. The manifesto exalted machines, speed, and war, which was defined as "the world's only hygiene." Marinetti eliminated all adjectives, adverbs, and punctuation from his plays and poems; he also proposed a break with metrical schemes, syntax, and every other convention of creative writing. Initially limiting these theories to literature, Marinetti soon extended them to painting, sculpture, architecture, and music. His works include *Mafarka the Futurist* (1910; Eng. trans., 1972) and *Zang Tumb Tumb: The Siege of Adrianople* (1914; Eng. trans., 1972).

Marion, Francis Francis Marion, b. Berkely County, S.C., *c.*1732, d. Feb. 27, 1795, known as "the Swamp Fox," was a guerrilla commander in South Carolina during the American Revolution. After the British captured Charleston in 1780, he and a band of irregulars roamed the coastal marsh country, raiding enemy outposts and disrupting British and Loyalist activities. In 1781 he commanded the militia at the Battle of Eutaw Springs. After the war, Marion served in the South Carolina legislature and the state constitutional convention of 1790.

marionette see PUPPET

Maris, Roger Roger Eugene Maris, b. Fargo, N.Dak., Sept. 10, 1934, d. Dec. 14, 1985, was an American professional baseball player who made history when he broke (1961) Babe Ruth's one-season home-run record with a total of 61. Ruth had hit 60 home runs during a 154-game season, whereas Maris's record was set in 162 games.

Maris joined the New York Yankees in 1960 and teamed with Mickey Mantle to form a high-powered hitting duo. He was named the American League's Most Valuable Player twice (1960 and 1961), and in 1961 he also led the league in runs batted in (142). Maris was traded to the St. Louis Cardinals in 1966 and retired in 1968.

Marisol [mair'-i-suhl] A leading American pop artist of Venezuelan ancestry, Marisol Escobar, b. Paris, May 22, 1930, known as Marisol, is noted for her witty sculptures that comment on the inanities of modern life. Her assemblages, which are group portraits, combine large, carved wooden figures, plaster casts, and real objects such as shoes or items of clothing. Often, all the members of the group resemble the artist.

Maritain, Jacques [mah-ree-tan'] Jacques Maritain, b. Nov. 18, 1882, d. Apr. 28, 1973, a French Roman Catholic philosopher, sought to interpret the philosophy of Saint Thomas AQUINAS in terms of the intellectual and practical problems of the modern world. The lectures of Henri BERGSON led him to abandon scientific materialism, however, and he was converted (1906) to Catholicism by the mystic poet Léon Bloy.

Philosophy begins, Maritain held, with the "intuition of being." Intuition, however, must be related to other sorts of knowledge. In *The Degrees of Knowledge* (1932; Eng. trans., 1937), his most important work, he discusses knowledge of the universe in three categories: mobile being (nature), quantity (mathematics), and "being as being" (metaphysics). The sciences discover within nature problems that go beyond experiment and mathematical analysis. Maritain strips Aquinas's five proofs of God's existence of examples taken from ancient physics and restates them in modern terms.

maritime climate see CLIMATE

maritime law Maritime law (also called admiralty law) is concerned with rights and duties stemming from the use of ships on the high seas and other navigable waters having outlets to the sea. As a separate body of law, it dates from ancient times.

By the late Middle Ages there were advanced sea codes in effect in several areas of Europe. Important in the Mediterranean was the *Consolat de Mar* (Consulate of the Sea), compiled in Barcelona in the 13th century. In northern Europe the 12th-century Rolls of Oléron, an Anglo-Norman or French compilation, were more influential. Other codifications included the Laws of Wisby and the Laws of the Hansa Towns (see HANSEATIC LEAGUE).

In England the tendency of maritime law to develop into a separate system was encouraged by the maritime disputes that were adjudicated by special courts attached to the office of the Lord High Admiral. In 1873 the functions of these courts were assumed by the high court of justice.

English admiralty law was brought to colonial America, and vice-admiralty courts were established. When the U.S. Constitution was drafted, there was virtually unanimous agreement that federal judicial power should extend, as Article III provides, to "all cases of admiralty and maritime jurisdiction" with the result that, in the United States, maritime law is under the exclusive jurisdiction of the federal courts, except for common law suits stemming from collision at sea.

Through the years the Supreme Court has taken an expansive view of admiralty jurisdiction. Contrary to earlier beliefs, the jurisdiction reaches not only coastal waters but also the Great Lakes and the principal rivers—indeed, any body of water connecting states or forming a channel to the sea.

International law, as distinguished from maritime law, has tended to concern itself with issues related to freedom of the seas (see SEAS, FREEDOM OF THE) and—in the second half of the 20th century—with exploitation of the resources of the sea, seabed, and territorial shelf (see SEA, LAW OF THE).

Maritime law, concerned principally as it is with oceangoing commerce, tends toward uniformity the world over, even in the absence of formal international agreement. In important areas, however, there have been international conventions as well. Perhaps the most notable example is the Hague Convention on Carriage of Goods by Sea (1921), ratified by practically the entire shipping world.

Maritime Provinces   The Maritime Provinces of NEW BRUNSWICK, NOVA SCOTIA, and PRINCE EDWARD ISLAND encompass the southeasternmost corner of Canada. With a combined area of 134,584 km^2 (51,963 mi^2), the Maritimes comprise less than 1.4% of the total national area. Lumbering, mining, and fishing dominate the economy; Prince Edward Island has particularly rich farmland. Once part of ACADIA, the Maritimes were caught between French and British control from their first sighting by the French in 1604 until the entire area was ceded to Britain in 1763.

Marius, Gaius [mar'-ee-uhs]   Gaius Marius, born of local gentry c.157 BC near Arpinum, rose to prominence in Rome through skillful manipulation of noble patrons and successful military commands, the first of which was in the war (109–105 BC) against JUGURTHA, king of Numidia.

By regularizing the recruitment of the landless poor, Marius unwittingly laid the basis for the growth of client armies that were loyal only to their commanders. Elected consul for five consecutive years (104–100), he also revised the organization, training, and equipment of Roman armies while repelling invasions of the Teutoni (102) and Cimbri (101). Political miscalculations in 100, however, forced him to abandon Rome.

Marius again commanded in the Social War (90–89),

but his progress was thwarted by Lucius Cornelius SULLA. In the struggle between the two for command in the war against MITHRADATES VI of Pontus, Sulla demonstrated the effects of Marius's reforms by marching on Rome and forcing Marius into exile. Raising his own client army, Marius joined Lucius Cornelius CINNA to capture Rome. Amid a bloody purge of his enemies, Marius was made consul for the year 86 BC, but he died soon after taking office.

Marivaux, Pierre Carlet de Chamblain de   [mah-ree-voh', pee-air' kahr-lay' duh shahm-blan' duh]   Pierre Carlet de Chamblain de Marivaux, b. Feb. 4, 1688, d. Feb. 12, 1763, the most important French playwright of the 18th century, wrote numerous comedies for La Comédie Française and La Comédie Italienne of Paris, the most famous of which are *The Game of Love and Chance* (1730; Eng. trans., 1923) and *Les Fausses Confidences* (1737; trans. as *False Confession,* 1958). The French word *marivaudage* signifies the flirtatious bantering tone characteristic of Marivaux's dialogue. He also published a number of essays and two important though unfinished novels, *La Vie de Marianne* (1731–41; trans. as *The Virtuous Orphan,* 1743) and *Le Paysan parvenu* (1734–35; trans. as *The Fortunate Peasant,* 1735).

marjoram [mahr'-juh-ruhm]   Marjoram, or sweet marjoram, is a perennial subshrub, *Origanum majorana,* of the mint family, Labiatae, cultivated for its fragrant leaves, which are used as a flavoring and aromatic. Native to western Asia and the Mediterranean region, marjoram is commercially cultivated in France, Chile, Peru, and California. Whole or ground marjoram is used with vegetables, lamb, sausage, stews, and poultry stuffing. Its essential oil is occasionally used in spice mixtures and perfumes.

Mark, Saint   In the Christian Bible, Mark was the son of Mary of Jerusalem (whose house was used as a gathering place by early Christians) and the cousin of Saint BARNABAS. Mark was his Roman surname; his first name was John (Acts 12:12). He accompanied Barnabas and Saint PAUL on their first missionary journey (Acts 12 and 13) but abruptly left them at Perga. Paul therefore refused to take Mark on the second trip, a decision that precipitated a break between the apostle and Barnabas (Acts 15:36–40). Paul and Mark later reconciled their differences (Col. 4:10; Philem. 24). Mark was also associated with Peter (Acts 12:12; 1 Pet. 5:13).

Mark, Gospel According to   Mark is the second Gospel in the New Testament of the BIBLE. It is the earliest and the shortest of the four Gospels. Papias, an early church father, ascribed this Gospel to Mark, an interpreter of Peter who is often identified with Mark, the cousin of Saint BARNABAS and companion of Barnabas and Saint PAUL on their first missionary journey. Irenaeus said that

Mark wrote this Gospel after Peter and Paul had died. Most scholars today, therefore, date the book AD 65–70.

The Gospel was probably written in Rome for a primarily Gentile audience, to convince them that Jesus of Nazareth, in spite of his sufferings and death, was the Son of God. It has been called a Gospel of action because it records 18 miracles (similar in count to Matthew and Luke) but only 4 parables (Matthew includes 18 parables and Luke 19). Jesus' victory over evil through his deeds and death receives emphasis. Much material in Mark is repeated in Matthew and in Luke, leading most scholars to conclude that Mark was written first and used independently by the other writers.

marketing   Marketing includes a variety of activities relating to the distribution and sale of goods or services. Simple marketing activities began with the development of a nonsubsistence economy and interregional trade, including caravan and maritime commerce. Village fairs, town markets, and peddlers were all involved in primitive marketing activities. Later, general stores, traveling salespeople, and, still later, the 20th-century chain store became the chief marketing agencies. Modern marketing has evolved into a complex and diverse field. This field includes a wide variety of special functions such as AD-VERTISING, MAIL-ORDER BUSINESS, PUBLIC RELATIONS, RETAILING and merchandising, SALES, TRANSPORTATION, WHOLESALING, marketing research, and pricing of goods.

Markham, Edwin   Edwin Markham is the pen name of Charles Edward Anson Markham, b. Oregon City, Oreg., Apr. 23, 1852, d. Mar. 7, 1940, an obscure California schoolteacher who achieved great fame in 1899 with his poem "The Man with the Hoe." Inspired by Jean François Millet's painting of the same title, Markham chose a resoundingly rhetorical and sonorous style to express his concern for the downtrodden. Later poems, notably "Lincoln, the Man of the People" (1901), were also popular. Markham was an outspoken critic of child labor, and his articles on the subject were collected in *The Children of Bondage* (1914).

Markov, Andrei Andreyevich [mahr'-kawf, ahn-dray' ahn-dray'-uh-vich]   The Soviet mathematician Andrei Andreyevich Markov, b. June 14 (N.S.), 1856, d. July 20, 1922, is best known for his work in probability and for the so-called Markov process.

A graduate (1878) of St. Petersburg University, where he began teaching in 1880, Markov applied the method of continued fractions, pioneered by his teacher Pafnuty Chebyshev, to probability theory. Markov gave particular emphasis to Markov chains—sequences of random variables in which the future variable is determined by the present variable but is independent of the way in which the present state arose from its predecessors. In 1923, Norbert WIENER became the first to treat rigorously a continuous Markov process.

Markova, Dame Alicia [marh'-koh-vuh]   Dame Alicia Markova, b. Lillian Alicia Marks, London, Dec. 1, 1910, was the first great British ballerina. She studied with Seraphima Astafyeva until she was 14, when she joined the Ballets Russes de Serge Diaghilev. Markova created the title role in the young George Balanchine's *Le Rossignol* (*The Nightingale*, 1926). In the 1930s, following Diaghilev's death (1929), she danced with the Ballet Rambert and the Vic-Wells Ballet (now the Royal Ballet). In 1935 she formed the Markova-Dolin Ballet with her frequent partner Anton Dolin.

Markova was prima ballerina (1938–41) of the Ballets Russes de Monte Carlo, appearing in works by Leonid Massine, such as *Seventh Symphony*. She danced (1941–44; 1945–46) with American Ballet Theatre and created the role of Juliet (1943) in Anthony Tudor's one-act *Romeo and Juliet*. In 1950 she and Dolin founded the London Festival Ballet. Until her retirement from performance in 1963, Markova continued to appear as a guest artist with numerous companies. She was noted above all for her *Giselle*.

marl   A sedimentary rock, marl is a white, gray, or brownish earthy mixture of fine-grained calcium carbonate and clay. Formed in both marine and freshwater environments, marl commonly contains fossil shells. It is used as a fertilizer and in the manufacture of insulation, portland cement, and bricks. Some marl, such as the potassium-rich glauconite, or green sand, marl, is used in water softeners.

Marlborough, John Churchill, 1st Duke of   John Churchill, 1st duke of Marlborough, b. May 26, 1650, d. June 16, 1722, was an English statesman and an outstanding general. He entered the army in 1667; he first distinguished himself by helping defeat (1685) the re-

John Churchill, 1st duke of Marlborough, was one of the greatest military commanders in history. He reached the zenith of his power during the reign of Queen Anne (1702–14), when he won numerous victories in the War of the Spanish Succession.

bellion of the duke of MONMOUTH. King JAMES II raised him to the peerage and promoted him to lieutenant general. Churchill soon shifted his allegiance, however, to William of Orange, who deposed James (1688; see GLORIOUS REVOLUTION) and ruled as WILLIAM III. Churchill then campaigned for William during the war against France (see GRAND ALLIANCE, WAR OF THE) in Flanders and Ireland. The king made Churchill earl of Marlborough, but Marlborough lost royal favor when it became known that he was in secret correspondence with the deposed James II.

In 1677 or 1678 Marlborough married Sarah Jennings, a favorite of ANNE, the younger daughter of James II. When Anne became queen in 1702, she appointed Marlborough commander in chief and first minister. During the long war against France (see SPANISH SUCCESSION, WAR OF THE), he won victories at Blenheim (1704), Ramillies (1706), Oudenarde (1708), and Malplaquet (1709). Anne raised him to a duke and had Blenheim Palace in Oxfordshire built for him. Gradually, however, Sarah's relationship with the queen worsened, and in 1711, Marlborough was ousted from all his offices. He was charged with financial fraud and went into exile the following year. He returned to England in 1714, remaining relatively inactive for the rest of his life. He was excessively ambitious and not particularly loyal, but he is acknowledged as a master military strategist.

Marlborough, Sarah Churchill, Duchess of

Sarah Churchill, b. Sarah Jennings, May 29, 1660, d. Oct. 18, 1744, a clever, mercurial beauty, was the confidante of Princess (later Queen) ANNE from childhood and in 1677 or 1678 married John Churchill, later duke of Marlborough. She reconciled Anne to WILLIAM III after he deposed the princess's father, JAMES II, in 1688. Although Sarah's husband was dismissed in 1692, Sarah remained in Princess Anne's employ. The couple returned to full favor when Anne became queen in 1702. The duchess's political intrigues, however, led to her dismissal in 1711.

marlin

Marlins, family Istiophoridae, are large oceanic fishes characterized by an elongation of the upper jaw (premaxillae and nasal bones) into a long, rounded, pointed bill, or spear. The complete function of the bill is not clear,

The blue marlin, found in warm and tropical seas throughout the world, is a favorite sport fish among deep-sea anglers.

but apparently it is used to stun the marlin's prey of fish and squid as the marlin slashes through their schools. Marlins can swim at speeds up to 65 km/h (40 mph).

Four species are frequently recognized. The black marlin, *Makaira indica*, of the Indian and Pacific oceans, is the largest, reaching 708 kg (1,560 lb). The blue marlin, *M. nigricans*, is found worldwide in warm waters. The striped marlin, *Tetrapturus audax*, inhabits the Pacific. The white marlin, *T. albidus*, of the Atlantic, is the smallest.

Marlowe, Christopher

Christopher Marlowe, baptized Feb. 26, 1564, d. May 30, 1593, an Elizabethan dramatist and poet second in greatness only to Shakespeare, is recognized for a handful of excellent plays—*Tamburlaine the Great*, *Doctor Faustus*, *Edward II*, and *The Jew of Malta*—along with his narrative poem *Hero and Leander* (1598) and the much imitated "Come live with me and be my love" (1599).

The son of a shoemaker, Marlowe attended King's School, Canterbury, and in 1581 matriculated at Cambridge. In 1587 he seems to have been employed on a confidential mission for Elizabeth I. By 1589, Marlowe was living in London and probably writing and producing his major plays. His companionships made him one of the University Wits. In 1592 he and Richard Baines were arrested in Flushing for counterfeiting. Because of Baines's testimony, Marlowe also was alleged to have been connected with Sir Walter Raleigh's so-called "school of night"—a group supposedly dabbling in the sacrilegious, alchemy, and the occult. On May 18, 1593, the Privy Council issued a warrant for Marlowe's arrest because certain heretical papers found in the possession of Thomas KYD were claimed by Kyd to be Marlowe's. Questioned and released, Marlowe was murdered by Ingram Frazier at Eleanor Bull's tavern in Deptford.

Marlowe's play *Tamburlaine the Great*, Parts 1 and 2 (published 1590) is drawn from histories of the Mongol conqueror; *Edward II* (published 1594) is based on English history; *The Massacre at Paris* (published 1600) makes use of contemporary pamphlets describing the Catholic-Huguenot conflict in France; *Doctor Faustus* (published 1604, 1616) is indebted to a translation of the German *Faustbuch*; and *Dido, Queen of Carthage* (published 1594) follows Vergil's *Aeneid*. Only *The Jew of Malta* (published 1633) lacks a known direct source.

In his studies of ambitious men, Marlowe dealt with the Renaissance "overreacher," revealing his heroism and strength of will while chronicling the loss of humanity occasioned by his unchecked abuse of power. In his mastery of blank verse—Marlowe's "mighty line"—in his successful development of the tragedy and the history play, and in his ability to handle themes as different as tragic love, self-destruction, suffering, and damnation, Marlowe sketched the way other English dramatists would follow.

Marmara, Sea of

[mahr'-muh-ruh] The Sea of Marmara, ancient Propontis, is an inland sea in northwest

Turkey. Formed about 2.5 million years ago, it connects with the Black Sea through the BOSPORUS (northeast) and with the Aegean Sea through the DARDANELLES (southwest). Only about 280 km (175 mi) long and 80 km (50 mi) at its widest point, the water has a small tidal range because of its lack of strong currents. Two island groups lie in the sea, the Princes' Islands (northeast) and Marmara Islands (southwest). ISTANBUL, Turkey's largest city, lies on both sides of the Bosporus at its junction with the Sea of Marmara.

marmoset [mahr'-muh-set]   Long-tailed monkeys, marmosets comprise the 4 genera and 33 species of the family Callithricidae, order Primates. They are among the world's smallest monkeys, often weighing less than 0.45 kg (1 lb) and measuring 20 to 35 cm (8 to 14 in) long, with a tail 25 to 40 cm (10 to 16 in) long. The fur is long and variable in color. Marmosets inhabit tropical forests of Panama and South America. They feed on fruit, insects, and spiders. The male assists in the birth of the young and carries them on his back between feedings.

The cotton-top marmoset, native to the rain forests of Colombia, is among the world's smallest primates, measuring 25 cm (10 in) in combined head and body length. This monkey's name is derived from its shaggy, white crest.

marmot [mahr'-muht]   Marmots are about 12 species of rodents in the genus *Marmota*. The largest members of the squirrel family, Sciuridae, marmots weigh between 3 and 8 kg (7 and 18 lb). The head-body length ranges from 30 to 60 cm (12 to 24 in); the bushy tail is 10 to 25 cm (4 to 10 in) long. Marmots live in burrows in open habitats where the vegetable matter they eat is plentiful. Among the best-known species are the GROUNDHOG, or woodchuck, *M. monax*, of eastern and central North America; the hoary marmot, *M. caligata*, of western North America; and the alpine marmot, *M. marmota*, of Europe.

Marne, Battles of the   see WORLD WAR I

Marne River   The Marne River, in northern France, rises in the Plateau de Langres and arcs northwest over a winding course of 525 km (326 mi) to join the SEINE RIVER at Charenton-le-Pont, an eastern suburb of Paris. Navigable for more than 354 km (220 mi), the Marne is connected by canals with the AISNE, RHINE, and SAÔNE rivers. During World War I the Allies twice repulsed German drives toward Paris at the Marne. Heavy fighting took place in the area again during World War II (1944).

Maronites   The Maronites are the largest Christian sect in Lebanon, where they constitute a large minority of the population. The sect first appeared in northern Syria during the 6th century but was driven into the Lebanon Mountains by Muslims in the 7th century. The Maronite patron saint is the Syrian monk Maro (Maron, d. *c.*410), but the sect's actual founder was Yuhanna Maro (d. 707), under whom the group developed a distinct political and communal organization. The Maronites claim to have always been Eastern Rite Christians (see EASTERN RITE CHURCHES) in union with Rome. It seems that until the 12th century, however, the community professed the doctrines of MONOTHELITISM. During the CRUSADES the Maronites allied themselves with the Roman Catholic church, and in 1964 the head of the Maronite church was made a cardinal by Pope Paul VI. The Maronites retain ancient Eastern rites and other religious customs and use Syriac for their liturgy.

In bloody conflict from earliest times with surrounding tribes and sects, the Maronites nevertheless prospered under a militant clergy. Under European protection, they became the dominant political sect in Lebanon, and since Lebanon's independence (1943), they have controlled many key governmental and military posts. Their dominance has repeatedly been challenged, however, by Lebanon's growing Muslim population.

Marquand, J. P. [mahr'-kwahnd]   John Phillips Marquand, b. Wilmington, Del., Nov. 10, 1893, d. July 16, 1960, was an American novelist whose major subject was the Boston upper-class elite. He was a novelist of manners who found in the tradition-bound lives of the descendants of an old aristrocracy material for satire and examples of the virtues of courtesy, honesty, and fairness. Marquand made this milieu his subject only after a long and successful career as a writer of slick adventure and cloak-and-dagger fiction (including works featuring the Japanese detective Mr. Moto). *The Late George Apley* (1937), for which he won a Pulitzer Prize, was his first novel about the customs and habits of Boston gentility.

Marquesas Islands [mahr-kay'-sahs]   The Marquesas Islands, 14 isles in the central Pacific Ocean about 1,450 km (900 mi) northeast of Tahiti, are part of FRENCH POLYNESIA. Their land area totals 1,274 km^2 (492 mi^2); Nuku Hiva is the largest island. The population, mostly Polynesian, of the 7 inhabited islands is 5,419 (1977). Volcanic in origin, the Marquesas have a hot, humid climate with rainfall of 635–1,400 mm (25–55 in) yearly.

Vanilla, coffee, tobacco, and breadfruit are grown in the mountain valleys. Copra and mother-of-pearl are exported.

Álvaro de Mendaña de Neyra was the first European to reach the Marquesas (1595). Later visited by British (1774) and American (1791) seamen, the islands came under French control in 1842. The painter Paul Gauguin worked and died on Hiva Oa, the second largest island. Herman Melville described the islands in his book *Typee* (1846).

marquetry [mahr'-kuh-tree]   Marquetry is a method of decorating furniture with floral, arabesque, or figurative designs formed of thin pieces of exotic or colored woods, metals, or organic materials, such as tortoiseshell, mother-of-pearl, and ivory. These designs originally were cut with a hand saw and glued directly to the surface of the furniture. By the mid-19th century, machine tools were used to saw, slice, or cut the materials in paper-thin layers. The pieces of the design were then fitted together, glued to the furniture, and fixed there with a hot marquetry iron and a hammer.

Marquette, Jacques [mahr-ket']   A Jesuit missionary, Jacques Marquette, b. France, June 1, 1637, d. May 18, 1675, explored the Great Lakes and the Mississippi River valley with Louis JOLLIET. He arrived in Quebec in 1666 and studied Indian languages for two years before leaving to work with other missionaries on the shores of Lake Superior. Marquette founded (1671) Saint Ignace mission on the north shore of the Mackinac Straits. In 1672, Jolliet arrived with orders to seek a great river to the west, which the Illinois Indians had described.

In May 1673 an expedition composed of Jolliet, Marquette, and five voyageurs (employed to carry traders and goods into and out of the fur-trapping country) set out by way of Green Bay and the Fox and Wisconsin rivers. They reached the Mississippi and descended it to the Arkansas before returning, convinced that the Mississippi flowed into the Gulf of Mexico. On their return, Marquette remained for a year at the mission of Saint Francis Xavier at De Pere near modern Green Bay. In 1674–75 he traveled to an Illinois Indian village but died while returning to the Saint Ignace mission.

marquis   see TITLES OF NOBILITY AND HONOR

Marquis, Don [mahr'-kwis]   A newspaper columnist for the *New York Sun* and *New York Tribune,* Donald Robert Perry Marquis, b. Walnut, Ill., July 29, 1878, d. Dec. 29, 1937, is best remembered for the poems of satire and humor ostensibly written by his twin creations, archy the cockroach (a reincarnated poet) and mehitabel the cat. The pieces were collected in such volumes as *archy and mehitabel* (1927), *archy's Life of mehitabel* (1933), and *The Life and Times of archy and mehitabel* (1940). Marquis also wrote short stories, plays, and other humorous verse.

Marrakech [mah-rah-kesh']   Marrakech (also Marrakesh) is a city in Marrakech province of southern Morocco. Its population is 1,425,000 (1987 est.). Located in the northern foothills of the High Atlas Mountains, Marrakech is the gateway to Morocco's interior. Renowned for its leather goods, the economy is now centered on tourism. The dominant landmark in the city is the 12th-century 67-m-high (220-ft) Kotubia minaret. The Dar Si Said palace (1591) houses the Museum of Moroccan Art.

Marrakech was founded in 1062 by the Almoravids. The Almohads made it their capital in 1147, and a series of conquerors occupied Marrakech from 1269 to 1554, when the Sadi sultans made it their capital. The city declined, and by the 17th century it was a slave-trading center. It was held by the French (1912–56) until Morocco became independent.

marriage   The institution of marriage is the socially recognized union between a man and a woman that serves to legitimate their children. In most societies of the world, husband and wife live together. Because a primary, although not essential, purpose of marriage is the procreation of children, sex is always recognized as a legitimate part of marriage (although in some cultures marriage is not the only institution for approved sexual activity).

All societies create around marriage a host of related cultural features having a lesser or greater degree of elaboration, which makes marriage superficially one of the most complex and varied of all human institutions.

Marriage: A Social Institution

A conventional marriage in most cultures follows a chain

The bride in a traditional Japanese wedding ceremony usually dresses in elaborate attire. The marriage rites culminate in a ceremonial feast at the groom's parental home, where the couple ritually drink three cups of sake.

In Hinduism the wedding ceremony initiates one of the four stages of life. Marriage rites include the recitation of traditional mantras by the bride and groom, who take seven steps together, symbolizing their journey through life.

of typical events in a predictable order. The initial stage involves some sort of courtship or, in some cultures, an arrangement by a marriage broker, which leads to a wedding of the bride and the groom. The wedding itself functions as a rite of passage (see PASSAGE, RITES OF). Particular details of the wedding ceremony and other activities associated with the event vary according to a particular culture's customs and, within socially accepted boundaries, the wishes of the principals or their kinfolk. After the wedding phase the marital relationship gradually matures and changes as the married pair age and as children are born and grow up. The termination of marriage, either with the death of one of the spouses or by divorce, marks the fourth and final stage. Widowed or divorced persons may or may not be allowed to remarry and go through the marital cycle once more.

Before Marriage. Marriages are either arranged between families (usually with some right of veto by the bride or groom) or are begun through a courtship in which the partners have found one another. Arranged marriages are predominant primarily in societies that place great importance on property inheritance, on linkages between lineages, or in which elders hold that young people are unable to make sound choices. China, India, and the Middle East are among the many parts of the world in which societies traditionally have practiced arranged marriages.

Arranged marriages, taken as a whole, work as well as any other form of marriage. The bride and the groom tend to expect far less, and the roles are far more clearly spelled out than in societies in which people select their own spouses.

The Wedding. The wedding is an occurrence before which the marriage union can be called off but after which the partners can be legally separated only by death, divorce, or annulment.

In traditional Eskimo culture the wedding is no more than the actual moving of bride and groom into the same household. In most societies, however, weddings are marked by celebration—a public statement that a marriage has been established. In the West a wedding must be performed by an official of the state or by a member of the clergy, who is declared an official of the state for this purpose. In some European countries a civil ceremony is required before a religious one is valid.

In traditional societies in many parts of the world, notably among the tribal peoples of Africa, the wedding occurs as a stage in a series of payments known as bride-price, or bridewealth (less commonly, in payments of groomwealth). Such payments are not to be confused with the gifts that are exchanged at weddings in many societies, or with DOWRY, which is the bride's property that she brings with her into the marriage. The exchange of bride-price in no way implies the selling of the bride. Rather, the payment is made for rights acquired in marriage to the bride, which may include the right to affiliate her children to the husband's lineage or clan, rights to property, sexual rights, and rights to labor. The latter may consist of the bride's labor in maintaining the household, to be interlinked with the work of other members of the household, as well as the rewards of labor performed by the bride outside the household. In theory, at least, such rights as those granted through the bride-price exchange are always reciprocated.

The Course of the Marriage. With the arrival of a child, the marriage partners face an important new set of roles—not just the roles of father and mother but those of coparent.

In some cultures the standard of behavior for parents is rigidly enforced by society and leaves little room for deviation. In others, as in modern Western society, such roles are less clearly defined, and questions of parenting can lead to considerable tension between the spouses or between the child's parents and grandparents. In some societies a person is not considered to have reached

In Western countries, church weddings, which solemnize the marriage by religious rites, are widely observed. The exchanging of rings and nuptial vows are integral aspects of the traditional American wedding ceremony.

adulthood before he or she marries, no matter at what age. In a few cultures, including that of the Tiv of Nigeria, a person is not considered fully an adult until he or she becomes a parent.

Plural Marriage. Although MONOGAMY, the marriage of one man and one woman at a time, is the rule in Western society, many other cultures allow plural marriage, or POLYGAMY. In many traditional African and Asian societies men are allowed to have more than one wife at a time, a practice called *polygyny*. The early books of the Old Testament contain many references to polygyny. A few societies—most of them in central Asia—traditionally allow a woman to have more than one husband at a time, called *polyandry*. In an extremely rare custom, known only from the Himalayan region, a few societies have allowed polygyny and polyandry simultaneously, a practice termed *polygyandry*.

People involved in plural marriages generally have sought different rewards in marriage from those sought in a monogamous union. In various polygynous cultures of Africa, for example, a man's having many heirs traditionally enhances his social position; the fact that a woman has many teammates results in greater cooperation both in agriculture or other domestic work and in seeing that all the wives get a fair share of the household property and benefits.

Divorce and Remarriage. In most cultures divorce is allowed, and divorced persons may, and often do, remarry. Some cultures, including that of the Brahman castes of India, do not allow widows to remarry. In various societies in which bride-price is paid as part of marriage, a widow may be inherited by one of her husband's kinsmen. If she is too old to bear children, she may elect not to be inherited. If she is inherited and does not like her new husband, called her *levir*, usually she is free to seek divorce. Early anthropologists wrote a great deal about the *levirate*—the term correctly refers to the inheritance of widows, but sometimes it is used to refer to the kind of polygyny in which a widowed woman marries her deceased husband's brother, as occurred among the ancient Hebrew tribes.

In a few places, if a young woman dies her sister is sent to replace her as wife; this custom, called the *sororate*, was common among various North American Indian peoples.

Marriage: A Legal Definition

Although the expression *the marriage contract* is often used in everyday speech, marriage is technically what is known as an anomalous contract and from a legal standpoint is not to be confused with other forms of contract. In the West marriage is a matter of family law, not contract law. Family law dictates whom one can marry and sets forth minimum ages for marriage. It governs the law of divorce and, to some degree, of property. Thus the terms of the so-called marriage contract are, with minor exceptions, set by usage and are not subject to change by individual contract. If the spouses wish to make a contract about division of labor, who looks after the children, and who pays for what, there is no reason why they should not do so; however, the stipulations in such contracts are almost never enforceable at law.

Common-Law Marriage. Although the term *common-law marriage* is often used to refer to a union in which no legally sanctioned wedding ceremony has taken place, it is in fact a misuse. During the early period of the common law of England, marriage by contract between the bride and the groom or between their kin was a recognized mode of marriage, even though neither church nor state had any direct involvement in it. Some U.S. states have declared by fiat that if two people live together for a certain period of time, an express or implied contract can be assumed, and therefore their union can be treated as tantamount to a marriage for legal purposes. Rights of persons living in such unions have recently been tested in court trials, including California's much-publicized *Marvin v. Marvin* (1979), considered a landmark decision because the court ruled that unwed partners possess certain property rights comparable to those assumed in marriage.

History of Legal Marriage. Among the Romans and other ancient Western peoples, marriage was not a legal matter; it was established and carried out by contract between families. The Christian idea of an officially sanctioned marriage derived ultimately from an ancient Judaic notion that sex should be confined to marriage. To define and also to enforce sanctions against the sin of adultery, the church had first to determine that the accused married person was in fact married. The response was to ritualize marriage by converting it into a sacrament.

Not until the Middle Ages, when much church usage was codified as canon law, did marriage become associated with legal codes in the Western world. During the Reformation, Martin Luther negated the papal notions about marriage as a sacrament but upheld its institutional connection with the law. In his view marriage was something that the secular government should control.

When the Constitution of the United States was drawn up, control over marriage law was placed under the jurisdiction of the individual states. A constitutional amendment would be required to allow federal law to alter marriage and divorce laws of the states.

See also: DIVORCE; FAMILY; KINSHIP; WOMEN IN SOCIETY.

Marriage of Figaro, The   see BEAUMARCHAIS, PIERRE CARON DE; MOZART, WOLFGANG AMADEUS

Mars (mythology)   In Roman mythology Mars was the god of war, of agriculture, and of the state. He was the parthenogenetic son of Juno, the husband of the goddess Bellona, and the lover of Venus. He was originally Mars Sylvanus, a god of spring vegetation. As Mars Gradivus, he was identified with the Greek war god ARES. His festivals in March (the month was named for him) and October marked the opening and closing of the military campaign season.

As Mars Quirinius, god of the state, he was the father of ROMULUS AND REMUS by the vestal virgin Rhea Silvia. He saved them from drowning in the Tiber and raised them with the help of the she-wolf and the sacred woodpecker Picus. The wolf, the woodpecker, the horse, and the color red were associated with him.

Mars (planet)   Mars, the red planet, is the fourth planet from the Sun; it is named for the Roman god of war. Easily distinguished in the night sky by its reddish appearance, it is 1.5 times farther from the Sun than the Earth and only about half as large as the Earth.

More than any other planet in the solar system, Mars has characteristics that make it an Earth-like world. Its period of rotation and the inclination of its axis are similar to Earth's. Its density indicates that it is made of rocky materials, although with proportionately less iron and more lightweight elements and volatiles than the Earth. Its atmosphere is thin enough to allow observation of the surface. Only the Earth and Mars among the terrestrial planets have satellites; the two very tiny bodies orbiting Mars were discovered in 1877 by Asaph Hall and named PHOBOS and DEIMOS.

Characteristics

The rotation period of Mars is only 37 minutes longer than the Earth's, a fact already determined in the late 1600s by watching the motion of surface features. The rotation axis is tilted with respect to the orbital plane by almost 24°, so that both planets experience significant seasonal differences in the amount of sunlight falling on a given hemisphere during the year. The difference between winter and summer is more extreme on Mars, due to the greater eccentricity of the martian orbit. The distance of Mars from the Sun ranges from 206.7 million km (128.4 million mi) at perihelion to 249.1 million km (154.7 million mi) at aphelion, a difference of 42.4 million km (26.3 million mi). By contrast the Earth's distance from the Sun changes by only about 2.5 million km (1.6 million mi). The red planet therefore receives about 40 percent more sunlight during southern summer, when nearest the Sun, than during southern winter, when the Sun is most distant. These conditions produce relatively hot southern summers and mild northern winters but cool northern summers and cold southern winters.

CHARACTERISTICS OF MARS

Mean distance from Sun	227,900,000 km (141,600,000 mi)
Length of year	687 days
Length of day	24 h, 37 min, 23 sec
Inclination of axis	23° 59'
Equatorial diameter	6,787 km (4,210 mi)
Mass compared to Earth	0.107
Specific density (water=1)	3.9
Atmosphere	95% CO_2, 2% Argon, 3% N_2
Mean surface temperature	−23° C (−19° F)
Satellites	2

Surface Appearance. Mars is a small planet and even at most favorable times is never closer to the Earth than 56 million km (35 million mi). This makes it difficult to observe details on the surface. Resolving surface features is made even more of a problem by the blurring effects of two atmospheres. One of the best examples of the resulting confusion is the case of the martian canals, first reportedly observed by the Italian priest Pietro Secchi in 1876. Giovanni Schiaparelli published a map of Mars in 1877 on which he assigned names to the recognized bright and dark features, but which also included a large number of straight linear features that he and Secchi called canali. The mistranslation of this term into "canal" instead of "channel" by English-speaking countries carried a totally misleading connotation of artificial construction that was never intended by the two observers. The view that canals were the work of a heroic, intelligent race trying to tap the melting polar ice for water to irrigate their equatorial crops was persuasively championed by Percival Lowell in his book of 1895. Not all observers agreed with the canal theory, but the idea that Mars could and probably did support some kind of life became established, with little scientific evidence, and persisted until the middle of the 20th century.

Changes take place in the surface features of Mars as the seasons change. The most obvious is the rapid spring shrinking of the polar cap from its large winter size, when it may reach 45° latitude. The polar cap grows back as summer turns to fall, reaching full size shortly before winter begins.

The darker areas of Mars, call *maria*, sometimes respond to seasonal change, becoming darker as the polar cap retreats during spring. This occurrence was originally thought to represent vegetation growing, as water from the melting polar cap becomes available. More recent studies indicate instead that the spring darkening is due to winds blowing fine bright dust off darker rocks. Telescopic observers have long known that dust blows about the martian surface; dust storms have been observed to grow out of the orange deserts and spread over the landscape, occasionally covering the entire planet in a featureless red haze.

Atmosphere. Telescopic measurements of the spectrum of Mars showed a thin atmosphere composed mostly of carbon dioxide. As early as 1940 it was known that oxygen and water vapor were extremely rare, but the true composition of the atmosphere, as with the true nature of the martian surface, became well known only when spacecraft began to explore the planet at close range. Nitrogen, argon, and small traces of oxygen and water vapor were found, and an atmospheric pressure of 7.5 millibars, compared to 1,000 millibars on Earth at sea level.

Exploring Mars

Flyby Results. MARINER 4 obtained the first close look at Mars in 1965. The carbon dioxide atmosphere was found to be exceptionally thin, only 1/100 that at sea level on the Earth. No magnetic field was detected. Twenty-two fuzzy pictures showed plains covered with large, flat-bottomed craters. In the 1 percent of the surface examined, no evidence of life, canals, or recent geologic activity was detected. Mars seemed more like the Moon than like the Earth.

Two more flyby spacecraft carrying high-resolution television cameras refined this picture in 1969. Cratered plains were again observed, the craters themselves being

(Below) *The extinct Martian volcano Olympus Mons is the largest known mountain in the solar system. It is 26 km (16 mi) high, or about three times as high as Mount Everest, and has a base nearly 600 km (370 mi) across.*

(Above) *Visible in this* Viking 1 *photograph of Mars are Argyre, an immense crater* (just below center) *and part of Vallis Marineris, a long canyon in the upper region.*

highly eroded; the worn-down rims and shallow, filled-in floors were evidence of the abrasive action of wind-blown dust. Because the atmosphere of Mars is so thin, wind velocities up to several hundred kilometers per hour are required to raise the dust particles during a dust storm, and these fast-moving particles erode structures with a sand-blasting effect. Featureless terrain was also observed as regions devoid of any surface detail, again suggesting ongoing erosion. Areas of jumbled blocks, perhaps resulting from subsurface collapse, were named chaotic terrain. The south polar cap was photographed during early spring, revealing frost-covered crater rims poking through the thicker deposits of frozen carbon dioxide. Temperatures over the ice fields were 160 to 170 K (about −170° F).

Orbiter Results. A new era of exploration of the planet Mars began when orbiter spacecraft were sent there, first in 1971 (*Mariner 9*) and again in 1976 (*Viking 1* and *2*). The advantage of an orbiter is the ability to map nearly all of the planet's surface, and to be able to do so repeatedly in order to look for seasonal and long-term changes in surface features.

When the entire surface of Mars came under examination, it became clear that in many respects Mars was similar to both the Earth and the Moon. Four huge shield volcanoes were observed on Mars, plus a great number of smaller ones like those found on the Earth. The largest volcano, Olympus Mons, reaches 24 km (15 mi) above a smooth plain. Most of the major volcanic structures are located in two particular regions of Mars, where the crust

has swelled upward. These crustal uplifts are also found on the Earth, but not on the Moon. Near the largest of the crustal swells, where the four extremely large shield volcanoes are located, is an immense crack in the crust of Mars. This rift valley is a series of canyons, each several hundred km long and up to 100 km (62 mi) wide, that spans a distance of 5,000 km (3,100 mi). Placed in the United States, it would stretch from San Diego, Calif., to Boston. Such rift valleys are well known on the Earth.

Despite these Earth-like geologic structures, most of Mars looks like the Moon. Elevated cratered plains dot the southern hemisphere, like the highlands of the Moon. The lower-lying northern hemisphere has smooth plains that seem to be similar to the dark volcanic maria of the Moon. About 80% of the martian surface indicates a history similar to that which ended 3 billion years ago on the Moon. In a few areas Mars began to experience more Earth-like geologic processes that modified the lunarlike surface.

Other processes have modified the martian surface. Several hundred long, winding channels exist on Mars with characteristics similar to those of dried-up river channels. The structure of these channels makes them seem like those stream beds cut by sudden runoff in desert regions on the Earth. Many observers regard the presence of these channels as strong evidence for liquid-water erosion, since lava and glacial erosion produce very different channels.

Viking Lander Results. The first detailed measurements of the surface and atmospheric conditions of the red

A photograph taken of the Martian surface from Viking Lander 2 *discloses a rock-filled plain. Many of the dark gray rocks are porous, indicating a volcanic origin. Both field and rocks are covered with red iron-oxide dust.*

planet began on July 20, 1976, when the VIKING *1* lander touched down on the rocky desert called Chryse Planitia ("plains of gold"), seven years to the day following the first Apollo landing on the Moon. During and after descent, the atmospheric composition and structure were measured. The atmosphere of Mars was found to consist of 95% carbon dioxide, 2 to 3% nitrogen, 1 to 2% argon, and tiny traces of oxygen and water vapor. Ozone to screen out ultraviolet light is almost nonexistent. Water vapor is almost totally absent near the winter polar cap, but in the summer hemisphere, where *Viking 1* landed, it exists in amounts about 5/100 of that found in the driest parts of the Earth. The atmospheric pressure at Chryse (which is a basin some 2 km/1.2 mi below an imaginary reference "sea level" on Mars) was about 7.5 millibars (sea-level pressure on Earth is about 1,000 millibars). Detailed analysis of the atmosphere provided evidence that in the past its pressure was probably higher, supporting the conclusions derived from the observations of dried-up river channels.

Temperatures at the Viking landing site depended on the time of day. After dark the *Viking 1* lander chilled to 187 K (−123° F), but warmed during the day to 244 K (−20° F). By contrast, polar temperatures are, during winter, 146 K (−197° F). Winds were surprisingly gentle, 6 to 8 mph with occasional gusts of 30 to 40 mph.

Surrounding the *Viking 1* lander was a dusty reddish plain littered with both dark and reddish rocks, including a large boulder. Drifting soil piles up near the rocks and formed a dune field not far from the lander. Much to the surprise of scientists, the martian sky is not deep, dark blue but a light pinkish gray, presumably due to fine dust

particles suspended in the atmosphere.

Dust was less common at the *Viking 2* landing site, also a rock-strewn plain, located 7,500 km (4,660 mi) from the Chryse site. Named Utopia, the region is much farther north and had at the time of landing nearly three times as much water vapor in the air as was observed over Chryse. Rocks were abundant at Utopia; most showed the same reddish stain seen at the *Viking 1* site, due to the presence of iron oxide. The soil of Mars where the Vikings landed is similar to basaltic lava but heavily enriched in iron and depleted in aluminum. The iron is in a highly oxidized state; results of analysis by the chemical and biological experiments suggest the presence of superoxides, peroxides, and ozonides. These unusual compounds, which contribute to the strong coloration of the martian deserts, are probably formed in the presence of a small amount of water vapor under the action of the ultraviolet light that reaches the surface of Mars. Remarkably little seismic noise was recorded on seismometers, indicating that Mars is less active than the Earth.

Search for Life. A major portion of the Viking effort was directed at searching for life processes based on a carbon biochemistry. Although the soil chemistry of Mars was found to be unusual and highly active, no conclusive evidence of biological activity has been found. The initial results of an experiment based on photosynthesis, for example, indicated that the martian soil is capable of breaking down carbon dioxide and making carbon compounds, as do green plants on Earth. A control sample, sterilized at high temperatures, showed no meaningful response. When the original experiment was repeated in the presence of water, which should have enhanced a biological process on a dry planet, the response again went to zero. Other experiments showed strong chemical reactions to nutrients used, and a test for organic compounds in the soil proved negative. Despite this, Mars remains the best candidate for Earth-like life in the solar system outside of the Earth itself. The question of life there remains open; the inability of the Vikings to detect life may simply mean that the experiments were designed incorrectly. Further studies of the martian surface are required. A number of international programs are planned for placing probes on Mars during the 1990s, possibly followed by a manned mission to the planet in the early 21st century.

See also: PLANETS AND PLANETARY SYSTEMS; SOLAR SYSTEM.

Mars (spacecraft)   The Mars probes are a series of Soviet spacecraft sent to the planet Mars between 1960 and 1973. Two basic types of spacecraft were used, one weighing 1 ton and the other 5 tons. The scientific results have been meager, and the program has been indefinitely suspended.

The *Mars 1* probe was successfully launched on Nov. 1, 1962, but went dead long before it reached Mars. *Mars 2* and *Mars 3* were inserted into orbit around Mars on Nov. 27 and Dec. 2, 1971, but entry probes dropped into the martian atmosphere returned no data. *Mars 4* missed the planet by 2,100 km (1,300 mi) in 1974 when its braking engine failed to operate. *Mars 5* was successfully injected into Mars orbit, but its few television pictures were inferior in quality to those obtained by *Mariner 9* in 1973. When the two landers *Mars 6* and *7* arrived near Mars a month later, one (*Mars 7*) missed the planet by 1,300 km (800 mi); the other entered the atmosphere but went dead during the final stages of the descent, after relaying some confusing atmospheric data.

In 1988 the Soviet Union sent two probes toward Phobos, the larger martian moon. Both probes failed, one soon after launch and the other near Phobos.

Marsalis (family) [mahr-sal'-uhs]   The name Marsalis became widely known to jazz enthusiasts in 1980, when trumpeter **Wynton Marsalis**, b. New Orleans, La., Oct. 18, 1961, joined Art Blakey and the Jazz Messengers, revealing his dazzling technique and genius at improvisation. The son of jazz pianist **Ellis Marsalis**, Wynton studied classical music at New York's Juilliard School. In 1982 he formed his own band with older brother **Branford**, b. New Orleans, Aug. 26, 1960, a brilliant tenor saxophonist (and an actor) who became music director of "The Tonight Show" in 1992. Wynton has won Grammy awards for both classical and jazz recordings, the only person to do so. Another brother, **Delfeayo**, b. New Orleans, July 20, 1965, is gaining renown as a producer of jazz recordings.

Marseillaise, La [mahr-say-yez', lah]   *La Marseillaise*, the French national anthem, was written and composed by Claude Joseph Rouget de Lisle, an amateur musician, on the night of Apr. 24, 1792. It became the great rallying call of the French Revolution and was given its current name after it was sung on the streets of Paris by troops from Marseille. *La Marseillaise* is musically one of the most sophisticated of national anthems; it has been quoted and adapted by a number of composers, including Tchaikovsky in his *1812 Overture*.

Marseille [mahr-say']   Marseille (or Marseilles) is the major port and second most populous city of France. It is located in the southeastern part of the country on the Mediterranean Sea near the mouth of RHÔNE RIVER. The population of the city proper is 800,550 (1990), and of the metropolitan area, 1,262,223.

Contemporary City. Trade continues to be the economic mainstay of Marseille, the most important port on the Mediterranean. Major imports include petroleum, wine, fruits, olive oil, hides and skins, and tropical agricultural products. Exports are dominated by wines, liqueurs, processed foods, cement, and metal products. Petroleum refining and shipbuilding are the principal industries, but chemicals, soap, glass, plastics, textiles, olive oil, pro-

cessed foods, and leather goods are also important products. Marseille is connected with the Rhône via a canal and thus has access to the extensive waterway network of France. Petroleum is shipped northward by pipeline.

History. Marseille is one of the oldest cities in France. About 600 BC, Greek mariners founded a settlement there called Massalia. It grew quickly and its residents colonized much of present-day southern France. In 49 BC it fell to Rome. From the 13th to the 15th century Marseille was a free republic. In 1481, Marseille became part of France. During the 18th and 19th centuries Marseille grew considerably as the major port serving the French colonies in the West Indies and North Africa. Marseille suffered severe damage during World War II, but much of the city has since been rebuilt.

---

marsh   see SWAMP, MARSH, AND BOG

Marsh, Othniel Charles   The American paleontologist Othniel Charles Marsh, b. Lockport, N.Y., Oct. 29, 1831, d. Mar. 18, 1899, discovered over 1,000 fossil vertebrates, mainly dinosaurs, during his many scientific explorations of the western United States. His collection of fossils (now in the Peabody Museum affiliated with Yale University) was unparalleled. Professor of paleontology (1866–99) at Yale and the first vertebrate paleontologist (1882–92) of the U.S. Geological Survey, Marsh was a pioneer in the field of vertebrate paleontology in the United States.

Marsh, Reginald   The American painter Reginald Marsh, b. Paris, France, Mar. 14, 1898, d. July 3, 1954, is known for his lively depictions of New York City life. He studied at Yale University and at the New York City Art Students League under Kenneth Hayes Miller and John

Why Not Use the "L"? (1930) exemplifies the vigorous style of the American artist Reginald Marsh, who began as a magazine illustrator and went on to create paintings, etchings, and lithographs of New York City life. (Whitney Museum, New York City.)

Sloan. Having begun his career as a commercial illustrator for *Harper's Bazaar,* the *New York Daily News,* and the *New Yorker,* Marsh found his favorite subjects in the crowds at Coney Island's beaches, boardwalks, and amusement parks and among the inhabitants of Bowery flophouses. He caught both the squalor and the energy of Manhattan during the Depression years, depicting those baser aspects of urban existence which often escaped the more gently romantic ASHCAN SCHOOL.

Marshall, George C.   George Catlett Marshall, b. Uniontown, Pa., Dec. 31, 1880, d. Oct. 16, 1959, an American army officer and diplomat, was chief of staff of the U.S. Army during World War II and the only person ever to be both secretary of state (1947–49) and secretary of defense (1950–51).

A 1901 graduate of the Virginia Military Institute, Marshall served in France in World War I and won recognition for his role in directing the St. Mihiel and Meuse-Argonne offensives. From 1919 to 1924 he was aide to Gen. John J. PERSHING. He became assistant chief of staff of the army (July 1938), deputy chief of staff (Oct. 1938), and then chief of staff (1939). Predicting American involvement in World War II, he was a strong advocate of military preparedness. During the war he supervised U.S. military activities and was the leading U.S. military spokesperson at Allied summit conferences. He became general of the army in December 1944.

In November 1945, President Harry S. TRUMAN made Marshall his personal representative in China, where Marshall unsuccessfully attempted to negotiate a settlement of the civil war between the Nationalists and the Communists. In 1947, Truman appointed him secretary of state. During Marshall's tenure, the United States adopted a strong anti-Soviet policy, the keystones of which were the Truman Doctrine of aid to nations threatened by Communism and the MARSHALL PLAN for the economic reconstruction of Western Europe, for which Marshall was awarded the Nobel Peace Prize in 1953. In ill health, Marshall resigned in 1949, only to be called back in 1950 as secretary of defense during the Korean War.

Marshall, James Wilson   James Wilson Marshall, b. Hunterdon County, N.J., Oct. 8, 1810, d. Aug. 10, 1885, discovered gold in California on Jan. 24, 1848, launching the GOLD RUSH of 1849. Arriving in California in 1845, he settled at Sutter's Fort, the present site of Sacramento. He found gold while building a sawmill near the fort. The sawmill failed, however, and Marshall did not benefit personally from his important discovery.

Marshall, John   John Marshall, b. Prince William (now Fauquier) County, Va., Sept. 24, 1755, d. July 6, 1835, the fourth chief justice of the United States, in large measure determined the shape of the American system of constitutional law. Marshall lived his early years close to the Virginia frontier and was only informally educated. He fought in the American Revolution alongside George Washington. After the war Marshall returned to Virginia, where he studied and began to practice law. He became active in Virginia state politics, serving several terms in the House of Delegates (1782–90, 1795–96) and emerged as a leader of the Federalist party in Virginia. He was a political rival of his distant relative Thomas Jefferson, who had already fallen out with the Federalists. In 1797, Marshall was sent by President John Adams to France to aid in the negotiation of the XYZ AFFAIR. The part he played there won him national popularity. In 1799 he was elected to the House of Representatives, and in 1800, Adams appointed him secretary of state.

In January 1801, two months before the Adams Administration was to expire, and with it rule by the Federalist party, Adams appointed Marshall Chief Justice of the United States. Adams made other "midnight" appointments, one of which resulted in an important Supreme Court case, MARBURY V. MADISON (1803). The court's decision in this case, written by Marshall, was the first in which the court declared an act of Congress unconstitutional. The decision established the practice of JUDICIAL REVIEW by the federal courts over acts of the other two branches of government.

In *Fletcher* v. *Peck* (1810) the court under Marshall's

George Catlett Marshall, a five-star American general, directed the operations of U.S. forces in both Europe and the Pacific during World War II. Marshall subsequently served as secretary of state (1947–49) and devised the European Recovery Program, or Marshall Plan.

(Right) *The early governmental career of John Marshall— diplomatic negotiator, congressman, and secretary of state—all occurred within a span of 4 years (1797–1801). His greatest achievements, however, were as a jurist, during his 35-year term (1801–35) as chief justice of the U.S. Supreme Court.*

leadership limited the states' ability to impair contracts and established the sanctity of private property rights. In DARTMOUTH COLLEGE V. WOODWARD (1816) the court upheld the inviolability of contracts from amendment by the states. In McCULLOCH V. MARYLAND (1819) the states were prohibited from taxing a federal instrumentality, the Bank of the United States, and the court upheld the right of Congress to establish such an instrument by interpreting the "implied powers" clause of the Constitution in a broad manner. In *Cohens* v. *Virginia* (1821) and GIBBONS V. OGDEN (1824), Marshall wrote opinions that established the unity of the federal court system and set the precedent for the assertion of federal authority over the states where their interests clashed.

In 1807, Marshall presided over the treason trial of Aaron BURR, in which, against the wishes of the Jeffersonians, Burr was declared innocent.

Marshall, Paule   The American writer Paule Marshall, b. Brooklyn, N.Y., Apr. 9, 1929, has established a reputation for powerful and perceptive stories of West Indian blacks and their struggle to enter the modern world without succumbing to its deadening spirit. Her first novel, *Brown Girl, Brownstones* (1959), deals with the maturation of its heroine in a Barbadian enclave in Brooklyn; her second, *The Chosen Place, the Timeless People* (1969), analyzes the failure of an American social project in a forgotten corner of a forgotten Caribbean island. *Praise Song for the Widow* (1972) was her next, highly praised novel. *Reena and Other Stories* was published in 1984.

Marshall, Thomas R.   Thomas Riley Marshall, b. North Manchester, Ind., Mar. 14, 1854, d. June 1, 1925, was the 28th vice-president of the United States (1913–21). As Democratic governor of Indiana (1909–13), he was a reformer, which led to his nomination as Woodrow WILSON's running mate. Popular and witty, Marshall is best known for saying "What this country needs is a really good five-cent cigar." His memoirs appeared in 1925.

Marshall, Thurgood   Thurgood Marshall, b. Baltimore, Md., July 2, 1908, became (1967) the first black member of the U.S. Supreme Court. He graduated from Lincoln University in 1930 and received his law degree from Howard University in 1933. He practiced law in Baltimore, specializing in civil rights litigation. In 1940 he became chief of the legal-defense section of the National Association for the Advancement of Colored People (NAACP). He argued 32 cases (winning 29) before the Supreme Court, among them the landmark school-segregation case of BROWN V. BOARD OF EDUCATION OF TOPEKA, KANSAS (1954). In 1965, President Lyndon Johnson appointed Marshall solicitor general of the United States, and in 1967 he nominated him to the Supreme Court. On the court, Marshall consistently took liberal stands on a wide range of issues, including abortion, religion, and the death penalty. He resigned from the court in 1991.

Marshall Islands   The Marshall Islands are a group of 34 islands located about 3,500 km (2,200 mi) southwest of Hawaii in the Pacific Ocean. The total area of the islands is 181 km^2 (70 mi^2), and the population is 43,417 (1990 est.). In 1947 they became part of the U.S.-administered Trust Territory of the Pacific Islands (see PACIFIC ISLANDS, TRUST TERRITORY OF THE).

The low-lying, coral islands are divided into two parallel chains some 200 km (130 mi) apart. Many of the Micronesian inhabitants fish and grow coconuts, cacao, taro, and fruits. Tourism and banking are of growing importance.

In 1526, Spaniards were the first Europeans to discover the islands, and in 1788 the British sea captain John Marshall visited them. The Marshalls were held by Germany from 1885 until 1914, when they passed to Japan. They were captured by the United States in 1944. Subsequently the islands of BIKINI and ENIWETOK were used to test atomic and hydrogen bombs. There is a U.S. missile testing range on Kwajalein.

The Marshall Islands became internally self-governing in 1979. A compact under which it would become a republic in "free association" with the United States was approved by the islanders in 1983; the United States proclaimed the compact effective as of Oct. 21, 1986.

Marshall Plan   The Marshall Plan, formally known as the European Recovery Program, was a program of U.S. economic and technical assistance to 16 European countries after World War II. Its aim was to restore the war-ravaged economy of Western Europe and to stimulate economic growth and trade there.

In early 1947, as the COLD WAR between the United States and the USSR began to take shape, U.S. policymakers concluded that Western Europe would require substantial economic aid to regain political stability. In an address at Harvard University on June 5, 1947, Secretary of State George C. Marshall proposed that the European countries draw up a unified plan for economic reconstruction to be funded by the United States. The USSR and other countries of Eastern Europe were invited to join, but they declined. The Economic Cooperation Administration was established by the United States to administer the plan, with Paul G. Hoffman as head. The 16 West European countries then formed the Organization for European Economic Cooperation to coordinate the program and received $13.15 billion in U.S. aid.

Marsilius of Padua   [mahr-sil'-ee-uhs]   Marsilius of Padua, c.1275–1342, was an Italian scholar whose *Defensor Pacis* (Defender of the Peace) is regarded as one of the most important works of political philosophy produced in the Middle Ages. Marsilius studied philosophy at Padua and medicine at Paris, where he was made rector of the university in 1313. In *Defensor Pacis*, which was published anonymously in 1324, he argued that all authority rests with the people and that the church is subordinate to the state, from which it derives all jurisdiction, both spiritual and temporal. When his authorship of the work became known in 1326, Marsilius fled Paris and took refuge with the German king LOUIS IV, who was embroiled in a political struggle with the papacy. In 1327, Pope JOHN XXII condemned five propositions taken from *Defensor* and excommunicated its author. In that year Marsilius accompanied Louis to Rome, where the latter was crowned (1328) emperor and an antipope was installed. Marsilius returned to Germany in 1329 and spent the rest of his life at Louis's court.

___

Marston, John   John Marston, baptized Oct. 7, 1576, d. June 25, 1634, was an English satirical poet and dramatist. He published the verse satires collected in *The Scourge of Villainy* (1598); his best-known play is *The Malcontent* (1604), mingling comedy and revenge tragedy. Other works include the comedies *Eastward Ho!* (1605), written in collaboration with Ben Jonson and George Chapman, and *The Dutch Courtesan* (1605); and the tragedy *Sophonisba* (1606). In 1609 he abandoned writing and became a clergyman.

___

marsupial [mahr-soo'-pee-ul]   Marsupials are a group of mammals constituting the order Marsupialia, which is divided usually into 8 or 9 families containing about 80 genera and 250 species. All but 70 species are found in the Australian region of the world; the remaining species are the opossums of North and South America. Marsupials range in size from the marsupial mouse, *Planigale subtilissima*, which rarely exceeds 95 mm (3.75 in) in total length—including its 50-mm (2-in) tail—and 10 g (about ⅓ oz) in weight, to the great gray kangaroo, *Macropus giganteus*, which may reach 2.5 m (8 ft) in total length and more than 70 kg (155 lb) in weight.

Marsupials are distinguished from other mammals by anatomical, physiological, and developmental differences. These distinctions are of such significance that the marsupials are placed in an infraclass of their own, Metatheria. The most obvious, but not the most important, characteristic is the presence of a pouch, or marsupium, which provides continued maternal protection to the undeveloped newborn young. Not all species of marsupials have pouches, however, and in some it develops only during the nursing period. Further, a nonmarsupial, the spiny anteater, or echidna, *Tachyglossus aculeatus*, also develops a pouch for its nursing young. Pouches range from simple folds of skin to well-developed sacs that can be closed by muscular action.

One of the most important marsupial characteristics is the presence in the female of two vaginas, which open to the outside through a single opening, the urogenital sinus. The two vaginas have not fused to form a single vagina, as in most other mammals, because the tubes (ureters) from the kidneys to the bladder pass between them. Although the vaginas serve as passageways for the sperm to the egg, the young are not born through the vaginal

passages, as in other mammals; instead, a new opening develops in the connective tissue between the vaginas and functions as the birth canal. In kangaroos this passageway becomes permanent after the birth of the first young. Male marsupials have forked penises, and the testes are located in a scrotal sac in front of the penis, rather than behind it (except in the marsupial mole, *Notoryctes*, in which the testes are internal).

The two other groups of living mammals are the egg-laying monotremes and the placental mammals. During pregnancy placental mammals develop a placenta through which the mother nourishes the unborn young. Despite the name given to this other group of mammals, marsupials also develop placentas. The marsupial placenta, however, is typically the primitive yolk-sac, or choriovitelline, type. The mammalian yolk sac, similar to that of birds and reptiles, contains no true yolk (except in the monotremes), but its walls join the lining of the mother's uterus to form the placental connection between mother and young. In three groups of marsupials, however—the koala, *Phascolarctos*; the wombat, *Vombatus*; and the bandicoots, family Peramelidae—there is an advanced chorioallantoic placenta analogous to that of the placental mammals. The allantois is a pouch that arises from the lower part of the gut of the embryo and serves as a storage place for wastes. In the chorioallantoic placenta the allantois enlarges and makes contact with the outer membranes (chorion) surrounding the embryo, and both are joined to the lining of the mother's uterus.

Marsupials are born hairless and blind in a very undeveloped state and essentially continue their embryonic development within the pouch. Gestation varies from a relatively brief 12 to 37 days, but pouch development may last for a considerable time—almost 8 months in the red kangaroo, *Macropus rufus*. Typically, the just-born young crawls from the birth-canal opening along its mother's fur and into the pouch, where it fastens onto a nipple. The nipple expands to "lock" the young in place. A special, but temporary, arrangement of the breathing passage allows the young to suckle and breathe at the same time. In marsupials without pouches the young simply fasten onto the exposed nipples.

Marsupials, like placental mammals, have undergone adaptive radiation, or the evolution of different types to meet changing ecological conditions. The kangaroo, for example, evolved as a fairly large, swift herbivore to exploit the vast grasslands of Australia, and even though greatly different in appearance, it is the ecological counterpart of the grass-eating antelopes and wild horses of other continents. Other marsupials closely resemble their ecological counterparts among the placental mammals. The marsupial mole, for example, resembles the placental mole.

Marsupial fossils have been found in North America, South America, Europe, Australia, and Antarctica. The earliest record, dating to the late Cretaceous Period, about 80 million years ago, is from North America. The fossil evidence suggests that placental and marsupial

Marsupials are mammals whose embryolike young are generally nurtured inside the mother's pouch. Gestation in marsupials is typically brief, but development in the pouch may be quite long, allowing the young to continue their growth processes on a nourishing diet in relative safety. Nine types of marsupials include the wombat; the South American woolly opossum; the numbat, or banded anteater; the marsupial jumping mouse; the marsupial mole; the Eastern Australian native cat, or quoll; the brush-tailed rock wallaby, a smaller relative of the kangaroo; the honey-glider possum; and the koala.

mammals evolved at about the same time from the primitive pantotheres, possibly as far back as the early Cretaceous, about 120 million years ago.

Marsupials became an important element in the fauna of South America during the Tertiary Period, from about 65 million to 3 million years ago. They reached Australia as early as the Oligocene Epoch, about 30 million years ago, and have been the dominant mammals of Australia for the past 2.5 million years. In 1982 the 40-million-year-old fossil remains of an extinct marsupial were discovered in Antarctica. This find confirmed theories that marsupials reached Australia from South America by way of Antarctica while these continents were still linked in the huge Gondwanaland landmass.

Marsyas [mahr'-see-uhs]   In Greek mythology Marsyas was a Phrygian SATYR. When ATHENA abandoned the double flute because playing it distorted her face, Marsyas took it up and became famous for his beautiful music. He challenged APOLLO to a musical contest, on the terms that the winner could do what he wished with the loser. At first both played equally well, but Apollo then challenged Marsyas to play his instrument upside down; this could be done on Apollo's instrument, the lyre, but not on the flute, so the Muses, who were judges, awarded the contest to Apollo. He hanged Marsyas from a pine tree and flayed him. Marsyas's blood, or the tears of his friends, is said to have formed the river Marsyas.

marten   Martens are eight species of usually arboreal, weasellike mammals of the genus *Martes* in the weasel family, Mustelidae. The genus includes the sable, *M. zibellina*, and the fisher, *M. pennanti*, as well as those animals commonly called martens. Martens range up to 60 cm (2 ft) long, plus a 30-cm (1-ft) tail, and reach 2 kg (4.5 lb) in weight. Their fur is soft and thick and commercially valuable. It ranges in color from golden brown to almost black, with a characteristic whitish yellow to reddish yellow patch on the throat and chest. Martens feed mainly on rodents, but also eat rabbits, birds, fruit, insects, and carrion. Martens display the phenomenon of delayed implantation, in which the fertilized ovum (egg) halts its development and remains free within the uterus for varying lengths of time; as a result, gestation in martens may last 7 to 9 months. Mating occurs in summer and the usually two to four young are born in early spring.

The American marten, *M. americana*, also called the American sable, is found from Alaska to eastern Canada south into the western United States. The Eurasian pine marten, *M. martes*, and the beech or stone marten, *M. foina*, have been overhunted and exterminated from many parts of their range.

The American marten inhabits North American forests, hunting squirrels and other prey in tree branches. Closely related to the mink, the marten is prized for its glossy brown fur.

Martha's Vineyard   Martha's Vineyard, an island in the Atlantic Ocean located 6 km (4 mi) off the coast of Cape Cod, is part of Massachusetts. It covers 280 km^2 (108 mi^2) and has a population of 11,541 (1990).

Edgartown and Vineyard Haven are the largest towns. Martha's Vineyard State Forest occupies much of the island. Brightly colored clay cliffs are located at the western tip. Martha's Vineyard was settled in 1642. During the 18th and 19th centuries it was a major whaling center.

Martí, José [mahr-tee', hoh-say']   The Cuban José Martí, b. Havana, Jan. 28, 1853, d. May 19, 1895, is remembered throughout the Spanish-speaking world as a literary and political revolutionary. He was so precocious a political rebel against the Spanish colonial regime that his first arrest and exile took place at age 16. This exile (1871–78) took him to Spain, France, Mexico, and Guatemala. A second, longer exile beginning in 1879 brought him into contact with the United States and Venezuela. His essays, collected in *Our America* (1891; Eng. trans., 1977), contain penetrating analyses of the sociopolitical problems of Latin America. During his final sojourn in New York, Martí founded (1892) the Cuban Revolutionary party.

As a writer, Martí is regarded as an important forerunner of *modernismo* (modernist movement), the Spanish equivalent of symbolism. Building on traditional sacred and profane oratorical styles, he elaborated a supple, architectural prose in sharp contrast to the reigning bombastic Spanish style. His poetry also helped turn Spanish verse away from its romantic excesses. Like his children's stories, collected in *La Edad de Oro* (The Golden Age, 1898), Martí's poetry is characterized by tenderness, sincerity, and directness. These qualities are especially evident in the *Ismaelillo* (1882) poems and in *Versos sencillos* (Simple Verses, 1891). Martí was killed fighting for Cuban independence in the battle of Dos Ríos.

Martial   Martial, the anglicized name of the Latin poet Marcus Valerius Martialis, AD c.40–c.104, was born and educated in Spain and went to Rome as a protégé of his compatriots Seneca and Lucan. *Epigrams*, more than 1,500 short poems collected in 14 books, form a lively, amusing, and often satirical commentary on the contemporary scene. Passionately interested in people, their weaknesses and follies, Martial liked especially to explore the seamier side of life.

martial arts   The all-purpose phrase *martial arts* is used for various fighting methods that evolved from ancient Asian combat skills. The present-day forms have a wide range of applications. These forms are practiced for physical fitness, recreation, and self-defense; as law-enforcement tactics; and as competitive sports. The teaching methods, selection of technique, style of performance, procedures of play or practice, and underlying concepts vary according to the specialty, the instructor, and the environment. Even in a single specialized branch of the martial arts, differences in style, techniques, attitudes, and objectives exist.

History

There is little agreement about the origins and history of the martial arts. Records—dating from at least 2000 BC—of similar fighting methods existing throughout the world have been uncovered, but the specifically Asian styles are generally acknowledged to have come to China from India and Tibet, where they were used by monks for exercise and as protection against bandits. From China the martial arts spread to the rest of Asia, reaching Japan last because of its geographical isolation. Although Japan was among the last of the Asian countries to acquire knowledge of the martial arts, they flourished there. In the Tokugawa era martial-arts training was reserved for warriors serving feudal lords and was forbidden to peasants, who practiced in secret. During the nationalistic period preceding World War II, martial arts were incorporated into Japan's military training programs. Practice of martial arts was banned after the war until the mid-1950s, when they were legalized.

Basic Techniques

Although hundreds of names exist for different styles and specialities of the martial arts, there is a relatively small group of techniques. All weaponless martial-arts methods consist of one or more of the following: hand blows (using the fist, knuckles, fingertips, or the side or palm of the hand); arm blows, blocks, and parries (using the wrist, forearm, and elbow); foot blows (using toes, instep, ball, side, or heel of the foot); knee kicks; throws, trips, and takedowns; grappling and immobilizations (holds, locks, twists, levers, chokes, and escapes). Weapons are used in some martial arts, alone or in conjunction with weaponless techniques. Weapons include stones, sticks, staffs, swords, spears, lances, bows and arrows, and thrown cutting objects.

(3) The elbow lock in aikido, a defense-oriented martial art, immobilizes an attacker. (4) A practitioner of kung-fu assumes a basic fighting stance.

(7) The kokutsu-daichi, or back leaning stance, is a basic defensive position of karate.

The illustrations demonstrate several basic martial-arts techniques and fighting postures. (1) The side blade kick, a karate blow, is commonly directed toward an opponent's chest or head. (2) The seio-nage, or shoulder throw, used in judo, can be used against an assailant attacking from behind.

(5) Following a takedown in karate, a choke hold may be applied to discourage the fallen opponent from attempting to break free. (6) The backhand blow of an attacker is warded off with a forearm block and countered with a kick to the shin. These techniques are common to several of the martial arts.

(8) The bent wrist lock, or "come-along," is used in jujitsu, another defense-oriented martial art, to control an opponent with a minimum of struggling.

Colored Belts. The designation of skill or rank by colored belts was first used in judo in the late 19th century. No standard belt-ranking system exists among the martial-arts specialties or among the different schools and styles of the same specialty. A white belt commonly indicates novice status; a brown belt is widely used for advanced rank; a black belt indicates expert proficiency. Many systems use blue, yellow, orange, green, and purple belts in varying patterns of progression for intermediate levels between white-, brown-, and black-belt ranks. In some systems belts are awarded solely through competition: winners are promoted. In other systems promotion is achieved by demonstration of technical skill in a series of fluid, dancelike movements called *kata*. Other systems require contests and formal demonstrations for ranking. Belt-rank promotions and demotions can be made at the discretion of the instructor, the *sensei*.

Karate and Kung Fu. These are probably the most widely known of the martial arts. The principal techniques are hand and foot blows. Kung fu is the earlier, Chinese form; *karate* is used as a generic term for many styles of hand-and-foot-fighting methods developed in Asian countries, but particularly the Japanese styles. Hundreds of karate and kung-fu styles and substyles exist, and all use similar hitting and kicking techniques; the differences among them are stylistic. Some styles (the "hard" schools) emphasize power and strength training. Other styles (the "soft" schools) train for speed and precision. In some, hand blows are preferred, whereas others stress foot blows. In some styles contests and tournaments are the favored training method; in others *kata* is preferred. Some practitioners also condition the striking areas of their hands to make them calloused and insensitive to pain.

Karate contests are not standardized. Points are usually awarded for unopposed hand or foot blows delivered to within a few inches of the target spots, which include the head, eyes, throat, solar plexus, groin, and kidneys. With few exceptions, deliberate contact blows are invalid and are penalized.

Judo. Judo is a relatively recent activity synthesized—from several jujitsu methods—by Jigoro Kano, a late-19th-century Japanese educator and sports enthusiast. Originally, it had two forms—one for self-defense and a separate, distinct form for physical conditioning. Today the word *judo* is applied almost exclusively to the sport variant. Throws and grappling are the principal techniques. Safety falls are practiced in a *dojo* (a special practice hall) so that skilled practitioners can receive a fast, high throw and fall onto the mat with little risk of injury. In contests points are awarded to *tori* (the thrower or initiator of the action) for throws performed with good technique; for putting *uke* (the receiver of the throw) on his or her side or back; for applying a hold or choke that immobilizes *uke* for 30 seconds or until he or she signals for release; or for a combination of throwing and grappling. In modern judo events there are qualifying matches, and contestants compete in weight classes. The first Olympic Games judo competition took place in 1964, and judo became a regular event in 1972.

Jujitsu. Although widely regarded as a specialty within the martial arts, *jujitsu* is a generic term referring to many systems with considerable differences among them. Some jujitsus favor hitting and kicking to such a degree that they cannot be distinguished from karate. Other styles of jujitsu bear a striking resemblance to judo.

Aikido. Aikido is a highly stylized form of jujitsu that employs wrist, elbow, and shoulder twists in a formal manner. As *tori* performs the maneuver, *uke* does not resist but rolls in a graceful arc, giving the appearance of having been thrown. Originally presented as a highly dangerous fighting method, aikido is now thought to be, after tai chi chuan, the most gentle of the martial arts. Currently, there is no competition in aikido; it is practiced in *randori* (free-style) and *kata* forms.

Tai Chi Chuan. Tai chi chuan, or t'ai chi, is a physical-conditioning exercise that enhances the flexibility of body movement. The slow, graceful, elegant gestures of *tai chi chuan* routines hardly resemble the original hand and foot blows and blocks and parries they represent. There is little likelihood that *tai chi chuan* could be used for practical, modern self-defense. In China it is widely practiced by individuals and by groups who gather in public squares to perform the movements in unison.

Kendo. This highly stylized sport is derived from ancient Japanese sword-fighting. In contests players use a *shinai* (a bamboo sword bound with leather and held with both hands). For training and practice a *bokuto* (wooden sword) is used. Technique is limited to a few actions executed in a formal manner. Points are scored by calling out and striking a target area: the head, the side of the body, the throat, or the wrists. Protective clothing and equipment and the rules of contest prevent injury. Kendo players wear a lightweight cotton jacket, a *hakama* (loose, flowing, full-cut pants), and head, throat, chest, and wrist protectors. *Kata* forms are practiced using the *bokuto* and a shorter, one-hand sword.

---

martial law   Martial law is the temporary substitution of military authority for civil rule, usually in time of war, rebellion, or natural disaster. It is distinguished from MILITARY JUSTICE, which is the legal system applied to those in military service, and also from military government imposed upon conquered territories. Martial law is not law in the formal sense but merely the substitution of military procedures for the usual procedures of law and the courts.

The U.S. Constitution makes no specific provision for the imposition of martial law. Article I, Section 9, however, allows the suspension of the privilege of HABEAS CORPUS when, because of rebellion or invasion, the public safety warrants it. States have the power to declare martial law when it is deemed necessary for the public safety. The president is empowered by law to declare martial law to protect states against invasion and—when a state so requests—against domestic violence (protections guaranteed by Article IV, Section 4, of the U.S. Constitution). This proclamation of martial law may be preventive or punitive—the latter only in cases when civil courts cannot function properly (see EX PARTE MILLIGAN).

Multicelled birdhouses are placed near gardens to attract insect-eating purple martins, to form colonies of up to 200 pairs.

martin   Martin is the common name for several birds of the swallow family, Hirundinidae. The purple martin, *Progne subis*, is the largest North American swallow (20 cm/8 in); the male is blue black over its entire body, the female dingy gray on the underside. Feeding on the wing, martins consume great numbers of insect pests, and for centuries humans have sought to lure them to yards and gardens, often by erecting multicompartmented structures, which the gregarious martins accept as a substitute for tree cavities, their usual nesting sites. The purple martin nests across the continent from southern Canada to Mexico and winters in South America.

Martin, Frank   The Swiss composer Frank Martin, b. Sept. 15, 1890, d. Nov. 21, 1974, studied in Zurich, Rome, and Paris. His music has a cool, personal style distinguished by smooth harmonies and clear, sophisticated counterpoint. A natural ease of declamation makes his vocal music outstanding, especially the opera *The Tempest* (1956) and the oratorios *Golgotha* (1948) and *Le Mystère de la Nativité* (1959). His instrumental works include a series of orchestral ballades, the well-known *Petite Symphonie Concertante* (1946), and chamber works.

Martin, John   An eccentric and visionary English painter, John Martin, b. July 19, 1789, d. Feb. 17, 1854, became one of the most popular and famous artists of his time despite his provincial origins and the adverse criticism of John Ruskin. The extraordinary imagery of his grandiose biblical scenes and his persistent interest in Utopian and futuristic schemes for the redevelopment of London earned him the undeserved sobriquet "Mad Martin." His last three major works—*The Last Judgment*, *The Great Day of His Wrath*, and *The Plains of Heaven*

(1851–53; Tate Gallery, London)—are remarkable examples of late English romanticism.

Martin, Joseph William, Jr.   The American politician Joseph W. Martin, b. North Attleboro, Mass., Nov. 3, 1884, d. Mar. 6, 1968, was the longtime Republican leader in the U.S. House of Representatives. Elected from Massachusetts, Martin served in the House (1925–67), where he was the Republican leader (1939–59) and Speaker (1947–49, 1953–55).

Martin, Luther   The American lawyer Luther Martin, b. New Brunswick, N.J., *c.*1748, d. July 10, 1826, served as a Maryland delegate to the Constitutional Convention (1787) and as attorney general of Maryland (1778–1805, 1818–22). Martin successfully defended (1807) Aaron BURR against a charge of treason and represented (1819) Maryland in McCULLOCH V. MARYLAND.

Martin, Mary   Singer and actress of the American musical stage, Mary Martin, b. Weatherford, Tex., Dec. 1, 1913, d. Nov. 3, 1990, gained widespread fame for her performance in the long-running (1949–51) *South Pacific*. Soon afterward, she became (1954) the quintessential Peter Pan. Aside from playing successfully in reprises throughout her long career, Martin earned critical acclaim for two other original roles: in *The Sound of Music* (1959; Tony and New York Drama Critics' awards) and *I Do! I Do!* (1966, 1967–68).

Martin du Gard, Roger   [mahr-tan' due gahr]   The French novelist Roger Martin du Gard, b. Mar. 23, 1881, d. Aug. 22, 1958, established his reputation with the eight-volume saga *Les Thibault* (1922–40; Eng. trans., 1939–41) and was awarded the Nobel Prize for literature in 1937. Written in the tradition of the 19th-century novel, *Les Thibault* explores the life of a bourgeois family at the turn of the century and shows the clash of generations that divided French society at the time of World War I. Martin du Gard also wrote the widely read novel *Jean Barois* (1913; Eng. trans., 1949) and memoirs of his friendship with André Gide.

Martin of Tours, Saint   Saint Martin, *c.*316–397, was bishop of Tours, missionary to Gaul, and one of the fathers of Western monasticism. Martin joined the Roman army but converted to Christianity and became convinced that a soldier of Christ ought not to bear arms against other Christians.

About 360, Martin joined Saint HILARY OF POITIERS and founded the monastery of Ligugé, the first in Gaul. In 371, despite his objections, he was acclaimed bishop of Tours. He founded there the monastery of Marmoutiers, where he resided and which became the training center for missions to the Celts.

Although he was a staunchly orthodox Christian, Martin withheld communion from the bishops who condoned the slaughter of the Priscillian heretics, and he attempted reconciliation with the latter. His efforts led some to suspect him of heresy. Saint Martin is the patron saint of France. Feast day: Nov. 11.

Martin V, Pope   Martin V, b. 1368, d. Feb. 20, 1431, was pope from 1417 until 1431. Born at Genazzano, Italy, he was originally named Oddo Colonna. His election as pope during the Council of Constance marked the termination of the Great Schism of the West, which had divided the Latin church since 1378.

Martin's principal achievement lay in engineering the restoration of the papal authority both at Rome and within the Papal States, on whose financial resources the papacy was to become, as the century wore on, increasingly dependent. He was less successful in his attempts to suppress the Hussites in Bohemia and to effect reunion with the Greek church.

Martineau, Harriet [mahr'-tin-oh]   The English writer Harriet Martineau, b. Norwich, June 12, 1802, d. June 27, 1876, deaf from childhood and in poor health throughout her life, was for a time forced to support herself by needlework. A series of educational works—notably the nine-volume *Illustrations of Political Economy* (1832–34), *Forest and Game-Law Tales* (1845), and *The Positive Philosophy of Auguste Comte* (1853)—that explained complicated economic and philosophical ideas in laymen's terms brought her widespread recognition. Martineau also wrote travel books, including *A Complete Guide to the English Lakes* (1855), and a remarkably frank autobiography (1877).

Martini, Simone   The Italian artist Simone Martini, active 1315–44, emerged from the school of Duccio to become one of the most distinguished and influential Sienese painters of the 14th century. The sumptuous, glowing color, the lavish use of gold, and the complex and rhythmic linear patterns that characterize Simone's paintings are apparent in his earliest dated works—the enormous fresco, *Maestà* (1315; almost 12 m/40 ft wide), painted on an end wall of the council chamber in Siena's Palazzo Pubblico, and a panel, *Saint Louis of Toulouse Crowning Robert of Anjou King of Naples* (1317; Museo di Capodimonte, Naples).

Simone's love of courtly elegance, in part a reflection of French Gothic art, is most extensively expressed in the frescoes of the Chapel of Saint Martin in the Lower Church of San Francesco, Assisi. Here also Simone demonstrates his mastery of perspective. In yet another fresco—a depiction of the Sienese warrior Guidoriccio da Fogliano painted in 1328 opposite the *Maestà* in Siena—Simone proves himself an innovator in landscape painting. The artist's most famous smaller work is *The Annunciation* (1333; Uffizi, Florence).

Simone spent his last years at the papal court in Avignon, where his presence is believed to have influenced the development of Western European painting.

Martinique [mahr-tin-eek']   Martinique, the largest of the Windward Islands in the eastern Caribbean, is an overseas department of France. Its population is 344,922 (1987 est.), and it covers 1,079 km^2 (417 mi^2). Fort-de-France is the capital and leading port.

Martinique is of volcanic origin and is primarily mountainous. The highest peak, Mount Pelée, 1,397 m (4,583 ft) high, last erupted in 1902.

Agriculture is the principal economic activity. Tourism is also important. Petroleum refining, rum making, and sugar processing are the major industries. The majority of the population is black or mulatto. The culture is a blend of French and African influences, and the local patois includes elements of French, Spanish, and African languages.

In 1502, Christopher Columbus landed on Martinique. In 1635 the first settlers, who were French, arrived. Soon sugarcane was introduced, and African slaves were brought to work on the sugar plantations. Subsequently, control of the island alternated between the French and British, until 1814, when the French gained permanent control. In 1946, Martinique was granted department status.

Martins, Peter   Peter Martins, b. Copenhagen, Oct. 27, 1946, is ballet master in chief of the New York City Ballet (NYCB). Martins entered the Royal Danish Ballet at the age of 18 and appeared with NYCB as a guest artist from 1967 until 1970, when he became a principal dancer. Martins frequently partnered Suzanne Farrell, notably in George Balanchine's *Chaconne* and *Divertimento #15* and Jerome Robbins's *In G Major, Dances at a Gathering*, and *Other Dances*. His choreography includes *Calcium Night Light* (1978), *Valse Triste* (1985), *Songs of the Auvergne* (1986), *Les Gentilhommes* (1987), and the Ray Charles ballet *A Fool for You* (1988). He retired as a dancer in 1984.

Martinů, Bohuslav [mahr'-tin-oo, baw'-hus-lahf]   The Czech composer Bohuslav Martinů, b. Dec. 8, 1890, d. Aug. 28, 1959, is best known for his orchestral and chamber music, although he also wrote 10 operas. Martinů was a pupil of Josef Suk's and Albert Roussel's. From 1932 he lived mainly in France and the United States, returning to Europe in 1953. His works, generally written in a postimpressionist idiom, include 6 symphonies, 13 ballets, and 6 string quartets, in addition to concertos for various instruments and *The Frescoes of Piero della Francesca* for orchestra (1956).

MARV   see MIRV missile

Marvell, Andrew   In his lifetime the English poet Andrew Marvell, b. Winestead-in-Holderness, Yorkshire,

Mar. 31, 1621, d. Aug. 18, 1678, was known as a Puritan member of Parliament who published political verse satires and a satirical prose argument, *The Rehearsal Transprosed* (1672), in favor of toleration. Today he is remembered for a small body of lyric poems not published until after his death, which have earned him a reputation matched only by John Donne's. "To His Coy Mistress" and "The Garden" perfectly embody qualities now treasured in 17th-century lyrics.

Like his older contemporary John Milton, Marvell was educated at Cambridge University. He spent some time abroad, acted as tutor to the daughter of Lord Fairfax and to a ward of Oliver Cromwell, and in 1657 was appointed assistant to Milton, the Latin secretary to Cromwell's government. From 1659 until his death, during which time his satires were published, he served as member of Parliament for Hull.

The kind of wit characteristic of Marvell's poems associates him with Donne; the cultural tradition that enriches them—Latin, European, and English—likens them to Ben Jonson's verse. The quality peculiar to the poems is a detachment, an elusiveness, a personal evasiveness with which Marvell frames the speakers in his "Mower" poems, or views "The Picture of Little T. C.," or balances moral estimates of Cromwell in "An Horatian Ode." This detachment allows multiple responses to the poems, which can be read as parodies or even burlesques of poetic conventions and which often end in brilliant anticlimax.

Marx, Karl   Karl Heinrich Marx, b. May 5, 1818, d. Mar. 14, 1883, was a German economist, philosopher, and revolutionist whose writings form the basis of the body of ideas known as MARXISM. With the aid of Friedrich ENGELS he produced much of the theory of modern SOCIALISM and COMMUNISM. Marx's father, Heinrich, was a Jewish lawyer who had converted his family to Christianity partly to preserve his job in the Prussian state. Karl himself was baptized in the Evangelical church. As a student at the University of Berlin, young Marx was strongly influenced by the philosophy of G. W. F. HEGEL and by a radical group called Young Hegelians, who attempted to apply Hegelian ideas to the movement against organized religion and the Prussian autocracy. In 1841, Marx received a doctorate in philosophy.

In 1842, Marx became editor of the *Rheinische Zeitung* in Cologne, a liberal democratic newspaper for which he wrote increasingly radical editorials on social and economic issues. The newspaper was banned by the Prussian government in 1843, and Marx left for Paris with his bride, Jenny von Westphalen. There he went further in his criticism of society. Ludwig FEUERBACH had written a book called *The Essence of Christianity* (1841; Eng. trans., 1854), arguing that God had been invented by humans as a projection of their own ideals. If religion were abolished, Feuerbach claimed, human beings would overcome their ALIENATION. Marx applied this idea of alienation to private property, which he said caused humans to work only for themselves, not for the good of their species. He called for a communist society to overcome

Karl Marx, German political philosopher and economist, was the founder of scientific socialism, or Marxism. The tenets of Marxism are outlined in The Communist Manifesto. *His theories are the basis for modern communism.*

the dehumanizing effect of private property.

In 1845, Marx moved to Brussels, and in 1847 he went to London. He had previously made friends with Friedrich Engels, who, like himself, had been a Young Hegelian. In *The German Ideology* (1932; Eng. trans., 1938), the two developed their materialistic conception of history. They argued that human thought was determined by social and economic forces, particularly those related to the means of production. They developed a method of analysis they called DIALECTICAL MATERIALISM, in which the clash of historical forces leads to changes in society.

In 1848, in the COMMUNIST MANIFESTO, Marx and Engels declared that all history was the history of class struggles. Under CAPITALISM, the struggle between the working class and the business class would end in a new society, a communist one. The outbreak of the REVOLUTIONS OF 1848 in Europe led Marx to return to Cologne, where he began publication of the *Neue Rheinische Zeitung*, but with the failure of the German liberal democratic movement he moved permanently (1849) to London. For many years he and his family lived in poverty. From 1851 to 1862 he spent most of his time in the British Museum, studying economic and social history and developing his theories.

Marx's ideas began to influence a group of workers and German émigrés in London, who established (1864) the International Workingmen's Association, later known as the First International (see INTERNATIONAL, SOCIALIST). By the time of the brief COMMUNE OF PARIS in 1871, Marx's name had begun to be well known in European political circles. A struggle developed within the International between Marx and the Russian anarchist Mikhail BAKUNIN, whom Marx eventually defeated and expelled, at the cost of the destruction of the International.

In 1867, Marx published the first volume of Das KAPITAL (Eng. trans., 1886). The next two volumes, edited by Engels, were published after Marx's death. The fourth volume was edited by Karl KAUTSKY. Marx's last years were marked by illness and depression. His wife died in 1881, and his eldest daughter in 1883, shortly before his own death.

The importance of Marx's thought extends far beyond the revolutionary movements whose prophet he became. His writings on economics and sociology are still influential in academic circles and among many who do not share his political views.

Marx Brothers Famous for their surrealistic attacks on middle-class morality, the Marx Brothers of New York City were a unique family of American vaudeville and film comedians. Chico, b. Leonard, Mar. 22, 1887, d. Oct. 11, 1961, specialized in Italian-dialect routines; Harpo, b. Adolph, Nov. 23, 1888, d. Sept. 28, 1964, performed in pantomime and played the harp; and Groucho, b. Julius, Oct. 2, 1890, d. Aug. 19, 1977, was the leering, bushy-browed, cigar-smoking, wisecracking leader of the trio. Two other brothers—Gummo, b. Milton, c.1892, d. Apr. 21, 1977, and Zeppo, b. Herbert, Feb. 25, 1901, d. Nov. 30, 1979—joined the act at different times but made no significant comic contribution.

The team's hallmark was a refusal to behave normally in a rational, complex society. After a false start as a teenage singing group, the boys switched to slapstick comedy and became popular vaudeville clowns. In 1924 they graduated to Broadway musical revues with *I'll Say She Is*, followed by *The Cocoanuts* (1925; film, 1929) and *Animal Crackers* (1928; film, 1930). Five Paramount comedies, including *Monkey Business* (1931), *Horse Feathers* (1932), and the now-classic *Duck Soup* (1933), were moderately popular, but after the brothers moved to MGM they found commercial success with *A Night at the Opera* (1935) and *A Day at the Races* (1937). They made *Room Service* (1938) for RKO.

The team disbanded in 1941. Brief screen reunions during the late 1940s, which resulted in the parody *A Night in Casablanca* (1946), were box-office failures, and only Groucho succeeded as a solo performer, mainly as the aggressive, double-talking host of the radio and television quiz show "You Bet Your Life" (1947–61).

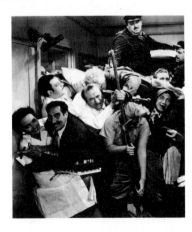

A ship's crowded stateroom in A Night at the Opera *(1935)* provided a classic situation for the zany comedy of the Marx Brothers. The team of former vaudevillians—Groucho, Chico, and Harpo—split up in 1941, after a series of successful films made the previous decade.

Marxism Marxism is a body of social, political, and economic thought derived from the writings of Karl MARX

and his collaborator, Friedrich ENGELS. Various schools of Marxism have emerged since Marx's death in 1883. Many of these remain influential today (see also SOCIALISM and COMMUNISM).

At the center of Marx's work is his analysis of CAPITALISM. Concentrating on the social and economic relations in which people earn their livings, Marx saw behind capitalism's legal facade a struggle of two main classes: the capitalists, who own the productive resources, and the workers, or PROLETARIAT, who must work for wages in order to survive. The main theories that make up this analysis—the theory of alienation, the labor theory of value, and the materialist conception of history—must all be understood with this focus in mind.

Marxism has its main intellectual origins in German philosophy, English political economy, and French utopian socialism. It is from G. W. F. HEGEL that Marx learned a way of thinking about the world, in all its fluid complexity, that is called "dialectics." Adam SMITH's and David RICARDO's view that the values of commodities express the amount of labor time that go into their production underlay Marx's own labor theory of value. From the French utopians, especially Charles FOURIER and the comte de SAINT-SIMON, Marx caught a glimpse of a happier future that lay beyond capitalism.

Marxist Theory

Marx's study of capitalism was grounded in a philosophy that was both dialectical and materialist. With dialectics, the changes and interactions that anything undergoes are brought into focus and emphasized, and special attention is devoted to whatever patterns emerge. This method enabled Marx, when examining a particular problem within capitalism, to keep in view both the broader interactions that made up the whole and the past and future development of present phenomena. In this way, capitalism as it unfolded as a system in history becomes the main object of his study.

Marx's dialectic was materialist. Marx was primarily concerned with capitalism as lived rather than as thought about, but people's lives also involve consciousness. Marx's materialism puts ideas back into the heads of living people and treats both as parts of a world that is forever being remade through human activities. In this dialectical process, ideas also affect the social conditions and behavior that more generally shape them. (See also DIALECTICAL MATERIALISM.)

Alienation. Marx's theories about capitalism are best understood as answers to his pointed questions about its nature, effects, and development. How do the ways and conditions in which people earn their living affect their bodies, minds, and daily lives? In the theory of alienation Marx gives his answer. The people who do the work in capitalism own none of the means (machines and raw materials, for example) that they use in their work. These are owned by the capitalists, to whom workers must sell their "labor power," or ability to do work, in return for a wage. The worker is thus alienated from his or her productive activity, playing no part in deciding what to do or how to do it. The worker is alienated from the product of that activity, having no control over what is made or what becomes of it. The worker is alienated from other human beings, with competition and mutual indifference replacing most forms of cooperation. Finally, the worker is alienated from the distinctive potential inherent in the notion of *human being.*

The severing of these relationships leaves on one side an individual who is physically weakened, mentally confused, isolated, and virtually powerless. On the other side of this separation are products and ties with other people, outside the control of the worker. In the marketplace the worker's products pass from one hand to another, changing names and form along the way—value, commodity, capital, profit, interest, rent, wage—eventually reentering the worker's daily life as the landlord's house, the grocer's food, and the boss's factory.

Theory of Value. What is the effect of the worker's alienated labor on its products? Smith and Ricardo used the labor theory of value to explain broad price ratios. Marx took this explanation more or less for granted; his labor theory of value is primarily concerned with the more basic problem of why goods have prices at all. In capitalism the distribution of what is produced is a function of markets and prices. Marx's explanation of this anomaly concentrates on the separation of the worker from his or her means of production and the sale of his or her labor power that this separation makes necessary. As a result of this separation, all the things that workers produce are produced with this exchange in mind. "Value" is the general social form taken by all the products of alienated labor (labor to which the four relations of alienated labor apply). Such products could sell (have "exchange values") and serve (have "use values") only in ways that express and contribute to this alienation.

Surplus value, the third aspect of value, is the difference between the amount of exchange and use value created by workers and the amount of value returned to them as wages. The capitalist's control over this surplus is the basis of their power over the workers and the rest of society. Marx's labor theory of value also provides a detailed account of the struggle between capitalists and workers over the size of the surplus value. Because of competition among capitalists, workers are constantly being replaced by machinery, enabling and requiring capitalists to extract ever-greater amounts of surplus value from workers remaining.

Paradoxically, the amount of surplus value is also the source of capitalism's greatest weakness. Because only part of their product is returned to them as wages, the workers, as consumers, cannot buy a large portion of what they produce; this leads to crises of "overproduction," capitalism's classic contradiction, in which people are forced to live on too little because they have produced too much.

Historical Tendencies. How did capitalism originate, and where is it leading? Marx answered this question with an account of the transformation of feudalism (see MANORIALISM) into capitalism. He focused on the contradictions that arose through the growth of towns, population, technology, and trade, which at a certain point burst asunder the feudal social and political forms in which production

had been organized. Relations of lord to serf based on feudal rights and obligations had become a hindrance to the further development of these productive forces; they were replaced by the contractual relations of capitalists to workers. With capitalists free to pursue profits wherever they might take them and workers equally "free" to sell their labor power to capitalists however they might use it, the productive potential inherent in the new forces of production, especially technology and science, was freed. If profit maximization leads to rapid growth when rapid growth maximizes profits, however, profit maximization restricts growth when growth proves unprofitable. According to Marx, the periodic and worsening crises of overproduction that began about 1830 attest to capitalism's growing inability to take full advantage of the potential for producing wealth that has grown up with it.

Within this framework the actual course of history is determined by class struggle. The capitalists' interests lie in securing their power and expanding profits. Workers, on the other hand, have interests in higher wages, safer working conditions, shorter hours, job security, and—because it is required to realize other interests—a new distribution of power. The class struggle involves everything that these two major classes do to promote their incompatible interests at each other's expense.

Marx believed that once most workers recognized their interests and became "class conscious," the overthrow of capitalism would proceed as quickly and democratically as the nature of capitalist opposition allowed. The socialist society that would emerge out of the revolution would develop the full productive potential inherited from capitalism. The final goal is the human one of abolishing alienation. Marx called the attainment of this goal communism.

Marxism Today

From its beginnings, Marxism has been under strong attack by critics. Many argue that with the advent of the welfare state and the relative prosperity of workers in much of the Western world, Marxism is no longer relevant. Marxists answer that the basic structures that set capitalism apart from other social forms—private ownership of industrial wealth and alienated wage labor—have changed very little in the past 100 years. Some point to the antidemocratic practices of many Communist countries and claim that authoritarianism is inherent in Marxist doctrine. Marxists respond that Marx concentrated on advanced industrial capitalism and never supposed that socialism could achieve its full promise in relatively poor nations.

Marxism, as defined here, has had its main influence among workers and intellectuals in the capitalist countries, especially in Europe, who have used it as a major tool in defining their problems and developing political strategies. In the Third World, Marxism—considerably modified by a strong dose of voluntarism—has clarified the nature of the enemy for many liberation movements. In the Communist countries, selected doctrines of Marx have been frozen into abstract principles and formulas to serve as the official ideology of the regimes. The influence of these three versions of Marxism is as different as their content.

Mary   Mary, the mother of Jesus Christ, has been accorded a special place of devotion especially in the Roman Catholic and Eastern Orthodox churches. The New Testament records that she was the cousin of Elizabeth, mother of John the Baptist, and that she was betrothed and, later, married to JOSEPH. After giving birth to Jesus in a stable at Bethlehem, where she had gone with Joseph to register for a government census, Mary returned to Nazareth to live quietly and humbly with her family (Luke 2:1–20). At his crucifixion Jesus asked his beloved disciple, John, to look after his mother. Little is known about Mary after this, although Acts 1:14, the last reference to her in the New Testament, places her among the disciples.

The New Testament states that Mary conceived Jesus by the HOLY SPIRIT and thus without losing her virginity (Matt. 1:18, 20; Luke 1:35). Despite biblical references to Jesus' "brothers," the idea of Mary's perpetual virginity appeared in the early church. Saint Athanasius used

Mary, here portrayed by the 13th-century Italian artist Cimabue in Madonna with Angels, *is the mother of Jesus Christ. Christian theology holds that Mary was a virgin when she gave birth.*

the term "ever virgin" to refer to Mary, and this view was apparently accepted by the Fathers of the Church from the 5th century on. It was formally established as a doctrine at the church's Lateran Council in 649. Although the VIRGIN BIRTH is a tenet of virtually all Christian churches, modern biblical criticism has questioned the authenticity of the accounts in Matthew and Luke. The doctrine of Mary's perpetual virginity is taught principally by the Roman Catholic and Orthodox churches.

Marian teachings received considerable impetus at the councils of EPHESUS (431) and Chalcedon (451), both of which upheld the title *theotokos* ("God-bearer," or Mother of God) as descriptive of Mary. The doctrine of Mary's bodily assumption into heaven can be traced to apocryphal documents dating from the 4th century, but this doctrine was not officially formulated and defined for Roman Catholics until 1950 (see ASSUMPTION OF MARY). The doctrine of Mary's IMMACULATE CONCEPTION was a matter of dispute throughout the Middle Ages. In 1854, however, Pope Pius IX declared that Mary was freed from original sin by a special act of grace the moment she was conceived in the womb of Saint Anne. (Tradition names Saint ANNE and Saint Joachim as Mary's parents.)

Pope Pius XII strongly promoted Marian piety during his reign (1939–58). Because Roman Catholic teaching holds that Mary is deserving of the "highest veneration," the church observes 17 Marian festivals each year, 5 of which are major: Immaculate Conception, Dec. 8; Purification, Feb. 2; Annunciation, Mar. 25; Assumption, Aug. 15; and Birth, Sept. 8. The ROSARY contains 50 Ave Marias ("hail Marys"), and devotion to the "immaculate heart" of Mary is popular in some circles.

Mary of Burgundy   Mary, b. Feb. 13, 1457, d. Mar. 27, 1482, was duchess of Burgundy and wife of the Austrian archduke Maximilian (later MAXIMILIAN I, Holy Roman Emperor). After the death of her father, CHARLES THE BOLD, in January 1477, Mary was threatened by LOUIS XI of France's seizure of Burgundy and Picardy and his imminent invasion of the Low Countries and the rest of her inheritance. In the same year she concluded her previously arranged marriage to the Habsburg heir, Maximilian, who helped her defeat Louis in 1479. The marriage ultimately gave the HABSBURGS control of the Burgundian territories, including the Netherlands.

Mary Magdalene [mag'-duh-lin]   In the New Testament of the Bible, Mary, who came from the town of Magdala near Capernaum, was closely associated with Jesus Christ. She was cured of seven demons by Jesus (Mark 16:9; Luke 8:2), ministered to him, went with him on his preaching mission in Galilee (Luke 8:2, 3), and was among those who followed Jesus on his last journey to Jerusalem (Mark 15:40, 41). Mary was present at the crucifixion (Mark 15:40), went to the tomb to anoint Jesus' body (Mark 16:1, Luke 23:55–24:11), reported the empty tomb to the apostles (Luke 24:10), and was the first person to see Jesus after the resurrection (John 20:11–18).

Tradition, but no solid evidence, identifies Mary as the sinful woman of Luke 7:36–50 who anointed the feet of Jesus. A legend, considered improbable, places her in southern France, living a life of penitence, during her last days. Feast day: July 22.

Mary and Martha

In the New Testament, Mary and Martha were the two sisters of LAZARUS who lived in Bethany, near Jerusalem. They are important disciples of Jesus in several Gospel passages, including those recording the resurrection of Lazarus (John 11:1–44) and the two sisters' different responses to Jesus' visit (Luke 10:38–42). In the latter passage, the active Martha prepares the meal while Mary listens at Jesus' feet with his disciples. Because of Jesus' approval of Mary's choice, she has come to symbolize the contemplative life. She is sometimes identified with Mary Magdalene. Feast days: July 22 (Mary); July 29 (Martha).

Mary I, Queen of England

Mary Tudor, b. Feb. 18, 1516, d. Nov. 17, 1558, ruled England as Queen Mary I from 1553 and earned the epithet Bloody Mary for the executions of Protestants that occurred during her reign. She was the daughter of HENRY VIII by his first wife, CATHERINE OF ARAGON. In 1533, Henry divorced Catherine because she had not borne him a male heir. The pope refused to recognize the divorce, however, and England broke with Rome in 1534. An increasingly Protestant Church of England was brought into being during the later years of Henry's reign, and Mary reluctantly declared her parents' union illegal and abjured Roman Catholicism. In private she retained her Catholic faith through the reign (1547–53) of her half brother, EDWARD VI. When Edward died, an attempt was made to divert the succession to a Protestant cousin, Lady Jane GREY, but it failed and Mary acceded to the throne.

Mary restored Catholicism, reestablishing the traditional services and the authority of the pope. In 1554 she married the future PHILIP II of Spain, son of Holy Roman Emperor Charles V. The last three years of Mary's reign were marred by the execution of about 300 Protestants. Hundreds of other Protestants spent the later years of her reign in exile on the Continent. In 1557, Philip induced Mary to ally with Spain in an unpopular war with France that cost England Calais, its last Continental possession. Mary never bore a child; at her death the throne passed to her younger half sister, ELIZABETH I.

Mary II, Queen of England

As queen of England, Mary II, b. Apr. 30, 1662, d. Dec. 28, 1694, ruled jointly with her husband, WILLIAM III. The eldest daughter of JAMES II, she married her cousin William, prince of Orange, in 1677 and lived with him in Holland. Mary supported William's invasion of England against James in 1688 (see GLORIOUS REVOLUTION). Although considered the legitimate heir to the throne, Mary insisted that her husband be joint sovereign with her, and in 1689 they were crowned together.

Mary, Queen of Scots

Mary, Queen of Scots, b. Dec. 8, 1542, d. Feb. 8, 1587, was a beautiful and controversial woman whose life was full of drama and intrigue.

Early Life. Mary Stuart was the daughter of JAMES V of Scotland and Mary of Guise (see GUISE family). Six days after her birth her father died, and she became queen of Scotland. Her French mother, chosen as regent, sent Mary to France in 1548.

In April 1558, Mary married the dauphin, Francis; she secretly agreed to bequeath Scotland to France if she should die without a son. In July 1559, Francis succeeded his father, becoming King FRANCIS II, and Mary became queen of France as well as of Scotland.

Many Roman Catholics also recognized Mary Stuart as queen of England after the Protestant ELIZABETH I succeeded to the throne in November 1558. Mary Stuart's claim to the English throne was based on the fact that she was the granddaughter of Margaret Tudor, sister of HENRY VIII. In December 1560, Mary's young husband, Francis II, died. Unwilling to stay in France under the domination of her mother-in-law, CATHERINE DE MÉDICIS, Mary decided to return to Scotland.

Return to Scotland. On Aug. 19, 1561, Mary landed at Leith and immediately took the advice of the moderates, James Stuart (her half brother, later earl of Moray) and William Maitland of Lethington, and recognized the Reformed (Presbyterian) church. The Protestant reformers, including John KNOX, were horrified because she had Mass in her own chapel, and the Roman Catholics were worried about her lack of zeal for their cause. For the next few years, Mary tried to placate the Protestants and befriend Elizabeth, while at the same time negotiating a Catholic marriage with Don Carlos, the son of PHILIP II of Spain. When refusals came on both the English succession and the Spanish marriage, Mary married her first cousin, Henry Stewart, Lord DARNLEY, on July 29, 1565.

Mary Stuart, queen of Scotland and a Roman Catholic, alienated and lost the support of the Protestant Scottish nobility by her political decisions and marriages. Forced to abdicate in 1567, she fled to England, where she was imprisoned. After repeated Catholic plots to make her queen of England, Mary was executed.

Plots and Intrigue. This union was unacceptable to the Protestants, and Moray raised a rebellion, which Mary quickly suppressed. After her marriage with Darnley soured, Mary turned to her Italian secretary, David Riccio, for comfort and advice. The Protestant lords disliked Riccio's influence because they suspected him of being a papal agent, and on Mar. 9, 1566, a group of Protestant lords, acting with the support of Darnley, murdered Riccio in Mary's presence at Holyrood Palace. Mary, who was six months pregnant, survived the horrible ordeal. In Edinburgh Castle on June 19, 1566, she gave birth to a son, James (later JAMES I of England).

By the end of 1566, Mary had befriended James Hepburn, earl of BOTHWELL, and was seeking a way to dissolve her marriage with Darnley. On Feb. 10, 1567, Darnley was murdered, but it seems unlikely that Mary was aware of the actual plot to eliminate him. At the time, Bothwell was believed to be the chief instigator. Nevertheless, he was acquitted after an all-too-brief trial. In April, Mary went off with Bothwell (perhaps a victim of abduction); early in May he obtained a divorce from his wife, and on May 15, 1567, he and Mary were wed according to the Protestant rite.

These events alienated even some of Mary's closest supporters. The nobles, many of whom disliked Bothwell, banded together to face Mary and her new husband at Carberry. The queen was forced to surrender, and Bothwell fled.

Mary was imprisoned at Lochleven Castle and on July 24, 1567, she was compelled to abdicate in favor of her son, who became King James VI of Scotland. With help from a few brave friends, Mary escaped from the castle and immediately rallied a large force behind her. They engaged in battle at Langside on May 13, 1567, and were soundly beaten by the army led by the Protestant lords.

English Captivity. Mary crossed the Solway into England and spent nearly 19 years in captivity; she never returned to Scotland. While she was incarcerated in England, numerous unsuccessful plots by English Roman Catholics and foreign agents evolved around her. The Babington plot, which called for the assassination of Elizabeth, was formed to trap Mary. Mary was found guilty of complicity and sentenced to be beheaded. Although reluctant to execute her cousin, Elizabeth gave the order that was carried out at Fotheringhay Castle.

Maryknoll Missioners   The Catholic Foreign Mission Society of America, commonly known as the Maryknoll Missioners, was founded in 1911 as a men's religious community by two Roman Catholic priests, James A. Walsh and Thomas F. Price. An affiliated community of women, the Maryknoll Sisters of Saint Dominic, was established by Mary Joseph Rogers in 1920. The Maryknollers' early missionary work was concentrated in the Far East, especially in China and Korea. Expelled from China after the Communist revolution of 1949, they were later active in Latin America, the Philippines, and East Africa.

Maryland   Maryland, one of the Middle Atlantic states of the United States, ranks 42d among the states in area and 19th in population and is a leading state in population density. CHESAPEAKE BAY, the largest bay in the continental United States, almost severs the state, dividing the Eastern Shore—which is located on the DELMARVA PENINSULA (shared by Delaware, Maryland, and Virginia)—from the Western Shore. The straight northern boundary with Pennsylvania is part of the MASON-DIXON LINE, which was established in 1769; the southern and western boundaries with Virginia and West Virginia, repectively, follow the Potomac River, except where the District of Columbia intervenes; Delaware lies to the east. The state capital is ANNAPOLIS, which lies within the metropolitan area of Baltimore, Maryland's largest city.

One of the 13 original states, Maryland was named for Queen Henrietta Maria, wife of Charles I of England.

Land and Resources

Maryland has three major physiographic divisions—the Coastal Plain, the Piedmont, and the Appalachian Mountains. The Coastal Plain occupies all of eastern Maryland. It is underlain by sedimentary rock, and elevations are lower than 30 m (100 ft) on the Eastern Shore and lower than 60 m (200 ft) on the more rolling Western Shore. Along the Atlantic coast a series of low, sandy barrier islands and vast stretches of swampy and tidal wetlands surround Chesapeake Bay. The Coastal Plain is bounded on the west by the FALL LINE.

West of the fall line is the PIEDMONT PLATEAU, which is part of the Appalachians and underlain mostly by igneous and metamorphic rocks. Elevations rise to 400 m (1,300 ft), and the rolling surface is well suited for agriculture except where cut by steep-sided valleys. The BLUE RIDGE MOUNTAINS begin west of Frederick and extend across the state as a prominent, forested ridge, with summits reaching about 520 m (1,700 ft). West of the Blue Ridge lies a broad plain known as the Great Valley, and farther west is a series of narrow parallel ridges and valleys known as the Ridge and Valley region. In far western Maryland rises the high edge of the APPALACHIAN MOUNTAINS, where Backbone Mountain, Maryland's highest point, reaches 1,024 m (3,360 ft).

Soils. The best agricultural soils occur on the Piedmont and in well-drained areas of the Coastal Plain. Soils in the Great Valley and western areas are of poorer quality.

Drainage. About 184 km (114 mi) of the 309-km-long (192-mi) Chesapeake Bay are within Maryland's borders. The bay, together with such broad indentations as the lower Potomac and Patuxent river valleys, is part of the lower Susquehanna drainage system. The Susquehanna River enters the northern end of the bay. Major rivers draining from the east are the Elk, Chester, Choptank, Nanticoke, and Pokomoke; draining from the west are the Patapsco, Patuxent, and Potomac, which are interrupted, respectively, by falls at Baltimore, Laurel, and Potomac (to the northwest of Washington, D.C.).

Climate. The Coastal Plain has hot summers and mild winters. Temperatures average above 1° C (34° F) in Jan-

MARYLAND

Land: Area: 32,135 km^2 (12,407 mi^2); rank: 42d.
Capital: Annapolis (1990 pop., 33,187). Largest city:
Baltimore (1990 pop., 736,014). Counties: 23.
Elevations: highest—1,024 m (3,360 ft), at Backbone
Mountain; lowest—sea level, at the Atlantic coast.

People: Population (1990): 4,798,622; rank: 19th;
density: 188.9 persons per km^2 (489.2 per mi^2). Distribution (1990): 81.3% urban, 18.7% rural. Average annual change (1980–90): +1.4%.

Government (1993): Governor: William Donald
Schaefer, Democrat. U.S. Congress: Senate—2 Democrats; House—4 Democrats, 4 Republicans. Electoral
college votes: 10. State legislature: 47 senators, 141
representatives.

Economy: State personal income (1989): $98.6 billion;
rank: 14th. Median family income (1989): $45,032;
rank: 4th. Agriculture: income (1989)—$1.3 billion.
Fishing: value (1989)—$52 million. Lumber production
(1991, with Delaware): 134 million board feet. Mining
(nonfuel): value (1988)—$363 million. Manufacturing:
value added (1987)—$14 billion. Services: value (1987)—
$24.9 billion.

Miscellany: Statehood: Apr. 28, 1788; the 7th state.
Nicknames: Old Line State, Free State; tree: white oak;
motto: *Fatti Maschii, Parole Femine* ("Manly Deeds,
Womanly Words"); song: "Maryland, My Maryland."

Baltimore
Oriole

Black-eyed
Susan

uary, and more than 23° C (74° F) in July; annual precipitation is generally more than 1,070 mm (42 in), and
snowfall is less than 510 mm (20 in). In the Piedmont
temperatures average 1° C (34° F) in January and 24° C
(76° F) in July; precipitation is less than 1,070 mm (42
in), and snowfall is moderate, between 510 mm (20 in)
and 760 mm (30 in). The mountainous west has severe
winters, with temperatures generally below freezing and
snowfall totaling between 1,020 mm (40 in) and 2,540
mm (100 in). Summers are cool, with the average temperature in July less than 21° C (70° F).

Vegetation and Animal Life. Forests and woodlands cover more than 40% of the state. An oak-hickory hardwood
forest dominates the Appalachian and Piedmont areas
and is common on the Western Shore. The lower Eastern
Shore has a Southern pine forest, with loblolly, pitch, and
Virginia pines. Occasional bears and bobcats are seen in
the mountains, and deer, foxes, opossums, and raccoons
abound throughout the state.

Chesapeake Bay is rich in oysters, clams, crabs, and
other marine animals. The bay is also part of the Atlantic
flyway and is visited by numerous migrating birds, wild
geese, and ducks. Game birds in the western uplands include quail, wild turkey, and ruffed grouse.

Resources. Maryland has limited natural resources.
Coal reserves in the western mountains are estimated at

more than 450 million metric tons (500 million U.S.
tons), but production has declined since the early 20th
century. Natural gas occurs in two small fields in the
west. The most important minerals are limestone, sand,
gravel, and clays and shales, which are used in brickmak-
ing. Extensive underground water resources are available
in the sedimentary rocks underlying the Coastal Plain, but
other regions must depend on surface water from rivers
and reservoirs for municipal and industrial water supplies.

People

Maryland has a population of 4,798,622 (1990). The
rate of increase for 1980–90 was 13.8%, compared with
a national average of 10.2%. Large areas are sparsely
populated, especially in the west, because more than
80% of the total population is concentrated in either the
BALTIMORE or Washington metropolitan area or the fast-
growing belt located between the two cities in what is
known as the Baltimore-Washington corridor. About 15%
of the population reside within Baltimore's city limits.
FREDERICK, HAGERSTOWN, and Salisbury are important cities located outside the Baltimore area.

African Americans have lived in Maryland since the
colonial period and now constitute about 25% of the
population, with most living in Baltimore. The principal
ethnic groups in the white majority are of British, Ger-

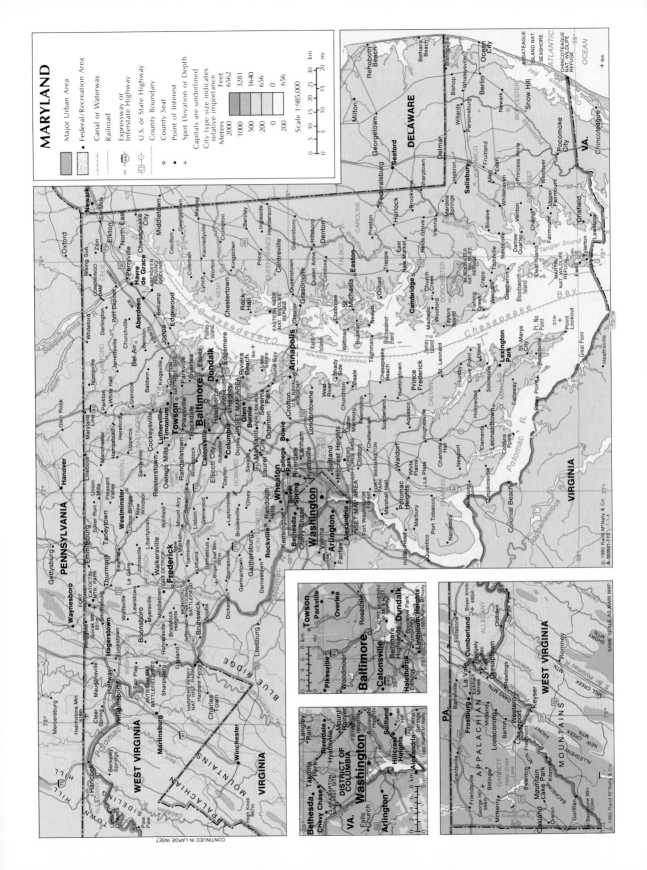

MARYLAND

Major Urban Area
Federal/Recreation Area
Canal or Waterway
Railroad
Expressway or Interstate Highway
U.S. or State Highway
County Boundary
County Seat
Point of Interest
Spot Elevation or Depth
Capitals are underlined
City type size indicates relative importance

Meters	Feet
2000	6562
1000	3281
500	1640
200	656
0	0
200	656

Scale 1:1,985,000

© 1980 Rand McNally & Co.   A-500501-712 \ -1-1-1

CONTINUED IN LARGE INSET

SAME SCALE AS MAIN MAP

man, Hispanic, Italian, Polish, and Russian descent. The population is approximately 32% Protestant, 24% Roman Catholic, and 10% Jewish.

Education. In 1826 a statewide education system was established. Black children were educated separately until the 1954 Supreme Court decision ended school segregation. Maryland has 47 institutes of higher education. The University of Maryland (1820), with its main campus at College Park, is the largest state institution. The JOHNS HOPKINS UNIVERSITY in Baltimore is the state's most distinguished private institution. The UNITED STATES NAVAL ACADEMY is located in Annapolis. The Peabody Institute in Baltimore is nationally renowned for the study of music. The Enoch Pratt Free Library, also in Baltimore, is considered one of the nation's finest municipal libraries.

Cultural Institutions. Most of Maryland's cultural institutions are concentrated in Baltimore. The Baltimore Symphony Orchestra and the Baltimore Opera Company are both highly rated nationally. Art museums in Baltimore are the Peale Museum, the Baltimore Museum of Art, and the Walters Art Gallery.

Historical Sites and Recreation. Nationally maintained places of historic interest include the Civil War Antietam National Battlefield site, near Sharpsburg; FORT MCHENRY National Monument, in Baltimore harbor, the defense of which during the War of 1812 inspired Francis Scott KEY to write "The Star-Spangled Banner"; Hampton, an elegant Georgian mansion begun in 1783 in Towson; and the Chesapeake and Ohio National Monument. Other historical sites include the restored waterfront of downtown Annapolis; St. Mary's City, the restored early colonial capital; the Star-Spangled Banner House, where the original flag commemorated in the national anthem was sewn by Mary Pickersgill; and the U.S.S. CONSTELLATION, in Baltimore harbor.

Catoctin Mountain Park near Thurmont includes within its borders the Camp David presidential retreat. The Appalachian Trail crosses the state, and 34 state parks and 9 state forests provide additional hiking and camping facilities. Ocean City is a popular summer resort on the Atlantic Ocean. The Chesapeake Bay area offers superior pleasure boating, and excellent duck hunting is available along its coastal wetlands.

Professional sports teams include the Baltimore Orioles (baseball) and two suburban Washington teams—the Washington Bullets (basketball) and Washington Capitals (hockey). Major horse-racing tracks are at Pimlico, home of the Preakness, in Baltimore, and in Laurel.

Communications. Maryland has 123 radio and 12 television stations (1984). The state's 14 daily newspapers have a combined circulation of 702,000. The Washington and Baltimore metropolitan areas dominate radio and television broadcasting within the state. Other towns with commercial television stations are Hagerstown and Salisbury. The most influential newspaper in the state is the *Baltimore Sun*.

Economic Activity

Maryland's colonial economy was based primarily on the cultivation and export of tobacco. After the Revolution,

shipbuilding developed, and Baltimore quickly grew to rival Boston, New York, and Philadelphia as a port and commercial center. Modern growth factors include proximity to the nation's capital and location within the much-traveled and heavily industrialized Eastern Seaboard transportation corridor, which links Boston, New York City, and Washington, D.C.

Manufacturing. Manufacturing is a principal economic activity of Maryland, with Baltimore the center of about a third of all manufacturing activities (by value). Other important industrial areas are found in Baltimore, Montgomery, and Prince George counties. Historically, metalworking has been a chief industry in the state and remains important. The Sparrows Point plant of Bethlehem Steel is one of the largest steel mills on tidewater in the nation. Large steel-using industries include auto assembly, production of electrical tools, aerospace manufacture, and shipbuilding. Other manufacturing activities include textiles and such port-related operations as spice processing, sugar refining, and flour milling.

Agriculture. Farming continues to be an important activity on the Eastern Shore and in the nonmetropolitan counties between Baltimore and Cumberland. The Eastern Shore is one of the country's leading producers of broiler chickens, and corn and soybeans are also widely cultivated. Southern Maryland still produces tobacco that has good burning qualities. Mixed dairy and crop farming is important on the Piedmont. Apples and peaches are a speciality in the valleys of western Maryland.

Fishing and Forestry. The principal commercial fishing area is the Chesapeake Bay. Shellfish accounts for the great majority of the volume and value of the fishing catch. Also of commercial importance are various types of finfish. The forestry industry is small; lumber, pulpwood, furniture veneers, and Christmas trees constitute the principal products.

Chesapeake Bay's fishing industry yields several million dollars annually and supports more than 18,000 fishing families. Shellfish, including crabs, oysters, and clams, are found in both natural and artificial beds.

Baltimore, the largest city in Maryland, was first settled as a tobacco port in the early 17th century. In 1904 a fire destroyed most of downtown, and the reconstructed city has incorporated modern urban planning and architecture.

Mining. Stone is the most valuable mineral produced and is quarried in Allegany, Baltimore, Cecil, Howard, and Montgomery counties. Coal, Maryland's only fossil-fuel resource, is mined in Allegany and Garrett counties. Sand and gravel are found statewide.

Transportation. Located within the Eastern Seaboard transportation corridor, Maryland is well provided with high-speed connections to New York City, Boston, and Washington, D.C. Major north-south and east-west highways focus on Baltimore. Rail transportation is provided by Amtrak, and the historically important Baltimore and Ohio railroad provides commuter service between Baltimore and Washington. A mass-transit subway line opened in Baltimore in 1983. The Chesapeake and Delaware canal, part of the Atlantic Intracoastal Waterway, provides direct water access to Delaware Bay and harbors farther north. Baltimore is one of America's busiest ports. The Baltimore-Washington International Airport is the major air terminal in the state.

Energy. Maryland is linked with the power grid of the eastern United States and has within its borders more than 20 generating plants. About half of the state's electricity is produced by coal-fired plants. The Calvert Cliffs Nuclear Plant, located in Lusby, produces about 30% of the state's electricity.

Government and Politics

Maryland's most recent constitution, adopted in 1867 and much amended, provides for a bicameral General Assembly with a 47-member Senate and a 141-member House of Delegates. Members of the assembly are elected to 4-year terms. The chief executive is the governor, who is popularly elected for a 4-year term and is limited to two consecutive terms. The state's 23 counties provide basic services such as road construction, schools, and police and are the principal form of local government. Maryland sends to the U.S. Congress two senators and eight representatives. It has ten electoral votes in national presidential elections. Long considered a Democratic stronghold, Maryland can no longer be counted on to vote for Democratic candidates in state and national elections.

History

Giovanni da VERRAZANO is thought to have visited the Atlantic coast near Chincoteague Bay in 1524. In 1526, Spanish explorers sailed into Chesapeake Bay and called it Santa María. In 1608, Capt. John SMITH of Virginia became the first authenticated European visitor. In late 1631, William Clairborne established a fur-trading post, which is regarded as the first permanent European settlement, on Kent Island (opposite Annapolis). At the time of early European settlement, the principal Indian groups were three Algonquian tribes—the Piscataway on the Western Shore, who left the area in 1697; and the Nanticoke and Pocomoke-Assateague on the Eastern Shore, who migrated westward in the 1740s. The Susquehannock also inhabited the area, but in 1675 they were carried into captivity by the Iroquois Nations.

In 1632, King Charles I of England granted George Calvert, 1st Baron Baltimore (see CALVERT family), settlement rights to lands between the 40th parallel and the south bank of the Potomac. Calvert died before the papers were complete, and the charter passed to his son Cecilius (Cecil) Calvert, 2d Baron Baltimore. In November 1633, 200 colonists set sail from England in the *Ark* and the *Dove*, which landed on Mar. 24, 1634, at Saint Clement (now Blakistone) Island at the mouth of the Potomac. They purchased the Indian village of Yaocomico, which they renamed St. Mary's (now St. Mary's City) and used for 60 years as the capital and center of the colony. Lord Baltimore, a Roman Catholic, sought religious freedom for the colony, and in 1649 the Colonial Assembly passed the Act Concerning Religion, the first statute in the colonies to provide freedom of worship for all Christians.

From 1692 to 1715, Maryland was a crown colony, ruled by royal governors. In 1694 the capital moved to Annapolis. The Baltimores regained control in 1715. At first the colony had a diversified agriculture, but by the end of the 17th century tobacco was the staple crop.

In the Revolutionary period, Maryland was one of the first colonies to repudiate the STAMP ACT (1765). On July 3, 1776, the state disavowed its allegiance to the king, and four months later was the first of the former colonies to adopt a state constitution. During the Revolutionary War, Maryland troops distinguished themselves in battles outside the state, but no fighting took place in the state. In 1788, Maryland became the seventh state to ratify the U.S. Constitution, and in 1791 it ceded to the nation 174 km^2 (67 mi^2) along the Potomac for construction of the District of Columbia.

Maryland's early years of statehood were spent in developing the state's resources. Shipping and trade expanded, and Baltimore, incorporated in 1797, grew rapidly as a port and a shipbuilding and industrial center. New transportation facilities integrated the growing trade of lands west of the Appalachians into the region. Among the more important routes were the NATIONAL ROAD (1818); the Chesapeake and Delaware Canal (1829) across the Delmarva Peninsula; the Chesapeake and Ohio Canal along the Potomac River to Cumberland and the coalfields of western Maryland; and the Baltimore and Ohio Railroad, the first U.S. passenger railroad, begun in 1828.

At the outbreak of the Civil War, Maryland had almost equal numbers of slaves and free blacks, and the state was sharply divided in its sympathies to North and South. However, when neighboring Virginia seceded, Maryland's presence within the Union became vital to the defense of Washington, D.C., and President Lincoln was forced to prevent secession by imposing military rule. Fierce battles fought on Maryland soil included the battles of South Mountain and ANTIETAM (both in 1862) and Monocacy (1864).

Manufacturing expanded after the Civil War and eventually emerged as the mainstay of the economy. Thousands of European immigrants, together with blacks migrating from rural counties, flocked to take jobs in Baltimore's textile and other factories.

In 1904, Baltimore was devastated by fire but recovered to grow rapidly as World Wars I and II increased demand for the city's industrial products. More recently, Washington-related research and other industries have increased the state's prosperity.

Race relations in Maryland were severely strained by the 1954 U.S. Supreme Court decision to end segregation, and widespread rioting occurred in the 1960s, mostly in Baltimore. Spiro T. AGNEW, Maryland's fifth Republican governor since 1895 (1967–69), was elected U.S. vice-president in 1968 and 1972. In 1973, however, he resigned the office during an investigation of charges of graft while he was a Maryland official. Governor Marvin Mandel, Agnew's Democratic successor, was convicted in 1978 on charges of mail fraud and racketeering and sentenced to jail. He was forced by Maryland law to resign, but in January 1979, his conviction was overturned on appeal, and he reassumed office for the 45 hours of his term remaining.

During the late 1970s and 1980s, Baltimore's downtown and harbor areas underwent major urban renewal.

Masaccio [mah-zah'-choh] The Florentine painter Tommaso di Ser Giovanni di Mone, b. Dec. 21, 1401, d. 1428, was nicknamed Masaccio ("Slovenly Tom") because he cared so little for his appearance and personal affairs and so much more for his art. Along with the architect Filippo Brunelleschi and the sculptor Donatello, he is universally considered to be one of the founders of the Florentine Renaissance.

Masaccio was the first artist to use the principles of Brunelleschi's linear PERSPECTIVE in a major painting when he executed his *Trinity* fresco (*c.*1425–27; Santa Maria Novella, Florence), in which he created the illusion of a chapel receding beyond the wall on which it is painted. Reinforcing this perspective effect is the placement of the figures of the donors, who are portrayed kneeling on a shelf that seems to project forward. The entire composition is constructed to lead the spectator's eye inexorably toward the focal point of the work, the pyramidal group composed of the Virgin and Saint John at the bases and God the Father and the crucified Christ at the apex. This astonishing visual tour-de-force marks the true beginning of the monumental and rationally ordered painting of the Italian Renaissance.

Masaccio's few other surviving works are equally daring in conception. In his *Madonna and Child Enthroned* (*c.*1426; National Gallery, London), the central panel of a polyptych executed for a church in Pisa, the painter illuminated the entire scene with a single source of light. The dramatic effects of light and shadow—called CHIAROSCURO—stand out even more in Masaccio's contributions to the frescoes decorating the Brancacci Chapel in the church of Santa Maria del Carmine in Florence, on which he collaborated (*c.*1425–27) with Masolino. There, in *The Expulsion of Adam and Eve*, Masaccio modeled in light and shadow the naked forms of the grief-stricken couple, who are shown striding hastily from the Gate of Paradise in one of the most animated and emotive renditions of the scene ever painted. Masaccio did not live to complete the Brancacci Chapel decorations. He died in Rome sometime in 1428, while still in his late twenties.

Masada [muh-say'-duh] The natural rock fortress of Masada, on the western shore of the Dead Sea in southeast Israel, was the final outpost of the Jewish ZEALOTS in their revolt against Rome during the 1st century AD. According to the historian Josephus, it was first built by the high priest Jonathan, the brother of Judas Maccabeus (r. 160–142 BC). Following the return of Herod the Great from Rome in 39 BC, a new fortress was built on the site, described in great detail by Josephus.

Little is known of Masada during the period following

Masada was an ancient Hebrew fortress located at the top of a mesa above the Dead Sea. The Judean king Herod the Great (r. 37–4 BC) was the chief builder of Masada. It was the last stronghold of the Zealot Jews, who captured it during the Jewish revolt (AD 66–73) against the Romans.

Herod's death in 4 BC, but by AD 66, at the beginning of the Jewish Revolt, it was held by a Roman garrison. This garrison was expelled by the Zealots, who maintained control of the fortress until 73, when it was finally conquered by the Romans. During the final siege, 960 Zealot resistors committed mass suicide.

Masai [mah-sy'] The Masai are a nomadic cattle-herding people of East Africa who have with determination clung to their traditional ways, rejecting the cash economy and refusing to settle or become farmers. One of the

The Masai, a nomadic pastoral people living principally in Kenya and Tanzania, were once famed as the ablest warriors of East Africa. Adult men continue to be initiated into a hierarchy of groups. The warrior age-group is responsible for protecting and herding the tribe's livestock.

tall, slender, Nilotic peoples, the Masai speak an Eastern Chari-Nile language of the Sudanic stock. Traditionally, the Masai ranged widely over the Kenya highlands in raiding expeditions, but after suffering famine and disease they were persuaded by the Kenya government to move to southern Kenya and Tanzania. They were estimated to number close to 300,000 in the late 1960s.

Cattle are the basis of the Masai economy, providing food, mainly in the form of milk and blood, and property for payment of bride-price. Masai also keep many sheep, and some goats and donkeys. Social features include descent through the father's line and multiple wives. Traditionally, Masai males have been age-graded in the stages of boy, warrior, and elder. A man may marry only after he has served as a warrior, at about age 30. Masai residence groups are divided into elders' and warriors' kraals, or villages.

Masanobu [mah-sah'-noh-boo] Okumura Masanobu, c.1686–1764, was a Japanese painter and printmaker who worked in the UKIYO-E style, a decorative mode depicting genre subjects associated with the world of popular entertainment. Masanobu experimented with techniques of Urushi-e, or lacquer prints, and he invented both the long, narrow "pillar print" and the Uki-e, or perspective print, a novelty popular in the 1740s. He also has been credited with introducing into Japanese art the color printing that after 1741 replaced the hand-coloring technique used by earlier printmakers. His elegant figure style set the vogue for bijin-ga, or portraits of famous beauties.

Masaryk, Jan [mah'-sah-rik, yahn] Jan Masaryk, b. Sept. 14, 1886, d. Mar. 10, 1948, son of Czech leader Tomáš Masaryk, was foreign minister in the Czech exile government in London during World War II and in the postwar coalition government of Eduard BENEŠ. He remained foreign minister after the Communist coup of Feb. 25, 1948, but committed suicide or was murdered a few weeks later.

Masaryk, Tomáš [toh'-mahsh] Tomáš Garrigue Masaryk, b. Mar. 7, 1850, d. Sept. 14, 1937, noted Czech philosopher, nationalist, and democrat, was the founding president (1918–35) of Czechoslovakia. His study of Plato's logic, Protestant rationalism, and British empiricism made Masaryk a pragmatist but also imbued him with a scrupulous regard for accuracy regardless of political consequences. He gained a professorship at the Czech University of Prague in 1882 and four years later helped expose as forgeries a group of ostensibly medieval Slavic manuscripts that had been underpinnings of Czech cultural nationalism. He also denounced expressions of Czech anti-Semitism.

An advocate of democratic reform and Czech autonomy within Austria-Hungary, Masaryk was twice elected (1891, 1907) to the Austrian parliament. In 1900 he founded the Progressive (or Realist) party. After the outbreak of World War I, Masaryk, with colleagues Eduard BeneŠ and Milan Stefánik, began working for Czech independence in union with Slovakia.

With the establishment of Czechoslovakia after the war, Masaryk was elected the republic's first president. Reelected three times, he had mixed success in his attempt to make his country a model democracy. Masaryk wrote many books, including *The Making of a State* (1925; Eng. trans., 1927).

Mascagni, Pietro [mahs-kahn'-yee] Pietro Mascagni, b. Dec. 7, 1863, d. Aug. 2, 1945, was one of the most important composers of Italian opera in the generation after Verdi's. His one-act *Cavalleria Rusticana* (1889), based on a play by Giovanni Verga, is a landmark in VERISMO, a school of Italian naturalism. This was Mascagni's first opera, written for a competition sponsored by the publishing house of Sonzogno. It not only won the prize but also quickly became a worldwide success. Mascagni's 17 later operas and operettas are varied in style and show gains in musical craftsmanship, but none match the dramatic power of his earliest work. The best known of these are *L'Amico Fritz* (1891), *Iris* (1898), and *Il Piccolo Marat* (1921).

In 1929 he became the musical director of La Scala, succeeding Arturo Toscanini. Mascagni was an active supporter of fascism, and at its defeat in 1945 his fortunes fell, and he died in poverty and isolation.

masculinity   see SEXUAL DEVELOPMENT

Masefield, John [mayz'-feeld] The English poet John Masefield, b. June 1, 1878, d. May 12, 1967, became the 15th poet laureate in 1930. After serving as a merchant seaman aboard a large sailing vessel, Masefield returned to England to make a living as a journalist. His volume of poetry *Salt-Water Ballads* (1902) and the long narrative poems *The Everlasting Mercy* (1911) and *Reynard the Fox* (1919) won him an enthusiastic audience. He also wrote verse dramas and three successful adventure novels: *Sard Harker* (1924), *Odtaa* (1926), and *Basilissa* (1940). Two early poems, "Sea Fever" and "Cargoes," are enduringly popular.

maser   The maser is a device that generates "well organized" or coherent light in the microwave region of the spectrum. Maser is an acronym for *Microwave Amplification by Stimulated Emission of Radiation*. In the early 1950s, Charles H. Townes of Columbia University isolated high-energy ammonia molecules using an electric field. The molecules contained electrons raised to high-energy states that then jumped to the ground state, emitting microwave photons, some of which would stimulate more electrons to jump to the ground state. This resulted in stimulated emission, or the spontaneous production of photons with identical wavelength and wave phase. In

1954, Townes, J. P. Gordon, and H. J. Zeiger succeeded in concentrating, or amplifying, such waves, producing the first maser.

When the high-energy molecules (the so-called population inversion) are contained in a partially mirrored chamber, they will strongly interact, emitting an extremely coherent beam from a small opening. Such powerful beams are usually obtained from LASERS, the visible-light analogs of masers. Masers are more commonly used in two applications: because maser light is given off in brief pulses at specific frequencies, it serves as the basis for very accurate clocks (see ATOMIC CLOCK); and because masers can amplify a microwave signal without generating electrical noise, they find important use as amplifiers of weak microwave signals from distant sources (see RADIO ASTRONOMY).

Maseru [maz'-uh-roo] Maseru (1986 est. pop., 106,000) is the capital and largest town of Lesotho. Located along the Caledon River near the South African border, Maseru is linked by rail with South Africa. Its industries produce light consumer goods. In 1869, MOSHESHWE I, chief of the Sotho nation, established Maseru as his capital.

Mashhad [mahsh-hahd'] Mashhad (also Meshed) is a city in the extreme northeast of Iran. Its population is 1,463,508 (1986 est.). Mashhad is an important market for the wool trade and is well known for carpet manufacturing. Tourism is also important to the economy; more than 100,000 Shiite Muslim pilgrims go to Mashhad annually to visit the tombs and shrines of the great Abbasid caliph HARUN-AL-RASHID and his son-in-law Ali al-Rida (d. 819), the 8th imam of the Twelver SHIITES.

Although Mashhad is an ancient settlement, it did not begin to grow until the 9th century when it became a pilgrimage center. (Its name means "place of martyrdom.") Partially destroyed in 1220 by Mongols and again during the 16th century by other Central Asian tribes, the city was much beautified by Shah ABBAS I (r. 1588–1629). From 1736 to 1747 under NADIR SHAH it served as the capital of Persia.

Masinissa [mas-in-is'-uh] Masinissa, b. *c*.238, d. 149 or 148 BC, founded the nation of NUMIDIA in North Africa west of Carthage. As a young tribal leader, he fought ably in Spain against the Romans during the Second PUNIC WAR (218–201 BC), but in 206 he changed sides, assisting SCIPIO AFRICANUS MAJOR in defeating Carthage at Zama (202). With Roman backing he established himself as king of Numidia, previously a collection of diverse, seminomadic tribes, and expanded his realm at Carthage's expense.

masks   Masks are artificial face coverings used in ritual and primitive theater to transform the wearers into—or

(Below) *This ancestor mask was formerly used in clan initiation rites in Borneo. Its wearer assumed the ancestor's power. (Nationalmuseet, Copenhagen.)*

(Above) *A Bamileke dancer in Cameroon wears a beaded mask. Ancestor worship dominates Bamileke religion, and heritage is celebrated with masked dance rituals.*

(Below) *This highly formalized mask is used in ceremonial initiation rites by the Senufo tribe, of Mali and the Ivory Coast. (Metropolitan Museum of Art, New York.).*

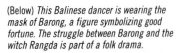

(Below) *This Balinese dancer is wearing the mask of Barong, a figure symbolizing good fortune. The struggle between Barong and the witch Rangda is part of a folk drama.*

The hideously distorted features and garish colors of this demon mask from Sri Lanka (Ceylon) are believed to ward off evil spirits responsible for disease.

This turquoise funerary mask (c.1300–1450), believed to be the Totec fertility god Quetzalcoatl, is an artifact of the Mixtec culture of Mexico. (British Museum, London.)

to identify them with the powers and properties of—animals or supernatural beings. In part the mask functions as a disguise, but this is a secondary characteristic, for in primitive societies the mask is only the focal point of a special costume that covers, and most often hides, the whole body.

Masks generally represent benevolent forces, but in Sri Lanka and among certain North American Indian groups, they portray the demons of evil or disease that SHAMANS are believed empowered to expel. In some Afri-

can societies, supreme power is given to a masked figure who maintains social order in the community and punishes major crimes with death.

The use of masks in the Western theater has a long history. Ancient Greek actors wore tragic and comic masks, the better to convey their emotions to audiences seated far from the stage. Medieval troupes of traveling players routinely wore masks, as did many of the actors in the religious dramas supported by the church. The use of masks continued in the Renaissance court MASQUE and

(Left) *This painted wooden mask was carved by a member of the Kwakiutl tribe,indigenous to British Columbia. Kwakiutl carvings are noted for their powerful rendering of totemic forces. (Denver Art Museum.)* (Right) *This face mask was used by the Bella Coola, a neighboring people of the Kwakiutl. Both masks were believed to possess animistic powers that became transferred to the wearer. (American Museum of Natural History, New York.)*

in its offshoot, the ballet, as well as in the Italian COMMEDIA DELL'ARTE productions of the 16th to 18th centuries. In the 19th century masks were associated principally with MIME AND PANTOMIME. In the 20th century they have been used to great effect by Gordon Craig in England, Vsevolod Meyerhold in Russia, Max Reinhardt in Germany, and Eugene O'Neill in the United States. In the Oriental theater, masks form an integral part of Japanese NO DRAMA; the intricate face painting used in KABUKI and in classical Chinese drama may also be considered a kind of mask.

See also: ACTING; THEATER, HISTORY OF THE.

Maslow, Abraham H. Abraham Harold Maslow, b. Brooklyn, N.Y., Apr. 1, 1908, d. June 8, 1970, championed HUMANISTIC PSYCHOLOGY. Maslow described the "hierarchy of prepotency" in human motivations. Observing that "man is a wanting animal" and that one desire is no sooner satisfied than another takes its place, he noted sense and order in the succession of motives. In the relatively rare individuals in whom all lower needs are satisfied a new motive can be observed, the drive for self-actualization—becoming everything that one is capable of becoming. Maslow distinguished self-actualized people from most people in being unusually healthy psychologically, perceiving everyday life realistically, and accepting it without defensiveness. In *Toward a Psychology of Being* (1962), Maslow examined the "peak experiences" of insight, joy, or intense awareness that self-actualizing people appear to have, or to have had.

masochism Masochism is the derivation of sexual pleasure from being hurt physically or mentally by a sexual partner or oneself. The pain, abuse, or humiliation may result in orgasm or may be used as a preliminary to other kinds of sexual activity. Masochism is the direct opposite of SADISM.

Masochism probably develops from feelings of shame and confusion about sexual relations. Masochists may treat pain as just punishment for their sexual desires; or they may use their ability to endure pain as a means of gaining attention. The term *masochism* was suggested by the Austrian Leopold von Sacher-Masoch, who depicted this aberration in his novels. The term is also used in a more general, nonsexual sense to describe the derivation of pleasure from being punished or dominated.

Mason (family) For most of the 19th century and part of the 20th, much of America's musical life was influenced by the Masons. The founder of this dynasty was **Lowell Mason**, b. Medfield, Mass., Jan. 8, 1792, d. Aug. 11, 1872. Convinced of the inferiority of American church music, he published in 1822 a collection of his own hymns (the first of some 1,200) based on European models and adaptations from Beethoven, Handel, Haydn, Mozart, and others. Its success—it went through 22 editions in the next 36 years—helped to make him superintendent of Boston church music in 1827 and, in 1838, of the music curriculum in Boston public schools, which set the pattern for music education throughout the United States.

Lowell's son **William Mason**, b. Jan. 24, 1829, d. July 14, 1908, a pianist, composer, and teacher, studied in Europe with Franz Liszt and other notable musicians and then concertized in Europe and America. Settling in New York in 1855, he led the city's musical life by appearing in concerts (occasionally with Louis Moreau Gottschalk) and establishing the first regular chamber-music series. His brother **Henry Mason** was cofounder of Mason & Hamlin, a piano manufacturer.

Daniel Gregory Mason, b. Nov. 20, 1873, d. Dec. 4, 1953, son of Henry, spread his views while a prominent faculty member (1910–42) of Columbia University and as an influential critic. Though a skillful composer, he lacked individuality. He espoused musical nationalism but interpreted it narrowly, accepting as true American music only that expressive of Anglo-Saxon New England and the gentility of the old South.

Mason, George   The American political leader George Mason, b. Stafford (now Fairfax) County, Va., Dec. 11, 1725, d. Oct. 7, 1792, was the principal architect of the Virginia Declaration of Rights (1776), a document that served as a partial model for the first section of the Declaration of Independence and for the federal Bill of Rights. Mason served (1758–61) in the Virginia House of Burgesses and later drafted Virginia's Non-Importation Resolutions (1769) against British goods as well as the Fairfax Resolves (1774), a definition of the colonies' constitutional position in relation to Britain. In 1776 he helped frame Virginia's constitution, to which his Declaration of Rights was attached.

From 1776 to 1788, Mason served in the Virginia House of Delegates. In 1787 he attended the CONSTITUTIONAL CONVENTION in Philadelphia, where he played a leading role in framing the new government. Despite this, he became an active and articulate opponent of the U.S. Constitution, largely because he felt that it vested too much ill-defined power in the national government. He refused to sign it and voted against its ratification. Mason declined (1790) an appointment as U.S. senator from Virginia.

Mason, James   James Mason, b. May 15, 1909, d. July 27, 1984, was a British actor whose brooding presence distinguished dozens of films after his initial success in *I Met a Murderer* (1939). He was especially effective as the domineering lover in *The Seventh Veil* (1945); an Irish Republican Army fugitive in *Odd Man Out* (1947); the Nazi general Erwin Rommel in *The Desert Fox* (1951); Brutus in *Julius Caesar* (1953); Judy Garland's dissipated husband in *A Star Is Born* (1954); and the smitten professor in the 1962 film version of Vladimir Nabokov's novel *Lolita*.

Mason, James Murray   James Murray Mason, b. Fairfax County, Va., Nov. 3, 1798, d. Apr. 28, 1871, was a U.S. and Confederate public official best known for his role in the TRENT AFFAIR. A U.S. representative (1837–39) and senator (1847–61), he drafted the Fugitive Slave Act (1850; see FUGITIVE SLAVE LAWS). In 1861, Confederate president Jefferson Davis made him a commissioner to Great Britain to obtain British help for the Confederacy. While aboard the British ship *Trent*, Mason and the Confederate commissioner to France, John SLIDELL, were taken into custody by Charles Wilkes, commander of the U.S. warship *San Jacinto*. Jailed until 1862, Mason went on to England but never won official British recognition.

Mason, John   John Mason, b. 1586, d. December 1635, was a British royalist officer under the Stuart kings and a founder of the colony of New Hampshire. While governor of Newfoundland (1615–21) he explored and mapped the island's coast.

Mason became Sir Ferdinando GORGES's chief associate in his colonization efforts in New England. In 1622 the Council for New England gave Gorges and Mason a huge land grant between the Merrimack and Kennebec rivers extending 97 km (60 mi) inland. In 1629 the grant was divided; Mason received the area, which he called New Hampshire, between the Merrimack and Piscataqua rivers. Following Mason's death, the Massachusetts Bay Colony claimed New Hampshire; Mason's heirs carried on a long campaign against Massachusetts to regain right to the colony. New Hampshire became a royal colony in 1679, but the dispute over the land claims continued. The family's remaining land rights were finally sold (1746) to a group of 12 prominent men of Portsmouth, the so-called Masonian Proprietors, who subsequently made numerous land grants in the colony.

Mason-Dixon line   The Mason-Dixon line is popularly considered the dividing line between the U.S. northern and southern states. It actually marks the border between Pennsylvania to the north and Maryland and West Virginia to the south. The eastern portion of the line was surveyed between 1763 and 1767 by the English astronomers Charles Mason and Jeremiah Dixon to settle a boundary dispute between Pennsylvania and Maryland. The surveying of the western extension was completed in 1784. During the debates over the MISSOURI COMPROMISE in 1820 and 1821, the line was used to designate the boundary between slave and free states. As a result, both during and after the Civil War it was considered the demarcation line between North and South. Most of the original stone markers can still be seen.

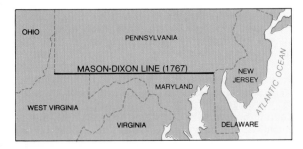

Masonic orders   see FREEMASONRY

Masorah   [muh-sohr'-uh]   Masorah, a Hebrew word meaning "transmission," refers to the work of Hebrew scholars throughout the centuries aimed at the establishment of a uniform and correct text of the Hebrew Bible, which traditionally lacked vowels and punctuation marks. The Masoretes compared manuscript copies then in existence, provided critical annotations and corrections, and pointed out obscurities and variants and discrepancies in spelling. Irregular or unusual spellings were recorded on special lists. All this was marked on the margins of scriptural copies or in separate pamphlets; the received text was left untouched. The marginal compilation was known as the small or Marginal Masorah; a compilation with notes at the top and bottom of the text was called the Great or Final Masorah. To safeguard correct pronunciation, systems of vowels, stops, and accents were devised.

Although oral transmission of grammatical and orthographic practice is very old, the written Masorah originated, at the latest, in the 7th century AD.

masque   *Masque,* a French word meaning "face-mask," refers to a form of indoor courtly entertainment popular during the Renaissance that was characterized by song, spectacular display, and dance. The term first appeared in the 16th century at the peak of the masque's popularity in Italy. The masque was designed for a specific occasion, usually some event associated with the life of the court, the Christmas season being the chief time for such revels. It derived its form in part from the medieval mumming play (a procession of masked persons) and the practice of disguising (a dramatized debate among masked participants). The costumed dancers in a masque danced first among themselves and then chose partners from among the spectators, blurring the distinction between actors and audience. Although the masque proper might last no longer than an hour, the dancing often continued for hours thereafter. In its use of spectacle, allegory, symbolism, and mythology the English masque shared some features with the civic pageant, but primarily it was an indoor show sponsored by the court.

The greatest period of the English court masque was from the accession (1603) of James I to the cessation of all dramatic activity by Act of Parliament in 1642. Perhaps the most important masque historically was *The Masque of Blackness* (1605), for it marked the beginning of the long and fruitful collaboration between the poet Ben Jonson and the architect and stage designer Inigo Jones, who created increasingly sophisticated and spectacular scenery, derived from Italian models. In the *Masque of Queens* (1609), Jonson introduced the "antimasque," a farcical, grotesque episode that mocked the orderliness or the subject of the main masque, and this element was included in most subsequent masques.

In the 17th century the typical masque contained a prologue, an antimasque, a debate, a resolution of the dramatic action, a presentation of the masquers, an invitation to dance, and a final song. One of the most expensive productions was James Shirley's *Triumph of Peace* (1634), rumored to have cost $20,000. The same year also saw the production of John MILTON's *Comus.* The last masque of the period was *Salmacida Spolia* (1640), designed by Jones and Sir William Davenant. Masques as dramatic entertainment and as court revel died out in the mid-17th century, later monarchs being apparently unwilling to expend money on them. The influence of the masque, however, can be seen in a number of plays of the early 17th century, Shakespeare's The TEMPEST among them; its most enduring legacies were the songs, dances, stage machinery, and set designs that were invented for the form.

Mass   The central religious service of the Roman Catholic church, Mass is the celebration of the sacrament of the EUCHARIST, the rite instituted by Jesus Christ at the LAST SUPPER. Some Lutherans and Anglicans also refer to the Eucharist as Mass. Based on the medieval Latin liturgy of Rome, the Mass takes its name from the Latin *missa* (dismissed), referring to the practice of dismissing the catechumens before the offertory. In the Eastern churches, the Mass is called the Holy Liturgy or the Offering. Catholics believe that consecration of the eucharistic elements of bread and wine transforms their substances into those of Jesus' body and blood; this doctrine is called transubstantiation. Catholics are required to attend Sunday Mass as a minimum of public worship.

The two chief parts of the Mass are the LITURGY of the Word and the Liturgy of the Eucharist. The first consists primarily of two or three Scripture readings, a homily following the Gospel reading, and general intercessions or prayers of the faithful. The main actions of the second part are the preparation of the altar and gifts, eucharistic prayer, breaking of bread, and communion. The LORD'S PRAYER is recited at the end of the eucharistic prayer and is followed by the exchange of the sign of peace. Introductory rites, including an entrance song, penitential rite, and opening prayer, precede the Word liturgy, and a concluding rite follows communion.

The structure of the Mass has remained fairly constant since the 2d century, although some local variations existed until modern times. In the Roman rite Mass was celebrated in Latin from an early period until the reforms of the Second VATICAN COUNCIL.

mass   (musical setting)   From about the 3d to the 11th century AD the mass in the Western (Roman) church evolved as a Latin ritual consisting of chants by the choir and recitation by the priest. The choir chants, which are the items of musical importance, fall into two categories: proper, or texts that vary from day to day according to festival and season; and ordinary, texts normally sung at every mass. The proper chants, derived in large part from the Eastern churches and the Jewish synagogue, consist primarily of psalms with interpolated antiphon and responsory verses (Introit, Gradual, Alleluia or Tract, Offertory, Communion). Codified mainly during the reign of Pope Gregory I (590–604), these chants, as well as others of later date, have come to be called "Gregorian." The ordinary evolved more slowly, achieving its final form in the 11th century (Kyrie, Gloria, Credo, Sanctus, Agnus Dei). Around 1300 these five chants began to be treated as a cycle, and the term *missa* applied to them as a group as well as to the entire liturgy.

Polyphonic settings are found from the 11th century on. At first the proper received more attention. After 1300, complete polyphonic ordinaries appear; the first by a single composer is the four-voiced *Mass of Our Lady* by Guillaume de MACHAUT, composed in the mid-1300s.

In the 15th and 16th centuries mass-ordinary cycles became the rule, their movements usually related by some musical theme, such as a common head motive or cantus firmus. Gregorian cantus firmi were preferred, but secular melodies were also used, notably the tune "L'homme armé" (The Armed Man). After 1500, "parody masses" were based on polyphonic motets, chansons, or madrigals rather than on single melodies.

Cycles of propers were also composed in the 15th and 16th centuries. A special type, combining elements of the proper and ordinary, is the REQUIEM (mass for the dead).

In the 16th century the Council of Trent (1545–63) attempted to diminish secular tendencies in Roman Catholic church music. The legend that a performance of PALESTRINA's *Missa Papae Marcelli* persuaded the Council not to banish polyphonic music from the church may have some basis in fact.

After 1600 the mass ceded to opera its position as the major large form of art music. Most baroque composers cultivated the concerted mass, incorporating obbligato instruments and orchestra, solo arias and ensembles, and polyphonic choruses, culminating in Johann Sebastian Bach's Mass in B Minor (1736).

Throughout the classical and romantic eras masses continued to be written in a contemporary style. A few significant masses have been written in the 20th century by Igor Stravinsky, Paul Hindemith, Francis Poulenc, Leoš Janáček, and Zoltán Kodály. The liturgical reforms of the Second Vatican Council (1964) have led to the composition of vernacular masses in a simple, often popular style. In a separate category are modern works that use the mass in a quasi-dramatic context; a noteworthy example is Benjamin Britten's *War Requiem* (1961).

Some Protestant churches employ the mass, or a variant of it. The Lutheran church uses a *Missa brevis* consisting of Kyrie and Gloria; the original version of Bach's Mass in B Minor, as well as his other masses, are of this type. The Anglican liturgy includes a Communion service in English.

—

mass (physics)   Every physical body has an inherent property called its mass. Mass may most simply be considered as the amount of substance in a body. Mass manifests itself in two ways that can be measured. One measurable quantity is the INERTIA of a body, inertia being the body's resistance to ACCELERATION. The other measurable quantity is the force of gravity that acts on a body when it is in a gravitational field (see GRAVITATION). Because humans live within the Earth's gravitational field, the concepts of mass and weight are sometimes confused. Weight is simply a measure of the force of gravitation acting on a body, and varies depending on the strength of that force. Thus a person weighs more on the Earth than on the much less massive Moon. The mass of that person, however, remains the same.

Inertial Mass. The greater the mass of a body is, the greater is its resistance to acceleration. To state it another way, when the same amount of force is applied to two different bodies, the force induces a smaller acceleration in the body with the larger mass. This relationship is expressed in Isaac Newton's second law of motion as

$f = ma$ (see LAWS OF MOTION). Here, f is the resultant force, m is the mass of the body, and a is the corresponding acceleration.

Gravitational Mass. The force of gravity that acts on a body is proportional to the mass of the body. This relationship is expressed by the formula $f_g = mg$, in which g represents the local intensity of a given gravity field. This Newtonian law means that the masses of two objects on the Earth's surface can be compared by using a lever balance to compare the force of gravity acting on the two objects. It also means that the acceleration imposed by gravity on an object is independent of the mass of the falling object, if the gravitational attraction is the only significant force that is acting on the object.

Equivalence of Mass and Energy. In classical mechanics the two above-mentioned manifestations of mass are usually considered in terms of Newton's separate laws of motion and of gravitation. In modern physics, however, inertial and gravitational mass are the same. That is, Albert Einstein's theory of gravitation (see RELATIVITY) replaces these concepts of mass with the concept of mass as affecting the curvature of the space-time continuum.

In fact, when the speed of an object becomes significant compared to the speed of light, Newtonian laws no longer apply. Instead, Einstein's theory predicts that mass increases as such speeds are approached. Another consequence of relativity is that mass and energy are equivalent, and one can be converted into the other. Einstein's famous formula, $E = mc^2$, shows the relationship in which E is the energy equivalent of mass m multiplied by the square of c (see ENERGY).

Measurement of Mass. The mass of an object can be measured in terms of acceleration effects, but this is difficult in practice. The common practice is to express mass in terms of its weight in the local gravitational field, that of the Earth. In the international system of units (see UNITS, PHYSICAL), the kilogram (kg) is the basic unit of mass. The standard kilogram—the only remaining physical standard among the basic units—is a platinum-iridium cylinder kept at the International Bureau of Weights and Measures in Sèvres, France. Many English-speaking countries continue to use the pound, as well, one pound being about 0.4536 kg. The slug, a unit used by engineers, is defined as the mass of a body that requires a force of one pound to provide an acceleration of 1 ft/sec². At sea level, a body's mass in slugs is about equal to its weight, in pounds, divided by 32.

See also: WEIGHTS AND MEASURES.

mass, center of   see CENTER OF GRAVITY

mass, law of conservation of   see CONSERVATION, LAWS OF

—

mass defect   The mass defect is the difference between the actual measured mass of an ATOM and its mass number, the total number of the protons and neutrons in its nucleus. About 99.98% of the mass of an atom is attributable to its nucleus. The remainder is attributable to its atomic electrons. The exactly measured mass of a given isotope is called its atomic mass, M. The whole number close to the mass is the isotope's mass number, A. In 1927, Francis Aston called the small but definite discrepancy between M and A the mass defect.

The explanation of the mass defect is found in Albert Einstein's equivalency of mass and energy ($E = mc^2$) and the concept of BINDING ENERGY. Any system of particles that is bound by mutually attractive forces has less total energy and therefore less mass than that of the same number of free particles. This decrease in mass is of appreciable significance only in the case of nuclei. Because of nuclear binding, the mass of any nucleus (except for the lightest isotopes) is about 1% less than the sum of the free masses of the neutrons and protons of which it is composed. The atomic mass unit as defined from carbon-12 is about 1% less than the mass of the neutron or the proton. Thus the mass of any isotope is close to a whole number in atomic mass units. Some modern authorities have redefined the mass defect as the difference between the mass of the atom and the sum of the masses of its free particles, in order to emphasize that its physical significance is the same as that of binding energy.

On June 14, 1985, a Lebanese hijacker held a gun to the head of TWA pilot John Testrake. For the millions who watched TV broadcasts from Beirut airport, this image became the emblem of all such events.

mass-luminosity relation   The mass-luminosity relation is a correlation between the mass and the luminosity of a STAR. It allows the luminosity of a star to be determined if the mass is known independently. Conversely, it allows the mass to be determined if the distance and the apparent magnitude of a star are known well enough to calculate its luminosity. For main-sequence stars like the Sun, it is found that mass is closely related to luminosity in the sense that the more massive the star, the more luminous it is. For stars of about one solar mass, luminosity rises steeply with mass (L ~ M^3). It rises even more steeply with mass for heavier stars (L ~ M^4). The correlation means that the more massive a star, the more rapidly it will consume its nuclear fuel (see STELLAR EVOLUTION).

The mass-luminosity correlation is good only for main-sequence stars, that is, for those which shine by converting hydrogen into helium in their cores, as does the Sun. It fails for giant stars that have evolved away from the main sequence and that generate energy in shells surrounding an inert helium core. It fails most dramatically for white dwarf stars that have no nuclear energy sources. The Sun deviates only slightly from the mass-luminosity correlation defined by nearby stars.

mass media   A medium, in the language of the field of COMMUNICATIONS, is a means of sending messages, or communicating. Mass media are the instruments by which messages are sent to large numbers of people. Whether a medium is mass or not depends on how it is used. Radio is a mass medium when used for broadcasting but not when used for communication among individuals, as in citizen's band and ham radio. The four major categories of mass media are print media (newspapers,

magazines, books), recordings (records and audio tapes, videocassettes and videodiscs), motion pictures, and radio and television broadcasts.

All forms of mass media share several characteristics. They usually employ professional communicators (the editors in a newspaper or publishing house, the programmers at a television station) who make choices about what their audiences will see, hear, or read. They use technologies that are costly and complex, requiring specialized engineers and technicians to operate them; they are therefore not freely available for use by private individuals. Communications from the mass media are mass-produced and are disseminated rapidly: multiple copies of the same newspaper are printed and distributed within hours and are bought and read by thousands. Radio and television can transmit news as soon as it happens. (Thirty-five minutes after the assassination of U.S. president John F. Kennedy in 1963 most Americans had received the news; it took more than eight months for the entire American public to learn of President Lincoln's assassination in 1865.) Most mass media are relatively inexpensive to buy or receive.

Mass-media communications are primarily one-way; audience members are rarely able to use the media for feedback. Moreover, the communicators are physically separated from their audience, and the individuals and groups that make up the audience are separated from one another.

History. The invention (1830) of the steam-powered printing press marks the beginning of the era of the mass media, making it possible for the first U.S. mass-circulation newspapers to be published in 1833. The first popular paperback books were produced in the 1850s; mass-circulation magazines began to appear in the 1860s.

During the 19th century two revolutionary new communication technologies were introduced. Photography was invented in the 1820s, and a method for reproducing photographs in the print media was perfected in 1880. Moreover, photography led to the development of a new mass medium, the motion picture, in the 1880s. The telegraph, introduced in 1844, was the first TELECOMMU-NICATIONS technology, followed by the telephone in 1876, the wireless telegraph in 1897, radio in 1906, and television in the 1920s.

During the 1950s television emerged as the dominant mass medium in the United States. Television's growth had adverse effects on the other mass media. Radio was forced to produce more specialized programming for smaller, single-interest audiences. Newspaper circulation per capita had already begun to decline in the 1930s as radio became a major news medium, and after the success of television the number of daily U.S. newspapers began to drop precipitously. Similarly, motion-picture attendance declined, and many general-interest magazines disappeared after television became the principal mass medium. Only the recording industry thrived, as radio stations turned to recorded music for much of their content.

The Mass Media Today. New technologies have continued to transform the mass media. Since the 1960s COM-MUNICATIONS SATELLITES have made instantaneous global communication a reality. During the 1970s CABLE TV became a popular alternative to broadcast television, the first home videocassette recorders and prerecorded tapes appeared, and videogames and personal computers were introduced. COMPACT DISCS, laser discs, TELETEXT, and VIDEOTEX also made their debut during the 1980s. The communications revolution shows no signs of slowing as new technologies, such as fiber optics and high-definition television, continue to appear.

Where the printed word once dominated mass communications, the major contemporary form is the visual image as it appears in television, movies, and photography. (Some believe that the primacy of the visual has been responsible for declining literacy rates.) Many older, mechanical technologies have been replaced by electronic ones: motion pictures use computer graphics, digital recording techniques are making old-style records obsolete, the print media now rely on word processing and electronic typesetting, and electronic versions of some print media are available through computer databanks and CD-ROM (see COMPUTER).

The mass media today have also been characterized by a movement toward concentrated ownership. Increasingly, more media of all types are owned by fewer and fewer persons or corporate entities. The largest media firms are enormous conglomerates with multinational, multimedia holdings that are used in combination to increase sales.

Advertising. Most U.S. newspaper and magazine publishers and radio and television stations make their profits from the sale of space or time to advertisers. In other words, the "products" that these media create and sell are audiences. The cost of buying space or time is added to the price of an advertiser's goods or services (although,

theoretically, increased sales as a result of advertising should result in lowered prices). A medium's dependence on advertising may force it to concentrate on attracting larger audiences rather than providing better content. Advertising may also influence media content: a magazine that runs cigarette ads may not be enthusiastic about printing an article on the dangers of smoking. Moreover, the distinction between advertising and other types of content is not always clear.

Information and Entertainment. The mass media are the most effective means of disseminating information to large numbers of people in a short period of time. Information in U.S. mass media often takes the form of entertainment, which draws the largest audiences and is therefore the most profitable. Psychologists suggest, however, that the media may provide role models whose behaviors are imitated by members of the audience. Violence in the media has been of particular concern, but other behaviors or attitudes may also be affected: sexual behavior, ideas about ethnic minorities, notions of masculinity and femininity, for example.

News and Politics. Because the mass media, especially television, are the only source of news for most, political or social biases in the media may have profound effects. Public dependence on the media may give them the power to set political agenda, to determine which issues should be the subject of public debate. Audiences' inability to verify news reports may make them vulnerable to propaganda.

Much of the news is devoted to "media events," events that might not occur without the presence of the media. Youthful demonstrators in the late 1960s chanted "The whole world is watching!" in front of the ever-present television cameras—in effect acknowledging a collaboration that provided both publicity and entertaining news.

There seems little doubt that television, in concert with the other mass media, has changed the focus of political campaigns from issues to images: the appearance and personality of the candidate. The media also enable candidates to communicate directly with the entire body of voters, thereby undermining political parties, and politicians with the ability to project a positive "image" through the television screen have an immense advantage, as Ronald Reagan demonstrated in 1980 and 1984. The effects of mass-mediated campaigns on audiences are often indirect, however. According to sociologist Paul Lazarsfeld's two-step flow theory, mass-mediated messages may be accepted, rejected, or modified by "opinion leaders"—knowledgeable audience members whom others turn to for advice and information.

Mass Culture, Global Culture. The liberalization of Communist societies of Eastern Europe and the cry for democracy in China—both trends of the late 1980s—attest to the power of the media to penetrate ideological walls, yet U.S. popular culture exerts a far greater attraction worldwide than Western intellectual ideas. U.S. movies, television, music, and magazines often stifle the development of native versions in many foreign countries. Those concerned with maintaining their own traditions have accused the mass media of "cultural imperialism." Imperialist or not, the mass media may eventually create a homogenized global culture decorated with the symbols of Western popular arts.

mass number   The mass number of an atomic nucleus, denoted by the symbol *A,* is the number of nucleons (protons and neutrons) present in the nucleus. Mass numbers may be suffixed to the names of elements to distinguish isotopes. For example, uranium-235 and uranium-238 are the most abundant isotopic components of natural uranium.

    See also: ATOM; ATOMIC NUMBER; ATOMIC WEIGHT; ISOTOPE.

mass production   see MANUFACTURING, HISTORY OF

mass spectrometry   Mass spectrometry is a widely used instrumental method of analyzing organic and inorganic molecules. It involves producing ions and separating them according to their mass-to-charge (*m/e*) ratios. Mass spectrometry is most often used in organic chemical applications such as compound identification, structure elucidation, mixture analysis, quantitative elemental analysis, and stable isotope determination. It may also be used in radioisotope half-life determination and free radical studies.

    Ionization is usually achieved by high-energy electron bombardment. The positively charged ions are accelerated from the ion source by a positive potential of a few thousand volts, focused through an ion-source slit, and separated by one of several methods, usually deflection by a magnetic field. Lighter ions are curved more by a given magnetic field strength than are heavier ones.

    A scan of varying magnetic field strength will eventually focus ions of every mass onto the collector, where the resulting signal is amplified and recorded. The "mass spectrum" produced is a plot of the relative abundance of the ions of each *m/e* ratio.

    Mass spectrometry has become an extremely sophisticated and complex technique. Computers and data-handling systems have been interfaced with mass spectrometers to provide rapid recording and analysis of data.

mass transit   see TRANSPORTATION

Massachuset   The Massachuset, an Algonquian-speaking North American Indian people, were a confederacy of related tribal groups that included the Massachuset proper, the Nauset, the Nipmuc, and the Wampanoag. These tribes occupied permanent towns in the valleys of the Charles and Neponset rivers, including the future site of Boston and of its suburbs.

    Although the Massachuset disappeared as a people before much could be recorded of their culture, they are known to have been horticulturalists, also heavily dependent on marine life for their subsistence, and to have numbered about 3,000 in early colonial times.

Wars with neighboring confederacies and diseases introduced by Europeans reduced the Massachuset peoples to only a small fraction of their former strength and power by 1618. By the 1640s the Massachuset ceased to exist as a separate, independent tribal group. In that decade the survivors were gathered into mission villages where they became known as "praying Indians," and they were eventually assimilated into the mainstream of colonial life.

Massachusetts   Massachusetts is a small state in the northeastern United States that has made contributions to the nation far greater than its size might suggest. Sixth smallest in area, it lies at the center of New England, with Vermont, New Hampshire, and Maine to the north and Rhode Island and Connecticut to the south. New York is to the west, and the Atlantic Ocean is to the east.

    The state, known legally as a commonwealth, was first permanently settled at PLYMOUTH in 1620. One of the 13 original states, it was the 6th to ratify the Constitution. BOSTON, the capital of Massachusetts, is the de facto capital of New England.

    The name *Massachusetts* is thought to be of Algonquian origin and means "near the great hill." The state has made many contributions to the nation in its cultural growth, its political activities, and its concern for social welfare.

Land and Resources

Massachusetts displays a wide variety of topography within its small area. The western border lies along the crest of the Taconic Mountains. Immediately to the east are the BERKSHIRE HILLS and the deep, narrow, north-south trending Berkshire Valley, eroded from soft limestones. Farther to the east is a high, rolling plateau of ancient crystalline rocks, deeply carved by Connecticut River tributaries.

    The plateau gives way abruptly to the nearly flat Connecticut River valley. Its soils are the state's most fertile. Between the valley and the Atlantic Ocean is a hilly region of forests, lakes, and a few low mountains. Elevations decrease from west to east. Near the shoreline the topography displays little relief.

    Southeastern Massachusetts is a low, sandy plain, interrupted by occasional glacial debris. CAPE COD is an extension of glacial materials that reaches far into the open ocean. It is composed entirely of sand and gravel. The coast of Massachusetts varies from an occasional rocky headland, such as Cape Ann, to long sandy beaches. MARTHA'S VINEYARD, NANTUCKET ISLAND, and the Elizabeth Islands lie offshore to the south.

    Massachusetts is underlain with Paleozoic or pre-Paleozoic rocks. Igneous and metamorphic rocks, such as granites, gneisses, and schists, are common. Only the major river valleys contain sedimentary rocks on a large scale.

    Soils. Massachusetts soils are derived in large part from glacial detritus. Soils are composed of glacial till and are thin, relatively barren of mineral nutrients, and choked with boulders. Pockets of loams were pressed into agricultural use in the 17th and 18th centuries, and the

AT A GLANCE

MASSACHUSETTS

Land: Area: 27,337 km² (10,555 mi²); rank: 44th.
Capital and largest city: Boston (1990 pop., 574,283).
Counties: 14. Elevations: highest—1,063 m (3,487 ft),
at Mount Greylock; lowest—sea level, at the Atlantic
coast.

People: Population (1990): 6,029,051; rank: 13th;
density: 296.4 persons per km² (767.6 per mi²). Distribution (1990): 84.3% urban, 15.7% rural. Average annual change (1980–90): +0.51%.

Government (1993): Governor: William F. Weld, Republican. U.S. Congress: Senate—2 Democrats; House—
8 Democrats, 2 Republicans. Electoral college votes: 12.
State legislature: 40 senators, 160 representatives.

Economy: State personal income (1989): $131.1
billion; rank: 10th. Median family income (1989):
$44,367; rank: 5th. Agriculture: income (1989)—$429
million. Fishing: value (1989)—$273 million.
Lumber production (1991): 45 million board feet. Mining (nonfuel): value (1988)—$192 million. Manufactur-
ing: value added (1987)—$35.8 billion. Services: value
(1987)—$41.4 billion.

Miscellany: Statehood: Feb. 6, 1788; the 6th state.
Nickname: Bay State; tree: American elm; motto: *Ense
petit placidam sub libertate quietem* ("By the sword we
seek peace, but peace only under liberty"); song: "All
Hail to Massachusetts."

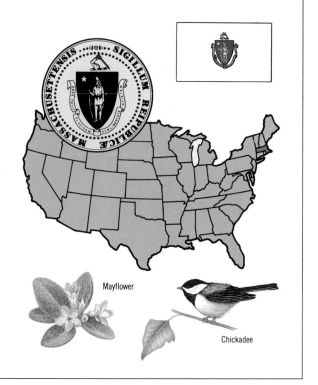

Mayflower

Chickadee

floodplains of the major river valleys—especially the Connecticut—are still extensively cultivated. The soils are often alluvial, rich in nutrients and relatively level. In areas
underlain by extensive glacial sand deposits, soils tend to
be dry and infertile.

Climate. Massachusetts has four distinct seasons. A
major climatic element is the proximity of the state to the
sea and the Gulf Stream. Much of eastern Massachusetts
has milder temperatures and receives less snowfall than
the central and western parts of the state. Massachusetts
has experienced many hurricanes.

Precipitation varies little within the state, averaging
1,067 mm (42 in) annually. Snow depths vary considerably, with the western mountains receiving 1.5 to 1.8 m
(5 to 6 ft) during the winter.

Because of its coastal location, Massachusetts has a
narrow temperature range. July mean temperatures range
from 22° C (71° F) in the west to 19° C (67° F) on Cape
Cod. In the winter the contrast is reversed, with the
coastal areas significantly warmer (−1° C/31° F) than the
interior (−4° C/24° F).

Drainage. The CONNECTICUT RIVER rises in Canada and
flows south across the state to Connecticut, providing extensive farmland as well as waterpower sites. The Merrimack rises in New Hampshire, its lower course entering

Massachusetts near LOWELL and passing eastward to the
sea at Newburyport.

Smaller streams include the HOUSATONIC RIVER, which
drains the southern portion of the Berkshire Valley, and the
Blackstone, Charles, Deerfield, and Taunton rivers. Rapids
and waterfalls are common along virtually all waterways.

Extensive tidal marshes lie between the beaches and
the mainland. These are important breeding grounds and
sources of food for marine life and waterfowl.

The largest body of water in Massachusetts is Quabbin
Reservoir. This lake provides fresh water to the residents
of greater Boston, 105 km (65 mi) to the east.

Vegetation and Animal Life. The vegetation in Massachusetts is diversified, containing both the deciduous
forests of oak, hickory, and maple common to the south
in Connecticut, as well as the coniferous forests of pine,
spruce, hemlock, and balsam fir found to the north. The
forests often display an understory of rhododendron, mountain laurel, witch hazel, shadbush, and dogwood.

Most indigenous wildlife has long since been driven
away by human settlement or diminished by three centuries of hunting. Small mammals such as foxes, rabbits,
raccoons, skunks, and squirrels are abundant, bears,
bobcats, and deer, somewhat less so. Birds—both terrestrial and waterfowl—are common.

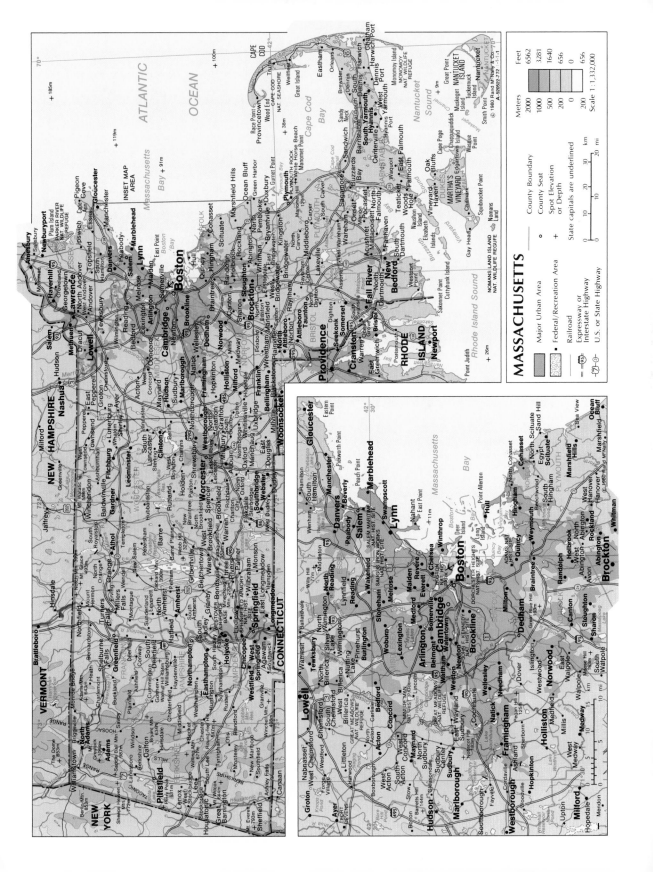

MASSACHUSETTS

		Feet
		6562
		3281
		1640
		656
		0
		656

Meters		
2000		
1000		
500		
200		
0		
200		

© 1980 Rand McNally & Co.
A-500622-772 -1-1-1

Scale 1 : 1,332,000

County Boundary
County Seat ○
Spot Elevation + or Depth
State capitals are underlined

Major Urban Area
Federal/Recreation Area
Railroad
Expressway or Interstate Highway
U.S. or State Highway

0 10 20 30 km
0   10   20 mi

Resources. Massachusetts has few endemic resources. In colonial days, small quantities of iron, silver, copper, and other metals were extracted and smelted. Charcoal was produced from the abundant hardwood forests, and waterpower sites for mills and forges were abundant. Granite, lime, sandstone, and sand and gravel are now the state's dominant mineral resources.

People

At the end of the American Revolution, Massachusetts was the 4th largest state in population. In 1990 it ranked 13th. The population is concentrated today in the eastern part of the state, particularly metropolitan Boston. The population grew by only 5.1% from 1980 to 1990, as compared with a national increase of 10.2% in that same period. WORCESTER, SPRINGFIELD, and Lowell have populations of more than 100,000, and the Boston metropolitan area has almost 2.9 million residents.

Population Composition. In its first 200 years, the population of Massachusetts was virtually pure English in composition. In the early 19th century large numbers of Irish came to the state, primarily to Boston. Later, southern Europeans, particularly Italians, arrived in Boston along with large numbers of Polish and Russian Jews, Portuguese, and French- and some English-speaking Canadians.

After World War II, Boston attracted increasing numbers of African Americans, most of whom live in the greater Boston area. In recent years, Massachusetts has experienced a steady influx of Puerto Ricans, Cubans, and other Caribbean nationals. The Chinese population is the most rapidly expanding component of its population.

Roman Catholics form the largest religious group. Membership in the United Church of Christ and the Episcopal church is also significant.

Education. Massachusetts has been a pioneer in education. The nation's first public secondary school, Boston Latin School, was founded in 1635 and the first college, Harvard, in the following year. The first vocational school was opened in 1821 and the first high school for girls in 1826. As early as 1642 laws were enacted to establish schools in cities and towns and to require compulsory education.

Since 1950 the state has begun a major program to expand and upgrade the state university and state colleges and to establish a statewide system of community colleges. The largest state institution is the University of Massachusetts (1863), with its main campus at Amherst. Among the leading private institutions of higher education are AMHERST COLLEGE, BOSTON UNIVERSITY, HARVARD UNIVERSITY, the MASSACHUSETTS INSTITUTE OF TECHNOLOGY, SMITH COLLEGE, WELLESLEY COLLEGE, and WILLIAMS COLLEGE.

Culture. Music has long been important in Massachusetts. The Handel and Haydn Society of Boston, founded in 1815, continues to perform. The BOSTON SYMPHONY ORCHESTRA is one of the finest in the country, and its associated BOSTON POPS ORCHESTRA draws large crowds to summer concerts. The Berkshire Music Festival at Tanglewood offers both instruction in music and performances for the public. The NEW ENGLAND CONSERVATORY OF MUSIC is located in Boston.

The colonial society of Massachusetts supported such painters as Gilbert STUART and John Singleton COPLEY and artisans like Paul REVERE. Many fine examples of their work are contained in the Boston Museum of Fine Arts. Other museums include the Gardner Museum and Peabody Museum of Archaeology and Ethnology in the Boston area, the Clark Art Institute in Williamstown, and the Worcester Art Museum.

Historical Sites. The state's 350 years of continuous settlement have left Massachusetts with many historical houses, forts, factories, and battlegrounds. Entire villages have been re-created with scrupulous care.

Boston's historic sites are linked by a Freedom Trail. Along the trail are the Old North Church, Paul Revere's house, FANEUIL HALL, and the Old State House. The early Plymouth settlement is memorialized by several monuments and a re-creation of the original primitive settlement.

The battle areas associated with Lexington and Concord have been designated a National Historic Park. Many cities and towns have established historic districts. Homes of famous authors open to the public include those of Herman Melville, Louisa May Alcott, Ralph Waldo Emerson, and John Greenleaf Whittier. The site of the Walden Pond cabin where Henry David Thoreau lived has recently been found and excavated.

Recreation and Sports. In the summer many residents and tourists enjoy the state's sandy beaches, particularly in the Cape Cod National Seashore. In the interior many lakes and ponds provide water recreation. Extensive hik-

Boston's Faneuil Hall (center foreground) *was established in 1742 as a meeting hall and public market. Boston began a series of urban renewal projects during the 1960s, emphasizing modern architecture harmonious with the traditional buildings.*

ing trails, some a part of the APPALACHIAN TRAIL, are open to all. Winter activities include skiing, skating, and tobogganing. Autumn travelers can view spectacular foliage from marked highway trails. The state supports many professional sports organizations, including the New England Patriots (football) and the Boston Bruins (hockey), Celtics (basketball), and Red Sox (baseball).

Communications. Massachusetts is well served by all forms of modern communications. Nearly every city has its own daily newspaper, and weekly papers serve small towns and rural areas. The internationally distributed *Christian Science Monitor* is headquartered in Boston. The *Boston Globe* is the state's most widely read newspaper. The Boston broadcasting station WGBH is a major producer of programming for the Public Broadcasting Service.

Economic Activity

An early start was given to manufacturing in Massachusetts by its numerous gristmills and sawmills and by its artisans and cottage industries. By the time of the American Revolution nearly every town produced leather and textile goods, metalware, and furniture.

The Industrial Revolution came early to Massachusetts, and the first half of the 19th century saw the flowering of nearly all of its present manufacturing cities. Textile weaving was the most important industry, followed by shoe manufacturing.

During the 20th century most of these low-value consumer-goods industries have moved elsewhere and have been replaced by industries of higher value such as electronics. Several major computer manufacturers are located in the state.

Energy. Petroleum provides the bulk of the state's power. Nuclear-power plants are located in Plymouth and Rowe.

Agriculture, Forestry, and Fishing. Massachusetts is not a major agricultural state. Dairying is a primary source of farm income along with poultry raising. Many farms now grow specialty crops such as cranberries, apples, tobacco, and vegetables.

Forest-related industries are negligible. Small quantities of hardwoods are cut for furniture and firewood, and there is some production of white-pine lumber.

Fishing has long been an important economic activity in Massachusetts; GLOUCESTER, NEW BEDFORD, and Boston are its major ports. In recent years Massachusetts has ranked highest among the New England states in the value of its commercial catch. Cod and lobster are among the major species caught.

Tourism. Tourism has grown in economic importance in Massachusetts since World War II. The state offers both a rich history and recreational opportunities. Many cities and towns have historic sites and exhibits for tourists.

Transportation and Trade. Transportation in Massachusetts relies heavily on the automobile and truck. The state has an excellent highway network. Many modern airports serve the state, and Boston ranks high in both the nation and the world in annual air passenger traffic. It is also an important shipping center. The state's once-fine railroad network has been radically reduced, but both Amtrak and Conrail have service within the state.

Located on the northernmost tip of Cape Cod, historic Provincetown is a flourishing artists' colony and resort town. Its harbor was the site of the Pilgrims' arrival in 1620 and of the signing of the Mayflower Compact.

Government and Politics

The constitution of Massachusetts was adopted in 1780. As amended, it provides for a governor and lieutenant governor who serve 4-year terms. The legislature is known as the General Court and consists of the 40-member Senate and the 160-member House of Representatives. Legislators are elected to 2-year terms.

The highest court in Massachusetts is the Supreme Judicial Court. A hierarchy of trial courts operates within the county structure. The 14 county administrative bodies in Massachusetts have relatively limited powers. Cities are usually governed by a mayor and a board of aldermen or city councillors. Towns, run by selectmen, hold many of the powers vested in counties elsewhere.

One unusual feature of Massachusetts government is the Metropolitan District Commission. This body maintains water supplies, sewerage disposal, recreation facilities, and certain highways in Boston and its environs.

A stronghold of the Democratic party, the state has 11 legislators in the U.S. House of Representatives, the great majority of whom are Democrats. The state legislature is also largely composed of members of that party. Since 1900, however, Republicans—including Calvin Coolidge—have served as governor more often than Democrats.

History

The pre-European population of Massachusetts was a small number of relatively independent native-American tribes. In the late 16th century, European ships explored the New England coast, led by Giovanni da VERRAZANO in 1524 and Bartholomew Gosnold in 1602.

The Colonial Period. Interest in the commercial exploitation of New England grew in Europe, especially in England. The first permanent settlers in Massachusetts, however, were not fortune hunters but the religious group known as the PILGRIMS. In December 1620 they landed at Plymouth, where they established a colony according to terms drawn up in the Mayflower Compact before debarking (see MAYFLOWER; PLYMOUTH COLONY).

The Pilgrims were soon followed by other English settlers. The Dorchester Company founded a colony at Gloucester (1623) on Cape Ann and, after Gloucester's failure, at Naumkeag (SALEM, 1626). In 1628 a party of Puritans led by John ENDECOTT settled at Salem under the auspices of the New England Company. The following year the MASSACHUSETTS BAY COMPANY was chartered as a successor to the New England Company; its first large group of Puritan settlers arrived in 1630 under the leadership of John Winthrop (see WINTHROP family).

PURITANISM was the overriding religiopolitical force in the Bay Colony. Citizenship (called freemanship) was restricted (until 1664) to church members. Religious dissenters, most notably Anne HUTCHINSON and Roger WILLIAMS, were banished from the colony. Within the framework of religious restriction, however, the colony developed representative institutions early on.

Throughout this period new immigrants arrived. Farming, lumbering, and fishing were the principal occupations. Movement into the interior brought conflict with the Indians, as in the Pequot War (1637). In 1643 the Bay Colony formed the New England Confederation with Plymouth, Connecticut, and New Haven colonies to coordinate defense. The confederation acted most effectively during KING PHILIP'S WAR (1675–76).

Continual disagreements arose between the colonists and the English government. In 1684 the colony's charter was revoked, and in 1686 the Massachusetts Bay and Plymouth colonies were included in the Dominion of New England under Sir Edmund ANDROS. News of the GLORIOUS REVOLUTION in England prompted uprisings against Andros and the dissolution of the Dominion in 1689. Two years later a royal charter was issued that incorporated Plymouth Colony and the Province of Maine within Massachusetts but placed the extended colony under a royal governor and removed the religious qualification for voting. The authority of the Puritan clergy, already much weakened, was further diminished as a result of the SALEM WITCH TRIALS of 1692.

Massachusetts experienced accelerated growth in the early 18th century. Mills were built along the smaller rivers and streams in the interior to grind grain, saw logs, forge iron, and process wool. Seaport towns grew and prospered as a lucrative overseas trade flourished. Ships carried timber and salt fish to the Caribbean and returned with molasses and sugar. Rum, distilled in Medford and Newburyport, was carried to West Africa along with cloth and simple utensils to be traded for slaves who were, in turn, carried to the Caribbean Islands and South America.

From the Revolution to the Civil War. The various taxes put forth by the British after 1730 were unpopular in thriving Massachusetts. The so-called Molasses Act, Sugar Act, and STAMP ACT, followed by the TOWNSHEND ACTS, stimulated colonial opposition that led to the BOSTON MASSACRE of 1770 and the BOSTON TEA PARTY in 1773. The British closed the port of Boston, and two years later, a search-and-destroy mission by British troops precipitated the Battles of LEXINGTON AND CONCORD.

Massachusetts was briefly the focus of attention at the start of the AMERICAN REVOLUTION. In June 1775 the Battle of BUNKER HILL proved to be a costly victory for the British. In 1776 they evacuated Boston, and fighting ended on Massachusetts soil.

Massachusetts patriots, including John ADAMS, Samuel ADAMS, and John HANCOCK, were leaders in the Revolution, and the state continued to provide leadership for the young American republic. General opposition to the WAR OF 1812 brought on talk of secession at the HARTFORD CONVENTION (1814–15).

The decades before the Civil War were prosperous ones. Farming spread into the farthest valleys of the Berkshires. Canals, toll roads, and railroads were built connecting all of the principal cities. Factories were built along the rivers. The textile industry, which was to dominate the state's economy for the next century, gained its initial momentum under capitalists like Francis Cabot LOWELL. Workers were first recruited from local farms and villages, but in the mid-1840s the first non-English immigrants, the Irish, arrived. The long British cultural hegemony was over. The mill cities grew rapidly. As water-power sites proved inadequate for large-scale factory expansion, steam engines powered by coal were used.

The Civil War was entered with great enthusiasm, especially because Massachusetts had a long history of ABOLITIONIST sentiment. The state was a major arsenal for the war, with guns, blankets, tents, and shoes produced in vast quantities.

Economic Change. The late 19th century was the state's greatest industrial period. Massachusetts was a national leader in the production not only of textiles and shoes but also of textile and shoemaking machinery, silverware, machine tools, glass, paper, rubber products, locomotives, guns, and fire engines. Then, from 1900 to 1910, many factories, which had become increasingly obsolescent, closed. Service industries, however, were beginning to assume a new role in the Massachusetts economy. Banking and insurance, important in the era of industrial expansion and transportation growth, reached out for new markets in the West. Retailing and wholesaling expanded to serve the new urban populations. Many office and clerical jobs were created in cities like Boston, Worcester, and Springfield.

The Depression of the 1930s was especially severe in those communities already hard hit by the closing of textile and shoe factories. World War II temporarily reversed this trend as the state became a leading producer of war materiel. The traditional industries of shipbuilding and machinery were greatly expanded, along with local development of new products such as radar, sonar, and jet engines.

In the post–World War II era Massachusetts has played a national leadership role in social and political activities. The presidency of John F. Kennedy recalled the long political tradition of the state. Beginning in the 1950s, Massachusetts's economy generally has been revitalized, with electronics, nonelectrical machinery, and computer-oriented industries stimulating growth. Service industries continue to expand, especially in the areas of banking, insurance, health care, and higher education. Democratic governor Michael DUKAKIS claimed credit for the state's apparently strong economy in his unsuccessful campaign for the presidency in 1988. In fact, the economy was faltering badly, and Massachusetts entered the 1990s in a recession.

Massachusetts Bay Company

The Massachusetts Bay Company was a joint stock trading company chartered by the English crown in 1629 to colonize a vast area in New England extending from 3 mi (4.8 km) north of the Merrimack River to 3 mi south of the Charles River. It was quickly taken over by a group of Puritans, under the leadership of John Winthrop (see WINTHROP family), who wished to establish a religious community in the New World. The first colonists sailed from England in 1630 and established the Massachusetts Bay Colony, with its center at Boston. Other settlers, almost all Puritans, joined them; by 1640 there were 20,000 settlers in Boston and neighboring towns.

The Puritan leaders had carried the company's charter with them to New England; this action enabled them to govern themselves and meant that they would not be controlled by governors and stockholders in England. Bending the charter to their own purposes, the Puritans transformed the company into a religious commonwealth. Their ambition had been to establish an ideal Christian community—a "city on a hill," as Winthrop called it—with the eyes of England and the entire world on it. Winthrop was reelected governor, and a theocracy was in fact established. In May 1631 the Puritan leaders agreed to recognize only church members as freemen (those entitled to vote and hold office). The company's officers became the colony's magistrates. The ministers of the church defined orthodoxy, and the colony's magistrates enforced it. Dissenters were suppressed or banished.

For about 50 years the Massachusetts Bay Colony developed into a Puritan commonwealth, with little interference from England. In 1684, however, the government of Charles II revoked the company's charter. The colony was merged briefly (1686–88) into the Dominion of New England, extending from New Hampshire to New Jersey. In 1691 the colony was unified with Plymouth and Maine into the royal colony of MASSACHUSETTS; the religious laws instituted by the Massachusetts Bay Company were largely repealed.

Massachusetts Institute of Technology

Established in 1861, the Massachusetts Institute of Technology (M.I.T.) is a private coeducational institution in Cambridge, Mass. It is both a land-grant and sea-grant school. Undergraduate and graduate degrees are granted in the schools of architecture and planning, humanities and social sciences, engineering, science, and management. M.I.T. operates on the laboratory method of instruction, with undergraduate and graduate students and professors partaking in research. It has many research facilities in the life, earth, space, and nuclear sciences and participates in programs at the Brookhaven National Laboratory in Upton, N.Y., and the Woods Hole (Mass.) Oceanographic Institution.

massasauga [mas-uh-saw'-guh] The massasauga, *Sistrurus catenatus,* is a rattlesnake reaching about 1 m (3 ft) in length. It is gray to grayish brown, with dark spots, blotches, or crossbars. It and the related pygmy rattlers are distinguished from other rattlesnakes, genus *Crotalus,* by having a set of nine large scales on the head. The massasauga is found from central New York and southern Ontario southwest to Coahuila, Mexico. It frequently inhabits swampy areas. The massasauga bears eight or nine living young.

Massasoit [mas-uh-soyt'] Massasoit (meaning "great sachem"), d. 1662, was the name used by early English colonists for the principal leader of the Wampanoag tribe, traditional inhabitants of present-day Massachusetts and eastern Rhode Island. His real name was Wawmegin, or "Yellow Feather." Introduced to the colonists by the Abnaki leader SAMOSET, Massasoit remained friendly and accommodating to the newcomers throughout his lifetime. However, his second son, Metagomet, who became known to the English as Philip of Pokanoket or King Philip, adopted a different policy. Philip led the major Indian assault on the English settlements in 1675–76, attempting to drive the colonists out of and away from tribal lands.

Masséna, André [mah-say-nah'] André Masséna, b. May 6, 1758, d. Apr. 4, 1817, was a French general in the FRENCH REVOLUTIONARY WARS and NAPOLEONIC WARS. Enlisting in 1775, he rose to divisional general in 1793. Masséna distinguished himself under NAPOLEON I, scoring a major success at Zurich in 1799, diverting the Austrian armies at Genoa in 1800, conquering the kingdom of Naples in 1806, and displaying great bravery at Aspern-Essling and Wagram in 1809. He was made a marshal (1804), duc de Rivoli (1808), and prince d'Essling (1810). Defeated by the duke of WELLINGTON in Portugal and Spain in 1810–11, he was dismissed.

Massenet, Jules [mah-suh-nay', zhuel] Jules Émile Frédéric Massenet, b. May 12, 1842, d. Aug. 13, 1912, was a French composer best known for his operas *Manon, Thaïs,* and *Werther.* He entered the Paris Conservatory at the age of 9, won the Grand Prix de Rome in 1863, and was appointed professor of composition at the conservatory in 1878. The central link in French opera between Gounod and the confirmed modernists, Massenet was a teacher of Gustave Charpentier and Gabriel Pierné.

Massenet was tremendously popular during his lifetime, and his influence was widely felt. His musical and dramatic style is a unique combination of religiosity and eroticism. Other Massenet operas revived in the late 20th century include *Esclarmonde* (1889), *Sapho* (1897), *Cendrillon* (1899), and *La Navarraise* (1894). In addition to his operas, Massenet wrote oratorios and cantatas, incidental music for plays, several orchestral works (including a piano concerto), piano pieces, and hundreds of songs.

Massey, Vincent [mas'-ee]   Charles Vincent Massey, b. Toronto, Feb. 20, 1887, d. Dec. 30, 1967, was the first native Canadian to serve as governor general of Canada (1952–59). President (1921–25) of his family's business, the Massey-Harris Company, he was appointed (1925) minister without portfolio by Prime Minister William Lyon Mackenzie King.

Massey was minister to the United States (1926–30) and high commissioner for Canada in Britain (1935–46). He headed (1949–51) the Royal Commission on National Development in the Arts, Letters, and Sciences and continued to promote development of the arts while governor general. He was the brother of the actor Raymond Massey.

Massey, William   William Ferguson Massey, b. Mar. 26, 1856, d. May 10, 1925, a staunch agrarian conservative and supporter of the British Empire, led New Zealand as prime minister for 13 years. He emigrated from Ireland in 1870. Elected to Parliament in 1894, he became leader of the conservative Opposition party in 1903, changing its name (1909) to the Reform party. In 1912 he became prime minister, an office he held until his death. He introduced liberal land reforms while crushing militant labor unions. At the outbreak of World War I, Massey sent an expeditionary force to Europe and served (1917–18) in the British war cabinet. During the war New Zealand was governed by a coalition (1915–19) of Massey's Reform party and Sir Joseph Ward's Liberals. Afterward Massey opposed the movement for a more independent dominion status within the Empire.

Massif Central [mah-seef' sahn-trahl']   The Massif Central is a region of mountains and plateaus in south central France covering about 90,700 km^2 (35,000 mi^2). These highlands rise from the Paris Basin on the north, the Rhône River valley on the east and southeast, and the Aquitaine Basin on the southwest. The highest peak is the extinct volcano Puy de Sancy (1,886 m/6,188 ft); the mean elevation is approximately 760 m (2,500 ft).

Composed of a core of ancient crystalline rock, the mountains are flanked by sedimentary deposits of more recent age. Headwaters or major tributaries of the LOIRE, the SEINE, and the RHÔNE rise in the region, making it a natural site for industrial centers (CLERMONT-FERRAND, LI-

MOGES, SAINT-ÉTIENNE, and Le Creusot) and hydroelectric stations. Coal and kaolin deposits are mined at Saint-Étienne, Alès, and Blanzy. Cattle and sheep are raised in the central uplands; vineyards and market gardens are found on gentler slopes.

Massine, Leonid [mah-seen', lay-oh-need']   Leonid Massine, b. Leonid Myassine in Russia on Aug. 8, 1895, d. Mar. 15, 1979, enjoyed worldwide renown as both a choreographer and a character dancer, especially in his own ballets. In 1915, under the tutelage of Serge DIAGHILEV, he completed his first ballet, *Soleil de Nuit*, and in 1917 he established himself as a choreographer of note with *Parade* and *The Good-Humored Ladies*. Even more successful, two years later, were *The Three-Cornered Hat* and *The Fantastic Toyshop*. In 1921 he left the BALLETS RUSSES DE SERGE DIAGHILEV but returned sporadically between 1925 and 1928. Subsequently he was chief choreographer and maître de ballet of Colonel W. de Basil's company (1933–38) and then of the Ballet Russes de Monte Carlo (1938–41; see BALLETS RUSSES DE MONTE CARLO). During this period he was the most influential choreographer in Western Europe and the United States. He later created the dance sequences in the films *The Red Shoes* (1948) and *Tales of Hoffmann* (1951). Only a handful of his works seem likely to survive, although his place in ballet history as a creator of innovative and comic works is secure.

Massinger, Philip [mas'-in-jur]   Philip Massinger, b. November 1583, d. March 1640, was a skillful and prolific English dramatist. He collaborated with John Fletcher (1579–1625) before working independently for the King's Men, the leading London theatrical company of the time. Fifteen plays by Massinger survive, of which the most celebrated is the comedy *A New Way to Pay Old Debts* (c.1625), memorable for its portrayal of the ludicrous scheming villain Sir Giles Overreach.

Masson, André [mah-sohn']   André Masson, b. Jan. 4, 1896, d. Oct. 28, 1987, was a French painter, illustrator, printmaker, and writer who played an important role in the surrealist movement of the 1920s. A deeply philosophical artist, he often invested his works with emotional and violent qualities that emerged from his exploration of the subconscious—a path that led him to use automatism in some of his paintings. Masson did influential work as a book illustrator, theatrical designer, sculptor, and writer. A wartime stay (1941–45) in the United States inspired him to delve into African American and American Indian myths. One of Masson's most admired paintings, *Battle of Fishes* (1926), is in the Museum of Modern Art in New York.

Massys, Quentin [mah-sees' kven'-tin]   Quentin Massys (also known as Metsys), b. Louvain, c.1465, d.

1530, was the first Flemish painter to integrate elements of late-15th-century Italian painting with the decorative Gothic tradition of Flemish art. Massys's synthesis of older Flemish forms with Italian Renaissance methods can be seen in one of his masterpieces, the triptych altarpiece of the Lamentation (1511; Musée Royale des Beaux-Arts, Antwerp). In this work a stark mountainous background and an expressionistic figure of Christ, both typical of the Flemish tradition, were combined with figures that were handled with a broadness and massiveness altogether unprecedented in Flemish painting of that time. The faces of the mourners are not idealized, but strikingly naturalistic. While they mourn, they carry on with the necessary small tasks of preparing Christ's body for entombment, just as people in real life might do. The wings of the triptych are even more overtly secular. *Herod's Feast* is really a thinly disguised contemporary aristocratic dinner party, and the *Martyrdom of Saint John* contains heads that are reminiscent of the contorted features in Leonardo's studies of human physiognomy. This realism is even more evident in Massys's *Ecce Homo* (1514–16; Prado, Madrid). The naturalism of Massys marks the beginning of an evolution in Flemish art away from the idealized Gothic style toward the work of Peter Bruegel.

mastaba [mas'-tuh-buh]   Mastaba (Arabic for "bench") is the name given to ancient Egyptian tombs with rectangular superstructures dating from the Early Dynastic period and the Old Kingdom (c.3100–2181 BC). The most elaborate mastabas were built for the kings of the 1st and 2d dynasties (c.3100–2686 BC); in dynasties thereafter PYRAMIDS came to be the typical royal tomb. Mastabas, however, continued to be used as the tombs for nobles and officials throughout the Old Kingdom.

mastectomy [mas-tek'-tuh-mee]   Mastectomy is surgical removal of the BREAST, usually because of CANCER in the female breast. In simple mastectomy only the breast tissue is removed, and the underlying muscles and sometimes the nipple are preserved. Radical mastectomy entails removing the breast, the lymph nodes near the collarbone and armpit, and sections of the arm and chest muscles. Mastectomy does not interfere with production of female hormones or with female functions. In some cases new surgical techniques and prosthetics allow reconstruction of the breast, using the nipple from the amputated breast. In other cases artificial breast forms may be fitted to the chest. After mastectomy, exercises are prescribed to "train" adjoining muscles to give strength to the shoulder and arm.

In the past, surgeons preferred the radical operation (along with X-ray treatments) in the belief that the chances of curing breast cancer were improved by removing as much normal tissue as possible. Recently, however, the trend is toward simple mastectomy in conjunction with hormone therapy and anticancer drugs (chemotherapy) designed to destroy cancer cells that may have spread (metastasized) from the breast to other parts of the body.

Masters, Edgar Lee   A leading figure of the Chicago Renaissance, Edgar Lee Masters, b. Garnett, Kans., Aug. 23, 1869, d. Mar. 5, 1950, although trained as a lawyer and the author of several novels and biographies, is primarily remembered for just one book of poems, the influential SPOON RIVER ANTHOLOGY (1915; play, 1963). His earlier books of verse were diffuse and conventional; later ones, such as *Domesday Book* (1920), *The Fate of the Jury* (1929), and *Poems of People* (1936), suggested that his one success owed much to good fortune. *Spoon River* seemed to prefigure Sherwood Anderson's WINESBURG, OHIO (1919), another volume that shattered the idyllic image of small-town America. Of his later works, a series of novels in the 1920s and several biographical studies of prominent American figures in the 1930s, the highly critical *Lincoln, the Man* (1931) was the most successful. Masters published *Across Spoon River: An Autobiography* in 1936.

Masters and Johnson reports   Gynecologist William Howell Masters, b. Cleveland, Ohio, Dec. 27, 1915, and his psychologist colleague Virginia Eshelman Johnson, b. Springfield, Mo., Feb. 11, 1925, developed polygraphlike instruments to measure human sexual response in the laboratory and wrote three pioneering reports of their findings. The first, *Human Sexual Response* (1966), described the physiological responses during four phases of erotic arousal for males and females. *Human Sexual Inadequacy* (1970) concerned the treatment of sexual problems such as impotence, premature ejaculation, and frigidity. *Homosexuality in Perspective* (1979) described the sexual responses of homosexual men and lesbians.

In the first book female orgasms were shown to progress through the same series of physiological changes no matter what the stimulus. The study of homosexuality found that homosexual couples can have mutually satisfying sexual lives.

The work of Masters and Johnson became a basis for reevaluating homosexual and female sexual response, but it also met with some suspicion, as did the earlier sexual research of Alfred C. Kinsey (see KINSEY REPORTS). The observation of sexual acts by scientists using machines may alter the acts, a point that they readily admit. Considerable criticism was also voiced over the general applicability of their experiences in converting homosexuals to heterosexuality.

Further controversy was aroused by their 1988 publication, *Crisis: Heterosexual Behavior in the Age of AIDS*, in which they forecast an epidemic spread of AIDS among heterosexuals. Masters and Johnson, who married in 1971, have trained thousands of SEX THERAPY workers in their St. Louis, Mo., laboratory.

mastersinger   see MEISTERSINGER

Masterson, Bat   William B. Masterson, b. Iroquois County, Ill., Nov. 24, 1853, d. Oct. 25, 1921, popularly known as Bat, was one of the legendary gunslingers of the American West. After his family moved (1871) to Kansas, Masterson was a scout, Indian fighter, buffalo hunter, and railroad worker before he became deputy sheriff of Dodge City in 1876. Forceful and fast with a six-gun, Masterson soon established his reputation in Kansas and later became a terror of lawbreakers in Deadwood, S.Dak., and Tombstone, Ariz. He often worked with his two lawmen brothers and sometimes assisted federal marshal Wyatt EARP. In 1902 he moved to New York City, where he worked as a sportswriter on the *Morning Telegraph*.

mastiff The mastiff is a huge, smooth-coated breed of dog with a large blocky head, blunt muzzle, drop ears, and a low-carried tail. For show, males must stand at least 75 cm (30 in) at the shoulder, whereas females must be a minimum of 68.75 cm (27.5 in). An adult male weighs at least 74.25 kg (165 lb). The mastiff gives the impression of immense strength: the chest is deep and broad, the back muscular and powerful. The coat may be fawn, apricot, silver, or brindle, with black muzzle and ears. The mastiff is a reliable guard.

The mastiff type of dog probably originated in Asia and was introduced into England as early as the 6th century BC. Invading Romans, impressed with its strength and fighting ability, used the breed to fight bulls, bears, lions, tigers, and gladiators in the arena. In Elizabethan times, the breed was used for baiting bears and lions.

The mastiff is a working dog bred in England. Mastiff-type dogs fought in the Roman circus and in the dogfights of Elizabethan England.

Mastigophora [mas-tig-ah'-fur-uh] Mastigophora is a diverse class of unicellular organisms belonging to the phylum PROTOZOA and characterized by having one or more flagella, which are used for propulsion and sometimes as food-gathering or sensory structures. Members of this class are either free-living, inhabiting fresh water or soil, or parasitic in animals and humans. Many species are colonial, growing into large blooms in salt or fresh wa-

ter. Reproduction is generally by binary fission.

At one time Mastigophora included many species, such as *Euglena,* that contain chlorophyll and can photosynthesize food, as well as species that are colorless and must feed on other organisms. Most authorities now classify the plantlike species in separate groups—such as Euglenophyta—or among the algae, so that according to most classifications the Mastigophora now include only the animallike species (zoomastiginia).

Mastigophora that cause parasitic disease include the trypanosomes, which cause African sleeping sickness and kala-azar; and the trichomonads, which cause vaginal infections in humans and abortion in cattle.

mastodon [mas'-tuh-dahn] The mastodon, an elephantlike mammal belonging to the order Proboscidea, was widespread from the Miocene through the Pleistocene epochs (26 million to 10 thousand years ago). Mastodons were in the mainline of proboscidean evolution, first appearing in the Early Oligocene (38 million to 26 million years ago). Their teeth, consisting of a series of paired conical cusps, seen in profile resemble a woman's breasts; hence the name *mastodon* was derived from the Greek for breast tooth.

Gomphotherium (also called *Trilophodon*) lived during the Late Miocene and the Early Pliocene (12 million to 3.5 million years ago). It resembled *Phiomia,* but the teeth were more breastlike and the trunk was more fully developed. Shovel-tusked mastodons such as *Amebelodon* developed broad, scoop-shaped lower tusks that were useful for digging vegetation. *Mastodon americanus,*

The mastodon, a browsing mammal somewhat smaller than a present-day elephant, became extinct only in the last 10,000 years.

common in North America during the Pleistocene Epoch and perhaps up to a few thousand years ago, was not as tall as modern elephants. Its strongly curved upper tusks were very large, and its body was covered with long, reddish brown hair.

See also: ICE AGES; LA BREA TAR PIT.

Mastroianni, Marcello [mahs-troy-ahn'-nee, mar-chel'-loh]   Marcello Mastroianni, b. Sept. 28, 1924, has starred in roles ranging from light comedy to heavy drama. He first won international recognition as the journalist in Federico Fellini's *La Dolce Vita* (1960). Mastroianni has since been successful in Michelangelo Antonioni's *La Notte* (1961); the comedies *Divorce Italian Style* (1962), *Yesterday, Today, and Tomorrow* (1963), and *Marriage Italian Style* (1964); as Fellini's alter ego in *8½* (1963); and as Camus's antihero in *The Stranger* (1967). For his portrayal of a persecuted homosexual in *A Special Day* (1977), Mastroianni won an Academy Award.

masturbation [mas-tur-bay'-shuhn]   Masturbation, or "autoeroticism," is any kind of sexual self-stimulation that leads to erotic arousal. Orgasm is a frequent, though not necessary, result. Masturbation is a common sexual activity among both males and females; most studies indicate that more than 90 percent of males and 60 percent of females masturbate at some point during their lives. Masturbation is the quickest, most successful method for many females to attain orgasm.

Despite myths and fallacies that have developed over the years regarding masturbation's supposed ill effects on physical and mental health, it is a normal sexual activity; indeed, it is a useful means of developing one's sensual capacities. Young children, adolescents, and young and old adults alike often engage in masturbatory activities. Mental health professionals discourage its practice only when it becomes the sole sexual outlet despite the ready availability of other outlets or when it is accompanied by excessive feelings of disgust, shame, or guilt.

Masudi, al- [mah-soo'-dee, ahl]   Abu al-Hasan Ali al-Masudi, d. *c.*956, an Arab historian and geographer from Baghdad, traveled north to the Caspian Sea, south to Madagascar, and east to India, Sri Lanka, and the China Sea. Much of his findings appeared in the encyclopedic *Meadows of Gold and Mines of Gems.* Al-Masudi was the first Arab historian to organize material in topics rather than in the traditional, more random annalistic form.

Masur, Kurt [muh-zoor']   The German conductor Kurt Masur, b. July 18, 1927, was named music director of the New York Philharmonic (effective 1992) in 1990. Previously chief conductor of the Dresden Philharmonic (1967–72) and of the Leipzig Gewandhaus Orchestra (1970–), Masur is known particularly for his interpretations of romantic music and for the distinctive sound of his orchestras. A prominent figure in Leipzig, he was credited in 1989 with helping avert bloody repression of the prodemocracy demonstrations in that East German city.

Masurian Lakes [muh-zoo'-ree-uhn]   The Masurian Lakes region (also called Masuria), located in northeastern Poland near the USSR border, contains more than 2,700 small lakes and numerous short rivers and covers about 260 km^2 (100 mi^2). Early in World War I the area, then part of East Prussia, was the scene of heavy fighting in which the Russians were defeated by German troops. The region remained part of Germany until 1945 when it was granted to Poland. Most of the German-speaking population was then expelled and replaced by Poles.

Mata Hari [mah'-tuh hah'-ree]   Mata Hari was the stage name of a Dutch dancer, Margaretha Geertruida Zelle, b. Aug. 7, 1876, d. Oct. 15, 1917, who was accused of spying for the Germans in France during World War I. An erotic dancer, she performed in Paris, Berlin, London, and Rome before the war and, as a neutral, continued to move about freely during the war. Among her many lovers were high-ranking Allied military officers, from whom she is alleged to have gleaned valuable information that she passed on to the Germans. Arrested in Paris in 1917, she was tried by court martial and executed by the French. Opinion is divided as to whether she was really a spy.

Mata Hari, a Dutch dancer and spy for the Germans during World War I, counted among her lovers many high-ranking Allied military officers. The French discovered her duplicity and arrested her in Paris in February 1917. She was shot by a firing squad on Oct. 15, 1917.

Matabeleland   see ZIMBABWE

match   A match is a small stick of wood or cardboard, tipped by a small bulb of a hardened substance that ignites when it is scraped across certain abrasive surfaces. The earliest matches were wood splinters dipped in melted sulfur and ignited by a spark struck with a flint and steel. The first friction matches, tipped with mixtures that included the incendiary chemical white phosphorus, were produced in the 1830s. They were easy to ignite, but the white phosphorus proved a deadly poison for workers in the match factories, and for all of those who happened to ingest the match head accidentally. The incidence of "phossy jaw," a bone malady caused by the chemical, was among the earliest of recognized occupational diseases.

The white phosphorus matches were of the "strike anywhere" variety; they could be ignited by friction against almost any surface, and even accidental friction was often sufficient to ignite the match and start a fire. In 1855 the safety match appeared; it could be ignited only by striking it on a surface containing red phosphorus. Cardboard book matches, first produced in the 1890s, were safety matches with the striking surface glued to the matchbook cover. Phosphorus remained a hazard in "strike anywhere" matches, however, until the development (1911) of phosphorus sesquisulfide, a nonpoisonous chemical.

Wooden matches today are die-cut from pine veneers, then dipped in liquid chemicals that produce an easily ignited, extinguishable tip. Book matches are made from paperboard that has been chemically treated to eliminate smoldering when matches are extinguished.

maté [mah-tay'] A beverage brewed from the dried young leaves and shoots of an evergreen tree, *Ilex paraguariensis*, of the holly family, maté has been used for centuries as a stimulant and restorative drink by the Indians of South America. Known also as yerba maté and Paraguay tea, the tealike liquid contains considerable amounts of caffeine and tannin. It is now popular throughout most of South America, often prepared in elaborate gourd-shaped cups and sipped through strawlike strainers.

materialism Materialism is a philosophical theory that maintains that all events, acts, and states of affairs are either subordinate to or may be completely reduced to material objects and their interrelationships. Materialism is a metaphysical theory; the colloquial usage, in which concern with physical and personal desires and their satisfaction is said to be materialistic, is technically called HEDONISM.

Although many of the pre-Socratic philosophers attempted to reduce phenomena to a single material principle, the earliest well-articulated materialism is that of DEMOCRITUS. In his theory of ATOMISM the basic elements of the world are indestructible particles (atoms) moving around in space. Thus, the distinction between the mind and the body is merely a distinction between different ways in which the basic atoms are combined.

Atomism was revived in the 17th century by the French scientist Pierre Gassendi, who sought to combine the theory with Christian doctrine, and by Thomas HOBBES, who formulated a mechanistic theory of psychology, arguing that sensations are corporeal motions within the brain. In the 18th century Baron d'HOLBACH expounded the theory that nature is a causally determined succession of arrangements of matter in motion. Materialism in this period was closely associated with the scientific and secularist movements of the day.

The scientific advances of the 19th and 20th centuries so reinforced the materialist position concerning the basic similarity of organic and inorganic matter that the focus of debate has shifted. In the 19th century materialism was incorporated into the DIALECTICAL MATERIALISM of Karl MARX, where it referred to the determinative role of material conditions on the intellectual, social, and political development of humanity. In contemporary philosophy, materialism is primarily concerned with the relation between the mind, the brain, and behavior.

materials technology Materials technology comprises the selection, production, and processing of materials to ensure that they ultimately have the desired shape and specified properties for optimum performance. Materials include plastics, glass, ceramics, metals, and semiconductors; they may be used alone or in combinations.

Engineering of Materials

To specify the required properties, a materials engineer must work with other engineers to anticipate the functional and service requirements of the final product. The materials engineer must be familiar with many fields of technology: chemistry, physics, metallurgy, ceramics, and so on. The guiding principles of materials technology are that (1) properties depend directly on the internal structure of the materials, and (2) any desired change in properties requires an appropriate change in the internal structure. Conversely, if service conditions change the internal structure, a corresponding change must be expected in the properties.

Properties of Materials

The engineer who designs machines, electrical products, buildings, refineries, nuclear reactors, and ships has to know whether the chosen materials will perform as required, and whether they will resist failure in service. Key properties include mechanical behavior, electrical and magnetic responses, thermal characteristics, and chemical stability.

Mechanical properties involve the response of materials to applied forces, or loads. Stress is the amount of load per unit of area. Materials respond to a stress with a strain, which is deformation per unit length. Typically, the initial strain is elastic; that is, the material resumes its original shape when the stress is removed. The amount of elastic strain is proportional to the applied stress. The ratio of stress to strain is a characteristic property of a material and is called the modulus of elasticity; its value is high for a rigid material such as steel, and much lower for flexible materials.

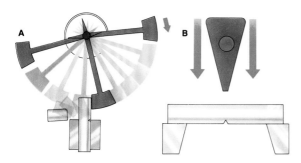

Impact tests measure the amount of impact energy that a notched metal bar can absorb before breaking. The Izod test (A) uses a notched vertical bar, and the Charpy test (B) employs a notched horizontal bar.

Common mechanical properties include strength, ductility, and toughness. Strength is the stress required for failure, ductility is the strain prior to fracture, and toughness is the energy required for fracture. Two different strengths are of interest: ultimate strength and yield strength. The ultimate strength indicates the maximum load a material can support when the original cross-sectional area is the basis for calculation. This strength is important in any design calculation, because the component proceeds to complete rupture when it is loaded in excess of this rating. Yield strength is the stress required to initiate plastic (permanent) deformation. This constitutes failure of a part if its shape or dimensions must remain unchanged in service. Stress and the various strengths have units of newtons/meter^2 or pounds/inch^2. Ductility is expressed as the percentage of elongation at fracture and is dimensionless. Toughness is measured in joules or foot-pounds. Testing for strength and ductility is conducted in a tensile machine that pulls a sample and records the amount of strain.

Electrical properties commonly encountered in materials technology are resistivity for conductors and relative dielectric constant for insulators. Resistivity is a property of a material independent of its shape. However, it is related to resistance because, in a uniform shape such as a wire, resistance equals the resistivity times the length divided by the cross-sectional area. The values of resistivity vary from approximately 10^{-5} ohm-cm for the metallic electrodes in a spark plug to more than 10^{12} ohm-cm for insulators, with values for semiconductors falling in between. The relative dielectric constant is more complex and indicates the charge displacements that are possible within an insulator without actual charge transport.

Thermal properties that are important for materials engineers are expansion and thermal conductivity. The former is the dimensional change that accompanies temperature change and may lead to stresses or failure, or both, of a product if appropriate design considerations are not incorporated. Thermal conductivity is difficult to measure directly. In metals (only), however, it is very closely related to electrical conductivity (the reciprocal of resistivity), which is easily measured.

CORROSION is the best-known chemical behavior of significance to the materials technologist. No product—even though it is made from sufficiently strong and tough materials—can last indefinitely if it is subjected to environments in which its materials undergo chemical alteration. Technological preventatives include (1) materials selection to avoid galvanic couples, (2) protective coatings such as glass, paint, or plated metals to isolate the surface from the environment, and (3) impressed currents from DC sources or from sacrificial anodes.

Control of the Materials Structure by Processing

Because the foregoing properties, as well as others, depend on the internal structure of the material, it is necessary to know how the structure of a material may be modified. In addition to the choice of composition, the internal structure may be controlled by solidification procedures, by mechanical deformation that accompanies reshaping operations, and by a variety of thermal treatments. In addition, some materials are subjected to radiation treatments.

Solidification is monitored to produce single crystals in the production of semiconductors. It may be performed sufficiently rapidly to avoid crystallization and therefore produce the structure of glass. In metals, this means cooling from above 1,000° C (1,832° F) to room temperature in less than a millisecond. (To produce ordinary silicate glasses, cooling may continue for many minutes.) Solidification processes are almost always designed to minimize segregation of the constituents and thus provide more uniformity in the product. An exception occurs in materials such as silicon for semiconductors. Since the silicon must have extreme purity, it is slowly crystallized so that the impurities remain in the final liquid, which is then discarded.

Mechanical processing commonly involves deforming the material beyond the elastic limit. Not only does this provide a new external shape, it also changes the atom-to-atom arrangement within the material. This deformation strengthens a ductile material. As a result, the ultimate strength always exceeds the yield strength. The engineer may make use of this added strength in a variety of ways.

Metal-hardness tests measure the indentation produced when a machine (left) presses a hard, standard-shaped material into the metal surface under a specific load. The Vickers test (A) uses a pyramid-shaped diamond indenter, and the Brinell test (B) a hardened steel ball. In the Rockwell test (C) a light and then a heavy load is applied to a diamond indenter; the difference in depth indicates hardness.

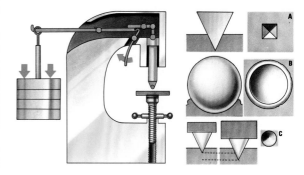

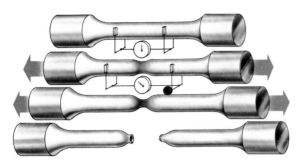

In determining the tensile strength of materials, standardized cylindrical specimens are stretched to the breaking point on special machines at a constant rate of elongation and temperature. Initially, the entire sample is uniformly elongated; the strain then is localized, and the sample breaks at a specific load and elongation.

For example, a car bumper is given added strength by a process called cold-working. Unfortunately, cold-working also makes a metal less ductile. Therefore, a compromise must be chosen between strength increase and ductility loss.

In addition, materials engineers must coordinate property requirements with the manufacturing engineers who will make the component. For example, a strip of steel for a bumper can be made exceptionally strong by cold-working it 90%—that is, to 10% of its original cross-sectional area. This is not done, however, because it would require massive equipment and large amounts of power to develop high strength by that means. Further, the loss of ductility could lead to cracking.

Thermal processing can remove the structural changes within the metal that lead to deformation strengthening. The deformation distorted the normal atomic coordination within a ductile material; given an opportunity, the atoms will rearrange themselves into their original, more stable patterns. The opportunity for rearrangement is facilitated by raising the temperature, so that the atoms in a material become more loosely bound into a structure. Thus, a cold-worked metal may be annealed (heated and slowly cooled) to soften and toughen it. Shorter annealing times are required at higher temperatures.

Thermal processing treatments may also be used to change the extent and distribution of residual stresses that affect the internal structure. The annealing of glass permits the distorted bonds between the atoms to return to their more favored positions. Conversely, hot glass may be tempered by cooling its surface more rapidly than its interior. This introduces compressive stresses among the atoms in the surface zone and thus increases the bending strength of the glass by several hundred percent.

mathematics   Mathematics is the study of numbers, sets of points, and various abstract elements, together with relations between them and operations performed on them. Mathematics deals with size, order, shape, and other relationships among quantities. For the history of this subject, see MATHEMATICS, HISTORY OF.

Aspects of Mathematics

Mathematics is variously considered a language, an art, a science, a tool, and a game.

A language is an agreed-upon set of symbols or sounds; mathematics may be considered the language used to express size and order. Equations and statements of inequality are mathematical sentences. Mathematical elements such as constants and variables are analogous to parts of speech. Notions of artistic beauty and harmony exist in the patterns, relationships, and symmetries of arithmetic and geometry. Developing new mathematical theories, concepts, and systems is aesthetically satisfying. The study of mathematics can be a rewarding endeavor in much the same sense as can the study of history, literature, or music.

Mathematics is the science of logical reasoning, in which valid conclusions are arrived at from a set of AXIOMS (see LOGIC). It involves a search for truth. It is rigorous and precise. Although some theories discovered 2,000 years ago are still valid, mathematics continues to change and develop.

Mathematics is a tool in that it contains the skills for PROBLEM SOLVING; organizing, simplifying, and interpreting data; and performing calculations that are necessary in subjects such as science, business, and industry. The development of modern COMPUTERS and CALCULATORS has enabled mathematicians to solve problems that previously were extremely difficult or impossible to solve. Some areas of mathematics were developed specifically to solve certain types of problems. One goal of mathematics is to solve a problem in a systematic way so that similar problems can be solved more easily in the same way.

With mathematics one can create a set of consistent rules and regulations (axioms) and proceed by logical reasoning to invent and play a game.

Branches of Mathematics

Some branches of mathematics were developed in order to solve certain physical problems or to explain physical phenomena. For example, in his study of astronomy, Johannes KEPLER found it necessary to develop new mathematics. On the other hand, mathematical calculations sometimes lead to the discovery of new physical phenomena. Deviations in the motions of Neptune from the predictions of the mathematical theory led to the discovery (1931) of the planet Pluto.

Mathematics today can be subdivided into pure mathematics and applied mathematics. Applied mathematics deals with solutions to practical problems in areas such as physics, economics, business, navigation, and astronomy. Pure mathematics deals with the study of the abstract properties of mathematical quantities and systems without regard to application. Computer science, PROBABILITY, STATISTICS, and operations research are often considered part of applied mathematics, whereas abstract algebra, number theory, and topology are usually considered part of pure mathematics.

Mathematics may also be divided into various branches, depending on the elements and axioms used. Some of the major branches can be further subdivided into several significant subbranches. Each branch usually consists of definitions, undefined terms, elements, axioms, operations, relations, and theorems.

ARITHMETIC deals with numbers and the fundamental operations (addition, subtraction, multiplication, and division) and the extensions of these (raising to powers and extracting roots). Arithmetic is sometimes called the art of computation.

ALGEBRA involves the operations of arithmetic. Unknown numbers are represented by symbols called variables. Open mathematical sentences (equations and inequalities involving variables) are solved for the "unknowns." Systems of equations are used to solve practical problems. Solution of systems of linear equations leads to the study of linear algebra, in which the elements are matrices and vectors. Abstract algebra is the study of systems that satisfy certain sets of axioms. Some of these structures are fields, rings, groups, and domains (see GROUP THEORY). The elements used in abstract algebra may be numbers, vectors, or even geometric transformations.

GEOMETRY is the branch of mathematics that deals with sets of points in a plane or in space. The study of plane curves, angles, polygons, and lines is called plane geometry. The study of space curves (in three-dimensional space) such as spheres, cones, cylinders, and polyhedra is called solid geometry. In about 300 BC, EUCLID established a set of axioms for geometry. In Euclidean geometry, all of these axioms are obeyed. NON-EUCLIDEAN GEOMETRIES have been developed by denying the validity of the famous fifth postulate (parallel postulate), which stated that "given a line and a point not on the line, one and only one coplanar line can be drawn through the point parallel to the given line."

ANALYTIC GEOMETRY is the study of geometry through algebraic methods. DIFFERENTIAL GEOMETRY applies techniques of calculus to geometry and studies such local properties as tangents and curvature. TOPOLOGY, which has been developed in the 20th century, is a study of generalized geometric elements and such properties as connectedness and compactness. Fractal geometry (see GEOMETRY, FRACTAL), which, like topology, includes structures that are non-Euclidean, has been applied in CHAOS THEORY.

TRIGONOMETRY is the branch of mathematics used in computing, rather than directly measuring, distances. The trigonometric functions (sine, cosine, tangent, cotangent, secant, and cosecant) can be defined as the ratios of lengths of sides of right triangles or in terms of coordinates of terminal points of arcs on the unit circle (circular functions).

Analysis is the name given to the branches of mathematics that use the concept of a LIMIT. CALCULUS is considered a branch of analysis; so are subjects that depend on the concepts of calculus, such as DIFFERENTIAL EQUATIONS, VECTOR ANALYSIS, real analysis, and complex analysis. DIFFERENTIAL CALCULUS involves derivatives. The definite integral—a quantity studied in INTEGRAL CALCULUS—can be used to find areas and volumes of irregular figures and to find lengths of curves.

NUMBER THEORY is one of the oldest branches of pure mathematics. The elements used are the integers, and the topics investigated include PRIME NUMBERS, factorization, and congruences.

mathematics, education in Mathematics has been regarded as essential to a liberal education at least since Plato maintained that proficiency in mathematics was a prerequisite for the study of philosophy. Today a good education in mathematics is important because of its usefulness in careers such as environmental studies, business, engineering, medicine, and psychology, as well as in the biological, mathematical, and physical sciences. Knowledge of mathematics also helps students understand CALCULATORS and COMPUTERS.

The goal of mathematics education is to encourage the use of precise and accurate thinking to solve problems. A minimal mathematics proficiency, educators believe, would require students to learn the arithmetic of whole numbers and rational numbers (with both decimal and fractional notation), to be able to measure in standard units and convert from one unit to another, to estimate and approximate, to use graphs and other methods of organizing and interpreting data to see patterns and trends, and to understand probabilistic ideas, the geometry of two and three dimensions, and the place of functions in science and mathematics.

In the United States, ARITHMETIC is taught from kindergarten through grade 8, introductory algebra and intuitive geometry usually in grades 7 and 8, ALGEBRA in grade 9, GEOMETRY in grade 10, intermediate algebra, statistics, precalculus, analytic geometry, and sometimes TRIGONOMETRY and PROBABILITY in grades 11 and 12. College mathematics usually begins with about 2 years of differential and integral CALCULUS and linear algebra and covers probability theory.

Nearly all American children study mathematics through grade 8, and most take some mathematics courses in high school. In the mid-1980s, in response to findings that indicated unacceptable levels of math literacy, many states increased mathematics requirements for high school graduation. Increasingly, in the United States, algebra and geometry are included with some probability and statistics and some work with calculators even before the 9th grade.

So-called new mathematics, emphasizing functions, set theory, and structures, was developed and taught in the 1950s and '60s, but many educators considered it too abstract for children and its classroom use has since declined. From the 1970s, trends have included teaching mathematics in relation to concrete situations, applying mathematics to consumer concerns, using computers along with mathematics, and using games, activities, and real problems to show the power of abstract thinking and mathematical systems.

mathematics, history of Mathematics is as old as civilization itself. By the Neolithic Period, as life became

The Greek philosopher Euclid summarized the mathematical knowledge of his day in a book, the Elements, *in which he set forth the principles of geometry and plane trigonometry.*

settled and villages began to appear, writing and counting became increasingly useful. With counting, the history of mathematics began. To count the passage of time, to weave intricate patterns in baskets or fabrics, and to apportion goods, crops, and livestock required a basic sense of arithmetic.

Egyptian, Babylonian, and Greek Mathematics

The earliest knowledge of mathematics is preserved in Egyptian papyruses, Babylonian cuneiform tablets, and Greek manuscripts. They indicate that the first mathematical concerns involved ARITHMETIC, ALGEBRA, GEOMETRY, and TRIGONOMETRY.

Arithmetic and Algebra. Among the earliest surviving mathematical texts is the famous Rhind papyrus (*c.*1750 BC). Arithmetic for the Egyptians was essentially additive; repeated doubling was used for multiplication. FRACTIONS were generally expressed as unit fractions of the form $1/n$.

Babylonian arithmetic, which made use of a place-valued sexagesimal system, made certain computations, such as multiplication and division, considerably easier than the Egyptian method. The Babylonian base 60 is still used in measuring time and the degrees of a circle.

The first major discoveries in Greek mathematics are ascribed to PYTHAGORAS OF SAMOS and his followers. Pythagorean arithmetic regarded numbers as sums of units or points and consequently has often been interpreted as an abstract form of atomism. A group centered around ZENO OF ELEA (5th century BC) opposed this Pythagorean atomism and formulated ZENO'S PARADOXES. The ultimate effect of Zeno's arguments was to stress the need to study the definitions and foundations of mathematics more closely. The PYTHAGOREANS also provided the first general proof of the so-called Pythagorean theorem (see PYTHAGORUS, THEOREM OF) and discovered the existence of IRRATIONAL NUMBERS, then known as incommensurable magnitudes.

The discovery of incommensurable magnitudes made it clear that Pythagorean arithmetic was insufficient to express such geometric quantities as the diagonal of a square. EUDOXUS OF CNIDUS later solved the dilemma by working out a theory of proportion. This trend was reinforced by PLATO, the teacher of Eudoxus, who regarded geometry as the model of certain reasoning.

Geometry and Trigonometry. The best-known mathematician of antiquity is EUCLID (fl. 3d century BC), whose *Elements of Geometry* provides a systematic treatment of geometry.

The greatest mathematician of ancient times, judged by the quality of his own original work, was ARCHIMEDES (287–212 BC), who applied the method of exhaustion to determine rigorously the areas and volumes of numerous geometric figures. Eudoxus, ARISTARCHUS OF SAMOS, HIPPARCHUS of Nicaea, and PTOLEMY made fundamental contributions in developing geometric models for planetary motions. The last of the noteworthy geometers of ancient times was Pappus (fl. 3d century AD).

In the *Almagest* Ptolemy introduced a kind of trigonometry, and also provided the rudiments of SPHERICAL TRIGONOMETRY.

Islamic and Medieval Mathematics

After the fall of the Roman Empire in the western Mediterranean, the Greco-Roman tradition was maintained and transmitted to the Latin West by Islamic scholars. Because Arabic science was greatly interested in astronomy, considerable attention was devoted to Ptolemy's *Almagest* and to the advance of trigonometry. The astron-

The mathematical tables and diagrams illustrated are from a 13th-century Arabic edition of the Almagest, *a scientific encyclopedia compiled by the Greek astronomer Ptolemy about AD 140.*

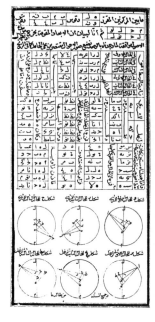
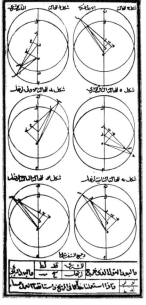

omer Al-Battani advanced the study of spherical trigonometry.

Leonardo Pisano, better known as Fibonacci, wrote his *Liber Abaci* (c.1202), bringing both the Arabic place-valued decimal system and the use of Arabic numerals to the Latin West.

The most striking advance in medieval mathematics was its innovative application of mathematics to physics, particularly to the problems of uniform and accelerated motion.

With the fall of Constantinople (1453) many Eastern scholars left for western Europe and brought knowledge of Greek manuscripts (and often the manuscripts themselves) with them. The astronomer Georg von Peuerbach began a translation of Ptolemy's *Almagest* that one of his students, Regiomontanus, completed. In Italy artists studied Vitruvius, applied geometry to the construction of great buildings, and pioneered in the mathematical study of perspective. Leonardo da Vinci and Leon Battista Alberti wrote on the mathematics of perspective.

Early in the 16th century great progress was made in algebra. In Italy Niccolò Tartaglia discovered general solutions for cubic equations, which were eventually published by Gerolamo Cardano in his *Ars magna* (1545). Cases involving imaginary roots were treated by Rafaello Bombelli in his *Algebra* (1572). In the late 16th century François Viète demonstrated the value of symbols by using plus (+) and minus (−) signs for operations, and letters to represent unknowns.

Throughout the 16th century, in keeping with the importance of bookkeeping and calculation, mathematicians sought better notation and quicker methods. With this incentive a Flemish mathematician, Simon Stevin of Bruges, introduced decimal fractions, and John Napier of Scotland invented logarithms.

Mathematics in the Seventeenth and Eighteenth Centuries

The mathematical discoveries of the 17th century were stimulated by the revolution in physics and astronomy. Galileo proved that the paths followed by projectiles were always parabolic. The 17th century also saw the birth of analytic geometry, calculus, number theory, and probability theory.

Analytic Geometry. In his *Discours de la methode* (*Discourse on Method,* 1637) the French philosopher René Descartes championed the logic of mathematics. He also brought algebra and geometry together in the form of analytic, or coordinate, geometry. Analytic geometry made possible for the first time the graphic representation of functions and allowed the properties of a wide variety of curves to be determined systematically and with considerable precision. An important early contribution of analytic geometry was its role in helping to solve the so-called problem of tangents, that is, the determination of a line that lies tangent to a given curve at a given point. Such mathematicians as Pierre de Fermat, Christiaan Huygens, Descartes, and William Wallace all worked on the subject.

Calculus. By about 1650 the essential components for calculus—analytic geometry, infinitesimal methods, the study of areas, and the problem of tangents—were all

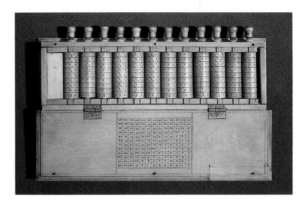

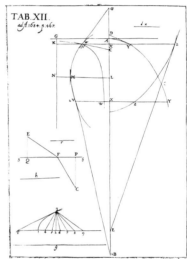

(Above) *A pocket-size mechanical calculator was invented in 1617 by John Napier, who also invented logarithms. It consists of a set of columns, each displaying the digits 0 to 9 and their multiples; multiplication is done by rotating the columns.* (Left) *Gottfried Wilhelm von Leibniz explained his system of differential calculus in 1684 in the journal* Acta Eruditorum. *The first page of his article is seen here.*

present. Within a decade of each other, Sir Isaac Newton and Gottfried Wilhelm von Leibniz discovered independently the fundamental features of the calculus, as well as the connection between integrations and differentiations.

Newton discovered his fluxional calculus in 1665–66, having studied Isaac Barrow's work and John Wallis's *Arithmetic.* Newton thought of curves as generated by the motion of points and viewed his derivatives as velocities. By contrast, the calculus of Leibniz, developed between 1673 and 1676, was influenced by the geometry of Descartes, Huygens, and Pascal. The first account of Leibniz's differential calculus was published in 1684, followed by his integral calculus in 1686. Leibniz invented symbols of such operational utility that they quickly became the standard notation for the new calculus. The symbols for differentials (*dx* and *dy*) and for the integral ($\int$) appear in papers that Leibniz published on the calculus.

Eighteenth-century mathematics was characterized by a further elaboration of the differential and integral calculus. In general, mathematicians abandoned Newton's fluxional calculus in favor of the new methods that Leibniz had presented. Jakob Bernoulli and his son Johann studied Leibniz's papers and assiduously developed the techniques of the calculus and the integration of ordinary DIFFERENTIAL EQUATIONS. By about 1750, Leonhard EULER, who also studied infinite SERIES, had established the well-known trigonometric identity $e^{ix} = \cos x + i \sin x$, and developed a theory of differential equations.

Greatly influenced by Euler's prodigious work, the French mathematician Joseph Louis Comte de LAGRANGE sought to improve the rigor of mathematics by providing purely analytic proofs. Lagrange rejected the method of LIMITS and instead approached the study of functions through their Taylor series. But difficulties with the CONVERGENCE of such series and the discovery of functions that had no Taylor series limited the success of his approach. By 1800, Pierre Simon de LAPLACE had established the Newtonian world system with the best mathematics of the day in his *Traité de mecanique céleste* (*Treatise on Celestial Mechanics,* 1799–1825).

Number Theory and Probability. There was also considerable interest in number theory and probability in the 17th and 18th centuries. Pierre de Fermat studied probability in the context of games of chance and eventually found important applications.

Nineteenth- and Twentieth-Century Mathematics

While mathematics continued to be applied to the standard problems of physics and astronomy, pure mathematics came to be increasingly studied. Calculus broadened into analysis (those areas making use of concepts of calculus such as the limit).

Analysis, Geometry, and Number Theory. In Germany the work of Carl Friedrich GAUSS covered most major areas of pure and applied mathematics. His most impressive single work, published in 1801, provided a thorough and innovative treatment of number theory. Gauss also succeeded in giving a physical interpretation to COMPLEX NUMBERS by representing them in terms of points on a two-dimensional plane. In applied mathematics Gauss studied geodosy and the motion of the planets and wrote a masterful treatise on the LEAST-SQUARES METHOD. Gauss's surviving notebooks and papers show that he had also discovered NON-EUCLIDEAN GEOMETRY.

The textbooks of Augustin Louis CAUCHY, published in 1821 and 1823 and designed for students at France's famous École Polytechnique (founded 1794), were concerned with developing the basic theorems of the calculus as rigorously as possible. Other French mathematicians who produced important books in connection with their teaching include A. M. Legendre and Gaspard MONGE.

Mathematical physics made rapid progress in the hands of such theoreticians as Lagrange, Monge, Joseph Fourier, S. D. Poisson, and Cauchy, as well as through the work of A. M. AMPÈRE. In carrying out a mathematical treatment of heat, Fourier established that any arbitrary function could be represented by a trigonometric series of specific form, the so-called Fourier series central to FOURIER ANALYSIS.

The German mathematician P. G. L. Dirichlet was the first to develop rigorously the use of the Fourier series. The most immediate influence of Dirichlet was on his student Bernhard RIEMANN. In his study of complex functions, Riemann introduced the concept of the Riemann surface, thus relating TOPOLOGY to analysis.

Riemann's discovery of a continuous, nondifferentiable function showed the inadequacy of geometric intuition as a guide in analysis; mathematicians had always assumed that any continuous function must possess derivatives. Among the most important mathematicians in the 19th century to stress the need for new methods of analysis was Karl Theodor WEIERSTRASS, who emphasized the rigor of proceeding arithmetically—defining, for example, irrational numbers as limits of convergent series. Leopold Kronecker was greatly opposed to the sort of analysis developed by Weierstrass and advocated, instead of infinite processes, the reduction of all mathematics to arguments involving only the integers and a finite number of steps.

Kronecker's opposition to any use of the infinite in mathematics left him adamantly opposed to transfinite SET THEORY, created by Georg CANTOR in the 1880s.

As analysis was making rapid progress in the 19th century, so, too, were geometry and the new fields to which it gave rise. PROJECTIVE GEOMETRY was simultaneously discovered early in the century by Joseph Gergonne and Poncelet. In the 1820s, August Ferdinand Möbius and Julius Plücker in Germany, Michel Chasles in France, and Arthur Cayley in England emphasized algebraic geometry. Möbius is also known for his pioneering efforts in topology, and for his MÖBIUS STRIP, a theoretical surface having only one side.

Among the most controversial discoveries of the 19th century were non-Euclidean geometries. Simultaneously, Nikolai Ivanovich LOBACHEVSKY and János BOLYAI realized (as had Gauss earlier) that alternative axioms could be introduced for which the resulting geometries were non-Euclidean but perfectly consistent. Topology, known as *analysis situs* in the 19th century, also grew out of geometry, as did the 20th-century concept of fractional dimensions (see GEOMETRY, FRACTAL).

Late in the 19th century, French mathematics came to rival that of Germany. Following Joseph Liouville's proof of the existence of TRANSCENDENTAL NUMBERS, Charles Hermite proved in 1873 that e was such a number, and in 1882, Ferdinand Lindemann established that π was also transcendental. Hermite came to be the leading exponent of analysis in France at the end of the century. Among his contemporaries and followers were figures such as René Baire, Émile Borel, J. S. Hadamard, H. L. Lebesgue, and C. E. Picard. The greatest mathematician in France at the end of the century was Henri POINCARÉ, whose interests covered nearly every field of creative mathematics. His observation that apparently deterministic systems could show chaotic behavior, for example, presaged the development of CHAOS THEORY in the later 20th century (see also CATASTROPHE THEORY).

Whereas analysis and geometry received great attention on the Continent, English mathematicians tended to pursue algebra and its applications to geometry. Continental mathematics was eventually promoted in England, however, by such mathematicians as Charles BABBAGE and Sir John HERSCHEL. Algebra in England also took the form of BOOLEAN ALGEBRA, promulgated by George BOOLE. Important contributions by Englishmen to symbolic LOGIC included the work of Bertrand RUSSELL and Alfred North WHITEHEAD in the 20th century.

Other branches of mathematics that led to important areas of activity in the 20th century include the study of tensor analysis and DIFFERENTIAL GEOMETRY, and abstract algebra, including the study of fields, groups, and rings. Group theory, with which names such as Evariste Galois and Camille Jordan are associated, was one of the great discoveries and unifying principles of the late 19th century. Group theory made possible the unification of geometry and algebra.

Philosophy of Mathematics. The discovery of paradoxes in set theory has led to attempts to ensure that mathematics be kept free of paradoxes and contradictions. Gottlob FREGE, Giuseppe Peano, Augustus De Morgan, and the English mathematicians Whitehead and Russell, working in the spirit of Boole, stressed logicism, which posits the priority of logic and assumes that mathematical objects can be defined within the framework of logic. Then the properties of these objects can be proven using normal logical methods.

A second approach followed the work of David HILBERT, who proposed to formalize relevant parts of mathematics with the aid of an artificial language of logic, and to prove by means of finite mathematics that no paradoxes can be derived in the formal system. Hilbert's work, known as formalism, was taken up by John VON NEUMANN and Kurt GÖDEL, among others, and was dealt a severe setback when Gödel proved in 1931 with his incompleteness theorem that no axiomatic approach could be sufficient to determine the consistency of any branch of mathematics. Another approach followed the work of Kronecker, who believed that mathematics should deal only with finite numbers and with a finite number of operations.

mathematics, new   see MATHEMATICS, EDUCATION IN

Mather (family) [math'-ur]   The Mather family exerted tremendous influence on the shape and direction of PURITANISM in Massachusetts for three generations. **Richard Mather**, b. England, 1596, d. 1669, left (1635) for the Massachusetts Bay Colony, where he was immediately recognized as a leader of the distinctive theology and church organization that was developing there. He served as minister in Dorchester, Mass., for 33 years and published the first careful explanation of CONGREGATIONALISM. He argued against those who wanted to form a regulating assembly, or presbytery, which could control local churches through its decisions. His defense of cooperating but independent church units formed the basic structure of the Cambridge Platform (1648), which shaped Congregationalist self-consciousness for centuries afterward.

One of Richard's six sons was **Increase Mather**, b. Dorchester, Mass., June 21, 1639, d. Aug. 23, 1723. As minister (1664) of Boston's Second Congregational Church (New North Church), he shaped the lives and val-

Cotton Mather, a 17th-century American Congregational minister and scholar, is remembered primarily for his apologetic accounts of the Salem Witch Trials and for several ecclesiastic histories that record the decline of Puritan orthodoxy in America.

ues of second-generation New England Puritans according to established traditional guidelines. At first he opposed the HALFWAY COVENANT compromise on church membership but later defended it. In 1688 he went to England where, after three years, he succeeded in negotiating a renewed charter for Massachusetts. Increase was president of Harvard from 1685 to 1701.

Another significant family member was **Cotton Mather**, b. Boston, Feb. 12, 1663, d. Feb. 13, 1728, son of Increase, named for his maternal grandfather, John Cotton. During his 43 years as preacher and pastor he wrote 450 books on a variety of topics. His long history, *Magnalia Christi Americana* (1702), is a classic memorial to early Puritan efforts to establish their version of Christianity in the Western Hemisphere. Cotton also helped initiate the Salem Witch Trials, but later he criticized the executions.

Sensitive to the decline of vital religion and intolerant of secularism, Cotton criticized New Englanders for their failings and attempted to revive the piety of earlier generations in an age when the old forms commanded less respect.

Mathewson, Christy   Christopher Mathewson, b. Factoryville, Pa., Aug. 12, 1880, d. Oct. 7, 1925, was an American professional baseball player whose pitching skills enabled him to win 373 games (with only 188 losses) during his career. The right-handed Mathewson, whose best pitch was the "screwball," played for the New York Giants from 1900 to 1916. In 1903 he won 30 games, the first of 3 consecutive seasons in which he won 30 or more games. Mathewson became the mainstay of the last-place Giants, and he led them to the pennant in 1904. For the next 10 years Mathewson was baseball's premier pitcher, winning 22 or more games each season. He was equally overpowering in World Series play and still holds records for most complete games (10) and for shutouts (4). When the Baseball Hall of Fame was founded in 1936, he was one of the first five players to be inducted.

Mathias, Bob [muh-thy'-uhs]   Robert Bruce Mathias, b. Tulare, Calif., Nov. 17, 1930, was the boy-wonder of track and field who won the Olympic Games decathlon at the age of 17. As a high school senior Mathias learned of the 10-event competition for the first time and was persuaded to try it. He astounded the world and won the 1948 Olympic decathlon.

Four years later he again won this coveted Olympic gold medal. His 1952 victory set a world-record point total for the event, the third in his short career. He retired at the age of 21, unbeaten in 10 decathlons. Mathias went on to serve several terms as a Republican congressperson, in addition to serving (1977–83) as the director of the U.S. Olympic Training Centers.

Matilda   The daughter of HENRY I of England and mother of HENRY II, Matilda, b. February 1102, d. Sept. 10, 1167, was frustrated in her ambition to become queen of England. She first married (1114) Holy Roman Emperor HENRY V. After his death (1125) she returned to England, where she was recognized (1127) as her father's heir. Matilda's waspish personality and her unpopular marriage (1128) to Geoffrey Plantagenet, count of Anjou, alienated her supporters. On Henry I's death in 1135, Matilda's cousin STEPHEN was proclaimed king, and she went to war to claim her inheritance. For a few months in 1141 she held the upper hand in the conflict, but she was never crowned. Matilda left England in 1148, spending her remaining years in Normandy. In 1154, however, Henry, her eldest son by Geoffrey, succeeded to the English throne.

Matilda of Tuscany   Matilda of Tuscany, known as the Grand Countess, b. 1046, d. July 24, 1115, was famous for her opposition to the Holy Roman emperors and her support of the papacy during the INVESTITURE CONTROVERSY. Orphaned as a child, Matilda was sole heir to the vast lands of the house of Canossa in central Italy. She was a staunch supporter of Pope GREGORY VII against Emperor HENRY IV, and her castle at Canossa was the site in 1077 of a meeting between them in which the pope accepted the emperor's penance. Matilda made large donations of jewels and land to the papacy but also willed property to Emperor HENRY V, thus provoking a quarrel between empire and papacy over the control of Tuscany after her death.

matins   see DIVINE OFFICE

Matisse, Henri [mah-tees']   Henri Matisse, b. Dec. 31, 1869, d. Nov. 3, 1954, ranks among the greatest painters of the 20th century. During the 1890s, Matisse met Charles Camoin, Georges Rouault, and Albert Marquet, painters of his age who, with Maurice Vlaminck, André Derain, and Georges Braque, were to join with him in forming the Fauve group (see FAUVISM). "Les Fauves," or "Wild Beasts," was a derogatory label applied to these artists when they exhibited together in Paris in 1905. Their imagery—composed of strokes of bright, often

The prolific output of the 20th-century French artist Henri Matisse—as in his still-life painting Flowering Ivy (1941)—is characterized by its bold and decorative use of vivid Fauvist color. (Private collection, New York City.)

clashing, color—defied all traditional canons of competent painting and shocked the general public. Recognizable subjects appear in the paintings of the Fauves—portraits, still lifes, and interiors are especially prevalent. However, these motifs are used as pretexts for pictorial innovation, sometimes tending toward pure abstraction. Typical of Matisse's painting during this period is *Woman with a Hat: Madame Matisse* (1905; private collection, California), in which the sitter's dress, skin, and feathered hat are rendered in an unnaturalistic pattern of energetically brushed greens, pinks, and lavenders. The masterpieces of his early work are a series of large canvases titled *The Dance* (1910; Museum of Modern Western Art, Moscow).

Under the influence of cubism, Matisse's palette became more somber and his shapes took on a geometrical severity—as in *The Moroccans* (1916; Museum of Modern Art, New York City) and *The Piano Lesson* (c.1917; Museum of Modern Art). During the 1920s his color brightened again and his patterns became more complex, especially in his *Odalisques*, female nudes against arabesques of North African fabrics.

Matisse carried the expressive freedom of his Fauve manner into sculpture, which first achieved distinctive individuality in the flowing, semiabstract forms of *La Serpentine* (1909; Museum of Art, Baltimore, Md.) and *The Back* (1909–30; Museum of Modern Art), a series of monumental figure studies. In 1931–33 he returned to an earlier theme in *The Dance*, a pair of large mural paintings, one of which is at the Barnes Foundation, Merion, Pa.

From 1944 to the end of his life, Matisse produced *découpés*, in which he cut shapes from colored paper and pasted them onto fields of white. These works, which achieve an ultimate blending of Matisse's vibrant color with the energetic flow of his line, are considered by many to be his best. Matisse's supreme accomplishment was to liberate color from its traditionally realistic function and to make it the foundation of a decorative art of the highest order.

matriarchy Matriarchy is a hypothetical system of social organization in which familial and political authority is held by women. Conceptions about matriarchy were developed by 19th-century evolutionists, anthropologists, and historians, whose ideas about society and social evolution were influenced by Darwin's theories of biological evolution. Their notions were based on conjecture and inference, not on study of an actual matriarchy. Arguing from logical principles rather than from direct evidence, they concluded that an earlier stage of social evolution must have been matriarchal.

The real-life type of social organization that most resembles the matriarchal society is matrilineal social organization, in which descent is traced through women (see KINSHIP). In such a society a household usually consists of a woman and her husband; their unmarried daughters and sons; and married daughters, their husbands, and their children. Authority over such a matrilineal household, however, is in the hands of a male, most commonly the brother of the oldest woman. In a matrilineal society, property and position are inherited matrilineally—by men who trace their relationship through women—passing from a man to his sister's son rather than to his own son. This situation occurs because fathers and sons belong to different matriclans (see CLAN), whereas maternal uncles and nephews belong to the same clan.

matrix (mathematics) see ALGEBRA

Matsu see QUEMOY

Matsuoka Yosuke [maht-soo'-oh-kah yoh-soo'-kay] Matsuoka Yosuke, b. Mar. 3, 1880, d. June 27, 1946, was a Japanese diplomat and statesman. After serving as president of the South Manchuria Railway, he became foreign minister (1940–41). In that capacity he concluded the Tripartite, or Axis, Pact with Germany and Italy in 1940 and a nonaggression pact with the USSR in 1941. An ardent war supporter who pressed for Japanese invasions of Southeast Asia and opposed Japanese-U.S. negotiations, Matsuoka was relieved of office in July 1941 by Premier KONOE FUMIMARO. He died in Tokyo while awaiting trial as a war criminal.

Matta Echaurren, Roberto Sebastián [mayt'-tah ek-har'-ren, roh-bair'-toh seh-bahs-tee-ahn'] Roberto Sebastián Matta Echaurren, b. Santiago, Chile, Nov. 11, 1912, is the last important painter of the surrealist movement (see SURREALISM, art). In 1934 he studied architecture under Le Corbusier in Paris, where he met the French surrealists, whose group he joined in 1937. In 1939, Matta went to the United States. At first he was influenced by Yves Tanguy, but in 1944 he met Marcel Duchamp, who had a more decisive impact on his art. Matta changed his painting style in the 1940s from one consisting of atmospheric effects and molten colors to a more linear style.

matter Matter is any substance that possesses MASS and occupies space. Thus, gases, liquids, solids, and plasmas are all different forms of matter. Because electromagnetic radiation is known to possess mass, it may be useful for some purposes to consider radiation also to be a form of matter.

The atomic theory of matter holds that all matter is made up of molecules, which in turn are composed of atoms; it has been established that about 100 distinct elementary atoms exist (see ELEMENTS) that can bind together to form myriad different molecules. Atoms themselves are composed of subatomic bits of matter (see FUNDAMENTAL PARTICLES). With the discovery of the electron, proton, and finally—in 1932—the neutron, it was thought that knowledge of the atom was complete. Beginning in the 1940s, though, a vast array of new particles was discovered, some produced by cosmic rays and some produced by high-energy accelerators. Most of these particles are unstable. Some of them are believed to play a role in the internal structure of the nucleus.

A possibility is now beginning to emerge that all matter may consist of a small number of more elementary particles. Some of these particles, called QUARKS, have fractional charges and other unusual properties. Neutrons and protons have an internal structure that involves three quarks and are therefore members of the class of particles called HADRONS. Electrons are members of another class of elementary particles: LEPTONS. A third type of elementary particle, BOSONS, are involved in the transmission of the fundamental forces of nature. The properties of hadrons, leptons, and bosons are described by the modern theories of QUANTUM ELECTRODYNAMICS and QUANTUM CHROMODYNAMICS. Scientists have found evidence for the existence of ANTIMATTER—composed of particles equal in mass but opposite in charge to their ordinary-matter analogues—but are uncertain as to its amount in the universe. They are also investigating the possibility of even finer structures in ordinary matter.

See also: FUNDAMENTAL INTERACTIONS; KINETIC THEORY OF MATTER.

Matterhorn The Matterhorn (French: Mont Cervin) is the third highest peak of the Alps and of Europe outside the USSR. It is located in the Pennine Range on the Switzerland-Italy border about 10 km (6 mi) southwest of Zermatt, Switzerland. Although only about 4,480 m (14,700 ft) high, it is difficult to climb because of its towering cliffs. More climbers have died on the Matterhorn than on any other Alpine peak.

Edward Whymper, a British explorer, led the first successful ascent on July 14, 1865. Four of the seven men in the expedition died on the way down, however, starting myths that the mountain was protected by spirits. The first ascent of the very steep and dangerous southeast side was made in 1911 by a party led by Mario Piacenza.

Matthew, Saint   In the New Testament of the Bible, Saint Matthew was the tax collector called by Jesus Christ to be one of the 12 apostles (Matt. 9:9). Matthew has often been identified with Levi, the son of Alphaeus, also a tax collector (Mark 2:14; Luke 5:27–28). Although traditionally he has been regarded as the author of the first Gospel, modern scholarship strongly disputes this attribution. Matthew's symbol as an evangelist is an angel, and in art he is often depicted with sword and money bag. Feast day: Sept. 21 (Western); Nov. 16 (Eastern).

Matthew, Gospel According to   The Gospel According to Matthew is the opening book of the New Testament of the Bible. Although first in canonical order, it is probably not the earliest Gospel. Besides drawing heavily from Mark, Matthew shapes material from other sources around Mark's narrative outline. One such source, commonly called Q (from the German *quelle,* "source"), is thought to have consisted primarily of sayings of Jesus; it was also used by Luke. Material unique to this Gospel relates to the birth of Jesus (1–2), the arrangement of the Sermon on the Mount (5–7), and Jesus' utterances on the end of the world (24–25).

Matthew is generally held to have been written about AD 80, although scholars have argued for dates as early as 65 and as late as 100. Tradition ascribes authorship to the apostle Matthew, but modern scholars, acknowledging Matthew as a source, contend that a disciple or school of disciples were responsible for its present form.

Matthew is the most topical of the Synoptic Gospels. The teachings and sayings of Jesus are gathered into five thematic discourses and structured around Mark's narrative framework. Each discourse is followed by a summary statement (7:28; 11:1; 13:53; 19:1; 28:1). A prologue and epilogue are added (1–2; 28:9–20). Because of the emphasis on law, teaching, and righteousness, scholars believe that Matthew was addressed to a predominantly Jewish audience, presumably in Palestine or Syria. Jesus is presented as the messianic fulfiller, especially in the role of king, and the teacher of the way of righteousness.

Matthews, D. H.   see PLATE TECTONICS

Matthews, Sir Stanley   The Englishman Sir Stanley Matthews, b. Feb. 1, 1915, is a legendary figure of soccer history. He played as a winger and possessed seemingly magical ball and body control. Matthews's professional career lasted an incredible 33 years. He began playing professionally in 1932, played for Stoke City and Blackpool, and retired in 1965, at the age of 50. That same year he became Sir Stanley Matthews, the first professional soccer player to be knighted. He was usually double-teamed and frequently fouled, but he bore it all stoically. When the European Footballer of the Year award was instituted in 1956, Matthews was the first winner.

Matthias, Saint   [muh-thy'-uhs]   In the New Testament, Matthias was the apostle chosen by lot to replace Judas Iscariot (Acts 1:15–26). According to one tradition, he preached the gospel in Ethiopia. Feast day: May 14 (Roman); Feb. 24 (other Western); Aug. 9 (Eastern).

Matthias, Holy Roman Emperor   Matthias, b. Feb. 24, 1557, d. Mar. 20, 1619, was Holy Roman emperor (1612–19), king of Hungary (1608–18), and king of Bohemia (1611–17). As the third son of Emperor MAXIMILIAN II, he had no dominions to rule for a long time. In 1577 he accepted the invitation of the States-General of the Netherlands to become governor-general, but he resigned in 1581. Between 1605 and 1611 he led the opposition to his elder brother RUDOLF II, whom he succeeded on the thrones of Hungary and Bohemia and, later, as emperor. Unable to cope with the Bohemian Protestant rebellion of 1618, which initiated the THIRTY YEARS' WAR, Matthias was pushed aside as king of Bohemia and Hungary by his cousin Ferdinand, who succeeded him as Emperor FERDINAND II on his death.

Matthias Corvinus, King of Hungary   [kor-vy'-nuhs]   Matthias Corvinus, also known as Matthias I Hunyadi, b. Feb. 23, 1440, d. Apr. 6, 1490, was king of Hungary (1458–90) and one of the great figures of Hungarian history. The son of the national hero János HUNYADI, Matthias was elected to the throne after the death of Ladislas V. An advocate of royal centralization, Matthias limited the power of the barons by relying on the lesser nobility and the burghers. He reorganized the government, built a large standing army, fostered manufacturing and commerce, and streamlined taxation. Matthias secured Hungary's southern frontiers and also conquered Moravia, Silesia, and much of Austria, with the goal of becoming Holy Roman emperor. Between 1469 and 1478 some of the nobility in Bohemia attempted to have him recognized as king of that country, but they failed. A great patron of Renaissance art and humanist learning, Matthias founded two universities—at Pozsony (now Bratislava) and Buda; his royal court at Buda emerged as the greatest Renaissance center east of Italy and Germany.

Matthiessen, F. O.   [math'-i-sen]   The noted American writer Francis Otto Matthiessen, b. Pasadena, Calif., Feb. 19, 1902, d. Apr. 1, 1950, was an important force in shaping scholarly criticism of American literature. Matthiessen's *American Renaissance: The Age of Emerson and Whitman* (1941) is a seminal survey. During his brilliant career Matthiessen produced books on Sarah Jewett (1929), Henry James (1944), and Theodore Dreiser (1951) and edited *The Oxford Book of American Verse* (1950). In the 1940s he became a tragic victim of right-wing anti-Communist crusaders, committing suicide at the age of 48.

matzo   see PASSOVER

Mau Mau [mow' mow]   The Mau Mau was an anti-European guerrilla movement among the KIKUYU people of British-ruled Kenya in the 1950s. European settlement and missionary work had led to widespread social disruption among the Kikuyu tribe. Disaffected Kikuyu began to advocate the expulsion of European farmers and to call for the restoration of their ancient African customs. They banded together by oath to achieve this aim.

After a lengthy period of unrest, dating at least from the 1930s, discontented Kikuyu took to guerrilla warfare. In 1952 the colonial government of Kenya declared a state of emergency. By 1956 about 100 Europeans and at least 2,000 Kikuyu "loyalists" had been killed. Government forces gradually hunted down the rebel gangs, killing more than 11,000, and in 1960 the state of emergency ended. The Mau Mau rebellion, however, helped to persuade the British to grant independence (1963) to Kenya. Jomo KENYATTA, supposedly the leader of the Mau Mau movement, became Kenya's first prime minister, although the guerrilla fighters of the forests benefited little from independence.

Mauchly, John William [mawch'-lee]   The American physicist John William Mauchly, b. Cincinnati, Ohio, Aug. 30, 1907, d. Jan. 8, 1980, made major contributions to the invention of electronic digital COMPUTERS. Mauchly studied physics at The Johns Hopkins University from 1925 to 1932, became head of the physics department at Ursinus College in Collegeville, Pa., in 1933, and joined the Moore School of Electrical Engineering of the University of Pennsylvania in 1941.

Mauchly's interest in developing computers began in his student days. At Ursinus he constructed an analog computer to analyze weather data. From 1942 to 1946 he collaborated with J. Presper Eckert and others at the Moore School to build the ENIAC computer. The first large electronic computer, ENIAC increased processing speeds a thousand times. With John VON NEUMANN, Mauchly and Eckert designed the EDVAC computer, which initiated the use of programs read into the computer to establish the sequence of operations.

Eckert and Mauchly formed a corporation to build computers in 1946. They began work on the UNIVAC I computer (see UNIVAC) in 1948 and completed it in 1951. Remington Rand absorbed the Eckert-Mauchly Corporation in 1950.

Maudslay, Henry [mawdz'-lee]   Henry Maudslay was an English maker of machine tools whose inventions spurred the growth of British industry in the early 19th century. Maudslay, b. Aug. 22, 1771, d. Feb. 14, 1831, learned his trade in the workshops of Joseph Bramah, where he helped to develop the slide rest, a lathe improvement that made metal turning faster and far more accurate. As an independent machinist, he invented a lathe for producing accurate screw threads, making possible for the first time the manufacture of screws and nuts in standard sizes. Maudslay's 44 special-purpose machines produced finished ship pulleys in what has been described as the first fully mechanized production line. Many brilliant English inventors trained in his shop, among them Sir Joseph Whitworth and James Nasmyth.

Maugham, W. Somerset [mawm]   William Somerset Maugham, b. Paris, Jan. 25, 1874, d. Dec. 16, 1965, was an English playwright and novelist and one of the most popular writers of the 20th century. The best of Maugham's 31 plays—*Our Betters* (1915), *The Circle* (1921), and *The Constant Wife* (1927)—are minor masterpieces. Classic English drawing-room comedies, they are perceptive stories of love, marriage, and adultery. Other notable comedies—*Lady Frederick* (1903), his first hit, and *Mrs. Dot* (1904)—deal with adultresses. These plays were followed by more serious but less successful ones. When *Sheppey* (1933) failed, he gave up playwriting. Maugham's best-known novel, *Of Human Bondage* (1915), is in part a fictionalization of his own unhappy youth. Among his other important novels are *The Moon and Sixpence* (1919), a thinly veiled life of the painter Paul Gauguin; *Ashenden* (1928), based on Maugham's work in wartime intelligence; *Cakes and Ale* (1930), a satire thought to portray Thomas Hardy and Hugh Walpole; and *The Razor's Edge* (1944), about a young American's mystical quest for fulfillment. The most famous of his short stories—many of which are set in the Far East—is "Miss Thompson," which describes a Puritan missionary's ruin by a prostitute; it was dramatized as *Rain* (1922). *The Summing Up* (1938) is Maugham's urbane memoir. *A Writer's Notebook* (1949) and *The Vagrant Mood* (1952) contain critical essays.

Somerset Maugham's most memorable work, the novel Of Human Bondage (1915), is a semi-autobiographical account of a crippled student's painful progress toward maturity.

Maui [mow'-ee]   Maui, second largest of the volcanic Hawaiian Islands, is situated between Molokai and Hawaii islands. It comprises 1,886 km² (728 mi²) and has a population of 100,374 (1990). The island is noted for its sugarcane and pineapple production, although tourism is also a major source of income. Maui consists of two dormant volcanoes linked by an 11-km-wide (7-mi) valley isthmus. The eastern peak, Haleakala, rising to 3,056 m (10,025 ft), has one of the world's largest craters (see HALEAKALA CRATER); the area is contained in Haleakala National Park. In western Maui are the island's largest towns—Wailuku, seat of Maui County; Kahului; and Lahaina.

Mauldin, Bill [mawl'-din]   William Henry "Bill" Mauldin, b. Mountain Park, N.Mex., Oct. 29, 1921, first gained fame with his World War II cartoons for *Stars and Stripes* and later with his editorial cartoons for the *St. Louis Post-Dispatch* and then the *Chicago Sun-Times*. He won Pulitzer Prizes for editorial cartooning in 1945 and 1959. *Up Front* (1945) is a collection of his war cartoons; *Back Home* (1947) treats problems of adjusting to civilian life. Two other collections, *A Sort of Saga* (1949) and *The Brass Ring* (1971), are autobiographical.

Maulpertsch, Franz Anton [mowl'-pairch, frahnts ahn'-tohn]   Franz Anton Maulpertsch, b. June 8, 1724, d. Aug. 8, 1796, was the foremost Austrian painter and etcher of the baroque period. The dynamic compositions and swirling forms in his ceiling frescoes seem to open the ceilings to the sky, a favorite baroque illusionistic device. Influenced by such Italian artists as Tiepolo, as well as by the Bavarian Asam brothers, Maulpertsch worked with a bold, rapid brush stroke. However, the Vienna Academy regarded his work as too daring and denied him support.

Mauna Kea [mow'-nuh kay'-uh]   Mauna Kea is a large dormant volcano and the highest mountain in the state of Hawaii. It is located on north central Hawaii Island, about 43 km (27 mi) northwest of Hilo. Measuring 4,205 m (13,796 ft) high above sea level, it extends an additional 5,547 m (18,200 ft) to the ocean floor. Thus, from base to peak it is the highest individual mountain in the world. It was last active more than 4,000 years ago; its snow-covered cone is the site of Mauna Kea Observatory. The mountain's upper slopes have caves where ancient Hawaiians dug basalt for tools. The lower slopes support large cattle ranches and coffee plantations. The mountain is regarded in Hawaiian legend as the home of the goddess Poliahu, who is the rival of Pele, the fire goddess of Mauna Loa.

Mauna Kea Observatory   Mauna Kea Observatory—founded in 1967 in affiliation with the University of Hawaii and located at the top of the dormant volcano for which it is named—is the site of an assortment of powerful astronomical instruments. A combination of dry, rarefied air and protection by clouds from lights below make Mauna Kea perhaps the best place in the Northern Hemisphere for nighttime observation. Its telescopes include

an 88-in (2.24-m) optical and infrared reflector, a 152-in (3.76-m) infrared reflector, and a 144-in (3.6-m) optical and infrared reflector. Under construction are a pair of millimeter- and submillimeter-range telescopes, as well as 2 optical telescopes, which when finished will be the world's largest. Called the Keck I and Keck II, respectively, each will have a 400-in (10-m) reflector composed of 36 hexagonal mirrors. Keck I will be operational in 1992, Keck II in 1996.

Mauna Loa [mow'-nuh loh'-uh]   Mauna Loa is a massive, active volcano that occupies most of the south central part of Hawaii Island. About 65 km (40 mi) southwest of Hilo, it is 4,170 m (13,680 ft) high, about 120 km (75 mi) long, and 105 km (65 mi) wide—the largest mountain in the world in cubic mass. Its principal active features, contained in the Hawaii Volcanoes National Park, include the summit crater, Mokuaweoweo, at an altitude of 4,115 m (13,500 ft); the 1,250-m-high (4,100-ft) KILAUEA crater with the fire pit Halemaumau on its crater floor; and the newly developed Mauna Ulu, active from 1969 to 1974.

Maupassant, Guy de [moh-pah-sahn', gee]   The French writer Guy de Maupassant, b. Aug. 5, 1850, d. July 6, 1893, is one of the world's most celebrated masters of the short story and the most widely translated French author. Born in Normandy, where he spent an unhappy childhood, he later served in the Franco-Prussian War, studied law in Paris, and entered the civil service—experiences frequently evoked in his stories. The most significant influence on his artistic career was that of Gustave Flaubert, a family friend who became the young writer's mentor, reading his first efforts and introducing him to important novelists such as Émile Zola and Henry James. It was in Zola's naturalist group that Maupassant made his name, when he submitted the story "Boule-de-Suif" (1880; Eng. trans., "Ball-of-Tallow," 1899) to a collection of war tales, *Les Soirées de Médan* (1880).

Most of Maupassant's fiction—which included six novels and about 300 short stories—was written in the decade that followed. His story collections include *La Maison Tellier* (1881; Eng. trans., 1932), *Mademoiselle Fifi* (1882; Eng. trans., 1922), and *Miss Harriet* (1884; Eng. trans., 1923). Among his novels the best known is the semiautobiographical *Bel-Ami* (1885; Eng. trans., 1891); an even better novel, however, is his *Pierre and Jean* (1888; trans. as *The Two Brothers*, 1890), an exercise in narrative objectivity, on a par with the best of his stories.

After 1891, Maupassant suffered increasingly from the syphilis that he had contracted in his youth. He died totally demented in an asylum.

Mauriac, François [mohr-ee-ahk']   A French Catholic novelist, playwright, essayist, and polemicist, François Mauriac, b. Oct. 11, 1885, d. Sept. 1, 1970, is known chiefly for his fictional treatment of the problem of sin

François Mauriac, a modern French Catholic man of letters, found success as a novelist, playwright, essayist, poet, and journalist. In 1952 he was awarded the Nobel Prize for literature.

and of the suffering that results from spiritual aridity. The 23 novels he published between 1922 and 1954—including *The Desert of Love* (1925; Eng. trans., 1929), *Thérèse* (1927; Eng. trans., 1928), *Vipers' Tangle* (1932; Eng. trans., 1933), and *A Woman of the Pharisees* (1941; Eng. trans., 1946)—mostly set among the bourgeois of his native Bordeaux, show him haunted by the conflicts between the spirit and the flesh, between *God and Mammon* (1929; Eng. trans., 1936), as a nonfictional statement of his beliefs is titled. Mauriac's plays *Asmodée* (1938; Eng. trans., 1939) and *The Egoists* (1945; Eng. trans., 1959), representing, respectively, a modern young Tartuffe and a sadistic old egocentric, were outstanding successes. Elected to the Académie Française in 1933, Mauriac received the Nobel Prize for literature in 1952.

Maurice, Saint [mohr'-is]

Saint Maurice, d. *c.*286, was the leader of the Theban Legion, a group of Egyptian Christians in the Roman army, which, according to a 5th-century source, was massacred by the Emperor Maximian in Gaul for refusing to sacrifice to Roman gods. Evidence exists that a group of soldiers, but not an entire legion, was martyred at Agaunum, now Saint-Maurice-en-Valais, Switzerland. Saint Maurice is the patron saint of infantry soldiers. Feast day: Sept. 22.

Maurice, Frederick Denison

One of the most controversial English theologians of his day, John Frederick Denison Maurice, b. Aug. 29, 1805, d. Apr. 1, 1872, was a founder of the Christian Socialist movement (see CHRISTIAN SOCIALISM). The first edition of his most important book, *The Kingdom of Christ,* appeared in 1838.

An influential preacher and educator whose liberal ideas attracted the young, Maurice helped found the Christian Socialist movement in 1848. Convinced that cooperation and not competition was the rule of the universe, his aim was to Christianize socialists and socialize Christians. Believing in education to change hearts and minds, Maurice founded Queen's College (1848) and the Workingmen's College (1854), both in London.

Maurice of Nassau, Prince of Orange

Maurice of Nassau, b. Nov. 13, 1567, d. Apr. 23, 1625, was a Dutch soldier and statesman. As leader of the armies of the emergent Dutch Republic, he won a series of victories (1590–1604) over the Spanish rulers of the Netherlands.

Maurice was the second son of WILLIAM I, prince of Orange. He was named stadholder (governor) in Holland and Zeeland after his father's assassination in 1584. Under the political guidance of the Land's Advocate of Holland Johan van OLDENBARNEVELT, he became (1589) stadholder in all the other provinces except Friesland. In 1618, Maurice officially became prince of Orange on the death of his elder brother.

As commander of the Dutch armies, Maurice instituted reforms that enabled him in 1597 to drive the Spanish from the territory of the United Provinces. After renewal of the war with Spain in 1621, Maurice's campaigns met with little success. His brother Frederick Henry succeeded him.

Mauritania [mohr-i-tayn'-ee-uh]

Mauritania, a nation located in northwest Africa, is a bridge between Arab Africa to the north and sub-Saharan Africa to the south. Mauritania's southern neighbor is Senegal. On the south-

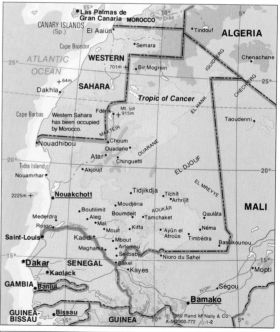

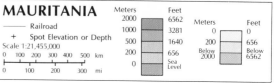

MAURITANIA	Meters	Feet		
—— Railroad	2000	6562	Meters	Feet
+ Spot Elevation or Depth	1000	3281	0	0
Scale 1:21,455,000	500	1640	200	656
0 100 200 300 400 500 km	200	656	Below 2000	Below 6562
0 100 200 300 mi	0	Sea Level		

AT A GLANCE

ISLAMIC REPUBLIC OF MAURITANIA

Land: Area: 1,030,700 km^2 (397,955 mi^2). Capital and largest city: Nouakchott (1987 est. pop., 600,000).

People: Population (1990 est.): 1,934,549. Density: 1.9 persons per km^2 (4.9 per mi^2). Distribution (1987): 34% urban, 66% rural. Official languages: French, Arabic. Major religion: Islam.

Government: Type: military rule. Legislature: none. Political subdivisions: 12 regions, district of Nouakchott.

Economy: GNP (1989): $953 million; $490 per capita. Labor distribution (1985): agriculture—66%; trade, government, and services—24%; manufacturing, mining, public utilities, and construction—10%. Foreign trade (1988): imports—$365 million; exports—$424 million. Currency: 1 ouguiya = 5 khoums.

Education and Health: Literacy (1985): 17% of adult population. Universities (1987): 1. Hospital beds (1984): 1,325. Physicians (1984): 170. Life expectancy (1990): women—49; men—44. Infant mortality (1990): 96 per 1,000 live births.

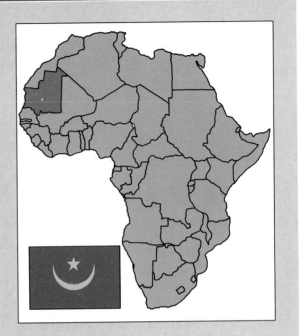

east and east Mauritania adjoins Mali, and on the northeast it borders Algeria. To the west Mauritania has a 700-km (435-mi) coastline on the Atlantic. To the northwest Mauritania borders Morocco and WESTERN SAHARA. Mauritania gained its independence in 1960.

Land

Mauritania's northern region covers two-thirds of the land and is part of the SAHARA. Its terrain consists of sand dunes and rocky plateaus, with altitudes ranging up to 915 m (3,002 ft) at Mount Idjil, the nation's high point. The smaller southern region, composed of the SAHEL and the northern portion of the SENEGAL RIVER valley, has an average altitude of 91 m (300 ft). Except for a few oases in the desert, the alluvial river valley soils provide the country's only arable land. Mauritania's rivers, all tributaries of the Senegal River, are located in the southwest.

Daytime temperature in the desert is usually above 38° C (100° F) for the six hottest months of the year; in the cooler season it is about 24° C (75° F). Rainfall in the desert is undependable and totals less than 100 mm (4 in) a year. In NOUAKCHOTT, the capital, temperatures reach about 33° C (92° F) in the warmest month and average about 13° C (56° F) in the coolest month; rainfall totals about 178 mm (7 in) a year. Rainfall at Sélibaby, in the extreme south, averages 635 mm (25 in) a year.

High-grade iron-ore deposits at Fdérik, in the Sahara,

are the country's principal resource. Copper is found at Akjoujt.

People

Mauritania's population is made up of light- and dark-skinned MOORS of Arab-Berber and African-Sudanic descent and black Africans. Four-fifths of the population live in the Senegal River valley and the Sahel. Traditionally, Moors are seminomads, whereas the black Africans are sedentary farmers. Slavery, officially abolished in 1980, still exists. Arabic and French are the official languages, but the Africans also use tribal languages. Islam is the religion of almost all the population.

The rate of population increase since independence has been almost 3%. Prolonged drought has led to a massive migration to urban areas; the nomadic population—some 83% of the total in 1963—was reduced to only 25% by 1986. Many former nomads live in tent camps at the edges of towns and cities and survive on food aid.

The government allocates a substantial portion of its budget to education, but only a small percentage of children attend school. The University of Nouakchott was established in 1983. Health-care facilities are limited, and average life expectancies are among the world's lowest.

Clans of priest-teachers called marabouts preserve and hand down the Arab-Islamic culture. Drought has caused the disbanding of many clans and the decline of traditional nomadic culture.

Economic Activity

Subsistence agriculture and livestock raising are pursued by some 60% of the population. Settled farming is confined to the Senegal River valley and the oases. Dams are being built along the Senegal River to increase the amount of arable land. The principal crops are millet, sorghum, peanuts, rice, sugarcane, and dates. Before the Sahel drought of 1969–74, Mauritania's farmers grew enough grain to feed the country; by the mid-1980s, however, most foodstuffs had to be imported. Due to drought and overgrazing, the desert is moving southward at about 6.5 km (4 mi) per year. Efforts to restore pastureland by digging wells and stabilizing dunes have met with little success.

The modern sector of the economy is dominated by iron mining (nationalized in 1974) and the rapidly growing fishing industry, which provide nearly all export earnings.

Government

The Military Committee of National Recovery, which assumed power in 1978, abolished the constitution, the National Assembly, the sole political party, and elections. The head of the committee functions as president.

History

Mauritania's first inhabitants were Africans and BERBERS. The ancient kingdom of Ghana gained control of the area in the 10th century but lost it to the invading Almoravids in the 11th century. Mauritanians were converted to Islam; most adopted the Arabic language and culture after conquest by the Beni Hasan in the 16th century. France controlled the area, part of French West Africa, from 1903 until independence in 1960. Mauritania became embroiled in a war with the Algerian-backed Polisario Front guerrillas of the Spanish Sahara, now Western Sahara, after it annexed (1976) the southern third of that former colony. These hostilities brought on a serious economic crisis and led to the overthrow of the government of Moktar Ould Daddah, president since independence, in July 1978. The new government relinquished the Mauritanian claim to Western Sahara in 1979; subsequently Morocco claimed the entire area. Muhammad Ould Haidalla, who became chief of state in 1980, formally recognized the Polisario government in 1984. Haidalla was overthrown in late 1984 in a bloodless coup led by Col. Maawiya Ould Taya. In 1989, a border incident with Senegal resulted in large-scale ethnic violence and the displacement of thousands from each country, including the expulsion of many black Mauritanians to Senegal.

Mauritius [mohr-ish'-uhs] Mauritius is an independent island state in the Indian Ocean, 805 km (500 mi) east of Madagascar. Its outlying territories include the is-

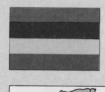
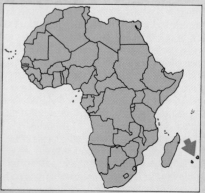

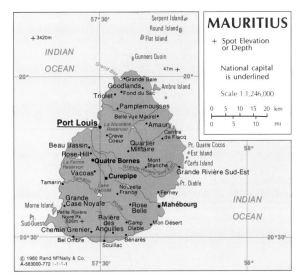

MAURITIUS

+ Spot Elevation
  or Depth

National capital
is underlined

Scale 1:1,246,000

© 1980 Rand McNally & Co.
A-583000-772-1-1-1

land of Rodriguez, situated 554 km (344 mi) eastward and covering 104 km^2 (40 mi^2), and two clusters of islets. Because of its location on ocean trade routes, Mauritius has experienced successive colonization and immigration by French, East Africans, British, Indians, and Chinese.

The island of Mauritius is volcanic and is surrounded by coral reefs. The heavily populated, narrow coastal plains give way to a high plateau (average elevation 500 m/1,650 ft) in the interior. Petite Rivière Noire Peak (826 m/2,710 ft) is the highest point in the country. The climate is tropical, with little seasonal variation in temperature. Rainfall is heaviest (5,080 mm/200 in) on the plateau.

The two largest ethnic groups are Indo-Mauritians (68%) and Creoles (mixed French and African descent, 27%). Chinese and Europeans constitute small minorities. Although English is the official language, Creole—a French patois—is most common. Following the eradication of malaria in the late 1940s, the growth rate increased dramatically. Primary and secondary education are free but not compulsory.

Sugar accounts for nearly 90% of agricultural land use and 40% of exports. To lessen dependence on sugar, the government successfully encouraged the cultivation of tea and food crops and the expansion of light industries (particularly knitwear), tourism, and offshore banking, leading to rapid economic growth in the 1980s and early 1990s.

Although it was explored by the Portuguese (1510) and Dutch (1598), Mauritius—previously uninhabited—was not permanently settled until 1721, when the French occupied the island, established sugar plantations, and brought East African slaves to work on them. In 1810 the British captured the island and brought Indian servants to work on the plantations. Since gaining independence in 1968, the country has claimed the BRITISH INDIAN OCEAN TERRITORY (administered by Mauritius until 1965). Members of the unicameral Legislative Assembly are both elected and appointed to ensure representation of all eth-

nic groups. A governor-general represents the British crown as head of state. Sir Seewoosagur Ramgoolam, prime minister from independence until his electoral defeat in 1982, served as governor-general from 1983 until his death (1985). Aneerood Jugnauth, who became prime minister in 1982, attempted unsuccessfully to make Mauritius a republic in 1990.

Maurois, André [mohr-wah', ahn-dray']   The French writer André Maurois, pen name of Émile Herzog, b. July 26, 1885, d. Oct. 9, 1967, first came to prominence as an interpreter of Anglo-French relations in the gently satirical *The Silence of Colonel Bramble* (1918; Eng. trans., 1927), based on his experiences in World War I. He later became known for his studies of English history and for his romanticized biographies of Shelley (1923), Disraeli (1927), Byron (1930), George Sand (1952), Hugo (1954), and Balzac (1963). Maurois's biography of Marcel Proust, *The Quest for Proust* (1949; Eng. trans., 1950), is among his finest works. His *Memoirs* (1948; Eng. trans., 1970) contains discerning analyses of the strains on the Anglo-French alliance during World War II. Maurois was elected to the Académie Française in 1938.

Maury, Matthew Fontaine [mohr'-ee, fahn-tayn']   The U.S. naval officer Matthew Fontaine Maury, b. Spotsylvania County, Va., Jan. 14, 1806, d. Feb. 1, 1873, was the first person to undertake a systematic and comprehensive study of the ocean. His work on oceanography and navigation led to an international conference (Brussels, 1853) that produced the International Hydrographic Bureau, established international standards of meteorological observations, and organized a uniform system of weather reporting at sea.

After a severe injury in a stagecoach accident in 1839 forced him from active service, Maury took charge (1842) of the Depot of Charts and Instruments in Washington, the predecessor of the U.S. Naval Observatory and the U.S. Naval Oceanographic Office. While in this office he undertook compilation of oceanographic data from old and current ship logs, and in 1847 he published the first (for the North Atlantic Ocean) of his *Wind and Current Charts*. During the Civil War he was a captain in the Confederate Navy.

Maurya [mow'-ur-yuh]   The Maurya dynasty of India dates from *c.*321 BC, when CHANDRAGUPTA MAURYA ascended to the throne of Magadha, the principal kingdom in what is now Bihar. By *c.*303 BC, Chandragupta controlled the Indus and Ganges plains as well as far northwestern portions of the Indian subcontinent. He abdicated in favor of his son Bindusara (r. *c.*297–273). Chandragupta's grandson ASOKA, who ruled *c.*272–232 BC, expanded the empire. Soon after Asoka's death the empire fell apart, although the dynasty lasted until *c.*185 BC, when the last Maurya, Brihadnatha, was assassinated by a member of the Sunga dynasty.

Mausolus [maw-soh'-luhs]   Mausolus, d. 352 BC, was a Persian satrap (governor) of the province of Caria, in present-day Turkey, from about 376 to 352 BC. An almost autonomous ruler, Mausolus is best known for his tomb at Halicarnassus, called the Mausoleum; it was one of the SEVEN WONDERS OF THE WORLD.

Mavrokordátos, Aléxandros [mahv-roh-kohr-dah'-tohs]   The Greek statesman Aléxandros Mavrokordátos, b. Feb. 11, 1791, d. Aug. 18, 1865, a member of a prominent Phanariot family, played a leading role in his country's independence movement. In August 1821, shortly after the outbreak of the Greek revolt against Turkish rule, he left Italy, where he was in exile, to join the insurgents. The first president (1822) of the Hellenic Republic, he later held various diplomatic and ministerial posts under King OTTO, including that of prime minister.

Mawson, Sir Douglas   An Australian geologist and explorer, Sir Douglas Mawson, b. England, May 5, 1882, d. Oct. 14, 1958, accompanied Sir Ernest Henry SHACK-LETON's Antarctic expedition of 1907–09 and helped in the ascent of Mount Erebus and in locating the south magnetic pole. In 1911–14 he headed the Australasian Antarctic Expedition, charting previously unexplored coastal regions and making numerous sled trips inland. Mawson also led (1929–31) an expedition, sponsored jointly by Great Britain, Australia, and New Zealand, that mapped portions of Antarctica now claimed by Australia.

Maxim (family) [mak'-sim]   A family of prolific and versatile inventors, the Maxims are best known for their contributions to military technology, especially the MACHINE GUN, smokeless powder, and the Maxim rifle silencer.

Hiram Stevens Maxim, b. Sangerville, Maine, Feb. 5, 1840, d. Nov. 24, 1916, was apprenticed at age 14 to a carriage maker. He became interested in automatic weapons and opened a workshop in London, where by 1884 he had produced the first practical automatic machine gun, the Maxim gun, which used the barrel's recoil to eject the spent cartridge and reload the chamber. He also developed cordite, a smokeless powder. Maxim guns became standard equipment for every army.

Hiram's younger brother **Hudson Maxim**, b. Orneville, Maine, Feb. 3, 1853, d. May 6, 1927, devoted his career to the development of explosives, first as a partner in Hiram's company, then in his own factory at Maxim, N.J. Hudson invented (with R. C. Schupphaus) the Maxim-Schupphaus smokeless powder, an artillery ammunition widely used in World War I, and the high explosive maximite.

Hiram Percy Maxim, b. Brooklyn, N.Y., Sept. 2, 1869, d. Feb. 17, 1936, son of Hiram Stevens Maxim, turned his energies to motor vehicles. He built a gasoline-powered three-wheeled automobile in 1895 and, as chief engineer of the Pope Manufacturing Company of Hartford,

Conn., designed an electric automobile, the Columbia, in 1897. Work on the automobile muffler led him to invent the rifle silencer. Maxim adapted the silencer principle to safety valves, air compressors and blowers, and other devices. An early HAM RADIO experimenter, he cofounded (1914) the American Radio Relay League.

Maximian, Roman Emperor [mak-sim'-ee-uhn]   Maximian (Marcus Aurelius Valerius Maximianus), c.240–310, a skilled general and military colleague of DIOCLETIAN, was made ruler of the West when Diocletian divided the Roman Empire in 286. In the political disruption that followed their joint abdication in 305, Maximian at first supported his son Maxentius in his struggle for power with Septimus SEVERUS (r. 306–07), GALERIUS, and CONSTANTINE I. With Maxentius, Maximian reclaimed the imperial crown in 306, and after defeating Severus and Galerius made an alliance with Constantine. After Maximian tried in vain to depose his son in 307, he abdicated (308) once more and took refuge with Constantine in Gaul. A revolt (310) against Constantine ended in his capture and suicide.

Maximilian, Elector and Duke of Bavaria [mak-si-mil'-yuhn]   Maximilian of Bavaria, b. Apr. 17, 1573, d. Sept. 27, 1651, was one of the leading figures of the THIRTY YEARS' WAR. In 1597 he succeeded to the duchy of Bavaria. He put together a fine army for the Catholic League of German Princes, which he formed in 1610 to oppose the Protestant Union. In 1620 his general, Johann Tserclaes, graf von TILLY, defeated the elector Palatine, FREDERICK V, who was the head of the Protestant Union, and restored Holy Roman Emperor FERDINAND II to the throne of Bohemia. In return, Ferdinand bestowed on Maximilian the Upper Palatinate (northern Bavaria) and Frederick's electorate.

Although Tilly won further victories, against both Frederick's generals and CHRISTIAN IV of Denmark, Maximilian feared that the emperor's growing military power would weaken his own position as leader of the Catholic League. Consequently, in 1630, Maximilian blackmailed the emperor into dismissing his successful general, Albrecht von WALLENSTEIN. For the same reason Maximilian concluded an alliance with France, the emperor's archenemy, in 1631. France, however, could do nothing to prevent its other ally, GUSTAV II ADOLF of Sweden, from devastating (1631–32) Bavaria after he had defeated Tilly at Breitenfeld on Sept. 17, 1631.

It was not until 1634 that Maximilian regained his realm. At the Peace of Westphalia in 1648 (see WESTPHALIA, PEACE OF), he maintained his electoral title and the Upper Palatinate. Ambitious and able though unscrupulous, Maximilian had won his personal objectives but at enormous cost to his subjects.

Maximilian, Emperor of Mexico   Maximilian, b. July 6, 1832, d. June 19, 1867, was the brother of Aus-

Emperor Maximilian of Mexico, formerly an Austrian archduke, became ruler of Mexico in 1864 through the efforts of Mexican conservatives seeking the overthrow of liberal president Benito Juárez. A liberal himself, he alienated his supporters by upholding the outsted leader's reforms.

trian Emperor FRANCIS JOSEPH and emperor of Mexico from 1864 to 1867. In 1857 he married CARLOTA, the daughter of Leopold I, king of the Belgians.

In 1862 the French invaded Mexico, and Mexican conservatives offered Maximilian the imperial crown. NAPOLEON III convinced him to accept, and in 1864, Maximilian and Carlota arrived in Mexico. The conservatives wanted Maximilian to annul the liberal reforms of the Benito JUÁREZ government, but instead, he pursued moderate policies. The liberals forcibly resisted him because his empire had been created by the French invaders. When Napoleon III withdrew the French army in 1867, Maximilian first prepared to depart but was later persuaded to remain and fight to retain his crown. The empire's forces were overwhelmed by the liberal armies, however, and Maximilian was captured and executed near Querétaro.

Maximilian I, King of Bavaria   Maximilian, b. May 27, 1756, d. Oct. 13, 1825, ruled Bavaria first as elector (as Maximilian IV Joseph, 1799–1806) and then as king (as Maximilian I, 1806–25). He was a constitutional monarch inspired by the ideals of the Enlightenment. Sympathetic to France, Maximilian made a separate peace with NAPOLEON I in 1801 and was rewarded by the creation of a Bavarian kingdom. He supported Napoleon until 1813, when he changed sides in the hope of protecting Bavaria against Austria and Prussia. Popular and genuinely democratic, Maximilian gave his country a parliament under the liberal constitution of 1818. His son, LOUIS I, succeeded him.

Maximilian I, Holy Roman Emperor   Emperor Maximilian I, b. Mar. 22, 1459, d. Jan. 12, 1519, was one of the most colorful of the HABSBURGS. He built a complex system of alliances that made his family a dominant power in 16th-century Europe.

The son of the ineffectual Holy Roman emperor FREDERICK III, whom he succeeded in 1493, Maximilian married (1477) MARY OF BURGUNDY, the daughter of Duke CHARLES THE BOLD and heiress of the Netherlands. Following a revolution after Charles's death in 1477, Maximilian reestablished ducal power in the Netherlands and defended his new domain against the designs of King LOUIS XI of France. After Mary's death in 1482, Maximilian fought with the estates of the Netherlands over the regency for his children, acquiring control in 1485.

Maximilian repeatedly intervened in European politics but usually with little success. His plans for the administrative reform of Germany were blocked, and he was defeated by the Swiss Confederation in 1499. He was much more successful in his "marriage diplomacy." His son Philip (later PHILIP I of Castile) married JOAN THE MAD, daughter of FERDINAND II of Aragon and ISABELLA I of Castile; his younger grandson and granddaughter married the daughter and son, respectively, of Ladislas II, king of Hungary. Through the first of these marriages, his grandson and successor, Holy Roman Emperor CHARLES V, received a vast territorial inheritance. Transformed in German folk legend into "the last knight," Maximilian was in fact a true Renaissance prince—in his politics, in his patronage of artists and scholars, and in his own poems.

Maximilian I, who became Holy Roman Emperor in 1493, increased the power of the Habsburg dynasty through his marriage to Mary of Burgundy and by arranging his son's marriage to the heir to Spain's throne.

Maximilian II, Holy Roman Emperor   Maximilian II, b. July 31, 1527, d. Oct. 12, 1576, was Holy Roman emperor (1564–76) and king of Bohemia (1562–76) and Hungary (1563–76). The nephew of Holy Roman Emperor CHARLES V and the eldest son of FERDINAND I, Maximilian was educated in Spain. After a dispute over the order of succession, the HABSBURG family agreed that Maximilian rather than Charles's son, Philip II of Spain, would succeed Ferdinand as emperor.

Maximilian disliked Spain and all it stood for; he leaned toward Lutheranism but agreed to remain a Roman Catholic in order to safeguard his succession. As emperor he advocated compromise and kept a balance between the two confessions, and he allowed the nobility of the Austrian duchies and of his kingdoms of Bohemia and Hungary freedom of worship.

Maximilian did not extend imperial authority nor was he successful against the Turks, but he maintained his crowns and possessions as well as peace in the empire. In 1573 he was offered the throne of Poland, but the proposal collapsed because of some Polish opposition. Maximilian was succeeded by his son RUDOLF II.

Maxwell, James Clerk

The Scottish physicist James Clerk Maxwell, b. Nov. 13, 1831, d. Nov. 5, 1879, did revolutionary work in electromagnetism and the kinetic theory of gases. After graduating (1854) with a degree in mathematics from Trinity College, Cambridge, he held professorships at Marischal College in Aberdeen (1856) and King's College in London (1860) and became the first Cavendish Professor of Physics at Cambridge in 1871.

Maxwell's first major contribution to science was a study of the planet Saturn's rings, the nature of which was much debated. Maxwell showed that stability could be achieved only if the rings consisted of numerous small solid particles, an explanation still accepted. Maxwell next considered molecules of gases in rapid motion. By treating them statistically he was able to formulate (1866), independently of Ludwig Boltzmann, the Maxwell-Boltzmann kinetic theory of gases (see KINETIC THEORY OF MATTER). This theory showed that temperatures and heat involved only molecular movement. Philosophically, this theory meant a change from a concept of certainty—heat viewed as flowing from hot to cold—to one of statistics—molecules at high temperature have only a high probability of moving toward those at low temperature. This new approach did not reject the earlier studies of thermodynamics; rather, it used a better theory to explain these observations.

Maxwell's most important achievement was his extension and mathematical formulation of Michael FARADAY's theories of electricity and magnetic lines of force. In his research, conducted between 1864 and 1873, Maxwell showed that a few relatively simple mathematical equations could express the behavior of electric and magnetic fields and their interrelated nature; that is, an oscillating

The Scottish physicist James Clerk Maxwell developed the mathematical explanation of the electromagnetic field. His work is often compared in importance to that of Sir Isaac Newton.

electric charge produces an electromagnetic field. These four partial differential equations first appeared in fully developed form in Maxwell's great treatise *Electricity and Magnetism* (1873). Since known as Maxwell's equations, they are one of the great achievements of 19th-century physics.

Maxwell also calculated that the speed of propagation of an electromagnetic field is approximately that of the speed of light. He proposed that the phenomenon of light is therefore an electromagnetic phenomenon. Because charges can oscillate with any frequency, Maxwell concluded that visible light forms only a small part of the entire spectrum of possible ELECTROMAGNETIC RADIATION.

May Day

The custom of celebrating May Day, May 1, can be traced to ancient spring rituals connected with fertility and growth. Although theoretically superseded by the Christian celebration of Easter, the holiday has survived in various forms. In 15th-century England, May Day festivities were celebrated with dances around the Maypole and were also tied to the figure of Robin Hood, whom local youths impersonated in MORRIS DANCES and dramatic performances.

May Day was designated a labor holiday by the Second Socialist International in 1889 and has since been celebrated—with parades, demonstrations, and speeches—by labor unions and political parties of the left. As International Workers' Day, it is a public holiday in many countries. May Day parades are often prominent displays of military strength.

Maya

[my'-uh]   The ancient Maya were a group of American Indian peoples who lived in southern Mexico, particularly the present-day states of Chiapas, Tabasco, Campeche, Yucatán, and Quintana Roo, and in Belize, Guatemala, and adjacent Honduras. Their descendants, the modern Maya, live in the same regions today. The ancestors of the Maya, like those of other New World peoples, crossed the BERING LAND BRIDGE from Asia more than 20,000 years ago, during the last ice age.

The Maya were the first people of the New World to keep historical records: their written history begins in 50 BC, when they began to inscribe texts on pots, jades, bones, stone monuments, and palace walls. Maya records trace the history of the great kings and queens who ruled from 50 BC until the Spanish conquest in the 16th century. All Maya "long count" calendar inscriptions fall between AD 292 and AD 909, roughly defining the period called Classic. Earlier Maya culture is called Formative or Preclassic (2000 BC–AD 300), and subsequent civilization is known as Postclassic (AD 900–conquest).

Protected by difficult terrain and heavy vegetation, the ruins of few ancient Maya cities were known before the 19th century, when explorers and archaeologists began to rediscover them. The age and proliferation of Maya writings have been recognized since about 1900, when the calendrical content of Maya hieroglyphic inscriptions was deciphered and the dates correlated with the Christian

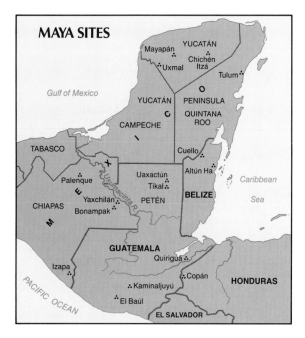

MAYA SITES

calendar. For most of the 20th century, only the extensive calendrical data of Maya inscriptions could be read, and as a result, Maya scholars hypothesized that the inscriptions were pure calendrical records. Because little evidence of warfare had been recognized archaeologically, the Classic Maya were thought of as peaceful timekeepers and skywatchers.

More recent scholarship changed the picture dramatically. In 1958, Heinrich Berlin demonstrated that certain Maya hieroglyphs, which he called emblem glyphs, contained symbols that varied according to location, indicating dynastic lines or place names. In 1960, Tatiana Proskouriakoff showed that the patterns of dates were markers of the important events in rulers' lives. The chronological record turned out to serve history and the perpetuation of the memory of great nobles. Subsequently, major archaeological discoveries, particularly at PALENQUE and TIKAL, confirmed what the writings said, and examination of Maya art has revealed not only historical portraiture but also a pantheon of gods, goddesses, and heroes—in other words, Maya religion and mythic history.

History of the Ancient Maya

By 5000 BC the Maya had settled along Caribbean and Pacific coasts, forming egalitarian fishing communities. Certainly by 2000 BC the Maya had also moved inland and adopted agriculture for their subsistence. Maize and beans formed the Maya diet then as today, although many other foodstuffs—squash, tomatoes, peppers, fruits, and game—were supplements. The word for maize—*wah*—is synonymous with food itself, and the maize god was honored from early times.

Preclassic Period. During the Early Preclassic (2000–900 BC), civilization began to take shape in parts of ME-

SOAMERICA. By 1200 BC the OLMEC of the Gulf Coast had risen to preeminence, dominating trade routes that extended from the modern Mexican state of Guerrero to Costa Rica, passing through Maya regions. At COPÁN, Honduras, and Cuello, Belize, around 1000 BC, local Maya leaders began to imitate Olmec styles of pottery and jades and adopted orthodox Olmec religious symbols for their own use.

The Maya began to develop intensive agriculture and sophisticated water management during the Middle Preclassic (900–300 BC), which may have helped support the population explosion of the Late Preclassic (300 BC–AD 300). During this same period, writing was invented in Mesoamerica, probably by the ZAPOTECS of Oaxaca.

During the Late Preclassic, Maya village life everywhere gave way to stratified society dominated by a small elite. The fruits of intensive agriculture and the profits of long-distance trade began to be concentrated in the hands of a few. Lowland Maya groups at El Mirador, Cerros, Lamanai, Uaxactún, and Tikal cleared small villages and replaced them with planned communities centered on massive ceremonial structures featuring enormous mask facades of a newly codified pantheon. In the highlands, at IZAPA, Abaj Takalik, El Baúl, and KAMINALJUYÚ, other Maya groups erected stone stelae on which Maya lords and deities were portrayed, sometimes in association with dates. Although they did not invent the "long count" calendar, the Maya were its greatest exploiters, and they used it to record history in their own languages.

Classic Period. By AD 250 or so, at Tikal, Uaxactún, Río Azul, and elsewhere in the lowlands, both monumental architecture and stelae with historical records were being erected, but on these monuments the Maya lords wear the images of the gods, and from this point until the end of the Classic period, the Maya rulers reigned as divine kings. Much religious ritual focused on ancestors. From the inscriptions, linguists believe that the Classic Maya spoke a language closely related to modern Chol, Yucatec, and Chorti. During the Early Classic (AD 250–550), the Maya also sustained profound contact with warriors and traders from TEOTIHUACÁN in central Mexico, the largest and most powerful state of the era. There is no evidence of conquest, but Maya adopted some foreign deities, modes of representation, and styles of clothing.

By the end of the Early Classic, powerful lineages had established cities and city-states throughout the lowlands. Following a period (AD 530–580) called the "hiatus," when few dated works of art or buildings were made, the Maya thrived during the Late Classic (AD 550–900), and art, architecture, and writing flourished at dozens of city-states. More than 2 million people may have lived in the Maya area, and Tikal, the largest center, may have had a population of 75,000–100,000. To support growing populations, the Maya expanded their systems of intensive agriculture.

No lowland Classic Maya domain survived into the 10th century. Ultimately, the system of rule that had served the Maya well for centuries failed. Faced with famine, foreign invasion, chronic warfare, and perhaps disease, an era ended in what is generally called the

(Above) *Maya painting has survived chiefly through ceramics. This vessel shows a priest performing a ceremony with a serpent.*

(Left) *The pyramid known as the Castillo is the most striking of the Maya structures at Chichén Itzá in the north central Yucatán Peninsula.*

Classic Maya collapse. Although the Maya continued to live in both highlands and lowlands, the period of their greatest splendor was over.

Postclassic Period. In the northern lowlands, civilization continued to thrive briefly at UXMAL and other sites in the Puuc hills and then well into the Postclassic at CHICHÉN ITZÁ. At the beginning of the Postclassic, speakers of Itzá or Putún Maya from the Tabasco coast probably ruled at Chichén Itzá, consolidating a powerful state sustained by trade, tribute, and war, and possibly developing a new system of administration, whereby three or four brothers may have shared power simultaneously. According to central Mexican and Maya annals, the TOLTEC king Quetzalcóatl (Feathered Serpent) fled in 986 from Tula, Hidalgo, to Yucatán, where he was known as Kukulcán, a Maya translation of his name. Chichén Itzá and Tula share common styles of art and architecture, and Toltec rulers may have held power briefly at Chichén Itzá. Tula was sacked at the end of the 12th century; Chichén Itzá was probably abandoned by then as well.

The Itzá founded a new capital at MAYAPÁN in the 13th century, 100 km (62 mi) to the west of Chichén Itzá, and they modeled their main buildings on those of their former capital. Unlike most other Maya cities, Mayapán was walled, and some 15,000 people lived close together inside the protective shield, a response to troubled and warlike times. In the mid-15th century, Mayapán fell to treachery and revolt.

Trading towns survived along the Caribbean coast, and in 1502, Christopher Columbus and his son Ferdinand encountered Maya traders plying high dugout canoes filled with cloth and other goods off the coast of Honduras. Wracked by strife and then by European diseases, the Maya of Yucatán broke up into tiny states at the time of the Spanish conquest. The Spanish took advantage of Maya division to take control in 1542, and they established their own capital at Mérida, on the site of a Maya city called Tiho.

During the Late Postclassic, the Highland Maya of Guatemala—Cakchiquel, Quiché, Pokomam, Tzutuhil—established fortified cities on hillside acropolises at Iximché, Utatlán, and Mixco Viejo, and fought for control of precious resources, such as obsidian. The Quiché had made alliances with the Aztecs, but the Cakchiquels aided the Spanish cause. In 1527 the Europeans established their own capital, now known as Ciudad Vieja. A few years later, a young Quiché nobleman wrote down the *Popol Vuh*, the greatest surviving Maya work of literature, in the European alphabet. The last Maya kingdom, Tayasal, in Lake Petén Itzá, was taken by the Spanish in 1697.

Ancient Maya Civilization

Although writing in the New World did not originate among the Maya, they gave writing its greatest refinements. The Maya wrote a mixed script, with ideographic and phonetic elements. About 80 percent of Maya glyphs can now be interpreted for their meaning; a smaller number can be sounded out phonetically and understood through Maya languages spoken today.

Most inscriptions survive on stelae, and they recount

the lives and deeds of nobles, the positions of heavenly bodies—particularly the Moon, Venus, and Jupiter—on the dates recorded (all the major events in the life of Chan Bahlum of Palenque, for example, coincided with the movements of Jupiter), associated mythic events, and occasionally, artists' signatures. Four Postclassic Maya screenfold, or pleated, manuscripts are known, and by sheer accident of survival, all are almanacs of the rituals, offerings, and auguries for the year. Scribes and artists were nobles; many may have been priests.

The Maya used several calendars simultaneously, and the "long count," a continuous record of days from a zero date that correlates to Aug. 13, 3114 BC, was as precise as the Julian-day number, a chronological system developed in Europe in 1582 for scientific calculations. They also kept track of the solar and lunar years and the cycles of visible planets. In their calculations, numbers were written with dots (for ones) and bars (for fives) in a vigesimal (based on the number 20) system. Their number system used a placeholder that functioned like zero, which allowed them to calculate enormous sums.

Across the Maya realm, as evinced in art and inscriptions, Maya nobility celebrated a ritual cycle: birth, heir designation, accession, warfare, ballgame (an athletic contest that was also a symbolic event), death. Blood was the mortar of Maya life, and offerings were made to seal these events. Male nobles drew blood from the penis, ear, or tongue; women drew blood from the tongue; blood was drawn from the ears, fingernails, and mouths of war captives before they were sacrificed.

When nobles died, the Maya believed that they became one with the gods, and that they dwelt in the night sky with them. In Classic times, pyramids were erected over the tombs of dead kings, shrines to the ancestors and the gods.

Architecture. Maya architectural forms were derived from domestic architecture: stone or earthen platform and wattle-and-daub shelter, covered by a hip roof of thatch. The shrine and platform of the pyramid grew from the house form, and the Maya corbel arch, often called a "false" arch, preserves the hip roof in stone. With these elements the Maya built palaces, pyramids, shrines, and even ballcourts.

Maya cities follow no grid. During the Postclassic, Chichén Itzá builders introduced new forms, particularly columns, and great colonnades were set in front of many administrative buildings. Palaces with galleries of columns opened onto private patios.

Sculpture and Painting. Early Classic stone sculpture usually features a single Maya ruler celebrating his reign in one of a limited number of formal poses. On the peripheries of the Classic realm at the beginning of the Late Classic, new modes of representation were introduced, and multifigure compositions became the rule. Scenes of bloodletting, warfare, and play in the ballgame were carved on lintels and panels as well as on stelae. Many fine carvings on small jades, shells, and bones were worn and used by nobles, and many objects bear their owner's name.

Few monumental paintings survive, but a complete program has been preserved at BONAMPAK. Undoubtedly the most complex representation known in Maya art, it features hundreds of nobles celebrating the installation of an heir in office and the subsequent battle and bloodletting that sealed the events in 790 and 792. During the 7th and 8th centuries many schools of vase painting thrived, and the surviving works are a window on Maya belief and ritual. No Classic books survive, but the fine-line painting on some pots may be comparable to manuscript illumination.

At Chichén Itzá, war, warriors, and sacrifice dominate the representations. From the *cenote*, or sacred well, gold disks, jades, and other precious objects have been retrieved.

The Modern Maya

The modern Maya live in roughly the same geography as did their predecessors, now divided by modern political boundaries. Some 4 million or so speak one of the 30 or more Maya languages and retain traditional customs, diet, dress, or housing. Many, particularly in Mérida and Cancún, have adopted an urban life, but most continue to live in rural areas.

During the Colonial period, Spanish slavers hauled thousands of Maya to the mines in northern Mexico, where most died, leaving the tropical lowlands virtually unpopulated. Now the Mexican government has granted many Tzeltal, Tzotzil, Chol, and Yucatec Maya new *ejidos*, or collective farms, there, where they raise coffee or cattle. In Guatemala, Kekchi and Mopan settlers have pushed into the Petén rain forest. Civil and racial strife in Guatemala in the 1970s and 1980s forced many Maya, particularly from the department of Quiché, to flee across the border to Mexico. The Mexican government moved a large number of refugees to a permanent settlement near Edzna, Campeche.

In both the highlands and the lowlands, the Maya have maintained age-old rituals for naming children, nurturing the agricultural cycle, marriage, sickness, death, and even auguring the future. In the northern lowlands, Chaac the rain god is worshiped, and in times of need a *chachaac*, or rainmaking ceremony, is performed. Before the conquest, the *uayeb*, or last five days of the year, was a dangerous time; most Maya now identify *uayeb* with Holy Week, and it and Carnival are carefully observed.

Maya rebellions were common until the 20th century. In Yucatán, Mexico established (1902) a separate territory, Quintana Roo on the east side of the peninsula, where many rebels fled. Made a state in 1974, Quintana Roo is now the location of Mexico's prosperous Caribbean resorts.

See also: INDIANS, AMERICAN; PRE-COLUMBIAN ART AND ARCHITECTURE.

Mayakovsky, Vladimir Vladimirovich [my-uh-kawf'-skee, vluhd-yee'-mir vluhd-yee'-mir-uh-vich]   Vladimir Mayakovsky, the leading Russian poet during the early years of the Soviet regime, b. July 19 (N.S.), 1893, d. Apr. 14, 1930, strove to shock through his unconventional verse and startling public pronouncements. He deliberately ignored natural beauty and instead extolled fabricated objects, as in his 1925 poem in honor of New York's Brooklyn Bridge. A signatory of the Russian futurist manifesto, provocatively entitled *A Slap in the Face of Public Taste* (1912; Eng. trans., 1971), he urged the destruction of Russia's cultural legacy, especially the hegemony of the symbolists. Mayakovsky was the first Russian poet to write exclusively accentual verse, that is, poetry with a fixed number of stresses per line but with any number of syllables, as in *A Cloud in Trousers* (1914–15; Eng. trans., 1965).

An early adherent of the Communist cause who celebrated the arrival of the revolution in an ode (1918) and a satirical verse play—the famous *Mystery-Bouffe* (1918; Eng. trans., 1933)—and who later eulogized its leader, Lenin, in a long poem (1924), Mayakovsky defiantly proclaimed his verse an activity "like any other," placing it at the service of the Soviet state. Accordingly, he also wrote primitive propaganda doggerel as well as advertising copy for Soviet products ranging from cigarettes to infants' pacifiers. Mayakovsky composed moving love lyrics, such as *I Love* (1922; Eng. trans., 1955), but in these, too, he deliberately avoided sentimentality by resorting to crude imagery and blasphemous similes.

Although Mayakovsky's loyalty to the Communist cause was sincere, his rebellious art made him suspect in the eyes of Soviet functionaries, who preferred the obedient and conventional writers who defined SOCIALIST REALISM. His fears of the bureaucratization and regimentation of Soviet society were in turn expressed in two comedies, *The Bedbug* (1928; Eng. trans., 1960) and *The Bathhouse* (1929; Eng. trans., 1963). Mayakovsky's apprehensions for the future, together with the government's refusal to allow him to travel abroad to see the woman he loved, contributed to his suicide.

Mayapán [mah-yah-pahn'] Mayapán, 40 km (25 mi) southeast of Mérida in northwestern Yucatán, Mexico, was the capital of a large MAYA state in late pre-Columbian times. During the 11th and 12th centuries it was a modest center, subordinate to the TOLTEC-Maya rulers of CHICHÉN ITZÁ. After a successful revolt against Chichén in 1187, Mayapán ruled northern Yucatán, holding provincial lords in the capital to ensure the continuing payment of tribute. The destruction of Mayapán in a revolt in the early 1440s ended centralized government in northern Yucatán.

Unlike other Maya centers, Mayapán was a true city, with about 10,000 residents and more than 4,000 roughly built houses, small palaces, shrines, and temples. The most prominent building is an inferior copy of Chichén's Kukulcán temple.

mayapple see MANDRAKE

Mayer, Louis B. [may'-ur] Louis Burt Mayer, b. Minsk, Russia, 1882 or 1885, d. Oct. 29, 1957, was a Hollywood film mogul who for many years headed the Metro-Goldwyn-Mayer Corporation, ruling his studio like a patriarch in order to make "decent, wholesome pictures for Americans." Initially a scrap-metal dealer, he made a fortune as a New England movie-theater owner before forming the Louis B. Mayer Pictures Corporation in 1918. Merging his company with Marcus Loew's Metro and the Goldwyn Company to found MGM in 1924, he became vice-president of the new company, acting as general manager of the Culver City studio until forced to retire in 1951.

Mayfield, Julian American novelist, essayist, playwright, actor, and black-power advocate Julian Mayfield, b. Greer, S.C., June 6, 1928, d. Oct. 20, 1984, served as aide to President Kwame Nkrumah of Ghana (1962–66) and Prime Minister Forbes Burnham of Guyana (1971–75) and was founding editor of the *African Review* (Accra, Ghana). His first two novels, *The Hit* (1957) and *The Long Night* (1958), were well received as realistic and humorous stories of black life in America. His third novel, *The Grand Parade* (1961), regarded as his best, offered a bleak look at the fate of a black mayor in U.S. politics.

Mayflower The English ship the *Mayflower* carried the Separatist Puritans, later known as PILGRIMS, to Plymouth, Mass., in 1620. The vessel was chartered by John CARVER, a leader of the Separatist congregation at Leiden, Holland, who had gone to London to make arrangements for the voyage to America. The ship was made ready at Southampton with a passenger list that included English Separatists, hired help (among them Myles STANDISH, a professional soldier, and John ALDEN, a cooper), and other colonists who were to be taken along at the insistence of the London businesspeople who were helping to finance the expedition.

In the meantime the Leiden Separatists, who had initiated the venture, sailed for Southampton on July 22, 1620, with 35 members of the congregation and their leaders William BRADFORD and William BREWSTER aboard the *Speedwell*. Both the *Speedwell* and the *Mayflower*, carrying a total of about 120 passengers, sailed from Southampton on August 15, but they were twice forced back by dangerous leaks on the *Speedwell*. At the English port of Plymouth some of the *Speedwell*'s passengers were regrouped on the *Mayflower*, and on September 16 the historic voyage began.

This time the *Mayflower* carried 102 passengers, only 37 of whom were from the Leiden congregation, in addition to the crew. The voyage took 65 days, during which two persons died. A boy, Oceanus Hopkins, was born at sea, and another, Peregrine WHITE, was born as the ship lay at anchor off Cape Cod. The ship came in sight of Cape Cod on November 19 and dropped anchor at Provincetown on November 21. That day 41 men signed the so-called Mayflower Compact, a "plantation covenant" modeled after a Separatist church covenant, by which they agreed to establish a "Civil Body Politic" (a temporary government) and to be bound by its laws. This agreement was thought necessary because there were rumors

The Mayflower, *a three-masted merchant ship originally constructed for transporting wine, was the vessel in which a group of Puritan Separatists reached Plymouth Bay, Mass., to found the first permanent English settlement in New England. The settlers who made the transatlantic voyage in 1620 have come to be known as the* Pilgrim Fathers, *a term popularized during the 19th century.*

that some of the non-Separatists, called "Strangers," among the passengers would defy the Pilgrims if they landed in a place other than that specified in the land grant they had received from the LONDON COMPANY. The compact became the basis of government in the PLYMOUTH COLONY. After it was signed, the Pilgrims elected John Carver their first governor.

After weeks of scouting for a suitable settlement area, the *Mayflower*'s passengers finally landed at Plymouth on Dec. 26, 1620. Although the *Mayflower*'s captain and part owner, Christopher Jones, had threatened to leave the Pilgrims unless they quickly found a place to land, the ship remained at Plymouth during the first terrible winter of 1620–21, when half of the colonists died. The *Mayflower* left Plymouth on Apr. 15, 1621, and arrived back in England on May 16.

A model of the *Mayflower* on display in Pilgrim Hall, Plymouth, gives the ship's dimensions as 90 ft (27.4 m) long, with a 64-ft (19.5-m) keel, 26-ft (7.9-m) beam, and a hold 11 ft (3.4 m) deep. In 1957 a close replica of the *Mayflower* was sailed from Plymouth, England, to Plymouth, Mass., where it is on view.

mayfly   Mayflies are primitive winged insects of the order Ephemeroptera, usually found near streams, rivers, ponds, and lakes. One of the most ancient insect groups, mayflies have left fossils up to 300 million years old. Typical adult mayflies are up to 2 cm (0.8 in) long, with bulging eyes and two or three long, slender tail filaments.

Immature mayflies (nymphs) live underwater, where they breathe through abdominal gills. Some mayfly nymphs prey upon smaller aquatic animals, and others eat plant fragments. Mayfly nymphs are an important food for fish and are excellent fish bait.

The adult mayfly (top) *is a slim, delicate insect whose brief life span is devoted to mating. It does not have a developed mouth for eating but lives on energy stored from eating during its 3 years as an underwater nymph* (bottom).

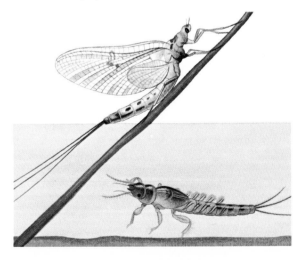

After up to three years in a nymph stage, the insects emerge from the water, usually at night, and molt (shed their skin) into a winged form that usually molts again into an adult mayfly. Mayflies are the only insects to molt after having wings. Adult mayflies cannot eat, and they live only a few hours or days, during which time they mate and females lay eggs. Huge swarms of mayflies may be attracted to lights and thus become a nuisance, especially near lakeside resorts.

Mayo   Mayo is a county in Connacht province in northwestern Ireland, on the Atlantic Ocean, with an area of 5,398 km^2 (2,084 mi^2). The population is 115,184 (1986). Mayo is characterized by a rugged coastline and mountainous terrain in the north. There are several lakes, including Loughs Mask and Carrowmore. Castlebar is the county town. Livestock raising is the mainstay of the economy. Taken by the Normans at the end of the 12th century, Mayo was finally brought fully under English control in the 16th century.

Mayo, Elton   George Elton Mayo, b. Adelaide, Australia, Dec. 26, 1880, d. Sept. 7, 1949, first served as a teacher in logic and philosophy at Queensland University. In 1923 he became research associate at the University of Pennyslvania; in 1926 he joined the Harvard Business School faculty in the area of industrial development, combining the philosophic analysis of human problems with technological and production techniques. Worker-management studies led to his key contribution to the Hawthorne studies, which are classical in industrial psychology. The Hawthorne studies led to a refinement in industrial psychology's experimental methods and human-problem conception and a reappraisal of oversimplified ideas of social motivation.

Mayo Clinic   Named in 1903, the Mayo Clinic originated as part of St. Mary's Hospital, which was opened in 1889 in Rochester, Minn., by the Sisters of St. Francis with the help of Dr. William Worrall Mayo. Mayo's two sons, also physicians, founded the clinic when they expanded the facilities to accommodate additional physicians and surgeons in order to further their father's practice. Initially only a surgical clinic, it became a full medical center in 1915. Today the Mayo Clinic is a private association of more than 900 physicians and surgeons. St. Mary's and Methodist hospitals, long affiliated with the Mayo Clinic, were merged with it in 1986. The Mayo Foundation administers the clinic, the Mayo Medical School, the Mayo School of Health Related Sciences, and the Mayo Graduate School of Medicine. Two branch clinics serve the communities of Jacksonville, Fla., and Scottsdale, Ariz.

mayor   A mayor is the head of a MUNICIPAL GOVERNMENT and usually serves as the chair of a municipal council. If there is no city manager, the mayor also acts as head of the executive branch of the city government. In the United States a mayor is usually popularly elected; in many European cities, however, the mayor is elected by the municipal council or appointed by the national government. In Great Britain the office is now little more than ceremonial. In the United States it is common to distinguish between strong-mayor city governments, in which the mayor presides over the council and has a veto power over its actions, and weak-mayor governments, in which the council is predominant.

Mayotte   [mah-yuht']   Mayotte (Mahorè), one of the Comoro Islands, lies between Africa and Madagascar. It has an area of 373 km^2 (144 mi^2) and a population of 67,167 (1985). France took possession of Mayotte in 1843. The people, of Arab, black African, and Malagasy descent, voted to remain attached to France when the Comoros gained independence in 1975. Two additional referenda in 1976 reaffirmed this decision.

Mays, Willie   Willie Howard Mays, Jr., b. Fairfield, Ala., May 6, 1931, was one of American professional baseball's most exciting and talented performers. For 21 years he played center field for the Giants, first in New York (1951–52, 1954–57) and later in San Francisco (1958–72), before finishing his career in 1973 as a member of the New York Mets. Best remembered as a home-run hitter—he ranks third in career home runs, with 660—Mays was a flawless center fielder and had an uncanny instinct for exploiting opponents' errors while he was on the base paths. When Mays was 19 years old, the Giants bought (1950) his contract from the Negro National League Birmingham Black Barons. In 1951, after hitting .477 in 35 games for Minneapolis of the American Association, he was called up to the major leagues, where he proceeded to win the National League (NL) Rookie of the Year award.

During his career Mays won 4 NL home-run crowns and 1 batting title, was the NL's Most Valuable Player twice (1954, 1965), and appeared in 24 All-Star Games

Willie Mays, the first player in professional baseball's National League to hit 600 home runs, made his debut with the New York Giants in 1951. Mays starred with the Giants as a center fielder for 21 seasons. He retired in 1973 after compiling career totals of 660 home runs and 3,283 hits.

and 4 World Series. Mays retired with 3,283 hits and a .302 batting average for his career. He was elected to the Baseball Hall of Fame in 1979, the first year he was eligible.

Maytag, Frederick Louis   Frederick Louis Maytag, b. near Elgin, Ill., July 14, 1857, d. Mar. 26, 1937, founded (1909) the Maytag Company in Newton, Iowa, which became the world's largest producer of washing machines. In 1911 he developed an electric washing machine and in 1922 introduced the aluminum tub machine. In later years the company produced a popular line of automatic washers and dryers. Maytag served in the Iowa Senate (1902–12) and as mayor of Newton (1923–25).

Mazarin, Jules [mah-zah-ran', zhool]   Jules Mazarin, originally Giulio Mazarini, b. July 14, 1602, d. Mar. 9, 1661, a French statesman and Roman Catholic cardinal, ruled France as the first minister of the regent ANNE OF AUSTRIA. He was born near Rome, studied at the Spanish university of Alcalá de Henares, and then entered the papal diplomatic service. On his journeys to France he impressed the ruling minister, Cardinal RICHELIEU. On Oct. 26, 1630, Mazarin attracted international attention by negotiating a truce between the French and Spanish armies as they were about to engage in battle at Casale. He settled in France in 1640 and the following year was made a cardinal on the recommendation of LOUIS XIII.

When Richelieu's death (1642) was followed by that of the king in 1643, Anne of Austria, regent for her five-year-old son LOUIS XIV, turned to Mazarin as her principal minister. A strong affection existed between them and it was rumored that they were secretly married. The cardinal continued Richelieu's policies, but, being a foreigner and less ruthless, he relied on subtlety and persuasion. Despite Mazarin's concessions, opposition from the judicial hierarchy and groups of dissident nobles led to the civil wars of the FRONDE in the years 1648–53. Mazarin emerged triumphant from these conflicts, forcing one of his main opponents, Louis II de Bourbon, prince de Condé (see CONDÉ family), to join the Spanish armies.

Mazarin's main achievements were in diplomacy. His negotiations at the end of the THIRTY YEARS' WAR in Germany led to the Peace of Westphalia (1648; see WEST-PHALIA, PEACE OF) and at the end of the war with Spain to the Treaty of the Pyrenees (1659). Mazarin died at Vincennes, leaving Louis XIV with the most powerful kingdom of continental Europe.

Mazatlán [mah-saht-lahn']   Mazatlán, a city and seaport, is located in the southern part of Sinaloa state in northwestern Mexico, at the mouth of the Gulf of California. It is Mexico's largest port on the Pacific Ocean and has a population of 199,830 (1980). Mazatlán exports the agricultural and mineral products of a large hinterland. A popular tourist resort, it is known for its excellent sandy beaches and good fishing.

Mazepa, Ivan Stepanovich [muhz-yay'-puh, ee-vahn' step-ah'-nuh-vich]   Ivan Stepanovich Mazepa, c.1644–1709, was a COSSACK leader who planned to create an independent Ukraine. In 1708, during the Great NORTHERN WAR, Mazepa concluded a secret alliance with CHARLES XII of Sweden, by which Ukraine was to become an independent state with Mazepa as hereditary ruler. The Russian victory over the Swedes at Poltava (July 8, 1709) put an end to this dream, however. Mazepa fled with Charles to Bendery in Moldavia, where he died. A popular legend about Mazepa's youth is the subject of Lord Byron's poem *Mazeppa*.

mazurka   The mazurka is a Polish folk dance in triple meter danced by couples in multiples of four, its few basic steps and positions allowing for much choreographic improvisation. Tempos range from moderately slow to quite fast with accents on the second and third beats.

During the 19th century the mazurka became a stylized instrumental dance form. Frédéric Chopin composed 52 mazurkas for the piano; other composers who wrote mazurkas include Mikhail Glinka, Modest Mussorgsky, and Peter Ilich Tchaikovsky.

Mazzini, Giuseppe [maht-tsee'-nee, joo-zep'-pay]   Giuseppe Mazzini, b. June 22, 1805, d. Mar. 10, 1872, was a political theorist and republican revolutionary who fought for Italian unification and independence. Influenced by romantic and liberal ideas and by hatred of oppression, Mazzini inspired Italy's RISORGIMENTO. In 1827 he joined the Carbonari, a secret society that advocated political freedom. He was subsequently jailed and then exiled to France.

In Marseille he founded (1831) Giovine Italia ("Young Italy"), a patriotic republican movement that aspired to unify Italy through popular initiatives. A prophet of nationalism, Mazzini dreamed of an eventual free association of European states. In 1834 he came under a death sentence for plotting a military expedition into territory of the House of Savoy. He finally made his way to England in 1837, where he tried to enlist English sympathy for Italian nationalism.

Mazzini returned to Italy during the REVOLUTIONS OF 1848. When Pope PIUS IX was driven out of Rome, Mazzini reached the high point of his career, becoming one of the governing triumvirate of the short-lived Roman Republic (February–July 1849). Thereafter, he escaped to London again.

Mazzini returned to Italy during the wars of 1859 and 1860 but took no joy in seeing the establishment in 1861 of a unified Italian kingdom rather than a republic. He was still hatching schemes for gaining Venice and Rome when he was arrested and imprisoned at Gaeta (August–October 1870) at the time VICTOR EMMANUEL II was taking Rome. In failing health, Mazzini retired to Pisa, where he died.

Mazzini's conception of nationalism and his austere,

moral philosophy of the "duties of man" influenced political thought long after his death. He wrote extensively and widely—on literature, philosophy, and politics. An English translation of his works appeared in 1890–91 (6 vols.).

Mbabane [muh-bah-bah'-nay]   Mbabane, the administrative capital of Swaziland, is situated in the northwestern part of the country, on the Highveld, 24 km (15 mi) east of the South African border. Its population is 52,000 (1986 est.). It is primarily a commercial and administrative center (nearby Lobamba is the legislative capital) and is a popular tourist attraction.

Mbini   see EQUATORIAL GUINEA

Mboya, Tom [muh-boy'-uh]   Thomas Joseph Mboya, b. Aug. 15, 1930, d. July 5, 1969, a Kenyan political leader and member of the Luo tribe, was one of the principal architects of Kenyan independence. From 1953 to 1963 he was general secretary of the Kenya Federation of Labor (KFL); in 1957 he was elected to the Kenya Legislative Council as the workers' candidate. Mboya was a cofounder in 1960 of the Kenya African National Union (KANU), which played a major part in the achievement (1963) of Kenya's independence. He participated in Jomo KENYATTA's government as minister of labor (1962), as minister of justice (1963), and as minister for economic planning (1964–69). His assassination set off widespread rioting.

Mbundu [em-boon'-doo]   The Mbundu, an African people speaking the Kimbundu language, occupied a part of the African interior early penetrated by the Portuguese during the 16th-century slave trade. The Mbundu kingdom of Ndongo was the farthest southwest area of the western Bantu-speakers. The title of their dynastic ruler, *ngola*, was adapted by the Portuguese as a name, Angola, for the greater area around the kingdom. In 1671 the Portuguese beheaded the reigning *ngola* and destroyed all vestiges of kingship. The Mbundu created a rich literature of protest against colonialism and forced labor; the Mbundu poet Agostinho António NETO became head of the liberation movement and founder (1975) of the independent nation of Angola. The Mbundu, who numbered nearly 2 million in the 1980s, are divided into various ethnic groups including the Ndongo, Dembo, and Pende.

Mc: names with this prefix are alphabetized as MAC

MDMA   MDMA is a synthetic drug that is also called "ecstasy." The letters MDMA are an abbreviation of its chemical name, methylenedioxymethamphetamine. The drug is related to the AMPHETAMINES and the HALLUCINOGENS. It was used legally by some psychotherapists in the 1970s and early 1980s for its effect in inducing a state of apparently enhanced self-awareness. After MDMA was found to be toxic to the nervous systems of laboratory animals, however, the U.S. Food and Drug Administration banned it from medical use. In the meantime MDMA had gained popularity as a recreational drug. Long-term effects on the nervous systems of MDMA abusers are not yet known, but side effects such as fatigue and sleeplessness are observed, and a few deaths have been reported.

---

mead   Mead is an intoxicating alcoholic beverage made by fermenting honey and water, sometimes with fruit and spices added as flavorings. Along with beer and ale, mead is one of the oldest European fermented drinks. It was made in ancient Greece and Rome and was thought to be the drink of the gods by early Teutonic tribes. Its production grew into an industry in 15th-century Germany, and throughout northern Europe mead consumption began to drop only toward the end of the 16th century. The Welsh drink Metheglyn is a highly spiced mead.

Mead, George Herbert   George Herbert Mead, b. South Hadley, Mass., Feb. 27, 1863, d. Apr. 26, 1931, was an important philosopher within the movement of American PRAGMATISM. Mead was greatly influenced by Darwinism, but he challenged many of the ideas of the crude BEHAVIORISM to which it led. Writing extensively on the theory of time and the nature of reality, he developed a view of emergence and novelty in natural processes. His social psychology, especially his theory of the self, has had a great influence on psychologists and social scientists. He published relatively little; large segments of his books are collections from his unfinished manuscripts and his students' notes.

Mead, Lake   Lake Mead, on the Arizona-Nevada border, is a reservoir that was formed in 1936 by the construction of HOOVER DAM across the Colorado River to the west of the Grand Canyon. The largest artificial lake by volume in the United States, it is 185 km (115 mi) long, up to 16 km (10 mi) wide, and has a capacity of 38,296,200,000 m³ (31,250,000 acre ft). It is part of the Lake Mead National Recreation Area.

Mead, Margaret   The American anthropologist Margaret Mead, b. Philadelphia, Dec. 16, 1901, d. Nov. 15, 1978, was a tireless publicist for and popularizer of cultural anthropology. She did fieldwork in the South Pacific, which resulted in the publication of her famous dissertation, *Coming of Age in Samoa* (1928). In this work she showed that, in contrast to modern Western society, adolescence in some societies is traditionally not an especially difficult time. Later she wrote *Sex and Temperament in Three Primitive Societies* (1935), which reported her observations on sex roles and aggression.

Mead was associated with the American Museum of Natural History in New York City from 1926 until her death. She was an early exponent of the use of photogra-

The American anthropologist Margaret Mead was noted for her studies of culture and psychology in both Oceanic and Western societies, predominantly in the areas of sexuality and sex roles, adolescence, race, and education.

phy in anthropological research. This emphasis, along with her desire always to reach a large audience, is commemorated in the annual Margaret Mead Festival of anthropological films at the Museum of Natural History.

In the 1980s, Mead's work, particularly her famous study of Samoa, became a subject of controversy. Her critics alleged that her belief in the overriding influence of culture in shaping personality led her to misread her evidence and overgeneralize. Her champions upheld her undeniably keen observations.

Meade, George Gordon   George Gordon Meade, b. Cádiz, Spain, Dec. 31, 1815, d. Nov. 6, 1872, was a Union general in the U.S. Civil War and the victor of the Battle at Gettysburg. A graduate of West Point (1835), he won a brevet in the Mexican War (1846–48) and started out in the Civil War as a brigade commander.

Meade was severely wounded in the PENINSULAR CAMPAIGN (1862) but performed well at the Second Battle of BULL RUN and, as a division commander, at the Battles of South Mountain, ANTIETAM, and FREDERICKSBURG. Promoted to corps command, he commanded effectively at CHANCELLORSVILLE (1863).

Named commander of the Army of the Potomac a few days before the opening of the Battle of Gettysburg (see GETTYSBURG, BATTLE OF), Meade showed skill in his handling of infantry, artillery, and cavalry and defeated the Confederates. He is sometimes criticized, however, for permitting Robert E. LEE and his army to escape. Following the war he commanded several military departments.

meadow saffron   Meadow saffron, *Colchicum autumnale,* is a perennial herb of the lily family, Liliaceae, native to Europe and North Africa but now found wild in North America. Its flowers resemble those of the unrelated spring-blooming crocuses, and meadow saffron is of-

ten called autumn crocus. In the spring the bulblike corm produces long, narrow leaves, up to 30 cm (1 ft) long, which die down before midsummer and are later followed by one to four large, long-tubed, lavender-to-white, leafless flowers in August or September. The dried corms are poisonous and are used as the drug colchicum and as the source of the alkaloid colchicine, both of which are used medicinally, for example, in the treatment of gout.

Meadowcroft Rockshelter   Meadowcroft Rockshelter, an archaeological site in southwestern Pennsylvania, provides evidence for the human occupation of North America dating before 12,000 years ago. Archaeologists at the site have claimed occupation dates going back 19,000 years, but the evidence has been widely disputed and no consensus has been reached. The site has yielded stone artifacts and other cultural remains from a long succession of intermittent occupations. Heaviest use of the area seems to have been from 2000 BC to AD 300.

meadowlark   Meadowlark is the common name for several upland birds in the genus *Sturnella,* family Icteridae, that are related to the American BLACKBIRDS. The two U.S. species, eastern, *S. magna,* and western, *S. neglecta,* meadowlarks, are very similar in size (25 cm/10 in) and appearance—mottled brown above with white outer tail feathers, and yellow below with a black crescent across the breast. Both are common farmland birds, each with its own cheerful, flutelike song. Feeding largely on insect pests, the meadowlark is helpful to humans.

The eastern meadowlark is a striking yellow-and-black-breasted songbird found widely in rural North America.

mean   see AVERAGE

meander, river   [mee-an'-dur]   RIVERS AND STREAMS that meander flow in a sinuous, or S-shaped, path. The main current swings toward the outer concave bank of the meander bend where the velocity and turbulence are at a maximum; this necessitates a return flow toward the convex inner bank, where coarse particles deposited by the water form the crescent-shaped point bar. Shallow sections (riffles) alternating with deep sections (pools) are characteristic of meandering rivers. Because of erosion on the outer bank, meandering rivers and streams tend to shift over their FLOODPLAINS and form OXBOW LAKES. Meanders also tend to lengthen a river and reduce its velocity.

The morphology and origin of meanders are related to flow discharge, channel slope, and composition of the entrained sediment. Meandering rivers pose environmental problems, such as bank erosion, that generally require engineering solutions.

Meany, George George Meany, b. New York City, Aug. 16, 1894, d. Jan. 10, 1980, successfully merged the American Federation of Labor (AFL) and Congress of Industrial Organizations (CIO) to form (1955) the AMERICAN FEDERATION OF LABOR AND CONGRESS OF INDUSTRIAL ORGANIZATIONS (AFL-CIO). Meany began work as a plumber at age 16, turning to the union movement full time in 1922. He became secretary-treasurer of the AFL in 1939 and president in 1952. After the merger with the CIO, he was elected president of the new federation, which at the time represented most of U.S. organized labor. He was consistently reelected thereafter.

Meany used his influence to support anti-Communist labor organizations in the Americas and elsewhere. In the 1960s he placed the AFL-CIO firmly behind the U.S. war effort in Vietnam. In 1972 he broke with AFL-CIO tradition by refusing to endorse the Democratic presidential nominee, George McGovern. In the late 1970s he was strongly critical of the economic program of the Democratic administration of Jimmy Carter. Meany retired in 1979.

George Meany, an American labor leader, was instrumental in the consolidation of the American Federation of Labor and the Congress of Industrial Organizations. He served as president of the AFL-CIO from its inception in 1955 until he retired in 1979.

Meares, John [meerz] John Meares, c.1756–1809, was a British naval officer and explorer. He served in the navy until 1783, then entered the merchant service and made several voyages to the northwest coast of North

America between 1786 and 1788. At Nootka Sound on Vancouver Island he erected a trading post and built the *North West America*, the first schooner launched on the Pacific Ocean north of Mexico. When the Spanish, who claimed the region, seized (1789) two of his vessels, Meares sought redress from the British crown, exaggerating both his claims and his losses; he thus precipitated a controversy that almost led to war between Britain and Spain. The issue was settled in 1790 by the Nootka Sound Convention, the first formal sign of the decline of Spain's American empire.

---

measles Measles, or rubeola, is a highly contagious viral disease. It usually affects children but can occur at any age in susceptible persons. The measles virus is not the same virus that causes GERMAN MEASLES.

The virus is transmitted by sneezing, coughing, and direct personal contact. The early symptoms—fever, malaise, sore muscles, headache, eye irritation, and sensitivity to light—occur about 11 days after infection. Nasal discharge, sneezing, and coughing develop rapidly. Two to four days after the first symptom, a characteristic skin rash appears, which fades after a few days. While not a particularly severe disease, measles does reduce normal resistance, making a patient susceptible to more serious secondary bacterial infections. In rare cases, the virus enters the brain to cause a form of encephalitis.

Measles was once common throughout the world. Explosive outbreaks would occur, particularly in institutional settings or military barracks. In 1963, however, the measles vaccine was introduced, which greatly reduced the incidence. Nevertheless, the 1980s saw a marked increase in measles cases in the United States. Experts believe that this rise may have resulted from the failure to vaccinate many infants at the age of 15 months. In addition, about 5 percent of vaccinated adults are not adequately protected by a single dose of vaccine. Physicians now recommend that everyone receive two doses of measles vaccine. Medical treatment consists of symptom relief and the use of antibiotics to prevent secondary infections. Infection confers lifelong immunity.

---

measurement Measurement is the process of obtaining quantitative information about the physical world. Methods for increasing the accuracy of measurements are intimately associated with the growth of technology. This article discusses the methods used for measuring particular fundamental quantities.

Units and Standards

Any measurement must involve the comparison of the measured quantity with a known standard unit. In absolute measurement, the unit may be the official unit for the quantity considered, such as the meter or the ampere. In relative measurement, a special reference unit is chosen for a given measurement; for example, the brightness of a star is expressed in terms of the brightness of another star.

A length of 3.6 meters means that the measured length is 3.6 times as large as a standard length, in this case the meter. Until 1960 the standard meter was equal to the length of a prototype meter bar kept in Paris. It was then redefined as 1,650,763.73 times the wavelength of the radiation emitted at a specified energy level by krypton-86. In 1983 it was redefined once again, as the length of the path traveled by light in a vacuum during a time interval of 1/299,792,458 of a second. This definition has the great advantage of being reproducible in any well-equipped laboratory, rather than depending on an actual object. The wide variety of units and standards employed worldwide are similarly based on physical quantities.

The presently agreed-on system of units used for scientific work in many countries, known as the International System of Units, or simply the SI system, is based on the mks (meter-kilogram-second) system and contains seven base units of length, mass, time, temperature (kelvin), luminous intensity (candela), amount of substance (mole), and electric current (ampere). The mole is a dimensionless chemical unit that cannot be measured directly; the others are directly measurable.

Measurement of Basic SI Nonelectrical Quantities

In addition to the basic dimensionally independent SI quantities, there are many other measurements closely related to these basic quantities. The survey below deals with the principles of measuring the standard quantities as well as certain derived quantities.

Length Measurements. Length measurements play a special role in measurement technology, because nearly all other analog measurements (those involving continuous—rather than stepwise, or digital—monitoring) may be reduced to measurements of length. The simplest measurement of this kind is carried out with a ruler, in which case an accuracy of approximately 1 mm can be achieved. A vernier caliper will correctly measure to 0.05 mm, while an accuracy of 0.01 mm is possible with a screw micrometer. Accurate length comparisons to 0.001 mm are possible with CALIPERS or end gauges. These are then used as length substandards, with which it is only possible to determine whether an object has the same dimensions as the substandard. The determination of such

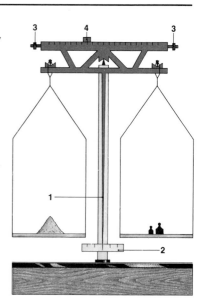

The determination of mass is most accurately performed by means of a two-pan balance. The object to be weighed is placed on the left pan of the balance, and weights of known mass are added to the right pan until the pointer (1) is centered on the scale (2)—at which point the weights on the two pans are equal. Screw nuts (3) are fitted on both ends of the balance beam for initial centering of the pointer. A small rider weight (4), which slides along a scale on the beam, is used to obtain more-accurate readings of mass.

quantities as angles, areas, deformation, and velocity depends on accurate measurement of length.

Mass Measurements. The mass m of an object is measured by means of the force W, or weight, exerted upon it by the Earth. This force is related to the mass through the expression $W = mg$, where g is the known acceleration of gravity. This acceleration may in turn be measured as the distance a falling object covers within a given time frame. The simplest means for measuring mass is to use a spring balance; however, such a device is inherently inaccurate. The measurement of mass is therefore usually carried out as a *null* measurement, in which one mass is compared to another, known mass. A BALANCE is used for this purpose. Comparison is made through the use of several standard weights, which generally cannot be lighter than several milligrams. Measurements of volume and density (mass per unit volume) are also closely related to determinations of mass.

Time Measurements. Time measurements are always based on counting periodic phenomena, such as oscillations of atoms and molecules, electromagnetic oscillations in oscillators, and sound or mechanical vibrations. The use of these time standards results in a variety of clocks (see CLOCKS AND WATCHES), including the ATOMIC CLOCK, the quartz crystal clock, and the common watch and pendulum clock.

Temperature Measurements. There are two fundamental laws on which temperature measurements may be based. The best-known law is that of Robert Boyle and J. L. Gay-Lussac (see GAS LAWS), according to which gas pressure depends on temperature. Temperature measurement thus becomes a pressure measurement that can be performed as a length measurement with the aid of a manometer.

The radiation law, according to which the quantity of radiation emitted by a substance depends on temperature, is less well known. The measurement in this case is

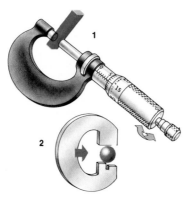

A micrometer caliper (1) is used by machinists to measure accurately external dimensions of parts. Metric micrometers usually measure to 0.01 mm (0.004 in), whereas those measuring in inches can be read to 0.001 in. (0.025 mm). For mass-production work in which a range of sizes is allowable, the component must pass the first but not the second step of a limit snap gauge (2).

that of the radiation intensity as determined by a bolometer. Several other methods of temperature measurement are also known. These make use of THERMOCOUPLES, THERMOMETERS, bimetals, and vapor-pressure thermometers.

The field of calorimetry is closely related to temperature measurement. It involves determination of the initial and final temperatures of a given, weighed amount of a liquid whose specific heat is known. Calorimetry forms the basis for a determination of specific heat, thermal conductivity, and energy, through the conversion of energy, or work, into heat in a calorimeter.

Measurement of Luminous Intensity. Luminous intensity may be determined by either absolute or relative measurements. Relative measurements involve comparison of the strength of an unknown light source to that of a known (and variable) light source.

This can be done very accurately through a visual null measurement by attenuating the light from the known source until both sources appear to be equally bright. Attenuation is possible through the use of a diaphragm or a light-absorbing prism, or by varying the distance to one of the light sources. Determination of the null point is then followed by the actual measurement.

Absolute light measurements are carried out by means of visual null comparison to a radiation standard, such as a piece of tungsten wire heated electrically to a specified temperature; the amount of radiation thus emitted is known from the radiation laws. Another type of absolute measurement makes use of calibrated radiation-absorption meters.

Measurement of Electrical Quantities

The measurement of electric current is chiefly based on the 19th-century discovery by Hans Christian Oersted and Michael FARADAY of the relationship between electricity and magnetism. The fundamental association is the phenomenon, first reported by Oersted in 1820, that an electric current passing through a conductor produces a magnetic field, which in turn exerts a force on other currents near it. Two currents thus always exert a force on each other (the law of Biot and Savart), and the measurement of the force exerted by one on the other gives a measure of the current. This fact is also used in the definition of the unit of current: one ampere is the current that gives rise to a force of 2×10^{-7} newtons between two perfect conductors of infinite length, in vacuo, carrying the current at a distance of one meter from each other.

In practical measuring instruments that make use of this phenomenon, the conductors consist of two coils with a large number of turns. By connecting these coils in different ways, such electrodynamometers as AMMETERS, VOLTMETERS, and wattmeters may be constructed, as well as a class of instruments known as Ferraris meters. Measurement with an electrodynamometer is based on determining the force acting between the two coils through which current flows. This is effected by measuring the deviation from equilibrium of a free-turning coil opposed by a small spring. In Ferraris meters the two coils are fixed with respect to a piece of metal that is free to turn, and the measurement is based on the eddy currents in-

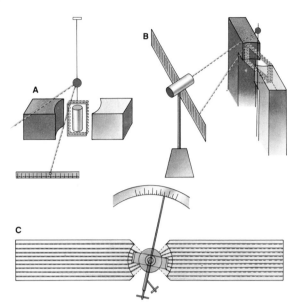

A moving-coil galvanometer measures electric currents. One version of this device (A) uses an iron core and a coil of wire suspended between the poles of a permanent magnet. A uniform magnetifc field is established that exerts a twisting force, or torque, on the coil when a current passes through it. A mirror attached to a flat metal strip reflects light from a source to a scale. When the coil is deflected (B), the spot of light on the scale is moved by an amount proportional to the current. In a portable version (C) the moving coil pivots between two jewel bearings, two hairsprings provide the restoring torque and current leads, and a pointer indicates the reading.

duced in the metal. In all of these two-coil instruments, the magnetic field is weak when the current intensity is low, so that these meters are not very sensitive. However, they can measure both direct and alternating currents.

Another widely used electromagnetic current-measuring instrument is the moving-coil meter, or GALVANOMETER, in which the current to be measured flows through a coil suspended in a strong magnetic field induced by a permanent magnet rather than by the current itself. Such instruments measure only direct current.

Transducer Measurements

When direct measurements of a particular quantity are impossible, some other measurable quantity can often be found that is linked to the former by some law. Many measuring instruments convert one form of energy into another. This is called transduction; the converter itself is called a TRANSDUCER. Although transducers as a group involve many forms of energy, in practice it is often convenient to convert a quantity into an electrically measurable one. The measurement signal is then available in the form of a current-to-voltage signal that can be processed in a number of different ways that are either impossible or very difficult to do with mechanical signals. Common electrical transducers include the photoelectric cell, the Geiger counter, the thermocouple, and the piezoelectric crystal.

Measurement Errors

The result of a measurement and the actual value of the quantity to be measured are often not precisely equal. The difference between these two values may be due either to random errors or to systematic errors. Random errors are those which occur in the act of measurement itself; systematic errors occur as a result of instrument faults and calibration mistakes. Repeating a measurement reduces the random error in the final result in proportion to $\sqrt{n}$, where n is the number of measurements taken. It is more difficult to estimate and reduce the magnitude of systematic errors.

See also: METRIC SYSTEM; UNITS, PHYSICAL; WEIGHTS AND MEASURES.

meat and meat packing   The term *meat* commonly refers to the skeletal muscle from the carcasses of animals—beef and veal (cattle), pork (hogs), and lamb (sheep). The general composition of such meat is approximately 70% water, 21% protein, 8% fat, and 1% ash (mineral). A cooked 85-g (3-oz) serving of beef contains approximately 200 calories, 9.4 g of fat (4.2 g of saturated fat), and 73 mg of cholesterol. POULTRY, fish (see FISHING INDUSTRY), and wild game are sometimes considered to be meat; they are not discussed here.

With sales in 1986 of more than $60 billion, the meat and meat-packing industry is the largest agriculture-based industry in the United States. It is concerned primarily with converting the flesh of livestock into edible meat items. The United States is the world's largest meat producer, followed by the USSR, Germany, France, Brazil, and Argentina.

Development of the Industry. The first meat packers in the United States were the colonial New England farmers, who packed meats in salt as a means of preservation. As the frontier moved westward, slaughter facilities were constructed near population centers, and livestock were driven overland or barged to these markets. Cincinnati, Ohio, was known as "Porkopolis" because of the large volume of hogs marketed and killed there. In the mid-1800s, with the development of refrigerated rail shipping, Chicago became the center for the collection and slaughter of livestock because of its central location as a railroad terminus. Most recently, the beef industry has left the large metropolitan areas to be near the large commercial feedlots in the central United States in such states as Texas, Oklahoma, Kansas, and Nebraska. The pork industry remains more centrally located in the Midwest, principally in Iowa, Illinois, Minnesota, Michigan, and Nebraska.

Scope of the Meat-Packing Industry. In the United States more than 2 million farmers and ranchers are engaged in raising livestock, which is slaughtered at approximately 4,000 federally inspected plants doing more than 96% of all processing (less than 1% is slaughtered at the farm for personal consumption without inspection, and the remainder is state inspected). As with many industries, there is a consolidation trend. Currently, three major

BEEF CUTS

FOREQUARTERS		HINDQUARTERS	
CHUCK:	Blade steak and roast Shoulder steak and roast Various other pot roast cuts Chuck short ribs Stewing beef Ground beef	**SHORT LOIN:**	Club steak (also called shell steak, New York steak) T-bone steak Porterhouse steak Tenderloin (filet mignon)
RIB:	Rib roasts, standing and rolled Rib steak Rib eye steak and roast (Delmonico)	**SIRLOIN:**	Pin bone steak Flat bone steak Wedge bone steak Tip steak and roast
		RUMP:	Rump roast
SHORT PLATE:	Short ribs Corned beef Stewing beef Ground beef	**ROUND:**	Top round and steak Bottom round and steak Eye of round Heel of round Cubed steak Ground beef Tip steak and roast
SHANK:	Cross cuts Stewing beef		
BRISKET		**FLANK:**	Flank steak Ground beef

packers process approximately 70% of the beef and 60% of the pork in the United States.

In addition to the sale of meat from the carcasses, by-products are an essential part of the meat-packing business. In the case of beef, as much as 15% of the value of the live animal may be in the form of by-products such as hides, inedible and edible tallow, meat and bone meal, and variety meats. Only about 62% of beef is consumed as beef cuts; 24% is ground for hamburger, and 14% is processed into bologna-type products. In the case of pork, more than 65% of the total is consumed in the form of processed meats such as ham, bacon, and sausage. A large proportion of these meat by-products are exported. The meat-packing industry also produces such products as pharmaceuticals, cosmetics, glues, and gelatins.

Slaughtering and Processing Procedures. The Humane Slaughter Act (1960) requires that prior to slaughter animals be rendered completely unconscious with a minimum of excitement and discomfort, by mechanical, electrical, or chemical (carbon dioxide gas) methods.

After being bled, skinned, and eviscerated (having the internal organs removed), the carcasses are chilled for 24 to 48 hours before being graded and processed. Meat items, such as the brain, kidneys, sweetbread (calf thymus gland), tail, and tongue, do not accompany a carcass and are considered edible by-products to be sold separately as specialty items. These parts, and all other items removed from the carcass, such as feet, hide, and intestines, are called offal.

Inspection and Grading System. Inspection takes place at practically every step of the livestock-procurement and meat-packing processes. Inspection attempts to ensure that harmful additives and ingredients are kept out of manufactured meat products, that sick and diseased animals are excluded from the market, that misleading labeling and packaging are eliminated, and that contaminated and unwholesome meats are prevented from reaching consumers. Federal meat inspection is administered by the Food Safety and Inspection Service (FSIS) of the U.S. Department of Agriculture (USDA). Meat that is to be used entirely within a given state need be inspected only by that state's department of agriculture, whereas all meats entering interstate commerce must be federally inspected.

Unlike inspection, which is mandatory, meat grading is a service offered to packers on a voluntary basis by the Agricultural Marketing Service of the USDA. Grading is funded from fees paid by the users. Grading establishes and maintains uniform trading standards and aids in the determination of the value of various cuts of meat.

Carcasses are given both a quality and a yield grade. Quality grades for beef carcasses are prime, choice, select, standard, commercial, utility, cutter, and canner. These grades are assigned on the basis of carcass marbling (fat flecks or streaks within the lean), color and texture of the lean, and maturity, which is determined according to the color, size, and texture of the cartilage bones. Although grading was not originally intended to provide estimates of palatability (taste and tenderness) for consumers, it has become a consumer rating for beef. Carcasses below the choice grade have rarely been stamped with a grade because they were thought to be less palatable. The belief held by some consumers that leaner meats (those with a lower fat content) are more healthful has led to an increased demand for the select grade, however. Yield grades classify carcasses on the basis of the proportion of usable meat to bone and fat and are used along with quality grades to determine monetary value of a carcass.

Other Aspects. Livestock marketing and prices are affected by weather, feed prices, federal import policies, and consumer demands. In the United States meat packing is a high-risk industry; government statistics indicate that workers in meat-packing plants have the highest injury rate of all U.S. industrial workers.

See also: CATTLE AND CATTLE RAISING.

Mecca [mek'-uh]   Mecca (Arabic: *Makkah*), the birthplace of MUHAMMAD, is the holiest city of the Islamic faith. Capital of the Hejaz province of Saudi Arabia, Mecca is located 72 km (45 mi) east of Jidda, its port on the Red Sea, and about 485 km (300 mi) south of Medina. Mecca's population is 550,000 (1980 est.). The city is located on the valley of the Wadi Ibrahim and is surrounded by hills from 60 to 150 m (200 to 500 ft) high.

Mecca is a holy city, and non-Muslims are not permitted to enter it. For Muslims, however, the pilgrimage to Mecca, or the *hajj,* is one of the basic tenets of the religion. Each year, over 1,000,000 people visit during the month of pilgrimage. The core of Mecca, including the commercial district, surrounds the al-Haram or Great Mosque, which can hold 300,000 people. Inside the mosque are the KAABA (a shrine enclosing a sacred Black Stone) and the well of Zamzam. They are the focus of the pilgrimage.

Even before Muhammad's birth (570), the city was an important commercial and religious center (the Black Stone was sacred in early Arabic religions). Muhammad began to preach in the city c.613 but was forced to flee to Medina in 622 (the Hegira). In 630 he returned with 10,000 men to conquer the city and establish it as the center of the Islamic world. The city was ruled by the armathians from 930 until 1269, when the Egyptian Mamelukes gained control. The Ottoman Turks ruled from

As the birthplace of Muhammad, Mecca is the most sacred city and pilgrimage center of the Muslim world. The al-Haram mosque is the core of the city and contains the Kaaba, the sacred building housing the venerated Black Stone. Shown here are pilgrims prostrating themselves before the Kaaba, the place toward which Muslims everywhere face while praying.

1517 until 1916, when the Hejaz region became independent, with Mecca as its capital. Mecca fell to Ibn Saud in 1924, and in 1932 Hejaz became a province of Saudi Arabia. In November 1979 a group of 200 Muslim zealots seized Mecca's Great Mosque; they were driven out by Saudi troops after 10 days, and many were executed. In 1987, Iranian pilgrims staged violent demonstrations in the city.

mechanical advantage   see SIMPLE MACHINES

mechanical drawing
A mechanical drawing is a graphical system in which separate views, arranged according to orthographic projection theory, show an object in detail. LEONARDO DA VINCI is known as the father of modern drawing. He practiced and taught a method of graphical description that conveyed and recorded ideas about mechanical objects and systems.

In the late 1700s, Gaspard MONGE, a French mathematician, introduced two planes of projection at right angles to each other for graphical description of solid objects. His system, known as orthographic projection, is used in modern mechanical drawing.

The rapid industrial growth of the 19th and 20th centuries led to acceptance of orthographic projection drawing, universal drawing standards, and more functional, less decorative drawings. Today, mechanical drawings are the means of communication between designers and builders.

Mechanical drawings are produced freehand or with instruments. Instruments are used for most finished mechanical drawings, which are usually made to scale and require such precision tools as T-squares, parallel bars, drafting machines, compasses, and irregular or French curves. These traditional tools are now being superseded by computers (see COMPUTER-AIDED DESIGN AND COMPUTER-AIDED MANUFACTURE).

Most mechanical drawings use the orthographic projection system. As shown in figure 1, separate views of the object are arranged to show all its details. The views, representing the top (plan) view, front (elevation) view, and right side view, are constructed as if a transparent box had been placed over the object and the object then projected onto the box's top, front, and right side. If the box sides were cut and laid flat, the object would then appear as an orthographic projection.

The pictorial view is a graphical presentation that presents an object much as the eye would see it. Pictorial representations are often used for presentation drawings and maintenance-book illustrations. Figure 2 shows an isometric pictorial drawing of the object in figure 1.

The engineering draftsman in the background works with the more traditional tools of the mechanical drafting trade—inclined table, triangle, and drafting machine. The draftsman in the foreground creates his drawings on a personal computer.

mechanical engineering
Mechanical engineering is concerned primarily with means of converting energy to useful mechanical forms. The specialty is machine oriented; the mechanical engineer's creations involve motion, in contrast to other branches of ENGINEERING where most creations are static.

Machines consist of two major types of subsystems. The prime mover converts energy, usually in the form of fuel, into simple mechanical form. The INTERNAL COMBUSTION ENGINE serves in this capacity, converting gasoline energy into the movement of a rotating shaft. The functional mechanism converts the output of the prime mover into useful work. In the automobile the functional mechanism converts the output of the engine into movement of the vehicle.

Mechanical engineering is concerned with the design of prime movers and functional mechanisms. Practitioners, however, invariably specialize, concentrating in such areas as the design of diesel engines or steam turbines, or the functional portions of such equipment as refrigerators or metal-cutting machines.

The development of mechanical engineering closely parallels the industrial revolution; in fact both received impetus from the STEAM ENGINE patented in 1769 by James Watt. Pioneering this field were millwrights and mechanics with little or no formal education. By the mid-19th century, however, a sufficient number of professional mechanical engineers existed to form (1847) the British Institution of Mechanical Engineers. The American Society of Mechanical Engineers was founded in 1880. Simultaneously, university curricula evolved to provide training.

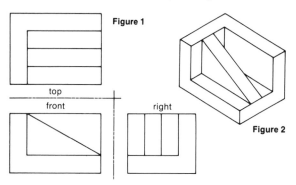

Figure 1

Figure 2

top

front

right

mechanics Mechanics, a branch of PHYSICS, describes the effect of FORCE on bodies at rest or in motion. Particles and solids are studied in DYNAMICS and STATICS, gases and liquids in FLUID MECHANICS, astronomical bodies in CELESTIAL MECHANICS, and subatomic phenomena in QUANTUM MECHANICS.

Mecklenburg [mak'-len-boork] Mecklenburg, officially Mecklenburg-Vorpommern, is a German state located on the Baltic Sea between the Elbe and Oder rivers in northeastern Germany. The state has an area of 23,838 km² (9,204 mi²) and a population of 1,960,000 (1991 est.). Dairying occurs, and fodder and grain crops are grown. ROSTOCK, Warnemünde, Schwerin (the capital), and Neubrandenburg are major cities.

The area was occupied by Slavs in about AD 600. The princes of Mecklenburg became vassals of the Holy Roman Empire in the 12th century and dukes in 1348. After various divisions and reunifications, the region was divided into the duchies of Mecklenburg-Schwerin and Mecklenburg-Strelitz in 1701. They became grand duchies in 1815 and members of the German Empire in 1871. The grand dukes were deposed in 1918, and the two states were united as Mecklenburg state in 1934. They were part of East Germany from 1945 to 1990, when Germany was reunified and the new state of Mecklenburg-Vorpommern was created in the region.

Mecklenburg Declaration of Independence [mek'-len-burg] The Mecklenburg Declaration of Independence was an alleged resolution passed by the citizens of Charlotte, in Mecklenburg County, N.C., on May 20, 1775. It supposedly asserted that they were a sovereign people independent of Great Britain—a year before the adoption of the Declaration of Independence. The Mecklenburg Declaration is not attested by any document earlier than 1819, however, and it is probably a garbled version of the Mecklenburg Resolves of May 31, 1775. The resolves declared that the authority of king and Parliament was "for the present wholly suspended" and replaced by the authority of the colonial legislatures.

medals and decorations Medals and decorations are conspicuous tokens of services rendered by an individual to a state or other governing entity. A medal usually consists of two parts: a badge bearing an inscription or design and a ribbon suspended from the badge. A decoration may involve several separate elements: a badge; a collar or chain from which the badge is hung; a sash in a distinctive color; and a large star or other distinctive shape, worn on or near the sash.

Medals and decorations may be divided into three classes. The oldest, dating from medieval times, is the decoration granted as the token of membership in a chivalric order. In later centuries this category of medal was joined by two others: awards for gallantry and campaign

awards. In the United States, the Congressional Medal of Honor is a famous example of a gallantry award; the Victory Medal that was given to participants in World War II is perhaps the best-known American campaign medal.

Ancient and Medieval Chivalric Decorations. Decorations have deep roots in history. The Greeks awarded a golden button for gallantry on the field. The Romans crowned outstanding soldiers with oak or laurel wreaths, and many Roman coins show the emperor so crowned.

During the Middle Ages, individual acts of heroism on the battlefield or of service in other capacities were sometimes recognized by gifts of swords or grants of land. Later medieval kings, searching for ways of binding a powerful nobility to an increasingly ambitious monarchy, created orders of CHIVALRY. The restricted membership of such an order received certain distinctive apparel, including sashes and badges, and could consider itself as enlisted in a distinguished elite.

The oldest surviving chivalric orders are probably those of Portugal, one of which dates from 1162. England's ambitious Edward III instituted the Most Noble Order of the Garter in 1348, during the Hundred Years' War with France. One of the most famous of all medieval orders, that of the Golden Fleece, was first awarded in Burgundy in 1429. Orders of chivalry spread throughout Europe in late medieval and early modern times. Their rise was predictable in any area where a prince sought to enlarge his powers. Thus, in Russia, chivalric orders were the innovation of two of Russia's most ambitious rulers, Peter the Great (r. 1682–1725) and Catherine the Great (r. 1762–96).

Campaign and Gallantry Awards. When the English defeated the Spanish Armada in 1588, the event was commemorated by a limited number of gold and silver medals, which were presented to prominent governmental and naval officers by Queen Elizabeth herself. In the 1640s, during the English Civil War, decorations began to be awarded for specific acts of bravery rather than as mere tokens of royal favor. Like the earlier Armada medals, these were oval and could be worn on a chain. In 1650, Oliver Cromwell awarded a special medal to all participants who had fought against the royalist Scots in the Battle of Dunbar.

American Awards. American medals and decorations are restricted to those for bravery or participation. No official hereditary chivalric orders are recognized, although during the nation's founding years one was almost adopted. In 1783 officers of the American Continental Army established the Society of the Cincinnati; membership was restricted to Revolutionary War officers and their eldest male heirs. The suggestion was made that the federal government take over the society, but republican sympathies prevented it, and the society remained a private organization.

The highest decoration for gallantry in the United States and the oldest official American medal that is still awarded is the Congressional Medal of Honor, instituted in 1861–62 and first awarded in March 1863 at the height of the Civil War. Second in distinction are the Distinguished Service Cross (U.S. Army, first awarded in 1918), the Navy Cross (1919), and the Air Force Cross

Medals and Decorations of the United States

Distinguished Service Cross

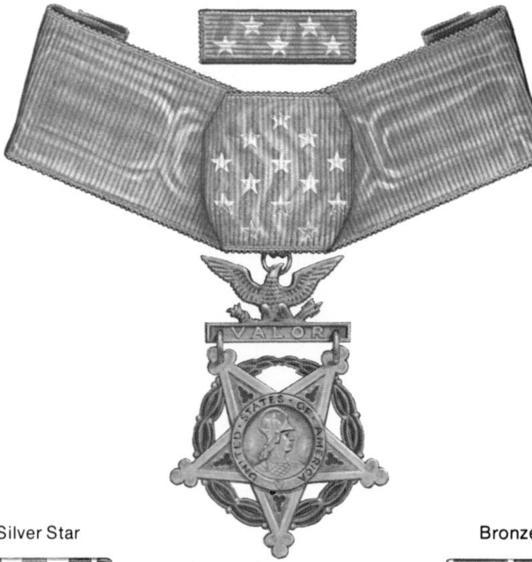

Congressional Medal of Honor
(Army)

Navy Cross

Distinguished
Flying Cross

Silver Star

Civilian Distinguished
Service Medal

Bronze Star

Purple Heart

European-African-Middle
Eastern Campaign Medal
(World War II)

Presidential
Unit Citation
(Army)

Legion of Merit
(Chief Commander)

Presidential
Unit Citation
(Navy)

Victory Medal
(World War I)

Medals and Decorations of the World

Knight Commander of the Order
of the British Empire
(United Kingdom)

Volunteer Service Medal
(Canada)

Commander of the Order of Pius
(Vatican)

Victoria Cross
(United Kingdom)

Star
(United Kingdom)

Iron Cross
(Germany)

Order of Merit 1st Class
(German Federal Republic)

Korean
Service Medal
(United Nations)

Vietnam Medal
(Australia)

Order of Lenin
(USSR)

National Order of Merit
(France)

Hero of the
Soviet Union
(USSR)

Croix de Guerre
(France)

Medal of
Supreme Bravery
(Israel)

(1960). Gallantry awards also include the Purple Heart, first instituted by George Washington in 1782 and reinstituted by Congress in 1932, the 200th anniversary of Washington's birth; the Silver and Bronze stars, dating from World Wars I and II, respectively; and the Distinguished Service Medal of the army, navy, and air force. Campaign awards have been given for participation in all major U.S. wars as well as for minor engagements. In common with many other countries, the United States issues "ribbon bars," which bear the same pattern as the ribbons worn with campaign medals and other decorations. These bars are worn in place of the medals, except on extraordinary state occasions.

European Awards. The most highly prized British gallantry award is the Victoria Cross, introduced in 1856. The bronze for this rather plain decoration came from a Russian cannon captured during the Crimean War. The French Revolution swept away all French chivalric orders, banning them as antidemocratic. The French Republic, nevertheless, wanted to find a method of honoring distinguished citizens in war and peace; in 1802, Napoléon Bonaparte (later Emperor Napoleon I) instituted the Légion d'Honneur, which in essence is a republican chivalric order. The badge of the Legion of Honor with its red ribbon is awarded in five classes. The Croix de Guerre, instituted during World War I, is France's highest award for gallantry.

Medan [may-dahn']   Medan, a city on the Deli River, is the capital of North Sumatra province, northeastern Sumatra, Indonesia. The largest city on Sumatra, it has a population of 2,110,000 (1985 est.). Medan is a transportation and trading center; Belawan, its port, is at the mouth of the river, on the Andaman Sea, 24 km (15 mi) away. Medan manufactures automobiles, machinery, and foodstuffs.

Originally settled as several Indonesian and Chinese villages around vast tobacco plantations, Medan was incorporated in 1886. The sultan of Deli's palace (19th century), a gift from the Dutch, is a historical landmark. Medan has two universities.

Medea [med-ee'-uh]   In Greek mythology Medea was the sorceress who helped JASON steal the GOLDEN FLEECE from her father, King Aeetes of Colchis. Fleeing from Colchis with Jason and the Argonauts, Medea allegedly dismembered her brother Apsyrtus to delay Jason's pursuers. By the time they reached Greece, Medea and Jason were married. She tricked King Pelias's daughters into murdering their father, Jason's uncle, thus securing the crown for Jason. When Jason repudiated her for Glauce (or Creusa), the daughter of King Creon of Corinth, Medea first sent a poisoned robe to his fiancée, then killed her own two sons and set fire to the palace, fleeing through the air on a chariot sent by Helios, Aeetes' father. Understood not as a kidnapped earth goddess but as an evil woman, Medea has fascinated tragedians, notably Euripides, Seneca, Pierre Corneille, and Jean Anouilh.

Medellín [may-dayl-yeen']   Medellín, capital of Antioquia department in west central Colombia, is the principal industrial center and the second largest city in Colombia. It has a population of 1,468,089 (1985 est.). Medellín is set in a valley of the Cordillera Central at an altitude of 1,525 m (5,000 ft). Manufactures include steel, textiles, metal products, processed foods, rubber goods, electrical equipment, and tobacco products. Drug trafficking also contributes to the economy: Medellín is home to Colombia's richest, most violent cocaine cartel.

Founded in 1675, Medellín was isolated until the completion of railroads during the 19th century. Of interest are a national mint, several 17th-century churches, and numerous orchid gardens. The University of Antioquia and Bolívar University are there.

Medes   see MEDIA

Medford   Medford (1990 pop., 46,951) is a city on Bear Creek, in southwestern Oregon, and the seat of Jackson County. It was founded in 1883 and has an economy dependent on tourism, lumber, and fruit canning. CRATER LAKE National Park is nearby.

Media [mee'-dee-uh]   Media was an ancient country of western Asia corresponding to the modern provinces of Azerbaijan, Kurdistan, and some of Kermanshah in northwestern Iran. The Medes were Indo-Europeans, related to the ancient Persians, who entered Iran after 1200 BC and came under ASSYRIA's domination. They probably secured their freedom about 625 BC, when their king Cyaxares unified the Median tribes. He then conquered the Persians in southwestern Iran and joined (621) BABYLONIA in an attack that destroyed (612) Nineveh and the Assyrian Empire. From their capital at Ecbatana (modern Hamadan), the Medes then ruled western Iran, northern Mesopotamia, and part of Anatolia. They were overthrown in 550 BC by the Persian CYRUS THE GREAT.

median   see AVERAGE

mediation   Mediation is the intervention of a third party in a dispute between two other parties in an attempt to reconcile their differences, usually upon their request. Mediation differs from ARBITRATION. Whereas an arbitrator usually has the power to make decisions that are binding on the parties, the mediator seeks to persuade them to agree. Mediation is often used in international conflicts (where it is also termed *conciliation*). The United Nations has established procedures for obligatory mediation for member states.

In labor-management disputes mediation is frequently used during the early stages in an attempt to avoid strikes. In the United States mediation is conducted by the Federal Mediation and Conciliation Service, which was established in 1947.

Medicaid   Medicaid is a health-care program, funded jointly by U.S. federal and state agencies, that provides medical payments for those whose monthly income falls below state-specified levels, and who are 65 or older, blind, disabled, or members of families receiving AFDC— Aid to Families with Dependent Children. Thirty-four states use the Supplemental Security Income (SSI; see SOCIAL SECURITY) rules as an income yardstick; the other states have more restrictive standards. (MEDICARE, the other major government-sponsored health-care program, is administered by the federal Social Security Administration primarily for elderly recipients of social security.)

Medicaid was established in 1965 by an amendment to the Social Security Act. It is under the general oversight of the Health Care Financing Administration of the U.S. Department of Health and Human Services, which monitors the quality of the services provided and provides information and technical assistance to state and local organizations.

medical ethics   Medical ethics, a branch of the philosophy of ETHICS, deals with moral decisions in medicine. Rapid progress in the medical application of basic biological knowledge has necessitated the ethical questioning of certain present-day and imminent medical practices. Professional codes of ethics, such as the HIPPOCRATIC OATH with its rules of conduct for physicians, may require augmentation because modern medical technology has created many situations that offer conflicting alternatives.

Life-saving technologies, such as kidney dialysis and organ transplants, for example, cannot be used in every medical situation that might demand them. Decisions on their allocation may depend on consideration of personal and family consequences and other factors. Many hospitals have established committees to deal with such so-called triage decisions. A closely related question is that of EUTHANASIA, ordinarily the termination of extraordinary treatment of so-called hopeless cases. Voluntary euthanasia may be requested by the affected individual, but if the patient is unable to do so, involuntary euthanasia depends on the family or attending physician. The ethical values of each party differ, and a process of cooperative decision-making may be required (see DEATH AND DYING).

In prenatal diagnosis the option of therapeutic ABORTION is offered, if genetic defects are detected. The ethics of abortion may be complicated by such questions as the permissibility of selecting certain genetic traits. Physicians engaged in genetic counseling (see GENETIC DISEASES) often must deal with these questions. Related to this issue is that of the morality of using tissues from electively aborted fetuses for medical research. The rapidly developing techniques for abetting human FERTILITY, in turn, have brought with them a number of ethical problems (see ARTIFICIAL INSEMINATION).

Questions of medical ethics also arise in the area of GENETIC ENGINEERING, which involves use of recombinant-DNA molecules. It is likely that ways will be found to correct many human genetic defects with recombinant DNA.

The ethical questions center on the growing ability to control evolution.

Another area of concern is that of brain interventions, which may place strict limitations on individual freedom. Implantation of electrodes in the brain and administration of psychoactive drugs may be considered reversible, whereas psychosurgery is irreversible. Frontal lobotomy, which surgically disrupts pathways between the frontal lobes and the midbrain, was once commonly used in attempts to control abnormal behavior. Other, less drastic procedures sever connections between more discrete parts of the brain or destroy only defined areas (see PSYCHOPATHOLOGY).

A further area of ethical concern is experimentation on human subjects, which may be the last stage prior to general use of a new drug or medical procedure. Informed consent from the subjects must be obtained by law. In cases involving highly esoteric research, however, truly informed consent may be difficult to obtain. The values of the research in relation to potential hazards to the subjects should be determined in a sensitive and consciously ethical manner.

See also: MALPRACTICE; SURROGATE MOTHERHOOD.

Medicare   Medicare is a system of U.S. government-provided health insurance for the elderly. Operated by the Social Security Administration and financed largely by SOCIAL SECURITY funds, it is designed for persons 65 years old and older, and for the severely disabled. Medicare helps to pay for the services of physicians, inpatient hospital care, some outpatient hospital services, and limited home care after the patient leaves the hospital. One of the most successful of President Lyndon Johnson's Great Society programs, Medicare was signed into law in 1965, along with MEDICAID, a program for the medically indigent. The two programs, between them, have allowed broad access to physician and hospital care for some of the poor, most of the disabled who receive social security benefits, and almost all the elderly.

Medicare covers 98 percent of the nation's 30 million elderly as well as another 2 million of the permanently disabled. Medicare Part A, which helps pay hospital costs, covers all enrollees. Part B, Supplementary Medical Insurance, is an optional plan for which a premium is charged. It pays 80 percent of the fee for each office visit to a doctor, although it will not pay more than "customary and reasonable" fees, and in 1989 it issued new fee standards that will increase payments for preventive medicine and reduce them for surgery and for such diagnostic specialties as radiology.

Medici (family) [med'-i-chee]   The Medici, the most famous of Italian dynasties, governed FLORENCE under a veiled despotism (1434–94, 1512–27) and as overt hereditary rulers (1530–1737). Its members were among the great patrons of the Italian Renaissance.

Originally merchants and bankers, the Medici were active in Florentine politics from the late 13th century on.

A detail from Benozzo Gozzoli's fresco Procession of the Magi *(1459) portrays the Florentine prince Lorenzo de'Medici at age 10. Called "il Magnifico," or the Magnificent, Lorenzo was not only a shrewd politician but also a noted poet, scholar, and patron of the arts. (Palazzo Medici-Riccardi, Florence.)*

Cosimo de'Medici, b. Sept. 27, 1389, d. Aug. 1, 1464, ruled Florence from 1434 until his death. Although Cosimo rarely held office in the city's highest magistracy, the priorate, he transformed the government into a despotism by ensuring that only his followers were eligible for important offices. At the same time, he managed Medici interests in banking, trade, and industry. Cosimo's major diplomatic achievement was the creation of a balance of power in Italy by alliance with Milan and Naples in 1454. He patronized the arts and founded (1450) the Platonic Academy in Florence. Soon after his death Cosimo was given the title *Pater Patriae* (the father of his country).

Cosimo was succeeded by his son, **Piero de'Medici**, 1416–69, who in turn was succeeded by his son **Lorenzo the Magnificent**, b. Jan. 1, 1449, d. Apr. 8, 1492. Educated by the Platonic philosopher Marsilio FICINO, Lorenzo created a brilliant court culture of painters, poets, and philosophers. Lorenzo's literary circle included Giovanni Pico della Mirandola and Luigi Pulci, and he patronized such artists as Sandro Botticelli, Domenico Ghirlandaio, Leonardo da Vinci, Fra Filippo Lippi, Michelangelo, and Andrea del Verrochio. In 1478, Lorenzo's brother, Giuliano, was killed in an assassination plot by the rival Pazzi family, supported by Pope SIXTUS IV. Lorenzo survived his wounds and restored order by the brutal extermination of his opponents.

Two years after Lorenzo's death, his son and successor, **Piero**, 1471–1503, was expelled from Florence by King CHARLES VIII of France. Florence was then a republic until the Medici regained control in 1512 under Lorenzo the Magnificent's grandson, **Lorenzo**, 1492–1519, who became duke of Urbino. Lorenzo's uncle Giovanni guided the government the first year until he was elected pope as LEO X and left for Rome. One of Giuliano's illegitimate sons, Giulio, also became pope, as CLEMENT VII, in 1523. Expelled from Florence again in 1527, the family was restored by Spain in 1530 and ruled thereafter by hereditary right. The true founder of this rule was **Cosimo I**, b. June 12, 1519, d. Apr. 21, 1574, who succeeded his relative Alessandro de'Medici as duke of Florence in 1537 and became grand duke of TUSCANY in 1569.

The Medici dukes continued to be influential in the dynastic politics of early modern Europe. The daughter of Lorenzo, duke of Urbino, was CATHERINE DE MÉDICIS, who married HENRY II of France. MARIE DE MÉDICIS, who became the second wife of HENRY IV of France, was the daughter of Cosimo I's successor, Francesco de'Medici. The last Medici duke died without a male heir in 1737.

---

medicinal plants   Primitive humans experimentally sampled many kinds of plants. Plants that were palatable were used for food; those with toxic or unpleasant effects were avoided or used against enemies; others that produced physiological effects such as perspiration, defecation, healing, or hallucination were saved for medicinal purposes and divination. Over a period of thousands of years, people learned to use a variety of plants as medicines for different ailments.

Use in History. More than 4,000 years ago, according to tradition, the Chinese emperor Qian Nong put together a book (herbal) of medicinal plants called *Bencao*. It contained descriptions of more than 300 plants, several of which are still used in medicine. During the same era and later, the Sumerians recorded prescriptions on clay tablets, and the Egyptians recorded exotic plant ingredients in *Ebers Papyrus*. The Greeks and the Romans derived some of their herbal knowledge from these early civilizations. Their contributions are recorded in *De Materia Medica* by Dioscorides and the 37-volume natural history written by Pliny the Elder. Some of these earlier works are known to us through translations into Arabic by Rhazes and Avicenna. The knowledge of medicinal plants was further nurtured by monks in Europe who studied and grew medicinal plants and translated the Arabic works.

The first "licensed" apothecary shops opened in Baghdad (now in Iraq) in the 9th century. By the 13th century, London became a major trading center in herbs and spices. Much adulteration occurred in this trade, because proper standards and quality controls had not been established. Poorly identified plants and substitutes for true medicinal herbs were sold everywhere. In 1753, Carolus Linnaeus introduced the binomial system of plant nomenclature, which helped in the identification of plants. With the subsequent publication of pharmacopoeias, the method of identification and the standard of quality for each drug were clearly defined.

The trend to replace crude plant drugs with their pure active principles started in the 18th century with the pioneering work of Karl Scheele, who isolated organic acids from plants. This achievement was followed by the isolation of morphine from opium by Friedrich Sertürner and quinine from cinchona bark by Pierre Pelletier and Joseph Caventou. These and similar discoveries opened the door to the field of phytochemistry. Today approximately 25 percent of all prescriptions contain one or more active ingredients from plants.

Active Ingredients. Numerous familiar examples can be given. The active ingredient in the toxic plants used in South America to poison arrow tips is curare, now used as a skeletal-muscle relaxant in surgery. The opium poppy produces morphine, an indispensable analgesic. Coca yields cocaine, a useful local anesthetic. The drug LSD (lysergic acid diethylamide) is chemically related to compounds obtained from the fungus ergot, which yields useful substances, some of which stop bleeding in childbirth or relieve migraine headaches.

Some plants of the nightshade family, Solanaceae, such as species of *Datura* and *Atropa*, contain fairly large amounts of the poisonous alkaloids atropine and scopolamine. These plants are toxic when consumed in large quantities but are invaluable medicinal agents when administered in proper amounts. The Chibcha Indians of Colombia used a variety of *Datura* species to sedate their human sacrifices; several tribes in Africa continue to use datura in initiation rites. The juice of the belladonna plant, *Atropa belladonna*, whose name in Italian means beautiful lady, was used by women in centuries past to dilate, or widen, the pupils of the eyes, a sign of beauty in those days. The active principle atropine is employed in modern medicine as a pupil dilator; scopolamine is used as a hypnotic and as an antispasmodic to reduce gastrointestinal contractions.

Foxglove, *Digitalis purpurea*, a common garden plant, is the source of digitalis, a drug used to treat dropsy, which often occurs in patients with congestive heart failure.

Snakeroot, *Rauwolfia serpentina*, contains an alkaloid, reserpine, now used in treating a variety of psychiatric disorders and hypertension. In a way *Rauwolfia* heralded the era of tranquilizers. Madagascar periwinkle, *Catharanthus roseus*, which belongs to the same family as *Rauwolfia*, contains the alkaloids vinblastine and vincristine, which are used in treating Hodgkin's disease and childhood leukemia, respectively.

When cortisone and other steroids, such as the sex hormones, were first isolated in the 1930s in minute amounts from glands of cattle, their usefulness as medicinal agents was apparent, but the cost of isolating them was prohibitive. Because the supply from animal sources was inadequate, a worldwide search for plant substitutes was undertaken. This search led to a variety of yams, *Dioscorea*, which now provide the starting material, diosgenin, for the production of several steroids.

---

medicine The practice of medicine is devoted to the maintenance of good health. This involves the detection and prevention of disease, the curing of those disorders for which treatment exists, and, in all cases, the amelioration of pain and minimizing of disabilities. Modern medicine has also assumed the task of improving PUBLIC HEALTH by promoting hygiene and advancing standards for nutrition and the environment. Medical science in the 20th century has experienced a rapid growth in its informational and technological resources. This growth has been accompanied by increasingly complex patterns of health-care delivery. The importance of health care in modern society is reflected in the fact that about 10 percent of the gross national product of technologically advanced nations is devoted to serving health needs. Society, in turn, has made increasing demands for greater access to health care and for greater accountability from the healing professions.

Scarcely a century ago, health care was primarily the task of the family or neighborhood physician, who diagnosed and treated patients with no assistance other than unskilled help. In contrast, the modern physician has become only one—although an essential—component in an enterprise that numbers among the largest enterprises in developed countries, both in terms of money and in terms of the number of persons employed. HOSPITALS, which are among the largest employers, account for the greatest proportion of health-care costs. Another large component is education (see MEDICINE, EDUCATION IN).

Modern medicine also requires ongoing research in various fields of science as well as the continuing development of clinical procedures and technologies. Much of this research and development is done in universities, medical schools, and governmental institutions. The PHARMACEUTICAL INDUSTRY is also a major contributor. A vast distribution system brings the products to pharmacies and hospital dispensaries.

The Branches of Medicine

In the United States and Canada, medicine currently is divided into 23 distinct areas, or specialties, each with its own rule-making and certifying body. The largest divisions are further divided into subspecialties that have additional requirements for training and certification. In the following description, these 23 divisions are grouped under the more general categories of nonsurgical, surgical, and hospital-based specialties, with family practice as a separate field. For a description of the fields of nursing, see NURSING.

Nonsurgical Specialties. The nonsurgical specialties that involve direct patient care include internal medicine, PEDIATRICS, allergy and immunology, DERMATOLOGY, preventive medicine, and PSYCHIATRY and NEUROLOGY.

Practitioners of internal medicine, or internists, are concerned with the diagnosis and treatment of adults

A patient is positioned for treatment in the water bath of a lithotripter, a device that breaks up kidney stones by using shock waves.

with diseases of the internal organs. Those called general internists are primary-care physicians, in that they have a direct relationship with patients on a long-term basis and refer them to other specialists only for specific problems. Many internists, however, specialize in a specific area of the body. This has led to the formation of nine subspecialties, as follows.

Cardiology is the care of patients with diseases of the heart and blood vessels. *Endocrinology and metabolism* is the care of patients who have problems related to glands of the body. *Gastroenterology* is the study of diseases of the gastrointestinal tract; it also deals with diseases of the liver and pancreas. HEMATOLOGY treats patients with diseases of the blood cells, bone marrow, and lymph nodes; hematologists also operate blood banks and manage patients with blood-clotting disorders. *Infectious disease* specialists are consulted chiefly in the treatment of severe or exotic infections, the selection and use of antibiotics, and the management of complications resulting from antibiotic use. Specialists in *nephrology* are experts in the diagnosis and treatment of kidney diseases, also managing blood-dialysis centers for patients who lack functioning kidneys. *Oncology* involves the treatment of cancer patients with chemotherapeutic agents; oncologists frequently act in the capacity of general internists for such patients. *Pulmonary disease* is concerned with diseases of the lungs and air passages. Finally, *rheumatology* specialists treat patients with joint diseases and joint-related systemic diseases.

Pediatrics is constituted much like internal medicine, but it deals instead with infants and children. The new field of adolescent medicine, however, has extended these traditional age limits. Recognized pediatric subspecialties include pediatric *cardiology, hematology/oncology, endocrinology*, and *nephrology.* These subspecialties differ from their adult counterparts, because infants and children have distinctive diseases and disease patterns. One subspecialty unique to pediatrics is *neonatal-perinatal medicine*, dedicated to the management of premature infants and ill newborns.

Allergy and immunology, besides dealing with hypersensitivity disorders such as asthma and food allergies, also treats immune-related problems such as patients with organ transplants and patients incapable of manufacturing components of the immune system.

Dermatology is the study of diseases of the skin. Since the majority of human diseases have at least some effect on the skin, this field of medicine intersects with many other specialties. The dermatologist must understand the systemic diseases likely to be responsible for a skin rash.

Preventive medicine studies means of improving the level of health in a community. Most work in this area is done under the aegis of a government, university, or institute. Two subspecialties exist: *occupational medicine*, devoted to detecting and measuring adverse effects of the workplace; and *aerospace medicine* (see SPACE MEDICINE).

Psychiatry and neurology is divided into two obvious subspecialties. *Psychiatry* is concerned with those brain functions expressed as behavior, mood, and intelligence, whereas *neurology* is concerned with organic diseases of the central nervous system, including the brain. In general, psychiatrists treat patients with nonorganic diseases of the brain, whereas neurologists treat those with organic diseases. Psychiatrists also spend much of their professional time treating emotional responses to chronic disease.

Surgical Specialties. SURGERY and the surgical specialties include general, plastic, colon and rectal, neurological, orthopedic, and thoracic surgery; otolaryngology; OPHTHALMOLOGY; and urology. OBSTETRICS and GYNECOLOGY exhibit important elements both of surgery and of general medicine.

General surgery deals with those conditions which require operative interventions not falling within the areas of the related disciplines listed above. If required, however, the general surgeon can deal with most surgical problems, having mastered the techniques basic to all the fields. The anatomical areas with which the general surgeon is most concerned are the abdomen and its contents; many surgeons specialize further, such as breast surgeons and thyroid surgeons. The subspecialties of general surgery are *pediatric surgery*, which deals with surgical problems of children, and *hand surgery.*

In PLASTIC SURGERY the surgeon is called upon both to improve body function by dealing with disfigurements and to prevent such disfigurements following accidents or disease. Thus, much of the surgery of the head and neck is performed by plastic surgeons. The extensive skin grafting necessitated by severe burns is also performed by plastic surgeons. Some surgeons, however, deal primarily with cosmetic surgery performed solely to improve appearance.

Colon and rectal surgery has developed because the colon and rectum are the site of a number of common diseases that routinely or occasionally require surgical therapy. General surgeons with a special interest in abdominal surgery also frequently treat malignant tumors at these sites.

Brain surgeons operate on a patient using a computerized robot arm, which calculates the angles at which the drill and biopsy needle it holds are to be directed into the brain. This advanced technique eliminates the need for general anesthesia.

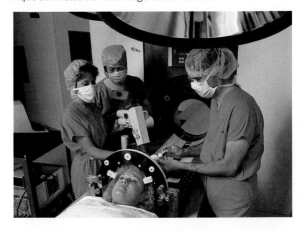

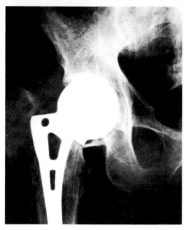

Orthopedic surgery may involve the fitting of artificial parts, or prostheses, into a patient. (Above) Using techniques of computer-aided design, a body part such as a hip joint can be built exactly to meet the needs of the patient. (Left) An X-ray photo shows the successful implantation of one such artificial hip.

Neurological surgery is concerned with patients who have surgical problems of the brain and spinal column, the peripheral nervous system, or the tissues that support these systems, including the blood vessels. The realms of the neurosurgeon and the orthopedic surgeon (discussed below) may overlap in the care of patients with certain kinds of back pain.

The field of otolaryngology is concerned with the ear, the nose and sinuses, and the throat, including the larynx, the pharynx, and related structures. Although the field is classified as a surgical specialty, the otolaryngologist also treats nonsurgical conditions of these structures.

The ophthalmologist treats medical and surgical eye conditions and is concerned with the prevention and treatment of blindness. Fitting patients with corrective lenses is done by ophthalmologists as well as by optometrists, who are nonphysicians devoted exclusively to the correction of refractive errors, such as myopia (nearsightedness).

Orthopedic surgery is concerned with diseases of the bones, joints, and muscles. Orthopedic specialists are also called in when an arm or leg must be amputated, and they are involved with the fitting of artificial body parts (prostheses) and in the training of amputees to operate the devices.

Thoracic surgery first emerged as a separate discipline for treating pulmonary diseases, such as abscesses or cancer of the lung or complications resulting from tuberculosis. The field expanded rapidly following the development of the heart-lung machine, which enables physicians to make a direct attack on diseases of the heart. The thoracic surgeon may also be called upon for cases involving neck surgery.

Urology treats surgical diseases of the kidneys and both medical and surgical conditions of the remainder of the urinary tract and the male genital system.

Physicians in the field of obstetrics and gynecology have increasingly come to regard themselves as providing primary care for women. That is, their patients come to them directly, rather than by referral from other physicians. Some of these specialists primarily practice obstetrics, or the care of women before, during, and after childbirth; others primarily practice gynecology, or the treatment of female patients with diseases or disorders of the genital tract.

Hospital-Based Specialties. The hospital-based specialist conducts highly technical but usually limited care in association with the physician of record. Specialties include anesthesiology, emergency medicine, NUCLEAR MEDICINE, PATHOLOGY, physical medicine and rehabilitation (see REHABILITATION MEDICINE), and RADIOLOGY.

The anesthesiologist renders a patient unconscious during surgery and also provides general care from some hours before the operation until the patient has fully recovered from the effects of anesthesia.

The emergency-medicine specialist must be able to care for a desperately ill patient brought into the emergency room of a hospital. Situations to be faced include the diagnosis and treatment of poisoning, illicit drug use, overmedication, attempted suicide, injury from accidents or assault, internal bleeding, and heart attacks. The physician must then also be prepared to marshal the resources of the hospital for more definitive therapy, as needed. Medical technicians trained to provide on-site emergency aid or otherwise assist specialists in emergency medicine are known as PARAMEDICS.

Nuclear medicine is a fairly recent field that involves placing radioactive materials inside the body and determining their location by means of appropriate detectors. In this way a physician practicing nuclear medicine can establish such situations as the integrity of the heart muscle, thyroid-gland function, and the existence of tumors at such sites as the liver.

Pathology is the study of tissues or body fluids for the presence of abnormal conditions or disease. The clinical pathologist examines blood and other body fluids in a search for abnormal levels of substances such as blood sugar, urea, hormones, and drugs, and may also supervise the microbiology laboratory, where microorganisms causing a patient's illness are identified and their sensitivity to available antibiotics determined. Some clinical pathologists are in charge of blood banking (see BLOOD BANK) or may direct hematology laboratories, where the numbers and types of blood cells in a sample are determined and the blood factors for clotting are measured. The forensic pathologist makes use of all the procedures and skills of pathology in an effort to aid the administration of justice. The anatomic pathologist examines tissues obtained during surgery or at an autopsy and also examines cells from body secretions.

The object of physical medicine and rehabilitation is to rehabilitate a patient who has had an injury or illness, using such physical modalities as exercise, baths, electrical stimulation, and heat. Such modalities are useful in a broad range of cases and are essential after a stroke that has left a patient with some degree of paralysis. Nonphysicians trained to work in the field are discussed in OCCUPATIONAL THERAPY and PHYSICAL THERAPY.

The specialty of radiology is divided into the areas of diagnostic radiology and therapeutic radiology. Diagnostic radiologists use NUCLEAR MAGNETIC RESONANCE imaging and other techniques to observe internal structures. In therapeutic radiology, radiation is used to cause the destruction of selected tissues.

Family Medicine. The explosive growth of medical specialties has come to be perceived by many persons as a loss of the continuing relationship between patient and physician. A movement in reaction to this perceived trend began shortly after the end of World War II, culminating in the development of the specialty called family practice. This specialty is intended to restore the patient-physician relationship and, simultaneously, to equip the practitioner with the knowledge and skills expected of a contemporary physician. A family-practice physician is expected to be able to care for most of the nonsurgical illnesses of adults and children, to use the continuing relationship with the patient and the patient's family to teach preventive medicine, and to have the acumen to refer the minority of patients with illnesses too complex for the family physician to an appropriate specialist.

Health-Care Facilities

The largest and most complex form of health-care facility is the hospital, which deals with the critically ill and with patients who need complex diagnostic procedures or must undergo major surgery. Care given to patients not confined to a hospital, called outpatient or ambulatory care, is ordinarily dispensed in a clinic or office. A clinic may be either freestanding or attached to a hospital.

The Hospital Team. Treatment in a hospital necessarily is a team effort, led by the physician or physicians directly responsible for a patient's welfare. Other physicians who may be involved in the care of a patient include anesthesiologists, pathologists, and radiologists, and, in teaching hospitals, the resident physicians. All of the hospital personnel support the work of the physicians in charge. Of these personnel, the nursing staff is the largest component.

As new machinery and new procedures are introduced into a hospital, members of the technical staff also must be increased in order to operate the equipment. Besides this, a hospital operates like a small village and must have cooks, cleaners, laundry personnel, carpenters, plumbers, bookkeepers, a police staff, and a cadre of administrators as well.

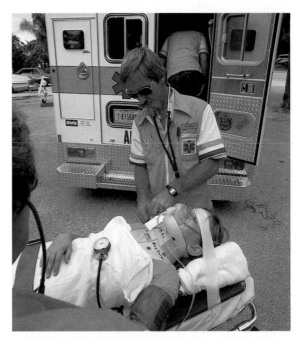

Paramedics play an essential role in the emergency medical services of a hospital. When a call is placed for an ambulance, one or more paramedics travel along to provide on-site aid.

Kinds of Hospitals. Hospital inpatient care devolves into either acute or chronic care. Acute-care hospitals are classified as primary, secondary, or tertiary institutions. The low-technology primary hospitals are usually located in rural areas and generally deal with emergencies and therapies that do not involve complex procedures. The secondary hospitals are more typical of hospitals in general, providing a greater range of physician skills and modern technology than the primary hospitals. Tertiary institutions are typified by the teaching hospitals of the major medical schools and are also called referral centers. Usually they are large, often with more than a thousand beds, and they provide most or all of the latest medical equipment available. Even more important, they have physicians and technicians on their staffs who are highly trained in all types of investigation and treatment. Most of the patients found in tertiary-care hospitals are similar to those in secondary centers, but the rest have been referred to such hospitals for special care such as therapy for severe burns, open-heart surgery, the attending of premature infants, or hip replacement. Tertiary-care hospitals are quite expensive, partly because of the advanced technology being employed but even more because of the size of the staff required. The ratio of employees to patients in a tertiary-care hospital may exceed five to one.

Other types of hospitals, called specialty hospitals, admit only those patients who fit a restricted group of diagnoses and, usually, who are due for a medium-to-long stay. Psychiatric hospitals are the most numerous specialty hospitals and the ones with the largest patient population.

Chronic-disease hospitals, also called long-term–care facilities, are typically the hospitals of last resort for persons too ill for any other alternative but for whom no known therapy exists that could justify their presence in expensive acute-care hospitals. Finally, the HOSPICE movement, devoted to caring for the terminally ill, generally makes use of the home environment but sometimes involves so-called hospice dwellings, commonly located within a hospital.

Standards of Practice

In the United States, medical licensure is controlled by each state, territory, and commonwealth. Licensure depends on satisfactory completion of the standard medical curriculum in an American or Canadian medical school, clinical experience, and satisfactory performance on an examination.

In theory, possession of a valid medical license entitles a physician to practice all branches of medicine and surgery within that jurisdiction. In actuality, further training is needed beyond receipt of the M.D. degree. Such training, called graduate medical education, is controlled by a quasi-autonomous nongovernmental body called the American Council on Graduate Medical Education. This body is made up of representatives from each specialty board and from hospitals, medical schools, specialty societies, and the AMERICAN MEDICAL ASSOCIATION (AMA), with one member appointed by the federal government. Working through committees and its constituent organizations, the council approves each hospital training program and endorses an examination given by the appropriate specialty board.

Most physicians in active practice have hospital privileges. That is, they are members of the medical staff of a hospital and are allowed to admit patients to that hospital. To practice at a hospital, however, the physician must meet requirements in addition to a license, which are mandated by the governing body of the institution.

In most nations other than the United States, licensure is a national rather than a provincial matter. Graduation from one of the schools within a country often entitles a physician to a license without further examination. In most countries, however, physicians are required to complete further examinations in order to be accredited as specialists.

The Economics of Health Care

The United States has no national health program that provides physician services, medications, and a hospital bed when required. A multiplicity of insurance plans exists instead, including voluntary nonprofit plans such as Blue Cross, commercial plans of the major insurance corporations, the national MEDICARE plan (primarily for those over 65), and MEDICAID, a federal-state scheme for those needing financial aid. In all of these insurance schemes a limit exists to coverage, and in most there is a copayment requirement for coverage of physician services (see HEALTH-CARE SYSTEMS).

One growing trend in this area is the development of health maintenance organizations, or HMOs. Enrollees in an HMO select a primary-care physician from the plan's panel. For a set fee, the enrollee is provided with primary-physician services, specialist services as needed, drugs, and hospital coverage. There is less choice of physician and hospital in an HMO than in an insurance plan, but the financial advantage both to the employer and to the employee are powerful motivating forces. That is, health-care costs in the United States are continuing to increase, and these costs are paid for either from the tax dollar (Medicare and Medicaid) or by health insurance, which as part of the wage package directly reduces the take-home pay of an employee. Consequently, there is great appeal in the notion of reducing costs without diminishing the amount of health care. Because the largest single item in the total health-care bill is hospital care, increasing emphasis has been placed on decreasing lengths of hospital stay and restricting the ease of admission into a hospital.

The pressure exerted on hospitals by insurers has resulted in a shorter length of stay for the average admission and in a heightened competition for admissions among hospitals. The result is that a patient currently admitted into a hospital is more acutely ill, on the average, than a patient in years past, thereby requiring more com-

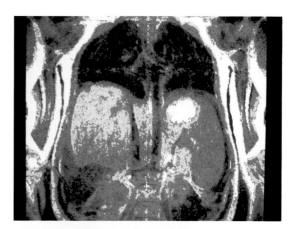

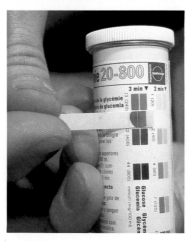

The diagnostic tools available to modern medicine range from sophisticated machines to systems that can be used in the home. (Above) A radiological image of the organs in the chest is obtained by magnetic resonance imaging. (Left) A person with diabetes can monitor blood-sugar levels by using this kit, which compares a test strip with a color chart.

plex and advanced and, inevitably, more expensive therapy. At the same time, since patients can no longer be admitted to hospitals solely for testing (insurers no longer pay the costs for such admissions), the trend has been established to do testing on an ambulatory basis. Ambulatory surgical centers have been developed in which procedures that once required days of hospitalization are done within an hour of the patient's entrance in the early morning.

Worldwide, systems of health-care financing range from the comprehensive schemes of the Scandinavian countries to nations that can or do provide little or no care.

Trends in Medicine

The rapid changes taking place in the U.S. medical-care system are likely to continue. Creation of a national health plan is considered less likely than expansion of insurance coverage to selected groups—for example, establishment of federal catastrophe insurance.

Medicine and the law are currently maintaining an uneasy relationship, as seen in the rising number of MALPRACTICE suits. Of equal moment are new medical dilemmas with strong ethical and legal overtones that have been brought about by the introduction of new therapies and techniques. These include the definition of death for purposes of organ transplantation or for cessation of care to the terminally ill (see DEATH AND DYING), SURROGATE MOTHERHOOD, and decisions as to who shall benefit from treatment modalities (see MEDICAL ETHICS).

On the whole, medical care in the United States, at its best, is unequaled anywhere else in the world. Such care, however, is not uniformly available. For example, infant mortality in the nation exceeds that of other technologically advanced countries. Although for much of the population the infant mortality rate is comparable to the low rates observed in Scandinavian countries, at the lowest socioeconomic stratum the infant mortality rate is comparable to those in Third World countries. Thus, the United States simultaneously enjoys the best and—in terms of developed countries—the worst of medical care.

See also: CHIROPRACTIC; DENTISTRY; GERIATRICS; OSTEOPATHIC MEDICINE; SPORTS MEDICINE.

medicine, education in   Education in medicine is the continuing process of acquiring and maintaining the skills needed to provide quality health care. Worldwide, two major systems exist for the education of physicians: the American system, followed in the United States and Canada, and the European system, which has been adopted by the rest of the world. The American system has four stages: a general collegiate education, which includes a grounding in chemistry, physics, and biology; undergraduate medical education (medical school), which teaches basic medical skills and awards the M.D. degree; graduate medical education (residency), where a specialty is acquired; and postgraduate education (continuing medical education), for keeping abreast of recent advances in medical science. In the European system, the student proceeds from secondary school directly to

medical school, where the appropriate college-level courses in chemistry and physics are taken. As a result, undergraduate medical education typically occupies six years.

Medical-School Education

In the United States, admissions to medical schools are made on the basis of college grades, performance on the Medical College Admission Test (MCAT), recommendations concerning the character of the applicant, and the applicant's extracurricular activities. Since the 1970s, efforts have been made to obtain a percentage of students from minority groups.

Most medical schools have a four-year curriculum, which is traditionally divided into basic-science and clinical-science components. The basic-science component consists of courses such as human anatomy, human physiology, biochemistry, pathology, microbiology, pharmacology, and human behavior. During the first two years, many medical schools also teach students how to interview and counsel patients, perform a physical examination, and diagnose. Instruction is carried out through lectures, self-paced training programs, laboratory experience, and actual patient encounters.

The second half of medical-school education consists of instruction in the clinical sciences: pediatrics, surgery, psychiatry, internal medicine, obstetrics, gynecology, and family practice. The student usually works with specialists in caring for patients and attends teaching sessions in each of these specialties. A student assigned to surgery, for example, might first take down a medical and social history from a patient, examine the patient, and report the findings to the patient's physician. The surgeon would verify the findings and then, working with the student and others on the medical staff, determine how best to care for the patient. If the care includes an operation, the student might work directly with the surgical team.

Recently, new areas of study, such as computer science, medical ethics, geriatrics, and decision analysis/ cost containment, have been added to medical-school curricula. There is also an increasing emphasis on primary care, ambulatory care, and family medicine.

In most countries, there are many more applicants to medical schools than there are places. This has resulted in applicants from wealthier nations seeking admission to foreign schools that grant valid degrees but that do not usually allow foreign nationals to be licensed in the host country. Such schools are of variable quality.

Graduate School Education

Almost all U.S. medical-school graduates seek further training in one of the 23 medical specialties approved by the American Board of Medical Specialties (see MEDICINE). During the training, which lasts from two to seven years, depending on the specialty, the student learns the specific skills needed for assuming responsibility for the independent practice of medicine. Nearly all learning occurs in the context of caring for patients.

Usually at the end of the first year of graduate education, or residency, the physician passes an examination to obtain a medical license from the state in which he or she is practicing. At the conclusion of residency, a physician who wishes to become a recognized specialist must complete an evaluation program directed by one of the 23 medical specialty boards. At this point, most physicians go into the private practice of medicine, but others teach, perform research, or administer programs. This structure for specialty training and certification is the pattern followed around the world.

Certain specialties have an absolute excess of practitioners, and government agencies predict an oversupply of physicians in the United States as well as in other leading industrial and scientific nations. In the United States this has resulted in pressure to decrease the number of medical-school admissions, to increase restrictions on U.S. citizens who are graduates of foreign medical schools, and to decrease the number of approved graduate (residency) positions. It is expected that competition for graduate-training positions will intensify as a result.

Postgraduate Education

Nearly all physicians participate in continuing medical education to keep up with the massive amount of information being discovered each year concerning human health. Two popular approaches are self-assessment programs and intense short-term courses. The former include self-administered examinations that simulate the types of problems that practicing physicians encounter, and learning materials designed to explain the correct approach to the questions posed. Intense short-term postgraduate courses are one- to seven-day learning experiences that take physicians away from their practices for only a few days. Many states require that physicians periodically prove that they have actively participated in continuing medical education in order to be reregistered to practice medicine. Many specialty boards now also request that those already certified in that specialty be reexamined periodically.

See also: NURSING; OSTEOPATHIC MEDICINE.

---

medicine, history of   Medicine is among the most ancient of human occupations. Evidences of the practice of ritual healing, combining religion and primitive science, are found in the earliest traces of communal living. Until the period of the Enlightenment, medical science and technology advanced at a relatively slow and steady rate in the world's major cultures. With the birth of modern science and the onset of the Industrial Revolution, the progress of medicine also began to accelerate. In spite of the breathtaking rapidity of developments in modern medicine, however, it is all of a piece. Hippocrates would quickly have appreciated that contemporary medical practices are founded on principles similar to medicine in his own day.

Primitive Medicine

Throughout the ages, SHAMANS and medicine men have discovered valuable information that then was handed down from generation to generation. Morphine, quinine, ephedrine, and rauwolfia, all used today, come from an-

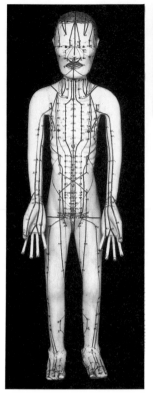

(Above) *A clay model of a sheep's liver was used by Babylonian priests to foretell the course of human illness, a procedure known as hepatoscopy. The sick person first breathed into the nostrils of a live sheep. A priest killed the sheep, removed its liver, and made a diagnosis by comparing the organ to markings on the clay model.* (Left) *Chinese acupuncture points are indicated on this 19th-century Japanese doll. In acupuncture selected points on the body are stimulated with needles to redirect the Chi, or life force. Invented more than 5,000 years ago, acupuncture is still routinely used in China.*

cient, prescientific lore. Primitive medicine men learned to set fractures; they even performed such complex procedures as trephination—boring holes in the skull to treat disease.

Egyptian Medicine

What is known of Egyptian medicine comes principally from two large fragments of writing, the Ebers papyrus and the Smith papyrus. These papyruses were written about 1600 BC; the Ebers text is a compilation from many sources, and the Smith is probably a copy of a text written about 2500 BC. The Ebers papyrus includes incantations for specific illnesses as well as invocations to the gods; careful case histories and valuable prescriptions, such as castor oil as a cathartic and tannic acid for burns, also were recorded. The Smith papyrus, on the other hand, includes surgical advice that remains pertinent today, such as the use of compression to stop bleeding, and sections on diseases of the eye and other organs.

Middle Eastern Medicine

About 2000 BC the Amorites unified the nations and tribes in the valleys of the Tigris and Euphrates rivers. They built Babylon, and science and learning flourished under their greatest king, Hammurabi. The Code of Hammurabi, which constitutes wide-ranging laws inscribed on a great stone pillar, includes definitions of the conduct of a physician—what he may treat, what his fee should be—

and also prescribes punishments for malpractice. The Hebrew civilization developing at about the same time placed strong emphasis on public health and sanitation. It codified these practices in the Pentateuch and Talmud as prescribed by Moses.

Oriental Medicine

The healing arts in the Orient have had a long and complex history. In several Oriental cultures, particularly India and China, forms of medicine involved elaborate theories encoded in multivolume series of texts. Such systems are now referred to as traditional medicine (see MEDICINE, TRADITIONAL).

India. Throughout much of their history, the Indians came into contact with the Persians, Greeks, and Chinese, with whom they exchanged information. About 900 BC the *Ayur-veda,* written in India, combined descriptions of disease with information on herbs and magic. The first great Hindu physician known, Charaka, practiced about 1000 BC. Susruta, in the 5th century AD, noted the relationship of malaria to mosquitoes and of plague to rats, knew of more than 700 medicinal plants, and described more than 100 surgical instruments. He treated fractures, removed tumors and kidney stones, and delivered babies by cesarian section.

China. The *Nei Jing,* or *Book of Medicine of the Yellow Emperor,* probably written in the 3d century BC, describes human anatomy, including the circulation of the blood. Much of the treatment at that time was based on the yin-yang principle; that is, the balance between active and passive, hot and cold, male and female. The most important role of a Chinese physician was to restore the harmony between yin and yang in a patient. The Chinese also developed massage and invented ACUPUNCTURE and immunization against smallpox. The physician Hua Tuo, in 300 BC, pioneered the use of anesthesia.

The *Bencao Gang Mu,* begun in the 3d or 4th century AD and completed in the 16th century, describes about 1,000 drugs, including croton oil, opium, rhubarb, iron, and ephedrine, all of which have been used in modern times. The pinnacle of Chinese medicine was reached during the reign of Emperor Qian Long, when all medical information was compiled in a 40-volume encyclopedia, *The Golden Mirror of Medicine* (1743). Within a few years, however, European ideas began to be introduced, resulting in modern and traditional medicine simultaneously being practiced.

Greek Medicine

The healing art of ancient Greece was associated with the worship of Apollo. According to legend, medicine, taught to Chiron by Apollo, was in turn passed on to Aesculapius, who may have been a real man who lived about 1200 BC but later was thought to be a god and was worshiped in temples of healing. Inscriptions on these temples record the treatment of disease, consisting of rest, exercise, diet, and magic.

Hippocrates. Among the more important principles stressed by the physician HIPPOCRATES (c.460–377 BC)

The Greek physicians Galen and Hippocrates, born centuries apart, talk together in this ancient fresco. Galen's theories on human physiology were considered authoritative for centuries. Hippocrates established guidelines for diagnosis and treatment.

were: (1) a physician should work not for personal gain but for love of humanity; (2) disease should be studied by meticulous observation, and cases should be carefully recorded and studied to establish a prognosis; (3) disease is often the result of environmental forces—diet, climate, and occupation; and (4) a physician should emphasize simple treatment supplemented with careful diet and surgical intervention when necessary. A physician's conduct is summarized in the HIPPOCRATIC OATH.

Aristotle. In the 4th century BC, ARISTOTLE, pupil of Plato and teacher of Alexander the Great, dissected many species, studied insect and animal behavior with great accuracy, laid the foundations for embryology, and suggested evolution. Aristotle's contribution lies in his belief that the scientific method—careful observation, experimentation, and study of cause and effect—could lead to greater scientific knowledge.

Roman Medicine

Roman medicine emphasized public health. Ancient Rome's sanitation, sewage disposal, and water system exceeded anything that followed in the Western world prior to the 19th century. Medical students were educated at public expense, and physicians were supplied for the poor.

The most important contributions to medicine during the Roman Empire were those of Celsus and GALEN. Aulus Cornelius Celsus (fl. AD 10–37), wrote an eight-volume encyclopedia on medicine, *De Re Medica.* Little recognized during its own time, the work was rediscovered in the 15th century when it had a great impact on scientific thought. Six of the eight books describe various diseases and discuss therapy using diet, drugs, and manipulation. The last two books treat topics in surgery, including operations for goiter, hernia, and bladder stone. Celsus also recommended treating fractures with splints and bandages stiffened with starch.

Galen (AD c.131–200) wrote 500 books, 80 of which

are extant. Although he stated that knowledge of human anatomy was fundamental for a physician, his anatomical facts were obtained from the dissection of animals and incorporated many errors when applied to human anatomy. Nevertheless, he explained the function of many nerves, discovered the sympathetic nervous system, and described almost all the structures of the brain visible to the naked eye.

Medicine in the Islamic Empire

Between the fall of Rome in the 5th century AD and the Renaissance in the 15th century, knowledge of medicine flourished in the Islamic empire. Islamic medicine was strongly influenced by Greek medicine, the medical writings of the Talmud, and astrologic teachings from Egypt and the Orient. Basic chemical processes, including distillation, crystallization, and sublimation, were discovered. Such words as *alkali, alcohol, syrup*, and *drug*—all of Arabic derivation—are now widely used.

The great physicians of the Islamic world included, in the eastern caliphate, Rhazes (AD *c.*860–930), a Persian who distinguished smallpox from measles, and AVICENNA, who tried to codify all of medicine while squaring its facts with the systems of Galen and Aristotle. In the western caliphate, under the Umayyad dynasty, the greatest clinicians were Avenzoar of Córdoba (d. 1162, in Seville) and MAIMONIDES.

The Islamic civilization also established several hospitals. The greatest were the ones at Damascus (1160), which remained active for three centuries, and the Al-Mansur Hospital in Cairo (1276). The latter was the first hospital to emphasize science, teaching, and social service.

The Medieval Period in Europe

During the Middle Ages the influence of Christian theology affected medicine in several ways. The Christian emphasis on charity and concern for the sick and injured led to the establishment of hospitals often related to and maintained by monastic orders. The concern of Christian theology, however, was to cure the soul rather than the body; disease usually was considered supernatural in origin and cured by religious means. As a result, scientific investigation was inhibited during this time.

Salerno. The first European medical school was founded at Salerno, near Naples, in the 8th century. The area was still part of the Byzantine Empire, so many Greek texts were available. The anatomy taught there was based on that of the pig, and the physiology and pathology followed that of Galen, but a spirit of investigation suffused the institution. By the 11th century it had become a center of medical knowledge.

In the 13th century the greatest medical schools of the renaissance, Bologna and Padua, were founded. At Bologna the physician Taddeo Alderotti (*c.*1223–1303) was a prime mover in establishing postmortem dissections and a developer of the *Consilia*, or medical case book, in which advice was given by the professor to younger or less sophisticated physicians. Thus was born the clinical case history.

Andreas Vesalius dissects the arm of a cadaver in this portrait from his 1543 treatise on human anatomy. Vesalius's investigations created an uproar in Europe's medical academies, where most knowledge was learned from ancient manuscripts.

Medicine of the Renaissance Period

The Renaissance revolutionized medical thought as it did all scientific, artistic, and other intellectual activity. The dissemination of knowledge was greatly aided by the development of printing. Andreas VESALIUS, born in Brussels, was a professor of ANATOMY in Padua, where he wrote *De Humani Corporis Fabrica* (*On the Fabric of the Human Body,* 1543). This work was the first accurate anatomy text and included masterful illustrations that corrected errors of Galen.

Ambroise Paré (*c.*1510–1590), a French physician, revolutionized surgery. He treated his patients humanely, using ligatures to stop bleeding from vessels instead of cauterizing them with boiling oil or hot instruments. Other men of this age included Aureolus PARACELSUS, a Swiss physician who rejected traditional schools of thought and advocated the use of such chemicals as laudanum (a preparation of opium) in treating disease.

The Seventeenth Century

William HARVEY, an English physician of the 17th century, studied in Padua and later taught anatomy in London. He published *De Motu Cordis* (*On the Motion of the Heart,* 1628), which describes the circulation of blood throughout the body. As the first application of the idea of measurement to a biological phenomenon, the book exhibited true science in its solution of a medical problem.

The Galenic idea that the heart was a source of heat and that the lungs were cooling devices for the heart gave way before the elegant experiments of English scientists Richard Lower (1631–91) and John Mayow (1640–79). Mayow passed venous blood through lungs and showed that the change from dark to bright red was associated with the uptake of some substance from the air—an observation all the more remarkable in that the substance, oxygen, had not yet been discovered. Perhaps the greatest clinician of the century was Thomas Sydenham (1624–

(Right) *A signboard from 17th-century England advertises the skills of a typical surgeon. Leeching and purging were his usual treatments.*

(Below) *A plate from William Harvey's book* On the Motion of the Heart, *published in 1628, illustrates the function of valves in the veins of the arm.*

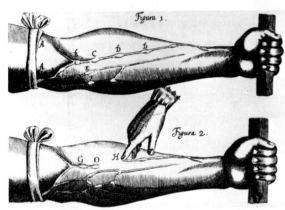

89), who showed concern for the effects of environmental factors on health and had a humanistic approach to the treatment of patients.

The century was also remarkable for the invention and development of the microscope. By using microscopes, a Dutch scientist, Antoni van LEEUWENHOEK, discovered red blood cells, bacteria, and protozoans; he also described the microscopic appearance of muscle. The greatest microscopist of the century, Marcello Malpighi (1628–94), described the embryology of the chick and was the first to observe capillaries.

Two philosophic schools of medicine arose in the century, both of which contributed to science but also slowed progress by their excessive rigidity. One, the iatrophysical school, regarded all physiological events as the rigid results of the laws of physics. Its greatest exponent was Italian scientist Giovanni BORELLI. Many of his studies were valid, but he also advanced such notions as that digestion was a purely mechanical process of grinding and crushing. The iatrochemical school, founded by Flemish chemist Johannes Baptista van Helmont (1579–1644), took on significance when propounded by English physicist Thomas Willis (1621–75), who analyzed urine and noted the presence of sugar in diabetic urine. Simi-

larly, Dutch physician Regnier de Graaf (1641–73) collected pancreatic juice and recognized its importance in the digestion of food by chemical rather than mechanical means.

During the 17th century the Royal Society of London, the Académie des Sciences in Paris, and the Collegium Naturae Curiosorum in Germany were founded and dedicated to the advancement of science. By means of these societies ideas were exchanged and journals published, thus spreading information throughout much of Europe.

The Eighteenth Century

During the 18th century Hermann Boerhaave (1668–1738), a Dutch physician, by means of his practice, teaching, and writings, influenced the development of Leiden into the world center for medicine. James Lind (1716–94), a British naval surgeon, cured scurvy, caused by a deficiency of vitamin C, by requiring sailors to drink lime and lemon juice. Edward JENNER demonstrated that vaccination with cowpox, a mild disease, would prevent smallpox. English physician William Withering (1741–99) discovered the use of digitalis, perhaps the most useful drug in the treatment of heart disease. Austrian physician Leopold Auenbrugger (1722–1809) found that by tapping gently on the chest, fluid in the chest cavity as well as other signs of disease could be detected. English surgeon John Hunter (1728–93) is notable for his emphasis on precise anatomical knowledge and his insistence on experimentation. Italian anatomist Giovanni B. Morgagni (1682–1771) founded pathologic anatomy, and French physiologist Marie François Bichat (1771–1802) developed histology.

The Nineteenth Century

Preceding the 19th century, medicine had advanced at a slowly increasing rate; the scientific basis of practice, however, aside from anatomy, was created during the

People vaccinated with cowpox metamorphose into actual cows in this cartoon of the late 1700s, lampooning the work of Dr. Edward Jenner. Despite ridicule, Jenner's treatment curbed deadly smallpox epidemics.

19th century. The basic medical sciences were founded, opening the way for immense strides during the 20th century.

Advances in Medical Science. During the 19th century Jacob Henle (1809–85) showed that the kidney contained tiny tubules responsible for the urine-forming function of that organ. His descriptions of the microscopic structure of the eye and brain also led to consideration of the relationship of structure (anatomy) to function (physiology). Rudolf Virchow (1821–1902), the founder of cellular pathology, was responsible for promoting the use of the microscope. He demonstrated that all body tissues and organs are made of cells and their products, that all cells are produced from other cells, that many diseases are the result of changes in cells, and that one could identify a disease by the appearance of the cells. His work became the basis for modern-day understanding of disease.

The science of microbiology was founded by Louis PASTEUR, who showed that certain pure chemical crystals could exist in two forms, differing from each other as an object differs from its mirror image. The importance to medicine of this work is that the building blocks of the body, such as amino acids and sugars, are usable in one form only and not in mirror-image form. Pasteur conducted a series of complex experiments proving that many plant and animal diseases are due to yeasts and bacteria. He discovered methods of immunization, a process that has saved more lives than all advances in all of previous medicine. Further, his work, developed by others after him, has resulted in safe milk (through pasteurization) and food, better methods of producing chemicals and drugs, and increased agricultural production.

The science of bacteriology developed rapidly in the last quarter of the 19th century, when the bacterial causes of many important diseases were identified. Robert KOCH, who along with Pasteur is considered the founder of scientific bacteriology, isolated the organisms that produce anthrax, tuberculosis, and cholera, and invented the gel-like medium used for many years on plates in bacteriology laboratories (a substance now replaced by agar). He also developed a set of rules (Koch's postulates) that, if followed, can prove that an organism is truly the cause of a disease.

The Rise of Modern Surgery. The 19th century made modern surgery possible by means of two great discoveries: safe anesthesia, and control of wound infection. A Boston dentist, William Morton, (1819–68), discovered that inhalation of diethyl ether would render a person unconscious and incapable of perceiving pain (see ANESTHETICS). As surgeons began using anesthesia to perform longer, more intricate operations, however, the benefits of Morton's discovery began to be diminished by wound infections. In Vienna, Hungarian physician Ignaz Semmelweis (1818–65) had been insisting that puerperal sepsis, a usually fatal infection experienced by some women after childbirth, was due to infection of the birth canal by the hands of hospital attendants. This theory was ridiculed, because at the time no scientific reason was known that supported it. When Pasteur showed that microorganisms in the air and on hands could produce disease, however,

Doctors and students at Massachuestts General Hospital in 1846 stand by an operating table as William Morton exhibits his ether-inhaling device. Safe general anesthesia marked the advent of modern surgery.

the British surgeon Joseph LISTER began his epochal work on infection. Published in 1867, this work showed that surgery was made safer by using antiseptics to sterilize equipment and the surrounding environment. The antiseptic process was thereafter gradually extended to make the operating room germfree by sterilizing all equipment and supplies, covering surgeons and attendants with sterile gowns, and draping the patient so that only the site of actual operation was exposed.

Psychiatry. The roots of modern PSYCHIATRY extend to the very last years of the 18th century, when French physician Philippe Pinel (1745–1826) was beginning to alter the treatment of persons suffering from psychoses. Such patients had been incarcerated in institutions and chained to walls until, in 1798, Pinel removed chains from patients at the Bicêtre Hospital in Paris and began to popularize the concept of psychotics as patients and psychiatry as a field of medicine rather than a branch of penology. These enlightened attitudes developed until, by the last quarter of the 19th century, psychiatry was dominated by two figures: Emil KRAEPELIN in Germany and Sigmund FREUD in Vienna. Kraepelin's work was important in demonstrating that the discipline of psychiatry could be subjected to the same rigorous standards of investigation as other medical disciplines, whereas Freud revolutionized understanding of the unconscious mind and the treatment of patients suffering from neuroses and anxiety.

The Twentieth Century

Medicine in the 20th century made enormous advances in the basic medical sciences. It also expanded to take full advantage of the equally rapid strides being made in all the other fields of science and technology. As a result, no synopsis of the achievements of medicine in the century can really be provided here. Individual entries on the various fields of medicine provide such current reviews.

Antibiotics. One major area of advance in 20th-century medicine has been in pharmaceuticals, and in particular the development of ANTIBIOTICS. A pioneer in this field was the German bacteriologist Paul EHRLICH, who discovered certain of the body's white blood cells and was able to stain the tubercle bacillus, a crucial step in identifying the tuberculosis-causing organism and developing means of controlling the disease. In 1909, Ehrlich synthesized arsphenamine, a drug that could destroy the syphilis-causing organism *Treponema pallidum.* With this accomplishment, Ehrlich ushered in the age of antibiotics and chemotherapy.

The German physician Gerhard Domagk (1895–1964), working 25 years after Ehrlich, developed the first useful SULFA DRUG, or sulfonamide, which was used to treat streptococcal disease. In 1929 the British bacteriologist Alexander FLEMING discovered PENICILLIN, which destroys various bacteria. In 1943 the microbiologist Selman WAKSMAN (1888–1973) discovered streptomycin, the first antibiotic effective against tuberculosis; it was also effective against a number of other bacteria not affected by penicillin. Many antibiotics are now in use.

Vaccines. The 20th century has seen the conquest of a number of diseases through immunization. Smallpox, has disappeared worldwide. In technologically advanced countries a number of childhood diseases such as poliomyelitis, rubeola (measles), rubella (German measles), diphtheria, and mumps now occur infrequently and sporadically. Vaccines against diseases such as influenza have also been developed, but influenza and a number of others remain difficult to control because of the many varieties of the virus and its capacity to mutate. Such difficulties surround current research on a vaccine against acquired immune deficiency syndrome (see AIDS). Research medicine is thus heavily involved in efforts to

Modern medical research makes use of advanced technology. Medical physicist Michel Ter-Pogossian is seen here with the cyclotron he installed in 1965 at the Washington University School of Medicine for research into the medical uses of short-lived radioisotopes.

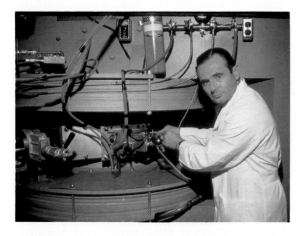

understand the immune system, not only with respect to AIDS but also because of other diseases such as rheumatic fever, rheumatoid arthritis, and lupus erythematosus.

Medical Genetics. Medical research at the cellular level, such as on the immune system, has been made possible through 20th-century advances in genetic techniques. The causes of many diseases have been traced to defective chromosomes or to specific genes on the chromosomes. The hope is that such diseases can eventually be treated through direct intervention, using the techniques of GENETIC ENGINEERING. By means of such techniques, several natural body chemicals have become available in quantity, including insulin, interferon, clot-dissolving enzymes, and human growth hormone.

Medical Technology. The contributions of other fields of science and technology to advances in 20th-century medicine and surgery have been so numerous that only one such field will be chosen here as an example: X-ray imaging. The discovery of X rays led rapidly to their employment in various diagnostic and therapeutic ways, and their use in medical research made possible the elucidation of the structure of molecules such as DNA, proteins, and vitamins.

medicine, traditional The term *medicine* generally evokes the concept of a modern discipline that uses advanced technology and that is integrated with large research efforts and high-technology hospitals and medical schools. Worldwide, however, many healing enterprises exist, at several levels of sophistication. Even in the most advanced cultures, for example, some forms of FOLK MEDICINE may be detected—suggested curative procedures that do not involve formal training and are passed on from person to person. In certain cultures another form of medicine exists, known as traditional medicine.

Traditional medicine constitutes various institutionalized and regularized procedures. Practitioners profess a common standard for which normal methods of training exist, and they often accept a common text as the source of knowledge. Whereas the oldest forms of traditional medicine are chiefly magical and religious in nature, some of the highly developed forms, such as those found in India and China, are comparable to Western medicine prior to the Scientific Revolution. These higher forms of traditional medicine characteristically went through a period of rapid development; established a set of texts, customs, and manners; and then ceased to develop. In some instances practitioners have initiated new research. Ancient texts have remained the guideposts, however, and such current efforts are directed mainly toward reinterpreting and justifying reliance on those texts.

Shamanism. The phenomenon of shamanism centers on the figure of the SHAMAN, a person believed to be supernaturally endowed to deal with the spirit world. In terms of medicine, shamanistic powers include the power to cure the ill. The word is derived from Ural-Altaic languages of Asia. Shamanism also crossed the Bering Strait in prehistoric times and is found among the Eskimos,

Ritual dancers in Sri Lanka wear this mask to chase the spirit of catarrh from a sick patient. In many tribal societies the psychological effects of such rituals are believed to have physiological results.

Aleuts, and American Indian tribes throughout North and South America. Closely allied systems occur in the Malay Peninsula, in Indonesia, and among the Australian Aborigines; until recent times, remote tribal groups in India and Korea maintained shamanistic systems as well. Among American Indians, shamans are known as medicine men; somewhat shamanistic figures in African cultures are called witch doctors.

A person is not accepted as a shaman until first instructed by shaman masters and then subjected to a series of trials. The person may wander, or remain for a long period in a tent or hut, and behave in a manner that in modern terms might be called "psychotic," finally ending the ordeal in a crisis that results in a self-cure. The entire rite of initiation is a symbolic form of death and resurrection. After being tortured by evil spirits and wandering in a netherworld, the shaman returns to Earth as the rightful intermediary between members of the tribe and supernatural forces. Sickness in such groups is conceived of as spiritual; in serious illnesses, the soul may have been taken to the netherworld by spirits and must therefore be rescued by the shaman and restored to its rightful body. In terms of modern medicine, the shaman practices primitive physical techniques but may be an expert herbalist and can also have strong psychological effects that can in turn influence the physical health of a patient.

Traditional Medicine in India. The subcontinent of India has a large and well-trained force of practitioners of modern medicine. In addition, it has several types of traditional medicine, the largest of which is called Ayurvedic medicine. The ancestry of this type can be traced back 3,000 years or so, but it evolved into its current form from about 500 BC to AD 500. Based on Sanskrit texts, it has a wide following. It is governmentally supported, has a defined curriculum, and has schools that grant degrees. Some of these schools are part of universities that may also have a modern medical school.

Like other major types of Asian traditional medicine, Ayurvedic medicine is based on humoral theories. That

is, the human body is considered a microcosm of the universe. The seven body substances—bone, flesh, fat, blood, semen, marrow, and chyle—are the product of three humors: *kapha*, or phlegm; *pitta*, or bile; and *vayu*, or wind. Health depends on the equilibrium of these humors, and sickness is a disequilibrium. The point of equilibrium depends on age, sex, temperament, climate, nutrition, and the nature of daily activities.

The basic texts of Ayurvedic medicine are the works of the physician Charaka, the *Charakasamhita*, which reached its present form around the 1st century AD, and those of Susruta, the *Susrutasamhita*, which, often rewritten, reached its present form in the 7th century AD. Later texts are essentially reworkings of these classics and the writings of Madhava and Vagbhata. In the texts, medicine is considered to be the science of living to a great age, and emphasis is placed on diet and the conduct of life. The works of Charaka express clearly that diseases are normally of natural origin. The Ayurvedic physician, or *vaidya*, requires great skill, knowledge, and experience to make a diagnosis. Treatment makes use of herbs, animal parts, manipulation of the patient, and modification of the diet. The list of medicines in the texts exceeds 700 plants.

Ayurvedic medicine arose with and is related to the development of the Hindu religion, substantially ceasing further growth when Hinduism reached its full flower. Because the Hindu religion forbade cutting a dead body, Ayurvedic knowledge of anatomy was fragmentary. Nonetheless, by Susruta's era, more than 120 surgical instruments made of steel were being used for specific tasks, and physicians were performing operations on the urinary bladder for the removal of stones. Indeed, plastic surgery in India was unrivaled anywhere in the world until the mid-18th century.

A smaller branch of traditional medicine on the subcontinent, and one common to Muslim areas, is known as Yunani or Unani. This is in fact the medicine of ancient Greece, translated into Arabic and Persian and then slowly modified by its practitioners, the *hakim*. The works of Galen are accepted literally and in detail. True to this Mediterranean tradition, the medicine has four humors: yellow bile, black bile, phlegm, and blood. These humors combine with the four primary qualities of heat, cold, moisture, and dryness. If the humors and qualities are in equilibrium, a person is healthy; if not, illness results. Yunani, like Ayurvedic medicine, prohibits dissection and autopsy, but innovations continue to be made in pharmacology. Therapy is by contrary medications; a "hot" disease, for example, is treated by administering a "cold" remedy.

Finally, it should be noted that whereas HOMEOPATHY has only a marginal existence today in Western countries, it has gained the status of a traditional form of medicine in India. Both Ayurvedic and Yunani practitioners add it to their therapeutic offerings, since the emphasis it places on decoctions of herbs has made it attractive to them. In contrast, an uneasy relationship is maintained with contemporary medicine.

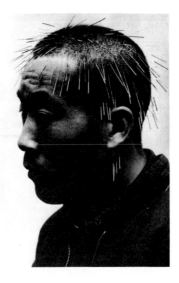

The traditional Chinese technique of acupuncture is used today to treat such ailments as arthritis, headaches, and ulcers. It has also been found effective as an anesthetic for some forms of surgery.

Traditional Medicine in China. Traditional Chinese medicine is deeply rooted in the Chinese view of the universe. The fundamental concept of the duality of all processes extends at least as far back as the 8th century BC. It is expressed as yang and yin; for example, yang is the heavens and yin the Earth, yang is hot and yin cold, yang is male and yin female. The universe is composed of five elements—metal, wood, water, fire, and earth—in varying proportions, but their interactions are in turn controlled by yang and yin. The two forces or essences are equal but in constant ebb and flow, causing continual changes. In medicine the primary role of the physician is to restore the balance between them. This requires the ability to control the levels of yang and yin. Twelve invisible channels, called *jin*, are assumed to carry the forces. These

Students in this biology class in Beijing examine a mammalian heart. Medicine has been among the most advanced of China's technical fields since the early 19th century; recently, emphasis on scientific education has increased the number of trained medical workers.

channels are deep in the muscle but not in communication with the blood vessels, and they communicate with three "burning spaces" that are analogous to reservoirs of yang and yin. Such theories are contained in several major texts of traditional Chinese medicine, including the *Nei Jing*, The Book of Medicine of the Yellow Emperor, which is presumed to have been written in the 3d century BC.

The first step in treatment of the ill is diagnosis. The methods involve interrogation and the use of the senses, each modality being described in exquisite detail. Inspection of the pulses alone can take three hours, since this is thought to be the single most valuable source of information about a patient. The pulse is said to vary with many factors, and 51 chief types of pulse are said to exist. Where the pulse is abnormal is where one of the 12 yang-yin channels is likely to be blocked. Diseases are diagnosed in this way, down to the specific organ involved and the future course of the disease.

The next step, therapy, involves methods affecting the unsatisfactory yang-yin balance. ACUPUNCTURE, or the insertion of long needles into the body channels, is thought to restore equilibrium. Proponents relate its supposed effectiveness to the blocking of pain-conducting nerves or to the local release of neurotransmitters called endorphins.

Moxibustion, another characteristic therapy of traditional Chinese medicine, is analogous to the blistering procedures found in many other traditional and folk medicines. Powdered leaves of a plant, *Artemisia*, are compressed into a pellet, placed at the desired site on the patient's skin, and ignited, forming a blister. Just as acupuncture charts point out where a needle is to be inserted, moxibustion charts identify where blistering is to take place for a desired effect.

The traditional Chinese physician also makes use of a large collection of therapeutic materials. The *Bencao Gang Mu*, The Great Herbal, was published at the end of the 16th century and contains some 1,900 prescriptions; it remains the standard in the field. Many of the medications are potent, and some have been acquired by modern medicine. Of these the best known is ephedrine, an effective medication for asthma.

Surgery was not much practiced in traditional Chinese medicine, although fractures were treated by bonesetters. The lack of interest in surgery was based on the yang-yin philosophy of harmony and on the Chinese consideration of the body as a sacred inheritance from ancestors, so that body injuries indicated a lack of filial piety.

Traditional Medicine in Japan. By the 7th century AD the influence of Chinese medicine had spread to Japan. At first the texts of this imported product were meticulously followed. In the 17th century, however, a "reformist" interpretation of Chinese medicine arose claiming that the only basis for medicine should be the *Shanghang Lun*, a Chinese treatise on fevers, as interpreted by Japanese authorities. This marked the beginnings of Japan's own school of traditional medicine, which continues to be a significant element in Japanese health care.

medicine man   SEE SHAMAN

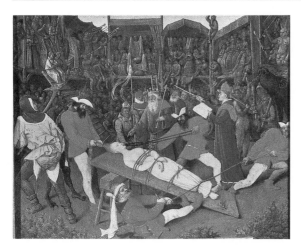

A mid-15th-century miniature, The Martyrdom of Saint Apollonia *by Jean Fouquet, shows the staging of a French mystery play in the period when drama moved from the church to the public square. (Musée Condé, Chantilly.)*

medieval drama [med-ee'-vul]   The distinguishing features of medieval drama are its Christian content and didactic purpose. Vernacular plays typically dramatized the lives of saints, Bible stories, or moral allegories. The biblical cycle plays, sometimes called mystery plays, were originally performed under church auspices but by the late 14th century were produced under the supervision of craft guilds (*mistères*) and performed in public places on the feast of Corpus Christi or during Whitsuntide.

Although they contained Old Testament and nativity sequences, the cycles were primarily devoted to portraying the life and passion of Christ, his harrowing of hell, his resurrection and appearances to his disciples and to the two Marys, and his ascension. Some cycles centered on the Virgin, but these were suppressed in Protestant countries during the Reformation. Typically the plays adhered as closely as possible—given their "translation" into verse—to the biblical narratives, but some are based on episodes left undeveloped in the Bible, such as the visit of the Shepherds or Balaam and his ass, or are derived from legendary sources, such as plays about the Antichrist. The cycle plays reached their greatest expansion in the 15th and early 16th centuries but in England were suppressed as "popish" in the 1570s.

Protestant antagonism also accounts for the disappearance of most of the miracle, or saints, plays. Only two are extant: the *Conversion of Saint Paul*, narrative history similar to the biblical cycles, and *Mary Magdalene*, which combines biblical-cycle elements with the framework of the morality.

The morality play was an allegory that depicted the fall of a representative Everyman, his life in sin and folly, and his eventual redemption. In the most elaborate of these, the *Castle of Perseverance* (c.1425), the soul of Humanum Genus resides in a castle encircled by the forces of good (God, His Angels, and other agents) and evil (the World, the Flesh, the Devil, Covetise and the other Seven Deadly Sins). The play follows his life, its climax being a battle in which the forces of good beat off the evil ones with a barrage of roses, symbols of Christ's passion. Not all morality plays were solemn, however; *Mankind* (c.1470) depicted the fall and life in sin of its protagonist in an often farcical manner.

The most famous morality play, EVERYMAN (c.1500), an English work probably derived from a Dutch original, is less typical of the genre in that it omits the fall and life in sin and instead dramatizes Everyman's summons by Death to account for his sins. These moralities were performed by professional and traveling troupes. The influence of the form can be seen in Christopher MARLOWE's *Doctor Faustus* (written 1588; publ. 1604, 1616) and in the Falstaff scenes of Shakespeare's *Henry IV*, as well as in other Renaissance plays.

See also: THEATER, HISTORY OF THE.

medieval music   The Middle Ages in music began in 313, when the Roman emperor Constantine the Great embraced Christianity. Emerging from underground, the church immediately established a schola cantorum in Rome for the training of musicians. Church music then consisted, as it had since pre-Christian Judaism, of PLAINSONG, liturgical texts chanted to flowing melodies without measured rhythm. The Roman liturgy became standard in Western Christianity due primarily to the efforts of Gregory I, pope from 590 to 604. The body of plainsong is known as Gregorian chant in his honor, although it seems not to have reached its final form until the 8th century.

Expansion of the Liturgy. Classical music theory, transmitted (6th century) by Boethius and studied by all aspirants to the clergy, equipped medieval musicians to use tropes—textual or musical additions—to extend the received texts and melodies of the plainsong Mass. These plainsong additions, newly composed to poetic texts, were

Pope Gregory I (left), under the inspiration of the Holy Spirit, is shown directing the collection and codification of plainsong, the liturgical vocal music of the medieval Roman Catholic church. Plainsong, also known as Gregorian chant in honor of Pope Gregory, greatly influenced all other music in the Middle Ages.

This illustration is from a manuscript containing works by Guillaume de Machaut, one of the foremost composers and poets of 14th-century France. Machaut played a major role in the development of polyphony and the increasing secularization of medieval music.

inserted between or even within the regular chants. Tropes could become quite lengthy, even theatrical. The *Quem queritis* ("Whom do you seek?") trope, composed early in the 10th century and depicting the scene at Jesus' empty tomb, is an ancestor of the late-medieval miracle, mystery, and passion plays.

The sequence, originally a mere tag to the Alleluia of the Mass, began around the same time and in the same way as the trope, but it eventually detached itself from particular chants to become an independent composition.

Development of Polyphony. Simultaneous with the "horizontal" elaboration by tropes came "vertical" elaboration by polyphony (more than one melodic line sounding simultaneously). This technique began modestly enough with the parallel organum of the 9th century, in which two singers began on different pitches, separated by the musical interval of a fourth or fifth, and sang the same melody "in parallel." Eventually, voices moved independently of the melody, and the original chant, the cantus firmus or "tenor" (literally, holder), had to be slowed down to accommodate the other voices' fantastic decorations. Leading schools in this florid organum were located at St. Martial in Limoges (1100–50) and Notre Dame in Paris (1175–1220), especially under the latter's two great masters, Léonin and Pérotin.

The Notre Dame school not only perfected organum, but derived new polyphonic forms from it. The clausula began as an elaboration of the phrase-ending in a chant, but grew into an independent composition. The conductus, a song with several stanzas, was not based on a chant at all. The fitting of new words, in Latin or in French, to some of the voice parts while leaving the original Latin in the tenor resulted in the MOTET. Combining text and (often ribald) commentary in the same piece, the motet was the most characteristic musical form of the great scholastic era in Paris.

Secular Songs. In SONG forms such as the lai, virelay, rondeau, and ballade, the troubadours of southern France celebrated the virtues of chivalry and courtly love. In northern France and Germany the trouvères and minnesingers followed the troubadours' example (see MINSTRELS, MINNESINGERS, AND TROUBADOURS). The somewhat earlier Latin songs (with vague musical notation) preserved in the *Carmina Burana* manuscript (1280) provide an earlier view of medieval life as it was lived by itinerant clerics and students.

Ars Nova. The early 14th century saw a flowering of rhythmic freedom and dissonant harmonies in polyphonic music. The composer and music theorist Philippe de VITRY gave the era its name in his treatise *Ars nova* (c.1323). As a composer, Vitry took second place to Guillaume de MACHAUT, a musician who overshadowed his century as Beethoven did the 19th. Machaut completed the merging of sacred and secular music by continuing the development of the motet and by introducing polyphonic versions of the troubadour song forms. About the same time (c.1330), the first polyphonic Italian music was composed, in courtly song forms such as the MADRIGAL, caccia (a form of canon), and ballata.

It is tempting to hear in Machaut's colorful music the approach of the Renaissance with its sensual, humanistic taste. Many 15th-century composers followed in his steps. England's John Dunstable, for example, is thought to have lived in Italy; his motets, songs, and sections of the mass are a significant synthesis of French learning and Italian warmth. France's Guillaume DUFAY took an important step by placing music on the same level of importance as text. As the first composer to create one unified musical work from the five parts of the mass, he set the musical agenda of the Renaissance.

medieval period   see MIDDLE AGES

Medina [muh-dee'-nuh]   Medina (Arabic: Al-Madinah), the second holiest city in Islam (after Mecca) and site of the tomb of MUHAMMAD, is located in HEJAZ region, western Saudi Arabia. The population is 198,196 (1974). All residents are Arabic-speaking Muslims.

Medina is noted for its pottery and date palms. The old walled city is surrounded by the pilgrim camping ground (Al Manakh) and the An Bariya Quarter, the former commercial district. Historical sites include the tombs of Aaron and Muhammad; the Mosque of Quba, the first mosque in Islamic history; the Mosque of the Two Quiblahs, commemorating Muhammad's changing of the direction to be faced while praying from toward Jerusalem to toward Mecca; and the Prophet's Mosque, which Muhammad helped to build. Medina is often visited by Muslim pilgrims en route to Mecca. Non-Muslims are forbidden access to all pilgrimage sites.

The first settlers of Medina were Jews expelled from Palestine by the Romans in AD 135. Muhammad arrived from Mecca in 622, and, although he first treated the Jews with indulgence, he soon drove them out of Hejaz and made Medina the administrative capital of his Islamic state, a position it maintained until 661. After 661 the Umayyads, Egyptians, and Turks controlled the city at various times until 1916, when the independent Arab kingdom of Hejaz was formed. In 1932, Hejaz became part of Saudi Arabia.

meditation   Meditation is the contemplation or reflective consideration of an object or a religious truth in order to arrive at a desired mental or spiritual state. It is an important part of Buddhism and Hinduism but also appears in Christianity and Islam. Although usually considered a means toward developing the spiritual life of a religious person, meditation is not necessarily a religious practice. Transcendental Meditation (TM), for example, is used by many people to attain peace of mind. TM is a version of yogic practices (see YOGA) that was introduced into the West by Maharishi Mahesh Yogi in the late 1960s. It does not have a doctrinal content and is practiced by both religious (of any persuasion) and nonreligious people.

A young Buddhist monk meditates in order to attain spiritual freedom, or Nirvana. Meditation is traditionally practiced by devoutly religious persons, such as Buddhist and Christian monks. Since the 1960s, however, many Westerners with no strong religious convictions have begun to meditate in order to achieve peace of mind.

Mediterranean Sea   The Mediterranean is the world's largest inland sea. It lies between the continents of Europe and Africa and is bounded on the east by the westernmost stretches of Asia. Its length is about 4,025 km (2,500 mi), its average width 805 km (500 mi), and its area about 2,965,500 km^2 (1,145,000 mi^2). The greatest depth, 5,092 m (16,706 ft), is in the Matapan Trench of the Ionian Basin. The mean depth is 1,525 m (5,000 ft).

The name of the sea is derived from the Latin *medius* ("middle") and *terra* ("earth," or "land"), indicating that the sea was once believed by certain civilizations to be at the center of the world. Countries that border the Mediterranean are, counterclockwise, Morocco, Algeria, Tunisia, Libya, Egypt, Israel, Lebanon, Syria, Turkey, Greece, Albania, Yugoslavia, Italy, Monaco, France, and Spain. Island states within the sea are Malta and Cyprus. Other large islands, from west to east, are the BALEARIC ISLANDS, CORSICA, SARDINIA, SICILY, and Crete, lying in the Ligurian, TYRRHENIAN, ADRIATIC, IONIAN, and AEGEAN seas. The Mediterranean is linked to the Atlantic Ocean by the Strait

of GIBRALTAR, to the Black Sea by the Turkish straits (DARDANELLES and BOSPORUS), and to the Red Sea by the SUEZ CANAL.

The Mediterranean shores were settled in prehistoric times. Ever since, many people have entered the region from the continental interiors. The entire coastline and continental shelves are littered with the ruins of earlier civilizations. Some of them developed into great empires, expanding far beyond the basin itself. For millennia, the products of the region have been exported throughout the known world, and the Mediterranean countries have, in turn, served as a vast receiving house for staples and luxury goods. Because of its critical location at the juncture of three continents, and because of the "stepping-stone" islands, the many fine harbors, and the rich cities and countries on its shores, the Mediterranean Sea has long been of strategic importance. The Strait of Gibraltar, the Turkish straits, and the Suez Canal are among the world's most important marine passageways.

Geology. The present Mediterranean Sea is a remnant of the ancient Tethys Seaway that once extended as far north as the Danube Basin and possibly as far east as the Aral Sea. The seabed is divided by a ridge into eastern and western basins, and then subdivided into several lesser basins and seas. The Adriatic, Ionian, and Aegean seas all have abyssal plains beyond the continental shelf, which averages less than 24 km (15 mi) in width. The smaller basins are separated by submarine ridges. The generally steep and rocky coasts are often deeply indented and interrupted by small, scattered plains. Although most streams entering the sea carry considerable amounts of sediment, the only large deltas are those of the NILE, RHÔNE, and PO rivers. Many of the islands are the peaks of volcanoes, some of which are still active. The entire Mediterranean basin is tectonically active with frequent earthquakes, particularly in Greece and Turkey.

Climate. The Mediterranean climate, one of the most distinctive in the world, is characterized by mild, wet winters and hot, long, dry summers. Precipitation generally decreases toward the south and east and ranges from more than 2,540 mm (100 in) per year near Dalmatia to less than 255 mm (10 in) annually in parts of North Africa. Temperatures also decrease toward the east and increase toward the south.

Hydrology and Marine Life. Of the numerous rivers that flow into the Mediterranean, the largest is the Nile in Egypt. Other important rivers are the EBRO in Spain; the Rhône in France; the ARNO, TIBER, Po, and Isonzo in Italy; Vardar, Strimán, and Nestos in Greece; and Gediz and Menderes in Turkey. All the water from rivers and rainfall, however, could not maintain the level of the sea, which would drop about 1,400 mm (55 in) per year without a great deal of inflow from the Atlantic. A surface current enters the Mediterranean through Gibraltar. Underneath, a smaller and slower current, about 305 m (1,000 ft) deep, flows into the Atlantic. Water balance is also maintained by a similar—although smaller—inflow and outflow through the Turkish straits. The general pattern of surface currents is counterclockwise. Only at Gibraltar and on the east coast of Tunisia is the tidal range greater

MEDITERRANEAN SEA

+ Spot Depth

Meters	Feet
0	0
200	656
2000	6562
Below 4000	Below 13124

Scale 1:25,437,000

© 1980 Rand McNally & Co.
A-558300-772

than 914 mm (3 ft). Surface temperatures vary seasonally, from about 5° C (41° F) in February in the northern Adriatic to 31° C (88° F) in August off the coast of Libya. Because of considerable evaporation, the water is much more saline than that of the Atlantic Ocean or the Black Sea.

The floor of the Mediterranean is covered with yellow brown sediments of lime, clay, and sand to an approximate thickness of 2,740 m (9,000 ft). Underlying this layer is blue mud. Fine riverine muds overlie these strata near river mouths.

The variety of climates, water depths, salinity, and landforms has produced a variety of flora and fauna, both in the sea and on its shores. More than 400 species of fish are found, along with shellfish, corals, sponges, and seaweeds.

Economy. From ancient times fishing has been an important economic activity in the Mediterranean basin. TYRIAN PURPLE dye, made from the Mediterranean rock whelk, was once an important product, as were sponges. Around the Mediterranean, agriculture has always been the basis of the economy. Manufacturing is becoming increasingly important, however, especially in the European countries and in Israel. Evidence exists of petroleum and natural gas deposits in the deep sediments of the basin floors.

Concern has been expressed that the Mediterranean may be "dying" due to pollution, most of which comes from municipal and industrial wastes on the European shore. International efforts to control pollution have begun.

History. The oldest civilizations along the Mediterranean were in Egypt (from 3000 BC), Crete and Greece (the AEGEAN CIVILIZATION in the 2d millennium BC), and Anatolia (the HITTITES during 1900–1200 BC). Subsequently, a number of maritime commercial states arose, including PHOENICIA, CARTHAGE, and the Greek city-states. Between the 3d century BC and the 1st century AD, Rome unified the entire basin under its rule. After the Roman Empire dissolved in AD 476, Arabs swept across North Africa into Iberia, and Germans and Slavs invaded from the north. Between the 11th and the 14th centuries, several commercial city-states developed, particularly in Italy. The Ottoman Turks had established their empire throughout the eastern Mediterranean and in North Africa by the 16th century. Increasing piracy and the discovery of new sea routes to India around Africa resulted in a decline in the maritime importance of the Mediterranean, but the opening of the Suez Canal in 1869 led to the sea's recovery as a major trade route.

medlar [med'-lur]   The medlar, *Mespilus germanica*, a member of the rose family, Rosaceae, is a small, twiggy tree growing from 3 to 6 m (10 to 20 ft) tall. It has finely toothed leaves and solitary white flowers. Native to Europe, it is grown there for the small, brown-colored, applelike fruit, which is eaten raw or in preserves. The fruit remains hard until frost, after which it is picked and kept in a cool, dry room until soft.

Medum [may-doom'] Medum (also Meidum, Meydum, or Maydum) is an Egyptian archaeological site northeast of AL-FAIYUM, mainly known for its oddly shaped PYRAMID. Probably begun late in the 3d dynasty (c.2686–2613 BC), it was originally built as a step pyramid about 94 m (398 ft) high. In the 4th dynasty, under Snefru (fl. 2600 BC), the structure was converted into a true pyramid by filling in its angles and casing it with limestone. Early 4th-dynasty tombs north of the pyramid contained fine examples of Egyptian painting, notably the mural known as the "Medum Geese."

Medusa [muh-doo'-suh] In Greek mythology Medusa was the only mortal of the three GORGONS, daughters of the sea god Phorcys and his sister-wife Ceto. Originally very beautiful women, they were transformed into ugly monsters, with serpents for hair, claws of bronze, and staring eyes capable of turning anyone who looked at them into stone. The hero PERSEUS killed Medusa by cutting off her head, and the winged horse PEGASUS sprang from her blood. Perseus used Medusa's head to petrify ATLAS (hence the Atlas mountains), but he later gave the head to ATHENA, who put it on her shield.

Medwall, Henry Henry Medwall (fl. c.1490), an English dramatist, was the author of the earliest known secular play in English, *Fulgens and Lucres*. A copy of the complete text was first discovered in 1919. The play tells the story of a woman's choice between two suitors and has a comic subplot.

meerschaum [mir'-shuhm] The very light, porous CLAY MINERAL meerschaum, or sepiolite ($H_6Mg_8Si_{12}O_{30}(OH)_{10}$ · $6H_2O$), is used chiefly as the bowl of often intricately carved tobacco pipes. As a weathering product of serpentine or magnesite, it occurs in many U.S. locations. Light-colored nodules with a fibrous structure are found in the stratified earthy or alluvial deposits at Eskişehir, Turkey (the chief commercial occurrence). Meerschaum may be scratched with a fingernail and is easily carved; it hardens on drying and may even float, giving the appearance to which the name *meerschaum* refers—German for "sea foam."

Meese, Edwin Edwin Meese III, b. Oakland, Calif., Dec. 2, 1931, was U.S. attorney general under President Ronald Reagan from 1985 to 1988. Meese, who earned his law degree in 1958, was an aide (1966–74) to Reagan as governor of California and later his counselor (1981–85) at the White House. Meese's appointment as attorney general was stalled for nearly a year because of allegations of improprieties. His resignation from that office coincided with a report from a special prosecutor who concluded that Meese had "probably violated criminal law" but that prosecution was unwarranted.

megalith [meg'-uh-lith] Megaliths (Greek, *megas*, "large," and *lithos*, "stone") are prehistoric structures built of massive stones, usually for religious or funerary purposes. Four principal types of megaliths can be distinguished: standing stones, row alignments, stone circles, and burial chambers. Most of them occur in Europe and date from the Late Neolithic Period and Early Bronze Age (4000–1000 BC). Megalithic burial chambers are also known in India dating from the 1st millennium BC and in Japan dating from early historic times. Standing stones have been erected even more recently by peoples in West Africa and by certain tribal groups of the northeast Indian state of Assam.

Standing Stones and Row Alignments. Isolated standing stones, or menhirs, are found at scattered sites throughout western and northern Europe and are common in Britain and Brittany (northwest France). The larger examples are probably prehistoric. Some of the smaller ones may have been erected in recent times as rubbing-stones for cattle.

Ancient stone alignments range from simple pairs of stones to complex arrays of multiple rows extending over a long distance, as at CARNAC in Brittany. Some of them may have had an astronomical significance; others, such as the stone avenue at AVEBURY, England, appear to be processional ways leading to a prehistoric sanctuary.

Stone Circles. Numerous circles or near-circular rings of standing stones exist, mainly in the British Isles. About one-third of these appear to have been laid out deliberately in noncircular shapes (such as ellipses, flattened circles, and egg-shaped circles); these may have been designed to achieve a whole-number ratio between the perimeter and principal diameter of the formation. Sites of this kind in Scotland (such as the Ring of Brodgar in Orkney) suggest the use of a common unit of measurement, the so-called megalithic yard, of 0.829 m (2.72 ft). If these interpretations are correct, they imply a

Stonehenge, on Salisbury Plain in Wiltshire, England, is a formation of holes and large stones surrounded by a ditch. Its earliest sections date from about 2800 BC.

(Above) *Carnac, a village in Brittany, is the site of prehistoric stone monuments. One, called the Ménec system (above), consists of 1,099 standing stones ranged in eleven rows.*

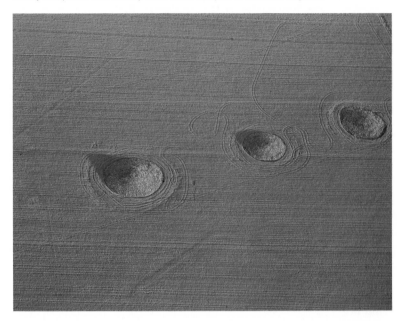

(Below) *Barrows, prehistoric burial chambers covered with mounds of earth or stone, are found in Britain and in many areas of Europe. These barrows (below) are located near Silbury Hill, part of the Avebury stone circle complex in Wiltshire, England.*

knowledge in prehistoric Europe of mensuration and geometry at a date much earlier than that given by documentary records from the early civilizations of Egypt and Mesopotamia. Some stone circles in Britain were enclosed within embanked earthworks, circular or oval in shape. These are known as henge monuments, a name invented from that of STONEHENGE in England.

Megalithic Tombs. The most frequently encountered class of megaliths consists of prehistoric stone-built burial chambers, which are widely distributed from southern Spain to southern Sweden. These are mostly collective tombs in which a number of individuals were buried at intervals over a long period, sometimes as much as 1,000 years.

Two basic types of burial chambers reflect different religious traditions. Passage graves, in which the burial chamber is reached by a lower and narrower stone-built passage, are usually covered by a BARROW (a round earthen mound) or a cairn (a pile of heaped stones); they occur mainly in coastal areas. Gallery graves have a broader axial chamber of constant width, sometimes divided transversely into segments and usually covered by long earthen mounds or cairns, often with a concave forecourt at the entrance. They tend to be distributed inland near the areas best suited for cultivation.

In France and Iberia such burial chambers are called *dolmens,* but in Britain this term is reserved for megalithic tombs denuded of their covering mound or cairn. In Wales and in the older British literature they are called *cromlechs.*

Formerly archaeologists supposed that the tradition of megalith building represented a religious movement spread by a small number of missionaries from the Mediterranean to Iberia and thence northward to Scandinavia. Radiocarbon dates have revealed that the earliest tombs are in Brittany, however, and that those of northern Europe form a separate group developed independently. The megalithic monuments in each of these geographic regions are now generally thought to represent the response of local Neolithic or Bronze Age populations to larger and stronger social ties and group interrelations with neighboring populations.

See also: ARCHAEOASTRONOMY; EUROPEAN PREHISTORY; STONE ALIGNMENTS.

megalopolis   A megalopolis is an extensive, heavily populated, continuously urban area that may include many cities. The term comes from the ancient Greeks, who in the 4th century BC began to build a grandiosely planned city called Megalopolis on the Peloponnesus. The modern term was introduced in 1961 by geographer Jean Gottman who, after two decades of research, published his book, *Megalopolis: The Urbanized Northeastern Seaboard of the United States,* on the urbanization between New Hampshire and northern Virginia. This almost continuous strip of urban and suburban development has also been called the "Main Street" of the country, or the Northeast Corridor, because it is linked by major highways and rail lines. Other emerging metropolis areas are Los Angeles–San Francisco and Dallas-Houston in the United States, the greater Paris and greater London areas, the Ruhr industrial basin, and the Tokyo-Osaka complex.

Megiddo [muh-gid'-oh] Ancient Megiddo, identified at the mound of Tell el-Muteselim on the Plain of Esdraelon in present-day Israel, was a major Canaanite city of northern Palestine. Mentioned in the annals of Tuthmosis III, it was the site of a great battle between the Egyptians and a Syrian confederation in 1486 BC.

Occupation levels date back to the 8th millennium BC. Following its conquest by Thutmose III in 1468 BC, Megiddo became a flourishing city. Found in its palace were two important hoards of ivories illustrating Canaanite art at its best.

Under Solomon in the 10th century BC, Megiddo became a strategic stronghold with a casemate wall with four-piered gateway. Completed under the 9th-century BC reign of Ahab, the city included a rock-cut shaft leading to a subterranean water supply. After the conquest by the Assyrian Tiglath-Pileser III (c.734 BC), a new city was erected on the site. Extensive excavations were undertaken in 1925-39.

Mehmed II, Sultan of the Ottoman Empire
[me-met'] Mehmed II, called the Conqueror, b. Mar. 30, 1432, d. May 3, 1481, sultan of the OTTOMAN EMPIRE (1444–46, 1451–81), extended Ottoman control to the Danube and of Anatolia to the Euphrates. His father, MURAD II, tried to abdicate when Mehmed was only 12 years old, but in the wake of the son's unsuccessful first reign, the father returned to power. When the more mature Mehmed ascended the throne once more (after Murad's death), he tried to create a world empire. After conquering Byzantine Constantinople in 1453, he rebuilt it into the prosperous capital of Istanbul. To counter the

Mehmed II, the Ottoman sultan whose capture of Constantinople in 1453 finally destroyed the Byzantine Empire, also unified Anatolia under Ottoman rule and completed the Ottoman conquest of the Balkans.

power of the Turkish aristocracy, Mehmed continued his father's policy of expanding the JANISSARY infantry corps. Mehmed conquered Serbia in 1459 and the Morea by 1460, extending the empire in Europe to the Danube and the Aegean. By 1461 he had conquered Anatolia as far as the Euphrates but failed to push further due to resistance from the MAMELUKES of Syria as well as from the White Sheep Turkmen of Iran. He was beginning new campaigns to capture Rhodes and southern Italy when he died suddenly. Mehmed was succeeded by his son, BAYEZID II.

Mehta, Zubin [may'-tuh, zoo'-bin] Zubin Mehta, b. Bombay, India, Apr. 29, 1936, achieved international stature as a conductor at an early age. His first conducting lessons were with his father, Mehli Mehta, director of the Bombay Symphony. He studied with Hans Swarowsky at the Vienna Academy of Music and won the first International Conductors Competition in Liverpool in 1958. In 1961, Mehta became music director of the Montreal Symphony, and in 1962 he took on the Los Angeles Philharmonic as well, which in 15 years he raised to international prominence. He made his Metropolitan Opera debut in 1965 and has since conducted at La Scala, Covent Garden, and the Vienna State Opera. He became music director of the Israel Philharmonic in 1969—and its director for life in 1981. From 1978 to 1991, Mehta also served as music director of the New York Philharmonic. He is a popular guest conductor; his flamboyant style is heard best in late romantic music.

Meier, Richard [my'-ur] The American postmodern architect Richard Meier, b. Newark, N.J., Oct. 12, 1934, is the most widely known of the group termed the New York Five (see POSTMODERN ARCHITECTURE). His neo–Le Corbusier white houses of layered screens, stairs, and ramps set in green landscapes made him instantly famous. His later work in commercial and institutional architecture espouses a hierarchy of building elements, sleek industrialized skins, and greater complexity in planning and massing. This is particularly evident in the Cornell University Undergraduate Housing (1974) in Ithaca, N.Y., the Atheneum (1979) in New Harmony, Ind., and the High Museum of Art in Atlanta (1983). In 1984 he received the Pritzker Prize.

Meighen, Arthur [mee'-uhn] Arthur Meighen, b. near Anderson, Ontario, June 16, 1874, d. Aug. 5, 1960, was prime minister of Canada (1920–21, 1926). A Manitoba lawyer, he was elected (1908) to the Canadian House of Commons and was secretary of state (1917) and minister of the interior (1917) in Sir Robert L. Borden's Conservative government. On Borden's resignation (1920), Meighen was chosen prime minister, but he lost the 1921 election. He formed another short-lived government in 1926 and sat (1932–41) in the Senate.

Meiji Restoration [may'-jee]   The Meiji Restoration of Jan. 3, 1868, returned authority to the Japanese emperor and brought an end to the military governments (see SHOGUN) that dominated Japan since 1185. Humiliated in 1854 when U.S. Commodore Matthew PERRY forced Japan to abandon its policy of seclusion, Japanese leaders resolved to transform the country into a modern, industrialized nation. Between 1854 and the restoration of 1868, opposition to the ruling TOKUGAWA family's authority increased, particularly from SAMURAI in the western domains of the Satsuma, Choshu, Tosa, and Hizen. The trade treaty of 1858, which granted foreigners rights to reside in Japan, conduct business, maintain diplomatic representatives, and remain immune to Japanese legal jurisdiction (the right of EXTRATERRITORIALITY), aroused opposition from both the *daimyo* (lords) and the imperial court. After 1858 the imperial court in Kyoto became the focus of national politics. From then until 1868 attacks on Tokugawa supporters increased.

With the restoration, Japan moved to a new form of unified national authority under the symbolic leadership of the young emperor Meiji (1852–1912), who gave his name to the period that lasted until his death. A conservative coalition of imperial princes, court nobles, daimyo, and samurai activists was brought together to form the new imperial government. In pursuit of the goals of *fukoku-kyohei*—rich country, strong army—the government was moved to Tokyo by 1873, the daimyo and samurai classes were abolished, a conscript army was established, and social equality was proclaimed.

Although political life was dominated by an oligarchy of former samurai, Japan was a constitutional monarchy by 1889, and representative government commenced in 1890. Among the leaders of the Meiji period were prime ministers ITO HIROBUMI and YAMAGATA ARITOMO; as finance minister during the 1880s, MATSUKATA MASAYOSHI placed Japan on a sound financial base. Japan's successful modernization was apparent from the ending of extraterritoriality in 1899, from its military victories over China (1895; see SINO-JAPANESE WARS) and Russia (1905; see RUSSO-JAPANESE WAR), and from the Anglo-Japanese alliance of 1902. Meanwhile, agriculture and industry prospered with government assistance. In a single generation Japan was transformed from a secluded and backward nation into a world power.

Mein Kampf   see HITLER, ADOLF

Meinecke, Friedrich [my'-nek-e, freed'-rik]   Friedrich Meinecke, b. Oct. 30, 1862, d. Feb. 6, 1954, was a noted German historian of ideas. He strove to write history that related political developments to broader cultural and intellectual currents. A fervent German patriot, Meinecke argued in *Weltbürgertum and Nationalstaat* (Cosmopolitanism and the Nation-State, 1907; Eng. trans., 1970) that the German state represented a unique synthesis of political power and culture. Later, however, disillusioned by World War I, he recognized in his book the *Idee der Staatsräson in der neueren Geschichte* (1924; trans. as *Machiavellism,* 1957) that such a synthesis was no longer possible in modern mass society. He nevertheless reemphasized in his last great work, *Die Entsehung des Historismus* (1936; trans. as *Historicism,* 1972), his belief in the positive contribution of classical German culture to modern Western civilization.

meiosis   see CELL

Meir, Golda [may-ir', gohl'-duh]   Golda Meir, b. May 3, 1898, d. Dec. 8, 1978, was prime minister of Israel from 1969 to 1974. Born into a poor Jewish family in Kiev, Ukraine, she emigrated to Milwaukee, Wis., in 1906. She married Morris Myerson in 1917, and the couple emigrated to Palestine in 1921. In the years before and during World War II, Meir held key posts in the Jewish Agency—the highest Jewish authority in British-administered Palestine—and in the World Zionist Organization. After Israel proclaimed its independence in 1948, she was appointed ambassador to the USSR by Prime Minister David Ben-Gurion, later serving as minister of labor (1949–56) and minister of foreign affairs (1956–66), as well as head of the Israeli delegation to the United States. Meir, who had adopted her Hebrew name in 1956, assumed the position of prime minister in 1969, after the death of Levi Eshkol. On Oct. 6, 1973, Egypt and Syria launched an attack, catching Israel by surprise. Although Israeli forces were able to rally and go on the offensive, Meir and her defense minister, Moshe Dayan, were criticized for being unprepared for the Arab attack. In the spring elections of 1974 the Labor party suffered a setback, and Meir—unable to form a government—resigned.

Golda Meir served as prime minister of Israel from 1969 to 1974. She resigned over her government's slowness to mobilize during the 1973 Arab-Israeli War, but she remained enormously popular after leaving office.

Meissen ware   see POTTERY AND PORCELAIN

Meissonnier, Juste Aurèle [may-sohn-ee-ay']   Juste Aurèle Meissonnier, b. *c.*1693, d. July 31, 1750, was a French goldsmith, interior designer, and architect often regarded as one of the originators of the 18th-century ROCOCO STYLE of decorative arts. From 1724 he worked as a goldsmith for Louis XV, who appointed (1726) him designer of the king's bedchamber and cabinet. The asymmetrical, swirling patterns of Meissonnier's designs are characteristic of the rococo. His metalwork and decoration were bold, imaginative, and facile.

meistersinger [my'-stur-sing-ur] The meistersingers, or mastersingers, were middle-class German poet-musicians who flourished especially in the 16th century and were the successors of the courtly minnesingers (love-singers) of the 12th through the 14th century. From about 1450, solo song was cultivated by craft guilds in many German towns and cities; guild members developed elaborate rules for their art, held contests, and awarded prizes. Their texts were mainly religious or didactic; their melodies, while resembling those of the minnesingers, often ended in florid cadences foreign to those of their predecessors. Richard Wagner's opera *Die Meistersinger von Nürnberg* (1868) vividly represents both the charm and the banality of the movement.

Meitner, Lise [myt'-nur, lee'-ze] The Vienna-born physicist Lise Meitner, b. Nov. 7, 1878, d. Oct. 27, 1968, together with her nephew Otto R. Frisch, published a theoretical interpretation of nuclear fission in 1939. After receiving (1906) her doctorate from the University of Vienna, Meitner began her research career in 1907 with the radiochemist Otto Hahn. In 1917 they discovered protactinium, the precursor substance from which actinium is formed. Meitner then became head (1917–38) of the physics department of the Kaiser Wilhelm Institute for Chemistry in Berlin. Fleeing Nazi persecution, she resumed her work at the Nobel Institute in Sweden. Her theoretical work helped to clarify the relationships between beta and gamma rays and stimulated Hahn and Fritz Strassmann in their discovery of the fission of heavy nuclei.

Meknès [mek-nesh'] Meknès, a city in Meknès province in northern Morocco, has a population of 704,000 (1987 est.). The walled medina and imperial compound are on the southeastern side of the Oued Bou Fekrane Wadi; the French-built new city is on the northeastern side. The city is a commercial center surrounded by rich farmlands; manufactures include carpets, leather, and pottery. Refineries process petroleum from nearby fields.

Founded in the 10th century as a trade center, Meknès was captured soon after by the Almoravids. Moulay Ismail of the Alouits made it his capital in 1673, building 24 km (15 mi) of walls and the largest palace in the world of that time, resulting in the city's being called the "Versailles of Morocco." The French used Meknès as the center of their colonization of Morocco in the 20th century.

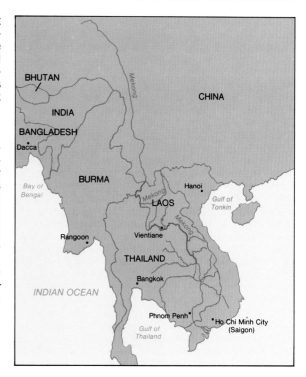

Mekong River [may'-kawng] One of the world's great rivers, the Mekong rises in the Tanggula Range in eastern Tibet, China, then flows southeastward for about 4,180 km (2,600 mi). It empties its silt-laden waters into the South China Sea through a complex delta south of Ho Chi Minh City, in southern Vietnam. The drainage basin covers approximately 795,000 km^2 (307,000 mi^2). In its middle course the river follows the boundary between Burma and Laos and between Laos and Thailand. The largest cities along it are Phnom Penh, in Cambodia and Vientiane, in Laos. The Mekong delta is navigable by shallow-draft vessels. The volume of sediment is so great that parts of the delta coastline advance as much as 38 m (125 ft) per year.

Melaka [muh-lak'-uh] Melaka (also Malacca) is the capital of the state of the same name in Malaysia; it is also a port city. Located on the west coast of the Malay Peninsula on the Strait of Malacca, the city lies about 130 km (80 mi) southeast of Kuala Lumpur. Melaka's population is 88,073 (1980). A trade center for the surrounding agricultural region, Melaka exports locally produced rubber and imports sugar and rice. The city's landmarks include Cheng Hoon Teng Temple (main hall built 1704), the oldest Chinese Buddhist temple in Malaysia; and Saint Paul's Church, built during the 16th century.

Melaka was a small fishing village by the early 15th century, when it became the capital of a Malay kingdom.

In 1511 the Portuguese conquered Melaka, which was by then a center of the SPICE TRADE. In 1641 the Dutch assumed control, and in 1795 the city passed to the British. Melaka became part of independent Malaysia in 1957.

Melanchthon, Philipp [muh-lank'-thuhn] Philipp Melanchthon, b. Feb. 16, 1497, d. Apr. 19, 1560, a German theologian and educator, worked with Martin LUTHER in leading the Protestant REFORMATION of the 16th century. His real family name was Schwarzerd (meaning "black earth"), of which Melanchthon is the Greek translation. Melanchthon's *Loci communes rerum theologicarum* (Commonplaces of Theology, 1521), which offered a systematic presentation of Lutheran teachings, was an important book revised and enlarged several times.

Melanchthon assisted Luther in university and school reforms and in organizing (1527) the visitation program to regulate the evangelical territorial churches. He was the chief author of the AUGSBURG CONFESSION (1530) and the *Apology,* a defense of the Augsburg Confession in response to the Catholic Confutation. In 1537 he wrote *Treatise on the Power of the Papacy,* which was added to Luther's Schmalkaldic Articles as a confession of faith. Like Luther, he stressed the justification of the sinner by faith in Christ as a gift of God's grace alone, as taught by Saint Paul. After Luther's death, Melanchthon assumed the leadership of the reform movement, but he bowed to compromise too easily in the interest of peace and became embroiled in dogmatic controversies with the staunch Lutheran party.

Melanesia [mel-uh-nee'-zhuh] Melanesia is one of three main island groups in OCEANIA. Its major island groups include the nations of FIJI, PAPUA NEW GUINEA, the SOLOMON ISLANDS, and VANUATU, along with the French dependency of NEW CALEDONIA. The islands were explored during the 18th century by the British navigator James COOK. The people of the region, known as Melanesians, number more than 2 million. Their languages are identified broadly as Melanesian (see OCEANIA, LANGUAGES OF). Great physical, cultural, and linguistic differences exist among Melanesian groups, and evidence suggests an admixture of Negroid and Australoid racial stocks, among others. Some groups show cultural affiliations with Polynesia and Micronesia. Most Melanesians are settled horticulturalists. Along the coasts are people skilled in sea travel using large carved canoes. Traditional types of social organization vary widely. Religious ritual traditionally focuses on ancestral and other spirit beings. Sacred flutes, masks, and weapons are among their many traditional craft objects, and great skill is lavished on their carvings (see OCEANIA, ART OF).

melatonin   see PINEAL GLAND

Melba, Dame Nellie   Nellie Melba was the stage name of the coloratura soprano Mrs. Helen Porter Armstrong, b. Helen Mitchell, Richmond, Australia, May 19, 1859. She died in Sydney on Feb. 23, 1931, five years after she retired from the stage and returned to her native country as president of the Melbourne Conservatory. A thoroughly trained musician and *prima donna assoluta* at London's Covent Garden and the Metropolitan Opera (debut in 1893), she set new standards for the performance of such roles as Gilda in *Rigoletto,* Violetta in *La Traviata,* and Rosina in *The Marriage of Figaro.* She was made a Dame of the British Empire in 1918; due to her enormous popularity Melba toast and peach Melba were named in her honor.

Melbourne   Melbourne, Australia's second largest city, is the capital of the southeastern state of Victoria. Sprawling along the shore of a large, naturally protected harbor on Port Phillip Bay, metropolitan Melbourne has a population of 2,964,000 (1987 est.); the city proper has only 63,388 inhabitants (1981). Melbourne is laid out with wide streets and a predominance of single-family dwellings; its population density is low. Melbourne's population was once overwhelmingly of British ancestry. Since World War II, however, there has been an influx of eastern and southern Europeans. Melbourne is noted as an industrial, financial, and administrative center. Ships, automobiles, clothing, metal, and rubber goods are

Melbourne, on the southeastern coast of Australia, is the capital of the state of Victoria and the nation's second largest city. The city was founded during the 1830s and grew dramatically during the Victoria gold rushes of the 1850s.

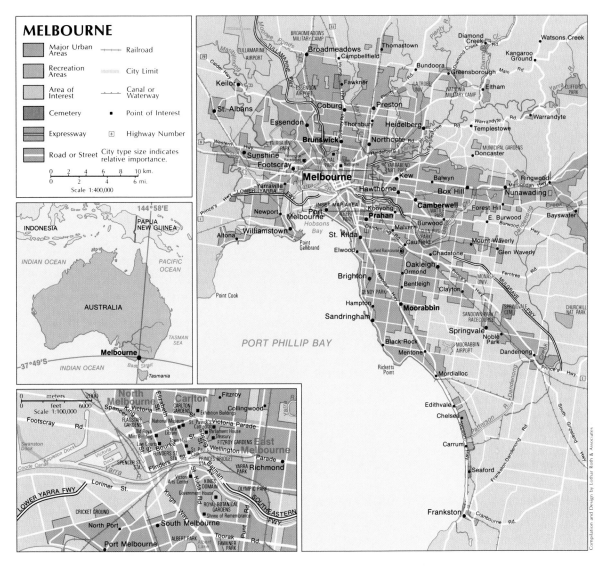

MELBOURNE

	Major Urban Areas	⊢⊢⊢⊢	Railroad
	Recreation Areas		City Limit
	Area of Interest		Canal or Waterway
	Cemetery	▪	Point of Interest
	Expressway	ⓢ	Highway Number
	Road or Street		City type size indicates relative importance.

0   2   4   6   8   10 km.
0   2   4   6 mi.
Scale 1:400,000

144°58'E

INDONESIA

PAPUA NEW GUINEA

INDIAN OCEAN

PACIFIC OCEAN

AUSTRALIA

TASMAN SEA

Melbourne

37°49'S

INDIAN OCEAN

Bass Strait

Tasmania

PORT PHILLIP BAY

Compilation and Design by Lothar Roth & Associates

---

among the principal products. The city is also a center for sea, land (especially rail), and air routes. About one-third of Australia's imports pass through the port, including petroleum, paper, timber, iron, steel, and chemicals. Its main exports are wool and agricultural products.

Traditionally a leader in arts and letters, Melbourne has a large public library, museums, and three universities: Melbourne (1855), Monash (1958), and La Trobe (1964). Its Flemington Racecourse is the scene of the Melbourne Cup horse race. Notable buildings include the State Parliament House and the Anglican and Roman Catholic cathedrals.

Since the beginning of permanent settlement in 1835, Melbourne has been a port for products from the interior. In 1851 it became the capital of the colony of Victoria. Following the gold rush in the 1850s, Melbourne became the largest city in Australia until it was surpassed by Sydney early in the 20th century. Between 1901 and 1927 it served as the federal capital. It was the site of the Summer Olympics in 1956.

Melbourne, William Lamb, 2d Viscount

As British prime minister, William Lamb, 2d Viscount Melbourne, b. Mar. 15, 1779, d. Nov. 24, 1848, served Queen VICTORIA as advisor and avuncular confidant during the first years (1837–41) of her reign. As home secretary (1830–34), Melbourne repressed agrarian rebels and trade unionists, but he supported the REFORM ACT of 1832.

A brief tenure as prime minister (1834) ended with his dismissal by King WILLIAM IV, who objected to Whig plans for church reform. Melbourne was returned to that office, however, in April 1835 and remained until September 1841. As prime minister, Melbourne pressed for urban improvements, penny postage, and liberalization of the Canadian government. He opposed parliamentary reorganization and repeal of the CORN LAWS. Melbourne's influence with Queen Victoria led to the Bedchamber Crisis in 1839 (Melbourne had resigned but returned to office when Victoria refused to allow the Tory Sir Robert PEEL to replace her Whig ladies-in-waiting with Tories); and the queen kept Melbourne's government afloat (1840–41) after he had lost much of his popular support. At Melbourne's request, Victoria dissolved Parliament in 1841, and the Conservatives attained power in the ensuing general election. Melbourne's marriage (1805) to the impetuous Lady Caroline Ponsonby was marked by several estrangements—one of which followed Lady Caroline's affair with Lord BYRON.

Melchites   see EASTERN RITE CHURCHES; ORTHODOX CHURCH

Meletius of Antioch, Saint [mil-ee'-shuhs, an'-tee-ahk]   Meletius, d. 381, bishop of Antioch and representative of the Antiochene tradition in theology, was appointed to the see in 360. Although a moderate in the controversy over ARIANISM, he immediately offended the Arian emperor Constantius II and was exiled. In his absence the supporters of Eustathius, a former bishop of Antioch, consecrated (362) Paulinus as bishop, creating a schism. Meletius returned in 363 but was exiled twice again (365–66 and 371–78) under Emperor Valens. Finally restored to his diocese in 378, Meletius was presiding over the First Council of Constantinople (see CONSTANTINOPLE, COUNCILS OF) when he died. Feast day: Feb. 12 (Eastern).

Méliès, Georges [may-lee-es']   A major contributor to the development of world cinema in its formative years, the Frenchman Georges Méliès, b. Dec. 6, 1861, d. Jan. 21, 1938, began his career as a conjurer. He was attracted to the cinema immediately after seeing the first Lumière showings in 1895 and soon developed his own distinctive studio-based style. Méliès was fascinated by the spectacle and trickery possible in the cinema, and his hundreds of little films, mostly dealing with fantastic subjects, are full of dancing girls and acrobatic devils, awe-inspiring disasters and miraculous transformations. For 10 years after 1896, Méliès's Star Film company was a dominant force in the film industry, producing such inventive and amusing short subjects as *A Trip to the Moon* (1902) and *New York–Paris by Automobile* (1908). His production methods and conception of film action as a sequence of tableaux, however, gradually became outdated. He ceased production in 1912 and was reduced to poverty.

Melilla [may-leel'-yuh]   Melilla (1982 pop., 54,741), a free port on the Mediterranean coast of Morocco, is an enclave governed by Spain as part of Malaga province. The economy is based on port activities and fishing; the city is also a Spanish military base. Known to the Phoenicians as Rusaddir, Melilla was successively held by the Carthaginians, Romans, Byzantines, and Moors until 1497, when it was captured by Spain. In 1936 it was the scene of an army revolt that started the Spanish Civil War. Morocco claims both Melilla and Ceuta.

Mellon, Andrew W. [mel'-uhn]   Andrew William Mellon, b. Pittsburgh, Pa., Mar. 24, 1855, d. Aug. 26, 1937, one of the wealthiest financiers of his day, served as U.S. secretary of the treasury from 1921 to 1932 under Presidents Harding, Coolidge, and Hoover. In 1882, with his brother Richard, he took control of the family banking business. Later he acquired interests in coal, aluminum, and oil. As treasury secretary he was instrumental in persuading Congress to lower wartime tax rates in order to spur business expansion. An art collector throughout his life, Mellon gave works valued at $35 million, together with $15 million in cash, to found the NATIONAL GALLERY OF ART in 1937.

Andrew W. Mellon, an American financier and public official, served as U.S. secretary of the treasury (1921–32) and as U.S. ambassador to Britain (1932–33). He donated (1937) his art collection, with the funds to house and maintain it, as the National Gallery of Art.

Mellon, Paul   One of the leading American art collectors and patrons of the 20th century, Paul Mellon, b. Pittsburgh, Pa., June 11, 1907, is the only son of financier Andrew W. Mellon. For much of his life, Paul Mellon has served as a trustee of the various foundations set up to disburse the vast Mellon fortune to art museums and other beneficiaries. In 1937 his father established the NATIONAL GALLERY OF ART in Washington, D.C., with an enormous gift of money and art holdings. It opened in 1941, and the younger Mellon became a trustee in 1945. He was its president (1963–79) and chairman (1979–85).

Through his interest in Anglo-American culture, Mellon came to collect 18th-century British art. This led to his establishment (1976) of the Yale Center for British Art and British Studies in New Haven, Conn. Another Mellon gift to the nation, the huge East Building of Washington's National Gallery, was designed by I. M. Pei to house contemporary art and the Center for Advanced Study in the Visual Arts; it was opened in 1978.

Mellon Foundation The Andrew W. Mellon Foundation was formed in 1969 by the merger of the Avalon Foundation, established in 1940 by Ailsa Mellon Bruce, with the Old Dominion Foundation, established in 1941 by Paul Mellon. It donates funds to higher education, cultural and environmental programs, population education and research programs, and the performing arts.

Other foundations established by members of the Mellon family include the A. W. Mellon Educational and Charitable Trust, formed in 1930, and the Richard King Mellon Foundation, established in 1947.

melodrama Melodrama is a rigidly conventionalized genre of popular drama, theatrical rather than literary, characterized by rapid and exciting physical action, sharply contrasted and simplified characters, and colorful alternations of violence, pathos, and humor. The central situation—victimization of helpless innocence by powerful evil forces—gives rise to four basic characters: the hero and the heroine, a comic ally who assists them, and the villain. Instead of tragic inevitability, melodrama uses coincidence and surprise to keep the action at high tension. Staggering effects and powerful emotional shocks build to frequent climaxes; scenes are of confrontation, pursuit, and escape, ending in striking tableaux.

Evolving out of sentimental and bourgeois drama, the GOTHIC ROMANCE, pantomime, and the opéra comique at the end of the 18th century, melodrama first appeared in France and England as a result of the battle between great and small theaters over restrictions limiting performances of spoken drama to licensed houses. The law was successfully circumvented by the use of music, which served as emotional commentary on the action and gave rise to the term *melodrama*, which combines the Greek words for song and play. Victorian melodrama was spectacular in staging, featuring sensational scenes of fires, explosions, avalanches, and shipwrecks and vivid depictions of city life, as in Dion BOUCICAULT's *The Corsican Brothers* (1852), Tom Taylor's *Ticket-of-Leave Man* (1863), and Augustin DALY's *Under the Gaslight* (1867).

melody A melody is a logical—as opposed to a random—succession of single tones of varying PITCH, having a recognizable musical shape or contour. Melody is often considered the horizontal aspect of music, as opposed to harmony, the vertical aspect. Inseparable from melody is RHYTHM, the durational organization of music. The same succession of pitches may create an entirely different emotional response in the listener if the rhythm is changed. Rhythmic manipulation of melody is a basic tool used by composers to create musical form. The range and variety of melodic styles is so vast that attempts to render the term more precise involve the elimination of one or more valid styles.

Melodies are frequently constructed of short melodic units. The smallest unit that comprises a melodic idea—which may be as few as two or three notes—is a motif.

Motifs are combined to form phrases—perhaps of 4-measure lengths—and phrases are combined to form periods, passages comparable in completeness to a full sentence.

The relationships between melody and other pitches determine musical texture. The texture is monophonic if the melody is unaccompanied; it is polyphonic when two or more melodies occur together; it is homophonic when a melody is accompanied by chordal harmony.

melon Melons, or muskmelons, *Cucumis melo*, of the Cucurbitaceae (cucumber) family, are a diverse group of annual, trailing-vine plants that are grown for their fruits. The plants originated in the region of Persia and were probably introduced into North America during the 16th century.

The botanical classification of melons differs in some respects from popular nomenclature. The large group of netted melons, *C. melo reticulatus,* are commonly called cantaloupes in the United States. (A larger cantaloupe type is often marketed as a "muskmelon.") The true cantaloupe, however, *C. melo cantalupensis,* is seldom grown in North America, although it is common in Europe. Unlike the American cantaloupe, its skin is not netted. The so-called winter melons, *C. melo inodorus,* while officially members of the muskmelon group, lack the typical musky odor and are usually larger than cantaloupes. The winter melon group includes the smooth-skinned, green-fleshed honeydew; the dark green, orange-fleshed Persian; the yellow-skinned, green- or white-fleshed casaba; and the Crenshaw, which has a dark green, wrinkled rind and pink flesh. Most melons grow best in a hot, dry climate, although a few cultivars have been developed that can be grown in more northerly regions.

See also: WATERMELON.

Muskmelons, also called canteloupes, have a hard rind that encases the juicy pulp, and flat seeds that form a netlike mass in the hollow center (detail, top). They grow on creeping vines that feature large, lobed leaves and yellow flowers.

Melos [mee'-lahs] Melos (Milos) is an island of Greece's CYCLADES in the Aegean Sea. Its population is 4,554 (1981). Its area is 150 km² (58 mi²), and its maximum elevation, Mount Prophet Elias, is 751 m (2,464 ft). Archaeological digging has uncovered ancient settlements dating from the Middle Bronze Age (c.3000–c.2000 BC). The *Venus de Milo*, now in the Louvre Museum, Paris, was found on the island in 1820. An ancient source of obsidian, Melos now exports gypsum, barium, sulfur, salt, wine, and cotton.

Melozzo da Forli [may-lawt'-tsoh dah fohr-lee'] The brilliant 15th-century Italian painter Melozzo da Forli, 1438–94, was known for his mastery of illusionism in ceiling and wall painting. He worked for a time (1465–75) in Urbino, where he may have come into contact with Piero della Francesca—a strong influence on his style. None of Melozzo's important decorative work survives intact, but it is clear from fragments of his apse fresco *Ascension* (1477–80), for the Church of Santi Apostoli, Rome—which are preserved in the Vatican and the Quirinale Palace, Rome—that his sophisticated depiction of figures moving freely in space must have had a significant impact on subsequent painters.

melting point The melting point is the sharply defined, reproducible temperature at which a pure solid substance, when heated, changes into a liquid. This temperature is the same as the freezing point of the liquid. At the melting point, solid and liquid exist together in equilibrium. Heating this mixture further will not raise its temperature but will cause more solid to melt. Depending upon the substance, the melt may have a greater or lesser density than the solid.

Impurities alter the melting point. In fact, the purity of a sample is often tested by observing the temperature at which it melts. Also, depending upon the substance, the application of pressure may raise or lower the melting point. Thus, pressure lowers the melting point of ice, allowing one to skate on it.

Melville, Andrew The Scottish scholar, educator, and reformer Andrew Melville, b. Aug. 1, 1545, d. 1622, was successor to John KNOX as the leader of Scottish Presbyterianism. Melville became principal of Glasgow University in 1574. In this position, and later as principal of St. Mary's College, St. Andrews, he encouraged the study of languages, science, and modern forms of philosophy and theology.

In 1578, Melville drew up the *Second Book of Discipline*, endorsed by the 1581 General Assembly, which excluded even a modified system of bishops for the Church of Scotland (see SCOTLAND, CHURCH OF). He quarreled with James VI's regent, the duke of Lennox, and later with James himself, when these rulers tried to retain some form of episcopacy in Scotland. For his forthright defense of Presbyterianism, Melville was once forced (1584) to flee Scotland. Later, after James had succeeded to the English throne (as James I), Melville was imprisoned (1607–11) in the Tower of London. He was released from the Tower to accept a post as professor of biblical theology at the University of Sedan, France, dying there 11 years later.

Melville, Herman Known primarily as the author of MOBY-DICK, Herman Melville, b. New York City, Aug. 1, 1819, d. Sept. 28, 1891, is regarded as one of America's greatest and most influential novelists. A major figure in the group of eminent pre–Civil War writers called the American Romantics or members of the American Renaissance who created a new and vigorous national literature, he is also one of the most notable examples of an American author whose work went largely unrecognized in his own time and who died in obscurity.

His father's death in 1832 obliged Melville to leave school. He first went to sea in 1839 as a cabin boy, an experience that furnished the materials for his novel *Redburn* (1849). In 1841 he embarked again on a whaling ship, which he deserted while in port in the South Seas. There he lived briefly with a primitive native tribe, then roamed about the islands before joining the U.S. Navy in 1843—an experience he put to use in *White-Jacket* (1850).

Typee (1846) and *Omoo* (1847), drawn from his adventures in the South Seas, had considerable success. His third novel, *Mardi* (1849), however, was a disaster: a blend of satire and allegorical romance written in an extravagantly wordy style.

By this time married and a father, Melville was compelled to lower his artistic ambitions for a time. Working quickly, he produced *Redburn* and *White-Jacket*, both written in a straightforward style different from that of *Mardi*. These two works, which Melville admitted to having written almost entirely for money, restored some measure of his popularity. More financially secure, in 1850 he left New York, where he had been living since his marriage, and moved to Pittsfield, Mass. He bought a farm there, began *Moby-Dick*, and formed a friendship with Nathaniel Hawthorne, to whom he dedicated the book. Published in 1851, Melville's masterpiece had modest sales, and although it was acclaimed by some, the critical response was largely negative, provoking in Melville a bitterness expressed in his next work, *Pierre* (1852).

The first of Melville's novels that takes place entirely on land, *Pierre* is a dark, eccentric work written in a strangely mannered style that angered and baffled its few readers. Those not put off by its style and wild philosophizings were offended by the seeming immorality of its story, which dealt openly with incest and explored with remarkable acuteness those psychological relationships which Freud would later term Oedipal. Although a failure in its own time, *Pierre* is now regarded as one of Melville's most important and self-revealing works. After *Pierre* he wrote a number of stories and sketches, notably "Bartleby the Scrivener" (1853) and "Benito Cereno" (1855), both of which appeared in *Putnam's* magazine, as well as a

Herman Melville, a 19th-century novelist and poet, was an instrumental figure in the development of a distinct American literature. Although Melville's complex nautical adventure Moby-Dick *(1851)* was critically rejected during his lifetime, the work is now recognized as a masterpiece.

short novel, *Israel Potter*, published serially in *Putnam's* in 1854–55 and appearing in book form in 1855.

Melville's last full-length novel, *The Confidence Man* (1857), is a brilliantly inventive satire; filled with mock philosophizing, it is virtually plotless and is written in a style even more eccentric than that of *Pierre*. It sold poorly, received uniformly hostile reviews, and—aside from the short novel *Billy Budd*—was Melville's final effort as a fiction writer. After 1857 he wrote mostly poetry, which has received increased attention in the 20th century. His most important verse is contained in the collection *Battle-Pieces and Aspects of the War* (1866) and in the long philosophical poem *Clarel* (1876). In 1863, Melville returned to New York City, where 3 years later he became a customs inspector, a job he held for 19 years. In 1888 he began work on *Billy Budd*, which was still in manuscript form when he died in 1891. It was published in 1924 as part of the revival of interest in his works that would finally give Melville the worldwide recognition denied him during his lifetime.

membrane chemistry   Natural and artificial membranes are special assemblies of molecules that serve to isolate or separate regions in liquids. Such membranes create and maintain concentration gradients of chemicals or define special microenvironments. Membrane chemistry is the study of the chemical properties and behavior of these systems.

Biological Membranes. In nature, biochemical reactions are often highly specific and efficient, and these properties are often due to the special chemistry of biological membranes. In general these membranes consist of layers of oriented phospholipid or glycolipid molecules (see LIPID), with embedded protein molecules. The lipids have a polar head group (see DIPOLE) and a hydrocarbon chain that resembles a tail. The polar region is hydrophilic (attracts water), whereas the tail is hydrophobic (repels water). The system appears as a sandwich, with the heads assembled on the top and bottom and the long tails oriented toward the center. The protein molecules that are often present in such systems serve as channels for the

selective flow of specific ions and molecules from one region to another in cellular fluids, sometimes in opposition to concentration gradients.

Biomimetic Membranes. Artificial systems can mimic the selectivity and efficiency of natural biological membranes. The field of membrane-mimetic chemistry is concerned with the production of special membranes and the technological applications of these materials. Surfactants or detergents (molecules with hydrophilic and hydrophobic regions) often assemble into spherical structures, termed micelles, whose interior regions promote or catalyze many specialized chemical reactions.

Several classes of organic molecules have structures that mimic the microenvironments achieved in membranes. Cyclodextrins are rings of simple sugars that resemble doughnuts. Their interior regions have special chemical and physical properties that catalyze particular reactions. These cavities may be capped or enlarged using modern techniques in synthetic organic chemistry. In each case, the unusual nature of the isolated microenvironment imparts new and striking chemistries to these artificial systems.

Industrial Applications. Semipermeable membranes have been developed commercially for application in such diverse processes as the separation of heavy ions and metals from water-supply systems; the removal of salt from seawater (see DESALINATION); the ultrafiltration of specific sizes of large molecules or particles for the chemical industry; and the separation of gases in processes ranging from refinery operations and enhanced oil recovery to food preservation. In addition, the range of catalytic processes has been expanded by the development of high-temperature metallic and ceramic membranes.

In the drug industry, biomimetic membranes and vesicles can be used as timed-release agents to administer ingested medicine, to regulate the dose from small bandages applied directly to the skin, and to lock in chemicals for long-term release (as in flea collars for pets). Another application is the encapsulation of cellular materials for drug production, using the techniques of molecular biology.

Memling, Hans   Among the most popular and successful painters of the early Renaissance, Hans Memling, c.1430–94, is admired today for the superb technique, harmonious composition, and glowing color seen in his portraits and religious works.

Memling's style changed so little during his career that historians have found it difficult to date his works. Probably among the earliest is the *Madonna Enthroned with Saints and Donors*, or *The Donne Altarpiece* (1468; National Gallery, London). His other religious works include the *Adoration of the Magi* triptych (1479) and the important *Shrine of Saint Ursula* (1489), both in the Hospital of Saint John, Bruges.

Memling excelled in portraiture, capturing the character of his sitters with startling sensitivity and tact. These pictures are also of interest because they reveal an evolu-

The devotional paintings of Hans Memling, exemplified by this diptych panel (1487) of the Virgin and Child, are characterized by attention to detail, subtle lighting, and balanced composition. (Musée Memling, Bruges, Belgium.)

tion in the treatment of the background space, which is initially flat and later opens up to include either an indoor corner or an outdoor landscape. These treatments are seen in the diptych *Martin van Nieuwenhove* (1487; Hospital of Saint John, Bruges) and *Portrait of a Man Holding a Coin of Nero* (c.1478; Musée Royale des Beaux Arts, Antwerp). Memling also gave the loving attention to texture—in fabrics, furs, and jewels—so characteristic of the Flemish masters.

Memminger, Christopher Gustavus

Christopher Gustavus Memminger, b. Württemberg, Germany, Jan. 9, 1803, d. Mar. 7, 1888, was secretary of the treasury (1861–64) for the CONFEDERATE STATES OF AMERICA during the U.S. Civil War. He sought to finance the war through taxation and bond sales, but prolongation of the conflict obliged him to adopt an inflationary program of paper-currency issues. Although Memminger lacked full support for his funding plans from the Confederate Congress, he was blamed for the collapse of the Confederacy's credit and was forced to resign.

Memnon

Memnon [mem'-nahn]   In Greek mythology Memnon, the son of Eos, goddess of dawn, and Tithonus, brother of Priam, was king of Ethiopia. He led his army to the defense of Troy in the TROJAN WAR, where he was killed by ACHILLES. At Eos's request, Zeus granted immortality to Memnon, according to one version of the myth. The Greeks called the statue of the pharaoh Amenhotep III near Thebes, Egypt, the colossus of Memnon because at dawn it emitted mysterious musical sounds that were thought to be Memnon's greeting to Eos.

Memorial Day

The U.S. holiday Memorial Day, or Decoration Day, is a day of remembrance for those who have died in the nation's service. The holiday was first widely observed on May 30, 1868, when flowers were placed on the graves of Union and Confederate soldiers. It is now celebrated in almost every state on the last Monday in May.

memory

Memory is the process of storing and retrieving information. Although popularly regarded as a single "faculty," human memory is more usefully considered as a whole range of processes, from those allowing the brief storage of sensory information during perception to the process underlying the retention of knowledge of a language or the recollection of a personal experience.

Sensory Memory. The process of perceiving often involves accumulating information during a period of time. Hearing a sentence, a word, or even a syllable requires the listener to integrate a changing pattern of auditory stimulation. This integration demands some form of temporary buffer storage, and it is fairly certain that perception relies heavily on such temporary memory stores. It is also clear that humans have long-term memory for sensory information—for the sound of a violin, the taste of an apple, or the color of a sunset. Such information is stored in some relatively permanent form; whether different sensory modalities are stored separately or whether they form part of a more general memory store is unclear.

Short-Term Memory. Short-term memory is the system used to remember information "in use," such as a telephone number while one is dialing it. Whether or not short-term memory represents a separate system, it does have certain clearly defined characteristics. It is limited in storage capacity: most people can repeat a 7- or 8-digit telephone number, but not 10 or 11 digits. Short-term memory appears to be related to speech: a string of similar-sounding consonants such as *B G C V T P* is less likely to be remembered correctly than a string of dissimilar consonants such as *K G R W F L*. This phenomenon is not due to hearing incorrectly, because the effect also occurs when the letters are presented visually. It does, however, seem to depend on some form of inner speech, because congenitally deaf children show the effect, provided they use speech reasonably well.

Long-Term Memory. The learner's role as an active organizer of material is very important in long-term memory. For instance, if an individual learns a list of words that happens to contain a number of animal names, he or she will tend to recall the animal names in a cluster, even though he or she originally heard them scattered throughout the list. This suggests that the learner actively attempts to place some form of organization on the material he or she learns. Even with lists of unrelated words, on successive learning trials, people tend to produce clusters of words in the same order—again suggesting that they are organizing words in some consistent manner. Instructing an experimental subject to sort words into categories of his or her own choosing leads to excellent retention, even if the subject had not expected to be tested, implying that organization leads to learning. The better the organization system is for items of information in memory, the more accessible the information is likely to be.

Inherent retrieval limitations may exist in human memory. Most people have experienced the "feeling of knowing"—trying to remember the name of an acquaintance, for example, without being able to produce it at the crucial moment. When someone else produces it, the name is recognized without difficulty. Hints or cues are often helpful, and indeed the process of recognition, under most circumstances, could be regarded as providing a particularly strong cue. Recognition may simplify the access problem but does not in itself guarantee retrieval; in some situations an individual may even fail to recognize a word he or she has been shown, and yet subsequently be able to recall it, given an appropriate cue.

Mnemonics are additional cues to help retrieve the appropriate information. For example, a mnemonic for remembering the order of the lines of the G-clef in music— E, G, B, D, F—uses the sentence "Every good boy does fine." The letters are elaborated into a meaningful sentence, providing a sequential organization not present in the order of the letters themselves.

The comprehension of language must depend on an individual's prior knowledge both of the language itself and of the characteristics of the world that the language is describing. The term *semantic memory* is used to refer to the system within which such knowledge of the world is stored. The character of this system is of great interest to cognitive psychologists, linguists with an interest in semantics, and computer scientists interested in designing more elegant and flexible COMPUTER MEMORY systems.

Forgetting. Forgetting is the process through which information in memory becomes inaccessible, either because the information is no longer stored or because it is stored but is not at that time retrievable. Forgetting is rapid at first and then gradually levels off.

Forgetting may be increased by interference from other material either learned beforehand (proactive inhibition) or subsequently (retroactive inhibition). In both cases the amount of forgetting increases with the amount of interfering material and with its similarity to the material being remembered. For example, if a cook is trying to remember a soup recipe, recall will be worse if it is one of six soup recipes just read. Reading a comparable amount about a different topic such as car maintenance would inhibit recall of the soup recipe less.

In remembering stories or events there is a tendency

for distortions to occur. People tend to remember what they regard as most important; they typically operate by attempting to reconstruct the incident using their existing knowledge, with the result that they may recall what would have been expected rather than what actually occurred. Perhaps the most popularly known explanation of forgetting is Sigmund Freud's theory that one forgets or represses incidents associated with anxiety. The experimental evidence for this is weak, however, and the theory is certainly not applicable to the enormous amount of forgetting of trivial detail that forms an important and indeed useful component of normal human memory. Other theories suggest that memory traces spontaneously decay, or that they are disrupted by interference from the traces produced by competing information.

The Physiological Basis of Memory. The long-term memory trace apparently depends on a combination of NEUROTRANSMITTER synthesis and new nerve-fiber growth, as demonstrated, for example, in extensive experiments over a 30-year period with *Aplysia californica*, a variety of sea slug. In a typical stimulus-response experiment (see BEHAVIORISM), researchers conditioned slugs by gently touching their syphon (breathing apparatus) and then, seconds later, giving their tails an electric shock. After a short period of training, the slugs took quick evasive action when just their syphons were touched, demonstrating that they had a memory of the shocks. Because *Aplysia*'s brain has only about 20,000 neurons (see NERVOUS SYSTEM), as opposed to the human brain's 100 billion neurons, researchers were able to chart which groups of neurons were producing neurotransmitters in response to the syphon touch and which in response to the tail shock. They also discovered that new nerve connections had grown between the two areas.

Researchers have also studied the growth of nerve connections in embryonic and developing brains and proposed, in the late 1980s, a physiological theory of BRAIN functions called neural Darwinism. According to the theory, as the developing brain is flooded with sensory input, groups of cells that electrochemically process this information strengthen their connections, whereas other groups of cells die off (in humans, about 70 percent by the age of eight months). Concurrently, new connections between cells are made, and areas of the brain are "mapped" for various functions, including memory.

The view of the process now emerging is that the brain not only somehow codes memories into "programs" to be acted on through a network of interconnected cells, but actually alters the structure of its interconnections to accommodate new memories. Computer scientists have joined with neurophysiologists in developing computer models of small sections of the brain (see NEURAL NETWORKS).

Valuable insights have also accrued through the study of damaged brains. Human memory processes may be disrupted following a blow to the head or the passage of an electric current through the brain. In both cases this is followed by a general disturbance of memory. This amnesia tends to "shrink," with earlier memories becoming available first. Often a residue of information acquired shortly before the disturbance never seems to come back. This might represent the failure of the memory trace to consolidate.

Different parts of the brain are almost certainly mapped for different aspects of memory. Hence, subjects with damage in a limited portion of the left cerebral hemisphere may show poor short-term memory but have quite normal long-term learning ability. Conversely, other patients with damage to the temporal lobes and hippocampus in both hemispheres of the brain may show a general, long-term memory deficit. Whether this is a learning deficit or a retrieval failure remains an open question.

Memphis (Egypt)   Memphis, on the west bank of the Nile, 25 km (16 mi) south of Cairo, was a major city of ancient Egypt. According to legend, Menes, the first king of united Egypt, built Memphis as his administrative capital at the juncture of Upper and Lower Egypt. Throughout the Old Kingdom (c.2686–2181 BC) Memphis served as the capital city of Egypt. Few remains at Memphis date from this period, although the pyramids and sphinx of GIZA as well as the necropolis of SAQQARA are nearby. Outside the modern village of Mitrahine lie scant traces of the once vast Temple of Ptah (begun c.3000 BC), built to honor the primary deity of Memphis.

From the 25th dynasty (716–656 BC) to the Roman occupation (from the 1st century BC) Memphis returned to prominence. Monuments include the palace of Apries, the fourth king of the 26th dynasty (664–525 BC), and, nearby, the ruins of stone tables used by the priests of the Late Period for embalming the APIS bulls that were buried at Saqqara. During the 27th dynasty (525–404 BC), when the Persians ruled Egypt, Memphis again served as the capital. The crafts flourished and a faïence industry remained active from this time well into the 2d century AD.

Memphis (Tennessee)   Memphis, the largest city of Tennessee and the seat of Shelby County, is located along the Mississippi River in the southwest corner of the state. The city has a population of 610,337 (1990), and the metropolitan area, 981,747. Memphis is the business center of the agricultural South and a major distribution hub for the south central area. It is an important barge-line port on the inland waterway system.

Contemporary City. Memphis has a larger proportion (about half) of blacks than any other major Tennessee city, and it is a city of strong Southern traditions. It has the largest spot-cotton market in the world: one-third of the domestic crop is traded through the Memphis Cotton Exchange. About 800 manufacturing plants are located in Memphis, and the city is the center of a wholesale and retail trade market. It has the world's largest inland hardwood lumber market and manufactures finished wood products, farm implements, chemicals, textiles, paper, drugs, and rubber products.

Memphis has a rich musical heritage. It is the birthplace of the "blues," immortalized in compositions by W.

Memphis, in the southwestern portion of Tennessee, is the state's largest city and one of the most important centers of commerce in the South.

C. Handy: "Beale Street Blues" and "Memphis Blues." Fans of Elvis Presley visit Graceland, his Memphis mansion. The city is a music-recording center and has a ballet, symphony, repertory theater, and opera. It is also a major convention city. There are several colleges and universities, including Memphis State University (1912), and the city has the largest medical center in the South.

History. The French built Fort Prudhomme within the present city limits in 1682. The fort came into British possession in 1763 and was ceded to the United States in 1797. The town of Memphis was laid out in 1819 by agreement between Andrew JACKSON and two partners and was named for the ancient Egyptian city. During the Civil War, Memphis was a Confederate center, but it fell to Union forces in 1862. Much of its progress in the 20th century took place under the direct or indirect administration of Edward H. "Boss" Crump (1874–1954), a powerful Democratic political figure until the 1940s. Civil rights leader Martin Luther King, Jr., was killed in Memphis in 1968.

Menander [min-an'-dur]   The Greek comic dramatist Menander, 342–292 BC, as the greatest exemplar of New Comedy, the genre that held the stage in Athens from the beginning of the Hellenistic period, can be considered the father of the COMEDY of manners and thus, indirectly, of modern romantic comedy. Of the more than 100 plays written by Menander, only the *Dyskolos* (*The Misanthrope*) has come down intact, but the survival of large portions of others has made possible the reconstruction of such favorites as *Perikeiromnê* (*The Rape of the Lock*) and *Epitrepontes* (*The Arbitration*).

Menander's plays were extremely popular in ancient times and, chiefly through his Roman adaptors, PLAUTUS and TERENCE, have exerted a profound influence on the history of European DRAMA from the Renaissance to modern times. Adept at inventing plots full of intrigue, variety, and surprise and at composing effortless-sounding but subtle verse, Menander dealt humorously and ironically—but always sympathetically—with the private domestic problems of traditional Athenian types, focusing on their ethical, social, and emotional dilemmas. The plays celebrate understanding, generosity, and respect for others as the highest social values.

Mencius [men'-shus]

The Chinese philosopher Mencius (Chinese: Mengzi), c.372–c.289 BC, was a leading exponent of CONFUCIANISM. Born in what is today Shandong province, he lived during the period of the Warring States (403–222 BC), when a handful of competing states were fighting against each other for the hegemony of China. Traveling from one state to another as a roving political advisor, Mencius spent 40 years trying to persuade the contending kings to be righteous rulers.

The chief doctrine of Mencius is the original goodness of human nature, which is bestowed by heaven and possessed by everyone. Mencius argued that every person has four innate feelings: commiseration, shame and dislike, respect and reverence, and right and wrong. These four feelings can be further developed into the four moral virtues: benevolence, righteousness, propriety, and wisdom.

Mencken, H. L. [menk'-en]

Henry Louis Mencken, b. Sept. 12, 1880, d. Jan. 29, 1956, was the most influential American editor, essayist, and social critic of the first half of the 20th century. A biting satirist, he enjoyed his greatest power in the 1920s during his editorship of the *American Mercury*. As editor of the *Mercury* (1924–33) and, earlier, of the *Smart Set* (1914–24), Mencken championed such bold new writers as Theodore Dreiser, James Branch Cabell, and Sinclair Lewis, helping liberate American literature from the Genteel Tradition.

The American journalist and social critic H. L. Mencken supported the works of such modern writers as Sinclair Lewis and Eugene O'Neill. His editorial columns often criticized the narrow scope of middle-class culture.

Mencken began to win national attention in 1914, when he and George Jean Nathan became coeditors of the *Smart Set*. In his newspaper and magazine essays, Mencken attacked virtually every aspect of American life—its culture (or lack of it), educational system, religious manias, politics, and the "booboisie," the word he coined to describe the great American public. Two of his best and most representative essays are "Puritanism as a Literary Force" (1917), in which he saw Puritanism as the root of most American problems, and "The Sahara of the Bozart" (1920), a severe indictment of Southern culture and literature, which ironically helped inspire the Southern literary renaissance of the 1920s and '30s.

Mencken's influence waned in the 1930s, partly because his iconoclasm was better suited to the prosperity of the 1920s and partly because he opposed Franklin D. Roosevelt and the New Deal. During this period Mencken continued to work on *The American Language* (1919, 1921, 1931, 1936, 1963; supplements, 1945–48), an ambitious, multivolumed work in which he demonstrated that American English is in many ways a different language from its British counterpart, and remained active as a newspaperman and commentator until a stroke silenced him in 1948.

Mencken's work includes the essays collected in the six-volume *Prejudices* (1919–27); book-length studies of George Bernard Shaw (1905), Friedrich Nietzsche (1908), women (1917), democracy (1926), and religion (1930); and the autobiographical trilogy: *Happy Days* (1940), *Newspaper Days* (1941), and *Heathen Days* (1943). Several volumes of his correspondence have been published, including that with Dreiser (1986) and with his wife, Sarah (1987), as well as *The Diary of H. L. Mencken* (1990), which he kept from 1930 to 1948.

Mende [mahnd]

The Mende, a West African people of Sierra Leone and Liberia, are noted for the importance of secret societies, particularly the men's Poro and women's Sande, in directing the conduct of daily life. Traditionally, they were a warring people living in villages and towns combined into chiefdoms. Chiefs were warriors and military protectors; war captives served the Mende as slaves.

The Mende speak a language of the Mandingo subfamily of the Niger-Congo stock; they numbered an estimated 2,500,000 in the 1980s. Descent and inheritance are traced through the father's line. Marriage is polygynous; the payment of bride-price is traditionally practiced. Secret societies prepare boys and girls for responsible adulthood, regulate sexual conduct, guide political and economic affairs, and operate social and medical services. Mende art forms are mostly woodcarvings: black-painted helmet masks worn by Sande dancers, human heads, and female figures associated with divination.

Mendel, Gregor Johann [men'-dul, gray'-gohr]

The first person to discover the basic laws of heredity and suggest the existence of genes was an Austrian monk, Gregor Mendel, b. July 22, 1822, d. Jan. 6, 1884. The

The Austrian monk Gregor Mendel discovered (1856–68) the basic principles of heredity through experimentation with peas in his monastery's garden. Mendel's statistical analysis of his data provided the mathematical basis for modern genetics.

importance of his work was not realized until 1900, at which time his findings laid the foundation for the science of genetics.

Born Johann Mendel in Heinzendorf, Austrian Silesia (now Czechoslovakia), he changed his name to Gregor in 1843 when he entered the Augustinian monastery at Brünn (now Brno). He was ordained a priest in 1847, and in 1851 was sent to the University of Vienna for training as a teacher of mathematics and natural sciences. He returned to Brünn in 1854, where he taught until 1868, when he was promoted to abbot.

In a monastery garden Mendel began (1856) the breeding experiments that led him to discover the laws of heredity. Working with garden peas, he studied seven characteristics that occur in alternative forms: plant height (tallness vs. shortness), seed color (green vs. yellow), seed shape (smooth vs. wrinkled), seed-coat color (colored vs. white), pod shape (inflated vs. wrinkled), pod color (green vs. yellow), and flower distribution (along length vs. at end of stem). Mendel made hundreds of crosses by means of artificial pollination. He kept careful records of the plants that were crossed and of the offspring. In 1865, Mendel reported his findings at a meeting of the Brünn Natural History Society. The following year his results were published as "Experiments with Plant Hybrids" in the society's journal.

Mendel summarized his findings in three theories. He asserted that during the formation of the sex cells—the egg and the sperm—paired factors segregate, or separate. Thus, a sperm or egg may contain either a tallness factor or a shortness factor, not both. This theory is called Mendel's first law, or the principle of segregation.

Mendel's second law, called the principle of independent assortment, stated that characteristics are inherited independently of each other; that is, the tallness factor may be inherited with any other factor, dominant or recessive. This law later was modified when Thomas Hunt Morgan discovered linkage, or the inheritance of two or more genes situated close to each other on the same chromosome.

The third theory, the law of dominance, stated that each inherited characteristic is determined by the interaction of two hereditary factors (now called genes), one from each parent. In the characteristics that he studied, Mendel found that one factor of the pair always predominated; for example, tallness always was dominant over shortness.

Mendele Mokher Sefarim [men'-duh-luh mawk'-ur sef'-uh-rim]   Mendele Mokher Sefarim was the pseudonym of Sholem Yakob Abramowitch, b. Minsk, Russia, Jan. 2, 1836, d. Dec. 8, 1917, who, along with his younger contemporaries Scholem ALEICHEM and Y. L. PERETZ, is one of the triumvirate of Yiddish classical writers. Orphaned at 13, Mendele came to sympathize with the poor and portrayed their nobility in the midst of suffering. He was a pioneer of the Hebrew literary renaissance and after 1863 wrote primarily in Yiddish. Of his early satires, the most popular was The Nag (1873; Eng. trans., 1955), an allegory of the Jews as the world's becudgeled nag that demanded justice, not pity. Mendele's major novels include Fishke the Lame (1869; Eng. trans., 1960), about Jewish beggars who remain pure at heart, and The Travels and Adventures of Benjamin III (1878; Eng. trans., 1949), a satire on impractical Jewish visionaries.

mendelevium [men-duh-lay'-vee-uhm]   Mendelevium is a radioactive chemical element of the ACTINIDE SERIES. Its symbol is Md (originally Mv), its atomic number is 101, and its atomic weight is 258 (stablest isotope). Mendelevium was first synthesized in 1955 by A. Ghiorso, B. G. Harvey, G. R. Choppin, S. G. Thompson, and Glenn T. Seaborg, who bombarded einsteinium-253 with helium ions. The element was named in honor of Dmitry Mendeleyev, the discoverer of the periodic system. The creation of mendelevium was the basis for the discovery of all the chemical elements with atomic numbers over 101.

Mendeleyev, Dmitry Ivanovich [min-dil-yay'-uhf, duh-mee'-tree ee-vah'-nuh-vich]   The Russian chemist Dmitry Ivanovich Mendeleyev, b. Feb. 8 (N.S.), 1834, d. Feb. 2 (N.S.), 1907, formulated the PERIODIC TABLE, one of the most useful and important generalizations of chemistry and of all science. Mendeleyev was born in Tobolsk, Siberia (now Tyumen Oblast), and graduated from the Faculty of Physics and Mathematics of the Main Pedagogical Institute in Saint Petersburg (now Leningrad) in 1855. In 1860, Mendeleyev discovered the concept of critical temperature and attended the first International Chemical Congress at Karlsruhe, Germany, where Stanislao CANNIZZARO's views on atomic weights planted the seeds for the concept of the periodic table.

Mendeleyev served as professor of chemistry at the Saint Petersburg Technological Institute (1864–66) and at the University of Saint Petersburg (1867–90). Because he found no suitable text for his students, he wrote his own—*Principles of Chemistry* (1868–71). The systematization of ideas required for this book led Mendeleyev to formulate the periodic table in March 1869.

After discovery of the elements gallium (1875), scandium (1879), and germanium (1886), whose existence was predicted by Mendeleyev in 1871, the periodic law and Mendeleyev's periodic table were universally accepted. Mendeleyev became famous and was showered with honors. In 1906 he missed winning the Nobel Prize for chemistry by one vote.

See also: CHEMISTRY, HISTORY OF.

The Russian chemist Dmitry Mendeleyev announced his discovery of the periodic law in March 1869, which stated that "elements placed according to the value of their atomic weights present a clear periodicity of properties."

Mendel's laws   see GENETICS

Mendelsohn, Eric [men'-duhl-suhn] Eric Mendelsohn, b. Mar. 21, 1887, d. Sept. 15, 1953, was a German architect who became internationally known for his contributions to the International Style and to expressionism in architecture. While serving in the German army (1917–19) he produced small sketches of monumental, dynamic building forms of great expressive force. When he returned from the war he established himself as an architect in Berlin, made enlarged posters of his sketches, and exhibited these visionary fantasies at the Cassirer art gallery under the title "Architecture in Steel and Concrete." The flowing shapes of his Einstein Tower (1924), an observatory in Potsdam, and the title of his earlier exhibition led many to assume that the structure was made of reinforced concrete. It was, in fact, conventional masonry stuccoed over. His Luckenwalde hat-factory buildings (1923), however, were built of concrete and drew considerable attention by their rational use of what was a relatively new material.

Mendelsohn's expansion of the *Berliner Tageblatt* newspaper building (1921–22) showed his characteristic emphasis on kinetic forms, continuity, and horizontal

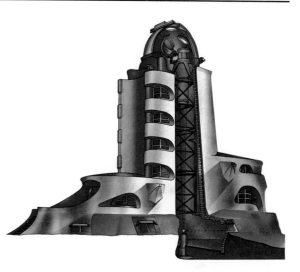

The sinuous forms of Eric Mendelsohn's Einstein Tower (1920–24; destroyed during World War II), an observatory and astrophysical laboratory in Potsdam, East Germany, are representative of the expressionist architecture of the post-World War I period.

bands of brick and glass—a style he used in other buildings of the 1920s. In Palestine he designed the Hadassah University Medical Center (1936), the Anglo-Palestine Bank (1937), and other major hospital and educational buildings. His completed American projects, all built between 1946 and 1954, include the Maimonides Hospital in San Francisco, synagogues in St. Louis, Cleveland, Grand Rapids, and Saint Paul, and the laboratories for the Atomic Energy Commission in Berkeley, Calif.

Mendelssohn, Felix Jakob Ludwig Felix Mendelssohn-Bartholdy, b. Hamburg, Feb. 3, 1809, was a major German romantic composer. He was the son of a banker and grandson of the philosopher Moses Mendelssohn. In 1812 the family moved to Berlin. Young Felix (along with his sister Fanny, a talented pianist and composer) received piano lessons from his mother; he subsequently studied with Ludwig Berger and Carl Friedrich Zelter.

Mendelssohn showed a surprising gift for composition at an early age. He wrote his famous overture to Shakespeare's *A Midsummer Night's Dream* when he was 17; by then he had also written 12 symphonies for string orchestra. Mendelssohn traveled extensively, especially to England, and in 1835 he became conductor of the Gewandhaus orchestra in Leipzig. In 1837 he married Cécile Jeanrenaud, the daughter of a French Huguenot clergyman (Mendelssohn, though of Jewish descent, was baptized a Protestant in 1824). In 1842–43, Mendelssohn organized the Leipzig Conservatory and made it known worldwide as a model music school. Shocked by the death of his sister Fanny on May 14, 1847, and exhausted from overwork, Mendelssohn died in Leipzig on Nov. 4, 1847.

The German composer Felix Mendelssohn was considered one of the foremost composers of the early 19th century. Within the confines of classical forms, he created lyrical expressions characteristic of the early romantic movement.

Mendelssohn excelled in all musical genres except opera. His most important symphonies are the *Reformation* (composed 1829–30, revised 1832), the sparkling *Italian* (1832–33), and the elegiac *Scotch* (sketched 1829–32, finished 1842). His programmatic overtures, of which the *Hebrides* or *Fingal's Cave* (1830, revised 1832) is best known, point the way to the symphonic poem. His violin concerto (1844) and octet for strings (written at age 16) stand out among many instrumental works. The *Songs Without Words* for piano were once popular as teaching pieces, and his *Variations sérieuses* (1841) is a distinguished set of variations. His six organ sonatas and the oratorios *St. Paul* (1832–36) and *Elijah* (1845-46) reflect the influence of J. S. Bach, whose *St. Matthew Passion* Mendelssohn conducted in 1829, the first performance of the work since Bach's time.

Mendelssohn's occasional lapses into sentimentality are offset by his elfin scherzos, elegiac moods, musical seascapes, and impeccable craftsmanship overall. His music is thought to reflect the middle-class culture of Germany before the revolution of 1848 and of early Victorian England.

Mendelssohn, Moses Moses Mendelssohn, b. Sept. 26, 1729, d. Jan. 4, 1786, became a major figure in German philosophy and literature while remaining faithful to his Jewish heritage. Thus, he encouraged those, both Jewish and Christian, who believed that Jews could accept modern Western culture without apostasy. Mendelssohn's most important philosophic work, *Phaedon* (1767), is concerned with immortality.

As an advocate of secular as well as religious education for Jews, Mendelssohn brought the ideas of the Enlightenment to his coreligionists by his activities as an editor and by his German biblical translations with Hebrew commentaries. In his essay *Jerusalem* (1783) he first defended the separation of religious and political authority and then argued for granting full civil rights to Jews. His personal character was so highly esteemed that his friend Gotthold Lessing immortalized him as the title character of the drama *Nathan the Wise* (1781).

Menderes, Adnan [men-dair-es' ahd-nahn'] Adnan Menderes, b. 1899, d. Sept. 17, 1961, organized (1946) the Democratic party of Turkey, becoming prime minister in 1950 after the party's electoral victory. He brought Turkey into NATO (1952) and initiated economic programs that raised the standard of living. His curbs on civil liberties provoked unrest, however, and in 1960 he was overthrown by the military. He was tried for unconstitutional acts and executed.

Mendoza, Antonio de [mayn-doh'-thah, ahn-tohn'-ee-oh day] A Spanish noble, Antonio de Mendoza, b. c.1490, d. July 21, 1552, served as the first viceroy of NEW SPAIN (1535–50) and as viceroy of Peru (1551–52). Mendoza laid the foundations for a colonial system that lasted for almost 300 years. An able administrator, he collected revenues for the crown with efficiency, pacified the Indians, developed agriculture and mining, and established the first mint in the Mexican territories. He brought the first printing press to the New World and prepared the groundwork for the University of Mexico, which was established in 1551. Mendoza was named viceroy of Peru in 1551 but died a short time after arriving in Lima.

Mendoza, Pedro de The Spanish conquistador Pedro de Mendoza, b. 1487, d. June 23, 1537, founded the city of Buenos Aires in 1536 and served as the first governor of the Río de la Plata region (modern Argentina). Ill and besieged by increasingly hostile Indians, Mendoza set sail (1537) for Spain but died at sea. His settlement was abandoned in 1541.

Menelaus [men-uh-lay'-uhs] In Greek mythology Menelaus, king of Sparta, was the son of ATREUS and the husband of HELEN OF TROY. When PARIS carried off Helen and much of his treasure to Troy, Menelaus and his brother AGAMEMNON led the army of Greek princes that won the TROJAN WAR and recovered Helen. On the return voyage, Menelaus lost most of his ships and was driven to Egypt. There, in one version of the story, he rescued Helen, who had been brought there by Hermes while the Greeks and Trojans were fighting over a phantom of her. Menelaus appears in Homer's *Iliad* and *Odyssey* and in plays of Aeschylus and Euripides.

Menelik II, Emperor of Ethiopia [men'-uh-lik] Menelik II, b. Aug. 17, 1844, d. Dec. 12 or 13, 1913, is considered the founder of the modern Ethiopian state. He served (1865–89) as king of Shoa (Shewa) province and succeeded Yohannes IV as emperor in 1889, after a period of bitter internal struggles. Menelik modernized the army and administration, encouraged education, and controlled the great feudal chiefs. In 1894 he granted a concession for building a railway from Addis Ababa to the French port of Djibouti.

Threatened by Italian claims to Ethiopia, Menelik effectively played Great Britain and France against the Italians. In 1896 he decisively defeated an Italian army at the Battle of Adowa, the first crushing reverse inflicted by an African people on a European colonial power. The Treaty of Addis Ababa (1896) recognized Ethiopia's complete independence.

Menem, Carlos Saúl [men'-em, kahr'-lohs sa-uel'] Carlos Saúl Menem, b. July 2, 1930, took office as president of Argentina on July 8, 1989, during a severe economic crisis. A Peronista who had been governor of La Rioja province, Menem took immediate steps to curb Argentina's hyperinflation and to effect other economic reforms. More controversially, he pardoned military men accused of human rights abuses and other offenses and also leftists suspected of subversion.

Menéndez de Avilés, Pedro [men-ayn'-deth day ah-vee-lays', pay'-droh] Pedro Menéndez de Avilés, b. Feb. 15, 1519, d. Sept. 17, 1574, established the Spanish colony of Florida and founded Saint Augustine, the oldest permanent city in the United States. When Philip II decided to settle Florida and evangelize the Indians, he selected Menéndez to lead the expedition. Menéndez's fleet arrived off the Florida coast in August 1565, and in September Menéndez authorized the construction of a fort at Saint Augustine. He massacred most of the French Huguenots settled at Fort Caroline, including their leader, Jean RIBAUT. Although Menéndez returned to Spain in 1567 and made only one further visit to the colony, he remained governor until his death and urged a "just war" against the Indians of Florida, who refused to accept the Christian message.

Menes, King of Egypt [mee'-neez] According to tradition, Menes, fl. *c*.3100 BC, was the first king of the 1st Egyptian dynasty. Ancient writers credited him with uniting Lower and Upper Egypt through war, establishing what is now known as the Old Kingdom, and founding Memphis as its capital. His tomb was discovered in 1897. Some historians have identified Menes as King Narmer or as a combination of several kings.

Mengistu Haile Mariam [men-gee'-stue hy'-lee mahr'-ee-ahm] Ethiopian army officer Mengistu Haile Mariam, b. 1937, was a key figure in the 1974 revolution that overthrew Emperor Haile Selassie. He became chairman of the ruling Provisional Military Administrative Council (Dergue) in 1977 and head of the newly formed Ethiopian Communist party in 1984. Mengistu became president under a new constitution in 1987. With Soviet and Cuban aid he battled secessionists in Eritrea and other regions. He also launched a controversial resettlement program in drought-stricken northern Ethiopia. Mengistu survived a violent coup attempt in May 1989.

menhaden [men-hay'-din] Menhaden, genus *Brevoortia*, comprise several species of fish in the herring family, Clupeidae. They inhabit the estuarine and coastal marine waters of the Atlantic and Gulf of Mexico coasts of North America. Menhaden are slab-sided, silvery, schooling fishes having numerous fine rows of gill rakers used to strain microscopic plant life from the water. The adults attain a length of 37.5 cm (15 in) and a weight of 0.5 kg (1 lb) or so during a 4- to 6-year life span.

Ménière's disease [muhn-yairz'] Ménière's disease is a disorder of the inner ear resulting in dizziness and loss of balance (vertigo), usually accompanied by ringing in the ears and loss of hearing. This condition most frequently occurs in adults. Episodes can be days or years apart and can last from hours to days. The immediate cause is an excess of endolymph, the fluid in the inner ear, but the reason for the excess is not known.

meningitis [men-in-jy'-tis] Meningitis is a potentially fatal inflammation of the meninges, or membranes, covering the brain and spinal cord. The causative organisms, usually bacterial or viral, gain access to the cerebrospinal fluid and follow the space around vessels. The epidemic disease called cerebrospinal meningitis is caused by the meningococcus bacterium, *Neisseria meningitidis*, a spherical organism that inhabits the nasopharynx of healthy human carriers but that sometimes infects the blood and cerebrospinal fluid. The most common cause of bacterial meningitis, however, is *Haemophilus influenzae* type B (see HEMOPHILUS). Meningitis may result from head injuries and infections involving the eyes, ears, or nose; it can also be a complication of systemic disorders such as pneumonia and syphilis. Transmission is by direct contact between people.

The initial symptoms of meningitis are extreme headache, rapidly rising fever, stiffness of the neck, and extreme irritability and drowsiness. Further progression depends on the causative agent and the health of the host. The patient may experience deafness, muscle weakness in the face, and other signs of nerve paralysis. Convulsions, mental retardation, and behavioral disturbances may also occur, and may remain in some cases. Many patients recover fully.

Diagnosis is often made by lumbar puncture (spinal tap), whereby direct access is gained to the site of infection. Special stains and culture of the extracted fluid will often identify the specific organism so that proper therapy may begin. Patients are treated with antibiotics, and a vaccine against *Haemophilus influenzae* type B was licensed for use in 1985.

Menkaure, King of Egypt [men-koo'-ray] Menkaure, also called Mycerinus, fl. *c*.2525 BC, was an ancient Egyptian king of the 4th dynasty (*c*.2613–*c*.2494 BC). The successor of Khafre, Menkaure built the third and smallest of the three Pyramids at Giza, which constitute the sole surviving example of the SEVEN WONDERS OF THE WORLD.

Menken, Adah Isaacs [menk'-en, ay'-duh]   Adah Isaacs Menken, b. Chartrain, La., June 15, 1835, d. Aug. 10, 1868, was one of the most notorious actresses on the American stage. The part that made her famous was the "pants role" (1863) of Mazeppa in a play based on Byron's poem, during the course of which she was bound, nearly naked, to the back of a horse that galloped about the stage. Though her acting ability was severely limited, she could drive audiences wild. Menken fascinated a number of writers, including Mark Twain and Charles Dickens.

Mennin, Peter [men'-in]   Peter Mennin, b. Erie, Pa., May 17, 1923, d. June 17, 1983, composed for most mediums, but he is known primarily for his symphonies and concertos. His music is often characterized by long, flowing melodic lines in a polyphonic texture and a mildly dissonant, neoclassical style.

Mennin taught composition at New York's Juilliard School of Music from 1947 to 1958, was director of the Peabody Conservatory in Baltimore from 1958 to 1962, and then returned to Juilliard as president, a post he held until his death.

Menninger (family)   **Charles Frederick Menninger**, b. Tell City, Ind., July 11, 1862, d. Nov. 28, 1953, and his son **Karl Augustus Menninger**, b. Topeka, Kans., July 22, 1893, d. July 18, 1990, founded the Menninger Clinic for psychiatry in Topeka in the 1920s. The clinic pioneered the idea of drawing together many specialists under one roof. Joined by Charles's other son, **William Claire Menninger**, b. Topeka, Oct. 15, 1899, d. Sept. 6, 1966, the family established the Menninger Foundation in 1941, which trains professionals in various mental-health specialties, provides treatment, and conducts psychiatric research.

Mennonites [men'-uhn-yts]   The Mennonites, a Protestant religious group descended from the 16th-century ANABAPTISTS, take their name from Menno Simons (1496–1561), a Dutch Roman Catholic priest converted to the Anabaptist faith. Menno was active in the Netherlands, and he also developed a following in Holstein and along the lower Rhine River and the Baltic.

The Mennonites rejected infant baptism, the swearing of oaths, military service, and worldliness. They practiced strong church discipline in their congregations and lived simple, honest, loving lives in emulation of the earliest Christians. As summarized by the Dordrecht Confession of 1632, Mennonite theological principles stress the direct influence of the Holy Spirit on the heart of the be-

An Amish couple travels a Pennsylvania road in the traditional open courting buggy. The Amish, who split with Swiss Mennonites during the 1790s, today live in North America, with significant numbers in Lancaster County, Pa.

liever and the importance of the Bible, with its message of salvation through the mystical experience of Christ's presence in the heart.

Because Mennonites refused to assume state offices, to serve as police or soldiers, or to take oaths of loyalty, they were considered subversive and as such were severely persecuted. These persecutions led at various times to the emigration of Mennonite groups: to the American colonies (1683), where they settled in Pennsylvania; to Russia (1788); and, in the 20th century, from Russia and North America to Latin America. In Europe they gradually gained a measure of toleration in Holland, Switzerland, the Palatinate, and northern Germany.

In the New World the Mennonites branched into several factions, of which the (Old) Mennonite Church—still the largest—is the parent group. Other groups include the General Conference Mennonite Church and the Mennonite Brethren Church. The Amish Church, named for Jacob Ammann, a 17th-century Swiss Mennonite bishop, remains insular and conservative. Old Order Amish avoid modern technology in farming and manufacturing, wear clothing fastened by hooks and eyes instead of buttons, worship in private homes, and continue to speak a German-English amalgam (see PENNSYLVANIA DUTCH). The Conservative Amish differ only in their adoption of English and Sunday schools.

Menominee [muh-nahm'-uh-nee]   The Menominee, or Menomini, an Algonquian-speaking North American Indian tribe, were the only Wisconsin Indians to avoid entirely the American removal policy of the 1830s. Their assigned reservation, in north central Wisconsin, lies within the territory they occupied when first contacted (c.1667) by the French fur trader Nicolas Perrot. Menominee means "good seed" or "wild-rice people," referring to their traditional heavy reliance on wild-rice collecting for subsistence. Originally, they inhabited the Menominee River area in northeastern Wisconsin, but participation in the fur trade led the Menominee to expand their range. Although before European contact their population may have been more than 1,500, by the time the first French arrived they were reduced by wars and diseases to an estimated 400 people. The present Menominee reservation population includes descendants of white traders and settlers who intermarried with the Indians as well as many landless POTAWATOMI who settled on the reservation in the 1870s. Under the U.S. government's policy of "termination," Menominee lands lost reservation status in 1961, but after much hardship and economic decline federal aid was restored a decade later.

menopause [men'-uh-pawz] Menopause, also known as climacteric, refers to the cessation of menstruation, and thus the end of the reproductive capacity, of a woman. This usually occurs at about age 50, but it may occur prematurely before age 45 or artificially by removal of the ovaries. The onset may be abrupt or slow; the length of the menstrual cycle increases, accompanied by decreased menstrual flow. As many as 10 years before menopause, the ovaries begin to cease normal function. During this perimenopausal period ovarian failure results in various basic physiological changes: infertility, or failure to ovulate; a decrease in the number of developing follicles and oocytes (see MENSTRUATION); a decreased level of ovarian hormones, notably estrogen and progesterone; and a rise in follicle stimulating hormone (FSH) and luteinizing hormone (LH).

Symptoms

Many of the symptoms that occur during menopause result from estrogen deficiency. It is difficult, however, to separate these symptoms from those caused by the normal aging process and from social and domestic pressures.

The major symptoms (and their possible causes) occurring during pre- and postmenopause can be divided into four main categories: changes in blood vasculature, the musculoskeleton, emotional status, and sexual activity.

Blood Vasculature. Nonsmoking women have a virtual immunity to coronary heart disease before menopause; unfortunately, after menopause the incidence of heart and vascular complications rapidly approaches that of men. During menopause, such temporary symptoms as hot flashes, night sweating, and tension or migraine headaches contribute to the overall irritability and insomnia that normally occur during this time. The years preceding the climacteric may be filled with patterns of irregular bleeding. Postmenopausal bleeding is a signal to seek immediate medical attention, because the incidence

of uterine or cervical cancer ranges from 15% to 30% in postclimacteric women.

Musculoskeleton. An increased laxity of ligaments as well as reduced muscle tone and strength contribute to many of the symptoms occurring after ovarian failure. Backache and pain in the shoulders, elbows, knees, and joints of the hands often occur. In addition, decreased muscle tone affecting the pelvic floor muscles, the bladder, and the urethra results in urine leakage and a need to urinate frequently. The lining of the vagina and urinary tract becomes less acidic, making menopausal women more prone to infections.

OSTEOPOROSIS, caused by severe or prolonged bone loss as a result of estrogen deficiency, affects 35% of women after a natural menopause. As bones become weaker and more brittle, fractures can be caused by even minor stress.

Emotional Status. Anxiety or depression or, usually, a mixture of both may not result directly from menopause but rather from the personal life of the individual. Many situations seem to coincide with the age of menopause, such as adolescence crisis in a child, departure or marriage of the children, declining sexual activity, a husband's frustrations and anxieties, parental loss or parental dependence, or loss of a husband or partner. Psychiatric therapy and help from an understanding sexual partner and supportive family members can be the most beneficial remedies.

Sexual Activity. About 20% to 25% of menopausal women experience pain or discomfort during intercourse. This problem usually arises from thinning of the vaginal wall and a lack of vaginal lubrication, both due to estrogen deficiency; it can be solved by using a lubricant. Emotional problems may cause declining sexual activity in some women. On the other hand, many women experience heightened libido.

Therapy

Hormone replacement therapy (HRT) is used to reduce the discomfort of menopausal symptoms and also to prevent osteoporosis and lower the risk of heart disease. Its early use, when estrogen alone was administered, was linked with uterine cancer. This risk has largely been offset by alternating low doses of estrogen with progestin (a form of progesterone). Thus, HRT mimics the hormonal cycle before menopause. Although a woman on HRT does not ovulate, the progestin does cause a monthly shedding of the uterine lining, resulting in monthly bleeding. This cyclic uterine-lining shedding protects the body against uterine cancer.

Menorca   see MINORCA

Menotti, Gian Carlo [may-noht'-ee, jahn kahr'-loh] The Italian-American composer Gian Carlo Menotti, b. Cadegliano, Italy, July 7, 1911, is widely regarded as the last of the operatic composers in the VERISMO tradition, which he has adapted to the English language. He was the sixth of ten children of a musical family. He moved in

The composer Gian Carlo Menotti is shown staging his Christmas opera Amahl and the Night Visitors *(1951), the first opera specifically composed for American television.*

his teens to the United States and studied at the Curtis Institute, Philadelphia, from 1927 until 1933. His first opera was *Amelia Goes to the Ball* (1937). *The Old Maid and the Thief* (1939) was the first opera ever commissioned for radio.

After *The Island God* (1942), Menotti began presenting his works on Broadway, in his own skillful stagings. These include his first popular success, *The Medium* (1946); the witty *The Telephone* (1947); his highly acclaimed *The Consul* (1950); *The Saint of Bleeker Street* (1954), perhaps his richest score; and *Maria Golovin* (1958). His Christmas work, *Amahl and the Night Visitors* (1951), was the first opera commissioned for television.

Menotti's later operas were less successful. With a sharp ear for American English, he has written all his own librettos, as well as two librettos for operas by his friend Samuel BARBER: *Vanessa* (1958) and *Antony and Cleopatra* (1966). Menotti helped organize and direct the Festival of the Two Worlds, so named because it was founded in Spoleto, Italy, in 1958 and expanded to include Charleston, S.C., in 1977.

mens rea [mens ray'-uh]   Mens rea (Latin, "guilty mind") is a concept used in Anglo-American criminal law to denote the element of criminal intent in an offense. All legal systems require a showing for most crimes that the criminal intended to commit a crime. In Anglo-American law, a criminal act is categorized in one of four ways, accordingly. An offender who acts "purposely" has an actual and conscious intent to commit a crime; "knowingly," is aware that the conduct will cause a crime; "recklessly," has a conscious disregard that the conduct may have criminal consequences; "negligently," acts with inadvertence to possible criminal harm to others.

Menshevism   see BOLSHEVIKS AND MENSHEVIKS

Menshikov, Aleksandr Danilovich, Prince
[men'-shi-kuhf, uhl-yik-sahn'-dur duhn-yee'-luh-vich]
Prince Aleksandr Danilovich Menshikov, b. Nov. 16

(N.S.), 1673, d. Nov. 23 (N.S.), 1729, was the real ruler of Russia during the reign (1725–27) of Empress CATHERINE I. A low-born but markedly able crony of Emperor PETER I, he rose to the rank of field marshal after the Battle of Poltava (1709). On Peter's death, he helped secure the succession of Catherine, Peter's second wife and Menshikov's former mistress, and became effective ruler. Plans to marry his daughter to the succeeding sovereign, Peter II, miscarried, and he was exiled to Siberia in 1727.

menstruation [men-stroo-ay'-shuhn]   Menstruation, the periodic monthly discharge of the inner lining of the uterus (endometrium), lasts about 4 to 5 days and occurs, on the average, every 28 days. During this period, known as the menstrual cycle, an egg (oocyte) matures and is ovulated. The uterus at this time prepares a suitable environment in which a fertilized egg could develop into a fetus.

Phases of the Cycle. The first day of menses, or the onset of menstrual flow, is considered the first day of the cycle. Although 28 days is considered an average cycle, the time may range from 21 to 35 days. Climate, emotional factors, age, and drugs can alter the length of the menstrual cycle.

Days 0 to 13 of the cycle are called the follicular phase. Women are born with about 2 million ovarian follicles—microscopic structures, each of which surrounds an egg. At the start of a menstrual cycle about 200 follicles enlarge and become filled with fluid. By day 5 or 6 of the cycle, one of them begins to grow, while the others disintegrate. At midcycle, day 14, the oocyte within this follicle matures, the follicle ruptures, and ovulation occurs with the release of the mature oocyte down the fallopian tube.

During the luteal phase, from days 14 to 28, the collapsed follicle transforms into a corpus luteum and secretes progesterone.

Hormonal Control. The menstrual cycle is under strict hormonal control. At the beginning of the follicular phase, there is an increase in the secretion of follicle-stimulating hormone (FSH) from the pituitary. This stimulates the growth of a follicle in one of the ovaries; other follicles cease to grow at this time. The pituitary gland also secretes luteinizing hormone (LH), which acts along with FSH to cause the growing follicle to secrete the female sex hormone estrogen. This ovarian hormone causes the uterine glands to grow and the lining of the uterus to thicken in preparation for implantation of the embryo, should fertilization occur.

As the pituitary gland releases more and more FSH, the growing follicle secretes more estrogen. The increased levels of estrogen in the blood exert an inhibitory effect on the FSH-releasing center in the brain, resulting in a decrease in the secretion of FSH. The increasing levels of estrogen also trigger a midcycle (day 14) LH discharge from the pituitary, which causes the follicle to ovulate the mature oocyte.

The oocyte is propelled to the ampulla, the region of the fallopian tubes where fertilization occurs. Fertilization usually takes place within 24 hours of ovulation, and the embryo is implanted in the uterus 6 to 7 days after ovulation. If fertilization does not occur, the oocyte degenerates and is reabsorbed by normal bodily processes.

After ovulation, LH causes the cells of the ruptured follicle to undergo a transformation into a mass of cells that are rich in blood vessels, the corpus luteum. The corpus luteum still secretes estrogen, but in a smaller quantity than was secreted prior to ovulation. More important, the corpus luteum secretes the second major female sex hormone, progesterone. Progesterone acts on the uterine lining, which has already been stimulated to thicken under the influence of estrogen.

Progesterone causes the glands in the uterine lining to mature and to begin to secrete substances that are essential for the survival and implantation of the fertilized egg. Progesterone also inhibits the FSH-releasing centers in the brain, preventing the release of FSH and the start of a new cycle.

Menses. In the absence of fertilization, the elevated levels of progesterone secreted by the corpus luteum begin to inhibit the LH-releasing centers in the brain, causing a decline in the levels of LH. Because LH is responsible for maintaining the secretion of progesterone from the corpus luteum, the corpus luteum begins to shrink and stops secreting progesterone as the LH level falls. As the progesterone levels decline, the hormonal support to the uterine lining is lost and the body begins to reabsorb the tissue that was built up during the follicular and luteal phases of the cycle.

More tissue, however, is present than can be reabsorbed. The menstrual flow, which consists of this excess uterine epithelium as well as blood, lasts approximately 4 to 5 days. The corpus luteum degenerates, and its hormone production ceases; the FSH-releasing mechanisms in the brain are freed from their inhibition, and FSH levels begin to rise, signaling the start of a new menstrual cycle, the growth of a new follicle and oocyte, and the buildup of the uterine lining.

Menarche and Menopause. The time at which the menstrual cycle begins in girls is called the menarche and depends on such factors as heredity, nutrition, climate, and other as yet unknown parameters. The average age of menarche in North America and Europe is 13 years, with a range between 10 and 16 years. These menstrual cycles continue until approximately age 50, with the average woman having about 400 cycles in her lifetime. The cessation of menstrual cycles and the accompanying loss of reproductive ability is termed MENOPAUSE.

Disorders. The absence of menstruation at any time during the reproductive life span of a woman, known as amenorrhea, has many causes. Among these are emotional stress, ANOREXIA NERVOSA, tuberculosis, thyroid disorders, diabetes, adrenal gland diseases, and brain and ovarian diseases. Amenorrhea may occur when the absence of menstruation is considered perfectly normal, such as preceding puberty, during menopause, during and immediately after pregnancy, and as a side effect of certain drugs. Amenorrhea occurring in the absence of any of these states, however, may be an indication of deep underlying pathology and should be brought to the attention of a physician.

Dysmenorrhea is abdominal or pelvic pain prior to or associated with menstruation. It is usually caused by an increased level of prostaglandin secretion and may be aggravated by emotional and environmental factors.

See also: HORMONE, ANIMAL; PREGNANCY AND BIRTH; REPRODUCTIVE SYSTEM, HUMAN.

▬
mental disorder   A mental disorder, or PSYCHOPATHOLOGY, is a dysfunction of mental ability that causes its sufferer undue distress or even disability. Some mental disorders result from environmental factors; others, such as mental retardation or ALZHEIMER'S DISEASE, may be the result of organic brain damage. Current research has uncovered much evidence that many mental disorders, such as SCHIZOPHRENIA and acute DEPRESSION, may be genetically transmitted from one generation to the next. The American Psychiatric Association currently recognizes some 250 categories of mental disorders.

Various treatment options include PSYCHOTHERAPY and PSYCHOANALYSIS, in which a patient discusses problems with, and follows suggestions of, a trained practitioner; BEHAVIOR MODIFICATION, which seeks to alleviate disorders through changing habitual behaviors; and drug therapy, which seeks to change a patient's perceptions through an alteration of brain chemistry.

See also: OBSESSIVE-COMPULSIVE DISORDER; PERSONALITY, MULTIPLE; PSYCHOSIS.

▬
mental retardation   Mental retardation is characterized by significantly subaverage levels of general intellectual functioning. Recent definitions have also emphasized such characteristics as its onset in the childhood years and impairments in adaptive behavior, but most researchers and professionals who work with the retarded continue to rely on subnormal INTELLIGENCE as the key definitional feature. Individuals scoring below 70 on standardized tests measuring intelligence quotient (IQ; see PSYCHOLOGICAL MEASUREMENT) are considered to be mentally retarded.

Retardation is thought to affect approximately 3% of the U.S. population, although some experts argue that a smaller percentage of individuals (1%) should receive the diagnosis. The large majority of retarded individuals fall in the mild range of retardation (IQ = 55–69), and smaller numbers are moderately (IQ = 40–54), severely (IQ = 25–39), or profoundly (IQ = 0–24) retarded. A disproportionate number of mildly retarded persons come from families of the lowest socioeconomic classes, whereas the more severe levels of retardation seem to affect all social classes to the same extent. More males than females are retarded, and retardation can coexist with psychological disorders (for example, AUTISM, SCHIZOPHRENIA) and physical disabilities (CEREBRAL PALSY, SPINA BIFIDA).

Organic and Familial Causes. The organically retarded, comprising less than half of the retarded population, suffer from retardation of known organic etiology. The factors that cause organic retardation can be genetic (DOWN'S SYNDROME, PHENYLKETONURIA), prenatal (rubella), perinatal (asphyxia), or postnatal (meningitis, head trauma) in origin. In all, more than 200 organic etiologies have been identified. Familial retarded individuals, comprising more than half of the retarded population, exhibit retardation for which there is no apparent cause. Familial retarded individuals are generally offspring of parents who are themselves of low intelligence; these individuals also spend their early years in impoverished environments. Thus, genetic or environmental factors, or some combination of the two, may cause familial retardation.

Genetic screening is now used to tell parents if their offspring will suffer from Down's syndrome or from a variety of other organic disabilities, even while the child is still unborn (see GENETIC DISEASES). Genetic counseling informs prospective parents in several high-risk categories (including older parents and parents who have already had a retarded child) of the chances that their next child will be retarded. Special dietary supplements have helped children with phenylketonuria—an inborn chemical imbalance—to avoid the progressive retardation that usually accompanies the syndrome if left untreated.

Education of Retarded Children. Research on older retarded children has shown that motivational factors play the major role in determining how productive and independent a retarded child ultimately becomes. Because retarded children face an increased number of failure experiences compared to normal children, however, they may develop traits that work against their achieving independence. They often become overly wary of adults and develop a lower expectancy of success (that is, they do not expect to succeed at challenging tasks). At the same time, retarded children are more likely to become dependent on adult approval and to accept adult (as opposed to their own) solutions to difficult problems. The net effect is that retarded individuals frequently perform below the level of their intellectual abilities on a variety of experimental and real-life tasks.

Changing Societal Perceptions of the Retarded. The prevailing attitudes toward the retarded throughout history have ranged from contempt to reverence. The care of retarded individuals has also varied considerably over time. Inspired by the rehabilitative efforts of Jean Itard (1775–1838) and his pupil Edouard Séguin (1812–80)—who were early advocates of the use of special educational methods to teach handicapped children—workers in the mid-19th century set out to improve the intellectual and social adjustment of the retarded. Their spirit of reform led to the establishment of numerous training schools in the United States and abroad.

In the years roughly between the 1870s and the 1920s, however, U.S. care for the retarded markedly regressed. Several states passed laws mandating sexual segregation and forced sterilization; popular writers emphasized the moral degeneracy of the retarded; and experts routinely recommended the institutionalization of all retarded children. The 1920s finally marked the beginnings of liberalized attitudes, as the first outpatient and community-service programs were begun.

Many higher-functioning retarded persons have been deinstitutionalized—that is, moved from larger institu-

tional settings into smaller group homes and independent living settings. Federal law now guarantees all HANDICAPPED PERSONS, including the retarded, the right to an education, and there is a strong movement to "mainstream" retarded children into classes with normal children. The effects of both deinstitutionalization and mainstreaming are the subjects of intense debate among experts in mental retardation.

—

Menuhin, Yehudi [men'-yoo-in, yuh-hoo'-dee]   The distinguished violinist Yehudi Menuhin, b. New York City, Apr. 22, 1916, of Russian-Jewish parents, was an outstanding prodigy who made his public debut with the Mendelssohn concerto at age 7. He studied in Europe with Adolf Busch and Georges Enesco and, from childhood, toured to great acclaim throughout the world. During World War II, Menuhin performed in concert for the Allied troops, and after the war he played in the newly liberated countries of Europe and in the USSR, raising money for refugee relief and other humanitarian causes. Menuhin's explorations of several musical traditions have led to collaborations with the Indian sitarist Ravi SHANKAR and the French jazz violinist Stéphane Grappelli.

—

Menzies, Sir Robert Gordon [men'-ziez] Sir Robert Gordon Menzies, b. Jeparit, Victoria, Dec. 20, 1894, d. May 14, 1978, prime minister of Australia from 1939 to 1941 and from 1949 to 1966, was the chief architect and coordinator of that nation's prosperity in the difficult years of the cold war and the Korean War. He was a barrister before entering provincial government (1928) and Parliament (1934). He became attorney general (1935–39) and succeeded Joseph LYONS as prime minister in 1939 but resigned in 1941. During 1944, while out of office, Menzies helped create the ideology of the Australian Liberal party. He won the 1949 election and again became prime minister. Thus began 23 years of Liberal party hegemony.

Under Menzies's direction, immigration from postwar Europe provided a basis for the remarkable economic and industrial expansion of Australia. Menzies was also a ma-

Sir Robert Menzies, an Australian statesman who served as prime minister for nearly 20 years, encouraged rapid economic growth during the 1950s through policies of his Liberal-Country party government.

jor figure in international politics, playing the role of peacemaker during the Suez Crisis (1956) and succeeding Jan Smuts as leader of the Commonwealth of Nations. He was almost solely responsible for directing Australian foreign policy toward the orbit of the United States. Menzies was knighted in 1963.

Mer de Glace [mair duh glahs] Mer de Glace (French: Sea of Ice), the second longest glacier in the Alps, is situated on the northern slope of Mont BLANC near Chamonix, France. It is approximately 6 km (3.5 mi) long. Formed by several smaller glaciers flowing together, it moves about 130 m (425 ft) per year. The glacier is continually replenished by the heavy snows on the upper mountain.

mercantilism Mercantilism was an economic policy of the commercial age preceding the Industrial Revolution. Governments in the 16th, 17th, and 18th centuries practiced mercantilism in an effort to build up their military and industrial strength. State intervention was an important part of mercantilism. Governments encouraged domestic industry, regulated production, controlled trading companies, placed restrictions such as tariffs and quotas on the importation of merchandise from other countries, and sought out raw materials and markets through COLONIALISM. Mercantilists believed that a country's exports were one measure of its strength and that economic success could be judged by the influx of gold, silver, and other precious metals from abroad. A further reason for acquiring gold and silver was that they could be used to purchase military supplies.

An influential advocate of mercantilism was Jean Baptiste COLBERT, who directed French economic policies under Louis XIV. Great Britain's mercantilist policies were embodied in the NAVIGATION ACTS of the 17th century. Mercantilist thinking was based on the assumption that the volume of trade was limited and that countries could expand their trade only at the expense of others. The notion was assailed by the PHYSIOCRATS, by Adam SMITH in his *Wealth of Nations* (1776), and by other classical economists in the 19th century. The triumph of Smith's FREE TRADE and LAISSEZ-FAIRE ideas in the early 19th century led to the demise of mercantilist policies.

Mercator, Gerardus [mur-kay'-tur, juh-rahr'-duhs] Gerardus Mercator, b. Mar. 5, 1512, d. Dec. 2, 1594, was a Flemish cartographer and geographer best known for his mapping work, especially the Mercator projection, which used straight lines to indicate latitude and longitude. Mercator studied in Louvain, Belgium, under Gemma Frisius, and in 1552 he became a mapmaker and lecturer at the University of Duisberg. His map of Europe (published in 1554) was the best of its kind for many decades. He produced a map of the British Isles in 1564 and in the same year was made court cosmographer to Duke William of Cleve. Mercator first used his cylindrical

projection on his world map of 1569. His great *Atlas*, in which he sought to describe the creation and history of the world, was printed, unfinished, in 1595.

mercenaries Mercenaries—professional soldiers who fight for pay in the armies of foreign countries—have been employed in armies since ancient times. Alexander the Great used them in his extensive conquests. In the Middle Ages, "free companies" were often hired to fight feudal wars. They frequently proved unreliable, however, selling their services to the highest bidder or turning to plunder at war's end. Mercenaries played a notable role in the many wars among the Italian city-states in the 14th and 15th centuries; their commanders, CONDOTTIERI, often acquired small states of their own.

In the 17th century, mercenaries were gradually replaced in European armies by standing volunteer forces. Swiss, German, and Dutch troops, however, were often employed by the rulers of other countries. HESSIANS fought for the British in the American Revolution. Swiss mercenaries fought in several European armies between the 15th and 19th centuries but were most important in France, where they served as personal guards to the kings. Such arrangements were prohibited by the Swiss government in 1874, an exception being made for the Swiss Guard of the Vatican, which was established in 1505 and continues to exist today. In recent times mercenaries have been employed in African civil wars. *Soldiers of Fortune,* a U.S. magazine, addresses contemporary mercenaries.

Mercer, Johnny Lyricist, songwriter, and singer John H. Mercer, b. Savannah, Ga., Nov. 18, 1909, d. June 25, 1976, helped write many of the most celebrated songs of the 1930s and '40s. Mercer wrote the lyrics and sometimes the music for a number of songs that became popular classics, including "Blues in the Night," "That Old Black Magic," "Jeepers Creepers," and "Come Rain or Come Shine." As president of Capitol Records, Mercer recorded such fledgling musicians as Peggy Lee and Nat "King" Cole. In 1946, "On the Atchison, Topeka and the Santa Fe" won him the first of four Academy Awards; the fourth (1962) was for "Days of Wine and Roses," written in collaboration with Henry Mancini.

Mercer, Mabel Among musicians, singers, and enthusiasts of classic American popular music, singer Mabel Mercer, b. Feb. 3, 1900, d. Apr. 20, 1984, was admired as the most sophisticated song stylist of her era. Born in England, Mercer began her singing career in Paris and was featured at the celebrated café Bricktop's in the 1930s. She arrived in the United States in 1938. In addition to her own elegant versions of cabaret and show songs, she was known for rediscovering arcane material, often from forgotten musicals. In 1983, Mercer received the Presidential Medal of Freedom from President Ronald Reagan.

Merchant of Venice, The *The Merchant of Venice,* first performed in 1596 and published in 1600, is one of SHAKESPEARE's most popular—though controversial—comedies. The plot is in part based on a story by the late-14th-century Italian writer Giovanni Fiorentino. Although the merchant Antonio is saved by Portia's legal efforts from rendering his "pound of flesh" for indebtedness to the Jewish moneylender Shylock, there is no happy ending for Shylock himself. Shakespeare's unflattering portrait of this character no doubt reflects Christian anti-Semitism and the medieval hatred of usury. The moving speech given Shylock in act 3, scene 1, nevertheless suggests the dramatist's attempt to transcend contemporary stereotypes. The play's two most famous scenes are the casket scene and the courtroom scene, in which Portia eloquently argues the superiority of mercy over malice and pleads for human understanding.

Mercia [mur'-shuh]   Mercia was one of the ANGLO-SAXON kingdoms of England. Located in central England, it was settled (*c*.500) by the Angles and first achieved prominence under King Penda (r. *c*.632–54). In the 8th century its kings, notably OFFA (r. 757–96), were acknowledged overlords of all England, but they lost their ascendancy to the kings of WESSEX.

Mercier, Honoré   Honoré Mercier, b. St. Athanase, Lower Canada (now Quebec), Oct. 15, 1840, d. Oct. 30, 1894, prime minister of Quebec from 1887 to 1891, was a noted defender of French-Canadian rights and provincial autonomy. He sat in the Canadian House of Commons (1872–74) and was elected to the Quebec legislature in 1879. Outraged by the execution (1885) of the rebel Louis RIEL, Mercier formed the *Parti national,* in which French-Canadian Liberals and Conservatives joined forces. After becoming prime minister, Mercier called (1887) an interprovincial conference at which five premiers discussed their grievances against the central government. In 1891, Mercier was charged with corruption and dismissed from office.

Merckx, Eddy [murks]   Eddy Merckx, b. June 17, 1945, a professional Belgian cyclist, is recognized by most authorities as the greatest road racer of all time. By the age of 28 he had set more records than any other racer, with more than 300 professional victories. He won the world amateur cycling championship in 1964, and in 1967 he captured the world professional cycling title. He became the first man to win all of the major scoring classifications in both the 1968 Giro d'Italia and the 1969 Tour de France. He also won an unsurpassed 5 Tour de France events.

Mercury (mythology)   In Roman mythology Mercury was the god of merchants and commerce, of science and astronomy, of thieves, travelers, and vagabonds, and of cleverness and eloquence. The messenger of the gods, he was represented in art as a young man with winged hat and sandals. He was identified with the Greek god HERMES.

Mercury (planet)   Mercury, the planet closest to the Sun, is a cratered world. It is the smallest of the inner planets, perhaps because the heat of the nearby Sun as Mercury formed, about 4.6 billion years ago, prevented most of the gases present in the vicinity from becoming part of the protoplanet. Mercury's surface is very hot, sometimes reaching extremes of more than 470° C (more than 1,380° F)—especially at two "hot spots" opposite one another on the equator. This heat and the planet's low gravity make it impossible for Mercury to retain any significant atmosphere, even though nighttime temperatures drop to −170° C (−270° F). Trace amounts of hydrogen, helium, and oxygen above the surface probably derive from the solar wind, while similar traces of sodium and potassium atoms may represent gases diffusing up through the planet's crust.

Astronomical Data. Mercury orbits the Sun once every 88 days at distances varying from 70 million to 46 million km (43 million to 29 million mi). Because of the great difficulty in observing this small and distant planet, which never appears more than 28° from the Sun in the sky, it was thought as late as the early 1960s that Mercury also rotated with an 88-day period, so that one hemisphere always faced the Sun. Radar observations have since shown, though, that the true rotation period is 58.6 days, or about ⅔ of the period of revolution. Mercury rotates three times for every two trips around the Sun, so that during every alternate perihelion passage the same face points directly at the Sun. The inclination of its rotation axis is 7°. The perihelion of Mercury's orbit advances 43 seconds of arc per century, an effect only fully explained by Einstein's general theory of relativity. Mercury has no known satellites.

Physical Characteristics. Mercury's equatorial diameter is 4,880 km (3,030 mi), about 40% that of the Earth, and its mass is about 6% of the Earth's. Its high density implies that there is a large iron or nickel-iron core inside the planet. Mercury is thought to contain a higher percentage of iron than the Earth does. Current computer models set Mercury's core radius at 1,800 km (1,100 mi)—75% of the radius of the planet. The Earth's core has a radius that is only about 55% of the planetary radius. This large iron core, part of which is probably molten, is undoubtedly responsible for Mercury's intrinsic magnetic field. Discovered in 1974 by the MARINER 10 spacecraft, the field is only about 1% as strong as the Earth's at the surface. This is enough, however, to disturb the solar wind as it streams past the planet.

Mariner 10 also provided the first close-up pictures of Mercury's surface, although only 40% of it has been photographed in detail. Extensive cratered highlands, which imply a very old surface where they exist, cover much of the observed crust and give it a lunar appearance. Dark, smooth plains apparently similar to the Moon's maria, or

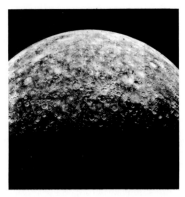

(Above) *Mercury appears in a photomosaic, or composite photograph, taken by Mariner 10, which approached to within 740 km (460 mi) of the planet on Mar. 29, 1974.* (Left) *A photomosaic of the landscape of Mercury reveals a cratered surface similar to that of the Moon. Scientists believe these craters were caused by the impact of meteors in the early years of the solar system.*

"seas," are also present. The reduced number of craters in these regions suggests that they are younger than the highlands. Some of the observed craters are giant impact basins like those found on the Moon. The largest, 1,300 km (800 mi) in diameter, is called the Caloris Basin because it is located at one of Mercury's "hot spots"—either of the two points where the Sun can be directly overhead when Mercury is nearest the Sun.

Mercury is quite different from the Moon, however. It is 40% larger, 4.5 times more massive, and much richer in iron. Even Mercury's surface is different from that of the Moon in two important ways. First, although heavily cratered, Mercury's highlands are not saturated with craters. Extensive, gently rolling plains predominate. These plains may represent the original crust of Mercury showing through the effects of cratering. Mercury's higher surface gravity prevents meteoric impacts from spreading their ejecta as far as they do on the Moon, so that some of the precratering surface may have remained intact. Second, there are large, long, and winding scarps, or one-sided ridges, that cross the surface of the cratered highlands for hundreds of kilometers. These scarps are thought to have formed during contraction of the crust as Mercury's large core cooled and partially solidified, much as an apple skin wrinkles as the apple begins to dry out. Thus, while externally Mercury looks like the Moon, internally it is more like the Earth in terms of its large iron core and related magnetic field. The formation and development of this core is what primarily distinguishes the evolution of Mercury from the evolution of the Moon.

See also: SOLAR SYSTEM.

mercury   The chemical element mercury is a shiny metallic liquid. Its chemical symbol, Hg, is derived from the Greek word *hydrargyrum*, meaning "liquid silver," or "quick silver." Although now obsolete, the word *quicksilver* has long been used as a synonym for mercury. The element shares Group IIB of the PERIODIC TABLE with zinc and cadmium. The atomic number of mercury is 80; its atomic weight is 200.59. Mercury is very dense, weighing 13.6 times as much as an equal volume of water. Stone, iron, and even lead can float on its surface.

Occurrence. Mercury constitutes 0.5 parts per million (ppm) of the Earth's crust, making it more plentiful than gold or silver. Mercury is found principally in the ore CINNABAR (mercury sulfide, HgS) but also in the uncombined state. The preparation of mercury from its ores is fairly simple. The ore is ground up and heated to about 580° C in the presence of oxygen. Mercury vapor escapes from the ores and sulfur dioxide is removed. The metal is condensed and purified by washing with nitric acid, followed by distillation.

Early Applications. Mercury was among the first metals known, and its compounds have been used throughout history. The Egyptians and the Chinese may have been using cinnabar as a red pigment for centuries before the birth of Christ. The alchemists thought that mercury had mystical properties and used it in their attempts to transmute base metals into gold. The Greeks used it as a medicine, and its compounds were used from about the 15th century to the mid-20th century to cure syphilis. Because mercury is extremely toxic and its curative effect is unproven, other syphilis medicines are now used.

Modern Uses. The usefulness of mercury is limited by its poisonous nature and scarcity. Mercury is used in electrical switches, which consist of a small tube with two contacts at one end. If the mercury collects at this end, then contact is made and the circuit is completed. If the tube is tilted, contact is broken. Mercury is highly suitable for use in thermometers because it does not moisten glass and its thermal expansion is uniform. It is used in pressure-measuring devices because, due to its high density, it requires less space. Mercury vapor lamps are powerful and economical sources of ultraviolet and visible light.

Amalgams are ALLOYS of mercury with other metals or with nonmetals such as tellurium. Silver and gold amalgams occur in nature, but most amalgams are artificially produced. The amalgam used in dental fillings contains tin and silver (and sometimes gold) dissolved in mercury. In the manufacture of mirrors, an amalgam of one part tin and three parts mercury is applied to glass.

Chemical Properties. Mercury is a fairly unreactive metal and is highly resistant to corrosion. When heated to near its boiling point (346.72° C), mercury oxidizes in air, and mercuric oxide, HgO, is formed. At 500° C, mercuric oxide decomposes into mercury and oxygen, a phenomenon that led to the discovery of oxygen by Joseph Priestley and Karl Scheele. Mercuric oxide is a constituent of mercury batteries, which have been invaluable as compact, efficient power sources in the exploration of outer space.

Mercury Compounds. The most useful mercury salts are the two mercury chlorides and mercury sulfide. Mercurous chloride, HgCl, or calomel, is a white, relatively insoluble salt. It is used in calomel electrodes for electrochemical cells, and in medicine as a cathartic and diuretic. Mercuric chloride, $HgCl_2$, or corrosive sublimate, is highly poisonous because it is so soluble. It was used for deliberate poisonings as early as the 14th century. It is now used as a disinfectant, in preparing other mercury compounds, and in antifungal skin ointments. Mercuric sulfide occurs in a red form and an amorphous black form. The red form (vermilion) is used as a coloring mate-

rial. Cinnabar is sometimes used to color tattoos red, but it causes skin irritations and obstructions of the lymphatic system. Mercuric fulminate, $Hg(ONC)_2$, is an explosive used in percussion caps for munitions. Mercurochrome is an organic mercury compound that is used on wounds as an antibacterial agent.

Mercury Poisoning. There are two types of mercury poisoning, acute and chronic. Acute mercury poisoning results from the ingestion of soluble mercury salts, which violently corrode skin and mucous membranes. Although cases have occurred in which persons have ingested elemental mercury without suffering permanent damage, mercury vapor aspirated into the lungs can cause severe pneumonia and death.

Chronic mercury poisoning occurs through the regular absorption of small amounts of mercury. This condition is often a disease of workers in mercury mines, laboratories, and industries that use mercury (see DISEASES, OCCUPATIONAL).

The most toxic mercury compounds are those which are fat-soluble, because this property assists in their distribution throughout the body. Methyl mercury compounds, such as dimethyl mercury, $Hg(CH_3)_2$, are among the most dangerous. Mercury salts released into the environment may frequently be converted by anaerobic bacteria into such compounds, which can then be carried through the food chain to humans—as in the disaster at Minamata Bay, Japan (see POLLUTANTS, CHEMICAL). Other microorganisms can convert methyl mercury compounds into the insoluble, and therefore harmless, mercury sulfide, HgS.

Mercury program   The Mercury program was the earliest U.S. project to put an ASTRONAUT into space. It utilized one-person, bell-shaped capsules that were boosted into orbits 161 to 283 km (100 to 176 mi) above the Earth. The capsules reentered the atmosphere ballistically, and parachutes were deployed on the final descent to ocean splashdown. The capsules were then re-

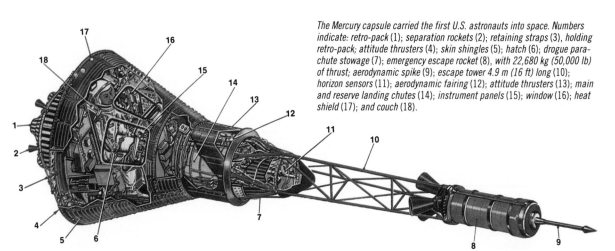

The Mercury capsule carried the first U.S. astronauts into space. Numbers indicate: retro-pack (1); separation rockets (2); retaining straps (3), holding retro-pack; attitude thrusters (4); skin shingles (5); hatch (6); drogue parachute stowage (7); emergency escape rocket (8), with 22,680 kg (50,000 lb) of thrust; aerodynamic spike (9); escape tower 4.9 m (16 ft) long (10); horizon sensors (11); aerodynamic fairing (12); attitude thrusters (13); main and reserve landing chutes (14); instrument panels (15); window (16); heat shield (17); and couch (18).

covered by U.S. naval vessels and helicopters. The project successfully flew two suborbital and four orbital manned missions.

From the time the prime contract for the Mercury spacecraft was awarded to the McDonnell Aircraft Corporation of St. Louis, Mo., on Jan. 12, 1959, through the landing of the fourth Mercury orbital capsule on May 16, 1963, the project cost slightly more than $400 million and involved the technical skills of more than 2 million men and women in the research, development, and testing of the spacecraft, its launch vehicles, and a worldwide tracking and communications network.

The Spacecraft

Although manned spaceflight had been studied since the late 1940s, serious development of a manned satellite was not considered by Congress until after the Soviet Union launched *Sputniks 1* and *2* in October and November 1957. In March 1958, Maxime A. Faget, Benjamine J. Garland, and James J. Buglia of the National Advisory Committee for Aeronautics (NACA) proposed a wingless, manned satellite that could follow a ballistic path to reenter the atmosphere without exposing the crew to excessively high temperatures or dangerous acceleration. The chief points of this proposal were incorporated into the Mercury program.

The size and weight of the Mercury spacecraft were dictated by the lifting capability of the Atlas D intercontinental ballistic missile (ICBM), the only reliable missile in the U.S. arsenal in the early 1960s powerful enough to boost a manned satellite into a 161-km (100-mi) orbit. The capsule was thus designed to weigh less than 1,350 kg (3,000 lb). It was 2.9 m (9 ft 7 in) high from the heat shield at the blunt end to the top of its cylindrical recovery section, housing a small drogue parachute and large ringsail parachutes.

The capsule was divided into three sections. The cylindrical section contained the radio antennas and sensors of the automatic control system in addition to the parachutes. The cabin, arranged like a fighter aircraft cockpit, was pressurized with pure oxygen at 0.3 atmospheres. The astronaut reclined on a contour couch designed to provide protection from accelerations of as much as 20 gravities. Behind the cabin was the bell-shaped heat shield and six solid-propellant rockets. Three of these rockets, with a thrust of 180 kg (400 lb) each, were fired to separate the capsule from the launch vehicle and to adjust the orbit of the capsule. Three more, with a thrust of 450 kg (1,000 lb) each, were fired in retrograde to brake the capsule out of orbit so that it would reenter the atmosphere.

The attitude, or position, of the capsule was controlled by an array of 18 hydrogen-peroxide gas thrusters. These could pitch the spacecraft up or down, yaw it left or right, or roll it. The pilot could fire them by means of a hand controller or leave attitude control to an autopilot.

Following the launch, the most critical part of the flight was the firing of the braking rockets. The pilot was required to put the capsule in a precise attitude for retrofire in order to land in the sea near the recovery ships.

U.S. astronaut Alan B. Shepard, Jr., and his Mercury capsule Freedom 7 *were shot into space and successfully recovered from the Atlantic Ocean on May 5, 1961. The entire flight lasted 15 minutes.*

Missions

During 1960–61, the Mercury capsule was launched by a Redstone missile on a series of suborbital flights that tested the integrity of its structure and the effectiveness of the steeple-shaped launch escape tower. The last of these, on Jan. 31, 1961, took a chimpanzee named Ham on a suborbital flight, from which he was recovered unharmed.

On May 5, 1961, Lt. Comdr. Alan B. SHEPARD, Jr., of the navy was launched 485 km (303 mi) downrange aboard Mercury-Redstone 3. The capsule, named *Freedom 7*, reached an altitude of 185 km (116 mi). During the 15-minute flight, Shepard tested the control system and reported that all systems worked well.

The second suborbital manned flight (July 21, 1961) launched Capt. Virgil I. "Gus" GRISSOM of the air force to an altitude of 190 km (118.3 mi). After the splashdown, 483 km (302 mi) from the Cape Canaveral launch site, Grissom narrowly escaped drowning when a hatch blew out prematurely and his capsule filled with water. He was rescued by a helicopter, but the capsule, *Liberty Bell 7*, sank and was not recovered.

Following a series of Mercury unmanned orbital test flights launched by the Atlas D, Lt. Col. John H. GLENN, Jr., of the marines flew a three-orbit (4 hr 55 min) mission (Feb. 20, 1962) in the spacecraft he named *Friend-*

Prior to his historic Mercury flight, John Glenn, the first American to orbit the Earth, was trained extensively in various flight simulators as well as the actual capsule that he rode into space. Such training was given to all astronauts in order to familiarize them completely with the nature and operation of all the spacecraft systems.

ship 7 (Mercury-Atlas 6). The first American to fly in orbit, Glenn received a hero's welcome on the same scale as that accorded Charles A. Lindbergh after his New York–Paris flight in 1927. A second three-orbit (4 hr 56 min) mission was flown on May 24, 1962, in *Aurora 7* (Mercury-Atlas 7) by Lt. Comdr. Scott M. Carpenter of the navy. Flight time was doubled by Comdr. Walter M. SCHIRRA, Jr., of the navy during the six-orbit mission of *Sigma 7* (Mercury-Atlas 8) on Oct. 3, 1962.

Project Mercury ended with the 22-orbit (34 hr 20 min) flight of Maj. Leroy Gordon COOPER, Jr., of the air force on May 15–16, 1963, in *Faith 7* (Mercury-Atlas 9). Four years and 10 months after the National Aeronautics and Space Administration (NASA) was created by an act of Congress on July 16, 1958, the first American manned space program had been completed.

See also: SPACE EXPLORATION.

Mercury Theatre   see WELLES, ORSON

mercy killing   see EUTHANASIA

Meredith, George [mair'-uh-dith]   George Meredith, b. Feb. 12, 1828, d. May 18, 1909, was an English novelist, poet, and essayist who ranks with George Eliot; Charles Dickens; Alfred, Lord Tennyson; and Robert Browning as one of the major literary figures of Victorian England. Meredith's early prose works, *The Shaving of Shagpat* (1856) and *Farina* (1857), were followed by his first novel, *The Ordeal of Richard Feverel* (1859), which adapts the framework of Shakespeare's *Romeo and Juliet* to an English aristocratic setting. The novel bewildered its first readers with its use of an ironic narrative technique that mimics the voices of the characters. *Beauchamp's*

Career (1875), which Meredith considered his finest work, concerns an idealistic radical politician whose views are tempered by experience.

Modern critics have generally agreed, however, that *The Egoist* (1879) is Meredith's masterpiece. Its hero, a fatuous and self-absorbed landowner, attempts to manipulate women to whom he is engaged, but he is finally discomfited by Clara Middleton, one of the most engaging portraits of a woman in the language. The novel proceeds almost entirely through conversation, with occasional interjections by the ironic narrator. *Diana of the Crossways* (1885) depicts a woman struggling for emancipation in a reactionary society.

In 1894, Meredith closed his career as a novelist with *The Amazing Marriage* (1895) but continued to write poetry. *Last Poems* (1909) was published posthumously. Meredith's poetry is characterized by subtle metrical control, a genius for metaphor, and a sustained lyrical tone—some of his greatest work is found in *Poems and Lyrics of the Joy of Earth* (1883). He was highly respected and widely quoted as a critic, and his *Essay on Comedy* (1877) offers a philosophical account of comedy as a social corrective.

George Meredith, today regarded among the major figures of Victorian literature, appears in a portrait by G. F. Watts. His most important novels include The Ordeal of Richard Feverel *(1859) and* The Egoist *(1879). (National Portrait Gallery, London.)*

Meredith, William   The poetry of William Morris Meredith, Jr., b. New York City, Jan. 9, 1919, has been called neo-Augustan because its unusual perceptions are so often framed in ordered, metrically regular verse. Meredith's collections include *Love Letter from an Impossible Land* (1944), *The Open Sea and Other Poems* (1958), *Earth Walk* (1970), *The Cheer* (1980), and *Partial Accounts: New and Selected Poems* (1987; Pulitzer Prize).

Merezhkovsky, Dmitry Sergeyevich [mair-i-sh-kawf'-skee, duh-mee'-tree sir-gay'-uh-vich]   A Russian writer and one of the founders of Russian symbolism, Dmitry Sergeyevich Merezhkovsky, b. Aug. 14 (N.S.), 1865, d. Dec. 7, 1941, won international recognition for his historical novels and studies of such writers as Tolstoy, Dostoyevsky, and Dante. Merezhkovsky and his wife, the poet Zinaida Hippius, were central figures in the intellectual and artistic life of Russia throughout the Silver Age (1895–1925). After the Bolsheviks came to power they emigrated to Paris. His trilogy *Christ and Antichrist* (1896–1905), comprising *Julian the Apostate, Leonardo da Vinci*, and *Peter and Aleksis*, was immensely popular and often translated. *Leonardo da Vinci* was a favorite of Sigmund Freud's, and *Peter and Aleksis*, set in the age of Peter the Great, best shows the power of Merezhkovsky's historical imagination.

merganser [mur-gan'-sur] Mergansers are several species of diving ducks whose slender, hook-tipped bills are serrated on the edges, providing an efficient tool for catching the fish that are their principal food. The common merganser, *Mergus merganser*, widespread in fresh waters throughout the Northern Hemisphere, is 63 cm (25 in) long; the drake (male) is white with a black back, black wings, and a green head with an inconspicuous crest. Females are grayer, with chestnut brown heads and prominent crests. In the slightly smaller red-breasted merganser, *M. serrator*, which inhabits both fresh and salt water, the female is similar to the common merganser but the drake is grayer, with a chestnut breastplate and a green crest. Other species include the Old World smew, *M. albellus*, sometimes placed in a different genus, *Mergellus*; the North American hooded merganser, *Lophodytes cucullatus*; the Brazilian merganser, *M. octosetaceus*; the Chinese merganser, *M. squamatus*; and the Auckland Island (New Zealand) merganser, *M. australis*. The last species is believed extinct.

The common merganser is a diving duck that uses its long, thin, serrated beak to catch fish.

Mergenthaler, Ottmar [mur'-guhn-tah-lur, oht'-mahr] Ottmar Mergenthaler, b. May 11, 1854, d. Oct. 28, 1899, was a German-American whose invention of the LINOTYPE machine made a significant contribution to the PRINTING industry. Apprenticed to a watchmaker in his native Germany at the age of 14, he emigrated to the United States in 1872. While employed in the Baltimore, Md., machine shop of August Hahl he worked on building a "writing machine" that later helped him solve the problems involved in mechanizing the tedious work of typesetting (see TYPE AND TYPESETTING). His machine used a keyboard to assemble lines of matrices prior to casting a one-piece slug in molten metal. The first machine was installed in the *New York Tribune* in 1886.

merger A merger, in business, is the acquisition of one or more companies by another and their operation as one firm. Companies may merge in several different ways. One company may purchase another's stock, two companies may exchange shares, or two or more companies may combine to form a new company. An alternative to the merger is the HOLDING COMPANY, which buys a controlling interest in another company and operates it as a subsidiary. Mergers have played an important part in the growth of U.S. business corporations; most large corporations have developed through the merging of smaller companies. In the United States antitrust laws have been passed in an effort to prevent monopolies (see MONOPOLY AND COMPETITION), which may be created by mergers.

Meri, La   see LA MERI

Mérida [may'-ree-dah] Mérida is the capital of Yucatán state in Mexico, at the northwestern tip of the Yucatán Peninsula. It is located 35 km (23 mi) south of its port city, Progresso, on the Gulf of Mexico. Mérida's population is 424,529 (1983 est.).

A manufacturing and commercial center, Mérida produces sisal, chicle, and processed foods. Tourism, important to the economy, is centered on Mérida's historic landmarks: the cathedral (built 1561–98), the Archaeological Museum, and nearby Maya sites including CHICHÉN ITZÁ and UXMAL. The University of Yucatán (first established 1624) is there.

During the 6th century a Mayan city, T'ho, was established there. In 1542 the Spanish founded the present city on the site. An 1848 uprising by the Maya Indians was quashed by military force nearby.

Meridian [muh-rid'-ee-uhn] Meridian (1990 pop., 41,036), the third largest city in Mississippi and seat of Lauderdale County, is located in the eastern part of the state. It is an important transportation and industrial center where lumber, furniture, textiles, transportation equipment, and processed foods are manufactured. Meridian was settled in 1831. In 1863, during the Civil War, it served briefly as the state capital, and in 1864 it was burned by Union forces.

meridian instruments   see TRANSIT CIRCLE

Mérimée, Prosper [may-ree-may', prohs-pair']
Prosper Mérimée, b. Sept. 28, 1803, d. Sept. 23, 1870,
famous as a prose stylist and master of short fiction, was
an important figure in French romanticism. An archaeologist and inspector general of historic monuments by
profession, Mérimée began writing as a hoax. *The Plays of
Clara Gazul* (1825; Eng. trans., 1825) is a collection of
ironic dramas about love and death that Mérimée claimed
were the work of an imaginary Spanish actress. His
chronicle play *La Jacquerie* (1828) and his novel *A
Chronicle of the Reign of Charles IX* (1829; Eng. trans.,
1830) are richly detailed studies of French history, inspired by the work of Sir Walter Scott. Mérimée is best
known, however, for his short stories and novellas—"Ma-
teo Falcone" (1829; Eng. trans., 1903), *Colomba* (1840;
Eng. trans., 1856), and *Carmen* (1845; Eng. trans.,
1878), on which Bizet's opera is based.

Merionethshire   see GWYNEDD

Merleau-Ponty, Maurice [mair-loh-pohn-tee', moh-
rees'] Maurice Merleau-Ponty, b. Mar. 14, 1908, d.
May 4, 1961, a French phenomenologist and social critic, is regarded as one of the finest phenomenologists to
have worked in the tradition of Edmund HUSSERL, a reputation that is based primarily on his two early works, *The
Structure of Behavior* (1942; Eng. trans., 1963) and *The
Phenomenology of Perception* (1945; Eng. trans., 1962).
Unlike Husserl, Merleau-Ponty focused on the world-re-
ferring structures of perception rather than the internal
organization of consciousness. His PHENOMENOLOGY is
unique in that he refutes certain idealistic suppositions
that characterize classical phenomenology.

After a period of political collaboration with Jean Paul
SARTRE, Merleau-Ponty argued (1955) that history was ir-
reducibly plural and that no single movement, not even
Marxism (with which he remained sympathetic), could be
regarded as the exclusive agency of historical progress.

Merlin   In stories of King ARTHUR AND ARTHURIAN LEG-
END, Merlin was a sorcerer and counselor of Uther Pen-
dragon and his son Arthur. It was on Merlin's advice that
Uther established the Round Table and found his true
heir through the sword-in-the-stone test. Merlin disappeared when the Lady of the Lake, using magic he taught
her, imprisoned him in an enchanted thornbush. Merlin
represents an amalgamation of a Celtic sky deity and a
Welsh or British bard of about AD 500.

mermaid   In European folklore a mermaid is a supernatural sea creature shaped like a woman from the waist
up but with the tail of a fish. The appearance of mermaids is generally associated with human catastrophe,

and, like the Greek SIRENS, they are sometimes said to
lure sailors to their deaths. Many folktales, however, tell
of romance or marriage between mermaids and mortal
men. Although mermaids probably originated in Celtic
mythology, in medieval symbolism they represented the
dual nature of Jesus Christ.

Merman, Ethel   Ethel Merman, stage name of Ethel
Zimmerman, b. Astoria, N.Y., Jan. 16, 1909, d. Feb. 15,
1984, was an American entertainer known for her brassy,
extroverted style and effortless ability to belt out energetic songs. Merman became an overnight star after appearing in the Broadway musical *Girl Crazy* (1930). Later
musical comedy successes included *Anything Goes*
(1934; film, 1936), *Du Barry Was a Lady* (1939), *Panama Hattie* (1940), *Annie Get Your Gun* (1946), *Call Me
Madam* (1950; film, 1953), and *Gypsy* (1959).

Merman also appeared frequently on television. She
won the New York Drama Critics Award three times and
Tony Awards in 1951 and 1972.

Meroë [mair'-oh-ee]   Meroë was an ancient African
kingdom and the capital city of CUSH, located on the east
bank of the Nile in the northern province of the Sudan,
north of Khartoum. The kings of Napata ruled there from
the mid-8th century BC until 300 BC, and the city-state
flourished until about AD 350. It was the center of an
iron-smelting industry and may have been a source of the
spread of iron-casting techniques in ancient Africa. Extensively excavated, the site revealed royal palaces, temples to Amon and Isis, and a group of pyramids.

Merovingian art and architecture [mair-oh-vin'-
jee-uhn]   Merovingian art and architecture comprises the
artifacts and structures created in the period from the
conversion to Christianity in 496 of CLOVIS and his Frankish followers, the new rulers of Roman Gaul (France and
some adjacent areas), until 751, when Clovis's last descendant of the Merovingian family was deposed by the
new Carolingian dynasty (see CAROLINGIAN ART AND ARCHITEC-
TURE). This little-documented period saw the gradual decay
of the Late Roman artistic tradition and the appearance
of new forms and techniques, some brought by the new
Germanic settlers and others imported from the creative
centers of the Near East, especially Egypt and Syria.

Architecture. Few buildings survive, but excavations
have established that most churches continued the various Early Christian types (see EARLY CHRISTIAN ART AND AR-
CHITECTURE), among which the BASILICA held pride of place,
although often betraying in details—such as chapels
flanking the apse—the influence of contemporary Syria.
Best preserved is the 5th-century Church of Saint Pierre
(now Musée Lapidaire Romain) at Vienne, in southeast
France. Similarly the 7th-century Baptistery of Saint Jean
at Poitiers, in west central France, incorporates forms of
classical architecture in a decorative but poorly integrated

fashion. The ornamentation of the Hypogée des Dunes (Crypt of the Dunes) at Poitiers—a 7th-century underground chamber serving as an abbot's mausoleum and memorial chapel—is a rich and fascinating mixture of Christian subjects with magical inscriptions and symbolic or protective carvings, often of fantastical animals.

Sculpture. During the Merovingian period workshops in Aquitaine continued to carve marble capitals of debased classical types that were shipped by water throughout France. The area east of Paris supplied stone sarcophagi for a wide area, of which the most impressive and interesting are three 7th-century sarcophagi in the crypt of the Abbey of Jouarre near Paris. That of the Abbess Theodechilde is covered with rows of seashells carved with great precision and elegance and has a long inscription of almost equally fine classical appearance.

Decorative Arts. Among the finest achievements of Merovingian art were objects of personal adornment buried with the dead, such as buckles, fibulae, and sword mounts. Those intended for royalty were made of heavy gold inset with jewels, and similar objects were executed in bronze and iron for less exalted personages. The same taste for brilliant color, rich materials, and simple, abstract form was also manifested in such works for the Christian church as large altar crosses, chalices, patens, book covers, and reliquaries, for example, the splendid reliquary casket of Teuderigus (late 7th century; Abbey Treasury, Saint Maurice d'Agaune, Switzerland).

Several monasteries founded by Irish monks—including those at Luxeuil and Corbie in France and Saint Gall in Switzerland—produced ILLUMINATED MANUSCRIPTS, in which the primary decorations are enlarged initial letters made of animals intertwined and combined in curious ways. The best works, such as the *Gellone Sacramentary* (c.790–95; Bibliothèque Nationale, Paris), exhibit familiarity with Mediterranean art as well as with the regional Germanic tradition.

Merovingians (dynasty)   The Merovingians were the first dynasty of FRANKS to rule most of what is today France and parts of western Germany and the Low Countries. The dynasty took its name from Merovech, a chief of the Salian Franks. He was the father of Childeric I (d. 481), whose son CLOVIS (r. 481–511) established Frankish rule over most of GAUL and converted to Roman Christianity.

When Clovis died, his kingdom was divided, according to Frankish custom, among his four sons: Theodoric (d. 534), Chlodomer (d. 524), Childebert I (d. 558), and Chlotar I (d. 561), who made their respective headquarters at Metz, Orléans, Paris, and Soissons. From 558 to 561 the Frankish territories were reunited under Chlotar I, but on his death the kingdom was divided again. His sons, Charibert I (d. 567), Sigibert I (d. 575), Guntran (d. 592), and Chilperic I (d. 584), received the territories of AQUITAINE, Austrasia, BURGUNDY, and Neustria, respectively. Sigibert and Chilperic began a long and savage war with each other, which was ultimately won by Chilperic's

family. Chiperic's grandson Dagobert I, king of all the Franks from 629 to 639, was the last Merovingian king of consequence. After Dagobert's death the kings of the Merovingian dynasty became captives of various magnate families. The most successful of these families, the CAROLINGIANS, finally overthrew the Merovingians in 751 and established their own dynasty.

Merrick, David   The most successful American theatrical producer of the mid-20th century, David Merrick, b. David Margulois in St. Louis, Mo., Nov. 27, 1912, was educated for the law but after 1954 devoted much of his life to the theater, producing more than 70 musicals and plays in little more than 20 years. These included such hits as *Fanny* (1954), *Becket* (1960), *Hello Dolly!* (1964), *Marat/Sade* (1965), *Travesties* (1975), and *42nd Street* (1980). Known for his business acumen and flair for creating publicity, Merrick has been described as the P. T. Barnum of Broadway producers.

Merrill, James   James Ingram Merrill, b. New York City, Mar. 3, 1926, has written numerous volumes of poetry and other works, including the novel *The (Diblos) Notebook* (1965). His poetry, which uses puns and allusions to capture a refined sensibility, exhibits dazzling wit. Merrill explores his childhood and problems of memory and identity: the self is haunted by contemporary history in *The Fire Screen* (1969) and by the richness of social life in *Nights and Days* (1966). The long poem *Divine Comedies* (1976) explores parapsychological phenomena. Merrill's later works include *The Changing Light at Sandover* (1982).

Merrill, Robert   The baritone Robert Merrill, b. Brooklyn, N.Y., June 4, 1917, first studied voice with his mother and then sang popular music on radio and in clubs before turning to opera. He made his debut at the Metropolitan Opera in 1945 as the elder Germont in Verdi's *La Traviata*, then subsequently sang most of the important roles for baritone with that company. Witty and eloquent, Merrill became a popular recitalist and a frequent guest on television talk shows.

Merrimack   see MONITOR AND MERRIMACK

Mersey, River [mur'-zee]   The River Mersey, formed by the confluence of the rivers Goyt and Tame, rising in the Pennines, begins at Stockport, England. Over its 113-km (70-mi) course, it flows west past the suburbs of Manchester to Liverpool, where it enters the Irish Sea. The river drains a 2,292-km^2 (885-mi^2) area. Its estuary, almost 5 km (3 mi) wide, is tidal to Warrington and open to oceangoing vessels. The river is an important commercial artery. A railroad tunnel and two road tunnels run under the river connecting Birkenhead to Liverpool.

Merton, Robert   The sociologist Robert King Merton, b. Philadelphia, July 5, 1910, has taught at Harvard (1934–39), Tulane (1939–41), and Columbia (1941–79) universities. In *Social Theory and Social Structure* (1949; rev. ed., 1968), his most influential work, Merton holds that anomie and deviant behavior result when a society does not offer individuals the means to realize the aspirations it has given rise to. His widely admired *On the Shoulders of Giants* (1965) is a witty and wide-ranging discourse on the nature of knowledge and the history of its transmission.

Merton, Thomas   A monk and a prominent writer, Thomas Merton, b. Prades, France, Jan. 31, 1915, d. Dec. 10, 1968, became one of the most famous American Roman Catholics of the 20th century. After teaching English for a while and working in a Harlem settlement house, Merton decided (1941) to become a monk, choosing the Trappist order for its discipline of silence and solitude. His writing, which includes poetry, meditations, and works of social criticism, brought him prominence in American letters. His autobiography, *The Seven Storey Mountain* (1948), became a best-seller. Merton gained permission to attend an ecumenical conference of Buddhist and Christian monks held in Bangkok, Thailand. While attending that meeting, he was accidentally electrocuted.

Merv [myairf]   Merv, an ancient city of central Asia, now in Turkmenia, USSR, flourished as a capital of Abbasid and Seljuk rulers in the Middle Ages. In Persian legend Merv was the birthplace of humankind. Situated in an oasis on the Murghab River, it was an important post on trade routes to the east from before the 3d century BC. Captured by Muslims in AD 651, it became a major center of Islamic learning under the ABBASIDS. Under Seljuk control from the 11th to the 13th century, Merv was destroyed by the Mongols in 1221. It was later under Turkmen control until it was occupied in 1884 by the Russians. The modern city, about 30 km (19 mi) from the ancient site, was renamed Mary in 1937.

Merwin, W. S.   William Stanley Merwin, b. New York City, Sept. 30, 1927, is one of America's most prolific poets and translators. His own poetry began conventionally, but with the publication of *The Lice* (1967) his style changed. The later style, heavily weighted with the concerns of the mythological imagination, presents an interior life obsessed with breaking through to its emotional foundations. Merwin's language is spare, almost toneless at times, recalling the neutral vocabulary of translators. His translations, highly acclaimed, are mainly of poetry in Romance languages. *Unframed Originals: Recollections* (1982) is an autobiographical prose work. *The Rain in the Trees* and *Selected Poems* (both 1988) are volumes of verse.

Meryon, Charles [mair-yohn', sharl]   The French artist Charles Meryon, b. Nov. 23, 1821, d. February 1868, was one of the greatest etchers of the 19th century. Meryon is best known for his cityscapes of Paris and Bourges, for example, *Eaux-Fortes sur Paris* (Etchings of Paris, 1852–54), which portrayed the brooding melancholy of the monuments of Paris with an almost photographic attention to detail, sharpened by strongly contrasting tonal qualities. The hallucinatory mood of the scenes reflected Meryon's deteriorating mental condition, which eventually led to his suicide.

Mesa [may'-suh]   Mesa (1990 pop., 288,091) is a suburban city in southwestern Arizona about 25 km (15 mi) east of Phoenix. Its principal industry is packing and shipping citrus fruit and vegetables grown nearby; electronics and airplane parts are also manufactured. Mesa was settled in 1878 by Mormons.

Mesa Verde National Park [may'-suh vair'-dee]   Mesa Verde National Park, located in southwestern Colo-

Mesa Verde National Park, in southwest Colorado, was established in 1906 to preserve the prehistoric Indian cliff dwellings. The most spectacular ruins are those of the Cliff Palace, with its multistoried apartments and subterranean sacred rooms, or kivas. It was occupied from c.1100 to 1300.

rado about 45 km (28 mi) west of Durango and encompassing an area of 210 km^2 (81 mi^2), is a major site of prehistoric cliff dwellings and open pueblos of the ANASAZI Indians. Its name (Spanish for "green table") is derived from the park's typical land formations of steep rock walls and flat tops (mesas). Established in 1906, the park is open to visitors all year.

Hundreds of ruins and artifacts document nearly 1,000 years of cultural development at the site. Archaeologists distinguish four periods. From some time after AD 1 until AD 400, the people called Basket Maker II lived in caves and pithouses. They grew beans, corn, and squash on the mesa tops and kept domesticated dogs and turkeys. The Basket Maker III period, in which pottery was introduced and house construction began, lasted from the 5th until the mid-8th century. During the Pueblo I and II periods, from the mid-8th until the 11th century, the inhabitants began to build pueblos, rectangular apartmentlike stone houses often arranged in several stories. The Pueblo III period, lasting from the 12th until the beginning of the 14th century, is noted for the construction of the Mesa Verde immense cliff dwellings, communal habitations built of stone, mud mortar, and wood on the ledges of the cliffs and protected by rock overhangs.

The most impressive of the ruins is the Cliff Palace, which was excavated in 1909. Other notable ruins are Balcony House, Spruce Tree House, and Square Tower House, all built during the 12th and 13th centuries.

After AD 1300 the inhabitants of Mesa Verde abandoned their villages and moved away, perhaps because of raids by hostile nomads, perhaps because of prolonged periods of extreme drought. For centuries the cliff dwellings were abandoned and forgotten, but at the end of the 19th century they were discovered by cowboys and subsequently excavated.

Mesabi Range [muh-sah'-bee] The Mesabi Range, a series of low hills in northeastern Minnesota, is a large iron-ore source. The range extends for about 160 km (100 mi), and its highest point reaches approximately 600 m (2,000 ft). High-grade hematite was discovered there in 1887 and was mined from open pits until the 1950s, when most had been removed.

mescaline see HALLUCINOGENS; PEYOTE

Meshed see MASHHAD

Mesmer, Franz Anton [mes'-mur, frahnts ahn'-tohn] Franz Anton Mesmer, b. May 23, 1734, d. Mar. 5, 1815, was an Austrian physician who believed that magnetism emanated from the stars and from animals, as well as from iron. Often accused of being a magician and charlatan, Mesmer treated neurotic patients using iron magnets and HYPNOSIS, which he originated. Hypnosis, or "mes-

merism," later became an accepted psychotherapeutic technique.

Mesoamerica [mes'-oh-uh-mair'-i-kuh] *Mesoamerica* is a term for the culture area occupied by the native peoples of central and southern Mexico, Guatemala, Belize, and western Honduras and El Salvador. They and their pre-Columbian ancestors—the AZTEC, MAYA, MIXTEC, OLMEC, TOLTEC, and ZAPOTEC, to name a few—also represent an ancient cultural tradition. Shared features of this tradition, largely obscured since the Spanish conquest, once ranged from farming systems and religious beliefs to specific types of buildings, tools, and artistic ornament.

See also: INDIANS, AMERICAN; PRE-COLUMBIAN ART AND ARCHITECTURE.

Mesolithic Period [mes-oh-lith'-ik] *Mesolithic* ("middle stone") refers to the period in European prehistory immediately following the Pleistocene Epoch, when microlithic (small) chipped stone tools became common and NEOLITHIC farming and herding practices had not yet replaced the traditional PALEOLITHIC subsistence pattern based on hunting and gathering. *Mesolithic* has also been used to refer to a wide variety of early Holocene (early post-Pleistocene) tool cultures outside of Europe that share some of the European Mesolithic traits; however, their diversity is such that the term is no longer widely used in this context.

The development of the European Mesolithic took place concurrently with major environmental changes starting about 8300 BC, according to radiometric age-dating. The onset then of the warmer climate of the Holocene brought the retreat of the glacial sheet from northern Europe, a rise in sea level, and the gradual replacement of the herbaceous steppes and tundras by forests.

The Mesolithic descendants of the late Pleistocene hunters and gatherers varied in their adaptation to the new environmental conditions. Those in southwestern, central, and southeastern Europe were apparently not particularly innovative, and the evidence recovered from sites in France of the Tardenoisian culture, for instance, has been interpreted by some investigators to indicate both a population decrease and a cultural impoverishment. In contrast, on the northern European plains the Maglemosian settlements, in particular, left evidence of the activities of pioneering and technologically inventive groups spreading within the recently deglaciated areas, especially along the Scandinavian coasts.

The major adaptive changes generally characteristic of the European Mesolithic included a shift from the hunting of herd animals such as the reindeer to the exploitation of more solitary woodland species such as the European elk and the deer. Evidence also indicates the increasing importance of fish, shellfish, crustaceans, seals, and seabirds. Unfortunately, few data have been pre-

An artist's reconstruction depicts the Mesolithic settlement at Lepenski Vir (c.5000–4600 BC), on a terrace beside the Danube River in the Iron Gates gorge in Yugoslavia. The inhabitants are believed to have been hunters and gatherers. The closely spaced trapezoidal houses faced the river; they had wood and stone walls and red or white plastered floors.

served on the use of plants.

The main technological feature of the European Mesolithic is the widespread use of geometric microliths and bladelets or microblades. These diminutive flints were inserted singly or in sets on arrows, spears, and sickles, as well as in other bone, antler, and wooden implements. Because flint yields a very hard and sharp edge when chipped, the manufacture of these microlithic tools, which are effectively all edge and which in addition could be replaced individually (as bits are changed in modern tools), constituted a major technological advance. New or improved implements in bone and antler were also produced at this time, especially in the north European settlements, and included spears, harpoon and leister heads, barbless fishhooks, needles, and mattock heads. New woodworking tools—such as axes and adzes with stone heads made by chipping, pecking, and polishing—were used to fashion dugout canoes, paddles, bows, and fletched arrows.

The few sites that have been sufficiently excavated seem to indicate prolonged occupation of the same locality. That the Mesolithic represents a successful ecological adaptation can best be seen from the fact that it persisted in several parts of northern Europe for at least 2 to 3 millennia after 6000 BC, when the farming of cereals and the herding of goats and sheep had already started to spread from the Near East.

meson [mee'-zahn]　A meson is a subatomic FUNDAMENTAL PARTICLE of the HADRON class. In current theory, mesons are composed of QUARK-antiquark pairs, held together by GLUONS, and are susceptible to all four of the FUNDAMENTAL INTERACTIONS. The existence of a meson was conjectured in 1935 by Hideki Yukawa of Japan to account for the cohesive force that binds nuclear constituents together. This meson, the pi meson, or pion, was discovered in 1947. It has a mass about 270 times greater than the electron yet is about seven times smaller than the proton. Its lifetime is about ten billionths of a second. Since then several other mesons have been discovered, including K-mesons, eta mesons, and omega mesons. Predictions and discoveries of mesons are closely tied to developments in quark theory. In 1983 the long-sought B-meson was discovered. It contains a very heavy b-quark, making it more than five times as heavy as a proton. Its lifetime is about one trillionth of a second.

Mesopotamia [mes-uh-puh-tay'-mee-uh]   Mesopotamia (Greek for "land between the rivers") refers to the region between the Tigris and Euphrates rivers, in what is now Iraq, northern Syria, and southern Turkey. The southern part of Mesopotamia was one of the areas in which civilized human societies first developed—a civilized society being one in which the dominant people live in cities, keep written records, and have a metal technology.

About 5500 BC, people in southern Mesopotamia learned to divert the waters of the Euphrates to irrigate the land for farming, which was necessary because of the area's low rainfall. Irrigation, it turned out, made the land much more productive than land watered by rainfall, thus generating an agricultural surplus that led to a concentration of wealth in the hands of a dominant class. Over time this surplus wealth was used to create the institutions characteristic of urban civilization. The people who developed this civilization were called Sumerians, and their country was known as SUMER.

The Protoliterate Period. The first cities, the most important of which was URUK, were established between c.3500 and 3100 BC. Toward the end of the period, a writing system developed, at first consisting of pictographic signs inscribed on small clay tablets and then more stylized signs, known today as CUNEIFORM. Sumerian, the language of these earliest written documents, is unrelated to any other known language. The ruling classes of this formative age used their accumulated wealth to construct large brick buildings, many of them apparently devoted to religious purposes. (For information on Mesopotamian religion, see MYTHOLOGY.)

The Early Dynastic Period. The period from about 3000 BC to 2300 BC is called the Early Dynastic period because it is the earliest time for which historians possess infor-

Mesopotamia, an ancient country of Asia, extended from the Persian Gulf northward to the mountains of Armenia. The "land between the rivers," bounded by the Tigris and Euphrates rivers, flourished from c.3000 BC until the Persian conquest in 539 BC.

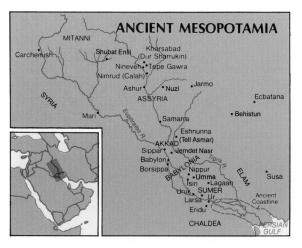

ANCIENT MESOPOTAMIA

(Above) *The law code of Hamurabi, king of Babylonia, is recorded on this stele, which also bears a relief portrait of the king standing before Shamash, the god of justice.* (Above, left) *A detail from the stele shows part of the code's text in cuneiform script.* (Left) *This black granite head is believed to be a portrait of the great lawgiver. (Louvre, Paris.)*

mation about the ruling dynasties of Mesopotamia. Cities now grew in size and were surrounded by walls, as more people from the surrounding villages moved into them.

The Early Dynastic period is divided into three phases. Later generations remembered Early Dynastic I (ending c.2700 BC) as a time of recovery from a disastrous flood, or DELUGE, the story of which is told in Mesopotamia epics as well as in the Bible. According to one theory, Early Dynastic Sumer was governed by a league of cities that met in the religious center of NIPPUR, near modern Baghdad, to decide issues democratically. In addition to Uruk and Nippur, other major cities of the period included KISH, LAGASH, UR, and Umma.

Early Dynastic II (c.2700–2500 BC) was a heroic age in which rulers, especially those of Uruk, were remembered as having had great adventures involving travel to distant places. GILGAMESH, a semilegendary figure who is one of the great heroes of Mesopotamian tradition, was one of these.

In Early Dynastic III (c.2500–2300 BC) the bureaucracy grew, tablets from Lagash revealing an administration that was bent on recording all its resources; they also show that much of the wealth of Lagash remained in private hands. At this time the symbols used in cuneiform writing, previously arranged in random order, began to be recorded in the order in which they were pronounced, a change that greatly increased the efficiency of the writing system.

The Old Akkadian and Neo-Sumerian Periods. Warfare and attempts at aggrandizement were frequent among the small states of southern Mesopotamia. The first systematic imperialist, the Akkadian king SARGON, came from farther north. About 2350 or 2300 BC he conquered the Sumerian cities, ruling from his capital, Agade or AKKAD, which gave its name both to his empire and to its Semitic language. The name Sargon (Sharruken), meaning "True King" or "the king is legitimate," was probably adopted to counter his image as a usurper.

Sargon imposed a bureaucracy on his empire and established centralized control. Archaeological remains from this period include large numbers of cuneiform tablets in Akkadian recording the activities of his administration. Later sources claim that Sargon campaigned as far up the Euphrates as modern Turkey, but contemporary evidence does not indicate such far-reaching conquests. The influence of his grandson, Naram-Sin, however, extended west into Syria and east as far as Susa in present-day Iran. Parts of the empire remained loyal to Sargon's heirs until c.2150 BC, when mountain tribespeople called the Gutians overthrew the Sargonic kingdom and imposed

This winged, human-headed bull, representing a guardian spirit, stood at the entrance to the palace of the Assyrian king Sargon II at Khorsabad. Unearthed in the 1840s by the pioneer Mesopotamian archaeologist Paul Émile Botta, it was one of the first examples of ancient Mesopotamian art to be discovered. (Louvre, Paris.)

their rule on part of the south.

Utu-hegal of Uruk claimed credit for expelling the Gutians, and one of his officials, UR-NAMMU of Ur, established an empire. Smaller but probably better organized than Sargon's realm, it is called the Neo-Sumerian empire because most of its royal inscriptions and administrative texts were written in the old language, Sumerian, rather than in Akkadian. However, Sumerian at this time may have survived only as a written, rather than a spoken, language. Ur-Nammu's son Shulgi (r. c.2094–2047 BC) systematized the administration, and from his reign until 2000 BC an exceptionally large number of documents, dealing with such things as legal decisions, taxation, prices paid by merchants, and the lives and salaries of

The discoveries of Paul Émile Botta and Austen Layard captured the imagination of 19th-century Europe. In this rendering, an illustrator of the time created a romanticized picture of life in the ancient Assyrian city of Nimrud (Calah), excavated by Layard from 1845 to 1851.

semifree persons who worked as serfs for the government, have been recovered.

The Neo-Sumerian period ended with another bid for autonomy by the subject city-states and another invasion by mountain peoples, who did not, however, establish any lasting domination over the south.

The Old Babylonian and Kassite Periods. The successors to the Ur dynasty were from a new ethnic group, the Amorites ("Westerners"), who spoke their own Semitic language but wrote in Akkadian and Sumerian. In the first phase of this period (*c.*2000–1763 BC), the rival southern kingdoms of Larsa and Isin maneuvered against each other and tried to form alliances with other cities. Larsa eventually emerged as the winner but was in turn defeated by HAMMURABI (r. *c.*1792–1750 BC), ruler of the hitherto obscure central Mesopotamian city of BABYLON, who founded the Old Babylonian empire, which extended as far north as MARI in present-day Syria. Hammurabi is best known as the author of the law code that bears his name, which was probably intended as a political document showing the king's wise decisions rather than as a codification for use in courts. After Hammurabi's death, his son soon lost control of the south, but Babylon remained a powerful state until the conquest of central Mesopotamia by the HITTITES *c.*1600 BC.

The Hittite invasion marks the beginning of the Dark Age of Mesopotamian history, a period of disorganization that probably lasted for about a century and a half. When order was reestablished after 1500 BC, Babylon reemerged as the dominant city of central and southern Mesopotamia, or BABYLONIA. The successors of the Old Babylonian kings were the KASSITES, a new ethnic group who, like the Sumerians, spoke a language not related to any other. They probably constituted a very small ruling class, and their goal was to carry on earlier Mesopotamian traditions. Their success is shown by the fact that they reigned longer than any other Mesopotamian dynasty, from about 1495 until 1155 BC.

From northern Mesopotamia around the modern city of Mosul, rulers of the city of Ashur began raiding into the south and west after 1363 BC and established themselves as a regional power. These Assyrians, along with the Kassites, corresponded with the kings of Egypt, who were interested in maintaining stability in Syria and Palestine. The Assyrian kings depicted themselves as warlike heroes, but with a couple of exceptions the pacific Kassite kings held their own against their incursions.

The latter part of the Kassite period witnessed the rise of ELAM in western Iran, which was centrally administered from the city of Susa. The most vigorous Elamite king, Shutruk-Nahhunte (r. 1165–1158 BC), waged war in Babylonia, and his successor eliminated the last Kassite king.

The Assyrian Empire. Around 1100 BC the ARAMAEANS, perhaps migrants from the Arabian desert, emerged in western Asia. They never formed large states, but their language permeated everywhere and became the lingua franca for trade and diplomacy in most of the region. The Aramaeans' arrival disrupted the power of ASSYRIA in northern Mesopotamia, but the Assyrians maintained their dynasty, and the heartland remained loyal to the kings. With the accession of ASHURNASIRPAL II in 883 BC, the Assyrians began to make sweeps south and west to plunder their neighbors' cities. The Assyrian army, trained in an ethic of egalitarianism between officers and men,

This photograph shows an excavated section of the palace area at Babylon that is identified by some authorities as the remains of the famous Hanging Gardens of Babylon. These gardens, constructed on artificial terraces, were classified by Greek writers as one of the Seven Wonders of the Ancient World. According to the Jewish historian Flavius Josephus, they were built by King Nebuchadnezzar II for his wife, a Median princess, to remind her of the green hills of her native land. Other ancient sources attribute the Hanging Gardens to Semiramis, a legendary queen of Assyria.

developed into one of the most effective siege instruments in history.

The army penetrated ever farther west, and the imperial ideology allowed it to incorporate smaller states into the Assyrian system. Most non-Assyrians opposed the process, and the picture of the Assyrians found in Amos and Isaiah is one that was shared by most peoples: they were viewed as horrible and dangerous, to be resisted if possible and negotiated with if necessary. Coalitions of states in the west resisted Assyrian expansionism, notably at Qarqar in Syria in 853 BC, but from 883 to 640 BC the trend was in Assyrias' favor.

The Assyrian king TIGLATH-PILESER III (r. 745–727 BC) intervened in kingdoms as far away as the Mediterranean. He was succeeded by a short-lived king, Shalmaneser V (r. 727–722 BC), whom the Bible credits with the destruction of the northern kingdom of ISRAEL (2 Kings 17). His successor (r. 722–705 BC) took the name SARGON II, probably because, like the first Sargon of Akkad, he was a usurper. He spent his life in the field, campaigning not only in the west but also in the north, in what is now eastern Turkey, against the kingdom of URARTU. In 714 BC he defeated Urartu and incorporated it into the Assyrian empire.

Subsequent kings, all descended from Sargon, expanded the provinces even farther. SENNACHERIB (r. 705–681 BC) sacked Babylon, and ESARHADDON (r. 680–669 BC) conquered Egypt. The last effective Neo-Assyrian king, ASHURBANIPAL (r. 668–626 BC), assembled a library for the use of his court diviners and perhaps for his own use.

To this library, discovered in 1850 by Sir Austen Henry Layard in the ruins of Ashurbanipal's capital at NINEVEH, the modern world owes a large part of its knowledge of Akkadian and Sumerian literature. It contained as many as 1,200 clay tablets. The king had Babylonian scribes copy old stories, and from this project came the fullest version of the Epic of Gilgamesh, the Early Dynastic ruler of Uruk. The major interest in the library was in texts about omens. The Assyrians, like earlier Mesopotamians, believed that the future could be predicted from ominous events; the most popular type of omen was derived from observing the livers of freshly sacrificed sheep.

Tablets from Ashurbanipal's library also included dictionaries that have proved important for the study of monolingual Sumerian texts; these lexical texts list Sumerian words and frequently translate them into Akkadian and sometimes give pronunciations of the Sumerian. The texts show that the Sumerian language continued to be read as a medium of knowledge, although, like Latin in the Middle Ages, it had ceased to be anyone's first language. It is likely that by the Neo-Assyrian period even Akkadian had been supplanted by Aramaic as a spoken language, though it remained the language of literature.

The Neo-Babylonian Empire. Assyria's decline began about 640 BC because of pressure from MEDIA, which had become the dominant kingdom east of Mesopotamia. The Medes attacked Assyria in 621 BC and, aided by the Babylonians and other allies, captured Nineveh, the Assyrian capital, in 612 BC.

Southern Mesopotamia was seized by Nabopolassar, a general who had worked for the Assyrians and now set himself up as king of Babylon; Nabopolassar was a Chaldean, that is, an Aramaic-speaking city-dweller of southern Mesopotamia (see CHALDEA). He controlled the south from 625 to 605 BC and was succeeded by his vigorous son, NEBUCHADNEZZAR (r. 605–562 BC), who asserted Babylonian claims to all the area previously dominated by the Neo-Assyrians in the southern half of western Asia. Nebuchadnezzar eliminated many kingdoms in the west, including the southern Jewish kingdom of JUDAH in 587 BC, and deported their leaders to Babylonia (see BABYLONIAN CAPTIVITY). He built temples and established a museum in Babylon for the trophies he had won. His most famous building project was the Hanging Gardens of Babylon, one of the SEVEN WONDERS OF THE WORLD.

Nebuchadnezzar's successors found themselves outmaneuvered by the Persian king CYRUS THE GREAT and lost control of more and more of their new empire. The last, Nabonidus (r. 555–539 BC), was defeated by Cyrus in 539 BC, and the Persians occupied Babylonia, thus ending the last independent kingdom of ancient Mesopotamia.

Mesopotamia under Foreign Domination. The ACHAEMENID Persian empire, greater in area than any previous Near Eastern empire, was accepted by most of the people of western Asia as a benign force; the Persians tried self-consciously to win the favor of their subject peoples and to respect local sensibilities. Uniting Iran, Mesopotamia, Syria, Anatolia, and Egypt, the new rulers created an economy that unified the whole region and led to unparalleled prosperity. Unfortunately, Mesopotamia was no longer at the center of this world, and its concerns were relatively neglected as they would be by all subsequent powers that conquered the area down to the Arab conquest of the 7th century AD.

Mesopotamian Cultural Legacy. The ancient Mesopotamians left a rich legacy to the Western world. The Babylonians were pioneers in mathematics and astronomy. The sexagesimal system of the Sumerians is used in

The Ziggurat of Ur was built by King Ur-Nammu in the Neo-Sumerian, or Ur III, period (c.2100–2000 BC). Dedicated to the moon god, Nannar, it exemplifies the classic temple tower of Mesopotamia, a type of architecture that endured for nearly 2,000 years.

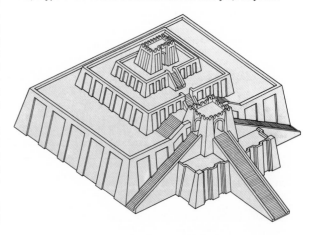

modern astronomy and timekeeping (60 seconds = one minute, 60 minutes = one hour). Mesopotamian literature had a strong influence on many portions of the Hebrew Bible and also contributed to Greek mythology.

Although Mesopotamian architecture has not endured so well as that of other ancient civilizations because of the mud brick of which it was constructed, the achievements of Mesopotamian architects were nevertheless impressive. Major development (c.3500 BC) was the creation of artificial terraces on which temples were built and which were probably meant to outline precincts considered sacred. The temple terrace evolved into a kind of pedestal for the temple, which in Akkadian was called a ZIGGURAT, or temple tower. Several of these temples have been preserved, the most impressive of which is at Ur. Because the temples that were once atop the ziggurats have eroded, it is not known how they actually looked.

Large palaces have been found at Mari on the Euphrates near the Syrian-Iraqi border and at Khorsabad in Assyria. Sargon II's palace, dating from about 715 BC, is a typical example built around courtyards and containing many smaller rooms that had various purposes.

Mesopotamian cities were first surrounded by walls in the Early Dynastic period (3000–2300 BC). Their gates were sometimes quite elaborate structures with several chambers designed to make it hard for attackers to take the gate in one rush. The most opulent was the Ishtar gate at Babylon, from the Neo-Babylonian period.

Mesopotamian art is attested in statuary, reliefs, murals, and cylinder seals. Statues of humans and animals from the Old Akkadian period (2300–2150 BC) begin to take on lifelike qualities. But probably nothing surpasses the Neo-Assyrian wall reliefs that decorated the royal palaces at Nimrud and Khorsabad. These depict the glories of the ruler and his skill at hunting and other lordly pursuits. Murals instead of reliefs decorate the earlier palace of Mari (c.1800 BC), where the king is shown at work and play in colors still vivid.

Cylinder seals were small stone cylinders carved so as to make an impression on clay tablets when rolled across them. They served as signatures for important Mesopotamians and sometimes reveal great ingenuity and grace on a very small scale. They often depicted the struggles of heroes and animals, or the seal owner as a worshiper being led before a god.

Mesopotamian Archaeology. Although earlier travelers to Mesopotamia had observed the existence of ruins and antiquities, the real investigation of sites began only with the work of European enthusiasts in the 19th century. Paul Émile Botta, French consul in Mosul in the 1840s, discovered in the ruins of Assyrian Khorsabad the colossal winged human-headed bulls that are now in the Louvre in Paris. A British officer, Henry Creswicke Rawlinson, scaled the cliff at BEHISTUN in Iran and accurately copied a trilingual cuneiform inscription of Darius I, the Persian and Akkadian parts of which he and others later deciphered. Austen Layard, a British diplomat, in 1849–51 uncovered at Kuyunjik (Nineveh) Ashurbanipal's library, which is now in the British Museum in London. By the end of the 19th century the earlier Sumerian civilization

The magnificent Ishtar Gate of Babylon, decorated with glazed tiles and animal reliefs, was built in the 6th century BC by Nebuchadnezzar II and reconstructed by the German archaeologist Robert Koldewey. (Staatliche Museen, Berlin.)

had been discovered, and since the early 20th century a more scientific approach to excavation and documentation has characterized archaeological expeditions in Mesopotamia.

mesosphere [mes'-uhs-feer]   The warm stratopause, about 0° C (32° F) in temperature and existing roughly 50 km (30 mi) above sea level, and the cold mesopause, about –90° C (–130° F) and 80 km (50 mi) above sea level, form the lower and upper boundaries of the mesosphere. The decrease of temperature with increasing altitude, as within the troposphere, is caused by absorption of solar radiation at the base (the ozone layer and the Earth's surface, respectively) and the adiabatic cooling of rising air parcels. The actual temperature at the mesopause behaves in a strange manner. Above the poles, the winter temperatures are about –30° C (–20° F), not much different from those at the polar surfaces. The upper mesospheric summer temperatures, however, can be as low as –140° C (–96° F), which are the lowest temperatures naturally occurring on Earth. Solar absorption apparently does not take place near the mesopause.

Mesozoic Era see EARTH, GEOLOGICAL HISTORY OF; GEO-LOGIC TIME

mesquite [mes'-keet] Mesquites are 25 to perhaps 40 species of spiny shrubs or trees of the genus *Prosopis,* in the pea family, Leguminosae. They are found in the warm, usually drier regions of the Americas, with one species in Africa and two in Asia. The common mesquite of the southwestern United States and northern Mexico is usually classified as *P. juliflora,* but some authorities believe that it actually should be classified as *P. glandulosa.* The common mesquite varies from a tree 15 m (50 ft) high, where water is adequate, to a small shrub in very arid locations. Its leaves are commonly divided into two stalks, each bearing many small leaflets. The greenish white flowers, produced in dense, narrow spikes, mature into long pods with seeds that can be made into flour.

Messene [mes-ee'-nee] Messene (also called Ithome), in the southwest Peloponnesus, Greece, was a heavily fortified city of ancient Arcadia founded (369 BC) by Epaminondas as part of a strategic barrier against Spartan expansion. Its remains include well-preserved walls that were famed as among the strongest fortifications of Greek antiquity. The ancient site (at the modern village of Mavromati) covered 9 km^2 (3.5 mi^2) including the acropolis (Mt. Ithome) and the surrounding farmlands. The walls, designed to protect against technically advanced artillery-and-siege warfare, withstood several Macedonian and Spartan attacks in the 3d century BC. Seven of the 30 towers are well preserved, as is the Arcadian Gate.

Messerschmitt, Willy Willy Messerschmitt, b. June 26, 1898, d. Sept. 15, 1978, was a German designer and manufacturer of aircraft. After service in World War I, Messerschmitt studied aviation and engineering in Munich and established an aircraft manufacturing company in 1923, later merging with Bayerische Flugzeugwerke (BFW). After the formation of the Nazi government, Messerschmitt expanded his production to embrace military aircraft as well, notably the Bf-108; Bf-109, the most widely produced warplane of World War II; Bf-110; Me-262, the world's first operational jet fighter; Me-323, a 6-engine transport capable of carrying 18 tons; and Me-410, a fighter-bomber. He was arrested (1945) for his involvement in the Hitler regime; tried by a German denazification court (1948), he was found to be a "reluctant beneficiary" of the regime. His company returned to aviation by the mid-1950s, engaging in the coproduction of a number of NATO aircraft. The expansion of Germany's reconstituted aerospace industry has witnessed, through mergers, the formation of the Messerschmitt-Bölkow-Blohm GmbH, a German aerospace conglomerate.

Messiaen, Olivier [mes-ee-ahn', oh-liv-ee-ay'] One of the foremost French composers of the 20th century,

Olivier Messiaen, b. Avignon, Dec. 10, 1908, d. Apr. 27, 1992, was the son of the poet Cécile Sauvage and a translator of English literature. He taught himself to play the piano and began to compose at the age of 8, and at age 11 he entered the Paris Conservatory where his teachers included Marcel Dupré and Paul Dukas. In 1931 he was appointed organist of La Trinité in Paris. While a prisoner of war (1940–42) in Germany, he composed *Quatuor pour la fin du temps* (Quartet for the End of Time) for violin, clarinet, cello, and piano. After his release he joined the faculty of the Paris Conservatory.

Messiaen's music sprang from his deep Catholic mysticism. He made use of widely disparate material—from Gregorian chant and Oriental scale patterns and rhythm to electronic sounds and bird songs, of which he made a study. His music is distinguished by great rhythmic subtlety and a highly developed sense of tone color. His major works include *Vingt Regards sur l'Enfant Jésus* (Twenty Views of the Child Jesus, 1944) for piano; *Turangalîla* (1948), a 10-movement symphony for piano and an orchestra featuring a number of exotic percussion instruments; and the 13-movement *La Transfiguration de Notre Seigneur Jésus Christ* (The Transfiguration of Our Lord Jesus Christ, 1969) for a chorus in 10 parts, 7 solo instruments, and an orchestra with a huge percussion section.

messiah [muh-sy'-uh] The term *messiah* comes from the Hebrew *mashiah* ("anointed"); the Greek equivalent is *christos* (Christ). In ancient Israel it was applied to the king, who was anointed with oil to symbolize his being chosen as ruler. After the kingdom was destroyed in the 6th century BC, the Jews hoped for its restoration, and the messiah became the man whom God would send to reestablish it, the chosen descendant of King David. Alongside this "restorative" concept of the messiah, a more apocalyptic version emerged in the course of time, in which the messiah's coming would be marked by a cataclysmic rupture in the normal processes of history, accompanied by great miracles and wonders; after this, human life and the laws of nature would be radically transformed.

During the second Jewish war with Rome (AD 132–35), the military leader BAR KOCHBA was declared a messianic figure by Rabbi AKIBA BEN JOSEPH. A great deal of messianic speculation occurred after the expulsion of the Jews from Spain in 1492; Rabbi Isaac ben Judah ABRAVANEL predicted the coming of the messiah in the year 1503. SABBATAI ZEVI, who claimed messianic status, attracted followers at the time of the persecutions of Polish Jewry in the 17th century; Jacob FRANK, who founded a messianic sect in the 18th century, claimed to be a reincarnation of Sabbatai.

In the Jewish mystical tradition known as KABBALAH, messianism focused more on the initial act of divine creation than on a future "end-time." One of the great kabbalistic books, the *Zohar,* views messianic redemption as a supernatural miracle involving the gradual illumination of the world (primarily through individual persons) by the light of the messiah.

Christianity inherited the idea of messiahship from Judaism. Christians believe that JESUS CHRIST is the messiah through whom God reveals himself to the world, and the early church adopted many messianic themes from its Jewish background. "The Son of Man," a name applied to Jesus in the New Testament, is a messianic image also used in the Jewish pseudepigraphic Book of Enoch.

Messier, Charles [mes-ee-ay']   The French astronomer Charles Messier, b. June 26, 1730, d. Apr. 11 or 12, 1817, compiled the well-known Messier catalog, a famous and still-used list of celestial objects (see ASTRONOMICAL CATALOGS AND ATLASES). He was the first in France to observe Halley's comet on its return in 1759, and in subsequent years he claimed the discovery of 21 new comets. Messier compiled his catalog of extended nebulous objects in order to distinguish them from comets; as first published (1774) it contained 45 objects, but this number was increased to 68 in 1780 and 103 in 1781. The list includes star clusters, nebulae, and galaxies.

Messina [mes-see'-nah]   Messina, a busy seaport and commercial center, is the capital of Messina province, Italy, situated in northeastern Sicily. It is situated only 5 km (3 mi) across the Strait of Messina from the Italian mainland. The city's population is 270,546 (1988 est.). Messina's industries include chemical, pharmaceutical, and preserved food and other food product manufacturing. Because Messina suffered serious earthquakes in 1783 and 1908, few old buildings remain. Messina's university was founded in 1548.
   Settled in the late 8th century BC by Greek colonists, the city was first known as Zancle and later as Messana in ancient times. It was almost completely destroyed by an earthquake in 1908. During World War II, Allied forces "raced" to capture Messina in 1943 but failed to reach it in time to prevent an Axis withdrawal across the strait.

Messina, Antonello da   see ANTONELLO DA MESSINA

Messina, Strait of   The Strait of Messina (ancient Fretum Siculum) separates the southern tip of Italy from Sicily. The strait also separates the Ionian Sea from the Tyrrhenian Sea. It is about 32 km (20 mi) long and from 3 to 16 km (2 to 10 mi) wide. The dangerous tidal current and whirlpools in the strait inspired the ancient legend of SCYLLA AND CHARYBDIS.

mestizo [may-stee'-soh]   *Mestizo* is a term of vague biological and cultural classification used in many parts of the Spanish-speaking world for persons of mixed Indian and white ancestry. In Latin America its definition varies from one country to the next, and it must be understood in different cultural contexts. The term always implies that the mestizo speaks Spanish or Portuguese and that the *indio* (Indian) does not, or does not speak it as well.
   In Peru, *cholo* expresses the general sense of mestizo

and defines people who are mixtures of predominantly Indian and predominantly white parents, who are themselves offspring of mestizo parents. In both Peru and Mexico, upper-class persons of mixed ancestry are called *criolle* or *cruzado* rather than mestizo. In Brazil, a *caboclo* is a person who speaks Portuguese, lives as a storekeeper or trader in the backwoods, deals with Indians, and is mestizo. The coastal *cariocas*, although also biologically mestizo, are socially superior to the *caboclo*.

Meštrović, Ivan [mesh'-troh-vich]   Ivan Meštrović, b. Croatia, Aug. 15, 1883, d. Jan. 16, 1962, was one of the first Yugoslav sculptors to move away from academic realism. After World War I he became director of the Zagreb Academy of Art in Yugoslavia and executed the *Monument of Gregory, Bishop of Nin* (1926), an elongated bronze figure done as a gift to the city of Split, and *Monument to the Unknown Soldier* (1935–38), a large mausoleum on Mount Avala near Belgrade. His dramatically grandiose style reflected the influence of cubism as well as of ancient Assyrian and Babylonian sculpture.

metabolism   Metabolism is the sum of all the chemical reactions in the living CELL that are used for the production of useful work and the synthesis of cell constituents. Almost all cellular reactions are catalyzed by complex PROTEIN molecules called ENZYMES, which greatly speed reaction rates.
   Many structures in the living cell are of great complexity and periodically must be replaced. This process of building new molecules is called anabolism. Structures that are worn out or no longer needed are broken down into smaller molecules and either reused or excreted; this process is called catabolism. Great quantities of energy are required not only to produce the work needed for the pumping of the heart, for muscular contraction, and for nerve conduction, but also to provide the chemical work needed to make the large molecules characteristic of living cells. Anabolism and catabolism are aspects of overall metabolism, and they occur interdependently and continuously.

Basal Metabolism

In the combustion of food, oxygen (O_2) is used and carbon dioxide (CO_2) is given off. The rate of oxygen consumption indicates the energy expenditure of an organism, or its metabolic rate. The metabolic rate of any given animal at any given time is highly variable and is influenced by many diverse factors, including amount of muscular activity; quality of diet; presence or absence of digestion, lactation, or pregnancy; time of day or year; period of the menstrual cycle; and emotional state. In order to fix a point of reference, a convention has been adopted to serve as the standard metabolic rate. The ideal standard established is the metabolism of an animal under the least physiologically demanding conditions. In the case of humans, other mammals, and birds, this minimal-rate-of-energy metabolism is usually termed the *bas-*

al metabolic rate (BMR): the rate of metabolism of a fasting animal at rest and under no thermal stress.

For humans the BMR is defined as the rate of oxygen consumed while the subject rests quietly, after a sleep of at least 8 hours; the last meal should have been at least 12 hours earlier; no exercise should have been performed for at least 30 minutes; and the environmental temperature should be between 16.7° and 30.6° C (62° and 87° F). By definition, then, the BMR represents the minimal amount of energy required by the body per unit time merely to keep the individual alive—that is, the energy needed to support muscle contraction for breathing, heartbeat, and muscle tone; to maintain such continuous synthetic processes as occur in various cells; and to support the electrical activity of the brain.

Cold-blooded animals have no metabolic state to which the term *basal* can be applied because their body temperature depends on the environmental temperature, and the rate of metabolism varies with the body temperature. For these animals the minimum metabolism of fasting individuals at a given environmental temperature is referred to as the *standard metabolic rate* (SMR). Whichever term is used, BMR or SMR, what defines minimal stress varies from species to species.

Bioenergetics

All organisms require a continuous supply of energy for (1) maintenance, including the repair and replacement of worn-out parts and the carrying out of specific cell functions, (2) growth, and (3) reproduction.

The energy that cells need comes from chemical reactions. Any chemical reaction that can go on spontaneously must do so by going from a more-energy-rich state to a less-energy-rich state, just as a ball on a hillside can roll to the bottom spontaneously but will never go up the hill unless it is pushed or carried. The difference in energy between the two states is released into the environment as work and heat. Of the energy released by a chemical reaction, only a certain percentage can be used to do work, no matter how efficient the process (see THERMODYNAMICS).

Coupled Reactions. "Uphill" reactions—that is, reactions whose products are at a higher energy level than the starting materials—cannot take place unless energy is supplied. The cell supplies it by first making a high-energy compound that, when broken down, will release more energy than is needed for the "uphill" reaction. The most frequently used of these high-energy compounds is adenosine triphosphate, or ATP (see ATP). Synthesis of the desired material and the breakdown of ATP are linked together so that the overall reaction is "downhill" and is thus energetically possible. This linkage can take place by many mechanisms. Suppose, for example, the reaction of two substances, *A* and *B*, forms two products, *C* and *D*. If the products are at a higher energy level than the reactants, the reaction cannot go on spontaneously. If, however, *D* can react with a substance *E* to produce substances *F* and *G* at a much lower energy level—that is, a reaction that goes on readily—then, if the energy production by the second reaction exceeds the energy requirement of the first reaction, the two coupled reactions will proceed.

Components of Living Organisms. All organisms capable of independent life (in other words, all except the viruses) are made principally of fats (see FATS AND OILS), proteins, CARBOHYDRATES, and nucleic acids. Fats and carbohydrates can be broken down to simpler compounds—fatty acids, glycerol, and simple sugars—which may be used for immediate energy production. Fatty acids in excess of immediate needs can be rebuilt into fat and stored in special cells making up adipose tissue. Sugars in excess of current needs are either converted to fatty acids and stored as fat, or formed into a giant polymer—in plants, a starch granule; in animals, a glycogen molecule. Protein is degraded to amino acids, which, if not used to make new protein, can be converted to derivatives of fatty acids or sugars and utilized accordingly.

Energy Production. The major source of energy in the cell is obtained from the oxidation of hydrogen. The greatest single source of hydrogen molecules for oxidation is the KREBS CYCLE, a series of chemical reactions that can be looked on as a machine for removing hydrogen from food.

The hydrogen is sent to the electron transport system (ETS), which is made up of large molecules within and on the inner membrane of the mitochondrion that are capable of rapidly alternating oxidation and reduction reactions. The electrons from the hydrogen molecules pass through a series of cytochromes (close relatives of hemoglobin), the last of which catalyzes the formation of water from the electrons, hydrogen protons, and oxygen derived from respired air. The entire series runs "downhill" and energy is produced. Any energy not used for chemical work is dissipated as heat.

Oxidative Phosphorylation. The energy produced by the ETS is used to form a chemical bond between adenosine diphosphate (ADP) and inorganic phosphate (P_i) to form ATP. In fully functional cells, electron transport is tightly coupled to oxidative phosphorylation. That is, if ATP synthesis is prevented (which would happen if there were a lack of P_i, ADP, or oxygen), electron transport will not take place. The ATP generated is used throughout the cell to drive most of the otherwise energetically unfavorable reactions.

In certain vertebrate tissues, notably skeletal muscle and the brain, an extra store of energy is maintained by using excess ATP to convert creatine to creatine phosphate, which is also a high-energy compound. Creatine phosphate can quickly transfer the phosphate group to ADP to reform ATP when the latter is needed. Invertebrates use phosphoarginine in a similar fashion.

Anaerobic Reactions. All cells can synthesize some ATP in the absence of oxygen by means of anaerobic reactions. Usually glucose, the most important sugar in the cell, is broken down to pyruvic acid, which is then converted to lactic acid and excreted from the cell. As an example, bacteria present in milk absorb milk sugar and convert it to lactic acid in a metabolic process that produces enough ATP to meet the bacteria's needs. The lactic acid is excreted and sours the milk.

Glycolysis. When oxygen is present the pyruvic acid obtained from glucose does not become lactic acid but is instead converted either to oxaloacetic acid or to acetyl coenzyme A, depending on the cell's needs at the moment. In either case it enters the Krebs cycle. The steps from glucose to pyruvic acid may be called glycolysis, the anaerobic pathway (*anaerobic* meaning not requiring oxygen), or, in honor of two of its discoverers, the Embden-Myerhof pathway. It must be stressed that the Krebs cycle is a much more efficient producer of ATP than is glycolysis.

Polymerization and Hydrogenation. In order for new cell constituents to be built, one or more of the following processes must take place. One process, polymerization, can involve the production of proteins by joining together large numbers of amino acids in specific arrangements; it can also involve the production of RNA or DNA from mononucleotides. Polymerization requires the presence of either ATP or certain other high-energy compounds, many of which are derived from ATP. Another process, hydrogenation, also called reduction, is the addition of hydrogen to a molecule. This process usually requires a carrier molecule, such as a pyridine nucleotide, and a hydrogen source, commonly supplied from the degradation of glucose. Most large molecules are built by chemical linkage of small molecules, a process whose immediate source of energy generally is ATP.

Plant Metabolism

Unlike animals—which typically obtain both energy and nutrients by eating plants or other animals—plants obtain the atoms for synthesis from atmospheric carbon dioxide and absorb water and simple salts of nitrogen, phosphorus, and potassium from the soil. The energy of sunlight is captured in a process called PHOTOSYNTHESIS by the chloroplast, an organelle in leaf cells that contains chlorophyll. The chloroplast synthesizes sugar, which is used as the basic raw material for all the compounds found in the plant cell. Energy for metabolism is obtained in catabolism of this sugar.

The chemical reactions by which plant constituents are formed, interconverted, and degraded constitute the complex of plant metabolism. Knowledge of plant metabolism is probably less complete than that of metabolism in animals or bacteria. New plant compounds are reported almost yearly, and each new compound requires long study to determine its function or mode of synthesis in the plant. Indeed, several thousand species of plants make substances that, despite years of investigation by plant physiologists and biochemists, have no discernible role in metabolism. These substances include rubber; such TERPENES as turpentine and menthol; such ALKALOIDS as morphine, caffeine, and nicotine; tannin; and many other substances useful to industry and medicine.

Nevertheless, careful investigations have shown that both the overall pattern of metabolism and the enzymes that catalyze individual chemical reactions are basically similar in plants, animals, and microorganisms. Basically similar, too, are the mechanisms that regulate plant and animal metabolism by means of plant hormones and animal hormones.

The Role of Photosynthesis. Unlike animals and many microorganisms, green plants are able to use photosynthesis to make all their basic foodstuffs. In photosynthesis plants combine CO_2, water, and the energy in sunlight to build carbohydrate, which then becomes the chief internal source of building materials and the energy to drive metabolic processes. The ability to make organic molecules from inorganic nutrients makes photosynthesizers the major link between the inorganic and organic worlds. Photosynthesis is also exhibited by certain bacteria, some protozoans, and the blue-green algae. A few chemosynthetic bacteria make their own organic food from carbon dioxide, water, and nitrate or ammonia in their surroundings; however, they derive the energy not from light but by oxidizing simple substances such as iron or sulfur.

Biochemical Activity. Plant nitrogen commonly originates from nitrates absorbed through the roots. Nitrates must be converted to ammonia before the nitrogen can be used in protein synthesis, and the reactions necessary for this conversion are initiated by oxidative processes of respiration. Hence, the application of nitrate boosts the demand for respiration—and overall respiration increases.

Almost all of the different plant compounds originate, one way or another, from sugar produced in photosynthesis. The bulk of the plant consists of modified sugars or their polymers, the polysaccharides: cellulose; noncellulose polysaccharides such as xylans and mannans; hemicellulose; pectins; and, in woody plants, lignin.

Energy Reserves. Many plants store sugar as sucrose, but most deposit reserve sugar as starch—a larger and more insoluble molecule than sucrose and therefore more stable. Starch is also stored in many seeds, where it serves as food during germination; in woody twigs, where it provides energy for the growth of buds; and in many tubers and roots, where it serves as food for new growth.

Starch is made by a series of reactions similar to those for its counterpart in animals, glycogen. When the demand for energy is sufficient, the process of converting plant starch back to glucose (which is then catabolized in respiration) is a simple one. Fat is also accumulated as long-term reserve material. It is most concentrated in fruits and seeds.

Animal Metabolism

Animal metabolism consists of the utilization of nutrients absorbed from the digestive tract and their catabolism as fuel for energy or their conversion into substances of the body. The molecules and even most cells of the body have brief lifetimes and are constantly replaced, whereas tissue as a whole maintains its characteristic structure. This constant rebuilding process without a net change in the amount of a cell constituent is known as dynamic equilibrium.

The basic building blocks of metabolism are glucose (sugar) derived from the digestion of dietary carbohydrate, amino acids (from dietary protein), and fatty acids and glycerol (from fats). Glucose is preferentially used by most cells if it is available, such as shortly after meals, but fat takes over as the major source a few hours later, and body tissues may be sacrificed for their protein content as fasting continues.

Energy Reserves. Excess nutrients not immediately used to meet energy needs are stored in a carbohydrate reserve called glycogen (mostly in the liver and skeletal muscle) and in a fat reserve called triglyceride, deposited in adipose tissue. Vertebrates can quickly convert excess carbohydrate to fat but not vice versa. In mammals, about 50% of glucose is normally oxidized completely to carbon dioxide and water; 5% is converted to glycogen; and 30% to 40% is converted to fat. The carbohydrate stored as glycogen is sufficient for energy needs for only a few hours, whereas the adult human has sufficient fat stored for several weeks of starvation.

Regulation of Metabolism. In order for an animal to function, cell metabolism must be integrated; equally important, the metabolism of the component cells must be coordinated. This latter task requires the exchange of information between cells, even in widely separated parts of the body. Most higher animals possess two major modalities for such communication: the nervous system, and many kinds of messenger substances. Of the latter the best known are the hormones (see HORMONE, ANIMAL), secretions of the endocrine glands that enter the bloodstream and are carried throughout the body. Each hormone affects the metabolism of cells that have receptors for that hormone. Sometimes the target cells may even be another endocrine gland, which in turn secretes another hormone affecting still other cells.

Another group of messenger chemicals characteristically acts quite locally. These chemicals include the prostaglandins, which are found throughout the body but tend to affect only those cells within the area from which they are released. Other such local messengers affect nervous tissue, and some chemicals are so localized that they are formed within a cell and affect enzymes contained there.

Hormones regulate cell metabolism either by changing the cell membrane's permeability to extracellular substances or by altering the activity of intracellular enzymes. Groups of enzymes are linked together in so-called metabolic pathways (chains of reactions), and hormones often act by increasing or decreasing the activity of "pacemaker" enzymes that control major pathways.

Thus, for example, glucose uptake by muscle cells is controlled by the permeability of the cell membrane to glucose and by the enzyme hexokinase; glycogen synthesis is controlled by the enzyme glycogen synthetase; glycogen breakdown to glucose, by the enzyme phosphorylase; and fat mobilization from fat deposits, by the enzyme lipoprotein lipase.

See also: HORMONE, PLANT; NITROGEN CYCLE.

——
metal   The most distinguishing physical characteristics of metals are an ability to conduct electricity (a property that diminishes with increasing temperature), an excellent conductivity of heat, and a high reflectivity of light from a polished surface, commonly known as metallic luster. In addition, most metals deform (change shape), rather than shatter, on impact or under pressure. Metals that can be hammered or beaten into sheets are called *malleable*; those which can be drawn into wire are called *ductile*. Certain properties, such as hardness and me-

chanical strength, are not shared by all metals; some metals are actually soft enough to be scratched by a fingernail or deformed by hand.

All metals share certain chemical properties. Many metal oxides react with water to form basic (alkaline) solutions; such substances are termed basic anhydrides or basic oxides. Metals characteristically combine with nonmetals to form ionic compounds in which the metal ion is always positive and the nonmetal ion is always negative.

Alloys. Different metals can often be fused with each other to yield new metallic substances called ALLOYS. Alloys of two or more metals can be formulated in a wide variety of compositions and usually have physical properties differing considerably from their components. By careful choice of composition, alloys can be made that have great hardness, toughness, mechanical strength, and resistance to corrosion.

Metalloids. Elements falling on the dividing line between metals and nonmetals in the periodic table are called metalloids, or semimetals, and have physical and chemical properties between the two extremes. The metalloids are the elements boron, silicon, germanium, arsenic, antimony, selenium, and tellurium. They often appear shiny and metallic to the eye, but are brittle and differ radically in their electrical properties. Silicon and germanium are SEMICONDUCTORS and have electrical conductivities that lie between the extremes of metals and nonmetal insulators. Unlike true metals, semiconductors become more conductive at high temperatures and are extremely sensitive to trace levels of impurities, a fact of central importance to the use of these substances in solid-state electronic devices.

Atomic Properties. Atoms of the metallic elements differ in several important ways from those of the nonmetals and the metalloids. Metal atoms in general give up electrons more readily than atoms of other elements, as shown by their low ionization potentials (see IONS AND IONIZATION). A closely related property is the large atomic diameters of metal atoms compared to those of other elements. Because the electrons of a metal atom are held more weakly, they have a greater range of motion, resulting in a larger size in proportion to the number of electrons present. Metal atoms have the lowest electronegativities of all elements, meaning that metal atoms bonded to other atoms attract electrons weakly.

Although the metallic elements vary greatly in their reactivity, all can be induced to give up electrons and form positive ions with relative ease; that is, almost all metals can be oxidized under mild conditions. This fact can be accounted for by a combination of factors, as the example of the easily oxidized metal sodium illustrates. The single-valence electron of a sodium atom is held loosely, only weakly binds atoms together in the metal, and contributes greatly to the volume of the atom as a whole. Little energy is needed to remove this electron, and the resulting sodium ion has a much smaller diameter. The energy spent in making the ion is more than regained in the combined effects of electron capture by the oxidizing species and the high electrical attraction between the small positive ion and either the negative ions in a solid or the very polar water molecules in a solution. Metals that are less easily oxidized than sodium have higher ionization potentials, are more tightly bound together in the metallic crystal, and show a less dramatic volume contraction when ionized.

The Metallic Elements. About three-fourths of the known chemical elements are true metals. Among the representative elements in the PERIODIC TABLE, all of the elements in Groups IA (the alkali metals, from lithium to francium) and IIA (the alkaline earth metals, from beryllium to radium) are metals. Also, the heavier elements in Groups IIIA (aluminum, gallium, indium, and thallium), IVA (tin and lead), and VA (bismuth) are metals. All of the 33 TRANSITION ELEMENTS in the eight B groups at the center of the periodic table are also metals, as are all of the LANTHANIDES and ACTINIDES.

Structure and Bonding in Metals. Many metals have remarkably simple arrangements of their atoms in the solid state (crystal structures), in which each atom is surrounded by as many neighbor atoms as is geometrically possible. Three such arrangements are very common: hexagonal closest packing (*hcp*), cubic closest packing (*ccp*), and body-centered cubic (*bcc*). Each is best visualized by imagining the atoms to be hard, identical spheres. In the first two structures the atoms are arranged in close-packed layers in a hexagonal or honeycomb pattern; in a given layer each atom has six nearest neighbors in contact with itself. In both structures the layers are stacked on top of each other so that every atom has, in addition to these six, three contact neighbors in the layer above and three in the plane below, for a grand total of 12. The hexagonal and cubic closest packing structures differ in the way that repeating layers are stacked relative to each other, but they are equally efficient in maximizing atom contacts and minimizing empty space.

The body-centered cubic structure does not arrange atoms quite as efficiently with respect to minimizing empty space, but it affords slightly more close contacts between atoms. Each atom is surrounded by eight contact neighbors arranged at the corners of a cube. There are six next-nearest neighbors directly across each cube face (the center atoms of the adjacent cubes) at a separation between atom centers only 15% greater than the contact distance, giving a total of 14 fairly close neighbor atoms. It is not uncommon for a metallic element to form crystals in one of these structures at a low temperature and in a different one at high temperature.

Because most metal atoms have few valence electrons and many contact neighbors in the solid state, it is clear that metallic crystals cannot be held together by single two-electron covalent bonds between each pair of atoms. The bonding in solid metals is very different from that in covalent and ionic substances. Most of the distinguishing properties of metals stem from these differences.

The simplest theory of the metallic bond is called the free-electron or electron-gas model. The metal atoms are imagined to be positive ions immersed in a negatively charged gas or sea of valence electrons, giving the entire structure electrical neutrality. The valence electrons in the sea are not associated with any given atoms and are free to move throughout the entire body of the solid metal.

This simple model accounts for many of the characteristic properties of metals. Metals can conduct electricity, which is simply a flow of electrons, because of the mobility of the free valence electrons. The electrical resistance of metals increases with temperature because the heightened vibrational motion of the metal atoms impedes electron flow. Layers of metal atoms can be shifted or displaced with respect to each other without disrupting the electron sea, with the result that metals are plastic under pressure or impact, allowing them the properties of malleability and ductility. Molten metals conduct electric current almost as well as the solids, because in the liquid state the positive metal ions, now mobile, are still immersed in the conducting free-electron sea. Finally, the free-electron metallic bond is nonspecific, which means that one type of metal ion can be substituted for another without changing the overall bonding in a major way, so that metals can form an incredible variety of solid solutions, or alloys.

A more quantitative and comprehensive theory of metallic bonding and of bonding in solids in general is called the band theory of solids (see SOLID-STATE PHYSICS). In the band theory all the electrons in a solid occupy allowed energy levels that are so closely spaced as to be practically continuous. These closely spaced levels or energy bands are separated by energy gaps of varying magnitude within which electrons are not allowed. Energy bands that are completely filled with electrons cannot conduct electrical current, so that insulators or nonconductors always have completely filled bands separated from any unoccupied bands by large energy gaps. In metals either an allowed band is only partially filled, or a filled band overlaps with an empty one (zero energy gap); in either case electrical conduction is possible.

The band theory accounts in an appealing way for the nearly total reflection of visible light from highly polished metal surfaces. The incoming visible-light photon excites an electron from the top level of its partially filled energy band to one of the continuum of unoccupied allowed higher levels in the same band. The excited electron then drops back down to the top filled level of the band, emitting a visible photon of exactly the same frequency and therefore "reflecting" the light.

Ferromagnetism, a property possessed by iron and a few other metals that allows them to become permanently magnetized (see MAGNETISM), is accounted for in the band theory by postulating that electrons of opposite spin (and hence opposite magnetic polarity) are distributed in unequal numbers in the allowed energy bands, giving the bulk solid metal a net magnetic moment.

metal detector   A metal detector is a device that reacts to the presence of metal and hence can be used to detect concealed metal objects. One kind is based on an electronic circuit that oscillates at a frequency determined by the inductance of the unit's search coil. The presence of metal near the coil alters the inductance of the coil and hence the frequency of oscillation. This change can be used to activate a flashing light or produce an audible tone.

---

metal fatigue   Metal fatigue is the tendency for a metal to break under the action of repeated cyclic stresses. Fatigue may occur for values of cyclic stress considerably less than the ultimate tensile strength of the material. A single application of the stress apparently does nothing detrimental to the structure; when enough of these seemingly harmless stresses are applied in a cyclic manner, however, they bring about a small crack that grows with continued loadings until complete fracture takes place. Since the small cracks may not be noticed, the metal may fracture with a suddenness that can be dangerous, as in high-speed machinery. Special inspection techniques have been developed to spot these small cracks.

Fatigue failures are due to the repeated application of tensile stresses or shear stresses, which tend to pull the material apart. However, a cycle that consists of alternating equal stresses in tension and compression, called a fully reversed cycle, is usually used to obtain the endurance limits of a particular material.

See also: METALLURGY.

metal ore   see ORE DEPOSITS

---

metallurgy   The term *metallurgy* refers to the science and technology of METALS. Extractive, or process, metallurgy concerns the extraction of metals from their ores and the subsequent refinement of these metals. Physical metallurgy concerns the physical and mechanical properties of metals, and how metals may be shaped into useful products by means of heat and mechanical processes. Iron and steel and their alloys are among the most important metals and are known as the ferrous metals; aluminum, copper, zinc, nickel, tin, silver, and gold are particularly important nonferrous metals.

Early History

Metals came into limited use 5,500 years ago when the Egyptians made and wore copper beads, and their rulers bathed in water conveyed by copper pipes from the river Nile to their private pools. Copper nuggets and meteoric iron, as well as gold and silver, were also used in that time. Gold, in the form of nuggets found exposed along riverbeds, was pounded into crude ornaments with a stone hammer. Silver nuggets were also used to make fine ornaments.

Some of the most sophisticated early metallurgical techniques evolved around the use of copper, the first industrial metal. The earliest use of natural copper involved an extremely limited Stone Age technique by which small, specially selected pieces of metal were made into beads, awls, pins, or hoops by cold forging, a technique that consisted simply of hammering the cold metal. Early attempts to cold-hammer small pieces of natural copper were able to give only a limited improvement to such pieces. The stone-working techniques (such as simple shaping) found greater success when smiths learned to produce copper of a more malleable form by the process of ANNEALING: exposing the copper to a slow, softening heat. Annealing was a step toward the subsequent melting, or smelting, of copper.

The first efforts to shape molten metal consisted of cutting forms in slabs of stone, or molding forms in clay. To fill these molds, the smith transferred the molten metal to a crucible, a process known as open-mold CASTING.

The art of smelting ores to produce metals, discovered near the end of the Stone Age, was applied not only to copper, but also to silver, lead, tin, and probably iron. The production of stronger and more easily shaped ALLOYS proceeded by trial and error. It was found that the addition of tin to copper formed the alloy bronze.

By the late 4th millennium BC, smiths were remarkably sophisticated in a practical way regarding the individual phenomena of metallurgy. They knew the effects on metals of hammering, annealing, oxidation, melting, and alloying; and they were aware of the phenomena of simple decomposition of ores, their reduction, double decomposition, and exchange of impurities.

The Iron Age dates from about 1500 BC, when iron ore is first known to have been smelted. During this era iron was used mainly for making coins, cooking utensils, and implements of war. The cementation process for making

This painting by John Ferguson Weir, Forging the Shaft: A Welding Heat *(1877), dramatizes a process of shaping and strengthening metal that has been used since ancient times. (Metropolitan Museum of Art, New York City.)*

steel and the art of quenching steel for hardening and TEMPERING of weapons were discovered early in the Iron Age. The progress of metallurgy moved slowly until about AD 1300, when the Catalan forge was developed in Spain. The forerunner of the modern open-hearth furnace (see OPEN-HEARTH PROCESS), it made possible the production of a sizable tonnage of iron in one heat. The forerunner of the modern BLAST FURNACE was the continuous-shaft furnace, developed in Germany about AD 1323, which produced the high-carbon product known as cast iron.

From Art to Science

The transition of metallurgy from an art to a science was slow compared to the technological progress in other fields. Its advance was hastened by the beginning of the power age. With the Industrial Revolution in England came a demand for larger quantities of metal and for greater production capacities. An iron works was erected at Glasport, Hampshire, where the processes for puddling and rolling iron were perfected in 1700. This marked the beginning of the rolling mill, in which iron and steel bars, shapes, and sheets are produced. The predominant structural metal at that time was WROUGHT IRON; it remained so until the invention of the Bessemer converter in 1855 by the English scientist Sir Henry BESSEMER.

Not until the 18th century did scientists begin to appreciate the complex chemistry of metallurgy. Metallography, the study of the structural and physical properties of metals, grew throughout the 19th century.

Modern Techniques

Modern extractive and physical metallurgy makes use of a combination of ancient and modern techniques. Each metal requires a unique process for separation from the ore. By far the most important is the production of pig iron from iron ore by smelting in a blast furnace. Steel is then produced from the pig iron by one of several processes, including the Bessemer process, the open-hearth process, the ELECTRIC-FURNACE process, and the oxygen-furnace process. Another important extraction process is the production of alumina from bauxite by the Bayer process, and the production of ALUMINUM from alumina by the Hall-Héroult process.

Once the metal is extracted the methods of physical metallurgy are employed to fabricate it into useful products. These include mechanical treatments such as rolling, drawing, forming, or extrusion, which change the shape of the metal; joining processes such as brazing and WELDING AND SOLDERING; and finishing techniques such as ELECTROPLATING and galvanizing.

The techniques of metallography are used to determine what metals are suitable for a particular purpose, or for analyzing deficiencies in metal products. Tension and compression tests are two important methods of testing the strength of metals (see MATERIALS TECHNOLOGY).

Among the most important advances have been techniques for joining metals together so that the junctures will be at least as strong as the parent metals themselves. The standard techniques of electric-arc and gas welding have now been joined by electron-beam welding, in which

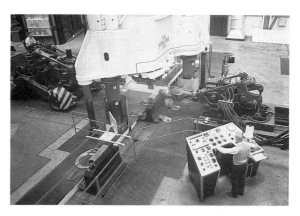

Modern techniques for shaping metal include forging on massive power presses. A hot ingot, or metal blank, is positioned on an anvil under this 1,500-ton press by a remote-controlled manipulator.

heat is produced by bombarding the metal with a dense beam of high-velocity electrons, and laser welding, which allows excellent control of the heat input for delicate work in the aerospace and electronics industries.

Among other new methods for strengthening or giving special properties to metals is a technique called rapid-solidification-processing (R-S-P), where a molten metal is cooled within seconds to a solid state, creating a material with a glasslike, or amorphous, structure. R-S-P metals possess highly magnetic properties useful in electric generators and electronic equipment. Ion implantation, a method of strengthening metals (as well as other materials, such as ceramics), involves "zapping" a metal with the charged ions of another element inside a vacuum chamber. A thin layer of an extremely hard, durable alloy is built up. Its properties may be totally different from those of the underlying metal.

---

metamorphic rock The recrystallization of the constituent minerals of SEDIMENTARY or IGNEOUS ROCKS, at elevated temperatures or pressures or under conditions different from those in which the rocks originated, produces metamorphic rocks. These rocks usually occur in zones, or orogenic belts—hundreds or thousands of kilometers long and tens or hundreds of kilometers wide—that were formed by movements and interactions of large continental and oceanic plates (see PLATE TECTONICS). Subduction of an oceanic plate under the edge of a continental plate creates new temperature and pressure conditions in the rocks along the boundary between the plates. The products of erosion and weathering of the rocks of the continents and of volcanism along the continental margins and in nearby island arcs are deposited in adjacent ocean basins to form sedimentary and volcanic piles that may later be subjected to folding, faulting, and metamorphism during orogenic movements of the plates. Examples of orogenic belts are such mountain ranges as the Cordillera and Appalachian mountains in North America, and the Alpine Range and Caledonides in Europe.

Metamorphic rocks are rocks that have undergone changes in composition under high pressure, high temperature, or both. Because pressure and temperature within the Earth are constantly changing, a large proportion of its rocks are metamorphic. Gneiss and schist (A) are produced by intense heat and stress acting on igneous rock, such as granite. Quartzite (B) is produced by metamorphosis of sedimentary sandstone. Slate (C) develops from shale; if further metamorphosis occurs, it becomes gneiss. Marble (D) forms from calcium carbonate.

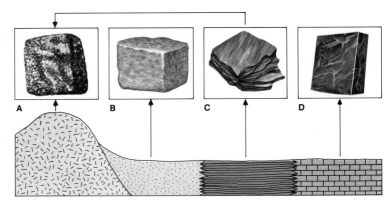

Composition

Metamorphic rocks are classified on the bases of their composition and the physical conditions under which they were recrystallized. Derivation of metamorphic rock from a particular rock type is indicated by the prefix *meta-*, as in the terms *metasediment, metavolcanic rock,* and *metagabbro.* Some metamorphic rock names, such as phyllite, SCHIST, and SLATE, have a strong textural connotation. The minerals of these metamorphic rocks are coarse- to fine-grained and have a strong parallel orientation.

The most common compositional groups of metamorphic rocks are those derived from pelitic (clayey) and calcareous (limey) sedimentary rocks, sandstones, and various intrusive and volcanic rocks. Pelitic rocks are rich in aluminum and silicon and contain some iron, magnesium, calcium, potassium, and sodium; their metamorphosed equivalents contain minerals such as quartz, micas, and various aluminum-rich silicates. Common minerals in metamorphosed calcareous sedimentary rocks are calcite, dolomite, epidote, tremolite, hornblende, diopside, and wollastonite. If the original rock is nearly pure calcium carbonate, metamorphic recrystallization changes it to MARBLE. SANDSTONES are recrystallized to various types of quartzite.

Metamorphosed igneous rocks are commonly grouped on the basis of their silica content, which ranges from 40 to 45% in the most basic (ultramafic) rocks to about 50% in common basic (mafic) rocks, about 60% in intermediate rocks, and 70% in acidic (silicic) rocks. When metamorphosed, the ultramafic rocks are converted to the hydrous magnesium silicates SERPENTINE and TALC. The mafic rocks are rich in magnesium, iron, calcium, and aluminum; their metamorphosed equivalents, metagabbro and metabasalt, are rich in minerals such as chlorite, amphibole, and epidote, which have a high content of these elements. Among the metamorphosed intermediate rocks, meta-andesites are extremely common. They contain more silica and calcium and less magnesium and iron than the metabasalts. High content of epidote and amphibole along with plagioclase is common. Together the meta-andesites and metabasalts form a part of rocks commonly called greenstones.

Conditions of Formation

Mineral assemblages of metamorphic rocks are important indicators of the physical conditions under which the rocks formed. Different mineral assemblages will crystallize from the same chemical composition at different pressures and temperatures. For example, andalusite (along with biotite, cordierite, and garnet) is common in aluminum-rich rocks recrystallized in the aureoles of plutons at shallow depths and medium temperatures. At high temperatures, sillimanite crystallizes instead of andalusite, and at high pressures kyanite is formed. All have the same chemical composition (Al_2SiO_5), but each has a different crystal structure.

Because temperature and pressure are dependent on geologic setting, the study of metamorphic rocks yields significant information on the geologic history of a region. Changes in the mineral assemblages in the rocks around intrusive masses of igneous rock are brought about mainly by changes in temperature, because the temperature of recrystallization in the surrounding rocks increases toward the intrusion, whereas the rock pressure stays about the same. On the other hand, the pressure gradient varies with depth in the Earth's crust, and, accordingly, affects the mineral assemblages that recrystallize at different levels and are later exposed by erosion and denudation. Metamorphic rocks can therefore be grouped into facies, each facies representing all the mineral assemblages that form from various chemical compositions under certain pressure and temperature conditions.

Metamorphoses [met-uh-mohr'-fuh-seez]   The *Metamorphoses* (c.AD 8), OVID's masterpiece, is a Latin poem in 15 books that recounts a series of transformations, largely of humans into animals, plants, and mineral forms. The stories range through history from the most remote mythic times to the foundation of the Roman Empire. Some of the most famous tales concern Apollo's pursuit of Daphne, who is transformed into a laurel tree; Echo's ill-fated love for the selfish Narcissus, who becomes a flower; and the hospitality of the devoted elderly couple Baucis and Philemon, who in recompense are changed by Zeus into interlocking trees. First translated (1565–67) into English by Arthur Golding, the *Metamorphoses* has served as a storehouse of classical myths since Chaucer's time.

metamorphosis

metamorphosis   Some animals go through a radical change in form or structure—a process called metamorphosis—during the development from egg to adult, resulting in a series of distinctive stages. Animals that undergo one or more metamorphoses as they develop are said to have complex life cycles. Early developmental stages are often termed larvae; sexually reproductive stages are termed adults.

The life cycle of the frog provides a simple example of metamorphic development. The tadpole (larval stage) that hatches from the egg is limbless and possesses external gills and a large tail. Tadpoles feed on aquatic algae and have a long, coiled intestine to process this type of food. After a period of time ranging from a few months to several years, depending on the species involved, tadpoles metamorphose to frogs (adult stage) over a few weeks. They absorb their tails. Hind limbs and then forelimbs soon develop. The eyes enlarge and the skeleton is altered. As the frog emerges from the pond, it breathes with the aid of lungs and feeds primarily on insects. To accommodate this shift from a herbivorous to a carnivorous feeding habit, the intestine of the frog is short and straight. The beginning of metamorphosis is triggered by the release of thyroid hormone.

The higher insects (such as beetles, flies, butterflies, and wasps) complete a more complicated series of metamorphoses as development proceeds from egg to adult. For the butterfly or moth the larva that hatches from the egg is called a caterpillar. The caterpillar is vermiform and feeds voraciously on plant matter. After completing four molts the larval butterfly has grown tremendously in size and undergoes a metamorphosis to the pupal (or chrysalis) stage. As its final act the caterpillar secretes a cocoon about itself. The larval growth and metamorphosis are controlled by juvenile hormone, which is produced by the corpora allata in the larval brain. Inside the cocoon the tissues of the PUPA are reorganized. Larval structures are broken down, and adult structures such as wings develop. When this metamorphosis is complete, the winged adult emerges from the cocoon.

Each of the stages is highly specialized for a limited series of functions. The slow-moving caterpillar is the feeding stage. Essentially all the increase in size (weight) is confined to this stage. The pupal stage is a complicated period of larval tissue breakdown and differentiation of the adult structures. Periods of inclement weather, such as winter, are often endured in the pupal stage. The adult stage does little feeding and does not grow, but it provides dispersal, selects an appropriate habitat to lay its eggs, and reproduces sexually.

Metamorphosis is considered complete when a clear distinction exists between larval and adult stage, such as from tadpole to frog and from larva to pupa to adult. Some animals undergo gradual, or incomplete, metamorphosis. The young resemble adults. Their form gradually changes into an adult through a series of molts. They undergo no pupal stage and no destruction of immature tissues. Examples of such animals are lobsters and cockroaches.

Many marine organisms, both invertebrates and fishes, begin life as minute planktonic larvae. These larval stages are responsible for dispersal and ultimately for habitat selection. The larvae must settle out of the water at a location suitable for growth of the juvenile to the adult.

Parasitic organisms are also characterized by complex life cycles with striking metamorphic changes. For parasites the different stages may be specialized for dispersal, host-seeking, attachment and penetration, feeding, and reproduction.

metaphor

metaphor   A metaphor, from a Greek word meaning "to carry over," is a FIGURE OF SPEECH in which a word properly belonging to a particular object is applied to an-

Grasshoppers undergo simple metamorphosis (A): *the young insects, or nymphs, usually resemble the adults, and wings develop with each molt. Butterflies undergo complete metamorphosis* (B): *the young, or larvae, enter a quiescent stage* (pupa) *before becoming adults.*

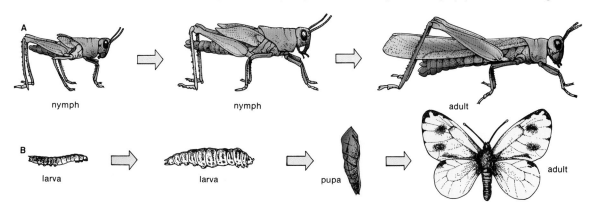

A   nymph   nymph   adult

B   larva   larva   pupa   adult

other. Metaphor is the single most important device of literary language and the principal means by which ordinary usage increases its range of definition. Language itself is profoundly metaphorical because people find it easier to grasp concepts when they are expressed by concrete analogy. Many words that were once used metaphorically for this reason, such as the "leg" of a table, the "hood" of a car, or the "summit" of an achievement, have now ceased to be figurative and are accepted as literal descriptions. Such expressions are called dead metaphors. The use of two incongruous metaphors in close proximity often results in the absurdity of a mixed metaphor.

Metaphor, an implicit analogy, is often distinguished from simile, an explicit comparison containing the word *like* or *as*. The difference is mainly linguistic, however, and both metaphor and simile are used to evoke concrete and abstract likenesses between disparate objects or areas of experience.

metaphysical poetry Metaphysical poetry is the name given to the work of certain early-17th-century English poets, including Richard CRASHAW, John DONNE, George HERBERT, Andrew MARVELL, Henry Vaughan, and Thomas Traherne. Religious and amorous themes constituted the subject of the poetry, which had an intricate intellectual quality achieved by elliptical writing. Metaphysical poems depended heavily on irony and paradox; they used the conceit, a metaphor linking disparate ideas or objects. A revival of interest in metaphysical poetry took place in the 20th century, led by T. S. ELIOT and F. R. LEAVIS.

metaphysics Metaphysics is that area of philosophy which concerns itself with the nature and structure of reality. It deals with such questions as the following. Are the objects we perceive real or illusory? Does the external world exist apart from our consciousness of it? Is reality ultimately reducible to a single underlying substance? If so, is it essentially spiritual or material? Is the universe intelligible and orderly, or incomprehensible and chaotic?

In its traditional meaning metaphysics has included cosmology, the study of the organization and origin of the universe, and THEOLOGY, the study of the nature and existence of God. Modern metaphysical inquiry includes the philosophy of mind or self (sometimes called rational psychology), which deals with such issues as the mind-body problem, free will and determinism, and personal identity. The term *metaphysics* itself was introduced by early editors of the works of ARISTOTLE to describe those writings which came after (and thus carried analysis beyond) his studies on physics.

Metaphysics began with the pre-Socratic philosophers who were concerned with whether reality was reducible to a single underlying substance. The MILESIAN SCHOOL took a monist position (see MONISM) on this question, whereas PYTHAGORAS OF SAMOS posited a dualistic or two-substance theory (see DUALISM) about the world, and ANAXAGORAS and EMPEDOCLES took a pluralistic position (see PLURALISM),

holding that reality was made up of many discrete particles. In the subsequent development of philosophy monism is represented by such philosophers as Baruch SPINOZA and G. W. F. HEGEL; dualism by PLATO, Rene DESCARTES, and Immanuel KANT; and pluralism by Gottfried von LEIBNIZ and some pragmatists.

Beyond the question of whether or not reality is composed of one or more than one basic substance lies the question, What kind of substance is it? On this issue metaphysics traditionally has been divided between materialists who believe that all reality is basically material or physical and idealists who believe that reality is spiritual or nonmaterial (see MATERIALISM and IDEALISM). Important materialists have included the pre-Socratic atomists (see ATOMISM), Thomas HOBBES, and Karl MARX. Among contemporary materialist theories, especially with respect to the nature of humanity, are analytical behaviorism and the neural identity theory of mind. Major idealists have included PARMENIDES, PLATO, George BERKELEY, Johann Gottlieb FICHTE, and G. W. F. HEGEL.

A third major metaphysical issue centers around the problem of permanence and change. Most philosophers have attempted to explain change in terms of either mechanism or TELEOLOGY. Materialists have tended to take a mechanistic view, explaining change as the action and reaction of physical particles with one another. Both idealists and theologians have taken a teleologic approach, appealing to a spiritual (usually supernatural) principle as the ultimate source and cause of all change.

The modern attack on metaphysics began with the skeptical EMPIRICISM of David HUME, who argued that ideas such as "substance," "reality," "mind," and "causality" were undemonstrable. Immanuel Kant, too, questioned the possibility of metaphysical knowledge in the traditional sense. In his view the ultimate nature of reality (things as they really are) is unknowable, for the human mind is limited to knowledge of phenomena or appearances. His several "critiques" of the speculative and practical functions of reason significantly altered the course of philosophy. After Kant philosophers such as Fichte and Hegel became more interested in the creative activity of the ego or reason itself than in the natural world. It was not long, however, before these newer systems came under severe attack from both Marx and the positivists (see POSITIVISM), an attack from which idealism and metaphysics in general have never fully recovered.

See also: EPISTEMOLOGY; ETHICS; PHILOSOPHY.

metastasis see CANCER

metatherian see MARSUPIAL

Metaxás, Ioánnis [may-tahk'-sahs, yoh-ahn'-is] Ioánnis Metaxás, b. Apr. 12, 1871, d. Jan. 29, 1941, a Greek general and statesman, ruled Greece as a dictator from 1936 until his death. Although chief of the general staff from 1915, he was exiled because of his pro-German sympathies when Greece entered (1917) World War I on the Allied side. A leading royalist, he was in and out of Greece during the 1920s. Appointed prime minister in 1936 by the restored king GEORGE II, Metaxás suspended the constitution that August and established a semi-Fascist regime. In 1940, however, Greece was invaded by the Italians, and Metaxás aligned his country with the Western Allies in World War II. Shortly after his death Greece was overrun by the Germans.

metazoan

metazoan [met-uh-zoh'-uhn] In informal usage, metazoans are simply animals having a multicellular plan of structure, in contrast to one-celled animals, such as the amoeba. In formal usage, metazoans are members of the Metazoa, one of the three subkingdoms of the animal kingdom, and are characterized by a true digestive cavity, that is, one lined with endodermal epithelium. Multicellular animals without a true digestive cavity are the sponges, making up the subkingdom Parazoa. The third subkingdom is the Protozoa, or one-celled animals. Metazoans comprise nearly every form of life generally considered "animals." Characteristic of the metazoan body plan is the specialization of cells for different functions. Similar cells become organized into tissues, and, in the higher animals, many of these tissues are formed into organs.

Zoologists believe that the Metazoa evolved from protozoans. Most think that these protozoans were flagellates, possessing hairlike flagella for locomotion, and that the intermediate stage consisted of a colonial association of individual flagellate cells in the form of a hollow sphere.

Metcalfe, Charles Theophilus Metcalfe, Baron

Metcalfe, Charles Theophilus Metcalfe, Baron [met'-kuhf] Charles T. Metcalfe, b. Calcutta, Jan. 30, 1785, d. Sept. 5, 1846, headed British colonial administrations in India, Jamaica, and Canada. As provisional governor general of India (1835–36), Metcalfe ended press censorship. He then served as lieutenant governor of India's Northwestern Provinces (1836–38). After leaving India, Metcalfe was effective as governor of Jamaica (1839–42), but as governor general of Canada (1843–45) he had a stormy tenure because of his resistance to the demand for responsible government (in which ministers are responsible to the legislature).

Metellus Pius, Quintus Caecilius

Metellus Pius, Quintus Caecilius The Roman general Quintus Caecilius Metellus Pius, d. c.63 BC, supported Lucius Cornelius SULLA in the civil war of 88–82 BC. The son of Metellus Numidicus, who had been exiled by the popular party, he helped achieve his father's return to Rome (c.98), thus earning the surname Pius (meaning filial devotion). Metellus Pius fought against Gaius MARIUS and Lucius Cornelius CINNA in 87 and fled to Africa until allying (83) with Sulla, for whom he campaigned successfully in southern Italy. Metellus and Sulla were consuls together in 80. With help from POMPEY THE GREAT, Metellus eventually defeated the forces of Quintus Sertorius in Spain after Sertorius was murdered (72). In 71, Metellus returned to a triumph in Rome.

meteor and meteorite

meteor and meteorite A meteor, also known as a shooting or falling star, is the streak of light produced by the vaporization of interplanetary particles as they enter the Earth's atmosphere. While still in space the particles are called meteoroids. A large and abnormally bright meteor is referred to as a fireball, and an exploding fireball is called a bolide. Larger meteors are not completely vaporized, and the particles that reach the Earth's surface are called meteorites. They may form METEORITE CRATERS, such as those found on the Moon, the inner planets, and the satellites of Mars and Jupiter.

Meteor Showers. Although a few meteors can be seen on any night, especially after midnight, during certain times of the year so many are visible that they are termed meteor showers. Records of meteor showers predate the 11th century. Until the present century, when the origin of such showers began to be understood, the phenomenon was usually the cause of considerable fear. Most meteor showers are believed to be produced by the debris of comets, which leave a trail of particles behind them as they orbit the Sun. When the Earth intercepts this stream of cometary debris, the small, low-density particles strike the atmosphere at speeds between 35 and 95 km/sec (22 and 60 mi/sec), causing them to vaporize and creating the visible meteor display. The average size of a meteor, which can be estimated from its brightness, height, and distance, is about the size of a grain of sand.

During a shower, meteors appear to radiate from a point in the sky, called the radiant, which can be associated with a particular constellation. These radiant points give each shower its name; thus the Perseids (July 25–August 18) appear to radiate from the constellation Perseus, and the Leonids (November 15–19) from Leo. During the height of the heaviest showers, from 30 to 70 meteors may normally be seen every hour, but on rare occasions in a spectacular display that number may be visible every second.

Meteorites. It has been estimated that micrometeorites, so small that they drift to the ground without vapor-

Meteorites are masses of interplanetary rock that survive passage through the Earth's atmosphere. The Willamette Meteorite, weighing 14 metric tons and measuring 300 cm (118 in) in length, was found in Oregon in 1902.

izing, may add 1,000 tons to the mass of the Earth each day. Micrometeorites are not associated with meteor showers, nor are the larger meteorites that form craters. Although 500 large meteorites may fall on the Earth each year, only about 1% of these are recovered. About 2,200 meteorites are known throughout the world.

Meteorites may be classified according to composition as irons (siderites), stony irons (siderolites), and stones (aerolites). Iron meteorites are extremely dense and consist of 90% iron and 10% nickel. Stone meteorites have only about 10% nickel-iron and consist chiefly of silicates. Stony iron meteorites, which are relatively rare, are composed of iron and silicates in about equal proportions. Most stone meteorites contain small, spherical particles, or chondrules, composed of the silicates olivine, pyroxene, or orthopyroxene. These are called chondrites to distinguish them from the few stones without chondrules, known as achondrites. While chondrites may contain 50 different minerals along with nickel-iron, achondrites contain mainly pyroxene and plagioclase. Nickel-iron is only rarely found in achondrites. It is not known if the glassy fragments found in certain regions of the Earth, known as TEKTITES, are related to meteorites. They have never been observed to fall. Iron meteorites are the type most often found, because of their unusual appearance. Stone meteorites are actually more numerous, but since they resemble ordinary rocks, they are not often found unless a fall is actually observed. Of all observed meteorite falls, 85% are chondrites, as are 95% of all stone falls.

A special class of chondrites of particular interest are the carbonaceous chondrites. The members of this class consist largely of the mineral serpentine, and they contain amino acids and other organic compounds believed to be of extraterrestrial origin. Very dark in color, they are extremely rare and constitute only about 2% of all stone falls.

A very few meteorites have been identified as lunar in origin, but most are believed to originate from large parent bodies that formed at the time of the formation of the solar system and later broke up.

Meteor Crater   Barringer Meteor Crater, a tourist attraction and astronaut training site in northern Arizona, is a bowl-shaped depression 180 m (600 ft) deep and 1.2 km (0.72 mi) in diameter, surrounded by a rim 50 m (160 ft) high. Although nearly 100 meteorite impact scars are now known on Earth, it was the first to be identified and remains the best preserved. It was created more than 25,000 years ago by an asteroidal body, probably 30 m (100 ft) in diameter, weighing 63,000 metric tons, and traveling 8–16 km/sec (5–10 mi/sec), that exploded upon impact, releasing energy equivalent to 3.5 million tons of TNT. Most of the meteorite vaporized, but about 30 tons of fragments have been collected. The shock was so intense that it formed microscopic diamonds and two polymorphs of quartz, the minerals COESITE and stishovite.

meteorite craters   Meteorite craters, circular depressions in the crust of planets and satellites, are created by the impacts of large bodies such as asteroids, comet heads, and giant meteorites. Modern space exploration has revealed impact cratering to be the dominant process that has sculpted the surfaces of the terrestrial-type planets and satellites since their creation.

The rate of impact, however, appears to have decreased since the early years of the solar system (between 4.6 and 3.6 billion years ago), when the early debris collided and combined with the larger planets.

The Explosive Potential of Giant Meteorites

Thousands of meteorites still continue to flash through the sky each night, but most are only the size of a sand grain and thus burn up while still in the upper atmosphere. Only a few score are large enough—1 kg (2 lb) or more—to crash to the ground as meteorites (see METEOR AND METEORITE).

Meteorites of about 100 tons bore percussion pits, or penetration funnels, in the ground upon impact. Meteorites much larger than this size explode upon striking the ground because of the great velocities at which they travel. A potential exploding meteorite, or bolide, moving, for example, at only 5 km/sec (10,800 mph) already has a kinetic energy equivalent to an equal mass of TNT. A giant meteorite striking the Earth can create a crater more than ten times wider than its own diameter.

Giant meteorites of a size that would create a crater 10 km (6 mi) across have been estimated to impact on Earth only three times per million years, and only one of these would be expected to strike a continental surface, whereas the other two would probably fall in the oceans. Two such craters of recent vintage have been recognized: the 1.3-million-year-old Lake Bosumtwi (also called Ashanti) crater in Ghana and the possibly 700,000-year-old Lake El'gygytgyn crater in northeastern Siberia. The theory that the catastrophic results of the impact of a giant

Meteor Crater, near Winslow, Ariz., was formed several thousand years ago by the impact of an iron-nickel meteorite.

meteorite, asteroid, or comet on the Earth's surface may have caused the mass EXTINCTION of life forms that took place 65 million years ago, at the end of the Cretaceous Period, is now gaining increasing respectability in the scientific community.

Identification of Meteoric Origin

At the present time only twelve localities having associated meteorite fragments are known; all other impact structures are recognized by such criteria as geomorphic and structural style and by the presence of shock-wave damage.

Structure. Unlike most natural landforms, meteorite craters are created almost instantaneously; they can therefore be experimentally scale-modeled without concern for the time factor. Both laboratory experiments and geologic observations indicate that the structure of a crater is largely related to its size.

Overall, the entire structure may bear a resemblance to the wave pattern created by dropping a stone into a pool of water. Accordingly, the ancient impact sites as they appear today are commonly marked by mountains rather than by depressions. The central upward bulge is presumed to develop by a combination of ground rebound immediately after hypervelocity impact (a period of rapid decompression) and an inward flow of the ground during the terminal stages of blast excavation. Central uplifts tend to form preferentially in shallow craters where the energy burst occurs near ground level.

Nearly all impact structures recognized on the Earth still retain an overall circular pattern. Most have a central depression filled with breccia (a type of fragmented rock) and display a vestigial rim. With the passage of time, however, erosion modifies the form of the original crater, which becomes filled with sediment or may be structurally distorted by movements in the Earth's crust. The old, worn-down scars that remain are called astroblemes (literally, "star-wounds"). Because of the long sweep of geologic time, astroblemes (about 80 are known) are more common than meteorite craters (about 20) on the Earth.

Shock-Wave Damage. Intense shock effects in the target rocks are especially useful for identifying astroblemes, where obvious evidence of neither the original crater nor the projectile remains. The study of lunar material, which is commonly shocked, has helped to establish criteria for recognizing the effects of shock-metamorphism.

Of unusual interest, and regarded as diagnostic of an impact event, is the presence of COESITE and stishovite, the two high-density polymorphs of quartz. Both of these rare minerals were detected for the first time in nature at Meteor Crater, after their presence was predicted by scientists. Apparently, intense shock equivalent to that delivered by a bolide impact is needed to convert common quartz to these high-pressure variants of silica.

Occurrence

The craters that have been identified with the most certainty as meteoritic in origin are those with which associated meteorite fragments have been found. Such craters must be only a few tens of thousands of years old at the most, because meteoritic materials weather rather rapidly in the terrestrial environment. The largest such crater, the more than 25,000-year-old METEOR CRATER (also called the Barringer or Canyon Diablo Crater) remains in a remarkable state of preservation because of its Arizona desert environment. Other craters whose meteoritic origin was identified between 1920 and 1950 include the 850-m-diameter (2,800-ft) Wolf Creek Crater in Australia (the second largest known site that contains definite bolide fragments), three other examples in Australia (Dalgaranga, Boxhole, and the Henbury group of craters); the Kaalijarv crater in Estonia; the El Aouelloul crater in Mauritania; and the Wabar crater in the Empty Quarter of Saudi Arabia.

In the United States, geologists have identified, in addition to Meteor Crater, three small craters near Odessa, Tex., and about a dozen astroblemes. Many large impact structures have been recognized in the ancient rocks of the Canadian Shield since the discovery (1950) of the New Quebec Crater in northern Quebec. Manicouagan Reservoir astrobleme in Quebec, for example, is a ring structure 70 km (40 mi) across, with an uplifted center surrounded by a depressed, annular, lake-filled ring.

---

meteorological instrumentation Meteorology is the study of the atmosphere. Although observations concerning weather and CLIMATE were made by early humans, quantitative measurements could not be made until the invention of various meteorological instruments. Separate articles discuss the BAROMETER, HYGROMETER, and THERMOMETER; these meteorological instruments measure, respectively, air pressure, humidity, and temperature. RADIOSONDES, small radio transmitters, are used to transmit measurements made in the upper atmosphere—from balloons, for example, to ground stations. Some other instruments are briefly discussed below.

Purpose of Instruments

Meteorological observations serve three purposes: (1) providing climatological averages, (2) providing data for WEATHER FORECASTING, and (3) providing microclimatologists (also called micrometeorologists) with detailed information about the atmosphere's lowest 100 m (330 ft): temperature and wind profiles, vertical flow of heat, momentum, water vapor, and pollutants.

Simple instruments such as rain gauges and weather vanes were invented more than 2,000 years ago. They were useful for climatological measurements but had little value for weather forecasting because the latter requires accurate values of air pressure, humidity, and temperature. Instruments for measuring these variables—the barometer, hygrometer, and thermometer—were invented about 1650. Weather forecasts based on data from a single station are usually very poor. For more accurate forecasts, synoptic data—data from many stations—must be relayed to a central station. Modern weather forecasting therefore developed after the inven-

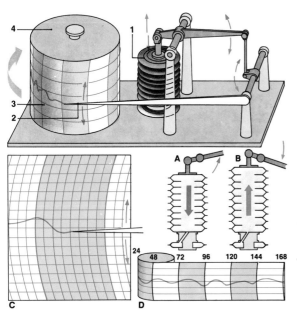

A barograph is a device for measuring atmospheric pressure. It consists of an aneroid barometer connected to a recording instrument. The barometer (1), a flexible metal chamber controlled by a spring, responds to changes in air pressure by contracting (A) and expanding (B). A stylus (2) records these movements on a graph (3) mounted on a turning cylinder (4). Any fluctuation in pressure is immediately registered (C). The cylinder completes one rotation weekly. The more sensitive microbarograph rotates once every 24 hours (D).

tion of the telegraph in the middle of the 19th century.

The accuracy of present-day instruments is excellent for climatological purposes, more than sufficient for synoptic purposes (weather forecasts fail for reasons other than instrumental errors), and marginal to good for micrometeorological investigations. Perhaps even more important than the accuracy and reliability of an instrument is that it be exposed correctly during the measurement. A nonshielded thermometer, for example, will absorb direct or diffuse sunlight and, consequently, indicate a temperature higher than the true air temperature.

Types of Instruments

Instruments for measuring precipitation, evaporation, sunshine duration, and solar radiational energy are discussed below.

Precipitation. The earliest meteorological instruments were probably rain gauges, because they are so easy to construct: if a vessel is exposed to precipitation and the horizontal cross section of the vessel is constant, a measuring stick will indicate the total amount of precipitation. The oldest recorded data are from India in the 4th century BC., where an extensive climatological network must have existed because averages are known for several areas. In 1663, Sir Christopher Wren, the architect of Saint Paul's Cathedral in London, constructed the first self-recording rain gauge.

Different countries have rain gauges with different sizes. The standard instrument in the United States has a cylindrical form. The orifice has a radius of 20 cm (8 in) and is 60 cm (24 in) above the ground.

Evaporation. The most reliable instruments to measure evaporation are lysimeters. They consist of a piece of natural soil (weighing several tons) with vegetation similar to the immediate surroundings. By weighing this piece at regular intervals, the evaporation can be determined after taking into account the gain of water by rainfall and irrigation and the loss of water by percolation. Very few of these huge instruments exist.

Sunshine Duration. The duration of sunshine can be measured with a Campbell-Stokes sunshine recorder. A solid glass sphere is used to focus the Sun's rays, so that a record is charred on specially printed cards; the beginning and end of sunny periods can be read off at the end of the day, at which time the old card is replaced by a new one. Basically the same instrument as the one designed by J. F. Campbell in the 1850s, it is still being used worldwide.

Solar Radiation. Instruments for measuring sunshine duration cannot distinguish between degrees of brightness. The general method of measuring the solar-radiation intensity is to have a black plate absorb all of the solar energy and then have this energy converted into heat in the plate. Because the variable air temperature also influences the temperature of the black plate, a similar white plate (reflecting the sunshine) is part of the instrument. The temperature difference between the two plates is a good indicator of the amount of incident solar radiational energy. Various instruments perform this measurement, for example, the ACTINOMETER, pyrheliometer, and solarimeter, but they all operate on similar principles.

Use of Radar

Liquid and solid particles, such as cloud droplets, raindrops, ice crystals, hailstones, and snowflakes, scatter microwave radiation, thus producing RADAR echoes. The scattering increases strongly with the increasing radius of the scattering particles and with the decreasing wavelength of the radar. A radar wavelength of 3 cm (1.2 in) is preferred for detecting light precipitation, and a 10-cm

The pluviometer, or rain gauge, measures precipitation. Its outer case (1) is a metal can designed to provide stability when embedded in the earth. Inside the can is a funnel (2), which channels rain, snow, and hail into a glass jar (3). The accumulated liquid is then poured into a graduated cylinder (4) to be measured.

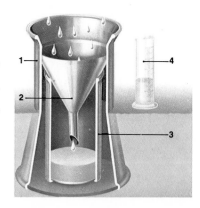

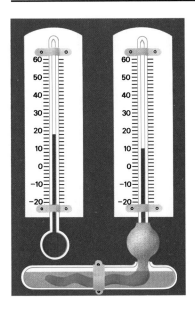

A psychrometer measures humidity in the air. It consists of two mercury thermometers mounted on a frame. The bulb of one thermometer (right) *is wrapped in a piece of wet cloth. As the water evaporates, this thermometer is cooled. The degree to which evaporation takes place is determined by the amount of water already present in the air: moist air will cause less evaporation, dry air will cause more. The difference between thermometer readings is checked against prepared charts to determine the relative humidity of the air.*

(4-in) wavelength for heavy precipitation. The echoes enable the meteorologist to identify areas with clouds, to identify the nature of the cloud elements, to estimate the precipitation rate, and (still experimentally) to detect the formation of a tornado 20 minutes before a funnel touches down.

meteorology   Meteorology is the study of the Earth's ATMOSPHERE and the variations in temperature and moisture patterns that produce different weather conditions. Some of the major subjects of study are such phenomena as PRECIPITATION (rain and snow), THUNDERSTORMS, TORNADOES, and HURRICANES.

The importance of meteorological events is felt in various ways. For example, a DROUGHT results in water shortages, crop damage, low river-flow rates, and increased wildfire potential. In addition, these effects may lead to restricted river travel, saltwater infiltration in aquifers and coastal bays, stress on various plant and animal species, population shifts, economic hardship, and even political unrest. The critical impact of weather on human activity has led to the development of the uncertain science of WEATHER FORECASTING.

The word *meteorology* derives from the Greek word *meteoron*, which refers to an astronomical phenomenon. Aristotle's *Meteorologica* (340 BC) concerned all phenomena above the ground. Astronomy, including the study of meteors, or "shooting stars," later became a separate discipline. The science of meteorology was restricted eventually to the study of the atmosphere. Various weather phenomena are still referred to as "meteors," such as hydrometeors (liquid or frozen water—rain, SNOW AND SNOWFLAKES, CLOUDS, FOG), lithometeors (dry particles—sand, dust, or smoke; see SANDSTORM AND DUST STORM), photometeors (optical phenomena—HALOS, MI-

RAGES, RAINBOWS), coronas, and electrometeors (electrical phenomena—LIGHTNING, SAINT ELMO'S FIRE).

Modern meteorology focuses primarily on the typical weather patterns observed, including thunderstorms, extratropical cyclones (see CYCLONE AND ANTICYCLONE), hurricanes, typhoons, and MONSOONS. Meteorology is usually considered to describe and study the physical basis for individual events; in contrast, climatology (see CLIMATE) describes and studies the origin of atmospheric patterns observed over time.

Scope

A complete description of the atmosphere requires an interdisciplinary approach, drawing on many fields of science and engineering. The atmosphere's motions, based on the fluid-dynamics equations for a compressible fluid (namely air) on the rotating Earth (see CORIOLIS EFFECT), are treated in dynamic meteorology. One important complication in studying the atmosphere is that the changes of atmospheric water among the three phases (solid, liquid, and gas) occur in a highly complex, nonlinear fashion. These changes profoundly modify the equations used in dynamic meteorology.

The behavior of water is also studied in its own right as part of physical meteorology (atmospheric physics), namely cloud physics, which deals with clouds, fog, and hydrometeors (see WEATHER MODIFICATION). Physical meteorology has a number of other specialties dealing with additional physical processes. For example, radiative transfer addresses the fundamental driving force in the atmosphere, incoming SOLAR RADIATION, and the problem of propagating radiant energy. Other specialized disciplines are atmospheric optics and atmospheric acoustics.

Some branches of meteorology take integrative views of typical phenomena at particular scales (or sizes). Successively larger scales (in space and time) are considered in micrometeorology (the study of phenomena in the lowest 1–2 km/0.6–1.2 mi of the atmosphere; see MICROCLIMATE), mesoscale meteorology (thunderstorms, sea breezes, mountain winds), synoptic meteorology (high and low pressure systems, FRONTS), and the study of general circulation (monsoons). Weather forecasting, the predictive aspect of meteorology, derives from these disciplines; each branch tries to apply the insights gained by all the others in an attempt to understand its own particular weather events.

Other branches of meteorology focus on phenomena in specific locations, such as equatorial areas, the tropics, maritime regions, coastal areas, the poles, and mountains. The upper atmosphere is also studied separately. Other disciplines concentrate on taking observations with particular technologies, including radio, RADAR, and satellites. Computer technology, including numerical weather prediction, interactive data analysis, and display systems, is applied extensively.

The chemical behavior of the atmosphere, studied in atmospheric chemistry, is rapidly gaining in importance due to inadvertent changes caused by humans in the molecular composition of the atmosphere. Changes in ozone (see OZONE LAYER) and carbon dioxide (CO_2) concentra-

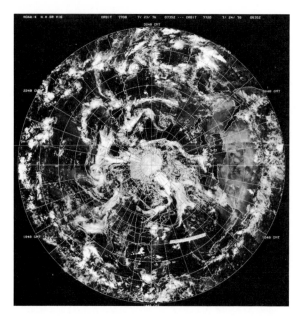

This global view of the weather is a mosaic of many photographs taken by orbiting meteorological satellites. Such mosaics enable meteorologists to study weather patterns affecting the entire planet.

tions, and increased levels of ACID RAIN, have gone beyond the status of local problems to become regional or global issues (see GREENHOUSE EFFECT; POLLUTION, ENVIRONMENTAL).

Meteorological studies are carried out in conjunction with several environmentally related fields. These include aeronautics, agriculture, architecture, ballistics, ecology, energy production, forestry, hydrology, medicine, and oceanography. Many of these related fields simply need to determine the weather's effects at a particular time and place, but some (hydrology and oceanography, for example) also affect meteorological events by modifying atmospheric conditions at the Earth's surface (see OCEAN-ATMOSPHERE INTERACTION).

Development of Modern Meteorology

Modern dynamic meteorology was born in 1948, when Jule Charney succeeded in reducing the dynamic equations of motion to a simple form. Development of the digital computer allowed weather forecasting to be based on an approximate solution to these equations.

Since 1948, technologies for remote sensing of the atmosphere have proliferated. By 1950 radar had been developed to the point where it could be used to delineate clouds by their suspended water droplets and thus indicate the internal structure of storms, especially thunderstorms. In the mid-1960s radar units that measure the Doppler shift (see DOPPLER EFFECT) were developed to provide velocity information, as well as reflectivity. After 1960 weather satellites began providing detailed observations of the entire Earth.

In the United States the first sustained governmental activity in meteorology came in 1870, when Congress di-

rected the army to organize a weather service to forecast storms over the Great Lakes and the coasts. After two decades this activity, conducted by the Signal Corps, was transferred to a new civilian Weather Bureau. Half a century later the growing need of aviators for frequent observations and short-term forecasts led to the bureau's transfer to the Department of Commerce. In 1965 the Weather Bureau became part of the new Environmental Science Services Administration (ESSA), with climatology separated into a new Environmental Data Service (EDS); five years later the Bureau became the NATIONAL WEATHER SERVICE.

Contemporary Meteorology

The field of meteorology is increasingly becoming computerized and automated as scientists seek how best to use the flood of observations from a wide variety of traditional and new instruments. For example, rapid processing of Doppler radar data is crucial to maximize the warning time for tornadoes and other severe local weather phenomena. The preparation of observations for use in large numerical global forecast models, the "timestepping" of these models, and the processing of the resulting output are too laborious for any but the most powerful computers.

New observing systems coming on-line in the early 1990s include the NEXRAD (Next Generation Radar) Doppler radar network, the Profiler wind-sensing network, and many new, powerful satellite sensors, such as the scatterometer, which can measure wind speeds at the ocean's surface.

Much of this information is passed around the world on the WORLD WEATHER WATCH, organized by the WORLD METEOROLOGICAL ORGANIZATION. In turn, a few centers around the world develop large models from the conditions observed, and send the resulting weather forecasts across the network. Two such centers are the National

This satellite photograph indicates the cloud temperatures of Hurricane Camille (1969). A computer translated the infrared brightness levels of the original photograph into color tones, which correspond to degrees of heat.

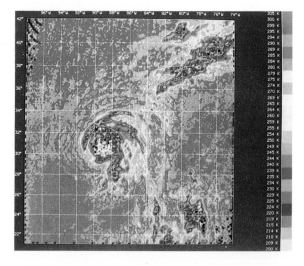

Meteorologists use computers to generate sophisticated models of tornadoes, based on atmospheric measurements in the hope of making accurate hourly forecasts of storm behavior. From these data they can construct three-dimensional models. Here the colors indicate rain densities at six different altitudes in a tornado, with red signifying the heaviest rainfall.

Meteorological Center (Suitland, Md.) and the European Center for Medium-Range Weather Forecasting (Bracknell, in the United Kingdom).

Another form of international cooperation is seen in various meteorological programs. For example, the Tropical Ocean Global Atmosphere project seeks to develop observations and theories revealing the links between tropical oceans and the entire world's atmosphere. The International Satellite Cloud Climatology Program is an attempt to quantify the effects of clouds on the atmosphere. Such international cooperation is crucial in addressing various global-scale phenomena.

See also: ATMOSPHERIC SCIENCES; WEATHER VARIATION AND EXTREMES.

meter (literature)   see VERSIFICATION

meter (music)   Meter is the pattern of regular time units (beats) employed for measuring music. In a score, meter is indicated by time signatures and measure bars. In time signatures, for example, $2/4$, $3/2$, $6/8$, or the like, the lower number names the kind of note (quarter, half, or eighth in the signatures shown here) that gets one beat; the upper number tells how many such beats fall into each measure of the piece or section. From the end of the Renaissance to the 20th century, a single meter has usually prevailed throughout a piece. Other music at times has had polymeters (several meters simultaneously) and multimeters (different meters successively). Metrical psalms (see HYMN) employ meter in the poetic sense of measuring the number of syllables in a line.

methadone [meth'-uh-dohn]   Methadone, a synthetic narcotic, was developed in Germany during World War II

as a measure against a decreased supply of opium, which was used medicinally. Its properties resemble those of morphine, except that it is more active when taken orally, and its duration of action is considerably longer. These attributes have made it an especially useful drug for treating patients afflicted with chronic pain, such as those suffering from cancer, who require a potent narcotic analgesic. Relatively small doses frequently suffice, although as tolerance develops, doses must be increased.

Because methadone behaves in most respects the same way as morphine and heroin do, it has become the preferred treatment for detoxification from these drugs in that it prevents severe withdrawal symptoms and circumvents the use of needles. Doses are given according to a patient's need until a stable state is reached in which methadone has fully been substituted for the other opiate. The methadone doses are then gradually reduced until the patient, in theory, is free from dependence. In practice, however, the methadone habit frequently simply replaces the previous habit.

Methadone maintenance is a controversial practice introduced as a treatment for heroin addicts in 1963. The theory behind this practice is that methadone addiction is not accompanied by the impairments of function that follow repeated intravenous doses of heroin. Furthermore, in theory, most patients can be managed with relatively low doses. In practice, methadone maintenance was originally initiated as a means of reducing the criminal behavior associated with heroin addiction. Cocaine and alcohol, however, are more frequently associated with crimes of violence than is heroin addiction, and methadone users often abuse those drugs.

methane [meth'-ayn]   Methane, or marsh gas, is a colorless, odorless gas that is the principal component (about 85%) of natural gas. Widely distributed in nature, methane is a major constituent of the atmospheres of the outer planets. With one carbon atom per molecule, methane (CH_4) is the simplest HYDROCARBON. The gas is nonpoisonous but inflammable, burning with a pale blue flame. In addition to its familiar use in natural gas for cooking and heating, methane is used to manufacture numerous organic chemicals including methyl alcohol, methyl and methylene chlorides, ammonia, acetylene, and formaldehyde.

methanol   see METHYL ALCOHOL

methemoglobinemia   see BLOOD

method acting   Acting that enters the inner thoughts and feelings of the character to be portrayed is known as method acting. It is usually contrasted with the mechanical-external system of acting, in which the mastery of technique is considered paramount. Method acting is also called the Stanislavsky system for its founder, the early-20th-century Russian director Konstantin STANISLAVSKY. The system became popular in the United States in the

1930s, largely through the efforts of the American Group Theatre, whose more prominent members included Lee Strasberg, John Garfield, Harold Clurman, Lee J. Cobb, Elia Kazan, and Sanford Meisner. Among the important contemporary actors who were trained in the tradition of method acting are Marlon Brando, Maureen Stapleton, and Eli Wallach.

Methodism   Methodism is the name given to a group of Protestant churches that arose from the 18th-century Wesleyan movement in England led by John and Charles Wesley (see WESLEY family) and George WHITEFIELD. The origins of Methodism are inseparable from the careers of the Wesley brothers. In 1738, influenced by the Moravians (see MORAVIAN CHURCH), they organized small "societies" within the Church of England for religious sharing, Bible study, prayer, and preaching. Doctrine was based on an Arminian (see ARMINIANISM) interpretation of the THIRTY-NINE ARTICLES but emphasized personal experience of conversion, assurance, and sanctification. The Wesleys and their associate Whitefield traveled widely, preaching to large and enthusiastic crowds of working people. The movement spread through most of England. A striking growth took place in Ireland and to a lesser extent in Wales and Scotland. To preserve personal fellowship, "bands" and "class meetings" were formed, and the whole was brought together (1744) by John Wesley in the British Conference.

When John Wesley died in 1791 the relationship between the Methodists and the Church of England was unclear, although Wesley's ordination of "clergy" for work in

John Wesley, an ordained minister in the Church of England, was the founder of Methodism. In 1738, Wesley formed a society within the Church of England that was devoted to the study of religion "by rule and method."

America made a breach likely. The separation was formalized when the Conference of 1795 asserted that Methodist preachers could administer sacraments without ordination by the Church of England.

A number of divisions soon took place among the Methodists. The Methodist New Connection, the Primitive Methodist Church, and the Bible Christians separated from the Conference between 1797 and 1815. They were reunited in two mergers (1907, 1932) with the main branch to form the Methodist Church in Britain, which today has a membership of about 450,000. The central organization is the British Conference. This church has recently engaged in ecumenical negotiations with the Church of England.

Whitefield conducted several preaching tours in North America and was an influential figure in the GREAT AWAKENING. Wesleyan Methodism was later established in America by unofficial lay missionaries such as Philip EMBURY, Barbara Heck, Robert Strawbridge, and Thomas Webb; and by missionaries appointed by John Wesley, of whom the chief were Francis ASBURY, Richard Boardman, Joseph Pilmore, and Thomas Rankin. In 1784, Wesley's actual ordination of two missionaries and appointment of Thomas COKE as "superintendent" for America led to the formation of the Methodist Episcopal Church in Baltimore.

In 1830, in a controversy over episcopal authority, the Methodist Protestant Church was formed by a strongly liberal minority. In 1843 the Wesleyan Methodist Church of America was started by a group of antislavery Methodists. The next year the General Conference split over issues related to slavery and episcopal authority, and the Methodist Episcopal Church, South, was formed at the Louisville convention in 1845. In 1860 came the Free Methodist Church, which was antislavery and theologically perfectionist. The Methodist Episcopal Church was troubled by controversy over sanctification and interpretation of the Bible (fundamentalism). Three large black churches were also organized, largely in protest against racial prejudice: the African Methodist Episcopal Church (1816), the African Methodist Episcopal Zion Church (1820), and the Colored (later Christian) Methodist Episcopal Church (1870).

With the formation of the Methodist Church in 1939 by the Northern and Southern branches and the Methodist Protestants, reunion was achieved. A racially identified central jurisdiction was abolished in 1968. In that year the church merged with the EVANGELICAL UNITED BRETHREN CHURCH to form the United Methodist Church.

Methuselah [muh-thoo'-suh-luh]   The biblical patriarch Methuselah, the son of Enoch and grandfather of Noah, died at the age of 969, according to Genesis 5. The expression *as old as Methuselah* is used to describe a very old person.

methyl alcohol   Methyl alcohol, CH_3OH, also known as methanol and wood alcohol, is a colorless, poisonous liquid originally obtained by the distillation of wood in the absence of air. It may be produced catalytically from carbon monoxide and hydrogen. It is water-soluble and undergoes all of the reactions of a primary ALCOHOL.

The consumption of methyl alcohol can cause blindness, and as little as 30 ml (1 oz) has caused death. Methyl alcohol is used as a solvent for plastics, paints, and varnishes; as an antifreeze; and in the manufacture of methyl compounds.

Methyl alcohol can be used as a motor fuel either by itself or in combination with gasoline in the mixture GASOHOL. Methyl alcohol–powered automobiles produce less carbon monoxide and reduce ozone formation, resulting in less air pollution. Because methyl alcohol corrodes engines, however, cars that run on gasoline must be redesigned to burn it.

Meton [mee'-tahn]   The Athenian astronomer Meton, fl. 450–400 BC, gave his name to a 19-year lunisolar calendaric cycle. This cycle of 6,940 days (19 solar years) was found to be almost equivalent to 235 lunar (synodic) months. The discovery of this cycle facilitated the intercalation of a 13th month in the Greek CALENDAR, which normally consisted of 12 lunar months (354 days).

metric system   The modern metric system of units and standards of measure is rooted in 17th- and 18th-century efforts to establish a simple, easily used, universally acceptable system of WEIGHTS AND MEASURES. These efforts were motivated by two guiding principles. In the first place, there were many who hoped for the definition of a single unit of measure that could serve as the basis for the logical construction of a complete and consistent system of units of measure; in the second place, there was also a growing number of people favoring decimal relationships for units of the same quantity.

The forces driving toward a change from diverse and essentially unrelated customary systems of measure included rapidly growing international commerce and the changing political structure of Europe and its colonial dependencies. It became necessary to accommodate many incompatible ways of doing business. Moreover, the growth of scientific investigation not only created new demands for accuracy and uniformity in measurements, it also provided the vision for a universally acceptable scientific basis for a system of measurements. The customary systems, handed down mainly from the Babylonians, Egyptians, Greeks, and Romans, were based on unrelated objects and phenomena, including human anatomy, with no practical hope for uniformity.

Origins of the Metric System

The birth of the metric system occurred in the climate of bold reform and scientific rationalization that prevailed in France during the latter part of the 18th century. The French Academy of Sciences organized committees to study the creation of a standard system of weights and measures. After scientific consideration of various possibilities, the committee recommended a new unit of length equal to one ten-millionth of the length of the arc from the equator to the North Pole, or a quadrant of the Earth's meridian circle. This unit was given the name *mètre,* derived from the Greek word *metron,* meaning "a measure." From the same word came the name of the new system. The unit of mass, the kilogram, was defined as the mass of water contained by a cube whose sides are one-tenth the unit of length. The unit of volume, the liter, was defined in the same way; thus the unit of length became the basis for the system. The new Republic of France adopted the recommendations of the French Academy in 1793.

Development of the System

The French Academy of Sciences also recommended that the primary reference standard for the unit of length be defined by a precise measurement of the arc of meridian between Dunkerque, France, and Barcelona, Spain. Platinum artifact reference standards for the meter and the kilogram were constructed in 1799 and deposited in the French National Archives in Paris. These two standards later came to be known as the Meter of the Archives and the Kilogram of the Archives.

The introduction of the metric system in France met with the usual resistance to change. In 1812 the old units of measure were restored by Napoleon I, emperor of France. In 1840 the metric system again became mandatory in France. The use of the metric system spread slowly to other European countries and to the United States, where it became legal, but not mandatory, in 1866. The international acceptance of the metric system was implemented by the Diplomatic Conference of the Meter, convened in 1875, and attended by delegates from 20 countries. This conference produced the Treaty of the Meter, signed in May 1875 by the delegates of 17 countries, including the United States.

The metric treaty provided the institutional machinery needed to promote the refinement, diffusion, and use of the metric system. The International Committee for Weights and Measures, widely known as CIPM *(Comité International des Poids et Mesures),* was established under the broad supervision of the General Conference on Weights and Measures, CGPM *(Conférence Général des Poids et Mesures),* consisting of delegates from member countries. The first General Conference met in 1889 to approve new international metric prototype reference standards to redefine length and mass. These prototypes were based on the Archives standards. The First CGPM also ratified the equality (within known uncertainties) of a number of national prototype standards for length and mass and distributed these standards to the member nations. This was the beginning of the diffusion of a uniform metric system throughout the world. The Metric Convention also established the International Bureau of Weights and Measures, BIPM *(Bureau International des Poids et Mesures),* to carry out the scientific work of the International System under the supervision of CIPM.

NAMES AND SYMBOLS FOR METRIC PREFIXES

Prefix	Symbol	Multiplier
exa (10^{18})	E	1,000,000,000,000,000,000
peta (10^{15})	P	1,000,000,000,000,000
tera (10^{12})	T	1,000,000,000,000
giga (10^9)	G	1,000,000,000
mega (10^6)	M	1,000,000
kilo (10^3)	k	1,000
hecto (10^2)	h	100
deka (10)	da	10
deci (10^{-1})	d	0.1
centi (10^{-2})	c	0.01
milli (10^{-3})	m	0.001
micro (10^{-6})	μ	0.000 001
nano (10^{-9})	n	0.000 000 001
pico (10^{-12})	p	0.000 000 000 001
femto (10^{-15})	f	0.000 000 000 000 001
atto (10^{-18})	a	0.000 000 000 000 000 001

The Metric System in the United States

In the United States, there was much official and scientific interest in the development of the metric system during the earliest days of the nation. President Washington urged Congress to take action toward uniform measurements. Thomas Jefferson and John Quincy Adams, during their terms as secretary of state, carried out comprehensive studies of a decimal measurement system. Following an additional special study by the newly organized National Academy of Sciences in 1866, Congress enacted legislation authorizing (but not mandating) the use of the metric system in the United States that same year.

The act of 1866 was an important turning point in the history of measurements in the United States. By making it lawful to employ the metric system, the act was a first step toward eventually harmonizing the U.S. measurement system with those of other nations. The act also defined by law the relationships to be used in calculating the values of customary units of measurement used in the United States from the corresponding metric units. Moreover, in that same year a joint resolution authorized and directed the secretary of the treasury to furnish each state with one set of standard metric weights and measures.

With the act of 1866 as a background, the United States was an important participant in the considerations leading to the Metric Convention of May 20, 1875. In 1893, metric prototypes were declared to be the U.S. Fundamental Standards for length and mass.

In 1901 the U.S. National Bureau of Standards was organized for the purpose of serving the worlds of science and technology; it made little progress toward a wider acceptance of metric units.

Following World War II, however, and particularly following the USSR's successful launching (1957) of the first space satellite, *Sputnik 1*—which opened the age of space exploration—a renewed interest in the metric system developed in the United States. By 1968 the spread of metric measurements throughout the world was nearly complete. Arguments for conversion based on expanding foreign markets were becoming increasingly persuasive. Recognizing these trends, in 1968 Congress authorized the secretary of commerce to undertake a new and intensive study over a period of three years in order to determine the advantages and the disadvantages of increased use of the metric system in the United States. The resulting report, *The U.S. Metric Study*, published in 1970–71, treated all aspects of the issue and considered the interests of consumers, educators, professionals, industry, and state and federal agencies. It concluded that the United States should join the rest of the world in the use of the metric system as the predominant common language of measurement.

Following the recommendation of *The U.S. Metric Study*, Congress enacted the Metric Conversion Act of 1975, which declared that "the policy of the United States shall be to coordinate and plan the increasing use of the metric system in the United States and to establish a United States Metric Board to coordinate the voluntary conversion to the metric system." The Office of Metric Programs replaced the U.S. Metric Board in 1982.

Despite such efforts on the part of the government to promote the metric system, the public resisted the use of this system of measurement. Popular use of the metric system in the United States in the 1980s remains limited, although some U.S. industries use metric units. Motor vehicles, farm machinery, and computer equipment are manufactured to metric specifications.

Base Units and Derived Units

When the metric system was first conceived, one of the goals was the definition of a single unit from which the essential system of measurements could be constructed. Indeed, it was thought that the unit of length, the meter, should be regarded in this way, and much scientific effort went into the careful selection of an acceptable definition. It was also necessary to rely on the properties of pure water in order to define a unit of mass, the kilogram. The measurement system required for trade and commerce in the 18th century rested on the definitions of two units, the meter (length) and the kilogram (mass); units for other necessary quantities, such as area and volume, were derived from them. The ultimate goal of a complete system of measurements logically derived from the definition of a single unit was not realizable when the metric system was first established, and it is not realizable today. Nevertheless, the fundamental idea persisted, and a modern metric system has been founded on six base units and designated by the 11th CGPM (1960) as the International System of Units with the international abbreviation SI (see UNITS, PHYSICAL). The SI base units—expanded to seven in 1971—are independent by convention, and are the meter, kilogram, second, ampere, kelvin, mole, and candela. It is possible, in principle, for industrial nations to maintain complete systems of measurement that are equivalent within acceptable limits of uncertainty by comparing national standards for the SI base units to those maintained by the International Bureau of Weights and Measures, BIPM *(Bureau International des Poids et Mesures)*, in Sèvres, France.

metropolitan area   A metropolitan area is the region encompassing a city, its suburbs, and the towns and rural areas that fall within the orbit of its social and economic influence. Since 1983 the U.S. Office of Management and Budget has designated such U.S. metropolitan areas as Metropolitan Statistical Areas (MSAs) and, for the largest metropolitan complexes, Consolidated Metropolitan Statistical Areas (CMSAs). The individual components of CMSAs are called Primary Metropolitan Statistical Areas (PMSAs). In 1988 there were 287 officially designated MSAs and CMSAs. Within just 37 of these areas reside 119 million people, nearly half the U.S. population. The New York metropolitan area, with 18 million people, is the largest, followed by Los Angeles, Chicago, San Francisco, and Philadelphia. Greater London, in England, and Japan's Tokyo-Yokohama complex are examples of other large metropolitan areas.

See also: CITY; MEGALOPOLIS.

Metropolitan Museum of Art, The   The Metropolitan Museum of Art, New York City, founded in 1870, is the largest art museum in the Western world. Its collections span 5,000 years of art history and cover almost every area of world art: the Ancient Near East, Egyptian, Greek and Roman, Islamic, and Far Eastern art; European painting, sculpture, and decorative arts; American painting, sculpture, and decorative arts; musical instruments; arms and armor; and costumes and textiles.

This comprehensive collection grew out of a small group of 174 paintings purchased in Paris in 1870 and was enlarged in 1874 by a significant collection of antiquities excavated in Cyprus by Luigi Palma di Cesnola, who

The exterior facade of the Metropolitan Museum of Art is the work of several architects. Richard Morris Hunt designed the Beaux-Arts exterior of the central wing (completed 1902); McKim, Mead, and White added the flanking wings (completed 1926).

later became the museum's director (1876–1914). The first permanent building, in Central Park, was designed (1874–80) by Calvert Vaux as a neo-Gothic structure; it was altered (1895) and incorporated into Richard Morris Hunt's neoclassic extension of the building along Fifth Avenue. Monumental wings were added by the architectural firm of McKim, Mead, and White (1905–26).

Among more recent additions to the museum's holdings are the Robert Lehman collection and the Rockefeller collection of primitive art, both now housed in their own wings, opened in 1975 and 1982, respectively.

Metropolitan Opera   The most prestigious opera company in the United States, the Metropolitan Operahouse Company, Ltd. in New York City first opened its doors to the public on Oct. 22, 1883, with a performance of Gounod's *Faust*. The original opera house, located at 39th Street on Manhattan's West Side, was designed by Josiah Cleveland Cady. The first season resulted in a deficit of $600,000, and a new directorial regime promoted 7 years of opera in German. A serious fire in 1892 necessitated another rethinking of the company's goals when the theater was reopened under the management of Henry E. Abbey and Maurice Grau.

The great days of the "Met" then began. Singers such as Lilli Lehmann, Emma Eames, Nellie Melba, and Lillian Nordica were engaged, and operas were sung in their original languages. Heinrich Conried, who succeeded Grau in 1903, engaged Enrico Caruso, Geraldine Farrar, Fyodor Chaliapin, and Gustav Mahler and defied Cosima Wagner by producing her husband's *Parsifal*. When the banker Otto Kahn bought out the company in 1908, Giulio Gatti-Casazza and Arturo Toscanini became general manager and musical director, respectively.

The Depression of the 1930s threatened the company's survival; its labor and financial problems persisted into the regimes of Edward JOHNSON (general manager 1935–50) and Rudolf BING (1950–72).

The company relocated in September 1966, when the new Metropolitan Opera House—designed by Wallace K. Harrison—opened at Lincoln Center with the world premiere of Samuel Barber's *Antony and Cleopatra*. Despite recent fiscal pressures and managerial turnover, the Metropolitan Opera remains an operatic mecca of the United States, reaching the entire nation with its radio and television broadcasts.

Metsu, Gabriel   [met'-soo, gah'-bree-el]   Gabriel Metsu, b. January 1629, d. October 1667, was a Dutch genre painter. A pupil of the Leiden painter Gerard Dou, Metsu was active in Leiden for the first part of his career. His work also reflects the influence of Jan Vermeer and Pieter de Hoogh. He had settled in Amsterdam by 1657 and spent the last decade of his short life there. Fascinated by rare and precious objects, Dutch interiors, and color and light, Metsu created a wide range of works, some painted quite broadly and some with the meticulous precision his teacher had made famous in Leiden. His

The 17th-century Dutch painter Gabriel Metsu was a master in portraying the contemporaneous middle class. The Sick Child *(1660), exemplifies his depiction of daily life. (Rijksmuseum, Amsterdam.)*

best-known painting, *The Sick Child* (c.1660; Rijksmuseum, Amsterdam), is noted for its simplicity and directness. The *Man Writing a Letter* and *Woman Reading a Letter* (both undated and both in the collection of Sir Alfred Beit, Blessington, Ireland) and the *Visit to the Nursery* (c.1660; Metropolitan Museum of Art, New York City) are other well-known examples of Metsu's skills.

Metsys, Quentin   see MASSYS, QUENTIN

▬

Metternich, Klemens, Fürst von [met'-ur-nik, klay'-menz, fuerst fuhn]   Prince Metternich, b. May 15, 1773, d. June 11, 1859, was the foreign minister (1809–48) and chancellor (1821–48) who guided Austria to victory in the NAPOLEONIC WARS and established its central position in 19th-century Europe. Born in the Rhineland, Klemens Wenzel Nepomuk Lothar von Metternich came from a family of imperial counts. As a student he witnessed the early violence of the French Revolution and became a champion of enlightened but decisive government.

In Vienna in 1795, Metternich married Eleanore von Kaunitz, granddaughter of the former Austrian chancellor Wenzel Anton von Kaunitz. Metternich then rose steadily in the Austrian diplomatic service and in 1806 became

ambassador to France. He came to admire NAPOLEON I, even while plotting war against him with the Austrian foreign minister, Johann Philipp von Stadion.

In 1809, Metternich succeeded Stadion as foreign minister. He then pursued a French alliance, his master stroke being the marriage (1810) of Marie Louise, the daughter of Emperor Francis I (formerly Holy Roman Emperor FRANCIS II), to Napoleon. After Napoleon's disastrous Russian campaign in 1812, Metternich tried unsuccessfully to persuade Napoleon to withdraw from central Europe without bringing the Russians in. At the Congress of Vienna (September 1814–June 1815; see VIENNA, CONGRESS OF), Metternich, who had been created prince in 1813, cut a brilliant figure. Supported by Lord CASTLEREAGH of Britain and Charles de TALLEYRAND-PÉRIGORD of France, he restricted the territorial aggrandizement of Prussia and Russia. He also created the GERMAN CONFEDERATION under Austrian presidency, thus keeping Prussia from the leading position in Germany. In Italy, Austria annexed Lombardy and Venetia and restored the Illyrian provinces. Thus Austria became the center of a loosely organized buffer zone between France and Russia.

Metternich's course became increasingly repressive, however. At the congresses of Troppau (1820), Laibach (1821), and Verona (1822), he favored intervention by the great powers against revolution, and he increasingly aligned Austria with Prussia and Russia in the so-called HOLY ALLIANCE against change. In internal Austrian affairs he was more progressive, but he had little influence on Emperor Francis or his successor, FERDINAND I. Deservedly or not, Metternich became a symbol of repression and a leading target of the REVOLUTIONS OF 1848, which drove him from office.

Austrian diplomat Prince Klemens von Metternich was Europe's leading statesman from 1815 to 1848. As the guiding spirit behind the Congress of Vienna (1814–15), Metternich sought to achieve a balance of power in Europe in order to attain a lasting peace. Metternich's methods were repressive, and in 1848 he was forced to flee Austria.

▬

Metz [mets]   Metz, the capital of Moselle department in northeastern France, is situated at the confluence of the Moselle and the Seille rivers about 40 km (25 mi) west of the German border. The population is 114,232 (1982). A strategic communications and transportation center, Metz is a major city in the important Lorraine iron-mining and industrial region. Textiles, machine tools, agricultural machinery, elevators, leather products, printing, brewing, and food processing are significant manufacturing activities.

Among the many old churches, monuments, and public buildings in Metz are the Gothic Cathedral of Saint Étienne (13th–16th centuries), the Palais de Justice begun in the 18th century, the 4th-century Church of Saint Peter, and the Porte des Allemands (13th–15th centuries).

Metz was the capital of the Mediomatrici, a Gallic tribe, and then a Roman military post until the 5th century when it was taken by the Franks. After the division of the Carolingian empire in the 9th century, it became the capital of Lotharingia. The seat of a powerful bishop, Metz was a free city within the Holy Roman Empire from the 12th century. Protestantism was adopted during the Reformation and, afraid of persecution, Metz accepted the protection of the French crown, which annexed it in 1552. The city withstood a long siege by Holy Roman Emperor Charles V in that year. The Treaty of Westphalia (1648) provided for the formal cession of Metz, with Toul and Verdun, to France. During the Franco-Prussian War (1870–71), Metz fell to the Prussians after a 2-month siege. At the end of the war it was ceded to Germany. The Peace of Versailles after World War I returned Metz to France, but it was occupied by the Germans during World War II. Metz suffered much destruction during both wars.

Meuse River [muz] The Meuse River (Flemish: Maes; Dutch: Maas) rises in northeastern France on the Langres Plateau. The river flows for about 930 km (580 mi) north and then east through France and through Belgium and the Netherlands to the North Sea. From Maastricht (Netherlands) to Maaseik (Belgium) the river follows the boundary between the two countries for a short distance. About 110 km (70 mi) past Venlo in the Netherlands, the river curves to the west and splits into two branches: one joins the Waal River, a channel of the Rhine; the other becomes the Hollandsch Diep, the river's mouth. Both branches empty into the North Sea. The chief towns along the river's course are Verdun, Sedan, and Mézières in France, Namur and Liège in Belgium, and Maastricht in the Netherlands. Navigable to Sedan, the Meuse supports many industries, especially in Belgium. A series of canals connects the river to Antwerp, Belgium, and Rotterdam, Netherlands.

Mexicali [may-hee-kah'-lee] Mexicali (1983 est. pop., 510,664) is the capital of Baja California Norte state in northwestern Mexico. It is located in the Mexicali Valley, an extension of the IMPERIAL VALLEY, directly south of the U.S. border from the city of Calexico, Calif. An important transportation and commercial center for the surrounding agricultural region, its principal industries are the processing of cotton, fruits, vegetables, and grains. The University of Baja California (1957) is there.

Mexican Americans see CHICANO

Mexican art and architecture see LATIN AMERICAN ART AND ARCHITECTURE

Mexican beaded lizard The common name of the Mexican beaded lizard, *Heloderma horridum,* is derived from its nonoverlapping, beadlike scales that typically form black-and-yellow patterns reminiscent of Indian beadwork. The Mexican beaded lizard is one of the two living members of the only poisonous lizard family, the Helodermatidae; the other is the Gila monster. The poison glands of the Mexican beaded lizard are in the lower jaw and empty into a groove in front of the teeth. A number of the upper and lower teeth have a single groove in front and often a shallow groove in back to transmit the poison, which is introduced into a wound by chewing. The Mexican beaded lizard is found in western Mexico and grows up to 90 cm (35 in) long, including its tail. It feeds on bird and reptile eggs and on nestling birds and mammals.

Mexican hairless dog The Mexican hairless dog is a small breed whose appearance suggests that of a chihuahua with a long muzzle. The origins of the Mexican hairless dog are uncertain. One theory holds that it is descended from an African breed of hairless dog and reached Mexico by way of the Orient; it was once known in Mexico as the "Chinese dog." Another theory is that it is descended from an older and larger Mexican hairless breed, the xoloitzcuintli, whose origins also are unknown.

The Mexican hairless dog reaches 30 cm (12 in) high at the shoulder and about 7 kg (15 lb) in weight. It has a slender head, erect ears, and a long tail. Its skin may be of any color, solid or mottled, but it is usually black, brown, gray, or pink. A sparse growth of hair may be present on the top of the head and at the tip of the tail.

The xoloitzcuintli, another hairless breed from Mexico, was once associated with a Mexican religious cult devoted to the god Xoloth, from whom its name is derived. The xoloitzcuintli stands 50 cm (20 in) high at the shoulder and reaches about 16 kg (35 lb) in weight. It has many features in common with the Mexican hairless dog, including tufts of hair on its head and tail tip and its skin color.

The Mexican hairless is a small dog of uncertain origin that has existed in Mexico for several centuries. The breed may have developed from large hairless dogs known in Mexico and Peru prior to the Spanish conquest or from Chinese hairless dogs brought to Mexico on merchant ships.

Mexican jumping bean Mexican jumping beans are the seedlike fruits, or nutlets (actually carpels, or segments of the fruit), of certain shrubs of the genus *Sebastiania* in the spurge family, Euphorbiaceae. A nutlet may contain the larva of a small moth, *Carpocapsa saltitans,* of the family Olethreutidae, the movements of which cause the nutlet to "jump."

Mexican salamander The Mexican salamander, *Ambystoma mexicanum*, in the family Ambystomatidae, is more commonly known as the axolotl, a name derived from the Aztec. Its native home is the Mexican plateau, and it was formerly abundant in Lake Xochimilco near Mexico City.

The Mexican salamander is dark in color and large, reaching 29 cm (11.5 in) in length. It is neotenic, normally reaching sexual maturity and breeding while still retaining larval characteristics such as gills.

Although the name *axolotl* usually pertains to the Mexican salamander, it is scientifically applicable to any sexually mature salamander retaining larval characteristics in any species of *Ambystoma*. Neoteny has been observed in nearly all of the approximately 20 species of *Ambystoma*.

Because it is normally neotenic but may metamorphose in nature or in the laboratory, the Mexican salamander has been the object of more intensive study than any other salamander. It is the most common non-mammalian vertebrate laboratory animal and has the longest purebred line.

Mexican War The Mexican War between the United States and Mexico began with a Mexican attack on American troops along the southern border of Texas on Apr. 25, 1846. Fighting ended when U.S. Gen. Winfield SCOTT occupied Mexico City on Sept. 14, 1847; a few months later a peace treaty was signed (Feb. 2, 1848) at Guadalupe Hidalgo. In addition to recognizing the U.S. annexation of Texas, defeated Mexico ceded California and New Mexico (including all the present-day states of the Southwest) to the United States.

Background

As with all major events, historical interpretations concerning the causes of the Mexican War vary. Simply stated, a dictatorial Centralist government in Mexico began the war because of the U.S. annexation (1845) of Texas, which Mexico continued to claim despite the establishment of the independent republic of Texas ten years before. Some historians have argued, however, that the United States provoked the war by annexing Texas and, more deliberately, by stationing an army at the mouth of the Rio Grande. A related interpretation maintains that the administration of U.S. president James K. POLK forced Mexico to war in order to seize California and the Southwest. A minority believes that the war arose simply out of Mexico's failure to

pay claims for losses sustained by U.S. citizens during the Mexican War of Independence.

Mexican Politics. At the time of the war, two diametrically opposed factions had arisen in Mexico: the Federalists, who supported a constitutional democracy; and the Centralists, who supported an autocratic government under a monarch or dictator. Various clashing parties of Centralists were in control of the government from 1835 to December 1844. During that time numerous rebellions and insurgencies occurred within Mexican territory, including the temporary disaffection of California and the TEXAS REVOLUTION, which resulted in the independence (1836) of Texas.

In December 1844 a coalition of moderates and Federalists forced the dictator Antonio López de SANTA ANNA into exile and installed José Joaquín Herrera as acting president of Mexico. Centralists immediately began planning the overthrow of Herrera, and the U.S. annexation of Texas in 1845 provided them with a jingoistic cause.

U.S. Policy. A joint congressional resolution (Feb. 28, 1845) providing for the U.S. annexation of Texas had caused considerable political debate in the United States. The desire of the Texas Republic to join the United States had been blocked for several years by antislavery forces, who feared that several new slave states would be created from the Texas territory. The principal factor that led the administration of John TYLER to take action was British interest in independent Texas. About the same time, the term MANIFEST DESTINY came into vogue to describe what was regarded as a God-given right to expand U.S. territory.

The Mexican Response and the Slidell Mission. The government of Herrera had already initiated steps, encouraged by the British, to recognize the independence of the Republic of Texas. In August 1845 the Herrera government indicated willingness to accept the loss of Texas, but it also hoped to lay to rest the claims question that had plagued U.S.-Mexican affairs since 1825. Herrera requested that the United States send a minister plenipotentiary to Mexico, and President Polk appointed John

General Antonio López de Santa Anna became president of Mexico for the third time soon after the outbreak (1846) of the Mexican War. He commanded Mexican forces in most of the key engagements of the war. Although exiled after the fall of Mexico City (1847), he returned to power in 1853.

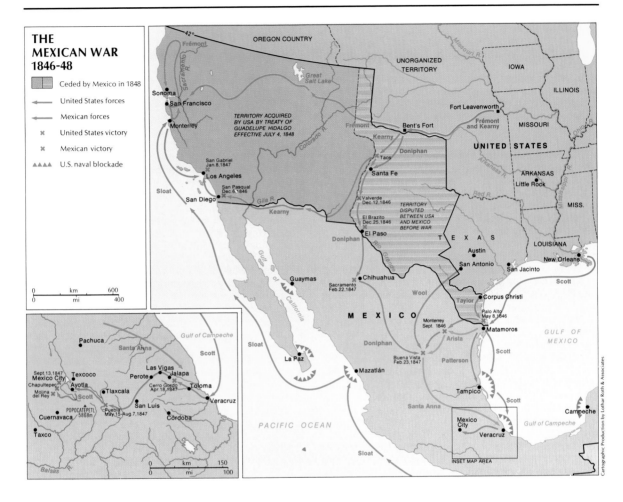

THE MEXICAN WAR 1846-48

- Ceded by Mexico in 1848
- United States forces
- Mexican forces
- × United States victory
- × Mexican victory
- ▲▲▲▲ U.S. naval blockade

SLIDELL. Slidell's authority, however, may have exceeded Herrera's intentions. Slidell was authorized to purchase California and New Mexico from Mexico and to settle the Texas boundary dispute. While the Republic of Texas had claimed the Rio Grande as its boundary, Mexico claimed the area north of the Rio Grande to the Nueces River.

When Slidell arrived, Herrera, afraid of being denounced for giving in to the Americans, refused to meet with him. On Jan. 2, 1846, Centralist leader Mariano Parades y Arillaga entered Mexico City at the head of an army. Herrera fled, and Parades, who assumed the presidency on January 4, ordered Slidell out of Mexico.

After the failure of the Slidell mission, Polk ordered Zachary TAYLOR to move his army to the mouth of the Rio Grande and to prepare to defend Texas from invasion. Taylor did so, arriving at the Rio Grande on Mar. 28, 1846. On April 23 the new dictator of Mexico issued a declaration of war.

Northern Mexican Campaign

On Apr. 25, 1846, Mexican troops crossed the Rio Grande and ambushed a detachment of American dragoons. On May 13, over the vigorous opposition of the abolitionists, the U.S. Congress voted to declare war on Mexico. In the meantime two more Mexican attacks had been made across the Rio Grande, and both had been repulsed. Mexican leaders clearly expected to win these battles as well as to recover Texas and win the war. Thus, the quick defeats north of the Rio Grande surprised and shocked the Mexican leadership and forced the evacuation of the Mexican garrison at Matamoros. Taylor occupied Matamoros on May 18, and in July he moved his base up the Rio Grande to Camargo. By August American strength on the Rio Grande had swollen to nearly 20,000 troops, but fevers, dysentery, and general debility were rampant, and the mortality rate from sickness was alarming. A determined Mexican attack in July or August would have proven disastrous to the Americans.

Mexican Rebellion. The Mexicans did not attack, because the Centralist government was collapsing. Rather than uniting Mexico, the war had given the Federalists an opportunity to rebel, and as Taylor moved to the Rio

Grande, he received increasing support from the rebels. The Centralist government fell on August 6, and soon thereafter Valentín Gómez Farías, a federalist, assumed temporary control of the government.

In the meantime, Santa Anna had returned to Mexico from Cuba. Perhaps the only leader capable of uniting the nation, he soon received command of the Mexican army; in December he was elected president by the Mexican Congress but did not formally assume office until the following March.

Monterrey and Buena Vista. In the meantime, Taylor began his attack on Monterrey on September 21. With about 2,000 men, Gen. William J. Worth captured the road between Monterrey and Saltillo and by noon was storming Federation Hill. Six companies of Texas Rangers charged up the hill, seized the enemy artillery, and turned the cannon on retreating Mexican forces. On the opposite side of the city a diversionary attack penetrated the town. On September 23, after bloody street-to-street fighting, the Mexican general Pedro de Ampudia requested and was granted a truce. On September 25 he was permitted to withdraw his forces from the city, and an eight-week armistice was agreed on.

Taylor was criticized both by the military and by President Polk for agreeing to an armistice. Taylor therefore informed Santa Anna, who had assumed command of the Mexican forces at San Luis Potosí, that the armistice would be terminated early. On November 16 he occupied Saltillo. His position was strengthened by an independent force under Gen. John E. Wood, which took Parras, to the west of Monterrey, on December 5.

In January 1847, Santa Anna moved north with about 20,000 men to dislodge Taylor who, outnumbered almost three to one, took up a position at the hacienda of Buena Vista, a few kilometers from Saltillo. The Mexican attack began on February 22, and by the next morning the main Mexican force had nearly overcome the U.S. defense. However, a dramatic charge led by Col. Jefferson DAVIS about noon and a determined artillery advance under Capt. Braxton BRAGG finally saved the day for the Americans. Santa Anna withdrew that night.

Gen. Zachary Taylor (mounted, center) and his staff survey the U.S. siege of Monterrey from a bluff overlooking the city.

Central Mexican Campaign

The decisive campaign of the war was Scott's advance from Veracruz to Mexico City. Scott assembled an army of approximately 12,000, which was transported by sea to a beach about 5 km (3 mi) south of Veracruz. Landing on March 10–11, it had surrounded the city by March 15. A combined naval and land attack forced the almost impregnable town to surrender on March 28.

Cerro Gordo and Puebla. Almost immediately Scott began the advance toward Mexico City. Only sporadic resistance was encountered until his army reached the village of Cerro Gordo about 80 km (50 mi) inland. The attack on Cerro Gordo was led by units under William J. Worth on April 18. The U.S. engineers, who included Robert E. LEE, George B. MCCLELLAN, Joseph E. JOHNSTON, and P. G. T. BEAUREGARD, found a trail that enabled the Americans to envelop and rout Santa Anna's forces. Pursuit was impossible, but Worth moved up the road to occupy the venerable Perote Castle on April 22. Scott and the main army had entered Jalapa on April 19. There the advance stopped for a month.

On May 14–15, Worth and John A. Quitman moved into Puebla, about 80 km (50 mi) closer to Mexico City. The town's leaders and the priests had decided to open Puebla to the Americans. Santa Anna had only about 2,000 cavalry, which the Americans easily routed. By July 15, with recent augmentations, Scott's forces numbered about 14,000. However, more than 3,000 were sick or convalescent.

Contreras, Churubusco, and Chapultepec. On August 7, Scott began his advance from Puebla. The first heavy fighting occurred on August 19–20 during the Battle of CONTRERAS, outside Mexico City. Heavy Mexican losses forced Santa Anna to fall back about 8 km (5 mi) to Churubusco, where he took up a defensive position in a fortified convent. Advancing under extremely heavy fire on August 20, Scott's men finally forced the convent's surrender, although Santa Anna and much of his command escaped. Fighting was renewed on September 7–8 at Molino del Rey, where the Americans forced the Mexican position. The final battle for Mexico City took place at the fortified hill of CHAPULTEPEC. American artillery bombardment on September 12 was followed the next day by an infantry assault. The citadel was heroically defended by cadets from the Mexican Military College, but they were forced to surrender before noon. U.S. troops entered Mexico City that afternoon, and shortly after midnight Santa Anna evacuated his troops.

The war was over. In little more than five months, Gen. Winfield Scott had done what many had considered impossible. Santa Anna fled the country, and the new acting president, Pedro María Anaya, began negotiations with the American peace commissioner Nicholas Trist (1800–74) in November. Trist had just been recalled to Washington, but he decided to negotiate without credentials.

Campaigns in the American West

While the crucial fighting was taking place in Mexico, vari-

U.S. forces commanded by Gen. Winfield Scott triumphantly enter Mexico City on Sept. 13, 1847, following the brilliant 6-month campaign that had begun with the successful landing at Veracruz.

ous U.S. expeditions effected the conquest of Mexico's territories in the American Southwest.

Kearny in New Mexico. Immediately after the declaration of war, Brig. Gen. Stephen Watts KEARNY, with an army consisting largely of Missouri volunteers and numbering fewer than 2,000 (though gloriously labeled the Army of the West), moved down the Santa Fe Trail into New Mexico in July 1846. The Mexican governor was unable to rally any resistance, and Kearny entered Santa Fe unopposed on Aug. 18, 1846.

Kearny then divided his command into three groups: one, under Sterling PRICE, was to occupy New Mexico; a second, under Alexander William Doniphan, was ordered to capture Chihuahua; the third, under his own command, headed for California. Price faced unrest and then rebellion in New Mexico in January 1847. Price fought three engagements with rebels, many of whom were Pueblo Indians, and by mid-February had the revolt under control.

Doniphan and the Missouri Volunteers struggled down the Rio Grande, reaching the vicinity of present-day El Paso, Tex., late in December 1846. On Christmas Day at El Brazito they routed a small detachment of Mexicans. On February 28 the Americans won a decisive victory at the crossing of the Sacramento River just outside Chihuahua. In May, Doniphan took his command eastward to Saltillo to join Taylor's forces.

Kearny set out for California on September 25 with only 300 dragoons. At Socorro, N.Mex., they met the famous guide Kit CARSON, who was returning from California. Learning that the conquest of California was virtually complete, Kearny sent 200 of his men back to Santa Fe and, led by Carson, continued to California.

Conquest of California. The American settlers in California had revolted against Mexican rule and established (June 1846) the Bear Flag Republic, under John C. FRÉMONT, before news of the war reached them. On July 2, U.S. Commodore John Drake Sloat landed at Monterrey. He proclaimed U.S. jurisdiction on July 7 and two days later occupied San Francisco. However, California was by no means under U.S. control. Mexican authority in Cali-

fornia was divided between two rivals, Pío Pico in Los Angeles and José Castro in Monterrey. Following the American landing, Castro headed south, apparently to attempt reconciliation with Pico and resistance to the United States. However, Commodore Robert STOCKTON, who replaced Sloat on July 23, sailed down the coast and landed troops under Frémont at San Diego and others near Los Angeles. Pico and Castro fled on August 10.

Heavy-handed martial-law administration precipitated a revolt in southern California in September. Led by José María Flores, the rebels had expelled the Americans from Los Angeles and San Diego by the end of October. On Dec. 6, 1846, Kearny, en route to San Diego, met the rebels in an indecisive action at the Battle of San Pascual. Joining Stockton, who had arrived at San Diego, Kearny defeated a rebel band near Los Angeles on the San Gabriel River on Jan. 8–9, 1847. On January 13, Frémont received the final surrender of the rebels and signed the Treaty of Cahuenga. With California secure, the U.S. Navy attempted the conquest of Mexican ports on the Pacific, capturing Mazatlán (Nov. 11, 1847), Guaymas (Nov. 17, 1847), and San Blas (Jan. 12, 1848).

Impact of the War in the United States

Despite the objections of the abolitionists, the war received enthusiastic support in all sections of the United States and was fought almost entirely by volunteers. The army swelled from a little more than 6,000 to more than 115,000. Of this total approximately 1.5 percent were killed in the fighting, and nearly 10 percent died of disease; another 12 percent were wounded or discharged because of disease or both. For years afterward, Mexican War veterans continued to suffer from the debilitating diseases contracted during the campaigns. The casualty rate was thus easily more than 25 percent for the 17 months of the war; the total casualties may have reached 35–40 percent if later injury- and disease-related deaths are added. In this respect the war was the most disastrous in American military history.

During the war political quarrels arose regarding the disposition of conquered Mexico. A strong "All-Mexico" movement urged annexation of the entire territory. Abolitionists opposed that position and fought for the exclusion of slavery from any territory absorbed by the United States. In 1847 the House of Representatives passed the WILMOT PROVISO, stipulating that none of the territory acquired should be open to slavery. The Senate avoided the issue, and a late attempt to add it to the Treaty of Guadalupe Hidalgo was defeated.

The Treaty of GUADALUPE HIDALGO was the unsatisfactory result of Nicholas Trist's unauthorized negotiations. It was reluctantly approved by the U.S. Senate on Mar. 10, 1848, and ratified by the Mexican Congress on May 25. Mexico's cession of California and New Mexico and its recognition of U.S. sovereignty over all Texas north of the Rio Grande formalized the addition of 3.1 million km^2 (1.2 million mi^2) of territory to the United States. In return the United States agreed to pay $15 million and assumed the claims of its citizens against Mexico. A final territorial adjustment between Mexico and the United States was made by the GADSDEN PURCHASE in 1853.

Mexico   Mexico is the third largest country in Latin America (after Brazil and Argentina). It is bordered by the United States on the north, Guatemala and Belize on the southeast, the Gulf of Mexico and the Caribbean Sea on the east, and the Pacific Ocean on the west and south.

Ancient empires—including those of the MAYA, TOLTEC, and AZTEC—flourished there for centuries before the Spanish conquest of 1519–21. Under the Spanish, Mexico became the core of NEW SPAIN and was ruled as a colony for more than 300 years. On Oct. 4, 1824, Mexico became a republic and assumed its present name, which is derived from the Méxicanos, one of seven Nahuatl tribes who inhabit the central regions of the country.

In the late 19th century, the dictator Porfirio DÍAZ brought a long period of stability and development by foreign interests. The 1910 Revolution signaled the beginning of a period of dramatic social change that led in 1938 to the nationalization of the country's basic industries. Vast new petroleum resources discovered in the 1970s and '80s raised hopes of expanded economic growth.

Land and Resources

Mexico rises to a high point of 5,747 m (18,855 ft) in the volcano Orizaba, located near Puebla in a chain of mountains called the Transverse Volcanic Sierra (or Volcanic Cordillera). This chain, which extends east-west, includes the volcanoes POPOCATÉPETL (5,452 m/17,888 ft), IXTACIHUATL (5,386 m/17,671 ft), and PARÍCUTIN (2,774 m/9,101 ft). Areas north of the Transverse Volcanic Sierra are structural continuations of U.S. landforms; areas south of the volcanic zone are structurally related to landforms in Central America and the West Indies.

Landforms. In the north the principal landform, covering almost 50% of the country's area, is the Mexican Plateau, a high tableland exceeding 2,130 m (7,000 ft) in elevation. It is divided by the Sierra Zacatecas range into the dry, sparsely settled Northern Mesa and the densely

---

AT A GLANCE

UNITED STATES OF MEXICO

Land: Area: 1,958,201 km^2 (756,065 mi^2). Capital and largest city: Mexico City (1989 est. pop., 10,355,347).

People: Population (1990 prelim.): 81,484,551. Density : 41.6 persons per km^2 (107.8 per mi^2). Distribution (1990): 66% urban, 34% rural. Official language: Spanish. Major religion: Roman Catholicism.

Government: Type: republic. Legislature: National Congress. Political subdivisions: 31 states, 1 federal district.

Economy: GDP (1989): $187 billion; $2,165 per capita. Labor distribution (1987): agriculture—25.8%; manufacturing—11.7%; public administration, defense, and services—11.1%; trade—7.9%; construction—5.9%; transportation and communications—3.1%; mining—2.3%; finance—1.9%; public utilities—0.5%; other—29.8%. Foreign trade (1989): imports—$23.3 billion; exports—$23.1 billion. Currency: 1 peso = 100 centavos.

Education and Health: Literacy (1988): 92.2% of adult population. Universities (1985): 82. Hospital beds (1984): 72,000. Physicians (1983): 74,640. Life expectancy (1990): women—76; men—68. Infant mortality (1990): 33 per 1,000 live births.

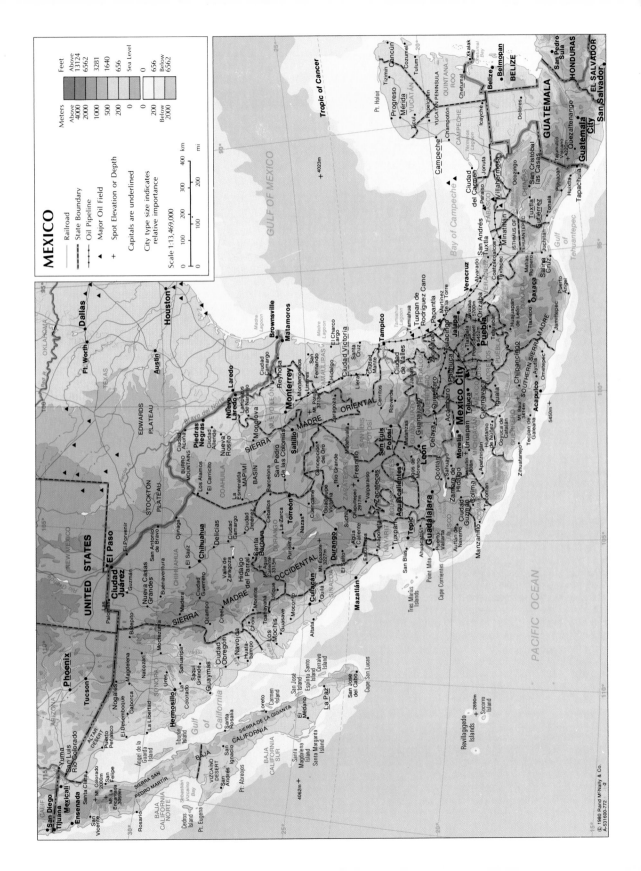

MEXICO

——————	Railroad
–·–·–·–	State Boundary
●	Oil Pipeline
▲	Major Oil Field
+	Spot Elevation or Depth

Capitals are underlined

City type size indicates
relative importance

Scale 1:13,469,000

Feet
Above 13124
6562
3281
1640
656
Sea Level
0
656
Below 6562

Meters
Above 4000
2000
1000
500
200
0
0
200
Below 2000

© 1980 Rand McNally & Co.
A-53160-772   -2

The city of Veracruz, located on the Gulf of Mexico, was founded in 1519 by Hernán Cortés. The city is a major seaport, important industrial center, and popular tourist resort. The Municipal Palace is shown here.

populated Central Mesa. The SIERRA MADRE ranges, southern extensions of the Rocky Mountains, border the Mexican Plateau. Coastal plains edge the mountains along the Gulf of Mexico and Pacific coasts. Separated from the mainland by the Gulf of California (see CALIFORNIA, GULF OF) is the BAJA CALIFORNIA peninsula.

South of the Transverse Volcanic Sierra and extending as far as the down-faulted lowlands of the Isthmus of TEHUANTEPEC, Mexico's narrowest point, are three prominent landforms. They include the Mixteco Shield (*Escudo Mixteco*) at the southern end of the Sierra Madre Occidental and the Zempoaltépetl region farther east; the rugged and ancient rocks of the Southern Sierra Madre, which descend steeply to the Pacific coast between Cape Corrientes and the Gulf of Tehuantepec; and the isolated Balsas River Basin, located between the volcanic zone and the Southern Sierra Madre. In the east, the YUCATÁN PENINSULA projects northward into the Gulf of Mexico as a limestone platform. Between the Yucatán Peninsula, the Isthmus of Tehuantepec, and neighboring Guatemala, the principal landforms are the Tabasco Plain, along the Gulf of Mexico; the Chiapas Highlands; the down-faulted Chiapas Valley, the Sierra Madre de Chiapas; and a narrow coastal plain along the Pacific Ocean.

Soils. Mexico's most fertile soils, along river valleys and on the Gulf and Pacific coastal plains, are alluvial in origin. Fertile soils inland include the lacustrine soils, formed on the dry beds of ancient lakes. Soils of volcanic origin are also generally productive. Arid soils, deficient in

humus, are found in the northern Mexican Plateau, in Baja California, and in the northern Yucatán Peninsula. Rendzina soils dominate the northern Gulf Coast plain and parts of the Balsas Basin and the southern Yucatán Peninsula. Laterites are common in nonalluvial areas along the coastal plains and on the humid northern slopes of the Chiapas Highlands.

Climate. Mexico's climate is hot and humid along the coastal areas and becomes increasingly arid toward the north. Temperatures decrease with increasing altitude. During the warmer half of the year, all of Mexico lies in the belt of Northeast Trade Winds, which blow from the Bermuda or Azores Subtropical High and bring heat and humidity from the Gulf of Mexico. In the cooler half of the year, the Bermuda Subtropical High dominates the climate of northern Mexico and brings clear skies with virtually no precipitation, while southern parts of Mexico remain under the influence of the Northeast Trades. The wettest areas, where rainfall varies between 1,500 and 3,500 mm (59 and 140 in) each year, include the mountainous slopes of southern and central Mexico. Drier conditions prevail in the north. The driest areas on the Mexican Plateau receive less than 305 mm (12 in) of precipitation a year; very dry areas along the northwest Pacific coast receive as little as 50 mm (2 in) a year.

Mexico has a number of altitudinal temperature zones. The hottest lands (*tierra caliente*) are along the coastal plains, in the Balsas Basin and in the Chiapas Valley. Temperatures there exceed 22° C (72° F). Semihot lands, with temperatures between 18° C (64° F) and 22° C (72° F), are found in the eastern slopes of the Sierra Madre Oriental and Occidental, while temperate conditions (*tierra templada*), with average temperatures between 12° C (54° F) and 18° C (64° F), are common over most of the Mexican Plateau. Cold temperatures (*tierra fría*), ranging between 5° C (41° F) and 12° C (54° F), dominate areas above 1,830 m (6,000 ft) in altitude, and very cold conditions (*tierra helada*) exist above 3,650 m (12,000 ft). Tropical cyclones bring heavy rains during the summer and early fall and are most common in September. In winter occasional outbursts of continental polar air from North America bring unusually cold winter temperatures.

Drainage. The six principal rivers draining to the Gulf of Mexico include the Río Bravo del Norte (RIO GRANDE), which follows part of the United States–Mexico border; the 700-km-long (438-mi) Grijalva in the southeast; the 966-km (600-mi) Usumacinta, which lies along part of the Guatemala–Mexico border; the 314-km (195-mi) Papaloapan; the 300-km (188-mi) Coatzacoalcos; and the 510-km (319-mi) Pánuco. The major rivers draining to the Pacific are the Colorado, which flows into the head of the Gulf of California; the 724-km (450-mi) Balsas; and the 927-km (579-mi) Lerma-Santiago river system—the longest in all Mexico—whose headwaters are diverted for use by Mexico City. The major rivers of the Mexican Plateau evaporate, disappear underground, or flow into lakes.

Vegetation and Animal Life. Rain-forest vegetation predominates in southwestern CAMPECHE, northeastern CHIAPAS, northern TABASCO, and southeastern VERACRUZ states, as well as in southern and eastern regions of the Yucatán Peninsula. Coniferous and oak-tree forests predominate in humid areas of the mild and semicold climate regions, including most of the mountainous ranges. Tropical savanna grasslands dominate much of the Yucatán Peninsula and some areas of the Pacific and Gulf of Mexico coastal plains. Thorny desert thickets and dry grasslands can be found in the Mexican Plateau, northeastern and northwestern parts of the country, and in Baja California. Mangrove swamps are common along the Gulf and Pacific coasts south of the Tropic of Cancer. Widely distributed fauna include deer, coyote, ocelots, sparrow hawks, buzzards, rabbits, skunks, badgers, pumas, and bears. The tropical areas are inhabited by armadillos, tapirs, monkeys, macaws, parrots, crocodiles, iguanas, and snakes.

Resources. Mexico has abundant petroleum resources, especially in the Reforma field of Chiapas and Tabasco states, developed since 1972, and offshore in the Bay of Campeche (discovered in 1978 and 1981). Additional new gas and oil fields were found in 1984. Natural gas, sulfur, and salt are found with the petroleum deposits. Other important minerals are coal, iron ore, silver, fluorite, gold, copper, lead, cadmium, manganese, antimony, zinc, mercury, and barites. Lands suitable for farming constitute only about 15% of the total land area, and lands for grazing about 38%. Forests cover 25% of the land. Fish are abundant in waters off both coasts. Hydroelectric-power sites are numerous along the steep edges of the Mexican Plateau.

People

The inhabitants of Mexico are ethnically diverse, but racial data have not been officially recorded since 1921. The basis for the identification of ethnic groups is now the primary language used. By this criterion, about 7% of the population are considered Indian and includes 4% who are bilingual and 3% who speak only an indigenous language. The most widely used languages other than Spanish are Nahuatl, used in east central Mexico; Maya, spoken primarily in the Yucatán; Zapotec and Mixtec, spoken in OAXACA state; and Otomi, spoken near Mexico City and in parts of PUEBLA and Veracruz states.

Religion. An estimated 97% of the population are Roman Catholics, and 2% are Protestants; there are about 100,000 Jews. Freedom of religion is constitutionally guaranteed, and only civil marriages are legal.

Demography. From just about 15 million persons in 1910, Mexico's population grew to 34 million in 1960, more than 66 million in 1980, and almost 88 million in 1990. With the annual rate of natural increase at 2.2%, the population is expected to reach 100 million by the mid-1990s. Since World War II, the infant mortality rate has decreased dramatically, and as a result, Mexico has a very young population—approximately half of the people are under 15 years of age.

The most densely populated areas are between latitudes 19° and 21° north in parts of the Mexican Plateau and Transverse Volcanic Sierra at altitudes above 1,000 m (3,280 ft). The most sparsely populated areas are the states of Baja California Sur, on the Baja California peninsula, and Campeche and QUINTANA ROO, on the Yucatán Peninsula. The largest city and the capital of Mexico, MEXICO CITY, is more than five times the size of second-ranking GUADALAJARA. Other large cities, in order of population size, are MONTERREY, Mexico City's suburb of Netzahualcoyotl, PUEBLA, LEÓN, CIUDAD JUÁREZ, CULIACÁN, MEXICALI, TIJUANA, MÉRIDA, and ACAPULCO.

Education and Health. Most children between 6 and 14 years old attend a 6-year, free, compulsory elementary-school program; few continue their education beyond this level. Of these, most go on to regional technological institutes, and only about 5% attend institutions of higher learning. Intensive adult education programs were begun in the 1970s to decrease illiteracy. Since 1931, when the first Law of Social Security was passed, health conditions in Mexico have improved dramatically under the aegis of the Mexican Institute of Social Security (IMSS).

The Arts. Famous Mexican writers are Mariano AZUELA, Carlos FUENTES, Octavio PAZ, Agustín YÁÑEZ, and Martín Luis Guzmán. Modern Mexican art is expressed in the work of such famous artists as José Clemente OROZCO, Diego RIVERA, David Alfaro SIQUEIROS, Rufino TAMAYO, and Juan O'GORMAN, whose politically inspired murals and mosaics decorate many of Mexico's modern buildings.

Among the nation's outstanding composers are Carlos CHÁVEZ and Silvestre Revueltas. Regional folk arts, derived from ancient Indian cultures, also flourish, and ceramics, woven items, silverwork, sandals, and hats are sold in large quantities to enthusiastic tourists.

Popocatépetl, the second highest mountain in Mexico (5,452 m/ 17,888 ft), derives its name from an Aztec word meaning "smoking mountain." The volcano last erupted in 1802.

Economic Activity

Mining and subsistence farming, the predominant economic activities during the colonial period, remain important today, although silver is now less important than petroleum, natural gas, and other industrial minerals. Commercial agriculture has been actively promoted by government-sponsored programs of agrarian reform, irrigation, and road construction. Manufacturing grew rapidly after 1940 to become today's fastest-growing sector of the economy. Tourism is Mexico's second largest net earner of foreign exchange (after the petroleum industry).

Depressed oil markets contributed to an economic crisis that started in the early 1980s and persisted. Following multiple devaluations of the peso, the nation faced bankruptcy. The government nationalized banks and subsequently imposed a broad austerity program.

Manufacturing. The principal iron and steel centers are located at Monterrey and Monclova. Most other industries are attracted to the densely populated urban areas in and around Mexico City, Guadalajara, Orizaba, and Puebla. In addition to steel, the main industries include food processing, petroleum refining, and the manufacture of petrochemicals, synthetic fibers, textiles, fertilizers, paper, pharmaceuticals, and the assembly of automobiles. Also important are the construction industry and the related manufacture of cement.

Mining. Petroleum, the production of which was nationalized in 1938 and is now controlled by the government agency PEMEX (Petróleos Méxicanos), is Mexico's principal mineral resource and leading export. In the 1920s, Mexico was second only to the United States in the production of petroleum. New finds, including those developed since 1974 in the Reforma and Campeche fields of the south, brought Mexico's total of proven oil and natural-gas reserves to more than 71 billion barrels in 1985. Natural gas produced in association with the petroleum is piped to Monterrey. Mexico's other minerals include silver, lead, and zinc, mostly produced from the old colonial mining centers of PACHUCA, SAN LUIS POTOSÍ (city), Guanajuato (city), La Paz, Parral, and Zacatecas (city); copper, worked at Cananea in the northwest and near Santa Rosalía on the Baja California Peninsula; and sulfur, first extracted in 1956 near Jaltipán in the Isthmus of Tehuantepec.

Energy. In 1987, Mexico produced an estimated 91 billion kW h of electricity. About three-quarters was generated in thermal plants fueled by petroleum, natural gas, and coal; one-quarter was produced in hydroelectric plants located on the steep southern and eastern edges of the Mexican Plateau.

Agriculture, Forestry, and Fishing. Most people employed in agriculture are subsistence farmers producing small amounts of corn and beans, while sometimes raising a goat, some chickens, or a pig. Commercial farming is concentrated in irrigated regions of the arid north, where cotton and wheat are the chief crops; along the Mayo, Yaqui, and Fuerte rivers, where tomatoes and melons are raised; and in southern, frost-free plains and highlands of JALISCO, Veracruz, Tabasco, Chiapas, and Oaxaca states, where coffee, sugarcane, bananas, cacao, and pineapples are major crops. Since the 1910 Revolution many large estates (*haciendas*) and coffee plantations (*fincas*) have been broken up and distributed as small holdings (*ejidos*) to landless farm workers. Cattle raising, an important colonial activity, is concentrated in the semiarid north; sheep are raised in drier parts of the Mexican Plateau, and goats in more rugged sections.

The forest industry is as yet small. The principal trees cut are pine, red cedar, holm oak, and *oyamel*. Fishing is a similarly underdeveloped but potentially profitable in-

Mexico City's Plaza de las Tres Culturas, or Square of Three Cultures, contains a reconstructed Aztec temple, a 16th-century Spanish church, and modern buildings. Founded in the 14th century, Mexico City is one of the world's most rapidly growing metropolitan areas.

dustry. Fish plays a minor role in Mexican diets, and most of the catch is exported.

Transportation. Despite the mountainous terrain, most parts of Mexico are now well served by a network of modern highways and by an extensive system of secondary roads. The road system focuses on Mexico City, the nation's cultural and economic hub, and includes among its major axes the 1,189-km (739-mi) PAN AMERICAN HIGHWAY (to Nuevo Laredo) and the 1,979-km (1,230-mi) Central Highway (to Ciudad Juárez). The nationally owned rail network is less extensive than the road system, but it is nonetheless vital, carrying millions of passengers and millions of tons of freight annually.

Numerous airports offer national and international flights. Air services now carry nearly as many passengers as the railroads and transport a significant amount of freight. The major Mexican airline is Compañía Mexicana de Aviación, and there are smaller regional airlines. Ferry systems operate across the Gulf of California between La Paz and Mazatlán, between Santa Rosalía and Cabo San Lucas on the Baja California peninsula, and Guaymas and Puerto Vallarta on the mainland. Among the principal ports are Tampico, Veracruz, and Coatzacoalcos along the Gulf of Mexico, and Mazatlán and Guaymas on the Pacific coast.

Trade. In recent years Mexico, unlike many developing nations, has had a favorable balance of trade. Petroleum is the most valuable export; other important export commodities include cotton, coffee, nonferrous metals, and foodstuffs. Mexican imports include machinery, equipment, industrial vehicles, and intermediate goods. Trade with the United States accounts for nearly three-quarters of all imports and exports. Tourism is also a vital earner of foreign exchange.

Government

Mexico's present constitution, adopted in 1917, provides for a division of powers between the central government and the 31 states and the federal district (Mexico City). The strong executive branch of government is headed by a directly elected president who is limited to one six-year term. Legislative power is vested in the bicameral National Congress, elected by universal adult suffrage, comprising a Chamber of Deputies, with 500 members, and a Senate, composed of two senators from each state and the federal district. Judicial powers are vested in the Supreme Court of Justice. The Institutional Revolutionary party (PRI) has dominated national politics since 1929. In December 1988 the PRI candidate Carlos SALINAS DE GORTARI, a principal architect of the government's economic policy, became president.

Mexico, history of Modern Mexican society has its roots in the interaction between two diverse civilizations, the American Indian and the Spanish. The Spaniards, the Indians, and their mestizos (mixed offspring) have shared a land limited in resources and a generally difficult climate. Their history has been characterized by poverty and struggle and by frequent and intense violence.

A Mayan stone relief (AD 772) from Yaxchilán, a site in Chiapas, Mexico, portrays a figure arrayed in elaborate ceremonial attire.

Mesoamerican Civilization

Prior to the arrival of the Spanish, two types of civilizations emerged in MESOAMERICA: the highland, characterized by states and empires with elaborate class structures, advanced architecture, bureaucracies, and densely settled agrarian areas; and the lowland civilizations of primitive aboriginal groups.

By the 1st or 2d millennium BC tribes of sedentary seed gatherers, the OLMEC, had settled in villages along the southwestern edge of the Gulf of Mexico. These small and simply structured communities planted corn, beans, and squash. The basic tools were the stone ax and the wooden digging stick.

The Classic Maya and Central Highland Civilizations. After about 400 BC the Indians developed more complex forms of social organization. Their social structure was dominated by a ruling class of priests, who, acting as the representatives of the gods, distributed land, allocated food surpluses, stored seed, sponsored trade, and employed skilled craftworkers. These theocracies reached their peak in the central highland cities of TEOTIHUACÁN and MONTE ALBÁN and in the great centers of the MAYA of southern Mexico.

Until about AD 750 these classic societies remained generally peaceful and nonexpansionist. A combination of natural disasters and overpopulation brought both the Maya and the Teotihuacán to an end. The growing opulence of the urban religious centers bred envy and then resentment in the hinterland villages. A spreading revolt probably interrupted trade, cutting off the food supply, and the great theocratic centers were either abandoned or conquered. Between 650 and 670 warlike peoples invaded, burned, and plundered Teotihuacán, and the collapse of Monte Albán and all the great Maya centers followed. By AD 900, the golden age of pre-Columbian civilization had ended.

The Toltec and Aztec. The new civilization that emerged has been called TOLTEC; it centered around the city of TULA on the central plateau. The Toltec developed a complex society based on warfare and military expansion, intensive agriculture, and a tight government control. They levied tribute on the agriculture surplus of their subject tribes and widely practiced human sacrifice. The Toltec flourished for three centuries, but by the 13th century, after a period of internecine struggle, Tula had fallen, and the Toltec peoples had dispersed.

During the 15th century the warlike AZTEC created a remarkable if short-lived empire. Three large cities, TENOCHTITLÁN (the capital), Tlacopán, and Texcoco, dominated their confederacy. The tribe organized itself into clans with stratified and pyramidal social hierarchies. At the top were the warriors and priests (about 3,000 in total), who dominated all high office and collected tribute from subordinate groups. Beneath these nobles existed a servile class of free peasants and a mass of serfs. The *pochteca,* a group of non-Aztec merchants living in Tenochtitlán's twin city, Tlatelolco, controlled trade.

The chief Aztec god, HUITZILOPOCHTLI, was a god of the Sun and of war. Prominent among the many lesser deities was QUETZALCÓATL, a serpent god of the arts and morality. According to Aztec legend he had been exiled, but his return was expected to herald the end of Aztec civilization. The Aztec believed that their world was frequently created and then consumed in recurrent disasters. Only constant warfare and human sacrifice would help to preserve their civilization. Aztec warriors captured males from the surrounding tribes for the needed sacrifices; other victims were obtained by tributes levied on subject tribes.

Spanish Conquest and Rule

The Spanish conquest of Mexico, launched from Cuba, resulted eventually in the creation of a new, hybrid culture. Spanish political control lasted for three centuries.

Conquest. Hoping to found a colony that might supply mineral riches and a cheap labor force, Cuban Governor Diego de VELÁZQUEZ DE CUÉLLAR sent a series of military expeditions to the mainland. The first, under Francisco Hernández de Córdoba (d. 1518?), reached the Yucatán Peninsula in 1517. The following year a second expedition, under Juan de Grijalva (d. 1527), reached the peninsula and explored the Mexican coast as far as the site of present-day Veracruz.

The third expedition, led by the Spanish CONQUISTADOR Hernán CORTÉS, succeeded in conquering the Aztecs in less than three years. Cortés landed in 1519, founded the town of VERACRUZ, and then proceeded inland. Many of the disgruntled Aztec subjects flocked to his side. He reached Tenochtitlán in November 1519 and soon captured the Aztec emperor MONTEZUMA II. After the Spaniards' initial successes, the Aztec besieged Tenochtitlán; on the night of June 30–July 1, 1520, known as *la noche triste* (the night of sadness), Cortés was forced to retreat, causing many casualties. The following summer, however, the Europeans sacked and besieged Tenochtitlán, and the Aztecs finally collapsed. Cortés named his conquest NEW SPAIN and sent out expeditions to extend Spanish power over the continent.

The Rise of New Spain. The Spanish crown rapidly sought to consolidate its new empire and slowly curbed Cortés's personal power. An AUDIENCIA (royal court) was established in 1528, and the first viceroy, Antonio de MENDOZA, took office in 1535. The followers of Cortés received ENCOMIENDAS, grants of Indian villages from which they could collect tribute. Many of the clergy objected to the *encomiendas*, the missionary Bartolomé de Las Casas being the most vocal. The Indians themselves revolted (1541) unsuccessfully against Spanish control and abuses of the *encomienda* system in the Mixtón War. The Spanish ruler, Holy Roman Emperor CHARLES V, attempted to abolish or curb the *encomiendas*—most notably by the so-called New Laws of the Indies of 1542. Twenty years later a group of leading colonists (led by Cortés's son) revolted in protest against attempts to diminish their power, but the viceroy put down the rebellion. The *encomienda* system declined gradually.

The Spanish crown sought to create a well-ordered colony, free of feudal privilege and religious dissent. The

The meeting (1519) of Hernán Cortés and the Aztec emperor Montezuma II, in which Cortés was received as a descendant of the god Quetzalcóatl, is depicted in this 17th-century Spanish painting. Cortés's conquest of the Aztec empire initiated Spanish rule on the North American continent. (British Embassy, Mexico City.)

Spanish religious orders (especially the Franciscans) capitalized on the similarities between Catholicism and Indian folk religion to carry out mass conversions and often built shrines on the sites of Indian idols. After the conversions, parish priests organized the Christian communities. Missions and monasteries came to dominate much of the countryside.

Silver mining underlay the colony's prosperity. Urban centers based on mining flourished at Zacatecas, Taxco, and Fresnillo (and later in Durango and Chihuahua). Large estates and ranches fed the mining centers. Other estates grew wheat, sugarcane, and indigo for export. Colonial merchants distributed such goods as cotton, silk, and dye that the Indians produced.

Period of Decline. In the 17th century the economy of New Spain collapsed. Disease and overwork had combined to wipe out much of the Indian population. By 1700 only a little more than 1 million Indians survived in New Spain—out of an estimated population of 11 million or more in the 1520s. Without labor the mines could no longer function. The population retreated into rural estates called *haciendas,* which became self-sufficient centers of political and economic power. The viceroyalty's frontiers continued to expand as friars and soldiers moved the borders into what are today the states of Texas and California.

Bourbon Reforms. In the 18th century a new Spanish dynasty, the Bourbons, reorganized the colonies. Political boundaries were reshuffled; the crown improved tax collection, reduced export and import duties, and appointed honest officials. Mining production rose fourfold, and agriculture and trade increased. Acapulco flourished as a center of trade with the Orient; Veracruz dominated the Caribbean and European trade. The colonists also developed textile, rope, tobacco, china, and pulque (an alcoholic beverage) industries. PUEBLA, GUANAJUATO, and GUADALAJARA became centers of wealth and industry. MEXICO CITY grew to a population of 170,000. It housed the viceroy, a great university, a school of mines, and an *audiencia.*

In 1800, New Spain's economy thrived. The population had grown to 6.5 million—about 42% Indian, 18% white, and 38% mestizo. The system contained, however, the roots of its own destruction. Native-born criollos (Creoles, or people of European descent born in Spanish America) resented Spanish monopolization of political power and an economic system that favored the Spanish-born. Spain's authority was also eroded as its position as a world power declined.

Independence to 1910

Mexican independence came about at the convergence of two revolts. The first was led by two poor priests, Miguel HIDALGO Y COSTILLA and José María MORELOS Y PAVÓN, and was directed against colonial officials. On Sept. 16, 1810, Hidalgo called for a new government and redistribution of land in his *Grito de Dolores* (Cry of Sorrows; a rousing speech made in the town of Dolores). Hidalgo's forces marched toward Mexico City, and in the meantime Morelos led guerrilla forces in the south; he assumed leadership of the revolution after Hidalgo was executed

Father Miguel Hidalgo, whose Crito de Dolores (Cry of Sorrows, 1810) became the battle cry of the first Mexican uprising against the Spanish, led a Mexican Indian army to initial victories before his defeat at Calderón in 1811. Hidalgo has become a powerful symbol of the Mexican independence movement.

(1811). The Spanish bureaucracy and rich criollos defeated the rebellion, however, and executed (1815) Morelos. The second revolt occurred when these same wealthy criollos, who feared that Spain (then dominated by liberals) would acquiesce to demands for land redistribution, under the leadership of Agustín de ITURBIDE declared (1821) Mexico independent. Iturbide was proclaimed Emperor Agustín I in 1822, but the following year unpaid troops rebelled and set up a republic with Guadalupe Victoria (1786?–1843) as its first president.

The Age of Santa Anna. Gen. Antonio López de SANTA ANNA, one of the leaders of the coup that had overthrown Iturbide and several times president of Mexico, was more a representative than a dominant figure. The government was saddled with an internal debt of millions of pesos incurred by Spain and Iturbide. Foreign loans could be obtained only at heavy rates of interest. Once the money reached Mexico, government officials spent it on secondhand war materiel or grafted it themselves. Bankrupt governments rose and fell.

During this turbulent era, two groups competed for dominance. Liberals representing regional power centers and free-trading interests sought to model the new Mexican nation on the United States. Their rivals, the conservatives, were supported by the army, the former colonial administrative centers, and some manufacturers. Santa Anna, sometimes a liberal, sometimes a conservative, moved in and out of power.

By the 1850s this chaos had led to disaster. Mining virtually stopped, agriculture declined, and trade and industry suffered from internal tariffs, foreign competition, banditry, and political violence. Texas had declared its independence on Mar. 2, 1836 (see TEXAS REVOLUTION), and by 1846, Mexico was embroiled in a war with the United States (see MEXICAN WAR). The disunited Mexicans were routed, and in the peace treaty of GUADALUPE HIDALGO, Mexico lost over half its territory, including the area of the present U.S. states of California and New Mexico as well as northern Arizona. In 1853, Santa Anna returned to power as "perpetual dictator" and sold south-ern Arizona to the United States for $10 million (see GADSDEN PURCHASE).

Liberal Reforms. In 1855 a brilliant group of liberals led by the pure-blooded Indian Benito JUÁREZ forced Santa Anna from power. The liberals decreed that the church had to sell most of its land and that Indian com-munal lands *(ejidos)* had to be distributed to individual peasants. The liberals also promulgated (1857) a new constitution. A new civil war erupted, however, called the War of Reform (1858–61). The conservatives sought for-eign help, and in 1862, NAPOLEON III of France sought to establish a Mexican empire under the Austrian prince Maximilian (see MAXIMILIAN, EMPEROR OF MEXICO). Al-though supported by French troops and Mexican conser-vatives, Maximilian could not consolidate his empire. The French withdrew in 1867, leaving the ill-fated emperor to meet his death. Juárez, then president, initiated various reforms to modernize Mexico, but he died in 1872.

The accomplishments of the liberals were impressive. They destroyed the power of the army, the church, and

(Above) *The execu-tion of Emperor Max-imilian, portrayed by Édouard Manet, fol-lowed the withdrawal of French troops from Mexico in 1867. (Stadtische Kunst-halle, Mannheim, W. Germany.)* (Right) *General Porfirio Díaz, who toppled the gov-ernment of Sebastián Lerdo in 1876, achieved rapid eco-nomic progress dur-ing his more than 30 years of rule.*

other conservative elements and institutionalized demo-cratic principles in the constitution of 1857. Their strug-gle against the French also created modern Mexican na-tionalism.

The Age of Don Porfirio. Juárez's liberal successors fal-tered, however, and in 1876 a general, Porfirio DÍAZ, seized power. Díaz established order and workable gov-ernment. Civil wars ceased, and eventually banditry dis-appeared from the countryside. The army became profes-sionalized. The *Rurales,* a militarized police force of sev-eral thousand, maintained order throughout the country. Díaz and the *Científicos,* the group of wealthy intellectu-als that advised him, adopted French positivism as a na-tional creed. Foreign investors rushed in; the results were phenomenal. Exports and national income increased; new highways, railroads, and telegraph lines crossed Mexico; and new industries dotted the countryside. Foreign in-vestment and technology revived mining and created ma-jor oil fields around Veracruz. Mexico became the model for much of the then developing world.

The urban and rural masses in Porfirian Mexico, how-ever, remained impoverished. Mexicans of all classes hated the increasing foreign economic dominance. Final-ly a politically ambitious younger generation came to re-sent the rule of the Díaz clique.

Modern Mexico

Two major strikes, political discontent, and financial dis-locations disturbed the last years of the Díaz dictatorship. The Revolution of 1910 and the regime's collapse, how-ever, amazed the entire Western world.

The Revolution. In 1908, Diaz told a U.S. journalist that Mexico would be ready for free elections in 1910. Inspired by this interview, the opposition began organizing and eventually coalesced around an eccentric northern land-owner, Francisco I. MADERO. Madero campaigned under the slogan "Effective suffrage and no reelection." Díaz rigged the election, however, and Madero then led a revolt that spread rapidly throughout the nation. As the corrupt Díaz military organization collapsed, the old dictator fled.

A moderate, Madero angered not only the radical pro-ponents of land reform and economic nationalism but also the landowners. With conservative support, yet an-other general, Victoriano HUERTA, overthrew Madero and had him executed.

Mexico again became engulfed in ruinous violence. In the north, Pancho VILLA, an ex-bandit, organized the local cowboys. In the south, Emiliano ZAPATA recruited an army of angry landless peasants. The U.S. government under Woodrow Wilson sent troops that occupied Veracruz for several months; Huerta, his army defeated, fled. In Au-gust 1914, however, Venustiano CARRANZA, a rich land-owner who had supported Madero, assumed executive power, and civil war broke out. In 1915 the U.S. govern-ment recognized Carranza as head of a de facto govern-ment, and in 1917, Carranza's forces prevailed. Zapata was murdered (1919), and Villa surrendered (1920).

The victors called a convention that legislated (1917) a new constitution embodying principles of anticlerical-ism, land reform, nationalism, and the protection of

Pancho Villa (right center), a Mexican bandit and revolutionary, became a folk hero for his elusive guerrilla attacks during the political turmoil that followed the 1910 revolution. His armed opposition contributed to the fall (1914) of Victoriano Huerta and persisted through the ensuing Carranza regime.

workers. In 1920, Carranza tried to prevent Gen. Álvaro OBREGÓN from succeeding him as president, but Obregón led a military coup that overthrew Carranza's government the following year.

The Northern Dynasty. The governments that ruled Mexico from 1921 to 1933 are known as the Northern Dynasty. The presidents Obregón, Plutarco Elías CALLES, Emilio Portes Gil (1891–1978), Pascual Ortiz Rubio (1877–1963), and Abelardo Rodríguez (1889–1967)—dominated by politicians from northern Mexico—sought to establish order while developing the economy. They faced bitter opposition from the clergy, landowners, foreign investors, and ambitious generals.

The northerners formed a new political party, the PNR (National Revolutionary party), which unified progovernment political forces. The land reforms of Calles and Portes Gil expanded the internal market and created peace in rural areas. Economic productivity rose, mining resumed, and MONTERREY became a center for steel production. Calles established cordial relations with the United States. The government and its labor allies, however, had become increasingly corrupt. Calles became more conservative, ending land reform and opposing strikes. Furthermore, the world depression that began in 1929 had halted the economic recovery.

Gen. Lázaro CÁRDENAS became president in 1934. He ended the policies of the Northern Dynasty and revived the revolutionary fervor of 1910. His government exiled Calles, carried out a vast land reform, reorganized the labor movement, and nationalized foreign oil companies. Cárdenas also established state-managed collective farms as the basis of Mexican agriculture.

Mexico since 1940. Manuel Ávila Camacho and his successor, Miguel Alemán Valdés, established policies that Mexico has followed since Cárdenas, emphasizing industrial growth while downplaying redistributive social reforms and economic nationalism. Economic issues, intellectual ferment, and government repression of labor led to the student strike of 1968, which was brutally suppressed by the government of Gustavo Díaz Ordaz.

The term of Luis ECHEVERRÍA ÁLVAREZ, who succeeded Díaz Ordaz, was marked by economic instability and political unrest. Under Echeverría's successor, José LÓPEZ PORTILLO, the nation exploited newly found oil reserves and entered a period of economic prosperity and growing international influence. The decline of the world oil market in the 1980s, however, plunged Mexico into an economic crisis. When Miguel DE LA MADRID HURTADO assumed the presidency in 1982, Mexico's economy was on the verge of collapse. The country suffered another setback in 1985 when earthquakes damaged the capital, killing thousands. In December 1988, Carlos SALINAS DE GORTARI became president following a controversial election. During 1989 the government liberalized Mexico's foreign-investment regulations to permit foreign ownership of business and negotiated a landmark agreement with foreign commercial bank creditors to lower Mexico's $54 billion debt. Also, in a governor's race the PRI conceded its first-ever election defeat.

México (state)   México is a Mexican state that lies on the central plateau and envelops the country's federal district. The capital is TOLUCA, and the state's population is 12,013,044 (1989 est.). The primary economic activity is agriculture, especially dairy farming, but mining is also important. Many archaeological sites, the most famous among them TEOTIHUACÁN, make México a popular tourist region. The state was occupied by U.S. forces during the Mexican war in 1847 and by the French in 1963.

Mexico, Gulf of   The Gulf of Mexico, an arm of the ATLANTIC OCEAN, is bounded by the United States on the north and east, Mexico on the west and south, and Cuba on the east. The gulf has two channels, each about 160 km (100 mi) wide; the Straits of Florida, south of the Florida peninsula, connect it to the Atlantic, and the Yucatán Channel runs between Mexico and Cuba to connect with the Caribbean.

The gulf, oval in shape, covers about 1,602,000 km² (619,000 mi²). It is generally shallow, with a maximum depth of 4,321 m (14,178 ft) below sea level at Sigsbee Deep. The shoreline, about 4,800 km (3,000 mi) long, is low and marshy, with many inlets and lagoons. The climate varies from subtropical to tropical, and hurricanes often form in the gulf from June to October. The major rivers entering the gulf are the Mississippi and the Rio Grande.

Mexico City

Mexico City   Mexico City (Spanish: México), the capital and leading industrial and cultural center of Mexico, is one of the world's fastest-growing urban areas. The population of the federal district (the administrative area

within which the city is located), grew from 3,050,000 in 1950 to 8,236,960 (1990). The entire metropolitan area, which extends into the adjoining state of México, had an estimated 1990 population of 22.2 million, making it the world's largest city. The site of the present-day city was originally the Aztec capital, Tenochtitlán, making Mexico City the oldest capital in Latin America.

Contemporary City. A major expansion of industry has occurred during recent decades. The city's manufacturing concerns are highly diversified and include food processing; production of textiles, garments, shoes, steel construction materials, and pharmaceuticals; petroleum refining; and automobile assembly. One of Mexico City's most serious problems is the tremendous air pollution resulting from overcentralization of industry in the Valley of Mexico.

Mexico City is the hub of Mexico's transportation network. Its airport is the major international link for the country, and it is connected by both rail and highway to Mexico's other cities and ports on both coastlines. This network enables the city to serve as the market and service center for a sizable tributary region.

Tourism contributes significantly to the economy of Mexico City. Among the numerous landmarks are the National Cathedral (begun 1573), the oldest and largest in Latin America; the Basilica of Guadalúpe; the National Palace (1692); the Zócalo, or main square; and the Plaza México, the world's largest bullring. The Paseo de la Reforma, a beautiful tree-lined boulevard, cuts a diagonal swath across the city to Chapultepec Park.

Mexico City is the nation's most important educational and cultural center. The National Autonomous University of Mexico (1551) is located at University City. The National Museum of History and the world-famous Museum of Anthropology (1964), both in Chapultepec Park, are the major museums. The Mexican Folklore Ballet performs in the Palace of Fine Arts.

History. Indians first settled along the shores of shallow Lake Texcoco by about 1500 BC. About 1325, the

(Above) *Mosaics by Juan O'Gorman adorn the exterior walls of the library at the National Autonomous University of Mexico in Mexico City. Outdoor sculptures appear in the plaza between the library and the University Museum of Sciences and Arts.* (Right) *Mexico City's twin-towered Metropolitan Cathedral has a mixed baroque and neoclassical facade. It is Latin America's largest church.*

Aztecs selected an island in the lake as the capital of their empire and named it Tenochtitlán. It was connected to the mainland by causeways. In 1521 the Spanish explorer Hernán CORTÉS captured and razed the city, building a Spanish city in its place. The new city, Mexico City, served as capital of that part of Spanish America extending as far south as Panama. During this period, the lake was drained and drainage canals built.

In 1821, Mexican revolutionaries under Gen. Agustín de ITURBIDE captured Mexico City. The city was occupied by the United States in 1847 during the Mexican War and by France for four years when MAXIMILIAN, archduke of Austria, was named emperor of Mexico by Napoleon III in 1863. During the Mexican Revolution (1910–15) the city was the scene of heavy fighting. In 1968, Mexico City hosted the Summer Olympic Games. A 1985 earthquake caused extensive damage.

Meyer, Adolf

Adolf Meyer, b. Sept. 13, 1866, d. Mar. 17, 1950, was one of the earliest and most influential American psychiatrists. Born in Niederweningen, Switzerland, Meyer emigrated to the United States in 1892 and held the chair of psychiatry at Johns Hopkins University from 1910 to 1941.

Meyer rejected simple biological explanations of mental illness. He argued, for example, that schizophrenia was a personality disorder. His psychobiological studies showed that thoughts and feelings affect a person's physiological state; he became the first American psychiatrist to compile case histories of his patients.

Meyer can be credited with giving psychiatry its pluralistic, pragmatic orientation; he also did significant medical research as a neurologist.

Meyerbeer, Giacomo

[my'-ur-bair, jah'-koh-moh] The German composer Giacomo Meyerbeer (originally Jakob Liebmann Beer), b. Berlin, Sept. 5, 1791, d. May 2, 1864, dominated the most brilliant period of French grand opera in Paris. In 1816 he went to Italy to study. His successful *Il Crociato in Egitto* (The Crusader in Egypt, 1824) was written in the style of Rossini. On the advice of his friend Carl Maria von Weber, Meyerbeer left Italy for France in 1826. Combining German musical discipline with Italian lyricism and French theatricality, he found his métier in his first French grand opera, *Robert le Diable* (1831), which enchanted Parisians with its historical fantasies and helped to save the Paris Opera from fiscal collapse. There followed *Les Huguenots* (1836), *Le Prophète* (1849), *L'Étoile du Nord* (North Star, 1854), *Dinorah, ou le Pardon de Ploërmel* (1859), and *L'Africaine*, begun in 1838 but not produced until 1865, a year after Meyerbeer's death. Meyerbeer's French operas are particularly notable for their spectacle and orchestral effects.

Meyerhold, Vsevolod Emilievich

[my'-ur-hohlt or mee-yir'-hohlt]   Vsevolod Emilievich Meyerhold, b. Feb. 9 (N.S.), 1874, d. Feb. 2, 1940, in his 40 years as a director and producer in Russia, succeeded almost single-handedly in revolutionizing the modern theater. At Konstantin Stanislavsky's invitation, he staged symbolist drama in the Moscow Art Theater's experimental studio. Meyerhold's account of this work appears in his seminal book *On Theatre* (1913; Eng. trans., 1969). From 1908 to 1919, Meyerhold directed opera and drama at the imperial theaters in Saint Petersburg but simultaneously staged experimental productions that drew on the improvisation, clowning, and acrobatics of the *commedia dell'arte* tradition.

Meyerhold staged the first "Soviet" play to be produced after the Bolshevik revolution, Mayakovsky's politically radical *Mystery-Bouffe* (1918). He headed his own Moscow theater until its closing in 1938. His idea of the theater as an autonomous art, however, caused his arrest (1939) as a "formalist" during the Stalinist era, and he died in custody.

There were few areas of theatrical life that remained untouched by Meyerhold's hand. Having dispensed with the use of a curtain in 1905, he turned auditorium and stage into a single, well-lighted area for his staging (1910) of Molière's *Don Juan*. A believer in total theater, he invited the collaboration of artists, musicians, and poets.

mezzo-soprano

The mezzo-soprano is the most common natural singing voice of women; its range lies between those of the soprano and contralto. The mezzo-soprano voice is heavier, darker, and less agile than the higher soprano voices, but it is valued for its great expressive quality. Low female solos in oratorio are suited to the mezzo-soprano voice because it blends well in the solo quartet. In opera the title role in Bizet's *Carmen* and the role of Suzuki in Puccini's *Madama Butterfly* are for mezzo-soprano.

mezzotint

Mezzotint is a technique of ENGRAVING in which the entire surface of the metal engraving plate is first covered with hundreds of small pricks, or burrs, and these are then burnished and scraped to create light or inkless areas. The technique was invented in the 17th century and was extensively used until the early 19th century, especially in England. Because it was the only method by which the many gradations of shading in oil paintings could be reproduced, the mezzotint (from the Italian *mezza tinta*, "half-tone") was the favored method for reproducing old masters.

mho

see OHM'S LAW

Mi Fei

[mee fay]   The Chinese scholar-painter Mi Fei, 1051–1107, also called Mi Fu, was one of the foremost artists working in the literati (*wenren*) tradition during the Northern Song dynasty (960–1127). A renowned calligrapher and painter, he wrote two major treatises on art and developed a distinctive style of landscape painting in

which clusters of flattened ink strokes (later called Mi dots) are used to form the rocks, trees, and the characteristically mist-shrouded mountain peaks. His son Mi Youren (1075–1151) painted in Mi's style, which influenced many later artists, notably Gao Kegong of the Yuan dynasty (1279–1368) and Dong Qichang of the Ming dynasty (1368–1644).

Miami (city in Florida)   Miami, a city in southeastern Florida, is located on Biscayne Bay. It is the seat of Dade County. The city's population of 358,548 (1990) makes Miami the second largest city in the state (after Jacksonville). Metropolitan Dade County, however, has a population of 1,937,094, making it by far the largest urban area in Florida and one of the largest in the South.

In the metropolitan area 17% of the population is African American, and about 40% is "Anglo"; roughly half the population is Hispanic—the highest percentage in any major U.S. city—more than two-thirds of whom are Cuban. Spanish has become the unofficial second language of the city. About 225,000 Jews, many elderly, live in the Miami area.

The city's climate and its proximity to the Atlantic

Hotels, condominiums, parks, and recreational areas cover the narrow island that is Miami Beach, which lies parallel to Miami. The city's primary source of income is the millions of tourists who come to enjoy the ocean, climate, and nightlife.

Ocean have made Miami one of the great North American tourist centers. The Orange Bowl is home of the Miami Dolphins, the city's professional football team, and the scene of the New Year's Day Orange Bowl game.

Miami has an international airport and is a major seaport. In addition to tourism, the city supports some manufacturing, including textiles, clothing, shoes, aviation equipment, and processed foods. During the 1960s, Miami emerged as a major center of finance and business with Latin America. The economy was further stimulated by the opening (June 1980) of a free-trade zone in the city.

Major educational institutions include the University of Miami (1925), in Coral Gables, and Florida International University (1965). Seaquarium is a tropical marine aquarium.

The Spanish established a Jesuit mission in the Miami area in the 1560s. In 1835, during the Seminole Wars, Fort Dallas was built on the site. The city of Miami was founded in 1870. Real growth occurred after 1895, when Henry M. Flagler began developing it as a resort area. The city experienced a great land boom in the 1920s and another in the 1950s. Many Cubans arrived after Fidel Castro came to power in 1959 and again in 1980. In the late 1970s many Haitians also arrived. Miami prospered in the 1980s, with various revitalization projects, including rapid-transit systems. In 1985, Xavier Suarez was elected the city's first Cuban-born mayor, and in 1989, Ileana Ros-Lehtinen became the first Cuban American to be elected to Congress from Dade County.

Miami (Indian tribe)   The Miami, a group of Algonquian-speaking North American Indian tribes, were one of the largest and most influential groups in the Ohio Valley during the 18th century. A horticultural people organized in six local bands, each under its own chief, they lived in large settled villages in summer and in hunting camps in winter. The Ojibwa Indians called them *Owmawmeg* ("people of the peninsula"); this name was adopted by the French and English as Miami. They called themselves *Twatwa*, a word for the cry of the crane, the symbol of one of their principal clans.

Originally from what is now northern Illinois and Indiana, the Miami were driven out of their homeland by marauding Iroquois (see IROQUOIS LEAGUE) war parties in the 1640s and began a series of migrations to present-day Wisconsin, Michigan, and Ohio before resettling in Indiana early in the 18th century. They played an important role in all of the Ohio Valley Indian wars until the end of the War of 1812. Soon thereafter, with their population much reduced, they ceded most of their land to the U.S. government. In the 1840s most remaining Miami, then estimated to number 1,000, were removed to Kansas and later to Oklahoma. A few thousand Miami now live in Indiana and Oklahoma.

Miantonomo [mee-an-tuh-noh'-moh]   Miantonomo, c.1600–1643, was a Narragansett Indian chief. Although he aided the Massachusetts Bay colonists in the Pequot

War (1637), they later accused him of treachery. Captured (1643) by the pro-English Mohegan tribe under Uncas, Miantonomo was turned over to the Puritan authorities and sentenced to death. His execution by the brother of Uncas was in effect a political murder, because Miantonomo was an ally of Roger Williams of Rhode Island, banished by the Puritans for radicalism.

mica [my'-kuh]   Mica is a generic name for a group of complex hydrous potassium-aluminum SILICATE MINERALS that differ somewhat in chemical composition; examples are biotite, lepidolite, muscovite, phlogopite, and vermiculite. Mica has a low coefficient of expansion, high dielectric strength, good electrical resistivity, a uniform dielectric constant, and capacitance stability; at one time it was the best electrical and thermal insulator known.

The iron content determines the color. Muscovite is generally gray, green, or brown; biotite, brown or black; lepidolite, pink or green; phlogopite, light brown to yellow; and vermiculite, brown. Muscovite has the greatest commercial value and is the mica that is ground and pulverized into pigment grades.

Large crystals of mica—ranging from less than 2 cm (0.8 in) up to 2 m (6.6 ft) in length—are generally found in granitic PEGMATITES. The largest resources of muscovite are in Brazil, Western Africa, and the Madras and Bihar areas of India. The Malagasy Republic is the major world source of phlogopite mica. Mica was first mined in the United States in New Hampshire. After about 1870 production of mica began on a large scale in North Carolina, which now produces more dry and wet ground mica than does any other state.

Small, dry, ground mica flakes are used as a thin coating on rubber surfaces to overcome tackiness and sticking. In exterior house paints dry ground mica adds body, reduces running and sagging, and improves weatherability. The addition of mica to all types of sealers for porous surfaces (such as wallboard, masonry, and concrete blocks) greatly reduces penetration and improves holdout. The inclusion of mica in road and highway paints

The mica group of minerals consists of complex aluminum-potassium silicates and varying amounts of other elements. Commonly found as flat plates or scaly aggregates with shining surfaces, micas have the remarkable property of peeling easily into thin, elastic sheets.

improves wearability, gives good adhesion, and reduces flaking and cracking. Micas are also used in caulking compounds, lubricants, greases, welding-rod coatings, and dry-powder fire extinguishers.

Wet ground mica is produced by grinding mica flakes in water until they are reduced to fine scales. Wet ground mica costs more than twice as much as dry ground mica and is used predominantly in paint and rubber, as well as in plastics and lubricants. Wet ground mica is also used to coat wallpaper, because it imparts an attractive silky or pearly luster.

Micah, Book of [my'-kuh]   Micah is the 6th of the 12 books of Minor Prophets in the Old Testament of the BIBLE. Composed of both dire warnings and encouraging promises, this small but important book records the prophet Micah's preaching in Judah in the late 8th century BC. Micah observed the Assyrians' conquest of northern Israel and predicted the destruction of Jerusalem as punishment for social injustice and corruption among the priests and political leadership. His call for justice is tempered by the promise of a messianic ruler from Bethlehem (5:2–6) whose reign would see swords beaten into plowshares (4:3). Most scholars believe that chapters 4–7 were written after the time of Micah.

Michael   Michael, which means "he who is like God," is the name of an archangel who is mentioned only four times in the Bible (Dan. 10:13 ff. and 12:1; Jude 9; Rev. 12:7–9) but is prominent in the apocryphal literature. Portrayed as Israel's guardian, a prince of heaven, and a great warrior (he overcomes Satan in Rev. 12), he came to be regarded as a key Christian saint. Feast day: Sept. 29 (with Gabriel and Raphael, Western); Nov. 8 (Eastern).

Michael Cerularius [sir-uh-lair'-ee-uhs]   Michael Cerularius, b. c.1000, d. Jan. 21, 1059, was patriarch of Constantinople (1043–58) in the period when the final schism between the Eastern Orthodox and the Roman Catholic churches occurred (1054). Rejecting Roman claims to ecclesiastical supremacy, and particularly pressure for liturgical conformity, Cerularius quarreled with the papal legate Cardinal Humbert. Humbert then delivered a bull of excommunication against the Eastern churches, and Cerularius responded by anathematizing the Western church.

Michael VIII, Palaeologus, Byzantine Emperor [pay-lee-oh-loh'-guhs]   Michael VIII, b. c.1225, d. Dec. 11, 1282, restored to the BYZANTINE EMPIRE some of the lands it had lost to the western Crusaders and founded the Palaeologus dynasty, which ruled the empire until 1453. In 1258, Michael usurped the throne from John IV Lascaris in Nicaea, seat of the exiled Byzantine court and had himself crowned emperor. He successfully defeated his chief rival, the despot of Epirus, and the weakened

Latin Empire of Constantinople (see CONSTANTINOPLE, LATIN EMPIRE OF) fell to him in 1261. With the capital city, Constantinople, restored, Michael had himself crowned emperor again (1261). His principal opponent was CHARLES I of Naples and Sicily. By negotiating a reunion of the Eastern and Western churches, Michael induced Pope Gregory X to restrain Charles. Later he financed a successful revolt, the SICILIAN VESPERS (1282), against Charles. Michael was succeeded by his son, Andronicus II.

Michael, Tsar of Russia Michael (Mikhail Fyodorovich Romanov), b. 1596, d. July 23 (N.S.), 1645, tsar of Russia (1613–45), founded the ROMANOV dynasty. To end the chaos of the TIME OF TROUBLES, the *zemsky sobor* (assembly of the land) offered the throne to Michael, a grandnephew of Tsar IVAN IV. Michael was dominated first by his mother, Ksenia Ivanovna Shestova, and later by his father, Fyodor Nikitich Romanov, who served as patriarch of the Russian Orthodox church and coruler until he died in 1633. Under Michael's rule domestic disorder was checked, and peace was established with Sweden (1617) and Poland (1618, 1634). He was succeeded by his son ALEXIS.

Michael the Brave Michael the Brave (Mihai Viteazul), b. 1558, d. Aug. 19 (N.S.), 1601, was the first Romanian prince who succeeded, albeit for only a year, in uniting Walachia, Transylvania, and Moldavia. He became prince of Walachia in 1593 and seized Transylvania two years later with the help of Holy Roman Emperor RUDOLF II. In May 1600 he successfully invaded Moldavia, but that autumn he lost Transylvania to Rudolf's troops and Moldavia to a Polish army. He was murdered the next year.

Michel, Robert H. [my'-kul] Robert Henry Michel, b. Peoria, Ill., Mar. 2, 1923, a Republican congressman from Illinois, was elected minority whip (1974) and then minority leader (1980) of the House of Representatives. After army service, Michel graduated (1948) from Bradley University in Peoria. First elected to Congress in 1956 and regularly reelected, he proved an orthodox conservative, consistently voting to cut social programs and supporting military spending. In his leadership positions, he demonstrated his mastery of parliamentary compromise.

Michelangelo [mik-ul-an'-juh-loh] The Italian Michelangelo Buonarroti, almost certainly the most famous artist produced by Western civilization and arguably the greatest, is universally viewed as the supreme Renaissance artist (see RENAISSANCE ART AND ARCHITECTURE). He created monumental works of painting, sculpture, and architecture and left an additional legacy of numerous letters and poems. Through this vast and multifaceted body of artistic achievement, Michelangelo made an indelible imprint on the Western imagination.

A member of an old and distinguished Florentine fam-

ily, Michelangelo was born near Arezzo, Italy, on Mar. 6, 1475, and he died on Feb. 18, 1564, in Rome—a record of longevity that was as unusual as his precocity as an artist. He saw himself primarily as a sculptor.

The Early Florentine Years. In his first relief, the *Madonna of the Stairs* (1489–92; Casa Buonarroti, Florence), executed while the artist was still less than 20 years of age, the *schiacciato* (flattened relief) style directly recalls Donatello's technique. The depiction of the Child's muscular right arm extended behind him, the compression of the space, and the mood of sadness that permeates the piece convey a compositional and psychological tension that marks much of Michelangelo's later

Michelangelo's commanding image (c.1515) of the Old Testament prophet Moses is one of his greatest sculptural works.

work. The relief remained unfinished in detail—another hallmark of the artist's more mature production.

Michelangelo's first response to the majesty of classical Roman art (see ROMAN ART AND ARCHITECTURE) is found in his larger-than-life statue of *Bacchus*, the god of wine (1496–97; Bargello, Florence). In this, his first mature masterpiece, Michelangelo amplified the classical ideal of beauty in a sensual and compositionally complex rendering of the human form that echoes Donatello's bronze *David* (c.1440–42; Bargello, Florence).

Michelangelo was above all a carver in marble whose ability to extract animate form from a block of stone remains unsurpassed. The *Pietà* (1498–1500; Saint Peter's Basilica, Rome) epitomizes a grace and finish that are unmatched even in his later work. The suppleness of Christ's naturalistically modeled torso is emphasized by the Virgin's flowing drapery, by the serene features of the two youthful faces, and by the large pyramidal composition that rises to a natural apex at the head of the Mother of God. The sweet tenderness of the *Pietà* gave way to power and monumentality in the marble *David* (1501–04; Accademia, Florence), a colossal (4.34-m/14.24-ft) evocation of athletic prowess and dynamic action. In this heroic work Michelangelo successfully fused classical inspiration with Florentine humanism and enhanced this fusion through his own depiction of the male nude.

Julius II and the Sistine Ceiling. The remainder of Michelangelo's career was largely controlled by his relationship with the papacy, and from 1505 to 1516 the Vatican became the focal point of his artistic endeavors. Initially called to Rome to sculpt an enormous tomb for Pope JULIUS II, Michelangelo completed only a fraction of the proposed sculptural program, including the magnificent *Moses* (c.1515; San Pietro in Vincoli, Rome) and the fascinating nude studies known as the *Dying Slave* and the *Rebellious Slave* (both c.1510–13; Louvre, Paris). A major reason for his inability to finish Julius's tomb was the immense project he undertook (1508–12) to execute on the ceiling of the SISTINE CHAPEL a pictorial cycle devoted to the biblical history of humanity.

Michelangelo's organization of the Sistine ceiling frescoes (see FRESCO PAINTING) represents perhaps the most complex composition in Western art. The space contains an intricate illusionistic architectural structure that serves as a frame for the disposition of the sculpturelike forms. Of the nine central narrative scenes illustrating events from the creation of the universe as told in Genesis, the most sublime scene is the *Creation of Adam*, in which Michelangelo's new vision of human beauty, first articulated in the *David*, attains pictorial form. In the four years that it took to complete the ceiling, Michelangelo realized the full potential of the High Renaissance style; in the process, he changed the artistic vision of another great High Renaissance master, RAPHAEL, and altered the course of Western art.

Disillusion and Maturity. The supreme statements of the potential nobility of human beings expressed in the *David* and the Sistine ceiling frescoes gave way after 1520 to more complex, agitated, and ominous artistic creations. To a profoundly religious and humanistic

Michelangelo the jolting breakup of the Roman church after 1517, the terrible sack of Rome by the troops of Holy Roman Emperor Charles V in 1527, and the final crushing of the Florentine Republic in 1530 came as disillusioning blows. A radical change in the artist's outlook is apparent in the masterwork of his middle age, the architectural and sculptural program of the Medici Chapel in Florence (1519–34). The overall architectural scheme of the chapel owes a great debt to Filippo BRUNELLESCHI's nearby Old Sacristy, but the overwhelming effect of Michelangelo's squeezed niches, crowded windows, and nonsupporting members is as subtle and disconcerting as the earlier design is clear and rationalistic. The statues atop the tombs of Lorenzo and Giuliano de'Medici retain the human dignity inherent in all of Michelangelo's works, but they strike a new note of sorrow and poignancy. In the intense spirituality of its overall design and the disturbing power of forms such as the figure of *Dawn* on one of the tombs, the Medici Chapel signals a dramatic shift in Michelangelo's outlook and style, which hereafter takes on the highly artificial ideals of beauty that played a key role in the development of MANNERISM.

The Final Years. Michelangelo's seemingly inexhaustible powers of artistic invention made it possible for him in his final three decades to create an even more personal style. This last phase of his artistic career, spent almost entirely in Rome, is characterized by a militant and all-encompassing religious outlook and a relative subordination of sculptural to pictorial and architectural efforts. In his last frescoes, the *Last Judgment* (1536–41; Sistine Chapel, Vatican), the *Conversion of St. Paul* (1542–45; Pauline Chapel, Vatican), and the *Crucifixion of Peter* (1545–50; Pauline Chapel, Vatican), he replaced the rational compositional unity and beauty of the Sistine ceiling frescoes with a visionary world in which the compression of the figures and the violence of their actions take place in a supremely spiritual world. His human forms are as powerfully modeled as ever, but they are now contorted in physical agonies that imply the necessity of human suffering for the salvation of human souls.

Perhaps Michangelo's most interesting works of this period are the architectural commissions he executed in Rome in the last years of his life. His completion of Antonio da Sangallo's Farnese Palace (1517–50) and his design for the Campidoglio, the plaza and its rebuilt classical structures atop the Capitoline Hill (begun 1538), both display an idiosyncratic reordering of the Renaissance architectural vocabulary around outsized and overwhelmingly powerful elements—the huge cornice of the Farnese and the gigantic, two-story Corinthian order of the Palazzo dei Conservatori on the Capitoline. This projection of awesome power also marks Michangelo's completion and reinterpretation of Donato BRAMANTE's plan for SAINT PETER'S BASILICA. Restoring Bramante's Greek-cross plan for the church, Michelangelo went on to design a powerful exterior unified by a colossal double Corinthian order, and the magnificent ribbed dome that crowns the structure. In his very last years the aging artist returned to his first love, sculpture, executing the *Pietà*, or *Deposition* (c.1550; Cathedral, Florence) that he intended to have

(Opposite page) The vast frescoes done (1508–12) by Michelangelo in the Sistine Chapel of the Vatican are universally judged his masterwork in that medium and a great achievement of High Renaissance painting. In this ceiling panel of the Creation story, Adam is being given life by God.

placed on his own tomb. Unfinished and partially mutilated by Michelangelo in a fit of depression, the aged and resigned features of the figure of Nicodemus supporting the dead Christ constitute a self-portrait.

Michelin, André and Édouard [meesh-lan', ahn-dray', ay-dwahr'] André Michelin, b. Jan. 16, 1853, d. Apr. 4, 1931, and his brother Édouard, b. June 23, 1859, d. Aug. 25, 1940, manufactured France's first pneumatic TIRES. In 1891 they offered experimental tires to a bicycle racer. The bicyclist won, and within a year some 10,000 others adopted the Michelin tire. In 1895 the brothers fitted their tires on a Daimler automobile that they drove in the Paris-Bordeaux auto race. Later the company introduced tire tread patterns (1905), demountable wheel rims (1906), low-pressure "balloon" tires (1923), steel-cord tires (1938), and steel-belted radial tires (1949).

Michelozzo [mee-kay-loht'-soh] The Italian sculptor and architect Michelozzo di Bartolommeo, b. 1396, d. Oct. 7, 1472, was the leading architectural designer in Florence in the generation after Filippo Brunelleschi. Like Brunelleschi, he received many commissions from Cosimo de'Medici, including those for the library of the Convent of San Marco (1436–43), and the Palazzo Medici-Riccardi (1444–59). In the Palazzo Medici-Riccardi, a traditionally rusticated three-story exterior is capped by a vast cornice that is classical in detail but irrational in its huge proportions. Half-classical and half-traditional Tuscan in design, the palazzo set the standard for Florentine town palaces for the next 100 years. Michelozzo also worked in Venice, Milan, and even Dubrovnik, spreading the vocabulary of Renaissance architecture far beyond Tuscany.

Michelson-Morley experiment In 1887 two American scientists, Albert A. Michelson (1852–1931) and Edward W. Morley (1838–1923), performed a classic experiment that contributed to the downfall of the concepts of absolute space and the ether (see ETHER, physics). The accepted theories of late-19th-century physics required space to be filled with a medium—the ether—through which light was thought to propagate. If the Earth moves through the ether, the speed of a light ray as measured on Earth would depend on its direction, much as the speed of a swimmer depends on whether he or she swims with, against, or across the current.

Michelson, who achieved fame for his accurate measurement of the velocity of light, designed an apparatus, called an INTERFEROMETER, which could detect this effect. Schematically, an interferometer consists of two straight arms set at right angles to each other. Each arm has a mirror at one end. At the intersection where the arms are joined a half-silvered mirror splits a light beam into two. Each half of the split beam travels down one arm and is reflected back by the mirror at the end of each arm. When the two beams are recombined, they interfere in such a way as to produce a characteristic pattern of fringes that depends on the difference in time required for the two beams to make the round trip. If the apparatus is rotated through 90°, the roles of parallel and perpendicular arms are reversed and the fringe pattern would shift.

The expected fringe shift was four-tenths of a wavelength; however, no shift as large as four-hundredths of a wavelength was observed. Many repetitions of the experiment by other researchers have confirmed this null result. Einstein's theory of RELATIVITY provides the only fully consistent explanation; it postulates that the speed of light is always the same, regardless of the motion of the observer, and therefore is the same in each direction along each arm of the interferometer.

Michener, James A. [mich'-nur] Best known for his novels about exotic places and people, the American author James Albert Michener, b. New York City, Feb. 3, 1907, is one of the most prolific authors of the 20th century. His first collection of stories, *Tales of the South Pacific* (1947; Pulitzer Prize, 1948), remains one of his most popular books, forming the basis of the musical *South Pacific* (1949). In such lengthy novels as *Hawaii* (1959), *The Source* (1965), *Centennial* (1974), *Chesapeake* (1978), and *The Covenant* (1980), Michener uses his lucid narrative style to present vast amounts of detailed information on various cultures. *Hawaii* proceeds from the geological creation of the islands and traces their story of successive racial migrations to the time of U.S. statehood. *The Source* encompasses 12,000 years of Palestinian history, and *The Covenant* describes the 500-year history of South Africa. In *Centennial* and *Chesapeake* Michener applies the same epic treatment to the American West and Chesapeake Bay area. More recent novels are *Space* (1982), *Poland* (1983), *Texas* (1986), and *Alaska* (1988). Michener's nonfiction includes *Kent State: What Happened and Why* (1971), *Sports in America* (1976), and *The World Is My Home* (1992), his autobiography.

Michigan [mish'-uh-guhn] The state of Michigan consists of two peninsulas formed by the Great Lakes—the large mitten-shaped Lower Peninsula and the smaller Upper Peninsula—plus numerous islands located within the Great Lakes. The state has land borders with Ohio, Indiana, and Wisconsin; water forms part of the state boundary with Wisconsin and all of it with Illinois and Minnesota. Canada and Michigan are joined for 1,160 km (720 mi) along the international boundary. Michigan ranks 11th among the U.S. states in area, with 250,738 km² (96,810 mi²). In addition, however, Michigan is responsible for managing a significant portion of the Great

MICHIGAN

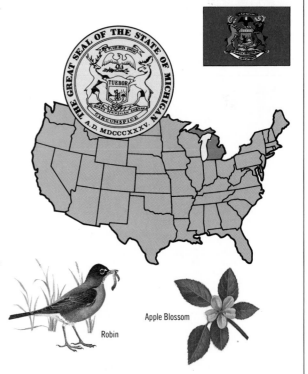

Land: Area: 250,738 km² (96,810 mi²); rank: 11th. Capital: Lansing (1990 pop., 127,321). Largest city: Detroit (1990 pop., 1,027,974). Counties: 83. Elevations: highest—603 m (1,979 ft), at Mount Arvon; lowest—174 m (572 ft), at Lake Erie.

People: Population (1990): 9,328,784; rank: 8th; density: 63.2 persons per km² (163.6 per mi²). Distribution (1990): 70.5% urban, 29.5% rural. Average annual change (1980–90): +0.07%.

Government (1993): Governor: John Engler, Republican. U.S. Congress: Senate—2 Democrats; House—10 Democrats, 6 Republicans. Electoral college votes: 18. State legislature: 38 senators, 110 representatives.

Economy: State personal income (1989): $161.8 billion; rank: 9th. Median family income (1989): $36,652; rank: 16th. Agriculture: income (1989)—$2.9 billion. Lumber production (1991): 313 million board feet. Mining (nonfuel): value (1988)—$1.6 billion. Manufacturing: value added (1987)—$60.26 billion. Services: value (1987)—$37.4 billion.

Miscellany: Statehood: Jan. 26, 1837; the 26th state. Nicknames: Wolverine State and Great Lake State; tree: white pine; motto: *Si quaeris peninsulam amoenam circumspice* ("If you seek a pleasant peninsula, look about you"); song: "Michigan, My Michigan."

Apple Blossom

Robin

Lakes water area (99,905 km²/38,575 mi²). Michigan's shoreline of 3,592 km (2,232 mi) is the longest of any inland state. The name *Michigan* is derived from two Algonquian words, *michi* ("large") and *gami* ("lake").

Land and Resources

The Michigan Basin bedrock underlying Michigan dates from the Precambrian and Paleozoic eras. The present shape of both the Great Lakes and Michigan's peninsulas was formed about 2,500 years ago as a result of glacial ice and meltwater action and elevation changes of the lakes' outlets.

The Upper Peninsula, also called the Northern Peninsula, extends for about 500 km (310 mi) in an east-west direction; its northern shore lies along Lake Superior, and the southern shore is along Lake Michigan. The Upper Peninsula upland covers its western half. The Porcupine Mountains reach 597 m (1,958 ft), and Mount Curwood in the Huron Mountains, at 603 m (1,979 ft), is the state's highest point. The Upper Peninsula lowland, in the east, has an average elevation of 213 m (700 ft).

The Lower Peninsula topography consists of lowland areas punctuated with glacial uplands. Lowlands formed from former glacial lake beds are located in the southeast, around Saginaw and Muskegon. Glacial moraines

form the thumb upland and the northern upland, which rises to 518 m (1,700 ft) near Cadillac. When the Pleistocene glaciers melted 10,000 to 16,000 years ago, glacial till was deposited throughout the peninsula, forming hilly moraines and plains.

Soils. Three soil types are found in Michigan: podzols, gray brown podzolics, and mixed organic bog soils. The podzols, the least fertile of the three, are mostly found in the Upper Peninsula and the northern two-thirds of the Lower Peninsula. The productive gray brown podzolics are found in the southern Lower Peninsula. The widely distributed mixed organic bog soils were created when inland lakes filled in with rich nutrients. Remains of ice-age mastodons and other extinct animals are sometimes found in the former bogs.

Rivers and Lakes. Michigan has more than 11,000 natural inland lakes. Houghton Lake is the largest, with an area of 80 km² (31 mi²). Most of Michigan's rivers are relatively short, but are useful for hydroelectrical power generation; they are also used for transportation and recreation. Numerous attractive waterfalls are found in the Upper Peninsula. The Grand is the longest river and flows 420 km (260 mi) in the southwestern part of the state. The Saginaw River system drains an area of nearly 15,540 km² (6,000 mi²).

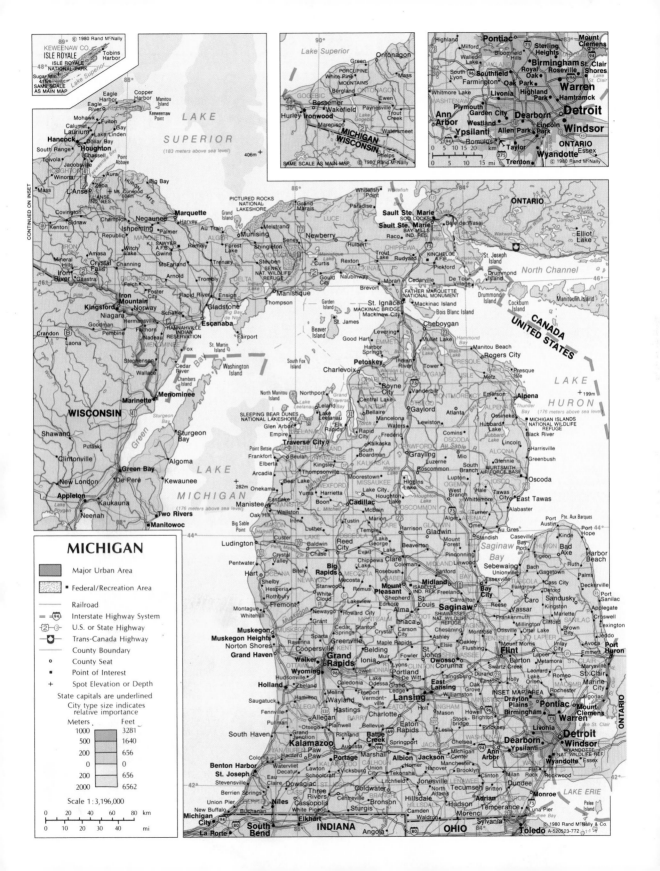

Visitors to the Warren Dunes State Park, on the southern tip of Lake Michigan, may imagine that they are looking upon a vast ocean rather than a freshwater lake. Michigan is the third largest of the Great Lakes and forms the western boundary of the state of Michigan.

Climate. Michigan is situated within the humid continental climate region. The Great Lakes, however, influence the temperature, the number of frost-free days, and the ratio of sunshine to cloudy days. Average annual temperatures vary between 10° C (50° F) at Detroit in the southeast and 4° C (39° F) at Marquette in the northcentral Upper Peninsula. The greatest range in annual temperatures occurs in the northern Lower Peninsula, with a record high of 44.4° C (112° F) and a record low of −46.1° C (−51° F). An average of 787 mm (31 in) of precipitation falls annually in the state. Snow, sleet, hail, and ice storms are common, and tornadoes and blizzards sometimes occur. Snowfall averages range from 762 mm (30 in) in the southeast to 4572 mm (180 in) in the Keweenaw Peninsula in the northern Upper Peninsula. Heavy cloud cover in the fall and early winter is common because the Great Lakes rarely freeze totally.

Vegetation and Animal Life. Pioneer settlers removed most of the native vegetation. Throughout southern Michigan, hardwood species are regenerating in the original forest associations of oak, hickory, and walnut on well-drained land and of maple, beech, and birch or elm, ash, and cottonwood on moist land. Mixed forests of both deciduous and coniferous trees were common in the Upper Peninsula and the northern Lower Peninsula. Most prized by early lumbermen were stands of white pine. Other commercial trees include ash, aspen, cherry, hemlock, spruce, cedar, and replanted red pine.

Several species of animals are native to the region including whitetail deer, black bear, moose, raccoon, red fox, bobcat, woodchuck, squirrel, beaver, muskrat, rabbit, skunk, porcupine, and the reintroduced elk. Eagle,

osprey, and the endangered Kirtland's warbler are less often seen; the wolverine, fisher, marten, and wild bison have vanished. Several species of fish have become rare, including white fish, sturgeon, herring, muskellunge, and lake trout. Sport fish found in the state include bluegill, crappie, perch, large and smallmouth bass, pike, and salmon. Common birds include the great blue heron, kingfisher, several duck species, geese, and gulls. Game birds inhabiting the area are the partridge, quail, and ringneck pheasant.

Mineral Resources. Deposits of copper and iron ore are found in the western Upper Peninsula. There are also small reserves of zinc, lead, nickel, cobalt, platinum, gold, silver, and uranium. Other minerals include limestone, rock salt and brines, gypsum, and coal. Reserves of natural gas and petroleum are found at several locations in Lower Michigan.

People

Michigan's 1990 population was 9,328,784. About 70% of all inhabitants live in urban areas. DETROIT (1990 pop., 1,027,974) is the largest city. GRAND RAPIDS, WARREN, Flint, LANSING, Sterling Heights, ANN ARBOR, and Livonia all have between 100,000 and 200,000 residents.

Between 1970 and 1980 Michigan recorded a slow rate of growth—4.3%; during 1980–90 it was even slower—0.7%. Historically, Michigan has experienced a net gain from migrations into the state; since the mid-1970s, however, a net out-migration has taken place. In 1990 African Americans made up about 14% of the population, Hispanics 2.2%, Asians and Pacific Islanders 1.1%, and American Indians 0.6%.

The Protestant religious denominations are most numerous in Michigan. The Roman Catholic church is the oldest denomination; the French established the first church at SAULT SAINTE MARIE in 1668. There is a fairly sizable minority of Jewish people, with most residing in the greater Detroit area.

Education and Culture. Michigan has long been a leader in public education. In 1837 the nation's first state primary school fund was created, and tuition-free primary schooling was enacted in 1869. The state has a particularly distinguished public higher-education system; institutions include Michigan State University (1855) at East Lansing and the University of Michigan (1817), with its main campus at Ann Arbor (see MICHIGAN, UNIVERSITY OF).

Michigan's museums include the Detroit Institute of Arts and Detroit Historical Museum; the Henry Ford Museum (of transportation and technology exhibits) located at Greenfield Village in Dearborn; historical museums at Lansing and Grand Rapids; the University of Michigan Museum of Art in Ann Arbor; and the Gerald Ford Museum (in Grand Rapids) and Presidential Library (in Ann Arbor). The Cranbrook Foundation, in Bloomfield Hills, is the site of a well-known art school. The National Music Camp at Interlochen and the Detroit Symphony are both well known throughout the country.

Michigan's historic sites include Mackinac Island, located in the Straits of MACKINAC, which is the site of a fortress built by the British in 1780; and Norton Indian Mounds in Grand Rapids (built between 110 BC and AD 280).

Communications. The state is served by numerous Sunday, daily, weekly, and semiweekly newspapers. The leading daily newspapers are the *Detroit News* and the *Detroit Free Press.* Radio stations WWJ (1920) and WJR (1922) are two of the nation's pioneering commercial broadcast stations. There are many other radio stations broadcasting in Michigan, as well as television stations.

Recreation and Sports. Michigan's many lakes, especially the Great Lakes, are the state's greatest recreational resource. Pictured Rocks National Lakeshore is an area of dramatic sandstone cliffs along Lake Superior; Sleeping Bear Dunes National Lakeshore extends for 55 km (34 mi) along the shores of Lake Michigan. Isle Royale National Park is a wilderness island in Lake Superior. Most major league sports are centered in Detroit (baseball and hockey) or at the nearby Pontiac Silverdome (basketball and football).

Economic Activity

Although Michigan (specifically, Detroit) is closely identified with the motor-vehicle industry, the state earns a good deal more from service industries than from the—nonetheless important—manufacturing industries. A critical economic problem for the state is developing sufficient diversification of industry, particularly in cities like Flint, to prevent unemployment when the auto industry is affected by a weakened national economy.

Agriculture. Michigan ranks in the midrange nationally in agricultural output, with most production concentrated in the southern half of the Lower Peninsula. A significant fruit-growing belt is located in the west along Lake Michigan, and the thumb region is a leading producer of beans and sugar beets. Michigan is a national leader in the production of tart cherries, cucumbers, dry beans, and blueberries. Other major crops include corn, wheat, soybeans, potatoes, hay, and table vegetables. Dairy and beef cattle, hogs, and laying chickens lead livestock production. Mint, red cloverseed, and grapes for wine are specialty crops.

Forestry and Fishing. Michigan's commercial timberlands cover 7.5 million ha (18.8 million acres) and are among the largest in the nation. The dollar value of the state's fisheries industry did not vary greatly after the opening of the St. Lawrence Seaway in 1959, although the size (in terms of weight) of the commercial fish harvest has declined considerably. Since the opening of the Seaway, sea lamprey have been reduced, and salmon have been introduced to help control alewife (a species of herring) and to create a sport-fishing industry in the state.

Mining. Mining roughly matches agriculture in economic importance in Michigan. The most valuable minerals are petroleum, iron ore, and natural gas. Fuels are tapped in the Lower Peninsula, and metallic ores are mined in the Upper Peninsula. Michigan is a leading producer of iron ore. Nonmetallic resources such as limestone, natural salines, sand, and gravel contribute importantly to mining revenue. Michigan no longer leads the nation in copper production, but the remaining low-grade deposits may be the largest in the nation. The state is the leading producer of peat in the United States.

Manufacturing and Energy. The metropolitan Detroit area is one of the world's foremost manufacturing regions. Approximately one-third of Michigan's industrial workers produce transportation equipment, including cars, trucks, and tractors. Motor vehicles are manufactured in DEARBORN, KALAMAZOO, Flint, Lansing, and Pontiac, as well as the Detroit metropolitan area. Parts manufacturing and auto-related research are provided mostly at JACKSON, SAGINAW, and Grand Rapids. Michigan is also an important producer of nonelectric machinery, fabricated metal products, and primary metals. Other leading industries are cereal and food processing, especially in BATTLE CREEK; chemicals and drug production, centered in Midland; and furniture manufacturing in MUSKEGON and Grand Rapids.

In 1886, Michigan's first petroleum well was drilled near Port Huron, and natural gas was tapped in 1927. Although new fields have continued to be productive, they are grossly inadequate for the state's needs; most of the state's fuel comes from outside sources. Michigan's power is generated largely by plants using coal, oil, or gas. There are also nuclear-powered energy installations and a few hydroelectric plants.

Tourism. Tourism, professional sports, and other leisure-time activities are linked to numerous businesses that employ many thousands of people. Out-of-state visitors are attracted by Michigan's plentiful outdoor recreation opportunities; water resources, including the Great Lakes and the thousands of inland lakes and streams, are particularly appealing for sports and nature enthusiasts.

Transportation. Michigan's transportation network consists of an extensive road and freeway system as well as railroads. Michigan and Canada are linked by bridges at Detroit, Port Huron, and Sault Sainte Marie. The Mackinac Bridge links the Upper and Lower peninsulas. Tunnels for railroad and auto use are located at Detroit and Port Huron. Detroit and several other cities have port facilities for ocean vessels, and freighters are used on the Great Lakes for the transport of bulk commodities.

Government and Politics

Michigan has been governed by constitutions of 1835, 1850, 1908, and currently 1964 as amended. The chief officer, the governor, is teamed with a lieutenant governor; they are elected to 4-year terms of office. Michigan's bicameral legislature is composed of a Senate, whose 38 members serve 4-year terms, and a House of Representatives, whose 110 members are elected every 2 years. Local government comprises 83 counties, which are divided into townships as well as incorporated villages and cities.

Whether the Republican party was established in 1854 at Jackson, Mich., "under the oaks," or at Ripon, Wis., may never be settled. Nevertheless, up to 1932 the state was a "citadel of Republicanism." Since then, neither major party has dominated state politics. After World War II, however, the Democratic party increased its influence significantly. In 1974, Gerald R. Ford, a Republican congressman from Grand Rapids (served 1948–73), became the 38th President of the United States.

Detroit's Renaissance Center is a complex of 4 office buildings, a 73-story hotel, restaurants, and shops on the banks of the Detroit River. The 13-ha (33-acre) complex has stimulated some regeneration of the downtown area.

Automobiles move down an assembly line in Detroit, known as "the automotive capital of the world." Detroit's auto industry employs a sizable proportion of Michigan's industrial workers.

History

Pre-European Settlement. Material from the oldest dated archaeological site in Michigan suggests that Paleo-Indian hunters inhabited the area north of Detroit about 11,000 years ago. After 500 BC the Hopewellian MOUND BUILDERS moved into the state. Subsequently the state was inhabited by three Algonquian tribes—the OJIBWA, the OTTAWA, and the Potawatomi—and an Iroquoian-speaking tribe, the Wyandot (Huron).

Colonial Period. The first European to explore the area that is present-day Michigan was Étienne BRÛLÉ, who visited the Upper Peninsula about 1620. In 1668, Father Jacques MARQUETTE founded the first permanent settlement, Sault Sainte Marie. Throughout this early period, fur trading with the Indians dominated the activities of the Euro-Americans. Forts Michilimackinac (1715) and later Mackinac (1780; both now reconstructed) became renowned as the center of fur trade. In 1701, Antoine de la Mothe CADILLAC established Fort Ponchartrain, which subsequently came to control the fur trade in the Lower Peninsula. In 1760, near the end of the FRENCH AND INDIAN WAR between the British and French, the British gained control of the area and governed it until 1796. During this period the British built Fort Lernoult (1779) at Detroit and Fort Mackinac (1780), neither of which American forces were powerful enough to seize during the Revolution. In hope of controlling part of the Great Lakes region, the Spanish entered the Lower Peninsula briefly in 1781.

The American Pioneer Period. In 1787 the area became part of the NORTHWEST TERRITORY; subsequently fighting broke out between Indians in the area (with British support) and the United States. After Gen. Anthony WAYNE's victory at Fallen Timbers (1794), Indian resistance was broken, and the British peacefully relinquished (1796) Detroit and Fort Mackinac under the terms of JAY'S TREATY. Michigan

Territory was established in 1805. During the WAR OF 1812, Michigan was temporarily lost to the British.

Michigan's pioneer land boom came in the 1830s and '40s. It was spurred by the completion of the ERIE CANAL (1825), road building, and the spread of favorable reports concerning the agricultural quality of the land. Michigan received statehood on Jan. 26, 1837. The mining boom in the Upper Peninsula began in the mid-1840s with the discovery of copper and iron ore. The demand for lumber in the Midwest and Plains laid the foundation for Michigan's nation-leading logging boom during the last half of the 19th century. The state's virgin forests were depleted because of astonishingly high cutting rates. During the Civil War and later years, Michigan farms became known for the production of wheat, potatoes, hops, and sheep.

Industrial Development. During the Civil War more than 90,000 Michiganians fought, and almost 14,000 died. Because of the wartime labor shortages and the trend to create labor-saving devices, the innovative foundation was laid for the evolution of the automobile industry. As early as 1886, R. E. Olds drove a steam car in Lansing. Henry Ford (see FORD family) established his company in 1903. The assembly-line production of about 15 million low-cost Model T cars between 1908 and 1927 coupled with Ford's $5-per-day minimum-wage policy set in 1914 (considered a high wage at the time) revolutionized Michigan's economy.

The Depression of the 1930s led to statewide economic hardship and also a labor-relations crisis of lasting magnitude. In 1935 the UNITED AUTO WORKERS union (UAW) was formed. Between 1935 and 1941, in a series of violent strikes involving the major automobile plants, the UAW won the right to negotiate company-wide labor contracts. With the outbreak of World War II, automobile production was halted and the plants were rapidly converted to the production of motor-related armaments, artillery, and ammunition. The Willow Run B-24 Bomber Plant produced 8,685 aircraft, more than any other plant in the nation. Following World War II automobile production began again and soon reached record levels. Employment in the motor-vehicle industry, however, dropped significantly after the Korean War, partly because of automation and decentralization of the industry.

Throughout the 20th century, black and white unskilled workers from the South relocated in Detroit and other industrial cities. Blacks became increasingly concentrated in the central cities, while whites moved to suburban areas. Although interracial riots had occurred in 1863 and 1943, the low point in civil strife came at Detroit in the summer of 1967 when a riot resulted in dozens of deaths and huge property losses.

Revitalization and Prospects for the Future. Since the urban turmoil of the 1960s, several African-American leaders have gained political power in Michigan; they include Coleman Young, mayor of Detroit. Mall projects in city centers have resulted in revitalization. Grand Rapids and Lansing have built community colleges in downtown locations. Detroit, in a dramatic move to revitalize its downtown, constructed the riverfront Renaissance Center, a complex of four 39-story office buildings surrounding a circular 73-story hotel (1977). Detroit's building projects continued through the 1980s.

The economy of Detroit—and the state—is exceptionally sensitive to national and international factors affecting the automobile industry. The economy suffered severely in the late 1970s and early 1980s but had recovered by the mid-1980s. Continuing the trend to diversify the economy and to reduce environmental damage of land and water resources remain the challenges facing Michigan's citizens.

Michigan, Lake Lake Michigan is the only one of the GREAT LAKES of North America to lie totally within U.S. territory. It is bounded by the states of Wisconsin on the west, Michigan on the north and east, Illinois on the southwest, and Indiana on the southeast. The third largest of the Great Lakes, Lake Michigan measures 494 km (307 mi) from north to south and has a maximum width of 190 km (118 mi). The surface area is about 57,750 km^2 (22,300 mi^2); the lake has a mean depth of 84 m (276 ft) and a maximum of 281 m (923 ft). In the north the lake discharges into Lake Huron through the Straits of Mackinac (see MACKINAC, STRAITS OF). Rivers draining into the lake include the Manistee, Pere Marquette, White, Muskegon, Grand, Kalamazoo, and Saint Joseph on the east. GREEN BAY, an inlet of the lake in Wisconsin, receives the Fox and Menominee. In 1900 the Chicago River was reversed to flow from the lake into the Des Plaines at Joliet, Ill.

Among the important cities on Lake Michigan's shores

are Chicago, Gary, Green Bay, and Milwaukee. Shipping is important on the lake, which is connected to the Atlantic Ocean via the St. Lawrence Seaway. The lake's first European discoverer was the French explorer Jean Nicolet, in 1634.

Michigan, University of   Founded in 1817 in Detroit, the University of Michigan moved to Ann Arbor in 1837. Its many colleges and schools include those of liberal arts, education, music, social work, law, medicine, dentistry, and architecture. The Gerald R. Ford Presidential Library; the Medical Center, with the nation's first university hospital; and the Kelsey Museum of Ancient and Medieval Archaeology are other features. Branches of the university are at Dearborn (1959), with programs in liberal arts, engineering, and education; and at Flint (1956), which offers the bachelor's degree.

Michoacán   [mee-choh-ah-kahn'] Michoacán is a state of mountainous terrain in west central Mexico, along the Pacific Ocean. The capital is Morelia, and the state's population is 3,424,235 (1989 est.). Elevations range from sea level to more than 3,050 m (10,000 ft) over an area of 59,863 km^2 (23,114 mi^2). Michoacán means "place that has fish," which probably refers to the abundant fish supply in the Pátzcuaro Lake. Agriculture, mining of minerals, and livestock raising account for the state's balanced economy. The area is home to the Tarascan Indians, who, because they were enemies of the Aztecs, accepted Spanish rule after little fighting during the 1520s.

Mickey Mouse   see Disney, Walt

Mickiewicz, Adam   [mi'-kuh-vich] Generally regarded as Poland's greatest poet, Adam Mickiewicz, b. Dec. 24, 1798, d. Nov. 26, 1855, was the leading figure of Polish romanticism and made the Polish national cause the central subject of his life's work. His first volume of poetry (1822) contained ballads and romances; the second (1823), the narrative poem *Grazyna* and parts two and four of *Forefathers' Eve*, a new type of drama based on the Belorussian folk rite of ancestor worship.

In 1823, Mickiewicz was arrested on charges of belonging to an anti-Russian conspiracy and was exiled to Russia, where he was able to publish two of his most important poetic works: *Crimean Sonnets* and the long narrative poem *Konrad Wallenrod* (trans., 1925). On leaving Russia he settled in Rome, where he learned of the outbreak of the November Insurrection of 1830, but by the time he reached the Prussian-Polish border the revolt had been crushed. Convinced his role was that of a spiritual leader, Mickiewicz joined the Poles streaming out of Poland seeking refuge in western Europe; he settled in Paris.

During his most creative period (1832–34), Mickiewicz published the great romantic drama *Forefathers' Eve, Part Three* (trans., 1926), *The Books of the Polish*

Nation and Pilgrimage, and the lyrical epic poem *Pan Tadeusz* (trans., 1917).

Micmac   [mik'-mak] The Micmac Indians of northeast North America are thought to have been the first native American society to encounter Europeans—the Norse Vikings who arrived about AD 1000. After John Cabot's visit in 1497, European fishermen and explorers regularly visited Micmac territory, which stretched from New Brunswick and Nova Scotia to Newfoundland.

The Micmac spoke an Algonquian language most closely related to Cree, but their closest political and social relations were with the Abnaki. As expert canoeists and sea navigators, they based their economy on the resources of the sea and its inlets, supplemented by hunting and collecting of plant foods. The Micmac became the first Indians to serve as middlemen in the European fur trade with interior tribes of North America. Missionized by the French in the early 1600s, they remained steadfastly loyal to France for a full generation after the British conquest of 1760. Contemporary Micmac communities are located in much the same territory they occupied five centuries ago. In 1987 their population was about 16,300.

microbiology   Microbiology is the study of organisms that cannot be seen by the naked eye. These organisms include bacteria, viruses, certain algae, fungi, and protozoans. The existence of microorganisms was first demonstrated in the 1660s, when Robert Hooke of England built compound microscopes and Antoni van Leeuwenhoek of Holland constructed powerful lenses, which these men used to study and illustrate various microbes. Further development of the light microscope in succeeding centuries enabled scientists to examine all but the smallest microorganisms, the viruses.

The French scientist Louis Pasteur often is considered the founder of modern microbiology. The German bacteriologist Robert Koch developed techniques that are now considered standard methods in studying microorganisms.

The field of microbiology was rounded out in the 1930s with the development of the electron microscope, which made possible the observation of viruses. The first virus to be isolated and characterized in detail was the tobacco mosaic virus (TMV). Later studies revealed that viruses basically are nucleoprotein chains of either DNA or RNA. From the mid-20th century on, almost all genetic research on the biochemical level has used viruses as the experimental organism of choice (see genetics). Besides its use in genetic research, modern microbiology has contributed significantly to the study of disease and to research in agriculture and environmental health.

See also: Algae; Bacteria; Fungi; Protozoa; Virus.

microcephaly   [my-kroh-sef'-uh-lee] Microcephaly is an abnormal smallness of the skull, the head circumference measuring at least 3 standard deviations below the mean head circumference for the individual's age. Microcephaly is thought to reflect either poor brain growth or premature fusing of the cranium and is generally associated with varying degrees of mental retardation. Although probably resulting from a variety of causes, including genetic and environmental factors—among the latter, excessive exposure of the fetus to X rays—in most cases the cause of the microcephaly is undetermined. It may occur in 1 in 1,000 births, alone or in association with other birth defects, or convulsions, or both.

microclimate Microclimate consists of the detailed thermodynamic structure of the air space between a surface, or interface, and a fluctuating, elevated boundary. It is the space where the heat and wind effects of a particular surface begin to blend with the general, local climatic conditions. The microclimate provides the aerial environment in which plants and animals live.

Different microclimates are created by different underlying surfaces or objects. Theoretically, microclimates can be as numerous as the number of different surfaces. The physical landscape thus is a complex mosaic of many changing microclimates—such as those of urban street canyons, vegetation canopies, deserts, and greenhouses, those over lakes and oceans, and those surrounding the skin of animals and humans. A local suburban area may include many microclimates—that over a small pond, that over housing, that surrounding animals and humans, and that under the vegetation canopy in a small wooded area.

Strictly speaking, microclimates not only occupy and show their influence in the air space above a surface but also reside in, control, and are controlled by the conditions at the surface of a body. The skin-clothing interface of a person, the epidermis of a leaf, the wall of a building, or even the solid itself (for example, soil layers, skin layers, wall layers) influence microclimate. This view of microclimates, which is gaining in acceptance, stresses cause-and-effect and process-and-response. Thus microclimates can be seen as spanning the soil-plant-atmosphere continuum and involving the energy, mass, and momentum exchanges so important to life on Earth.

microcomputer see COMPUTER, PERSONAL

microeconomics see SUPPLY AND DEMAND

microelectronics The branch of electronics that emphasizes the miniaturization of both individual electronic components and complete electronic circuits is called microelectronics. The most notable achievement of microelectronics is the INTEGRATED CIRCUIT. Some components, such as certain resistors and capacitors, cannot be reduced to the size that is required for an integrated circuit and must be incorporated into a PRINTED CIRCUIT.

microfilm It is possible to photograph documents in a reduced size; such a reproduction is called a microcopy

or microform, and the process is called microphotography. Microcopies can be arranged in various ways; common arrangements include microfilm and microfiche.

Microfilm. In microfilm each page of the material is microphotographed in order on a roll of film. This process can be done quickly and automatically with special cameras. To see a given page the microfilm is placed in a special viewer and turned to the desired frame of film by rotating a reel on which the film has been wound. The viewer produces an enlarged image of about full size. A related machine called a printer can also photograph the enlarged image.

Microfilming began in banks in the 1920s. Before then, bank clerks recorded by hand the information from each check they had processed; banks now keep microfilm records of all checks. After the process had been perfected, many companies stored their records on microfilm. Libraries have found microfilming to be particularly useful for duplicating the pages of dissertations and reference materials that are used relatively infrequently. Back copies of newspapers, journals, magazines, and catalogs are often recorded on both microfilm and microfiche.

Microfiche. One drawback of the microfilm format is that the reel must be gone through frame by frame until the desired item is reached. With microfiche, each microphotograph is taken at an even greater reduction, and the frames are arranged in a rectangular pattern, which makes them more readily accessible. The photographs can be made frame by frame directly on a film of microfiche by a special microfiche camera, or strips of microfilm can be mounted in rows to form microfiche. Standard microfiche format is a 10×15-mm (4×6-in) card onto which pages are reproduced in a 20 to 1 ratio.

micromechanism Micromechanisms, sometimes called micromachines, are machines that are only 10 to 100 microns (0.0004 to 0.004 in) wide. Micromechanisms are fabricated of silicon or silicon compounds in much the same way that some INTEGRATED CIRCUITS are. A silicon layer is built up upon a substratum, and selected parts of the layer are etched away by a photolithographic process. The process is repeated until a finished component is realized. Microcomponents such as gears have also been made from nickel.

Extremely sensitive diaphragms have been developed for pressure sensors and chemical sensors (see THIN-FILM TECHNOLOGY).

Once perfected, micromechanisms could be cheaply manufactured in large batches and fabricated, perhaps, on the same microchips as the electronic components that would control them. Many commercial applications have been predicted. In medicine, for example, tiny devices might be built that could be injected into the bloodstream and could detect and destroy blood clots, viruses, or even cancer cells.

micrometer A micrometer is an instrument used to measure precisely the dimensions of solid objects. It has a C-shaped frame and a spindle that opens and closes the jaw by means of the rotation of a screw. An object is inserted in the jaw and measured by turning the handle to move the spindle until the object is held tight. The distance the spindle moves with one turn of the screw is known. Fractional measurements are given on the sleeve of the micrometer.

Micronesia [my-kroh-nee'-zhuh]   Micronesia, one of the three major divisions of Oceania, includes GUAM, KIRIBATI, NAURU, the MARSHALL and Northern MARIANA islands, PALAU, and the Federated States of Micronesia. The more than 2,000 islands are primarily coralloid in origin; some inhabited atolls are as small as 2.5 km^2 (1 mi^2).

The people, known as Micronesians, are of Polynesian and Australoid stocks. They numbered an estimated 262,000 in the early 1980s; about 33 percent live on Guam. Traditionally a farming and fishing people, they live in scattered hamlets, with extended families or lineages as residential units. Skilled navigators, the Micronesians made long sea voyages in fleets of canoes. World War II, with Japanese and then U.S. military occupation, brought devastation to these islanders. In the aftermath of the war many traditional aspects of Micronesian culture disappeared.

Micronesia, Federated States of   The Federated States of Micronesia (FSM), a Pacific island grouping in the eastern CAROLINE ISLANDS, comprises YAP, Truk, Ponape (Pohnpei), and Kusaie (Kosrae). Formally part of the U.S.-administered United Nations Trust Territory of the Pacific Islands (see PACIFIC ISLANDS, TRUST TERRITORY OF THE) from 1947 to 1990, the FSM became internally self-governing in 1979. On June 21, 1983, island voters approved a compact under which the FSM would become a sovereign state in "free association" with the United States; the United States would retain responsibility for its security and defense and provide it with financial aid. The United States declared the compact effective Nov. 3, 1986.

microphone   A microphone is a device that transforms acoustical energy (sound) into electrical signals. The signals can then be transmitted, amplified, and reconverted back into sound. Microphones are used in RADIO AND TELEVISION BROADCASTING, SOUND RECORDING AND REPRODUCTION, TELEPHONES, and public-address systems.

Operation. All microphones contain a thin membrane, or diaphragm, that forms a part of an electroacoustic transducer. The membrane vibrates in response to the impinging sound. The transducer generates an electrical signal that is analogous to the vibrations and hence to the acoustic signal in frequency and amplitude (see SOUND AND ACOUSTICS). The structure encasing the microphone not only protects the mechanism but also affects the directivity of the device—the variation of sound pickup with direction.

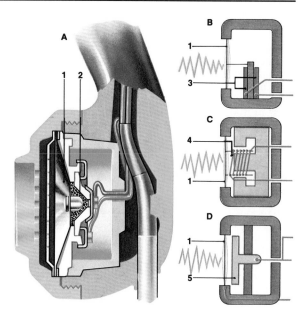

A microphone consists of a diaphragm (1), which vibrates in response to sound waves, and an attached transducer, which converts the vibrations into a corresponding variable current. The varying current may be obtained by a change in: (A) electrical resistance of carbon granules (2); (B) voltage induced by deformation of a piezoelectric crystal (3); (C) voltage induced in a coil (4) moving in a magnetic field; and (D) capacitance between diaphragm and fixed plate (5).

Types. Microphones may be classed by operating principle, the main types being the carbon, piezoelectric, dynamic, and capacitor microphones. The most widely used type, the carbon microphone, like the telephone transmitter, consists of an insulated cup containing carbon granules adjacent to the diaphragm.

In the PIEZOELECTRIC, or crystal, microphone the diaphragm is linked to a transducer crystal. The deformation of the crystal generates a small electrical signal. In the dynamic microphone the diaphragm is attached to a coil of wire that moves within the magnetic field of a permanent magnet. As it moves, the coil generates the signal voltage by means of ELECTROMAGNETIC INDUCTION.

In the capacitor microphone, the diaphragm is stretched close and parallel to a fixed metal electrode. Sound waves generating vibrations in the diaphragm cause a small alternating voltage (the signal) to be developed across the charged capacitor.

microprocessor   see COMPUTER; COMPUTER, PERSONAL

microscope   The microscope is an instrument that focuses light or other radiation through one or more lenses to form a magnified image of a specimen. The microscope has revolutionized the study of biology and medicine, revealing the tremendous quantity of activity that could never have been determined otherwise. The instrument has applications in all other scientific and technical areas as well. The ELECTRON MICROSCOPE is analogous in principle to the light microscope.

Historical Development. Magnification by simple lenses has been known from ancient times, but the development of the modern microscope dates from the construction of compound-lens systems, which occurred sometime in the period between 1590 and 1610. The credit should probably go to the Dutch lensmakers Hans and Zacharias Janssen (father and son), who in about 1600 constructed a simple instrument made of a pair of lenses mounted in a sliding tube. A compound-lens system using a convex lens in the eyepiece was described by Johannes Kepler in 1611, probably deriving from the Janssens' work.

Initial improvements in the microscope included the addition of a condenser lens to concentrate light on specimens, a specimen stage, and the control of tube movement. By the 1680s microscopists had discovered cells, capillaries, blood corpuscles, protozoans, and bacteria, one of the most important explorers in this field being the English scientist Robert HOOKE. The man generally considered the founder of microbiology, however, the Dutch biologist Antoni van LEEUWENHOEK, did his remarkable work with the use of a large number of single lenses that he ground himself.

Only a gradual improvement in microscope design took place during the next 150 years. In the early 1800s interest in anatomical fine structure inspired the development of effective specimen preparation techniques and, simultaneously, designers learned how to overcome the lens aberrations that had previously limited image quality. By 1900 the compound microscope had essentially evolved to its present form.

Basic Principles. The magnifying power of a microscope is determined by multiplying the magnification of the ocular (eyepiece) and the objective lens. For example, a low-power objective might have a magnification of 4x

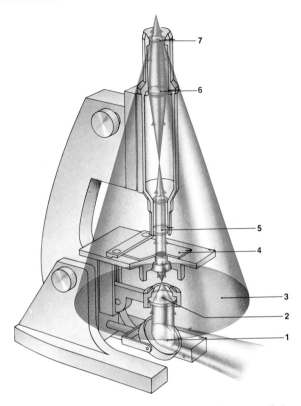

A compound optical microscope is an instrument that produces a magnified image of a small object. A typical microscope consists of a mirror (1) that reflects light from an external source through a condenser lens system (2) that concentrates and uniformly illuminates an object on a stage (4). An objective lens system (5) produces a real image (6) of the object that is then magnified by an eyepiece lens system (7). The final greatly enlarged image seen by the eye appears to lie in a plane (3). The magnification obtained is equal to the product of the magnifications produced by the objective and eyepiece lenses.

An early-18th-century microscope (left) and a modern binocular microscope differ greatly. In addition to internal lighting and camera systems, present microscopes have revolving turrets for selecting magnifying objectives.

and a high-power oil-immersion objective 100x. If each is used with an ocular of 10x magnifying power, magnifications of 40x and 1,000x are obtained. The smallest object that can be seen in an optical microscope is limited by the wave character of light to a size the order of one light wavelength. Under optimal conditions, using an oil-immersion lens, in which a drop of oil is placed on the slide and the lens is dipped into the drop, objects as small as 200 nanometers (nm) can be resolved. This limit is reached with a magnification of about 1,000x. Additional magnification is valuable only insofar as it contributes to ease of viewing.

Specimens for microscopy are mounted on rectangular glass slides and covered by a thin glass coverslip. Fine particulate materials such as powders and blood smears can be examined without further mechanical preparation, but most specimens are too thick to be seen in this way and are instead prepared as sections. A biological specimen is first preserved and hardened by infiltration of a chemical fixative such as formaldehyde. The fixed material is then dehydrated by a series of solvents, embedded in a wax or other medium for cutting, and mounted in a microtome. This is an instrument in which embedded tissue can be held at a chosen orientation for cutting to a thin, reproducible thickness by an extremely sharp knife. The sections, which are no thicker than 100 micrometers, may be stained with dyes to reveal various features.

Advanced Microscopes. Modifications of the basic microscope are numerous. Dissecting microscopes use a single-imaging system for wide-area, low-magnification imaging of relatively large objects. Zoom optics produce a continuous range of magnifications by varying lens element positions. Binocular eyepieces permit both eyes to be used for viewing.

At the forefront of advanced technology in microscopes that use visible light is the near-field optical microscope. Conventional light microscopes are not able to view specimen details that are smaller than the wavelength of visible light. This resolution can be extended by about ten times, however, by illuminating only a small part of the specimen and using a beam less than one wavelength wide.

Microscopes at Other Wavelengths. Microscopes have been developed that can observe objects in other regions of the electromagnetic spectrum, ranging from infrared light to X rays. Some of these microscopes are reflectors that make use of a mirror instead of a lens system.

Ultraviolet microscopy is used for the study of tissue elements such as nucleic acids that are invisible under ordinary light but that absorb light of wavelengths 250 to 400 nm. The image can be seen on a fluorescent screen and recorded on a photographic plate. In fluorescence microscopy, illumination is by ultraviolet or short-wavelength visible light. Certain specimens can be stained with dyes that absorb this light and reradiate at visible wavelengths so that the image of organisms such as tuberculosis bacilli stands out clearly.

X-ray wavelengths (0.01–100 nm) are comparable to those associated with electron beams. Using the "soft" X rays provided by SYNCHROTRON RADIATION, microscopes to exploit this resolving power have been developed. Scientists use computers to formulate three-dimensional images in both X-ray and light microscopy.

microseism

microseism [my'-kroh-syzm] Microseisms are low-amplitude seismic waves that continually travel across the Earth's surface. Although fundamentally the same as the more intense waves radiated by EARTHQUAKES, microseisms are caused, not by earthquakes, but by the interaction of wind and ocean waves with the Earth's crust, by erupting volcanoes, and by human sources such as motor vehicles and industry. Their amplitudes are greatest after periods of stormy weather, especially at locations near the seashore. Because microseisms, like other wave phenomena, propagate, they can be detected far from their sources, and are thus recorded as background noise on the seismograms of distant earthquakes.

microsurgery see SURGERY

microwave oven

microwave oven A microwave oven uses radiation in the short-wave region of the radio spectrum to cook (or defrost) food rapidly. The radiation, generated by a MAGNETRON (a kind of electron tube), is commonly scattered by a small fan to the oven's metal walls for uniform heating. It can pass through paper and glass and most kinds of china but causes molecules—primarily liquid—in the food to vibrate, producing heat. Simple foods cook better, because liquid portions of more complex dishes are cooked faster than drier portions; also, basic microwave ovens cannot brown foods.

The U.S. Food and Drug Administration limits permissible radiation leakage from a microwave oven to five milliwatts per square centimeter of a surface 5 cm (2 in) away. No ill effects have been observed from use of these ovens, but the effects of repeated exposure to low-level microwave radiation are a subject of controversy and current research.

microwaves

microwaves Microwaves consist of ELECTROMAGNETIC RADIATION in a particular range of wavelengths and frequencies. The wavelengths are in the centimeter range, and the frequencies are about 3 to 300 GHz (1 GHz = 10^9 Hz). Microwaves have a wavelength that is shorter than the radiation used in commercial radio broadcasting but longer than the wavelength of infrared radiation, but these boundaries between various ranges of frequencies are arbitrary.

Applications. Microwaves have a number of applications, such as RADAR, microwave ovens, and telecommunications. In the field of TELECOMMUNICATIONS, microwaves are used to carry information for telephone and television systems. One advantage of microwaves over ordinary radio waves is that microwaves, which have a higher frequency, can carry more information because information capacity is proportional to frequency. A drawback of microwaves is that they pass directly through the upper atmosphere without being reflected back to the Earth, so a signal from a transmitter cannot normally be picked up by a receiver beyond the horizon. Transmission of microwaves beyond line-of-sight distances requires the construction of a network of microwave relay stations placed about 40 km (25 mi) apart on top of tall towers situated on hilltops, or the use of communications satellites as relay stations to give an unobstructed path between the stations.

Generation. Microwaves are usually generated in special types of ELECTRON TUBES. Like the triode—the ordinary three-electrode tube—microwave tubes contain a cathode, anode, and grid inside an evacuated envelope. Ordinary electron tubes can operate at frequencies up to about 30 MHz (1 MHz=10^6 Hz). In the UHF (ultrahigh frequency) range (300–3,000 MHz) and in the microwave range, tubes must be designed to operate in an entirely different manner, because the frequency is comparable to the electron transit time—the time needed for electrons to travel between electrodes. Three important microwave tubes are the MAGNETRON, TRAVELING-WAVE TUBE, and klystron.

Transmission and Reception. Microwaves, like other

electromagnetic radiation, will travel, or propagate, through space. In some applications, however, the microwaves must be directed or guided. A structure for guiding microwaves is called an antenna. It performs the same function as the more common types of ANTENNAS but is different in construction. It may contain components such as WAVEGUIDES, horns, lenses, and reflectors. A receiving antenna similar to a transmitting antenna is used to receive microwave radiation, which is then directed to appropriate instruments for further processing.

Dangers. Microwave radiation is generated and used for a number of purposes. Most people are exposed to low-level microwave radiation, and those in certain locations and occupations may be exposed to considerably higher levels.

For microwaves, as with many other new technologies and materials, it is difficult to determine biological effects, for example, the long-term effect of low-level microwave radiation on people. The U.S. Environmental Protection Agency recommends an exposure limit of 10 milliwatts per square centimeter (10 mW/cm^2) for microwave sources in general. (Stricter limits have been set for microwave ovens, in particular.) Some critics hold that this standard is insufficient. Soviet research, for example, claims to have found evidence of damage caused by much lower exposures.

---

mid-oceanic ridge Winding sinuously through all of the oceans of the world, the mid-oceanic ridge is the greatest mountain range on Earth. It is a continuous, 60,000-km-long (36,000-mi) feature that commences in the ARCTIC OCEAN and extends through the ATLANTIC, the INDIAN, and the South PACIFIC oceans.

Description

Although the mid-oceanic ridge is a single connected system, two types of elevation can be distinguished: high relief (for example, the Mid-Atlantic Ridge) and low relief (for example, the East Pacific Rise). The Mid-Atlantic Ridge almost precisely follows the median axis of the Atlantic Ocean and extends throughout its length. It is abruptly offset by numerous TRANSFORM FAULTS and fracture zones, which, combined with numerous volcanoes, create a rugged topography. The central axis of the ridge is marked by a steep-walled RIFT VALLEY, usually about 40 km (25 mi) wide and 2 km (1 mi) deep, that is marked by high heat flow and earthquake activity.

The East Pacific Rise, lying along the eastern margin of the Pacific Basin, is a vast low bulge on the ocean floor. This rise stands about 3 km (2 mi) above the adjacent ocean floor and averages about 3,000 km (1,800 mi) across. The rise intersects North America in the Gulf of California, and a segment reappears off Oregon, with the SAN ANDREAS FAULT bridging the gap.

The mid-oceanic ridge is almost everywhere deeply submerged. Exceptions include Iceland, a so-called hot spot where enormous volumes of magma have poured out from the Earth's mantle, and the Saint Paul Rocks in the central South Atlantic Ocean, an upthrust outcrop of ul-

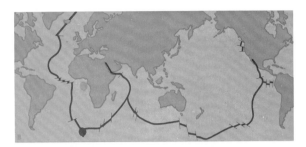

The purple line on this simple map indicates the huge range of underwater mountains that constitute the mid-oceanic ridge. The lines that break the course of the range at irregular intervals are fracture zones.

trabasic subcrustal rocks from a fracture zone. Many central oceanic islands, such as the Azores and Saint Helena, are volcanoes superimposed on the mid-oceanic ridge.

Formation

The mid-oceanic ridge can be explained in terms of seafloor spreading. The central rift is where dikes of basalt are emplaced while opposing plate edges (see PLATE TECTONICS) recede from each other at a rate of 1 to 10 cm (0.4 to 4 in) per year. The dikes gradually cool, but their center remains hotter and weaker than the chilled edges. The dikes are thus continuously split, with one-half being welded to each of the opposing plates.

The elevation of the mid-oceanic ridge is a thermal effect. A newly created and hence hot crust, being less dense than previously formed, cooler material, will stand high because of its buoyancy, in accordance with the principle of ISOSTASY.

Not all of the mid-oceanic ridge is a spreading ridge. For example, the leg between the South Atlantic Ocean and the central Indian Ocean is predominantly a transform fault—a crustal plate boundary dominated by shearing. Excluding such segments would give the ridge an overall length of 45,000 km (27,000 mi). Spreading ridges and transform faults, together with OCEANIC TRENCHES, constitute the three types of boundaries separating the crustal plates that cover the surface of the Earth.

The fact that the ridge occupies a truly mid-oceanic position in the Atlantic Ocean but not in the Pacific reflects the different circumstances under which the two ocean basins developed. The Atlantic Ocean was created by the splitting apart 190 million years ago of the universal continent of Pangea (see CONTINENTAL DRIFT). Because the generation of oceanic crust by seafloor spreading is a symmetrical process, the growing Atlantic ridge will remain forever in mid-ocean. In contrast, the Pacific ridge did not initially rupture a continent but arose from beneath the ancient world-encircling ocean called Panthalassa, of which the Pacific is now a collapsing remnant. The Pacific ridge was thus never constrained to occupy a median position with respect to surrounding landmasses.

See also: EARTH, GEOLOGICAL HISTORY OF; OCEAN AND SEA.

Midas [my'-duhs] In Greek mythology Midas was a Phrygian king whose touch turned everything into gold. Two stories are told of him. In the first, he insisted that MARSYAS (or PAN, in some versions) was a better musician than APOLLO, and Apollo gave Midas the ears of an ass. He concealed the ears under a turban, permitting no one but his barber to see them. The barber, sworn to silence, whispered the secret into a hole in the ground and then filled in the hole; but reeds grew from the hole and whispered Midas's secret in the wind.

In the second story, DIONYSUS gave Midas the gift of golden touch as a reward for a favor. After a brief period, during which his food, drink, and daughter were all turned into gold, he regretted his wish and asked to be released from it. He was allowed to wash his hands in the Pactolus River, and, ever after, the sands of that river were gold.

midden Midden, in archaeology, is a general term for the heaps of domestic refuse discarded from habitation sites at all periods in the past. Middens normally consist primarily of food remains, usually either animal bones or shells. From these the archaeologist can make inferences about the diet of the societies that discarded them and about species of animals that were exploited, animal diseases of the time, times and methods of slaughter, and sometimes the fauna that grew in the vicinity of the settlement. Pollen grains preserved in middens can provide information about the plants that were cultivated and about the environment that prevailed when the settlement was occupied. Human coprolites can provide data on both diet and disease. Often middens also contain a wide variety of artifacts, especially those that have been discarded as broken or useless.

middle age Middle age, the period of life between young adulthood and old age, has come to be recognized as a distinct period of human life only during the last few decades. This recognition is due to a trend toward the earlier departure of children from the parental home and to increases in the human life span. The actual onset of middle age is often heralded by one or more important events. In addition to the departure of children, these occurrences include MENOPAUSE, the closing of options for career change, career peaking, the prospect of retirement, gradual but noticeable decline in body function, and increasing responsibility for older family members. Because such events do not follow a definite timetable, the age boundaries for middle age must be set rather arbitrarily. The usual age range is 40 to 65, although scholars may vary the beginning from age 35 to 45. Studies of class differences report that the working and lower classes perceive middle age as starting earlier and finishing earlier, whereas the middle and upper classes see the period as starting later and lasting longer.

Entry into middle age is disruptive for some persons. Researchers speak of a mid-life crisis or transition that occurs in the later thirties or early forties. The goals and values held during the earlier years may need to be reassessed. Men and women often reach their peak in power and prestige at this time. Heightened authority is particularly evident among those who have followed a relatively "straight-line" career development, with few detours. For women who have remained in the home, control over the children may be decreasing, but the "empty-nest" phase of family life can give a woman the opportunity to restore control over her own life.

For both men and women life in the middle years is a time of increasing personal freedom. Carl JUNG portrayed the challenge as developing one's own potentials and interests, now that the responsibilities and obligations to build and support a family have begun to moderate. Often for the first time in adult life people can afford to think about what they themselves would like to do and be.

Jung speaks of a process of individuation that occurs in mid-life, and research provides supporting evidence: the increasing propensity for mid-career shifts in occupational interests is an example, as is the voluntary reentry of women into educational systems and the job market. Another example is the tendency of men to feel freer to express the less conventional masculine side of themselves, and for women to become more assertive and dominant. Those who ignore the opportunities for individuation—who grimly hang on to their children, for example—may find themselves unhappy and increasingly frustrated.

Relations with the younger generations are particularly critical for successful personal development. From the perspective of Erik ERIKSON, the major crisis of the middle years involves "generativity"—the willingness to guide and counsel—versus "rejectivity"—the exclusion of some persons from one's concern. A danger in middle age is that people may become overly concerned with themselves to the exclusion of others. Overuse of rejectivity leads directly to ego stagnation and indirectly to problems during later middle age or early old age in accepting one's life as having been productive and meaningful.

Generativity may help with another crisis: that prompted by an increasing awareness of personal mortality. During the middle years friends and acquaintances begin to die from so-called natural causes instead of accidents. On a more personal level are signs of bodily change such as declining physical energy, lessened sexual vigor, a receding hairline, or a developing paunch. Although the physiological changes are relatively minor and are more than compensated for by the greater experience and expertise of the middle-aged person, they are disturbing. Exercise, diets, face-lifts, hair transplants, and sexual escapades can help to foster the illusion of youth—but not the reality. With parents showing signs of dependency, and ultimately dying, most middle-aged persons begin to confront the fact that they are next in line to grow old and die.

An individual's experience of middle age appears to depend on how the events associated with that period are interpreted. The problem—and the challenge—is to be open to the new experiences potentially available, and not to attempt to carry on with outdated life structures.

See also: OLD AGE; YOUNG PEOPLE.

Middle Ages   Renaissance humanists gave the name Middle Ages to the period between the end of the Roman Empire and their own time—the 15th century—which they believed was a rebirth of the civilization of Greece and Rome.

Basic Periods

Within the thousand years of the Middle Ages, historians have recognized subperiods; the Early Middle Ages, to 900 or 1000; the High Middle Ages, from then to about 1300; and the Later Middle Ages, the 14th and 15th centuries. The Middle Ages, especially the early period, were also known as the DARK AGES, but historians today generally reject that term.

The Early Middle Ages. The Early Middle Ages was the period of the decline and fall of the Roman Empire, the invasions of the barbarians, and the triumph of Christianity. The Western Empire was broken up into barbarian kingdoms, until on Christmas Day, 800, the Frankish king, CHARLEMAGNE, was crowned emperor of the West by

the pope. By 900, however, the empire had broken up into a myriad of duchies, counties, margravates, bishoprics, abbacies, and other lordships whose rulers exercised more power than kings and emperors. At that same time the frontiers of Western Europe were being devastated from the north by Vikings, from the south by Muslims, and from the east by Magyars.

The High Middle Ages. In the 10th century Europe began to revive. Organized according to the rules of FEUDALISM, the Western Europeans were able to drive off the invaders and gradually to take the offensive. In 1099, the Crusaders captured the Holy Land from the Muslims, and in 1204 they seized the Eastern Empire from the Byzantines. Both were lost again by 1291, but more lasting was the Christian reconquest of Spain from the Moors. The hegemony of the Mediterranean Sea and its islands also was won by Western Christians, and missionaries brought the kingdoms of Scandinavia as well as of Poland, Bohemia, and Hungary into the orbit of Western civilization. Meantime, the economy and the society recovered and achieved heights unknown even under the Roman Empire. The church was reformed and revitalized. Splendid Romanesque art developed into glorious Gothic, and many great works of literature were written. Rediscovery of the works of Greek and Hellenistic philosophers, espe-

The map indicates the major political divisions of Europe about 1100. While relations deteriorated between the pope and the Holy Roman emperor and religious friction between western (Roman Catholic) and eastern (Orthodox) Christendom intensified, Islamic power increased in the east at the expense of the Byzantine Empire.

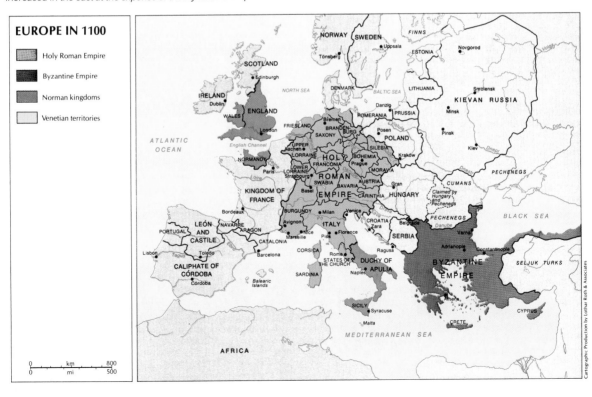

EUROPE IN 1100

- Holy Roman Empire
- Byzantine Empire
- Norman kingdoms
- Venetian territories

In this 15th-century miniature, Charles VII of France presides over the Parlement of Paris, the French high court, during the treason trial of Jean II, duc d'Alençon. During the reign of Charles VII the first provincial parlements were created.

cially Aristotle, provided the spark for SCHOLASTICISM, the great philosophic system of the Middle Ages.

The Later Middle Ages. In the 14th and 15th centuries, Europe suffered great famines, the catastrophic Black Death (see BUBONIC PLAGUE), and the HUNDRED YEARS' War. Those who survived, however, often had a better life, especially the peasants of Western Europe, who won both greater freedom and greater prosperity. The classic style dominated Italian art, while the north of Europe developed Flamboyant Gothic. Among the great writers of the period were Giovanni BOCCACCIO and DANTE ALIGHIERI; Geoffrey CHAUCER and Thomas MALORY; and Guillaume de Mauchaut and François VILLON.

Political Structure

The Imperial Idea. Despite the failure of the Carolingian empire the imperial idea remained strong in medieval Europe. In 961, OTTO I, king of Germany, made himself king of Italy and the following year obtained papal coronation as emperor. In the next century the kingdom of Burgundy was bequeathed to CONRAD II, and the emperors thereafter held the three realms. To the east the Poles, Bohemians, and Hungarians would sometimes admit that their kings were vassals of the emperor; but the kingdoms of France, Spain, England, and Scandinavia were never

more than nominal members of this HOLY ROMAN EMPIRE. The emperor was the most dignified of all lay rulers in medieval Europe but not always the most powerful.

Both empire and kingdoms were ruled by elected monarchs in the 10th century; only gradually were hereditary monarchies established and then not everywhere and always subject to dynastic failure.

Feudal Powers. The authority of the emperor and the kings was thought to derive from God. Power, however, had largely escaped from their hands into those of lesser lords. Effective government in medieval Europe depended heavily on the cooperation of these lords, and that cooperation was achieved by making their power over their territories and subjects hereditary as long as they performed the political and military services due from their fiefs. The vassals who held fiefs of an emperor or king could claim that that ruler was bound by the feudal contract not to disturb their rights in their fiefs. Thus the English barons obtained from King JOHN the MAGNA CARTA of 1215, guaranteeing to them the preservation of their rights and liberties. Strong rulers like King WILLIAM I (the Conqueror) of England and Holy Roman Emperor FREDERICK I (Barbarossa) even encouraged feudalism to obtain power for their states.

The Papacy. More dangerous to the authority and the power of medieval monarchs were the claims of churchmen, particularly the increasing secular power of the PAPACY. If popes and prelates crowned emperors and kings, why should not the churchmen claim superiority as

A miniature from the Limbourg brothers' Très Riches Heures du Duc de Berry *(1413–16) portrays peasants laboring outside the walled palace and village. (Musée Condé, Chantilly, France.)*

vicegerents for God? Pope NICHOLAS I did so as early as the 9th century, but it was Pope GREGORY VII in the 11th century who precipitated a great quarrel with Emperor HENRY IV over the relative authority and dignity of popes and emperors (see INVESTITURE CONTROVERSY). In the 12th and 13th centuries the popes won the leadership of Europe by preaching the CRUSADES, first against the Muslims, then against such heretical groups as the ALBIGENSES, and finally against Emperor FREDERICK II. Papal power reached its zenith under the reign (1198–1216) of INNOCENT III. It reached its lowest point during the so-called Babylonian Captivity (1309–78), when the popes were removed to Avignon and were under the domination of the French kings.

As successor to Saint Peter the pope claimed jurisdiction over all Christians, but his claim was recognized only in the Western, or Latin, church and then only in matters of CANON LAW. The hierarchy of the church had been organized with metropolitan archbishops, diocesan bishops, archdeacons, rural deans, and parish clergy. The pope could send orders down through this chain of command, and cases in ecclesiastical law could be appealed up through it to Rome. In addition to the secular clergy in the hierarchy, members of religious orders—monks, nuns, canons, friars, teaching or nursing brothers and sisters—constituted the regular clergy, who were, in fact, largely exempt from local jurisdiction and subject only to papal discipline.

The Towns. In addition to popes and emperors and kings and barons, yet another contestant for power appeared with the rise of the towns and the townspeople. Their wealth made it possible for them to buy arms, and their town levies became important military forces everywhere. With such wealth and military might, all of them sought increased liberties and became as self-governing as possible. The wealthiest and most powerful towns—those in Flanders, south Germany, and northern Italy—became independent COMMUNES. The most aggressive then set about conquering their neighbors and establishing city-states—Venice, Milan, and Florence were the most successful.

Representative Institutions. During the 12th and 13th centuries the towns and the religious orders developed representative institutions. By 1300 princes were making use of representatives of towns and churchmen to add strength to their feudal councils.

In England the king summoned representatives of each shire and borough to Parliament and proctors of the clergy in each diocese to meet in convocation. In France the States General, in Spain the Cortes, and in Germany the Diet all had similar representatives in their membership. Their principal power lay in consent to taxation, and when in the Later Middle Ages they found it easier to give such consent in advance, the kings lost much of their reason for calling these representative assemblies into session. The way was then open for the age of absolutism.

Society and Economy

The Court. The courts of princes and siegneurs were the natural centers for the social life of the noble class.

A miniature depicts a merchant measuring a bolt of fabric. The textile industry flourished during the Middle Ages, with the city of Bruges controlling much of the wool trade.

There they thronged for the great feasts of the Christian year: Christmas, Easter, and Pentecost. There they went for military expeditions, whether war, tourney, or Crusade. There they were summoned for judgment in their own cases or those of their peers. There also they gave counsel to their lords. Because they fought exclusively on horseback, they became the cavalry, the CHIVALRY of Europe.

Manorialism. The great majority of the people lived in the country, where they were divided into two main classes: lords and villagers. The villagers, who might legally be either free or serf, cultivated the land—whether their own or their lord's. The lord often had rights to services as well as monetary rents. The tenants commonly owed him a specified number of days of labor each year. He collected inheritance taxes and commanded his villagers' use of his mill, oven, and winepress; above all, the tenants were subject to the jurisdiction of his manorial court. The system of relationships between a lord and his tenants is called MANORIALISM. Serfs, who were bound to the land, might buy manumission, or if they fled to a town and lived there for a year and a day, they were free of all manorial claims. The example of the towns encouraged some villagers to form rural communes and obtain liberties of self-government from their lords.

Agriculture. Agricultural techniques greatly improved during the Middle Ages. Crop rotation, the replacement of oxen by the more efficient horses, and the use of the iron-tipped plow all helped to increase production. The cultivation of field peas and beans provided a new source of protein for European diets, but the main crops remained the cereal grains—rye, barley, oats, and wheat—from which were made the staple bread and ale. Cheese was made with milk from cows, goats, and ewes, and eggs were eaten. Most villagers had little meat, however; that was the privilege of the lords.

Trade, Industry, and the Towns. With the end of inva-

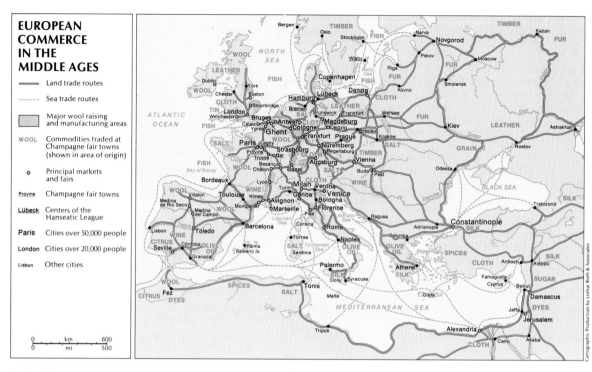

EUROPEAN COMMERCE IN THE MIDDLE AGES

— Land trade routes

----- Sea trade routes

▨ Major wool raising and manufacturing areas

WOOL Commodities traded at Champagne fair towns (shown in area of origin)

o Principal markets and fairs

Provins Champagne fair towns

L̲ü̲b̲e̲c̲k̲ Centers of the Hanseatic League

Paris Cities over 50,000 people

London Cities over 20,000 people

Lisbon Other cities

By the 14th century an extensive trade network had developed in Europe. The Italian city-states, particularly Venice and Genoa, domi- nated Mediterranean trade, whereas the cities of the Hanseatic League monopolized commerce in northern Europe.

sions in the 10th century, European merchants began to play a significant role in long-distance trade. Led by the Venetians, Italian merchants imported more and more goods from the East—spices, especially pepper, silks, and cottons. In return they needed goods the East would buy. They found them in amber, furs, and timber prod- ucts bought mainly from the Baltic and North Sea re- gions. The exchange of Mediterranean goods for northern European goods took place in the famous fairs of Cham- pagne. In addition to leather and metal industries, largely producing goods for home consumption, a woolen indus- try developed in the Low Countries and in northern Italy.

The merchant and the artisan needed freedom of movement, freedom from arbitrary demands for services or taxes, and protection from marauders. All these were found in the towns that were formed with remarkable ra- pidity during the High Middle Ages. There the merchants organized their GUILDS as voluntary associations to provide help to each other in time of need and together to de- mand from the lords the freedoms they needed. The ma- jority of the townspeople were little better off materially than the country people. They had greater legal freedom, however, and there were always plenty of migrants from the country to the town.

Church and Learning

Outside the walls of the towns lay the monasteries. Mo- NASTICISM came to Western Europe in the 4th century, and

many people had fled to the cloisters before Saint BENE- DICT of Nursia founded Monte Casino in southern Italy in 529. The rule of Saint Benedict was to spread throughout Latin Christendom.

A new monastery founded in 910 at CLUNY in French Burgundy became the mother house of a reformed order that spread throughout Europe. In its turn it was suc- ceeded by more radical reformers like the CISTERCIANS or the regular canons under a rule attributed to Saint Au- gustine (see AUGUSTINIANS). In the 13th century the friars (see DOMINICANS; FRANCISCANS) abandoned the cloister en- tirely and with the healing and teaching orders of brothers and sisters entered into the service of the world while still committed by vow to obedience, poverty, and chastity.

During the collapse of the Roman Empire the monas- teries had become the principal repositories of learning. When the barbarians were converted to Christianity, mon- asteries were founded by the missionaries to teach not only the faith but also the learning needful to Christians. That learning was considerable, including virtually all the extant classical Latin authors and the Fathers of the Church. It was increased from the 10th century onward by contact with Arab and Greek scholars. More of the works of Aristotle were discovered along with their Arabic commentators; Greek and Arabic scientific works were translated for Western use; and above all, the Arabic mathematics including Hindu notation was imported.

The new learning was brought into the classical curriculum taught in the schools: the seven liberal arts divided into the trivium of grammar, rhetoric, and logic, and the quadrivium of arithmetic, geometry, astronomy, and music. Monastic schools primarily taught young monks. Most of the education given to girls was received at home. As more and more students became concentrated in one place, there was demand for more teachers. In time a guild of teachers at Paris, a guild of students at Bologna, and a guild of doctors at Salerno called themselves universities and began to establish statutes and demand liberties from church and state alike, thus sowing the seeds of academic freedom. Soon other universities were founded at which a young man could become a master of arts and receive a license to teach, or he could go on to study theology, law, or medicine. In the Later Middle Ages students attended the universities for their intellectual and social life, whether or not they wished to become clergy or to teach or to practice a profession. This emphasis on knowledge for its own sake was a central strand of the HUMANISM that led to the RENAISSANCE.

See also: BYZANTINE ART AND ARCHITECTURE; BYZANTINE EMPIRE; FRANCE, HISTORY OF; GERMANY, HISTORY OF; GOTHIC ART AND ARCHITECTURE; GREAT BRITAIN, HISTORY OF; ITALY, HISTORY OF; MEDIEVAL DRAMA; MEDIEVAL MUSIC; PORTUGAL; ROMANESQUE ART AND ARCHITECTURE; RUSSIA/UNION OF SOVIET SOCIALIST REPUBLICS, HISTORY OF; SPAIN, HISTORY OF.

middle class   see CLASS, SOCIAL

Middle East   The Middle East is the region where Asia, Africa, and Europe meet. The area's precise boundaries are difficult to define. The term *Middle East* was first used in 1902 by the U.S. naval writer Alfred Mahan to refer to the western and northern approaches to India. Current usage began during World War II when the Allies used the term *Middle East* to refer to the region stretching from South Asia to North Africa. Gradually *Middle East* replaced older terms such as NEAR EAST or the LEVANT in popular usage.

The modern countries that make up the Middle East can be divided into four groups: Northeast Africa (Egypt and Libya); the Fertile Crescent (Syria, Lebanon, Jordan, Iraq, and Israel); the Arabian Peninsula (Saudi Arabia, Yemen, Kuwait, Bahrain, Qatar, the United Arab Emirates, and Oman); and the Northern Tier (Turkey and Iran). This area of about 9,000,000 km^2 (3,475,000 mi^2) has a population of nearly 246,000,000 persons (1990 est.). Other areas such as North Africa, Sudan, Afghanistan, Pakistan, Greece, Cyprus, and Muslim areas of Soviet Central Asia, are sometimes considered part of the Middle East.

Geographic factors help define the Middle East, but historical experience has been crucial in creating a regional identity. Early civilizations emerged in the valleys of the Nile and Tigris-Euphrates rivers and spread to the surrounding areas. By the 2d millennium BC the interaction between these areas created a regional context that transcended local differences. This unity later took political form in great empires. In the 6th century BC the area from western Egypt to northern India was united under the rule of the Persian Empire. Subsequent empires ruled large portions of the region at various times and had constant contact. Following the rise of Islam during the 7th century AD the entire Middle East was again unified by the creation of the Arab-Muslim empires of the UMAYYADS and ABBASIDS. The modern Middle East roughly coincides with the areas included in these empires. As Islamic empires expanded and contracted the sociocultural borders of the region changed. The later expansion of Islam created a larger Islamic world, of which the Middle East is just one part.

Land

Mountains, dry plateaus, and deserts dominate the landscape of the Middle East. A mountainous belt stretches

(Left) *Passengers sail along the Nile River in feluccas, vessels developed in Egypt. More than 95% of all Egyptians live along the flood plain of the Nile River.* (Below) *Salt-encrusted formations protrude from the surface of the world's saltiest body of water, the Dead Sea, along the Jordanian-Israeli border.*

across the Northern Tier. In Turkey, the Pontic (or North Anatolian) Mountains and the TAURUS surround the Anatolian Plateau of central Turkey and combine in rugged eastern Turkey. The mountain belt divides again in Iran, surrounding the dry Iranian plateau. To the north are the ELBURZ MOUNTAINS containing Mount Demavend (5,610 m/18,406 ft), the highest peak in the Middle East; to the south are the ZAGROS MOUNTAINS.

The area south of the mountainous Northern Tier consists of plains and divided plateaus. Lower mountains run north and south along the Mediterranean coast of Syria, Lebanon, and Israel. West of the Red Sea the land rises gradually to interior plateaus containing the Libyan and Western Egyptian deserts (see LIBYAN DESERT). East of these mountains, an arid lowland area extends from the Taurus to the coast of Oman.

Some of the world's major continental plates meet in the Middle East, and their interaction produced the characteristic geographic features of the region. Frequent earthquakes occur along the major plate boundaries, especially in Turkey and Iran.

Drainage. Because of limited rainfall, river systems are an important water source. There are two great permanent river systems, the NILE RIVER and the TIGRIS and EUPHRATES system. A number of smaller rivers have year-round flow, including the JORDAN RIVER and the Litani (in Lebanon), but many rivers dry up completely during dry seasons or contain water only after rare rainstorms.

Climate. The Middle East is generally characterized by aridity. Much of the region has hot, dry summers, with limited rainfall coming in the cooler winter season. Areas south of the northern mountains generally receive less than 250 mm (10 in) of rainfall annually. The mountain areas in Yemen and Oman, coastal areas of Syria, Lebanon, and Israel, and the coasts of the CASPIAN and BLACK seas receive higher rainfall. Summer temperatures are high throughout the region, with mean daily temperatures in July of more than 30° C (86° F) in the deserts and along the PERSIAN GULF and RED SEA coasts. In winter only the Anatolian Plateau and northern mountain areas have mean daily temperatures of less than 0° C (32° F).

Soils. Red desert soils cover virtually all of Libya, Egypt, and the central plain from the Taurus to the Indian Ocean. Gray desert soils cover much of northern and central Iran. The most important soils for agriculture are the alluvial soils of the Nile and Tigris-Euphrates valleys. Prairie, chestnut, and brown soils support agriculture in parts of Iraq and Syria, while terra rossa soils provide rich farming areas along the Mediterranean coasts of Turkey, Syria, Lebanon, Israel, and Libya.

Vegetation and Animal Life. Prehistoric forests have been greatly reduced by humans. Evergreens, herbs, and shrubs are found in the coastal regions. The Northern Tier has lush forests on the southern coasts of the Black and Caspian seas and steppe and desert vegetation in the plateaus. The largest vegetation zones are the desert and semiarid steppe areas.

Under pressure from humans, some animals that were once common, such as the lion, have disappeared, while others have been reduced in numbers. Still others (such as some forms of the mongoose, reptiles, and rodents) have adapted themselves to city and village environments. The Bactrian (two-humped) camel and the dromedary (one-humped camel) have been domesticated, as have sheep and goats. In the Nile Valley crocodiles and other distinctive riverain animals are found. The rest of the region contains animals of the Ethiopian region, such as baboons and ostriches.

Resources. The most important natural resources in the Middle East are its vast petroleum reserves, concentrated in the countries along the Persian Gulf. Gold, silver, copper, and iron have been mined since ancient times. Today the most important minerals are iron (Iran, Libya, Syria, and Turkey); chrome (Turkey); copper (in small deposits throughout the region); phosphate (Egypt, Jordan, Israel, and Syria); sulfur (Iran, Iraq, and Turkey); and rock salt (Yemen).

People

Middle Eastern society is a complex mosaic of peoples and cultures. Throughout history various groups moving into the region from surrounding areas have been integrated into the larger society while maintaining their own distinctive identity. In addition, small communities have maintained separate communal existences in geographically sheltered locales.

The three major groupings are SEMITES, TURKS, and Indo-Europeans (ARYANS). The major modern Semitic groups are the ARABS and the JEWS, while the Persians are the largest Indo-European group. Turkic peoples constitute the majority in modern Turkey. In Egypt ancient Nilotic elements and Nubians have maintained special identities. Other distinctive groups are KURDS (Iran, Iraq, and Turkey); the great Iranian tribes, BAKHTIARI, BALUCH, Lurs, and Qashqais; and many smaller groups.

Language and Religion. Language and religion are key elements in both Middle Eastern diversity and identity.

This petroleum-refining complex on the Persian Gulf in Saudi Arabia is the terminus of a pipeline leading to the oil fields of Dharhan. The nations of the Middle East contain most of the world's known petroleum reserves.

A farmer guides a cattle-drawn plow past two sculptured deities, remnants of ancient pharaonic Egypt, on a field near Thebes, in the central portion of the nation.

The major languages of the region are ARABIC, Persian (Farsi; see INDO-IRANIAN LANGUAGES), and Turkish (see URAL-ALTAIC LANGUAGES). Each of these is further differentiated into regional dialects. Among Semitic languages, other than Arabic, are HEBREW and ancient languages spoken in small communities throughout the region. Nubians, Armenians, Kurds, Azerbaijanis, and other groups have maintained their own languages.

The major monotheistic traditions of Middle Eastern origin—CHRISTIANITY, ISLAM, and JUDAISM—are represented by a variety of communities. Islam is now the dominant religion, and its Sunni tradition (see SUNNITES) is followed by the great majority of inhabitants throughout the Middle East. The Shia tradition of Islam (see SHIITES) is important in Iran, Iraq, Syria, and Lebanon. Other spe-cial Muslim groups include the Alawis of Syria and the DRUZES of the western Fertile Crescent. The largest Christian groups are the Copts (see COPTIC CHURCH) in Egypt, the Maronites in Lebanon, and the Greek Orthodox found in various countries. A remarkable number of other church communities have survived, including Armenians, Chaldeans, Nestorians, and Syriac or Jacobite groups (see ARMENIAN CHURCH; EASTERN RITE CHURCHES; JACOBITE CHURCH; NESTORIAN CHURCH). Judaism, the official religion of Israel, is also represented by smaller groups (such as the Karaites and Samarians). Other Middle Eastern religions include Yazidis in northern Iraq, ZOROASTRIANS in Iran, and BAHA'IS, who are found in many countries.

Demography. The nations of the Middle East are experiencing rapid population growth after a long period of relative stability or even decline. Current birthrates are not expected to decline in the near future, but death rates have fallen significantly, contributing to an annual rate of population increase of 1.6% to 4.3%. At least 45% of the total Middle Eastern population are younger than 15 years of age.

Throughout the Middle East the population is unevenly distributed, with large, virtually uninhabited desert areas, transitional zones where nomads live, and crowded agricultural areas. The contrast is most vivid in Egypt where more than 95% of the population live in the Nile Valley, which is only about 5% of the total land area. While rural villagers still constitute the majority of the population, the process of urbanization is rapid. In addition, the traditional nomadic populations are settling in villages or cities.

Economy

Agriculture. A majority of the population is engaged in agriculture although only about 14% of the surface is arable and about 6% of the land is cultivated. The two forms of principal agriculture are dry farming (dependent

These Libyans retain the nomadic, pastoral way of life that is vanishing in many parts of the Middle East.

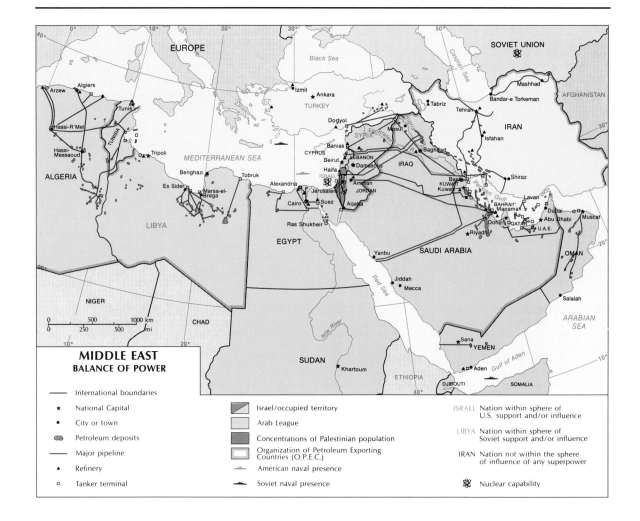

MIDDLE EAST
BALANCE OF POWER

— International boundaries
★ National Capital
• City or town
⬭ Petroleum deposits
— Major pipeline
▲ Refinery
□ Tanker terminal

▨ Israel/occupied territory
▢ Arab League
▤ Concentrations of Palestinian population
▢ Organization of Petroleum Exporting Countries (O.P.E.C.)
⌁ American naval presence
⬲ Soviet naval presence

ISRAEL Nation within sphere of U.S. support and/or influence
LIBYA Nation within sphere of Soviet support and/or influence
IRAN Nation not within the sphere of influence of any superpower
☢ Nuclear capability

on seasonal rainfall) in large areas of the Northern Tier and eastern Mediterranean coasts and irrigated farming in the river valleys and desert oases. In marginal areas nomadic groups herd sheep, goats, and camels.

Major food crops in the north are wheat, barley, and rye, with maize, millet, and rice being important in the southern areas. Dates are a major product of the oases. A wide variety of fruits are grown in the Mediterranean-climate area. The major cash crops are cotton (Egypt, Turkey, and Syria), tobacco (Turkey), and coffee (Yemen).

Traditional communal land ownership is being replaced by private or state control. Large landowners (often absentee landlords) controlled a large part of the arable land during much of the 20th century. Many governments, with varying degrees of success, have introduced land-reform programs that limit the amount of land an individual can own and that distribute land to peasants.

Mining. The leading extractive industry in the Middle East is petroleum. About 57% of the world's proven oil re-

serves are located there, and in 1986 petroleum reserves totaled almost 4 billion barrels. The most important oil fields are located in Saudi Arabia, Iran, Iraq, and the smaller states around the Persian Gulf and in Libya, with smaller known reserves scattered throughout the region.

Mining of resources other than petroleum tends to be limited. Turkey is an important producer of antimony, mercury, and magnesite and exploits significant deposits of coal and iron ore. Israel, Jordan, and Syria are major producers of phosphate.

Industry. Traditional craft and small-scale industries have declined in importance in the modern era, although some, such as carpet weaving, continue to be important. Modern industrial activities center on processing agricultural products, petroleum-related industries, and textile production. Throughout the entire Middle East production for domestic markets and import replacement is a major focus of industry. Significant industrial development has occurred in Turkey, Egypt, Israel, and Iran, and, to a lesser extent, everywhere in the region. Heavy capital goods are largely imported, but major assembly plants now exist for vehicles and machinery in Turkey, Egypt, Iran, and Israel. Iron and steel production is significant in Turkey and Egypt, and Turkey is one of the world's leading producers of cement.

Fishing and Forestry. Significant production of roundwood and sawtimber takes place only in Turkey and Iran. The Persian Gulf fishing industry was disrupted by the major oil spill that occurred during the 1991 GULF WAR. The leading fishing nations are Turkey, Egypt, and Yemen.

Transportation. The region's central location means that intercontinental transportation has long been important. Overland routes like the SILK ROAD from China and water travel in the region's seas have been significant since ancient times. The SUEZ CANAL, built between 1859 and 1869 to link the Red and Mediterranean seas, has long been one of the world's major shipping arteries. The Middle East has become important in interregional air transport because of its location.

Transportation within countries is not as well developed. Camels, donkeys, and other draft animals remain important means of transport, although they are gradually being replaced by motor vehicles. Great river boats haul freight and are becoming motorized.

Although the first railroads were built as early as 1851 (in Egypt), the rail systems are not well developed. The largest networks are in Turkey, Iran, and Egypt; the highest density is in Israel. Dirt roads are common, but road systems are being expanded and few areas remain isolated. The largest system of paved roads is in Turkey; Israel has the highest percentage of surfaced road. Internal airways are of growing importance, especially in larger countries.

Trade. Trade has long been a major part of the economic scene. Middle Eastern cities of ancient and medieval times were great commercial and trading centers. Twentieth-century trade has been dominated by the petroleum industry. Saudi Arabia, Iran, Iraq, Kuwait, the Gulf states, and Libya are leaders in the ORGANIZATION OF PETROLEUM EXPORTING COUNTRIES (OPEC), which has often played a significant role in setting world oil prices and controlling production. Before Iraq's August 1990 invasion of Kuwait, petroleum and petroleum products constituted more than 90% of the exports of Bahrain, Iraq, Iran, Kuwait, Libya, Oman, Qatar, Saudi Arabia, and the United Arab Emirates. An international boycott halted Iraqi and Kuwaiti oil exports in August 1990. Allied bombing during the Gulf war damaged many Iraqi oil facilities, while Kuwaiti oil wells were systmatically set ablaze by retreating Iraqi soldiers, permanently reducing output at some fields and causing extensive environmental damage. Agricultural products and raw materials make up most of the rest of the exports, with cotton being an important export of Egypt, Syria, Yemen, and Turkey. Only in Israel is a significant proportion of exports made up of industrial products, including polished diamonds. Manufactured goods are a major part of Middle Eastern

imports. Despite the large role of agriculture in local economies, foodstuffs are another major import.

While there is some significant intraregional trade, efforts to create regional trade communities have not been successful. Most Middle Eastern imports come from the countries of the developed world. Even excluding petroleum exports, which go predominantly to Western Europe, Japan, and the United States, customers for exports tend to be outside of the region. Cooperation and ties have developed between the United States, the European Community (EC) and Turkey, Israel, and selected Arab states. The influx into the region of vast oil revenues was changing this picture, as the oil-rich states became markets for Middle Eastern products and invested in the region. Social dislocations caused by economic modernization contributed to the rise of Islamic fundamentalism in the area, and the regional economy was disrupted by the Gulf war, particularly in nations with large numbers of expatriate workers in Iraq and the Gulf states and in Jordan, where the port of Aqaba was virtually closed by the boycott. The long-term economic and social consequences of the war, which exacerbated tensions between the region's haves and have-nots, remained unclear.

See also: separate articles on nations of the Middle East.

Middle English   *Middle English* is the name given to the ENGLISH LANGUAGE in use during the period extending from the Norman Conquest of 1066 to the introduction of printing in England in 1476. It connects the earliest form of the language, OLD ENGLISH, with the latest, Modern English. The major dialect areas distinguished for Middle English are Northern (spoken in Scotland and northern England), Midlands, and Southern. Each area, however, had many subdialects, so that on the basis of its spellings alone a particular Middle English document often can be localized to an area of a few miles' radius.

At the beginning of the Middle English period, English was still a highly inflected language with a word-stock almost wholly Germanic. By the end of the period, however, all but a handful of the inflections had been lost, and words of French origin made up a substantial part of the English vocabulary. The simplification and loss of inflections had begun in Old English times and continued unabated until the early 15th century, when final *e* ceased to be pronounced. The Norman Conquest made it inevitable that French words would come to be used in English, but the borrowing did not begin in earnest until the 13th century. Before that time the two languages developed largely in isolation: the Anglo-Norman aristocracy spoke French, their subjects English. After 1204, when King John lost Normandy, the Anglo-Normans finally started to learn English, and in so doing they quite naturally retained many of their familiar French words.

Old English had a standard literary dialect, late West Saxon, written throughout the country. Early Middle English lacked such a dialect because most educated people used French or Latin. By the close of the 14th century, however, English had reestablished itself as a written language, and the prevalent literary dialect—exemplified in the work of Geoffrey CHAUCER—was that of the capital, London. London English took most of its features from the East Midlands but incorporated elements from other dialect areas as well. The third-person-singular verbal inflection -s, for example, comes from the north; the East Midlands used -eth.

The printing press ensured the dominance of London English. People in all parts of the country became accustomed to seeing words spelled the way they were spelled (and pronounced) in London and eventually gave up their own spelling conventions and adopted those of the capital. The London spellings were then able to exert a subtle but constant pressure on pronunciation. Largely as a result of printing and broadcasting, the great dialectal diversity that characterized Middle English has gradually disappeared during the Modern English period.

middle schools and junior high schools

Middle schools and junior high schools in the United States, which usually encompass three consecutive years within grades 5–9, follow PRIMARY EDUCATION and precede SECONDARY EDUCATION but are otherwise difficult to define.

The Junior High School. Unlike either the primary or the high school, the junior high has 20th-century origins; the first were opened c.1909–10 in Crawfordsville and Madison, Ind.; Ogden, Utah; Columbus, Ohio; and Berkeley, Calif. Expediency was one reason for their development. The junior high school in Berkeley, for example, was founded as an efficient and inexpensive way to eliminate overcrowding in the high schools. In many school systems, fluctuations in enrollment have led to the establishment of junior high or middle schools and to the shortening or lengthening of the junior high school period of schooling. The need to eliminate racial segregation also led to revisions of the educational system during the 1950s and '60s.

An important rationale for the development of the junior high school was provided by the doctrine of "social efficiency" current during the early years of the 20th century. Some educators claimed that it was unreasonable to expect all students in grades 7, 8, and 9 to pursue the same studies and that, in order to justify offering a variety of courses, it would be necessary to enroll large numbers of students in junior high or other intermediate schools. Others claimed that the junior high school could serve the interests of society by differentiating students according to their probable social roles, preparing some for academic study in high school and others for VOCATIONAL EDUCATION. Some proponents of social efficiency saw the junior high school as the terminal educational experience for most children and urged that it emphasize the duties of citizenship. The few opponents of the junior high school and early differentiation of students argued that it would limit progress and equality of opportunity.

Some educational reformers believed that the junior high school would be able to design a curriculum uniquely suited to the interests of adolescents. For the most part, however, the junior high school has not been able to break free from educational traditions and the domination of college academic requirements. In the junior high school, students are usually introduced to specialized teachers and distinct subjects (as opposed to a self-contained classroom with one teacher) and a variety of extracurricular activities. The expectation that the junior high school would reduce schooling from 12 to 11 or even 10 years was rarely fulfilled.

The Middle School. The middle school is a post–World War II development in U.S. education. It typically enrolls students at the 5th or 6th grade level and usually ends at the 7th or 8th grade. Educators who favor the middle school claim that a school that is especially sensitive to the physical and psychological processes of children between the ages of 10 and 14 is necessary. Thus the appearance of the middle school may reflect the fact that children now reach puberty about 2 years earlier than did their grandparents.

The rapid development of middle schools beginning in the 1960s can be ascribed to several causes: the interests of preadolescent and adolescent children; the need to provide a transition between primary and secondary education more effective than the junior high school; the need for remedial work to decrease failure rates in high school; the opportunity to provide early subject-matter specialization and an integrated curriculum; and an attempt to strengthen the high school by reincorporating in it the 9th grade. Middle schools were also established to facilitate school desegregation plans; to make better use of existing school buildings; and to ease crowded conditions in some elementary schools.

Some middle schools have been more successful in revising teaching methods and curricula than were the junior high schools. The core curriculum proposed for the junior high school in the 1940s and '50s, which attempted to integrate language arts and social studies into one unit and mathematics and science into another, has been further modified in some middle schools. In such instances teams of four teachers (language arts, social studies, mathematics, and science) are assigned to classes of 100 to 125 students. This arrangement requires teachers to plan jointly, allows them to show students how subjects relate to each other, and allows students to receive individualized instruction.

Middle Stone Age   see MESOLITHIC PERIOD

Middlebury College

Established in 1800, Middlebury College is a private coeducational liberal arts school in Middlebury, Vt. The college is basically an undergraduate one but offers master's degrees in sciences and in its well-known summer language program, which is offered both at Middlebury and at overseas campuses. The Bread Loaf School of English and the Bread Loaf Writers' Conference are held each summer at the college.

Middlemarch

A novel by George ELIOT often considered her masterpiece, *Middlemarch* (1871–72), subtitled "A Study of Provincial Life," explores the moral growth of two principal characters. Dorothea Brooke, a highly intelligent young woman, marries Casaubon, an elderly scholar who has spent his life on the study of mythology. Dorothea believes that she is devoting her life to a great cause but after the marriage learns that Casaubon is petty, vindictive, and not even a capable scholar. In the novel's second major plot, a young physician, Lydgate, foolishly marries a silly, mercenary young woman. To support her he must compromise his medical standards. Through their sufferings Dorothea and Lydgate come to a greater understanding of themselves and others.

Middlesex   Middlesex, a former English county, is now part of Greater London. Mesolithic remains have been found there. Following Roman occupation, Saxons colonized the area. Part of Middlesex was taken over by the county of London in 1889; the rest was absorbed in 1965.

Middleton, Thomas   The English dramatist of the Jacobean period Thomas Middleton, b. Apr. 18, 1580, d. July 4, 1627, was a prolific writer of satirical and romantic comedies. His powerful tragedy *The Changeling* (1622), written in collaboration with William Rowley, shows the corruption of its heroine by an illicit passion. The mores of city dwellers are the subject of the comedies *A Trick to Catch the Old One* (1608), *A Mad World, My Masters* (c.1606), and *A Chaste Maid in Cheapside* (1630). Middleton also wrote an anti-Catholic political satire, *A Game at Chess* (1624), and numerous masques.

midge   The term *midge* is often used for all small, fragile flies. Technically, however, this term refers to three families in the order Diptera. Nonbiting midges (family Chironomidae), often called harlequin flies, resemble mosquitoes. They are seen in groups performing their mating dance, usually over water during the summer months.
  Biting midges (family Ceratopogonidae), which are barely visible, are bloodsuckers. They attach themselves to a wide variety of animals, including mosquitoes, and produce wounds that cause a painful itch. Some species carry parasitic worms that cause disease in humans and animals. Species of the bloodsucking genus *Phlebotomus*, often called sand flies, act as vectors of such human diseases as LEISHMANIASIS.
  Gall midges (family Cecidomyidae) are so named because many of their larvae cause and live in plant galls; some of these midges may feed on plants without causing galls. Others feed on insects and decaying matter. The larvae of the Hessian fly bore into wheat stems, causing much damage.

Midianites [mid'-ee-uhn-yts]   Supposed descendants of Abraham and therefore "cousins" of the ancient Israel-ites, the Midianites in biblical times were nomadic tribes-people who inhabited a part of northern Arabia to the east of Palestine. Biblical tradition holds that MOSES married a daughter of the Midianite priest Jethro (Exod. 2); thus, the Midianites may have influenced Judaism at a formative stage. Later, the Midianites made successful raids on the Israelites newly settled in Canaan, until they were stopped by Gideon's dramatic victory (Judg. 7).

Midland   Midland (1990 pop., 89,443), a city in west Texas on the southern edge of the Staked Plains, is the seat of Midland County. The center of a large ranching area, Midland was founded in 1881 as a station on the Texas and Pacific Railway equidistant from Fort Worth and El Paso. The city boomed after a vast petroleum basin was discovered nearby in 1923, and now many petroleum company headquarters are located there. Within the city are the Museum of the Southwest and the Permian Basin Petroleum Museum.

Midlands   The Midlands refers to the central counties of England and includes DERBYSHIRE, NOTTINGHAMSHIRE, LEICESTERSHIRE, NORTHAMPTONSHIRE, WARWICKSHIRE, STAFFORDSHIRE, and the West Midlands. With an area of about 15,581 km^2 (6,016 mi^2), the Midlands has a population of 9,141,000 (1988 est.). The chief cities that form the West Midlands conurbation are BIRMINGHAM, NOTTINGHAM, STOKE-ON-TRENT, Walsall, and Wolverhampton. Other major cities in the Midlands include COVENTRY, DERBY, and LEICESTER. This most heavily industrialized section of England produces heavy metals, electrical equipment, textiles, chemicals, and light goods.

Midler, Bette [bet]   Bette Midler, a popular American singer, b. Honolulu, Dec. 1, 1945, sang in the Broadway musical *Fiddler on the Roof* for three years (1966–69) before transferring her talents to nightclub and concert performances. Combining an outlandish stage presence—she has described herself as "trash with flash"—with considerable vocal ability, Midler perfected her nightclub act, consisting of highly idiosyncratic interpretations of songs from the 1940s, '50s, and '60s, in 1970. Her best-selling album, *The Divine Miss M.* (1972), was followed by *Bette Midler* (1973), *Broken Blossom* (1977), *Thighs and Whispers* (1979), and *No Frills* (1984). Midler's films include *The Rose* (1979), *Divine Madness* (1980), *Down and Out in Beverly Hills* (1986), *Ruthless People* (1986), *Outrageous Fortune* (1987), *Beaches* (1988), and *Stella* (1990).

midrash   The Hebrew word *midrash* ("search," "exposition") is used to designate (1) a method of interpreting Scriptures; (2) an instance of this method; and (3) a literary compilation of midrashic material. Midrash is an attempt to penetrate beneath the obvious meaning of a biblical passage and elicit further implications. It was used by Jews both for the elaboration of law (HALACHAH) and as a technique of preaching (*haggadah*). The method flourished in the centuries immediately before and following the beginning of the Christian era; many examples are found in the TALMUD and in the first three Gospels. The collections of midrash literature were made from about AD 300 until late in the Middle Ages.

Midsummer Night's Dream, A

William SHAKE-SPEARE's comedy *A Midsummer Night's Dream* (written c.1595) shows his enormous skill in articulating complex plots. There are at least four actions in the play: Duke Theseus and his impending marriage to Hippolyta, Queen of the Amazons; the lovers—Lysander and Hermia, Demetrius and Helena—lost in the wood; Oberon and Titania and the world of the fairies; and Bottom and his crew of artisans, who put on the play *Pyramus and Thisbe*, which parodies romantic love. The play also has a strong connection with the festivities traditionally associated with midsummer's eve (June 23).

Midway

Midway (1989 est. pop., 453), an unincorporated possession of the United States, is located in the central Pacific Ocean about 1,850 km (1,150 mi) northwest of Honolulu. It consists of two islets, Eastern and Sand, surrounded by a coral atoll that has a circumference of about 25 km (15 mi).

Midway was discovered by Americans in 1859 and annexed in 1867. It was a cable station and, after 1935, an airplane refueling stop. As a naval base in World War II, Midway was vital to U.S. Pacific defense. On June 4, 1942, a U.S. naval force under Adm. Chester W. Nimitz defeated a Japanese force under Adm. Yamamoto Isoroku off Midway. Four Japanese aircraft carriers were sunk in what proved to be the turning point of the war in the Pacific.

midwife

A midwife, traditionally a woman, attends an expectant mother during childbirth. Worldwide most babies—probably 75 percent—are delivered by midwives. Midwifery became uncommon in most developed nations as physicians assumed responsibility for maternity care. In the 1960s, however, a growing demand for midwives began in the United States, especially among those interested in natural childbirth and a more home- and family-centered approach to childbirth.

Midwife training varies from simple apprenticeship in many parts of the world to organized training programs for lay midwives and for nurse midwives. In the United States the latter may become certified nurse midwives (C.N.M.); more than 15 U.S. universities now offer midwifery as a nursing specialty.

Professional midwives, who may practice in the home, at maternity-care centers, or in hospitals, work with an obstetrician for consultation and referral of all complicated cases. They are adept at handling normal pregnancies and deliveries. Certified nurse midwives may perform episiotomies (surgical widening of the vaginal opening), but they may not use obstetrical forceps or perform cesarean deliveries.

See also: PREGNANCY AND BIRTH.

midwife toad

The midwife toad, *Alytes obstetricans*, is a member of the primitive frog family, Discoglossidae. This species occurs only in Europe. It is found from near sea level up to more than 2,000 m (6,500 ft) elevation. A related species is the Spanish midwife toad, *A. cisternasii*. In contrast to most frogs, midwife toads breed on land, not water, and the males carry and care for the eggs. During the breeding season, which extends from April to August, the male attracts a female by calling from his refuge under a rock or from a burrow in the ground. When a female appears, the male clasps her with his front legs and strokes her cloaca with his hind legs, inducing her to lay 20 to 60 eggs in a string. The male fertilizes the eggs as they are extruded, pushing his hind legs through the egg mass until the strings become entangled around his thighs. He emerges from his hiding place by night to moisten the eggs by entering the water or by allowing dew to condense on them. In about a month the male enters the water, where the tadpoles hatch and finish their development.

Mies van der Rohe, Ludwig

[mees vahn dair roh' e, loot'-vik] The German architect Ludwig Mies van der Rohe, b. Aachen, Mar. 27, 1886, d. Aug. 17, 1969, was one of the principal founders of MODERN ARCHITECTURE. Working primarily in Germany and the United States, he created a number of starkly beautiful glass-and-steel buildings that have made his name synonymous with the functionalist aesthetic of 20th-century design.

Like Le Corbusier and Walter Gropius, the other founders of modern architecture, he was apprenticed (1908–11) to the remarkable Peter Behrens, whose Berlin studio was a prolific source of architectural innovation. After his release (1919) from the German army, Mies began to move to the forefront of German avant-garde architecture with a series of striking projects, including several all-glass skyscrapers and a number of expansive country houses whose spirit owed much to Frank Lloyd Wright. By the mid-1920s, Mies's reputation was such that when the German Werkbund, an association of industrialists and artists, decided to build (1927) a full-scale architectural exhibition in Stuttgart called the Weissenhofsiedlung, he was chosen to prepare the overall plan, to select the architects for the more than 30 buildings, and to personally design a major housing block for the project. More than any other event in post–World War I Europe, the Weissenhof project established and made respectable the ideas and forms of modern architecture.

Mies was selected to design the German Pavilion for

The apartment houses at 845–860 Lake Shore Drive, Chicago, embody Ludwig Mies van der Rohe's "less is more" principle of architecture. Mies is considered one of the principal founders of modern architecture.

the 1929 International Exposition in Barcelona. Although the Pavilion was dismantled after the exposition closed, its design remains one of the high points of 20th-century architecture, as is the Tugendhat House (1930; Brno, Czechoslovakia), which Mies also designed. For both structures he also designed modernistic furniture using chromium-plated steel, leather, glass, and marble. These furniture designs, which are still being produced, incorporate most of the features found in Mies's building designs: unarticulated surfaces, careful proportions, and a functionalist design of austere elegance.

During the early 1930s the Mies–Gropius–Le Corbusier school of architecture, designated the INTERNATIONAL STYLE, triumphed in Europe while the Nazis were forcing the closing (1933) of the BAUHAUS—the Dessau center of modern design, which Mies had headed since 1930. Like many of his colleagues, Mies emigrated to the United States, becoming (1938) director of the School of Architecture at Chicago's Armour Institute, which was later renamed Illinois Institute of Technology (I. I. T.). Perhaps the most spectacular of all Mies's high-rise structures is the Seagram Building in New York City (1958), a 38-story tower clad in bronze and bronze-tinted glass. In such metal-and-glass towers Mies strove always to refine de-

tails and proportions. His maxim that "less is more" was never more beautifully realized than in the New National Gallery in Berlin (1968), a monument of steel, glass, and marble that enclosed a clear space filled only with light and art.

Miescher, Johann [mee'-shur, yoh'-hahn]   The Swiss biochemist Johann Friedrich Miescher, b. Aug. 13, 1844, d. Aug. 26, 1895, is credited with the discovery of the substance now known as deoxyribonucleic acid, or DNA. In 1869, while working with white blood cells in pus, Miescher isolated a substance from the nuclei of the cells that he called nuclein. Five years later Miescher isolated purer nuclein and, after recognizing its acidic properties, renamed it nucleic acid.

Mifflin, Thomas   Thomas Mifflin, b. Philadelphia, Jan. 10, 1744, d. Jan. 20, 1800, a major general in the American Revolution, later became the first governor of the state of Pennsylvania. A member of the First and Second Continental Congresses, he became an officer in the Continental Army in 1775 and was appointed that year to the post of quartermaster general—a post that he held (except for a few months in 1776) until 1778. Serving on the congressional board of war, Mifflin backed (1777) the CONWAY CABAL in an unsuccessful attempt to displace George Washington as commander in chief. Again a member of Congress (1782–84), he was its president (1783–84) and later served as a delegate to the Constitutional Convention of 1787. Mifflin was governor of Pennsylvania from 1790 to 1799.

MiG   A series of aircraft designed by or under the jurisdiction of Artem I. Mikoyan and Mikhail I. Gurevich at the Russian Design Bureau were given the designation MiG. The MiG–1 was a single-seat, single-engine, high-altitude monoplane fighter-interceptor of 1940; this was later produced in large numbers, until the autumn of 1941, in an improved version known as the MiG–3. Mikoyan-Gurevich continued single-seat fighter design during World War II with the development of various prototypes. In 1946 the MiG–9 (NATO code name Fargo) ground-attack fighter, the first of the MiG jet fighters, entered service with the Soviet air force. The MiG–15 (Fagot) all-metal stressed-skin mid-wing monoplane of 1947 was the first operational Soviet swept-wing aircraft. During 1953 the MiG–19 (Farmer) succeeded the MiG–17 as the first mass-produced Soviet aircraft capable of exceeding the speed of sound (Mach 1). The MiG–21 (Fishbed), a short-range fighter capable of a speed of Mach 2.1, was fitted with mid-delta wings. Variable-geometry wings constituted the main feature of the MiG–23 (Flogger), which appeared in 1967 and could attain Mach 3. That year also marked the first public showing of the MiG–25 (Foxbat), an all-weather, high-altitude interceptor and low-level strike fighter,

(Top) *The Soviet MiG-15 single-seat jet fighter, shown with North Korean markings, first appeared in service during the Korean War and is considered to be the USSR's first truly innovative jet plane. Called "Fagot" by NATO, the MiG-15 could fly, climb, and dive faster than previous Soviet aircraft. It had a top speed of 1,075 km/h (668 mph) and could climb to 15,545 m (51,000 ft).*

(Middle) *The Soviet MiG-21MF single-seat fighter, shown with Egyptian Air Force insignia, is known as "Fishbed" by NATO and is only one of several different versions of a model developed in the late 1950s on the basis of the MiG-15 Korean combat experience. Considered the most widely used combat aircraft in the world in the 1970s, it has a top speed of Mach 2.1, or 2,070 km/h (1,285 mph), a ceiling of 18,000 m (59,050 ft), and a range of 1,800 km (1,118 mi).*

(Bottom) *The Soviet MiG-25, shown with Russian markings and known as "Foxbat" by NATO, is an all-weather, long-range, single-seat, twin-jet supersonic aircraft. Considered one of the world's best interceptors, it can fly at an estimated speed of Mach 3.2 (3,380 km/h; 2,100 mph), climb to 24,400 m (80,000 ft), and has a combat range of at least 1,130 km (700 mi). It carries two radar-controlled and two infrared-homing air-to-air missiles.*

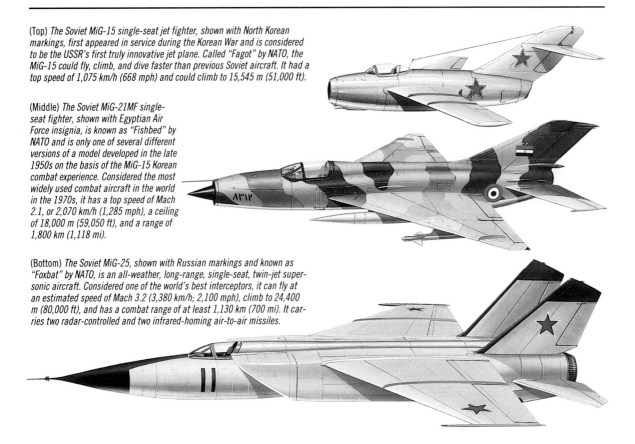

powered by two jet engines. On Sept. 6, 1976, an interceptor version of the MiG-25 was flown to Japan by a defecting Soviet pilot, Lt. Viktor Belenko, giving Japanese and U.S. technicians an opportunity to examine it. The MiG-27 is a development of the MiG–23. Early in 1978 there were reports of the MiG–29, a new Russian twin-engine, twin-fin, general-purpose fighter comparable to the American F–16 and F–18.

migraine   see HEADACHE

---

migrant labor   Migrant labor refers to workers who move from different parts within a country or from country to country to take advantage of seasonal or temporary employment opportunities. Given their frequent moves, they usually do not have any status in or major loyalty to a particular community. Migrant labor exists in many areas of the world, including Africa, Australia, Europe, and the United States.

Migrant laborers are used when the short-term demand for workers exceeds the available local supply. Agricultural businesses—the principal employers of migrant laborers—depend on these workers to help them cope with the unequal supply-and-demand problem that occurs when large amounts of crops must be harvested im-

mediately. These workers may arrive at their own initiative or be brought in by a contractor hired by the farmer.

Sometimes migrant workers are used to bypass the minimum-wage laws. In these cases companies may use illegal aliens (workers who are not citizens of the country in which they are employed and have not received permission to work in the host's country) to keep costs down. These companies not only may exploit these workers—the labor laws of the country do not protect illegal aliens—but also may acquire an unfair competitive advantage relative to other firms that rely on more highly paid labor. In some countries—the United States is one example—attempts have been made to prevent and control the use of illegal migrant workers. The major immigration reform bill that Congress passed in 1986 gives legal status to illegal aliens who worked in agriculture for at least 90 days from May 1, 1985, to May 1, 1986. Employers of illegals are subject to civil penalties.

In the United States the federal government has taken some steps to try to improve the difficult living and working conditions of the migrant-labor force. Also, for the first time, unionization of migrant labor in the United States became a reality in the 1960s through the efforts of Cesar CHAVEZ, who organized migrant workers in California. These efforts resulted in the creation of the National Farm Workers Association in 1962 (renamed United Farm Workers in 1972), its association with the AFL-CIO, and the negotiation in the 1970s of contracts with farmers.

Mihajlović, Draža [mee-hy'-loh-vich, drah'-zhah]

Dragoljub (called Draža) Mihajlović, b. Mar. 27, 1893, d. July 17, 1946, was a Yugoslav army officer and a Serbian nationalist and royalist. During World War II, after the conquest (1941) and partition of Yugoslavia by the Axis Powers, he organized underground *chetniks,* resistance forces in Serbia. Meanwhile a rival resistance organization controlled by the Yugoslav Communist party and led by Josip Broz (who adopted the name TITO) was operating— mainly in Bosnia and Montenegro. Tito's forces increased, while Mihajlović's *chetniks* gradually lost the support of the Allied Powers. In 1946, Mihajlović was captured by Tito's partisans, found guilty of "treason" in a show trial, and shot.

Mikan, George

George Lawrence Mikan, b. Joliet, Ill., June 18, 1924, is considered the first outstanding tall center in American professional basketball. A star at DePaul University, after beginning as a bespectacled teenager, he helped his team win the 1945 National Invitation Tournament (NIT). As a professional, mostly with the Minneapolis Lakers, he is regarded by basketball historians as the game's first superstar. Mikan, 2 m 8 cm (6 ft 10 in) tall, led his team to 5 National Basketball Association (NBA) titles. In 9 seasons as a professional (1947–56), he averaged 22.6 points per game. After his retirement, Mikan in 1967 became the first commissioner of the now-defunct American Basketball Association (ABA). He was inducted into the Basketball Hall of Fame in 1959.

Mikoyan, Anastas Ivanovich [mee-kuh-yan', uh-nuh-stas' ee-vahn'-uh-vich]

Anastas Ivanovich Mikoyan, b. Nov. 25, 1895, d. Oct. 21, 1978, served for more than 50 years in the Soviet government. A Communist party member from 1915, Mikoyan held various local administrative posts in the Caucasus before becoming (1926) commissar of trade under Joseph Stalin. He served Stalin and later Nikita Khrushchev in a variety of posts, becoming an expert in international trade. Mikoyan was a member of the politburo (1935–66), first vice-chairman of the Council of Ministers (1955–64), and chairman of the presidium of the Supreme Soviet (1964–65). He remained in the presidium until 1975.

Milan [mi-lahn']

Milan (Italian: Milano) is the capital of Lombardy region and Milan province, Italy. Milan (1988 est. pop., 1,478,505) is the second largest city in Italy. Located in the basin of the Po RIVER about 480 km (300 mi) northwest of Rome, it is connected by canals to the Adda River on the east and Ticino River on the west. The ancient Roman city of Mediolanum forms the core of present-day Milan. Most industrial development has taken place in Milan's suburbs, far from the central city.

Contemporary City. Milan is Italy's chief commercial, financial, and industrial center and its most modern city. It is the home of Italy's leading banking institutions and major stock exchange. Its industries manufacture steel, textiles (particularly silk), clothing, machine tools, aircraft, automobiles, railroad equipment, agricultural machinery, chemicals, printed materials, pharmaceuticals, furniture, and foodstuffs. Milan is also a major transportation center.

Among Milan's universities is the University of Milan (1923). The city's museums and galleries include the Poldo-Pezzoli Museum and the Natural History Museum. Art galleries are also contained in the Ambrosiana Library and the Brera Palace. The Church of Santa Maria delle Grazie (1465–90) houses Leonardo da Vinci's *The Last Supper.* Important historical buildings include the Milan Cathedral (a Gothic structure begun in 1386), Sforza Castle (1456), Ospedale Maggiore (1456), the Basilica di Sant' Ambrogio (386), and the Basilica di San Lorenzo (6th century). Milan is also the home of LA SCALA, one of the most prestigious opera companies.

History. Milan was probably founded by the Celts in about the 3d century BC. The city was taken by Rome in 222 BC, and from AD 305 until 402 it served as capital of the Western Roman Empire. During the 5th and 6th centuries Milan was repeatedly subjected to invasions by Huns, Goths, and Lombards and was reduced to only a village. The city was rebuilt, however, during the late 9th century and later became the seat of an archbishopric. In the 12th century Milan became a free commune, or republic. In the 13th century the city fell under the rule of its two great ducal families, the VISCONTI and the SFORZA. The Visconti ruled until 1447, and the Sforza dominated from 1450 until 1535.

After 1535 the city came under foreign domination for 400 years. Spain ruled it from 1535 until 1713, when— following the War of the Spanish Succession—it passed

Milan, Italy's second most populous city, rises from the plains of northern Italy between the Po River and the foothills of the Alps.

to Austria. France ruled Milan from 1796 until Austria regained control in 1815. In 1859, Milan became part of the Kingdom of Sardinia and subsequently part of unified Italy in 1861.

After World War I, Milan became the center of Benito Mussolini's National Fascist party; from Milan Mussolini sent his followers on the march to Rome in 1922. The city was badly damaged during World War II.

Milankovitch theory   see ICE AGES

Milarepa

[mil-uh-rep'-uh] Milarepa, 1040–1123, was a Tibetan Buddhist saint and poet who was also reputed to possess magical powers. Initiated into Buddhism by Marpa, the first patriarch of the Kargyupa sect, Milarepa in turn transmitted his teachings to sGam-po-pa, whose own disciples founded six famous schools under the umbrella of Kargyupa doctrine. With these schools, TIBETAN BUDDHISM came into its own, relying less and less on its historical link with India.

mildew

Two families of fungi, known as powdery and downy mildews, are parasites that grow on surfaces of plants, causing disease. The powdery mildews, family Erysiphaceae, produce a white, powdery mass of mycelia on leaves of such plants as cereal grains, roses, lilacs, and willows. Important genera of powdery mildew are *Microsphaerea, Uncinula,* and *Erysiphe.* Downy mildews, family Peronosporaceae, include such species as *Peronospora parasitica,* which affects members of the cabbage family; *Plasmopara viticola,* which affects grapes; and *Pseudoperonospora cubensis,* causing disease in members of the cucumber family. Another group of mildew, known as dark mildew, family Perisporiaceae, also parasitizes higher plants. *Mildew* is also a term referring to molds that grow on paper, cloth, leather, paint, and plastic. These fungi include such genera as *Aspergillus* and *Penicillium.*

Miles, Nelson A.

Nelson Appleton Miles, b. near Westminister, Mass., Aug. 8, 1839, d. May 15, 1925, was an officer in the Union Army during the U.S. Civil War and took part in campaigns against the American Indians. While with the Army of the Potomac, he reached (1865) the rank of major general of volunteers and was four times wounded. At the end of the Civil War, Miles accepted a commission as colonel in the regular army. Assigned to the West, he served in various Indian campaigns: in the Red River War (1874–75) against the Cheyenne, Kiowa, and Comanche in Texas; against the Sioux leaders SITTING BULL and CRAZY HORSE (1876–77); against the Nez Percé chief JOSEPH (1877); and against the Chiracahua Apache GERONIMO (1886). He also led troops that were called out to quell disorders accompanying the Pullman Strike of 1894. Miles was placed in command of the U.S. Army in 1895 and led the forces that occupied Puerto Rico during the Spanish-American War (1898).

Milesian school

[mil-ee'-zhuhn] The "Milesian school" refers to three early Greek philosophers—THALES OF MILETUS, ANAXIMANDER, and ANAXIMENES—who lived in the Ionian city of Miletus, on the coast of Anatolia, in the 6th century BC. The Milesians explained natural phenomena by reference only to observable entities (except in the case of Anaximander's *apeiron,* the "boundless" or "indefinite"). They also sought to discover the natural, impartial laws governing growth and change. Because of their methodological approach, the Milesians are called scientific or philosophical and are considered to have created the first true works of Greek philosophy.

Miletus

[my-lee'-tuhs] Miletus, an ancient Greek city of Anatolia, situated at the mouth of the Meander River, owed its importance to its position on trade routes. Highly prosperous, it founded many colonies and was the home of the MILESIAN SCHOOL of philosophy. In 499 BC, with other cities of Ionia, Miletus rebelled against the Persians, who sacked (494) it in retaliation. Captured by Alexander the Great after a siege in 334 BC, Miletus remained an important trade center into Roman times.

Milhaud, Darius

[mee-oh', dahr-ee-ues'] The prolific French composer Darius Milhaud, b. Sept. 4, 1892, d. June 22, 1974, was a prominent member of a group of composers with neoclassical tendencies known as Les Six, which also included Francis Poulenc and Arthur Honegger. Milhaud completed his studies at the Paris Conservatory under Vincent d'Indy and Paul Dukas, among others. A sojourn (1917–18) in Brazil as secretary to Paul Claudel and later tours in the United States brought Milhaud in touch with Latin American music and jazz. The jazz idiom permeates the ballet *The Creation of the World,* first performed in 1923, predating by a year George Gershwin's *Rhapsody in Blue.*

Although a notable exponent of polytonality, Milhaud

Darius Milhaud, a 20th-century French composer, wrote more than 400 works, including operas and ballets. Milhaud's music shows the influence both of Brazilian folk and popular music and of American jazz.

normally wrote in a readily accessible melodic style, as in *Protée* (1919). He was admired for his careful craftsmanship and the expressive clarity of his instrumentation. Many of his better-known compositions are characterized by Gallic wit, as in *Le boeuf sur le toit* (1919). Several of his important works, including the opera *Christopher Columbus* (1928) and the opera-oratorio *Saint Louis, King of France* (1970–71), are based on texts by Paul Claudel. He also wrote 12 symphonies in addition to ballets, suites, and incidental music to numerous plays; concertos for various instruments; choral works; chamber music, including 15 string quartets; numerous songs; and music for films and radio.

Milhaud taught at Mills College, Oakland, Calif., from 1940 to 1947, after which he returned to France to become professor of composition at the Paris Conservatory. He returned annually, however, to teach at Mills College until he retired in 1972.

military justice   Military justice establishes rules, structures, and procedures by which members of a nation's armed forces who transgress civil or military law may be apprehended, tried, and punished. Military justice during peacetime is usually restricted to the adjudication of military offenses; in wartime, civil offenses committed by military personnel may also become subject to military justice. Systems of military justice can be traced at least as far back as ancient Rome, but organized, modern military justice dates back to 17th-century English legislative enactments and articles promulgated by Gustavus Adolphus of Sweden.

In the United States the Constitution (Article I, Section 8) provides for Congress "to make rules for the government and regulation of the land and naval forces." In Ex parte Milligan (1866) the Supreme Court reaffirmed the separate nature of military justice and the limitation of the right to trial by jury in the administration of military law. Recently the Supreme Court has held that for crimes to fall under military jurisdiction they must be "service connected," although the definition of this term has remained murky.

The Uniform Code of Military Justice was enacted by Congress in 1950 to regularize military law for all the armed forces and to correct certain abuses of justice that had occurred during World War II. The code established three types of COURT-MARTIAL: general, special, and summary. All three may be convened by the president, a secretary of a service branch, or an appropriate commanding officer. General and special courts may be composed of commissioned officers or—when an enlisted man on trial demands it—officers and enlisted men.

General, special, and summary courts differ as to jurisdiction. The general court is used for capital and other serious offenses and may impose a wide range of sentences. A sentence of death requires a unanimous vote. The special court has jurisdiction over noncapital offenses, but the punishments that the court may administer are restricted. It may not, for example, order confinement for more than six months. The summary court also has juris-diction over noncapital offenses, but the punishments it may mete out are even more restricted than those of the special court.

Military personnel accused of code violations or other offenses may not be forced to incriminate themselves. They are also protected against cruel and unusual punishment (they may not be flogged, for example) and DOUBLE JEOPARDY. They have the right to obtain witnesses and documents essential for an adequate defense and the right to employ private counsel or have counsel appointed for the defense.

Review of court-martial decisions goes first to the convening authority, then to Courts of Military Review in the appropriate judge advocate's office, and, finally, under certain circumstances, to the United States Court of Military Appeals—a civilian, three-judge court appointed by the president for 15-year terms. In general, the rulings of courts in the military justice system are not reviewable in the civil courts except on questions of jurisdiction—and even there the power of the courts is limited (*Schlesinger* v. *Councilman*, 1975). Federal courts do have the power to review actions of military courts in cases of petitions for writs of HABEAS CORPUS when the assertion is that military courts had no jurisdiction or where constitutional rights may have been violated (*Calley* v. *Callaway*, 1975).

military police   Military police are the constabulary units of a nation's armed forces. These units are charged with maintaining order on military installations; they also have jurisdiction in areas near military bases when infractions involved military personnel. Additionally military police maintain security and discipline in a war zone. Each of the armed forces of the United States, for example, has its own trained police force. In the Army and the Marines, police duties are carried out by the Military Police, or MPs; in the Navy and the Coast Guard, by the Shore Patrol; and in the Air Force, by the Security Police.

military rank   see RANK, MILITARY

military strategy and tactics   see STRATEGY AND TACTICS, MILITARY

military warning and detection systems
Until the 20th century, military warning and detection methods lagged far behind the tactics of surprise. Scouts and sentries were the backbone of early warning systems. The balloon was the first application of technology to the problem; despite some isolated examples of success in the American Civil War, the Spanish-American War, and World War I, the balloon's role in warning and detection was short-lived and of little significance. A major factor in the withdrawal of the observation balloon from military service was the initiation of airplane reconnaissance missions. The airplane itself rapidly developed into such a powerful offensive weapon that it presently constitutes a most serious threat (second only to ballistic missiles) to the national security of all nations. Most countries, there-

fore, have some type of system to warn of an impending attack, to detect approaching aircraft, and to direct and control defensive countermeasures.

Because an air attack can come from any direction and can develop with great rapidity, it is not unusual for two or more nations to have cooperative arrangements for mutual air defense. An example is the U.S.–Canadian DEW (Distant Early Warning) System, a series of radar installations stretching across northern Canada and Alaska. Another system, NADGE (NATO Air Defense Ground Environment), ranks as a monument to international effort and collaboration.

The main elements of an air defense system are (1) sensors, (2) command and control, (3) communications, and (4) defensive weapons. The most common type of sensor is RADAR, which provides information on target range and bearing. Three-dimensional and height-finder radars give data on target altitude and identify aircraft targets. Airborne search radars such as the AWACS (see AIRBORNE WARNING AND CONTROL SYSTEM) may also be linked with the air defense system to provide an extended range of coverage and "look-down" capability for the detection of low-flying targets.

Direct reconnaissance from the air has been possible since the launching (1952) of the first U-2 (see U-2) aircraft, which photographed Soviet bomber bases and nuclear test sites. Reconnaissance by satellite has been possible since 1960, when the United States succeeded in recovering the film-containing reentry capsules of its DISCOVERER satellites. The SAMOS series of reconnaissance satellites was also launched beginning in that year. The USSR initiated its COSMOS series in 1962. Since that time the abilities of spy satellites have grown exponentially. Satellites equipped with infrared detectors that sense the heat generated in missile launches can signal warning of nuclear attack. The IMEWS series are equipped with cameras that transmit photos of detected missiles. VELA satellites can detect nuclear explosions, and the Teal Ruby satellite sensor detects aircraft in flight.

The newest generation of U.S. military satellites were launched beginning in the late 1980s by the Space Shuttle and by powerful new rockets. The satellites use radar to produce high-resolution images of Earth. They are equipped with powerful photographing telescopes. Some are capable of detecting Earth objects as small as 1 m (3 ft) across. They can "see" through clouds. And their orbital lives may last up to nine years.

■

military-industrial complex The term *military-industrial complex* was popularized by U.S. president Dwight D. Eisenhower in his farewell address to the American people in January 1961: "In the councils of government, we must guard against the acquisition of unwarranted influence, whether sought or unsought, by the military-industrial complex." He was warning against the conjunction of interests and the great potential influence wielded by a large military establishment working with a large arms industry.

Some historical antecedents exist for this concern,

most notably the *merchants-of-death* concept that was prevalent in the United States in the early 1930s. This term refers to the assumption that the U.S. financial and industrial community had been responsible for dragging the United States into war in 1917. To prevent a possible recurrence, efforts were directed toward preventing war profiteering in the event of some future war. The high point of these concerns was reached during the Senate Munitions Investigating Committee inquiry of 1934–36 headed by Sen. Gerald P. Nye, which looked into the role of munitions makers, bankers, and exporters in the U.S. decision to enter World War I. The committee failed to prove that there was any connection. Although the merchants-of-death thesis continues to exert some influence, it has yet to be proved that the armaments industry has been responsible for persuading any country into war.

Since Eisenhower's speech, the military-industrial complex has usually been discussed in terms of the deleterious effects defense spending has had on the U.S. economy and on domestic, social, and welfare programs. The tangled relationships between the government and weapons-making corporations are also seen as a problem. Members of the military-industrial complex include the U.S. Defense Department and its four military services, the various defense industries, certain influential members of Congress (especially those who sit on the Armed Services committees), research institutions, and the scientists and technologists who work in military research and in weaponry.

■

militia An organization of trained citizens—enlisted or conscripted—who are mobilized in periods of emergency is called a militia. Militias have existed at least since the time of the Greek city-states. Based on the concept that every able-bodied free male has the right and duty to defend his imperiled community or nation, the militia from the beginning has had democratic implications. This is reflected in the 2d Amendment to the U.S. Constitution, which relates to the maintenance of state militias.

In Anglo-Saxon England, the *fyrd* was the levy of all able-bodied freemen, locally organized and controlled. Similar militias developed in other European countries. Eventually, militias declined as a result of a the rise of an aristocratic military class and, later, the creation of large standing armies in the 18th and 19th centuries. During the 19th century compulsory military service generally replaced militias, although Switzerland continues to maintain a citizen-militia defense force. During World War II, Britain's Home Guard was a militia. In strife-torn Lebanon of the 1980s, factional armies were often termed *militias*.

The use of voluntary militiamen, including the MINUTEMEN, was widespread during the American Revolution. Earlier on—Virginia began in 1611—the colonies had instituted general levies of their able-bodied men, and the U.S. Militia Act of 1792 authorized the states to continue this practice. After the War of 1812 militia service became largely voluntary. In 1903 the volunteer units were organized as the NATIONAL GUARD.

milk A white liquid secreted by the mammary glands of female cows, goats, sheep, and other MAMMALS, milk is a highly nutritious substance that is widely consumed both in its natural form and in such dairy products as BUTTER and CHEESE. (For a discussion of human milk and its importance, see BREAST and BREAST-FEEDING.) This article deals with the processing of milk after it leaves the farm. The processes involved in cow-milk production are described in the DAIRYING article.

Nutritional Content. When it arrives at the processing plant, milk may contain up to 4% milk fat, which is suspended as minute globules in the serum, or skim milk, fraction. Because these globules weigh less than the serum, they gradually rise and form a top layer of cream. In addition to its fat, milk consists of several nutritionally important proteins, including casein; the unique milk sugar, lactose; calcium; phosphorus; salts; and vitamins, principally A and D.

Lactose comprises about 5% of milk. A carbohydrate, it is the sweetener of milk and is a major source of energy. Most infants readily digest lactose, but with increasing age persons of Asian and African descent often lose much of their ability to synthesize lactase, a lactose-splitting enzyme, and are thus unable to digest milk without becoming physically uncomfortable. In the manufacture of cultured buttermilk, yogurt, sour cream, and other fermented milk products, the fermenting bacteria break down some of the lactose; such products are more readily digested by many people than is whole milk.

Processing. At a dairy plant, milk is tested to determine its milk-fat content. Different batches may then be blended to adjust the fat content. To meet U.S. standards, fresh whole milk sold in stores must contain a minimum of 3.25% milk fat. Depending on the end use, therefore, bulk milk may be skimmed of much of its fat in a mechanical cream separator. Cream and skim milk, which are produced by separation, are then mixed in different proportions to produce lowfat milk (0.5% to 2.0% fat), whole milk, half-and-half (10.5% fat), coffee cream (18% fat), and whipping cream (30% fat).

Raw milk will sour quickly because of the presence of bacteria that convert lactose to lactic acid. PASTEURIZATION—the heating of milk to at least 71.7° C (161° F) for 15 seconds—destroys these bacteria, and refrigerated pasteurized milk will remain fresh for a week or more. Ultrapasteurization, at 137.8° C (280° F) for 2 seconds, allows milk products to be stored at room temperature for several weeks.

To prevent formation of a cream layer, most whole milk undergoes HOMOGENIZATION, a process in which hot milk is pumped through valves to break up and permanently disperse the fat globules. Off-flavors that may have developed in the milk if the cows have eaten succulent weeds, such as wild onion, are removed by subjecting the hot milk to a vacuum in a closed chamber, volatilizing the feed flavors.

Vitamins A and D are contained in the cream component of milk, and both of these vitamins must be added to skim and lowfat milk. One quart of milk supplies 100% of the U.S. recommended daily adult requirement of vitamin D.

Milk Products. In addition to butter and cheese, the most important dairy products include ICE CREAM, YOGURT, dried nonfat milk, and condensed and evaporated milk. Dried milk is made from skim or whole milk that is concentrated through vacuum evaporation until it contains about 40% milk solids. It is then heated and sprayed into a drying chamber at a temperature of about 193° C (380° F). The resulting milk powder can be reconstituted by adding water.

Both condensed and evaporated milk are made by evaporating moisture from milk to produce a thickened, concentrated milk. Sweetened condensed milk contains more than 40% added sugar, which helps to preserve it. Evaporated milk is preserved by sterilizing the milk in cans, although this changes its flavor greatly.

milk snake The milk snake, *Lampropeltis triangulum* or *L. doliata*, in the family Colubridae, has one of the most extensive ranges of any snake, from southeastern Canada to Ecuador. The snake's common name is erroneously derived from the myth that it sucks milk from cows. Milk snakes are smooth-scaled and generally tricolored in a banded or blotched pattern of red or brown, bordered by black, on a background of gray, white, or yellow. The black-bordered red distinguishes milk snakes from CORAL SNAKES, *Micrurus*, in the United States, where the red is bordered by yellow. Milk snakes kill prey by constriction and feed on rodents, birds, and other reptiles. Adults average between 0.5 and 1.0 m (1.5 and 3 ft) in total length. Milk snakes are sometimes called KING SNAKES.

Milk snakes, such as L. triangulum, *feed on other snakes, including the poisonous rattlesnake. The milk snake often kills its prey by coiling around the victim's body and constricting.*

milkweed Milkweeds comprise about 200 species of widely distributed, mostly perennial herbs of the genus *Asclepias* in the milkweed family, Asclepiadaceae. They are characterized by often having a thick, milky sap; paired, unlobed leaves; and fruit pods filled with silky tufted seeds. Their small but complex flowers are borne in rounded clusters and vary from white or yellowish to red or purplish. The toxic properties of the milky sap of the common milkweed, *A. syriaca,* are destroyed by boiling, and the young shoots, tender top leaves, flower buds, and hard, unripe seedpods can be boiled (with several changes of water) and eaten. Another milkweed, *A. tuberosa*, known as the butterfly weed, is poisonous.

milkwort   Milkworts are 500 or more species in the genus *Polygala* in the milkwort family, Polygalaceae. They are mostly perennial herbs widely distributed through the warmer regions of the world. Their flowers, borne in rounded or spikelike clusters, resemble those of the pea family. They have five sepals, two enlarged into wings, and typically three small petals.

Milky Way   see GALAXY, THE

mill   A mill is a machine that applies power to perform various types of work: grinding, crushing, stamping, and pressing. The term *mill* also refers to the building that houses such a machine. For many centuries, most mechanical work was performed by WATERWHEELS and windmills, and thus the word *mill* eventually became a synonym for any workplace where machinery was used. The term *milling* is now used to describe a large number of processes performed by MACHINE TOOLS.

The earliest mills were hand-powered devices for grinding grain, such as the quern, in which an upper

Windmills began to be used in western Europe about the 12th century. Although they are now used to drive pumps for drainage or irrigation purposes, windmills were first developed for grinding grain. A typical 18th-century tower mill consisted of a tower of brick or stone on which was mounted a rotatable cap (1). The cap carried the main drive shaft and the wooden slatted sails (2). A fantail (3) turned the cap automatically so that the sails always faced into the wind. A system of gears connected to the drive shaft turned the upper grindstone (4), which ground the grain against a lower, fixed stone. The ground grain was then poured through a chute (5) into a storage bin below.

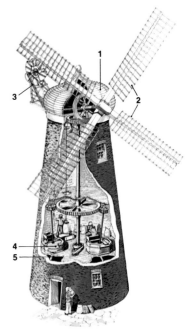

Watermills have been used for grinding grain into flour since ancient times. In this rendering of a typical watermill—whose basic form remained essentially unchanged in Europe for many centuries—a fast-flowing millrace turns a vertical paddle wheel (1) that is connected by a system of wooden gears to the upper, rotating stone of a pair of enclosed grindstones (2). Grain poured into the hopper (3) falls through a chute into the space between the stones and is ground into flour. The flour moves through another chute into storage sacks (4).

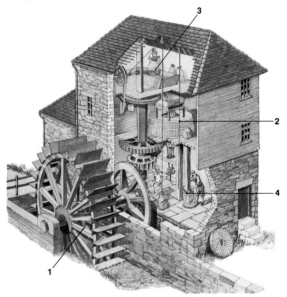

grinding stone with a handle is rotated inside a nether stone containing the grain. Although humanpower continued to be used to turn treadmills, draft animals soon began to provide the power for the larger grinding and pressing mills. The watermill, powered by a horizontal wheel, was probably first used in the West by the Greeks. The first efficient waterwheel, however, was a Roman invention. The Roman wheel, which was vertical, used a sophisticated system of gearing to transmit the motion of the waterwheel to a grinding stone that moved on a horizontal plane; by changing the diameter of the gear wheels, the speed of the stone's rotation could be changed.

From the Roman era and for well over a millennium waterwheels were the major source of mill power in Europe. Efficient windmills were a later development, achieving their greatest use only after the 15th century. Windmill technology grew increasingly complex, and windmills were used not only for grinding but also to saw wood, ventilate mines, and pump water.

In 1784, London's large flour millers, the Albion Mills, began to use steam power for their milling. Within the following century the steam engine transformed the landscape of Europe as the thousands of windmills and waterwheels that had provided most of the continent's power gradually fell into disuse and were dismantled.

The new steam-powered factories, with their machines and machine tenders, were totally unlike the older workplaces, but old language habits persisted, and they too were called "mills." (For a discussion of the contemporary rediscovery of wind power as an economic energy source, see WINDMILLS AND WIND POWER.)

Mill, James

Mill, James   James Mill, b. Apr. 6, 1773, d. June 23, 1836, was a Scottish utilitarian philosopher and historian, and one of the leading British intellectuals of the early 19th century. His long association with the British East India Company resulted from his important *History of India,* published in 1817.

As an intimate of the social philosopher Jeremy BENTHAM, Mill became a leader among Bentham's circle of friends, all of whom were committed to social and economic reform along the utilitarian lines advocated by Bentham. Mill's most lasting contribution to the movement, however, was probably his own son, John Stuart, whose education Mill personally undertook so as to provide him with the background necessary to assume leadership of the movement.

James Mill's most important philosophic work was *Analysis of the Phenomena of the Human Mind* (1829), which further developed a theory of the mind previously outlined by David Hume and David Hartley. In this, by showing how the principles of association at work in the mind operate on the materials thrown up by sense experience to generate new, or derived, mental phenomena, Mill provided the psychological basis for the ethics required by UTILITARIANISM.

Mill, John Stuart

Mill, John Stuart   John Stuart Mill, b. May 20, 1806, d. May 8, 1873, was the most influential British social and political thinker of the mid-Victorian period. The son of philosopher James Mill, John Stuart was introduced early to the Philosophical Radicals, or Benthamites, who actively pursued various social and political reforms along the utilitarian lines laid down by Jeremy BENTHAM. James Mill personally undertook the education of his precocious son, beginning with Greek at age 3, with the aim of preparing him intellectually for eventual leadership of the group. The account of this educational experience appears in the younger Mill's *Autobiography* (1873).

In his early twenties Mill experienced a "mental crisis," in which he was overcome by intense depression and plagued by doubts concerning the causes to which he had previously been devoted. Although this period passed, it left a permanent imprint on Mill. Although he remained a Benthamite, he revised his earlier beliefs in important respects.

In 1830, Mill was introduced to Harriet Taylor, a woman who was married and the mother of several children. They developed a deep, unconventional, and probably platonic friendship that resulted in marriage 21 years later, following the death of her husband. Mill attributed to his wife, who died in 1858, a decisive influence on all his later work.

Mill's earliest important philosophical work, *System of Logic* (1843), contains a valuable discussion of the epistemological principles underlying EMPIRICISM. Mill is mainly remembered today, however, for his contributions to ethical and social theory, in which his writings continue to exert an important influence. *Utilitarianism* (1863) was his effort to state and defend the view that "the great-

John Stuart Mill, a 19th-century English philosopher and economist, advocated utilitarian reforms in his many writings and as member of Parliament. A child prodigy, Mill had mastered Greek by the age of 7 and studied economics at the age of 13.

est happiness of the greatest number" should be the aim of personal and legislative conduct. He revised Bentham's version of UTILITARIANISM, however, by enriching the concept of pleasure. Although both Mill and Bentham believed that pleasure constituted happiness, Bentham had argued that all pleasures, physical or intellectual, were of equal value; Mill argued for the superiority of the "higher" pleasures of the mind. The earlier *On Liberty* (1859) was his statement of the principle that self-protection alone can justify either the state's tampering with the liberty of the individual or any personal interference with another's freedom. Mill particularly urged this point of view with respect to freedom of thought and discussion. *The Subjection of Women* (1869), a topic on which Mill and Harriet Taylor had collaborated as early as 1832, is a classic essay on all aspects of female emancipation.

Millais, Sir John Everett

Millais, Sir John Everett [mil-ay']   The British painter Sir John Everett Millais, b. Southampton, June 8, 1829, d. Aug. 13, 1896, was one of the founders (1848)

Ophelia, painted by the British artist Sir John Everett Millais in 1852, shows traits of his youthful Pre-Raphaelite style: sumptuous color, an accurate rendering of natural detail, and unconventional composition. (Tate Gallery, London.)

of the Pre-Raphaelite Brotherhood (see PRE-RAPHAELITES) and later a very popular genre painter. With William Holman Hunt and Dante Gabriel Rossetti, he joined in a movement dedicated to painting with truth to nature and sincerity of feeling. In choosing the name *Pre-Raphaelites* the three young painters expressed their rejection of what they saw as the artificial and classicist canons that had dominated Western painting since Raphael. Inspired by this doctrine, Millais executed a series of marvelously detailed and brilliantly colored masterpieces, including *Christ in the House of His Parents* (1850; Tate Gallery, London), *Lorenzo and Isabella* (1849; Walker Art Gallery, Liverpool), and *Ophelia* (1852; Tate Gallery). His *Return of the Dove to the Ark* (1851; Ashmolean Museum, Oxford) attracted special notice at the Paris Exhibition of 1855. In his later works, a more sedate treatment of anecdotal and sentimental themes appealed to average Victorian taste. Such subjects as *The Boyhood of Raleigh* (1870; Tate Gallery) proved to be great popular favorites, and the use (1885) in a soap advertisement of his picture of a small boy blowing bubbles created a sensation. He was made a baronet in 1885.

Millay, Edna St. Vincent [mil-ay'] An American poet who has been praised for her intensely lyrical and technically faultless verse, Edna St. Vincent Millay, b. Rockland, Maine, Feb. 22, 1892, d. Oct. 19, 1950, became one of America's most accomplished sonneteers. With the publication of her first volume, *Renascence and Other Poems* (1917), she moved to Greenwich Village and for several years lived a bohemian life, writing poetry, verse plays, and articles and becoming involved in political and social causes. The poetry of these years, as in *A Few Figs from Thistles* (1920) and *Second April* (1921), possesses a tone of cynicism that hardened into bitterness with the approach of World War II. The title poem of *The Harp Weaver and Other Poems* (1923) won the Pulitzer Prize. Later works, such as *Make Bright the Arrows* (1940), express her continuing involvement in contemporary affairs. Millay's *Collected Sonnets* appeared in 1941 and *Collected Lyrics* in 1943.

Edna St. Vincent Millay, an American lyric poet, was at the peak of her popularity during the 1920s, when her brittle poetry and rebellious wit were most in tune with the time. Millay's later work reflects political disillusionment, concern with mortality, and a belief in the futility of human effort.

millenarianism [mil-en-air'-ee-uhn-izm] In its narrowest sense *millenarianism* refers to belief in the SECOND COMING OF CHRIST and the establishment of his kingdom on Earth as predicted in the Book of REVELATION. More generally, the term refers to any religious movement that prophesies the imminent destruction of the present order and the establishment of a new order, usually reversing the relative status of the oppressed and the oppressor.

Christian millenarian beliefs were derived from Jewish apocalyptic traditions current in the centuries before and after Jesus Christ. Some scholars have, in fact, suggested that in its origins Christianity was related to such millenarian groups as the ESSENES. As Christianity developed into a stable community in the centuries after Jesus, millenarian activity became primarily a fringe movement, associated with such reform movements as MONTANISM and, in the 13th and 14th centuries, Joachimism and radical Franciscan movements. With the upheavals brought on by the Reformation in the 16th century, millenarianism increased and was found, for example, among the ANABAPTISTS.

In the 18th century, Independents in England (for example, Joseph Mede) and Pietists in Germany advocated millenarian views. Among contemporary Protestant groups believing in the millennium are the Seventh-Day ADVENTISTS, the CHRISTADELPHIANS, the JEHOVAH'S WITNESSES, and the PLYMOUTH BRETHREN.

Miller, Arthur A leading American playwright, Arthur Miller, b. New York City, Oct. 17, 1915, has made a reputation for dealing with contemporary political and moral issues. In 1937, during Miller's senior year at the University of Michigan, one of his plays was presented in Detroit by the Federal Theatre Project. In 1944 *The Man Who Had All the Luck* won a New York City Theatre Guild prize. With his first successes—*All My Sons* (1947; film, 1948), winner of the Drama Critics Circle Award, and *Death of a Salesman* (1949; film, 1952), winner of both the Drama Critics Circle Award and the Pulitzer Prize— Miller condemned the American ideal of prosperity on the grounds that few can pursue it without making dangerous moral compromises.

The keen social conscience evident in these plays has continued to manifest itself in Miller's writing. In the Tony Award-winning *The Crucible* (1953), for instance, he wrote of the witch-hunts in colonial Salem, Mass., and implied a parallel to the congressional investigations into subversion then in progress. The probing psychological tragedy *A View from the Bridge* (1955) questions the reasonableness of U.S. immigration laws. *After the Fall* (1964), which includes a thinly disguised portrayal of Miller's unhappy marriage to film actress Marilyn Monroe, offers a second, candid consideration of the congressional investigations in which Miller had been personally involved. Two one-act plays, *Incident at Vichy* (1964) and *The Price* (1968), deal with the universality of human responsibility and the guilt that often accompanies survival and success. Miller's later dramatic works include *The Creation of the World and Other Business* (1972), a play that seemed too openly didactic

Arthur Miller, the American dramatist, finds heroic tragedy in the ordinary person. In Death of a Salesman *(1949) and other plays, Miller reveals insight into and compassion for the individual struggling to ascertain an identity.*

for both critics and audiences.

Miller's writings outside the theater have been prolific and varied. His novel *Focus* (1945) is an ironic tale of anti-Semitism. The screenplay for *The Misfits* (1961) is only one of several he has written. In 1969 he wrote *In Russia*, a travel piece with illustrations by his wife, the photographer Inge Morath. *Chinese Encounters* (1979) is another traveler's tale, while *Salesman in Beijing* (1984) is an account of the production of his play in Chinese. *The Theater Essays of Arthur Miller* were collected in 1978. In 1987, Miller published *Timebends: A Life*, his autobiography.

Miller, Glenn   The trombonist and bandleader Glenn Miller, b. Clarinda, Iowa, Mar. 1, 1904, was a popular swing musician during the late 1930s and early '40s. Miller's band, organized in 1938, specialized in immaculate ensemble work, lush arrangements that featured velvety reeds, and a "sweet" rather than "hot" approach to swing. Miller entered the armed forces in 1942, directing a service band that played his arrangements for troops throughout the world. On Dec. 16, 1944, his plane was lost en route from England to France.

Miller, Henry   The American writer Henry Miller, b. New York City, Dec. 26, 1891, d. Jan. 7, 1980, achieved both notoriety and a lasting international reputation with his early novels, *Tropic of Cancer* (1934) and *Tropic of Capricorn* (1939), which shocked genteel taste by their graphic presentation of sexuality and frank, often obscene, language. Banned from the United States until 1961, these books became the center of the fight against censorship and in their final triumph vindicated their author's revolutionary honesty.

After years of struggle Miller freed himself from what he regarded as the puritanical restrictiveness of his Germanic background to become a writer of fiction. In 1930, encouraged and partly supported by his second wife, June Edith Smith, he took up residence in Paris. There he wrote the novels and short stories that would later make him famous and that won the recognition of T. S. Eliot and Anaïs Nin.

A visit to Greece in 1939 provided him with the material and inspiration for *The Colossus of Maroussi* (1941), a lyric celebration of the Greek spirit that many critics regard as Miller's finest book. After returning (1940) to the United States at the outbreak of World War II he began to write such philosophical, meditative essays as *The Air-Conditioned Nightmare* (1945) and became associated with a community of writers living in Big Sur, Calif. There he wrote the trilogy *The Rosy Crucifixion,* comprising *Sexus* (1949), *Plexus* (1953), and *Nexus* (1960), and also cast his influence over the writers of the BEAT GENERATION.

The American writer Henry Miller introduced an earthy sexuality into modern fiction. Acclaimed as a satirist but denounced as a pornographer, Miller was one of the most applauded and censored of modern novelists.

Miller, Jonathan   The English physician Jonathan Wolfe Miller, b. July 21, 1934, is better known as a comic, a writer, and a director of plays and operas. Miller had acted in student revues at Cambridge and was a practicing neurologist when he collaborated with Peter Cook, Alan Bennett, and Dudley Moore in their celebrated satirical comedy revue *Beyond the Fringe* (1959). For BBC television he produced a controversial version (1966) of *Alice in Wonderland* and the documentary series "The Body in Question" (1987), among many other memorable programs. He has written *The Body in Question* (1978), from his TV series; *Darwin for Beginners* (with coauthor Borin Van Loon, 1982); *States of Mind: Conversations with Psychological Investigators* (1983); and *The Human Body* (1983) and *The Facts of Life* (1984)—both elegantly written, sophisticated pop-up picture books.

Miller, Samuel Freeman   The American jurist Samuel Freeman Miller, b. Richmond, Ky., Apr. 5, 1816, d. Oct. 13, 1890, practiced medicine before becoming a lawyer and eventually serving as an associate justice of the U.S. Supreme Court. Miller, mildly abolitionist, moved (1850) from Kentucky to Iowa, where he became active in the Republican party. In 1862, President Abraham Lincoln appointed him to the Supreme Court, on which he served for 28 years. Miller wrote the majority opinions in *Ex parte*

Yarbrough (1884), which upheld black voting rights, and in the Slaughterhouse Cases (1873).

Miller, William   Originally a Baptist convert, William Miller, b. Pittsfield, Mass., Feb. 15, 1782, d. Dec. 20, 1849, became convinced from his reading of the Bible that the SECOND COMING OF CHRIST would occur sometime around 1843. Thousands, converted by his teaching after 1831, began to prepare for Christ's return. As 1843 passed without incident, Miller specified first Mar. 21, 1844, and later Oct. 22, 1844, as dates for the event. The failure of these predictions was a serious setback to the movement, but Miller and some devoted followers continued to preach the imminent return of Christ. Seventh-Day Adventism (see ADVENTISTS) grew out of the millennial excitement caused by the Millerites.

Millerand, Alexandre [meel-rahn', ahl-ek-sahnd']   Alexandre Millerand, b. Feb. 10, 1859, d. Apr. 7, 1943, a French Socialist minister (1899–1902) in René WALDECK-ROUSSEAU's cabinet, later moved to the Right politically and served (1920–24) as president of the French Third Republic. He was the first French Socialist to hold government office. As minister of commerce, Millerand was criticized by other Socialists for his participation in a non-Socialist government. He left the Socialist party after 1905 and served in various offices before he became president.

Milles, Carl [mil'-is]   The Swedish-American sculptor Carl Emil Wilhelm Anderson, known as Carl Milles, was born in Lagga, Sweden, on June 23, 1875, and died on Sept. 19, 1955. His early works show the influence of the impressionistic style of Auguste Rodin, but his mature style became more severe and angular, as shown in his stone monument to Sten Sture in Uppsala (completed 1925). Of his many monuments in Sweden, the *Poseidon* fountain (1927; Göteborg) and *Orpheus* fountain (1936; Stockholm) are perhaps the most renowned. After emigrating (1931) to the United States, Milles taught at the Cranbrook Academy in Cranbrook, Mich., and executed such well-known and highly praised works as the *Peace* monument (1936; Saint Paul, Minn.) and the *Meeting of the Waters* fountain (1940; St. Louis, Mo.). The entire range of his art is represented in the Millesgården, a public park in Stockholm.

millet   Millet includes several members of the grass family, Graminae, such as bread millet, or broomcorn, *Panicum miliaceum*; pearl millet, *Pennisetum americanum*; and foxtail millet, *Setaria italica*. It is grown as a major food grain in Africa, Asia, and the USSR. Millet seeds grow on long spikes, or panicles, at the ends of stalks that range in height from 0.3 to 3 m (1 to 10 ft). The strongly flavored grain is ground and eaten as porridge or in flat breads. Because millet will grow in rela-

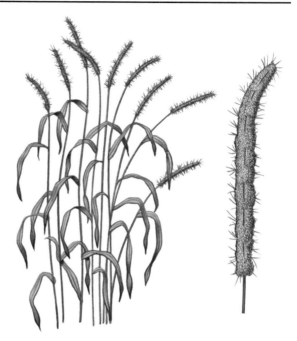

Foxtail millet, a species of millet that has been cultivated for centuries, is primarily used as poultry and livestock feed.

tively infertile soil, has a high tolerance to drought, and matures in only 6 to 12 weeks, it is widely cultivated as a food crop in less developed agricultural regions.

Millet, Jean François [mee-lay', zhawn frahn-swah']   Jean François Millet, b. Oct. 4, 1814, d. Jan. 20, 1875, was a French painter noted for his depictions of peasant life. Millet was the son of a Normandy farmer. In 1837 he received a scholarship to study in Paris,

The French painter Jean François Millet's The Gleaners *(1857) expressed the dignity and nobility of the peasant's toil with powerful realism and somber color. (Louvre, Paris.)*

where he became a pupil in the studio of Paul Delaroche. Despite his dislike of urban life, Millet remained in Paris until 1849, when he moved to the small village of Barbizon in the forest of Fontainebleau.

Flemish artists of the 17th century had depicted peasants at work, but Millet was the first painter to endow rural life with a dignity and monumentality that transcend realism and make the peasant an almost heroic figure. His subject matter frequently brought upon him the charge of socialism, and only after his death was he regarded as an original and important painter.

Many of his most popular and striking works, which include *The Winnower* (1848) and *The Angelus* (1857–59), now hang in the Louvre, Paris.

Millett, Kate [mil'-et]   An influential American feminist, Kate Millett, b. Saint Paul, Minn., Sept. 14, 1934, came to national prominence with the publication of her first book, *Sexual Politics* (1970). A formidable study of patriarchal institutions that argues that nearly all relations between men and women are determined by the male establishment's need to preserve its power over women, the book in its original form served as Millett's doctoral dissertation at Columbia. Active in the women's movement since 1966, Millett has also published a memoir, *Flying* (1974), which deals with the emotional traumas of celebrity and bisexuality, as well as two novels, the autobiographical *Sita* (1977) and *The Basement: Meditations on a Human Sacrifice* (1979).

Millikan's oil-drop experiment   The famous oil-drop experiment of the American physicist Robert Millikan (1868–1953) not only provided physicists with the first reliable determination of *e*, the electric charge on an electron, but also provided convincing evidence that electric charge comes in fundamental, natural units—the charge of a single electron. Millikan's experiments, started in 1906, used the straightforward method of measuring the force exerted by an electric field on a minute oil droplet that was electrically charged. Oil was used instead of water to avoid errors due to evaporation.

Millikan performed the experiment numerous times and included variations in which he radiated the apparatus with X rays while a drop was being observed, so that its charge could be increased or decreased almost at will. He found that the charge on a drop is never less than a certain minimum value and always an integral multiple of this value. He concluded that all electrons bear this same amount of charge, which he calculated as 4.770×10^{-10} electrostatic units (esu), very close to the modern value. For this work, as well as for his work on the PHOTOELECTRIC EFFECT, Millikan received the Nobel Prize for physics in 1923.

See also: ATOMIC CONSTANTS.

millipede   Millipedes, class Diplopoda, are elongate arthropods with many body segments and two pairs of legs on most segments. They are circular in cross section

Millipedes, or thousand leggers, differ from centipedes in having two (not one) pairs of legs per segment.

and have short antennae. Millipedes usually live in damp places in temperate and tropical regions and feed mainly on decaying plant material. They are slow-moving and harmless to humans, but for protection some give off an ill-smelling and sometimes irritating fluid. Most species are a few centimeters in length, but some tropical millipedes grow to be 30 cm (1 ft) long.

Mills, C. Wright   Charles Wright Mills, b. Waco, Tex., Aug. 28, 1916, d. Mar. 20, 1962, was a U.S. Marxian sociologist who is best known for his book *The Power Elite* (1956). Basing his theories on Karl Marx and Max Weber, Mills asserted that arbitrary, self-interested power in U.S. society was held by a ruling capitalist and military group, also called the MILITARY-INDUSTRIAL COMPLEX. A professor at Columbia University (1945–62), Mills was concerned that social scientists take an active, responsible role in society.

Mills, Robert   Robert Mills, b. Charleston, S.C., Aug. 12, 1781, d. Mar. 3, 1855, proclaimed himself to be the first native-born American architect trained for the profession. He made his reputation primarily by designing churches and major public buildings executed in the Greek Revival style. Mills's principal innovation in architecture was the auditorium church, a structure designed to accommodate the country's appetite for religious oratory. The most famous of these are the Circular Church (1804–06) in Charleston; the Sansom Street Baptist Church (1808) in Philadelphia, a round structure seating 4,000 people; the octagonal Unitarian Church (1811–13) in Philadelphia; and the Egyptian Revival Monumental Church (1812) in Richmond, Va.

A spokesman for indigenous American architecture, Mills achieved national prominence after being appointed (1836) architect and engineer to the federal government, in which capacity he designed for Washington, D.C., the Treasury Building (1836–41), the Patent Office (1837–42)—splendidly refurbished to house the National Portrait Gallery and the National Collection of Fine Arts—and the Post Office (1839)—all executed in stately variations of Greek Revival. His most notable work for the government was the Washington Monument, which he designed (1838) in the form of an Egyptian obelisk more than 168 m (550 ft) tall. The actual construction of the monument began in 1848 and was not completed until 1884, almost 30 years after the architect's death.

Mills, Wilbur D.   Wilbur Daigh Mills, b. Kensett, Ark., May 24, 1909, d. May 2, 1992, served as Democratic representative from the Second District of Arkansas between 1939 and 1977. From 1958 he chaired the highly influential House Ways and Means Committee, where he was admired by his colleagues for his conscientiousness and encyclopedic knowledge of pending legislation. Because of his scandalous, public involvment with a striptease dancer and his admitted alcoholism, he did not seek reelection in 1976.

Mills College   Established in 1852, Mills College in Oakland, Calif., is a private liberal arts college for women. The graduate program, leading to a master's degree, is coeducational.

Mills Cross   SEE RADIO ASTRONOMY

Milne, A. A. [miln]   The English author Alan Alexander Milne, b. Jan. 18, 1882, d. Jan. 31, 1956, is known primarily for his children's books, widely regarded as among the most delightful of all time. His major works are two books of verse, *When We Were Very Young* (1924) and *Now We Are Six* (1927), and the stories about Christopher Robin (in real life Milne's son, Christopher) and his toys—WINNIE-THE-POOH (1926) and *The House at Pooh Corner* (1928). The stories give life to the toys—Pooh Bear, Piglet, Tigger, Owl, Rabbit, Eeyore the Donkey, Kanga, and Roo—each with a distinct personality. Ernest Shepard's pen-and-ink drawings, including a map of Christopher Robin's world, form an integral part of the book. Milne, a frequent contributor to *Punch* magazine, also wrote essays; comic dramas, such as *Mr. Pim Passes By* (1920); and a detective novel, *The Red House Mystery* (1921).

A. A. Milne, creator of such classic children's books as Winnie-the-Pooh *(1926) and* The House at Pooh Corner *(1928), appears in this pen-and-ink drawing by P. Evans.*

Milner, Alfred Milner, Viscount [mil'-nur]   Alfred Milner, b. Mar. 23, 1854, d. May 13, 1925, was a British colonial governor best known for his role in the events surrounding the SOUTH AFRICAN WAR. In 1897 he was appointed British high commissioner for South Africa. His rigid stance in bargaining with President Paul

KRUGER of the Boer republics helped lead to the outbreak of the South African, or Boer, War (1899–1902). Milner stayed on in South Africa until 1905 to guide the economic and political reconstruction of the Transvaal and the Orange Free State. During World War I he was made (1916) a member of the British war cabinet; especially as secretary of war (1918), he played a prominent part in the direction of the British war effort.

Milnes, Sherrill [milnz]   The baritone Sherrill Milnes, b. Downers Grove, Ill., Jan. 10, 1935, studied with Rosa Ponselle and Boris Goldovsky, joined the New York City Opera in 1964, and became one of the leading baritones of his generation. His performances of roles in Verdi's *La Traviata, Il Trovatore,* and *Don Carlos* have been highly praised. He made his Metropolitan Opera debut in 1965 as Valentin in Gounod's *Faust* and has been an important member of that company ever since.

Milo [my'-loh]   Milo, or Milon, was a Greek athlete who lived in the last part of the 6th century BC. He won many prizes as a wrestler at the Olympic and Pythian games and led the army of his native city, Croton, to victory over Sybaris c.510 BC. Many legends arose about his strength; he was said, for example, to have carried a 4-year-old heifer through a stadium and then to have killed it and eaten all of it in a single day. He himself was said to have been eaten by wolves while his hands were caught in the crack of a tree that he was trying to tear apart.

Miloš, Prince of Serbia [mil'-awsh]   Miloš Obrenović, b. Mar. 18 (N.S.), 1780, d. Sept. 26 (N.S.), 1860, was an illiterate peasant who became prince of Serbia and founded the Obrenović dynasty. A leader of the first Serbian insurrection (1804–13) against the OTTOMAN EMPIRE, he quarreled with another leader, Karageorge Petrović, the founder of the Karadjordjević dynasty, who was proclaimed (1808) hereditary chief. In 1815, Miloš began a second, more successful revolt. Turkey recognized Miloš as "supreme prince and ruler of the Serbian nation," and in 1817, Miloš had Karageorge assassinated, which started a long feud between their dynasties. Miloš abdicated (1839) in favor of his son Milan and then a younger son, Michael, but in 1842, Alexander Karadjordjević became prince. Miloš was recalled to the throne in 1858.

Miłosz, Czesław [mee'-wawsh, ches'-wahv]   The Polish poet and novelist Czesław Miłosz, b. Vilnius, Lithuania, June 30, 1911, spent World War II in Warsaw, where he was active in the resistance. He served as a diplomat in the postwar Polish government but sought political asylum in Paris in 1951 and emigrated to the United States in 1960. In his social history, *The Captive Mind* (1952; Eng. trans., 1953), he described Communist repression of cultural life; the novel *Seizure of Power*

(1955) is about the resistance. Miłosz has translated English poets' works into Polish, and his many publications in English include a history of Polish literature (1969); a volume of poems, *Bells in Winter* (1978); and an autobiographical novel, *The Issa Valley* (1955; Eng. trans., 1981). Miłosz won the Nobel Prize for literature in 1980.

Milstein, Nathan [mil'-styn] The Russian-born American violinist Nathan Milstein, b. Odessa, Dec. 31 (N.S.), 1904, studied at the Odessa Music School and the conservatory in Saint Petersburg, where he was a pupil of Leopold Auer. Early in his career he gave concerts with the pianist Vladimir Horowitz. At the age of 21, Milstein went to Paris, where he built his reputation. He made his debut in the United States with the Philadelphia Orchestra in 1929 and has since become known particularly for his sensitive renditions of classical violin concertos.

Miltiades [mil-ty'-uh-deez] The Athenian general Miltiades, *c.*554–*c.*489 BC, was the victor in the Battle of Marathon. Born into a noble Athenian family, the Cimonids, he inherited a tyranny in the Chersonese (the Gallipoli Peninsula) shortly after 524. As a Persian vassal he was obliged to accompany Darius I to Scythia about 513; later he joined in the Ionian revolt (499–494). He then fled (493) from the Persians to Athens, where he was acquitted of tyranny and elected one of the ten Athenian generals for 490. He persuaded the Athenians to oppose the Persians at Marathon and initiated the battle. In 489 he attempted to conquer the island of Paros. Prosecuted because of his failure, he was fined and imprisoned; shortly thereafter he died of a wound sustained during the expedition.

Milton, John The English poet John Milton is one of the major figures of Western literature. His Christian epic PARADISE LOST ensures his stature as the finest nondramatic poet of the Renaissance, the worthy successor to Homer, Vergil, Dante, and Tasso.

John Milton was born on Dec. 9, 1608, into a prosperous London family in which his gifts were recognized and encouraged. His father, a proficient musician, provided private tutors and sent him to Saint Paul's School, so that even before he matriculated (1625) at Cambridge, Milton was proficient in Latin, Greek, and Hebrew. After receiving an M.A. in 1632 he retired to his father's country home near Windsor to study independently until, in 1638, he made a yearlong journey through France, Switzerland, and Italy.

When he returned to London, Milton began tutoring schoolboys, and in 1642 or 1643 he married 17-year-old Mary Powell. His published works already included a brief tribute to Shakespeare, printed in the second folio edition (1632) of the playwright's works; the masque *Comus*, performed in 1634; and "Lycidas" (1638), a pastoral elegy on the death of a fellow student, Edward King. Within

John Milton, a 17th-century English scholar and classical poet, is best known for his epic poem Paradise Lost *(1667), which recounts humanity's fall from divine grace.*

the conventions of the classical pastoral (see PASTORAL LITERATURE), Milton uses the young man's fate as an occasion to meditate on the uncertainty of life, his own purpose, and the failings of the clergy.

In 1641, Milton became embroiled in political and religious controversy by writing the antiprelatical tract *Of Reformation Touching Church-Discipline in England*, the first of his many polemical pamphlets. He also published—soon after his young wife left him—a series of tracts arguing for the legality of divorce, including *The Doctrine and Discipline of Divorce* (1643). Together with *Areopagitica*, an eloquent oration advocating freedom of the press from government censorship, these controversial writings won him public recognition and notoriety as a spokesperson for liberty and an opponent of monarchic government.

During the English Civil War he published *Poems of Mr. John Milton* (1645). The volume was largely ignored, although it contained "On the Morning of Christ's Nativity," an ode written when Milton was 21, and the charming companion poems "L'Allegro" and "Il Penseroso." Some of the poems in the volume are youthful exercises, but the collection as a whole demonstrates Milton's assimilation of English and classical literary traditions as well as his thorough preparation for the vocation of poet. As early as 1628, in a student exercise, Milton had avowed his intention to compose an epic poem in English, but contemporary events required that he temporarily forgo it.

During the trial of Charles I, Milton wrote *Of the Tenure of Kings and Magistrates* (1649), arguing that monarchs can rule only with their subjects' consent. He then became secretary to the Council of State under Oliver Cromwell and was entrusted with writing in Latin a defense of the execution of the king, *Eikonoklastes* (The Image Breakers, 1649), the last major project on which he labored with the remnant of his failing eyesight. In 1652 he became completely blind and was tempted, as he confessed in the moving sonnet "When I consider how my light is spent," to despair of ever accomplishing his life's work. The consolation that he found in his marriage (1656) to Katherine Woodcock gave way to new grief when she died in childbirth in 1658. With the help of a series of amanuenses he continued in his post until the restoration of the monarchy (1660), when he was imprisoned and fined and then allowed to retire.

With the Restoration the cause for which Milton had labored was defeated, but his last poems manifest a remarkable rebirth of creative energy after profound personal disappointment and testify to his indomitable will. Having retired from public life, Milton married (1663) his third wife, his former nurse Elizabeth Minshull, and lived with her and with the daughters that Mary Powell had borne after their reconciliation. He enlisted the girls in the work of reading and transcribing. Abandoning his long-standing plans for a patriotic epic on King Arthur, he took up the subject of Satan's rebellion, "man's first disobedience" of God, and the banishment of Adam and Eve from paradise. *Paradise Lost* appeared in 1667. It was followed four years later by *Paradise Regained*, a "brief epic" in a more austere style that dramatizes the Son of God's resistance to the temptations of worldly power, an act of heroism that surpasses that of Achilles and Odysseus, the heroes of classical epic. With *Paradise Lost*, this work holds out the possibility of recovering a "paradise within." In his last work published in his lifetime, *Samson Agonistes*, Milton recast a biblical folktale into classical tragic form, bestowing on the figure of Samson a moral stature that dignifies his violent revenge on the Philistines. During his final years Milton listened to his relatives and friends reading and continued to take pleasure in music. He died, probably of complications arising from gout, on Nov. 8, 1674.

Milwaukee

Milwaukee [mil-waw'-kee]   Milwaukee, seat of Milwaukee County and the largest city and industrial center in Wisconsin, is located on the shore of Lake Michigan, approximately 130 km (80 mi) north of Chicago. The city has a population of 628,088 (1990); that of its metropolitan area is 1,432,149. Milwaukee is located along a natural harbor formed by the Milwaukee, Menominee, and Kinnickinnic rivers as they enter Lake Michigan.

Milwaukee's economy is based on heavy industry and the manufacture of durable goods. Milwaukee is the country's leading manufacturer of diesel engines; power-generating equipment, mining machinery, agricultural equipment, auto parts, outboard motors, and motorcycles are also important products. Three of the four largest brewers in the nation—Miller, Pabst, and Schlitz—are headquartered in Milwaukee, resulting in the nickname Beer Capital. The city has a very active grain market. The Milwaukee area is served by extensive transportation facilities. The Port of Milwaukee, now part of the St. Lawrence Seaway system, has undergone considerable expansion since the seaway was opened (1959). Exports include grain, processed food, machinery, and equipment.

Milwaukee is the home of the Milwaukee Symphony Orchestra, the Milwaukee Repertory Theatre, and the Florentine Opera Chorus, all housed in the Performing Arts Center. Local fans support Milwaukee's professional baseball and basketball teams.

Five major educational institutions are headquartered in Milwaukee, including the University of Wisconsin—Milwaukee and Marquette University. The domed Mitchell Park Horticultural Conservatory, the Annunciation Greek Orthodox Church designed by Frank Lloyd Wright, and the War Memorial Center of Eero Saarinen are sources of pride to residents.

Milwaukee was settled in 1818 by Solomon Juneau, a French fur trader. The city's first inhabitants came from the eastern United States, but after 1840, European immigrants formed the largest group of settlers. Civil War needs accelerated the industrial development of Milwaukee. Its mayor-council government is unusual in that it has been led by socialists three times in this century.

mime and pantomime

mime and pantomime   Mime and pantomime, popular theatrical forms since antiquity, are dramatic performances in which a story is told or a theme developed through expressive bodily or facial movement. The comic and satiric mimes of ancient Greece and Rome were popular performers whose bawdy masked presentations, alternating buffoonery with sentimentality, were accompanied by a chorus, musicians, and the speech of the mime actor himself. Although outlawed with the rise of Christianity, the tradition nevertheless survived in part among the court jesters and wandering minstrels of the Middle Ages and was drawn upon in the MASQUES and court ballets that developed in Europe in the 16th century. The COMMEDIA DELL'ARTE, the Italian masked comedy of the 16th–18th centuries, which improvised with stock characters in standard situations, can be traced back to the wandering minstrels.

In France the Harlequin character from the *commedia dell'arte* became the white-faced figure Pierrot, played in the 19th century by the pantomime performer Jean Gaspard Deburau. Through his successors, Deburau's influence can be seen in the characters developed by Marcel MARCEAU, Charlie CHAPLIN, and Buster KEATON.

As distinct from *pantomime*, the term *mime* has come

The contemporary French actor Marcel Marceau brought new life to the tradition of mime with his creation of Bip, a stock character who appears as a white-faced clown. In mime and pantomime, a dramatic theme is developed silently through movement, gestures, and facial expressions.

to mean the 20th-century development of the art by Éti-enne Decroux, called the "father of modern mime," and Jacques Lecoq. Decroux's students include Marceau and the actor Jean Louis Barrault. *Pantomime* refers more specifically to the white-faced and illusionistic style derived from 19th-century sources.

mimeograph   The mimeograph, also called a stencil duplicator, is a device for producing copies from a prepared image surface or carrier. The image is produced on a special waxed paper called a stencil by removing the wax. The stencil is fastened to a porous drum, and as the drum is rotated the ink penetrates the areas of the stencil from which the wax has been removed, and is transferred to a sheet of paper. Early mimeograph machines were used with manually produced images, but use of the TYPEWRITER improved the quality of text reproduction. The process has been almost completely replaced by electrostatic copiers and offset duplicators (see ELECTROSTATIC PRINTING).

mimicry   The word *mimicry* comes from the Greek *mimos*, "imitator." In its biological sense, mimicry is the detailed, superficial resemblance in color, pattern, and shape between two or more species that occur together, resulting from the fact that one or all of them thereby gain protection from predation. The definition of mimicry can also be broadly interpreted to include various behavioral adaptations. For example, certain species of fruit fly exhibit behavioral mimicry when confronted by one of their predators, the jumping spider. By flapping their patterned wings, the flies are sufficiently able to resemble the territorial display of another spider to discourage the predator.

Mimicry in general is considered part of the larger category called adaptive coloration (see COLORATION, BIOLOGICAL), which includes all organisms that blend with backgrounds in various ways. Two general types of mimicry are recognized: Batesian and Müllerian.

Batesian Mimicry

Mimicry was first explained by the English naturalist H. W. Bates in 1862 as a result of his observations of butterflies during 11 years of research in the Amazon Valley. His studies led him to believe that some species of insects are unpalatable to would-be predators and that other species gain protection by being mistaken for them. This relationship, now called Batesian mimicry, occurs when a relatively rare, palatable species has diverged in appearance from its relatives and has evolved to look like an abundant, unpalatable species that is rejected as food by predators. The inedible species is the model, and the one that looks like it is the mimic. Bates assumed the mimics were palatable to predators because he saw their nonmimetic relatives eaten in the wild by birds.

Batesian mimicry demonstrated Darwin's controversial theory of evolution by natural selection, which had appeared in print a few years earlier. Predators could be invoked as the selective agents that brought about the evolution of Batesian mimicry, by choosing as food variants

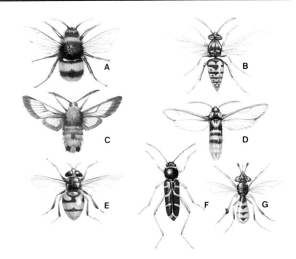

(Above) *The bumblebee* (A) *and wasp* (B), *both stinging insects, are mimicked by such harmless species as the bee hawkmoth* (C); *hornet clearwing moth* (D); *hoverfly* (E); *wasp beetle* (F); *and thick-headed fly* (G). (Below) *The unpalatable* Archonias bellona (H) *and palatable* Heliconius xanthocles (I), *both butterflies, and the palatable moth* Pericopis phyleis (J) *form a mimicry complex in tropical South Africa.*

(Below) *The nonpoisonous scarlet king snake* (K) *and the dangerously venomous coral snake* (L), *both of the southeastern United States, possess similar color patterns.*

of a mimic species that did not look sufficiently like the model to deceive them. The incipient mimics thus survived to reproduce more like themselves, whereas nonmimetic individuals died.

Examples of Batesian mimicry can be found among vertebrates such as birds and fishes, but the best-known instances occur among the insects. One such long-standing example, found in North America, is the monarch butterfly, *Danaus plexippus*, which is a tough, strong model that owes its noxious qualities to the presence of poisons it derives from its larval food plant, the milkweed. The toxins pass from the larva to the pupal and adult stages. Enough poison is contained in the abdomen of one monarch to cause emesis (vomiting) in a bird that has ingested it. The bird remembers this unpleasant experience and will reject other monarchs. The monarch serves as the model for the viceroy, *Limenitis archippus*, which has evolved a color pattern like that of its model. If a viceroy is offered to a bird that has recently ingested a monarch, the bird will reject it on sight alone. Offered to a naive bird, a viceroy will usually be acceptable food, indicating its inherent palatability. Research completed in Florida in 1991, however, may indicate that this classic example is not purely Batesian because not all viceroys are palatable. Therefore, the species-wide similarity between monarch and viceroy is most likely a combination of Batesian mimicry and another type, called Müllerian, discussed in the following section.

Müllerian Mimicry

A second kind of mimicry, also observed by Bates, was explained in 1879 by Fritz Müller, another entomologist working in Brazil. In this instance, mimetic resemblances occur between several species, all of which are unpalatable. The selective force of Müllerian mimicry, as it is called, is the reduction of mortality for members of each species involved in a shared mimetic color pattern. Each predator must learn what is edible and what is not. By pooling their numbers in a common appearance, the unpalatable species reduce their individual losses to naive predators, which must learn to reject only one color pattern for each Müllerian resemblance.

Müllerian mimicry is well demonstrated by the so-called tiger-striped complex of South American butterflies; several subfamilies, including the Heliconiinae, Danainae, and Ithomiinae, display a nearly identical pattern of orange, black, and yellow stripes that advertises to predators their shared unpalatability.

Evolution and Natural Selection

Like all adaptations, mimicry involves the inheritance of genetic traits, but mimicry operates under the particular influence of visual selection by predators. An initial understanding of the evolution of mimicry was provided by R. A. Fisher in 1958, and this understanding was expanded by the genetic studies of two other British researchers, C. A. Clarke and P. M. Sheppard, on the African mimetic butterfly *Papilio dardanus*. This mimetic species has numerous female forms, each of which re-

sembles a different model. The female forms are called morphs. Each morph is controlled by a so-called supergene, which in turn is regulated by modifier genes. The gene complex of each morph is adapted to its particular model. Two important findings from the research were that mimetic color patterns are controlled by the interaction of many genes, adapted over time to restrict variability and to increase mimicry, and that if a model becomes rare, mimicry begins to break down, with an increase in nonmimetic variants.

Although mimicry appears to break down in nature when a model becomes rare, experimental studies have shown that where a predator was supplied with adequate alternative food, a significant proportion of mimics (17 percent) escaped predation when the mimics outnumbered the models by as much as nine to one. This discovery means that the regulation of Batesian mimicry depends on several factors, including how noxious the model is and how hungry the predator is, as well as on the relative numbers of models and mimics.

Because of the deceptive nature of Batesian mimicry, it is to a predator's advantage to discriminate visually and to pick out a mimic; selection will therefore favor keen discrimination in a predator. In response to this trait, any genetic variation that improves mimetic resemblance and tends to drive a mimic toward more perfect resemblance to its model will also be favored by natural selection.

Mimir [mee'-mir]   In Norse mythology Mimir was a sea giant who guarded the well of wisdom, located beside the root of Yggdrasil that extended into Jötunnheim. He was called "the Wise" because he knew the past and the future. ODIN gave up one of his eyes to Mimir in order to drink from the well.

---

mimosa   Mimosa is the common name both for a number of trees and for a genus in the pea family, Leguminosae. The genus *Mimosa* comprises about 450 species mainly of herbs and small shrubs but also includes some trees and woody vines. These plants are native mostly to tropical America, with several species originating in Africa or Asia. Among the most interesting is the sensitive plant, *M. pudica,* a small spiny shrub of tropical America now found throughout the tropics of the world. Its stems grow to about 1 m (3 ft) long and bear divided leaves; the upper part of each leaf stalk (petiole) is usually divided into four branches (secondary petioles), each bearing up to 25 pairs of leaflets. At the bases of the paired leaflets, secondary petioles, and petiole are swollen joints called pulvini (singular, pulvinus). Touching or shaking the plant stimulates the pulvini, causing each pair of leaflets to close upward against one another, the secondary petioles to close against each other, and the main leaf stalk to drop about 60°. The plant remains in this position for a short time before slowly opening. It also assumes this closed position at night.

Mimosa is also the common name for certain other trees of the same family but in different genera. These include the Texas mimosa, *Desmanthus illinoensis*; several acacias, such as the Egyptian mimosa, *Acacia nilotica*; and an albizzia, *Albizzia julibrissin*. The last, also called the silk tree, is native to Asia but has been widely planted and naturalized in the milder parts of the United States.

Minamoto Yoritomo   see YORITOMO

---

minaret   A minaret, from the Arabic *manar* ("lighthouse"), is a tower, located near a MOSQUE, from which a Muslim crier (muezzin) calls the faithful of Islam to prayer five times a day. The ceremony of a call to prayer is as old as Islam itself and, in the Prophet Muhammad's time, took place from the roof of the Prophet's house in Medina. The earliest known mosques were generally without minarets, especially in cities with a predominantly Muslim population. By the beginning of the 8th century in Damascus, then a predominantly Christian city, the towers in the area of the old Roman temple (which had been converted into a mosque) were being used for the call to prayer. The minaret thus came to serve both a specific function for the Muslims and as a symbol to others of the presence of Muslims.

Most minarets in the Arab world are square and rather sober in appearance. An exception are the Cairo minarets, in which a variety of shapes are superimposed in each story. Iranian minarets are generally round and heavily decorated with brickwork or tiles.

See also: ISLAMIC ART AND ARCHITECTURE.

Mindanao [min-duh-nah'-oh]   Mindanao is the most southerly and second largest of the 11 main Philippine islands. It covers 94,631 km^2 (36,537 mi^2) and has a population of 10,986,000 (1989 est.). Its principal cities are DAVAO and Zamboanga. Mindanao is generally mountainous, and Mount Apo (2,954 m/9,690 ft) is the highest point in the Philippines. Relatively level regions include the broad, fertile valleys of the Mindanao and Agusan rivers.

Mindanao's economy is based on agriculture and exploitation of its rich natural resources. Crops include pineapples, corn, rice, abacá (used for rope making), coconuts, cotton, and coffee. Coal, nickel, iron, manganese, and copper are mined, and timber is a major export.

Southern Mindanao and Sulu (see SULU ARCHIPELAGO) have long been the traditional homeland of Filipino Muslims (Moro). The Moro resisted assimilation by conquerors, including Spain and the United States, for 300 years. In the 1960s and '70s rapid development and heavy immigration creating pressure on Moro land led to violent conflict in Mindanao.

Mindszenty, Jozsef [mind'-sent-ee, yoh'-zef]   The Hungarian cardinal Jozsef Mindszenty, b. Mar. 29, 1892,

d. May 6, 1975, became a symbol of political and religious resistance to communism in the 1950s and '60s. He was appointed bishop of Vszprém in 1944 and that same year was arrested by the Hungarian Nazis for protesting the persecution of the Jews.

As the highest-ranking Hungarian church official, Mindszenty became a target of the postwar Communist regime. In 1949 he was convicted of treason and sentenced to life imprisonment. Freed during the Hungarian Revolution of 1956, he took refuge in the U.S. embassy in Budapest. In 1971, Mindszenty left Hungary for Rome.

---

mine   A mine is an encased explosive charge fitted with a detonating device that is triggered by contact, by sound, by pressure, or by a magnetic field. Mines are used on land against personnel and vehicles—especially tracked vehicles such as tanks—and at sea against ships. Because of the relatively small possibility that any one mine may be triggered, mines are laid down in quantity to achieve a high density in the mouth of a harbor, for example, or over a land track that is likely to be used by an enemy. The process of discovering and removing land and naval mines is difficult and hazardous, and the accidental explosion of undetected mines has been a problem in post–World War II Europe and in Vietnam.

Naval Mines. Primitive naval mines were used, unsuccessfully, during the American Revolutionary War, when beer kegs filled with black powder were floated down the Delaware River against the British fleet (January 1778). Mines containing both explosives and a detonator were first used during the Crimean War. Until about 1870 the terms *mine* and *torpedo* were interchangeable.

Naval mines were widely used in World War I, when Germany mined the entrances to British and American ports and, in turn, the Allies mined the approaches to the North Sea and the harbors used by German submarines. World War II accelerated mine and minelaying technology: mines were laid by surface ships, through the torpedo tubes of submarines, and from aircraft.

The conventional direct-contact mine was gradually replaced by more sophisticated detonation systems: mines were triggered by the permanent magnetic field of a ship (magnetic mine), by the drop in water pressure that occurs when a ship passes nearby (pressure mine), and by the sound of a ship's propellers (acoustic mine).

Moored mines are attached to the ocean floor by an anchored cable and float just below the water's surface. Bottom mines are laid in shallow waters and are usually pressure mines designed to explode directly under a ship's hull. A controlled mine is connected by a cable to a control station on land and is triggered from the station. Such mines are used only in harbor defense.

Land Mines. Both antipersonnel and antitank mines were developed during World War II. Antitank mines are buried just below the ground surface and are triggered by the weight of a passing tank.

Antipersonnel and antitank land mines are buried beneath the ground and set off by the weight of people or vehicles passing on the ground surface. The U.S. antipersonnel bounding-type mine (A) is buried with the tips of the prongs (1) showing and the locking safety pin (2) set in a released position. Weight on the prongs releases the firing pin (3), which detonates the igniter (4). It, in turn, detonates the propelling charge (5) that fires the metal container (6) 2 m (4 ft) into the air, where it explodes, sending off deadly shrapnel. A modern conventional antipersonnel mine (B) is armed by the rotation of the safety clip (7) from the "safe" position (8) to the "armed" position (9). Pressure applied to the pressure plate (10) pushes the firing pin (11) onto the detonator (12), which explodes the charge (13). A heavy antitank mine (C) is armed by inserting the fuse (14) and rotating the arming plug (15). The pressure of a tank on the pressure plate (16) activates the fuse, which ignites the booster (17). This sets off the charge (18). Activation wells (19) contain auxiliary fuses to ensure an explosion.

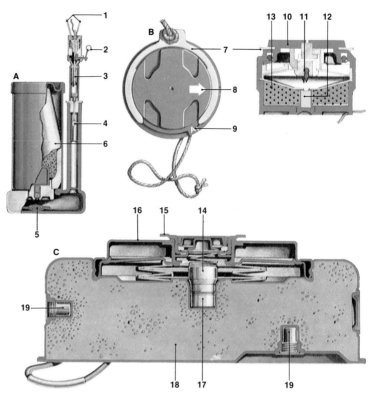

Antipersonnel mines are also triggered by weight. They may be a one-stage, simple blast type, or a two-stage fragmentation mine that first fires a container into the air and then releases a fragmenting explosive charge. Illuminating mines, when tripped, either burn in place or launch a flare that lights up a wide area.

mineral A mineral is a natural, homogeneous, inorganic solid with a crystalline atomic structure. Crystallinity implies that a mineral has a definite and limited range of composition, and that the composition is expressible as a chemical formula. Some substances that do not satisfy all these conditions, such as metallic liquid mercury, are commonly considered in the mineral realm but are more properly designated mineraloids. The word *mineral* may have different meanings in other sciences. In nutrition, it may mean any nonorganic element. In economics and economic geology, minerals may be practically anything of value extracted from the Earth, including petroleum and natural gas (which are neither inorganic nor solid).

Minerals comprise the vast majority of the material of the solid Earth. Aside from air, water, and organic matter, practically the only nonminerals in the Earth as a whole are molten rocks (magmas) and their solid glassy equivalents. Crystalline rocks themselves, and even soils for the most part, consist of aggregates of minerals. Almost all inorganic substances that are used by or of value to hu-

mans are derived from minerals. Over 3,000 minerals are currently known, and about 50 new ones are now discovered each year. Most GEMS are minerals, though some, such as opal, are mineraloids.

Mineralogy

Mineralogy is the study of the nature and origin of minerals. Although it is not one of the fundamental sciences, it was one of the first scientific fields to be developed, and curiosity about minerals led to many discoveries in physics and chemistry.

The science of crystallography, an offshoot of mineralogy, was founded by René Just HAÜY, who theorized in the late 18th and early 19th century that CRYSTALS are formed by stacking of identical structural blocks, now called unit cells, and showed that, as a consequence, the intercepts that the crystal faces make on a set of carefully chosen axes are always rational numbers when divided by an appropriate common factor. Next, the invention of the polarizing microscope and the use of thin sections made it possible to identify minerals by means of their optical properties. In the 20th century the discovery (1912) of X-ray diffraction made it possible to determine the internal atomic structures of crystals, while the invention of the electron microprobe helped standardize chemical analyses. The development of high-speed electronic computers has further facilitated determining the crystal structures of minerals.

Crystallography and Crystal Chemistry

Crystals consist of unit cells in the shape of parallelepipeds, stacked like bricks to form a homogeneous solid. The unit cell is not a physically separable entity, such as a molecule; it simply describes the repeat pattern of the structure. In fact, most minerals cannot be separated into molecules; the chemical bonds in the structure form a continuous network. The dimensions of unit cells are on the order of a few angstroms (10^{-8} cm), and the number of atoms contained in the volume of a unit cell is usually between two and a few hundred. The crystal lattice is the collection of unit-cell corners, and the crystal axes are usually considered to be parallel to the unit-cell edges. Crystals have varying amounts of symmetry, that is, repetition of the basic structural elements by symmetry operators such as rotation axes and mirror planes. All crystals may be assigned to one of 230 space groups, or possible combinations of symmetry elements in crystal lattices. In terms of the symmetry of the external faces and the physical properties, however, only 32 combinations, called crystal classes, are possible. These are further divided into six (or seven) crystal systems.

The objectives of mineralogical crystallography are to determine the crystal symmetry, the size and shape of the unit cell, and the arrangement of atoms within the unit cell of each mineral. This is now done almost entirely by X-ray diffraction.

Crystal chemistry is the study of the principles of the atomic structures of crystals. Different principles are applicable depending on the type of CHEMICAL BOND between the atoms of the mineral. Oxides and silicates have predominantly ionic bonding, with some admixture of covalent bonding; the important silicon-oxygen bond is considered to be about half ionic and half covalent.

Chemical Mineralogy

The compositions of minerals were formerly determined by so-called wet-chemical analysis, in which the mineral is dissolved, usually in an acid solution, and either its constituent elements are separately precipitated out and weighed, or else their concentrations in solution are determined by spectroscopic methods. For this type of analysis, a pure sample of the mineral must be separated from the rock in which it occurs; this separation may require the use of toxic heavy liquids.

A more versatile method is the electron microprobe, in which a beam of electrons is directed onto a polished surface of the mineral sample. This bombardment by electrons causes each element in the sample to emit X rays of characteristic wavelength. The intensity of each of these different X rays is then measured and compared with those given off by a standard material of known composition, under the same conditions of bombardment. If the standard is a natural mineral, it must have been analyzed previously by wet-chemical or some other method. The electron beam can be focused to a diameter of about 1 micrometer; thus, exceedingly small mineral grains, or different parts of the same grain, can be analyzed without separating them from the rock in which they occur.

The composition of most minerals varies within limits. This variation is known as isomorphous solid solution between two or more end members. The term *isomorphous* (see ISOMORPH) signifies that the end members have essentially the same crystal structure. For example, olivine is a solid solution between the end members forsterite (Mg_2SiO_4) and fayalite (Fe_2SiO_4); its general formula can be written $(Mg,Fe)SiO_4$. The elements Mg and Fe are said to substitute isomorphically for one another; they occupy the same position in the crystal lattice of the mineral. The composition of solid solutions can often be determined by measurement of physical properties, such as refractive index, density and unit-cell size, as well as by direct analysis. Because they are often dependent on the conditions of crystallization, particularly temperature, the compositions of minerals can be important in determining the geologic history of a rock.

Mineral Identification

The description of the physical properties of minerals is usually made with a view toward identification. There are three principal approaches to identifying minerals: hand specimen methods, optical methods, and X-ray diffraction.

Hand Specimen Methods. Essentially all minerals possess attributes that can be determined by sight or with simple tools. These attributes include color; LUSTER, the general appearance of the surface in reflected light, such as metallic, resinous, vitreous, or greasy; streak, the color of the powder when the mineral is rubbed on a white porcelain plate; habit, the general shape of the crystal or aggregates of crystals, such as acicular, tabular, or bladed; morphology, the external structure of mineral crystals, such as a cube, octahedron, or prism; twinning, the intergrowth of two or more crystals of the same mineral with certain regular geometric relationships; cleavage, the preferential breaking of a mineral on crystallographic planes of weakness; parting, the breakage along a plane of junction between closely related crystals, such as exsolution or twin planes; and fracture, the character of a broken, noncleavage surface, such as conchoidal (shell-like or curving), fibrous, or hackly. HARDNESS is usually measured comparatively, by means of a scale of ten minerals—the Mohs scale—ranging from talc (1, the softest) to diamond (10, the hardest).

Some properties, such as FLUORESCENCE, MAGNETISM, asterism, chatoyancy, and iridescence, are not present in all minerals but may aid identification in individual cases. Other physical properties, such as PIEZOELECTRICITY, heat conduction (see HEAT AND HEAT TRANSFER), electrical conductivity (see CONDUCTION, ELECTRIC), and MELTING POINT, have important applications in geological and geophysical research and in industry but are usually not useful for identifying minerals because they are difficult to measure.

Optical Methods. Every mineral has one or more characteristic refractive indices. The refractive index of a material is c/v, where c is the velocity of light in a vacuum and v is the velocity of light in the material (always less than c). If two transparent materials have greatly differing refractive indices, a beam of light is refracted as it passes through the interface, so that any irregularities on the

Among the more than 2,000 known minerals are: iron-stained hexagonal prisms of calcite (1), or calcium carbonate; rounded green masses of smithsonite (2), or zinc carbonate; yellow prismatic crystals of adamite (3), a complex arsenate of zinc; agate (4), made up of various colored bands of fine-grained quartz; labradorite (5), a feldspar from Labrador that exhibits a characteristic luster, or schiller; green, three-sided columnar crystals typical of tourmaline (6); and brass-yellow, striated cubes of pyrite (7), an iron sulfide.

mutual surface are accentuated by light and shadow, or brought into relief. Refractive indices can be measured accurately by the immersion method, in which small grains of a transparent mineral are observed under the microscope in liquids of various known refractive indices, until a match is obtained between liquid and mineral. This match is confirmed when the relief vanishes; that is, the mineral grains seem to disappear in the liquid.

The refractive index of minerals not belonging to the ISOMETRIC SYSTEM varies with the direction of oscillation of the incident light rays. This variation gives rise to more complicated phenomena, such as birefringence, interference colors, and interference figures, which may be observed with a polarizing petrographic microscope. These effects are also characteristic for each mineral. In the thin-section method, slices of rock 0.03 mm (0.0012 in)

thick are mounted on glass slides. Most common minerals can be identified rapidly from an estimate of the refractive index on the basis of the surface relief shown, the interference color, and other properties.

X-Ray Diffraction. The X-ray powder method is also a powerful tool for identification. The atoms in the crystal structure of the powdered sample diffract, or reflect, the incident X-ray beam, but only at certain angles, depending on the size and shape of the unit cell. The diffracted rays can be recorded on photographic film, or they can be measured with a radiation counter in a powder diffractometer. Each mineral produces a characteristic diffraction pattern when placed in an X-ray beam.

Naming and Classifying Minerals

The names of minerals may be derived from physical

Included above are: mixed crystals (8) of brown platelike siderite, an iron carbonate, and six-sided columns of quartz, a silicon oxide; blue and green masses of turquoise (9), an aluminum-and-copper-phosphate gemstone; yellow platelets of autunite (10) and green tabular crystals of torbernite (12), both phosphates of uranium; gray needlelike masses of stibnite (11), an antimony sulfide; purple hexagonal crystals of amethyst (13), a gem variety of quartz; and rounded yellow masses of prehnite (14), a calcium-aluminum silicate.

properties, often expressed in Latin or Greek; from chemical composition; or from the name of a person or locality.

Many classification schemes have been devised, but the one most prevalent, attributable to James Dwight DANA, is primarily a chemical classification based on the dominant anion or anion group. Classes are arranged in order of increasing complexity of the anion group. Within each class, minerals are often grouped according to structure type. This is especially important in SILICATE MINERALS, which are by far the most common minerals. Silicon is always bonded to, or coordinated by, four oxygen atoms. In some silicates, called nesosilicates, or island silicates, each oxygen is bonded to only one silicon, so that the silicate units are units of SiO_4^{4-}. In other groups, some or all of the oxygen atoms are bonded to two silicon atoms, so that the silicon and oxygen form larger units, or polymers (see POLYMERIZATION), which may take the form of "sisters" (sorosilicates), rings (cyclosilicates), chains (inosilicates), sheets (phyllosilicates), or continuous frameworks (tectosilicates). The group names are generally derived from Greek words describing the type of polymer, but some alternate, occasionally used names are derived from Jons Jakob BERZELIUS's older chemical classification based on fictitious silicic acids: for example, orthosilicates, from orthosilicic acid, H_4SiO_4.

Synthetic Mineralogy

An important part of mineralogy in the 20th century has been the synthesis of minerals in the laboratory, with the principal objective of learning the conditions of temperature and pressure and the nature of liquid or gaseous phases present during the formation of natural minerals.

Minerals are also synthesized to obtain pure specimens for determination of properties, to supply substitutes for scarce minerals of economic importance, and to manufacture gemstones.

Synthesis has traditionally been achieved using furnaces with tungsten- or platinum-wire heating elements, and large steel presses or hydraulic apparatus for attaining high pressure. The sample is taken to high pressure and temperature, held for a time until the reaction is complete, and then quenched and examined.

Extremely high pressures corresponding to those in the Earth's mantle have recently been attained with the diamond anvil, a compact apparatus in which the sample is placed between the faces of two diamond crystals and compressed with a thumbscrew. The device is small enough to fit on a microscope stage, and the sample can be observed through the transparent diamond faces. A laser beam can be projected through the microscope to heat the sample.

Mineral Occurrence

The core of the Earth consists of iron-nickel metal, as deduced from the presence of a magnetic field and from the overall density of the Earth. The upper mantle, as judged by fragments brought up in volcanic rocks, consists primarily of olivine and pyroxene. In the lower mantle, high pressures are thought to cause the breakdown of these complex silicates to simpler oxides, such as $(Mg,Fe)O$ and SiO_2. The oceanic crust is of basaltic composition, consisting primarily of pyroxene and plagioclase feldspar. The continental crust also has abundant plagioclase but in addition contains quartz, alkali feldspars, and other minerals.

Surface Mineral Environments. Minerals in IGNEOUS ROCKS crystallize from molten silicate liquids, or MAGMAS. BASALTS normally consist of plagioclase feldspar and pyroxene with subsidiary ilmenite and apatite. ZEOLITES often form from low-temperature alteration of basalts. GRANITES consist primarily of feldspar—both plagioclase and alkali feldspar (orthoclase and albite) and quartz—with subsidiary mica or amphibole, or both; zircon; minor iron oxides; and other minerals. PEGMATITES represent the last liquids to crystallize from granitic magmas and often contain large crystals of rare minerals. Alkalic igneous rocks, which have an abundance of sodium and potassium and a deficiency of silicon with respect to more-common rocks, are very rare but nevertheless furnish an abundance of mineral species.

METAMORPHIC ROCKS represent solid-state recrystallization of sedimentary or igneous rocks during deep burial in the crust. The most common minerals include quartz, feldspars, micas, amphiboles, epidote, garnet, and such aluminum silicates as andalusite, sillimanite, and kyanite. Metamorphosed siliceous carbonate rocks (MARBLE) provide an especially rich variety of minerals, most of which contain calcium and silicon.

Hydrothermal ORE DEPOSITS of minerals precipitate from hot aqueous solutions. The sulfide minerals, such as chalcopyrite, galena, molybdenite, pyrite, and sphalerite,

are found in this environment, although small amounts of pyrite may be found in any environment. Nonsulfide gangue minerals, such as barite, calcite, and fluorite, also occur here. On exposure to surface conditions, the sulfides are oxidized, resulting in the formation of metal sulfate minerals and oxides.

Minerals in SEDIMENTARY ROCKS and soils are of two types: detrital, grains remnant from weathered igneous or metamorphic rocks; and authigenic, grains that actually form in the sediment, normally as precipitates from low-temperature aqueous solutions. CLAY MINERALS are authigenic and are usually important constituents of soils, marine sediments, and sedimentary rocks, although detrital quartz and feldspar may often dominate. Some tropical soils, called LATERITES, are so deeply weathered that the only remaining minerals are the insoluble aluminum and/or iron oxides and hydroxides. These soils (bauxite) may be ores of aluminum. Halide minerals and the sulfates gypsum and anhydrite, as well as borate minerals, are found primarily in EVAPORITE deposits formed either from desert lakes or from receding seas. LIMESTONE consists of the mineral calcite, which has most often been precipitated by marine organisms, as evidenced by the presence of abundant fossils, which are themselves usually calcite or aragonite. The mineral dolomite also forms carbonate rocks, the precise origin of which is uncertain. Most economic concentrations of iron are sedimentary deposits consisting of the minerals hematite and magnetite. Other minerals of economic importance, such as gold, platinum, rutile, cassiterite, and ilmenite, are often concentrated in PLACER DEPOSITS.

Extraterrestrial Minerals. From the study of meteorites, many of which may be remnants of a hypothetical fifth inner planet, and the examination of the samples returned by lunar astronauts, the minerals of the Moon and Mercury, Venus, and Mars appear to be generally similar to those of the Earth. There are, however, differences. The principal minerals on the lunar surface are plagioclase feldspar and pyroxene, as on the Earth's surface, but the Moon appears to lack a metallic core and to be deficient in volatile materials such as alkalis and water, so that minerals containing these materials, such as micas, are absent.

See also: OCEANIC MINERAL RESOURCES.

mineral deposits   see ORE DEPOSITS

———

mineral oil   A product of the distillation of petroleum, mineral oil is a clear, colorless liquid, without odor or taste, that is used medicinally as a lubricant and laxative, as an oil base in cosmetics, and as an ingredient of paints and varnishes. It is also called liquid paraffin or liquid petrolatum. In a thicker, semisolid form mineral oil becomes petrolatum or petroleum jelly, used in ointments and dressings.

mineral resources, oceanic   see OCEANIC MINERAL RESOURCES

mineral water   Natural mineral water is spring water containing a higher than average percentage of mineral salts. It has long been believed to possess great curative powers, and well-known medicinal spas have been built around such mineral springs as Aix-les-Bains in France, Wiesbaden in Germany, Bath in England, and White Sulfur Springs, W.Va. At these spas visitors faithfully "take the waters" in the hope of relieving gout, liver trouble, indigestion, rheumatism, and many other ailments.

Mineral springs are generated deep underground, where, under intense heat and pressure, calcium, iron, potassium, sodium, and other minerals are leached from the surrounding rock. Natural mineral water can be either still or effervescent (impregnated with carbon dioxide gas), and it is often bottled and sold commercially.

miner's lung   see BLACK LUNG

Minerva   In Roman mythology Minerva was the goddess of wisdom, of arts and crafts, and of war. Originally, Minerva had been an important Etruscan deity of the dawn. She was the daughter of Pallas, a giant, whom she killed when he tried to rape her. After the Romans identified Minerva with the Greek goddess ATHENA, she was said to have sprung fully armed from the head of JUPITER.

Ming   (dynasty) The Ming dynasty, which ruled China from 1368 to 1644, was founded by a low-born Buddhist monk, Zhu Yuanzhang (1328–98), who led a peasant army to victory over the MONGOLS. Bracketed in history by alien dynasties—the YUAN of the Mongols and the QING of the Manchus—the Ming dynasty was purely Chinese, and its period of rule brought economic and social stability as well as cultural elaboration.

Hongwu (Zhu's reign title) became a cruel despot whose reliance on eunuchs and other attendants in the palace diminished the power of the civil bureaucracy and set a precedent for Ming absolutism. Beijing was rebuilt on a grand scale by the third Ming emperor, YONGLE (r. 1403–24). As part of his design for reasserting Chinese supremacy Yongle expanded overland trade with central Asia, established tributary relations with Japan and several Southeast Asian kingdoms, and sent the eunuch admiral ZHENG HE on maritime expeditions as far as the eastern coast of Africa.

Peace and economic expansion were accompanied by a flowering of intellectual and cultural life. Among those active in this period were the philosopher Wang Yangming; the painter and art theorist DONG QICHANG; the dramatist Tang Xiandu, who wrote *The Peony Pavilion*; and the Jesuit missionary Matteo RICCI. The painted porcelain of the Ming period is regarded as a high point in Chinese ceramics.

Ming power began to decline in the reign (1573–1620) of Wanli. By 1644 the empire was bankrupt, and the rebel leader LI ZICHENG took Beijing. The local Ming general called upon the Manchu tribes for help. The Manchus retook Beijing but would not relinquish control, ending the Ming dynasty.

Mingus, Charles   [ming'-guhs]   Charles Mingus, b. Nogales, Ariz., Apr. 22, 1922, d. Jan. 5, 1979, was a string bassist, pianist, and composer who had a considerable influence on modern jazz. Starting in the 1950s, his experiments with atonality and dissonance made him a leading figure among modern jazz composers, and his brilliant use of the bass elevated that instrument to solo status. Mingus's jazz workshops attracted a generation of younger musicians, including the singer and composer Joni Mitchell, with whom he collaborated in 1978. His autobiography, *Beneath the Underdog*, was published in 1971.

miniature painting   The term *miniature painting* was derived from work done in *minium*, a red lead pigment used most often in the lettering of early medieval manuscripts. By association, the term came to embrace manuscript illustration (see ILLUMINATED MANUSCRIPTS) and then to signify small-size separate portraits of the later medieval era.

The art of the miniature flourished in most of the world's civilizations; for information on non-European miniature painting, which lies outside the scope of this article, see the articles ISLAMIC ART AND ARCHITECTURE, INDIAN ART AND ARCHITECTURE, and PERSIAN ART AND ARCHITECTURE.

In the West the development of miniatures in illuminated manuscripts progressed greatly during the 15th century, when they were executed with as much care as panel paintings. Realism was taken to great lengths on the borders of some manuscripts, as in those by the Master of Mary of Burgundy and by the LIMBOURG BROTHERS, in which flowers, jewels, and feathers are painted so realistically that it almost seems possible to pick them up. Actual portraits now began to appear in manuscripts such as the *Bedford Book of Hours* (before 1422; British Muse-

Isaac Oliver, seen in a miniature self-portrait, was one of the foremost English miniaturists of the late 16th and early 17th centuries. In his precise yet naturalistic portraits Oliver extended the decorative traditions of medieval manuscript illumination. (National Portrait Gallery, London.)

Rembrandt Peale (1795), a miniature by the subject's uncle, James Peale, exemplifies the artist's delicate, linear style and subtle characterization. James Peale, the younger brother of the painter Charles W. Peale, was active in miniature portraiture during the last two decades of the 18th century. (Yale University Art Gallery, New Haven, Conn.)

um, London), in which portraits appear within initials, and in the *Chroniques de Hainaut* (mid-15th century; Bibliothèque Royale, Brussels), by the Flemish Master Girart de Roussillon, which contains a portrait of Philip the Good. From the execution of tiny portraits in manuscripts it was but a step to miniature portraits in separate lockets, and frames.

Underlining this relationship between miniatures and jewelry was the 16th-century miniaturists' practice of calling their colors by the names of gems: amethyst for purple, ruby for red, emerald for green, topaz for yellow. Early masters of these jeweled miniatures included Jean FOUQUET and Jean Clouet (see CLOUET family), two French artists who capitalized on the tradition of miniature art in the late-medieval Burgundian period.

At first, portrait miniatures, like illuminated manuscripts, were painted on vellum, then usually pasted on cards to give them strength and to prevent them from cockling (wrinkling). Such miniatures, executed in fine stippling with the minutest attention to detail, are best exemplified by the works of Hans HOLBEIN THE YOUNGER, Isaac Oliver, and Samuel Cooper in the 16th, early 17th, and late 17th centuries, respectively. From the end of the 17th century, ivory generally replaced vellum as a ground—an innovation sometimes attributed to the Venetian miniaturist Rosalba CARRIERA, who has also been credited with introducing a more painterly and free technique into miniatures. Beginning with Carriera the stippled technique was largely replaced by transparent washes, through which the translucence of the ivory was permitted to show.

Miniature painting ceased to have widespread appeal after the introduction of photography in the mid-19th century.

miniature pinscher   The miniature pinscher is a smaller version of the medium-sized German pinscher. The miniature pinscher, called a minpin by its breeders, originated in Germany perhaps as long ago as the late 1700s. Its naturally hanging ears are cropped to be erect and pointed, and its tail is docked short. Its short, glossy coat is usually a solid reddish brown or a black with reddish or tan markings. According to the American Kennel Club, which recognized the breed in 1929, ideal size is between 28 and 29 cm (11 and 11.5 in) high at the shoulder. Such dogs should weigh from 3.5 to 4.5 kg (8 to 10 lb).

minicomputer   see COMPUTER

minimal art   Minimal art, also known as primary structure and ABC art, is a diverse movement in sculpture that originated in New York City in the 1960s. The outstanding quality of all minimal art is its impersonality, which is a reaction against the expressive function and the emotional, spontaneous gestures of the MODERN ART of the 1950s. Works of minimal art are often constructed mechanically from the artist's plans in commonplace, industrial materials, such as plastic, steel, and concrete. Alexander CALDER used organic forms for primary structures, but such other sculptors in the movement as Anthony CARO and Tony SMITH concentrated on architectonic shapes—cubes, spheres, and beams. By avoiding subjective content and visual complexity, they emphasized the concrete, physical presence of their work and its relation to the surrounding space. These attributes of minimal art are exemplified by Robert MORRIS's *Untitled* (1967; Guggenheim Museum, New York City), a symmetrical arrangement of nine identical steel units placed on a floor.

The term *minimalist* has also been used to refer to the hard-edge painting of Ellsworth KELLY, Frank STELLA, and Kenneth NOLAND, whose work attempts to create anonymous forms devoid of aesthetic significance.

minimalism   (music)   The American musical movement called minimalism might be seen as a reaction to the complexity of modern music. Its basic principle is the repetition of a musical phrase with subtle, slowly shifting tonalities and a rhythmic structure (if there is one—some minimalist music is written without a beat) that remains the same for long periods. Electronic music allows minimalist composers to experiment with new sounds and new techniques for achieving repetition. Much of minimalist inspiration comes from the repetitive patterns of Asian music and the extended rhythms of African drum music. Among minimalism's major exponents are the composers La Monte Young (*Trio for Strings*, 1958), Terry Riley (*In C*, 1964), Steve REICH (*Drumming*, 1971), Philip GLASS (*Akhnaten*, an opera, 1984), and John Adams (the opera *Nixon in China*, 1987).

minimum wage   A minimum wage is a lower limit established by law for the wages employers may pay. In the United States the Fair Labor Standards Act (1938) set a minimum wage (25 cents per hour) for many workers engaged in interstate commerce. The law was intended to prevent competitive wage cutting by employers during the Depression. After the law was passed, however, wages began to rise as the economy turned to war production. Wages and prices continued to rise, and the original minimum wage ceased to be relevant. Accordingly, it was raised by Congress to 75 cents an hour in 1950 and after a series of additional increases reached $3.35 in 1981. Federal legislation passed in 1989 further increased the minimum hourly wage to $3.80 by April 1990 and to $4.25 by April 1991. The law's scope has been broadened to include millions of workers not originally covered. Small businesses—those with annual gross income of less than $500,000—are exempt.

The statutory minimum wage was first legislated in New Zealand in 1894. British trade boards fixed minimum wages in low-wage industries in 1910. In the United States, minimum-wage laws were first enacted by the state of Massachusetts in 1912.

---

mining and quarrying Mining is the working of pits or excavations from which minerals, such as coal, metals, and salt, are extracted from ORE DEPOSITS or large aggregations. Gems and fertilizers are also mined, as well as petroleum and natural gas. Increasingly, the ocean is being mined for other minerals.

Quarrying is the extraction of stone, either in blocks or as aggregate (sand and gravel), from open excavations.

This article discusses the history and present technologies associated with mining and quarrying in general. Descriptions of the special techniques used to mine a particular substance will be found in the article on that substance (for example, COAL AND COAL MINING; GOLD; PETROLEUM).

Since ancient times mining has had a fundamental political impact on society. Wars have been fought to acquire minerals. Colonization of many areas of the world was in part due to the need of Europe to acquire metals. Today, world politics and world trade are shaped in large measure by the locations of mineral and energy reserves.

Development of Mining Technology

Mining is one of the oldest human activities. Archaeologists in South Africa (one of the leading mineral producers in the world) have reported evidence that an iron mine there was worked 43,000 years ago. The earliest metals used by Neolithic peoples were probably gold and copper, for they occur "free" of other chemicals. Bronze, a mixture of copper and tin, was the first commonly used alloy, appearing about 3000 BC. Iron smelting began between 1900 and 1400 BC. (See BRONZE AGE; IRON AGE.)

Early mining was probably for the most part alluvial—that is, from free metals that had been washed out of gravel occurring on or near the surface. Underground mining was undertaken by 1300 BC in the Nubian desert. Underground mines in the Tyrol were worked from about 1600 to 400 BC. Both the Greeks and Romans carried on intensive mining activities, but after the fall of the Roman Empire, European mining experienced a decline from which it did not recover until the 11th century.

Medieval mining techniques had probably changed little from Roman practice, but when the first books on the subject appeared in the 16th century (notably, Agricola's *De re metallica*, 1556), they showed that basic mining operations—draining and ventilating the mines, carrying the ore to the surface, and crushing and washing it preparatory to working it—were all undergoing mechanization. Drainage was improved through the use of waterpower. The first useful STEAM ENGINE was developed (1699) to drain mines.

As coal mines grew deeper after 1750, the problems of draining water, ventilation, and getting the ore to the surface all increased. Improved steam engines solved the drainage problem. Ventilation was handled by auxiliary shafts for better circulation and by fires in the mines to draw in fresh air and expel the old heated air. Coal and other ores were removed from the face by picks and blasting. Ore was still transported through the mines by human (and sometimes animal) power during the mid-19th century.

There were few changes in metal mining techniques between 1750 and 1850, but from 1875 to 1900 the tonnage of the five leading nonferrous base metals (copper, lead, zinc, nickel, tin) rose from 268,000 to 1,955,000. Power drills for making shot holes for explosives were used in hard-rock mines after the 1860s.

After 1900, diesel locomotives were used to haul ores underground; the Leyner water drill (1907) reduced the dust caused by drilling; tungsten carbide-tipped drills during the 1930s increased efficiency at the work face.

Strip mining—that is, stripping away the shallow overlay to get at ore from the surface—has become widespread for coal and other ores as powerful machines have become available.

Prospecting

Since the 18th century increasingly more sophisticated scientific principles have been applied to prospecting. Most of the ore outcrops—telltale deposits on or near the Earth's surface—have already been discovered, and modern prospecting relies heavily on geological techniques that suggest the presence of underground ores.

A geological survey begins with mapping the area of exploration. On the basis of the maps, target areas are selected for evaluation. Test holes are drilled, and core samples are evaluated.

Geophysical testing techniques include seismic surveys, which test the elapsed time between the firing of an explosive charge in a surface feature and the detection of the resulting sound waves as they are reflected back from rock beds or other mineral deposits. Measurements are carried out on the ground or, very often, from specially equipped airplanes.

In 1972 the National Aeronautics and Space Administration (NASA) launched the satellite *Landsat 1*, which began a program of remote sensing of earth-resource data. With images covering up to 33,675 km^2 (13,000 mi^2), the more recent Landsat D series of satellites scans for several different wavelengths simultaneously.

Mining Methods

Ore deposits vary greatly in their physical characteristics.

Ore may be excavated by means of a series of horizontal, vertical, or inclined workings in veins and in more irregular ore deposits, or by openings, known as rooms, in flat deposits.

Stoping. The mining methods that can be applied to a given ore body, known as *stoping*, depend on the nature and size of the supports required to maintain the backs and the walls of an excavation, and on the requirements for permanently supporting the overlying and surrounding rocks and overburden to prevent movement and subsidence.

Some mines are naturally supported and need little extra aid. Artificially supported stopes use additional measures to support the mine opening, shafts, and working areas. In cut-and-fill stoping, the ore is excavated by working upward in vertical or steeply dipping veins. As the broken ore is removed, waste rock, sand, or some other filling material is run into the opening, leaving sufficient room so that further mining can be done. In narrow veins timber may be used for support. In square-set stopes, the walls and back of the working area are supported by regular framed timbers forming a skeleton enclosing a series of contiguous rectangular spaces and providing continu-

(Right) *Despite safety improvements provided by technology, underground coal mining remains a hard and sometimes hazardous and unhealthy occupation.*

(Below) *Coal is mined at the surface by auger drills that can bore as much as 33 m (100 ft) into a coal seam.*

ous support in all directions. The ore is excavated so as to provide just enough room for installing the next set of timbers. In block caving, a thick block of ore is partly cut off from surrounding blocks by a series of drifts (mine openings). The block is then undercut and caves in under its own weight.

The actual mining involves drilling, blasting, mucking (material removal), and the various operations on the surface necessary to remove the ore and to transport the miners. In recent years improvement in these processes has come largely through seeking greater energy efficiency, higher labor productivity, more continuous production methods, increased durability of equipment, and operating flexibility. Drilling shot holes and blasting the ore is still a standard process.

Continuous mining machines are found primarily in the working of coal where a single machine cuts, breaks, and loads the coal. Broken ore may be removed from the mine by railroad cars or by hoists pulled up the mine shaft.

Surface Mining. The two chief methods of surface mining are placer and open-pit, or strip, mining. Placer mining is used today primarily for gold or tin recovery out of stream beds. (PLACER DEPOSITS, by contrast, are underground mineral deposits—especially gold, diamonds, and titanium—originally formed by the action of water on rock.) Because the mined material is heavier than the debris surrounding it, washing stream-bed gravel will cause it to settle out of the water.

Open-pit methods are applied to ore deposits that are exposed or near ground surface. Overlying waste materials must be removed prior to mining the ore, an operation known as stripping. The mining site itself is basically a series of interconnected, slope-sided bench steps or mounds.

Open-pit mining follows the same sequence of operations as underground mining: drilling, blasting, and loading and removing of waste and ore. Notably missing are the support systems required in underground mining. Drilling is accomplished with drills similar to those used for oil-field work, although they are smaller in size. The holes range up to 0.3 m (1 ft) in diameter and are loaded with bulk explosives. After the blast the broken material is loaded onto rail cars, trucks, or conveyor systems. Truck and power-shovel combinations are usually used for clearing the rubble. Large shovels are capable of digging up to 47 m³ (60 yd³) per bite. Trucks with 120-ton capacity are common, but continuous-hauling techniques featuring conveyor systems used in conjunction with in-pit crushers are beginning to be used.

The destruction of large land areas that are often agriculturally productive, the vast amount of spoil, the enormous amounts of water often needed to process the ores, and increasing public environmental sensitivity make strip mining a continuing problem of public policy.

Quarrying

Quarrying is the method used to surface-mine such rock as marble, sandstone, granite, and limestone. When the rock is removed in blocks, it is called "dimension" stone, and

(Left) *Granite blocks are surface mined at this quarry near Concord, N.H. Such "dimension" stone quarries typically are steep sloped and have vertical-faced benches from which rock is removed nonexplosively.*

(Right) *Diamond mining, as with many other types, requires its own set of techniques. Diamonds are usually found in deep, narrow volcanic pipes. As seen in this aerial view, the pipe at this South African mine is exposed by a series of stepwise excavations.*

the quarries that are created by dimension cutting characteristically have steep faces transversed by stepped-down benches. Dimension stone is normally split off the face, rather than blasted, to preserve its shape and strength.

Aggregate quarry mining is done by blasting and produces a rubble, different sizes of which are useful for different purposes. The components of an aggregate plant would include a mechanism (perhaps conveyor belts) to bring the rubble to the "scalper," which screens it to remove waste, a crusher to reduce the rubble to a number of useful dimensions (fine, medium, and coarse sand, for example), screens to sort the several dimensions, a washer to clean the aggregate, and storage facilities for the finished product.

Water seepage, land restoration, and waste disposal create environmental problems for both types of quarries. Aggregate quarries also have dust, noise, and blasting vibration problems, as these works must be located near markets, typically large metropolitan areas.

Mining Worldwide

Although the United States is a net importer of minerals, it dominates the world's mineral production and produces more than 50% of the world total of industrially important mine products. Industrially useful minerals, especially the more exotic metals used in specialty steels and in fiber optics and electronics, now possess great strategic importance.

U.S. production of nonfuel minerals increased during the late 1980s, while the mining of metals—such as nickel, iron ore, and molybdenum—declined. Extraction of the minerals used in construction—aggregate, sand and gravel, gypsum, and crushed stone—increased, as did the mining of cement components.

All 50 states contribute to mining production; the leading states in the total amount of materials handled are Florida, Arizona, Minnesota, and Texas. Most extraction now takes place in surface mines.

Worldwide, hydraulic cement is the leading mineral commodity by weight. Others include iron ore, peat, and salt. Mineral production around the world is remarkably concentrated. Seventy percent of the world's supply of minerals is produced by fewer than 200 mines. Leading producers include Canada for silver, nickel, and zinc; the United States for lead and molybdenum; South Africa for platinum, vanadium, and gold; the USSR for chromium, tungsten, and manganese; Zaire for cobalt; and Turkey for boron.

Mine-safety issues continue to be a source of contention in the United States, as they are throughout the world. Critics of the Mine Safety and Health Administration (MSHA), which promulgates safety rules for U.S. mines, say that it must be more rigorous in its inspection standards and in its approval of the safety plans designed by mine owners. The toxic wastes produced by mining and smelting operations also present major safety problems.

ministry, Christian   Ministry means "service," which is an ideal for all Christians; the image of Christ as servant (Phil. 2:5–7; Mark 10:45) has been extended to the Christian church as a whole. From the beginning, however, certain individuals have been designated to perform spiritual functions within the church. Those ordained to these special ministries, which are usually full-time occupations, are now called ministers or PRIESTS. The Gospels agree that the first ministers received their commission directly from Jesus Christ, but their ministry was set within the context of the church. The APOSTLES went out from Jerusalem to preach, baptize, and establish churches.

As the church spread and became more institutionalized, local ministries emerged, presided over by prominent converts appointed by the apostles. The original offices were those of BISHOPS (overseers) and presbyters (elders), although to begin with these were not clearly distinguished. Presbyters came to be called priests. Ministers such as Stephen and his companions were also appointed to deal with administrative matters and leave the apostles free for preaching (Acts 6:1–6), although Stephen also preached. They have been taken as prototypes of deacons, although not actually called by this name.

During the 2d century the peripatetic ministries of apostles, evangelists, and prophets gradually died out and were replaced by a settled ministry situated in various towns and cities. Early in the century, Ignatius of Antioch testified to the increasing power and influence of the bishops, who came to be regarded as the successors to the apostles. Especially in cities where the churches had been founded by apostles, chronological lists of bishops were drawn up, and their unbroken line of succession from an apostolic founder was claimed to be a guarantee of the authenticity of their teaching, as against heretical teachers lacking such pedigree (see APOSTOLIC SUCCESSION).

The threefold ministry of bishops, priests, and deacons has been maintained in the Catholic tradition of the church, but at the Reformation most Protestant churches abolished the order of bishops and called their presbyters ministers. These ministers might be assisted by elders or deacons. In the Roman Catholic church a special worldwide ministry is exercised by the pope, or bishop of Rome.

Entry to the full-time ministry now entails a course of theological and practical training leading to ordination, the process by which the candidate is received into the ministerial order. In the Catholic tradition, ordination is by a bishop. In nonepiscopal Protestant churches, ordination is usually by a collective of ministers acting together. The Catholic tradition emphasizes the priestly and sacramental aspects of ministry, whereas the Protestant churches stress preaching and teaching.

See also: HOLY ORDERS.

mink   Mink are two species of semiaquatic mammals of the weasel family, Mustelidae. The American mink, *Mustela vison*, ranges from Alaska to the Gulf of Mexico. The European mink, *M. lutreola*, was once widely distributed in Europe and Asia but has been exterminated from much of its former range. American mink are raised commercially for their fur and are available in many color varieties. They also have been introduced into or escaped from fur ranches in Britain, Europe, and Asia, where they are displacing the native mink; in Britain there is considerable concern regarding their effect on native animal populations. Wild mink have lustrous, rich brown fur, with white markings on the chin, throat, and upper lip. They grow to 50 cm (20 in) in length, plus a 20-cm (8-in) tail, and about 1.5 kg (3.5 lb) in weight. Mink are twilight and

The mink M. vison *is a nocturnal carnivore related to the weasel. An excellent swimmer, it feeds on fish and amphibians in addition to birds and small rodents. The wild mink's deep brown coat is highly valued.*

nocturnal hunters and feed on a wide variety of animals. Breeding occurs in late winter. Commonly 5 to 8 young are born after a gestation period of usually 6 to 7 weeks.

Minkowski, Hermann   The Russian-born German mathematician Hermann Minkowski, b. June 22, 1864, d. Jan. 12, 1909, developed a new view of space and time. He considered three-dimensional space and time, which was formerly thought to be independent of space, to be coupled together in a four-dimensional space-time continuum. This idea provided a framework for all later mathematical developments in RELATIVITY, and it also aided Albert EINSTEIN in developing the general theory of relativity.

Minkowski was especially interested in quadratic forms, which are homogeneous, second-degree polynomials. His most original achievement, however, was his "geometry of numbers," which also led to his studies of convex bodies and to questions related to packing problems—the ways in which figures of a given shape can be placed within another given figure.

Minneapolis   Minneapolis, the largest city in Minnesota, is located in the southeastern part of the state, mostly on the west bank of the Mississippi River near its confluence with the Minnesota River. The population is 368,383 (1990). The city of SAINT PAUL is located on the east bank, and together Minneapolis and Saint Paul are known as the Twin Cities. The population of their metropolitan area is 2,464,124. Minneapolis is the seat of Hennepin County.

Situated at the head of navigation on the Mississippi, Minneapolis is a port of entry and a major rail junction, serving as the transportation, commercial, and industrial center for its fertile agricultural hinterland. It has long been known as the flour-milling capital of the world, although this industry has been surpassed by linseed-oil production. Agricultural machinery, computers, and electrical equipment are manufactured, and the city has large food-processing and publishing industries. Its grain market is one of the largest in the world.

The University of Minnesota (1851) is the leading educational institution there. Cultural institutions include the Minnesota Orchestra and the Minneapolis Institute of Arts. The Tyrone Guthrie Theater is the home of a prestigious regional acting company. Minneapolis has more than 20 lakes and approximately 150 parks, including Minnehaha Park, where Minnehaha Falls, of Longfellow's *Hiawatha*, is located.

In 1819, Fort Saint Anthony (renamed Fort Snelling in 1825) was established. The village of Saint Anthony on the east bank was incorporated in 1855. The village of Minneapolis, which took its name from the Sioux *minne* ("water") and the Greek *polis* ("city"), was incorporated on the west bank in 1856, and the two merged as the city of Minneapolis in 1872. Minneapolis became a lumber and then a grain-milling center. These industries attracted large numbers of Swedish and Norwegian immigrants.

In 1967 the Twin Cities Metropolitan Council was established to coordinate certain governmental functions of the units in the Minneapolis-Saint Paul metropolitan area. Each municipality retains its own executive, and governmental operations in Minneapolis are administered by a mayor and chief administrative officer.

Minnelli, Liza [muh-nel'-ee, ly'-zuh] A talented singer and actress, Liza Minnelli, b. Hollywood, Calif., Mar. 12, 1946, won an Academy Award for her role as Sally Bowles in the film *Cabaret* (1972). The daughter of director Vincente Minnelli and singer Judy GARLAND, Minnelli exhibits much of her mother's vocal power and gaminelike charm. Her work on Broadway has earned three Tony Awards, for *Flora, the Red Menace* (1965), *Liza at the Winter Garden* (1973), and *The Act* (1977). She has played leading parts in the films *The Sterile Cuckoo* (1969), *Tell Me That You Love Me, Junie Moon* (1970), *New York, New York* (1977), *Arthur* (1981), and *Arthur 2: On the Rocks* (1988).

The American film and stage actress Liza Minnelli established during the 1970s an international reputation as a singer and dancer. She received an Academy Award for her portrayal of an American cabaret singer in the film Cabaret *(1972).*

Minnelli, Vincente The Hollywood director most often associated with the most imaginative musicals of the 1940s and 1950s was Vincente Minnelli, b. Chicago, Feb. 28, 1910, d. July 25, 1986. Beginning with *Cabin in the Sky* in 1943, Minnelli set new standards for the musical genre with such films as *Meet Me in St. Louis* (1944), *The Pirate* (1948), *An American in Paris* (1951), *The Band Wagon* (1953), and *Gigi* (1958), which won nine Academy Awards. The visual dynamism and stylish decor of these films can also be seen in such nonmusical Minnelli efforts as *The Clock* (1945), *The Bad and the Beautiful* (1952), and *Lust for Life* (1956). His autobiography, *I Remember It Well*, appeared in 1974.

minnesingers see MINSTRELS, MINNESINGERS, AND TROUBADOURS

Minnesota Minnesota, located close to the center of the North American continent, contains the northernmost point in the continental United States, the Northwest Angle. Much of the boundary of Minnesota is outlined by natural waterways. A large portion of the north and northeast is separated from Manitoba and Ontario by Lake of the Woods, Rainy River, Pigeon River, Lake Superior, and numerous other lakes that stretch in an almost unbroken chain. Lake Superior and the Saint Croix and Mississippi rivers follow most of its eastern boundary with Wisconsin; to the west, the Red River of the North and Big Stone and Traverse lakes separate Minnesota from the Dakotas. The state is bordered by Iowa to the south.

It has been said that Minnesota's way of life seems permanently positioned in the middle of the American dream. This dream brought many immigrants to the state, bending people to the plow with the promise of a life of plenty, peace, and dignity in return for their honest labor. Minnesota received its name from the largest river that lies wholly within its boundaries; the Sioux called the river the Minnesota, meaning "clouded water," because of the light-colored clay it carried in suspension.

Land and Resources

More than two-thirds of Minnesota is nearly flat or gently rolling, with a mean elevation of 366 m (1,200 ft) above sea level. This central region is surrounded by areas of dissimilar topography. In the northeast, both the lowest and highest points in Minnesota are found in Arrowhead Country. This area is structurally part of the CANADIAN SHIELD, underlain with granite, gneiss, and schist. The flat prairies of the northwest and west were once part of the ancient Lake Agassiz basin and overlie limestone and shale. To the southeast, the Driftless Area is marked by incised streams and cross-cutting valleys.

During the Pleistocene Epoch all but the southeastern corner of the state was subjected to the action of glaciers. The last advance is largely responsible for the present physical landscape.

Soils. The prairie soils of the southern part of the state

MINNESOTA

Land: Area: 225,182 km² (86,943 mi²); rank: 12th. Capital: St. Paul (1990 pop., 272,235). Largest city: Minneapolis (1990 pop., 368,383). Counties: 87. Elevations: highest—701 m (2,301 ft), at Eagle Mountain; lowest—183 m (602 ft), at Lake Superior.

People: Population (1990): 4,387,029; rank: 20th; density: 21.2 persons per km² (55 per mi²). Distribution (1990): 69.9% urban, 30.1% rural. Average annual change (1980–90): +0.8%.

Government (1993): Governor: Arne Carlson, Republican. U.S. Congress: Senate—1 Democrat, 1 Republican; House—6 Democrats, 2 Republicans. Electoral college votes: 10. State legislature: 67 senators, 134 representatives.

Economy: State personal income (1989): $76.9 billion; rank: 20th. Median family income (1989): $36,916; rank: 14th. Agriculture: income (1989)—$6.5 billion. Lumber production (1991): 95 million board feet. Mining (nonfuel): value (1988)—$1.27 billion. Manufacturing: value added (1987)—$23.3 billion. Services: value (1987)—$19 billion.

Miscellany: Statehood: May 11, 1858; the 32d state. Nickname: North Star State; tree: red pine; motto: *L'Etoile du Nord* ("The Star of the North"); song: "Hail! Minnesota."

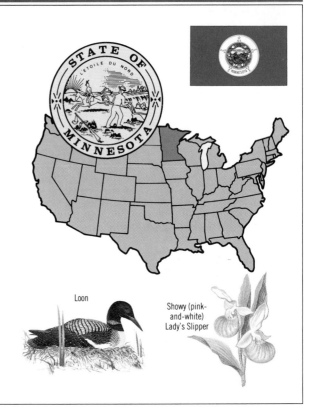

Loon

Showy (pink-and-white) Lady's Slipper

and the chernozems of western Minnesota are the most fertile. The northeast corner of the state is dominated by lithosols that have developed over resistant rock formations. Much of this area is forested and unsuitable for cultivation. Most of northern Minnesota's soils are podzols.

Drainage. Three major drainage basins are found within Minnesota. Only 9% of the state is drained by eastward-flowing streams emptying into Lake SUPERIOR. The Red River of the North, the Rainy, and other northerly flowing rivers drain 34%, and the MISSISSIPPI RIVER system, 57%. The Mississippi begins its 3,779-km (2,348-mi) course to the Gulf of Mexico at Lake Itasca.

Minnesota's automobile license plates claim the state is the "Land of 10,000 Lakes." Lakes with areas of 4 ha (10 acres) or more actually number 15,291. Within the state are about 40,200 km (25,000 mi) of streams and approximately 145,000 km (90,000 mi) of lake and river shoreline.

Climate. A humid continental climate dominates the state, but considerable variation occurs within its borders. Minnesota is susceptible to outbreaks of cold polar air from the north as well as occasional warm moist air from the Gulf of Mexico. The January mean temperature ranges from –17° C (1° F) in the northwest to –9° C (16° F) in

the southeast. July mean temperatures vary between 15° C (59° F) in the northeast and 23° C (74° F) in the southwest. Precipitation amounts of 813 mm (32 in) in the extreme southeast decrease to 483 mm (19 in) in the northwestern corner. Although snow and rain are equally common in Minnesota, most of the precipitation falls as rain, averaging 635 mm (25 in) yearly. The average annual snowfall is 1,143 mm (45 in).

Vegetation and Animal Life. The natural vegetation of the south and west was once extensive grasslands. Approximately 40% of the state was covered with prairie grass with gallery forests lining the water courses and the edges of lakes. Forested areas of the state were of two major types: in the east central and northern parts lay forests of spruce, balsam, and pines, whereas between the grasslands and the coniferous northern woods grew hardwood forests.

In the remote northern areas, moose are seen, while deer and smaller wild animals can be found throughout the state. More than 140 fish species have been sighted in Minnesota's waters, and the annual catch exceeds 11 million kg (25 million lb).

People

Since the 1950s, Minnesota has grown at a slower rate

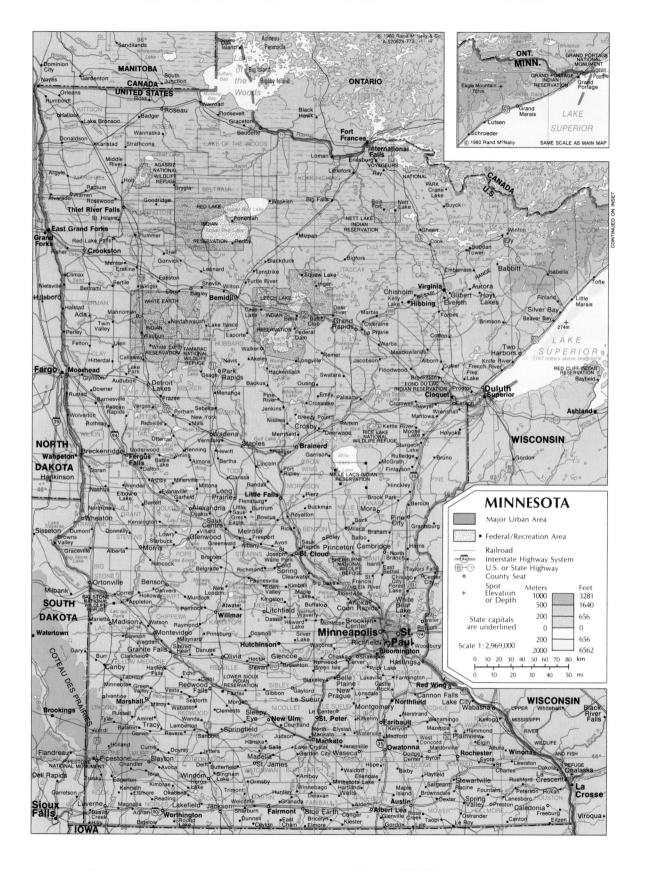

(Above) *Minnesota's state capitol in Saint Paul, a marble-domed structure patterned after Saint Peter's Basilica in Rome, was designed by Cass Gilbert and completed in 1904.*

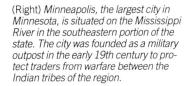

(Right) *Minneapolis, the largest city in Minnesota, is situated on the Mississippi River in the southeastern portion of the state. The city was founded as a military outpost in the early 19th century to protect traders from warfare between the Indian tribes of the region.*

than the nation as a whole. With a population of 4,387,029 (1990), the state has less than 2% of the total U.S. population. The heaviest population concentration is found in the southeastern part of the state near MINNEAPOLIS and SAINT PAUL, but other major concentrations are found in DULUTH, Rochester, and Bloomington—all with populations exceeding 70,000.

Minnesota's 1987 birthrate of 15.3 was slightly below the national average of 15.7; the state's death rate of 8.1 was also lower than the national average (8.7). Minnesota ranks second to Hawaii in the estimated life expectancy of its population.

Minnesota's population includes some Indian, Yankee, and Canadian groups, but the origins of most Minnesotans can be traced directly to European countries. Sweden, Norway, and Germany have been the dominant sources of immigrants. Racial minorities form a small part of the total population.

Education. In 1849 the territorial legislature enacted the first law pertaining to education. Common schools were to be open to all persons between the ages of 4 and 21 years. In 1851 only three schools, privately operated, existed in Minnesota, with an enrollment of 250. Today, children must attend school from age 7 to age 16. Minnesota has one of the lowest high school–dropout rates in the nation. Institutions of higher education located in the state range from the University of Minnesota, with its large enrollment,

to smaller private institutions such as CARLETON COLLEGE, Macalester College, and St. Olaf College.

Contributions to the nation's culture have been made by many noted Minnesotans. Sinclair Lewis, born in Sauk Centre, used his hometown as a model for his famous novel, *Main Street*. The novelist F. Scott Fitzgerald was also a native.

The Minneapolis–Saint Paul area is the home of the Minneapolis Institute of Arts, the Science Museum of Minnesota, and the Walker Art Center. The Tyrone Guthrie Theater provides entertainment in the performing arts, and the Minnesota Symphony Orchestra is world renowned.

Communications. The metropolitan area of Minneapolis and Saint Paul dominates the news media in the state. Of particular broadcasting interest in the 1980s was the national impact made by Minnesota public radio's Garrison Keillor and his tales of the fictitious Minnesota town, Lake Wobegon.

Economic Activity

Minnesota is highly industrialized, with many of the nation's giant business enterprises operating within its borders. In the past few decades manufacturing has displaced farming as the major source of income.

Agriculture. Minnesota is among the leading U.S. farm states, ranking high in the production of hay, oats, sugar beets, flaxseed, spring wheat, sunflower seed, soybeans, and rye. The state is a leading producer of milk, much of which is made into cheese and butter. Beef cattle, turkeys, and hogs are also valuable sources of farm income. Major farm areas are in the south, southwest, and Red River Valley.

Forestry. Forestry is also an important industry. Because more than half of Minnesota's commercial forestland is publicly owned, the state has the opportunity to determine the pattern competing land uses will take.

Mining. The state is the nation's primary source for domestic iron ore and low-grade taconite (rock containing 20–30% iron). The Mesabi Range supplies two-thirds of domestic production. Lack of demand for iron ore led to a severe slowdown in operations in 1983, but production has since increased somewhat. Limestone is found along the banks of the Mississippi and its tributaries. The finest granite is quarried near Saint Cloud, but other deposits are found in the Minnesota Valley. Sand and gravel are also produced in the state.

Manufacturing and Services. Minnesota's leading industry is the food-processing industry. Other valuable manufactures are nonelectrical machinery, fabricated metals, and electrical and electronic equipment. Computers are among the state's most important products.

Service companies such as insurance and financial institutions are important in the Minneapolis–Saint Paul area, and the Mayo Clinic is a major employer in Rochester.

Tourism. Tourism is important to Minnesota. Through state parks, recreation areas, and scenic and natural areas wind trails for snowmobiling, hiking, and cross-country skiing. Canoeing and boating are popular summer activities. National parklands include Voyageurs National Park along the Canadian border, Grand Portage National Monument on Lake Superior, and Pipestone National Monument in the southwest. Among other tourist attractions are the statues of Paul Bunyan and Babe in Brainerd and Bemidji and the annual Saint Paul Winter Carnival. The Minneapolis–Saint Paul area supports professional baseball, football, and hockey teams.

Transportation. Minnesota is served by several rail lines, including Amtrak. The state also has an interstate highway system, and a number of municipalities maintain mass-transit systems. Several ports on Lake Superior and on the Mississippi and Minnesota rivers complete the transportation network. Depending on the observer's perspective, Duluth is the beginning—or the end—of the St. Lawrence Seaway. The state's major airport is Minneapolis–Saint Paul International Airport.

Energy. Minnesota is more dependent on petroleum than its neighboring states. Within the state substantial variation exists in the types of fuel used for home heating. Several hydroelectric plants are located on the Minnesota, Mississippi, Rainy, St. Croix, and St. Louis rivers. The state also has nuclear power plants.

Government and Politics

Minnesota is governed under its original (1858) constitution, as amended. The governor is elected for a 4-year term. The bicameral state legislature consists of 67 senators elected for 4-year terms and 134 representatives with 2-year terms.

The state's judicial system is headed by the Supreme Court, composed of nine judges. The state also has a court of appeals and district, county, and municipal courts.

The greater Minneapolis–Saint Paul area is under the supervision of the Metropolitan Council, extending over a multicounty region. Public services such as water and sewage are coordinated by the Council.

Iron ore is extracted from this open-pit, or strip, mine in the Mesabi Range of northeastern Minnesota. Although mining is of diminishing importance as the high-grade ores are depleted, Minnesota remains first among U.S. states in the production of iron ore.

Although strongly Republican at the time of statehood (1858), Minnesota developed potent Populist traditions in the later 19th century. The Granger movement, the POPULIST PARTY, and the NONPARTISAN LEAGUE all attracted substantial support in Minnesota. The FARMER-LABOR PARTY, founded in 1920, became a major political force in the state. In 1944 this party merged with the Democrats to form the Democratic-Farmer-Labor (DFL) party. U.S. vice-presidents Hubert H. HUMPHREY, Jr., and Walter F. MONDALE are among the political leaders produced by the DFL. Other nationally known politicians from Minnesota include Harold STASSEN, three times Republican governor of the state (1939–43), and Eugene McCARTHY, a U.S. senator (1959–71) and anti–Vietnam War candidate for the Democratic presidential nomination in 1968. Today party allegiances in Minnesota tend to be split between agricultural and big-business Republicans and urban and blue-collar Democrats, operating under the DFL standard.

History

The Kensington Rune Stone, discovered near Alexandria in 1898, purports to record the visit of VIKINGS in 1362. Continuous recorded history, however, indicates that those who opened the territory included the Frenchmen Samuel de CHAMPLAIN; Daniel Greysolon, Sieur DULUTH; Louis HENNEPIN; Robert Cavelier, Sieur de LA SALLE; Jean NICOLET; Pierre Esprit RADISSON; and Medard Chouart, Sieur des Groseilliers.

Through their efforts, the great northern wilderness was claimed as part of the French Empire in North America. France yielded its North American territories to Great Britain by the 1763 Treaty of Paris, and the Union Jack replaced the French tricolor in the territory east of the Mississippi. After the American Revolution the area became a part of the United States. The territory west of the Mississippi came to the United States as part of the LOUISIANA PURCHASE.

Settlement of the territory began with the building in 1819 of Fort Anthony, renamed Fort Snelling in 1825, at the junction of the Mississippi and Minnesota rivers. The first white people to make permanent homes in Minnesota were farmers who lived in and around the fort. Many were French-Canadian *voyageurs,* carried west by their work in the fur trade. A few men and women had come from the east as traders, missionaries, or soldiers. Also present were a handful of Europeans—mostly Swiss and Scottish—who had fled the dangers and hardships of life in the Selkirk Colony RED RIVER SETTLEMENT to the north. When lands of the Sioux and Chippewa were placed on sale, many families from the eastern United States settled, along with French Canadians. Germans, Swedes, and Norwegians arrived beginning in the late 1840s.

On Mar. 3, 1849, the Territory of Minnesota was created. Its northern, eastern, and southern boundaries were the same as those of today, but its western limits extended to the Missouri and White Earth rivers—encompassing most of present-day North Dakota. During the 1850s, Indians relinquished their claims to areas within the territory, and in 1858, Minnesota was admitted to the Union.

The state experienced no fighting within its borders during the Civil War, but Minnesota did contribute soldiers to the Union effort. During 1862 a Sioux uprising in the state, brought about by a lack of food and money for the reservation inhabitants, resulted in the death of more than 400 settlers.

The state's economy was centered on wheat farming, milling, and lumbering. Beginning in the 1880s, however, the exploitation of iron ore became significant. Steel production at the U.S. Steel Corporation plant in Duluth began in 1915. Twentieth-century agriculture in Minnesota has moved from a concentration on wheat growing to dairying, with stress placed on the manufacture of butter and cheese.

The opening of the St. Lawrence Seaway in 1959 made Duluth a world port, enabling the state's products to be shipped easily. Industrial development has taken its toll, however. In recent years a court battle has been waged over the environmental hazards of dumping mineral wastes into Lake Superior and the releasing of toxic fumes into the atmosphere. Minnesotans must weigh the environmental costs of increased development in their state.

---

minnow   A *minnow* is technically a freshwater fish of the family Cyprinidae. Fishes of the family Umbridae are known as mudminnows and those of the families Cyprinodontidae and Poeciliidae are called topminnows. The family Cyprinidae contains about 275 genera and 1,600 species found in North America, Eurasia, and Africa. Minnows are typically 15 cm (6 in) or less in length, with a full body, large head, and soft fins. They lack jaw teeth, but many have pharyngeal, or throat, teeth located on the gill arches. Most species are omnivorous, eating both plants and small animal organisms. Less typical is the largest minnow, the mahseer, *Barbus* (or *Puntius*) *tor,* of India, which may reach a length of 2.7 m (9 ft), weigh well over 45 kg (100 lb), and have hand-sized scales. The carp, *Cyprinus carpio,* the largest minnow in Europe, has a spiny dorsal fin and may reach 36 kg (80 lb) in weight. The Colorado squawfish, *Ptychocheilus lucius,* the largest American minnow, may exceed 1.2 m (4 ft) in length and 32 kg (70 lb) in weight. The majority of North American minnows, 101 species, belong to the genus *Notropis* and are popularly called shiners because of their bright, reflective sides. Many species are popular aquarium fishes.

The eastern mud-minnow is found along the eastern seaboard of the United States from New York to Florida.

Minoan scripts   see LINEAR B

Minoans   see AEGEAN CIVILIZATION

---

minor   A minor is a person who is under the age of legal competence. Until recently that age was considered to be 21, but most states of the United States have lowered the legal age of adulthood to 18.

Minors are not ordinarily held responsible for contracts made with adults and can void such contracts if certain legal requirements are met. In traditional English law a minor under the age of 7 was presumed to be incapable of criminal activity. This presumption also held for a minor between the ages of 7 and 14 but could be rebutted with competent evidence. A minor between the ages of 14 and 21 was presumed to have criminal capacity. Many U.S. states now judge minors on a case-by-case basis.

Minors lack the right to vote, to hold public office, and to sue and be sued in their own right. They are, however, responsible for civil wrongs they commit, although their age and inexperience may be taken into consideration.

See also: CHILDREN'S RIGHTS; JUVENILE DELINQUENCY.

minor planet   see ASTEROID

Minorca [min-ohr'-kuh]   Minorca is one of Spain's Balearic Islands, located in the western Mediterranean Sea. It covers 668 km² (258 mi²), and the population is 58,727 (1981). The largest town, Mahon, located on the southeastern coast, has one of the finest natural harbors in the Mediterranean. Although much of the island is flat, it reaches 358 m (1,174 ft) at Toro Hill. Irrigation is necessary for cultivation. Goats, sheep, and cattle are raised, fishing takes place along the coast, and shoe manufacturing is the major industry. Tourism is becoming increasingly important.

Stone towers, built during the 2d millennium BC, are found on Minorca. Held by a succession of rulers, in the 13th century it came under Spanish control. In 1708 it was taken by the British, but it was returned to Spain in 1802.

minorities   see ETHNIC MINORITIES

Minos [my'-nuhs]   In Greek and Roman mythology Minos was both the ruler of Crete and, after his death, a judge of the underworld. Along with his twin brother, Rhadamanthus, Minos was the son of EUROPA, who had been impregnated by Zeus in the guise of a white bull. After becoming king of Crete with the aid of POSEIDON, Minos used his powerful navy to rule over an extensive Aegean empire. The Minoan civilization, which flourished on Crete from about 3000 to 1450 BC, was subsequently given his name; the palace at Knossos is popularly thought to be his palace, within which Minos confined the deadly MINOTAUR in an elaborate labyrinth built by Daedalus.

Minot [my'-nuht]   Minot (1990 pop., 34,544) is a city in north central North Dakota, located about 85 km (53 mi) south of the Canadian border. It is the seat of Ward County. Minot is a commercial and distribution center for wheat and livestock produced in the surrounding agricultural region. Food products, agricultural machinery, and

construction materials are manufactured. Lignite and petroleum fields and Minot Air Force Base are nearby. Minot State College (1913) is there. Minot was settled in 1886 as a construction camp for the Great Northern Railway.

Minotaur [min'-uh-tohr]   A Greek mythological monster, half man and half bull, the Minotaur was the offspring of Pasiphaë, wife of King MINOS of Crete, and a beautiful white bull. Poseidon had caused Pasiphaë to fall in love with the bull as a punishment to Minos for failing to offer the bull in sacrifice to the gods. Kept in the labyrinth designed by Daedalus, where 14 youths were annually sacrificed to him by Minos, the Minotaur was finally killed by the Athenian hero THESEUS, with the help of ARIADNE, daughter of Minos.

Minsk [meensk]   Minsk is the capital of BELORUSSIA, in the USSR, and the administrative center of Minsk oblast. The city's population is 1,612,000 (1989). Minsk is a major industrial and transportation center located on the Svisloch River and on the main railroad and highway linking Moscow with Warsaw. The city's factories produce heavy trucks, farm tractors, motorcycles, radios, and a wide range of machinery products. Minsk is the home of the Belorussian Academy of Sciences and Belorussian University (1921). An important cultural center, it has an opera house and Belorussian and Russian drama theaters.

One of Russia's oldest cities, Minsk was first mentioned as a trading settlement at the beginning of the 11th century. The seat of an early Russian principality, it passed to Lithuania at the start of the 14th century, to Poland in 1569, and to Russia in 1793. After the Bolshevik Revolution it was made the capital of the newly constituted Belorussian SSR in 1919. Minsk was heavily damaged in World War II and subsequently rebuilt.

minstrel show   see MUSIC HALL, VAUDEVILLE, AND BURLESQUE

minstrels, minnesingers, and troubadours

Minstrels (*menestrels*) of 10th-century France were members of the jongleur profession, which comprised itinerant entertainers who sang, played the fiddle, danced, and did acrobatics and juggling. Minstrels of sufficient talent and culture could obtain permanent positions in feudal households, thereby attaining a higher social status. None of their music survives, but some of their poetry is extant in the form of chansons de geste. In the 12th and 13th centuries they provided musical accompaniment for the verses of the troubadours, the poet-musicians of southern France. The troubadours, mostly members of the nobility, preserved their songs in manuscripts—called *chansonniers*—which are the earliest musical settings of a vernacular language (Provençal, or langue d'oc) to survive. The texts are concerned primarily with COURTLY LOVE, although politics and religion are also treated. Of the approximately 2,600 extant troubadour poems, about 260 have music, all monophonic melodies.

The trouvères were from northern France and originally imitated the art of the troubadours, translating the texts into their own dialect (Old French, or langue d'oil). The movement flourished from about 1150 to 1300 and included both the aristocracy and commoners. ADAM DE LA HALLE, the greatest of the trouvères, also composed some polyphonic songs and musical plays called pastourelles. More trouvère art has survived than that of the troubadours—approximately 4,000 poems, about 1,400 with melodies.

The Germans imported the troubadour-trouvère tradition in the mid-12th century, giving rise to the minnesinger movement, comprising aristocratic poet-musicians who cultivated monophonic songs of love (Minne) and other subjects. The movement reached its high point during the mid-13th to early 14th century before yielding to the MEISTERSINGERS in the 15th. TANNHÄUSER was an important minnesinger.

See also: MEDIEVAL MUSIC.

mint   Mint is the common name of approximately 25 perennial species of the genus *Mentha* of the Labiatae family, which grow throughout most temperate regions. The name is sometimes used to refer to any member of the Labiatae, often called the mint family because many plants within the family are characterized by their aromatic foliage (see BASIL; OREGANO). The true mints, however, are restricted to a much smaller group and its many hybrids. True mints can be propagated from seed; mint hybrids are sterile but can be easily propagated by replanting the stolons or through cuttings. Mints are cultivated as sweet herbs, whose leaves may be dried and used as flavorings, and for their essential oils, which are extracted and used in flavoring essences and for perfume and medicinal fragrances.

The common garden mint is SPEARMINT, *M. spicata*, which has a sweet, strong scent and is widely used in

Spearmint is a perennial herb and one of the most strongly flavored herbs of the mint family. It is widely cultivated both for its essential oil and for culinary purposes.

candies, chewing gum, herbal teas, and other products. PEPPERMINT, *M. piperita*, yields an essential oil that is composed primarily of menthol and menthone and is used to flavor candies, pharmaceutical preparations, and liqueurs. Apple mint, *M. villosa*, has rounded leaves and is often cultivated in home gardens.

mintage   Mintage is a process for coining metal MONEY by a government. The United States manufactures, or mints, coins at Philadelphia, Denver, San Francisco, and West Point.

The coin-manufacturing process has several steps: melting the metal bullion and casting it into bars; rolling the bars into strips or ribbons; cutting out the round disks, or planchets; adjusting their weight; rolling their rims; treating them with acid; striking the impressions on the planchets; and weighing each finished coin.

The Coinage Act of 1965 signaled the first major change in U.S. coinage in more than 100 years. Through 1964, U.S. silver coins were 90% silver and 10% copper. The act eliminated silver from the dime and quarter and greatly reduced the half-dollar's silver content. In 1970 the Bank Holding Company Act required that the last silver be removed from the half-dollar as well as the dollar. General-use dollars, half-dollars, quarters, and dimes now contain 91.67% copper and 8.33% nickel. The unpopular 1979 Susan B. Anthony dollar had the same metal content and was only slightly larger than the quarter. Nickels are 75% copper and 25% nickel. The most widely-circulated U.S. coin, the penny, was formerly 95% copper; due to rising costs it is now 97.6% zinc, with a thin coating of copper. Special provisions allow the mint to continue to strike limited numbers of dollars and half-dollars for coin collectors that are 60% copper and 40% silver. The first $10 gold coin in more than 50 years, also designed for collectors, was struck in 1983.

minuet [min-yoo-et']   The minuet, or menuet (from the Latin *minitus*, meaning "small" or "neat"), a measured, gliding dance in 3/4 time, dominated French and English social dancing roughly from 1650 to 1800, with its refined encapsulation of the epoch's courtly attitudes. Less a dance than an expression of polite deportment, it consisted basically of four movements, linked by a tiptoe walk and executed in an S, later a Z, pattern. Its rustic origins in the *branle* of Poitou vanished in Louis XIV's court, where each couple imbued its daintiness with stylized elegance. Jean Baptiste LULLY composed the first minuet in 1653.

Minuit, Peter [min'-u-it]   Peter Minuit, b. Wesel (now in Germany), c.1580, d. June 1638, was an early colonizer for the Dutch in North America. The first director general of the colony of NEW NETHERLAND, he arrived in 1626 and immediately legalized the position of the Dutch settlers by buying Manhattan Island from the Indians for trinkets valued at 60 guilders (later computed as the equivalent of $24). At the southern tip of the island he built a fort that he called New Amsterdam, from which modern New York City evolved. Recalled to Holland in 1631, Minuit later entered Swedish service. In 1638 he established the colony of New Sweden in what is now Delaware.

Minuteman missile   Minuteman was one of the earliest intercontinental ballistic missiles (ICBMs) developed in the United States. Of the four versions of Minuteman developed, only Minuteman II and III are still in service. A deployment of 450 Minuteman IIs and 550 Minuteman IIIs, together with 54 Titan ICBMs, represents the full strength of the U.S. land-based strategic nuclear force. Both versions are 18 m (59.7 ft) long and have a maximum diameter of 1.8 m (6 ft), but the Minuteman III is somewhat heavier at 34,500 kg (76,000 lb) and has a MIRV (multiple independently targeted reentry vehicle) payload instead of the single warhead used on the Minuteman II missile (see MIRV MISSILE). The Minuteman IIIs are stored ready for launch in individual silos about 24 m (80 ft) deep and more than 4 m (13 ft) wide. In 1986 advanced MX MISSILES began to be installed in modified Minuteman silos in Wyoming.

minutemen   In the American Revolution the minutemen were special militia units that supposedly could be called to arms "at a minute's notice." The first of these units, organized by the Massachusetts provincial congress in 1774, fought at the Battles of LEXINGTON AND CONCORD in 1775. Later, other colonies formed units of minutemen.

In the 1960s a small group of right-wing extremists in the United States who called themselves the Minutemen stockpiled arms for guerrilla warfare against what they believed to be the impending Communist takeover of the country. The organization was banned as subversive in some states and by the end of the decade had gone underground.

Miocene Epoch   see EARTH, GEOLOGICAL HISTORY OF; GEOLOGIC TIME

Mir   see SALYUT

Mirabeau, Honoré Gabriel Riqueti, Comte de
[mee-rah-boh', oh-nohr-ay' gah-bree-el' ree-ke-tee']
Honoré Gabriel Riqueti, comte de Mirabeau, b. Mar. 9, 1749, d. Apr. 2, 1791, was one of the ablest leaders of the FRENCH REVOLUTION. He was a powerful orator whose policies were based on both serious study and hard experience.

In 1789, Mirabeau entered the STATES-GENERAL as a delegate for the third estate (commons). He fought for the fusion of the three estates into a single assembly, his most famous action being his open defiance of King LOUIS XVI's attempt (June 23, 1789) to close the session after the third estate had proclaimed itself the National Assembly. He believed strongly in constitutional parliamentary monarchy and consequently sought to effect a sound distribution of power among the king, the assembly, and

the electorate. Frustrated by the assembly's tendency to monopolize power and refusal to allow deputies to become ministers, Mirabeau tried (1790) to achieve his purpose by surreptitious dealings with the court. The marquis de LAFAYETTE, however, thwarted his efforts; although Mirabeau accepted payment to advise the court, his plans were wasted on the evasively obdurate king.

When Mirabeau died, he was widely mourned as a champion of the people. His body was placed in the Panthéon, but it was removed a few years later, after evidence of his dealings with the king had come to light.

miracle   A miracle is an event occurring within human experience in which the hitherto observed operations of nature appear to be overruled or suspended; such events are usually ascribed to the intervention of divine power. In Judaism and Islam miracles are regarded as signs of the omnipotence of God. Many events are recorded in the Old Testament that are considered miraculous. One in particular, the Exodus from Egypt, became the symbol of all God's deliverances in history, the theme of much Jewish literature, and the hope of the Jewish future.

The New Testament records numerous miracles, frequently acts of healing, performed by Jesus Christ. They are presented by the Gospel writers as *gesta Christi*, the works of the Messiah, and were regarded as part of the proclamation of the kingdom of God, designed to awaken repentance and turn people toward God rather than to provoke mere wonder. The supreme miracles of Christianity are the INCARNATION (God becoming man) and the RESURRECTION (the raising of Jesus Christ from the dead). On these two miracles rests the historic faith of the Christian church.

Roman Catholic orthodoxy teaches that miracles still take place, as in every previous century. Certain places, such as LOURDES, are associated with miraculous healings. The Roman Catholic church also requires attestation of miracles as a basic condition for CANONIZATION.

miracle play   see MEDIEVAL DRAMA

Mirage   France's most notable range of modern warplanes, the Mirage, built by Dassault-Breguet, originated in 1955 as a single-seat jet fighter. The first prototype was developed into the larger Mirage III series, which was in turn scaled up to produce (1959) the IVA, a two-seat, high-speed bomber capable of delivering a French atomic bomb.

As of the mid-1980s, the range of Mirage aircraft also included versions of the F1, the Mirage 50 (1975), and the Mirage 2000 (1983), a single-engine, air-defense interceptor design. The Super Mirage 4000, under development, is fitted with two turbojets and contains composite structural materials.

mirage   The refraction of light through air layers of different density produces a mirage—a distortion of size, shape, or position of images. The bending of light by refraction in air is a regular occurrence but ordinarily is not noticeable over short distances. The amount of bending increases as vertical differences in air temperature, and therefore air density, increase.

The image of a distant object is always displaced, with respect to the viewer, from its true position toward the warmer, less dense air; that is, the colder, denser air lies within the curve made by the bending light path. When the air temperature is greatest near the ground, the image of a distant object is displaced downward, producing an inferior mirage, which may be inverted. The appearance of water over heated plains is actually a displaced image of the sky. If the air temperature increases with height, as for example above a body of water or a cool land surface, the image is displaced upward to form a superior mirage, usually much distorted. (See also FATA MORGANA.)

Miranda   Miranda, the innermost and smallest of the major moons of the planet URANUS, was discovered in 1948 by the Dutch-born American astronomer Gerard Kuiper. When VOYAGER 2 flew by Uranus on Jan. 24, 1986, Miranda was found to have a diameter of 484 km (301 mi); orbiting at a distance of 104,350 km (64,825 mi) above Uranus's cloud surface, the moon takes 1.41 days to circle the planet. Photographs revealed a bizarre surface in which old, heavily cratered terrain is interspersed with three nearly rectangular regions of younger terrain characterized by parallel, concentric grooves around their edges. Proposed explanations of Miranda's appearance range from tidal effects of other Uranian moons in the far past to the total fragmentation and reassembly of Miranda's materials through ancient collisions with moon fragments.

Miranda, Francisco de [mee-rahn'-dah]   The Venezuelan revolutionary Francisco de Miranda, b. Mar. 28, 1750, d. July 14, 1816, was an early participant in the movement for Latin American independence. He served as a captain in the Spanish army from 1772 to 1782, fighting against the British in Florida and the Bahamas during the American Revolution. Between 1783 and 1806 he traveled extensively, trying to persuade such political leaders as Alexander Hamilton and Catherine II of Russia to aid a revolution in the Spanish colonies. When the revolution began in 1810, Miranda returned to Venezuela from England. Working with Simon BOLÍVAR, he became a general in the revolutionary army and assumed dictatorial powers after the Venezuelan congress declared independence on July 5, 1811. During a battle in 1812, Miranda agreed to lay down arms if the Spanish promised to spare Venezuelan lives and property. The Spanish broke their promise, and Bolívar, convinced that Miranda was a traitor, handed him over to the royalists. He died in a Spanish prison.

Miranda v. Arizona   In the case of *Miranda* v. *Arizona* (1966) the U.S. Supreme Court held that unless a criminal suspect is informed of the right to counsel and the right against SELF-INCRIMINATION during police interrogation, evidence so obtained may not be used to prosecute the suspect. Ernesto Miranda, an indigent 23-year-old of limited education, had kidnapped and raped an 18-year-old girl. At the police station the victim picked Miranda out of the police lineup, after which he was interrogated for 2 hours. Within a short time Miranda gave a detailed oral confession and then wrote and signed a brief statement admitting and describing the crime. This procedure was accomplished without any effective warnings to the accused by the police. Miranda was then convicted with his confession used as evidence. Speaking through Chief Justice Earl Warren, the Supreme Court reversed Miranda's conviction, holding that evidence obtained during custodial interrogation is inadmissible when the suspect is not informed of his or her constitutional rights, including the right to counsel and the right to remain silent.

Miró, Joan [mee-roh', hoh-ahn']   Joan Miró, b. Montroig, Spain, Apr. 20, 1893, d. Dec. 25, 1983, was a

The playful, inventive images of Spanish surrealist Joan Miró often have cryptic poetic titles, such as Personages and a Dog in Front of the Sun *(1949). (Kunstmuseum, Basel.)*

foremost exponent of abstract and surrealist art. Although he enjoyed close contact with his countryman Pablo Picasso after moving to Paris (1919), Miró was influenced much more by the Fauves and the primitivism of Henri Rousseau than by the rigors of cubism. His first paintings in Paris combined extreme realism and geometrical abstraction, often inspired by the austere Catalan landscape of his homeland. Contacts with the Dadaist poets in the early 1920s acquainted Miró with surrealism, and he began to experiment with hallucinatory and dream-inspired art. From 1924 on he was a key figure in the circle of André Breton and other surrealists. Miró brought to the surrealist movement a humorous sense of fantasy and a startlingly fresh palette, as in his poetic and colorful *The Harlequin's Carnival* (1924–25; Albright-Knox Art Gallery, Buffalo, N.Y.) and *Dog Barking at the Moon* (1926; Philadelphia Museum of Art).

Throughout the late 1920s and '30s, Miró experimented with ever freer compositions whose organization results from the interplay of their individual elements rather than from a schema imposed from the outside. In works such as *Painting* (1933; Museum of Modern Art, New York City) his debt to collage art is noticeable in the loose organization of the composition. After executing a group of paintings reflecting the anguish and tragedy of the Spanish Civil War, Miró turned his intensely individualistic style to ceramics, tapestry design, and mural painting—fields to which he made significant contributions since World War II.

mirror   A mirror is a device that forms an optical image by reflection, as distinguished from a lens, which forms an image by refraction. Any flat, polished material reflects at least some light and thus acts as an elementary mirror.

The familiar hand mirror, or looking-glass, has been known from ancient times. The earliest mirrors were crudely fashioned by polishing disks of metal such as bronze. These simple mirrors became dull in time due to abrasion and oxidation by the atmosphere. More serviceable mirrors were developed by backing glass with thin sheets of metal foil, a process that was well known in the Middle Ages. Silver, which is the best reflector, was commonly used for this purpose. The method of chemical deposition of silver on glass was first used (1835) by the German chemist Justus von Liebig. This process, known as silvering, is still used in the manufacture of the common household mirror.

Most of the mirrors used for scientific and technical purposes are now made by a method of vacuum evaporation. In this process, the substance to be used for the reflecting surface is vaporized by heating it in a vacuum chamber and subsequently made to condense as a thin film onto a supporting substrate of glass or some other material. Aluminum is commonly used for the reflecting film because it is almost as efficient as silver and is much more resistant to oxidation and tarnishing. The aluminum coating is often further protected from oxidation by evaporating onto it a very thin, transparent layer of silicon monoxide, a process called overcoating. Astronomical re-

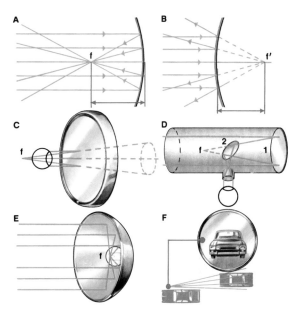

Parallel rays of light are reflected by a concave mirror (A) through a common focus f but are reflected and diverged by a convex mirror (B) as if they came from a focus f' behind the mirror. Concave shaving mirrors (C) produce magnified upright images when one looks into the mirror in front of its focus. A Newtonian telescope (D), consisting of a concave mirror (1) and a 45-degree mounted flat mirror (2), reflects light from the concave mirror to a focus outside the telescope tube. In car headlights (E) a bulb is placed at the focus of a concave mirror to produce a parallel beam of light. Car rearview convex mirrors (F) produce small and erect images of objects behind the driver.

flecting telescopes generally employ overcoated aluminum-on-glass mirrors. For scientific applications requiring the utmost precision, fused quartz, rather than glass, is usually used because of its very low thermal expansion.

Optical mirrors are of three basic types: the ordinary flat, or plane, mirror; the inward-curved, or concave, mirror; and the outward-curved, or convex, mirror. Concave mirrors are also called converging mirrors, because they cause light reflected by them to come to a focus. The magnifying shaving mirror is of this type. Convex mirrors spread out their reflected light and are thus also called diverging mirrors.

The formation of images by mirrors is conveniently treated by means of ray diagrams. Rays from a point source, which may be a single point or any one point on the surface of a luminous object, strike a plane mirror and are reflected. Each ray obeys the law of reflection, which states that the incident and reflected rays make equal angles with the mirror. As a consequence, the reflected rays appear to originate from the image point, which is located symmetrically with respect to the mirror surface and the object. The image is called a virtual image, because the light rays do not actually originate from it; they only appear to do so.

Ray diagrams for the formation of images by a concave mirror show that there are two cases that depend on the

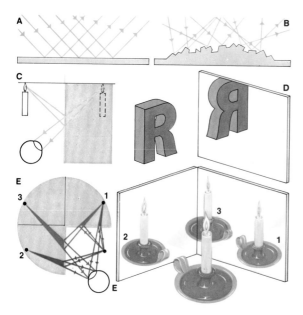

A smooth, flat surface (A) reflects parallel light rays in the same direction, whereas an irregular surface (B) reflects the light in different directions. A plane mirror (C) produces an upright image that is the same size as the object reflected. The image appears to be at the same distance behind the mirror as the object is in front. An object also appears to be perverted, or reversed (D), in a flat mirror. Three images of an object can be seen in two mirrors placed at right angles to each other (E). Images 1 and 2 are formed by a single reflection from a mirror. Image 3, produced after reflection by both mirrors, is doubly perverted and so looks exactly like the object.

mirror curvature and the location of the object. In either case, the image is magnified. A real image will be formed if the object is located at a distance from the mirror greater than half the radius of curvature of the mirror surface, and a virtual image will be formed if the object distance is less than this. If the mirror-to-object distance is p, and the mirror-to-image distance is q, then the two distances are related to the mirror's radius of curvature R by the equation $1/p + 1/q = 2/R$. This is called the *mirror equation*. Positive values of q indicate a real image, and negative values correspond to virtual images. If the object distance p is infinitely large so that the incoming rays are parallel, then the corresponding image distance will be $R/2$. This is called the *focal length* of the mirror; it is the distance at which parallel light rays are brought to a focus.

The image formed by a diverging or convex mirror is always virtual, upright, and reduced in size, whereas the virtual image in a concave mirror is always magnified.

When a spherical mirror (a mirror whose surface is a section of a sphere) is used to bring a beam of parallel rays into a focus, the rays that strike the central part of the mirror converge at a different focal point than do rays that strike the outer portions of the mirror. This defect, characteristic of any optical element having a spherical surface, is termed *spherical aberration*. For a mirror, this aberration can be corrected by making the mirror's sur-

face parabolic rather than spherical.

See also: OPTICS; REFLECTION; TELESCOPE, OPTICAL.

MIRV missile   The multiple independently targeted reentry vehicle (MIRV) is a ballistic missile equipped with multiple reentry vehicles (MRVs) that can be independently aimed at separate military targets. Although each reentry vehicle follows a ballistic path that can be modified by only a limited amount from that followed by a single warhead, a MRV payload can be more effective than a single large warhead delivered to the center of a given area. By employing a Post Boost Vehicle (PBV), which can be powered and maneuvered after the midcourse phase of the flight of an intercontinental ballistic missile (ICBM) or a submarine-launched ballistic missile (SLBM), a greater dispersion of MIRVs is possible. Onboard propulsion, navigation, and guidance systems enable individual MIRVs to make the final maneuvers necessary to strike specific designated targets. In this way a single ICBM or SLBM can attack a number of separate targets. U.S. strategic missiles equipped with MIRVs are the Minuteman III ICBM, the MX ICBM, the Polaris SLBM, the Poseidon SLBM, and the Trident SLBM. The Soviet inventory includes strategic ICBMs that have MIRV capability.

For several years U.S. researchers have been developing the MARV, or Maneuvering Reentry Vehicle, which—like MIRV—is a missile carrying one or more separate, pretargeted warheads. The difference lies in a MARV warhead's ability to make one evasive maneuver in the last part of its trajectory, to avoid enemy attack.

See also: NUCLEAR STRATEGY.

---

miscarriage   see PREGNANCY AND BIRTH

---

misdemeanor   A misdemeanor, in criminal law, is a crime of less serious nature than a FELONY. In the United States a misdemeanor is defined as a crime punishable by a fine or short term of imprisonment. Gambling, assault and battery, reckless driving, and petty larceny are examples of misdemeanors. In old English common law—but not in modern England—the difference between felonies and misdemeanors was more apparent. Felonies resulted in forfeiture and sometimes in capital punishment, whereas misdemeanors rarely involved forfeiture and were never punished by death.

Misérables, Les   [mee-zay-rahb'-luh, lay]   Victor HUGO's gigantic social novel *Les Misérables* (Eng. trans., 1862) presents the unfortunate adventures of Jean Valjean, a victim of social injustice whose goodness and generosity remain unshaken by a corrupt world. The novel is well constructed, suspenseful, and at times lyrical in its passionate plea for pity and humanitarianism toward the poor and suffering. Always immensely popular, the novel nevertheless suffers from digressions, a simplified psychology, and perhaps from Hugo's overzealous judg-ments. It is at its best in its descriptions of post-Napoleonic Paris.

Mishima Yukio [mee'-shee-mah yoo'-kee-oh]   The Japanese novelist and playwright Mishima Yukio, b. Hiraoka Kimitake, Jan. 14, 1925, d. Nov. 25, 1970, became a legend after his suicide following an attempt to foment rebellion among the ranks of his country's Self Defense Force. Eroticism—particularly homosexual—martyrdom, and conservative politics pervade even his first novel, *Confessions of a Mask* (1949; Eng. trans., 1958); but in his later works such concerns pale before his burning obsession: when and how to die. In novels such as *The Temple of the Golden Pavilion* (1956; Eng. trans., 1959) and in essays such as *Sun and Steel* (1968; Eng. trans., 1970) he widened his fascination with death to include nihilism, narcissism, and aestheticism.

Mishnah [mish'-nuh]   Mishnah, a Hebrew term meaning "repetition" or "study," is the name given to the oldest postbiblical codification of Jewish Oral Law. Together with the Gemara (later commentaries on the Mishnah itself), it forms the TALMUD.

Between 400 BC and the beginning of the Christian Era, the biblical laws (see TORAH) were intensively studied, applied to new situations, and supplemented by traditions of popular observance and by precedents established by prominent leaders. This material, long transmitted by word of mouth and known as the Oral Torah, defined the meaning of biblical laws. After the fall of Jerusalem and the destruction of the Temple in AD 70, the Jewish scholars and teachers called *tannaim* continued to elaborate and systematize the Oral Torah. About AD 200, Rabbi JUDAH HA-NASI promulgated a collection of the most reliable traditions. This work, the Mishnah, became the official text out of which further Jewish legal development occurred.

The Mishnah consists of six orders (*sedarim*): *Zeraim* ("Seeds"), treating agricultural laws; *Moed* ("Seasons"), Sabbath and festivals; *Nashim* ("Women"), marriage, divorce, and family law; *Neziqin* ("Damages"), civil and criminal jurisprudence; *Qodashim* ("Holy Things"), sacrificial cult and dietary laws; and *Tohorot* ("Purifications"), ritual defilement and purification. These are divided into 63 treatises. The Mishnah includes some nonlegal material, notably the *Pirke Avot* ("Chapters of the Fathers"), a collection of wise sayings that forms the final treatise of the *Neziqin*.

Miskito [mis-kee'-toe]   The Miskito are an ethnically mixed "Indian" people living in the river valleys and along the MOSQUITO COAST of eastern Nicaragua and Honduras. They speak a native American language related to Chibchan and numbered approximately 150,000 in 1980. The Miskito retain a strong sense of ethnic identity and have been significantly influenced by English-speaking foreigners, including missionaries of the MORAVIAN

CHURCH. Traditionally, they have been isolated from and hostile to the Hispanic heartland of Nicaragua and Honduras. Until recently the Miskito lived in numerous small villages. Women cultivated a variety of subsistence and cash crops and men sought jobs with foreign-owned lumber, mining, or banana companies. In recent years, due to Hispanic intrusions into their territory associated with the Sandinista revolution in Nicaragua, thousands of Nicaraguan Miskito have fled as refugees to Costa Rica and Honduras.

Miskolc [mish'-kawlts]   Miskolc, the second largest city in Hungary, is located in the northeastern part of the country, along the Sajó River. The population is 208,000 (1989 est.). It has important rail and road connections and is a major industrial center producing iron and steel, cement, chemicals, glass, and textiles. Lignite is mined in the vicinity. Landmarks include Saint Stephen's Church (13th century), Avas Reformed Church (15th century), and the 13th-century Diòsgyör castle. The city's Herman Ottó Museum has a collection of Scythian artifacts dating from the 6th century BC.

Miskolc was firmly established before the 13th century. It has endured repeated invasion throughout its history—by Mongols, particularly in 1241 when they nearly destroyed the city, Ottomans during the 16th and 17th centuries, and Germans during the 17th and 18th centuries.

missile   see ROCKETS AND MISSILES

missions, Christian   The Gospels record the command of Jesus Christ that his disciples go forth and teach all nations (Matt. 28:19); Christian missions are the response to this command. The history of missions is, to a large extent, the history of Christianity, because missionary efforts are recorded in the ACTS OF THE APOSTLES and have continued to the present.

Saint PAUL was the first great missionary to the Gentiles, and as a result of his efforts the church spread until, by the end of the 1st century, it had reached most of the great Mediterranean cities. By the beginning of the 4th century Christianity had become a dominant force in Greek culture, and in 313 it became an official religion of the Roman Empire. By the end of the 4th century it had extended as far as India in the east and Ireland in the west. In the following centuries the church expanded into northern Europe, and the evangelization of Germany and Scandinavia continued through the early medieval period. Saint BONIFACE, the apostle of Germany, Saint PATRICK, Ireland's apostle, and Saint AUGUSTINE OF CANTERBURY were notable missionaries of that era.

The great voyages of discovery in the 15th and 16th centuries and the expansion of European trade and colonization marked the beginning of a new surge of missionary activity. Among the religious orders, the FRANCISCANS, the DOMINICANS, the CARMELITES, and the JESUITS all undertook missions—some to combat heresy, others to establish Christianity in new lands. Jesuit missionaries sent

Throughout its history Christianity has been a missionary religion, undertaking pastoral as well as evangelizing tasks. In this photograph, a Baptist nurse and a Roman Catholic priest minister to children in Karachi, Pakistan.

to India and the Far East included Saint FRANCIS XAVIER, Matteo RICCI, and Roberto DE NOBILI. The Recollects (French Franciscans) were the first missionaries to Canada; they were followed by the Jesuits, whose explorations of Canada and the Upper Mississippi are recorded in the *Jesuit Relations.* The Franciscans and Jesuits, both of whom accompanied the Spanish conquerors in Central and South America, were the most important orders in Mexico and in the Spanish territories that later became part of the United States—Florida, California, and the Southwest. Roman Catholic missions were, and are, overseen by the Sacred Congregation for the Propagation of the Faith (founded 1622), known as the Propaganda, which was set up to settle disputes between rival missionary orders.

Although Protestant missionaries such as John ELIOT and Roger WILLIAMS ministered to the Indians in New England in the 17th century, Protestant churches lagged behind the Roman Catholics in missionary initiative. Protestant missions began in India with the arrival (1706) in Tranquebar of two German missionaries under the patronage of the king of Denmark.

The great era of expansion, however, took place in the 19th century when missionary societies were established in both Europe and the United States and when European colonialism was at its peak. Both Protestants and Roman Catholics sent missionaries to almost every country on Earth, and medical missionaries began to provide medical and educational assistance in conjunction with spiritual help. Evangelization is increasingly assumed by native Christians in their own regions.

See also: CHRISTIANITY; ECUMENICAL MOVEMENT.

Mississippi   The state of Mississippi borders Arkansas on the northwest, Louisiana on the southwest, Tennessee in the north, and Alabama in the east. In the southeast, Mississippi has a coastline on the Gulf of Mexico that is 71 km (44 mi) long. The state stretches for 530 km (330 mi) from north to south and 290 km (180 mi) from east to west. Mississippi ranks 32d in area among the U.S. states and 31st in population.

The first European settlement was established by the French in 1699 near present-day Oceansprings. Controlled by the British for the latter part of the 18th century, Mississippi became part of the United States after the Revolutionary War. The state takes its name from the Mississippi River, which forms most of its western boundary.

Land and Resources

Almost the entire state lies within the eastern Gulf Coastal Plain, which is divided into subregions. The flat Mississippi River Delta stretches along the east bank of the river. The Bluff Hills are located just east of the delta. East of the Bluff Hills three different areas span the state from north to south: the north central hills in the north, the Jackson Prairie in the center, and the Piney Woods in the south. The Black Prairie lies east of the north central hills. In the northeasternmost corner of the state are the Tennessee River Hills, including Woodall Mountain (246 m/806 ft), the highest point in the state. Elevations average 60–155 m (200–510 ft).

Soils. Mississippi soil types trend north-south approximating the physiographic regions. Alluvial soils compose the delta, and loess soils occupy the bluff region. The interior is composed of sandy and clay loams interspersed with loams and black prairie soils.

Rivers and Lakes. The major rivers include the YAZOO and the Big Black, which drain into the MISSISSIPPI RIVER; and the TOMBIGBEE, Pearl, and Pascagoula, which flow into the Gulf. Marshes exist along the coast. The major lakes are artificial. The state has extensive groundwater resources.

Climate. Mississippi's climate is subtropical. Average annual precipitation ranges from 1,676 mm (66 in) along the coast to 1,219 mm (48 in) in the north. Mean annual temperatures vary from 16° C (61° F) in the north to 20° C (68° F) along the coast. Summer maximum temperatures average 35° C (95° F), and winter minimums vary from 0° C (32° F) in the north to 11° C (44° F) in the south. Mississippi is subject to thunderstorms in midsummer and hurricanes in late summer and early autumn. Snow and sleet are rare.

Vegetation and Animal Life. About 55% of the state is covered with forests, which include several species of oak, hickory, and pine. In the alluvial areas cypress, gum, pecan, bays, elms, and willows grow. Decorative trees, such as the magnolia and live oak, also abound. Game animals include squirrel, deer, rabbit, wild turkey, and quail.

Resources and Environment. Mississippi has large forest resources because much of the state is covered with species that are suitable for lumbering, such as slash

MISSISSIPPI

Land: Area: 125,443 km² (48,434 mi²); rank: 32d. Capital and largest city: Jackson (1990 pop., 201,000). Counties: 82. Elevations: highest—246 m (806 ft), at Woodall Mountain; lowest—sea level, at the Gulf coast.

People: Population (1990): 2,586,443; rank: 31st; density: 20.5 persons per km² (53.1 per mi²). Distribution (1990): 47.1% urban, 52.9% rural. Average annual change (1980–90): +0.26%.

Government (1993): Governor: Kirk Fordice, Republican. U.S. Congress: Senate—2 Republicans; House—5 Democrats. Electoral college votes: 7. State legislature: 52 senators, 122 representatives.

Economy: State personal income (1989): $30.7 billion; rank: 33d. Median family income (1989): $24,448; rank: 50th. Agriculture: income (1989)—$2.3 billion. Fishing: value (1989)—$44 million. Lumber production (1991): 2.3 billion board feet. Mining (nonfuel): value (1988)—$103 million. Manufacturing: value added (1987)—$10.5 billion. Services: value (1987)—$5.6 billion.

Miscellany: Statehood: Dec. 10, 1817; the 20th state. Nickname: Magnolia State; tree: magnolia; motto: *Virtute et Armis* ("By Valor and Arms"); song: "Go Mississippi."

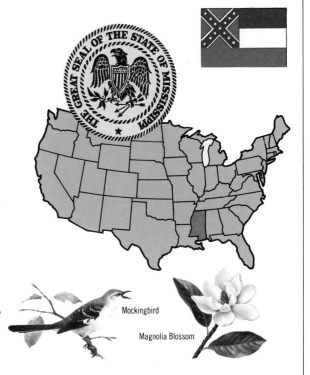

Mockingbird

Magnolia Blossom

People (continued)

pine and loblolly pine. Tung trees, introduced from China in 1905, are cultivated for their oil. The state's mineral-resource base is small, with only petroleum and natural gas being of national significance, although the deposits of sand, gravel, limestone, and clay are significant to the local economy. Lakes formed by dams on the Yazoo, Pearl, and Tennessee rivers provide important recreation and hydroelectric facilities.

Mississippi has set up an air- and water-pollution-control commission that is responsible for conserving and maintaining the potability of water supplies. Major efforts are devoted to undoing and preventing soil erosion and stream siltation and to reforestation. The damage caused by Mississippi River floods is an ever-present threat.

People

Mississippi's population is 2,586,443 (1990). The growth rate of 2.6% between 1980 and 1990 was substantially below the 10.2% growth rate for the nation as a whole. The most significant change in the composition of the population is the degree of urbanization. Before World War II the majority of the inhabitants were rural (80% in 1940), but by the late 1980s more than half of all Mississippians lived in urban areas. The leading cities in order of population are JACKSON, BILOXI, Greenville, Hatties-

burg, MERIDIAN, and GULFPORT. The percentage of Mississippi's white population decreased slightly from 1980 to 1990, while that of its black population increased.

Of the total population about 35% are black. Other nonwhite groups, including Choctaw Indians, make up less than 1% of the population. The Baptists are the leading religious denomination. There are also Protestants of various other denominations. Roman Catholics and Jews constitute very small percentages of the population.

Education and Cultural Activity. The first schools in Mississippi were private academies. By 1817 nine academies had received state charters and two of them later developed into colleges. In 1830, Presbyterians founded Oakland College, which is now Alcorn State University. The University of Mississippi was established in 1844 at Oxford. The Industrial Institute and College was founded in 1884 as the nation's first state-supported college for women. Today it is known as Mississippi University for Women. Many Mississippi public schools were battlegrounds in the struggle to desegregate tax-supported schools following the BROWN V. BOARD OF EDUCATION OF TOPEKA, KANSAS Supreme Court decision of 1954. Today Mississippi's public school system is well integrated. Mississippi's museums include the State Historical Museum in Jackson; the University Museums in Oxford, housing anthropological and archaeo-

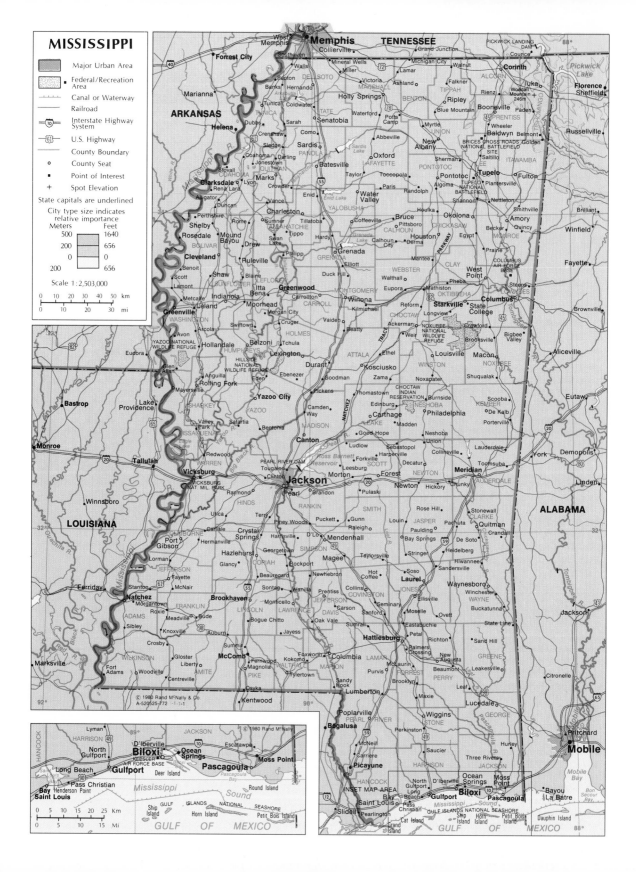

logical collections; and Beauvoir in Biloxi, the former home of Jefferson Davis.

Historical Sites. Mississippi has five registered National Historical Landmarks. Rowan Oak, the home where William Faulkner did most of his writing, is located at Oxford. The Warren County Courthouse in Vicksburg now serves as a Confederate museum. Longwood, an antebellum home, is located at Natchez and is a classic example of a southern plantation. Grand Village is an excavated Natchez Indian site. Indian mounds are located near Greenville and in the Lake George–Holly Bluff area. Civil War National Battlefields are located at VICKSBURG, Brices Cross Roads, and Tupelo.

Recreation and Sports. Mississippi offers opportunities for camping, fishing, and other outdoor activities in its state parks and national and state forests. The Natchez Trace, which began as a series of wilderness trails used by Indians and settlers, is now a national recreational highway.

Communications. The state's first newspaper, the *Mississippi Gazette*, began publication in 1799 in Natchez. Of the daily newspapers now published, the *Jackson Clarion-Ledger* (morning) and the *Jackson News* (evening) together have the largest daily circulation in the state. Mississippi is also very adequately served by television stations and by scores of radio stations.

Economic Activity

Reflecting the national economic picture, Mississippi earns more from service industries than from any other sector. Manufacturing, however, is the single largest source of income in Mississippi. Heavy capital-intensive industries—producing transportation equipment, chemicals, and electrical machinery and engaged in metalworking and shipbuilding—are located along the Gulf Coast, navigable waterways in the northeast, and in the port cities along the Mississippi River. Food processing is increasing in importance. Light industry, such as clothing manufacture, is found in the interior and the northeast. The lumber-and-wood-products industry is declining in economic significance, but sizable amounts of wood pulp, fiberboard, boxes, and naval stores are still produced.

In 1988, 25.1 billion kW h of electricity were pro- duced. Most of Mississippi's electricity is thermal power, and electricity is also transmitted into the state from Tennessee Valley Authority generating stations.

Agriculture and Foresting. Cotton and soybeans are the leading crops; hay, corn, rice, and wheat are also significant. Cattle, calves, and broilers make up a substantial part of livestock farming. Swine, milk, eggs, and orchard crops (fruit and pecans) compose a much smaller segment of the agricultural economy.

Earlier in this century forests had been seriously overcut, necessitating a major reforestation program. Large acreages of scientifically managed tree farms and woodlands of both softwoods and hardwoods are run on a sustained-yield basis.

Fishing. Various species of catfish, bass, bluegill, crappie, and perch are freshwater game fish. The primary catch of the marine fishery is white trout, shrimp, spotted sea trout, flounder, red drum, and ground mullet in the inshore area. The outshore region catch is mainly mackerel, lemonfish, bonito, bluefish, marlin, wahoo, sailfish, tuna, oysters, and shrimp.

Tourism. Gulf Coast beaches are a major year-round attraction due to Mississippi's mild winter climate. Those areas experiencing the greatest growth in tourism include the Natchez-Vicksburg area, the Gulf Coast, and the region south of Memphis, Tenn.

Transportation. Mississippi's major traffic arteries focus on Jackson, Meridian, the Gulf Coast, and the Mississippi River cities of Natchez, Vicksburg, and Greenville. Eleven railroads operate throughout the state. Water traffic is significant along the Gulf Coast and Mississippi River ports. Pascagoula and Vicksburg are the two largest ports. The Tennessee-Tombigbee Waterway, completed in 1984, connects the Tennessee River, in northeast Mississippi, with the Gulf of Mexico at Mobile, Ala., via a 377-km-long (234-mi) system of canals and locks along the Tombigbee River.

Government and Politics

Mississippi adopted its first constitution in 1817 and the present constitution in 1890. The legislature is bicameral, with a 122-member house of representatives and a 52-member senate. The governor is elected for a 4-year

The Mississippi River deposits fertile alluvial soils along the floodplain of its lower course, sometimes called the Mississippi alluvial plain.

term and may not serve successive terms. The judicial branch is composed of a supreme court, whose 9 judges serve 8-year terms, and chancery courts, whose 36 judges serve 4-year terms.

From 1876, when Reconstruction ended, until the presidential election of 1960 the electorate voted Democratic. After 1960, Democratic strength began to decline. The state voted for Democratic presidential candidate Jimmy Carter in 1976 but supported the Republicans under Ronald Reagan in 1980 and 1984 and George Bush in 1988.

History

Settlement. Prior to European exploration, Mississippi was occupied by the CHICKASAW, CHOCTAW, NATCHEZ, Biloxi, and Pascagoula. In 1540, Hernando DE SOTO was the first European to visit the region. Robert Cavelier, sieur de LA SALLE, claimed (1682) the Mississippi River valley for France 150 years later and named it Louisiana. In 1699, Pierre Le Moyne, sieur d'IBERVILLE, established the first permanent French settlement near present-day Oceansprings. In 1717 the financier John LAW launched the MISSISSIPPI SCHEME to bring settlers and commercial development to the French-held Mississippi River valley. Although the plan collapsed in 1720, it brought large numbers of settlers to the region. Following the French and Indian War (1754–63) the region passed to the British.

The second Spanish period began in 1781 and lasted until 1795, when the region became part of the United States. The territory of Mississippi, with its capital at Natchez, was organized in 1798, and in 1817 Mississippi became the 20th state. By 1832 most of the Indians had been moved to the Indian Territory (present-day Oklahoma), opening new areas to settlement.

From 1832 until secession the state experienced, in succession, a period of prosperity based largely on cotton cultivation and the use of slaves, depression, and war with Mexico. It was also a period of growing controversy over slavery. On Jan. 9, 1861, Mississippi seceded from the Union and became the second state to join the Confederate States of America. Jefferson DAVIS, a Mississippi politician, became the president of the Confederacy. Several Civil War battles were fought in the state, including the VICKSBURG CAMPAIGN (November 1862–December 1863).

Modern Era. The defeat of the Confederate States ushered in the RECONSTRUCTION era. In 1870, Mississippi was readmitted to the Union. In 1890 a new constitution was

(Above) *Linden is one of the many preserved mansions in Natchez built during the prosperous antebellum period.*

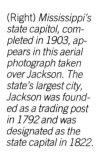

(Right) *Mississippi's state capitol, completed in 1903, appears in this aerial photograph taken over Jackson. The state's largest city, Jackson was founded as a trading post in 1792 and was designated as the state capital in 1822.*

adopted, which, in part, institutionalized segregation of the races (see JIM CROW LAWS). In the 1890s much in Mississippi seemed little changed from the 1830s. Population distribution was the same, cotton dominated the economy, and blacks—although now free—became economically trapped in the sharecropping system and experienced little change in their status.

During the tenure (1916–20) of Governor Theodore Bilbo, legislation was enacted that altered the economic, political, and social face of the state by improving state services. Nevertheless, Mississippi entered the 1920s as a rural, agrarian state with rigid segregation and a black majority. A devastating Mississippi River flood in 1927 weakened the economy. The Depression of the 1930s was the most trying economic period for the state. To induce industrial growth, and thereby improve the economic climate, the state initiated a program called Balancing Agriculture With Industry (BAWI). The discovery of petroleum (1939 and 1940) introduced a major new industry.

World War II brought Mississippi into the modern era by opening it to the outside world and introduced its people to prosperity. Farmers diversified their crops, becoming less reliant on cotton. With the advent of mechanization, small sharecropping plots were no longer economically viable. Industrialization grew, and by the 1960s employment rolls listed greater numbers of employees in the manufacturing sector than were involved in agriculture.

During the 1960s, Mississippi was a center of the CIVIL RIGHTS movement. Despite the 1954 Supreme Court decision making segregated schools illegal, the state did not quickly institute racial INTEGRATION. In 1962 a black student, James Meredith, attempted to attend the University of Mississippi law school. His admission was blocked, and during the subsequent violence, federal troops were sent to restore order. Violent incidents against blacks took place as the struggle for integration continued. After passage of the Federal Voting Rights Act (1965) many blacks were able to register and vote. In 1969, Charles Evers (see EVERS family) was elected mayor of Fayette and became the first black mayor in the history of the state.

Mississippi's economic base is now a composite of that of the nation, and social trends are in the direction of national norms rather than southern regionalism.

Mississippi River   The Mississippi River, 3,779 km (2,348 mi) long, is the second longest river, after the Missouri, in the United States. Its triangular drainage area, covering about 40% of the country and including all or part of 31 states, is approximately 3,250,000 km^2 (1,250,000 mi^2), the third largest in the world. The Mississippi rises in Minnesota and then flows south, following the boundaries between the states of Minnesota, Iowa, Missouri, Arkansas, and Louisiana on the west, and Wisconsin, Illinois, Kentucky, Tennessee, and Mississippi on the east. The river, whose name means "father of waters" in the Algonquian language, has long been an important transportation artery of North America.

Course of the River. Rising at an elevation of 446 m (1,463 ft) in Lake Itasca, Minn., the Mississippi flows through several glacial lakes to Minneapolis–Saint Paul, where it passes over a series of rapids and is joined by the Minnesota River. After this confluence the Mississippi is fringed by 60–90-m-high (200–300-ft) bluffs on both sides.

Between Minneapolis and St. Louis, Mo., the chief tributaries are the Illinois, Chippewa, Black, Wisconsin, Saint Croix, Iowa, Des Moines, and Rock rivers. The MISSOURI RIVER, joins the Mississippi at St. Louis. It is the longest tributary, constituting more than 40% of the Mississippi system drainage area and furnishing about 20% of the total discharge. At Cairo, Ill., the Mississippi is joined by the OHIO RIVER.

South of Cairo the Mississippi enters a wide (64–113 km/40–70 mi), low valley that was once an embayment of the Gulf of Mexico. Sediment has filled this area, and through the centuries the river has extended its mouth to the present location 966 km (600 mi) downstream. This lower part of the Mississippi's course is contained within natural levees formed by flood-deposited sediments. Beyond the levees lie low floodplains often at a lower elevation than the river itself. Another feature of the river is its meandering. The channel route from Cairo to New Orleans is almost three times as long as the valley. Major tributaries in the lower section are the ARKANSAS, RED, and White rivers.

The Mississippi enters the Gulf of Mexico (see MEXICO, GULF OF) about 160 km (100 mi) downstream from New Orleans, through a 26,150-km^2 (10,100-mi^2) delta. Because almost 550 million metric tons (500 million U.S. tons) of sediment are deposited annually, the delta extends about 91 m (300 ft) each year.

Flood Control. In its lower section the Mississippi is subject to disastrous flooding. Efforts at containing the river have been especially vigorous since a catastrophic flood in 1927. The federal government has built artificial levees 5–7 m (15–24 ft) high and dredged waterways that release the floodwater laterally to the Gulf of Mexico.

Navigation and Economic Use. The lower river, which has a relatively narrow but deep channel, is navigable for oceangoing ships upstream to Baton Rouge, La. About 24,150 km (15,000 mi) of the entire river system are presently navigable, and traffic has experienced significant growth in recent years. Cargoes consist mainly of petrochemicals from the Gulf of Mexico and grain from the Midwest.

Exploration and Development. The first Europeans to see the river inland were Hernando DE SOTO and his party in 1541. In the late 17th century the Frenchmen Jacques MARQUETTE and Louis JOLLIET (1673) and the sieur de LA SALLE explored the river from the north; La Salle, who reached the mouth of the Mississippi in 1682, claimed the whole valley for France. The western part of the basin was purchased from France by the United States in 1803 (see LOUISIANA PURCHASE) and was explored by the LEWIS AND CLARK EXPEDITION. Among the original Indian tribes living along the Mississippi were the OJIBWA, WINNEBAGO, FOX, SAUK, CHOCTAW, CHICKASAW, NATCHEZ, and ALABAMA.

The river system formed the pathways for much of the

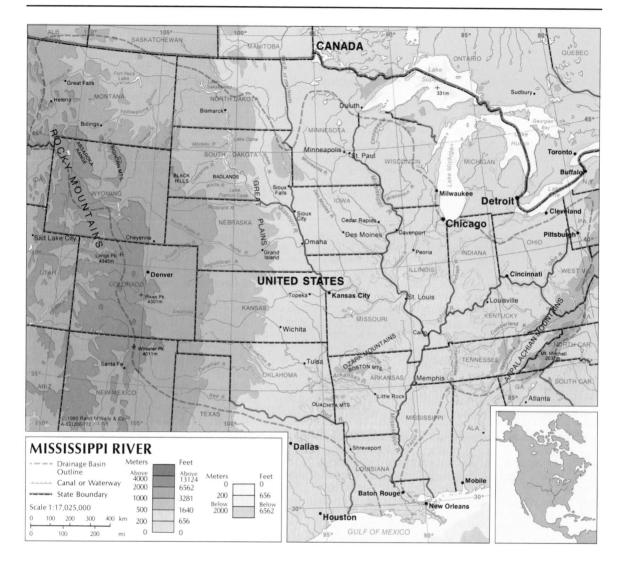

MISSISSIPPI RIVER

- – – Drainage Basin Outline
- Canal or Waterway
- – – State Boundary

Scale 1:17,025,000

Meters	Feet
Above 4000	Above 13124
2000	6562
1000	3281
500	1640
200	656
0	0

Meters	Feet
0	0
200	656
Below 2000	Below 6562

settlement of the central United States. The advent of the steamboat in 1812 brought dependable transportation, and river traffic increased rapidly. During the Civil War control of the river was a major strategic objective; the VICKSBURG CAMPAIGN (1863) achieved that goal for the Union armies.

Mississippi Scheme   The Mississippi Scheme of 1717–20 was a grandiose project devised by the Scottish financier John Law to generate private prosperity and state income in France through colonial commercial exploitation of French Louisiana. The French government, under the regent Philippe II, duc d'ORLÉANS, chartered (1717) Law's Company of the West, and frenzied private investment drove up shares from 500 to 18,000 *livres*. Many speculators became millionaires, France's colonial

and national economies were stimulated, and the company eventually absorbed (1719–20) all the other French trading companies, the state's tax collection, coinage, and debt, and Law's national bank. Although the scheme resulted in a large influx of settlers into Louisiana, the expected profits did not materialize. Panic selling of shares burst the "Mississippi bubble" in October 1720.

Mississippian Period   see GEOLOGIC TIME

Missoula   Missoula (1990 pop., 42,918), the seat of Missoula County, is a city in western Montana. Lumber and paper, sugar refining, and dairy industries are located there, and copper, gold, and lead are mined nearby. The University of Montana (1893) is in Missoula. The city was first settled in 1860 as a trading post.

MISSOURI

Land: Area: 180,546 km² (69,709 mi²); rank: 21st.
Capital: Jefferson City (1990 pop., 35,481). Largest
city: Kansas City (1990 pop., 435,146). Counties: 114.
Elevations: highest—540 m (1,772 ft), at Taum Sauk
Mountain; lowest—70 m (230 ft), at the Saint Francis
River.

People: Population (1990): 5,137,804; rank: 15th;
density: 28.7 persons per km² (74.3 per mi²). Distribution (1990): 68.7% urban, 31.3% rural. Average annual
change (1980–90): +0.4%.

Government (1993): Governor: Mel Carnahan, Demo-
crat. U.S. Congress: Senate—2 Republicans; House—6
Democrats, 3 Republicans. Electoral college votes: 11.
State legislature: 34 senators, 163 representatives.

Economy: State personal income (1989): $84.1 billion;
rank: 16th. Median family income (1989): $31,838;
rank: 32d. Agriculture: income (1989)—$3.9 billion.
Lumber production (1991): 249 million board feet. Mining (nonfuel): value (1988)—$968 million. Manufactur-
ing: value added (1987)—$25.9 billion. Services: value
(1987)—$25.25 billion.

Miscellany: Statehood: Aug. 10, 1821; the 24th state.
Nickname: Show Me State; tree: flowering dogwood; motto: *Salus populi suprema lex esto* ("The welfare of the
people shall be the supreme law"); song: "Missouri
Waltz."

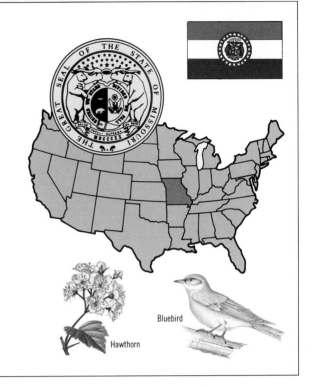

Bluebird

Hawthorn

Missouri   Missouri is a midwestern state of the United
States, located near the country's geographic center at
the confluence of the two longest rivers in the United
States—the Mississippi and the Missouri. Situated where
North meets South and where the industrial East gives
way to the plains of the West, Missouri exhibits characteristics of all these areas. It is bordered on the north by
Iowa; on the east by Illinois, Kentucky, and Tennessee;
on the south by Arkansas; and on the west by Nebraska,
Kansas, and Oklahoma. During the 19th century, Missouri served as a springboard for countless westward-
bound settlers. *Missouri*, an Algonquian word meaning
"people with big canoes," was the name given to the Indians living near the mouth of the Missouri River.

Land and Resources

The terrain of Missouri varies from flat plains to rough
hills. The lowest elevation, 70 m (230 ft), is along the
Saint Francis River in the southeast, and the highest
point, 540 m (1,772 ft), is Taum Sauk Mountain in the
Saint François Mountains south of St. Louis.

Physiographic Regions. Missouri has three major physiographic regions: the Ozark Highland, the Plains, and the
Mississippi Alluvial Plain. The Ozark Highland has an average elevation of about 300 m (1,000 ft); it covers the

southern portion of the state from St. Louis and Jefferson
City on the Missouri River to Oklahoma and Arkansas. The
region is famous for more than 5,000 caves and many
large springs. One, Big Spring, in the south central part of
the state, is among the largest springs in the United States.
The Ozarks retain the rolling surface of a plateau near
Springfield and in some of the central areas, but elsewhere
swift-flowing streams have dissected the plateau, forming
steep, narrow-crested hills. Relief reaches 230 m (750 ft)
in the most rugged areas (see OZARK MOUNTAINS).

North and west of the Ozarks is the Plains region, rising gradually from 200 m (650 ft) near St. Louis to more
than 380 m (1,250 ft) in the extreme northwest. Parts of
the northeast are nearly flat, but in most places erosion
by streams has resulted in hills and valleys. In a belt
about 80 km (50 mi) wide along the Missouri River, the
dissected plains are thickly mantled with loess. South of
the Missouri River, along the Kansas border, the Osage
Plains are more open and undulating.

The third major physiographic region, the Mississippi
Alluvial Plain, or Bootheel, consists of the seven southeastern counties. The flat surface slopes slightly southward from the foot of the Ozark Escarpment.

Soils. Missouri's most productive soils are those of the
loess belt along the Missouri River and the alluvial soils of
the Bootheel. Soil erosion, once a widespread problem,

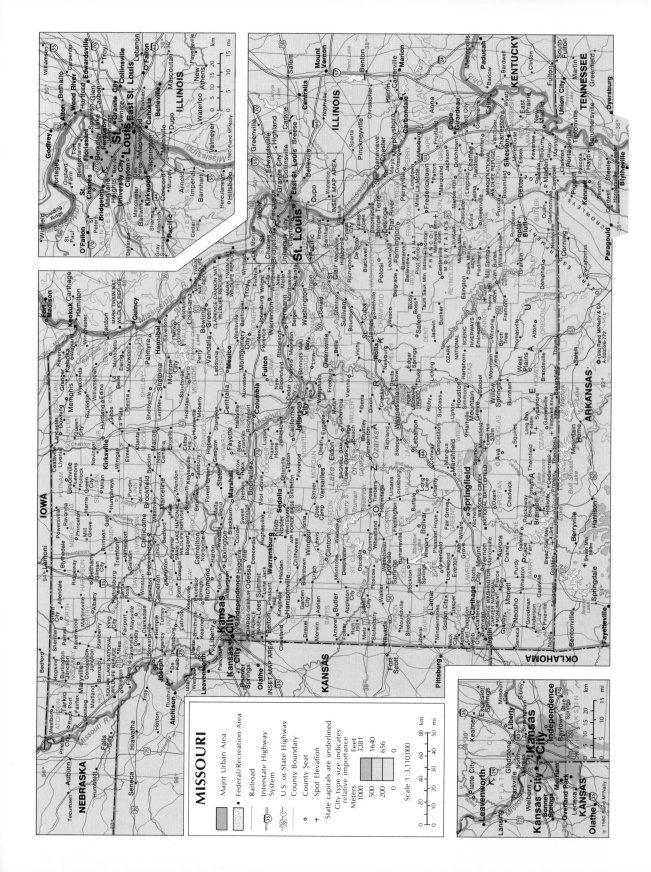

MISSOURI

Major Urban Area

Federal/Recreation Area

Railroad

Interstate Highway System

U.S. or State Highway

County Boundary

County Seat

+ Spot Elevation

State capitals are underlined

City type size indicates relative importance

Meters	Feet
1000	3281
500	1640
200	656
0	0

Scale 1:3,110,000

© 1980 Rand McNally

(Below) *St. Louis's Gateway Arch (completed 1964), a 192-m (630-ft) stainless-steel arch designed by Eero Saarinen, symbolizes the city's role as gateway to Missouri and the western American frontier.*

(Above) *This view of the St. Louis skyline was photographed from the Gateway Arch. Busch Memorial Stadium* (left) *is the home of the city's professional baseball and football teams. The Old Courthouse* (center) *was the scene of the first Dred Scott trial.*

has largely been controlled with improved management practices.

Rivers and Lakes. The MISSISSIPPI and MISSOURI rivers dominate the state's drainage system. The streams of northern Missouri flow generally southward across the till plain to these rivers. In southern Missouri streams flow away from the crest of the Ozark Highland in all directions. Ozark streams are fed by a complex network of underground drainage systems.

Missouri's largest lakes are artificial. The Lake of the Ozarks, formed by damming on the Osage River, is one of the world's largest artificial lakes. Groundwater is abundant.

Climate. Missouri has a continental climate with hot, humid summers and cold winters. The clash of contrasting air masses in spring and fall may set off violent thunderstorms, some of which are accompanied by tornadoes.

The average January minimum temperatures range from −10° C (14° F) in the northwest to −1° C (30° F) in the southeast. July maximum temperatures average 33° C (92° F) throughout the state. Mean annual precipitation ranges from 813 mm (32 in) in the northwest to 1,270 mm (50 in) in the southeast. Average annual snowfall is 508 mm (20 in) in the northwest and 130 mm (6.5 in) in the southeast.

Vegetation and Animal Life. At the time of white settlement, the flatter parts of the Plains region were covered with tall prairie grass. The more dissected parts were covered with hardwood forests. In the Ozarks an oak and hickory forest prevailed, with shortleaf pine intermixed in the east. The Mississippi Alluvial Plain had a forest of bald cypress, tupelo, and sweet gum. At present, new-growth commercial forests are gaining importance, and only in the Bootheel and the Osage Plains have farms and pastures blocked reforestation. The wildlife of Missouri includes deer, wild turkeys, and bears.

Mineral Resources. Missouri has about 13.6 billion metric tons (12.3 billion U.S. tons) of coal reserves in the Plains region. The state also has vast reserves of TAR SANDS in its western counties, but no economical method of mining this petroleum has yet been found. Missouri is the leading lead-mining state in the United States, with deposits in the eastern Ozarks. East central Missouri is an important producer of barite, which is used as a pigment. Clays are mined in central Missouri, and extensive iron-ore deposits are found in the eastern Ozarks. Limestone, marble, granite, and sandstone are quarried for construction purposes.

People

Missouri's population density slightly exceeds the national average of about 27 persons per km² (70 persons per mi²), but rural regions in the Ozarks and in north central Missouri have fewer than 4 persons per km² (10 per mi²). During the 1980s, KANSAS CITY overtook ST. LOUIS as the largest city in Missouri, but its metropolitan-area population remains second in size to metropolitan St. Louis. Other large cities are SPRINGFIELD, INDEPENDENCE, SAINT JOSEPH, and Columbia. About two-thirds of Missourians live in metropolitan areas. The population of Missouri is growing very slowly, a result of net migration out of the state.

Missouri has one of the nation's highest percentages of persons over 65 years of age. African Americans, concentrated in the large cities, constitute about 10.7% of the state's population. Roman Catholics constitute the largest single religious group, but Protestants, representing many denominations, form the majority of church members.

Education. Free public education became widely available after the Civil War. Education is at present supervised by a state department of education. The University of Missouri, founded in 1839, was the first state university west of the Mississippi River. Today it has four campuses. Eight state universities and colleges have been established along with Lincoln University, founded in 1866 as the first state college for blacks. Private institutions include St. Louis University (1818) and Washington University (1853), both in St. Louis.

Culture. The St. Louis Art Museum, the William Rockhill Nelson Gallery and Atkins Museum of Art in Kansas City, as well as the plant collections of the Missouri Botanical Garden in St. Louis are renowned. The St. Louis Symphony, established in 1880, is the second oldest symphony orchestra in the United States.

Historical Sites. The most visited historical site in the state is the Gateway Arch in the Jefferson National Expansion Memorial. Designed by Eero SAARINEN, it is located on the original riverfront town site of St. Louis and symbolizes the city's role as gateway to the West. The region surrounding HANNIBAL is closely associated with the life and work of Mark TWAIN. Saint Joseph was the eastern terminus of the famed but short-lived PONY EXPRESS.

Recreation. The Ozark National Scenic Riverways, the first national riverway, encompasses the Current and Jacks Fork rivers in the eastern Ozarks. Large tracts of the Ozarks are in national or state forests and are increasingly used for recreation. Professional baseball, football, and ice-hockey teams are supported in St. Louis and Kansas City.

Communications. The *St. Louis Post-Dispatch,* founded by Joseph PULITZER, and the *Kansas City Star* and *Times* are leading newspapers. The world's first school of journalism was founded at the University of Missouri-Columbia in 1908.

Economic Activity

Although Missouri is often considered an agricultural state—and in fact is one of the nation's leading farming states—manufacturing has assumed a more prominent economic role in Missouri than farming.

Agriculture. Missouri's principal crops are soybeans and corn, followed by winter wheat, cotton, and hay. Missouri usually ranks among the ten leading states in the production of each of these commodities. The loess belt and the Bootheel are the foremost row-crop areas, but agriculture is successful throughout the Plains region and western Ozarks. Most farm grains are used for livestock feed. This helps explain why Missouri is a major livestock state, habitually ranking high among all U.S. states in the production of beef cattle, hogs, and dairy cattle. Dairying is concentrated in southwestern Missouri. The distinctive agricultural economy of the Bootheel was once based on large cotton farms, but soybeans, corn, wheat, alfalfa, and rice have displaced much of the cotton.

Manufacturing. Missouri's largest industry is the manufacture of transportation equipment, especially automobiles, with production ranking second in the nation; aircraft, spacecraft, and railroad equipment follow. Other major industries include food processing (primarily brewing, flour milling, and meat packing), printing and publishing, and the manufacture of chemicals, fabricated metal products, machinery, and electrical equipment.

Tourism. Tourist facilities are concentrated at the Lake of the Ozarks and in the White River region of the southwest. All of the Ozarks offer hiking, cave exploring, camping, boating, canoeing, fishing, and hunting. Many small Ozark communities are economically dependent on tourism.

Transportation. Missouri's central location and its economic vitality spurred the development of a large network of roads, highways, and railroad track. The most heavily used transportation corridors are those between St. Louis and Kansas City and St. Louis and the southwest. Com-

(Right) *Union Station is Kansas City's historic central railroad station; it opened in 1914. Kansas City is Missouri's largest city and an active industrial center.*

(Below) *Lake of the Ozarks, located in central Missouri, is the state's largest lake. Created by the impounding of the Osage River by Bagnell Dam in 1931, the lake is 209 km (130 mi) long.*

mercial barge traffic on both the Missouri and Mississippi rivers makes St. Louis one of the nation's busiest inland river ports. Both St. Louis and Kansas City are national air and trucking centers.

Although large artificial lakes are conspicuous in the state's landscape, hydroelectric power provides only a small amount of Missouri's electricity production. Coal-fueled plants furnish approximately 90%.

Government and Politics

Missouri has had four constitutions: 1820, prior to statehood; 1865 and 1875, in the aftermath of the Civil War; and 1945. The Missouri general assembly is composed of a senate of 34 members serving 4-year terms, and a house of representatives, with 163 members who serve 2-year terms. The governor is elected for 4 years and may be reelected once.

The chief judicial officers are the 7 supreme court judges. The Missouri Plan for selecting judges, adopted in 1945, has become a nationwide model for the nonpartisan assignment of judges. Each of Missouri's 114 counties is governed by elected local officials. St. Louis functions as an independent city with county status.

Since World War II the Democrats, strongest in the cities and the Bootheel, have more often controlled the legislature, state offices, and Missouri's representation in the U.S. Congress. Missouri's Democrats tend to have a more conservative political philosophy than Democrats nationally. Republicans retain strength in suburban regions and in the southwestern part of the state.

History

Among the early Indian inhabitants of Missouri were MOUND BUILDERS, whose earthenwork monuments can be seen throughout the state. The most important regional tribes were the OSAGE, SAUK, FOX, and MISSOURI. Most had moved from the area by the time of European settlement.

European exploration began with the passage of Father Jacques MARQUETTE and the trader Louis JOLLIET down the Mississippi in 1673. In 1682 the Mississippi Valley was claimed for France by Robert Cavelier, sieur de LA SALLE, who named the territory Louisiana. The first permanent white settlement in what is now Missouri was made by the French at Sainte Geneviève in 1732.

French settlement in the 18th century was based on lead mining and fur trading, of which St. Louis (founded 1764) became the center. France ceded the region to Spain in 1762; Spain retroceded the region to France in 1802, and in 1803 Missouri, along with the rest of the Louisiana territory, was sold to the United States (see LOUISIANA PURCHASE). Missouri was made a U.S. territory in 1812.

Statehood was achieved in 1821 by way of the MISSOURI COMPROMISE (1820), which permitted Missouri's entry into the Union as a slave state. In 1837 the six northwestern counties were purchased from the Indians and added to the state by the Platte Purchase.

Because of its central location and its access to navigable rivers, Missouri served as the departure point for western trails and expeditions. The LEWIS AND CLARK EX-PEDITION began near St. Louis in 1804. The SANTA FE TRAIL opened a thriving trade with the Southwest in 1821, and the OREGON TRAIL, beginning in the 1830s and '40s, was used by thousands of settlers to the Northwest. Both trails originated at Independence, Mo. Steamboat traffic on the Mississippi and Missouri rivers became important by the 1820s. Later access to the West took place via the overland Butterfield Trail, the pony express, and the railroads radiating from St. Louis and Kansas City. The famous Missouri mule was specially bred for the arduous Santa Fe Trail.

Missouri was primarily a rural, agricultural state. In the Ozarks a subsistence farmer-woodsman economy was established. The Boonslick district in the state's center developed into the richest agricultural region, based in part on a small-scale slave plantation system.

The Civil War and Economic Growth. By the mid-19th century slavery was becoming uneconomical, and immigrants from free states and from Europe, especially Germany and Ireland, had modified the social structure. Nonetheless, slavery remained a controversial issue in the state. The case of DRED SCOTT V. SANDFORD, which reached the U.S. Supreme Court in 1856–57, began in Missouri. The moderate antislavery stance of Missouri's longtime (1821–50) senator, Thomas Hart BENTON, cost him his political career.

Despite the strong block of proslavery sentiment, a Missouri state convention voted against secession in 1861. Several major Civil War battles took place in the state, however, and guerrilla fighting was bitter, bloody, and statewide. Violence continued after the war in the activities of such outlaws as Jesse JAMES.

After the Civil War, railroad building and the renewed westward movement of Americans encouraged industry and urban growth. Following a new influx of foreign immigrants, St. Louis grew to become the nation's fourth largest city in 1900.

Economic development in the West fostered Kansas City's growth in agricultural and cattle-based industries. Missouri's peak rural-farm population was reached in 1900. Its economic and social growth was depicted in the murals of Thomas Hart BENTON, grandnephew of the senator.

The 20th Century. In the period from 1880 to 1920 lumbering companies exhausted the best of the Ozark timber. In southeastern Missouri large-scale forest clearing, levee building, ditching, and draining of swamps encouraged cotton farming and attracted thousands of laborers, many of whom were black. The Tri-State Mining District, centered on Joplin, was the nation's largest zinc-producing region, and the lead mines of the Saint François region boomed in the 1920s. Political power inexorably shifted from rural areas to the urban centers, as Missouri's cities expanded in response to the growing economy. The Depression of the 1930s temporarily slowed economic growth, World War II further drained the rural work force, which left the farms in favor of employment in the cities. Industries continued to expand in the 1950s. By the 1960s, however, depopulation of the inner part of each metropolitan area had begun. Urban deterioration lingers as one of the more intractable problems facing Missouri.

Missouri agriculture remains sound and efficient. A vigorous program of road improvement has broken down the isolation of the Ozarks and has encouraged the revival of Ozark crafts and folk culture. Missouri, because of its centrality in the nation and its diverse resources, continues to attract manufacturing and commerce, as well as developing more than its national share of retirement communities and tourists.

Missouri (Indian tribe)

The Missouri Indians of North America traditionally inhabited the lower Missouri River region of the prairie. Their Siouan language is closely related to that of the WINNEBAGO. Sometimes called Southern Siouans, the Missouri exhibited a mixture of Plains and Woodlands cultural traits. They lived along the river in permanent villages composed of earthern lodges and played lacrosse, a game typical of the Woodlands area. During seasonal expeditions into the plains they hunted bison and lived in tepees. For river travel the Missouri used skin boats, and for overland travel dog travois.

Like other southern Siouans, they were divided into totemic clans and traced descent through the male line. By 1830 white homesteaders were displacing the Missouri from the prairie. In 1843 the tribe numbered 931. Today, the Missouri live in Oklahoma on federal trust lands that they share with the OTO. The Missouri are not numerous—there are probably only several hundred of them.

Missouri Compromise

The Missouri Compromise of 1820–21 was an attempt to solve the sectional disputes between free and slave states in the United States. In 1818, Missouri Territory, where many settlers owned slaves, applied to join the Union. Bitter controversy ensued, because many Northerners wished to limit the addition of new slave states. Rep. James Tallmadge of New York added an amendment to the Missouri statehood bill that would gradually eliminate slavery there. The amendment was defeated in the U.S. Senate, and Congress adjourned without passing the statehood bill. In the next session of Congress, while the status of Missouri was still undecided, Alabama was admitted (1819) to the Union as a slave state. The free and slave states were now equally represented in the Senate.

In the midst of this conflict, Maine applied for admission to the Union, enabling Speaker of the House Henry CLAY to push through the series of measures that came to be called the Missouri Compromise. Missouri and Maine were to be admitted as slave and free states, respectively. Moreover, the Missouri Enabling Act of Mar. 6, 1820, forbade the creation of further slave states north of latitude 36° 30', Missouri's southern boundary. (The KANSAS-NEBRASKA ACT of 1854 repealed this law.) An additional controversy arose over Missouri's first constitution,

which excluded free blacks from the state. Congressional antislavery advocates challenged this clause and blocked Missouri's admission until it had been modified. Missouri became a state on Aug. 10, 1821.

Missouri River

The largest tributary of the Mississippi River, the Missouri originates at the junction of the Jefferson, Madison, and Gallatin rivers in southwestern Montana and flows 4,368 km (2,714 mi including its longest headstream) to join the Mississippi. It is the longest river in the United States. Its drainage basin covers about 1,371,100 km^2 (529,400 mi^2).

The upper Missouri River flows eastward across the high plains of Montana and joins the Yellowstone River near the North Dakota border. It then flows southward across the high plains of North and South Dakota. Its course marks the approximate southern limit of continental glaciation.

Tributaries flowing from the west are the Little Missouri, Cheyenne, White, and Niobrara rivers. The James and Big Sioux rivers enter from the north. The Missouri continues southeastward and meets the PLATTE RIVER near Omaha, Nebr., and Council Bluffs, Iowa. The river flows on to Kansas City, where the Kansas River enters from the west. The river's course turns eastward across Missouri to St. Louis, where it joins the Mississippi (see map at MISSISSIPPI RIVER).

The Missouri River, the longest river in the United States, flows through seven states. Because of its large load of suspended sediment, the Missouri has been nicknamed "Big Muddy."

The average discharge of the Missouri is about 1,810 m³ (64,000 ft³) per second at its mouth. Sediment load from erosion is heavy, suggesting its nickname, "Big Muddy."

Early inhabitants of the Missouri valley included the CHEYENNE, CROW, Mandan, PAWNEE, and SIOUX Indians. In 1673 the French explorers Jacques MARQUETTE and Louis JOLLIET were the first white people to see the Missouri. The upper river was explored (1738) by Pierre Gaultier de Varennes, sieur de La Vérendrye.

After the Louisiana Purchase of 1803 the area was explored by the LEWIS AND CLARK EXPEDITION in 1804–06.

Efforts to control the Missouri started in 1933–40 with construction of the Fort Peck Dam in Montana. The dams of the Missouri River Basin Project, begun in 1944, include the Canyon Ferry Dam (1954) in Montana, the Garrison Dam (1956) in North Dakota, and the Oahe (1963), Big Bend (1967), Fort Randall (1956), and Gavins Point (1956) dams in South Dakota. Such projects provided flood control, power, and irrigation. The river is navigable upstream to Sioux City, Iowa.

The common European mistletoe is traditionally hung over doorways during the Christmas season. The belief that it has magical powers dates back to early Nordic and Celtic legends.

mist   Mist is a suspension of tiny water droplets that hang in the atmosphere like a thin veil, decreasing visibility. Mist is intermediate between haze and FOG; the suspension is termed fog when visibility falls to less than 1 km (0.6 mi). A light rain of tiny droplets is called mist in the United States; in Scotland, a combination of fog and heavy drizzle is called mist.

mistletoe   Mistletoes are typically small, green-leaved shrubs of the mistletoe family, Loranthaceae, commonly semiparasitic on trees. They are widely known for their decorative use during the Christmas season and because they can cause serious injury to certain trees. Mistletoes penetrate the bark of the host tree and attach to the conducting tissues (xylem) by suckerlike organs called haustoria, which are generally considered to be modified roots. Mistletoes contain chlorophyll and can manufacture their own food by photosynthesis, but they extract water and nutrients from the host.

The American mistletoes comprise about 200 mostly tropical species in the genus *Phoradendron* and are found from the northern United States to central Argentina. They usually appear as bunched tufts or leafy, perennial evergreen shoots that stand out when the host has shed its leaves. A few species form long, hanging tufts or spreading, fountainlike masses. The mature fruit is commonly a translucent whitish berry, sometimes shaded with green or yellow. Birds eat the berries and spread the seeds by wiping them off their bills onto branches or by depositing them in their droppings. *P. serotinum,* with green, jointed stems that reach up to 30 cm (1 ft) long and small, leathery leaves and yellow flowers, is the common American Christmas mistletoe. Western American Indians used to boil the berries of certain species as food, and a tea made from the leaves was believed to have con-

traceptive and abortive qualities. Mistletoe may be toxic to browsing livestock, however, and the raw berries of eastern species have proved fatal to children.

mistral   [mis'-trahl]   A mistral, which is a cold, dry, northwesterly wind that blows in southern France, is created when air from an inland high-pressure zone passes through the Alps-Pyrenees gap and funnels down the Rhône Valley toward a low-pressure area in the northwestern Mediterranean Sea. The wind velocity, strengthened because of the funneling effect, often reaches 100 km/h (60 mph). The mistral, called a bora on the Adriatic coast, is strongest and most frequent in the winter and spring, when it may blow for several days at a time, sometimes causing severe crop damage and reaching heights of up to 3 km (2 mi) within the troposphere.

Mistral, Frédéric   [mee-strahl' fray-day-reek']   Frédéric Mistral, b. Sept. 8, 1830, d. Mar. 25, 1914, was the leading figure in the revival of PROVENÇAL LITERATURE. His genius for depicting rural life, his lyric and imaginative gifts, and his passionate love of Provence gave him an international stature, recognized by the Nobel Prize for literature awarded him in 1904.

Mistral's verse romance *Mirèio* (1859; Eng. trans., 1867) was immediately recognized as a masterpiece and later adapted by the composer Charles Gounod as an opera, *Mireille. Nerto* (1884), based on a medieval legend, was almost equally popular. Mistral's other works include an epic, *Lou Pouèmo dóu Rose* (1897; trans. as *The Song of the Rhône*, 1937) and collections of shorter poems. He also compiled a Provençal dictionary (1878–86) and set up (1904) a museum in Arles illustrating Provençal life.

Mitchell, Arthur   Arthur Mitchell, b. New York City, Mar. 27, 1934, is the founder and codirector of the

DANCE THEATRE OF HARLEM (DTH). As a principal dancer (1959) with the New York City Ballet (1956–71), Mitchell won international fame as the first black to achieve such rank in a major American ballet company. Begun with classes in a church basement in 1968 following the assassination of Dr. Martin Luther King, Jr., DTH has developed under Mitchell's direction into a full-scale professional ballet company. The earlier repertoire consisted of a nucleus of George Balanchine's works (*Agon, Concerto Barocco*) and Mitchell's own choreography of jazz and ethnic ballets, such as his *Rhythmetron,* which combines ritualistic and jazz steps with classical ballet.

In 1971, Mitchell collaborated with Balanchine to create *Concerto for Jazz Band and Orchestra,* a ballet involving dancers from both the New York City Ballet and DTH. By 1978, DTH had added new Balanchine repertoire and other classical works, many choreographed by Mitchell.

Mitchell, Billy   William Lendrum "Billy" Mitchell, b. Nice, France, Dec. 29, 1879, d. Feb. 19, 1936, was a U.S. army officer who was an early advocate of air power and of a strong, independent air force. Mitchell commanded the U.S. Army air forces in World War I, rising to the rank of brigadier general. In 1919 he became assistant chief of the Army Air Service, organizing a series of tests (1921–23) in which aircraft sank battleships.

Mitchell's increasingly strong advocacy of an independent air force led to open disagreements with his superiors, and in 1925 he was court-martialed for insubordination. Sentenced to five years' suspension from active service, he resigned his commission. As a civilian he continued to lobby for a strong air force; many of his ideas were accepted and put into effect in World War II, but he did not live to see this.

Mitchell, George J.   George John Mitchell, b. Waterville, Maine, Aug. 20, 1933, became Democratic (majority) leader of the U.S. Senate in 1989. A former federal judge, he was appointed to a Senate vacancy in 1980, winning election to the seat in 1982 and 1988. Mitchell gained prominence during the IRAN-CONTRA AFFAIR hearings.

Mitchell, John N.   John Newton Mitchell, b. Detroit, Sept. 5, 1913, d. Nov. 9, 1988, served as attorney general of the United States under President Richard M. Nixon in 1969–72. In March 1972 he became chairman of the Committee to Re-elect the President; his involvement in the ensuing WATERGATE scandal led to his conviction in January 1975 on charges of conspiracy, obstruction of justice, and perjury. After his release from prison in January 1979 he lived quietly in Washington, D.C.

Mitchell, Joni   Singer-composer Joni Mitchell, b. Roberta Joan Anderson in Fort MacLeod, Alberta, Canada, on Nov. 7, 1943, is a notable figure in the field of contemporary folk music. She has a vocal range of two and one-half octaves, a talent for incisive and powerful lyrics, and a unique guitar style. Her early recordings include *Clouds* (1969), for which she won a Grammy award, *Ladies of the Canyon* (1970), and *Blue* (1971). Her later work showed more jazz and rock influence, especially the collaborative *Mingus* (1979). Other releases are *Dog Eat Dog* (1985) and *Chalk Mark in a Rainstorm* (1988).

Mitchell, Margaret   Margaret Mitchell, b. Atlanta, Ga., Nov. 8, 1900, d. Aug. 16, 1949, published one novel, GONE WITH THE WIND (1936). This Pulitzer Prize–winning romance about the destruction of the old South during the Civil War became the best-selling novel ever and the basis for an equally famous film (1939).

Mitchell, Maria   Maria Mitchell, b. Nantucket, Mass., Aug. 1, 1818, d. June 28, 1889, was the first woman astronomer in America. Her discovery (1847) of a new comet brought her world fame. Mitchell was the first professor of astronomy (1865–88) at Vassar Female College and directed the college's observatory. She was the first woman elected to the American Academy of Arts and Sciences. The Nantucket Maria Mitchell Association (founded 1902) maintains an observatory, science library, and natural science museum in her honor.

Mitchell, Mount   Mount Mitchell, in western North Carolina, with an elevation of 2,307 m (6,683 ft), is the highest peak in the United States east of the Mississippi River. It is in the Black Mountains, a range of the Appalachian Mountains, and is part of Pisgah National Forest and Mount Mitchell State Park.

mite   Mites, of the order Acari (or Acarina), class Arachnida, usually are less than 1 mm (0.04 in) long. Adults characteristically have eight legs. The mouthparts and the first two pairs of legs are on the forward part of the body. The abdomen, which is typically unsegmented and shortened, bears the last two pairs of legs; there may be no evident division between the two body sections. Mites usually respire through tracheal pores and tubes, but in some, oxygen diffuses through the thin body cover-

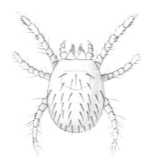

The harvest mite, also known as a chigger, lives off animals during its larval stage, drops off, and goes underground to pupate. A human infested by harvest mites experiences severe itching because of chemicals in the mite's secretions.

ing. The heart is often absent.

Perhaps more than 20,000 species of mites occur worldwide, in almost every habitat. Many species are parasitic, some being so only during a part of the life cycle. Most species lay eggs, but some bear living young. The newly hatched mite, called a larva, has only three pairs of legs. When the fourth pair is acquired after the first molt, the mite is known as a nymph; it becomes an adult after additional molts.

Mites have considerable economic significance: plant-eating species are among the most destructive of horticultural and agricultural pests. Others, such as chiggers, are human and animal pests.

Mitford (family)   Of the six spirited daughters of David Mitford (Baron Redesdale), an eccentric English aristocrat, five left a mark through their literary, social, or political activities. The eldest, **Nancy**, b. Nov. 28, 1904, d. June 30, 1973, became a successful comic novelist with such romps as *Wigs on the Green* (1935), *The Pursuit of Love* (1945)—for which her father served as model for the dundering Uncle Matthew—*Love in a Cold Climate* (1949), and *Don't Tell Alfred* (1960). **Diana**, b. June 17, 1910, one of the great beauties of the 1920s whose antics as a leader of the Bright Young Things inspired Evelyn Waugh's early novels, was first married (1929) to the millionaire Bryan Guinness and subsequently (1936) to Sir Oswald Mosley, founder of the British Union of Fascists. **Unity**, b. Aug. 8, 1914, d. May 28, 1948, was an outspoken admirer of nazism and an intimate of Hitler who attempted to kill herself the day war broke out. **Jessica**, b. Sept. 11, 1917, who became a Communist during the Spanish Civil War and was first married (1937) to Winston Churchill's "Red" nephew, Esmond Romilly, established herself as a trenchant critic of American society through such exposés as *The American Way of Death* (1963), *The Trial of Dr. Spock* (1969), and *Kind and Usual Punishment* (1973). The youngest sister, **Deborah**, b. Mar. 31, 1920, is by marriage the Duchess of Devonshire, and as such mistress of Chatsworth, England's stateliest home.

Mithradates VI, King of Pontus   (Mithradates the Great) [mith-ruh-day'-teez]   Mithradates VI Eupator, *c.*132–63 BC, was Rome's most dangerous opponent in Anatolia. His dynasty in PONTUS, founded by Mithradates I about 337 BC, had become an ally of Rome. After Mithradates VI succeeded to the throne in 120, however, he built support against Rome. By rescuing Greek cities of the Crimea from Sarmatian and Scythian attacks, he achieved control of the entire north coast of the Black Sea. Soon afterward he occupied Armenia Minor, eastern Pontus, and Colchis. By 104 BC, Mithradates had also occupied GALATIA and Paphlagonia. His attempt to seize CAPPADOCIA finally provoked Roman intervention (*c.*95, 92). Beginning in 88, Mithradates took over most of Anatolia, the Aegean Islands (except Rhodes), and much of Greece. While so doing, he instigated a massacre of 80,000 Romans and other Italians in Anatolia.

In three Mithradatic Wars (88–84, 83–81, 74–63), Roman armies destroyed Mithradates' ambitions to dominate the East. Although a brilliant leader and a master of guerrilla tactics, the Pontic king nevertheless could not withstand the imperial armies, led in the first war by Lucius Cornelius SULLA, in the second by Lucius Licinius Murena, and in the third by Lucius Licinius LUCULLUS and POMPEY THE GREAT. Avoiding capture, Mithradates fled to the Crimea, where he ordered a soldier to kill him.

Mithraism [mith'-ruh-izm]   Mithraism, the worship of the ancient Indo-Iranian god of light, Mithra, became early Christianity's most serious rival as the mystery cult rapidly spread from Syria and Anatolia throughout the western Mediterranean and into Gaul and Britain. Its cultic origins remain obscure. Although the Persian god Mithra, the chief ally of Ahura Mazda, the force of good in later ZOROASTRIANISM, is identical with the Roman deity, Western worship of Mithra had few connections with Zoroastrianism apart from its emphasis on the eternal struggle between good and evil. There were seven grades of initiation into the cult, completion of which conferred immortality. The most important ritual was the slaying of the bull, a reenactment of Mithra's killing of the cosmic bull of creation, which symbolized the conquest of evil and death. Astrology and sun worship also played a role in Mithraism.

Introduced into the West in the 1st century AD by Roman soldiers who had fought against the Parthians, the cult remained particularly popular among the military—the god embodied such soldierly values as victory, courage, and loyalty—and merchant classes. Women were excluded from the cult. One of the most powerful religious movements in the Roman Empire by the 4th century, Mithraism suffered persecution and died out after Christianity became dominant.

Mitla [meet'-lah]   Mitla, an archaeological site 40 km (25 mi) southwest of Oaxaca, Mexico, was the residence of the ZAPOTEC high priest at the time of the Spanish conquest. The site was first occupied in the 6th century BC, but the oldest surviving palaces belong to the period AD 200–900, the time when the Zapotec still ruled the Valley of Mexico from their capital at MONTE ALBÁN. Some time after 1000, at the time of the first MIXTEC invasions, the hill to the west of Mitla was converted into a fortress.

With the northern part of the Valley under Mixtec control, Mitla became one of the main centers of southern Zapotec culture. New palaces were constructed after 1200, decorated with elaborate raised geometric designs made of small, individually carved pieces of stone. These mosaics show Mixtec influence, as do frescoes in the same style as the famous Mixtec painted manuscripts.

mitochondrion [my-toh-kahn'-dree-uhn]   Mitochondria are cytoplasmic organelles that play a role in providing energy for CELL activities. They house the respiratory enzymes that convert oxygen and the products of carbohydrate, fat, and protein METABOLISM into adenosine triphosphate (see ATP) and guanosine triphosphate (GTP), chemicals that have high-energy bonds. Mitochondria generally measure 5 to 10 micrometers long and 0.5 to 1 micrometers wide. They have a smooth outer membrane and a highly folded inner membrane. The fluid matrix within these folds, or cristae, contains ribosomes, ribonucleic acid (RNA), deoxyribonucleic acid (DNA), and numerous enzymes.

mitosis   see CELL

—

Mitre, Bartolomé [mee'-tray, bar-toh-loh-may']   Bartolomé Mitre, b. June 26, 1821, d. Jan. 18, 1906, was president of Argentina from 1862 to 1868 and played a vital role in unifying his country. He served in the Uruguayan army and became a leading polemicist among the exiled opponents of the Argentinian dictator Juan Manuel de Rosas. In 1851 he joined the army of Justo José de Urquiza, which overthrew (1852) Rosas. Mitre then returned to his native Buenos Aires, where he led that province in revolt against Urquiza's federal constitution of 1853. After defeat in 1859, Buenos Aires joined the federation. In 1861, however, Mitre defeated Urquiza's forces. Mitre was then elected president.

Mitre's presidency marked a new beginning in Argentina. The economy, the legal system, communications, and education grew rapidly. Mitre commanded forces in the war with Paraguay that began in 1865. He later served in the Senate and founded (1870) the newspaper *La Nación*.

—

Mitropoulos, Dimitri [mee-troh'-poo-lohs, dee-mee'-tree]   Dimitri Mitropoulos, b. Mar. 1, 1896, d. Nov. 2, 1960, was an American conductor, composer, and pianist of Greek birth, particularly noted for his performances of 20th-century music. After studies in Athens and Berlin, he conducted the Athens Conservatory Orchestra from 1927. Following his U.S. debut (1936) in Boston, he led the Minneapolis Symphony (1938–49); from 1949 to 1958 he directed the New York Philharmonic Orchestra. A competition for conductors was established (1963) in his memory.

—

Mitterrand, François [mee-ter-rahn', frahn-swah']   François Maurice Marie Mitterrand, b. Oct. 26, 1916, elected president of France in 1981 and reelected in 1988, is the first Socialist president of the French Fifth Republic. After serving in the resistance during World War II, Mitterrand entered politics as a liberal outside the major parties and held several cabinet posts under the Fourth Republic. He opposed Charles de Gaulle's return to power and the creation of the Fifth Republic in 1958. In 1965 he united the Left behind his presidential candidacy, and in 1971 he became the leader of the Socialist party.

As candidate of the Union of the Left, Mitterrand defeated (1981) incumbent president Valéry Giscard

François Mitterrand has been president of France since 1981. A Socialist, he has changed the image of the French Fifth Republic, which was previously dominated by Gaullists and conservatives.

d'Estaing. Shortly afterward, the Socialists won a parliamentary majority, enabling Mitterrand and his prime minister, Pierre Mauroy, to carry out a series of sweeping reforms, including large increases in welfare programs and nationalization of several major banks and corporations. Economic problems, however, prompted the government to reverse course in 1982, freezing wages, curtailing welfare benefits, and halting further reforms. Mitterrand replaced Mauroy with Laurent Fabius in 1984. In 1986 the Right regained control of the Assembly, forcing Mitterrand to govern with opposition leader Jacques CHIRAC in an uneasy arrangement known as "cohabitation." Despite a rightward shift in the French political mood, Mitterrand won reelection in May 1988 and appointed a Socialist, Michel ROCARD, to the premiership. Rocard was succeeded in 1991 by Edith Cresson, also a Socialist.

—

Mix, Tom   Tom Mix, b. Mix Run, Pa., Jan. 6, 1880, d. Oct. 12, 1940, was the popular star of more than 170 short and feature-length Westerns between 1910 and the mid-1930s. Allegedly a former U.S. marshal, he was generally featured as a lawman in roles capitalizing on his horsemanship. He and his horse, Tony, left films for circus life in 1935.

—

mixed economy   In a mixed economy private enterprise and government both play an important role in the allocation and distribution of resources. All Western industrialized economies today are mixed. The reasons frequently cited to justify the substantial role government plays are: the desire to redistribute income and wealth; the feeling that government must deal with the problems of unemployment and inflation; the desire to regulate certain economic sectors for the public interest; and the perceived inability of competitive markets to provide such social goods as health care or to deal with such problems as environmental pollution. (See GOVERNMENT REGULATION.)

—

Mixtec [mis'-tek]   The Mixtec are a Mesoamerican Indian people living in the mountainous country of OAXACA in southern Mexico. Surviving pre-Spanish documents trace the history of individual Mixtec city-states to the 7th century AD. The Mixtec were artisans famous for their gold jewelry, manuscript painting, stone carving, and turquoise mosaic work.

For centuries the political activities of the Mixtec dynasties were confined to their homeland, but in the 13th and 14th centuries, by a combination of force, diplomatic marriages, and political alliances, they infiltrated ZAPOTEC territory and came to control most of the Valley of Oaxaca. To this period belongs one of the richest archaeological treasures unearthed in Mexico, Tomb 7 at MONTE ALBÁN. Discovered (1932) by Mexican archaeologist Alfonso Caso, it was built by the Zapotec but reused for the burial of a Mixtec nobleman.

Most of Mixtec territory was incorporated into the AZTEC empire between 1486 and 1519. The Mixtec were later defeated by an alliance of the Zapotec, the Aztec, and the Spanish CONQUISTADORS. The Mixtec population, estimated at 500,000 to 700,000 at the time of the Spanish conquest, today numbers about 300,000.

Mizoguchi, Kenji [mee'-zoh-goo-chee, ken'-jee]   The Japanese film director Kenji Mizoguchi, b. May 16, 1898, d. Aug. 24, 1956, is best known for his *jidai-geki,* or "period dramas," with their portrayal of the horrors of war, the lives of courtesans, and male-female relationships. His films (about 80) are wrought with a beauty and clarity unparalleled in Japanese cinema. Early productions dealt with the sufferings of women; his later efforts, such as *Saikaku Ichidai Onna* (The Life of Oharu, 1952), *Ugetsu Monogatari* (1953), and *Chikamatsu Monogatari* (1954), reflect his meditative style, which is characterized by long takes, a virtually immobile camera, few close-ups, and slow dissolves.

Mnemosyne [nee-mahz'-i-nee]   In Greek mythology Mnemosyne, the daughter of URANUS and GAEA, was goddess of memory. She slept with ZEUS for nine nights and gave birth to the nine MUSES. She appears in Hesiod's *Theogony*, but in most accounts she is a personification of memory rather than an actual character.

moa   Moas, order Dinornithiformes, are extinct flightless land birds that inhabited New Zealand. They ranged from about 1 to perhaps 3 m (3 to 10 ft) in height, and the largest specimens may have weighed more than 250 kg (550 lb). They had massive hind limbs, long necks, and small heads. The wings were reduced to tiny vestiges, and the breastbone, or sternum, was flattened, lacking the downward-projecting keel of flying birds. Their skeletal structure indicates that moas are perhaps most closely related to the small, flightless kiwis of New Zealand. Crop remains show that moas ate grasses, leaves, berries, and seeds. When the Maori colonized New Zealand about a thousand years ago, they developed a culture heavily dependent on moa hunting. This may have been a factor

in the decline of the birds. It is uncertain when the last moas became extinct. They existed at least until the 1600s, and a few eyewitness reports suggest that at least one small species may have survived until the 1800s.

The earliest fossil remains of moas are from the transitional time between the Late Miocene and Early Pliocene Epoch, about 12 million years ago.

Moas, flightless birds resembling ostriches, probably became extinct because of hunting and the clearing of vegetation on which they fed. Native to New Zealand, they were hunted by the Maori.

Moab [moh'-ab]   Moab was an ancient kingdom located to the east of the Dead Sea in what is now Jordan. Information about Moab comes primarily from the Old Testament and the Moabite Stone (discovered at Dibon in 1868), an inscribed slab erected by the Moabite king Mesha in the 9th century BC. A flourishing kingdom even before biblical times, this rich agricultural and grazing region was the home of a people closely related to the Israelites. During the reign of King David (early 10th century BC), Israel effectively dominated its eastern neighbor, but in the following centuries intermittent warfare occurred between Moab and both Judah and Israel. Moab declined in the 8th century BC and disappeared as a state about 600 BC.

Mobile   Situated in southwestern Alabama on Mobile Bay at the mouth of the Mobile River, Mobile is the seat of Mobile County and the state's second largest city. It has a population of 196,278 (1990), with 476,923 in the metropolitan area. Mobile is the state's only seaport and a major shipping, commercial, and industrial center. Manufactures include refined petroleum, food products, textiles, and paper. Tourism also plays a significant role in the city's economy. Its annual Azalea Festival and the Mardi Gras carnival are among the South's most popular events. The city's numerous antebellum mansions are open for public tours.

Mobile was founded in 1711, when floods forced Jean Baptiste Le Moyne, sieur de Bienville, to move his colony there from a bluff on the Mobile River. Mobile flourished as the capital of French Louisiana from 1711 to 1720 and was held by the British from 1763 to 1780, when Bernardo de Gálvez took the town for Spain. In 1813, Gen. James Wilkinson seized Mobile for the Americans, and it prospered as riverboats laden with cotton came down the Tombigbee and Alabama rivers to Mobile's port. During the Civil War, ships from Mobile evaded a federal blockade until Adm. David Farragut's victory at Mobile Bay in 1864. The city itself fell to Union forces in April 1865.

mobile   A mobile, or moving sculpture, is a form of KI-NETIC ART—in which movement is a major element. Between 1910 and 1920, Russian constructivists began to introduce movement into their art. Aleksandr Rodchenko is credited with having designed the first mobile when, in 1920, he suspended wooden structures that were designed to move in air currents. Alexander CALDER—influenced by Marcel Duchamp's ready-mades, the color and curving images of Joan Miró, and the geometry of Piet Mondrian's paintings—developed the mobile and made it a popular and significant sculptural form.

See also: CONSTRUCTIVISM.

mobile home   see HOUSING

Mobile River   The Mobile River, in Alabama, begins at the junction of the ALABAMA and TOMBIGBEE rivers and flows over a winding course of 72 km (45 mi) southward through the delta region to Mobile Bay, an arm of the Gulf of Mexico. The Tensaw River parallels the Mobile and has the same beginning and ending locations. With its tributaries, the Mobile drains an area of 109,557 km² (42,300 mi²). The city of Mobile, the chief city on the river, is located at its mouth.

Möbius strip [mur'-bee-us]   A Möbius strip is a two-dimensional surface with unusual properties. It can be

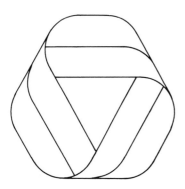

visualized in part by constructing a three-dimensional model as follows. Take a long, thin, rectangular piece of paper, give one of the narrow ends a half twist (180°) with respect to the other, then glue or tape the ends together. The edge of the loop thus formed is found to be a single closed curve, whereas if the paper had not been twisted before joining the ends it would have formed a cylinder with two edges. The surface of the strip is also "one-sided," in that any two points on its surface can be joined by a line that does not cross a midline drawn down the strip, as above. The Möbius strip was named for German mathematician August Ferdinand Möbius (1790–1868), and it demonstrates some interesting dimensional aspects of the field of mathematics called TOPOLOGY.

Mobutu Sese Seko [moh-boo'-too say'-say say'-koh]   Mobutu Sese Seko (Joseph Désiré Mobutu), b. Oct. 30, 1930, became president of Zaire (the former Belgian Congo) in a 1965 coup. Mobutu joined the independence movement in 1956, and after the Congo gained independence, he became secretary of state for national defense in the government of Patrice LUMUMBA. In September 1960 he led a successful coup against Premier Lumumba and President Joseph KASAVUBU. In February 1961 he returned Kasavubu to power and was named commander in chief of the army. The West-leaning Mobutu overthrew Kasavubu in 1965, became prime minister in 1966, and became president in 1967. Mobutu suppressed uprisings in SHABA in 1977 and 1978 and has created a sense of nationhood during his long rule, but he has been accused of corruption, economic mismanagement, and human-rights abuses.

Moby-Dick   Herman MELVILLE's stupendous novel of the sea, *Moby-Dick* (1851), combines factual scientific prose (especially in the chapters about whales and whaling), highly poetic passages, dramatic scenes, transcendental symbols, and structural counterpoint. Ostensibly the story of Captain Ahab's maniacal search for revenge against Moby-Dick, the beautiful, deadly white whale that had maimed him, on another level the book is an exploration of the themes of pride, leadership, tolerance, free will, fatalism, compassion, appearance versus reality, natural ambiguity, and "inscrutable malice."

moccasin   Moccasin is a soft-skin shoe traditionally worn by North American Indians. The word *moccasin* is derived from Algonquian dialects of the East, including those of the Massachuset, the Narragansett, and the Powhatan. The two basic types of moccasins are the one-piece, consisting of a single piece of soft leather with a seam at the instep and heel, worn principally by various western or Plains Indians, and the two-piece, a moccasin with a thick, rawhide sole sewn to a soft leather upper, worn by various Eastern Indians. Boot or "legging moccasins" were traditional from Alaska to Arizona and New

Mexico. They are still part of the woman's costume among certain Pueblo peoples of the Southwest, where leggings consist of white tanned deerskin wrapped around the calf. Moccasins are often decorated with beads or dyed porcupine-quill embroidery.

Mochica [moh-chee'-kuh]   The Mochica, or Moche, culture was a major early pre-Columbian American culture that flourished on the north coast of Peru between about 100 BC and AD 700. It is known for its modeled polychrome ceramic vessels portraying scenes from daily life and for its highly realistic effigy jars shaped in the form of human heads and thought to portray actual individuals. Finely crafted gold jewelry was among the artifacts in an important tomb find north of Trujillo announced in 1988. Other Mochica achievements lay in irrigation works and textile production.

The Mochica culture was originally centered in the Moche valley but later gained control of several neighboring coastal valleys to the north and south. Many Mochica monuments appear to have been religious in nature, notably the colorfully painted so-called Pyramid of the Sun and Pyramid of the Moon, south of Trujillo in the Moche valley. The combination of religious and military attributes in representations of persons of apparent authority suggests that the Mochica kingdom may have been a theocracy.

mock epic   The mock epic is a kind of satiric writing in which commonplace subjects are described in the elevated, heroic style of classical EPIC. By parody and deliberate misuse of heroic language and literary convention the satirist emphasizes the triviality of the subject, which is implicitly measured by the highest standards of human potential and made ridiculous.

The earliest surviving mock epic is the *Batrachomyomachia* (The Battle of the Frogs and Mice), a classical parody of Homer's *Iliad.* Mock-epic satire is characteristic of NEOCLASSICISM and thus flourished in the 17th and 18th centuries. Among the best-known mock epics of the period are Samuel Butler's *Hudibras* (1662–78), John Dryden's *MacFlecknoe* (1682), Nicolas Boileau's *Le Lutrin* (The Lectern, 1674–83), and Alexander Pope's *The Rape of the Lock* (1714) and *The Dunciad* (1728).

Mock-epic style has also been used during other periods and appears in Geoffrey Chaucer's *Sir Thopas* (c.1387), one of *The Canterbury Tales,* and in Lord Byron's *Don Juan* (1819–24). Although the mock-epic mode is most commonly found in poetry, it is also used by prose writers—notably Miguel de Cervantes in DON QUIXOTE (1605) and Jonathan Swift in *The Battle of the Books* (1704).

See also: BURLESQUE AND TRAVESTY.

mock orange   Mock oranges are shrubs of the genus *Philadelphus* in the saxifrage family, Saxifragaceae. Most of the 65 species are erect shrubs with curving or drooping branches and white flowers, which resemble orange blossoms. One of the popular cultivated forms is *P. coronarius,*

The common mock orange shrub is a fragrant ornamental bush widely cultivated for its flowers, which look like orange blossoms. Mock orange shrubs are planted behind herb or flower borders and in shrubberies or hedges.

native to Europe and southwestern Asia. It grows to 3 m (10 ft) high and bears small clusters of fragrant flowers. It is grown in many varieties, including dwarfed and double-flowered types. The Osage orange, *Maclura pomifera,* is sometimes also called a mock orange.

mockingbird   Mockingbirds comprise about 16 species of mostly tropical New World birds, family Mimidae, with the ability to mimic familiar sounds. The northern mockingbird, *Mimus polyglottos,* is slim and long-tailed and about 28 cm (11 in) long overall. It is gray, darker above than below, and has white patches on its wings and tail. It feeds mainly on insects but also eats fruits and seeds. Native to the southeastern United States, Mexico, and the West Indies, the northern mockingbird was once uncommon to rare above the Mason-Dixon line but more recently has extended its range northward to Wyoming and southeastern Canada.

The mockingbird has a melodic and varied song composed of twice-repeated phrases that are mimicked from other birds' songs, animal calls, and other common sounds.

ILLUSTRATION CREDITS

The following list credits or acknowledges, by page, the source of illustrations used in this volume. When two or more illustrations appear on one page, they are credited individually left to right, top to bottom; their credits are separated by semicolons. When both the photographer or artist and an agency or other source are given for an illustration, they are usually separated by a slash. Those illustrations not cited below are credited on the page on which they appear, either in the caption or alongside the illustration itself.